THE BRITISH YEAR BOOK OF
INTERNATIONAL LAW

THE
BRITISH YEAR BOOK OF
INTERNATIONAL LAW
1989

SIXTIETH YEAR OF ISSUE

OXFORD
AT THE CLARENDON PRESS
1990

Oxford University Press, Walton Street, Oxford OX2 6DP

Oxford New York Toronto
Delhi Bombay Calcutta Madras Karachi
Petaling Jaya Singapore Hong Kong Tokyo
Nairobi Dar es Salaam Cape Town
Melbourne Auckland
and associated companies in
Berlin Ibadan

Oxford is a trade mark of Oxford University Press

The British Year Book of International Law is an annual
publication, starting with Volume 52 (1981). Orders for
subscriptions or for individual volumes can be placed through
a bookseller or subscription agent. In case of difficulty please
write to the Retail Services Dept., Oxford University Press
Distribution Services, Saxon Way West, Corby, Northants
NN18 9ES, UK

British Library Cataloguing in Publication Data
The British year book of international law.
1989 : sixtieth year of international law
I. International law—Periodicals
341'.05   JX1
ISBN 0-19-825431-8

Computerset by
Promenade Graphics Ltd.,
Cheltenham, Glos.

Printed in Great Britain
by Biddles Ltd.,
Guildford and King's Lynn

CONTENTS

IN MEMORIAM

PROFESSOR MICHAEL AKEHURST, 1940–89

MICHAEL Akehurst, a member of the Editorial Committee, and a loyal contributor to the *Year Book*, died on 4 October 1989. His early demise at the age of 49 came as a shock to friends and colleagues. He has been fairly described by a colleague as 'a very private man, difficult to get to know and describe', and no doubt he could be quirky and was not adept at self-advertisement.

His contribution to the literature of the law was on a considerable scale, and wide-ranging. Apart from his regular chronicle of the decisions of the Court of Justice of the European Communities in the *Year Book* (1967–88), and his pioneering work on *The Law Governing Employment in International Organisations* (Cambridge, 1967), his work was in the field of general international law. This contribution took two forms. First, he published *A Modern Introduction to International Law*, which appeared in six editions (1970–87). This was a concise but highly readable account of the main areas of public international law. The book was enormously successful, and was translated into Spanish, Portuguese and Japanese. A student text, it was nonetheless recognized as a reliable source, and was often cited. Akehurst's other major writing consisted of substantial articles, of durable quality, on important areas of general international law, including the sources, and the bases of jurisdiction, most of which were published in the *Year Book*.

He spent most of his career in the Department of Law at Keele University, where he was a successful teacher. His eminence in his field was recognized by the award of a personal chair, and it was a colleague, Christina Lyon, who contributed a most graceful and well-informed tribute to *The Independent* newspaper of 9 October 1989.

I. B.

PROFESSOR COLONEL G. I. A. D. DRAPER, 1914–89

GERALD Draper, who died on 3 July 1989, was a member of the Advisory Committee of this *Year Book* from 1983. His unusual title of 'Professor Colonel' reflected the nature of his contribution to international law: he was both a memorable teacher and, as a result of his Army service, became a significant contributor to the development of the content of the humanitarian law of armed conflict.

Gerald Irving Anthony Dare Draper, OBE, was born on 30 May 1914. He attended King's College, London, where he was a Law Prizeman in 1933, and obtained his LL B in 1935 and his LL M in 1938. He entered professional life as a solicitor in 1936. During the Second World War he served in the Irish Guards.

Draper's first major experience in international law came at the close of the war when he moved to the Judge-Advocate-General's Office and became active as a Military Prosecutor in the trials of war criminals in Germany. From 1950 until his retirement with the rank of Colonel in 1956 he was a Legal Adviser in the Directorate of the Army Legal Staff, in which capacity he worked closely with Sir Hersch Lauterpacht in the revision of that Part of the *Manual of Military Law* dealing with 'The Law of War on Land' (published in 1958). In his Foreword, Sir Hersch paid tribute to the value of Draper's 'practical experience of military law and the trials of persons accused of war crimes' and 'his wide knowledge and painstaking energy, at the numerous stages of consultation with and between the authorities concerned'.

Upon his retirement from the Army in 1956 (with the rank of Colonel) Draper entered the second highly productive phase of his life as a teacher of, and writer on, international law. To his regular academic commitment, first at King's College, London and then at the University of Sussex (where he was Reader from 1967–76 and thereafter Professor of Law till his retirement in 1979) Draper added a constant succession of visits to academic institutes all over the world. He was widely known as a vigorous, often indeed outspoken, articulate and witty lecturer. Although he found time to maintain an extensive circle of friends, he was a prodigiously hard worker. He was a member of the British Delegation to the International Red Cross Conferences between 1957 and 1973 and was Legal Adviser to the British Delegation at the Geneva Conference on the Law of War, 1974–7. His interest in the law of war was manifested first in his pioneer study, *The Red Cross Conventions* (1958), which he further developed in two series of lectures at the Hague Academy in 1965 and 1979. He also produced an extensive series of some fifty articles on various other aspects of humanitarian and general international law ranging from 'The Origins of the Just War Tradition' through 'The Interaction of Christianity and Chivalry' and then on to the position of United Nations forces and the status of Jerusalem.

Gerald Draper will be remembered as a man of intellectual vigour, great kindness and considerable fortitude. For over forty years he suffered a particularly immobilizing form of arthritis resulting from the severe strain to which he subjected himself in the pursuit and prosecution of war criminals at the end of the War. In battling this affliction, as in all else that he did, he was immensely supported by the patient and continuous care of his wife, Julia.

E. L.

Professor Ben Atkinson Wortley, 1907–89

In June 1989 the *Year Book* lost one of its longest-serving members of the Editorial Committee when Professor B. A. Wortley, CMG, OBE, QC, LL D, died peacefully at his home in Wilmslow.

After a distinguished degree in law from Leeds University (1928), and a First in the Law Society's Finals (1929), 'Ben' practised as a Solicitor for two years before beginning his teaching career at the LSE. He moved to Manchester University in 1933, then to Birmingham in 1934, but back again to Manchester in 1936. There he stayed until retirement, save for the war years (he became Instructor Commander in the Educational Branch of the Royal Navy). In 1946 he assumed the title of Professor of International Law and Jurisprudence at Manchester, and he held that Chair for the remainder of his academic life.

The transition from a practising solicitor to an academic lawyer owed much to his fluency in French. He spent a year in France as a boy, and throughout his life his facility with the French language enabled him to play a useful role in international conferences and to lecture in French. He became part of the UK Delegation at conferences on private international law at The Hague in 1951, 1956, 1960 and 1964, and at New York in 1955 and 1958. He also served on the Council of UNIDROIT, in Rome, from 1950–75. His visits to France were frequent, and he acquired many friends there, friends who reciprocated by visiting Manchester to the great benefit of his students. He was an honorary Docteur en Droit of both Rennes and Strasbourg. He became an Associé of the Institut de Droit International in 1956, and a full Membre in 1967.

As a teacher Ben had a 'magisterial' style. Soft-spoken, but tall and handsome, he held firm views about the relationship between teacher and student. He taught, and they listened: not for him the notion of a 'shared, learning experience' which became current in the 1960s. Nevertheless, students readily recognized his great kindness and his deep, moral commitment to the values which underpinned the law. If his lectures lacked something in structure, they made up for this in idealism and conviction.

Ben was a devout Roman Catholic, and his belief moulded his approach to law. Thus his lectures on Jurisprudence dealt with topics such as anarchy, justice (Book V of the Nichomachean Ethics was a set book for his course) and human rights. In his teaching on international law he remained a fervent advocate of human rights, and his belief in the United Nations as a source of hope for mankind remained unimpaired. It was he who began the Schill Lectures, with the first series ('The UN—The First Ten Years' (1957)) of lectures to commemorate the tenth anniversary of the founding of the UN.

As a colleague Ben was friendly, hospitable and loyal (his hospitality aided by a marvellous wife, Peggy). Indeed, whilst this writer left Manchester in 1960, it was his privilege to count on Ben's friendship for the rest of his life. Even after retirement, not a year would pass without some note of news, or brief poem, from Ben.

Ben's published work cuts across his different fields of interest. His lectures in The Hague (1939, 1947, 1954 and 1958) were largely on private international law, and he was part-editor of *Dicey* for one edition in 1949. His monograph on *Expropriation in Public International Law*, published in 1959, was largely on public international law (with a marked insistence on the human right to property!), but by no means divorced from considerations of private international law. He edited a series of articles on the Common Market in 1974, and in 1967 published a textbook on *Jurisprudence*. This last reflected very much the content of his lecture course—with its emphasis on fundamental values, on human rights, and on the virtues of justice over anarchy: the writings of St. Thomas Aquinas and Aristotle figure prominently. It was never destined to be a popular book, used nation-wide, but it remains a challenging and stimulating piece of writing, however unorthodox.

In many ways Ben attempted too much. Few academic lawyers would today even pretend to a mastery over public international law, private international law and jurisprudence. Perhaps Ben himself did not achieve real mastery of all three. But he strove for breadth of knowledge and abhorred 'technical' mastery over detail within a narrow compass. Certainly this *Year Book* will miss his contributions, and there are many, many students whose lives are the richer for having known him.

D. W. B.

THE LAW AND PROCEDURE OF THE INTERNATIONAL COURT OF JUSTICE
1960–1989*

PART ONE

By HUGH THIRLWAY‡

* © Hugh Thirlway, 1990.
‡ Principal Legal Secretary, International Court of Justice.

INTRODUCTION

A regular feature of this *Year Book* from 1950 to 1959 was a series of articles by Sir Gerald Fitzmaurice analysing the judgments and advisory opinions of the International Court of Justice in terms of the statements of legal principle made therein, and the principles implicitly underlying the findings made. That series came to an end when Sir Gerald was himself elected a Member of the Court in 1960, though some of the same ground was covered in his tribute to 'Hersch Lauterpacht: The Scholar as Judge' which appeared in instalments in the *Year Books* for 1961 to 1963. Nor was Sir Gerald able to resume the series when he retired from the Court in 1973.

It is now thirty years since the last article of the original series appeared; and though time has not dimmed the lustre of Sir Gerald's achievement, there has been sufficient opportunity for scholars of greater distinction than myself to step forward to carry on the work. Whether the fact of their not having done so lessens or increases the degree of presumption shown in my undertaking the task must be left to the reader to judge; it is, at all events, a tribute to the scientific value of Sir Gerald's system of analysis that the Editors of the *Year Book* have considered it well worth resuming even though it must now come from a less distinguished pen.

The purpose in view remains as it was defined by Fitzmaurice in his first article: he noted that the Court had 'produced a considerable volume of authority on points of general interest to international lawyers', and continued:

It is the purpose of the present study to call attention to the existence of this body of statements of principle, by extracting and assembling in classified form, and with such comment as may be necessary to explain their bearing and effect in the context in which they were made, all the conclusions and findings of the Court (and, within certain limits, of individual Judges) presenting features of general interest from the standpoint of international law and procedure. It follows that the object is both a specialized and a limited one: in particular, it is not the intention to give an account of, or to comment on, the cases *as such* with which the Court has been called upon to deal. So far as the present study goes, these cases are the framework within which the Court has made general statements of principle. A good deal will naturally emerge as to the actual decisions in the cases themselves, but this will be incidental. Frequently, the decision or opinion of a judicial tribunal has no interest except in relation to the particular facts of the case. What is of *general* interest is the underlying principle: the immediate decision or opinion itself may turn simply on how that principle is to be applied to the circumstances of the case, or to the terms of the treaty provision under consideration.

The present series of articles is thus intended to take up where Sir Gerald Fitzmaurice left off, and the period covered may be stated to be the years 1960 to 1989. It is, however, difficult to mark the starting point with complete precision: the cycle of articles planned by Sir Gerald to cover the period 1954–59 was never completed, and his subsequent articles on 'Hersch Lauterpacht: The Scholar as Judge' covered only some of the missing ground.

In terms of decisions of the Court examined in the present series, the first is the judgment on the merits in the case of the *Right of Passage over Indian Territory* in 1960, and the last is the judgment of the Chamber of the Court formed to deal with the *Elettronica Sicula (ELSI)* case in 1989. At the same time, reference will occasionally be made to points discussed in decisions dating from 1954–59 where it appeared that Sir Gerald had not found the opportunity to discuss those decisions from the particular angle presently under consideration. In principle, although the series will take some years to complete, no attempt will be made to deal with decisions after 1989; as it is, the author fears the fate of Tristram Shandy, who found that he could not write his account of his life fast enough to keep up with his living of it![1]

The articles of Sir Gerald were devoted to successive four-year periods and were published not long after the expiration of the relevant period. This had two advantages (at least): the issues were fresh, and a four-year crop of decisions presented a manageable amount of material. The main disadvantage was one which only made itself felt as the cycles succeeded each other, and were eventually collected into two volumes. As Sir Gerald himself explained in the Preface to these volumes:

What was clearly needed, after the accumulation of a sufficient amount of material, was a fusion or blending of all those passages in the various articles that considered the same principle or rule, though in the context of different cases.[2]

---

[1] Lawrence Sterne, *The Life and Opinions of Tristram Shandy* (1759–67), vol. 4, ch. 13.
[2] *The Law and Procedure of the International Court of Justice* (hereinafter *Collected Edition*) (Cambridge, Grotius Publications Ltd., 1986), p. xxxi.

For this reason, the possibility of dividing up the period since 1959 into a number of periods for the purpose of the present articles was rejected, after brief consideration; it seemed wrong to throw away, for this period, the advantages of unity of treatment which had not been available to Sir Gerald for the period 1947–59.

On the other hand, I have had to contend with the correlative disadvantages stemming from the sheer volume of material (some 6,500 pages of the Court's *Reports* series), and from the lapse of many years since the earlier decisions treated were rendered. As a consequence I have thought it advisable to give less exhaustive coverage than did Sir Gerald to the numerous separate and dissenting opinions of Members of the Court, though these will not be neglected where they raise matters of principle not touched on by the Court, or approach the same principle in an original way. The existence of a vast published literature, in the various fields covered, commenting on the Court's decisions during the period, is both an advantage and a disadvantage: the reaction of scholars to a Court decision is sometimes enlightening, but it has obviously not been possible for me to review all the published material on the work of the Court during the period covered.

A special problem is posed by Sir Gerald Fitzmaurice's own separate or dissenting opinions as a Member of the Court, which often take up and develop themes previously outlined in his series of articles. To quote them as fully as their own merits deserve would hopelessly overload the present series; and since they exist in readily accessible form, this would perhaps be a work of supererogation. I shall endeavour to indicate, in relation to each specific matter discussed in these articles, at least the existence of any individual examination of it by Sir Gerald, which will always repay study; and I quote, sparingly, from Sir Gerald either when such quotation seems particularly illuminating, or when it appears to me useful to criticize the view he advances.

The size of the undertaking has had one particular practical consequence, namely the impossibility of planning the series in advance in anything more than broad outline. It appears from internal references that when the first article of a cycle from Sir Gerald's hand appeared in print, the structure of the remainder of the cycle was already foreseen; and Sir Gerald could therefore announce with confidence that such-and-such a point would be dealt with in such-and-such a later section. In the case of the present series, however, if the publication of the first part were delayed until all the subsequent parts were in a comparable state of readiness, the period covered would by then have slipped still further into the past. This means also that the structure of the series may prove to be lacking in architectural perfection; later articles may have to find room for afterthoughts, points which might have been well placed in this first article but only make their presence felt in the context of the later article.

The general arrangement of the various subjects considered is, so far as possible, based on that employed by Sir Gerald Fitzmaurice. Other systems of organization might commend themselves, but do not appear to present advantages outweighing the convenience of relating the treatment of a particular point in this series to Sir Gerald's handling of the same point, to which a footnote at the beginning of each section will refer.

Any discussion of matters dealt with in the decisions of the Court poses first the problem of the extent to which it is necessary to outline the factual background, and secondly that of the amount of direct quotation of the decisions, as opposed to paraphrase, summary or reference. The objective I have aimed at has been to produce a study which is self-contained, in the sense that sufficient facts are given, even in well-known cases, for the legal argument to be understood; and that argument is best expressed, at least initially, in the words used by the Court, even if the result is that these articles are, as the old lady said of *Hamlet*, 'all quotations'.

*　　*　　*

The following *caveat* has to be prefixed to any publication of mine, in view of my position as an official of the Registry of the International Court of Justice:

I should make it clear, first that the views which I have expressed are purely personal, and cannot of course be taken as reflecting the views, or having the approval, of the International Court of Justice, or of the United Nations; and secondly that my comments on the judgments and advisory opinions of the Court are based solely on published material, and not on any information of a confidential character to which I may have had access in the course of my duties. Accordingly, any comments of mine on the significance of any particular decision, or of any particular form of words in a judgment, advisory opinion, or separate or dissenting opinion, carry no more weight than those of any other student of the jurisprudence of the Court.

Chapter I:

Good Faith and Related Principles

1. *The Principle of Good Faith*

During the period under review, the concept of good faith, which had previously only been referred to by individual judges and not employed by the Court in its decisions,[3] developed into a notable element in the judicial armoury. The Court's statements on the subject are, however, at first sight somewhat contradictory. The period may be said to be framed, not merely chronologically but jurisprudentially, by the following two quotations:

---

[3] See Fitzmaurice, this *Year Book*, 27 (1950), p. 12; 30 (1953), p. 52; 35 (1959), pp. 206–7; *Collected Edition*, I, pp. 12, 183; II, pp. 609–10.

Just as the very rule of *pacta sunt servanda* in the law of treaties is based on good faith, so also is the binding character of an international obligation assumed by unilateral declaration.[4] (1973)

The principle of good faith is, as the Court has observed, 'one of the basic principles governing the creation and performance of legal obligations' . . .; it is not in itself a source of obligation where none would otherwise exist.[5] (1988)

The explanation for the apparent contradiction is, it is suggested, that the Court has used the expression 'good faith' to convey two different ideas; for clarity, these will be treated separately.

(1) *Good faith* lato sensu: *creation of a* 'servandum'

(a) *The* Nuclear Tests *cases*

The most far-reaching effects yet attributed to the concept of good faith were those declared by the Court in the *Nuclear Tests* cases. These cases, as the Court found,[6] had been brought with the sole intention of putting an end to the nuclear tests in the atmosphere being conducted by France in the Pacific; and while the proceedings before the Court were in progress, the French Government made it known, by various unilateral announcements, that no more atmospheric tests would be held. The proceedings brought could therefore be regarded as having achieved their object,[7] provided France was legally bound to conform to the line of conduct announced, and was not free to change its mind and resume atmospheric testing. The relations between France and the two applicant parties were such that no element of synallagmatic contract could be identified; was France to be held bound by purely unilateral declarations?

The Court responded on this point in terms which show that it was consciously making a broad statement of principle:

It is well recognized that declarations made by way of unilateral acts, concerning legal or factual situations, may have the effect of creating legal obligations. Declarations of this kind may be, and often are, very specific. When it is the intention of the State making the declaration that it should become bound according to its terms, that intention confers on the declaration the character of a legal undertaking, the State being thenceforth legally required to follow a course of conduct consistent with the declaration. An undertaking of this kind, if given publicly, and with an intent to be bound, even though not made within the context of international negotiations, is binding. In these circumstances, nothing in the nature of a *quid pro quo* nor any subsequent acceptance of the declaration, nor even any reply or reaction from other States, is required for the declaration to take effect, since

---

[4] *Nuclear Tests, ICJ Reports*, 1973, p. 268, para. 46.

[5] *Border and Transborder Armed Actions (Nicaragua v. Honduras), ICJ Reports*, 1988, p. 105, para. 94.

[6] There was strong dissent on this and other issues, but for purposes of discussion it may be assumed that the Court was correct in this view.

[7] Whether, even so, the Court was entitled to put an end to the proceedings *ex officio* is a point to be discussed in a later article.

such a requirement would be inconsistent with the strictly unilateral nature of the juridical act by which the pronouncement by the State was made . . .

Of course, not all unilateral acts imply obligation; but a State may choose to take up a certain position in relation to a particular matter with the intention of being bound—the intention is to be ascertained by interpretation of the act. When States make statements by which their freedom of action is to be limited, a restrictive interpretation is called for.[8]

After explaining that international law laid down no requirements of form for such declarations, the Court continued:

One of the basic principles governing the creation and performance of legal obligations, whatever their source, is the principle of good faith. Trust and confidence are inherent in international co-operation, in particular in an age when this co-operation in many fields is becoming increasingly essential. Just as the very rule of *pacta sunt servanda* in the law of treaties is based on good faith, so also is the binding character of an international obligation assumed by unilateral declaration. Thus interested States may take cognizance of unilateral declarations and place confidence in them, and are entitled to require that the obligation thus created be respected.[9]

This finding of the Court has been much criticized;[10] and one of its features which may inspire doubt is the creative role given to good faith. To some extent, however, the matter may be no more than one of terminology. What the Court is talking about here is something which would not normally be referred to as 'good faith'. The rule of *pacta sunt servanda* is based on a very fundamental idea or principle, and it may be that that fundamental idea can justify attaching legally binding effect to something which, lacking two-sidedness, is not a *pactum*; but 'good faith' is perhaps not the best name for it. It is instructive to consider Fitzmaurice's discussion of the basis of the *pacta sunt servanda* rule:

Consent may indeed be the foundation of the rules of customary international law. But the obligation to conform to these rules requires something more, namely the existence of a principle to the effect that the giving of consent, whether express or implied, creates obligation. This principle is the principle *pacta sunt servanda*. But strictly this is not a rule or principle of international law. It is, for international law, a postulate lying outside the actual field of international law. The system of international law cannot be clothed with force by a principle that is part of the system itself; for unless the system already had force that principle itself would have no validity, and there would be a *circulus inextricabilis* or *viciosus*. A principle exterior to the system must be sought. Such a principle is the rule *pacta sunt servanda*; and if the principle is to do what is required of it, it must, in relation to international law, be regarded not as a principle but as a *postulate*—an assumption

  [8] *ICJ Reports*, 1974, p. 267, paras. 43–4.
  [9] *ICJ Reports*, 1974, p. 268, para. 46.
  [10] See Zoller, *La Bonne Foi en droit international public*, pp. 340 ff.; Macdonald and Hough, 'The Nuclear Tests Case Revisited', *German Yearbook of International Law*, 20 (1977), p. 337; Rubin, 'The International Legal Effects of Unilateral Declarations', *American Journal of International Law*, 71 (1977), p. 1.

that has to be made before the system can work or have any meaning. In this sense, the principle *pacta servanda* becomes the postulate on which the whole system is founded, and becomes the theoretical foundation of international law and its binding force.[11]

It is the principle 'to the effect that the giving of consent'—consent to be bound—'creates obligation' which the Court appears to have had in mind in 1973, and to which it gave the inappropriate designation of 'good faith'. Avoiding the misleading implications of this term, what is the contribution so made by the Court to the development, or to the clarification, of international law?

Despite the assertion by the Court that 'It is well recognized that declarations made by way of unilateral acts . . . may have the effect of creating legal obligations',[12] this cannot be said to have been clearly established as a legal rule prior to the Court's pronouncement.[13] At all events, the conditions enunciated for a unilateral declaration to have a binding character have not previously been stated systematically. Let us take them one by one, as stated in the *Nuclear Tests* judgments.

(i) *The intention of the declarant State*

When it is the intention of the State making the declarations that it should become bound according to its terms, that intention confers on the declaration the character of a legal undertaking . . .

Speaking very generally, when for the purposes of any system of law it is necessary to determine whether a statement (apparently of the nature of a promise, undertaking or commitment—but to use any of these terms would beg the question) is to be regarded as placing its maker under an obligation for the future to conform its conduct to that statement, the enquiry may be regarded as one into the nature of the intentions of the maker of the statement; but at a more direct and concrete level, it is necessary to apply a number of criteria to see whether the statement fits one or other of them. Thus: was the statement made in exchange, retrospectively or prospectively, for some statement (promise, undertaking) made in favour of, or benefit conferred on, the maker of the statement (contract situation)? Was the statement made in a form defined by the legal system as sufficient in itself to prove intention, or deemed intention, to create obligation (e.g., promise under seal: see below)?

The enquiry may, however, range wider than the actual intention of the maker of the statement: it may be asked whether the circumstances are such that the addressee of the statement could properly have supposed that the statement was intended to create a commitment (acquiescence). The passage quoted from the *Nuclear Tests* judgment shows that it justifies the

---

[11] This *Year Book*, 35 (1959), pp. 195–6; *Collected Edition*, II, p. 597.
[12] *ICJ Reports*, 1974, p. 267, para. 43.
[13] See Rubin, loc. cit. above (n. 10), at p. 24.

enforceability of a unilateral declaration, in terms of the underlying principle of intention: this differentiates the legal situation from such hypotheses as estoppel, where the emphasis is on the reaction and expectations of the addressee of the declaration rather than the intentions of its maker.[14]

(ii) *The context of the statement*

An undertaking of this kind, if given publicly, and with an intent to be bound, even though not made within the context of international negotiations, is binding.

The reference to international negotiations is presumably to emphasize that the Court is here consciously laying down a broader ruling than that of the Permanent Court with regard to the Ihlen declaration in the *Eastern Greenland* case, which was specifically found to be a 'response to a request by the diplomatic representative of a foreign Power'.[15]

It is unclear whether it is, in the Court's thinking, an essential condition that the undertaking be 'given publicly'. The statements made on behalf of the French Government in the *Nuclear Tests* cases were of course made publicly rather than being addressed to the applicant governments directly; but one would have thought that it would be sufficient, as a general rule, for the declaration to have been made in such a way that it in fact became known to the State seeking to rely on it. To require that it should have been *addressed* to a particular State or States would, in the circumstances of the *Nuclear Tests* cases, have been asking more than France could give, and thus made it impossible to give effect to the declaration; but in general it is difficult to see why the legally binding effect of a declaration should depend on, *inter alia*, the fact of its having been made publicly.

A later paragraph of the judgment refers to the unilateral statements of the French authorities as having been made 'publicly and *erga omnes*',[16] which appears to add an additional element.[17] One cannot but recall the Court's *dictum* in the *Barcelona Traction* case, four years earlier:

. . . an essential distinction should be drawn between the obligations of a State towards the international community as a whole, and those arising vis-à-vis another State in the field of diplomatic protection. By their very nature the former are the concern of all States. In view of the importance of the rights involved, all States

---

[14] Zoller, op. cit. above (n. 10), pp. 341–3, draws attention to the Court's references to 'trust and confidence' in this context, and suggests that the 'good faith' involved may be that of the addressee, which must not be abused. A similar view is expressed by Carbone, 'Promise in International Law: a Confirmation of its Binding Force', *Italian Yearbook of International Law*, 1 (1975), p. 169. In view of the emphasis on the intentions of the maker of the declaration, however, it seems that these references are intended only to buttress the moral or ethical attractiveness of the principle propounded.

[15] *Legal Status of Eastern Greenland, PCIJ*, Series A/B, No. 53, p. 53.

[16] *ICJ Reports*, 1974, p. 269, para. 50.

[17] A curious fact is that 'publicly' in the earlier paragraph is translated by 'publiquement' in the French text of the judgment, but here the expression used is 'en dehors de la Cour et *erga omnes*'. The idea seems to be not so much the publicity given to the statements as that they were made outside the framework of the proceedings before the Court: cf. *Polish Upper Silesia, PCIJ*, Series A, No. 7, p. 12; *Free Zones, PCIJ*, Series A/B, No. 46, p. 170.

can be held to have a legal interest in their protection; they are obligations *erga omnes*.[18]

Does a unilateral declaration made *erga omnes* necessarily give rise to an international legal obligation *erga omnes*? If so, it would appear to follow that if France had recommenced atmospheric nuclear tests, proceedings could have been brought against it by any other State which could assert a title of jurisdiction, whether or not it was affected by the fall-out from the tests.[19] Furthermore, if this is an essential aspect of the law of unilateral declarations, it must apply whatever the degree of international importance of the subject-matter of the declaration. An obligation not to carry out atmospheric nuclear tests might rank in the scale of gravity not far short of the obligations *erga omnes* which the Court in 1970 presented as examples:

> Such obligations derive, for example, in contemporary international law, from the outlawing of acts of aggression, and of genocide, as also from the principles and rules concerning the basic rights of the human person, including protection from slavery and racial discrimination.[20]

It is not difficult, however, to think of examples of subjects to which a declaration—made publicly, and with intent to be bound—might relate, which would be of limited interest and minor significance, so that commitment *erga omnes* would be disproportionate.

(iii) and (iv) *No* quid pro quo *or acceptance needed*

In these circumstances, nothing in the nature of a *quid pro quo* nor any subsequent acceptance of the declaration, nor even any reply or reaction from other States, is required for the declaration to take effect, since such a requirement would be inconsistent with the strictly unilateral nature of the juridical act by which the pronouncement by the State was made.[21]

(iii) The Court here excludes anything corresponding to the requirement in English law of 'consideration' for an otherwise unilateral commitment to be legally enforceable.[22] It does more, however: the unqualified statement that 'nothing in the nature of a *quid pro quo* . . . is required' appears also to exclude anything corresponding to what French law refers to as 'la cause d'une obligation'. This concept to some extent parallels the English requirement of consideration: in a synallagmatic contract, the obligation of each party may be, and normally will be, the *cause* of the other; in the case of donations, wills, etc., the *cause* is the intention of conferring a

---

[18] *ICJ Reports*, 1970, p. 32, para. 33. To be discussed below, pp. 93–4.

[19] This reading of the *Nuclear Tests* judgments seems to be adopted by Weil, 'Towards Relative Normativity in International Law?', *American Journal of International Law*, 77 (1983), p. 432.

[20] *ICJ Reports*, 1970, p. 32, para. 34.

[21] *ICJ Reports*, 1974, p. 267, para. 43.

[22] This may be regarded as already established as far as treaties are concerned; 'it appears that the doctrine of consideration finds no room in international law': Mann, 'Reflections on a Commercial Law of Nations', this *Year Book*, 33 (1957), p. 30; cf. Lauterpacht, *Private Law Sources and Analogies of International Law*, pp. 177, 178.

benefit. A unilateral act of a contractual nature which is without a *cause* is invalid. Except in the special case of negotiable instruments, and similar commercial paper, an abstract promise, i.e., a promise unsupported by a *cause*, does not create an obligation.

It is not necessary to seek in comparative law the essence of a 'general principle' to appreciate that a confrontation of the International Court's conception of a unilateral act as productive of legal obligation with domestic law rules of legal commitment shows that the Court's conception is, to say the least, by no means a necessary deduction from the basic principle which underlies *pacta sunt servanda*. If English law has developed the doctrine of consideration, and French law the concept of the *cause*, it is because in neither system was it found appropriate that the mere assertion *in vacuo* of an intent to be bound should in all circumstances give rise to a binding obligation.[23]

In the terminology of the *Nuclear Tests* decision, 'good faith' alone does not, in municipal systems, necessarily require that an 'obligation assumed by unilateral declaration' should be legally enforceable.

(iv) An 'acceptance' of a unilateral declaration, if it were required for the enforceability of the obligation assumed, would impart a synallagmatic character into the legal relationship, and adulterate the purity of the concept of unilateral commitment.

(v) *The question of form*

With regard to the question of form, it should be observed that this is not a domain in which international law imposes any special or strict requirements.[24]

In particular, the Court observes, 'Whether a statement is made orally or in writing makes no essential difference . . . '.[25] In view of the general tolerance of international law in the matter of forms,[26] this is in itself neither surprising nor controversial; but it prompts further reflection. The English rule whereby a promise made under seal is valid and binding without proof of consideration may appear no more than an historical anomaly, but its significance in modern law is surely that the need for the specific form (the seal) draws the attention of the maker of the promise to the fact that he is entering into a binding commitment. When the Court lays down that, at the international level,

When it is the intention of the State making the [unilateral] declaration that it should become bound according to its terms, that intention confers on the declaration the character of a legal undertaking . . .[27]

---

[23] Carbonnier (*Droit civil*, vol. 2 (1964)) quotes the Italian writer Gorla (*Il contratto* (1955), vol. 1, section 4 ff., section 22) as advancing the view that the essential purpose of the *cause* is to limit the principle that consent alone can give rise to obligation.

[24] *ICJ Reports*, 1974, p. 267, para. 45.

[25] Ibid.

[26] Cf. the well-known *dictum* in the *Mavrommatis* case, PCIJ, Series A, No. 2, p. 34.

[27] *ICJ Reports*, 1974, p. 267, para. 43.

a gloss that should, it is suggested, be added is that it must have been the intention of the State concerned not merely to 'become bound according to its terms', but to become bound *unilaterally* according to its terms. A unilateral declaration which was intended to produce a response—in the *Nuclear Tests* cases, perhaps the discontinuance of the proceedings—may well entail an intention to become bound on the assumption, or indeed on the condition, that the response is forthcoming. This hypothesis is excluded from the Court's definition of the modalities of binding unilateral commitment.

The seal in English internal law further affords the necessary evidence of the nature of the intention of the author of the instrument; the question of proof is clearly more delicate, and more difficult, in the international sphere.

(vi) *Ascertainment of intention*

. . . the intention [of being bound] is to be ascertained by interpretation of the act. When States make statements by which their freedom of action is to be limited, a restrictive interpretation is called for.[28]

The meaning of the last sentence is presumably that unilateral statements by States should be interpreted restrictively in the sense that there should be a presumption against an intention to create a binding obligation, which would restrict the State's freedom of action. Whether there was such an intention is 'to be ascertained by interpretation of the act'; but the Court gives no guide as to how this might be done. In particular it is not clear whether the intention must appear on the face of the act, or whether the circumstances of its making are to be taken into account. Normally in interpreting a legal act, one guide as to the intention of the party or parties to it will be the presumed reason why the act was performed—in terms of treaty-interpretation, the treaty's object and purpose. In the case of a unilateral declaration, as envisaged in the *Nuclear Tests* judgment, the exclusion of any need for a *quid pro quo*, or indeed any reaction, makes this approach difficult, to say the least. However, when examining the actual statements made by the French Government, the Court did in fact find that 'they must be held to constitute an engagement of the State having regard to their intention *and to the circumstances in which they were made*'.[29] Further the Court considered that it was 'entitled to presume . . . that these statements were not made *in vacuo*, but in relation to the tests which constitute the very object of the present proceedings'.[30]

It was perhaps not to be expected that the Court would spell out in any detail the requirements by reference to which a unilateral act might be interpreted as constituting a binding obligation. Some guidance might

[28] Ibid., para. 44.
[29] *ICJ Reports*, 1974, p. 269, para. 49 (emphasis added).
[30] Ibid., para. 50.

however be expected from the way in which the Court approached the specific instance before it: from what was it able to deduce that the declaration of cessation of atmospheric nuclear tests was intended to bind France internationally not to carry out any further such tests? This is perhaps the most obscure and least satisfactory aspect of the judgment.[31]

One of the relevant circumstances would appear to be the identity of the person making or issuing the statement on behalf of the State concerned. Thus the Court said:

> Of the statements by the French Government now before the Court, the most essential are clearly those made by the President of the Republic. There can be no doubt, in view of his functions, that his public communications or statements, oral or written, as Head of State, are in international relations acts of the French State. His statements, and those of members of the French Government acting under his authority, up to the last statement made by the Minister of Defence (of 11 October 1974), constitute a whole. Thus in whatever form these statements were expressed, they must be held to constitute an engagement of the State, having regard to their intention and to the circumstances in which they were made.[32]

The emphasis here seems to be less on the question of who was entitled to commit the French Government at the international level than on the essential credibility of statements made at this level.

Two paragraphs further on, the Court gives the essence of its thinking on the point:

> In announcing that the 1974 series of atmospheric tests would be the last, the French Government conveyed to the world at large, including the Applicant, its intention effectively to terminate these tests. It was bound to assume that other States might take note of these statements and rely on their being effective. The validity of these statements and their legal consequences must be considered within the general framework of the security of international intercourse, and the confidence and trust which are so essential in the relations among States. It is from the actual substance of these statements, and from the circumstances attending their making, that the legal implications of the unilateral act must be deduced. The objects of these statements are clear and they were addressed to the international community as a whole, and the Court holds that they constitute an undertaking possessing legal effect. The Court considers that the President of the Republic, in deciding upon the effective cessation of atmospheric tests, gave an undertaking to the international community to which his words were addressed. It is true that the French Government has consistently maintained . . . that it 'has the conviction that its nuclear experiments have not violated any rule of international law', nor did France recognize that it was bound by any rule of international law to terminate its tests, but this does not affect the legal consequences of the statements examined

---

[31] Judge de Castro dissented on this point; he interpreted the statements made as showing only 'that the French Government has made up its mind to cease atmospheric nuclear testing from now on and has informed the public of its intention to do so. But I do not feel that it is possible to go farther. I see no indication warranting a presumption that France wished to bring into being an international obligation possessing the same binding force as a treaty . . . ' (*ICJ Reports*, 1974, p. 375).

[32] *ICJ Reports*, 1974, p. 269, para. 49.

above. The Court finds that the unilateral undertaking resulting from these statements cannot be interpreted as having been made in implicit reliance on an arbitrary power of reconsideration. The Court finds further that the French Government has undertaken an obligation the precise nature and limits of which must be understood in accordance with the actual terms in which they have been publicly expressed.[33]

The approach underlying this finding betrays, it is suggested, a shift between the two concepts of good faith discussed above. The Court took it as unquestionable that when the French Head of State announced the cessation of atmospheric tests, he was speaking in good faith, in the sense that he was correctly and honestly stating what was at the time the firm policy of the French Government. But was he at the same time guaranteeing that policy was immutable? The Court's reference to an 'arbitrary power of reconsideration' suggests that the reservation of such a power would be unusual and would have to be spelled out; but it is surely the irreversible unilateral commitment which is exceptional. In the sense first mentioned, the President's statement was fully entitled to 'confidence and trust'; and he was both entitled and bound to believe that it would be so received. But the more fundamental aspect of good faith, the principle whereby a unilateral commitment may rank as a '*servandum*' to be respected, requires the good faith intention to enter into such a commitment.

One element in the situation which was capable of importing this latter kind of good faith was one which the Court had ruled out of consideration, as a matter of principle, though its presence was detectable later in the reasoning. However '*erga omnes*' the statements were, they were obviously aimed at Australia and New Zealand in particular; and they were obviously related to the proceedings before the Court. If the parties had been in direct negotiation, the applicants would have been unlikely to agree to discontinue the proceedings in exchange for a cessation of atmospheric tests unless the respondent committed itself by way of legal obligation to make no more such tests.[34] Therefore, if the unilateral declaration was to achieve anything, it would have to be, and be intended to be, equally creative of obligations.

In conclusion, the *Nuclear Tests* judgments may be said to have contributed to the corpus of international law the development of the idea of a unilateral *servandum*, a legally enforceable obligation assumed purely unilaterally. The use of the concept of 'good faith' as a peg on which to hang this development is perhaps unfortunate, since what is operative here is a more fundamental principle, allied to the philosophical basis of *pacta sunt*

[33] *ICJ Reports*, 1974, pp. 269–70, para. 51.

[34] Cf. the very realistic discussion of the Belgian/Spanish negotiations for a discontinuance in the *Barcelona Traction* case, *ICJ Reports*, 1964, pp. 22–4. It should not be overlooked that if Australia and New Zealand had discontinued proceedings, they could not have brought a fresh case, since the jurisdictional titles had been withdrawn in the meantime — a point that throws some doubt on the Court's finding that the unilaterally created obligation to cease tests gave the applicants full satisfaction.

servanda. Furthermore, in order to apply the principle of the unilateral obligation to the particularly recalcitrant facts of the case, the Court had to state the principle in a dangerously wide formulation—excluding any need for any acceptance of the unilateral undertaking, or indeed any sort of two-way relationship, or any *cause* in the sense of Continental law. In any future development of the law of the unilateral act as source of obligation, it may however be expected that some of the characteristics stated in *Nuclear Tests* will be tempered or modified.

(b) *The* WHO *advisory opinion*

In its advisory opinion on the *Interpretation of the Agreement of 15 March 1951 between the WHO and Egypt*, the Court had occasion to consider Article 56 of the Vienna Convention on the Law of Treaties and the corresponding provision of the ILC draft articles on treaties between States and international organizations, or between international organizations; it commented:

These provisions . . . specifically provide that, when a right of denunciation is implied in a treaty by reason of its nature, the exercise of that right is conditional upon notice, and that of not less than twelve months. Clearly, these provisions also are based on an obligation to act in good faith and have reasonable regard to the interests of the other party to the treaty.[35]

This *dictum* however prompts some doubts. The nature of the treaty postulated is such that a right of denunciation is to be implied: that is to say that if the treaty is *interpreted* in good faith, it will be recognized that a right of denunciation must have been intended. A right of instant denunciation without previous warning, and effective immediately, would not, save perhaps in exceptional cases, have been intended; the parties would have assumed a reasonable period of notice, and the Vienna Convention lays down, as a practical solution, 12 months. But the basis for this is not 'an obligation *to act in good faith*'; it is *an interpretation in good faith* of the terms of the treaty 'in the light of its object and purpose'.[36]

Thus the *WHO* advisory opinion is not an authority for the proposition that good faith in itself can be a source of obligation.

(c) *The* Nicaragua v. United States of America *case*

In the case concerning *Military and Paramilitary Activities in and against Nicaragua,* the Court underlined the close relationship between a unilateral act, giving rise to binding obligations, and a *pactum*, both of which are therefore *servanda*. The United States had suggested that its policies and activities toward the Government of Nicaragua might be justified by alleged breaches by that Government of 'solemn commitments

---

[35] *ICJ Reports*, 1980, p. 95, para. 47.
[36] Cf. Waldock in *Yearbook of the ILC*, 1963, vol. 2, p. 67.

to the Nicaraguan people, the United States, and the Organization of American States'.[37] These commitments were supposed to have been undertaken through unilateral declarations in 1979 by the Nicaraguan Junta of National Reconstruction. After observing that the matters claimed to be covered by the commitment were questions of domestic policy, the Court observed that

the assertion of a commitment raises the question of the possibility of a State binding itself by agreement in relation to a question of domestic policy, such as that relating to the holding of free elections on its territory. The Court cannot discover, within the range of subjects open to international agreement, any obstacle or provision to hinder a State from making a commitment of this kind.[38]

No specific reference was made, in the Court's discussion of the matter, to 'good faith' as the justifying principle whereby a unilateral statement could give rise to obligation; but the passage quoted shows that the Court was, as in the *Nuclear Tests* cases, concerned to enquire whether there was an intention to undertake a commitment which would render any subsequent reneging an act contrary to good faith. Similarly, in the question of a commitment to hold free elections, the Court concluded:

But the Court cannot find an instrument with legal force, *whether unilateral or synallagmatic*, whereby Nicaragua has committed itself in respect of the principle or methods of holding elections.[39]

It should not be overlooked that the United States was not in fact claiming[40] that there existed an obligation *erga omnes*; the specific beneficiaries of the obligation were, as noted above, stated to be the Nicaraguan people, the OAS and the United States. This differentiates the legal situation sharply from that contemplated in the *Nuclear Tests* cases where, it will be recalled, the Court avoided any suggestion that the French statements were addressed to the applicant States by referring to a simple requirement that the undertaking should have been 'given publicly'.[41]

(d) *The* Frontier Dispute *case*

In the *Frontier Dispute* between Mali and Burkina Faso the question of the legal effects of a unilateral statement again arose, and in this case the statement was found to have been made *erga omnes*, or at least to have been

---

[37] *ICJ Reports*, 1986, p. 130, para. 257.

[38] Ibid., p. 131, para. 259.

[39] Ibid., p. 132, para. 261 (emphasis added).

[40] The Court also stated, curiously enough *after* examining the US contentions on the legal merits, that 'these justifications, advanced solely in a political context . . ., were not advanced as legal arguments' (ibid., p. 134, para. 266).

[41] In respect of alleged human rights violations, the question of obligations *erga omnes* did arise in the case; but these obligations were not alleged to rest on good faith observance of unilateral acts, and are therefore dealt with elsewhere in this article (pp. 99–102, below).

'not directed to any particular recipient'.[42] The Chamber took the opportunity to clarify the meaning of the *Nuclear Tests dicta*[43] on a number of points.

The unilateral statement relied on by Burkina Faso was a statement by the President of Mali whereby, in Burkina Faso's interpretation, Mali 'proclaimed itself already bound' by a report to be made by a Mediation Commission concerning the position of the frontier. The statement in question had been made at a press interview, and was to the effect that even if the commission decided that the frontier line passed through the Malian capital, the Government of Mali would comply with the decision.[44] The Chamber based its rejection of the Burkina Faso contention essentially on the point that this was hardly a normal way of undertaking a legal commitment to accept a decision as binding, and it could therefore not be interpreted as having been intended as creating such a commitment.

The Chamber first indicated why each case had to be considered on its own facts:

the Court . . . made clear in those cases that it is only 'when it is the intention of the State making the declaration that it should become bound according to its terms' that 'that intention confers on the declaration the character of a legal undertaking' . . . Thus it all depends on the intention of the State in question, and the Court emphasized that it is for the Court to 'form its own view of the meaning and scope intended by the author of a unilateral declaration which may create a legal obligation'.[45]

It then indicated why the French statements in the *Nuclear Tests* cases could, in the special circumstances of those cases, be regarded as a normal, indeed the only possible, way of creating a legal obligation:

In order to assess the intentions of the author of a unilateral act, account must be taken of all the factual circumstances in which the act occurred. For example, in the *Nuclear Tests* cases, the Court took the view that since the applicant States were not the only ones concerned at the possible continuance of atmospheric testing by the French Government, that Government's unilateral declarations had 'conveyed to the world at large, including the Applicant, its intention effectively to terminate these tests' *(ICJ Reports 1974*, p. 269, para. 51; p. 474, para. 53). In the particular circumstances of those cases, the French Government could not express an intention to be bound otherwise than by unilateral declarations. It is difficult to see how it could have accepted the terms of a negotiated solution with each of the applicants without thereby jeopardizing its contention that its conduct was lawful.[46]

---

[42] *ICJ Reports*, 1986, p. 574, para. 39. The authentic French text is perhaps clearer: 'une déclaration unilatérale privée de tout destinataire précis'.

[43] The Chamber included two Members of the Court who had taken part in, and voted in favour of, the *Nuclear Tests* decisions.

[44] *ICJ Reports*, 1986, p. 571, para. 36.

[45] Ibid., 1986, p. 573, para. 39.

[46] Ibid., p. 574, para. 40.

After thus explaining the special nature of the *Nuclear Tests* cases, the Chamber continued:

The circumstances of the present case are radically different. Here, there was nothing to hinder the Parties from manifesting an intention to accept the binding character of the conclusions of the Organization of African Unity Mediation Commission by the normal method: a formal agreement on the basis of reciprocity. Since no agreement of this kind was concluded between the Parties, the Chamber finds that there are no grounds to interpret the declaration made by Mali's head of State on 11 April 1975 as a unilateral act with legal implications in regard to the present case.[47]

(e) *The* Border and Transborder Armed Actions *case*

The most recent attempt to build a legal obligation out of good faith and nothing more was made in the case of *Border and Transborder Armed Actions*, brought by Nicaragua against Honduras. Honduras had argued that under the provisions of the Pact of Bogotá, the jurisdictional title asserted by Nicaragua, and upheld by the Court, Nicaragua was debarred from having recourse to the Court so long as the 'pacific procedure' constituted, in the view of Honduras, by the Contadora Process, had not been concluded. The Court, without ruling on whether the Contadora Process was or was not a 'pacific procedure' as contemplated by the Pact of Bogotá, held that it had in any event been concluded by the time the case was brought to the Court.

The further argument of Honduras, and the Court's finding on it, was as follows:

The Court has also to deal with the contention of Honduras that Nicaragua is precluded not only by Article IV of the Pact of Bogota but also 'by elementary considerations of good faith' from commencing any other procedure for pacific settlement until such time as the Contadora process has been concluded. The principle of good faith is, as the Court has observed, 'one of the basic principles governing the creation and performance of legal obligations' *(Nuclear Tests, ICJ Reports 1974*, p. 268, para. 46; p. 473, para. 49); it is not in itself a source of obligation where none would otherwise exist. In this case however the contention of Honduras is that, on the basis of successive acts by Nicaragua culminating in the Esquipulas Declaration of 25 May 1986 . . ., Nicaragua has entered into a 'commitment to the Contadora process'; it argues that by virtue of that Declaration, 'Nicaragua entered into a commitment with which its present unilateral Application to the Court is plainly incompatible'. The Court considers that whether or not the conduct of Nicaragua or the Esquipulas Declaration created any such commitment, the events of June/July 1986 constituted a 'conclusion' of the initial procedure both for purposes of Article IV of the Pact and in relation to any other obligation to exhaust that procedure which might have existed independently of the Pact.[48]

---

[47] Ibid., p. 574, para. 40.
[48] *ICJ Reports*, 1988, pp. 105–6, para. 94.

The Esquipulas Declaration here referred to was one made by the Presidents of the five Central American countries indicating willingness to sign the Act of Contadora, and to comply with it. *Vis-à-vis* any other Government, this might be considered to be a unilateral act; but as between the five signatory Governments, it would seem, despite its form, to be essentially synallagmatic. Whether or not the Declaration is to be so regarded, the argument of Honduras was not so much that good faith had created an obligation on Nicaragua's part, as that the admitted commitment to the Contadora Process entered into by Nicaragua entailed an undertaking not to resort to judicial settlement procedures, such recourse being inconsistent with performance in good faith of the admitted obligation. Hence the question raised in this case—but not examined by the Court, for the reasons stated—was one of good faith execution of an obligation, good faith *stricto sensu*, to which we may now turn.

(2) *Good faith* stricto sensu

In its more traditional and established form, the principle of good faith is, as the Court pointed out in 1988, not creative of obligations, but rather governs the way in which existing obligations are carried out or existing rights exercised.

Fitzmaurice's own definition is as follows:

The essence of the doctrine is that although a State may have a strict right to act in a particular way, it must not exercise this right in such a manner as to constitute an abuse of it; it must exercise its rights in good faith and with a sense of responsibility; it must have bona fide reasons for what it does, and not act arbitrarily or capriciously.[49]

Good faith has of course a role to play in the interpretation of treaties and other instruments, as indicated in Article 31 of the Vienna Convention on the Law of Treaties; but consideration of this aspect of the matter will be reserved for a later article, in the context of treaty interpretation and treaty law.

A field in which recourse to the term good faith has been frequent in the period under review has been in the context of the conduct of negotiations directed to settling a dispute or establishing the extent of the rights of the parties. The source of the obligation to negotiate, found in a number of recent decisions of the Court, will be examined elsewhere in these articles; for the present, attention will be addressed to what the Court has had to say concerning the way in which such negotiations are conducted.

(a) *Negotiations and good faith*

In the first of the series of modern cases in which the Court has had to grapple with problems of maritime delimitation, the *North Sea Continental*

---

[49] This *Year Book*, 27 (1950), pp. 12–13; *Collected Edition*, I, pp. 12–13.

Shelf cases of 1969, it discerned 'certain basic legal notions which . . . have from the beginning reflected the *opinio juris* in the matter of delimitation' of the continental shelf. These were:

that delimitation must be the object of agreement between the States concerned, and that such agreement must be arrived at in accordance with equitable principles.[50]

The court continued with an explanatory sentence which began with the following words:

On a foundation of very general precepts of justice and good faith, actual rules of law are here involved which govern the delimitation of adjacent continental shelves . . .[51]

The sentence, which is of phenomenal length, contained *(inter alia)* the following prescription:

(*a*) the parties are under an obligation to enter into negotiations with a view to arriving at an agreement, and not merely to go through a formal process of negotiation as a sort of prior condition for the automatic application of a certain method of delimitation in the absence of agreement; they are under an obligation so to conduct themselves that the negotiations are meaningful, which will not be the case when either of them insists upon its own position without contemplating any modification of it;

(*b*) . . .[52]

Taking this passage as a whole, it appears that the prescription last quoted is in fact a definition—though probably not a limitative one—of what the Court considered to be the content of an obligation to negotiate in good faith.[53] Such an obligation had in fact been defined in not dissimilar terms in 1957 in the *Lake Lanoux* arbitration.[54]

The idea of negotiations in good faith played an important part in the judgments of the Court in the two *Fisheries Jurisdiction* cases in 1973–4. The claim before the Court was simply that Iceland was not entitled under international law unilaterally to extend its fishery limits; but the Court found it necessary to go into the question of the preferential fishing rights of Iceland as a coastal State particularly dependent on its fisheries.[55] In this context, the Court found that 'The most appropriate method for the solution of the dispute is clearly that of negotiation';[56] and in the course of the negotiations which would take place between the parties on the basis of the judgment,

---

[50] *ICJ Reports*, 1969, p. 46, para. 85.
[51] Ibid., pp. 46–7.
[52] Ibid., p. 47, para. 85.
[53] In this sense, Zoller, op. cit. above (n. 10), pp. 62–3.
[54] 24 ILR 101.
[55] This approach was criticized by some Members of the Court, and its justification will be examined in a later article.
[56] *ICJ Reports*, 1974, p. 31, para. 73.

The task before them will be to conduct their negotiations on the basis that each must in good faith pay reasonable regard to the legal rights of the other . . .,[57]

the objective being 'an equitable solution derived from the applicable law'.[58]

In the *United Kingdom* v. *Iceland* case an interim arrangement had been entered into pending the Court's decision, which had still some time to run, but this was not so in the case brought by the Federal Republic of Germany. The Court therefore found it appropriate to include in its judgment in the latter case a special paragraph referring to the situation between delivery of the judgment and conclusion of the negotiations. After noting that the provisional measures indicated under Article 41 of the Statute would cease to have effect from the date of the judgment, the Court continued:

Notwithstanding the fact that the Parties have not entered into any provisional arrangement, they are not at liberty to conduct their fishing activities in the disputed waters without limitation. Negotiations in good faith, which are ordered by the Court in the present Judgment, involve in the circumstances of the case an obligation upon the Parties to pay reasonable regard to each other's rights and to conservation requirements pending the conclusion of the negotiations.[59]

This is a further development of the concept of good faith in relation to negotiations; previously good faith merely governed the manner in which negotiations are conducted, but the Court here considers that good faith in negotiating a settlement of a dispute may also require the temporary nonexercise of the rights asserted by the one or the other party to the dispute, or at least restraint in their exercise.

It is, however, noteworthy first that the pronouncement quoted above was made in relation to the observation that the provisional measures indicated by the Court were about to lapse on delivery of the judgment, and secondly that there is a specific reference to 'conservation' of the fish stocks. The purpose of provisional measures under Article 41 of the Statute is 'to preserve the respective rights of either party'. It appears therefore that this enlarged obligation deriving from good faith was justified by the fact that overfishing in the area while the negotiations were going on could cause irreparable harm to the fish stocks, the very subject-matter of the negotiations.[60] It can therefore be said that good faith in this particular instance required that neither side should press its rights while the negotiations were

---

[57] Ibid., p. 33, para. 78.

[58] Ibid.

[59] Ibid., p. 202, para. 70.

[60] Cf. also the provisions of the United Nations Convention on the Law of the Sea for the delimitation of the exclusive economic zone (Art. 74) and the continental shelf (Art. 83): delimitation is to be effected 'by agreement on the basis of international law', and

'3. Pending agreement as provided for in paragraph 1, the States concerned, in a spirit of understanding and co-operation, shall make every effort to enter into provisional arrangements of a practical

going on; but it does not follow that the same is true in all circumstances where there is an obligation to negotiate in good faith. In the absence of the element of potentially irreversible damage, good faith may restrain only acts of deliberate provocation or attempts to establish a *fait accompli* capable of prejudicing the outcome of the negotiations.

In the case of the *Continental Shelf (Tunisia/Libyan Arab Jamahiriya)* the Court had been asked not only to define the 'principles and rules of international law' to be applied for the delimitation of the continental shelf, but also to 'specify precisely the practical way in which the aforesaid principles and rules apply in this particular situation'.[61] In its 1982 judgment the Court referred to the delimitation as 'to be effected by agreement in implementation of the present Judgment',[62] and gave detailed indications as to how this was to be done; it did not refer either to negotiations or to 'good faith'.[63]

The concept of negotiations in good faith for the purpose of delimitation of continental shelf boundaries, as an obligation imposed by the law on the subject, was however reiterated by the Chamber formed to deal with the *Gulf of Maine* case in 1984. While differing from the *North Sea Continental Shelf* judgment in a number of respects, the *Gulf of Maine* judgment nonetheless laid down what it regarded as the 'fundamental norm' in the matter as follows:

What general international law prescribes in every maritime delimitation between neighbouring States could therefore be defined as follows:

(1) No maritime delimitation between States with opposite or adjacent coasts may be effected unilaterally by one of those States. Such delimitation must be sought and effected by means of an agreement, following negotiations conducted in good faith and with the genuine intention of achieving a positive result. Where, however, such agreement cannot be achieved, delimitation should be effected by recourse to a third party possessing the necessary competence.

(2) . . .[64]

The advisory opinion on the case of the *Interpretation of the Agreement of 25 March 1951 between the WHO and Egypt* has already been referred to. The Court there found that, for the purposes of a transfer of the WHO Regional Office from Egypt, the Organization and Egypt were under a duty 'to consult together in good faith as to the question under what conditions

nature and, during this transitional period, not to jeopardize or hamper the reaching of the final agreement. Such arrangements shall be without prejudice to the final delimitation.'

The conservation aspect is not treated, but is covered by the general prescription in Article 193 that the sovereign right of States to exploit their natural resources is to do so 'in accordance with their duty to protect and preserve the marine environment'.

Whether there is any distinction between good faith and 'a spirit of understanding and co-operation' is not clear.

[61] *ICJ Reports*, 1982, p. 21.

[62] Ibid., p. 92, para. 133.

[63] But note the observations of Judge Gros in his dissenting opinion on the effects of the principle of good faith on the implementation of the judgment: ibid., p. 145, para. 4.

[64] *ICJ Reports*, 1984, p. 299, para. 112.

and in accordance with what modalities' such transfer might be effected.[65] Curiously, no reference was made to good faith as regards the duty, also found by the Court, to consult and negotiate 'regarding the various arrangements needed to effect the transfer from the existing to the new site in an orderly manner and with a minimum of prejudice to the work of the Organization and the interests of Egypt'.[66] The Court did however go on to say that:

the paramount consideration both for the Organization and the host State in every case must be their clear obligation to co-operate in good faith to promote the objectives and purposes of the Organization as expressed in its Constitution; . . .[67]

Yet the commentator must wonder: does it in fact add anything to an obligation to negotiate, or to consult, to include the words 'in good faith' in its definition? Where an obligation, legal or conventional, is defined by specific words, good faith requires respect not only for the words but also for the spirit;[68] but to negotiate otherwise than in good faith is surely not to negotiate at all.

(b) *Abuse of rights*

Despite some *dicta* by individual judges, to which Fitzmaurice in his articles drew attention, no theory of abuse of rights in the international sphere has taken real shape in international practice and jurisprudence.[69] The matter may to a limited extent be one of terminology: it may be sufficient to employ the concept of good faith, in the two senses outlined above.[70]

It has of course to be accepted that if a right or discretion exists, it may be abused. An interesting observation in this connection was made by President Klaestad in his dissenting opinion in the case concerning the *Constitution of the Maritime Safety Committee of IMCO*. The majority of the Court had held that the eight 'largest ship-owning nations' had to be elected

---

[65] *ICJ Reports*, 1980, p. 95, para. 49, and p. 97, para. 51 (2)(*a*).

[66] Ibid., p. 95, para. 49, and p. 97, para. 51 (2)(*b*).

[67] Ibid., p. 96, para. 49.

[68] Reuter has suggested that the concept of negotiations involves, as one of its minimum obligations 'l'obligation de se comporter en négociateurs', and continues: 'Le principe dominant est ici celui de la bonne foi; les négociateurs s'interdisent certains agissements parce que ces agissements sont incompatibles avec une intention loyale de négocier': 'De l'obligation de négocier', *Communicazioni e studi*, 14 (1975), pp. 717–18.

[69] In this sense, Ago, Second Report on State Responsibility, *Yearbook of the ILC*, 1970, vol. 2, p. 193, para. 48. The study in this *Year Book*, 46 (1972–3), by Taylor, 'The Content of the Rule against Abuse of Rights in International Law', draws extensively on arbitral precedents and other international tribunals, but finds little in the jurisprudence of the ICJ.

[70] Fitzmaurice considered that 'there is little legal content in the obligation to exercise a right in good faith unless failure to do so would, in general, constitute an abuse of rights': this *Year Book*, 30 (1953), p. 52; *Collected Edition*, I, p. 183. 'Contra legem facit, qui id facit quod lex prohibet, in fraudem vero, qui salvis verbis legis sententiam eius circumvenit': Digest, I, 3, 29, quoted by Judge de Castro in the *Namibia* case, *ICJ Reports*, 1971, p. 183.

to the Committee by virtue of Article 28 of the IMCO Convention despite the idea of choice or discretion implied in the word 'elect'. For the Court,

The argument based on discretion would permit the Assembly, in use only of its discretion, to decide through its vote which nations have or do not have an important interest in maritime safety and to deny membership on the Committee to any State regardless of the size of its tonnage or any other qualification. The effect of such an interpretation would be to render superfluous the greater part of Article 28 (a) and to erect the discretion of the Assembly as the supreme rule for the constitution of the Maritime Safety Committee.[71]

President Klaestad took the opposite view, and replied to the majority argument as follows:

It cannot rightly be argued against my interpretation of Article 28(a) that such a discretionary power vested in the Assembly might, in a hypothetical case, lead to abuse or arbitrariness. That is no valid argument against the existence of a discretionary power as such. The possibility that a discretionary power of appraisal vested in a political body may, in extreme and hypothetical cases, be abused by that body, does not of course prove that no such discretionary power exists. A power or a right may in certain cases be abused. Nevertheless, that power or right exists.[72]

Mention should be made in this connection of the extremely interesting suggestion made in the dissenting opinion of Judge Gros in the *Namibia* case as to the legal means of enforcing against South Africa the obligations of the Mandate. Taking up a suggestion in the dissenting opinion of Judge De Visscher in the 1950 *Status of South West Africa* case, he considered that although the Court in its advisory opinion in that case had not found that South Africa was obliged to conclude a trusteeship agreement for the territory, its conclusions did contain an implication that there was an obligation of South Africa and the United Nations to negotiate with a view to the conclusion of such an agreement. His analysis of the position was as follows:

In 1950 the Court was unable, in its Opinion, to envisage the hypothesis that difficulties might arise over the implementation of the obligation to observe a certain line of conduct which it found incumbent on South Africa in declaring that an agreement for the modification of the Mandate should be concluded; hence its silence on that point. But the general rules concerning the obligation to negotiate suffice. If negotiations had been begun in good faith and if, at a given juncture, it had been found impossible to reach agreement on certain precise, objectively debatable points, then it might be argued that the Opinion of 1950, finding as it had that there was no obligation to place the Territory under trusteeship, prevented taking the matter further, inasmuch as the Mandatory's refusal to accept a draft trusteeship agreement could in that case reasonably be deemed justified: 'No party can impose its terms on the other party' (*ICJ Reports 1950*, p. 139). But the facts are otherwise: negotiations for the conclusion of a trusteeship agreement never began, and for that South Africa was responsible. The rule of law infringed herein is the obligation to negotiate in good faith.[73]

[71] *ICJ Reports*, 1960, p. 10.
[72] Ibid., p. 175.
[73] *ICJ Reports*, 1971, p. 344, para. 43.

For Judge Gros, the appropriate legal consequences (which he did not specify) could thus have been based on a 'judicial finding that there had been a breach of the obligation to transform the Mandate by negotiation as the 1950 Opinion prescribed'.[74]

The Court was in fact asked in 1985 to make a finding that a State had not acted in good faith, in a rather different context. By its 1982 judgment in the case of the *Continental Shelf (Tunisia/Libya)* the Court had defined the delimitation line between the continental shelves of the two parties with a certain degree of precision, but had, in accordance with the Special Agreement, reserved the final definition of the line for experts appointed by the parties. Following a certain amount of negotiation, Tunisia brought before the Court a request for revision and interpretation of the 1982 judgment, under Articles 60 and 61 of the Statute of the Court.

However, the Special Agreement had contained the following provisions for the implementation of the Court's judgment:

Article 2

Following the delivery of the Judgment of the Court, the two Parties shall meet to apply these principles and rules in order to determine the line of delimitation of the area of the continental shelf appertaining to each of the two countries, with a view to the conclusion of a treaty in this respect.

Article 3

In case the agreement mentioned in Article 2 is not reached within a period of three months, renewable by mutual agreement from the date of delivery of the Court's Judgment, the two Parties shall together go back to the Court and request any explanations or clarifications which would facilitate the task of the two delegations to arrive at the line separating the two areas of the continental shelf, and the two Parties shall comply with the Judgment of the Court and with its explanations and clarifications.[75]

Libya objected to the admissibility of Tunisia's request for interpretation of the 1982 judgment, on the grounds that:

the jurisdiction of the Court to entertain a request for interpretation under Article 60 is subject to a condition requiring the exhaustion of the alternative interpretation procedure, by joint application to the Court, instituted by Article 3 of the Special Agreement;[76]

and Tunisia, according to Libya, had 'neither endeavoured in good faith to implement the Court's judgment, nor indicated the precise points of difference'[77] of views between the parties; it had 'not made a bona fide attempt to

---

[74] Ibid., p. 345, para. 45.
[75] *ICJ Reports*, 1985, p. 214, para. 41.
[76] Ibid., p. 215, para. 42.
[77] Ibid., para. 41.

agree on points of explanation or clarification for the purpose of a joint request to the Court under Article 3'.[78]

The Court, however, did not deal with the alleged failure of Tunisia to act in good faith; it found that on a correct interpretation of the special agreement, this instrument did not require prior recourse to the procedure laid down by Article 3 as a precondition to a request for interpretation under Article 60 of the Statute. Judge Ruda dissented on this point: he considered that, because of the position taken up by Tunisia, 'there has never been a serious effort to try to settle between the Parties what were the points that needed explanation or clarification'.[79] However, since he considered that Libya had waived its objection based on this ground, he did not pursue the question of what consequences would flow from this failure.

An observation of the Court in the case of *Military and Paramilitary Activities in and against Nicaragua (Nicaragua* v. *United States of America)* suggests that the Court will be slow to assume an abuse of rights in other than flagrant cases. Nicaragua asserted that the United States reliance on collective self-defence was no more than a pretext:

> It has alleged that the true motive for the conduct of the United States is unrelated to the support which it accuses Nicaragua of giving to the armed opposition in El Salvador, and that the real objectives of United States policy are to impose its will upon Nicaragua and force it to comply with United States demands.[80]

The Court's finding was, however:

> if Nicaragua has been giving support to the armed opposition in El Salvador, and if this constitutes an armed attack on El Salvador and the other appropriate conditions are met, collective self-defence could be legally invoked by the United States, even though there may be the possibility of an additional motive, one perhaps even more decisive for the United States, drawn from the political orientation of the present Nicaraguan Government. The existence of an additional motive, other than that officially proclaimed by the United States, could not deprive the latter of its right to resort to collective self-defence. The conclusion to be drawn is that special caution is called for in considering the allegations of the United States concerning conduct by Nicaragua which may provide a sufficient basis for self-defence.[81]

In (for example) French administrative law, if an administrative power or discretion has been exercised for some object other than that for which the power or discretion was conferred, there will be a *détournement de pouvoir*.[82] The choice whether or not to exercise a right, even that of

---

[78] Ibid., para. 42.

[79] Ibid., p. 235.

[80] *ICJ Reports*, 1986, pp. 70–1, para. 127.

[81] Ibid.

[82] Cf. Brabant, *Le Droit administratif français* (1984), p. 525; Brown and Garner, *French Administrative Law*, p. 131. A similar charge (*eccesso di potere per sviamento del fine*) was at one time pressed by the Elettronica Sicula company *vis-à-vis* the Italian authorities (*ICJ Reports*, 1989, p. 73, para. 123), but was not part of the United States case before the Court.

self-defence, is not strictly to be assimilated to the exercise of a discretion; yet an interesting parallel is to be found in a decision of the French Conseil d'État, in a case in which an administrative act was done for more than one reason, and one of the reasons was improper. It decided that provided the act would have been done, even if that reason had not existed, on the basis of the remaining reasons, then the act was good;[83] i.e. the improper reason was treated as an 'additional motive' in the terminology of the *Nicaragua* v. *United States of America* decision.

2. *Estoppel, Preclusion and Acquiescence*

(1) *The nature of the concepts*

Another legal institution or concept which has suddenly sprung into prominence during the period under review is the notion of estoppel, with its companion or linked ideas of acquiescence and preclusion, derived, according to the Chamber in the *Gulf of Maine* case, from 'fundamental principles of good faith and equity'. While in his articles covering the period 1947 to 1959 Sir Gerald Fitzmaurice found it necessary to mention only one or two passing allusions to estoppel in individual opinions of judges,[84] one of the first cases in which he himself sat as a Member of the Court, the *Temple of Preah Vihear* case, afforded him the opportunity of examining the application of estoppel in international law in a separate opinion;[85] and the concept has played a part in the arguments in a number of other cases since 1959.

The essential aspect of a claim based on estoppel as distinguished from a claim based on acquiescence was brought out by Fitzmaurice in that separate opinion. A claim of estoppel may—and indeed frequently does—relate to the existence, non-existence or deemed existence of a particular state of mind of the respondent State, and in particular its acceptance of, or consent to, a particular matter; but while a claim of acquiescence asserts that the State concerned *did* accept or agree on that point, a claim of estoppel accepts, by implication, that the respondent State did *not* accept or agree, but contends that, having misled the applicant State by behaving as though it did agree, it cannot be permitted to deny the conclusion which its conduct suggested. As Fitzmaurice observes:

Thus it may be said that A, having accepted a certain obligation, or having become bound by a certain instrument, cannot now be heard to deny the fact, to 'blow hot and cold'. True enough, A cannot be heard to deny it; but what this really means is simply that A is bound, and, being bound, cannot escape from the obligation merely by denying its existence. In other words, if the denial can be shown to be false, there is no room or need for any plea of preclusion or estoppel.

---

[83] Conseil d'État, 12 janvier 1968, *Dame Perrot*.
[84] This *Year Book*, 27 (1950), p. 12; 37 (1961), p. 47; *Collected Edition*, I, p. 12; II, p. 680.
[85] *ICJ Reports*, 1962, pp. 62–5.

Such a plea is essentially a means of excluding a denial that might be *correct*—irrespective of its correctness. It prevents the assertion of what might in fact be *true*.[86]

There will obviously in many cases be a fairly fine line between the two analyses as applied to a particular situation; the same facts concerning the respondent State's conduct may be regarded as showing the attitude it did adopt, or as estopping it from denying that it had adopted that attitude, even if it had not. Hence the two contentions—acquiescence and estoppel—may be employed in parallel, and as a result the distinction between them may become blurred. Thus in the *Gulf of Maine* case, as the Chamber noted, Canada referred to estoppel as 'the alter ego of acquiescence'.[87] The Chamber itself kept the distinction firmly in mind, and stated it as follows:

The Chamber observes that in any case the concepts of acquiescence and estoppel, irrespective of the status accorded to them by international law, both follow from the fundamental principles of good faith and equity. They are, however, based on different legal reasoning, since acquiescence is equivalent to tacit recognition manifested by unilateral conduct which the other party may interpret as consent, while estoppel is linked to the idea of preclusion. According to one view, preclusion is in fact the procedural aspect and estoppel the substantive aspect of the same principle.[88]

Preclusion also carries the notion of being prevented from asserting what is in fact true: thus the Chamber's distinction corresponds to that drawn by Fitzmaurice, and correctly presents, it is submitted, current international law on the subject.

(2) *The cases*

Before pursuing the present analysis of the jurisprudence of the Court in this field, it may be useful to outline the facts and contentions of the parties in the cases in which questions of acquiescence, preclusion or estoppel have arisen. The first of these, the case concerning the *Arbitral Award made by the King of Spain on 23 December 1906*,[89] illustrates the narrow distinctions between acquiescence, preclusion, estoppel, and recourse to the subsequent conduct of the parties as a means of interpretation of a treaty. Nicaragua advanced a number of reasons why the designation of the King of Spain as arbitrator in the frontier dispute with Honduras, pursuant to the Gómez-Bonilla Treaty of 7 October 1894, was invalid, one of which was that the Treaty had lapsed before the King of Spain had signified his acceptance of the office of arbitrator. The Gómez-Bonilla Treaty was, according to its terms, to 'be in force for a period of ten years', but there were two possible interpretations of the Treaty as to the date from which the ten years was to run.

---

[86] Ibid., p. 63.
[87] *ICJ Reports*, 1984, p. 304, para. 129.
[88] Ibid., p. 305, para. 130.
[89] *ICJ Reports*, 1960, p. 189. The decision in this case was taken after the death of Judge Lauterpacht, but before the election of Judge Fitzmaurice.

The Court took the view, reading a number of the articles of the Treaty together, that, contrary to the contentions of Nicaragua, the intention of the parties had been that the ten-year period should begin to run from the date of the exchange of ratifications. It continued:

> That this was the intention of the Parties is put beyond doubt by the action taken by the two Parties by agreement in respect of the designation of the King of Spain as arbitrator.[90]

The Court, however, summed up its conclusion on the various Nicaraguan arguments for the nullity of the arbitration procedure as follows:

> Finally, the Court considers that, having regard to the fact that the designation of the King of Spain as arbitrator was freely agreed to by Nicaragua, that no objection was taken by Nicaragua to the jurisdiction of the King of Spain as arbitrator either on the ground of irregularity in his designation as arbitrator or on the ground that the Gómez-Bonilla Treaty had lapsed even before the King of Spain had signified his acceptance of the office of arbitrator, and that Nicaragua fully participated in the proceedings before the King, it is no longer open to Nicaragua to rely on either of these contentions as furnishing a ground for the nullity of the Award.[90]

Thus Nicaragua's agreement to the designation of the King of Spain as arbitrator was both conduct confirming the interpretation of the Gómez-Bonilla Treaty' which validated the appointment, and conduct disentitling Nicaragua from relying on *(inter alia)* the contention that the appointment was invalid as out of time, on grounds of acquiescence or preclusion.[91]

The Court did not, in the *King of Spain* case, mention the possibility of estoppel, though this was raised—and rejected—by the Judge *ad hoc* (Urrutia Holguin) appointed by Nicaragua, in his dissenting opinion.[92] He emphasized the need to show reliance by the one party on the apparent acquiescence of the other; and it is true that Honduras did not prove any effective reliance on the conduct of Nicaragua in this respect, let alone any change of position to its detriment. What the Court relied on, as is shown by the passage quoted above, was a broader concept of preclusion.

In addition to its argument directed to showing the *ab initio* nullity of the arbitral procedure, Nicaragua argued also that the award made by the King of Spain was invalid or incapable of execution. The Court's finding on this aspect of the case was as follows:

> In the judgment of the Court, Nicaragua, by express declaration and by conduct, recognized the Award as valid and it is no longer open to Nicaragua to go back upon that recognition and to challenge the validity of the Award. Nicaragua's failure to raise any question with regard to the validity of the Award for several

---

[90] Ibid., p. 208.

[91] The same cumulation of arguments is to be found in the arbitral decision in the *Costa Rica/Nicaragua Boundary* case (Moore's *International Arbitrations*, vol. 2, p. 1945), cited in Bowett, 'Estoppel before International Tribunals and its Relation to Acquiescence', this *Year Book*, 33 (1957), p. 176 at p. 198.

[92] *ICJ Reports*, 1960, pp. 222, 236.

years after the full terms of the Award had become known to it further confirms the conclusion at which the Court has arrived. The attitude of the Nicaraguan authorities during that period was in conformity with Article VII of the Gómez-Bonilla Treaty which provided that the arbitral decision whatever it might be—and this, in the view of the Court, includes the decision of the King of Spain as arbitrator—'shall be held as a perfect, binding and perpetual Treaty between the High Contracting Parties, and shall not be subject to appeal'.[93]

Despite the reference to the terms of the Treaty, it does not appear that the Court was here thinking in terms of interpretation of the Treaty by reference to the subsequent conduct of the parties. It would be stretching this doctrine beyond its limits to suggest that, because the parties had agreed that the award should rank as a treaty, a failure to challenge the award would amount to an implied interpretation of the award as a valid treaty. The Court's conclusion however makes perfect sense if interpreted as a finding of preclusion.

The underlying facts, so far as material, in the case of the *Temple of Preah Vihear* were as follows: by a treaty of 1904, Thailand—then known as Siam—and France, as Protecting Power of Cambodia, had agreed that the frontier between the two countries should follow the watershed between two specified river-basins, and that the delimitation should be carried out by Mixed Commissions composed of officers appointed by the two countries. A Mixed Commission was set up, and maps were eventually produced, and printed and published by a French firm; the relevant map showed the frontier as leaving the temple of Preah Vihear to Cambodia. It was later established that the line of the watershed ran the other side of the temple, so that if the mapped frontier line had followed the watershed, as contemplated by the 1904 treaty, the temple would have been left to Thailand. The map had apparently been produced by French officers on the instructions of the Mixed Commission, but the Commission had never approved it—indeed, the Commission had ceased to meet before the map was produced.

France handed over copies of the maps to Siam, and they were also given wide publicity. The Court found specifically that the circumstances of the delivery of the maps:

were such as called for some reaction, within a reasonable period, on the part of the Siamese authorities, if they wished to disagree with the map or had any serious question to raise in regard to it. They did not do so, either then or for many years, and thereby must be held to have acquiesced. *Qui tacet consentire videtur si loqui debuisset et potuisset.*[94]

Before turning to the second aspect of the case, we may note that there was initially no estoppel in any strict sense. The Court made no finding that

[93] Ibid., pp. 213–14.
[94] *ICJ Reports*, 1962, p. 23.

Cambodia (or France) had, in the early years, acted on the faith of Siam's apparent acceptance of the map, so as detrimentally to change its position. On the other hand, Siam was precluded from asserting that there had been no consent, by reason of its silence in face of the indication on the map of the frontier line. A finding of acquiescence of this kind is a finding of *deemed* consent: if there is evidence to show that a State has in fact given consent on a particular matter, there is no need to resort to the concept of acquiescence.

The Court did not, however, rest its decision solely on the conduct of Siam when, and immediately after, it received the map. It also took into account the many years of inaction, in the sense of lack of protest, which followed. It held that:

> Even if there were any doubt as to Siam's acceptance of the map in 1908, and hence of the frontier indicated thereon, the Court would consider, in the light of the subsequent course of events, that Thailand is now precluded by her conduct from asserting that she did not accept it. She has, for fifty years, enjoyed such benefits as the Treaty of 1904 conferred on her, if only the benefit of a stable frontier. France, and through her Cambodia, relied on Thailand's acceptance of the map . . . It is not now open to Thailand, while continuing to claim and enjoy the benefits of the settlement, to deny that she was even a consenting party to it.[95]

Fitzmaurice, in his separate opinion, was clear that the principle of preclusion 'is quite distinct theoretically from the notion of acquiescence', but continued:

> But acquiescence can operate as a preclusion or estoppel in certain cases, for instance where silence, on an occasion where there was a duty or need to speak or act, implies agreement, or a waiver of rights.[96]

Judge Wellington Koo, who dissented, assimilated preclusion to estoppel, since in his view the legal basis of the principle of preclusion:

> is that one party has relied on the statement or conduct of the other either to its own detriment or to the other's advantage.[97]

Judge Sir Percy Spender also emphasized the fact that 'the principle of preclusion is . . . quite distinct from the concept of recognition (or acquiescence) . . .',[98] the distinction being an important element in his dissent, for reasons to be examined in a moment. Like Judge Wellington Koo, he defined preclusion in terms which assimilate it wholly to estoppel:

> In my opinion the principle operates to prevent a State contesting before the Court a situation contrary to a clear and unequivocal representation previously made to it by another State, either expressly or impliedly, on which representation the other State was, in the circumstances, entitled to rely and in fact did rely, and

---

[95] Ibid., p. 32.
[96] Ibid., p. 62.
[97] Ibid., p. 97.
[98] Ibid., p. 131.

as a result that other State has been prejudiced or the State making it has secured some benefit for itself.[99]

In the *North Sea Continental Shelf* cases, Denmark and the Netherlands asserted that the equidistance rule for delimitation of the continental shelf, employed in the 1958 Geneva Convention on the subject, had become binding on the Federal Republic of Germany (which was not party to that Convention), *inter alia* on the basis of conduct of the Federal Republic. After examining the details of the conduct relied on by the applicants, and stating that the Federal Republic had not become bound by the Convention as such, the Court concluded:

> Having regard to these considerations of principle, it appears to the Court that only the existence of a situation of estoppel could suffice to lend substance to his contention,—that is to say if the Federal Republic were now precluded from denying the applicability of the conventional régime, by reason of past conduct, declarations, etc., which not only clearly and consistently evinced acceptance of that regime, but also had caused Denmark or the Netherlands, in reliance on such conduct, detrimentally to change position or suffer some prejudice. Of this there is no evidence whatever in the present case.[100]

An argument in the *Gulf of Maine* case which was based on estoppel related to the conduct of the parties in granting sea-bed exploration permits over disputed areas of the Georges Bank. Canada claimed that it was known to the United States that Canada had issued such permits, and that the United States had not protested or shown any reaction; and while the United States also issued permits in the disputed area it did nothing to inform Canada of this. Canada thus relied on the conduct of the United States as conveying the clear—even if incorrect—message that it accepted the Canadian claims. The essence of the Chamber's decision on these arguments was as follows:

> . . . while it may be conceded that the United States showed a certain imprudence in maintaining silence after Canada had issued the first permits for exploration on Georges Bank, any attempt to attribute to such silence, a brief silence at that, legal consequences taking the concrete form of an estoppel, seems to be going too far.

> . . . From 1965 onwards, as we have seen, the United States also issued exploration permits for the northwestern portion of Georges Bank, that is to say the area claimed by Canada. Here again it would have been prudent for the United States to inform Canada officially of those activities, but its failure to do so does not warrant the conclusion that it thereby gave Canada the impression that it accepted the Canadian standpoint, and that legal effects resulted. Once again the United States attitude towards Canada was unclear and perhaps ambiguous, but not to the point of entitling Canada to invoke the doctrine of estoppel.[101]

Canada also based its claim that the United States had acquiesced in the

---

[99] Ibid., pp. 143–4.
[100] *ICJ Reports*, 1969, p. 26, para. 30.
[101] *ICJ Reports*, 1984, p. 308, paras. 140–1.

idea of adopting a median line as the boundary between their respective maritime jurisdictions on the conduct of United States officials, and in particular a letter which came to be known as the 'Hoffman letter' from the name of its signatory, as amounting to an estoppel. In that letter, enquiring about the position of certain Canadian concessions in relation to the median line, Mr Hoffman, an official of the Bureau of Land Management of the Department of the Interior, explained that he had no authority to commit the United States as to the position of a median line.[102] The Chamber rejected the Canadian contentions, essentially for the following reason:

The Chamber considers that the terms of the 'Hoffman letter' cannot be invoked against the United States Government. It is true that Mr Hoffman's reservation, that he was not authorized to commit the United States, only concerned the location of a median line; the use of a median line as a method of delimitation did not seem to be in issue, but there is nothing to show that the method had been adopted at government level. Mr Hoffman, like his Canadian counterpart, was acting within the limits of his technical responsibilities and did not seem aware that the question of principle which the subject of the correspondence might imply had not been settled, and that the technical arrangements he was to make with his Canadian correspondents should not prejudge his country's position in subsequent negotiations between governments. This situation however, being a matter of United States internal administration, does not authorize Canada to rely on the contents of a letter from an official of the Bureau of Land Management of the Department of the Interior, which concerns a technical matter, as though it were an official declaration of the United States Government on that country's international maritime boundaries.[103]

When Nicaragua, in the case concerning *Military and Paramilitary Activities in and against Nicaragua (Nicaragua v. United States of America)*, sought to rely on its pre-war acceptance of the jurisdiction of the Permanent Court in order to bring proceedings against the United States of America, the United States argued that that acceptance was ineffective, or that, if it was effective so that Nicaragua could invoke it, 'Nicaragua's conduct in relation to the United States over the course of many years estops Nicaragua from doing so'.[104]

Having, it is argued, represented to the United States that it was not itself bound under the system of the Optional Clause, Nicaragua is estopped from invoking compulsory jurisdiction under that Clause against the United States. The United States asserts that since 1943 Nicaragua has consistently represented to the United States of America that Nicaragua was not bound by the Optional Clause, and when the occasion arose that this was material to the United States diplomatic activities, the United States relied upon those Nicaraguan representations.[105]

The Court, however, considered that Nicaragua's conduct over the period

[102] Ibid., p. 306, para. 133.
[103] Ibid., pp. 307–8, para. 139.
[104] Ibid., p. 413, para. 48.
[105] Ibid.

in question was, on the contrary, 'such as to evince its consent to be bound' by its pre-war declaration 'in such a way as to constitute a valid mode of acceptance of jurisdiction'.[106] The Court could not regard the particular incidents relied on by the United States, which were apparently inconsistent with Nicaragua's general conduct, 'as sufficient to overturn that conclusion, let alone to support an estoppel'.[107]

(3) *Analysis of estoppel*

For purposes of analysis of the concept of estoppel as reflected in the cases, we may take a phrase, already quoted, from the judgment of 1969 in the *North Sea Continental Shelf* cases to serve as a working definition of estoppel:

. . . only the existence of a situation of estoppel could suffice to lend substance to this contention,—that is to say if [the respondent State][108] were now precluded from denying the [fact asserted by the applicant State], by reason of past conduct, declarations, etc., which not only clearly and consistently evinced acceptance of that [fact], but also had caused [the applicant State], in reliance on such conduct, detrimentally to change position or suffer some prejudice.[109]

The elements of an estoppel here identified may thus be enumerated:
—conduct of the respondent State
—clearly and convincingly evincing assertion or acceptance
—of what must, according to the applicant State, be treated as a fact,
—relied on by the applicant State, which was thereby induced
—to change its position or suffer some prejudice.

(a) *Conduct of the respondent State*

As in the case of any conduct by which a State is to be held to have undertaken an obligation, the conduct must be that of the State, acting through its appropriate organs or officials.[110] Consistently with the underlying concept, whereby what matters is the effect produced on the respondent State, the constitutional niceties of the position of a given official are less important than the impression produced *ab extra* as to his competence to speak for the State. Yet there must be some degree of authority to speak vested in the person concerned.[111]

---

[106] Ibid., p. 414, para. 51.

[107] Ibid.

[108] For convenience of discussion, it will be assumed that in all cases an applicant is claiming that a respondent is bound by an estoppel; in the *North Sea Continental Shelf* cases, brought by special agreement, the parties were in fact not in the position of applicant or respondent.

[109] *ICJ Reports*, 1969, p. 26, para. 30.

[110] In the *Temple of Preah Vihear* case, there was the problem whether the estoppel or preclusion relied on to prevent Thailand from disputing the frontier line as mapped could prevail over the provisions of the frontier treaty; could a variation of a treaty be agreed to by anyone other than the persons who could sign the treaty? See below, pp. 47–9.

[111] Cf. the Court's observations, quoted above, p. 15, in respect of the statement made on behalf of the French Government in the *Nuclear Tests* cases, which had to be 'held to constitute an engagement of the State' (*ICJ Reports*, 1974, p. 269, para. 49).

In the *Temple of Preah Vihear* case, some emphasis was laid by the Court on the rank and functions of those who were known or presumed to have seen and accepted the map of the frontier line.[112] In the *Gulf of Maine* case, as the passage quoted above shows, the Court was unable to regard the Hoffman letter as creating an estoppel in view of Mr Hoffman's position and duties. The Court's rejection of the United States contentions as to estoppel in the Nicaragua case do not appear to be based on any doubts in this respect: the alleged assurances were given by the Nicaraguan Foreign Minister and the Nicaraguan Ambassador in Washington.[113]

It should also be noted that where a reaction—or more commonly an absence of reaction—is relied on as showing an estoppel, the governmental level at which the conduct occurred which should have provoked the reaction may also be relevant. The United States in the *Gulf of Maine* case rejected an alleged estoppel based on its failure to react to the grant by Canada of sea-bed exploration permits in the disputed area (see next section), which had been made public, claiming that:

the issue of offshore permits under Canadian legislation was not common knowledge, and merely constituted an internal administrative activity incapable of forming the basis of acquiescence or estoppel at the international level. Before any effect could result at this level it would, at least, have been necessary for the Canadian Department of External Affairs to send a diplomatic communication to the United States Department of State.[114]

In the jurisdictional phase of the *Barcelona Traction* case, it was argued for Spain that Belgium had by its conduct misled Spain about the import of the discontinuance of the proceedings before the Court, giving the impression that the discontinuance was final and the suit would not be re-started. The Court rejected this argument for a number of reasons, of which the first was that:

it is not clear whether the alleged misleading conduct was on the part of the Applicant Government itself or of private Belgian parties, or in the latter event, how far it is contended that the complicity or responsibility of the Applicant Government is involved.[115]

(b) *Clear and convincing indication of acceptance*

It would seem that one of the clearest forms of indication of acceptance or recognition of a particular state of affairs is when the respondent State has, possibly in another context, urged the existence of that state of affairs, in order to found its own interests. Thus in the *Temple of Preah Vihear* case Thailand had used the contentious map, or other maps showing the Temple as lying in Cambodia, 'even for public and official purposes', without

---

[112] *ICJ Reports*, 1962, p. 25.
[113] *ICJ Reports*, 1984, pp. 413–14, paras. 49–50.
[114] Ibid., p. 305, para. 131.
[115] *ICJ Reports*, 1964, p. 24.

raising any query; and this the Court regarded as significant.[116] Other examples of such a situation to have come before the Court relate to representations of law, as to which different considerations apply (see next section).

The time element may be relevant in this respect. In the *Temple* case the Court referred to the fifty-year period between the delivery of the map in 1908 and its being challenged in 1958; and in the *Gulf of Maine* case the Chamber emphasized that the United States silence relied on was a 'brief silence' only.

A claim of estoppel is, theoretically, based on the fact that the respondent State has done something; but it is, if anything, more common for a claim to be that a State has not done something which, on certain postulates, it might have been expected to do, and that this was a representation that the facts are otherwise. This was the position, as noted above, both in the *Temple* and the *Gulf of Maine* cases. The Chamber formed to deal with the case of *Elettronica Sicula SpA (ELSI)* observed that:

> although it cannot be excluded that an estoppel could in certain circumstances arise from a silence when something ought to have been said, there are obvious difficulties in constructing an estoppel from a mere failure to mention a matter at a particular point in somewhat desultory diplomatic exchanges.[117]

With due respect to the Chamber, the reference to a situation 'when something ought to have been said' corresponds more to an application of the principle *qui tacet consentire videtur . . .* than to an estoppel. It is submitted that for purposes of estoppel the question is not whether there is a duty to speak, but simply, did the silence or non-action amount in the circumstances to a suggestion or representation of a certain fact?

(c) *Conduct pointing to what must be treated as a fact*

Estoppel elevates a sort of legal fiction to the status of fact for the purposes of the relations between the parties. What then if the 'fact' which the respondent State is alleged to have suggested by its conduct is not a fact, but a legal assertion or conclusion?[118]

One view of estoppel is that it is part of a wider category of concepts, including tacit agreement, acquiescence, preclusion, etc., which can relate to matters of fact or of law. In his dissenting opinion in the *Temple of Preah Vihear* case, Judge Sir Percy Spender expressly included 'situations of law' in the sphere of operation of concepts of this kind:

> A State may of course recognize—or acquiesce in—any fact or situation either of

---

[116] *ICJ Reports*, 1962, pp. 27, 19.
[117] *ICJ Reports*, 1989, p. 44, para. 54.
[118] This was not so in the *ELSI* case, when it was sought to exclude the application of the rule of exhaustion of local remedies on the grounds of an estoppel; the Chamber treated the matter as an alleged representation, not that the local remedies rule was inapplicable, but that local remedies had been exhausted, a matter of fact, or of national law treated as fact.

law or fact and its intention to do so may be evidenced expressly or by implication. The recognition may become the source of a legal right or obligation to the extent to which it provides an essential element in the establishment of a legal right or obligation, as for example in preclusion or prescription. It may provide evidence of a fact or a state of facts, the probative value of which depends upon all the surrounding circumstances. It may afford aid in the interpretation of a document or conduct.[119]

The *Nicaragua* v. *United States* case has already been referred to; in that case the claim of the United States was that:

Having . . . represented to the United States that it was not itself bound under the system of the Optional Clause, Nicaragua is estopped from invoking compulsory jurisdiction under that Clause against the United States.[120]

Whether or not the pre-war Nicaraguan declaration of acceptance of jurisdiction of the Permanent Court was effective after the coming into force of the 1946 Statute, so that Nicaragua could itself have been sued, on that basis, by any other State having deposited a declaration, was a question not of fact but of law. As the Court stated in the *Border and Transborder Armed Actions (Nicaragua* v. *Honduras)* case:

The existence of jurisdiction of the Court in a given case is . . . not a question of fact, but a question of law to be resolved in the light of the relevant facts,[121]

and for that reason there could be no burden of proof, to show that there was, or that there was not, jurisdiction. The Court, however, continued: 'The determination of the facts may raise questions of proof.'[122]

In the *Nicaragua* v. *United States* case, it must be taken that the starting point of the United States argument was that Nicaragua's pre-war declaration *was* valid so that in the post-war optional clause system it *was* bound; this, as shown above, is essential to a claim of estoppel. Nicaragua had, it was said, 'consistently represented to the United States of America that Nicaragua was not bound by the Optional Clause, and . . . the United States relied upon those Nicaraguan representations'.[123] The reason why there was doubt as to the status of Nicaragua *vis-à-vis* the optional clause was because Nicaragua had never ratified the Protocol of Signature of the Statute of the Permanent Court. If Nicaragua had represented to the United States that it had not ratified that Protocol when in fact it had, then an estoppel could, it is suggested, have arisen whereby the Court would resolve the question of law, its jurisdiction in relation to Nicaragua, on the basis of the 'pseudo-fact' that the Protocol of Signature had not been ratified. But Nicaragua had accurately presented the facts to the United States; it had however accompanied that presentation with a statement of its

---

[119] *ICJ Reports*, 1962, p. 130.
[120] *ICJ Reports*, 1984, p. 413, para. 48.
[121] *ICJ Reports*, 1988, p. 76, para. 16.
[122] Ibid.
[123] *ICJ Reports*, 1984, p. 413, para. 48.

opinion—for it could be no more than that—that in consequence of those facts it was not bound by a subsisting declaration under the optional clause.

In the *Border and Transborder Armed Actions* case brought by Nicaragua against Honduras, an even more striking instance of an alleged estoppel of this kind was put forward, but not examined by the Court, which based its judgment on other grounds. Honduras had in 1960 accepted the jurisdiction of the Court under the Optional Clause 'for an indefinite term'. In May 1968, shortly before Nicaragua instituted proceedings, Honduras deposited a fresh declaration containing reservations which would—apparently—have excluded Nicaragua's claim from the purview of the declaration. Nicaragua claimed that the 1960 declaration, being 'for an indefinite term', was irrevocable, or revocable only on notice, and that Nicaragua could therefore found jurisdiction upon it. In support of its case, Nicaragua was able to point to a protest made by Honduras itself when in 1973 El Salvador sought to withdraw and replace a pre-war declaration of acceptance of jurisdiction made without limit of time.

Possibly to the embarrassment of Honduras, Nicaragua was able to quote the very terms of Honduras' letter of protest:

Leading authorities on international law take the position that a declaration not containing a time limit cannot be denounced, modified or broadened unless right to do so is expressly reserved in the original declaration and that, accordingly, new reservations cannot be made unless this requirement has been fulfilled.

To say otherwise would mean accepting the notion that a State can unilaterally terminate its obligation to submit to the jurisdiction of the Court whenever that suits its interests, thus denying other States the right to summon it before the Court to seek a settlement of disputes to which they are parties. This could well undermine the universally applicable principle of respect for treaties and for the principles of international law; . . .[124]

The implications of treating a statement of this kind as an estoppel, committing Honduras in respect of its own acceptance of jurisdiction, as urged by Nicaragua, are somewhat disturbing. Apart from the fact that the statement was not addressed to Nicaragua, and Nicaragua did not apparently act on it to its detriment, is it acceptable that a State which has once publicly expressed a view of the law on a particular point should be held to it even if it is incorrect?—and for purposes of estoppel it must be assumed to be so.

Against this it may be recalled that in the *Asylum* case in 1950,[125] Colombia was able to cite official Government communiqués issued in 1948 by Peru expressing the same view of the law (as to the right of the State granting asylum to qualify the offence) as was being advanced by Colombia in the proceedings and disputed by Peru in 1950.[126] Peru similarly referred to

---

[124] Reproduced in Rosenne, *Documentation on the International Court of Justice* (1979), p. 362; quoted in the counter-memorial of Nicaragua, para. 80.

[125] Discussed by Fitzmaurice, this *Year Book*, 29 (1952), p. 58; *Collected Edition*, I, p. 127.

[126] *Pleadings*, vol. 1, pp. 37–9.

a Report prepared by the Colombian Foreign Ministry, inconsistent with Colombia's stand in the proceedings. The Court dismissed all these pieces of evidence as irrelevant, with the brief statement that:

> The Court, whose duty it is to apply international law in deciding the present case, cannot attach decisive importance to any of these documents.[127]

Whether the idea of acquiescence or the idea of preclusion is applied, it is difficult to accept that a State is bound in its own affairs by a view of the law which it asserted against another State on a previous occasion. Curious consequences for the development of customary law would follow. Suppose that a State has protested against an extension of maritime jurisdiction claimed by another State at a time when that extension is gaining ground but has not yet become recognized by general customary law; once that recognition has been achieved, is the State which protested to remain, so far as regards its own maritime jurisdiction, locked into the previous customary-law regime?

In his separate opinion in the *Nuclear Tests* case Judge Gros drew attention to the fact that the proceedings brought by Australia against France to bring about the cessation of nuclear tests were inconsistent with Australia's earlier attitude to, and co-operation with, similar tests carried out by the United Kingdom on Australian territory.[128] Judge Gros did not however draw the conclusion that Australia was estopped from objecting to the French tests: his view was that

> Active participation in repeated atmospheric [nuclear] tests over several years in itself constitutes admission that such tests were in accordance with the rules of international law.[129]

This, it is suggested, is a more convincing analysis. Particularly in a field governed by customary law, where State practice is constitutive of law, the conduct of the applicant State is at least as valuable as that of any other State as evidence in support of a particular rule. It may however be dangerous to succumb to the temptation to give it more weight, simply because it emanates from the applicant State. Considerations of good faith in an individual case—rejection of a policy which blows first hot and then cold—must not be allowed to distort the development of general customary law.

It may be suspected that the dissenting opinion of Judge Lachs in the *North Sea Continental Shelf* cases fell into this trap. The question was whether the Federal Republic of Germany was bound by the equidistance rule in Article 6 of the 1958 Geneva Convention on the Continental Shelf, to which it was not a party. Judge Lachs attached decisive importance to a

---

[127] *ICJ Reports*, 1950, p. 278.
[128] *ICJ Reports*, 1974, pp. 279–81. The Australian Government had, with remarkable frankness, explained in its application that the change of attitude resulted from a change of government: ibid., pp. 279–80, para. 5.
[129] Ibid., p. 281, para. 8.

Proclamation made by the German Government on 22 January 1964, which referred to 'the development of general international law, as expressed in recent State practice and in particular in the signing of the Geneva Convention on the Continental Shelf'.[130] Judge Lachs commented on this:

> Here an opinion is expressed as to the character and scope of the law on the continental shelf. It constitutes in fact a value-judgment on the state of the law on the subject. Indeed it is emphatically implied that the mere signing of that instrument, at a time when it had not yet entered into force, was evidence of general international law. The Federal Republic viewed its own signature as a constituent element of that evidence, thus attaching to it far more importance than is normal in the case of signatures to instruments requiring ratification. If words have any meaning, these could be understood solely as the recognition by the Federal Republic that the Geneva Convention reflected general international law . . .
>
> The proclamation is, therefore, as binding upon the Federal Republic today as it was at the time it was made. A value-judgment of so final a nature may not be revoked. It should therefore be viewed as an unequivocal expression of *opinio juris*, with all the consequences flowing therefrom. Indeed, if it may be claimed that the *opinio juris* of certain other States is in doubt or not fully proven, this is certainly not the case of the Federal Republic. This is a decisive point in the present cases.[131]

The last two sentences quoted suggest that Judge Lachs was not convinced that the equidistance rule in the Geneva Convention had become a matter of general customary law, despite his reference to that Convention as having 'attained the identifiable status of a general law'.[132] Could Germany become bound, otherwise than by acquiescence or estoppel, by a purported rule which had not yet attained full customary-law status?

This brings out an aspect of estoppel which has not been specifically noted in the judicial treatment of it at the international level. One of its essential features may apparently be that the fact which is in issue must be one peculiarly in the knowledge of the person or the State against which estoppel is relied on.[133] In the cases before the International Court now being reviewed, this fact has usually been the subjective attitude, in particular the consent, of the respondent State—than which nothing could be more peculiarly or exclusively within the knowledge of that State. If however the question of fact which it is sought to resolve by estoppel is one which the applicant State could perfectly well resolve by itself, then the

---

[130] *ICJ Reports*, 1969, p. 233.

[131] Ibid., pp. 235–6.

[132] Ibid., p. 232.

[133] Cf. the duty, which Fitzmaurice suggested should be universal in international relations, to act *uberrimae fidei*, a duty which, as he conceded, is applicable in English law only 'when one of the parties in order to assess the risk or other material factors involved, is obliged to rely on information supplied by the other party and lying peculiarly, or exclusively within that party's knowledge': Fitzmaurice, this *Year Book*, 35 (1959), p. 210; *Collected Edition*, II, p. 614. See also *Recueil des cours*, 92 (1957–II), pp. 54–5.

respondent State may retort *'solvitur ambulando'*, and repudiate any estoppel.[134]

In short, the problem whether estoppel can relate to a question of law may be resolved by the wider rule that the matter to which the estoppel relates must be one where the applicant State had to, and did, rely on the respondent State.[135] If the facts are known to both States, each can form its own assessment of the legal situation which results from them, and the assertion by one of them that the legal situation is thus and thus—which means no more than that it is the *opinion* of that State that such is the legal situation—cannot be relied on to support an estoppel to that effect.

In the case brought by Nicaragua against the United States the argument of estoppel as applicable to a statement of opinion as to the law was also hinted at as against the United States. The Court was dealing with the question of the effect of Article 36, paragraph 5, of the Statute, and in particular the question whether it operated to validate the pre-war Optional Clause declaration of Nicaragua. The cases of the *Aerial Incident of 27 July 1955*, in one of which the United States had been applicant, were referred to in argument. The Court in the later case explained why its judgment in the *Aerial Incident* case had related to a different point, so that it did not consider that that decision 'provides any pointer to precise conclusions on the limited point now in issue'. It immediately added, however:

> The most that could be pointed out on the basis of the discussions surrounding the *Aerial Incident* case is that, at that time, the United States took a particularly broad view of the separability of an Optional-Clause declaration and its institutional foundation by contending that an Optional-Clause declaration (of a binding character) could have outlived by many years the court to which it related. But the present case also involves a problem of separability, since the question to be decided is the extent to which an Optional-Clause declaration (without binding force) can be separated from the institutional foundation which it ought originally to have possessed, so as to be grafted onto a new institutional foundation.[136]

It is by no means apparent what conceivable weight in the discussion could be attached to the fact that the United States, as litigant in a different case many years previously, had taken a 'particularly broad view' on a matter bearing some tenuous relationship with that under discussion. The passage quoted is no more than a debating point and, it is to be hoped, an isolated *lapsus curiae*.

---

[134] Cf. the application by Tunisia for the revision of the 1962 judgment in the *Continental Shelf (Tunisia/Libya)* case, where the Court rejected the 'new fact' relied on by Tunisia—the exact co-ordinates of a particular Libyan concession in the area—and took into account 'whether the circumstances were such that means were available to Tunisia to ascertain the details of the co-ordinates of the concession from other sources; and indeed whether it was in Tunisia's own interests to do so' (*ICJ Reports*, 1985, p. 205, para. 23). The Court's discussion of what was required by 'normal diligence', in paragraph 27 of its 1985 judgment, could, it is suggested, be transposed to a situation where estoppel was asserted.

[135] In this sense Martin, *L'Estoppel en droit international public* (1979), pp. 293, 322–3.

[136] *ICJ Reports*, 1984, pp. 405–6, para. 29.

(d) *Action by the applicant State in reliance on the statement to its detriment*

In the *Temple of Preah Vihear* case, one of the grounds on which Judge Sir Percy Spender dissented was that he considered that France did not rely upon any conduct of Thailand in relation to the frontier map, but on the accuracy of the surveys—made by French officers—on which the map was based. In his view, France 'had not the slightest interest in how Siam reacted to [the map]; there was no reaction she would have expected'.[137] For him, therefore, this essential element of an estoppel was lacking.

The requirement was analysed in the *Barcelona Traction* case, in the 1964 judgment on the preliminary objections, where the Court was strict in requiring that the applicant State should somehow be in a worse position than if it had not acted in reliance on the representations allegedly made by the other State. Spain claimed to be worse off as a result of having refrained from objecting to the discontinuance of the earlier proceedings on the faith of the representation, allegedly made by Belgium, that no further proceedings would be brought.

Without doubt, the Respondent is worse off now than if the present proceedings had not been brought. But that obviously is not the point, and it has never been clear why, had it known that these proceedings would be brought if the negotiations failed, the Respondent would not have agreed to the discontinuance of the earlier proceedings in order to facilitate the negotiations (the professed object); since it must not be overlooked that if the Respondent had not so agreed, the previous proceedings would simply have continued, whereas negotiations offered a possibility of finally settling the whole dispute. Given that without the Respondent's consent to the discontinuance of the original proceedings, these would have continued, what has to be considered now is not the present position of the Respondent, as compared with what it would have been if the current proceedings had never been brought, but what its position is in the current proceedings, as compared with what it would have been in the event of a continuation of the old ones.[138]

This aspect was also a major flaw in any assertion of an estoppel in the *North Sea Continental Shelf* cases; whatever contradictory indications the Federal Republic might have given of its attitude to the 1958 Geneva Convention, there was no evidence of Denmark and the Netherlands having relied on such indications to their detriment.[139]

The same aspect of estoppel may have been present to the mind of the Court in the *Continental Shelf (Tunisia/Libya)* case in 1962 when it took care to make clear that it was not making a finding of estoppel[140] when it attached decisive importance to the '26° line' dividing the petroleum con-

---

[137] *ICJ Reports*, 1962, p. 145.
[138] *ICJ Reports*, 1964, pp. 24–5.
[139] *ICJ Reports*, 1969, p. 26, para. 30, *in fine*.
[140] *ICJ Reports*, 1982, p. 84, para. 118.

cessions granted by the two parties.[141] While the concessions actually granted by each party produced a 'de facto line dividing the concession areas which were the subject of active claims',[142] there was no evidence at all that Libya, the second in time to grant a concession extending to the '26° line', had done so because the Tunisian concession ran up to that line, let alone that it had understood Tunisia to be implying that that was the maximum area claimed.

In the *Temple* case the Court referred to Thailand as having 'for fifty years, enjoyed such benefits as the Treaty of 1904 conferred on her, if only the benefit of a stable frontier'.[143] It is submitted that there is here some departure from the requirements of an estoppel, at least on a strict interpretation of those requirements. The benefit to Thailand is not material; what is required is a change in the relative positions of the parties, as on a see-saw, whereby the one profits from the other's detriment. France, and Cambodia, equally with Thailand enjoyed the benefit of the 1904 treaty. Furthermore, the benefit which would be relevant is not the benefit *of the treaty*, which Thailand would have had in any event, but the separate benefit *of the representation* that Thailand accepted the map.[144]

(4) *Relationship between estoppel, preclusion and acquiescence*

The cases examined support the view expressed by the Chamber in the *Gulf of Maine* case that

acquiescence is equivalent to tacit recognition manifested by unilateral conduct which the other party may interpret as consent, while estoppel is linked to the idea of preclusion.[145]

The close relationship between the two is accentuated in such cases by the circumstance that, even where estoppel was pleaded or discussed, what was sought to be established was an acceptance or consent of the respondent State. Estoppel is however not in principle limited in this way: the fact which the respondent State is to be precluded from denying can be any fact within its actual or presumed knowledge, and does not have to be a fact as to its own state of mind. There is here a radical difference, at the theoretical level, between estoppel and acquiescence, one, however, which has not manifested itself in practice during the period under review.

The other essential distinction is that pointed out by Fitzmaurice, and quoted at the beginning of this section, namely that acquiescence presumes a consent to have existed, on the basis of the factual circumstances, but the

---

[141] As emerged during the proceedings on the subsequent application for revision and interpretation, the Court was given, and acted upon, a rather over-simplified picture of the position; but the discrepancies later highlighted do not affect the present discussion.

[142] *ICJ Reports*, 1982, p. 84, para. 117.

[143] *ICJ Reports*, 1962, p. 32.

[144] Cf. the Court's analysis of the 'change of position' requirement in the *Barcelona Traction* case (p. 44, above).

[145] *ICJ Reports*, 1984, p. 305, para. 130.

presumption may be overturned by proof of the contrary;[146] whereas estoppel recognizes the possibility that the consent (or other fact) was non-existent—indeed virtually takes it for granted that that was so—but excludes any proof which would defeat the estoppel.

In the *Temple* case, as we have seen, the Court in effect found both an initial acquiescence and a subsequent estoppel.[147] The *King of Spain* case is more difficult to categorize: the Court in the judgment did not use any of the terms estoppel, preclusion or acquiescence. Judge *ad hoc* Urrutia Holguin apparently classifies the Court's finding as one of acquiescence,[148] and observes also that 'the theory of estoppel cannot be invoked against Nicaragua'.[149] The Court refers to 'the fact that the designation of the King of Spain as arbitrator *was freely agreed to* by Nicaragua . . . ',[150] which is a finding of acquiescence; but the same paragraph concludes that 'it is no longer open to Nicaragua to rely on' its procedural objections, which is terminology more appropriate to preclusion. Similarly, with regard to the question of the validity of the award, the Court found that 'Nicaragua, by express declaration and conduct, recognized the Award as valid', but continues 'and it is no longer open to Nicaragua to go back upon that recognition'.[151] Bearing in mind that the Court does not discuss any reliance by Honduras on Nicaragua's conduct resulting in a change of position, it was appropriate to regard the case as one of acquiescence.

The time element is likely to be more material in cases of acquiescence than in cases of estoppel. If there has been reliance on a statement leading to a change of the relative position of the parties, the time it has taken for this to occur is not relevant; but it may not be easy to say how many years of silence justify a conclusion of acquiescence.

The curious aspect of the *King of Spain* case is that although more than fifty years elapsed between the arbitral award being made by the King and the matter being brought to the International Court, the validity of the King's designation was in fact challenged less than six years after the award. The time taken before proceedings were taken to settle the dispute seems to

---

[146] Thus in the *Temple* case, Sir Percy Spender in his dissenting opinion regarded the conduct of Siam in relation to the frontier map as no more than evidence of a possible admission, and continued: 'Were any such admission the only evidence in this case it could well be conclusive. But it is not the only evidence. There is a great deal more. The task of the Court is to ascertain the true facts. It may in doing so be influenced by an admission established by the conduct of Siam. It cannot however be controlled by it if other evidence negatives or modifies or is inconsistent with the admission which a recognition may establish. The recognition is not conclusive' (*ICJ Reports*, 1962, p. 131). He made it clear that if the elements of an estoppel had been present, the recognition would have been conclusive: but in his view they were not.

[147] Conceptually this is an inconsistency, but the structure of the judgment is the not uncommon one of 'belt and braces', whereby arguments are cumulated in order to attract the strongest possible majority.

[148] *ICJ Reports*, 1960, p. 228, heading (*b*).

[149] Ibid., p. 236.

[150] Ibid., p. 209.

[151] Ibid., p. 213.

have carried some weight in the Court's thinking: as A.L.W. Munkman points out,

it might be thought that excessive stress was laid on a failure to protest against an award for five and a half years—a relatively short period—and a considerable delay in instituting proceedings for settling the dispute.[152]

It may be, however, that the five and a half years amount to a 'relatively short period' only in comparison with the subsequent 45 years of inaction; if the five and a half years were, in the circumstances, enough to support a finding of acquiescence, subsequent delays are irrelevant.

(5) *Estoppel in relation to treaty commitments*

When the question which it is hoped to resolve by appeal to the concepts of acquiescence or estoppel is one of treaty interpretation, application of these concepts overlaps with the established rule of recourse to the subsequent practice of the parties as a means for interpretation of the treaty. As we have seen, this occurred in the *King of Spain* case, in connection with the definition of the date from which the ten-year period of validity of the treaty should run..

A major complicating factor in the *Temple* case was the relationship between the map, to which Thailand was bound by either acquiescence or preclusion, and the 1904 treaty, which provided for the frontier in the disputed area to follow the watershed, which the line on the map, it was generally recognized, did not. Could the treaty between the parties be varied by a deemed consent derived from application of the principle of preclusion? The Court's answer to this was that the acceptance of the map by the parties 'caused the map to enter the treaty settlement and to become an integral part of it'.[153] The obvious difficulty with this view was that the map contradicted the treaty; for this reason, it was not possible to appeal, as in the *King of Spain* case, to the rule as to interpretation of a treaty by subsequent practice of the parties. However, in the Court's view:

It cannot be said that this process involved a departure from, and even a violation of, the terms of the Treaty of 1904, wherever the map line diverged from the line of the watershed for, as the Court sees the matter, the map (whether in all respects accurate by reference to the true watershed line or not) was accepted by the Parties in 1908 and thereafter as constituting the result of the interpretation given by the two Governments to the delimitation which the Treaty itself required. In other words, the Parties at that time adopted an interpretation of the treaty settlement which caused the map line, in so far as it may have departed from the line of the watershed, to prevail over the relevant clause of the treaty.[154]

---

[152] 'Adjudication and Adjustment — International Judicial Decision and the Settlement of Territorial and Boundary Disputes', this *Year Book*, 46 (1972–3), p. 96.

[153] *ICJ Reports*, 1962, p. 33.

[154] Ibid., pp. 33–4.

The point is explained perhaps more clearly by Judge Sir Gerald Fitz-maurice:

. . . I cannot accept the plea so eloquently urged on behalf of Thailand that any adherence to the Annex I line would have involved a departure from a solemn treaty obligation. This surely begs the question; for as the Judgment says, it is always open to governments, in their bilateral relations, to agree on a departure of this kind, provided they do so knowingly, or (as I think was Thailand's case here) in circumstances in which they must be held to have accepted, and as it were dis-counted in advance, the risks or consequences of lack, or possible lack, of know-ledge. In the present case, the conduct of each Party, over what was an important matter of common concern to both, was, in my opinion, evidence of, or amounted to, a mutual agreement to accept a certain line as the frontier line. What seems to me therefore really to have occurred was not in the legal sense a departure from the treaty provision concerned, but the mutual acceptance of a certain result as being its actual outcome, irrespective of the precise conformity of that outcome with the treaty criterion.[155]

This and some further arguments used by the Court pertain to the sub-ject of treaty interpretation, and will, as such, be discussed in a later article. For present purposes, dealing with acquiescence and preclusion, the fol-lowing may be said.

One interpretation of the silence of Siam is to read it as saying, on the basis that the treaty provided that the frontier was to follow the watershed, two things: (1) the line on the map follows the watershed; (2) I accept the map line as the treaty frontier. An alternative interpretation is to substitute the following: (1) the line on the map does not follow the watershed; (2) but since the line is otherwise an appropriate line, I accept the map line as the treaty frontier. The third interpretation is that of the Court: I accept the map line, whether or not it follows the watershed, as the treaty frontier.

The difficulty with the first interpretation is that (1) is an incorrect rep-resentation, not of Siam's attitude, but of geographical fact, the truth or otherwise of which was perfectly ascertainable by Cambodia, so that it did not need to rely on the representation by Siam. The second interpretation is perfectly workable; but it does not correspond to the historical facts, since the discrepancy between the map line and the watershed line was apparently not discovered until a survey in 1934–5. The problem with the third interpretation is: how could Cambodia—or the Court—tell that it was this third interpretation that Siam was conveying by its conduct, since outwardly the three would be indistinguishable?

It was in fact argued by Thailand that from 1908 to 1935 it believed that the map line and the watershed line coincided, and therefore that if it accepted the map line, it did so only in that belief. The Court rejected this argument on the facts, since the claim was inconsistent with other claims by Thailand.[156] Had these other claims not been made, however, and had the

[155] Ibid., p. 56.
[156] Ibid., p. 33.

Court considered that Thailand was under a misapprehension of this nature, the problem referred to above would have required to be solved.

Thailand also contended that an error was committed, an error of which the Siamese authorities were unaware at the time they accepted the map. The Court rejected this contention also:

> It is an established rule of law that the plea of error cannot be allowed as an element violating consent if the party advancing it contributed by its own conduct to the error, or could have avoided it, or if the circumstances were such as to put the party on notice of a possible error.[157]

The Court found as a fact that on the face of the map, 'to anyone who considered that the line of the watershed at Preah Vihear ought to follow the line of the escarpment' (which the map line did not), there was everything to put such a person upon enquiry.[158]

There is here a slight, but interesting, extension of the rules as to error in this connection. It is reasonable to expect that a State, before taking the step of giving its consent to some act or instrument, will scrutinize it properly, and it is therefore reasonable that if the circumstances are such as to put the State on notice of a possible error, it is bound to investigate, or lose the opportunity of invoking the error. In sum, this rule is itself a form of presumed acquiescence or preclusion. But where there is in fact no meditated act of acceptance, which ought to have been preceded by such enquiry, but a deemed acceptance attributed to the State on account of silence, it becomes somewhat artificial to pile preclusion on preclusion, as it were, and exclude a plea of error.

3. *The Role of Equity in International Law*

During the period under review there has been a striking increase in references to equity in the work of the Court—not only in the pleadings of the parties, but in the judgments themselves; so much so that one observer has felt able to declare that 'After fifty years of hesitation the World Court has clearly accepted equity as an important part of the law that it is authorized to apply'.[159] Concepts of equity have certainly had a very extensive influence in one particular domain—that of the delimitation of maritime areas; but it is probably premature to see in the decisions of the Court even in that specific field the application of any consistent and mature theory of equity. In matters unconnected with maritime delimitation, equity has been referred to and applied sporadically, but in ways which paradoxically are easier to reconcile with classical concepts of equity than the specialized use of it in disputes over maritime areas.

It had been the writer's intention, when planning this cycle of articles, to

[157] Ibid., p. 26.
[158] Ibid.
[159] Sohn, 'The Role of Equity in the Jurisprudence of the International Court of Justice', *Mélanges Georges Perrin* (1984), p. 311.

include in the first of the series an extended treatment of the concept of equity as it has appeared and taken shape in the decisions of the Court during the period under review. It became apparent, however, on fuller study of the question, that such a treatment would necessarily involve concentration on the particular field of law in which equitable considerations have played an extremely prominent part—the law of maritime delimitation—and would in addition need to be very long. The writer therefore came to the conclusion that it would make for a better balanced structure of the series of articles to reserve the examination of equity in this specialized context for a later chapter. The present section will therefore be confined to a few observations outlining some of the issues arising on this topic, and mention of some instances of equity having been invoked outside the field of delimitation of maritime territories.

(1) *Equity and* ex aequo et bono

If there is one thing on which the numerous scholars who have written on the subject agree, and one observation which the Court has made over and over again, with—it would seem—the unanimous support of its Members, however much they may disagree on other aspects of equity, it is that a decision in application of equity is not the same thing as a decision *ex aequo et bono*, contemplated by Article 38, paragraph 2, of the Statute as possible with the agreement of the parties.[160] Whether the distinction between the two is in practice as clear as this repeated *dictum* would suggest is another matter, and was doubted as early, in the context of boundary delimitation, as 1972.[161] In 1977, E. Lauterpacht considered that

> It must be appreciated that whether we are discussing a decision *ex aequo et bono* (in traditional terms, a decision completely outside the law) or whether we are considering equity in the new sense of 'equity within the law', we are talking about a situation in which the court is being asked to apply a subjective or discretionary element. The court is not applying the law; it is creating the law for the parties.[162]

For the Court, however, the distinction is vital, in view of the requirement in Article 38, paragraph 2, of the Statute that a decision of this type be taken only with the agreement of the parties.

Judge Sir Robert Jennings, in an extra-judicial capacity, has taken an opposite view to that of Lauterpacht, and emphasized the reality and importance of the distinction between equity and *ex aequo et bono*. His submission is that

there is indeed a difference of great importance between the two kinds of equity,

---

[160] *ICJ Reports*, 1969, p. 21, para. 17; p. 48, para. 88; 1982, p. 60, para. 71; 1984, p. 278, para. 59; 1985, p. 39, para. 45; 1986, p. 567, paras. 27–8; p. 633, para. 149.

[161] See Munkman, 'Adjudication and Adjustment—International Judicial Decision and the Settlement of Territorial and Boundary Disputes', this *Year Book*, 46 (1972–3), p. 88.

[162] 'Equity, Evasion, Equivocation and Evolution in International Law', *Proceedings of the American branch of the ILA*, 1977–8, p. 45. Judge Koretsky was of the same view in 1969: *ICJ Reports*, 1969, p. 166. Cf. also Weil, *Perspectives du droit de la délimitation maritime* (1988), pp. 180–1.

which may be expressed shortly in the following way. A decision *ex aequo et bono* could well be made without the need of specifically legal training or skill; indeed may perhaps be made better by one with a different skill. On the other hand, a decision according to equity as part of the law should mean the application to the case of principles and rules of equity for the proper identification of which a legal training is essential. The appreciation and application of equity so conceived is essentially juridical. And this is surely the kind of decision that parties seek, when they have not agreed to ask for a decision *ex aequo et bono*, and when they seek instead a decision according to law, albeit one that is also in accordance with the requirements of equity.[163]

The distinction here made is an interesting one, to which we shall return in a later article; but the essential point here is that both Sir Robert Jennings individually and the Court collectively regard *ex aequo et bono* as an extra-judicial activity, and equity as part of the law. A problem to be studied is therefore whether equity, while part of the law, is somehow different from the rest of law: whether equitable principles, while contained in the body of legal principles, yet have a special character which sets them off from other principles in that wider category.

(2) *Equity as part of the law*

The Court's first general enunciation of the position of equity in international law was made in the *North Sea Continental Shelf* cases, in a celebrated passage[164] which, however, one could have wished more lucidly expressed:

The Court comes next to the rule of equity. The legal basis of that rule in the particular case of the delimitation of the continental shelf as between adjoining States has already been stated.

This is a reference to the finding earlier in the judgment that one of the 'basic legal notions' which 'have from the beginning reflected the *opinio juris* in the matter of delimitation' was that agreement on delimitation 'must be arrived at in accordance with equitable principles'.[165]

It must however be noted that the rule rests also on a broader basis. Whatever the legal reasoning of a court of justice, its decisions must by definition be just, and therefore in that sense equitable.

This appears to exclude the possibility of an international tribunal having to apply a rule in circumstances in which its results were unjust or 'inequitable'; but it may mean no more than that a judicial decision is deemed, *ex definitione*, to be a just decision.

Nevertheless, when mention is made of a court dispensing justice or declaring the law, what is meant is that the decision finds its objective justification in

---

[163] 'Equity and Equitable Principles', *Schweizerisches Jahrbuch für internationales Recht*, 42 (1986), p. 30.
[164] *ICJ Reports*, 1969, p. 48, para. 88.
[165] Ibid., p. 46, para. 85.

considerations lying not outside but within the rules, and in this field it is precisely a rule of law that calls for the application of equitable principles.

The concept seems to be that there is a body of ideas which may be designated 'equitable principles', which can, in some legal circumstances but not in all, be made use of because there is a rule of law which authorizes their use. According to the literal meaning of the text, the body of ideas is not necessarily itself part of the corpus of law: the 'considerations lying . . . within the rules' are, apparently, not what is invoked (equitable principles) but the invoking mechanism (a rule of law). Thus a rule of international law might call for a matter to be decided by reference to equitable principles, just as a rule of international law might call for a matter to be decided by reference to a system of national law.[166]

> There is consequently no question in this case of any decision *ex aequo et bono*, such as would only be possible under the conditions prescribed by Article 38, paragraph 2, of the Court's Statute.

The reference to *ex aequo et bono* emphasizes *a contrario* that the Court is, in applying equitable principles, exercising its normal powers. It also suggests, however, that there is, at least, some kinship between the application of equitable principles and *ex aequo et bono*, even though while equitable principles are part of the law and legitimate, *ex aequo et bono* was born on the wrong side of the blanket.

The twofold basis referred to by the Court for the application of equitable principles in the *North Sea Continental Shelf* cases is to be noted, as it is at the root of some, at least, of the confusion which has subsequently surrounded the question. According to the Court, a customary law rule had arisen from State practice whereby the continental shelf was to be delimited by agreement in accordance with equitable principles. There was no *a priori* reason why the principles applied for the delimitation should have had to have anything legal about them; a customary rule could have arisen whereby delimitation was to be effected according to geological principles (natural prolongation?) or geometrical principles (equidistance?). In the context of, for example, the Truman Proclamation—the *fons et origo* of the expression—'equitable principles' probably meant no more than 'on a fair-shares basis'.[167]

The Court could have left it at that: once it had found that there was a customary-law rule of specified content, it had no need to justify the content of the rule in any way. However it went on to offer a 'broader basis' for the rule, first by referring to the duty of a Court to give decisions which are just 'and therefore in that sense equitable'; but the role of the Court was not in question; it was for the parties to arrive at an agreement 'in accordance

---

[166] Judge Morelli, though his approach is a different one, expresses the point as the *'renvoi* to equity by the legal rule': ibid., p. 213.

[167] Judge Koretsky thought that the reference in the Truman Proclamation 'means nothing more than calling upon neighbouring States to conclude agreements': ibid., p. 166.

with equitable principles', and while the Court regarded itself as entitled to give some guidelines,[168] it was not itself deciding what the result—which should be equitable—should be. The Court then reverted to the 'rule of law that calls for the application of equitable principles'—by the parties, not by the Court—, namely the existence of a custom to that effect.

Up to this point it should have been clear that the 'equitable principles' were not part of the *depositum juris* being applied by the Court; they were in a separate box, so to speak, which the Court was authorizing or directing the parties to open, and to employ its contents so as to agree their delimitation. However, when giving 'some degree of indication as to the possible ways in which [equity] might be applied in the present case',[169] the Court was clearly influenced by ideas of *legal* equity, not merely layman's equity—general fairness: in particular some of its observations[170] suggested the role of equity as corrective of injustice resulting from the application of rigid rules—eminently a jurisprudential concept.

This aspect, as well as the distinction between 'equitable principles' and legal rules, was underlined in the separate opinion of Judge Ammoun, who linked for this purpose international law with Roman law:

Thus it is necessary to make a distinction between the principle of equity in the wide sense of the word, which manifests itself, in the phrase of Papinian, *praeter legem*, as a subsidiary source of international law in order to remedy its insufficiencies and fill in its logical lacunae; and the settlement according to independent equity, *ex aequo et bono*, amounting to an extra-judicial activity, in the expression of the same jurisconsult, *contra legem*, whose role is, with the agreement of the parties, to remedy the social inadequacies of the law.[171]

However, Judge Ammoun considered that on this point he was differing from the judgment which, in his view, was envisaging 'abstract equity'.[172]

The possibility of the Court deciding in equity was raised, in a very different context, in the *Barcelona Traction* case; the circumstances of that case will be examined elsewhere.[173] What may be noted for present purposes is that the Court, while making no pronouncement of principle on the role of equity, and rejecting Belgium's claim based on equity, did apparently recognize that in certain circumstances a right of diplomatic protection might be based on 'considerations of equity',[174] which therefore (presumably) would form part of international law.

In the *Fisheries Jurisdiction* cases, the Court found the existence of an obligation on the parties to negotiate to bring about 'an equitable apportionment of the fishing reserves' in the disputed area, and added:

---

[168] Ibid., p. 50, para. 92.
[169] Ibid.
[170] Ibid., p. 49, para. 89; p. 49, para. 91.
[171] Ibid., p. 139, para. 37.
[172] Ibid.
[173] Below, p. 59.
[174] *ICJ Reports*, 1970, p. 48, para. 92.

it is not a matter of finding simply an equitable solution, but an equitable solution derived from the applicable law.[175]

Once again the Court held that international law directed the parties to a box marked 'equity', the contents of which might or might not themselves form part of the law;[176] and it was sufficient that the solution *derived from* the applicable law.

In the case concerning the *Continental Shelf (Tunisia/Libyan Arab Jamahiriya)*, the Court was not merely asked, as in the *North Sea* cases, to indicate the relevant principles and rules of international law, but also to 'clarify the practical method for their application'; in fact, it virtually drew the parties' line for them. Furthermore, it was expressly directed in the Special Agreement to 'take its decision according to equitable principles'.[177]

After discussing the 'equitable principles' which it considered it was bound to apply, the Court, made the following general statement of its conception of equity:

Equity as a legal concept is a direct emanation of the idea of justice. The Court whose task is by definition to administer justice is bound to apply it. In the course of the history of legal systems the term 'equity' had been used to define various legal concepts. It was often contrasted with the rigid rules of positive law, the severity of which had to be mitigated in order to do justice. In general, this contrast has no parallel in the development of international law; the legal concept of equity is a general principle directly applicable as law. Moreover, when applying positive international law, a court may choose among several possible interpretations of the law the one which appears, in the light of the circumstances of the case, to be closest to the requirements of justice. Application of equitable principles is to be distinguished from a decision *ex aequo et bono*. The Court can take such a decision only on condition that the Parties agree (Art. 38, para. 2, of the Statute), and the Court is then freed from the strict application of legal rules in order to bring about an appropriate settlement. The task of the Court in the present case is quite different: it is bound to apply equitable principles as part of international law, and to balance up the various considerations which it regards as relevant in order to produce an equitable result. While it is clear that no rigid rules exist as to the exact weight to be attached to each element in the case, this is very far from being an exercise of discretion or conciliation; nor is it an operation of distributive justice.[178]

It is clear from this passage that the 'equity' or 'equitable principles' which have to be applied to achieve a delimitation are no longer imported from outside the law, by way of the operation of *renvoi*; they are part of the equity within the law itself. It is possible that the increased role which the

---

[175] *ICJ Reports*, 1974, p. 33, para. 78; p. 202, para. 69. Judge de Castro considered that it was within the powers of the Court itself to 'decide according to principles of equity' and indicate the solution, but that to do so would not be 'a wise course': p. 103.

[176] E. Lauterpacht, loc. cit. above (n. 162), p. 4, criticizes the Court for failing to indicate why, in terms of applicable law, it was necessary to 'reach an equitable solution'. The answer probably lies in the feeling that the solution to a dispute must *ex definitione* be equitable – cf. the *North Sea dictum* as to the decision of a court of justice.

[177] *ICJ Reports*, 1982, p. 23 (Libyan translation of the Special Agreement).

[178] Ibid., p. 60, para. 71.

Court was requested to play in the delimitation has something to do with this. There is in the first place the magnetic attraction of the corpus of equity (of ill-defined content) contained within international law in matters other than maritime delimitation. What is more, it is no longer a matter of parties agreeing on what they think is fair, in the light of suggestions from the Court, but of the Court applying equitable principles. Admittedly, it was directed to do so by the Special Agreement; but there is no hint in the judgment that this was regarded as a direction to apply some sort of *lex specialis* which would otherwise have been outside its reach.

There is some confirmation of this movement from laymen's equity to lawyer's equity to be found in the judgment in the case of the *Continental Shelf (Libyan Arab Jamahiriya/Malta)*. The Court there reproduces 'a much-quoted *dictum*' from the *North Sea* cases:

In fact, there is no legal limit to the considerations which States may take account of for the purpose of making sure that they apply equitable procedures, and more often than not it is the balancing-up of such considerations that will produce this result rather than reliance on one to the exclusion of all others. The problem of the relative weight to be accorded to different considerations naturally varies with the circumstances of the case.[179]

To which it adds the following gloss:

Yet although there may be no legal limit to the considerations which States may take account of, this can hardly be true for a court applying equitable procedures. For a court, although there is assuredly no closed list of considerations, it is evident that only those that are pertinent to the institution of the continental shelf as it has developed within the law, and to the application of equitable principles to its delimitation, will qualify for inclusion. Otherwise, the legal concept of continental shelf could itself be fundamentally changed by the introduction of considerations strange to its nature.[180]

In short, States may determine their delimitation on a basis of *ex aequo et bono*, but the Court, even when applying equitable principles, must confine itself to what is within the body of law.

With the judgment of the Chamber formed to deal with the *Frontier Dispute*, the presence of equity *within* the body of international law became the subject of explicit judicial declaration:

It is clear that the Chamber cannot decide *ex aequo et bono* in this case. Since the Parties have not entrusted it with the task of carrying out an adjustment of their respective interests, it must also dismiss any possibility of resorting to equity *contra legem*. Nor will the Chamber apply equity *praeter legem*. On the other hand, it will have regard to equity *infra legem*, that is, that form of equity which constitutes a method of interpretation of the law in force, and is one of its attributes.[181]

The Chamber quotes the sentence from the *Fisheries Jurisdiction* judgments

[179] *ICJ Reports*, 1969, p. 50, para. 93.
[180] *ICJ Reports*, 1985, p. 40, para. 48.
[181] *ICJ Reports*, 1986, pp. 567–8, para. 28.

referring to the need to find 'an equitable solution derived from the applicable law'. What that solution was will be noted elsewhere.

(3) *Equity as corrective or constitutive of law*

If equitable principles are part of the corpus of law, it may be asked what distinguishes them from other rules of law—what is the mark of an equitable rule as distinct from a legal rule? As the Court observed in 1969, the decisions of a Court, based on law, are to be regarded as just, and in that sense equitable.

One possible answer is that equitable rules do not and cannot operate independently, to create rights and obligations; they are a moderating or correcting mechanism in relation to 'strict' rules of law. This is an interpretation of equity which has a respectable ancestry, back to the Ethics of Aristotle—the idea of equity as 'a correction of law where it is defective owing to its universality'.[182] It is the sense of equity *praeter legem* referred to by Judge Ammoun, in the passage quoted above, and by the *Frontier Dispute* Chamber. It is also deeply rooted in English law, as Sir Gerald Fitzmaurice recalled in his separate opinion in the *Barcelona Traction* case[183] where he quoted the definition of equity given in Snell.[184] Sir Robert Jennings, in the article quoted, suggests that one of the lessons which international law stands to learn from the experience of English law is 'that the rules of equity in a developed form are seen as additional to, and complementing rules of law, and thus refining it in its application to particular cases or for particular new purposes'.[185]

Chronologically, the next case in which equity was considered was the *Barcelona Traction, Light and Power Co.* case in 1970; but since this raises somewhat different aspects of equity, consideration of it will be deferred for the moment.

When the 1982 judgment in the *Tunisia/Libya* case was given, only three Members of the 1969 Court, which had given the *North Sea* judgment, were still sitting (Judges Forster, Gros and Lachs). One of them, Judge Gros, attached a dissenting opinion in which he complained that 'the way the Court set about the search for an equitable delimitation' was 'contrary to the concept of the role of equity in the delimitation of the continental shelf adopted by the Court in its 1969 Judgment'.[186] For Judge Gros, 'A court of justice only has recourse to equitable principles if faced with a legal situation such that the result obtained by applying the rules of law on the delimitation . . . appears inequitable on account of . . . geographical features'.[187] He continues:

A court of justice does not modify a delimitation because it finds subjectively

---

[182] 'ἐπανόρθωμα νόμου, ἧ ἐλλείπει διὰ τὸ καθόλου'.
[183] *ICJ Reports*, 1970, p. 85, para. 36.
[184] *Snell's Principles of Equity* (26th edn. by Megarry and Baker, 1966), pp. 5–6.
[185] Loc. cit. above (n. 163), p. 28.
[186] *ICJ Reports*, 1982, p. 148, para. 9.
[187] Ibid., p. 149, para. 13.

that it is less advantageous to one party than to the other, for this would be to embark upon the vain task of equalizing the facts of nature; it notes, having taken into consideration all the factors contemplated by the applicable law, that some of those factors, which are relevant, have disproportionate or inordinate effects which, perhaps, may generate inequity—which remains to be demonstrated. Only then, after this has been shown to be the case, comes the problem of balancing the equities as between the two Parties . . . and their application to the construction of the delimitation line.[188]

Somewhat further on in his opinion, Judge Gros declares: 'Equity is not a sort of independent and subjective vision that takes the place of law'.[189]

The passage in the judgment on which his dissent presumably focused was the statement that the Court did not consider that it was required

as a first step, to examine the effects of a delimitation by the equidistance method, and to reject that method in favour of some other only if it considers the results of an equidistance line to be inequitable.[190]

In other words, for Judge Gros, the function of equity, as contemplated in the 1969 judgment, was essentially corrective rather than constitutive; it was necessary to apply equitable considerations where the results to which the legal rules pointed seemed to be lacking in fairness.[191] This conception of the operation of equity in the international field was however flatly contradicted by Judge Jiménez de Aréchaga in the *Tunisia/Libya* case. He referred to the contention

that equity is to be viewed as a discretionary or moderating influence superadded to the rigour of formulated law; that it consists of the correction of a general rule when that rule, by reason of its generality, works hardship in a concrete case and produces results which are felt to be unfair,[192]

and commented:

There is no denying that this is a current conception of equity, which may be a correct one in the municipal law field. However, it is not the conception of equity applicable to continental shelf delimitation, as proclaimed by the Court in 1969 and developed by the [Anglo-French] arbitral tribunal in 1977.[193]

Judge Jiménez de Aréchaga's own view of the role of equity, at least as regards maritime delimitation, was as follows:

To resort to equity means, in effect, to appreciate and balance the relevant circumstances of the case, so as to render justice, not through the rigid application of

---

[188] Ibid., p. 150, para. 13.
[189] Ibid., p. 153, para. 19.
[190] Ibid., p. 79, para. 110.
[191] This was also the view of Ch. De Visscher, writing in 1972 (*De l'équité dans le règlement arbitral ou judiciaire des litiges de droit international public*, p. 5): 'La fonction de l'équité apparaît tantôt comme corrective, tantôt comme supplétive de la règle du droit.'
[192] *ICJ Reports*, 1982, p. 105, para. 19.
[193] Ibid., para. 20. The same view is firmly stated in Jiménez de Aréchaga's paper on 'The Conception of Equity in Maritime Delimitation', *International Law at the Time of its Codification* (Milan, 1987), vol. 2, p. 238.

general rules and principles and of formal legal concepts, but through an adaptation and adjustment of such principles, rules and concepts to the facts, realities and circumstances of each case. As was well stated by the 1977 Court of Arbitration, equity is 'to be looked for in the particular circumstances of the present case' . . . In other words, the judicial application of equitable principles means that a court should render justice in the concrete case, by means of a decision shaped by and adjusted to the relevant 'factual matrix' of that case. Equity is here nothing other than taking into account of a complex of historical and geographical circumstances the consideration of which does not diminish justice but, on the contrary, enriches it.[194]

The judgment of the Chamber formed to deal with the *Gulf of Maine* case does not advance the present discussion: it concentrated strictly on the law of maritime delimitation, and did not comment in any general way on the role of equity in the law. It defined what it regarded as the 'fundamental norm' established by customary law in this field, and this contains the element that the delimitation is to achieve 'an equitable result'.[195] Judge Gros again dissented, and stated in his dissenting opinion that he incorporated into it a number of paragraphs of his dissenting opinion in the *Tunisia/ Libya* case, including the passages from that opinion quoted above.[196]

Thus in the field of maritime delimitation any conception of equity as a corrective mechanism has tended to fade away in the face of a conception of equitable principles as specially flexible rules of law. We are therefore driven back to the query: why equity, rather than an adjustment of the law?

(4) *Why equity?*

If international law in a particular field comprises a number of clearly established rules, and a case arises which is not covered by any of those rules, but in which considerations of fairness point to a particular conclusion, why can the law not be extended by analogy? Why is it necessary to invoke the idea of equity in order to justify extending or adapting the law to the particular case? A possible answer may be the reluctance of the international judge to give even the appearance of legislating. Where law derives from the practice of States creative of custom, States in a particular situation not directly covered by practice and precedent may be induced by considerations of analogy, and indeed of fairness and justice, to adopt a novel solution, which, as an element of practice, contributes to the growth of law in an equitable direction.[197] But it is a bolder step for an international judge to assert that in the circumstances before him, States would

---

[194] *ICJ Reports*, 1982, p. 106, para. 24.
[195] *ICJ Reports*, 1984, p. 300, para. 112.
[196] Ibid., p. 378, para. 28.
[197] Schwarzenberger, 'Equity in International Law', *Year Book of World Affairs*, 1972, p. 346, considers that 'The movement from primitive and archaic legal systems to mature and developed legal systems tends to be accompanied by a change in emphasis from *jus strictum* to *jus aequum*', and that this is paralleled in the development of international law. The *jus aequum* however remains a *jus*, not a system of equity, even if more imbued with ideas of reasonableness and good faith than the *jus strictum*.

have reacted in such a way, since the very existence of the dispute is there to show that the two States before him did not—or at least one of them didn't. A judge cannot openly anticipate custom; if he is to go where custom has not yet gone, he needs an embodiment of his sense of justice to bolster his conclusions—and that is equity. Thus purely fortuitous circumstances may dictate whether a given development of the law in a particular field will come to pass as a development of customary law—as State practice—or as an equitable complement to the law—by judicial decision.

It is of course true that the absence of a rule of customary law may be other than fortuitous. It may be that, on closer examination, the lack of rule is in fact a negative rule, that States have shown, if only by inaction, that they did not consider it appropriate to adopt the rule which, to the judge, seems to be dictated by equity. Even if there is no 'negative practice' of this kind, the judge must tread warily.

In the *Barcelona Traction* case, the point in issue, expressed in simplest terms, was whether, in the event of injury by State A to a corporation (specifically, a limited liability company) whose national State was State B, State A could be required to make reparation to State C for the damage suffered by its nationals, shareholders in the corporation. For the purposes of discussion, it is to be assumed that no (or insufficient) practice, in the sense of successful diplomatic claims in comparable circumstances, could be relied on to found a customary-law rule of diplomatic protection of shareholders.[198]

The Court dismissed the claim, in effect on the basis that there was no right of action in the circumstances—which is, as noted above, a finding that there *is* a legal rule to the effect that there *is not* a right of action. Although the Court observed that 'International law may not, in some fields, provide specific rules in particular cases',[199] its finding was in no way equivalent to a *non-liquet*.[200]

The Court did in addition examine the question whether 'considerations of equity do not require that [Belgium] be held to possess a right of protection' of its shareholder nationals.[201] In its Memorial, Belgium had observed:

Mais ce n'est pas seulement l'application des règles précises déduites ci-avant de la pratique et de la jurisprudence internationales, qui qualifie le Gouvernement belge pour l'introduction de la présente demande, c'est aussi l'équité,[202]

---

[198] There is in fact some evidence of relevant practice, in particular lump-sum settlement agreements involving shareholders' claims; and this aspect of the judgment was vigorously criticized by Lillich, who accuses the Court of having been 'perfunctory' in its efforts 'to ascertain and apply customary prescriptions': 'The rigidity of Barcelona', *American Journal of International Law*, 65 (1971), p. 525. The practice had already been discussed by Judge Wellington Koo at the preliminary objection stage of the case: *ICJ Reports*, 1964, p. 63.

[199] *ICJ Reports*, 1970, p. 38, para. 52.

[200] This aspect will be considered further below, at pp. 81 ff.

[201] *ICJ Reports*, 1970, pp. 48–50, paras. 92–101.

[202] Memorial of Belgium, para. 328, *Pleadings*, vol. 1, p. 161.

and the Memorial went on to quote a passage from an arbitral award of Max Huber:

Le droit international qui, dans ce domaine, s'inspire essentiellement des principes de l'équité n'a établi aucun critère formel pour accorder ou refuser la protection diplomatique à des intérêts nationaux liés à des intérêts appartenant à des personnes de nationalités différentes.[203]

This reliance on equity disappeared subsequently from the arguments of Belgium, following the presentation of the Spanish preliminary objections; the suggestion seems however to have been that equity is part of the law on diplomatic protection, not merely required to correct or supplement it.

The Court first ruled that Belgium had no *jus standi* to exercise diplomatic protection of shareholders where no rights (as distinct from interests) of the shareholders had been prejudiced; this part of the judgment will be considered later. The Court then turned to 'considerations of equity', and observed:

it has been maintained that, for reasons of equity, a State should be able, in certain cases, to take up the protection of its nationals, shareholders in a company which has been the victim of a violation of international law. Thus a theory has been developed to the effect that the State of the shareholders has a right of diplomatic protection when the State whose responsibility has been invoked is the national State of the company. Whatever the validity of this theory may be, it is certainly not applicable to the present case, since Spain is not the national State of Barcelona Traction.

On the other hand, the Court considers that, in the field of diplomatic protection as in all other fields of international law, it is necessary that the law be applied reasonably. It has been suggested that if in a given case it is not possible to apply the general rule that the right of diplomatic protection of a company belongs to its national State, considerations of equity might call for the possibility of protection of the shareholders in question by their own national State. This hypothesis does not correspond to the circumstances of the present case.

In view, however, of the discretionary nature of diplomatic protection, considerations of equity cannot require more than the possibility for some protector State to intervene, whether it be the national State of the company, by virtue of the general rule mentioned above, or, in a secondary capacity, the national State of the shareholders who claim protection.[204]

The two stages in the *Barcelona Traction* judgment, whereby equity was turned to only after the law had been found not to afford the Belgian Government a remedy, suggest that the Court was influenced by the idea of equity as corrective or supplemental in effect, the view which later decisions seem to have banished—at least so far as maritime delimitation is concerned. But it remains unclear why if 'it is necessary that the law be applied reasonably', it could not be held simply that the law itself might

---

[203] *Ziat, Ben Kiran* case, *UN Reports of International Arbitral Awards*, vol. 2, pp. 729–30, quoted in Memorial of Belgium, loc. cit.

[204] *ICJ Reports*, 1970, p. 48, paras. 92–4 (numbering omitted).

provide protection for shareholders in appropriate cases. One explanation may be that tentatively advanced above: the difficulty of finding the existence of a customary-law rule in the absence of specific practice.

It may be significant that Judge Jessup, in his separate opinion, apparently makes no distinction between rules of international law deriving from equitable considerations and rules of international law *tout court*. Judge Jessup recognizes three 'exceptions' to a general rule providing for diplomatic protection of the corporation itself: where the corporation has the nationality of the respondent State; where the corporation has been wound up; and in case of direct injury to the shareholders.[205] Of these three, Judge Jessup observes that the rationale of the first 'seems to be based largely on equitable considerations', and adds that 'the result is so reasonable it has been accepted in State practice'.[206]

Still more striking is the remarkably prudent attitude displayed in the separate opinion of Sir Gerald Fitzmaurice. He there recognized that

the present state of international law leads to the inadmissible consequence that important interests may go wholly unprotected, and that what may possibly be grave wrongs will, as a result, not be susceptible even of investigation.[207]

After quoting authority to support the view that 'international law is to be applied with equity', he referred to the Court's judgment in the *North Sea Continental Shelf* cases as having introduced 'the considerations which led it to found its decision in part on equitable considerations' and added '*as it might well have done in the present case also*'.[208] The commentator is left wondering why it didn't, or at least why Judge Fitzmaurice did not dissent, holding that it should have done.

In conclusion, we may revert to the distinction, advanced above, between the development of customary law by extension of practice, which only States can do, and completion of customary law by equitable filling-in, which is the role of the judge. The judge must state and apply customary law as he finds it; he cannot, if the *Barcelona Traction* judgment reflects general judicial law, apply, as custom, what he thinks would be a good practice but which States apparently have not yet got round to adopting. The two spheres of action are so far distinct; but can equity form a part of customary law? May States by custom create law which requires recourse to equitable considerations? It is difficult to say that they cannot, but it is a thesis worth exploring that it is better that they should not. This does not mean that States may not be guided by concepts of fairness and justice in deciding how to act where the law leaves them a discretion; but it is the act in itself, as an element of practice, that makes the contribution to international customary law. The role of equitable principles is to push the

---

[205] Ibid., pp. 191–4, paras. 50–6.
[206] Ibid., pp. 191–2, para. 51.
[207] Ibid., p. 84, para. 35.
[208] Ibid., p. 85, para. 36 (emphasis added).

custom-created law in an appropriately just direction; they are not themselves part of that law.

The obvious instance is the Truman Proclamation, as interpreted and
applied in the *North Sea Continental Shelf* cases. When the Proclamation
declared that the boundary of the shelf 'shall be determined by the United
States and the State concerned in accordance with equitable principles', it
was in effect looking forward to an accumulation of practice which would
implement the vague idea of 'equitable principles' and produce customary
law. Unfortunately, when the Court was called upon in 1969 to say what
was that customary law, it was unable to find that the application of equity
had, up to that time, produced anything concrete which had attained sufficient acceptance to rank as customary law. The Court was therefore
forced back on the very terms of the Proclamation, and allowed the 'equitable principles' (of undefined content) to move from the sphere of influence
on the making of law into the sphere of law proper. This must have
appeared justified—indeed, the judgment did so justify it—on the grounds
that the application of equitable principles in appropriate circumstances
was a normal judicial function. What may have been overlooked was that it
was precisely that—a judicial function, not one appropriate for consensual
law-making by the subjects of law, if only because what is equitable is such
a subjective matter—one State's equity is another State's inequity.[209] To
this may be ascribed many of the difficulties that have subsequently arisen
in marine delimitation—but that is another story.[210]

4. *Application of Certain General Legal Maxims*

(1) *The possession of rights involves the performance of the corresponding obligations*

This principle was mentioned by Fitzmaurice in his very first article,[211]
by reference to the *dictum* in the advisory opinion on the *International
Status of South West Africa* that 'To retain the rights derived from the
Mandate and to deny the obligations thereunder could not be justified'.[212]
In the opinion in the *Namibia* case, the Court reverted to this principle,
but in a different form, when, referring to the relationship established
between the United Nations and each Mandatory Power with the entry into
force of the Charter, it stated that

One of the fundamental principles governing the international relationship thus
established is that a party which disowns or does not fulfil its own obligations can-

---

[209] A similar point — or the same point seen from a different angle — is made by Prosper Weil in his
brilliant study *Perspectives du droit de la délimitation maritime* (1988), pp. 118–23; as he observes, 'La
différence entre [les] deux visages de l'équité — celle des gouvernements qui négocient une délimitation
et celle du juge qui la décide — est fondamentale' (p. 122).

[210] To be considered further in a later article.

[211] This *Year Book*, 27 (1950), p. 8; *Collected Edition*, I, p. 8.

[212] *ICJ Reports*, 1950, p. 133.

not be recognized as retaining the rights which it claims to derive from the relationship.[213]

While this is a logical development, or corollary, of the 1950 *dictum*, its precise scope is less well-defined. To take treaty law as a parallel, there can be no doubt that a party to a treaty cannot claim to retain the rights it derives from the treaty while at the same time denying its obligations thereunder; but it is less certain in what circumstances to disown or fail to fulfil such obligations will have the effect of bringing about a forfeiture of the treaty rights.

The Court in fact transferred the debate on to the terrain of treaty relationships. After reciting the relevant parts of General Assembly Resolution 2145(XXI), it continued:

In examining this action of the General Assembly it is appropriate to have regard to the general principles of international law regulating termination of a treaty relationship on account of breach. For even if the mandate is viewed as having the character of an institution, as is maintained, it depends on the international agreements which created the system and regulated its application.[214]

Thus the Court does not elaborate on the practical implications, outside the realm of treaty law, of the general principle it enunciated. Whatever the academic interest of such an elaboration might have been, it has to be conceded that it would probably be of little practical impact, since examples of relationships involving rights and obligations which are not in some way conventional or treaty-derived do not spring to mind.[215]

(2) Pacta tertiis nec nocent nec prosunt

Good faith, in the broad sense requiring the observance of *pacta*, reaches the limit of its application when the *pactum* in question was concluded by the States other than the State whose conduct is in issue: hence the principle that *pacta tertiis nec nocent nec prosunt*.

In considering the application of this principle, it will be convenient to begin with the most recent case in which it has been considered in a decision: the judgment of the Chamber formed to deal with the *Frontier Dispute* case between Burkina Faso and Mali. The section of frontier between those two States which the Chamber was asked to define terminated to the east where it met the frontier of Niger. Mali contended that

the tripoint Niger–Mali–Burkina Faso cannot be determined by the two Parties

---

[213] *ICJ Reports*, 1971, p. 46, para. 91. Unusually in the Court's practice, this sentence constitutes a discrete numbered paragraph in itself, which suggests that the Court regarded it as an important statement of principle.

[214] *ICJ Reports*, 1971, p. 46, para. 94.

[215] Another interesting speculation is whether the *déchéance* of the Mandatory's rights for failure to meet its obligations would necessarily be irreversible, or whether South Africa might have had a *locus paenitentiae*, and on putting its house in order, could resume *de jure* control of the territory.

without Niger's agreement, nor can it be determined by the Chamber, which may not affect the rights of a third State not a party to the proceedings.[216]

The Chamber, after first satisfying itself that the Special Agreement, on a proper interpretation, did give expression to a common intention of the parties that the Chamber should define the frontier throughout the whole of the disputed areas, found as follows:

> The Chamber also considers that its jurisdiction is not restricted simply because the end-point of the frontier lies on the frontier of a third State not a party to the proceedings. The rights of the neighbouring State, Niger, are in any event safe-guarded by the operation of Article 59 of the Statute of the Court, which provides that 'The decision of the Court has no binding force except between the parties and in respect of that particular case'. The Parties could at any time have concluded an agreement for the delimitation of their frontier, according to whatever perception they might have had of it, and an agreement of this kind, although legally binding upon them by virtue of the principle *pacta sunt servanda*, would not be opposable to Niger. A judicial decision, which 'is simply an alternative to the direct and friendly settlement' of the dispute between the Parties (*PCIJ*, Series A, No. 22, p. 13), merely substitutes for the solution stemming directly from their shared inten-tion, the solution arrived at by a court under the mandate which they have given it. In both instances, the solution only has legal and binding effect as between the States which have accepted it, either directly or as a consequence of having accepted the court's jurisdiction to decide the case.[217]

While this may appear a novel extension of the *pacta tertiis* principle, it is in fact no more than a wide interpretation of the concept of *pactum*. If two States agree on a frontier line which has been defined by, e.g., the recommendation of a conciliator, it is their agreement which gives the line whatever validity it has, and that cannot include validity as against a third State not party to the agreement. If the same two States agree that a Court shall define the frontier, the only difference, from the point of view now under consideration, is that the agreement precedes the definition of the line, instead of following it;[218] it is still the agreement which gives the line validity.[219]

In this sense, it could well be contended that the provision of Article 59 of the Statute, in so far as it limits the binding force of a judgment to the parties to the case, is itself an application of the *pacta tertiis* principle.

The Chamber did also examine the question 'whether in this case, con-siderations related to the need to safeguard the interests of the third State concerned require it to refrain from exercising its jurisdiction to determine the whole course of the line';[220] this, however, was an issue relating to the

---

[216] *ICJ Reports*, 1986, p. 576, para. 44.

[217] Ibid., pp. 577–8, para. 46.

[218] Cf. Zafrulla Khan in *ICJ Yearbook*, 1971–2, pp. 129–30.

[219] Even for the parties the decision of the Court need not be accepted, but may be set aside by a further agreement between the parties; see the remarks on *jus cogens* and *jus dispositivum* in Chapter II, section 3, below.

[220] *ICJ Reports*, 1986, p. 578, para. 48.

proper exercise of the powers of the Court rather than to the *pacta tertiis* rule, and will therefore be examined in a later article.

Apart from this aspect, the *dictum* in the *Frontier Dispute* case is a classic instance of the *pacta tertiis* principle in straightforward circumstances. Greater difficulty arises when the *pactum* of the parties is imbued by international law with a special, status-creating, character, as in the case of agreements delimiting the continental shelf. The Chamber in the *Frontier Dispute* case referred to this aspect, in order to 'distinguish' it; but before quoting the passage, it will be convenient to retrace the history of the problem.

In the *North Sea Continental Shelf* cases, it will be recalled that the relative positions of Denmark, the Federal Republic of Germany and the Netherlands were such that an equidistance line could be drawn between the two 'outer' States—Denmark and the Netherlands—from a point on the median line between the three States and the United Kingdom, on the other side of the North Sea, up to a point fairly close inshore, where the line would have to bifurcate into an equidistance line Denmark/Federal Republic of Germany and an equidistance line Federal Republic of Germany/Netherlands.[221] The 'outer' States had concluded a delimitation agreement establishing this line, and claimed that it was opposable also to the Federal Republic of Germany,[222] as an equidistance line, on the basis either of the 1958 Geneva Convention on the Continental Shelf or of customary international law. The Court however found that the agreement was not so opposable, both because Denmark and the Netherlands were neither 'opposite' nor 'adjacent' States as contemplated by the Geneva Convention, and because the equidistance provision in the Convention was not opposable to the Federal Republic of Germany.[223]

Pausing there, we may note that the *pacta tertiis* rule was, apparently, considered so fundamental that it did not need to be mentioned: for the Court it was clear that the validity of the delimitation agreement against the Federal Republic of Germany was *entirely* dependent on the opposability to the Federal Republic of Germany of the equidistance rule. The Denmark/Netherlands *pactum* was injurious to the interests of the Federal Republic of Germany if it had a lawful claim to the areas which the *pactum* divided between the parties to it.

The Chamber in the *Frontier Dispute* case referred in its judgment to this aspect of the *North Sea* cases. After observing that

The legal considerations which have to be taken into account in determining the location of the land boundary between parties are in no way dependent on the position of the boundary between the territory of either of those parties and the

---

[221] See the map (No. 3) on p. 16 of *ICJ Reports*, 1969.

[222] In fact they went further, and claimed that it was valid *erga omnes*, but no other State would have had an interest in challenging it.

[223] *ICJ Reports*, 1969, pp. 27–8, paras. 35–6.

territory of a third State, even where, as in the present case, the rights in question for all three States derive from one and the same predecessor State,[224]

the Chamber went on to say that

On the other hand, in continental shelf delimitations, an agreement between the parties which is perfectly valid and binding on the treaty level may, when the relations between the parties and a third State are taken into consideration, prove to be contrary to the rules of international law governing the continental shelf (see *North Sea Continental Shelf, ICJ Reports 1969*, p. 20, para. 14; pp. 27–28, paras. 35–36). It follows that a court dealing with a request for the delimitation of a continental shelf must decline, even if so authorized by the disputant parties, to rule upon rights relating to areas in which third States have such claims as may contradict the legal considerations—especially in regard to equitable principles—which would have formed the basis of its decision.[225]

The Chamber was apparently here alluding to the problems that had arisen in the case concerning the *Continental Shelf (Libyan Arab Jamahiriya/Malta)* as a result of the unsuccessful attempt to intervene in the proceedings. The issues involved were not simple; and in the present article that case will be considered only in so far as it has some relevance to the *pacta tertiis* principle.

In the proceedings on the application of Italy to intervene, Italy had urged 'the impossibility, or at least the greatly increased difficulty of the Court effecting a delimitation between Libya and Malta in the absence of Italy from the proceedings'.[226] It had pointed out that 'the terminal points of the delimitation ultimately to be effected between the Parties will lie in the high seas, and it may prove that they will have to be tripoints or even quadripoints'[227]—i.e., that the delimitation would link up with delimitations with Italy or Tunisia. So far as the intervention was concerned, the Court held that this was irrelevant:

. . . the question is not whether the participation of Italy may be useful or even necessary to the Court; it is whether, assuming Italy's non-participation, a legal interest of Italy is *en cause*, or is likely to be affected by the decision;[228]

and the Court held that it was not. However, the Court also stated that it 'cannot wholly put aside the question of the legal interest of Italy as well as of other States of the Mediterranean region, and they will have to be taken into account' in the eventual judgment.[229] A little further on in its decision the Court said:

The future judgment will not merely be limited in its effects by Article 59 of the Statute: it will be expressed, upon its face, to be without prejudice to the rights and

---

[224] *ICJ Reports*, 1986, p. 578, para. 47.
[225] Ibid.
[226] *ICJ Reports*, 1984, p. 24, para. 39.
[227] Ibid.
[228] Ibid., p. 25, para. 40.
[229] Ibid., para. 41.

titles of third States. Under a Special Agreement concerning only the rights of the Parties, 'the Court has to determine which of the Parties has produced the most convincing proof of title' (*Minquiers and Ecrehos*, *ICJ Reports 1953*, p. 52), and not to decide in the absolute; similarly the Court will, so far as it may find it necessary to do so, make it clear that it is deciding only between the competing claims of Libya and Malta.[230]

At this stage, therefore, the Court appeared to be contemplating that by the effect of Article 59, and the *pacta tertiis* principle underlying it, whatever the Court decided would leave Italy free to press such claims to continental shelf areas as it saw fit, including any areas which the Court might, with all due verbal reservations, have allocated to Malta or Libya.[231] This emerges in particular from the dissenting opinion of Judge Sir Robert Jennings, where he criticized the Court's 'very broad interpretation' of Article 59, whereby '. . . every decision is to be analogous to a bilateral agreement, and *res inter alios acta* for third States . . . ',[232] and asks:

does this mean that the Court in effect disables itself from making useful and realistic pronouncements on questions of sovereignty and sovereign rights (and the latter is what we are in fact dealing with in this case)? 'Sovereign rights' that are opposable only to one other party comes very near to a contradiction in terms. A relative decision on continental shelf rights would seem especially odd coming from a Court which laid down 'non-encroachment' as one of the governing principles of the applicable law (*ICJ Reports 1969*, para. 101 C (1)); and lays it down, moreover, specifically in relation to delimitation by agreement.[233]

Against this, and in support of the Court's approach, it may be urged that the point is not that 'sovereign rights' are only opposable to one other party, but that, however valid such rights are *erga omnes*, the Court can only declare them to be valid, with binding effect as *res judicata*, in relation to the other party or parties to the proceedings. That is the whole sense of Article 59. This does not mean that the Court is necessarily obliged to word its judgments in that fashion: it may declare, as it did in the *Minquiers and Ecrehos* case, that 'sovereignty' over a defined area 'belongs to' a particular State;[234] but that does not prevent a third State from subsequently disputing that sovereignty.

This may be the normal operation of the principle; but the law of the continental shelf has developed in ways that complicate the matter not a little.[235] In the first place, there is the emphasis laid from the outset—the Truman Proclamation—up to and including the Montego Bay Convention,

---

[230] Ibid., pp. 26–7, para. 43.
[231] The Court was not called upon to draw a delimitation line, but it was required by the Special Agreement to say how the principles and rules which it found applicable should in practice be applied.
[232] *ICJ Reports*, 1984, p. 158.
[233] Ibid.
[234] *ICJ Reports*, 1953, p. 72.
[235] The development of the law of maritime delimitation in general will not be treated exhaustively in this series of articles; but we shall have more to say on it in later sections or later articles.

on the primary role of agreement in determination of continental shelf boundaries. Recourse to a Court is therefore, in a special sense, no more than a substitute for direct settlement, as the Permanent Court observed;[236] but paradoxically judicial settlement of continental shelf disputes is thereby made the more difficult because the Court is expected to put itself in the place of the parties, and write their agreement for them. *Pace* Sir Robert Jennings, this is a reason for insisting on the non-opposability to third States of judicial solutions in such cases. Secondly, the parties, and therefore the Court, are required to have regard to all relevant circumstances; and as Sir Robert trenchantly remarks, 'it is difficult to imagine a more relevant circumstance than the legal rights of a geographically immediate neighbour'.[237] Thirdly, if considerations of proportionality come into play, the area in which they do so has to be defined, which may involve looking at surrounding claims or interests.[238]

The essential difference, it is suggested, between an agreement between two States on a particular matter, and a judgment given in proceedings between the same two States on the same matter, lies not in the effect of the agreement or the judgment, but in the considerations that go to its making. If two States, A and B, agree that sovereignty over a given territory belongs to State A, they may choose to disregard—because neither of them accepts them—the rival claims of State C to that territory. This does C no injury, because the agreement is *res inter alios acta*. If however the Court is asked to decide, in proceedings between A and B, in which C does not participate, whether A has sovereignty, then the Court cannot ignore C's claims if they are before it, through an intervention or otherwise.

Another circumstance which must be taken into account by any tribunal which has to adjudicate upon a claim to sovereignty over a particular territory, is the extent to which the sovereignty is also claimed by some other Power.[239]

It is for this reason that Judge Sir Robert Jennings was entirely right in pointing to the impact which the Court's judgment would inevitably have on the interests of Italy, Article 59 of the Statute notwithstanding.[240]

Whether, or how far, the Court is obliged to give consideration to the possible claims of States not parties to the proceedings is not clear; in the *Eastern Greenland* case quoted above, the context shows that the only other Power which the Permanent Court of International Justice had to consider as a possible claimant was the other party to the case.

The case of the *Monetary Gold Removed from Rome in 1943*, though it related to ownership of moveable property, might suggest that there could be circumstances in which sovereignty claimed by a third State 'would not

---

[236] *PCIJ*, Series A, No. 22, p. 13, quoted in the *Frontier Dispute* judgment (p. 64, above).
[237] *ICJ Reports*, 1984, p. 154, para. 21.
[238] See the *Continental Shelf (Tunisia/Libya)* judgment, *ICJ Reports*, 1982, p. 91, para. 130.
[239] *PCIJ*, Series A/B, No. 53, p. 46; quoted in *ICJ Reports*, 1984, p. 26, para. 43.
[240] *ICJ Reports*, 1984, p. 158, paras. 28–9.

only be affected by a decision, but would form the very subject-matter of the decision',[241] so that jurisdiction could not be exercised; but the parallel appears doubtful to say the least. It was not Albania's title to the gold which was in question before the Court, but 'whether Albania has committed any international wrong against Italy'[242] justifying Italy in intercepting the gold: and it was this that the Court could not decide without the consent of Albania.

The Chamber in the *Frontier Dispute* seems to have had no qualms about competing claims by Niger in the neighbourhood of the eastern terminus of the frontier line, apparently because no indication had been brought to its notice that there were any such claims; and the general satisfaction with its judgment expressed in African circles suggests that it was justified in the course it took.

When the Court, having excluded the intervention of Italy, gave its decision in the *Malta/Libya* delimitation in 1985, the chickens came home to roost. The Court noted that it was informed of the claims of Italy, and that it had virtually promised Italy that its interests would be safeguarded; it noted also that both parties agreed

in contending that the Court should not feel inhibited from extending its decision to all areas which, independently of third party claims, are claimed by the Parties to this case, since if the Court were to exclude any such areas as are the subject of present or possible future claims by a third State it would in effect be deciding on such claims without jurisdiction to do so.[243]

It decided, however, to limit the area to which its judgment would be addressed, on the following grounds:

The Court notes that by the Special Agreement it is asked to define the legal principles and rules applicable to the delimitation of the area of continental shelf 'which appertains' to each of the Parties. The decision of the Court will, by virtue of Article 59 of the Statute, have binding force between the parties, but not against third States. If therefore the decision is to be stated in absolute terms, in the sense of permitting the delimitation of the areas of shelf which 'appertain' to the Parties, as distinct from the areas to which one of the Parties has shown a better title than the other, but which might nevertheless prove to 'appertain' to a third State if the Court had jurisdiction to enquire into the entitlement of that third State, the decision must be limited to a geographical area in which no such claims exist.[244]

The Court's response to the request of the parties not to limit its judgment in this way was, more or less, 'Vous l'avez voulu, Georges Dandin'; having opposed the intervention sought by Italy, they had only themselves to

[241] *ICJ Reports*, 1954, p. 32.
[242] Ibid.
[243] *ICJ Reports*, 1985, p. 25, para. 20.
[244] Ibid., para. 21.

thank if the eventual judgment was more restricted than they would have wished.

This latter argument was also used to meet the obvious objection that the result of the Court's restraint was to enable a third State to restrict the scope of the proceedings:

It has been questioned whether it is right that a third State—in this case, Italy—should be enabled, by virtue of its claims, to restrict the scope of a judgment requested of the Court by Malta and Libya; and it may also be argued that this approach would have prevented the Court from giving any judgment at all if Italy had advanced more ambitious claims. However, to argue along these lines is to disregard the special features of the present case. On the one hand, no inference can be drawn from the fact that the Court has taken into account the existence of Italian claims as to which it has not been suggested by either of the Parties that they are obviously unreasonable. On the other hand, neither Malta nor Libya seems to have been deterred by the probability of the Court's judgment being restricted in scope as a consequence of the Italian claims. The prospect of such a restriction did not persuade these countries to abandon their opposition to Italy's application to intervene . . .[245]

The reference to 'the special features of the present case' is heartening; for it is submitted that it would be unfortunate if the reasoning in this decision were to be treated as a general rule of judicial propriety for cases where there are competing claims by States not before the Court.

Even so limited in its impact, however, the reasoning prompts doubts, particularly the suggestion that a decision 'stated in absolute terms' could only be made in respect of an area in which no rival claims existed.[246] A first point is that it is difficult to understand the distinction, in the context of the continental shelf delimitation, between areas which 'appertain' to a State and 'areas to which one of the Parties has shown a better title than the other'. Both the distinction and the whole idea of a 'better' title seem inconsistent with the whole underlying concept of the rights *ab initio* over the natural prolongation of the land territory. More material to the present discussion is the idea that outside influences can prevent the Court from stating its decision 'in absolute terms'. It was in effect urged above that the Court should, indeed must, state its decision in every case in absolute terms; but that the principle underlying both the *pacta tertiis* rule and Article 59 of the Statute operates to ensure that its effects are not absolute.

The *Frontier Dispute* Chamber was, it is suggested, in the right of it when it referred to a 'presumption' that the parties have exclusive sovereign rights up to the limit of their claims, and added:

However, this is no more than a twofold presumption which underlies any boundary situation. This presumption remains in principle irrebuttable in the

---

[245] Ibid., p. 28, para. 23.
[246] On the factual level, it is worth noting that the Court was not fully informed as to Tunisian claims.

judicial context of a given case, in the sense that neither of the disputant parties, having contended that it possesses a common frontier with the other as far as a specific point, can change its position to rely on the alleged existence of sovereignty pertaining to a third State; but this presumption does not thereby create a ground of opposability outside that context and against the third State. Indeed, this is the whole point of the above-quoted Article 59 of the Statute.[247]

The Court had also to deal with the question of the effects of a judgment on third parties in the case concerning *Military and Paramilitary Activities in and against Nicaragua (Nicaragua* v. *United States of America)*; this was, however, in the special context of the United States 'multilateral treaty reservation' which referred to a class of States parties to a multilateral treaty which were 'affected by the decision'.[248] Since if even one State were to be 'affected', this would suffice to bring the reservation into effect,[249] the Court concentrated its attention on the position of El Salvador. It found that El Salvador would be 'affected' by a decision of the Court on the claims of Nicaragua based on the United Nations Charter:

> The Court has to consider the consequences of a rejection of the United States' justification of its actions as the exercise of the right of collective self-defence for the sake of El Salvador, in accordance with the United Nations Charter. A judgment to that effect would declare contrary to treaty-law the indirect aid which the United States Government considers itself entitled to give the Government of El Salvador in the form of activities in and against Nicaragua. The Court would of course refrain from any finding on whether El Salvador could lawfully exercise the right of individual self-defence; but El Salvador would still be affected by the Court's decision on the lawfulness of resort by the United States to collective self-defence. If the Court found that no armed attack had occurred, then not only would action by the United States in purported exercise of the right of collective self-defence prove to be unjustified, but so also would any action which El Salvador might take or might have taken on the asserted ground of individual self-defence.[250]

The significant sentence in this passage is that in which the Court stated that it would not make any finding on whether El Salvador could lawfully exercise the right of individual self-defence; the Court might have added that in any event, Article 59 would prevent that question being determined by the Court's decision on the United States claim of self-defence. It might even be said that *legally* El Salvador would not, in view of the effect of Article 59, be 'affected' in any event; but the multilateral treaty reservation had to be interpreted as intended to have some effect, and too strict an application of Article 59 would have rendered it meaningless.

---

[247] *ICJ Reports*, 1986, p. 579, para. 49.
[248] Text of reservation in *ICJ Reports*, 1984, pp. 421–2, para. 67. The interpretation whereby it was the 'treaty' and not the 'parties' to which the word 'affected' applied might have been attractive, but was unfortunately found to be unsustainable: ibid., p. 424, para. 72.
[249] *ICJ Reports*, 1986, p. 34, para. 48.
[250] Ibid., p. 36, para. 51.

(3) *Approbation and reprobation*

It has been suggested[251] that this equitable doctrine, or a principle of international law analogous to it, played some part in the decision of the Court on the reservation to the accession of Greece to the 1928 General Act in the *Aegean Sea Continental Shelf* case. The doctrine in equity is, broadly, that a party who bases its claims on a particular deed or instrument must take the instrument as he finds it, and cannot rely on such part of it as supports his case, while inviting the Court to disregard some other part of it which he considers less favourable.

The Court had to determine whether a dispute over the continental shelf said to be appurtenant to Greek islands in the Aegean fell within a reservation excluding jurisdiction over disputes 'relating to the territorial status' of Greece. Greece had relied on the intertemporal principle to assert that the term 'territorial status' could not have been intended to refer to the continental shelf which, as a legal concept, was unknown at the date of the reservation (1931). The Court had however already found,[252] when it reached the stage in its judgment at which it discussed this argument, that the expression 'territorial status' had been used 'as a generic term denoting any matters comprised within the concept of territorial status under general international law' so that

the presumption necessarily arises that its meaning was intended to follow the evolution of the law and to correspond with the meaning attached to the expression by the law in force at any given time.[253]

The Court then noted that the asserted basis of jurisdiction was Article 17 of the General Act, referring to disputes as to the 'respective rights' of the parties, and continued:

If the Greek Government is correct, as it undoubtedly is, in assuming that the meaning of the generic term 'rights' in Article 17 follows the evolution of the law, so as to be capable of embracing rights over the continental shelf, it is not clear why the similar term 'territorial status' should not likewise be liable to evolve in meaning in accordance with the 'development of international relations' (*PCIJ*, Series B, No. 4, p. 24).[254]

The Court also noted that the islands involved in Greece's claim included some which had only been ceded to Greece subsequently to the date of the reservation, and observed that

In consequence, it seems clear that, in the view of the Greek Government, the term 'rights' in Article 17 of the General Act has to be interpreted in the light of the geographical extent of the Greek State today, not of its extent in 1931. It would then be a little surprising if the meaning of Greece's reservation of disputes relating

---

[251] Sinclair, *The Vienna Convention on the Law of Treaties* (2nd edn., 1984), p. 126: cf. Elias, 'The Doctrine of Intertemporal Law', *American Journal of International Law*, 74 (1980), p. 301.

[252] This finding will be discussed below, in connection with the intertemporal principle in general.

[253] *ICJ Reports*, 1978, p. 32, para. 77.

[254] Ibid., p. 33, para. 78.

to its 'territorial status' was not also to evolve in the light of the change in the territorial extent of the Greek State brought about by 'the development of international relations'.[255]

Although the language used by the Court at this point in its judgment is perhaps ambiguous, it seems clear from the context that the operation in which the Court was engaging was that of seeking to determine the intention of Greece as author of the reservation, for purposes of its interpretation. In other words, the Court was not rejecting the Greek submission on the grounds that it involved a simultaneous approbation and reprobation; nor was it saying that it is impermissible, in a unilateral instrument of this kind, so to draft the text that the substantive scope of the instrument will be defined by the law in force at the time of its being invoked, and at the same time to define an exception in terms which tie it to the state of the law at the time of its adoption. It was saying that it is unlikely that such a result would have been intended, and therefore it can be assumed that it was not intended.[256]

Whether the rule excluding approbation and reprobation is part of international law must, for the present, be regarded as unsettled.

(4) States will be presumed to use the most appropriate means of creating rights or obligations

This principle, which does not appear to have received earlier judicial endorsement, is one eminently of good sense rather than equity: it may be stated more briefly and vividly as postulating that when the door is open, entry by the window is to be presumed improper, or at least unlikely.

Fitzmaurice did in his first article formulate a general principle that

where a particular process is contemplated for achieving a given result, whether in consequence of a treaty obligation or of an obligation arising from a general rule of international law, the result in question cannot properly be arrived at by substituting a different process for the one contemplated, even though it is due to the default of one of the parties subject to the obligation that the regular process cannot be employed.[257]

He was however addressing himself more to situations in which the intention of the States concerned was not in doubt, but the validity of the step taken was questionable—the specific instance he had in mind being the constitution of the Commissions in the *Peace Treaties* case—, in other words whether entry by the window is permissible when the door is shut. The approach in the cases now to be examined has been more concerned with

[255] Ibid.

[256] The next following paragraph, which compares the reservation under examination with another reservation to the same accession, is more clearly worded:

'. . . the Court can see no valid reason why one part of reservation (*b*) *should have been intended* to follow the evolution of international relations but not the other, *unless such an intention should have been made plain by Greece at the time*': ibid., p. 33, para. 79 (emphasis added).

[257] This *Year Book*, 27 (1950), p. 8; *Collected Edition*, I, p. 8.

establishing the intentions of a State which is alleged to have employed an unusual means to a particular end.

In the *North Sea Continental Shelf* cases, Denmark and the Netherlands argued that the Federal Republic of Germany, which had signed but not ratified the 1958 Geneva Convention on the Continental Shelf, had become bound by that Convention

in another way, —namely because, by conduct, by public statements and proclamations, and in other ways, the Republic has unilaterally assumed the obligations of the Convention; or has manifested its acceptance of the conventional régime; or has recognized it as being generally applicable to the delimitation of continental shelf areas.[258]

The Court first approached this contention on the basis that what was being suggested was that the conduct relied on showed that the Federal Republic intended by this means to become bound by the Convention (it turned later to the possibility—not here material—of an estoppel, i.e., that whatever the Federal Republic had intended, its conduct had created an impression of an expectation). On this assumption,

—that is to say if there had been a real intention to manifest acceptance or recognition of the applicability of the conventional régime—then it must be asked why it was that the Federal Republic did not take the obvious step of giving expression to this readiness by simply ratifying the Convention. In principle, when a number of States, including the one whose conduct is invoked, and those invoking it, have drawn up a convention specifically providing for a particular method by which the intention to become bound by the régime of the convention is to be manifested— namely by the carrying out of certain prescribed formalities (ratification, accession), it is not lightly to be presumed that a State which has not carried out these formalities, though at all times fully able and entitled to do so, has nevertheless somehow become bound in another way.[259]

The Court buttressed its argument with what must have appeared a *reductio ad absurdum*:

Indeed if it was a question not of obligation but of rights,—if, that is to say, a State which, though entitled to do so, had not ratified or acceded, attempted to claim rights under the convention, on the basis of a declared willingness to be bound by it, or of conduct evincing acceptance of the conventional régime, it would simply be told that, not having become a party to the convention it should not claim any rights under it until the professed willingness and acceptance had been manifested in the prescribed form.[260]

The same principle was applied by the Chamber formed to deal with the *Frontier Dispute* between Burkina Faso and Mali. It was faced with the

---

[258] *ICJ Reports*, 1969, p. 25, para. 27.

[259] Ibid., p. 25, para. 28.

[260] Ibid., pp. 25–6, para. 28. The Court also argued that even if the FRG had ratified the Convention, it could have entered a reservation excluding the equidistance rule, but as Judge Lachs (dissenting) pointed out, the statements relied on referred to 'the Convention as a whole with no exception or reservation' (ibid., p. 236).

argument of Burkina Faso that Mali, as a result of a unilateral statement by its Head of State,[261] had committed itself to accepting in advance as binding the report on the disputed frontier to be produced by a Mediation Commission. The Chamber referred to the special circumstances in which, in the *Nuclear Tests* cases, a unilateral declaration had been held to create a binding obligation, and explained:

The circumstances of the present case are radically different. Here, there was nothing to hinder the Parties from manifesting an intention to accept the binding character of the conclusions of the Organization of African Unity Mediation Commission by the normal method: a formal agreement on the basis of reciprocity.[262]

In the meantime, however, the same—or a closely analogous—principle had been appealed to, without success, by the United States in the jurisdictional phase of the case concerning *Military and Paramilitary Activities in and against Nicaragua (Nicaragua v. United States of America)*. Nicaragua had argued that

Nicaragua's conduct over a period of 38 years unequivocally constitutes consent to be bound by the compulsory jurisdiction of the Court by way of a recognition of the application of Article 36, paragraph 5, of the Statute to the Nicaraguan Declaration of 1929. Likewise the conduct of the United States over a period of 38 years unequivocally constitutes its recognition of the essential validity of the Declaration.[263]

To this, the United States objected that the contention of Nicaragua was

flatly inconsistent with the Statute of the Court, which provides only for consent to jurisdiction to be manifested in specific ways: . . . The Statute provides the sole basis on which the Court can exercise jurisdiction under Articles 36 and 37. In the particular case of Article 36, paragraph 5, the Statutes of the two Courts provide a means for States to express their consent, and Nicaragua did not use them.[264]

In effect, what the United States was saying was that if Nicaragua really consented to the jurisdiction, it should have made a new declaration under Article 36, paragraph 2, the normal means of doing so, rather than relying on a precarious structure of recognition of the continuing validity of an expired declaration. It is interesting in this connection to recall the Court's *reductio ad absurdum* in the *North Sea Continental Shelf* cases, its observations on the position of a State which actively claimed *rights* which it could have obtained by the normal means, but which it asserted on the basis of an alternative legal construct. Although in form Nicaragua was asserting that it was bound by its 1929 declaration, what it was in effect doing was relying on that declaration in order to assert a right to sue the United States.

---

[261] This statement has already been examined in relation to the question of good faith as the source of the validity of unilateral declarations at p. 19, above.

[262] *ICJ Reports*, 1986, p. 574, para. 40.

[263] *ICJ Reports*, 1984, p. 411, para. 43.

[264] Ibid., para. 44.

The Court did not accept the United States contention; it based its reasoning essentially on a finding that Nicaragua's situation had been 'wholly unique'. It referred to Nicaragua's absence of protest 'against the legal situation ascribed to it by the publications of the Court, the Secretary-General of the United Nations and major States':

Hence, if the Court were to object that Nicaragua ought to have made a declaration under Article 36, paragraph 2, it would be penalizing Nicaragua for having attached undue weight to the information given on that point by the Court and the Secretary-General of the United Nations and, in sum, having (on account of the authority of [its] sponsors) regarded [it] as more reliable than [it] really [was].[265]

The United States argument brings out the fact that the principle now under discussion can be given two interpretations: constitutional or volitional. Where there is a recognized means of achieving a particular end, it may be said that no other method is permitted by law; or it may be said that it will be presumed that States who wish to achieve that end will use the means provided, and there is a presumption against the conclusion that a State which acted in some other way was intending nevertheless to achieve the same end. The Court's finding in the *North Sea Continental Shelf* cases appears to be based at least primarily on the second interpretation, though the language used suggests that both ideas were in the Court's mind. In particular, the *reductio ad absurdum* mentioned above seems to be based on the idea that, no matter what the intentions of the State concerned had been, it would not be *allowed* to claim rights by the back door, as it were.

The United States argument in the *Nicaragua* case leans much more heavily on the constitutional conception, that what Nicaragua claimed to do was forbidden, or at least not permitted, by the Statute. The Court, however, answered it, in effect, on the consent basis, by saying that what would otherwise have been odd behaviour, from which consent or intention to be bound could not properly be deduced, was not so odd in view of the unique situation in which Nicaragua found itself.

Chapter II:

International Rights and Obligations

1. *The Completeness of the Law and the Nature of Legal Rights: International Law as Constitutive or Regulatory of such Rights*

During the period under review, the Court had to deal with a number of questions on which not only was the law uncertain, but it was unclear

---

[265] Ibid., p. 412, para. 46. The French text makes clear that it is the information (*informations* in French) of which the reliability was in question, not the sponsors. The English, by using the plural, apparently to follow the French, suggests the opposite.

whether international law had reached the areas in issue at all. Its decisions in these cases are therefore of great interest from the standpoint of the development of international law, both by the Court's own decisions and by the growth of custom. Two aspects will have to be considered: the question whether there are in fact areas where the law lays down no rights or obligations—the problem of *lacunae* in the law; and the question whether international legal rules are restrictive against a background of State freedom of action, or justificatory against a background of restriction of action—the *Lotus* problem.[266] Each problem arises when the Court is faced with a case *primae impressionis*.

The definition of a case *primae impressionis* is not, in the international field, as simple as it looks: for present purposes, we may perhaps define such a case as one in which the question is not whether the facts are such as to attract the application of a recognized rule of law, nor the modalities of application of such a rule, but one where the applicant has to rely on an alleged new rule or the application by extension or by analogy of an existing one.

(1) Lacunae *in the law and the question of* non-liquet

In general, when an international tribunal is faced with such a case there are a number of courses it can follow. A court in such circumstances may accept the applicant's contention that an existing rule may apply by analogy or extension. It may also find that a new rule has come into existence through the normal customary law processes, and that all that has been lacking is a definition of its crystallization, which a court decision can supply. It can also reject the claim on the ground that there is no rule justifying it, which is tantamount to saying that there *is* a rule of international law excluding an applicant from recovery in such circumstances. Thus in the case of *Military and Paramilitary Activities in and against Nicaragua (Nicaragua* v. *United States of America)*, when the Court stated that

in international law there are no rules, other than such rules as may be accepted by the State concerned, by treaty or otherwise, whereby the level of armaments of a sovereign State can be limited . . .,[267]

it was in effect declaring the existence of a rule that a State is free to determine for itself its level of armaments. Finally a Court may—according to one view, not universally accepted—decide that the claim must be dismissed because international law simply does not regulate the issues in question: i.e., declare a *non-liquet*.

The attitude of the Court in the *North Sea Continental Shelf* cases suggests that it was guided by a presumption against the existence of gaps in

---

[266] Cf. Fitzmaurice, this *Year Book*, 30 (1953), pp. 7–17; *Collected Edition*, I, pp. 138–48, under the heading 'The Bases and Foundation of State Rights. International Law as Constitutive or Merely Regulatory of Such Rights'.

[267] *ICJ Reports*, 1986, p. 135, para. 269.

the law. It was, as it found, faced with a situation in which the major international convention on the matter was not applicable, because one of the parties to the case was not a party to the convention; and the delimitation method provided for in the convention was not applicable as a mandatory rule of customary law.[268] The Court's examination of State practice, from which the latter conclusion had been drawn, had shown the comparative paucity of practice, and the difficulty of drawing conclusions from it as to the existence of a 'general practice accepted as law'.[269] In these circumstances, it was at least arguable that, outside the ambit of the 1958 Geneva Convention,[270] there was no legal regulation of the delimitation of continental shelf areas. The Court, however, stated firmly:

> But as between States faced with an issue concerning the lateral delimitation of adjacent continental shelves, there are still rules and principles of law to be applied; and in the present case it is not the fact either that rules are lacking, or that the situation is one for the unfettered appreciation of the Parties. Equally, it is not the case that if the equidistance principle is not a rule of law, there has to be as an alternative some other single equivalent rule.[271]

The customary law rules which the Court found established may be criticized as somewhat tenuously supported,[272] but this is not necessarily to be explained by a firm position of principle as to the propriety of a *non-liquet*. Independently of the question whether, as a matter of general legal theory, an international tribunal has the power to declare a *non-liquet*, it is evident that for the Court to have done so in the *North Sea* cases would have been both a severe blow to its prestige and a severe setback to the law of the sea.

In the *North Sea Continental Shelf* cases, a finding that there was no established customary law governing the delimitation of the continental shelf, i.e., a *non-liquet*, was perfectly possible in theory. In view of the form in which the matter was brought before the Court, this would indeed have constituted an unusually pure form of *non-liquet*, since both parties would have been left exactly where they were. In cases of a more normally adversarial nature, a *non-liquet* may be barely distinguishable in its effects from a rejection of the plaintiff's claim on the grounds that no rule supports it, which is tantamount, as we have seen, to a finding that there *is* a rule

---

[268] *ICJ Reports*, 1969, p. 46, para. 83.

[269] Ibid., pp. 43–5, paras. 75–80.

[270] The existence of a multilateral convention laying down rules in a particular field, unless expressly or impliedly codificatory, in itself suggests a lack of regulation of that field, prior to the Convention, or as between non-parties.

[271] *ICJ Reports*, 1969, p. 46, para. 83.

[272] Essentially, the Court's finding was that the '*opinio juris* in the matter of delimitation' was reflected in the principles

'that delimitation must be the object of agreement between the States concerned, and that such agreement must be arrived at in accordance with equitable principles' (ibid., p. 46, para. 85).

It is difficult to see how practice could support an *opinio juris* that agreement was a matter of obligation (cf. ibid., para. 78 *in fine*); and subsequent developments have shown the almost infinite flexibility which can be given to the idea of 'equitable principles'. This aspect will be examined further in a later article.

which *does not* endorse it. This may be illustrated by reference to the *Barcelona Traction* case. Before considering this aspect, however, the *Frontier Dispute* case will be considered, since it raises the possibility of another pure form of *non-liquet*, that of the inadequacy of the available material to support any legal conclusion justifiable by reference to the applicable law.

The frontier which the Chamber had in that case to establish was agreed by the parties to be identical with the pre-independence colonial boundary; and it was equally an agreed postulate that such boundary had been determined and existed throughout the whole of the disputed area. The Chamber had however to grapple with inadequate or conflicting records and maps in its search for the boundary, and it had to bear in mind that, where the parties advanced two different versions of the line, it could well be that neither was correct. Thus the Court declared:

> The Special Agreement of 20 October 1983 by which the case was brought before the Court deals with the question of the burden of proof only in order to make it clear that it is not prejudged by the written procedure there provided for (Art. 3, para. 2). In any event, however, in a case such as this, the rejection of any particular argument on the ground that the factual allegations on which it is based have not been proved is not sufficient to warrant upholding the contrary argument. The Chamber has to indicate the line of the frontier on the basis of the documents and other evidence presented to it by the disputant Parties. Its task is further complicated by the doubts it has expressed above regarding the sufficiency of this evidence.[273]

A particularly thorny problem was the location of a pool referred to in the documents as a reference point and called the pool of Kétiouaire; other documents referred to a pool called Kébanaire. After exhaustive analysis of the evidence, the Chamber concluded that 'there is insufficient information available to the Chamber for it to identify or to locate either of these two pools'.[274] The Chamber's dilemma was that it had as a matter of law to determine the position of the French administrative frontier of the colonial period, which the parties insisted was complete and completely delimited; but the evidence simply did not enable it to determine what had been the position of a particular sector of that frontier.[275] The Chamber was then faced with essentially the same problem as was encountered by the King of the Netherlands in 1831 in the arbitration concerning the *North Eastern Boundary*[276]—that the available evidence did not enable him to lay down the boundary in accordance with law. Like the arbitrator in that case, the Chamber did not pronounce a *non-liquet*, but proceeded to determine the boundary in the way which seemed most appropriate.

---

[273] *ICJ Reports*, 1986, p. 588, para. 65.
[274] *ICJ Reports*, 1986, p. 629, para. 141.
[275] *ICJ Reports*, 1986, p. 629, para. 142.
[276] Moore, *International Arbitrations*, vol. 1, pp. 119–36; discussed in Lauterpacht, *The Function of Law in the International Community* (1934), pp. 127–30. Cf. the *Guatemala/Honduras Boundary* arbitration, where the problem was, as in the *Frontier Dispute*, to determine the line of the *uti possidetis*: *UN Reports of International Arbitral Awards*, vol. 2, p. 1325.

The Chamber was in fact able to refer to an agreement concluded at local level in 1965,[277] and in the application of equity[278] to take account, not of the agreement itself, which had not been ratified at Governmental level, but 'of the circumstances in which the agreement was concluded'.[279] Had it not been for the fortuitous existence of the 1965 Agreement, what course could the Chamber have adopted? Neither side had proved its case for drawing the line in a particular position, and the evidence did not enable the Chamber to reach a firm conclusion on any other position. Should it have followed the example of the King of the Netherlands, and drawn a compromise line in an open exercise of its discretion, or should it have declined to indicate the frontier line in that area? The latter course would, it is suggested, have been preferable, unless a *non-liquet* is excluded for reasons of principle.[280] The parties could have been left to agree a line, or to conclude a new special agreement giving the Chamber power to decide *ex aequo et bono*.

Before leaving the subject of *non-liquet*, the *Northern Cameroons* case may also be noted. The Republic of Cameroon claimed that the United Kingdom had committed breaches of the Trusteeship Agreement for the Trust Territory of the Northern Cameroons; it was however recognized that that Agreement had been validly terminated by General Assembly resolution before the proceedings were instituted. The Court found that it could not adjudicate upon the merits of the claim, essentially because any judgment it gave would be not susceptible of any compliance or execution. When the Court thus declined to entertain the claim because the judgment could not have any 'forward reach',[281] its action may perhaps, without too great a stretch of the imagination, be assimilated to the category of *non-liquet*. A *non-liquet*, if permissible at all, would be justified by the 'silence of the law'. The Court observed that

in this case there is a dispute about the interpretation and application of a treaty—the Trusteeship Agreement—which has now been terminated, is no longer in force, and there can be no opportunity for a future act of interpretation of that treaty in accordance with any judgment the Court might render.[282]

It is arguable that the law has nothing to say about the interpretation of an extinct treaty, so that the Court was being asked to judge in a field where there was no longer any law to be declared.[283] This is, however, admittedly, an extension of the *non-liquet* concept; and the Court was probably wise to base its decision on considerations of the 'proper limits of its judicial

---

[277] *ICJ Reports*, 1986, p. 631, para. 146.
[278] Ibid., p. 633, para. 149.
[279] Ibid., *in fine*.
[280] See the Lauterpacht/Stone controversy, referred to below.
[281] *ICJ Reports*, 1963, p. 37.
[282] Ibid.
[283] On the other hand, the Court in *Western Sahara* did regard its opinion on the status of the territory in 1884 as 'based on law': *ICJ Reports*, 1975, p. 37, para. 73.

function'.[284] In this latter respect, the judgment will be further studied in a later article.

In the *Barcelona Traction* case, already outlined above, the Court's approach took as starting point the idea that an international claim could be brought by a State on behalf of a national if a right, not a mere interest, of that national had been infringed. One of the ways in which Belgium expressed its contentions was as follows; it argued that

there exists no rule of international law which would deny the national State of the shareholders the right of diplomatic protection for the purpose of seeking redress pursuant to unlawful acts committed by another State against the company in which they hold shares.[285]

The reply of the Court contains two separate strands of argument, not wholly consistent with each other. The first is that there can be no diplomatic protection unless a right under municipal law has been infringed; and shareholders have no right, in that law, to redress for injury done to the company. The other strand is that 'the position of the company rests on a positive rule of both municipal and international law'.

Paragraph 42 of the judgment has this to say on shareholders' rights:

If the shareholders disagree with the decisions taken on behalf of the company they may, in accordance with its articles or the relevant provisions of the law, change them or replace its officers, or take such action as is provided by law. Thus to protect the company against abuse by its management or the majority of shareholders, several municipal legal systems have vested in shareholders (sometimes a particular number is specified) the right to bring an action for the defence of the company, and conferred upon the minority of shareholders certain rights to guard against decisions affecting the rights of the company vis-à-vis its management or controlling shareholders. Nonetheless the shareholders' rights in relation to the company and its assets remain limited, this being, moreover, a corollary of the limited nature of their liability.[286]

In paragraph 52, the Court rejects the Belgian argument on this ground:

In the concrete situation, the company against which allegedly unlawful acts were directed is expressly vested with a right, whereas no such right is specifically provided for the shareholder in respect of those acts. Thus the position of the company rests on a positive rule of both municipal and international law. As to the shareholder, while he has certain rights expressly provided for him by municipal law as referred to in paragraph 42 above, appeal can, in the circumstances of the present case, only be made to the silence of international law. Such silence scarcely admits of interpretation in favour of the shareholder.[287]

This latter passage may be merely somewhat over-condensed and elliptic; but it does give cause to suspect a confusion of thought. Shareholders are

---

[284] Ibid., p. 38.
[285] *ICJ Reports*, 1970, p. 37, para. 51.
[286] Ibid., p. 35, para. 42.
[287] Ibid., p. 38, para. 52.

subjects of law in their own, and indeed probably in virtually all, municipal legal systems, but not in international law. There is no reason in theory why States should not previously have taken up the cause of nationals oppressed in their capacity as shareholders, but—on the premises of the judgment—this was not the case. Companies too are subjects of law in municipal legal systems; and diplomatic and judicial claims had been successfully made on behalf of companies. But the rights of shareholders discussed in paragraph 42 are of a kind that only a municipal system could confer, because they are rights of a constitutional or quasi-constitutional nature 'to protect the company against abuse by its management or the majority of the shareholders'. If an international action were brought on these lines, it not only could but—it is submitted—must terminate in a *non-liquet*. The weakness of this paragraph of the judgment is, in short, that it confuses the absence of a rule in a given field with the presence of a rule that there is no right of action in that field.

Furthermore, the law of international responsibility and of diplomatic protection is of customary origin, and a tribunal cannot declare the existence of a customary rule which might exist but does not yet exist.[288] But is it a sufficient answer to the Belgian contention to say (as the Court in effect does) that while there have been numerous successful claims for injuries to companies, there have been none for injury done to shareholders in analogous circumstances? The interpretative principle of *analogia legis*[289] has, as Fitzmaurice has observed,[290] been recognized by the Court; applying it, one might argue that the essence of the customary-law rule is the recognition of diplomatic protection where nationals of the protecting State have suffered harm by the action of the respondent State; and that the nature, in municipal law, of their interests which have been harmed is a secondary element.

The Court concedes that 'it may at first sight appear surprising that the evolution of law has not gone further and that no generally accepted rules in the matter have crystallized on the international plane'.[291] The judgment of the Court thus goes some way to recognize that the state of international law as regards protection of shareholders' rights is not entirely satisfactory: and Judge Fitzmaurice, in his separate opinion, was quite open about this: 'International law must in consequence be regarded as deficient and under-

---

[288] '. . . the Court, as a court of law, cannot render judgment *sub specie legis ferendae*, or anticipate the law before the legislation has laid it down': *Fisheries Jurisdiction, ICJ Reports*, 1974, pp. 23–4, para. 53.

[289] Cf. Gény, *Méthodes d'interprétation et sources en droit privé positif* (2nd edn.), vol. 1, pp. 304 ff.; Zajtay, 'Sur le raisonnement par analogie comme méthode d'interprétation du droit', *Liber Amicorum B.C.H. Aubin*, p. 307.

[290] This *Year Book*, 27 (1950), p. 18; *Collected Edition*, I, p. 18.

[291] *ICJ Reports*, 1970, p. 47, para. 89. It is in fact ironic that the judgment which contains a broad hint of disagreement with the 1966 judgment in the *South West Africa* case — see below — should in fact be capable of being summarized in a sentence from that judgment: 'Rights cannot be presumed to exist merely because it might seem desirable that they should': *ICJ Reports*, 1966, p. 48, para. 91.

developed in this field . . .';[292] and he indeed suggests that the law ought to provide:

an enlightened rule [which], while recognizing that the national government of the company can never be *required* to intervene, and that its reasons for not doing so cannot be questioned even though they may have nothing to do with the merits of the claim, would simply provide that in such event the government of the shareholders may do so—particularly if, as is frequently the case, it is just because the shareholding is mainly foreign that the government of the company feels that no sufficient national interest exists to warrant intervention on its own part.[293]

As Rosalyn Higgins has trenchantly observed, Judge Fitzmaurice:

seems to regard it as no part of his, or the Court's, function to develop law so as to provide 'an enlightened rule' rather than a 'deficient and under-developed' one . . . International law can never develop beyond the rudimentary state if the Court feels that the distinction between *lex lata* and *lex ferenda* forever prevents it from applying international law in a progressive manner in hitherto untested situations.[294]

However, what is also striking about the position taken up by Fitzmaurice and, less overtly, by the Court is its resemblance to the scenario postulated by Lauterpacht for a Court confronted with the need to choose between applying an unsatisfactory rule or pronouncing a *non-liquet*. In his paper entitled 'Some Observations on the Prohibition of "Non-Liquet" and the Completeness of the Law', Sir Hersch discussed in detail the possibility that, rather than pronounce a *non-liquet*, an international tribunal should apply a rule of law recognized to be unsatisfactory, and couple its decision with a recommendation for its improvement.

Is it in conformity with the judicial character of a pronouncement that, while leaving no doubt as to the law as declared by it and as indisputably binding upon the parties, it should—if it deems it necessary—draw attention to the shortcomings of the law thus declared and the necessity of its amendment? Is it consistent with its function that it should indicate directly—or indirectly by the manner of its reasoning—what ought to be the substance of any such change?[295]

Lauterpacht's view, though expressed in guarded terms, was that these questions should be answered in the affirmative.

The *Barcelona Traction* decision, however, also attracts the criticism expressed by Professor Julius Stone in his reply to Lauterpacht's paper.[296]

---

[292] *ICJ Reports*, 1970, p. 78, para. 25.

[293] Ibid., pp. 77–8, para. 24.

[294] Rosalyn Higgins, 'Aspects of the Case Concerning the Barcelona Traction Light and Power Co. Ltd.', *Virginia Journal of International Law*, 11 (1970–1), p. 341.

[295] *Symbolae Verzijl* (1958), p. 212; cf. also Fitzmaurice, this *Year Book*, 37 (1961), pp. 16–17; *Collected Edition*, II, pp. 649–50.

[296] Stone, '*Non Liquet* and the Function of Law in the International Community', this *Year Book*, 35 (1959), p. 124.

He points out that in effect Lauterpacht was regarding it as a likely situation

> that the Court would disapprove of the content of the rule which it has itself fashioned to deal with the case. For in the characteristic case where the *non liquet* issue is worth discussing the context of the rule to be applied, and therefore the result to be reached, would *ex hypothesi* be sufficiently absent or indeterminate to give the court ample room for choice.[297]

This is evidently exactly the criticism addressed by Rosalyn Higgins to the 1970 judgment as glossed by Fitzmaurice.

(2) *International law as constitutive or regulatory of States' rights*

The question whether there may be areas of international relations which are not regulated, or fully regulated, by international law was also in the background of the two *Fisheries Jurisdiction* cases; the claims presented to the Court in these cases involved the question whether it is sufficient justification for a State to show that an action which has been challenged is 'not contrary to international law'[298] rather than having to show that the action is authorized or permitted by a positive rule of international law.

The United Kingdom and the Federal Republic of Germany had each asked the Court to declare that Iceland's claim to a zone of exclusive fisheries jurisdiction extending 50 miles from baselines round its coasts was 'without foundation in international law and invalid' (United Kingdom) or 'has, as against the Federal Republic of Germany, no basis in international law'.

The decision of the Court was expressed in terms of the non-opposability of the Icelandic extension of fisheries jurisdiction to the two applicant States, because of the existence of established fishery rights enjoyed by them. From the discussion in Chapter I, section 3(2), above, it will be apparent that even if the Court had chosen to express its decision in more absolute terms, this would have been without legal effect in the relations between Iceland and any other State that chose to object to the extension.[299] The characteristic of the judgment as rendered which was regarded by a number of Members of the Court as vital[300] was not in fact the way in which the operative clause was expressed, but the reasoning underlying that clause. The key passages in the judgment are these:

> The provisions of the Icelandic Regulations of 14 July 1972 and the manner of

---

[297] Loc. cit. (previous note), at p. 148.

[298] The expression used in the operative part of the judgment in the *Fisheries* case (*ICJ Reports*, 1951, p. 143), and criticized by Fitzmaurice.

[299] In fact, as Judge Ignacio-Pinto pointed out, it need not even have led to a different effective decision, since the Court could, after stating that Iceland's extension of jurisdiction was invalid as a matter of general law, have gone on to devise a solution based on Iceland's exceptional situation: *ICJ Reports*, 1974, p. 36.

[300] See the Joint Separate Opinion of Judges Forster, Jiménez de Aréchaga, Nagendra Singh and Ruda, ibid., p. 45.

their implementation disregard the fishing rights of the Applicant . . . The Applicant is therefore justified in asking the Court to give all necessary protection to its own rights, while at the same time agreeing to recognize Iceland's preferential position. Accordingly, the Court is bound to conclude that the Icelandic Regulations . . . are not opposable to the United Kingdom, and the latter is under no obligation to accept the unilateral termination by Iceland of United Kingdom fishery rights in the area.[301]

That the Court could have gone further and considered the general validity of the Icelandic Regulations is indicated by the opening words of the following paragraph 'The findings stated by the Court in the preceding paragraph *suffice to provide a basis for the decision of the present case* . . .'.[302] What the Court was saying in effect is: whether or not the Icelandic Regulations are contrary to general international law, they certainly cannot be invoked against the applicants, so we do not need to consider the wider issue.

For this reason, the judgment itself did not have to tackle the question of principle whether the rules of international law are prohibitory against a background of freedom, or permissive against a background of restriction of action. Nevertheless, the *Fisheries Jurisdiction* cases are of interest in this respect, particularly as regards the nature and status of the legal rule asserted at various periods, and in various forms and fora, fixing the limit of the territorial sea, or of fishing or exclusive economic zones, at a defined distance from appropriate baselines—3 miles, '6 miles + 6 miles', 12 miles, 50 miles, or still higher figures.[303]

Lauterpacht, writing in 1950, when the trend towards wider and wider claims by coastal States was just beginning, took the view that there was a prohibitive rule determining the limit at which the high seas began, and therefore the limit of coastal State claims, and that this was virtually a matter of *jus cogens*. Discussing the role of protest with regard to unilateral claims to submarine areas, he suggested that, in general, protest against claims going beyond recognized limits was not necessary 'if the action of the state claiming to acquire title is so wrongful in relation to any particular state or so patently at variance with general international law as to render it wholly incapable of becoming the source of a legal right'; and the instance he gives is directly in point:

Thus, for instance, if a state were to proclaim an exclusive right of navigation, jurisdiction or exploitation on what is regarded by the generality of states as part of the high seas, the absence of protest would hardly make any difference to the legal position—in the same way as the manifest illegality of any other action would

---

[301] Ibid., p. 29, para. 67.

[302] Ibid., para. 68 (emphasis added).

[303] It should be emphasized that the present discussion is not intended to describe how the law of the sea has developed, but merely to consider, in the context of that law, the theoretical problems associated with the development of law in the light of observations made by the Court and its Members during the period under review.

preclude it from becoming a valid basis for precedent. *Ab injuria jus non oritur.* There are acts which are so tainted with nullity *ab initio* that no mere negligence of the interested state will cure it.[304]

If correct, this view would signify the near-impossibility of any development of customary law in the direction of extended claims of the coastal State. It is not clear whether Lauterpacht would have regarded as valid express agreements between States recognizing a claim to exclusive rights of a coastal State over part of the high seas. If such agreements were valid *inter partes*, a succession of them could presumably constitute a recognition that claims of this kind, while not valid *erga omnes*, were no longer an *injuria* incapable of producing rights; at that point, absence of protest would begin to be significant and effective for the development of customary law.

Subsequent developments of the practice of coastal State claims would seem to exclude the possibility of a rule of *jus cogens* which would deprive of even potential validity any purported extension beyond the established limit, having a paralysing effect on the development of customary law in the field. A rule which has itself developed by way of practice reaching further and further, as a rule of customary law, can hardly be assumed to provide that no further development in the same direction is possible. It would however be an over-simplification of the development of the law of the sea to regard it as a steady outward push by coastal States at the expense of the *res communis*.[305]

When discussing the *Fisheries* case in 1954, Fitzmaurice suggested by way of fundamental principle that

a State the legal validity of whose action is challenged must be prepared to show *either* that the action is justified by international law . . . *or* that the action is in a field which international law does not purport to regulate at all.[306]

Referring to the celebrated *dictum* in the judgment in that case that

The delimitation of sea areas has always an international aspect; it cannot be dependent merely upon the will of the coastal State as expressed in its municipal law . . .[307]

he observed that the delimitation of sea areas outside the recognized limits of territory could not be said to be 'a field which international law does not purport to regulate'; and that accordingly it was not sufficient to show that a claimed delimitation was 'not contrary to international law'.

---

[304] 'Sovereignty over Submarine Areas', this *Year Book*, 27 (1950), pp. 397–8. For reasons which he explained, Lauterpacht did not in fact consider that this was the case as regards proclamation of sovereignty over *submarine* areas, which he considered to be 'not inconsistent with existing law'; but this was his approach as regards exploitation of the sea itself.

[305] See, for example, O'Connell, 'Trends in the Law of the Sea', *Proceedings and Papers of the Fifth Commonwealth Law Conference* (1977), p. 415.

[306] This *Year Book*, 30 (1953), pp. 10–11; *Collected Edition*, I, pp. 141–2.

[307] *ICJ Reports*, 1951, p. 132.

In such situations as this, the controversy surrounding the Permanent Court's decision in the *Lotus* case is not yet resolved or exhausted. Is the approach to cases in which the law appears unsettled or dubious to be that 'restrictions upon the independence of States cannot . . . be presumed';[308] that 'the rights of States [have], by virtue of their sovereignty, to be regarded as absolute except in so far as restricted by some positive prohibition of international law' as Fitzmaurice expressed it; or is the position rather, as he himself held, that such an approach

leads in the final analysis to anarchy, since in the absence of any clearly proved restricting rule it makes the rights and actions of States dependent in the last resort on their own will and nothing else.[309]

The question of the applicability of the *Lotus* principle—or its antonym—in the field of extensions of maritime jurisdiction into high seas areas was specifically discussed by Judge Dillard in the *Fisheries Jurisdiction* cases, who saw them as raising questions of 'State autonomy and freedom of State action and presumptions flowing from such concepts'.[310] He described the attitude of Iceland as equivalent to a contention that

Because of the wide divergence in State practice, . . . there is no law or at least a lacuna in the law. viewed as a body of restraints on State conduct, and therefore the law does not prevent the extension by each State of its exclusive fisheries jurisdiction.[311]

So interpreted, this would amount to a philosophy of freedom of State action except where there can be shown to be a prohibitive rule (which may of course be deduced from the existence of a permissive rule in favour of some other State, the rights conferred by such permissive rule having a counterpart in the obligations of the prohibitive rule). Judge Dillard however goes on to re-express the presumed Icelandic approach in somewhat different terms:

She is not claiming an exception to an *established* rule, but a different kind of rule, namely a permissive rule which, in the absence of a specific rule to the contrary, permits the coastal State in a special situation to extend unilaterally its jurisdiction to an extent that it deems reasonable.[312]

The reference to a 'special situation' is in fact only consistent with a permissive rule; conceptually, if States are free to extend their fisheries jurisdiction unless there is a conflicting right or prohibitive rule, this must be the general case, and the restriction must be the exception or 'special situation'.

---

[308] *PCIJ*, Series A, No. 10, p. 18. Lauterpacht indeed thought that the principle so stated was almost a tautology: *The Development of International Law by the International Court*, p. 361.

[309] This *Year Book*, 30 (1953), p. 9; *Collected Edition*, I, p. 140.

[310] *ICJ Reports*, 1974, p. 59.

[311] Ibid., pp. 58–9.

[312] Ibid., p. 59.

Judge Dillard went on to express his own position on the question of States' freedom of action:

Borrowing from Lauterpacht, I would put the matter as follows: if the exercise of freedom trespasses on the interests of other States, then the issue arises as to its justification.[313]

The difficulty with this approach is the definition of the 'interests of other States';[314] they are presumably not rights,[315] but they are apparently something entitled to protection. If they are so protected, then there must be a correlative obligation to respect them; from which it must be concluded that there is a prohibitive rule in existence.

Judge de Castro came to 'the pessimistic conclusion that there is in international law no binding and uniform rule fixing the maximum extent of the jurisdiction of States with regard to fisheries' but continued: 'From this conclusion it has been deduced that there is a legal vacuum, but in my opinion this deduction is not based on conclusive reasons.'[316] Further on in his opinion, he apparently based himself on an implied presumption against State freedom of action in this domain:

The high seas are regarded as *res omnium communis*, and the use of them belongs equally to all peoples. The appropriation of an exclusive fishery zone in an area hitherto considered as part of the free seas is equivalent to deprivation of other people of their rights. The extension of its jurisdiction over the adjacent sea by a coastal State presupposes a reduction of the freedom of fishing of other States, and such respective increase and loss of power *calls for legal justification*.[317]

Judge de Castro's escape from the dilemma presented by the

conflict which is emerging between the principle of the freedom of the high seas with regard to fisheries, and the trends in favour of extension of the zone of jurisdiction of coastal States[318]

was to extend the scope of custom to find a place for the concepts of 'special rights, preferential rights and historic rights':

In order to be binding as a legal rule, the general conviction (*opinio communis*) does not have to fulfil all the conditions necessary for the emergence of a custom.[319]

The joint separate opinion of five judges (Judges Forster, Bengzon, Jiménez de Aréchaga, Nagendra Singh and Ruda) in the *Fisheries Jurisdiction* cases, however, held that a general practice had developed around a proposal made at the 1960 Conference on the Law of the Sea, whereby 'an

---

[313] Ibid.; the reference is to *The Development of International Law by the International Court*, p. 361.

[314] The expression appears in the 1958 Geneva Convention on the High Seas, by which States, in exercising their freedom of fishing, are to 'pay reasonable regard to the interests of other States'.

[315] Cf. the distinction made in the *Barcelona Traction* judgment, *ICJ Reports*, 1970, p. 36, para. 46.

[316] Ibid., p. 95.

[317] *ICJ Reports*, 1974, p. 97 (emphasis added).

[318] Ibid., p. 97.

[319] Ibid., p. 100,

exclusive fishery zone beyond the territorial sea has become an established feature of contemporary international law'.[320] They continued:

> It is also true that the joint formula voted at that Conference provided for a 6 + 6 formula, i.e., for an exclusive 12-mile fishery zone. It is however necessary to make a distinction between the two meanings which may be ascribed to that reference to 12 miles:
> (a) the 12-mile extension has now obtained recognition to the point that even distant-water fishing States no longer object to a coastal State extending its exclusive fisheries jurisdiction zone to 12 miles; or, on the other hand,
> (b) the 12-mile rule has come to mean that States cannot validly extend their exclusive fishery zones beyond that limit.
> . . . In our view, the concept of the fishery zone and the 12-mile limit became established with the meaning indicated in . . . (a) above . . .[321]

What, however, is the significance of a 'limit' of a defined number of miles from baselines round the coasts being set by international law?

Whatever limit may be set by general international law, unless this is to be treated as a matter of *jus cogens* (which, as noted above, seems to be no longer a tenable view), it will always remain open to the coastal State to conclude agreements with other States as to their action, or refraining from action, in a further area outside the limit, tantamount to a recognition of a special status for that further area, or of rights—of a treaty-law nature—of the coastal State over it.[322] In their joint opinion in the *Fisheries Jurisdiction* cases, the five judges in fact list a number of examples.[323]

It must follow, however, that what can be done by specific agreement can equally be done by tacit acceptance; that a State which enters into an agreement of restraint, implying special rights of a coastal State over an area beyond some 'established' limit set by international law, can equally, if it so wishes, simply refrain from protest if the coastal State asserts a claim to such rights over that area. Accordingly, the coastal State must equally be free to assert such a claim, not as being in conformity with existing law (though the coastal State may, by way of 'window-dressing', assert that it is), but so that it can take its chance of acceptance or protest on the part of other States interested.

---

[320] Ibid., p. 46.

[321] Ibid., pp. 46–7; a similar distinction is made by Judge de Castro, ibid., pp. 86, 90.

[322] This would, however, appear to be no longer the case as regards 'the sea-bed and ocean floor and subsoil thereof, beyond the limits of national jurisdiction', the definition of the 'Area' in the United Nations Convention on the Law of the Sea (Art. 1 (1)), since not only is the Area proclaimed to be 'the common heritage of mankind' (Art. 136), but Article 311(6) provides that
> 'States parties agree that there shall be no amendments to the basic principle relating to the common heritage of mankind set forth in Article 136 and that they shall not be party to any agreement in derogation thereof'.
Whether or to what extent the Convention is generally binding as a reflection or crystallization of customary law is a question not here examined.

[323] *ICJ Reports*, 1974, p. 50, footnote. The five judges also point out that certain particularly influential coastal States can offer more inducements to enter into such agreements than others; they therefore reject such evidence as practice in support of an alleged customary-law rule.

When the five judges in their joint opinion discuss the possibility that the 12-mile rule might mean 'that States cannot *validly* extend their exclusive fishery zones beyond that limit', the question remains: what is the sense of the word 'validly'? The 1958 Geneva Convention on the High Seas had already provided that 'The high seas being open to all nations, no State may *validly* purport to subject any part of them to its sovereignty'.[324] If we exclude the possibility of a rule of *jus cogens*, which would strike down the agreements listed by the five judges for extension of fishery limits by conventional (in the sense of treaty-law) means, the meaning must be that an extension of jurisdiction beyond the established limit will have no intrinsic validity, so as to be opposable *erga omnes*; its validity will, at least initially, be relative, within a finite number of bilateral relationships, between the coastal State and individual consenting—or non-protesting—States.

It must follow further, *a contrario*, that if the established limit has any meaning at all, it must be the furthest distance to which jurisdiction may be extended in a way which *does* have intrinsic validity; the furthest extension which is not dependent on acceptance or lack of protest by other States considered individually.[325] It is thus in a sense a *minimum* limit rather than a *maximum*, though it must also remain open to the coastal State to claim jurisdiction over a more restricted area if it so wishes.

This is the view expressed in the separate opinion of Judge Sir Humphrey Waldock in the *Fisheries Jurisdiction* cases, that ever since the failure of the Hague Codification Conference of 1930,

> The prevailing opinion was that . . . the 3-mile limit remained a limit which could be said to be generally accepted and, therefore, *ipso jure*, valid and enforceable against any other State; but that a claim in excess of that limit could no longer be said to be *ipso jure* contrary to international law and invalid *erga omnes*; and that the validity of such a claim as against another State would depend on whether it was accepted or acquiesced in by that State . . . In the absence of clearly established general rules, the legal issue has continued to present itself in terms of the opposability of the claim to each other State rather than of the absolute legality or illegality of the claim *erga omnes*; in other words, in terms of the acceptance or acquiescence of other States.[326]

The use of such an expression as 'not contrary to international law' may therefore be, at the very least, a linguistic convenience to convey the difference between asserted extensions of jurisdiction within and without the

---

[324] Emphasis added. However, the term 'high seas' was defined to mean 'all parts of the sea that are not included in the territorial sea or internal waters', which would appear to be what Sir Ian Sinclair has, in another context, called an 'ambulatory' or 'shifting' definition ('The Concept of a Continental Shelf', *Proceedings and Papers of the Fifth Commonwealth Law Conference* (1977), p. 450); if the generally-recognized territorial sea were to expand, presumably the high seas as so defined would shrink, and the Convention regime remain formally intact. In this sense see also Judge de Castro in *ICJ Reports*, 1974, pp. 92–3.

[325] For simplicity's sake, this leaves out of account the position of the 'single recalcitrant State' — the State which has stood out consistently against a developing rule, and retains exemption from it, as was the case of Norway in the *Fisheries* case.

[326] *ICJ Reports*, 1974, pp. 119–20, paras. 34–5.

established limit. An extension within the limit, which may not legally—or 'validly'—be opposed, may be said to be one which is supported by a rule of positive international law. An extension which goes beyond the established limit is not contrary to international law, in the sense that the act of asserting the extension is not a breach of international law; but no rule of positive international law requires other States to respect it.

In the course of Fitzmaurice's discussion of the *Fisheries* case, he regarded it as an important point that

so soon as it is admitted that international law governs the question of the breadth of the territorial sea, it follows automatically that international law must also prescribe *a* standard maximum breadth, universally valid and obligatory in principle, even though variations may be allowed in particular cases, e.g. on the basis of long continued (historic) usage. If this is not so, then international law would *not* govern the question of the extent of the territorial sea, since there is no practical difference between saying that international law prescribes no standard breadth for that sea, and saying that States are free to determine the breadth as they please.[327]

This can be accepted, in the light of subsequent developments, only on the basis that the word 'obligatory' refers to the duty of third States to accept the standard maximum breadth, not to a duty of the coastal State not to purport to go beyond it. It is doubtful, however, whether this was what Sir Gerald had in mind.

Although the Court, by dealing with the *Fisheries Jurisdiction* cases in terms of opposability, did not have to tackle the *Lotus* controversy directly, it made a *dictum* which is of much greater significance in this respect than might appear. To appreciate this, reference has first to be made again to Fitzmaurice's article of 1954, in which he took the view that a positive permissive rule of law must be shown to exist. One of Fitzmaurice's reasons for thinking this was that if the presumption were in favour of unfettered sovereignty, 'the outcome of a great many disputes would depend largely on the accident of which side was plaintiff and which defendant';[328] the defendant would only have to show that its action was 'not contrary to international law'. It is suggested however that this argument is not conclusive, since the reverse situation would arise if it were essential that the State challenged be able to show that its action was justified by a positive rule of law. In the field of unsettled legal regulation where our hypothesis is laid, any presumption places either the plaintiff or the defendant in a position of strength. The conclusion must surely be that such presumptions as to the

---

[327] This *Year Book*, 31 (1954), p. 385; *Collected Edition*, I, p. 215. This passage was regarded by Judge de Castro as so rigid as to be a *reductio ad absurdum*: *ICJ Reports*, 1974, p. 95.

[328] This *Year Book*, 30 (1953), p. 11; *Collected Edition*, I, p. 142. An argument on these lines had in fact been advanced by Sir Eric Beckett as counsel for the United Kingdom in the *Fisheries* case, but it was there addressed to the problem of the burden of proof: *Pleadings*, vol. 4, pp. 32–3. Beckett did also contend that there should be a presumption in favour of freedom of the seas, which was equivalent to requiring Norway to prove the legality of its baseline system; ibid., pp. 33–4.

existence or otherwise of a rule of law, while possibly valuable as an aid to legal ratiocination, cannot be used, or can only in the last resort be used, as a basis for decision; and this is the essential justification of the principle *jura novit curia*.

In fact the Court in the *Fisheries Jurisdiction* cases, when commenting on the difficulties resulting from the absence of the respondent from the proceedings, observed that

> The Court however, as an international judicial organ, is deemed to take judicial notice of international law, and is therefore required in a case falling under Article 53 of the Statute, as in any other case, to consider on its own initiative all rules of international law which may be relevant to the settlement of the dispute. It being the duty of the Court itself to ascertain and apply the relevant law in the given circumstances of the case, the burden of establishing or proving rules of international law cannot be imposed upon any of the parties, for the law lies within the judicial knowledge of the Court.[329]

By thus dismissing the application of the concept of the burden of proof, the Court was also debarring itself from resting its decision on the application of a presumption. If a presumption is to be employed as an element in the reasoning of a decision, then—unless it is an absolute presumption, in which case it is itself a rule of law—the question whether or not the party against whom it operates has succeeded in reversing it is a question of burden of proof.[330] If therefore the Court asserts that 'the law lies within the judicial knowledge of the Court', and that it will not impose a burden of proof, it cannot then find that there is a presumption either of the legal or of the illegal character of the conduct of the respondent to which the claim is directed. Unless the law is in fact found to be certain, the only course remaining would appear to be a *non-liquet*; and the *Fisheries Jurisdiction* judgments therefore seem, perhaps surprisingly, to suggest that the Court would contemplate declaring a *non-liquet* if circumstances so required.

2. *International Legal Obligations* erga omnes *and the* actio popularis

This concept may be said to have developed wholly within the period under review, at least as far as its recognition and application by the Court

---

[329] *ICJ Reports*, 1974, p. 9, para. 17. Fitzmaurice regards the latter sentence as a 'rather startling remark', and explains it as follows:

'The intended meaning (though not well expressed) must have been that the law is the law, and is whatever it is, whether or not the party concerned manages to establish its propositions, whereas the onus of establishing allegations of fact lies on the party making them and failure to do so may *per se* be deemed to negative the allegations':

'The Problem of the "Non-Appearing" Defendant Government', this *Year Book*, 51 (1980), p. 108, footnote 7.

[330] The rejection of the burden of proof as a possible determining factor also excludes another approach which might have been of particular applicability in the *Fisheries Jurisdiction* cases, that of the proof of change in the law. Whether or not the *Lotus* approach is adopted in a situation where the

are concerned.[331] Fitzmaurice's first set of articles did contain a brief section devoted to 'Obligations Owed to the International Community at Large, not to any Particular State as Beneficiary',[332] but this was devoted only to examination of a suggestion by Judge Alvarez in his dissenting opinion in the *Status of South West Africa* case,[333] and a brief discussion whether, for example, the obligation to recognize a new State or government might be regarded as an obligation toward the international community at large.

There is of course a sense in which many (though not all) of the obligations of States in general international law may be said to be obligations *erga omnes*. Thus the requirements of the law concerning the treatment of aliens oblige a State to treat the nationals of all other States in accordance with that law, so that there is, at least, an obligation *in posse* owed to all States. Such obligation however only takes on effective existence when a particular alien is alleged to have been improperly treated; and the obligation is then owed only to the State of his nationality.[334] The essence of the obligation *erga omnes* as developed by the Court since 1970 is that its breach confers a *locus standi in judicio* not merely on the State which has, or whose national has, been injured, but on all States. It is perhaps not so much an obligation *erga omnes* as an obligation of which the breach opens responsibility *erga omnes*.

The key pronouncement on the subject was made in the judgment in the *Barcelona Traction* case. Referring to the obligations of a State concerning the treatment of aliens in its territory, the Court said:

These obligations, however, are neither absolute nor unqualified. In particular, an essential distinction should be drawn between the obligations of a State towards the international community as a whole, and those arising vis-à-vis another State in the field of diplomatic protection. By their very nature the former are the concern of all States. In view of the importance of the rights involved, all States can be held to have a legal interest in their protection; they are obligations *erga omnes*.

Such obligations derive, for example, in contemporary international law, from the outlawing of acts of aggression, and of genocide, as also from the principles and rules concerning the basic rights of the human person, including protection from slavery and racial discrimination. Some of the corresponding rights of protection have entered into the body of general international law (*Reservations to the Convention on the Prevention and Punishment of the Crime of Genocide, Advisory*

law in the relevant domain has never been settled with certainty, it might be reasonable to expect that where the law was established with reasonable clarity, but one party asserts that a new rule of law has come into existence, that party should bear the burden of proving it.

[331] In this sense, Seidl-Hohenveldern, for whom the *actio popularis* was unknown in general international law prior to the *Barcelona Traction* judgment: 'Actio popularis im Völkerrecht?', *Communicazioni e studi*, 14 (1975), p. 805. On the other hand, it has been suggested that the concept, analogous to that of 'absolute rights' in some continental legal systems, has always been part of international law, but has been obscured by the voluntarist approach: Ruiz, 'Las obligaciones *erga omnes* en derecho internacional publico', *Homenaje al Professor Miaja de la Muela* (1979), p. 222; *sed quaere*.

[332] This *Year Book*, 27 (1950), pp. 14–15; *Collected Edition*, I, pp. 14–15.

[333] *ICJ Reports*, 1950, p. 177.

[334] The point is clearly made in a jurisdictional context in the separate opinion of Judge Morelli in the *Northern Cameroons* case, *ICJ Reports*, 1963, p. 146.

Opinion, ICJ Reports 1951, p. 23); others are conferred by international instruments of a universal or quasi-universal character.[335]

The essential distinction, in the Court's thinking, between such obligations *erga omnes* and other obligations of international law appears from the next paragraph of the judgment:

Obligations the performance of which is the subject of diplomatic protection are not of the same category. It cannot be held, when one such obligation in particular is in question, in a specific case, that all States have a legal interest in its observance. In order to bring a claim in respect of the breach of such an obligation, a State must first establish its right to do so . . .[336]

The implication *a contrario* is clear: a claim may be brought by any State against any State alleging a breach of an obligation towards the international community as a whole, without the applicant State having to show that it has itself, directly or through its nationals, suffered injury from the alleged breach.

Since there was no suggestion in the *Barcelona Traction* case that Spain had violated any obligation of this character, the passage quoted above must be regarded as an *obiter dictum*; furthermore, from the practical point of view, for this reason neither the facts in the case nor the remainder of the Court's judgment give any further enlightenment as to the application of the principle stated. Such enlightenment can however be gained, paradoxically, from study of an earlier decision, the 1966 judgment in the *South West Africa* cases; it is more or less an open secret that the passage in the *Barcelona Traction* judgment—with its specific reference to 'protection from . . . racial discrimination',[337] was intended as a public disavowal, by the Court in its 1970 composition, of at least one element in the controversial decision given by the (barest) majority of the judges sitting in 1966.[338]

The title of jurisdiction relied on by the applicants in the *South West Africa* cases was Article 7, paragraph 2, of the Mandate for South West Africa, which read:

The Mandatory agrees that, if any dispute whatever should arise between the Mandatory and another Member of the League of Nations relating to the interpret-

---

[335] *ICJ Reports*, 1970, p. 32, paras. 33–4.

[336] Ibid., p. 32, para. 35. The distinction is based, as Seidl-Hohenveldern points out, on a definition of the 'basic rights of the human person' which excludes rights to personal property, notwithstanding the inclusion of the right to property in the Universal Declaration of Human Rights: 'Actio popularis im Völkerrecht?', *Communicazioni e studi*, 14 (1975), p. 804.

[337] An interesting explanation put forward for the inconsistency between the *South West Africa* judgment and the *Barcelona Traction dictum* is that the UN Convention on the Elimination of Racial Discrimination had come into force in the meantime: Miaja de la Muela, 'El interés de las partes en el proceso ante el Tribunal internacional de justicia', *Communicazioni e studi*, 14 (1975), p. 558.

[338] See for example Gross, *The Future of the International Court of Justice*, vol. 2, pp. 748–50. Rosalyn Higgins, after noting the apparent inconsistency, comments drily 'One is aware, of course, that the composition of the Court has changed somewhat': 'Aspects of the Case Concerning the Barcelona Traction Light and Power Co. Ltd.', *Virginia Journal of International Law*, 11 (1970–1), p. 330, footnote 8.

ation or the application of the provisions of the Mandate, such dispute, if it cannot be settled by negotiation, shall be submitted to the Permanent Court of International Justice provided for by Article 14 of the Covenant of the League of Nations.[339]

South Africa had contended (Third Preliminary Objection) that the conflict or disagreement which the applicants sought to bring before the Court—essentially over whether the respondent was failing to observe the requirements of the Mandate as regards its treatment of the native inhabitants and administration of the Territory—was not a dispute as envisaged in Article 7, 'more particularly in that the said conflict or disagreement does not affect any material interests of the applicant States or their nationals'.[340]

In support of this proposition, the Respondent contends that the word 'dispute' must be given its generally accepted meaning in a context of a compulsory jurisdiction clause and that, when so interpreted, it means a disagreement or conflict between the Mandatory and another Member of the League concerning the legal rights and interests of such other Member in the matter before the Court; that 'the obligations imposed for the benefit of the inhabitants would have been owed to the League on whose behalf the Mandatory undertook to exercise the Mandate'.[341]

The response of the Court in 1962 to this argument was as follows:

The Respondent's contention runs counter to the natural and ordinary meaning of the provisions of Article 7 of the Mandate, which mentions 'any dispute whatever' arising between the Mandatory and another Member of the League of Nations 'relating to the interpretation or the application of the provisions of the Mandate'. The language used is broad, clear and precise: it gives rise to no ambiguity and it permits of no exception. It refers to any dispute whatever relating not to any one particular provision or provisions, but to 'the provisions' of the Mandate, obviously meaning all or any provisions, whether they relate to substantive obligations of the Mandatory toward the inhabitants of the Territory or toward the other Members of the League or to its obligation to submit to supervision by the League under Article 6 or to protection under Article 7 itself. For the manifest scope and purport of the provisions of this Article indicate that the Members of the League were understood to have a legal right or interest in the observance by the Mandatory of its obligations both toward the inhabitants of the Mandated Territory, and toward the League of Nations and its Members.[342]

At the close of its 1962 judgment, the Court included in its summing-up its conclusion that 'the dispute is one which is envisaged in the said Article 7 . . . Consequently the Court is competent to hear the dispute on the merits'. Its formal finding in the operative clause of its judgment was 'that it has jurisdiction to adjudicate upon the merits of the dispute'.[343] The decision was adopted by majority vote; and among the judges voting

[339] Quoted in *ICJ Reports*, 1962, p. 335.
[340] Ibid., p. 343.
[341] Ibid.
[342] Ibid.
[343] Ibid., p. 347.

against it was Sir Gerald Fitzmaurice, who filed a lengthy dissenting opinion, of which the authorship was shared with Sir Percy Spender.[344]

The context of the 1962 judgment was the question of jurisdiction, and the Court's finding was solely one of jurisdiction. Whether an applicant has a legal right or interest in the subject-matter of the proceedings is normally regarded as a question of admissibility, and was so treated in the *Barcelona Traction* case. Nevertheless the Court, in its 1962 judgment in the *South West Africa* case, had made a *dictum*, if not a finding, that the obligations of the Mandatory in respect of its conduct were owed not only to the League of Nations as an institution, but also to the members individually, and were backed by the jurisdictional clause of Article 7. An obligation owed to the other members of the League is not an obligation *erga omnes*, despite the vocation to universality of membership which characterized the League; but the Court's 1962 interpretation of Article 7 shared one essential feature with the later definition of obligations *erga omnes*. Each of the States to which the obligation was owed would not have, or would not necessarily have, a direct interest in compliance with it, in the sense of direct injury to the State,[345] or to its national, resulting from failure to comply with it.

The 1966 judgment of the Court[346] was based squarely on the question of the existence of a legal right or interest of the applicants appertaining to the subject-matter of the claim. The contention that that question had already been settled by the 1962 judgment was rejected by the Court in a couple of brief paragraphs.[347]

The Court at the outset drew a distinction between two categories of obligations of the Mandatory under the mandate: the duty to respect the special interests of the individual States in the territory (which in the case of the class 'C' Mandate for South West Africa meant no more than respect for the rights of missionaries)—the 'special interest' clauses—and the obligations as to treatment of the natives and administration of the territory

---

[344] In that opinion, the two judges summed up as follows their view on the Third Preliminary Objection:

'This view is, *first*, that Article 7 must be understood as referring to a dispute in the traditional sense of the term, as it would have been understood in 1920, namely a dispute between the actual parties before the Court about their own interests, in which they appear as representing themselves and not some other entity or interest; and *secondly*, that Article 7 in the general context and scheme of the Mandate, was intended to enable the Members of the League to protect their own rights and those of their nationals, and not to enable them to intervene in matters affecting solely the conduct of the Mandate in relation to the peoples of the mandated territory' (ibid., pp. 558–9).

They did not express any view on the implications of the Court's statement that the League Members 'were understood to have a legal right or interest in the observance by the Mandatory' of *all* its obligations under the Mandate.

[345] It would of course be fair to express the matter also by saying that, where *erga omnes* obligations are concerned, the fact that all States are interested in their observance means that each State suffers a symbolic or moral injury from their breach. This does not however affect the point here made.

[346] According to McWhinney (*The International Court of Justice and the Western Tradition of International Law*, p. 39), Sir Gerald Fitzmaurice is 'known' to have been the principal author of the majority judgment: cf. also ibid., p. 69.

[347] This aspect of the case raises questions of *res judicata* and the relationship between jurisdiction and admissibility, to be examined in a later article.

under the supervision of the League—the 'conduct' clauses. The importance of this was that if there had been no 'special interest' clauses, the jurisdictional clause in Article 7 could only have referred to the 'conduct'
clauses; and it would have made no sense to give a procedural right of
action before the Permanent Court unless a substantive right or interest was
conferred by the Mandate, which the procedure right would protect. As it
was,

Having regard to the situation thus outlined, and in particular to the distinction
to be drawn between the 'conduct' and the 'special interests' provisions of the various instruments of mandate, the question which now arises for decision by the
Court is whether any legal right or interest exists for the applicants relative to the
Mandate, apart from such as they may have in respect of the latter category of provisions;—a matter on which the Court expresses no opinion, since this category is
not in issue in the present case. In respect of the former category—the 'conduct'
provisions—the question which has to be decided is whether, according to the
scheme of the mandates and of the mandates system as a whole, any legal right or
interest (which is a different thing from a political interest) was vested in the members of the League of Nations, including the present Applicants, individually and
each in its own separate right to call for the carrying out of the mandates as regards
their 'conduct' clauses;—or whether this function must, rather, be regarded as having appertained exclusively to the League itself, and not to each and every member
State, separately and independently.[348]

The Court's conclusion was that no such right or interest was vested in
individual members of the League.

The most material part of the judgment for present purposes was, however, that in which it dealt with what it called the 'necessity' argument. The
details of that contention are not here material, but in essence the suggestion was that judicial control of the 'conduct' obligations was a necessary
part of the system and could only be secured by reading Article 7 in a wide
sense as conferring individual enforcement rights on the members of the
League. When rejecting this, the Court said:

. . . the Court, bearing in mind that the rights of the Applicants must be determined by reference to the character of the system said to give rise to them, considers that the 'necessity' argument falls to the ground for lack of verisimilitude in
the context of the economy and philosophy of that system. Looked at in another
way moreover, the argument amounts to a plea that the Court should allow the
equivalent of an 'actio popularis', or right resident in any member of a community
to take legal action in vindication of a public interest. But although a right of this
kind may be known to certain municipal systems of law, it is not known to international law as it stands at present: nor is the Court able to regard it as imported by
the 'general principles of law' referred to in Article 38, paragraph 1(c), of its
Statute.[349]

---

[348] *ICJ Reports*, 1966, p. 22, para. 14.
[349] Ibid., p. 47, para. 88.

To what extent was this finding contradicted by the *dictum* of the Court four years later?

It was not in fact claimed by the applicants that the alleged right of enforcement, being derived from an article of the Mandate which referred to members of the League, was exercisable by any State whatever; if it was asserted to be a 'right resident in any member of a community', that community could only be that of the members of the League of Nations, not the community of States. Furthermore, what was in question was the interpretation of an instrument concluded in 1920; the 'necessity' argument was founded on what was claimed to be an essential part of the structure of the mandate system as originally conceived. Yet the Court specifically stated that its finding was based upon contemporary international law: it refers to 'international law as it stands at present'.[350]

This paragraph of the Court's judgment therefore appears, despite the statement that the 'necessity' argument is simply being 'looked at in another way', to be addressed to a different and wider contention, which had not been specifically advanced, namely that certain at least of the Mandate's 'conduct' obligations were capable of enforcement by a true *actio popularis*, in short, that they were obligations *erga omnes*;[351] and it was thus this contention also that the 1966 judgment summarily rejected.

The *dictum* in the *Barcelona Traction* judgment in 1970, though *obiter*, thus clearly signalled a *revirement de jurisprudence* on this question. The subsequent judicial involvement with the fate of South West Africa, in the request for advisory opinion on the *Legal Consequences for States of the Continued Presence of South Africa in Namibia (South West Africa) notwithstanding Security Council Resolution 276 (1970)*, did not however require the hint given in 1970 to be followed up, since action to enforce what were seen as the obligations of the Mandate was taken by the political organs of the organization, in place of the organs of the League, rather than by States which had been members of the League.

In connection with the concept of international legal obligations *erga omnes*, it is however appropriate to refer also to the declaration made by the Court in the *Namibia* case that

the termination of the Mandate and the declarations [by the Security Council in resolution 276] of the illegality of South Africa's presence in Namibia are opposable to all States in the sense of barring *erga omnes* the legality of a situation which is maintained in violation of international law: . . .[352]

In the context of the question put to the Court as to the 'legal consequences

---

[350] See the discussion of the intertemporal law principle below, pp. 128 ff. Presumably however the non-existence of an *actio popularis* in the time of the League would have been regarded as an *a fortiori* case.

[351] Mbaye ('L'Intérêt pour agir devant la Cour internationale de Justice', *Recueil des cours*, 209 (1988–II), pp. 316–18) rejects the identification of the right to rely on an obligation *erga omnes* with an *actio popularis*.

[352] *Legal Consequences for States of the Continued Presence of South Africa in Namibia (South West Africa) notwithstanding Security Council Resolution 276 (1970)*, *ICJ Reports*, 1971, p. 56, para. 126.

for States' of the situation in Namibia, the practical question to which the above finding was addressed was that of the consequences for non-members of the United Nations.[353]

In the operative part of its advisory opinion, the Court indicated in succession the legal consequences for South Africa, for member States and for non-member States; South Africa was declared to be 'under obligation to withdraw its administration from Namibia immediately . . .'. One possible view of the declaration quoted above is that South Africa was under an obligation *erga omnes*, of the kind contemplated in the *Barcelona Traction* judgment, to withdraw from Namibia, such that any State could seek the enforcement of that obligation, without being required to show an individual legal interest in the matter. In the absence of any subsisting jurisdictional provision binding on South Africa, however, the point could not be tested.

The *Barcelona Traction dictum*, however, found an echo when in 1986 the Court was occupied with the case concerning *Military and Paramilitary Activities in and against Nicaragua (Nicaragua v. United States of America)*. Before considering the judgment in that case it is, however, necessary to revert a moment to two passages in the *Barcelona Traction* judgment, one of which was quoted above, but the implications of which have not yet been considered. After listing examples of what the Court saw as international obligations *erga omnes*, the Court continued:

Some of the contemporary rights of protection have entered into the body of general international law (*Reservations to the Convention on the Prevention and Punishment of the Crime of Genocide, Advisory Opinion, ICJ Reports 1951*, p. 23); others are conferred by international instruments of a universal or quasi universal character.[354]

Later in its judgment it added a further qualification:

With regard more particularly to human rights, to which reference has already been made in paragraph 34 of this Judgment, it should be noted that these also include protection against denial of justice. However, on the universal level, the instruments which embody human rights do not confer on States the capacity to protect the victims of infringements of such rights irrespective of their nationality.[355]

There are thus, it seems, two mutually exclusive classes of rights of international protection: those which are conferred by 'international instruments of a universal or quasi-universal character',[356] and those which have

---

[353] The action taken by the General Assembly and the Security Council and the obligations of member States will be discussed in a later article under the heading of international organizations.

[354] *ICJ Reports*, 1970, p. 32, para. 34.

[355] Ibid., p. 47, para. 91.

[356] The term 'quasi' is often useful legal shorthand, but this is an instance where more precision would have been desirable. The Court goes on to refer to the European Convention on Human Rights, which is hardly of a 'universal' character, unless the meaning is universality within a particular group of States of some homogeneity.

entered into the body of general international law. The latter do confer on States the capacity to protect victims of infringement irrespective of their nationality; the former do not—or at least, whether they do or not depends on the specific provision of the instruments referred to. Why this distinction should exist is not clear, nor is the relationship of the two categories: for example, would the conclusion of a new universal or quasi-universal instrument providing only for protection by the national State of the victim destroy or restrict a pre-existing universal right?

In view of this apparent withdrawal on the question of human rights, and of the existence of 'international instruments' of at least a 'quasi-universal character' dealing with the other subjects mentioned by the Court—slavery, racial discrimination—it may be doubted whether these passages can be relied on to support any customary-law right to invoke an *erga omnes* obligation, except in the case of genocide.[357] If this is so, the 1970 *dictum* is little more than an empty gesture. A right of protection conferred by a multilateral treaty derives its validity from the treaty, not from a principle that 'in view of the importance of the rights involved', all States have 'a legal interest in their protection'.[358]

In the 1986 judgment in the case brought by Nicaragua against the United States, the Court, when discussing allegations made in United States Government circles against the Government of Nicaragua which, to some extent, appeared to have been advanced as justifying the actions of the United States against the latter Government, noted 'that Nicaragua is accused . . . of violating human rights'.[359] Let it be recalled that in 1970 the Court had given, as one of its examples of international legal obligations *erga omnes*, those deriving 'from the principles and rules concerning the basic rights of the human person'.[360] Consistently with this approach, in 1986 the Court continued:

> This particular point requires to be studied independently of the question of the existence of a 'legal commitment' by Nicaragua towards the Organization of American States to respect these rights; the absence of such a commitment would not mean that Nicaragua could with impunity violate human rights.[361]

The Court thus appeared to be suggesting that Nicaragua was subject, along with all other States, to an international obligation *erga omnes* to

---

[357] Even in the case of genocide, it does not appear necessarily to follow that because, as the Court stated in 1951, 'the principles underlying the [Genocide] Convention are principles which are recognized by civilized nations as binding on States, even without any conventional obligation', the principles may be invoked by any State to bring a claim alleging genocide, even if no national of the applicant State has been harmed.

Leo Gross observes on the other hand that

'If the pronunciamento were to be taken seriously'—a striking qualification—'it would be difficult to imagine anything more likely to discourage States from accepting the compulsory jurisdiction of the Court': *The Future of the International Court of Justice*, vol. 2, p. 749.

[358] *ICJ Reports*, 1970, p. 32, para. 33.

[359] *ICJ Reports*, 1986, p. 134, para. 267.

[360] *ICJ Reports*, 1970, p. 32, para. 34.

[361] *ICJ Reports*, 1986, p. 134, para. 267.

respect human rights, not dependent on the existence of a specific treaty commitment. The United States, which was not appearing in the proceedings, had however not presented any formal counterclaim against Nicaragua on this (or any) ground. However, in the next sentences of its judgment, the Court apparently resiled from any suggestion of a customary-law right of action in this field:

However, where human rights are protected by international conventions, that protection takes the form of such arrangements for monitoring or ensuring respect for human rights as are provided for in the conventions themselves. The political pledge by Nicaragua was made in the context of the Organization of American States, the organs of which were consequently entitled to monitor its observance. The Court has noted above . . . that the Nicaraguan Government has since 1979 ratified a number of international instruments on human rights, and one of these was the American Convention on Human Rights (the Pact of San José, Costa Rica). The mechanisms provided for therein have functioned. The Inter-American Commission on Human Rights in fact took action and compiled two reports . . . following visits by the Commission to Nicaragua at the Government's invitation. Consequently, the Organization was in a position, if it so wished, to take a decision on the basis of these reports.[362]

This paragraph is capable of two distinct interpretations. The more restrictive view would be that the Court is in effect saying that, in respect of protection of human rights, the only obligations *erga omnes* are those created by universal or quasi-universal international conventions. The alternative interpretation is that there exists an obligation *erga omnes* in this field, but that if in respect of a particular State it is embodied in a convention providing mechanisms for ensuring its observance, no claim can be brought parallel to the operation of those mechanisms.

It was—unfortunately for commentators—unnecessary for the Court to spell its meaning out further, as the matter was before it only in the context of the possibility of human rights violations by Nicaragua being pleaded as a justification of the actions of the United States. The Court continued:

In any event, while the United States might form its own appraisal of the situation as to respect for human rights in Nicaragua, the use of force could not be the appropriate method to monitor or ensure such respect.[363]

Either interpretation of the Court's approach in fact points up a certain lack of coherence in the system propounded in the *Barcelona Traction* judgment. If the rights involved are of such importance that 'all States can be held to have a legal interest in their protection', then the existence or otherwise of an international convention is irrelevant unless, first, it provides for enforcement of the rights in question and, secondly, participation in it is not merely quasi-universal but universal. This was not even true of the

---

[362] Ibid.
[363] Ibid., para. 268.

Genocide Convention of 1951, and is not true today of any relevant convention.

The conclusion which has, it appears, to be accepted is that obligations *erga omnes* as to which 'compulsory rights of protection have entered into the body of general international law' may still be—with the possible exception of the obligation not to commit genocide—a purely theoretical category.

3. Jus cogens *and* jus dispositivum

(1) Jus cogens *and reservations to multilateral conventions*

In the *North Sea Continental Shelf* cases, the Court was faced with a contention that the 'equidistance principle' in the delimitation provisions (Article 6) of the 1958 Geneva Convention on the Continental Shelf had, through positive law processes, come to be regarded as a rule of customary international law; it regarded its negative conclusion on this point as confirmed by

the fact that Article 6 is one of those in respect of which, under the reservations article of the Convention (Article 12) reservations may be made by any State on signing, ratifying or acceding—for, speaking generally, it is a characteristic of purely conventional rules and obligations that, in regard to them, some faculty of making unilateral reservations may, within certain limits, be admitted;—whereas this cannot be so in the case of general or customary law rules and obligations which, by their very nature, must have equal force for all members of the international community, and cannot therefore be the subject of any right of unilateral exclusion exercisable at will by any one of them in its own favour. Consequently, it is to be expected that when, for whatever reason, rules or obligations of this order are embodied, or are intended to be reflected in certain provisions of a convention, such provisions will figure amongst those in respect of which a right of unilateral reservation is not conferred, or is excluded.[364]

As the present writer has pointed out elsewhere,[365] there is here some apparent confusion between the generality of a rule of law and its classification as *jus cogens* or otherwise. While it is true that 'general or customary law rules and obligations' must 'by their very nature . . . have equal force for all members of the international community', in the sense that if they do not, they cannot be general rules at all, but at most rules of local or special customary law, this requirement is satisfied if the rules in question are generally recognized as such by the members of international community; it does not also imply that they must in all cases be observed, and can in no circumstances be waived or excluded by agreement between two or more States. The whole significance of the distinction between *jus dispositivum*

---

[364] *ICJ Reports*, 1969, pp. 38–9, para. 63.
[365] *International Customary Law and Codification*, p. 120. In the same sense: Zemanek, 'Die Bedeutung der Kodifizierung des Völkerrechts für seine Anwendung', *Festschrift Verdross*, p. 584; Lang, *Le Plateau continental de la Mer du Nord*, p. 98.

and *jus cogens* is that rules of law falling within the former category may freely be varied or excluded by agreement in the relations between two or more States, provided the position of third-party States is in no way prejudiced.

(2) Jus cogens *and the decision of a court*

Is a decision of an international tribunal, or, more specifically, of the International Court of Justice, necessarily a matter of *jus cogens* so far as regards its statement of the law between the parties? The generally recognized declaratory, rather than constitutive, nature of an international judicial act would suggest that the law as declared by the Court is binding on the parties to the same extent after the judgment as it was before; all that has changed is that any doubt as to what that law is has been dissipated. Clearly, neither party can unilaterally choose to act otherwise than in accordance with the judgment, but it must be open to the parties to compromise their rights, and indeed to set aside the judgment altogether if such be their common wish.

A different view was, however, expressed by Judge Gros in the case of the *Continental Shelf (Tunisia/Libyan Arab Jamahiriya)*. The special agreement by which the Court was seised in that case, after entrusting to the Court the task of indicating the principles and rules of international law to determine the parties' respective continental shelves, and of clarifying the practical method for their application, went on to provide in Article 2 that 'the Parties shall meet to apply these principles and rules in order to determine the line of delimitation . . . with a view to the conclusion of a treaty in this respect'.[366] Article 3 provided that if agreement was not reached the parties could go back to the Court for explanations and clarifications.

During the oral proceedings, Judge Gros put a question to both parties, which appears to have somewhat disconcerted them. He asked each Agent to explain the position of his government on the question of the binding force of the judgment, with regard to (a) the principles and rules of international law which might be indicated by the Court, (b) the circumstances which characterized the area, regarded by the Court as pertinent, and (c) any equitable principles which the Court might take into account.[367]

The Agent of Tunisia gave what turned out to be the correct answer: that the Court's judgment on these questions was binding on the parties, in accordance with Article 94, paragraph 1, of the Charter, Article 59 of the Statute, and Article 94, paragraph 2, of the Rules of Court; it would also be final and without appeal in accordance with Article 60 of the Statute.[368] The reply of Libya, however, made no reference to these texts; it began with the words 'Bearing in mind that Libya and Tunisia have agreed in

---

[366] Libyan translation of the original Arabic: *ICJ Reports*, 1982, p. 23.
[367] *Pleadings*, vol. 5, p. 244.
[368] Ibid., p. 349.

Article 3 of the Special Agreement . . . to "comply with the judgment of the Court and with its explanations and clarifications" . . .', and then stated that 'The Judgment to be given by the Court in accordance with the Special Agreement will have binding force with regard to the principles and rules of international law found to be applicable . . .'.[369]

Judge Gros interpreted the absence of reference to the Charter and Statute in Libya's reply as deliberate, because to refer to the obligation of compliance deriving from those texts

would have undermined its contention that the Special Agreement provides for referral, after the Court has delivered judgment, to an unfettered agreement between the Parties which could then adjust the terms of the Judgment.[370]

On the basis of this interpretation, Judge Gros's conclusion is as follows:

The point is that by taking up such a position, contradicted by Tunisia, Libya was interpreting the Special Agreement as if that instrument were capable of amending the rules of the Charter and Statute, and that is something which goes to the heart of the Court's judicial role. It has been argued that two States can always agree by treaty to modify their legal situation and that the judgment could not make an exception to this rule. This is a somewhat simplistic view of things when what the situation calls for is a decision whether the Court, being thus warned of the intentions of a party, can keep silent in the face of such an opinion. The question was whether, before the judgment which the Parties asked the Court to deliver and which must be binding on them, the Special Agreement could validly have reserved for them the right wholly or partly to modify the Court's jurisdictional act. That is an unacceptable notion for the Court, which does not give States opinions but declares to them, with binding force, what it holds to be the law applicable to the dispute submitted to it. And, having been warned that one of the States felt able to disregard this, while the other State took the opposite position, the Court ought to have asked itself whether it might not thereby be prevented from properly exercising its judicial function.[371]

The majority of the Court was not convinced by this argument; and it is submitted that the majority view is the better one. The distinction between the *Free Zones* case and the *Continental Shelf* case is that in the former case what was asked for was 'a judgment which either of the Parties may render inoperative' (*PCIJ*, Series A, No. 24, p. 14), whereas in the latter case the parties were merely recognizing in advance that the solution to their problem of delimitation dictated by the strict application of the law might, in their shared view, be more satisfactory if subjected to some adjustment. The parallel might more appropriately be drawn with the Special Agreement in the *Serbian Loans* case, which provided not merely for the parties to negotiate on the basis of the Court's judgment, but for the one side or the other to make concessions required by 'considerations of equity'—which,

---

[369] Ibid., p. 501.
[370] *ICJ Reports*, 1982, p. 144, para. 2.
[371] Ibid.

presumably, the Court was considered not capable of taking into account in giving its legal judgment.[372]

In the *Northern Cameroons* case, the Court did refer to the fact that, after the judgment is given, the parties 'are in a position to take some retroactive or prospective action or avoidance of action, which would constitute a compliance with the Court's judgment or a *defiance thereof*';[373] but it would be reading too much into this passage to suppose that the Court regarded any action not in accordance with a judgment as necessarily 'a defiance thereof'.

4. *Universality and Uniformity of the Rules of International Law*

The creation of a considerable number of new States through the process of decolonization gave rise to a controversy, now somewhat abated, over the question whether existing rules of general international law are automatically binding on new States. According to one view such a State, having had no part in the formation of customary law rules, was entitled, on attaining independence, to select the rules which it was willing to accept as binding and to reject the rest.[374]

It has never been pleaded before the Court that a given customary rule relied on by one party is unenforceable against the other because the latter, being a new State, has not consented to its application; but an observation of the Chamber in the *Frontier Dispute* case suggests some sympathy with this approach. The Chamber attached considerable importance to the applicability on the African continent of the principle of *uti possidetis juris*, which it classified as 'a principle of a general kind which is logically connected with [this form of] decolonization wherever it occurs'.[375] At the same time, however, the Chamber emphasized the act of will of African States, emphasized by the well-known 1964 Cairo Resolution of the Conference of African Heads of State and of Government, to apply the principle in Africa.

The essential requirement of stability . . . has induced African States judiciously to consent to the respecting of colonial frontiers, and to take account of it in the interpretation of the principle of self-determination of peoples . . .[376]

Indeed it was by deliberate choice that African States selected, among all the classic principles, that of *uti possidetis*.[377]

---

[372] *PCIJ*, Series A/B, Nos. 20/21, pp. 15–16.

[373] *ICJ Reports*, 1963, pp. 37–8 (emphasis added). See also *Fisheries Jurisdiction*, p. 134 below.

[374] Cf. separate opinion of Judge Ammoun, *Barcelona Traction, Light and Power Company, Limited, ICJ Reports*, 1970, pp. 329–30; and see Tunkin, 'Remarks on the Juridical Nature of Customary Norms of International Law', *Columbia Law Review*, 49 (1961), p. 428; Sereni, 'I Nuovi Stati ed il Diritto internazionale', *Rivista di diritto internazionale*, 50 (1967), pp. 14–15.

[375] *ICJ Reports*, 1986, p. 566, para. 23; the bracketed words do not correspond to anything in the authentic French text, and may have been left over from an earlier draft.

[376] Ibid., p. 567, para. 25.

[377] Ibid., para. 26.

There is a logical difficulty here, of which the Chamber indeed seems to have been aware.

> . . . it may be wondered how the time-hallowed principle [of *uti possidetis*] has been able to withstand the new approaches to international law as expressed in Africa, where the successive attainment of independence and the emergence of new States have been accompanied by a certain questioning of traditional international law.[378]

For the Chamber, the problem is one of reconciling two principles of equal validity: the principle of *uti possidetis* and that of the self-determination of peoples. The latter principle would presumably, in the Chamber's thinking, have required the creation of boundaries which better respected the ethnic divisions in Africa. Clearly a requirement, if such there be, that a new State accept the existing rules of general international law cannot require it to accept two mutually contradictory principles. It is, however, not only from a purely academic and jurisprudential standpoint that one may doubt whether general international law can, or does, contain principles which contradict each other.

On a more direct and practical level, it may be observed that if the African States represented at Cairo had the option to adopt or reject the principles of *uti possidetis*, the same option must have been available to States which were not so represented, particularly those which attained independence subsequently. The principle of *uti possidetis* is however of such a nature that it must be applied universally (or at least universally within a continent) or not at all. More weight should therefore be attached to the Chamber's declaration of the universality of the principle than to its interpretation of the application of the principle in Africa as a matter of State consent.

The Chamber also proceeded on the basis that the principle declared at the Cairo conference and the pre-existing principle of the *uti possidetis* were identical. This may however not be so. The touchstone is the applicability of the principle to maritime boundaries; if the colonial power had not claimed or fixed such boundaries, it is difficult to see how the *uti possidetis* principle could apply to them. It has, however, been authoritatively stated that the Cairo pledge applies 'not just to those borders established by treaty or existing on dry land'.[379] It is in any event questionable whether the *uti possidetis* principle applies to boundaries between colonial possessions of one State and the territories, or colonial possessions, of another State. The essence of the *uti possidetis* principle is that it resolves the problem of boundaries which, prior to independence of the State concerned, were purely internal and administrative.

---

[378] Ibid., pp. 566–7, para. 25.

[379] Jiménez de Aréchaga, separate opinion, *Continental Shelf (Tunisia/Libya)*, *ICJ Reports*, 1982, p. 131. See also the disputed arbitral award between Guinea-Bissau and Senegal in the pending case of the *Arbitral Award of 31 July 1989*.

5. *The Limits of Reaction to Unlawful Conduct*

This heading is intended to refer to a question which is wider than that of the concepts of retorsion and reprisals in international law, and which arose in such wide form before the Court in the period under review. The question is: in what circumstances, and to what extent, may what would otherwise be an unlawful act by State A against State B be justified by the previous commission by State B of an unlawful act, against State A or otherwise? In the tortuous wording of the International Law Commission's draft on State Responsibility, the underlying principle is expressed as follows:

> The wrongfulness of an act of a State not in conformity with an obligation of that State towards another State is precluded if the act constitutes a measure legitimate under international law against that other State, in consequence of an internationally wrongful act of that other State.[380]

Although dealt with by the ILC under the heading of State responsibility, this is a question of general international law; it is clearly distinct from the problem in treaty-law of termination or suspension of the operation of a treaty by one party as a consequence of its breach by the other party, dealt with in Article 60 of the Vienna Convention on the Law of Treaties, and comes under the heading of 'State Responsibility' only because of the idiosyncratic approach to the subject by the ILC Special Rapporteurs.

In the *Barcelona Traction* case, the Court based its 1970 judgment on the lack of Belgian *jus standi* to bring the claim, and had therefore no need to examine the merits of the Belgian claim and the Spanish defence. It however included in its judgment a final paragraph in which it stated:

> In the course of the proceedings, the Parties have submitted a great amount of documentary and other evidence intended to substantiate their respective submissions. Of this evidence the Court has taken cognizance. It has been argued on one side that unlawful acts had been committed by the Spanish judicial and administrative authorities, and that as a result of those acts Spain has incurred international responsibility. On the other side it has been argued that the activities of Barcelona Traction and its subsidiaries were conducted in violation of Spanish law and caused damage to the Spanish economy. If both considerations were substantiated, the truth of the latter would in no way provide justification in respect of the former.[381]

The Spanish allegations of violations of Spanish law by the Barcelona Traction group were the subject of a penetrating question from the bench put by Sir Gerald Fitzmaurice. After pointing out that if the Spanish Government contended that the actions of its authorities and its courts involved no violations of law, the past conduct of the company had no relevance at all, he continued:

---

[380] Text and commentary in *Yearbook of the ILC*, 1979, vol. 2, pt. 2, p. 115.
[381] *ICJ Reports*, 1970, pp. 50–1, para. 102.

Secondly, there is the contrary view put forward on behalf of the Belgian Government, that the acts of the Spanish authorities and courts were irregular. This the Spanish Government denies. But does it, while maintaining its denial, invoke the past conduct of the company as an element which would, in law, justify irregularities on the Spanish side should any have occurred? If this is *not* the Spanish attitude, then again what is the exact relevance of this conduct, juridically, the conduct of the company, except indirectly, as affording an explanation of matters that might otherwise be obscure?

Finally, there is the line taken by Professor Jiménez and to some extent, though in a slightly different way, by Professor Weil, namely that the company's conduct precludes or estops the Belgian Government from complaining at what happened and that its claim should be rejected on that ground alone. Taken to its logical conclusion, this approach would involve the rejection of the Belgian claim irrespective of the truth of the allegations of irregularity made against the Spanish courts and authorities—and even if these allegations should be true. In short, on this view, it would, strictly, become irrelevant to enquire into the correctness of these allegations since, whether they were correct or not, the Belgian claim could not succeed.[382]

A first reply to this question was given by the Spanish Agent, Mr Castro-Rial, who emphasized that Spain had denied that any violation of laws had been committed by the Spanish courts and authorities.[383] He also emphasized in what respect the conduct of the Barcelona Traction group had directly influenced the events complained of as unlawful acts of Spanish authorities. He continued however:

Le Gouvernement espagnol estime en effet qu'en droit international la conduite répréhensible du particulier protégé peut, dans certaines circonstances, conduire à rendre irrecevable la protection diplomatique exercée par l'Etat de ce dernier . . . Néanmoins, le Gouvernement espagnol n'a pas, en l'occurrence, soulevé une exception préliminaire supplémentaire faisant appel à la doctrine dite des *clean hands*. La force des autres moyens développés par le Gouvernement espagnol dans ce procès le dispense, en effet, de demander à la Cour de rejeter la demande belge pour le motif que la société n'aurait pas les mains propres.[384]

A further reply to Sir Gerald's question was given by Mr Jiménez de Aréchaga, who explained that the reason why the conduct of the Barcelona Traction undertaking had been discussed was the following:

It is our contention that in this case such conduct is relevant to the decision whether or not the Spanish authorities did commit those violations of international law for which they stand accused.

Mr Lauterpacht cited the *Massey* case . . . against such a view. But that case can be distinguished. There, the alleged misconduct of the victim had no influence on the course of the judicial proceedings, which were in the premises rightly branded as a 'denial of justice'. Here, the conduct of the enterprise directly influenced the administrative decisions and the shape and sequence of the Spanish judicial pro-

---

[382] *Pleadings*, vol. 9, p. 671.
[383] Ibid., vol. 10, p. 371.
[384] Ibid., p. 372.

ceedings. If we are to have recourse to authority, I wish to cite the opinion of the Belgian author Mr Salmon. After an analysis of no less than 55 arbitral awards he reaches the opposite conclusion to Mr Lauterpacht. He writes 'l'indignité ou la conduite blâmable du réquérant peut conduire le tribunal international à repousser sa demande au fond ou à ne lui accorder qu'une indemnité réduite'. ('Des mains propres comme condition de recevabilité des réclamations internationales', *Annuaire français de droit international*, vol. X, 1964, p. 265.) He also states that this is 'un moyen de défense au fond' (ibid., p. 261).[385]

He emphasized that this contention was being put forward, not as a belated preliminary objection, but as a 'defence on the merits'.

The question here of interest is: did the Spanish argument, irrespective of whether it was to be classified as a preliminary objection or defence on the merits, amount to a contention that the actions of the Spanish authorities were justified, or 'cured', by the wrongful behaviour in Spain of the Barcelona Traction group? Taking a broad view, it might be said that if conduct of the complainant State (or its protected nationals) can validly be set up to block an international claim before a judicial tribunal, it effectively operates to invalidate that claim; if conduct otherwise wrongful cannot legitimately be complained of by the State where nationals have suffered from it, it is arguable that it is not 'wrongful' in any meaningful sense.[386]

However, whether this is so or not in general, in the particular circumstances of the *Barcelona Traction* case, the distinction between a procedural bar and a ground of exculpation of the Spanish authorities was clear. This was because, as Mr Lauterpacht, counsel for Belgium, pointed out,[387] the Spanish authorities were not aware of the allegedly wrongful conduct of the Barcelona Traction group until after the events complained of by Belgium. Counsel for Belgium quoted Bin Cheng to the effect that it is

a principle of logic as well as of law that something which is not known at the time of an action or decision, but only learned of subsequently, cannot be invoked as a motive for such action or decision.[388]

In this light, the *dictum* of the Court in the *Barcelona Traction* judgment—which at first sight appears to be a remarkable foray into the merits which the Court had found it could not examine—proves to be unrelated to

---

[385] Ibid., pp. 507–8.

[386] If a digression be permitted: a question which might be pursued as of considerable theoretical interest is whether there may exist in international law obligations analogous to the 'obligations naturelles' of French law—obligations which cannot be enforced through the courts, but nevertheless have a recognized existence in law (see Carbonnier, *Droit civil*, vol. 2, pp. 288–90). For example, the debtor who voluntarily pays a debt which is time-barred cannot claim his money back on the ground that there was no debt; he continued, after the period of prescription expired, to be under an 'obligation naturelle'. In addition, 'Ce peut être pareillement une obligation naturelle que de réparer un dommage que l'on a causé à autrui dans des conditions qui excluaient l'existence d'une responsabilité juridique . . .': Carbonnier, op. cit., p. 289.

[387] *Pleadings*, vol. 10, p. 254.

[388] *General Principles of Law as applied by International Courts and Tribunals*, p. 90.

the actual issue between the parties, and of no assistance in determining what, in the Court's view, are the limits of infringement of international law rendered permissible by way of reaction to illegal conduct of another State.

In the case of *United States Diplomatic and Consular Staff in Tehran*, the Court was able without difficulty to find that Iran had committed serious breaches of its obligations toward the United States under the 1961 and 1963 Vienna Conventions on Diplomatic and Consular Relations. It then turned to the fact that 'on the Iranian side, in often imprecise terms, the idea has been put forward that the conduct of the Iranian Government . . . might be justified by the existence of special circumstances'.[389] The Iranian Foreign Minister had written a letter to the Court claiming that the question brought before it by the United States

only represents a marginal and secondary aspect of an overall problem, one such that it cannot be studied separately, and which involves, *inter alia*, more than 25 years of continual interference by the United States in the internal affairs of Iran, the shameless exploitation of our country, and numerous crimes perpetrated against the Iranian people, contrary to and in conflict with all international and humanitarian norms.[390]

He also attributed to the United States an alleged complicity on the part of the CIA in the *coup d'état* of 1953 and the restoration of the Shah to the throne of Iran.

The Court first noted that these allegations had not been properly pleaded, nor presented as a counterclaim, and no evidence had been presented in support of them. It then continued, however:

In any case, even if the alleged criminal activities of the United States in Iran could be considered as having been established, the question would remain whether they could be regarded by the Court as constituting a justification of Iran's conduct and thus a defence to the United States' claims in the present case. The Court, however, is unable to accept that they can be so regarded. This is because diplomatic law itself provides the necessary means of defence against, and sanction for, illicit activities by members of diplomatic or consular missions.[391]

The Court pointed out that a diplomat who abuses his function can be declared *persona non grata*, and that there is also the 'more radical remedy' of breaking off of diplomatic relations.

The rules of diplomatic law, in short, constitute a self-contained régime which, on the one hand, lays down the receiving State's obligations regarding the facilities, privileges and immunities to be accorded to diplomatic missions and, on the other, foresees their possible abuse by members of the mission and specifies the means at the disposal of the receiving State to counter any such abuse. These means are, by

---

[389] *ICJ Reports*, 1980, p. 37, para. 80.
[390] Ibid., p. 8, para. 10.
[391] Ibid., p. 38, para. 83.

their nature, entirely efficacious, for unless the sending State recalls the member of the mission objected to forthwith, the prospect of the almost immediate loss of his privileges and immunities, because of the withdrawal by the receiving State of his recognition as a member of the mission, will in practice compel that person, in his own interest, to depart at once.[392]

This is a very elegant construction; but, with respect, it somewhat misses the main point raised by the Iranian letter. Iran's complaint was not so much against the individual diplomats whom it seized—in fact it admitted that some of them might be found innocent of the crimes it alleged[393]—nor even entirely against the Embassy itself, as a 'nest of spies'. It was objecting to the alleged interference by the United States in its affairs, conducted to some extent, but not exclusively, through the Tehran Embassy. Thus its main complaint did not fall within the ambit of 'diplomatic law' at all.

The Court in fact almost appears to be reasoning as though the intangibility of diplomats were justified by the possibility of declaring them *persona non grata* if they misbehave (or, indeed, even if they don't). The true position is surely the reverse: as the Court itself observes, 'the principle of the inviolability of the persons of diplomatic agents and the premises of diplomatic missions is one of the very foundations of this long-established régime . . .'[394] and the possibility of getting rid of an undesirable diplomat by a declaration of *persona non grata* is a corollary of this principle, not the other way round.

What is missing from the judgment in the *United States Diplomatic and Consular Staff in Tehran* case, in that part of it devoted to the Iranian theses, is a clear statement that the attack on the Embassy and the seizure of the diplomats could not be justified by any 'crimes' attributed to the United States, whether such 'crimes' were committed through the agency of the Tehran Embassy, or of individual diplomats stationed there, or not. It is, however, possible to attach some significance to the Court's silence on the point, in view of the declared position of Judge Tarazi, one of the judges who dissented on the major provisions of the operative part of the judgment. In his dissenting opinion Judge Tarazi suggested that by permitting the ex-Shah of Iran to enter its territory, the United States had committed a 'serious fault'; and he quoted French law to suggest that this fault absolved the defendant from responsibility.[395] This daring construction seems to have been tacitly rejected by the majority of the Court.

In the same case, the Court considered that it could not 'let pass without comment'[396] the attempted rescue operation set in motion by the United States on 24–25 April 1980, while the case was pending before the Court.

[392] Ibid., p. 40, para. 86.
[393] *Pleadings*, pp. 89; 130; 202, 203.
[394] *ICJ Reports*, 1980, p. 40, para. 86.
[395] Ibid., p. 62.
[396] Ibid., p. 43, para. 93.

This operation was presented by the United States as an exercise of its inherent right of self-defence, and was reported to the Security Council as such.[397] The Court commented on it with disfavour in so far as it was undertaken during pending judicial proceedings, and contrary to the terms of an Order indicating provisional measures; the Court regarded it as 'an operation . . . of a kind calculated to undermine respect for the judicial process in international relations'.[398] The Court was however careful to emphasize

that neither the question of the legality of the operation of 24 April 1980, under the Charter of the United Nations and under general international law, nor any possible question of responsibility flowing from it, is before the Court.[399]

The Court thus rejected the view expressed by Judge Morozov in his dissenting opinion that 'the Applicant has forfeited the legal right as well as the moral right to expect the Court to uphold any claim for reparation'.[400]

Since the Court regarded the legality of the operation as outside its purview, it will not be commented on here, save to remark that its characterization by the United States Government as an act of self-defence—which is not entirely self-evident—suggests that that Government would not with confidence have advanced the view that the operation was justified by the Iranian seizure and retention of the hostages, independently of the question of self-defence.

In the case concerning *Military and Paramilitary Activities in and against Nicaragua (Nicaragua v. United States of America)*, however, the United States, which in its turn was to decline to appear and present its case on the merits before the Court, did advance some arguments (in addition to its central plea of collective self-defence, the Court's treatment of which will be examined in a later article) partaking of the nature of retaliation.[401] The Court's finding on proportionate counter-measures involving the use of force requires to be quoted in full:

248. The United States admits that it is giving its support to the *contras* in

---

[397] *Pleadings*, p. 486.
[398] *ICJ Reports*, 1980, p. 43, para. 93.
[399] Ibid., para. 94.
[400] Ibid., p. 53.
[401] Before dealing with possible United States claims to retaliation, mention may be made of an obscure sentence in the judgment which appears to relate to the matter now under discussion. The Court records the existence of two organizations carrying on armed struggle against the Sandinista Government of Nicaragua, the FDN and the ARDE. Later in the judgment, after declaring that the Court 'considers as established the fact that certain transborder military incursions into the territory of Honduras and Costa Rica are imputable to the Government of Nicaragua', it adds:
   'The Court is also aware of the fact that the FDN operates along the Nicaraguan border with Honduras, and the ARDE operates along the border with Costa Rica' (*ICJ Reports*, 1986, p. 187, para. 164).
No conclusion is drawn from this, but the text seems designed to suggest that the presence of these bodies on the borders might constitute a justification, or at least a mitigating circumstance. Such quasi-findings by implication are, it is suggested, out of place in a judicial judgment.

Nicaragua, but justifies this by claiming that that State is adopting similar conduct by itself assisting the armed opposition in El Salvador, and to a lesser extent in Honduras and Costa Rica, and has committed transborder attacks on those two States. The United States raises this justification as one of self-defence; having rejected it on those terms, the Court has nevertheless to consider whether it may be valid as action by way of counter-measures in response to intervention. The Court has however to find that the applicable law does not warrant such a justification.

249. On the legal level the Court cannot regard response to an intervention by Nicaragua as such a justification. While an armed attack would give rise to an entitlement to collective self-defence, a use of force of a lesser degree of gravity cannot, as the Court has already observed . . . produce any entitlement to take collective counter-measures involving the use of force. The acts of which Nicaragua is accused, even assuming them to have been established and imputable to that State, could only have justified proportionate counter-measures on the part of the State which had been the victim of these acts, namely El Salvador, Honduras or Costa Rica. They could not justify counter-measures taken by a third State, the United States, and particularly could not justify intervention involving the use of force.[402]

The Court thus recognizes the legality of recourse to 'proportionate counter-measures' provided these are taken solely by the State which has been the victim of the acts requiring response, and provided they do not amount to 'intervention involving the use of force'. When the counter-measures are a response to a use of force, the significance of the term 'proportionate' becomes doubtful. The Court seems to have come near to saying that a response to the use or threat of force must either fulfil the condition of legitimate self-defence or be illegal; but some intermediate action remains as at least a theoretical possibility.

By way of alternative justification of United States support of the *contras* it was suggested that 'the present Government of Nicaragua is in violation of certain alleged assurances given by its immediate predecessor'.[403] The Court found that these assurances related to matters *prima facie* within the domestic jurisdiction of Nicaragua, and that the assurances were not intended to amount to a legal undertaking, and that they were not given to the United States, but to the Organization of American States. As though these reasons were not enough, the Court added:

Moreover, even supposing that the United States were entitled to act in lieu of the Organization, it could hardly make use for the purpose of methods which the Organization could not use itself; in particular, it could not be authorized to use force in that event. Of its nature, a commitment like this is one of a category which, if violated, cannot justify the use of force against a sovereign State.[404]

This also suggests that there are *some* commitments the breach of which would justify the use of force, otherwise than in self-defence.

---

[402] *ICJ Reports*, 1986, p. 127, paras. 248–9.
[403] Ibid., pp. 88–9, para. 167.
[404] Ibid., p. 133, para. 262.

CHAPTER III:

RELATIONSHIPS BETWEEN LEGAL ORDERS

1. *The Relationship between International and National Law*

(1) *Supremacy of international law*

The question of the relationship between international law and the various systems of national law was dealt with by Fitzmaurice under the heading of 'The supremacy of international over national law',[405] such supremacy being treated as a principle, to which exceptions were, indeed, only apparent. The wider title used for the present section does not imply any questioning or weakening of the principle of such supremacy;[406] but in the period under review a number of cases have raised questions of the content, or the applicability, of national law in circumstances in which the supremacy principle was not of direct relevance.

The Court has however not lacked opportunities of giving effect to the supremacy principle, but in most cases that principle has been so evident a foundation for the determination of the case that it has not been found necessary to state it. Thus, for example, in the *Fisheries Jurisdiction* cases, the extension of fisheries jurisdiction by Iceland complained of by the United Kingdom and the Federal Republic of Germany was effected by an Icelandic legislative text—the 'Regulations concerning the Fishery Limits off Iceland'. It was, however, an unquestioned postulate throughout the case that, so far as the Court, deciding in international law, was concerned, the rules of international law prevailed over the precepts of Icelandic legislation.[407]

---

[405] This *Year Book*, 30 (1953), p. 25; 35 (1959), p. 183; *Collected Edition*, I, p. 156; II, p. 587.

[406] Fitzmaurice in fact was strongly of the view that, since international law and national law are each supreme *in their own sphere*, the question of the supremacy of the one over the other did not really arise, and was part of the monist/dualist controversy which for him was 'largely sterile'. As he explained in his course at the Hague Academy in 1957:

'The very question of supremacy as between the two orders, national and international, is irrelevant, as is also that of the existence of some superior norm or order conferring supremacy. National law is not and cannot be a rival to international law in the international field, or it would cease to be national and become international, which, *ex hypothesi*, it is not. National law, *by definition*, cannot govern the action of, or relations with, other States. It may govern or fetter the action of its own State in such a way that the latter cannot fulfil its international obligations, but again, by definition only at the national level and without legal effect or operation beyond it. Formally, therefore, international and domestic law as *systems* can never come into conflict. What may occur is something strictly different, namely a conflict of *obligations*, or an inability for the State on the *domestic plane* to act in the manner required by international law' (*Recueil des cours*, 92 (1957-II), p. 79, quoted in Fitzmaurice, this *Year Book*, 35 (1959), p. 187; *Collected Edition*, II, p. 591).

[407] In 1969 the Althing (the Icelandic parliament) in fact recognized this when, in its seminal Resolution of 5 May 1969, it declared that 'recognition'—i.e., international recognition—should be obtained of Iceland's rights to a 12-mile fishing zone (*ICJ Reports*, 1974, p. 12, para. 24). On the other hand in 1971 the Prime Minister of Iceland asserted that 'Since there are no generally agreed rules of the width of the territorial limit, it must be in the power of every State to decide its territorial limit within a reasonable distance': quoted in *Pleadings*, vol. 2, p. 230.

In the case concerning the *United States Diplomatic and Consular Staff in Tehran*, a still more striking example of this unquestioned assumption of the supremacy of international law is to be found in the Court's judgment. Iranian militants, after invading the US Embassy, were holding members of the diplomatic staff as hostages, and had threatened to have some of them submitted to trial before a court or some other body. The Court declared:

These threats may at present merely be acts in contemplation. But the Court considers it necessary here and now to stress that, if the intention to submit the hostages to any form of criminal trial or investigation were to be put into effect, that would constitute a grave breach by Iran of its obligations under Article 31, paragraph 1, of the 1961 Vienna Convention. This paragraph states in the most express terms: 'A diplomatic agent shall enjoy immunity from the criminal jurisdiction of the receiving State.'[408]

Thus no matter what Iranian legislation might provide, international law precluded any criminal trial of the diplomatic staff.

In the *Barcelona Traction* case in 1970 Judge Gros, in a separate opinion, disagreed with the analysis of the relationship between international law and national law employed in the majority judgment, on the ground that it resulted in establishing 'a superiority of municipal law over international law, which is a veritable negation of the latter'.[409] It will however be more convenient to examine this view after the position of the majority in that case has been expounded, in the following section.

In the advisory opinion on the *Applicability of the Obligation to Arbitrate under Section 21 of the United Nations Headquarters Agreement of 26 June 1947*, the Court took, indeed seized, the opportunity of re-emphasizing the supremacy of international law over municipal law. The underlying legal question to which the action of the United States had given rise was the compatibility of United States legislation aimed at closing the office of the PLO Observer Mission with the obligations of the United States under the United Nations Headquarters Agreement. Clearly if there was a conflict, then in the international law sphere the Headquarters Agreement, as a treaty, should prevail. The United States Permanent Representative had however stated in a letter to the Secretary-General that the United States measures against the PLO Observer Mission were taken 'irrespective of any obligations the United States may have under the [Headquarters] Agreement'.[410] This looked very like an attempt to set up municipal legislation as a defence to an allegation of breach of treaty, which could be condemned on the basis of the supremacy of international law; but the Court was not seised of that question. It had only been asked whether there was an

---

[408] *ICJ Reports*, 1980, p. 37, para. 79.
[409] *ICJ Reports*, 1970, p. 272, para. 9.
[410] *ICJ Reports*, 1988, p. 22, para. 24.

obligation to arbitrate the question of conflict between the measures taken against the PLO Observer Mission and the Headquarters Agreement.

The Court however dealt with the point in the final paragraph of its advisory opinion. After stating its conclusion that 'the United States is bound to respect the obligation to have recourse to arbitration under Section 21 of the Headquarters Agreement', and quoting the Permanent Representative's statement, it continued:

> If it were necessary to interpret that statement as intended to refer not only to the substantive obligations laid down in, for example, sections 11, 12 and 13, but also to the obligation to arbitrate provided for in section 21, this conclusion would remain intact. It would be sufficient to recall the fundamental principle of international law that international law prevails over domestic law.[411]

The United States had given no other indication that it regarded its internal legislation as exempting it from the commitment to arbitration under Article 21. It is possible to doubt whether the *dictum* quoted was strictly necessary to the Court's advisory opinion; but this in its turn suggests that the Court regarded the supremacy principle as one of such importance that no opportunity should be let pass to emphasize it in the context of cases in which it appeared that it might be threatened.

Judge Oda, in a separate opinion, in fact expressed the view that the real issue was not the 'interpretation or application of the Headquarters Agreement (the terms of Article 21)', but 'whether in operative effect, precedence will be given to the uncontested interpretation or application of that Agreement or to the Anti-Terrorism Act . . .',[412] and regretted that the Court had not had to consider any argument on the 'crucial point' of the supremacy of international law.

Most recently, the supremacy of international law, specifically of treaty law, over national law was an element in the decision of the Chamber formed to deal with the case of *Elettronica Sicula SpA (ELSI)*. It was asserted by the United States that certain action of the Italian public authorities in relation to the ELSI company was contrary to a treaty provision whereby nationals of one party were not to be subjected, in the territory of the other, to 'arbitrary or discriminatory measures'.[413] The argument of the United States rested upon, *inter alia*, the contention that the action in question was 'under both the Treaty and Italian law, . . . unreasonable, and improperly motivated' and that it was 'found to be illegal under Italian domestic law for precisely this reason'.[414] There was some obscurity as to whether it had in fact been 'found to be illegal under Italian domestic law'; but the Chamber's view was in any event that

the fact that an act of a public authority may have been unlawful in municipal law

---

[411] Ibid., p. 34, para. 57.
[412] Ibid., p. 41.
[413] *ICJ Reports*, 1989, p. 72, para. 120.
[414] Ibid., p. 73, para. 123.

does not necessarily mean that that act was unlawful in international law, as a breach of treaty or otherwise. A finding of the local courts that an act was unlawful may well be relevant to an argument that it was also arbitrary; but by itself, and without more, unlawfulness cannot be said to amount to arbitrariness. It would be absurd if measures later quashed by higher authority or a superior court could, for that reason, be said to have been arbitrary in the sense of international law. To identify arbitrariness with mere unlawfulness would be to deprive it of any useful meaning in its own right. Nor does it follow from a finding by a municipal court that an act was unjustified, or unreasonable, or arbitrary, that that act is necessarily to be classed as arbitrary in international law, though the qualification given to the impugned act by a municipal authority may be a valuable indication.[415]

The unusual aspect of this finding is that it operates in favour of the State whose national law is in question. The principle of the supremacy of international law has developed in the form of findings that a State cannot rely on its own national law as a defence on the international law level. In the *ELSI* case, on the other hand, the fact that the domestic courts censured an action affecting foreign nationals was not regarded as sufficient to support a claim of breach of treaty.

(2) *Reference by international law to national law: specific systems or 'municipal law' in general?*

In the *Barcelona Traction, Light and Power Company, Limited* case, the Court was faced with the question whether Belgium could claim reparation from Spain for allegedly unlawful treatment by Spain of a Canadian-registered company in which Belgian nationals were shareholders. The point was originally raised by way of preliminary objection, to the effect that:

the claim advanced by the Belgian Government . . . is definitively inadmissible for want of capacity on the part of the Belgian Government in the present case, in view of the fact that the Barcelona company does not possess Belgian nationality and that in the case in point it is not possible to allow diplomatic action or international judicial proceedings on behalf of the alleged Belgian shareholders of the company on account of the damage which the company asserts it has suffered.[416]

This objection was joined to the merits by the Court's judgment of 1964; but when it was argued as part of the merits, it continued to be treated as a matter of *jus standi*, rather than as a question of the unlawfulness or otherwise, in international law, of Spain's actions. The complications arose because to say whether the actions of Spain were unlawful involved determining *vis-à-vis* what entity they were unlawful. For present purposes, the starting point may be taken to be the assumption that if what was done to the Barcelona Traction company had been done to an individual of Belgian nationality, Belgium would have had a clear international right of action.

The Court first observed that, in order to bring a claim in respect of a breach of an obligation the performance of which is the subject of diplomatic

---

[415] Ibid., p. 74, para. 124.
[416] *ICJ Reports*, 1964, p. 12.

protection, a State must first establish its right to do so; quoting the *Reparation for Injuries* case the Court stated that the rules on the subject rest on two suppositions:

The first is that the defendant State has broken an obligation towards the national State in respect of its nationals. The second is that only the party to whom an international obligation is due can bring a claim in respect of its breach.[417]

The Court then continued:

In the present case it is therefore essential to establish whether the losses allegedly suffered by Belgian shareholders in Barcelona Traction were the consequence of the violation of obligations of which they were the beneficiaries. In other words: has a right of Belgium been violated on account of its nationals' having suffered infringement of their rights as shareholders in a company not of Belgian nationality?[418]

The last sentence contains a latent ambiguity. The 'right' of Belgium referred to must clearly be a right conferred by international law. As the Permanent Court observed:

. . . by taking up a case on behalf of its nationals before an international tribunal a State is asserting its own right, that is to say, its right to ensure in the person of its nationals, respect for the rules of international law.[419]

Are the 'rights' of the Belgian nationals as shareholders, however, to be read as rights conferred by international law or rights conferred by a relevant system of national law? The latter was the position as seen by the Permanent Court in *Chorzów Factory*:

Rights or interests of an individual the violation of which rights causes damage are always on a different plane to rights belonging to a State, which rights may also be infringed by the same act.[420]

As observed above, the starting point for discussion must be that the respondent State has committed some act, as a result of which nationals of the applicant State have suffered damage. Whether the applicant State has *jus standi* and whether the act committed constitutes a breach of international law are two faces of the same coin.

The Court's approach was to determine this question by asking whether the nationals of the applicant State have suffered injury to a right, as distinct from prejudice to an interest. As the Court recognizes (para. 54), the distinction is to be determined by a system of law; but which?

In the *Oscar Chinn* case, the claim of the United Kingdom was founded

---

[417] *ICJ Reports*, 1949, pp. 181–2.
[418] *ICJ Reports*, 1970, pp. 32–3, para. 35.
[419] *Serbian Loans, PCIJ*, Series A, Nos. 20–1, p. 17.
[420] *PCIJ*, Series A, No. 17, p. 28.

partly on the assertion that Belgium had breached general international law by acting in such a way as to injure the acquired rights of Mr Chinn. In his dissenting opinion Judge Sir Cecil Hurst (who agreed with the Court on this point) spelled out the relevant distinction. The effect of the Belgian Government's action was to enable Chinn's rival, the Belgian company Unatra, enormously to undercut the rates he could offer for river transport.

Chinn possessed no right, either under the Treaty of Saint-Germain or under general international law, which entitled him to find customers in the Congo, i.e. people who were desirous of contracting with him. If the individuals with whom Chinn would have liked to make contracts found that they could get better terms elsewhere for the transport of their merchandise or the repairing of their ships, they had just as much right to contract with persons other than Chinn, as Chinn had to make contracts with them. Consequently, the fact that these other individuals found it to their advantage not to contract with Chinn, involved no violation by them of a right belonging to him. Similarly, the decision of the Belgian Government which rendered it more profitable for these persons to make contracts elsewhere and not with Chinn interfered with no acquired right of his.

If it could be shown on behalf of Chinn that some right which he had already obtained to carry the goods of a particular merchant or to repair the ships of some particular merchant had been infringed by the Belgian Government, as, for instance, if he had had in existence a contract to carry all the goods of such and such a person and the Belgian Government had stepped in and prevented that person, no matter how much he wished to do so, handing over his goods to Chinn to transport, it would be right to say that an acquired right of Chinn had been interfered with, but the facts do not show any such position. Chinn's right to fulfil existing contracts for the transport of goods or the repair of ships, or to secure new contracts to that effect if he could, was never interfered with.[421]

What however did Sir Cecil mean by 'some *right* which he had already obtained'? Presumably, what he had in mind was a contract between Chinn and his customer which would have been (had the Belgian Government not interfered) enforceable under the law of the Congo and in the courts of the Congo. It is difficult to see in what other sense Chinn could be said to have acquired a 'right'.

Thus in 1934, the Court was of the view that economic damage suffered by a national at the hands of a foreign State could not ground an action on the international plane unless a right enjoyed by the national had been interfered with; and in the light of Sir Cecil Hurst's opinion, it seems that the definition of a 'right' in this context is afforded by the appropriate system of national law.

But what is the 'appropriate' system of national law? For Judge Morelli, in his separate opinion in the *Barcelona Traction* case, the answer was evident: it is the law of the respondent State. In his view, each State is required by international law to afford judicial protection to the rights of

---

[421] *PCIJ*, Series A/B, No. 63, pp. 121–2.

foreigners, and to respect those rights; and the rights in question are those which the State itself confers on foreigners within its own municipal order.

This provides an indirect way of determining what interests the international rule is intended to protect, given that this rule only protects the interests of foreign individuals or foreign collective entities if those interests already enjoy a certain degree of protection within the municipal legal system. This means that the international rule refers to the municipal legal order in that, to impose upon a State a particular obligation, it presupposes a certain freely adopted attitude on the part of the legal order of that State . . .

There is nothing abnormal in this reference of an international rule to the law of a given State.[422]

Applying this to the situation of a company or corporation having legal personality recognized by the State concerned:

. . . there is on the one hand a set of rights conferred by the municipal order on the company and, on the other hand, within the same legal order, another, quite distinct set of rights conferred on the members. Each set of rights is entitled to its own, distinct international protection.

As has been seen, both these protections afforded by the international legal order presuppose a certain attitude on the part of municipal law, namely a certain manner in which it deals with the rights of the company, on the one hand, and those of the members on the other. In the present case, the State legal order to be considered is the Spanish legal system, that is to say the legal order of the State whose international obligations have to be determined.[423]

Judge Morelli found no difficulty in applying these principles to the case:[424] since Spanish law recognized the legal personality of the Barcelona Traction company, and did not recognize any shareholders' rights over the corporate property, Belgium on behalf of the shareholders could only have claimed for injury done to the rights of the shareholders *vis-à-vis* the company, not for injury done to the Canadian company or to the 'interests' of the shareholders (not amounting to rights in the Spanish legal order) in the company.

Thus for Judge Morelli the relationship of international law to municipal law in this field was one of *renvoi* or reference:[425] in order to ascertain to what extent the nationals of the State exercising protection could be the subject of international protection, it was necessary simply to consult the municipal law of the respondent State to see what rights that law granted to the foreign nationals concerned. Presumably even if the State of incorporation of the company and the respondent State had different rules as to the

---

[422] *ICJ Reports*, 1970, pp. 233–4.

[423] Ibid., p. 235.

[424] Ibid., p. 236, para. 6.

[425] This approach was criticized by Judge *ad hoc* Riphagen in his dissenting opinion, ibid., p. 338. The term *'renvoi'* is not strictly correct (see next note).

relationship between shareholders and company, it would be the law of the respondent State which would be the subject of the reference.[426]

This was not however the approach taken in the majority judgment of the Court, which began its analysis of the applicable international law with the following introduction:

In turning now to the international legal aspects of the case, the Court must, as already indicated, start from the fact that the present case essentially involves factors derived from municipal law—the distinction and the community between the company and the shareholder—which the Parties, however widely their interpretations may differ, each take as the point of departure of their reasoning. If the Court were to decide the case in disregard of the relevant institutions of municipal law it would, without justification, invite serious legal difficulties. It would lose touch with reality, for there are no corresponding institutions of international law to which the Court could resort. Thus the Court has, as indicated, not only to take cognizance of municipal law but also to refer to it. It is to rules generally accepted by municipal legal systems which recognize the limited company whose capital is represented by shares, and not to the municipal law of a particular State, that international law refers. In referring to such rules, the Court cannot modify, still less deform them.[427]

The penultimate sentence of this passage is clearly an important statement of principle. Setting aside for the moment the question of its implications, we may first enquire what is the legal status of the principle involved: is it a 'general principle of law', or a norm of customary international law?

The Court gives no indication of the nature or source of the principle it states. It does not appear that the principle is necessarily a general one, independent of custom and practice: in the first place, it is by no means inevitable or self-evident, as the different view taken by Judge Morelli makes clear; and secondly, it could in theory be deduced from the practice of State claims, or more pertinently, from the practice of international judicial and arbitral bodies. There are, however, indications that it was not in fact so derived.

In his separate opinion Judge Fitzmaurice mentions an objection:

that in so far as the doctrine of a right of intervention on behalf of foreign shareholders in a locally incorporated company unable to act for itself, or rendered incapable of so doing, may depend on a number of precedents deriving from cases decided by international tribunals, it will be found on a careful examination of those cases that the 'company' that was concerned was usually more in the nature of a firm, partnership, or other similar association of persons, than of a true separate corporate entity distinct from those persons . . . Where on the other hand, so it is said, a corporate entity really was involved, the capacity to claim on behalf of

---

[426] It could be that the Courts of the respondent State could apply the law of the State of incorporation to the question of the rights and relationship of the shareholders and the company: this would be true *renvoi* in the sense of the term in private international law.

[427] *ICJ Reports*, 1970, p. 37, para. 50.

shareholders resulted from the express terms of the treaty, convention or 'compromise' submitting the case to the tribunal,—consequently these cases cannot be cited as implying recognition of any general principle of law allowing of such claims.[428]

Fitzmaurice comments on this:

It may be true that the exact *rationale* of a number of the decisions concerned is not very easy to determine precisely, and lends itself to much controversy, as the course of the written and oral proceedings in both phases of the present case have amply demonstrated.[429]

The Court's justification for its approach appears in effect to be that it is merely applying existing international law to new developments, of a social and economic nature, of which it has to take account as matters of fact. There is however a great difference between applying existing law to, for example, modern technological developments, such as satellites, and applying it to new concepts which only have a meaning or indeed existence in the context of a system of legal relations.

The weakness of the *Barcelona Traction* judgment is that it treats 'municipal law' not as a concept which, to be meaningful, has to be attached to a specific national legal order, but as a sort of pool of legal ideas common to municipal legal systems, to be dipped into when international law itself does not include or directly recognize particular legal institutions.[430]

In this field international law is called upon to recognize institutions of municipal law that have an important and extensive role in the international field. This does not necessarily imply drawing any analogy between its own institutions and those of municipal law, nor does it amount to making rules of international law dependent upon categories of municipal law. All it means is that international law has had to recognize the corporate entity as an institution created by States in a domain essentially within their domestic jurisdiction.[431]

It is of course true that most legal systems recognize and provide for the creation of corporate entities which are treated as having a legal existence distinct from the persons who have brought them into being, supplied them with assets and directed their affairs. In this sense it is true that international law may have to recognize institutions of municipal law; but in the resolution of any specific dispute, it is impossible to remain on this level of abstraction.

The Court's approach to the question of the protection of shareholders in the *Barcelona Traction* case appears to have been dictated by the desire to

---

[428] Ibid., p. 74, para. 17.

[429] Ibid., para. 18. The precedents and practice are discussed by Belgium in *Pleadings*, vol. 1, pp. 153–61, vol. 5, pp. 663–88, vol. 8, p. 504, and by Spain in ibid., vol. 4, pp. 723–46, vol. 9, p. 627.

[430] As a Spanish commentator on the judgment observes,
'The company, as an institution, is not comprehensible without its legal framework, and it is to this that the Court refers when it has to define the legal position of the company and its shareholders, and the rights of the former and the latter': Ruiloba Santana, 'Virtualidad del derecho interno en el caso de la Barcelona Traction', *Revista española de derecho internacional*, 23 (1970), pp. 500–1.

[431] *ICJ Reports*, 1970, p. 33, para. 38.

achieve universality in its ruling. This attitude is in fact betrayed by the terminology used from the outset of the judgment. After referring to corporate personality, in historical perspective, as representing 'a development brought about by new and expanding requirements in the economic field', the Court observes, in the French text, which is the authentic text, of its judgment:

> Il est cependent inutile d'examiner les multiples formes que prennent les différentes entités juridiques dans le droit interne car la Cour ne doit se préoccuper que de celle dont la société en cause dans la présente affaire, la *Barcelona Traction*, offre un exemple—à savoir la société anonyme, dont le capital est représenté par des actions.[432]

It is simply incorrect to say that *Barcelona Traction* was a 'société anonyme'—a creature of French law—, any more than it was an *Aktiengesellschaft* or a *Naamelooze Vennootschap*; it was a limited liability company created under the law of Canada.[433] True, for convenience it had been referred to throughout the case in French—the language of the pleadings and that used by the majority of counsel at the hearings,— as a 'société anonyme'; but it is to be regretted that the Court should have fallen into the trap of supposing that there is no legal difference between the various 'entités juridiques' possessing, under specific systems of municipal law, legal personality.

Thus right from the start the Court was revealing an intention to lay down a principle applicable not only to the effects, in international law, of the relationships between a Canadian company and its shareholders, but to the effects of the parallel relationship involving any municipal-law entity having a legal personality distinct from that of its members or investors. What might thus have been expected was an analysis of the problem in terms of the municipal legal systems involved—those of Spain and Canada—and the identification of the distinction made in those systems between the personality of the corporation and its shareholders, and the absence of an individual right of action of shareholders for the protection of their interests, as the features relevant for determination of the question of international law to be resolved.[434] The solution would thus be capable of generalization to the extent that other systems of municipal law exhibit similar features; but the municipal law to which the Court would have found it necessary to refer would have been an individual existing system,

---

[432] Ibid., p. 34, para. 40.

[433] The Letters Patent incorporating the company under the Canadian Companies Act, 1906, were produced as Annex 5 to Chapter I of the Spanish Counter-Memorial (not reproduced in the *Pleadings*).

[434] Kearney ('Sources of Law and the International Court of Justice', *The Future of the International Court of Justice*, vol. 2, pp. 679–80) considers that the Court, like its predecessor, was
'deciding that a particular legal statement represented a general principle of law, whether specifically so denominated or not, rather than attempting to determine the "proper law" of the issue under consideration'.

rather than a hypothetical lowest-common-denominator system having a more than usually conceptual existence.[435]

The reason for the approach adopted by the Court may lie in the manner in which the case was pleaded. The question had its origin in a preliminary objection to Belgium's *jus standi*, which focused attention less on the rights to be protected, or the injury suffered, than on the procedural precedents, or lack of them, for an international claim brought on behalf of shareholders. The distinction in municipal law generally between corporate person and shareholders was therefore treated on both sides as axiomatic, as a sort of postulate of the problem; so that it seems that no one ever really stopped to ask *which* system of municipal law was relevant. Professor Virally, during the oral proceedings, put his finger on the weakness when he summed up his understanding of this part of the case presented by Spain as follows:

> . . . un Etat ne peut être rendu internationalement responsable que s'il a porté atteinte aux droits des particuliers. Ces droits sont évidemment définis par l'ordre juridique étatique puisque, sauf exception, l'individu n'est pas un sujet du droit international. En l'espèce, pour que la Belgique puisse intervenir, il faudrait donc qu'il y ait eu violation des droits des actionnaires belges tels que les définit le droit national compétent, dont il n'est d'ailleurs pas précisé si, en l'espèce, c'est le droit canadien, droit de la société, ou le droit espagnol, droit du for.[436]

Nor, in the enormous documentation of the case, does there appear to be any evidence of what Canadian law actually provided on the subject of the rights of shareholders in the event of injury to the company; it appears to have been taken for granted[437] that there is a universal, or quasi-universal, rule that shareholders do not have any right of action or redress in the case of injury to the company.

Judge Gros, in his separate opinion, rejected the view of the majority that, in his words:

> an international court must fall back on [*renvoyer*—the English text does not have

---

[435] Ruiloba Santana (loc. cit. above (n. 430), p. 514) suggests, as a precedent for the recognition of a body of 'generally accepted rules' as a *tertium genus* lying between international law and individual systems of municipal law, the reference in the judgment of the Permanent Court of International Justice in the *Serbian Loans* case to the conflict of laws:

'The rules thereof may be common to several States and may even be established by international conventions or customs, and in the latter case may possess the character of true international law governing the relations between States' (*PCIJ*, Series A, Nos. 20–1, p. 51).

However, as the words 'in the latter case' make clear, it is the convention or custom which confers international status on such rules; and whether a rule of this kind was 'common to several States' or existed (before being taken up into a convention) only in the law of a single State is without legal relevance.

[436] *Pleadings*, vol. 8, p. 512. Cf. Ago, vol. 10, p. 653.

[437] The eminent French conflicts lawyer Franceskakis observes drily that there is no trace of the Court having carried out a study of comparative law on the point, 'tant ces règles paraissaient semble-t-il évidentes': 'Lueurs sur le droit international des sociétés de capitaux; l'arrêt "Barcelona" de la Cour internationale de justice', *Revue critique de droit international privé*, 59 (1970), p. 642.

the idea of *renvoi*] concepts of municipal law when seeking to define the legal relationships between the company and the shareholder[438]

since, in his view:

the *renvoi* to municipal law leads eventually, as in the present case, to the establishment of a superiority of municipal over international law which is a veritable negation of the latter . . . To consider as a ground for exonerating a State from international responsibility for an alleged denial of justice the fact that its municipal law, or some systems of municipal law, do not feature a shareholder's right of action is not admissible; . . .[439]

Judge Gros refers to 'some systems of municipal law' because he contended that, as a matter of fact, the distinction between shareholder and company, fundamental to the Court's decision, was not such a universal feature of national systems of law.[440]

This however is the key to the divergence of views between Judge Gros and his colleagues. Had it been a question (as it was for Judge Morelli) of the national law of the respondent State failing to furnish a remedy, the basic rule, sometimes referred to as the rule of supremacy of international law, could have found application. This basic rule is however better explained, not as the supremacy of one system over the other, but, in the words of the Permanent Court, as providing that a State 'cannot rely on her own legislation to limit the scope of her international obligations'.[441] For the majority of the Court, however, what mattered was not the provisions of Spanish law, but the fact that, generally if not universally, a shareholder was not considered to have rights to redress under municipal law in the event of injury to the company.

(3) Renvoi *to pre-existing law: the* Frontier Dispute *case*

The idea that international law may in appropriate cases effect a *renvoi* to municipal law was referred to in the judgment of the Chamber formed to deal with the *Frontier Dispute* between Mali and Burkina Faso. It was common ground that the frontier between the two States was defined by the boundary between the two French colonies of Upper Volta and Sudan immediately prior to their accession to independence (application of the principle of the *uti possidetis*):

The line which the Chamber is required to determine as being that which existed in 1959–1960, was at that time merely the administrative boundary dividing two former French colonies, called *territoires d'outre-mer* from 1946; as such it had to be defined not according to international law, but according to the French legislation which was applicable to such *territoires*.[442]

[438] *ICJ Reports*, 1970, p. 272, para. 9.
[439] Ibid.
[440] Ibid., p. 273, para. 11.
[441] *Free Zones of Upper Savoy and the District of Gex, PCIJ*, Series A/B, No. 46, p. 167.
[442] *ICJ Reports*, 1986, p. 568, para. 29.

The Chamber however found it necessary to add a 'clarification':

> International law—and consequently the principle of *uti possidetis*—applies to the new State (as a State) not with retroactive effect, but immediately and from that moment onwards. It applies to the State *as it is*, i.e., to the 'photograph' of the territorial situation then existing. The principle of *uti possidetis* freezes the territorial title; it stops the clock, but does not put back the hands. Hence international law does not effect any renvoi to the law established by the colonizing State, nor indeed to any legal rule unilaterally established by any State whatever; French law—especially legislation enacted by France for its colonies and *territoires d'outre-mer*—may play a role not in itself (as if there were a sort of *continuum juris*, a legal link between such law and international law), but only as one factual element among others, or as evidence indicative of what has been called the 'colonial heritage', i.e., the 'photograph of the territory' at the critical date.[443]

This passage seems to have been inspired by a desire not to suggest that reference to French colonial boundaries signified any approval or legitimation of the colonial system,[444] but its scope and significance as a matter of legal argument are obscure. The idea seems to be that the moment when international law begins to govern the matter—the moment of independence—is also the moment when colonial law is spent, so that there is a breach of continuity. The *uti possidetis* principle is thus deemed to act upon the 'frozen' territorial title, which presents itself as a purely factual circumstance. This view however does not take account of the nature of a territorial boundary as a purely legal and immaterial concept: even if a boundary is constituted by a precise natural feature like a river, or defined on the ground by markers—or even a fence—its status *as a boundary* is conferred by a legal system, national or international as the case may be. If therefore colonial law ceases to operate at or before the moment international law begins to apply, there is no 'boundary' for the *uti possidetis* principle to act on.

The Chamber returned to the point later in its judgment when discussing an item of French colonial legislation—an Order of 31 August 1927, to which an erratum had been issued on 5 October 1927. The Chamber first observed that

> if the Chamber's task were to interpret and apply the Order as amended on 5 October 1927 as a regulative text, for the purpose of establishing the boundaries of Upper Volta in 1932, it would have to examine its scope and appraise the relevance of the initial text of 31 August 1927, and of any *travaux préparatoires*, in the light of the particular rules of the legal system from which the Order derives its force as a regulation, i.e., French colonial law.[445]

After emphasizing that the Order (which in fact related to the border

---

[443] Ibid., para. 30.
[444] As is clear from the separate opinion of Judge Abi-Saab, ibid., p. 659.
[445] Ibid., p. 590, para. 69.

between Upper Volta and Niger) was relevant only as evidence of the intentions of the colonial power, the Chamber continued:

from a more general perspective, the Chamber has already had occasion to emphasize . . . that if colonial law has any role to play in this case it does so not in its own right, by way of a renvoi from international law to colonial law, but solely as evidence of the situation which existed at the time when the two States Parties achieved independence. The Chamber is therefore free to examine in this light the two successive versions of the 1927 Order, while nonetheless attributing greater weight to the text as modified by the erratum as a reflection of the definitive intentions of the colonial authorities, and to take the *travaux préparatoires* into consideration if this proves to be necessary.[446]

It appears from the pleadings[447] that the significance of this passage is to discount an argument advanced by Mali, that the Order of 31 August 1927, even as amended, was null and void as a matter of French administrative law, and therefore should not be taken into account by the Chamber.[448] The general consideration advanced by the Chamber in response to this, in the passage just quoted, is open to the same objection as was suggested in respect of the earlier passage in the judgment: the 'definitive intentions of the colonial authorities' as to the course of an administrative boundary are to be expressed in an administrative act. If such an act is, by its own applicable law, a nullity, it may nevertheless cast some light on the views of the authorities as to where the boundary could or should be, but it is not evidence of where the boundary actually *was*.[449]

(4) *Municipal law as a source of analogy*

The use of analogies drawn from municipal law to illustrate, explain or expand rules of international law is a judicial practice of the utmost respectability, its bible being Lauterpacht's magisterial *Private Law Sources and Analogies of International Law* (1927). Overt use of it by the Court itself in its decision is, however, not particularly common; it is rather individual judges who have resorted to parallels in municipal law to throw light on a particular question. Judge Dillard, for example, was fond of using this technique; and the frequent reference in the opinions of Judge de Castro to Roman law afford a striking demonstration of the perennial freshness and applicability of certain basic legal conceptions.

Individual judges are often in a good position to draw analogies from the specific national systems of law with which they are most familiar. The Court as a whole tends more to refer to municipal law in general, *en bloc*, sometimes, as in the *Barcelona Traction* case, with unhappy results.[450]

[446] Ibid.
[447] Counter-Memorial of Mali, paras. 5.16–5.17.
[448] See paras. 71–2 of the judgment.
[449] A similar argument, distinguishing between 'evidence' or 'information regarding the views or intentions' of the authorities, and an act effective in colonial administrative law, is in fact employed by the Chamber in relation to a different instrument: see para. 80 of the judgment.
[450] See above, subsection (2).

There is of course a narrow line between reference to private law in quest of illuminating analogies, and recourse to the 'general principles of law' referred to in Article 38 of the Statute. It is therefore not surprising that the Court should buttress its conclusions with reference to a widespread consistent usage in municipal systems of law, even if no specific appeal is made to 'general principles'.

An appeal to municipal law, unspecified, by way of analogy is to be found in the advisory opinion given in the case of *Certain Expenses of the United Nations*. It had been argued, in support of the view that the expenditures under discussion were not 'expenses of the Organization' within the meaning of Article 17, paragraph 2, of the Charter, that those expenditures should have been authorized by the Security Council, not by the General Assembly. The Court observed:

If it is agreed that the action in question is within the scope of the functions of the Organization but it is alleged that it has been initiated or carried out in a manner not in conformity with the division of functions among the several organs which the Charter prescribes, one moves to the internal plane, to the internal structure of the Organization. If the action was taken by the wrong organ, it was irregular as a matter of that internal structure, but this would not necessarily mean that the expense incurred was not an expense of the Organization. Both national and international law contemplate cases in which the body corporate or politic may be bound, as to third parties, by an *ultra vires* act of an agent.[451]

The Court went on to point out that

In the legal system of States, there is often some procedure for determining the validity of even a legislative or governmental act, but no analogous procedure is to be found in the structure of the United Nations[452]

and that accordingly each organ must determine its own jurisdiction.

It is however striking that the Court refers to 'cases in which the body corporate or politic may be bound, *as to third parties*, by an *ultra vires* act of an agent'; this is perfectly correct,[453] but what was in issue was not the effect of General Assembly resolutions 'as to third parties', but as to member States which regarded them as *ultra vires*.

2. The Doctrine of Intertemporal Law

(1) The principle stated and applied

The principle was stated in conveniently lapidary form by Fitzmaurice:

In a considerable number of cases, the rights of States (and more particularly of

---

[451] *ICJ Reports*, 1962, p. 168.
[452] Ibid.
[453] In the context of English Company law, the rule in *Royal British Bank* v. *Turquand* (1855), 5 E & B 248, springs to mind, as more directly relevant than matters involving an 'agent'. This rule is however for the protection of those outside the company, not those inside (cf. *Pennington's Company Law* (5th edn., 1985), p. 140).

parties to an international dispute) depend or derive from rights, or a legal situation, existing at some time in the past, or on a treaty concluded at some comparatively remote date . . . It can now be regarded as an established principle of international law that in such cases the situation in question must be appraised, and the treaty interpreted, in the light of the rules of international law as they existed at the time, and not as they exist today. In other words, it is not permissible to import into the legal evaluation of a previously existing situation, or of an old treaty, doctrines of modern law that did not exist or were not accepted at the time, and only resulted from the subsequent development or evolution of international law.[454]

It should however perhaps be observed that the principle in fact comprises two branches, originating in slightly different logical or legal considerations. When it is a question of interpretation of a treaty or other instrument,[455] given that the basic objective is to determine the intentions of the party or parties at the time the instrument was brought into existence, it must in the nature of things be a normally irrefragable presumption that the intention was to create rights and obligations in the context of the law as it then stood. More generally, it is appropriate to consider the evidence of the intentions of the parties against the factual and legal background contemporary with the instrument. In the *Temple of Preah Vihear* case, Judge Sir Percy Spender dissented from the majority on the basis of a different interpretation of the events of the early years of the century; he warned that: 'It is easy to fall into the error of judging the events of long ago by present-day standards'.[456] It was the applicability, and the effective application, of this principle which was at the heart of the long-fought controversy over the Mandate for South West Africa.

Where however the issue in controversy is that of rights, or a legal situation, existing at some time in the past and not deriving from a treaty or similar act of will, it is because, objectively, the only rights which could exist at the time were the rights recognized by the international law of the time that that law has to be applied to the exclusion of subsequent or present-day law. This distinction was to emerge with some clarity in the *Aegean Sea Continental Shelf* case.

A fairly obvious application of the second aspect of the rule, but one which is still worth stating, is that when a rule is created conditioning the validity of a legal act or instrument on the performance of some formality, an act performed before the rule came into effect is valid without compliance with the formality required. Thus in the *South West Africa* cases it was contended that, if the Mandate for South West Africa was a treaty, it was rendered unenforceable by Article 18 of the Covenant, which provided that no treaty or international engagement should be binding if not registered in accordance with that article. The Court rejected this contention,

[454] This *Year Book*, 30 (1953), p. 5; *Collected Edition*, I, p. 135.
[455] *ICJ Reports*, 1975, p. 38, para. 77.
[456] *ICJ Reports*, 1962, p. 128.

inter alia because it held that the Mandate antedated the Covenant.[457]
There is of course no reason why a treaty should not provide for more retrospective effect, if the parties so wish, and in the special field of declarations
of acceptance of jurisdiction under the Optional Clause referring to disputes arising after a particular date, somewhat unexpected complications
can arise in this respect,[458] which however do not need to be gone into here.

The question of the application of the intertemporal law principle to the
interpretation of a treaty arose in the case of *Right of Passage over Indian
Territory*, where Portugal relied on a treaty dating from 1779. India
objected that that treaty was not validly entered into, and never became in
law a treaty binding on the Maratha rulers of India; it drew attention to the
existence of divergent texts, and the absence of any authentic text accepted
by the parties. The Court dealt with the point as follows:

> The Court does not consider it necessary to deal with these and other objections
> raised by India to the form of the Treaty and the procedure by means of which
> agreement upon its terms was reached. It is sufficient to state that the validity of a
> treaty concluded as long ago as the last quarter of the eighteenth century, in the
> conditions then prevailing in the Indian Peninsula, should not be judged upon the
> basis of practice and procedures which have since developed only gradually.[459]

As this incident demonstrates, however, the intertemporal law principle
is only adjective law—it is a technique for applying the appropriate law to
the facts, not itself a rule of substantive law. Thus to exempt the 1779
treaty from compliance with modern requirements of form and procedure
would not in itself justify a conclusion that it was valid and binding; that
remained to be established, in the light of eighteenth-century practice in
the Indian subcontinent. The Court therefore went on to find that

> The Marathas themselves regarded the Treaty of 1779 as valid and binding upon
> them, and gave effect to its provisions. The Treaty is frequently referred to as such
> in subsequent formal Maratha documents, including the two *sanads* of 1783 and
> 1785, which purport to have been issued in pursuance of the Treaty. The Marathas
> did not at any time cast any doubt upon the validity or binding character of the
> Treaty.[460]

The same case prompted observations by the Court on the wider question of the assessment of a claim under general international law in the light
of the nature of that law at the relevant time. Portugal's claim to a right of
passage from its territories to enclaves surrounded by Indian territory had
been upheld by the Court on the basis of a local custom binding on India,
but the Court found on the facts that the right did not extend to the passage
of police, armed police or soldiers, or arms and ammunition. Portugal had

---

[457] Ibid., p. 332.
[458] See the present writer's article in *Netherlands Yearbook of International Law*, 15 (1984), p. 97 at
pp. 121–8.
[459] *ICJ Reports*, 1960, p. 37.
[460] Ibid.

based its claim not only on a special or local custom, but also on 'general international custom' and 'the general principles of law recognized by civilized nations'. So far as the general right of passage was concerned, the Court saw no need to consider these bases of claim, since the claim under special custom was sufficient to lead to the same result.

As regards armed forces, armed police and arms and ammunition, the finding of the Court that the practice established between the Parties required for passage in respect of these categories the permission of the British or Indian authorities, renders it unnecessary for the Court to determine whether or not, in the absence of the practice that actually prevailed, general international custom or the general principles of law recognized by civilized nations could have been relied upon by Portugal in support of its claim to a right of passage in respect of these categories.

The Court is here dealing with a concrete case having special features. Historically the case goes back to a period when, and relates to a region in which, the relations between neighbouring States were not regulated by precisely formulated rules but were governed largely by practice. Where therefore the Court finds a practice clearly established between two States which was accepted by the Parties as governing the relations between them, the Court must attribute decisive effect to that practice for the purpose of determining their specific rights and obligations. Such a particular practice must prevail over any general rules.[461]

The principle of application of the contemporary law to a practice of a customary nature is evidently sound. What is perhaps surprising is the emphasis on the historical background in relation to a practice which had continued, if not up to the date of the dispute (1954), at the least up to the end of British rule in India. The implication appears to be that once the practice became firmly established, its continuance had a petrifying effect not merely on the actual rights and obligations of the parties, but also on the inter-relation, so far as these rights and obligations were concerned, of special custom and general custom, special custom and general principles. The Court's *dictum* is frustratingly cryptic; did it consider that there was at the date the judgment was given a wider principle which would have given States in the position of Portugal a more extensive right of transit? Would such wider principle have prevailed over contemporary special practices? If so, why did the historical background to Portugal's right prevent this? These must remain matters for speculation.[462]

A comparatively non-controversial,[463] yet unusual, application of the principle was required in the *Western Sahara* case. The unusual feature was that the request for advisory opinion addressed to the Court asked for assessment of the legal situation in the territory later known as Western Sahara 'at the time of colonization by Spain', a time which the Court

---

[461] Ibid., pp. 43–4.

[462] The reference to the relationship between practice and 'precisely formulated rules' is also thought-provoking, and will be reconsidered in a later article devoted to custom and other sources of law.

[463] But see the argument of the representative of Algeria, M Bedjaoui, discussed below, pp. 138–9.

decided was the period beginning in 1884.[464] The Court's decision to accede to the request for an opinion on this provoked, in the dissenting opinion of Judge Petrén, the trenchant observation that:

> The Court is the principal judicial organ of the United Nations; it is not an historical research institute . . . no one would think of submitting to the Court the question, for example, of the authenticity of the will of the Emperor Trajan, or whether the invasion of Britain by William the Conqueror was justified.[165]

Judge Petrén's doubts were, however, related to the proper exercise by the Court of its power to give advisory opinions (to be considered in a later article); he did not, apparently, contest that the law applicable to his hypothetical questions would be that of the Roman Empire and of eleventh-century Europe, respectively.

The first question put to the Court—whether the territory had been *terra nullius* at the relevant period—could be answered without too much difficulty by reference to the practice of States contemporary with the Spanish colonization. The Court began its examination of the question with a classic statement of the intertemporal principle:

> Turning to Question I, the Court observes that the request specifically locates the question in the context of 'the time of colonization by Spain', and it therefore seems clear that the words 'Was Western Sahara . . . a territory belonging to no one (*terra nullius*)?' have to be interpreted by reference to the law in force at that period. The expression '*terra nullius*' was a legal term of art employed in connection with 'occupation' as one of the accepted legal methods of acquiring sovereignty over territory. 'Occupation' being legally an original means of peaceably acquiring sovereignty over territory otherwise than by cession or succession, it was a cardinal condition of a valid 'occupation' that the territory should be '*terra nullius*'—a territory belonging to no one—at the time of the act alleged to constitute the 'occupation' (cf. *Legal Status of Eastern Greenland, PCIJ*, Series A/B, No. 53, pp. 44 f. and 63 f.).[466]

The second question was 'what were the legal ties between this territory and the Kingdom of Morocco and the Mauritanian entity', again at the time of colonization. As the Court noted,

> The scope of this question depends upon the meaning to be attached to the expression 'legal ties' in the context of the time of the colonization of the territory by Spain. That expression, however, unlike '*terra nullius*' in Question I, was not a term having in itself a very precise meaning.[467]

Normal application of the principle of intertemporal law would suggest that what the Court would have to determine was whether there were any (and if so, what) ties which would have been regarded by lawyers of 1884 as 'legal ties'—presumably in the sense of ties recognized as significant for

---

[464] *ICJ Reports*, 1975, p. 38, para. 77.
[465] Ibid., p. 108.
[466] Ibid., pp. 38–9, para. 79.
[467] Ibid., p. 40, para. 84.

international law. It would however probably not be too hardy a supposition that no ties short of territorial sovereignty would have been considered at that time as of any legal relevance.

The passage quoted above from the Court's advisory opinion in fact continues:

> Accordingly, in the view of the Court, the meaning of the expression 'legal ties' in Question II has to be found rather in the object and purpose of General Assembly resolution 3292(XXIX), by which it was decided to request the present advisory opinion of the Court.[468]

From an examination of the context of the resolution—the question of decolonization of the territory—the Court was able to identify an underlying controversy concerning

> pretensions put forward, on the one hand, by Morocco that the territory was then a part of the Sherifian State and, on the other, by Mauritania that the territory then formed part of the Bilad Shinguitti or Mauritanian entity.[469]

The Court deduced that what the General Assembly was referring to was 'such "legal ties" as may affect the policy to be followed in the decolonization of Western Sahara'.[470] Thus the Court allowed respect for the actual intention of the requesting organ to prevail over any too rigid application of the intertemporal law principle; but in doing so it left the status of the adjective 'legal', as applied to the ties, floating uncertainly between the centuries. Apart from the question whether international or local law was contemplated, were the ties to be identified legal only in the sense of relevant to the legal process of decolonization, or had they to have had some legal status in 1884? While the Court made no specific comment on the point, the alleged 'ties' it in fact examined, other than the territorial sovereignty claimed by Morocco, did not have a specifically international-law character, but were placed firmly in the context of the late nineteenth century.

(2) Application to future acts

The normal use of the intertemporal principle is by reference to acts performed, and law applicable, at a particular time: but essentially it simply requires that to each legal event should be applied the law as it stands at the time.[471] Thus it may also be said of an event which is to occur in the future that the law applicable to it will be the law as it stands then, not the law as it is at the moment the observation is made (subject of course to any question of acquired rights). Since the function of a Court does not normally require

---

[468] Ibid.
[469] Ibid., p. 42, para. 85.
[470] Ibid.
[471] Thus a Court is tacitly applying the intertemporal principle in every ordinary case by determining the dispute by reference to the law as it stands, rather as Molière's M. Jourdain was speaking prose without being aware of it.

it to look into the future, instances of this can be expected to be rare; but it did occur in the *Fisheries Jurisdiction* cases.

In the two *Fisheries Jurisdiction* cases, the Court was clearly preoccupied by the speed with which the law of the sea was developing and changing: it referred in particular to 'present endeavours, pursued under the auspices of the United Nations, to achieve in a third Conference on the Law of the Sea the further codification and progressive development of this branch of the Law' and observed that 'the Court, as a court of law, cannot render judgment *sub specie legis ferendae*, or anticipate the law before the legislator has laid it down'.[472]

When indicating that the parties were required by international law to negotiate in good faith to bring about an equitable apportionment of the fishing resources, the Court observed that the negotiations involved

an obligation upon the Parties to pay reasonable regard to each other's rights and to conservation requirements pending the conclusion of the negotiations. While this statement is of course a re-affirmation of a self-evident principle, it refers to the rights of the Parties as indicated in the present Judgment. It is obvious that both in regard to merits and to jurisdiction, the Court only pronounces on the case which is before it and not on any hypothetical situation which might arise in the future. *At the same time, the Court must add that its Judgment cannot preclude the Parties from benefiting from any subsequent developments in the pertinent rules of international law.*[473]

(3) *Problems of ascertaining the applicable law*

The intertemporal law principle presupposes that, for its application, it will in fact be possible to determine what international law provided at the time in question. Normally this should present no problem; but it is not inconceivable that a Court might be asked to determine, by reference to a past age, a question which had not at that time ever arisen for settlement,— a sort of retrospective case of first impression. In the context of municipal law rather than international law, this was a problem faced by the Chamber formed to deal with the case of *Elettronica Sicula SpA (ELSI)*. The facts on which the claim was based had occurred twenty years earlier, and in order to deal with an objection based on non-exhaustion of local remedies the Chamber was asked to say that a particular remedy did exist and was not used. The Chamber resolved the difficulty as follows:

It thus appears to the Chamber to be impossible to deduce, from the recent jurisprudence cited, what the attitude of the Italian courts would have been had Raytheon and Machlett brought an action, some 20 years ago, in reliance on Article 2043 of the Civil Code in conjunction with the provisions of the FCN Treaty and the Supplementary Agreement. Where the determination of a question of municipal law is essential to the Court's decision in a case, the Court will have to weigh the

---

[472] *ICJ Reports*, 1974, p. 192, para. 45. See also pp. 148–50, below.
[473] Ibid., pp. 202–3, para. 70 (emphasis added), *Federal Republic of Germany* v. *Iceland*. The last sentence appears also, in a slightly different context, in the *United Kingdom* v. *Iceland* judgment.

jurisprudence of the municipal courts, and 'If this is uncertain or divided, it will rest with the Court to select the interpretation which it considers most in conformity with the law' (*Brazilian Loans, PCIJ*, Series A, Nos. 20/21, p. 124). In the present case, however, it was for Italy to show, as a matter of fact, the existence of a remedy which was open to the United States stockholders and which they failed to employ. The Chamber does not consider that Italy has discharged that burden.[474]

Should this dilemma arise in respect of a question of international law, however, the rule of the burden of proof is unlikely to be of assistance.

(4) *Intertemporal* renvoi

So long as the intertemporal principle relates to the creation of rights or obligations by the operation of the rules of law current at the relevant time, there can be no room for argument but that it was those rules, and not those of a later period, which should be applied. So soon however as a subjective element is introduced, so soon as it is required to interpret the intentions of the parties to an instrument effected by an act of will—an *acte juridique* as opposed to a *fait juridique*—, the possibility exists of an intention to subject the legal relations created to such law as might from time to time thereafter become effective.

This process was identified for the first time in a decision of the Court in the advisory opinion given in the *Namibia* case;[475] but the simplest and most convincing example of its operation was in fact exemplified in the later case of the *Aegean Sea Continental Shelf*. The jurisdictional title invoked in that case was the 1928 General Act for the Peaceful Settlement of International Disputes, to which the applicant, Greece, had acceded in 1931, subject to a reservation referring to the 'territorial status' of Greece. In order to resist the assertion of this reservation against it by Turkey, by way of reciprocity, Greece argued, *inter alia*, that the concept of the continental shelf was unknown in 1931.

The Court observed as follows in relation to this argument:

The Greek Government invokes as a basis for the Court's jurisdiction in the present case Article 17 of the General Act under which the parties agreed to submit to judicial settlement all disputes with regard to which they 'are in conflict as to their respective rights'. Yet the rights that are the subject of the claims upon which Greece requests the Court in the Application to exercise its jurisdiction under Article 17 are the very rights over the continental shelf of which, as Greece insists, the authors of the General Act could have had no idea whatever in 1928. If the Greek Government is correct, as it undoubtedly is, in assuming that the meaning of the generic term 'rights' in Article 17 follows the evolution of the law, so as to be capable of embracing rights over the continental shelf, it is not clear why the similar term 'territorial status' should not likewise be liable to evolve in meaning in

[474] *ICJ Reports*, 1989, p. 47, para. 62.
[475] *Legal Consequences for States of the Continued Presence of South Africa in Namibia (South West Africa) notwithstanding Security Council Resolution 276 (1970)*.

accordance with 'the development of international relations' (*PCIJ*, Series B, No. 4, p. 24).[476]

It would of course be absurd to interpret the General Act as only creative of jurisdiction in respect of disputes over rights which existed in 1928; and the analysis of the Court is clearly correct in attributing to the authors of that instrument the intention that the term 'rights' should cover all rights existing, or asserted to exist, at the time the dispute was submitted for settlement. But, as the *Namibia* case had already shown, the same technique of interpretation could produce results which were more controversial. Before studying the *Aegean Sea* case further, we will resume the chronological order of decisions in this field, and examine the *Namibia* advisory opinion.

The Court in that case had to consider the (by then) familiar argument that, among the mandates conferred by the League of Nations, 'C' mandates were in a qualitatively different category from 'A' and 'B' mandates, as being, according to the contemporary intention of the members of the League, 'in their practical effect not far removed from annexation'.[477] The evidence that 'C' mandates were so regarded was implicitly accepted by the Court. The Court began its consideration of the point with a deferential gesture in favour of the intertemporal principle, but continued with a bold application of the interpretation technique just explained:

> Mindful as it is of the primary necessity of interpreting an instrument in accordance with the intentions of the parties at the time of its conclusion, the Court is bound to take into account the fact that the concepts embodied in Article 22 of the Covenant—'the strenuous conditions of the modern world' and 'the well-being and development' of the peoples concerned—were not static, but were by definition evolutionary, as also, therefore, was the concept of the 'sacred trust'. The parties to the Covenant must consequently be deemed to have accepted them as such. That is why, viewing the institutions of 1919, the Court must take into consideration the changes which have occurred in the supervening half-century, and its interpretation cannot remain unaffected by the subsequent development of law, through the Charter of the United Nations and by way of customary law.[478]

The conclusion to which this line of argument led was that 'the Court is unable to accept any construction which would attach to "C" mandates an object and purpose different from those of "A" and "B" mandates'.[479]

The doubts prompted by this line of argument do not relate to the legal logic, but to the basic finding, as to the intentions of the States concerned in 1919, upon which it is built. There must be a danger, when applying this line of approach, of confusing what, on the basis of the available evidence, may be found to have been the actual intention of the parties concerned,

---

[476] *ICJ Reports*, 1978, p. 33, para. 78.
[477] *ICJ Reports*, 1971, p. 28, para. 45.
[478] Ibid., p. 31, para. 53.
[479] Ibid., p. 32, para. 54.

and what is judged, with the benefit of hindsight, to be what *ought* to have been their intention. In the particular case of the *Namibia* advisory opinion there is reason to wonder whether this may not have happened. In the passage quoted above, it is to be observed that the Court did not find as a fact that the parties to the Covenant contemplated that the concepts in Article 22 should acquire a different content with the development of international law, but that, because the concepts were, in the Court's view, 'by definition evolutionary', they 'must consequently be deemed to have accepted them as such'. Not only is no evidence referred to that the parties had such an intention; none is offered to show that the concepts were *at the time* regarded as evolutionary.

Doubts as to whether the distinction between contemporary intention and subsequent benevolent hindsight was observed are reinforced by the immediately following passage in the opinion:

Moreover, an international instrument has to be interpreted and applied within the framework of the entire legal system prevailing at the time of the interpretation. In the domain to which the present proceedings relate, the last fifty years, as indicated above, have brought important developments. These developments leave little doubt that the ultimate objective of the sacred trust was the self-determination and independence of the peoples concerned. In this domain, as elsewhere, the *corpus iuris gentium* has been considerably enriched, and this the Court, if it is faithfully to discharge its functions, may not ignore.[480]

It may be objected that the 'entire legal system prevailing' at the time of the *Namibia* opinion includes the principle of intertemporal law, so that the first sentence quoted rather evades than meets the difficulty. Furthermore, the ultimate objective of the sacred trust was what it was in 1919; subsequent developments might make clearer what it had been, but could not retrospectively make it something other than what it was.

In his dissenting opinion, Fitzmaurice did not question the intellectual construction whereby recourse to the intertemporal principle may lead to the application of modern law, through the 'evolutionary' intention of the States concerned. He did however actively combat the finding that, in the case of the 'C' mandates, there could have been such an intention. Referring to the assurances given that the 'C' mandates would give 'ownership in all but name', he observed:

Whether this attitude was unethical according to present-day standards (it certainly was not so then) is juridically beside the point. It clearly indicates what the *intentions* of the parties were, and upon what basis the 'C' mandates were accepted. This does not of course mean that the mandatories obtained sovereignty. But it does mean that they could never, in the case of these territories contiguous to or very near their own, have been willing to accept a system according to which at the will of the Council of the League, they might at some future date find themselves

---

[480] Ibid., pp. 31–2, para. 53.

displaced in favour of another entity—possibly a hostile or unfriendly one—(as is indeed precisely the intention now). No sovereign State at that time—or indeed at any other time—would have accepted the administration of a territory on such terms.[481]

The same passage quoted above from paragraph 53 of the advisory opinion, referring to interpretation and application 'within the framework of the entire legal system prevailing' at the time of the interpretation, was taken up by the *Institut de droit international* in its Resolution of 'The Intertemporal Problem in Public International Law', adopted at Wiesbaden in 1975. Paragraph 4 of the Resolution provided:

> Wherever a provision of a treaty refers to a legal or other concept without defining it, it is appropriate to have recourse to the usual methods of interpretation in order to determine whether the concept concerned is to be interpreted as understood at the time when the provision was drawn up or as understood at the time of its application. Any interpretation of a treaty must take into account all relevant rules of international law which apply between the parties at the time of application.[482]

During the discussion of the text, Sir Gerald Fitzmaurice proposed the deletion of the second sentence, but while his proposal obtained some support, it was defeated on a vote.[483]

In the *Western Sahara* case, an ingenious argument was put forward by the representative of Algeria, M Bedjaoui, whereby the term '*terra nullius*' in the question put to the Court would not be interpreted according to the accepted meaning given to it by European States in 1884, but otherwise, by application of the technique of 'intertemporal *renvoi*' used in the *Namibia* case. After quoting the passage from the advisory opinion in that case which has been set out (in two halves) above, he continued:

> Mais dans le cas présent, il s'agit moins d'une adaptation que de la substitution d'une norme exactement inverse. Cette substitution est plus que légitime; elle est impérative dès lors que le droit des peuples à disposer d'eux-mêmes relève du *jus cogens* et se situe par conséquent au-dessus de toute autre norme juridique d'une part et traduit d'autre part une irréductibilité de principe au système d'occupation de territoires peuplés, c'est-à-dire exprime une incompatibilité radicale avec la théorie de la *terra nullius*.[484]

The idea of substituting, on an intertemporal law basis, the norm of self-determination of peoples for the concept of *terra nullius* appears somewhat startling; however the brief quotation above does not, of course, do full justice to M Bedjaoui's subtle and learned argument. Since the Court, as we have seen, did not adopt it, it falls outside the strict scope of the present

---

[481] Ibid., p. 277, para. 85.
[482] *Annuaire de l'Institut*, 1975, p. 339.
[483] Ibid., pp. 367–70.
[484] *Pleadings*, p. 493.

survey, in which space does not permit of so lengthy a digression as would be needed to examine it in full.[485]

The question of intertemporal law which arose in the *Aegean Sea Continental Shelf* case concerned, as noted above, the interpretation of the reservations attached by Greece to its accession to the 1928 General Act for the Pacific Settlement of International Disputes, the basis of jurisdiction which Greece relied on in the proceedings which it brought against Turkey. One of these reservations excluded from judicial settlement under the General Act

disputes concerning questions which by international law are solely within the domestic jurisdiction of States, and in particular disputes relating to the territorial status of Greece, including disputes relating to its rights of sovereignty over its ports and lines of communication.[486]

The question was whether a dispute with Turkey over the delimitation of the continental shelf fell within the category of 'disputes relating to the territorial status of Greece'.

Greece advanced two arguments on this point which partook of the nature of arguments of intertemporal law. First, it maintained

that a restrictive view has to be taken of the meaning of the expression 'disputes relating to the territorial status of Greece' in reservation (*b*) by reason of the historical context in which that expression was incorporated into the reservation.[487]

For reasons which it is not necessary to go into here, the essential contention of Greece was that such an expression as 'territorial status' in the 1920s was to be given 'a restrictive interpretation limited to the maintenance of the status quo established by treaties, normally as the result of post-war settlement'.[488]

The Court rejected this contention, but it did so essentially on the ground that 'the historical evidence adduced by Greece does not suffice to establish that the expression "territorial status" was used in the League of Nations period, and in particular in the General Act of 1928, in the special, restricted, sense contended for by Greece'.[489]

What is however material to the present discussion is that the Court did not disagree with Greece's contention in principle that the historical context should govern the interpretation of the reservation. Referring to the

---

[485] It may be observed, however, that the main weakness of the appeal to intertemporal *renvoi* was that, while reference was made in the General Assembly resolution to the 'time of colonization', the resolution itself was contemporary, so that the idea of an intention, at some moment in the past, that the meaning of a concept employed shall follow the development of the law, was wholly inapplicable. M Bedjaoui also did not, unfortunately, spell out what answer should, on the basis of his contentions, be given to Question I.

[486] *ICJ Reports*, 1978, p. 21, para. 48.

[487] Ibid., p. 28, para. 69.

[488] Ibid., p. 30, para. 72.

[489] Ibid., p. 31, para. 74.

decisions of the Court and of the Permanent Court of International Justice relied on by Greece[490] the Court stated:

According to this jurisprudence it is indeed clear that in interpreting reservation (b) regard must be paid to the intention of the Greek Government at the time when it deposited its instrument of accession to the General Act . . .[491]

The second argument put forward by Greece in this connection was more radical. It contended that there could be no question of the applicability of reservation (b) to a dispute over the continental shelf, because

the very idea of the continental shelf was wholly unknown in 1928 when the General Act was concluded, and in 1931 when Greece acceded to the Act.[492]

Essentially, this contention was advanced as a matter of the intention of Greece at the time of its accession; it was stated in the Memorial in the following terms:

. . . la notion même de plateau continental étant inconnue en 1931, il serait inconcevable que la Grèce ait pu avoir l'intention à cette date d'exclure les différends relatifs au plateau continental.[493]

It is however suggested that the point is not only one of actual or presumed intention; if the law of 1931 is to be applied, it is apparent that a dispute over the delimitation of the continental shelf was a legally meaningless concept, since the doctrine of the continental shelf had not yet been stated.[494]

The Court, however, rejected this contention of Greece also. It repudiated the parallel which Greece had sought to draw with the well-known *dictum* in the arbitral award in the case of *Petroleum Development Ltd.* v. *Sheikh of Abu Dhabi*,[495] on the following ground:

While there may well be a presumption that a person transferring valuable property rights to another intends only to transfer the rights which he possesses at that time, the case appears to the Court to be quite otherwise when a State, in agreeing to subject itself to compulsory procedures of pacific settlement, excepts from that agreement a category of disputes which, though covering clearly specified subject-matters, is of a generic kind. Once it is established that the expression 'the territorial status of Greece' was used in Greece's instrument of accession as a generic term denoting any matters comprised within the concept of territorial status under general international law, the presumption necessarily arises that its meaning was intended to follow the evolution of the law and to correspond with the meaning attached to the expression by the law in force at any given time. This presumption,

---

[490] *Anglo-Iranian Oil Co., ICJ Reports*, 1951, p. 104; *Rights of Minorities in Upper Silesia, PCIJ*, Series A, No. 15, p. 22; *Phosphates in Morocco, PCIJ*, Series A/B, No. 74, pp. 22–4.

[491] *ICJ Reports*, 1978, p. 29, para. 69.

[492] Ibid., p. 32, para. 77.

[493] *Pleadings*, p. 258.

[494] Whether, with the benefit of hindsight, one can say that States in 1931 did in fact have rights over the continental shelf without knowing it (cf. the Court's statement in 1969 that such rights 'exist *ab initio*' – *ICJ Reports*, 1969, p. 22, para. 19), or whether such rights only came into existence in the late 1940s is probably a sterile debate, but not without philosophical interest.

[495] 18 ILR 144, 152.

in the view of the Court, is even more compelling when it is recalled that the 1928 Act was a convention for the pacific settlement of disputes designed to be of the most general kind and of continuing duration, for it hardly seems conceivable that in such a convention terms like 'domestic jurisdiction' and 'territorial status' were intended to have a fixed content regardless of the subsequent evolution of international law.[496]

The Court therefore pursued its argument:

It follows that in interpreting and applying reservation (b) with respect to the present dispute the Court has to take account of the evolution which has occurred in the rules of international law concerning a coastal State's rights of exploration and exploitation over the continental shelf. The Court is, therefore, now called upon to examine whether, taking into account the developments in international law regarding the continental shelf, the expression 'disputes relating to the territorial status of Greece' should or should not be understood as comprising within it disputes relating to the geographical—the spatial—extent of Greece's rights over the continental shelf in the Aegean Sea.[497]

Its conclusion on this point was that, taking into account the particular circumstances of the dispute, that dispute was one which related to the territorial status of Greece within the meaning of reservation (b), and the Court declined jurisdiction on that ground.

One of the arguments advanced by the Court in support of its position has already been quoted: the interpretation of the 'rights' in Article 17 of the 1928 General Act. What is it about the term 'rights' which enables the Court's conclusion—wholly convincing as regards this specific term—to be drawn? A possible answer is that the 'evolution of the law' has no influence on the impact of a provision referring to a future conflict as to the respective 'rights' of the parties, because the term 'rights' in this context is one which necessarily extends to the whole of the 'rights' of the party at a given time. Like the term *'patrimoine'*, its content is *ex definitione* both fluctuating and universal.[498] It is for this reason that its peculiar operation with regard to intertemporal law has not attracted attention; it is too obvious to be stated. It is however more than questionable whether a term like 'territorial status', particularly in the context of a reservation—by definition, a text intended to have a limiting effect—can properly be attributed this chameleon-like character.

The Court went on to point out that some of the islands to which the claim of Greece related had only been acquired by it by cession in 1947, and were thus not in its possession in 1931. The Court commented:

In consequence, it seems clear that, in the view of the Greek Government, the term 'rights' in Article 17 of the General Act has to be interpreted in the light of the geographical extent of the Greek State today, not of its extent in 1931. It would

---

[496] *ICJ Reports*, 1978, p. 32, para. 77.

[497] Ibid., p. 34, para. 80.

[498] The same may probably be said of the expression 'the strenuous conditions of the modern world', given an 'evolutionary' interpretation by the Court in the *Namibia* case: see above, p. 136.

then be a little surprising if the meaning of Greece's reservation of disputes relating to its 'territorial status' was not also to evolve in the light of the change in the territorial extent of the Greek State brought about by 'the development of international relations'.[499]

This is however no more than a restatement of the same argument: the category of 'rights' contemplated in Article 17 of the General Act, because of its necessarily fluid yet universal character, could as well assimilate rights over a later-acquired territory as it could rights which were legally non-existent (or undiscovered) at the time the term was used. The fact that the variation in extent of rights is, in this instance, geographical is a purely incidental aspect, so that to argue that 'territorial status' must have been intended to undergo similar variation is, with all respect, no more than a debating point.

The basic weakness in the Court's argument in both the *Namibia* and the *Aegean Sea* cases however lies, it is suggested, in a shift between the two types of intertemporal law rule to which attention was drawn at the beginning of the present section. The Court's discussion proceeds on the basis that a term used in a legal text *can*, the intertemporal principle notwithstanding—or more precisely, by a more sophisticated application of intertemporality—, have a content which is referable to the law as it stands at the time when the term comes to be interpreted, because that was the parties' intention. From this, the conclusion is drawn that a term which *can* operate in this way *does* do so, as a matter of intertemporal law, as though it were an application of the other—non voluntarist—intertemporal rule. But the question is one of the interpretation of a text emanating from a State or States, i.e., of ascertaining the intentions of that State, or those States.[500]

In the case of the Mandate for South West Africa, the intention of the League and its members was the subject of fierce controversy. In the *Aegean Sea* case, there is nothing in the Court's discussion of the point which wholly convinces the reader that Greece *intended* the meaning of the expression 'territorial status' to be referable to the current state of the law. The material produced by Greece to throw light on the background to the text of its reservation—though it did not convince the Court that 'territorial status' was intended to have a more limited meaning than that generally accepted at the time—does not suggest that it was the intention of Greece that it should have, at least potentially, a wider meaning.

The third argument used by the Court at this stage in its reasoning was:

Furthermore, the close and necessary link that always exists between a jurisdictional clause and reservations to it, makes it difficult to accept that the meaning of the clause, but not of the reservation, should follow the evolution of the law. In the present instance, this difficulty is underlined by the fact that alongside Greece's

---

[499] *ICJ Reports*, 1978, p. 33, para. 78.

[500] It does not appear that the Court intended to scramble the two rules to the extent advocated by McWhinney ('The Time Dimension in International Law: Historical Relativism and Intertemporal Law', *Essays in International Law in honour of Judge Manfred Lachs* (1984), p. 179).

reservation of disputes relating to its 'territorial status' in reservation (*b*) is another reservation of disputes relating to questions of 'domestic jurisdiction', the content of which, as the Court has already had occasion to note, is 'an essentially relative question' and undoubtedly 'depends upon the development of international relations' . . . Again, the Court can see no valid reason why one part of reservation (*b*) should have been intended to follow the evolution of international relations but not the other, unless such an intention should have been made plain by Greece at the time.[501]

It is unfortunate that the Court here did not quote the 'domestic jurisdiction' reservation more fully, since it in fact refers to 'disputes concerning questions which *by international law* are solely within the domestic jurisdiction of States'. The reference to international law is surely more than sufficient to show an intention that the interpretation of 'domestic jurisdiction' should follow the evolution of the law. It is therefore hardly appropriate to require that Greece should have 'made plain . . . at the time' an opposite intention as regards the 'territorial status' reservation.

To sum up, the concept of terminology capable of giving rise to an 'intertemporal *renvoi*' used by the Court in the *Namibia* and *Aegean Sea* cases, though undoubtedly a valid one, is to be used with caution; it must be referred to the actual or legitimately deduced intention of the author or authors of the relevant text, and it is essential to avoid reading back into the intentions of the States concerned at the time they adopted this text considerations which, however firmly established they may be in present-day law, and however desirable it might have been had they been foreseen at the outset, were not in fact present to the minds of those concerned. To stretch the intertemporal principle in this way would be to falsify its whole nature.

3. *The Relationship between Sources of Law*

(1) *The nature of the rules governing the relationship between sources*

In broad terms, the relationship between the various sources of international law may be regarded as fairly well defined. At least for purposes of its application by the Court, the enumeration of its sources to be found in Article 38, paragraph 1, of the Statute of the Court can in practice be treated as an indication of a hierarchy, or order of priority of sources. International conventions in force between the parties, as *lex specialis*, exclude the application of rules of customary law covering the same ground as the treaties.[501a] An exception to this which has become recognized in more recent years is the concept of *jus cogens*: precepts of general (and presumably customary) international law which are regarded as so fundamental or so essential that attempts to derogate from them by treaty are ineffective. The 'general principles of law' constitute a concept the definition of which

---

[501] *ICJ Reports*, 1978, p. 33, para. 79.
[501a] Cf. *Military and Paramilitary Activities in and against Nicaragua, ICJ Reports*, 1986, p. 137, para. 274.

remains controversial, but it is generally understood to be one to which recourse is necessary only if neither treaties in force nor custom afford rules for the settlement of the dispute. Finally, the Statute itself provides, in sub-paragraph (*d*) of paragraph 1 of Article 38, that judicial decisions and legal teaching are no more than 'subsidiary means for the determination of rules of law'.

It was obviously contemplated, when the Statute was drawn up, that the Court would be able, in all cases before it, to have recourse to all the recognized sources in its quest for the rules applicable to the dispute. That this has not always been the case has been the result of the need to respect the limitations of the jurisdictional title by which the Court has been seised in a particular case, and the unforeseen restrictiveness of many such titles. It may occur, and it has occurred, that the Court is limited to the application of treaty law, to the exclusion of customary law in the same field, or—though the hypothesis might seem less probable—to the application of customary law to the exclusion of the provisions of a treaty currently in force between the parties, and containing relevant provisions.

The first situation arises when the Court is seised under the compromissory clause of a treaty in the common form whereby it is expressed to confer jurisdiction over disputes concerning the interpretation or application of the treaty. The disputed articles of the treaty may, to a greater or lesser extent, overlap with the customary law; but the Court is not empowered under a clause of this type to determine the rights and obligations of the parties under customary law, but only the rights and obligations (which may prove to be identical) under the treaty. This was the position in the case of *United States Diplomatic and Consular Staff in Tehran*, where the jurisdictional title invoked was purely conventional, primarily the Optional Protocols to the Vienna Conventions on Diplomatic and Consular Relations. As we shall see (subsection (2)(*c*) below), the Court in that case went somewhat beyond the strictly treaty-law scope of the jurisdiction. The second situation has so far arisen only in the case of *Military and Paramilitary Activities in and against Nicaragua* (discussed in subsection (2)(*d*) below), as a result of the application of the so-called 'multilateral treaty reservation' attached to the United States declaration of acceptance of jurisdiction under Article 36, paragraph 2, of the Statute.

A preliminary question which suggests itself at the outset of any examination of the Court's case law in this field is: what is the nature of the rules which determine the relationship *inter se* of the various sources or types of international law rules? Even setting aside the provisions of Article 38 of the Statute, it is universally accepted that, for example, as between the parties to a treaty the rules of the treaty displace any rules of customary law on the same subject. If it were not so, if treaty rules were powerless to modify the relationship resulting from customary law, there would indeed be no point in entering into treaties at all. But is this rule itself a rule of customary law?—it is obviously not a rule of treaty origin. Or is it a general principle of law, of the kind contemplated by Article 38, paragraph 1 (*c*), of the Statute? Or is it some kind of basic constitutional rule of the whole international legal order, lying outside the hierarchy of sources or norms stated in Article 38?

An example of the sort of question of the relationship between sources of law which may arise in practice is afforded by the *North Sea Continental Shelf* judgment. Discussing the possibility that the equidistance rule in Article 6 of the 1958 Geneva Convention on the Continental Shelf might represent or have become a rule of customary international law, the Court suggested that since

general or customary law rules and obligations . . . by their very nature, must have equal force for all members of the international community,

such rules will, when embodied in a convention

figure amongst those in respect of which a right of unilateral reservation is not conferred, or is excluded.[502]

Now it may be said that this is a rule of treaty interpretation, a field governed, except where the Vienna Convention on the Law of Treaties finds application, by customary law.[503] It would certainly be very difficult to trace a pedigree in State practice for a rule of interpretation on the lines of the above *dictum*.[504] In fact, however, it is not a rule of treaty interpretation: it is a rule destined to guide the judge in determining whether an asserted rule of law is or is not an accepted rule of customary international law. In order to ascertain whether States regarded it as such—the *opinio juris*—it is relevant to see how they treated it in a multilateral convention in which it was embodied or restated. The purpose is not to interpret the treaty to determine what were the rights and obligations of the parties to it, but to use the treaty as evidence of a particular view of customary law. The rule or technique proposed by the Court might therefore be treated as no more than a 'meta-principle';[505] but the point of interest here is whether it forms part of customary international law. It is perhaps not inconceivable that a practice might become established governing the relationship between treaty obligations and obligations themselves established by practice in the routine of custom; but it is doubtful if this can in fact be demonstrated. As O'Connell puts it, canons of treaty interpretation in general are 'no more than logical devices for ascertaining the real area of treaty interpretation', so that the effect of the provisions of the Vienna Convention on

---

[502] *ICJ Reports*, 1969, pp. 38–9, para. 63.

[503] Cf. the *dictum* of the Court in the *Military and Paramilitary Activities in and against Nicaragua* case discussed below, p. 147.

[504] The more so since, as we observed in Chapter II, section 3(1) above, it may in any event perhaps be based on a confusion of universality and force as *jus cogens*.

[505] Cf. Koskenniemi, 'General Principles: Reflections on Constructionist Thinking in International Law', *Oikevstiede-Jurisprudentia*, 18 (1985), p. 133.

the Law of Treaties concerning interpretation is that 'of transforming logical positions into rules of law'.[506]

The fact of the matter is that 'general international law' and 'customary international law' are not synonymous categorizations; there must be a place for (*inter alia*) rules which govern the relations between categories of international legal norms, and such rules must themselves form part of international law. The question was examined by Fitzmaurice in 1958, and his conclusion was that

the sources of international law cannot be stated, or cannot fully and certainly be stated, in terms of international law itself, and that there are and must be rules of law that have an inherent and necessary validity, in whose absence no system of law at all can exist or be originated. Such a rule, for instance, is the rule *pacta sunt servanda*.[507]

The question whether such rules are 'within' or 'without' the body of international law itself is a philosophical conundrum not without interest;[508] but all that needs to be noted here is that there must be 'legal' rules (whatever that means) determining the relations between different sources of law—or, of more practical impact, the relations between the products of different sources of law.

Another example of the sort of *dictum* of the Court which falls into this class is to be found in the judgment on the merits in the case of *Military and Paramilitary Activities in and against Nicaragua*. Again the Court was engaged, for reasons to be examined in a moment, in considering the relations between rules embodied in a multilateral treaty and rules, covering the same subject-matter, of customary international law. The Court there stated, as a general principle,

there are no grounds for holding that when customary international law is comprised of rules identical to those of treaty law, the latter 'supervenes' the former, so that the customary international law has no further existence of its own.[509]

It is significant that when the Court goes on to give a number of reasons for this ruling, these are of an intellectual or hypothetical nature and do not purport to be a statement of practice supporting a customary rule.[510]

Turning now from the nature of the rules governing the relationship between treaty law and customary law to the content of the rules themselves as declared by the Court, we may first consider the significance in this context of provision for reservations in a multilateral treaty. While, as observed above, the mere generality of a rule of customary law does not militate

---

[506] *International Law*, vol. 1, pp. 252–3.

[507] 'Some Problems regarding the Formal Sources of International Law', *Symbolae Verzijl* (1958), p. 164.

[508] See the observations of the present writer in *International Customary Law and Codification* (1972), pp. 37–9, and the important article of Maarten Bos, 'The Recognized Manifestations of International Law', *German Yearbook of International Law*, 20 (1977), p. 9, particularly pp. 72–3.

[509] *ICJ Reports*, 1986, p. 95, para. 177.

[510] Ibid., para. 96.

against the possibility of States agreeing by treaty to derogate from it or apply a different rule, it is certainly the case that if a rule is not only a general rule of customary law, but also a matter of *jus cogens*, it would be to be expected that a provision in a multilateral treaty stating the rule should not be one to which reservations under the treaty would be permitted.

The reverse relationship has in fact been considered by the Court in its judgment on the merits in the case of the *Military and Paramilitary Activities in and against Nicaragua*. When considering whether the prohibition of the use of force expressed in Article 2, paragraph 4, of the UN Charter is a principle of customary international law, the Court found confirmation that this was so

in the fact that it is frequently referred to in statements by State representatives as being not only a principle of customary international law but also a fundamental or cardinal principle of such law,

and the Court quoted allusions to the principle as being one of *jus cogens*.[511] The principle operating here may seem to be one which is conceptually self-evident: if a rule is one of *jus cogens*, it cannot be other than a general rule without self-contradiction. (An interesting theoretical question is whether a rule of *jus cogens* is necessarily customary in origin or authority, or whether a 'general principle', unsupported by practice, could have this status.[512])

(2) *Rights and obligations with a double foundation: overlap of treaty and customary law*[513]

It is universally accepted that—consideration of *jus cogens* apart—a treaty as *lex specialis* is law between the parties to it in derogation of the general customary law which would otherwise have governed their relations. Thus if a treaty provides that the parties, in their mutual relations, shall not be obliged to do something which customary law would otherwise have required of them, it is trite law that the obligation so set aside does not form part of the law between the parties. On the other hand, where the treaty is silent, general international law continues to apply. There is however the intermediate possibility, that some or all of the rights and obligations provided for in the treaty correspond exactly to those existing under customary law. If so, with which legal prescriptions are the parties complying when they give effect to those rights and obligations; and if it is the treaty they are complying with, what has become of the customary law

---

[511] Ibid., pp. 100–1, para. 190.

[512] The acceptance by the international community contemplated by Article 53 of the Vienna Convention on the Law of Treaties does not seem to require practice in support, and, according to some authors, need not be unanimous. On the influence in this field of codifying conventions, see Fois, 'La funzione degl accordi di codificazione nella formazione dello *jus cogens*', in *International Law at the Time of its Codification*, pp. 287 ff.

[513] Cf. Fitzmaurice, this *Year Book*, 30 (1953), pp. 57 ff.; *Collected Edition*, I, pp. 188 ff.

requirements? Are they ousted, along with the provisions of customary law which conflict with the treaty; or are they suspended; or do they continue to be present on the scene, invisibly as it were?

(a) *The* Fisheries Jurisdiction *case*

The question of the co-existence, between the same two States, of treaty law and customary international law governing the same questions arose in two different forms in the *Fisheries Jurisdiction (United Kingdom* v. *Iceland)* case in 1973.

The United Kingdom contended that the 1972 Icelandic Fishing Regulations, asserting exclusive fishing rights of Iceland over an area extending 50 miles from baselines round its coasts, were contrary to general international law. During the currency of the proceedings before the Court, the two parties had entered into an interim agreement regulating fishing by British vessels in the disputed area for a period of two years from 13 November 1973.

Counsel for the United Kingdom was asked whether that agreement definitively regulated, for the period indicated, the relations of the two Parties, so far as the fisheries in question were concerned, or whether it would be possible for the Court to replace that regulation with another. The reply was that the judgment would state the rules of customary international law between the Parties, defining their respective rights and obligations. However, that would not mean that the judgment would completely replace the interim agreement with immediate effect in the relations between the Parties, for, as the British Government saw the matter, the agreement would remain as a treaty in force. In any event, the Parties would be under a duty fully to regulate their relations in accordance with the terms of the judgment as soon as the interim agreement ceased to be in force, i.e., on 13 November 1975, or at such earlier date as the Parties might agree. On the other hand, the judgment would have immediate effect in so far as it dealt with matters not covered in the agreement.[514]

The difficulty which resulted, in the view of Judge Petrén, who had raised the question, was the following:

What the United Kingdom is requesting of the Court is to state the law which would have been applicable to the relations between the Parties in the event that they had not concluded that agreement. Yet the essence of the judicial function is to declare the law between the Parties as it exists, and not to declare what the law would have been if the existing law had not existed. The conclusion of the interim agreement has therefore had the effect of rendering the Application of the United Kingdom without object so far as the period covered by the agreement is concerned.[515]

Judge Petrén did not consider that there were any 'matters not covered in

---

[514] Dissenting opinion of Judge Petrén, *ICJ Reports*, 1974, p. 156.
[515] Ibid., pp. 156–7.

the agreement' to which the judgment could be of immediate application. Nor did he consider that the Court could or should endeavour to declare what the state of customary law was going to be on the date of expiration of the interim agreement, in view of the imminence of a further Law of the Sea Conference and the general state of flux in this domain.[516] For Judge Petrén,

if the dispute concerned the interpretation of a treaty, an interim agreement concerning its application over a given period would not hinder the Court from ruling before the end of that period on the interpretation and future application of the treaty,[517]

presumably because the treaty-law régime established by that treaty would remain unchanged during the currency of the interim agreement.

Judge Petrén's argument is based upon the implied premiss that the existing law between two States is solely that which is directly applicable, and that if general law is displaced (in matters of *jus dispositivum*) by the conclusion of a treaty, then that law ceases to exist as law between the parties. It was true, as Judge Petrén stated, that 'it is only on 13 November 1975 that customary international law will again govern the conditions under which fishing is carried out in the disputed area';[518] but does it follow that the customary international law applicable to fishing rights and the law of the sea ceased to exist between the parties in November 1973, to revive again in November 1975?

The judgment of the Court treated the point rather as one of the powers of the Court than as a matter of principle as to the relationship between treaty law and customary law. It emphasized the danger, if Judge Petrén's argument were adopted, of discouraging States from interim arrangements, and thus running contrary to the purpose of the Charter as to peaceful settlement of disputes.[519] The essential point of its ruling was as follows:

The Court is of the view that there is no incompatibility with its judicial function in making a pronouncement on the rights and duties of the Parties under existing international law which would clearly be capable of having a forward reach; this does not mean that the Court should declare the law between the Parties as it might be at the date of the expiration of the interim agreement, a task beyond the powers of any tribunal. The possibility of the law changing is ever present: but that cannot relieve the Court from its obligation to render a judgment 'on the basis of the law as it exists at the time of its decision'. In any event it cannot be said that the issues now before the Court have become without object; for there is no doubt that the case is one in which 'there exists at the time of the adjudication an actual controversy

---

[516] Judge Petrén observed that no difficulty would have arisen if the interim agreement had been drawn to expire on the date of the judgment; unfortunately, this possibility had been excluded by Iceland's boycotting of the proceedings before the Court.

[517] Ibid., p. 159.

[518] Ibid.

[519] Ibid., p. 20, para. 41.

involving a conflict of legal interests between the Parties' (*Northern Cameroons Judgment, ICJ Reports 1963*, pp. 33–34).[520]

As a matter of practical administration of justice, the Court's approach is undoubtedly sound; but the teasing point remains: Can the Court be said to be giving judgment 'on the basis of the law as it exists at the time of its decision', when the parties have mutually released each other from compliance with that law until the expiration of their agreement?[521] Certainly customary international law continues to exist and to develop 'behind', as it were, the treaty, but is it 'law' for the parties to the treaty so long as the treaty endures?

An aspect of the case which was closely examined by Judge Sir Humphrey Waldock, but to which the same significance was not attached in the judgment, was the continuing effect of an Exchange of Notes between the parties in 1961. This was, as Judge Waldock found, that

> Iceland and the United Kingdom agreed in 1961 that the 12-mile limit, which was the only fishery limit that had come near to general acceptance at the 1960 Conference, should thereafter constitute the limit of Iceland's fishery jurisdiction as between themselves. They further agreed that this 12-mile limit should remain in force between them unless and until an extension of Iceland's fishery jurisdiction should become opposable to the United Kingdom in accordance with the final clause in the Exchange of Notes. . . .[522]

In the view of Judge Waldock, Iceland by totally disregarding the provision of that final clause (whereby the lawfulness of any extension was to be determined by the Court) violated the terms of the Exchange of Notes.

> Iceland in effect tore up the assurance which she had given in 1961 and sought unilaterally to impose the new extension upon the United Kingdom. It follows that Iceland's extension of her fishery jurisdiction promulgated in 1972 does not comply with the conditions laid down in the compromissory clause of the 1961 Exchange of Notes. It further follows, in my opinion, that the extension is not opposable to the United Kingdom in the present proceedings.[523]

Thus if there was at the time of the judgment a rule of customary law which invalidated any purported extension of fisheries jurisdiction beyond 12 miles,[524] as the United Kingdom claimed, Iceland would be simultaneously in breach both of a customary-law obligation and a conventional obligation. More interesting, and more dubious, is the position if, on the contrary, general customary law had developed to the point at which a 50-mile limit was valid *erga omnes*; was Iceland to be permanently excluded,

---

[520] Ibid., pp. 19–20, para. 40.

[521] This aspect was emphasized, as Judge Petrén pointed out, by the fact that the Court in effect found that the parties were under a duty to negotiate, whereas the facts surrounding the conclusion of the interim accord, in Judge Petrén's view, showed that there was agreement not to negotiate again until the expiration of the interim accord.

[522] Ibid., p. 114, para. 22.

[523] Ibid., p. 117, para. 28.

[524] On the difficulties of interpreting customary rules in this domain, see Chapter II, section 1 above.

at least *vis-à-vis* the United Kingdom, from the happy throng of coastal States enjoying such an extension, as a result of its non-compliance with the procedures of the 1961 Exchange of Notes?[525]

(b) *The* Nuclear Tests *cases*

The claim of Australia and New Zealand in these cases was that 'the carrying out of further atmospheric nuclear weapon tests in the South Pacific Ocean is not consistent with applicable rules of international law', and the Court was asked to order that France 'shall not carry out any further such tests'.[526] In short, the contention was that, as a matter of general customary international law, France was obliged to stop the tests. The Court made no finding on the validity of this claim; but it found that France had entered into a binding unilateral obligation to stop the tests, so that the proceedings had become without object.

The unilateral obligation was, while not being a *pactum*, certainly a *servandum*;[527] and whether or not it partook of the nature of quasi-treaty law, it was certainly peculiar to France, and, though apparently an obligation *erga omnes*,[528] not a matter of general customary law. On the assumption therefore that the applicants' contentions were correct—and the Court was careful to leave the point entirely open—France would have been under two distinct obligations requiring identical conduct. The unilateral obligation, being *lex specialis*, presumably prevailed; what then was the position in general customary law? The question is of course something of a *hypothèse d'école*, but not without interest for all that.

In particular, the following point may be noted here, though to do so trespasses to some extent on later developments on the powers of the Court to declare a case without object.

The Court had not yet determined its jurisdiction to entertain the claim of Australia and New Zealand on the merits; as it expressly stated it had therefore to refrain from entering into the merits of the claim.[529] For purposes of its decision, therefore, the question remained entirely open whether France was under an obligation, under general international customary law, to put an end to atmospheric nuclear tests. The basis of the Court's decision was that the object of the claim had disappeared, so that there was nothing on which to give judgment.[530] The basic postulate was that, as a result of the French unilateral statements, the situation had changed.

---

[525] See also the present writer's *Non-Appearance before the International Court of Justice*, pp. 72–5.

[526] Submissions of Australia, *ICJ Reports*, 1974, p. 253; the New Zealand submissions were that the conduct of the tests 'constitutes a violation of New Zealand's rights under international law' (ibid., p. 460).

[527] See the discussion above, Chapter I, section 1(1).

[528] See above, pp. 11–12.

[529] *ICJ Reports*, 1974, p. 259, para. 22.

[530] Ibid., p. 272, para. 59.

But what was that change? The Court emphasized that the unilateral statements constituted 'an undertaking possessing legal effect', so that the French Government had 'undertaken an obligation'.[531] That obligation was an obligation to do what it had said it would do: stop the atmospheric tests. But if it was already bound by general international law to stop the tests, the new obligation merely paralleled the existing obligation, and there was no change in the situation justifying the conclusion that the case had become moot. The situation had only changed if the French Government was not previously under an obligation of general international law; but the Court had refrained from ruling on this, because it constituted the merits.

The situation would have been otherwise if the French statements had been, or could have been interpreted to be, an admission of the existence of an obligation of general law, and an undertaking to comply with it in future. This element would have constituted the change in the situation justifying a finding that the claim was without object. It was, however, impossible to interpret the French statements in that way.

Now it might be argued that the change in the situation which justified the Court's decision was that, whether or not there was an obligation to cease testing before the French declarations, after them there was an *admitted* obligation to do so. However, it was not the admission which was the object of the claim; it was the legal assurance that further tests would constitute the breach of an obligation.

It does not appear that the Court was conscious that the implied basis of its judgment was a finding on the merits which it recognized that it was not entitled to make at that stage (and with which some of its members might well not have agreed). The obligation created by the unilateral declarations seems to have been seen as somehow qualitatively different from the obligation of general law which Australia and New Zealand claimed to exist, and which could not be excluded as possibly existing.

(c) *The case of* United States Diplomatic and Consular Staff in Tehran

A further case before the Court in which questions of the relationship between customary law and treaty law were germane to the decision was that of the *United States Diplomatic and Consular Staff in Tehran*. The Court was there seised primarily on the basis of the Optional Protocols to the Vienna Conventions on Diplomatic and Consular Relations, whereby it had jurisdiction over 'disputes arising out of the interpretation or application of' the relevant convention. At first sight, therefore, the Court was limited to determining the dispute between the parties so far as it involved interpretation or application of the two Conventions, and was not called upon to rule on their relations under customary international law.

However, when finding that the Iranian Government had failed to

[531] Ibid., pp. 269–70, para. 51.

comply with a number of obligations imposed by the two Conventions, the Court went on to say:

> In the view of the Court, the obligations of the Iranian Government here in question are not merely contractual obligations established by the Vienna Conventions of 1961 and 1963, but also obligations under general international law.[532]

The Court was thus ruling on a question which was to assume particular importance in the case of *Military and Paramilitary Activities in and against Nicaragua*: whether, between two parties to a multilateral convention, obligations of customary law which have been incorporated into the convention regime may be said still to exist as customary-law obligations.

The Court found, later in its judgment, that

> ... Iran, by committing successive and continuing breaches of the obligations laid upon it by the Vienna Conventions ... and the applicable rules of general international law, has incurred responsibility towards the United States.[533]

This lays to rest one doubt which one might otherwise feel at the co-existence of a customary obligation and a treaty obligation: if the two require identical conduct, breach of the two obligations is only a single internationally wrongful act, and involves only a single duty of reparation.

This being so, the question remains why the Court thought it appropriate to mention the existence of the obligation of customary law. One reason may be the emphasis which the Court wished to lay on 'the extreme importance of the principles of law which it is called upon to apply in the present case';[534] the Court thought it desirable to make it clear that the Iranian Government had not merely breached a treaty (an act which in itself may range in gravity from the tremendous to the trivial) but had acted in a way likely

> to undermine the edifice of law carefully constructed by mankind over a period of centuries, the maintenance of which is vital to the necessity and well-being of the complex international community of the present day.[535]

Another reason (though this is speculation) may be hinted at by the reference to 'continuing breaches' of Iran's obligations. If, before the situation of the hostages was regularized, Iran were to denounce the Vienna Conventions and the Optional Protocols, it might claim that (at least) it was no longer in breach of a treaty obligation which no longer bound it. By emphasizing the customary-law backing of the obligation, the Court would do all it could to demolish this excuse in advance.

Whether the Court was entitled, on the basis of a title of jurisdiction referring to 'disputes arising out of the interpretation or application of' a

---

[532] *ICJ Reports*, 1980, p. 31, para. 62.
[533] Ibid., p. 41, para. 90.
[534] Ibid., pp. 42–3, para. 92.
[535] Ibid., p. 43.

treaty, to go into questions of customary law at all is a question to be examined in a later article in this series.

(d) Military and Paramilitary Activities in and against Nicaragua
(Nicaragua v. United States of America)

The complications arising from a reservation attached to the United States acceptance of jurisdiction under the Optional Clause placed the Court in the very curious position, in the case concerning *Military and Paramilitary Activities in and against Nicaragua (Nicaragua* v. *United States of America)*, of having to decide the case in disregard of treaty rights and obligations known to exist between the parties to the case, and known to be relevant to the solution of the affair.

The so-called 'multilateral treaty reservation' attached to the United States declaration—one of the most impenetrably obscure pieces of drafting which the Court has had to tackle—had the effect, as the Court found, that the jurisdiction conferred upon it by the declaration did not permit the Court to entertain claims of Nicaragua that the United States had breached certain articles of the United Nations Charter and the Charter of the Organization of American States, since other States parties to those instruments which might be affected by the decision were not parties to the proceedings;[536] this finding was however 'without prejudice either to other treaties or to the other sources of law enumerated in Article 38 of the Statute'.[537] The United States contended that the claim of Nicaragua based on 'customary and general international law' could also not be heard, because they

cannot be determined without recourse to the United Nations Charter as the principal source of that law, [and] they also cannot be determined without reference to the 'particular international law' established by multilateral conventions in force among the parties.[538]

As the Court explained further:

The United States contends that the only general and customary international law on which Nicaragua can base its claims is that of the Charter: in particular, the Court could not, it is said, consider the lawfulness of an alleged use of armed force without referring to the 'principal source of the relevant international law', namely, Article 2, paragraph 4, of the United Nations Charter. In brief, in a more general sense 'the provisions of the United Nations Charter relevant here subsume and supervene related principles of customary and general international law'. The United States concludes that 'since the multilateral treaty reservation bars adjudication of claims based on those treaties, it bars all of Nicaragua's claims'. Thus the effect of the reservation in question is not, it is said, merely to prevent the Court from deciding upon Nicaragua's claims by applying the multilateral treaties in

---

[536] *ICJ Reports*, 1986, p. 38, para. 56.
[537] Ibid., p. 92, para. 172.
[538] Ibid., p. 92, para. 173.

question; it further prevents it from applying in its decision any rule of customary international law the content of which is also the subject of a provision in those multilateral treaties.[539]

The objection of the United States raised a number of distinct problems. The first was whether there could be said to be a set of rights and obligations, deriving from customary law, in force between the United States and Nicaragua, in the areas of law governed by the articles of the Charter invoked by Nicaragua. If the existence of the conventional relationship deriving from the Charter had the effect of superseding or excluding the customary-law rules in the same field, or putting them into abeyance between the parties, then the Court could not find the United States in breach of customary-law obligations, however flagrant its violation of the Charter.

Even assuming that such customary-law obligations did exist, the Court was placed by the multilateral treaty reservation in something of a dilemma. If the rules of customary law relating to non-intervention, the use of force, etc., were identical to the norms in the United Nations Charter, it was difficult to refute the contention that, by deciding on issues according to customary law, it would in effect be deciding at the same time what was the law of the Charter on them, in contravention of the multilateral treaty reservation. If however the customary-law rules and the treaty-law rules diverged markedly from each other, then the same difficulty would arise as in the *Fisheries Jurisdiction (United Kingdom* v. *Iceland)* case, that the Court would be purporting to determine the dispute by reference to rules of law which were not those applicable between, and binding upon, the parties.

The Court's solution to the problem was as follows:

> The Court does not consider that, in the areas of law relevant to the present dispute, it can be claimed that all the customary rules which may be invoked have a content exactly identical to that of the rules contained in the treaties which cannot be applied by virtue of the United States reservation. On a number of points, the areas governed by the two sources of law do not exactly overlap, and the substantive rules in which they are framed are not identical in content.[540]

In the following paragraph of its judgment, the Court gave some examples to show that the areas governed by treaty law and by the Charter 'do not overlap exactly'. (In passing, it may be questioned whether these findings themselves might not be regarded as a trespass into the forbidden ground of 'disputes arising under a multilateral treaty'.) However, the Court did not evade the issue; it continued:

> But in addition, even if a treaty norm and a customary norm relevant to the present dispute were to have exactly the same content, this would not be a reason for the Court to take the view that the operation of the treaty process must necessarily deprive the customary norm of its separate applicability. Nor can the multilateral treaty reservation be interpreted as meaning that, once applicable to a given

[539] Ibid., pp. 92–3, para. 173.
[540] Ibid., pp. 93–4, para. 175.

dispute, it would exclude the application of any rule of customary international law the content of which was the same as, or analogous to, that of the treaty-law rule which had caused the reservation to become effective.[541]

The Court addressed much of its argument in the judgment on this point to demonstrating that

customary international law continues to exist and apply, separately from international treaty-law, even when the two categories of law have an identical content.[542]

This however would hardly have required demonstration—as the Court itself observed, it was already implicit in much of the *North Sea Continental Shelf* judgment[543]—had it not been for the near-universality of membership of the United Nations, which renders the idea of separate customary law identical with Charter law virtually meaningless in practical terms.

The question is not whether customary law and treaty law to the same extent exist side by side *in general*, but whether they can continue to exist side by side *as between the same parties*. If the United Nations Charter had been acceded to by every State of the world, the question whether customary law continued to exist on matters dealt with in the Charter would have become academic. So long as that is not the case, however, the question is whether two States bound *vis-à-vis* each other by a treaty obligation identical to a precept of customary law are also bound by that precept.

The question of the co-existence of customary and treaty rights had arisen previously in the case concerning *Rights of Nationals of the United States of America in Morocco* in 1952.[544] It was claimed by the United States in that case that rights of consular jurisdiction enjoyed by it by treaty, and through the operation of a most-favoured-nation clause, had also come to have an independent foundation in custom, so that when the treaty rights were terminated, the customary rights continued to subsist. The custom had, it was asserted, come into existence after the relevant treaties had been in operation for some time.

The Court rejected the contention for two reasons; one was that the custom relied on was a local custom which, under the rule laid down in the *Asylum* case,[545] had to be proved, and there had not been sufficient evidence to convince the Court of the existence of the custom. The other reason was stated as follows:

This was the case not merely of the United States but of most of the countries whose nationals were trading in Morocco. It is true that there were Powers represented at the Conference of Madrid in 1880 and at Algeciras in 1906 which had no

[541] Ibid., p. 94, para. 175.
[542] Ibid., p. 96, para. 79.
[543] *ICJ Reports*, 1969, p. 39, para. 63, quoted in *ICJ Reports*, 1986, p. 95, para. 177.
[544] *ICJ Reports*, 1952, p. 176; discussed by Fitzmaurice, this *Year Book*, 30 (1953), pp. 58–69; *Collected Edition*, I, pp. 188–99.
[545] *ICJ Reports*, 1950, p. 276.

treaty rights but were exercising consular jurisdiction with the consent or acquiescence of Morocco. It is also true that France, after the institution of the Protectorate, obtained declarations of renunciation from a large number of other States which were in a similar position. This is not enough to establish that the States exercising consular jurisdiction in pursuance of treaty rights enjoyed in addition an independent title thereto based on custom or usage.[546]

Fitzmaurice interprets this passage as not amounting to a denial by the Court of 'the principle that, apart from treaty, an independent basis of right, founded on custom and usage, might exist', but as a holding of fact 'that United States rights in Morocco were based solely on treaty and not all on custom or usage'.[547]

---

[546] *ICJ Reports*, 1952, pp. 199–200.
[547] This *Year Book*, 30 (1953), p. 65; *Collected Edition*, I, p. 195.

STRAITS USED FOR INTERNATIONAL NAVIGATION: A COMMENTARY ON PART III OF THE UNITED NATIONS CONVENTION ON THE LAW OF THE SEA 1982*

By s.n. nandan *and* d.h. anderson‡

I. Introduction

The UN Convention on the Law of the Sea was the product of a detailed re-examination of all issues relating to the law of the sea extending over a period of more than twelve years. In the words of its preamble, the Convention was seen as 'an important contribution to the maintenance of peace, justice and progress for all peoples of the world'. The Convention contains numerous significant provisions, amongst which must be included Part III concerning straits used for international navigation. The formulation of the articles in Part III was an important element in the overall solution, reached at the conference, to the question of maritime limits, since establishing 12 nm as the maximum breadth of the territorial sea was acceptable to many delegations only on the basis of a satisfactory regime for passage through straits used for international navigation. At the same time, Part III represents a balance between the interests of States bordering busy straits in such matters as security, safety and protection of the environment, and the interests of other States in the freedom of communications. The purpose of this article is to provide insights into the terms of Part III as a whole, as well as a detailed commentary on the individual articles.

(a) *The Evolution of the Law on International Straits 1894–1970*

Unlike several parts of the Convention (including Part II concerning the territorial sea and contiguous zone and Part VII concerning the high seas), the wording of Part III was not based on any of the Conventions on the Law of the Sea adopted by the First UN Conference on the Law of the Sea of 1958. This is not to say that Part III did not have antecedents: Part III is

---

* © S.N. Nandan and D.H. Anderson, 1990.

‡ S.N. Nandan was Leader of the Fiji Delegation to the Third UN Conference on the Law of the Sea and Rapporteur of the Second Committee. He is currently Under-Secretary-General and Special Representative of the Secretary-General of the UN for the Law of the Sea. D.H. Anderson was a member of the UK Delegation to the Conference, and is currently Second Legal Adviser, Foreign and Commonwealth Office, London. The views expressed in this article are the personal views of the authors and do not represent the views of any government or institution with which they are or have been associated.

the latest of several attempts by international lawyers and governmental conferences to set down in the form of articles the rules of law applicable to straits. The first attempts were made by the Institut de Droit International and the International Law Association (ILA) between 1894 and 1906 in their 'Rules relating to territorial Waters'. In the form adopted by the ILA in 1906 the Rules contained the following about straits:—

ART. 10.—Les dispositions des articles précédents s'appliquent aux détroits dont l'écart n'excède pas douze milles, sauf les modifications et distinctions suivantes:

1° Les détroits dont les côtes appartiennent à des États différents font partie de la mer territoriale des États riverains, qui y exerceront leur souveraineté jusqu'à la ligne médiane.

2° Les détroits dont les côtes appartiennent au même État et qui sont indispensables aux communications maritimes entre deux ou plusieurs États autres que l'État riverain font toujours partie de la mer territoriale du riverain, quel que soit le rapprochement des côtes. *Ils ne peuvent jamais être barrés.*

3° *Dans les détroits dont les côtes appartiennent au même État, la mer est territoriale bien que l'écartement des côtes dépasse douze milles, si à chaque entrée du détroit cette distance n'est pas dépassée.*

4° Les détroits qui servent de passage d'une mer libre à une autre mer libre ne peuvent jamais etre *barrés.*

ART. 11.—Le régime des détroits actuellement soumis à des conventions ou usages speciaux demeure réservé.

(The words in italics were the modifications made by the ILA to the Rules adopted by the Institut in 1894.)[1]

The League of Nations Conference of 1930 marked another attempt to formulate articles: the Hague Conference considered the question of the territorial sea in its Second Committee. The report of Sub-Committee No. II discussed the question of straits and included the following:—

PASSAGE OF WARSHIPS THROUGH STRAITS

Under no pretext whatever may the passage even of warships through straits used for international navigation between two parts of the high sea be interfered with.

According to the previous Article the waters of straits which do not form part of the high sea constitute territorial sea. It is essential to ensure in all circumstances the passage of merchant vessels and warships through straits between two parts of the high sea and forming ordinary routes of international navigation.[2]

The question of the law of international straits was reviewed fully in a learned treatise by Brüel, written in the late 1930s and published in English in 1947. His conclusion was that such straits had a legal position which was

---

[1] *Annuaire de l'Institut de Droit International, Abridgement* (1928–9), vol. 3, p. 393; *Report of the Seventeenth Conference of the ILA* (1906), pp. 114–16.

[2] Conference on the Progressive Codification of International Law, *Publications of the League of Nations V: Legal Questions,* 1930. The Report also appears in *American Journal of International Law,* 24 (1930), Supplement: Official Documents, p. 234 at p. 253.

sui juris, i.e. separate from the law of innocent passage through the territorial sea.[3]

The law was clarified in 1949 by the International Court of Justice: in its judgment in the *Corfu Channel* case, the Court held that:

. . . States in time of peace have a right to send their warships through straits used for international navigation between two parts of the high seas without the previous authorization of a coastal State, provided the passage is innocent. Unless otherwise prescribed in an international convention, there is no right for a coastal State to prohibit such passage through straits in time of peace.[4]

The Court thus stated some basic rules of customary law about passage through straits used for international navigation, rules which applied to all ships and which did not depend upon the precise legal status of the waters forming such a strait.

The wide significance of this decision was not fully reflected in the draft articles of the International Law Commission[5] which formed the basic proposal at the Geneva Conference on the Law of the Sea. As a result, the question of passage through straits was treated in the Convention on the Territorial Sea and the Contiguous Zone of 1958 as an incidental aspect of the right of innocent passage through the territorial sea. Thus Article 16(4) provided that:

There shall be no suspension of the innocent passage of foreign ships through straits which are used for international navigation between one part of the high seas and another part of the high seas or the territorial sea of a foreign State.

This paragraph was described by a participant in the Conference as 'a universally recognised rule of general international law';[6] but the question of straits was not dealt with generally and even less as a separate topic.

(b) *The UN Committee on the Peaceful Uses of the Sea-Bed ('the Sea-Bed Committee')*

The change in approach adopted at the Third Conference was prompted by the wider acceptance of the twelve-mile limit for the territorial sea which had become apparent in the 1970s. The change first found expression in the draft articles on the breadth of the territorial sea and straits submitted to the UN Sea-Bed Committee in 1971 by the United States. Draft Article II provided that:

[3] Brüel, *International Straits* (1947), vol. 1, pp. 38–9. Another leading authority is Baxter, *The Law of International Waterways* (1964), esp. pp. 159 ff. For a modern authority, see O'Connell, *The International Law of the Sea*, vol. 1 (1982), p. 327.

[4] *ICJ Reports*, 1949, p. 4, at p. 28. In the authentic French text, the key phrases are 'le droit de faire passer leurs navires de guerre par les détroits qui servent, aux fins de la navigation internationale, à mettre en communication deux parties de haute mer . . .'.

[5] Report of the ILC, in *Yearbook of the ILC*, 1958, vol. 2, pp. 254 ff., esp. draft Article 17(4).

[6] Fitzmaurice, 'Some Results of the Geneva Conference', *International and Comparative Law Quarterly*, 8 (1959), p. 73 at p. 101. See also Article 5(6) of the Convention on the Continental Shelf: the reference to 'recognized sea lanes essential to international navigation' includes straits used for international navigation.

In straits used for international navigation between one part of the high seas and another part of the high seas or the territorial sea of a foreign State, all ships and aircraft in transit shall enjoy the same freedom of navigation and overflight, for the purpose of transit through or over such straits, as they have on the high seas.[7]

In 1972, the Soviet Union made a similar proposal (but confined to straits linking two parts of the high seas) which went on to elaborate more detailed rules for the exercise of the freedoms of navigation and of overflight through straits.[8] Later that year, the 'List of Subjects and Issues relating to the Law of the Sea' adopted by the Sea-Bed Committee included item 4:

Straits used for International Navigation
4.1 Innocent Passage
4.2 Other Related Matters including the Question of the Right of Transit.[9]

The List of Subjects and Issues was, in effect, the substantive agenda for the Third Conference and the inclusion of a separate item about straits marked a significant development. In the Sea-Bed Committee (and indeed during much of the Conference), the views were pressed that there was no separate body of law about straits and that the rules about innocent passage through the territorial sea applied to them (subject to some qualifications). However, those views did not prevail: the predominant opinion was that the question of passage through straits used for international navigation should be treated separately from that of passage through the territorial sea. It is that opinion, based on customary law and the needs of the contemporary situation, which finds expression in Part III.

(c) *The Work of the Fiji/UK Group*

At the Conference, rival proposals were tabled which would have given expression to these two different approaches. Supporting the approach of separate treatment for straits, the UK put forward a set of draft articles in two parts, one on territorial sea and the other on straits;[10] and separate proposals on straits were tabled by Bulgaria and certain other States.[11] The UK's proposals on straits put forward the concept of the right of transit passage, which, though an extensive right in content, was not the same as freedom of navigation and overflight, as had been proposed by the US in 1971 and the Soviet Union in 1972. Supporting the other approach, a

[7] Report of the Committee on the Peaceful Uses of the Sea-Bed and the Ocean Floor beyond the Limits of National Jurisdiction, A/8421, p. 241. Article I provided for a maximum breadth of the territorial sea of 12 nm.

[8] Report of the Committee, A/8721, p. 162.

[9] Report to the General Assembly, A/8721, p. 5. (Item 2 concerned the territorial sea and Item 3 the contiguous zone.)

[10] A/CONF. 62/C.2/L. 3. Some amendments were proposed by Denmark and Finland (ibid., L. 15).

[11] Ibid., L. 11. Bulgaria *et al.* put forward proposals about passage through the territorial sea in ibid., L. 26. Algeria proposed 'free transit' in straits for ships other than warships which were to enjoy the right of innocent passage (ibid., L. 20). Iraq proposed 'freedom of navigation' in straits customarily used for navigation (ibid., L. 71).

group of delegations led by Malaysia[12] proposed to deal with straits in the context of the territorial sea, applying to straits the regime of innocent passage with modifications. The proposals by Fiji[13] were stated to be without prejudice to the Conference's decision on the issue of the approach; but, significantly, the point of departure in the Fiji paper was that submarines might pass in straits under water, thereby accepting a distinction between the territorial sea in general and straits—a distinction which formed the basis for the later compromise between the Fijian and British proposals. The Fijian proposals also dealt in detail with the question of the legislative powers of straits States. The two different approaches, as well as the Fijian proposals, were reflected in the document entitled 'Main Trends', produced by the Second Committee in 1974.[14]

Informal consultations had been held in 1974 between the British and Fijian delegations about questions of navigation and, in particular, the formulations of the rules on innocent passage in their respective sets of draft articles. In 1975 it was decided after further consultation to create a group of delegations from the different regional groups under the joint chairmanship of Mr Nandan (Fiji) and Mr Dudgeon (UK), the so-called 'Private Working Group on Straits used for International Navigation' or the 'Fiji/UK Group'. Attendance was by joint invitation of the Co-Chairmen who sought a cross-section of moderate opinion, drawn from all regional groups and including straits States and delegations with a particular interest in sea-borne trade or questions of limits of the territorial sea and EEZ. The first meeting on 25 March 1975 was attended by 14 delegations: Argentina, Bahrain, Denmark, Ethiopia, Fiji, Iceland, Italy, Kenya, Lebanon, Nigeria, Singapore, the UK, United Arab Emirates and Venezuela. (Subsequent meetings were attended also by Australia, Bulgaria and India.)[15] The objective was explained as being to continue to seek accommodation between the proposals of Fiji and the UK on straits, in order to achieve a sound balance between the interests of States bordering straits and maritime nations.

In the discussion, it was noted that unimpeded passage of straits was one

---

[12] Ibid., L. 16. The group consisted of Malaysia, Morocco, Oman and Yemen and the proposal was sometimes referred to in the Second Committee as 'the Oman draft'. A similar approach to that of L. 16 was implicit in the proposals by Spain (ibid., L. 6) and Iran (ibid., L. 72). The difference between the 'two different schools of thought' was brought out clearly in a statement by Mr Lacleta (Spain) during the 14th meeting of the Second Committee (*UNCLOS III Official Records* (hereinafter *Official Records*), vol. 2, pp. 136–7).

[13] A/CONF. 62/C.2/L. 19, repeating with modifications proposals advanced in Sea-Bed Committee in 1973 (A/AC. 138/SC II/242). Fiji's proposals of 1973 influenced those of the UK about passage through the territorial sea in A/CONF. 62/C.2/L. 3. In tabling the revised proposals in ibid., L. 19, Fiji indicated in an Explanatory Note an open mind about 'the regime or regimes applicable to the passage of foreign ships through straits'.

[14] *Official Records*, vol. 3, p. 107 at p. 115. A footnote reads: 'For some delegations, straits used for international navigation which are part of the territorial sea of one or more states, fall, except for some specific rules . . . under the same legal regime as that of any other portion of the territorial sea.'

[15] Nordquist (ed.), *United Nations Convention on the Law of the Sea 1982: A Commentary*, vol. 1 (1985), p. 107, gives the same list but excluding Ethiopia and Lebanon whose representatives did not attend the final meetings of the Group.

of three major issues, the others being the twelve-mile territorial sea and the 200-mile EEZ. Whilst passage should be unimpeded, it was pointed out that the cases of merchant ships, surface warships, submarines and nuclear-powered vessels (civil or military) would have to be considered, as well as overflight. The distinction was brought out between the regime of navigation and overflight, on the one hand, and the nature of the waters, on the other. Another distinction drawn was between straits linking two parts of the high seas/EEZ and those linking the high seas/EEZ to the territorial sea, on the grounds that the balance of interests differed between the two situations. The view was expressed that even in the first type of situation, complete freedom of navigation could not be accepted although freedom in the sense of non-discrimination should be granted. Concern for the interests of developing States was voiced. Responding to these points, the Co-Chairmen pointed out that the UK and Fiji draft articles had not proposed complete freedom of navigation such as existed on the high seas since passage had to be, for example, expeditious, without threat to the straits States and in compliance with international regulations. All types of vessels required to make passage; but passage must be effected in a way which did not prejudice the interests of coastal States in the narrow stretches of water forming straits. The question of nuclear vessels was being considered elsewhere in the conference. The need for submerged passage had to be considered in the context of its powerful backing and the safeguards offered to straits States.

After discussing the issues, the members of the Group agreed at the end of the first meeting to continue work on the basis that there should be a regime for straits which was separate from the regime of innocent passage applicable to the territorial sea in general. The members of the Group then proceeded to discuss the nature of the regime for straits during seven subsequent meetings ending on 18 April 1975. Between meetings, individual members of the Group held detailed informal discussions with many interested delegations outside the Group. In particular, in view of the link with the question of archipelagic States, close contacts were maintained with Indonesia and Malaysia: at the same time, major maritime powers such as the Soviet Union, the United States, France, Japan and the FRG were consulted, as well as straits States such as Morocco. The Co-Chairmen were especially active in those discussions.

On 30 April 1975, the Co-Chairmen circulated to all delegations the set of draft articles[16] which resulted from the Group's work and which represented what they described as a 'broad consensus' of the members. They explained that 'the principal basis of our work' had been 'the straits chapter of document A/CONF. 62/C.2/L. 3'; but several substantive changes were made by the Group, notably those concerning the definition of transit passage, the legislative powers of States bordering straits, the designation of

[16] Platzoder (ed.), *Third United Nations Conference on the Law of the Sea: Documents*, vol. 4 (1983), p. 194.

sea lanes and the status of the waters forming straits, as well as minor changes of wording.

The Chairman of the Second Committee took account of the Group's work in preparing his informal single negotiating text.[17] His main changes affected the structure of the draft articles, including the introduction of three sections (general provisions, transit passage and innocent passage) which brought greater clarity to the text. Whilst this part of the ISNT remained controversial, the subsequent changes to the text were minor and the Conference accepted what became Part III as part of the overall solution to the issue of limits.[18]

(d) *The Categorization of Straits in Part III*

The Conference attempted to make provision for navigation in all straits. However, circumstances of history and geography vary greatly from one strait to another, and so it was found appropriate to make different provision for different situations. For these reasons, the Convention in effect divided straits into several categories, with rules which may be summarized as follows:

(a) Straits not used for international navigation;
(b) 'Broad straits' which have a high seas/EEZ route through them; and
(c) Straits subject to their own long-standing regimes;

Not subject to Part III. Part II may apply to those areas in such straits which are territorial sea and Parts V, VI and VII apply to areas beyond the territorial sea.

(d) Straits not covered by (b) or (c) and used for international navigation:

Part III applies to the question of passage.

(i) Straits between two parts of the high seas/EEZ, apart from those subject to the exception in Article 38(1),

Part III, Section 2 applies, i.e. transit passage.

(ii) Straits between the high seas/EEZ and the territorial sea of a foreign State, and
(iii) Straits excluded from Article 38(1).

Part III, Section 3 applies, i.e. non-suspendable innocent passage.

Two further points may be noted: first, those straits which are situated

---

[17] A/CONF. 62/WP.8/Part II, Articles 34 to 44.
[18] Statements were made about different aspects of Part III upon signature of the Convention by Finland, Greece, Iran, Iraq, Oman, Spain and Sweden.

within an archipelagic State are subject to Part IV; and, secondly, there is no reference in Part III to the idea of 'historic straits' to parallel the reference to historic bays in Part II.

(e) *The Interpretation and Application of Part III as a Whole*

In construing and applying Part III, the normal rules of international law on the interpretation of treaties, as set out in the Vienna Convention on the Law of Treaties,[19] are applicable. At the same time, there are some general points which may be noted:

1. The way in which geographical factors should be approached;
2. The question of what is meant by the expression 'a strait used for international navigation';
3. The differences between transit passage, archipelagic sea lanes passage and innocent passage.

1. *Geographical factors*

Part III contains several important geographical references, such as those to straits 'formed by an island' and 'mainland', as well as to straits 'between one part of the high seas' and another. In putting forward their proposals at Caracas,[20] the UK delegation had available a set of 'chartlets' illustrating such features as the wide strait (with or without a suitable route beyond twelve-mile limits throughout its length), the strait giving access to the territorial sea of a foreign State, the strait lying between the mainland and an island of the coastal State, and so on. Geographical factors are of crucial importance in construing the provisions of Part III and, indeed, in deciding what constitutes 'a strait', since the term was not accompanied by a formal definition. The *Concise Oxford Dictionary* defines the word to mean a 'narrow passage of water connecting two seas or larger bodies of water'; it comes from the Latin root '*strictus*'. The definition's use of the word 'passage' is worthy of special note.

How, then, should geographical factors be approached? The best approach is to take into account the terms of the articles as well as all the relevant geographical and other factors, i.e. to adopt something of a 'common-sense' interpretation. A strictly literal (or 'mechanical') interpretation could well be found to be inappropriate in certain settings. Each geographical situation is unique and many published maps are drawn to a small scale which does not permit the inclusion of every natural feature. At the same time, some features may not be relevant to the question of how to apply Part III. It may be the case, to take the last example, that a strait is formed by a mainland and two islands of a coastal State, with the mainland on one

---

[19] Articles 31 to 35 set out rules of international law.

[20] Notably, at the time when the Second Committee considered Agenda Item 4: see the statement by Mr Dudgeon (UK) on 22 July 1974 (*Official Records*, vol. 2, pp. 125–6). A set of chartlets is appended to this article.

side and the two islands on the other. In such a case, the fact that there are two islands rather than one is hardly a material factor for the purposes of Article 38(1). To take another example, if a mainland is masked by an elongated island close to the coast so that strictly a strait is formed between that island and another belonging to the same State, it would be consonant with the intention behind Part III to assimilate the elongated island to the mainland for the purpose of applying Part III. An overly mathematical approach to straits would appear to be out of harmony with the principles of Part III. Its terms have to be construed in their context, which has to do with questions of passage—something reflected in the dictionary definition of the word 'strait'. This approach is also consistent with that of the ICJ in the *Fisheries* case (*UK* v. *Norway*),[21] as well as more recently in the *Libya/ Malta* case.[22]

2. *The question of 'use'*

The second issue—that of a strait's use for international navigation—is also crucial: it was a source of much discussion and even controversy at the Conference. The test of 'use' comes from the ICJ's decision in the *Corfu Channel* case and the Court's analysis of the idea retains its value. It will be recalled that after appraising certain evidence, the Court continued:

The Albanian Government does not dispute that the North Corfu Channel is a strait in the geographical sense; but it denies that this Channel belongs to the class of international highways through which a right of passage exists, on the grounds that it is only of secondary importance and not even a necessary route between two parts of the high seas, and that it is used almost exclusively for local traffic to and from the ports of Corfu and Saranda.

It may be asked whether the test is to be found in the volume of traffic passing through the Strait or in its greater or lesser importance for international navigation. But in the opinion of the Court the decisive criterion is rather its geographical situation as connecting two parts of the high seas and the fact of its being used for international navigation. Nor can it be decisive that this Strait is not a necessary route between two parts of the high seas, but only an alternative passage between the Aegean and the Adriatic Seas. It has nevertheless been a useful route for international maritime traffic.[23]

The Court concluded that 'the North Corfu Channel should be considered

---

[21] *ICJ Reports*, 1951, p. 116. In its judgment the Court stated that the rule whereby baselines must 'respect the general direction of the coast' was 'devoid of any mathematical precision' (at pp. 141–2).

[22] *ICJ Reports*, 1985, p. 13. The Court found that weighing up the relevant considerations in adjusting an equidistance line in order to achieve an equitable result was 'not a process which can infallibly be reduced to a formula expressed in actual figures' (at p. 52).

[23] *ICJ Reports*, 1949, p. 4 at p. 28. This aspect of the judgment was criticised by Brüel in an article entitled 'Some Observations on Two of the Statements concerning the Legal Position of International Straits'. Brüel recalled his conclusion in *International Straits* (1947) that 'only those straits that are of some, not quite inconsiderable, importance to the international sea-commerce, enjoy the peculiar legal position of straits', and went on to argue that 'the Corfu Channel fulfils none of these conditions'. Brüel described

as belonging to the class of international highways through which passage cannot be prohibited by a coastal state in time of peace'.

There exists a temporal problem with the word 'used'. In French, the equivalent is '*servant*', a present participle, or 'serving', which suggests that use at the time when the question arises is what really matters. If so, evidence of past use, whilst relevant in showing a pattern, is of lesser significance. In the normal case, very slight or short-lived use would be insufficient; but in certain circumstances limited use brought about by, say, an oil discovery may quickly put a strait into the category of those used for international navigation. Purely potential use would not appear to be sufficient: there should be actual use when the question falls to be decided. Taking the English and French texts together, 'used' and '*servant*' can be said to be in the present continuous.

Finally on 'use', it has to be remembered that proposals at different times to insert an adverb such as 'normally', 'customarily' or 'traditionally' before 'used' have been rejected. The ILC expressed 'the opinion that it would be in conformity with the Court's decision [in the *Corfu Channel* case] to insert the word "normally" ',[24] but this formulation was not accepted by the First UN Conference on the Law of the Sea.[25] Proposals were put forward at the Third Conference by Algeria and others[26] and by Iraq[27] employing the term 'customarily used'. Canada proposed a definition of 'international strait' which included the qualification that it 'has traditionally been used for international navigation'.[28] Chile spoke in favour of 'traditional use' in the Second Committee on 23 July 1974[29] and a similar proposal was advanced by Canada, Chile and Norway in an *aide-mémoire* dated 30 April 1975,[30] commenting upon the Fiji/UK Group's draft articles. However, the Chairman of the Second Committee did not include 'customarily', 'traditionally', or any similar qualification upon the word 'used' in framing his ISNT.[31] In contrast, Article 53 ('Right of Archipelagic Sea Lanes Passage') provides for that right to apply in 'all *normal* passage routes used as routes for international navigation or overflight' (paragraph 4): if an archipelagic State does not designate sea lanes or air routes, the right 'may be exercised through routes *normally* used for international navigation' (paragraph 12) (emphasis added). This contrast is significant since in many other respects

the Corfu Channel as a typical 'détroit latéral' or water dividing an island from a mainland 'the importance of which can never be sufficient to qualify them as "international" ' (*Festschrift für R. Laun* (1953)). This distinction has now been recognized in Articles 38(1) and 45 of the Convention, but the application of those Articles to the particular case of the Corfu Channel is not entirely clear.

[24] *Yearbook of the ILC*, 1956, vol. 2, p. 273.

[25] A/CONF. 13/C.1/SR. 34.

[26] A/CONF. 62/C.2/L. 44.

[27] Ibid., L. 71.

[28] Ibid., L. 83.

[29] *Official Records*, vol. 2, p. 138 (14th meeting).

[30] Platzoder, op. cit. above (n. 16), p. 223.

[31] A/CONF. 62/WP.8/Part II.

the right of archipelagic sea lanes passage is set out in the same terms as the right of transit passage. The omission of 'normally' from Part III means that any type of use may be relevant: no evidence of use is to be excluded *a priori*, e.g. as non-traditional or exceptional. Use which is recent or novel, as well as use in the more remote past, may be taken into account. Use does not have to be regular or to reach any predetermined level. It may be civil or military, or both, so long as the military use does not threaten the coastal State. Secondary or subsidiary straits which are not indispensable for international navigation may nevertheless count as ones used for international navigation so long as they connect two parts of the high seas/EEZ. The exact regime of passage through such a strait is, of course, a separate question and it is to be anticipated that international tribunals would have regard to all the relevant considerations of law and fact, including geography, in coming to a decision.

The reference to 'international navigation', taken together with references to the high seas/EEZ, exclude use of a strait for cross traffic between ports on the strait, even if shipping moves thereby from one State's territory to another's.

3. *Differences between the regimes of passage*

Turning to the differences between the regimes of transit passage, archipelagic sea lanes passage and innocent passage, these emerge from detailed comparisons of the texts of Parts III, IV and II. On the broader level, the differences between the right of transit passage and the right of innocent passage are of great significance, especially in their strategic aspect. Both are regimes of passage: in other words, under either regime ships may in principle pass. However, the right of innocent passage may be suspended in certain circumstances; it is not available to aircraft, and submarines are required to pass on the surface. Transit passage may not be suspended; it is available to aircraft, and may be exercised by submarines submerged. The distinctions are justified by the consideration that transit passage exists where there is no alternative route or none of equal convenience. The differences between the right of transit passage and that of archipelagic sea lanes passage are not so marked: indeed, much of the wording of Article 53 was taken verbatim from what became Part III. Article 53 contemplates the possibility of there being designated sea lanes and air routes which traverse the whole of an area of archipelagic waters, whereas Part III makes no provision for the designation of air routes in straits and sea lanes need not run for the entire length of a strait. The distinction arises from the geographical circumstances in the two cases. Whereas a strait is a relatively narrow strip of water, an archipelago often has islands more than 24 nm apart between which international sea routes pass. It was necessary, therefore, to devise a system which would confine the exercise of archipelagic sea lanes passage within certain limits. In practice, however, the differences between these two regimes of passage may be insignificant since ships and aircraft in transit can be expected to remain within the bounds of routes normally used for international navigation.

(f) *Part III and Customary Law*

Part III represents both codification and progressive development of customary law. The fundamental principles laid down by the ICJ in the *Corfu Channel* case have been retained and elaborated: this was achieved in the context of a consensus that 12 nm should be accepted as the maximum breadth of the territorial sea.[32] Many of the detailed rules take account of modern developments such as sea lanes and traffic schemes, and these rules too contain elements of codification and development of the law. The article attempted to strike a balance between the interests of coastal States and other States; between the security and other interests of the former and the general interest in freedom of commerce and communication; between self-protection and self-defence, on the one hand, and freedom of the seas and the freedom of communications on the other. The coastal State on a strait would not be justified in seeking to take advantage of its geographical situation in order to interfere with international communications; but, at the same time, its legitimate interests are safeguarded in relation to its coasts and waters within the strait. Although the precise balance proposed during the first part of the Conference was resisted by several States bordering straits, the terms of Part III—which resulted from long debates— eventually achieved consensus[33] and so represent negotiated solutions in the overall context. It is likely, therefore, that Part III will influence the practice of States even before the entry into force of the Convention.[34]

---

[32] A good number of straits used for international navigation are less than 24 nm wide. Of the 33 examples in the study prepared for the First UN Conference on the Law of the Sea in 1958, 32 are less than twice 12 nm wide and so are made up of territorial sea if the maximum permissible breadth of the territorial sea is taken by the coastal State(s) concerned (A/CONF. 13, *Official Records*, vol. 1, pp. 114 f.). In the State Department's table of 'Widths of Selected Straits and Channels', 108 out of 136 straits are less than 24 nm wide (*Geographic Bulletin*, No. 3, 1965).

[33] Although votes were taken on proposals by Spain to amend Articles 39 and 42 (*Official Records*, vol. 16, pp. 132–3, 176th plenary meeting).

[34] The following is a recent example:

JOINT DECLARATION BY THE GOVERNMENT OF THE UNITED KINGDOM AND THE GOVERNMENT OF THE FRENCH REPUBLIC

On the occasion of the signature of the Agreement relating to the Delimitation of the Territorial Sea in the Straits of Dover, the two Governments agreed on the following declaration:

The existence of a specific regime of navigation in the straits is generally accepted in the current state of international law. The need for such a regime is particularly clear in straits, such as the Straits of Dover, used for international navigation and linking two parts of the high seas or economic zones in the absence of any other route of similar convenience with respect to navigation.

In consequence, the two Governments recognise rights of unimpeded transit passage for merchant vessels, state vessels and, in particular, warships following their normal mode of navigation, as well as the right of overflight for aircraft, in the Straits of Dover. It is understood that, in accordance with the principles governing this regime under the rules of international law, such passage will be exercised in a continuous and expeditious manner.

The two Governments will continue to co-operate closely, both bilaterally and through the International Maritime Organisation, in the interests of ensuring the safety of navigation in the Straits of

II. PART III OF THE CONVENTION: TEXT AND COMMENTARY

SECTION I: GENERAL PROVISIONS

Article 34
Legal status of waters forming straits used for international navigation

1. The regime of passage through straits used for international navigation established in this Part shall not in other respects affect the legal status of the waters forming such straits or the exercise by the States bordering the straits of their sovereignty or jurisdiction over such waters and their air space, bed and subsoil.
2. The sovereignty or jurisdiction of the States bordering the straits is exercised subject to this Part and to other rules of international law.

Section 1, which consists of three articles, deals with several general points of a miscellaneous nature.

Article 34 stands in relation to Part III as Article 2 stands in relation to Part II: both define the legal status of the waters to which the respective Parts apply.

The formal proposals made to the Second Committee about straits used for international navigation[35] included Article 1(3)(*b*) of the draft articles of Bulgaria and other co-sponsors to the effect that 'the provisions of this Article . . . shall not affect the sovereign rights of the coastal States with respect to the surface, the sea-bed and the living and mineral resources of the straits'. During informal discussions in the Fiji/UK Group, disquiet was expressed about the possible effects of the proposals submitted by the UK upon other aspects of the waters forming straits. In particular, concern was expressed about possible prejudice to the coastal State's sovereignty over its internal waters and territorial sea within a strait, including its jurisdiction over such matters as fisheries. In order to allay these fears, the Group developed the wording which became Article 34. The wording was included by the Chairman of the Second Committee in his ISNT[36] and retained in subsequent texts.[37]

Article 34(1) makes it clear that Part III applies only to the question of

Dover, as well as in the southern North Sea and the Channel. In particular, the traffic separation scheme in the Straits of Dover will not be affected by the entry into force of the Agreement.

With due regard to the interests of the coastal states the two Governments will also take, in accordance with international agreements in force and generally accepted rules and regulations, measures necessary in order to prevent, reduce and control pollution of the marine environment by vessels.

2 November 1988

---

[35] A/CONF. 62/C.2/L. 3 (UK) (and amendments in L. 15 (Denmark and Finland), L. 6 (Spain), L. 11 (Bulgaria *et al.*), L. 16 (Malaysia *et al*), L. 19 (Fiji), L. 20 (Algeria), L. 71 (Iraq) and L. 72 (Iran), as well as definitions in L. 44 (Algeria *et al.*) and L. 83 (Canada)).

[36] A/CONF. 62/WP 8/Part II, Article 34(1) and (2).

[37] Despite some criticism (e.g. Spain, A/CONF. 62/WS/12) and some informal amendments (C2/Informal Meeting 4 (Spain), 17 (Greece) and 22 (Morocco), none of which were accepted).

passage through straits used for international navigation. It does not apply to such questions as whether the waters within such a strait are territorial sea, or high seas, or internal or archipelagic waters, nor to any questions of fishing, baselines, delimitation and the like. In other words, although it is entitled 'straits used for international navigation', Part III does not in fact apply to all aspects of such straits: it is confined to the question of passage in such straits. Article 34(1) speaks about 'the regime of passage . . . established in this Part': this is a reference to the right of transit passage (Section 2) and the right of innocent passage (Section 3) in the different types of straits used for international navigation. The regime of passage affects 'the legal status of the waters forming' straits used for international navigation to the extent that the waters are subject to that regime in accordance with Part III.[38] But in all other respects, the legal status of the waters is not affected. Equally unaffected is the exercise by the States bordering straits of their sovereignty or jurisdiction over the waters (including the sea-bed and subsoil and the air space) forming the straits.

Article 34(2) provides that (i) the sovereignty of a State bordering a strait over its internal waters and territorial sea within a strait, and (ii) its jurisdiction over any areas of its EEZ or continental shelf within a strait, have both to be exercised subject to (a) Part III as regards passage through the strait, and (b) other rules of international law, e.g. those on the non-use of force or delimitation.[39] In other words, in so far as non-navigational questions may arise, other rules of international law, including other Parts of the Convention, apply. Amongst other provisions in the Convention, Article 233 (safeguards with respect to straits used for international navigation) may be noted: this permits a State bordering such a strait to take appropriate enforcement measures in the case where a merchant ship has violated the State's laws and regulations, thereby causing or threatening major damage to the marine environment of the straits.

Article 35
Scope of this Part

Nothing in this Part affects:
  (a) any areas of internal waters within a strait, except where the establishment of a straight baseline in accordance with the method set forth in article 7 has the effect of enclosing as internal waters areas which had not previously been considered as such;
  (b) the legal status of the waters beyond the territorial seas of States bordering straits as exclusive economic zones or high seas; or
  (c) the legal regime in straits in which passage is regulated in whole or in part by

---

[38] In Article 49(4), the comparable provision in Part IV (Archipelagic States), there appears additionally a reference to the resources contained in the sea-bed, etc.: there can be no doubt that Article 34(1) also applies to any resources in the subsoil etc.

[39] Similar provisions are contained in Articles 2(3) concerning the territorial sea and 49(3) concerning archipelagic waters. The precise meaning of the reference to 'other rules of international law' may not always be entirely clear in practice.

long-standing international conventions in force specifically relating to such straits.

Article 35 sets out three separate saving provisions for cases not intended to be affected by Part III: in brief, they are (a) internal waters, (b) the status of waters beyond the territorial sea and (c) straits in which passage is regulated by existing treaties.

Case (a)

The origins of sub-paragraph (a), which concerns certain areas of water which are *ex*cluded, can be traced to proposals describing which straits were *in*cluded. Thus, Article 1(3) of the UK's proposal[40] was that transit passage should apply 'to any strait or other stretch of water, whatever its geographical name which (a) is used for international navigation and (b) connects two parts of the high seas'. A Canadian definition[41] of straits required that they should be 'naturally formed', should lie within the territorial sea and should have been 'traditionally used for international navigation'. In 1975, the Fiji/UK Group considered the definition: the resulting text applied to '. . . any strait (which term includes any naturally-formed stretch of water whatever its geographical name) . . .'.[42] In an *aide-mémoire*[43] dated 30 April 1975, Canada, Chile and Norway pointed out that on the basis of the *Corfu Channel* case and Article 16(4) of the Convention on the Territorial Sea and the Contiguous Zone of 1958 (hereinafter the CTSCZ), the law on straits applied to 'only those that lie within the territorial sea of one or more States' and that the proposed wording would negate the regime of internal waters behind straight baselines drawn by many States. In his ISNT, the Chairman of the Second Committee tried to take account of the three delegations' concerns[44] by excluding from the application of Part III 'any areas of internal waters which had been considered as part of the high seas or territorial sea prior to the drawing of straight baselines'.[45] Subject to drafting changes, this approach was accepted by the Conference in Article 35(a).

In the result, sub-paragraph (a) means that the rules about passage in Part III do not affect any areas of internal waters within a strait, unless those areas become internal waters as a result of the drawing of straight baselines in accordance with the method set forth in Article 7. Internal waters are defined by Article 8(1), i.e. waters on the landward side of the baseline of the territorial sea, and in the normal case there are no rights of passage, whether innocent or transit passage, through such waters. The exception implies that straight baselines may be drawn within or across

[40] A/CONF. 62/C.2/L. 3.

[41] A/CONF. 62/C.2/L. 83.

[42] Platzoder, op. cit. above (n. 16), p. 194. The rest of the definition followed the language of L. 3.

[43] Ibid., p. 223.

[44] A/CONF. 62/WP.8/Part II, Article 35(a).

[45] In accordance with the rules in Article 7.

straits so long as the criteria set out in Article 7 are satisfied. The exception is consistent with the rule in Article 8(2) concerning the maintenance of the right of innocent passage. Articles 8(2) and 35(a) both use the formula 'in accordance with the method set forth in Article 7': this wording was intended to be capable of applying to baselines drawn in the past, as well as to ones to be drawn in the future, so long as the *method* set out in Article 7 was followed.

Case (b)

This sub-paragraph was intended to clarify the position with regard to areas of water lying within a strait and beyond but surrounded by the territorial sea of the coastal State(s), the so-called 'pockets' of high seas or EEZ. This situation is found in longer, broader straits such as the Straits of Malacca, and it provoked questions from Malaysia in particular. The wording originated in Article 9 of the UK's proposals[46] to the effect that 'pockets' of high seas within a strait were not affected by the other provisions about passage in the strait. The Chairman of the Second Committee included in his ISNT similar wording as Article 36(b);[47] but he also made clear that 'pockets' of EEZ were equally not affected by the provisions about straits. Subject to changes made in the Drafting Committee (notably the insertion of the word 'legal' before 'status' in the interests of consistency), his approach was accepted.

Sub-paragraph (b) makes clear that the provisions of Part II do not affect the legal status of any areas of water within a strait lying beyond the outer limit of the territorial sea of the State or States bordering a strait: these 'pockets' may be EEZ, or high seas if the States concerned have not claimed EEZs (whether generally or in the strait). As such, they would be subject to the regime of freedom of navigation and overflight in accordance with Parts V and VII.[48] Sub-paragraph (b) is to similar effect as Article 34(1).

Case (c)

This sub-paragraph excludes from the application of Part III a small number of straits in regard to which there exists in each case a regime of passage specifically related to that strait.

By way of background, it may be recalled that Article 25 of the CTSCZ stated:

The provisions of this Convention shall not affect conventions or other international agreements already in force, as between Parties to them.

This approach was followed in the UK's proposals about straits[49] which included the following Article 10:

The provisions of this Chapter shall not affect obligations under the Charter of

---

[46] A/CONF. 62/C.2/L. 3: 'Nothing in this Chapter shall affect any areas of high seas within a strait.'
[47] A/CONF. 62/WP.8/Part II, Article 36(b).
[48] Especially relevant are Articles 58 and 87.
[49] Loc. cit. above, n. 40.

the United Nations or under conventions or other international agreements already in force relating to a particular strait.

A slightly different approach was put forward by Bulgaria and other States: thus Article 1(3)(c) of their proposals read:

> The provisions . . . (c) shall not affect the legal regime of straits through which transit is regulated by international agreements specifically relating to such straits.[50]

A clear example under both approaches was the Montreux Convention relating to the Bosphorus and Dardanelles. Denmark and Finland submitted a proposal[51] (in the form of an amendment to the UK's draft articles) advocating the maintenance of the regime of non-suspendable innocent passage in straits having a width of less than 6 nm, i.e. twice 3 nm. Sweden supported this approach on the grounds that 'it was not fair to ask coastal States to give up the control over passage through narrow straits that they had exercised for hundreds of years in accordance with the rules of international law'.[52]

Whilst the idea of excluding some particular cases found a positive response in the Fiji/UK Group, concern was expressed about the imprecise effects of the formulation which had been proposed by the UK. Denmark was especially concerned with this question in view of the regime in the Baltic Straits. As a result of discussions, some revised wording, derived largely from that of the Bulgarian proposal, was produced, as follows:

> The provisions of this Chapter shall not affect the legal regime in straits in which passage is regulated in whole or in part by long-standing international conventions in force specifically relating to such straits.[53]

In preparing his ISNT, the Chairman of the Second Committee accepted the results of the discussions in the Group; but, instead of making a separate article, he incorporated the formula into his Article 35[54] and he changed the term 'legal regime' to 'legal status'. The Chairman's approach in the ISNT was eventually accepted by the Conference as Article 35(c) of the Convention, but the term 'legal regime' was reinstated.

Sub-paragraph (c) means that Part III does not affect the legal regime in certain straits. This regime may be made up of the terms of the relevant convention and the practice of States (including of course that of the coastal State) and would include the regime of passage. The straits concerned are those in which passage is regulated by long-standing conventions relating specifically to those straits. The conventions may be bilateral or multilateral

---

[50] Ibid., L. 11.

[51] Ibid., L. 15.

[52] *Official Records*, vol. 2, p. 129 (12th meeting, 22 July 1974). Similar statements had been made by Denmark and Finland in introducing their amendment (L. 15) at the 11th meeting earlier that day (ibid., pp. 124–5).

[53] Article 10 of the draft articles produced by the Group, in Platzoder, op. cit. above (n. 16), p. 194.

[54] Loc. cit. above (n. 44).

and may be any kind of treaty. The regulation may be extensive, as in the case of the Montreux Convention of 1936 about the Turkish straits, or may be partial, as in the cases of the Treaty of Copenhagen of 1857 about the Danish Straits and the Treaty of 1881 between Argentina and Chile about the Straits of Magellan. The term 'long-standing international conventions in force' was chosen with those examples in mind:[55] a brand new convention about another strait somewhere in the world was not intended to count. In those straits to which Part III does not apply by virtue of Article 35(c), the local, existing regime was expected by the Conference to persist.

Article 36
High seas routes or routes through exclusive economic zones through straits used for international navigation

This Part does not apply to a strait used for international navigation if there exists through the strait a route through the high seas or through an exclusive economic zone of similar convenience with respect to navigational and hydrographical characteristics; in such routes, the other relevant Parts of this Convention, including the provisions regarding the freedoms of navigation and overflight, apply.

Article 36 was derived from Article 1(4) of the UK proposals,[56] which read:

Transit passage shall apply in a strait only to the extent that:
(a) an equally suitable high seas route does not exist through the strait; . . .

The intention was that the right of transit passage should not exist through

. . . what might be described as a broad strait: if the strait was rather more than 24 miles wide, and had a good and wide enough high-seas route down the middle, it was unnecessary to provide a special right of transit passage since ships and aircraft could navigate on the high seas through the strait . . .[57]

The Fiji/UK Group modified the wording of the proposal and referred to the absence of a high seas route of similar convenience . . . through the strait.[58] 'Similar convenience' was considered a better test than 'equal suitability' in the original proposal since exact equality may never be found at sea.

The Chairman of the Second Committee accepted the gist of the Group's proposal, but recast it as a separate article of general application. Thus, his Article 36 read:

The provisions of this Part shall not apply to a strait used for international navi-

---

[55] In signing the Convention, Finland and Sweden each stated their understandings that 'the exception from the transit passage regime provided for in Article 35(c) of the Convention is applicable to the strait between Finland (Aaland Islands) and Sweden' and that 'the present legal regime in that strait will remain unchanged after the entry into force of the Convention'. The strait is subject to the regime created by the Convention of 20 October 1921 on the Non-Fortification and Neutralization of the Aaland Islands, which includes rules about passage through the archipelago.

[56] A/CONF. 62/C.2/L. 3.

[57] *Official Records*, vol. 2, p. 125 (Mr Dudgeon, UK).

[58] Platzoder, op. cit. above (n. 16), p. 194.

gation if a high seas route or a route through an exclusive economic zone of similar convenience exists through the strait.[59]

As will be seen, the Chairman introduced two new elements: first, the article referred not solely to the right of transit passage but rather to Part III as a whole; and, secondly, the article applied also to a route through waters having the status of EEZ as well as to high seas routes.

In informal discussion in 1975, it was pointed out that the word 'convenience' was too broad a test by itself and needed qualification by reference to conditions of navigation and hydrography, i.e. objective criteria. Thus the questions were posed: similar to what? and convenient for whom? The similarly convenient route was intended to be the one through the territorial sea in the strait and the convenience was that of the user, not the coastal State. In revising the ISNT, the Chairman of the Second Committee accepted the need to clarify the scope of the words 'similar convenience'[60] by adding the words 'with respect to navigational or hydrographic characteristics'. In interpreting the phrase as a whole, regard may be had to factors such as distance, safety, the state of the sea, visibility, depth of water (including the presence of shallows or shoals) and ease of fixing a ship's position. The balance may vary between, say, a very large crude carrier and smaller coasters.

In further informal discussion in 1978, Yugoslavia suggested the addition to the end of the words: 'in such routes freedom of navigation and overflight shall be maintained unimpeded'.[61] A modified formula[62] was circulated in 1980, but there were doubts as to the need for it since Parts V and VII would apply to the waters in question by virtue of their own terms. None the less, the Chairman of the Second Committee endorsed a further modified version of the concluding phrase at the end of Article 36 and this secured consensus at the Conference.

As a result, Article 36 excludes from the application of this Part every strait where there is a similarly convenient route through the strait in the high seas or an EEZ. The justification for transit passage or non-suspendable innocent passage does not exist if there is a route through the strait where ships of other States can remain outside the territorial sea and can exercise rights of navigation under the regime of the high seas or of the EEZ. But this route must be similarly convenient both in terms of navigation (e.g. overall distances, position-fixing, and the route's breadth and straightness) and in terms of hydrography (e.g. depth and lack of natural obstructions). A similar proposition is contained in Article 38(1).

In extending its territorial sea to twelve nm, Japan has, by special

---

[59] A/CONF. 62/WP.8/Part II.

[60] A/CONF. 62/WP.8/REV. I/Part II, Article 35.

[61] Amendment C2/Informal Meeting/2.

[62] Ibid., Rev. 2: 'Parts VII and V respectively, including the provisions on freedom of navigation and overflight, apply.'

provisions, not extended it in certain straits, so as to leave a route through the straits which can be used without entering the territorial sea.[63] Sweden has also made similar arrangements[64] for certain areas in waters lying between Sweden and Denmark but outside the traditional Danish straits regulated by the Treaty of Copenhagen of 1857.

SECTION 2. TRANSIT PASSAGE

Article 37
Scope of this section

This section applies to straits which are used for international navigation between one part of the high seas or an exclusive economic zone and another part of the high seas or an exclusive economic zone.

Section 2, which consists of nine articles, sets out the regime of transit passage.

Article 37, which defines the scope of Section 2, was put forward by the Chairman of the Second Committee in his ISNT[65] when the Part of the draft Convention about straits was first sub-divided into three sections. The Chairman followed the general approach to the question adopted by the Fiji/UK Group[66] whose Article 1(1) had applied the right of transit passage to 'any strait (which term includes any naturally formed[67] stretch of water whatever its geographical name) which: (*a*) is used for international navigation and (*b*) connects two parts of the high seas'. The Chairman omitted the references to straits being 'naturally-formed' and to the irrelevance of a strait's name, no doubt because both points were considered self-evident. He inserted references to the EEZ in line with the remainder of his proposed ISNT. Subject to minor drafting changes, the Chairman's text was accepted by the Conference.

As a result, the regime of transit passage applies only in straits which (i) are used for international navigation and (ii) connect areas of sea which have the status of high seas or EEZ. If a strait leads only to territorial sea or internal waters, then Section 2 does not apply: Section 3 (providing for non-suspendable innocent passage under Article 45) applies instead.

Article 37 must, of course, be read together with Section 1 which contains several exclusion clauses, as well as with Article 38(1) which creates a second exceptional type of strait to which Section 3 applies.

---

[63] Law No. 30 of 2 May 1977: *UN Legislative Series*, ST/LEG/SER. B/19. The territorial sea remains at 3 nm in the Soya, Tsugaru, Osumi and Tsushima Straits.

[64] Amendments of 1 January 1980 to the Law of 1 July 1979 extending generally to 12 nm: Department of State, *Limits in the Seas: National Claims to Maritime Jurisdictions*, No. 36 (5th Revision, 1985).

[65] A/CONF. 62/WP.8/Part II.

[66] Platzoder, op. cit. above (n. 16), p. 194.

[67] The words 'naturally formed' had been put forward by Canada in A/CONF. 62/C.2/L. 83 in order to make absolutely clear that canals were not included in the definition of what constituted a strait.

Article 37 employs the two key criteria—a strait must be 'used for international navigation' and must connect two parts of the high seas/EEZ—laid down in the judgment of the International Court of Justice in the *Corfu Channel* case.[68] The wording of Article 37 must be interpreted in the light of that judgment. The meaning of the term 'used for international navigation' has been analysed above. In deciding whether a strait 'connects two parts' of the high seas/EEZ, there may be difficulty where one part is very small in extent. Here again, a 'common-sense' rather than a mechanical or mathematical interpretation is called for. If such a 'pocket' of high seas is surrounded by territorial sea and is not used as part of a route, there is insufficient justification for applying Section 2: instead, Section 3 would apply.

Article 38
Right of transit passage

1. In straits referred to in article 37, all ships and aircraft enjoy the right of transit passage, which shall not be impeded; except that, if the strait is formed by an island of a State bordering the strait and its mainland, transit passage shall not apply if there exists seaward of the island a route through the high seas or through an exclusive economic zone of similar convenience with respect to navigational and hydrographical characteristics.

2. Transit passage means the exercise in accordance with this Part of the freedom of navigation and overflight solely for the purpose of continuous and expeditious transit of the strait between one part of the high seas or an exclusive economic zone and another part of the high seas or an exclusive economic zone. However, the requirement of continuous and expeditious transit does not preclude passage through the strait for the purpose of entering, leaving or returning from a State bordering the strait, subject to the conditions of entry to that State.

3. Any activity which is not an exercise of the right of transit passage through a strait remains subject to the other applicable provisions of this Convention.

Article 38 is a key provision in the Convention. Against the background of acceptance of 12 nm as the maximum breadth of the territorial sea, Article 38 provides for a regime of transit passage in certain straits used for international navigation. This link was described in the following terms:

Acceptance of a territorial sea of 12 miles would result in a large number of straits forming essential links for international navigation, both by sea and air, ceasing to have a strip of high seas down the middle. Hence the need to ensure that unrestricted navigation through those vital links in the world network of communications should remain available for use by the international community.[69]

The origins of Article 38 can be found in the separate proposals of the UK[70] (which, as indicated above, formed one starting point for the work of

---

[68] *ICJ Reports*, 1949, p. 4.
[69] Mr Dudgeon (UK), *Official Records*, vol. 2, p. 125 (para. 17).
[70] A/CONF. 62/C.2/L. 3, Article 1.

the Fiji/UK Group[71]) and of Bulgaria *et al.*[72] as well as in those of the Chairman of the Second Committee.[73] In introducing its proposals, the UK delegation put forward this explanation of the concept of transit passage:

Article 1 sets out the concept of transit passage through straits connecting two parts of the high seas. The concept his delegation had tried to describe corresponded to what it believed to be the best international practice at that time. It proposed that ships and aircraft exercising the right of transit passage should not be impeded or hampered during their passage. At the same time the right was given 'solely for the purpose of continuous and expeditious transit of the strait'.[74]

No doubt, the practice which the delegation had in mind was that whereby passage had been exercised in certain straits on the basis of freedom of navigation and overflight, rather than on the basis of the right of innocent passage as defined in the CTSCZ[75] and irrespective of whether the coastal States' claims had left a central 'corridor' of high seas/EEZ in the strait. The proposals attracted much interest and some opposition, especially from States which supported the application of the regime of innocent passage to all straits.[76]

Paragraph 1 makes clear that all ships and aircraft, including therefore warships and military aircraft, enjoy the right of transit passage. The references to aircraft (which were included in both the UK's proposal[77] and, as regards straits 'traditionally used' for overflights, that by Bulgaria *et al.*[78]) proved controversial; objections were advanced to the effect that these proposals were inconsistent with the Chicago Convention. An amendment by Spain[79] to remove all reference to aircraft was, however, not accepted by the Conference. It is a right the exercise of which may not be impeded by any agency, whether the coastal State (the duties of which are stated also in Article 44) or the ships or aircraft of third States. The right applies in principle in all straits used for international navigation between two parts of the high seas/EEZ (Article 37). At the same time, the right is subject to (i) the qualifications in Section 1 of Part III, and (ii) the exception in paragraph 1 of the present article.

The exception excludes from the ambit of Section 2 the strait which runs

[71] Draft Articles of 30 April 1975, in Platzoder, op. cit. above (n. 16), p. 194.

[72] A/CONF. 62/C.2/L. 11.

[73] A/CONF. 62/WP.8/Part II, Article 38.

[74] *Official Records*, vol. 2, p. 125 (para. 18).

[75] Special provisions about straits are to be found in the legislation of several States bordering straits used for international navigation, notably France (24 December 1971, Article 3: ST/LEG/SER.B/18, p. 17); Japan (1 July 1977: ST/LEG/SER.B/19, p. 56); Morocco (2 March 1973, Article 3: ST/LEG/SER.B/18, p. 29); Oman (10 February 1981); and Sweden (1 January 1980). As regards the Straits of Gibraltar, see Colombos, *International Law of the Sea* (1967), p. 220; O'Connell, *International Law* (1970), vol. 1, p. 567; and Truver, *The Strait of Gibraltar and the Mediterranean Sea* (1980), esp. chapter 5.

[76] Spain, China, Egypt, Albania, Iran, Greece and PDR Yemen were notable in this regard, making particular reference to the Chicago Convention of 1944.

[77] Loc. cit. above, n. 70.

[78] Loc. cit. above, n. 72.

[79] Amendment C2/4 of 1978 (Spain).

between an island of the coastal State and its mainland[80] if there exists a
route seaward of the island through the high seas or EEZ which is of 'similar convenience with respect to navigational and hydrographical characteristics'. That expression bears the same meaning as in Article 36 and the
commentary on that article need not be repeated here. An example of such
a strait is the Pemba Channel off Tanzania. The Corfu Channel[81] is a less
clear case since part of the strait lies between Corfu and Albania. The application of the exception in particular geographical situations (e.g. where
there is an archipelago as in the Aegean or where there are several islands
lying together, or where it is not clear what is a State's 'mainland') may not
be free from difficulty; but the words should not be interpreted too mecha-
nically. Instead, all the relevant geographical and other circumstances[82]
should be taken into account and a 'commonsense' interpretation given, as
described above.

The underlying rationale of the exception is clear: in a place where there
exists an alternative route to seaward of the island of similar convenience,
the interest of the international community in freedom of communication is
not as strong as in the place where there is no such alternative route, and a
different balance was struck between that interest and the interest of the
coastal State. In those instances where a strait is excluded by Article 38(1)
from the regime of transit passage, the strait is subject to that of innocent
passage by virtue of Article 45.

Paragraph 2 defines the concept of 'transit passage'. It is the exercise of
'the freedom of navigation and overflight', freedoms to be found also in
Article 87 (Freedom of the High Seas). However, whilst in principle the
freedoms in paragraph 2 are of the same order as those in Article 87, paragraph 2 contains significant qualifications. First, the right of transit passage
must be exercised in accordance with Part III, not Part VII. Secondly, the
right must be exercised for a single purpose, namely transit from one part
of the high seas/EEZ to another part of the high seas/EEZ. Thirdly, the
purpose of the navigator (vessel or aircraft) must be that of 'continuous and
expeditious' transit of the strait. This means that hovering, loitering or conducting manoeuvres (all of which are part of the freedom of navigation on
the high seas) are not allowed when exercising the right of transit passage.
There are at least two parallels between Article 38(2) and Article 18: the
latter defines the meaning of (innocent) 'passage' in terms of specified purposes and also calls for passage to be 'continuous and expeditious' (subject
to safety requirements, *force majeure*, distress or humanitarian duty[83]).

To the requirement of continuous and expeditious transit of the entire

---

[80] An informal suggestion by Poland to refer to 'continental territory' was not accepted, but the
French text refers to '*le territoire continental*' nevertheless.

[81] In introducing the proposal, the UK representative referred to the case of 'a strait formed by an
island lying less than 24 miles off the coast'.

[82] A relevant factor may be the existence of an IMO traffic scheme: compare Article 53 (archipelagic
sea lanes passage).

[83] These are covered by Article 39(1)(c) in relation to straits.

length of a strait, there is a qualification for the case of transiting part of a strait, passing the coasts, say, of States A and C in order to enter, leave or return from the port or airport of State B which also borders the strait. A vessel or aircraft entering, etc., State B remains subject to its conditions of entry. An example of a State in the position of State B is Singapore. In introducing this part of its proposal, the UK representative in the Second Committee spoke as follows:

His delegation also had in mind the situation of the long strait which had more than one country bordering one side of the strait. Assuming a strait which had two countries on the western side, States A and B, and one country on the eastern side, State C, the United Kingdom draft proposed first, a right of transit should the ship or aircraft be going all the way northwards or southwards through the strait; secondly, a right of transit if the ship or aircraft was proceeding down the first part of the strait between States A and C with a view to calling at a port or airport of State B.[84]

The substance of the proposal was accepted in the second sentence of Article 38(2). The wording was refined during the course of the Conference and cast as an exception to the rule of 'continuous and expeditious' passage.

Paragraph 3 first appeared in the draft articles prepared by the Fiji/UK Group on Straits, dated 18 April 1975.[85] It was intended to make clear that any activity, including navigation in or over straits, which does not amount to an exercise of the right of transit passage as defined in Article 38 remains subject to the other provisions of the Convention. These include Article 34 (legal status of waters forming straits used for international navigation) and other articles in Part III, as well as Article 2 (legal status of the territorial sea, etc). In other words, if a vessel or aircraft is present in a strait used for international navigation but is not exercising the right of transit passage, then the vessel or aircraft is subject to provisions in the Convention other than those in Part III which regulate transit passage.

Proposals by Spain and Morocco[86] to add to the end of the paragraph the words 'and to other rules of international law' were not accepted. The proposals were advanced at a time when there remained controversy about overflight, it being argued by the proposers that it was contrary to rules of general international law contained in the Chicago Convention of 1944 on International Civil Aviation. The opposition to the proposals had a tactical element. Notwithstanding the rejection of the proposals, those rules of international law which are not excluded by the terms of the Convention (either expressly or implicitly—as are the rules in the Chicago Convention) would continue to be applicable. Reference to 'other rules of international law' was included in Article 34(2) concerning qualifications upon the sovereignty or jurisdiction of States bordering straits.

---

[84] *Official Records*, vol. 2, p. 125.
[85] Platzoder, op. cit. above (n. 16), p. 194.
[86] Amendment C2/4 of 1978 (Spain) and Amendment C2/22 of 1978 (Morocco).

Article 39
Duties of ships and aircraft during transit passage

1. Ships and aircraft, while exercising the right of transit passage, shall:
   (*a*) proceed without delay through or over the strait;
   (*b*) refrain from any threat or use of force against the sovereignty, territorial integrity or political independence of States bordering the strait, or in any other manner in violation of the principles of international law embodied in the Charter of the United Nations;
   (*c*) refrain from any activities other than those incident to their normal modes of continuous and expeditious transit unless rendered necessary by *force majeure* or by distress;
   (*d*) comply with other relevant provisions of this Part.

2. Ships in transit passage shall:
   (*a*) comply with generally accepted international regulations, procedures and practices for safety at sea, including the International Regulations for Preventing Collisions at Sea;
   (*b*) comply with generally accepted international regulations, procedures and practices for the prevention, reduction and control of pollution from ships.

3. Aircraft in transit passage shall:
   (*a*) observe the Rules of the Air established by the International Civil Aviation Organization as they apply to civil aircraft; state aircraft will normally comply with such safety measures and will at all times operate with due regard for the safety of navigation;
   (*b*) at all times monitor the radio frequency assigned by the competent internationally designated air traffic control authority or the appropriate international distress radio frequency.

Article 39, which specifies the duties of ships and aircraft during their exercise of the right of transit passage, is based upon the initial proposals of the UK.[87] The article applies, in principle, to all ships and aircraft, irrespective of their status (public or private, civil or military).

Paragraph 1 imposes four duties on ships and aircraft alike. They are, first, to proceed 'without delay', an expression in harmony with the requirements of 'continuous and expeditious transit' in Articles 38(2) and 39(1)(*c*). Navigators should proceed at their normal speed, having regard to all relevant factors, including safety requirements, weather conditions, the presence of other ships or aircraft in the strait, etc. Secondly, they are to refrain from the threat or use of force against the States bordering the strait. This wording applies the general obligation contained in Article 2(4) of the Charter of the United Nations[88] specifically to ships and aircraft in transit, whilst at the same time confining the beneficiaries of the obligation to the bordering States. The terms 'threat' and 'use' of force should be interpreted in the same way as in the Charter. A warship or a military aircraft does not

---

[87] A/CONF. 62/L. 3, Chapter Three, Article 2.
[88] The wording of Article 39(1)(*b*) is based on Article 2(4) of the UN Charter. The addition of the word 'sovereignty' adds little or nothing to 'territorial integrity'.

represent a threat of force by reason only of its presence in or over a strait.

Thirdly, and in many ways most importantly, ships and aircraft in transit are to 'refrain from any activities other than those incident to their normal modes of . . . transit'. In other words, ships and aircraft are to behave in their ordinary manner and do what is usual to effect their passage, and nothing else. In putting forward this approach, the intention was to avoid the need for a long list of prohibited activities such as the list of 'non-innocent' activities appearing in Article 19(2). Anything which is not incidental to transit in the normal mode is impermissible: clearly, most if not all the activities listed in Article 19(2) are not incidental. The term 'normal mode' was intended to mean, for example, that submarines could make their transits submerged, aircraft would fly at their normal altitudes, and surface vessels would follow their normal operating procedures whilst in transit. Regard would be had to all relevant circumstances, including in the case of submarines the depth of the water. The reference to 'the normal mode' avoided the need for a formula such as 'submarines may pass under water', which would have raised questions in the case of submersibles and other underwater vehicles which may come along in the future. This possibility of submerged transit took account of the fact that it is often much safer for a modern submarine to proceed dived. This approach was accepted in the Fiji/UK Group[89] and by the Chairman of the Second Committee.[90] It was challenged in the Second Committee's Working Group by certain delegations, notably Spain and Morocco who tabled amendments:[91] however, these were not accepted by the Conference. Others questioned the discretion which they understood was given to navigators in the phrase 'normal mode', for example in the case of an aircraft carrier or a flotilla, but they did not press their point and the term 'normal mode' was accepted. It may be noted that the term appears also in Article 53(3) concerning the rights of archipelagic sea lanes passage: the term carries the same meaning in both articles.

There is an exception to the obligation to refrain from non-incidental activity: Article 39(1)(c) accepts that a ship or aircraft in transit may have to slow or stop or take special action if this is made necessary by *force majeure* (e.g. collision or hurricane) or distress.

Finally, paragraph 1(d) obliges ships and aircraft to comply with the other relevant provisions of Part III: these include the obligations to respect sea lanes and traffic schemes in Article 41(7) and to observe applicable laws and regulations in Article 42(4), as well as obligations in the other provisions of Article 39. Paragraph 1(d), which originated in the Fiji/UK Group,[92] makes explicit a point which was left unstated in the UK's initial proposals.

Paragraph 2 specifies certain duties for ships in transit passage, arising

[89] Draft Articles of 30 April 1975 in Platzoder, op. cit. above (n. 16), p. 194.
[90] A/CONF. 62/WP.8, Part II, Article 39.
[91] Amendment C2/4 (Spain, 1978) and C2/22 (Morocco, 1978).
[92] Platzoder, op. cit. above (n. 16), p. 194 (Article 2(1)(d)).

from 'generally accepted international regulations, procedures and practices'. That expression was cast in deliberately wide terms and was intended to connote, in the first place, international conventions adopted for example under the auspices of the International Maritime Organization (IMO) which have secured wide acceptance within the world community, as well as subsidiary or related instruments and decisions. To such 'international regulations' must be added generally accepted 'procedures and practices', which include those normally followed by mariners. The duties specified are in two fields: safety and pollution. Ships in transit are to comply with international safety rules, including the International Regulations for Preventing Collisions at Sea. The current version of these Regulations is annexed to the Convention on the International Regulations for Preventing Collisions at Sea of 1972.[93] In particular, the regulations take account of sea lanes and traffic schemes, many of which relate to straits. Ships in transit are also to comply with international rules for the prevention, reduction and control of pollution: again, the IMO has adopted several conventions about marine pollution, notably the MARPOL Convention[94] of 1973.[95]

Paragraph 3 specifies similar duties for aircraft, designed to ensure safety. Aircraft in transit are to observe the Rules of the Air established by the International Civil Aviation Organization for civil aircraft: this means that military aircraft are to observe those Rules whilst in transit. The concept arose in the context of negotiations on an archipelagic regime. The US insisted on freedom of overflight for all aircraft. The Indonesians objected to this, stating that there was no place for such provision in the law of the sea and that it was a matter for ICAO. However, if such a provision was to be introduced then Indonesia wanted all aircraft, including military aircraft, to be subject to ICAO rules. This the US would not agree to. Eventually Fiji proposed the compromise whereby civil aviation would be subject to ICAO rules and military aircraft would normally comply with those rules. For strategic reasons the US did not want military aircraft to be subject to reporting requirements at all times. The normal practice is for military aircraft to observe and comply with ICAO rules, even though strictly they apply only to civil aircraft. The rules are applied worldwide. The relevant part of the Rules, according to a statement made by the UK delegation during discussions in the Second Committee's Working Group, is that relating to the high seas. In a study dated 20 January 1984, the Secretariat of ICAO noted that Article 39(3) would extend the legislative jurisdiction of the ICAO Council from the high seas to the air space above straits used for international navigation.[96]

Sub-paragraph (b) supplements the foregoing duties. Aircraft in transit are obliged to monitor either the radio frequency assigned by the air traffic

[93] In force 15 July 1977: IMO Publication 904. 85. OIE.
[94] International Convention for the Prevention of Pollution from Ships, London, 2 November 1973.
[95] See also Article 211(1).
[96] C-WP/7777, Secretariat Study of 20 January 1984.

control authority designated for the area concerned by ICAO (i.e. the authority listed in the local Regional Air Navigation Plan, as approved by the Council of ICAO), or the international distress radio frequency. This radio frequency is the one referred to in Annex 10 to the Chicago Convention, Aeronautical Communications, i.e. 121.5MHz. It has been argued by the ICAO Secretariat that aircraft are under a duty 'according to firmly established practice and international standards adopted by the ICAO Council' to monitor *both* the frequency assigned by the ATC authority *and* the distress frequency; that Article 39(3) contains an error in allowing alternatives; and that the relevant standards are *lex specialis* which will be complied with in practice.[97] It may well be true that those standards will always be complied with in practice: however, Article 39(3) is also a *lex specialis* for the overflight of straits by aircraft of all types and it should not be thought to contain errors. Aircraft in transit are to operate at all times with reasonable regard for the safety of navigation and so should be capable of knowing about other aircraft in the vicinity. In the case of State aircraft, the obligation to maintain continuous listening watch of the local air traffic control arises from requirements of safety and paragraph 3, rather than from the Rules of the Air. Standard 3.6.5.1 requires continuous listening watch in the case of a controlled flight and similar requirements exist in the visual flight rules (Standard 4.7, Annex 2) and in the instrument flight rules (Standard 5.3.2, Annex 2). Proposals by Morocco[98] to impose more specific restrictions and duties on aircraft in transit were not accepted by the Conference.

Article 40
Research and Survey activities

During transit passage, foreign ships, including marine scientific research and hydrographic survey ships, may not carry out any research or survey activities without the prior authorization of the States bordering straits.

The idea of this article was first put forward in the proposals of Fiji[99] in the twin contexts of innocent passage and passage through straits. The present wording first appeared in the Informal Composite Negotiating Text,[100] in the light of informal discussions. In effect, it supplements the general rules in Article 39 by adding specific rules about research and survey activities on the part of ships exercising the right of transit passage. The prior authorization of the State(s) bordering a strait is required for such activities. Where an agreed maritime boundary exists in a strait, the consent

---

[97] Ibid., paragraph 9.12.

[98] Amendment C2/22 of 1978. Restrictions proposed were no exercises, use of weapons, photography, refuelling in flight, dive-bombing and interference with the coastal State's telecommunications— many of which are excluded by virtue of paragraph 1 of Article 39. Greece proposed (in amendment C2/17 of 1978) to make the duty 'to comply' with the ICAO Rules, but this too was not accepted.

[99] A/CONF. 62/C.2/L. 19, Article 5(5).

[100] A/CONF. 62/WP.10; *Official Records*, vol. 8, Article 40. The ICNT's draft article began with the words 'In their': the words were changed to 'During transit' by the Drafting Committee.

of the appropriate coastal State is needed for activities in that part of the strait under its sovereignty or jurisdiction. The relevant activities are marine scientific research (a subject regulated by Part XIII of the Convention) and hydrographic surveying. Both activities are mentioned in Article 19(1)(j) concerning the meaning of innocent passage; and Article 40 (like Article 39) applies by virtue of Article 54 to ships exercising the right of archipelagic sea lanes passage.

Article 40 adds little to what is implicit in Article 39: it appears to have been included largely for the avoidance of doubt. It may have particular relevance in long straits, for example those of Malacca, and archipelagic waters.

Article 41
Sea lanes and traffic separation schemes in straits used for international navigation

1. In conformity with this Part, States bordering straits may designate sea lanes and prescribe traffic separation schemes for navigation in straits where necessary to promote the safe passage of ships.
2. Such States may, when circumstances require, and after giving due publicity thereto, substitute other sea lanes or traffic separation schemes for any sea lanes or traffic separation schemes previously designated or prescribed by them.
3. Such sea lanes and traffic separation schemes shall conform to generally accepted international regulations.
4. Before designating or substituting sea lanes or prescribing or substituting traffic separation schemes, States bordering straits shall refer proposals to the competent international organization with a view to their adoption. The organization may adopt only such sea lanes and traffic separation schemes as may be agreed with the States bordering the straits, after which the States may designate, prescribe or substitute them.
5. In respect of a strait where sea lanes or traffic separation schemes through the waters of two or more States bordering the strait are being proposed, the States concerned shall co-operate in formulating proposals in consultation with the competent international organization.
6. States bordering straits shall clearly indicate all sea lanes and traffic separation schemes designated or prescribed by them on charts to which due publicity shall be given.
7. Ships in transit passage shall respect applicable sea lanes and traffic separation schemes established in accordance with this article.

Article 41 gives further recognition in international law to the institution in recent times of traffic schemes for promoting the safety of shipping.[101] The article is based upon proposals made by the UK[102] and Fiji[103] and incorporates modifications and additions suggested by other delegations during informal discussions. In introducing the proposals, the UK

[101] Traffic schemes are also dealt with in Articles 22 (territorial sea) and 53 (archipelagic waters), as well as in the Collision Regulations and the Convention for the Safety of Life at Sea.
[102] A/CONF. 62/C.2/L. 3, Article 3.
[103] A/CONF. 62/C.2/L. 19, Article 5(6) to (10).

representative noted there was often a concentration of shipping in straits and continued: 'In view of the general interest of the international community in navigation through straits, we propose that traffic separation schemes should be fully considered before their promulgation.'[104]

The article has two parts: first, paragraphs 1 to 6 specify the rights and duties of States bordering straits in the matter of traffic schemes; and, secondly, paragraph 7 imposes a corresponding duty upon ships exercising the right of transit passage to respect such schemes.

Paragraph 1 confirms that States bordering straits are competent to designate sea lanes and to prescribe traffic separation schemes, including the making of laws and regulations,[105] where this is necessary to promote the safe passage of ships in straits. The necessity will often arise in straits used for international navigation and many traffic schemes already exist in such straits. The schemes take account both of ships in transit and local traffic, including traffic across a strait. There are also schemes which take account of the existence of shallows or shoals in a strait by defining 'deep draught routes'. Although the express reference to 'depth separation schemes' in the proposals by Fiji[106] was not incorporated in Article 41, they are covered as a type of traffic separation scheme. On 28 April 1982, a letter and statement were circulated to the Conference about the Straits of Malacca and Singapore by the delegations of Malaysia, Indonesia and Singapore:[107] this statement, although made with particular reference to Article 233 (safeguards with respect to straits used for international navigation), contained the point that traffic separation schemes could include 'the determination of under keel clearance for the Straits provided in Article 41'. The statement met with wide support.[108] Since then an agreement about under keel clearance has been drawn up by Indonesia, Malaysia, Singapore and Japan, making provision for the special characteristics of the Straits of Malacca.

Paragraph 2 recognizes that circumstances in a strait may change (e.g. natural changes such as silting may take place, or changes in traffic such as the introduction of large tankers following an oil discovery). Where the new circumstances require a change in the traffic scheme, a substituted scheme may be prescribed or designated. However, the coastal State has to respect the terms of the article and in particular give appropriate publicity to the change.

Paragraphs 3 and 4 take account of the worldwide interest in the safety of navigation in straits by requiring that traffic schemes conform to generally

---

[104] Statement by Mr Dudgeon (UK), *Official Records*, vol. 2, pp. 101–2.
[105] See Article 42(1)(a).
[106] A/CONF. 62/C.2/L. 19, Article 5(6).
[107] A/CONF. 62/L. 145 (Letter by Malaysia).
[108] A/CONF. 62/L. 145, Add. 1 to 8 (Indonesia, Singapore, France, UK, USA, Japan, Australia and FRG).

accepted international regulations, notably the Collision Regulations and the Safety of Life at Sea Convention.[109] Whereas Article 22 gives wide discretion to the coastal State with regard to traffic schemes in the territorial sea generally, Article 41(3) contains a safeguard for the international community in the particular case of traffic schemes in straits. Paragraphs 3 and 4 were the products of the Fiji/UK Group which sought to find a balance between the interests of States bordering on straits and other States.

In the initial proposals of the UK,[110] a State bordering a strait would have been in a position to designate or prescribe a traffic scheme 'only as approved by' the competent international organization (i.e. the IMO). This went too far for delegations such as Singapore and Fiji, which wished the role of the IMO to be purely advisory. Paragraph 4 represents a compromise between these approaches (which was worked out in the Fiji/UK Group). The procedure is as follows: first, the State(s) bordering a strait has to submit its proposals to the IMO; the latter may, secondly, adopt a scheme only in agreement with that State(s) (i.e. modifications have to be agreed); finally, the State bordering a strait may then proceed to designate or prescribe the traffic scheme. The same procedure applies to substitutions.

Paragraph 5 was first proposed in the Fiji/UK Group. It makes explicit provision for cases where there exist two or more States bordering the same strait and requires the States concerned to co-operate in formulating proposals in consultation with the IMO (i.e. the procedures indicated in paragraph 4).[111]

Paragraph 6 requires a State bordering a strait to mark on charts the traffic schemes which it has prescribed in the strait and to give appropriate publicity to the charts. It is similar to Article 53(10) concerning traffic schemes in archipelagic waters and Article 22(4) concerning sea lanes and traffic schemes in the territorial sea. Unlike Article 16 concerning charts depicting baselines, there is no obligation to deposit a copy of each chart with the Secretary-General of the United Nations.

Paragraph 7 requires ships to 'respect' sea lanes and traffic schemes. For example, they must not sail along a sea lane in the wrong direction. Whilst the paragraph does not in terms confine the exercise of the right of transit passage to sea lanes, in practice ships in transit can be expected to follow them. To 'respect' a scheme includes respecting its operating rules as well as the lines on the chart, although the obligation is less precise than one to 'comply with' a scheme.

---

[109] Convention on the International Regulations for Preventing Collisions at Sea, 1972 (referred to in Article 39(2)(a)).

[110] A/CONF. 62/C.2/L. 3, Article 3(3).

[111] Amendment C2/4 (1978) by Spain would have added a sentence requiring the agreement of all the States bordering the strait in the IMO before the scheme could be prescribed. However, this amendment was not adopted.

Article 42
Laws and regulations of States bordering straits relating to transit passage

1. Subject to the provisions of this section, States bordering straits may adopt laws and regulations relating to transit passage through straits, in respect of all or any of the following:

(a) the safety of navigation and the regulation of maritime traffic, as provided in article 41;

(b) the prevention, reduction and control of pollution, by giving effect to applicable international regulations regarding the discharge of oil, oily wastes and other noxious substances in the strait;

(c) with respect to fishing vessels, the prevention of fishing, including the stowage of fishing gear;

(d) the loading or unloading of any commodity, currency or person in contravention of the customs, fiscal, immigration or sanitary laws and regulations of States bordering straits.

2. Such laws and regulations shall not discriminate in form or in fact among foreign ships or in their application have the practical effect of denying, hampering or impairing the right of transit passage as defined in this section.

3. States bordering straits shall give due publicity to all such laws and regulations.

4. Foreign ships exercising the right of transit passage shall comply with such laws and regulations.

5. The flag State of a ship or the State of registry of an aircraft entitled to sovereign immunity which acts in a manner contrary to such laws and regulations or other provisions of this Part shall bear international responsibility for any loss or damage which results to States bordering straits.

Article 42 contains three elements: the powers of States bordering straits to prescribe laws and regulations relating to transit passage (paragraphs 1, 2 and 3); the duty of foreign ships in transit (paragraph 4); and the enforcement of laws, especially in the case of ships and aircraft entitled to sovereign immunity (paragraph 5).

In the UK's initial proposal,[112] the power to prescribe laws was confined to two matters: the implementation of traffic schemes and international regulations regarding discharges of oil. It was made clear that:

Foreign ships exercising the right of transit passage would have to conform with the regulations; should they fail to comply, the possibility of legal proceedings would arise in the case of merchant vessels. In the case of . . . vessels entitled to sovereign immunity . . . there would be liability on the international level or, in other words, state responsibility.[113]

In Fiji's proposal,[114] a much longer list was given of matters on which the State could legislate: this list applied both to straits and to the territorial sea generally. The Fiji/UK Group reviewed these and other proposals over a series of meetings. Suggestions were made to expand the UK's list in order

---

[112] Article 4 of A/CONF. 62/C.2/L. 3.

[113] *Official Records*, vol. 2, Summary Record of the 11th meeting of the Second Committee, paragraph 23, p. 125.

[114] Article 5 of ibid., L. 19.

to meet the legitimate concerns of States bordering straits. It was pointed out that a ship in transit might commit a pollution offence, or engage in fishing or smuggling, thereby giving rise to a need for the State to protect its interests. Waiting for a suspected ship to enter port would not be enough. It was also pointed out that a navigation offence might be committed which was not to do with sea lanes or traffic schemes, or a pollution offence which did not lead to damage so much as expense on the part of the State concerned. After detailed discussions, the list in the UK proposal was expanded and wording similar to Article 42(1) was accepted by the Group.[115]

The Group's text struck a balance between (i) the wish of States bordering straits to have specific regulatory powers (broadly the same as those in Article 21) so as to ensure safety and to protect their coastal interests along the shores of the strait, and (ii) the wish of flag States to see their ships pass through straits without interference from or the imposition of special rules by the bordering States. The Group's text on this issue formed the main basis for Article 41 of the ISNT proposed by the Chairman of the Second Committee;[116] and this text, with minor modifications made in the light of subsequent discussions, eventually became Article 42 of the Convention. Several amendments, the general effect of which was to broaden the powers of States bordering straits, were tabled in 1978;[117] but these amendments were not accepted by the Conference.

Paragraph 1 specifies under four headings the content of the legislation which States bordering straits may adopt about transit passage. First is the safety of navigation and the regulation of traffic, in the terms set out in Article 41. In concrete terms, such a State may give effect within its legal order to a scheme for sea lanes or traffic regulation which satisfies Article 41's requirements. It may do so for all foreign ships exercising the right of transit passage, so that in effect internationally adopted schemes for a strait may be made applicable to all ships in transit passage there regardless of their flags, i.e. even if the flag State has not enacted legislation for ships flying its flag. Secondly, in order to prevent, reduce and control pollution, legislation may be adopted giving effect to those applicable international regulations (such as the Convention on Marine Pollution, 1973) which prohibit the discharge of oil, oily wastes and other noxious substances[118] close to shore and therefore in straits. Similarly, this legislation can be applied to ships flying the flag of States which have not ratified the relevant

---

[115] Platzoder, op. cit. above (n. 16), p. 194.

[116] A/CONF. 62/WP.8/Part II, Article 41.

[117] Amendment C2/4 (Spain) would have broadened powers in regard to pollution and protection of facilities etc., and imposed requirements concerning liability. Amendment C2/17 (Greece) would have extended paragraph 1(a) to encompass laws about air traffic. Amendment C2/22 (Morocco) would have included in the list of legislative powers the protection of navigational aids, other installations, cables and pipelines; the conservation of living resources; and research and hydrographic surveys.

[118] Annex 1 to the Convention of 1973 concerns the discharge of oil and oily wastes, whilst Annex 2 deals with other noxious substances. Proposals in the Drafting Committee to replace 'applicable' by 'generally accepted' and to delete 'oily' before 'wastes' were not reflected in the text as adopted.

regulations. Thirdly, fishing vessels may be prohibited from fishing in straits, as well as from sailing with their gear unstowed in straits since failure to stow gear would be taken as prima facie evidence of a violation of the straits State's fishing laws. Finally, the legislation of a State bordering a strait prohibiting the loading or unloading of goods, currency or persons may be applied to ships exercising the right of transit passage. In short, the four headings envisage the adoption of legislation about traffic safety and the prevention of pollution, fishing and smuggling in straits, all issues of special concern to States bordering straits. The legislative powers are, however, 'subject to the provisions' of Section 2 of Part III—including, therefore, the rules in Article 44 (duties of States bordering straits).

Paragraph 2 excludes from the legislation any discrimination between foreign ships, as well as any measures in implementation or application of legislation which in their practical effect would deny, hamper or impair the right of transit passage. The rule of non-discrimination was proposed by both the UK and Fiji:[119] its content appears to be similar to that of Article 24(1)(b), although its wording is less specific as regards cargo. The rule about the application of laws and regulations was formulated in the Fiji/UK Group following several discussions of the question of the enforceability of legislation in straits. On the one hand, it was pointed out that there was a need to deter vessels, as well as to compensate anyone who had suffered damage, for example from pollution. On the other hand, it was noted that the terms of Articles 38(2) and 39(1)(c) contained safeguards for States bordering straits; that to give a right of arrest in a strait would undermine the right of transit passage (arrest in port, in an appropriate case, in respect of something done in a strait, was a different matter); and that, in the case of a warship, there was no power (comparable to that in Article 30 in relation to the territorial sea) to require it to leave a strait immediately so long as it was exercising the right of transit passage. The question of enforcement arose in the context of laws and regulations about the prevention of pollution, a topic also then being considered by the Third Committee and now dealt with in Article 233. That article makes clear that if a vessel not entitled to sovereign immunity violates legislation about the safety of navigation or the prevention of pollution (as referred to in Article 42(1)(a) and (b)) and thereby causes or threatens major damage from pollution, a State bordering a strait may take appropriate enforcement measures in relation to the vessel. Such a case would be an exceptional one: enforcement measures in a strait could well create hazards and are not contemplated in Article 42(2).

Paragraph 3 requires appropriate publicity to be given to any laws and regulations of a State bordering a strait and applying there.

Paragraph 4 contains the important obligation of foreign ships in transit passage, whether warships or merchant ships, to comply with laws and regulations made in accordance with paragraph 1.

---

[119] Article 4(2) of A/CONF. 62/C.2/L. 3 and Article in ibid., L. 19.

Paragraph 5 recognizes that whilst such legislation cannot be enforced through the courts against a warship (or other vessel or aircraft entitled to sovereign immunity), the coastal State should not be left without a remedy. The paragraph confirms that international responsibility is borne by the flag State for any loss or damage resulting from acts contrary to such legislation and incurred by States bordering straits. The same rule applies to acts contrary to Part III, including therefore Article 39, which result in loss or damage. The proposal of the Fiji/UK Group[120] to refer also to damage incurred by other States 'in the vicinity of the strait' was not included in Article 42 on account of its vagueness: in such a case, the general rules on State responsibility would apply.

Article 43
Navigational and safety aids and other improvements and the prevention, reduction and control of pollution

User States and States bordering a strait should by agreement co-operate:
(*a*) in the establishment and maintenance in a strait of necessary navigational and safety aids or other improvements in aid of international navigation; and
(*b*) for the prevention, reduction and control of pollution from ships.

This article, which seeks to promote co-operation between States bordering straits and the flag States of vessels and aircraft using straits, is based on a proposal by the UK.[121] The proposal recognized that the international interest in navigation through straits used for international navigation imposed certain restrictions on the rights of States bordering straits and therefore sought to foster co-operation as far as appropriate between those States and the flag States of vessels and aircraft using the strait over such matters as safety aids and the avoidance of pollution from ships. The article, which was put forward with the case of shipping passing through straits such as Malacca particularly in mind, aroused little comment and no controversy. In informal discussions in the Fiji/UK Group and later in the Second Committee Working Group when it was discussing the ISNT,[122] it was noted that the article was cast in conditional, non-mandatory terms: informal suggestions (*a*) to make it obligatory for user States to co-operate and (*b*) to make it clear that decisions about safety aids were for the straits State to make, were not pressed. In 1978, Morocco put forward an amendment[123] designed to make the article obligatory and to extend its scope to

---

[120] In their Article 4(5). Similarly, their Article 4(6), concerning the responsibility of a State bordering a strait for loss or damage to foreign ships or aircraft resulting from actions contrary to Part III, was not included in the Convention. The matter is governed by the general rules of international law.

[121] A/CONF. 62/C.2/L. 3, Article 5.

[122] A/CONF. 62/WP.8/Part II, Article 42.

[123] Amendment C2/22, reading: 'User States and States bordering a strait shall co-operate, by agreement, in the establishment and maintenance in the strait of necessary safety and environmental protection installations and navigation aids, as well as any other device calculated to safeguard the exercise of the right of transit passage in accordance with the provisions of this Part and of other rules of international law.'

cover safety installations and other devices; but this amendment was not accepted by the conference.

Sub-paragraph (*a*) would form a basis for international co-operation to defray the cost of such things as new lighting or buoying schemes, as well as the dredging of new channels for deep draught vessels, particularly if the new facilities were intended to benefit the ships of third States rather than those of the State(s) bordering the strait.[124] Sub-paragraph (*b*) would form a basis for co-operation in the provision of navigational aids in order to prevent the grounding or collision of vessels. That course would reduce the risks of pollution. As a whole, the article should encourage co-operation, whether on a bilateral or a wider basis, between States bordering straits and flag States.

Article 44
Duties of States bordering straits

States bordering straits shall not hamper transit passage and shall give appropriate publicity to any danger to navigation or overflight within or over the strait of which they have knowledge. There shall be no suspension of transit passage.

This article, which specifies three important duties on the part of States bordering straits, follows closely the wording of a proposal by the UK.[125] That proposal was similar in certain respects to Article 1(2)(*e*) and (*f*) of the proposals by Bulgaria and other States, to the effect that:

(*e*) No state shall be entitled to interrupt or suspend the transit of ships through the straits, or engage therein in any acts which interfere with the transit of ships, or require ships in transit to stop or communicate information of any kind.

(*f*) The coastal state shall not place in the straits any installations which could interfere with or hinder the transit of ships.[126]

The UK proposal was put forward with the decision of the ICJ in the *Corfu Channel* case[127] in mind: the Court found that States were obliged to give notice of dangers to navigation in waters under their sovereignty. This duty was codified in Article 15 of the CTSCZ and is repeated in Article 24 of the present Convention. Those articles also contain the concept of not hampering passage, whilst Article 16(4) of the CTSCZ contained a prohibition against the suspension of passage through straits used for international navigation between two parts of the high seas.

In discussions in the Second Committee in 1974, Denmark pointed out, with reference to paragraph 2(*f*) of the proposals by Bulgaria and its co-

---

[124] Some suggestions were voiced during the Conference that lighting, buoying and dredging should be paid for by the imposition of tolls. However, these suggestions were rejected. Japan has agreed to defray the cost of certain dredging work in the Straits of Malacca.

[125] A/CONF. 62/C.2/L. 3, Article 6. It appeared as Article 6 of the Fiji/UK Group's proposed text and as Article 43 of the ISNT.

[126] A/CONF. 62/C.2/L. 11, Article 1(1)(*e*). A similar proposal was contained in Article 3(2)(*d*) about overflight.

[127] *ICJ Reports*, 1949, p. 3.

sponsors, that Denmark's main island was separated from other parts of the country and from Sweden by narrow straits and that it was of vital social and economic importance to be able to build bridges and tunnels across those straits. Denmark's plans 'took full account of the obligation not to hamper the free passage of ships in transit'.[128]

In the Fiji/UK Group, the questions were raised of the difference between 'impede' and 'hamper' and of whether building a high bridge would amount to hampering, even if navigation was not affected. In reply, it was pointed out that the article was designed to forbid activities which could have the incidental effect of inhibiting passage. It was decided to retain the word 'hamper' in the Group's draft articles on that basis.

In subsequent discussions in the Second Committee, the draft article was not subject to much questioning or opposition. Suggestions to qualify the word 'hamper' by the adverb 'unduly' were not accepted, no doubt because it would have weakened the duty and introduced great scope for subjective interpretations. Suggestions about the liability of the flag State of a warship for loss or damage were not pressed in this article.[129] A suggestion about prior notification or authorization was not accepted by the Conference. In 1978, Spain put forward an amendment[130] to delete reference to overflight, but this failed to achieve the requisite support. Morocco tabled proposals specifying certain duties of States making use of straits[131] (insurance requirements and the liability of ships and aircraft for damage caused to the State bordering a strait); but again these proposals were not accepted in the form presented.

Article 44 contains three elements. The first—not hampering passage—means that movement has not to be obstructed by material obstacles or retarded, hindered or 'impeded' (a word used in Article 38). A State bordering a strait may not seek to impose legislative requirements which would in effect retard or prevent passage, nor seek to arrest ships in transit,[132] nor allow the construction of works or installations which would impede ships or aircraft in transit. The second element—notification of dangers—is confined to matters within the knowledge of the State bordering a strait. It was probably not intended to extend the duty of such a State beyond waters under its sovereignty: where, for example, two such States are on opposite sides of a strait, each is responsible for the waters on its side of the boundary running through the strait. Notification is effected by Notices to Mariners and other appropriate means. The third element—non-suspension—is a rule to which no exceptions are made in the Convention. This rule reflects the special status of straits used for international navigation.

[128] *Official Records*, vol. 2, p. 124 (Second Committee, 11th meeting, 22 July 1974).
[129] But see Article 42(5).
[130] Amendment C2/4.
[131] Amendment C2/22.
[132] To attempt an arrest in the middle of a busy strait may be a hazardous operation, e.g. in the case of a large tanker. Arrest in port is a different matter, as is the policing of fishing operations or illicit traffic in narcotics by small boats.

SECTION 3. INNOCENT PASSAGE

Article 45
Innocent passage

1. The regime of innocent passage, in accordance with Part II, section 3, shall apply in straits used for international navigation:

(a) excluded from the application of the regime of transit passage under article 38, paragraph 1; or

(b) between a part of the high seas or an exclusive economic zone and the territorial sea of a foreign State.

2. There shall be no suspension of innocent passage through such straits.

Section 3, which contains a single article, deals with those types of straits used for international navigation in which the basic regime of passage is not transit passage but rather innocent passage.

Article 45 was derived from proposals by the UK[133] and by Bulgaria and others.[134] Both sets of draft articles proposed the regime of non-suspendable innocent passage in the case of a strait used for international navigation between the high seas and the territorial sea of a foreign State. This was the rule in Article 16(4) of the CTSCZ.[135] The UK also proposed the same regime of non-suspendable innocent passage for certain types of straits connecting two parts of the high seas which were excluded from its proposals concerning transit passage, i.e. 'broad' straits through which a good high seas route existed and straits formed by an island of the coastal State to seaward of which a good high seas passage existed. In addition, the rules about traffic schemes in straits (now Article 41) were to apply in such straits. These proposals were accepted by the Fiji/UK Group on Straits.[136] In his ISNT, the Chairman of the Second Committee followed those proposals for the most part. He accepted the main elements, but added references to the EEZ and altered the structure, no doubt in order to give the article greater clarity. This ISNT made two other changes. It removed completely the 'broad' strait from the application of Part III, by means of the new Article 36 (high seas routes, etc.); and, secondly, it did not apply the proposed rules about traffic schemes in other straits (now Article 41) to the straits covered by section 3.

In discussion of the ISNT, the proposal attracted criticism on various

---

[133] A/CONF. 62/C.2/L. 3, Article 8.

[134] A/CONF. 62/C.2/L. 11, Article 2.

[135] In introducing the proposals, the UK delegation (Mr Dudgeon) stated: 'With regard to straits used for international navigation between one part of the high seas and the territorial sea of a foreign State, the interest of the International Community in free navigation is not so strong as in the case of straits linking two parts of the high seas. This difference is recognized by Article 8 of our proposals. Straits linking the high seas with the territorial sea of a foreign State would be subject to the regime of innocent passage as defined in Chapter 2 of our proposals instead of to the regime of transit passage described in Chapter 3 but, because no alternative way of sailing to the territorial sea of the State concerned would exist, we propose that the regime of innocent passage would not be subject to suspension. What we propose in short corresponds with the present position in such straits.'

[136] Article 7 of its Draft Articles. In discussion, it was noted that account should be taken in referring to the 'high seas' of the concept of the EEZ, then under active discussion in the Conference.

grounds, as well as much support. The article was criticized because it divided straits into different categories and did not treat them equally: against this, it was pointed out that different considerations applied to straits connecting two parts of the high seas from those connecting the high seas to the territorial sea of a foreign State.[137] The prohibition against suspension was criticized; but this position attracted little support, probably because it ran counter to Article 16(4) of the CTSCZ. The proposals of Malaysia and its co-sponsors,[138] to the effect that non-suspendable innocent passage should be the regime in all straits used for international navigation, were recalled; but this was in effect a criticism of the whole of section 2 and did not attract much support. The UK again put forward its proposal that the special rules about traffic schemes in other straits should apply also to section 3: although some support was voiced, this proposal was not accepted, with the result that the rules in Article 22 about sea lanes and so forth in the territorial sea apply as part of the regime of innocent passage to straits covered by Article 45. A UK drafting suggestion to make paragraph 1(a) of the article into a simple cross-reference to Article 38(1) was, however, accepted in the ISNT and now appears as Article 45(1)(a). Three informal proposals to the effect that in straits to which Article 45 applies the coastal State could (a) require prior notification or authorization for the passage of foreign warships, (b) confine the passage of research or survey ships, tankers and ships carrying nuclear materials to designated traffic lanes, and (c) require prior notification of the passage of foreign nuclear powered ships, were not accepted by the Conference. Finally, attention was drawn to the need to adopt similar methods for establishing baselines in straits where two States were adjacent or opposite each other before tackling the issue of delimitation; however, this subject is regulated by Part II (Territorial Sea), not by Part III (Straits).

Article 45 applies to two types of strait used for international navigation:

(a) a strait which is formed by an island of the State bordering the strait and its mainland and which is situated in a place where there exists seaward of the island a route through the high seas or EEZ of similar convenience; such a strait is excluded from the transit passage regime by Article 38(1);

(b) a strait connecting the high seas or EEZ and the territorial sea of a foreign State; 'foreign' means the same as in Article 16(4) of the CTSCZ, i.e. a State situated beyond the coastal State(s) bordering the strait. The French text uses the formulation '*d'un autre état*', consistent with that meaning, as is the Spanish '*de otro Estado*'.

In those types of strait, the regime of innocent passage as it is defined in

[137] The questions raised by the *aide-mémoire* of Canada, Chile and Norway of 30 April 1975 (Platzoder, op. cit. above (n. 16), p. 223) about the categories of strait put forward in the Fiji/UK Group's proposals were raised again in these discussions in the Second Committee's working group. These questions were no doubt prompted by particular geographical configurations in those States. The situation in the Aegean Sea was also alluded to by the coastal States concerned.

[138] A/CONF. 62/C.2/L. 16, Part II.

Part II applies in all its respects, subject to the exception that the right of innocent passage through such straits may not be suspended.[139]

APPENDIX

Set of chartlets derived from those made available in the Second Committee by the UK Delegation in 1974. (The numbers of the articles correspond with those in the Convention.)

[139] Article 25(3) permits temporary suspension of the right of innocent passage in specified areas of the territorial sea. Article 45(2) prohibits suspension in straits where it would prevent passage through them.

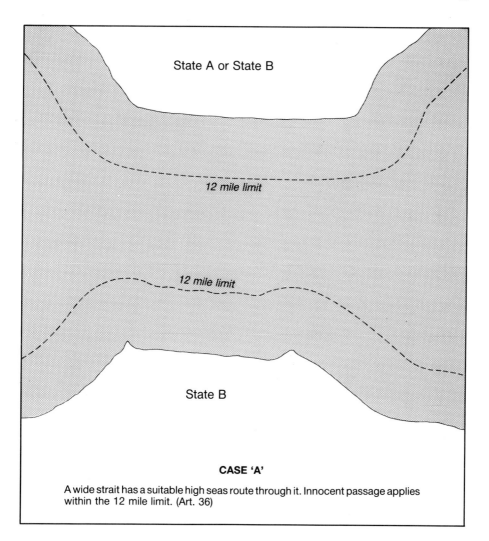

State A or State B

12 mile limit

12 mile limit

State B

CASE 'A'

A wide strait has a suitable high seas route through it. Innocent passage applies within the 12 mile limit. (Art. 36)

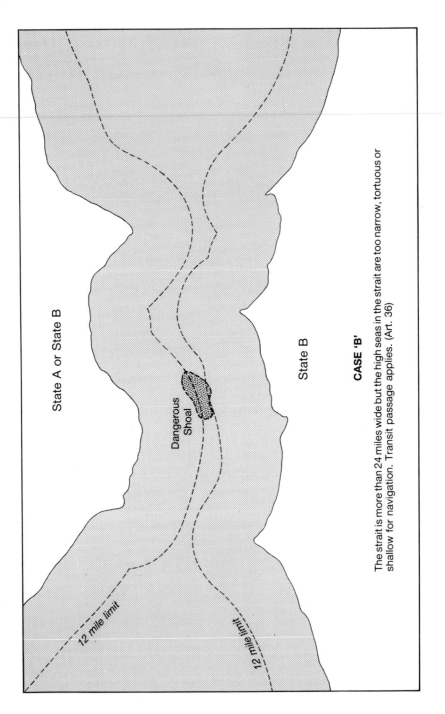

State A or State B

Dangerous
Shoal

State B

12 mile limit

12 mile limit

CASE 'B'

The strait is more than 24 miles wide but the high seas in the strait are too narrow, tortuous or shallow for navigation. Transit passage applies. (Art. 36)

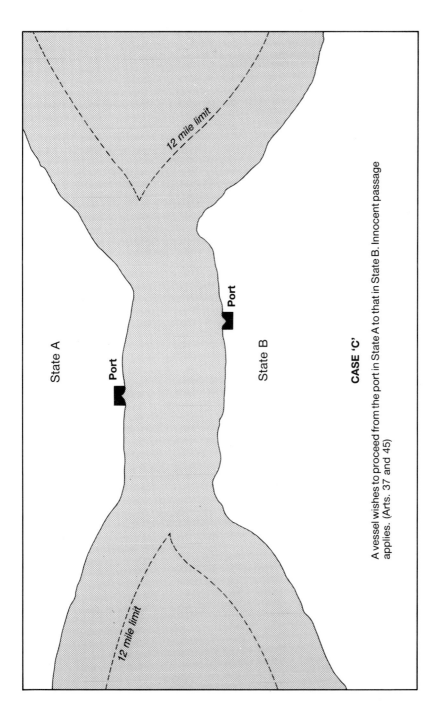

CASE 'C'

A vessel wishes to proceed from the port in State A to that in State B. Innocent passage applies. (Arts. 37 and 45)

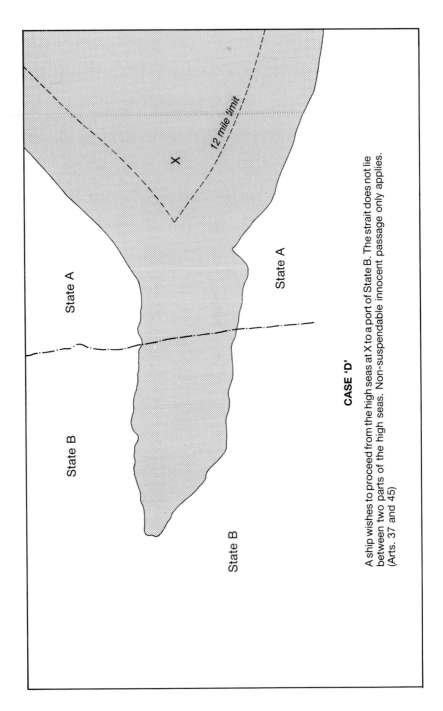

CASE 'D'

A ship wishes to proceed from the high seas at X to a port of State B. The strait does not lie between two parts of the high seas. Non-suspendable innocent passage only applies. (Arts. 37 and 45)

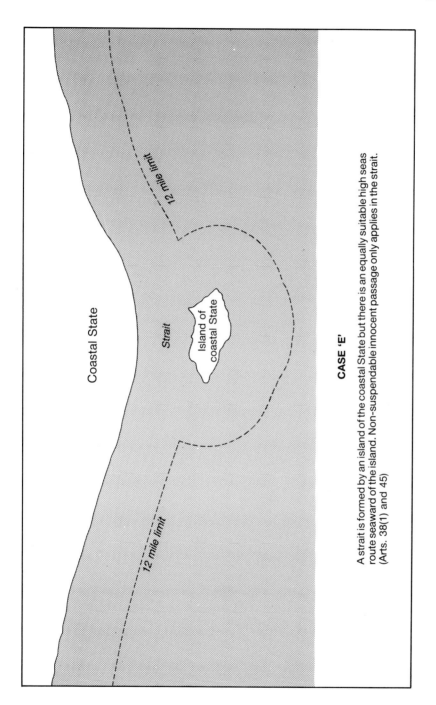

CASE 'E'

A strait is formed by an island of the coastal State but there is an equally suitable high seas route seaward of the island. Non-suspendable innocent passage only applies in the strait. (Arts. 38(1) and 45)

Coastal State

Strait

Island of coastal State

12 mile limit

12 mile limit

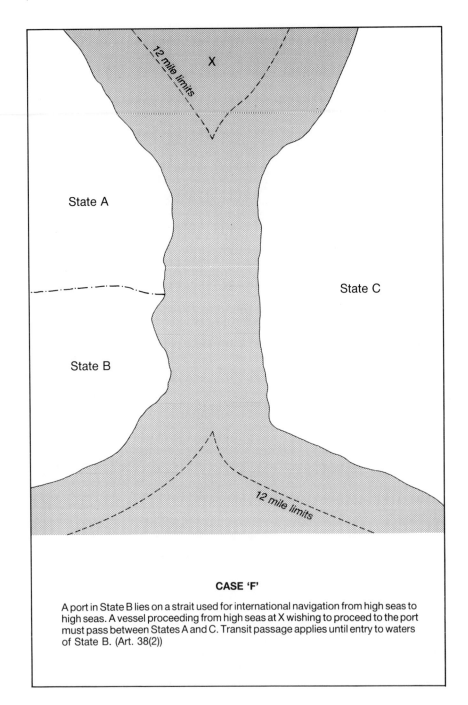

CASE 'F'

A port in State B lies on a strait used for international navigation from high seas to high seas. A vessel proceeding from high seas at X wishing to proceed to the port must pass between States A and C. Transit passage applies until entry to waters of State B. (Art. 38(2))

THE LEGAL SIGNIFICANCE OF MAPS IN BOUNDARY QUESTIONS: A REAPPRAISAL WITH PARTICULAR EMPHASIS ON NAMIBIA*

By SAKEUS AKWEENDA‡

I. INTRODUCTION

THE significance of map evidence in boundary questions has developed. Notwithstanding this development, this subject has been neglected by writers. Maps are often very briefly mentioned. For these reasons a reappraisal is needed. Some of the questions analysed in this article are as follows. How are maps classified in international law? What are the functions of maps in international law? What is the difference between 'incorporation' and 'mere mention' of maps in treaties or other instruments? What is the legal effect of a disclaimer on a map? The official United Nations map of Namibia contains a very interesting disclaimer, and therefore the present writer will examine it in detail. Further, the writer intends to consider the relationship between maps and the conduct of States. The writer is particularly concerned with a complex situation where there is a discrepancy or indeed discrepancies between a line on the ground and a line described in the instrument. Thus, two questions may be raised: first, where did the parties treat the boundary as being located? and second, when can maps be the basis of the legal principle of estoppel? As a case study the writer will refer to the Botswana-Namibia alignment commonly known as the southern boundary of Caprivi Strip. This line runs from 21° E to the junction of the Chobe (Linyanti) River with the Zambezi River. With regard to maps mentioned or incorporated in delimitation treaties the present writer will place special emphasis on instruments respecting the boundaries of Namibia. The practice of tribunals has been examined at length to illustrate various legal issues regarding map evidence. Recently, the question of maps was central to the *Frontier Dispute* case (Burkina Faso/Mali) (1986)[1] and the *Taba* award (Egypt/Israel Arbitration Tribunal) (1988).[2] These cases will be discussed in due course.

* © Dr Sakeus Akweenda, 1990.

‡ LL B, LL M, Ph.D (London). The writer is grateful to Professor Rosalyn Higgins, QC, of the London School of Economics and Political Science, University of London, who read the first draft of this study and offered invaluable comment; and to Mrs Jane Pugh and Mr Gary Llewellyn, Cartographers of the London School of Economics and Political Science, for their most helpful advice on the preparation of maps. The writer alone is responsible for the opinions expressed in the text.

References containing the abbreviations CAB, CO, FO and MPI are to documents in the Public Record Office, London.

[1] *ICJ Reports*, 1986, p. 554.

[2] *International Legal Materials*, 27 (1988), pp. 1421–1538.

II. Definition and Classification of Maps

A 'map' is often referred to as a 'chart', 'sketch map' or 'sketch'. According to Professor Hyde, a map 'is a portrayal of geographical facts, and usually also of political facts, associated with them; for a cartographer commonly endeavours to reveal not only what nature has wrought, but also what states have decreed with respect to her works'.[3] This means that the cartographer depicts not only mountains, rivers, cities and bays, but also the political entity with which they are associated, and the names that they bear.[4]

Maps are classified into two classes: private and official. Prima facie, the former indicates that the map has been prepared by a private individual, whereas the latter refers to a map prepared by an official surveyor or cartographer of a State, its agent or by any person under its auspices. The leading case on the character of an official map is the *Clipperton Island* case (*France* v. *Mexico*) (1931).[5] In an attempt to support its contention, Mexico produced a geographical map printed from the Archives of the Mexican Society of Geography and Statistics, where the island in dispute figures as comprised within the 'Political Military Governments of Spain in North America'. The Arbitrator stated:

> But the official character of this Map cannot be affirmed, because it is not certain that it was drawn by order and under the care of the state, or because the manuscript memorandum which one reads there, namely, that it was used at the Royal Tribunal of the Consulate of Mexico, does not confer official character.[6]

The description to be deduced from this paragraph is that an official map is 'drawn by order and under the care of the state'. But in some cases the dividing line is very thin. The mere fact that the official surveyors or cartographers prepared the map or compiled the data relating to it while in the course of their duties may not necessarily be sufficient to render the map official. Certain additional constitutional requirements have to be complied with. The Canadian case of *Price Bros. & Co.* v. *R* (1924)[7] may illustrate this point clearly. In that case Messrs Beaubien and Tache, respectively the Commissioner and Assistant Commissioner of Crown Lands, prepared certain Departmental maps in 1870 and 1880 depicting the disputed Lake Metis. In addition to these, further maps of the disputed territory were prepared by that Department until 1916. Some of these maps were erroneous,

---

[3] Hyde, 'Maps as Evidence in International Boundary Dipustes', *American Journal of International Law*, 27 (1933), p. 311; Hyde, *International Law Chiefly as Interpreted and Applied by the United States* (2nd edn., 1947), vol. 1, p. 492. See generally Murty, 'Boundaries and Maps', *Indian Journal of International Law*, 4 (1964), p. 367; Lamb, 'Treaties, Maps, and the Western Sector of the Sino-Indian Boundary Dispute', *Australian Yearbook of International Law*, 1 (1965), p. 37; Cukwurah, *The Settlement of Boundary Disputes in International Law* (1967), p. 216.

[4] Hyde, 'Maps as Evidence in International Boundary Disputes', loc. cit. (previous note), p. 311.

[5] *American Journal of International Law*, 26 (1931), p. 390.

[6] Ibid., p. 393.

[7] [1924] 3 DLR 817.

in that they showed only one lake, Metis, instead of three. Mr Justice Gibsone held that none of those departmental maps could bind the Crown, since they had not been sanctioned by an Order in Council.[8] A map prepared by an officer of the State or by his order for private use is not an official map.[9] In determining whether a given map is private or official, the printers are of less significance, since both classes of maps are usually printed by cartographical firms. The publication and printing of maps is a technical work, and some governments do not possess adequate technology.[10]

III. FUNCTIONS OF MAPS IN INTERNATIONAL LAW

As Professor Brownlie states, official and unofficial maps are sources of evidence 'material for the purpose of determining the existence of an alignment and its status in terms of acceptance and recognition by the states concerned'.[11] In matters of evidence, Professor Brownlie points out, logic and common sense are the best guides. Therefore, 'a map has probative value proportionate to its technical qualities'.[12] In this context, a privately published map may have as much significance as an official map if its technical quality is high.[13] The photographs and maps of an aerial survey may

[8] Ibid., p. 840.

[9] See *Duke of Beaufort* v. *Smith* (1849), 154 ER 1290; *Hammond* v. *Bradstreet* (1854), 156 ER 496 at 497; *Daniel* v. *Wilkin* (1852), 155 ER 1016.

[10] See *Temple* case, *ICJ Reports*, 1962, at p. 20; *Frontier Dispute* case, ibid. 1986, p. 554 at p. 584.

[11] Brownlie, *African Boundaries: A Legal and Diplomatic Encyclopaedia* (1979), p. 5. Brownlie states that other sources of evidence of boundaries may emerge from: international agreements, unilateral declarations by governments or individual officials, press releases, statements by ministers in debates of national assemblies, resolutions of the UN organs or regional intergovernmental organizations such as the OAU or the Arab League, archive material, administrative reports of Lands and Surveys departments, boundary descriptions and other references in national legislation, national constitutions, adminstrative practice, the views of experts in the form of monographs and evidence of acquiescence in relation to the boundary.

[12] Ibid., p. 5.

[13] Ibid. The dispute regarding the location of Rietfontein (Lower Rietfontein)—a farm situated between the Orange and the Nossob Rivers—demonstrates the significance of both private and official maps in the settlement of boundary disputes. The circumstances that led to this dispute may be summarized as follows. In 1865 Chief Vilander (Philander) and his following occupied Rietfontein and the adjacent territory. Vilander died on 25 August 1888, and was succeeded by his son David. On 16 December 1889, David set the farm Rietfontein apart as a Mission Station. After the conclusion of the Anglo-German Agreement in 1890, David petitioned the Commissioner of German South West Africa enquiring whether Rietfontein was under British or German sovereignty. See Memorandum from British Embassy, Berlin, 10 August 1894; Despatch No. 88 from Kayser to Gosselin, 17 August 1894, in FO 64/1334. In 1891 Moorees, late Surveyor-General of British Bechuanaland, demarcated the boundary from the Orange to about 26 miles north of the farm Rietfontein by posts and beacons. The result of that demarcation showed Rietfontein as within British Bechuanaland. However, on Herr Kiepert's private map, published in 1892, marked 'Deutscher Kolon Atlas für den amtlichen Gerbranch in den Schutzgebieten', Rietfontein was depicted situated within the German Protectorate. Britain protested, claiming that Kiepert's Map was based on wrong information. The German Authorities surveyed the area and published an official map in 'Mittheilugen aus den deutschen Schutzgebieten' corresponding with Kiepert's Map, placing Rietfontein about 19°45' E, that is, in German South West Africa. Britain eventually accepted the location depicted on these maps. In the present circumstances, Kiepert's privately published map had as much significance as an official map. For a detailed account

register an exact portrayal of utmost value to a commission or a tribunal burdened with the task of ascertaining the location of the boundary. This opinion was expressly stated in the *Frontier Dispute* case (1986). The Chamber, having discovered that all the important official maps were missing, observed that it was 'confronted with the unusual situation which does not ease its burden'.[14] The photographs in particular are the best means of disclosing every physical aspect of the area in question of which the commission or tribunal may seek to examine.

Professor Hyde states that in the course of a boundary arbitration 'the most obvious function of an official map issued under the auspices of a particular litigant may be that of holding that litigant in leash'.[15] Maps may illustrate the interpretation put on instruments by States concerned. This function was stressed by the Judicial Committee of the Privy Council in the *Labrador Boundary* case (1927):

> The maps here referred to, even when issued or accepted by departments of the Canadian Government, cannot be treated as admissions binding on that Government; for even if such an admission could be effectively made, the departments concerned are not shown to have had any authority to make it. But the fact that through a long series of years, and until the present dispute arose, all the maps issued in Canada either supported or were consistent with the claim now put forward by Newfoundland, is of some value as showing the construction put upon the Orders in Council and statutes by persons of authority and by the general public in the Dominion.[16]

Maps are often annexed to the delimitation treaties, reports of commissions demarcating the boundaries and arbitration awards, in order to illustrate the course of the boundary. However, in some cases the maps are not only annexures, they are incorporated into the texts. In the former case the primary function of the map is to illustrate the text, whereas in the latter it defines the delimitation. However, in both instances the maps cannot be taken as conclusive evidence in the determination of disputes that may arise concerning the location of the boundary.[17] Sometimes the course of the boundary is described solely by the map. A classical example of this case is the Convention between Britain and China of 6 August 1898 respecting the extension of Hong Kong.[18] In that Convention, the territory leased to Britain for the period of ninety-nine years was described only by the map. The Convention, so far as material, provides that 'the limits of British territory shall be enlarged under lease to the extent indicated generally on

see J.F. Herbst, 'Report on the Rietfontein Area' (1908), Cd.4323; Despatch No. 84 from Sir Edward Malet to Lord Kimberley, 13 August 1894, and Despatch No. 92 from British Embassy, Berlin, to Lord Kimberley, 21 August 1894, in FO 64/1334.

[14] *ICJ Reports*, 1986, p. 584; see also Hyde, 'Maps as Evidence in International Boundary Disputes', loc. cit. above (n. 3), p. 316; Chao, 'East China Sea: Boundary Problems Relating to the Tiao-Yu-T'ai Island', *Chinese Yearbook of International Law*, 2 (1982), p. 45 at pp. 51–6.

[15] Hyde, op. cit. above (n. 3), vol. 1, p. 495.

[16] [1927] 2 DLR 401 at 427.

[17] See Sandifer, *Evidence Before International Tribunals* (revised edn., 1975), p. 230.

[18] *British and Foreign State Papers* (hereinafter *BFSP*), 90 (1897–8), pp. 16–18 (text).

the annexed map. The exact boundaries shall be hereafter fixed when proper surveys have been made by officials appointed by the two Governments."[19] The practice whereby the contracting parties rely solely on the map in defining the boundary is extremely rare. It appears that it is usually adopted as a temporary measure, that is, pending the drafting of the text. A good example in this respect is the above-mentioned Convention regarding Hong Kong. It can be criticized on the ground that the boundary defined by the map alone lacks precision, with the exception perhaps of boundaries constituted by meridians, parallels and straight lines joining defined points. Therefore, under such circumstances, the map evidence cannot be treated as conclusive proof.

IV. Incorporation and Mere Mention of Maps in Instruments

In some cases maps are expressly made an integral part of the text to which they are attached, whereas in others they are merely referred to or mentioned as instruments consulted by the negotiators. In the former case the map employed should be completely identified in the text, and a mere mention is insufficient.[20] Further, it is only the former which may be said to assume the character of primary or original evidence. Professor Sandifer states that in such cases the 'supposed territorial limits' may be sought in the map itself.[21] Moreover, Sandifer continues, 'a map of this character will take precedence over any other maps that may be introduced as evidence and will be accepted as the best source collateral to the text of the treaty itself for the determination of the boundary'.[22] A classical example of this type of map is the map of the Zambezi River descriptive of the Namibia-Zambia alignment.[23] This map was prepared by a Joint Boundary Commission consisting of representatives of the Union of South Africa—the then Mandatory Power—and Northern Rhodesia, which determined the main channel of the Zambezi in August 1931. Having identified the main channel the Commission depicted the course of the boundary and the islands on this map. The Commission signed it and annexed it to their report. The Exchange of Notes between the Union and Northern Rhodesia which delimited the Zambezi incorporated this map in these words: 'His Majesty's Government in the Union are prepared . . . to agree that the map referred to in the above-quoted report, signed at Katima Molilo [sic] on the 8th of August, 1931, should be accepted for the purpose of defining the position of the "thalweg".'[24] The official character of this map can easily be

---

[19] Ibid., p. 17.
[20] Jones, *Boundary-Making: A Handbook for Statesmen, Treaty Editors and Boundary Commissioners* (1945), p. 64.
[21] Sandifer, op. cit. above (n. 17), p. 230.
[22] Ibid.
[23] See *South African Treaty Series*, 1933.
[24] Ibid.

ascertained: it bears the signatures of the Commissioners, it was drawn in the Surveyor General's Office in Pretoria and it was printed by the Government Printer, and the aerial survey was conducted under the authority of the Union Government.[25]

The present author maintains that if a map has been mentioned in an instrument, recourse may always be had to it in order to ascertain or confirm the real intention of the parties. Thus, such a map may be considered as a supplementary means of interpretation or *travaux préparatoires*. Significantly, the United States Supreme Court in *US* v. *State of Texas* (1895)[26] stated that 'the map to which the contracting parties referred is to be given the same effect as if it had been expressly made a part of the treaty'.[27] Four official maps regarding the boundaries of Namibia fall into the category under consideration. The first is the 'Intelligence Division of the War Office Map' of 1889 referred to in Article III (2) paragraph 4 of the Anglo-German Agreement of 1890. This treaty delimited the British and German spheres of influence in Africa. The above-mentioned article defined the boundary of German South West Africa, as Namibia was known at that time, following the 20° E, 22° S, and 21° E. The article in question provides that 'The course of the above boundary is traced in general accordance with a Map officially prepared for the British Government in 1889'. The three other examples are as follows. The Anglo-Portuguese Boundary Commission which drafted the Ruacana Agreement respecting the delimitation of the disputed boundary between Angola and the SWA Protectorate on 5 July 1920 attached three maps to the agreement. However, these maps were not incorporated in the text. These maps are: (*a*) map of Owambo—Northern Namibia—and Southern Angola illustrating the territory claimed by Germany and Portugal;[28] (*b*) sketch of the Ruacana Falls on the Kunene River;[29] and (*c*) sketch of the eastern end of the gorge at the Ruacana Falls showing the position of the boundary beacon agreed to by the British and Portuguese Boundary Commissioners on 5 July 1920.[30] The signatories—Great Britain and Portugal—agreed that they should not be part of the instrument. These official maps are still of immense importance to the Angola-Namibia boundary. The Boundary

---

[25] Article 3 of the Lateran Treaty—the Treaty of 11 February 1919 between the Holy See and Italy which created the Vatican City—incorporates a map in these words: 'The confines of the Vatican City are indicated on a plan which constitutes the first appendix to the present treaty of which it forms an integral part': *American Journal of International Law*, 23 (1929), Supplement, p. 187. On the status of the Holy See and the Vatican City as subjects of international law see Kunz, 'The Status of the Holy See in International Law', ibid. 46 (1952), p. 308; Rosalyn Higgins, *Conflicts of Interest, International Law in a Divided World* (1965), pp. 11–39; H. Wright, 'The Status of the Vatican City', *American Journal of International Law*, 38 (1944), p. 452; Mr Koeck's statement at the UN Conference on Succession of States in respect of Treaties in 1977, Doc. A/CONF. 80/16.

[26] 162 US 1.

[27] Ibid., at p. 37; see also *Noonan* v. *Braley* (1863), 67 US 2 Black, 499; *Jefferis* v. *East Omaha Land Co.* (1890), 134 US 178.

[28] FO 371/5515.

[29] Ibid.

[30] FO 371/4402, pp. 347–53.

Commission depicted the point at the Ruacana Falls from where the boundary commences running eastwards along a parallel to the Okavango River on the above-mentioned maps (*b*) and (*c*). The Ruacana Agreement did not enter into force.[31] Interestingly, Article 2 of the Portuguese-South African Agreement of 22 June 1926 which eventually settled the boundary question provides that the boundary follows 'the middle line of the Kunene River . . . up to a point at the Ruacana Falls, above the crest or lip where the said middle line crosses the parallel of latitude, passing through the beacon placed on the left bank of the said river in July 1920, by a commission appointed by the British and Portuguese Governments'. Thus, in order to ascertain the precise location of this point, recourse may always be had to these maps.

In some cases there may be discrepancies or contradictions between the express terms of the treaty and the map which has either been mentioned or incorporated in the text. In such circumstances, it may be extremely difficult to decide which of the two documents should override the other. Some treaties, however, contain express provision to this effect.[32] In such circumstances the express clause is decisive. If, however, the treaty is silent on this issue the rules of interpretation will be applied to both the map and the text in order to elicit the real intention of the parties. There is no intention at this juncture to give a detailed analysis of this problem: it is more properly examined under a separate heading.[33]

V. THE LEGAL SIGNIFICANCE OF A DISCLAIMER ON A MAP

A disclaimer on a map, as Professor Brownlie points out, has the particular effect of avoiding any assertion that the government or international organization publishing the map has become bound to accept the alignments shown by virtue of the legal concepts of estoppel, admission, acquiescence or recognition.[34] Further, this writer maintains that a disclaimer is an excellent warning to those consulting the map that certain issues are uncertain or that they do not fall within the scope of the map. The presence of disclaimers on maps 'will not reduce their value as expert evidence, at least in any substantial degree'.[35] A disclaimer may expressly indicate that

---

[31] The issue was settled by the Agreements between Portugal and the Union of South Africa of 22 June and 1 July 1926.

[32] Article 29 of the Peace Treaty of Versailles (1919) is a good example. Having clearly identified the boundaries of Germany on the map, namely those 'drawn in red on a one-in-a-million map' which was annexed to the Peace Treaty, this Article provides that 'in the case of any discrepancies between the text of the Treaty and this map or any other map which may be annexed, the text will be final': *BFSP*, 112 (1919), p. 27.

[33] Below, pp. 237–44; 246–51.

[34] Brownlie, op. cit. above (n. 11), p. 5.

[35] Ibid.

the map in question is not intended to be an authority on the lines delineated.[36]

The official UN map of Namibia contains a very interesting disclaimer concerning the international boundaries depicted on that map. The legal effect of this disclaimer on the alignments depicted on the map, as well as its effect on the question of title to Walvis Bay and the Penguin Islands, will be examined in due course.[37] Further, the disclaimer on a map which was invoked by Germany in the *Walfish Bay Boundary* case will be discussed later.[38] The 'Map Illustrating the Partition of Africa, 1870–1913, scale 1:16,093,500', published by Stanford's Geographical Establishment in London, contains a disclaimer concerning the Botswana-Namibia boundary. It states: 'the boundary of the Caprivi Finger is approximate only.'[39]

VI. The Practice of Tribunals regarding Maps

Until fairly recently, map evidence was admitted by international tribunals with a good deal of hesitation. Indeed, as the Tribunal observed in the *Beagle Channel* award *(Argentina v. Chile)* (1977),[40] 'the evidence of a map could certainly never *per se* override an attribution made, or a boundary-line defined, by Treaty,—and even where such an attribution or definition was ambiguous or uncertain, map evidence of what it might be was accepted with caution'.[41] Tribunals admitted map mainly for illustrative purposes.[42] The practice of tribunals on the subject of map evidence has developed. Map evidence has also been submitted in municipal courts.

Map evidence was invoked in the English courts as early as 1854. In *Hammond v. Bradstreet* (1854)[43] the plaintiff alleged that the defendants took certain goods from his dwelling-house in the county of Norfolk, which was situated on the north side of an estuary called Breydon Water formed by the junction of the rivers Waveney and Wensum. The defendants pleaded that they took them from the county of Suffolk. At the trial, in

---

[36] See, for instance, a map annexed to the Exchange of Notes between the UK and His Highness Sir Muda Hassanal Bolkiah, Sultan and Yang Di-Pertuan of Negara Brunei Darussalam, concerning the arrangements for a UK Force in Negara Brunei Darussalam, of 22 September 1983, descriptive of the land, premises, training area and other facilities occupied by the British Forces in Negara Brunei. The disclaimer provides that the 'map is not considered by either Government as an authority on the delimitation of international boundaries': *UK Treaty Series*, No. 31 (1984), Cmnd. 9207. This map was referred to in para. 5(2) of the Annex to the Exchange of Notes.

[37] Below, p. 251.

[38] Below, p. 216.

[39] MPI/377; CAB 29/1.

[40] HMSO, London, 1977.

[41] Ibid., p. 82.

[42] In the *Behring Sea* arbitration (*Great Britain v. USA*) (1893), for instance, Britain submitted maps illustrating resort and migration routes of sea fur seals in the North Pacific, and the area frequented by seals in the period extending from 15 July to 16 August 1891: *Behring Sea Arbitration, Papers Relating to the Proceedings of the Tribunal of Arbitration* (in 4 vols.), vol. 3 (HMSO, London, 1893), Maps 2 & 3.

[43] 156 ER 496.

order to show that the house in question was situated in Norfolk, the plaintiff tendered in evidence an ancient map, printed on paper from an
engraved copperplate, and having on the face of it, as part of the original
impression, the following words and figures: 'A new map of the county of
Suffolk, taken from the original map published by John Kirby, in 1736,
who took an actual and accurate survey of the whole county; now repub-
lished, with corrections and additions, by Joshua and William Kirby, sons
of the author, 1766, and engraved by John Ryland.'[44] Judge Coleridge challenged the authenticity of this map in these words:

> But assuming it to be what the inscription upon it declared it to be, a map pre-
> pared in 1766, in part from an older map in 1736, by Joshua and William Kirby,
> sons of John Kirby, who made the survey in 1736, at the utmost, this was only a
> declaration by Joshua and William, that they believed the boundaries to be as des-
> cribed by them, or, that they were as described by them . . . . They do not appear
> to have been deputed to make the map by any persons interested in the question,
> nor to have any knowledge of their own on the subject, nor to have been in any way
> connected with the district, so as to make it probable that they had such know-
> ledge.[45]

For the reasons stated in this paragraph the evidence of this map was
declared inadmissible. This case illustrates the fact that courts scrutinize
maps which are not 'original' or 'primary' with extreme care. Furthermore,
in this case, the cartographer's source of information was a matter of primary importance. This is almost always the case in every boundary question.[46] This caution is necessary because private persons depend to a large
extent upon information obtained from general and unauthoritative
sources.[47]

In *USA* v. *Rio Grande Dam and Irrigation Company* (1899), map evidence was admitted to illustrate whether the Rio Grande was navigable and
whether the diversion of this river was causing serious injury to other ripar-
ian States.[48] The United States, the plaintiff, brought proceedings to
restrain the defendants from constructing a dam across the Rio Grande in
the territory of New Mexico and appropriating the water of that river for
the purpose of irrigation. The plaintiff alleged that the impounding of the
waters by the construction of the dam and reservoir, and the diversion of
the waters for irrigation, would so deplete and prevent the flow of the
river through its channel as to seriously obstruct its navigable capacity

---

[44] Ibid., p. 497.
[45] Ibid., p. 499.
[46] See *Labrador Boundary* case (1927), [1927] 2 DLR 401 at 427; *Pollard* v. *Scott*, 170 ER 66; *R* v.
The Inhabitants of Milton, 174 ER 711; *Mercer* v. *Denne* (1902), [1904] 2 Ch. 534, at 544–7; Holdich,
'Geographical Problems in Boundary Making', *Geographical Journal*, 47 (1916), p. 421; Leverson,
ibid. 13 (1899), p. 478; Sandifer, op. cit. above (n. 17), p. 239.
[47] See consideration of *R* v. *Price Brothers*, below.
[48] 174 US 690.

throughout its entire course.[49] The court examined an official map of New Mexico and the USA showing the source, trend, course and mouth of the Rio Grande and concluded that the river was not navigable within the territory of New Mexico.[50]

Map evidence played a major part in *R* v. *Price Bros. & Co.* (1925),[51] where the Supreme Court of Canada had to determine the limits of a lake called Metis. This case requires a detailed examination, since it involves the legal significance of maps of unsurveyed areas or incorrect surveys, as well as private maps. The material facts of the case may be summarized as follows. A grant was made in 1693 by Frontenac, Intendant of New France, upon the request of Augustin Rover, for and in the name of his son Louis Rover, for the concession of Lake Metis, which discharged itself into a river of the same name. After various changes of ownership, the respondents, Price Bros. & Co., became the proprietor in 1922. The respondents alleged that at the time of the grant the bodies of water were considered only as a single lake. But the modern maps depicted three lakes connected by channels under the names Metis, Lac à La Croix and Lac à l'Anguille, these being respectively the upper, middle and lower lakes. There was no evidence except from the grant and maps as to what these lakes were called at the time of the grant. The respondents produced a number of maps which were admitted in evidence. These maps came originally from various sources, but were mostly selected from the collection of maps at the Dominion Archives. The earliest were of the date 1755; and in all these maps down to 1863 there was a single lake shown at the head of the river Metis. However, none of these maps purported to be from actual survey of the locality; those who drew them relied on information supplied by travellers.[52] In one Holland's map the lake was depicted under the name Metis, surrounded by lines presumably to represent the boundaries of the grant, but the lake was, according to the scale, somewhat less than ten miles in length and had an extreme breadth of upwards of five miles. Some of the official maps printed by the Department of Crown Lands represented the seigniory in accordance with the respondents' contention; others adopted that of the Crown. It was urged on behalf of the Crown that none of the departmental maps cited by the respondents had been made official by Order in Council, and consequently they could not bind the Crown.[53] Mr Justice Newcombe noted:

Maps are from their nature of very slight evidence. Geographers often lay them down upon incorrect surveys or information, copying the mistakes of one another. This may be illustrated by reference to Holland's map of 1803, where it is said,

[49] Ibid., 692.

[50] Ibid., 694, 698.

[51] *Canada Law Reports* [1926] SCR 28; appeal from the decision of Quebec Superior Court (Gibsone J), [1924] 3 DLR 817.

[52] For the list of maps see [1924] 3 DLR at pp. 828–30, note a.

[53] [1924] 3 DLR at 840.

under the figure of Lake Metis, surrounded by lines to represent the boundaries of the seigniory, that these lakes are laid down not from actual survey but from information of travellers.[54]

Newcombe stressed that Holland's map was certainly drawn 'without any reliable information'.[55] He continued:

[T]hese are all maps of an unsurveyed district, and they are really of little or no value to prove the facts which they depict or represent; they may however be useful as admissions against the party who produces them; and, in this aspect, the inference which they support is that, until the time of Ballantyne's survey, everybody, both cartographers and the persons from whom they got their information, were under the impression that the river Metis had its source in one lake only.[56]

On the subject of a map prepared by a private person, Mr Justice Newcombe, with whom Chief Justice Anglin and Mr Justice Mignault concurred, had this to say:

Maps, when they have no conventional or statutory significance, should be regarded merely as representing the opinions of the persons who constructed them, they furnish at best no adequate proof, and none when it appears that they are founded upon misleading or unreliable information or upon reasons which do not go to establish the theory or opinion represented, and when they have not the qualifications requisite to found proof of reputation.[57]

Further, the Court held that although some of the private maps were filed with the provisional government, they were not admissible as public documents against the Crown. Thus the Court could not apply the principles of admission and estoppel against the Crown, merely because the Crown issued them. The maps were not intended for the purpose of establishing facts or as admissions: they were merely illustrative, and the proof must come from sources outside them. Neither the Minister nor the Governor in Council could in the reasonable course of administration consider and conclude all the particulars or details which were depicted on the map, or all the questions which, if the map imported admission or proof, it might be used to determine. Newcombe declared that the map makers of the department 'use the information which is available, and they in turn, no matter how carefully they execute their work, are not proof against oversight or errors, the consequences of which might be very serious if these erroneous representations are to be taken as determining the facts with relation to pending claims'.[58] The Court held that the grant should be limited to one lake, the upper one, as upon the evidence, including the maps, the grant

[54] Ibid., p. 44.
[55] Ibid.
[56] Ibid.
[57] Ibid., p. 45.
[58] Ibid., p. 46.

could not be given an interpretation of wider import than a restricted literal meaning of the language used carried with it.[59]

Maps published by the interested parties during the 'critical date'—period of delimitation—are of special significance: they assist the tribunal in tracing the limits of hills, valleys, plateaux and other geographical facts referred to in the treaty. As Paul-Honoré-Vigliani, the Arbitrator in the *Manica* case *(Great Britain v. Portugal)* (1897), noted, the location of such places must have been 'under the eyes' of the negotiators.[60] One of the principal questions in that case was the meaning of the expression 'Plateau of Manica' employed in Article II of the Anglo-Portuguese Agreement of 11 June 1891 which delimited the 'sphere of influence' of the two States in east and central Africa. Vigliani placed reliance on maps in order to establish the intention of the plenipotentiaries as to the limits of the plateau:

> It is in reality to the whole extent of this territory, formed by a series of highlands connected with the ancient plateau of Manica, that the geographical maps published in the two countries interested at the time when the treaty was drawn up, applied the designation 'plateau' of Manica in reference both to the text of Article II and to the intention of the negotiators.[61]

Clearly, map evidence in the *Manica* arbitration contributed to the location of geographical names.[62] Similarly, maps and charts as evidence played a significant part in the *Walfish Bay Boundary* arbitration (1911) in interpreting the phrase 'including the plateau' which had been adopted by Dyer in the Proclamation of 12 May 1878.[63] Germany claimed that, till 1885, it was admitted by the British authorities that the district situated between Scheppmansdorf and Ururas, then claimed by Britain, did not belong to the territory of Walvis Bay. Germany invoked maps drawn before 1885, where the southern boundary was shown as terminating at Scheppmansdorf. However, maps published by the Admiralty had a disclaimer: 'approximate boundaries of the station of Walfisch Bay'. Germany maintained that the disclaimer was intended to refer 'to the circumstance that the proposal put forward by the Angra Pequeña and West Coast Mixed Commission was then awaiting a decision, the object of the proposal being to change the word "Rooibank" employed in Dyer's Proclamation and substitute for it the word "Rooikop" '.[64] Thus the disclaimer, according to

---

[59] Mr Justice Duff, in his dissenting opinion, noted that the fair inference to be drawn from the evidence of maps appeared to be that at the beginning of the nineteenth century, the whole chain of lakes was the subject designated by the term 'Lake Metis', according to the use of those familiar with the locality. Duff admitted that that was by no means necessarily conclusive as to the construction of the grant of 1693, but it was sufficient to establish a prima facie case in favour of the suppliants on the question of fact as to what was the subject or what were the waters designated in 1693 by the appellation '*Lac Métis*': ibid., p. 39.

[60] Moore, *International Arbitrations* (1898), vol. 5, p. 4985 at p. 4991.

[61] Ibid., p. 4991.

[62] See *Palmas* case, *UN Reports of International Arbitral Awards* (hereinafter *UNRIAA*), vol. 2, p. 829 at p. 852; *Costa Rica–Panama Boundary* case (1914), ibid. vol. 11, p. 528.

[63] The facts of this case are not examined in this work.

[64] *UNRIAA*, vol. 11, p. 263 at p. 277.

Germany, had no significant effect on the Admiralty maps. In that case the Cape Colony requested Wrey to survey the area. After the completion of his work, he drew up a report dated 14 January 1886, accompanied by a map on which he depicted the boundary of Walvis Bay, by means of thirteen pillars designated by letters.[65] The key issue was whether the boundaries marked on Wrey's map were those intended by Captain Dyer who annexed the territory on 12 March 1878. Wrey's map was indeed recognized in a joint report of the mixed commission of January 1889, consisting of Dr Goering and Colonel Philips, respectively representatives of Germany and Britain, as representing 'accurately the position and topographical features of the ground'.[66] Throughout the proceedings, Professor Prida, the Arbitrator, described the contentions of the parties with reference to this map, because of its accuracy. The employment of maps clearly lessened the Arbitrator's burden in tracing the limits of various claims:

That a mere glance at the map is enough to show that, taking the harbour at Walfish Bay as the centre, the radius which connects it with Nuberoff is longer than the one connecting it with the mission buildings at Rooibank and a little shorter than the one connecting it with Ururas, for which reason Captain Dyer's delimitation, supposed to be in excess of his instructions, would affect both extremities of the territory without his anxiety to justify his action in one case, and not in the other, being explained.[67]

In an attempt to demonstrate the accuracy of the demarcation carried out by Wrey, Great Britain argued, *inter alia*, that at the time of annexation of Walvis Bay by Captain Dyer, on 12 March 1878, the latter had no map of the interior, therefore he 'could not define with accuracy particular spots'.[68] Germany submitted two copies of Dr Stapff's Map of the lower valley of Kuisip—part of the disputed territory;[69] but it did not have much influence on the Arbitrator.

In the *Misiones Boundary* case *(Argentina v. Brazil)* (1889), the Tribunal had to determine title to the territory popularly called Misiones.[70] The dispute as to sovereignty over this tract grew out of a difference as to the position of the two rivers. It was admitted that the line between the two countries began, at the north, at the River Parana, opposite the mouth of the Iguaqua, and followed the course of the latter river for some distance eastwards; that farther to the south it followed the course of the Uruguay, and between these rivers it was formed by two connecting or practically connecting streams. But the two countries, Argentina and Brazil, were

---

[65] For Wrey's map, see *British Parliamentary Papers*, 1911, vol. 52, p. 745 (Africa No. 1, 1911) (Cd. 5857).

[66] *UNRIAA*, vol. 11, p. 272. In 1885 the Angra Pequeña and West Coast Mixed Claims Commission declared that the eastern boundary of Walvis Bay marked on Hahn's map, published in 1879, and copied in Juta's map of 1885, was incorrect: ibid., pp. 269, 288.

[67] Ibid., p. 306.

[68] Ibid., p. 284.

[69] Ibid., p. 286.

[70] Moore, *International Arbitrations* (1898), vol. 2, pp. 1969–2026.

unable to agree on the positions and courses of these streams: the latter maintained that they were the Santo Antonio and Pepiry-Guaçû, and the former claimed that they were San Antonio-Guazú and the Pepiry or Pequiry-Guazú situated more to the east. Brazil claimed that the correct names of the rivers mentioned by Argentina were Chapecó and Chopim. By a Treaty of 7 September 1889 Argentina and Brazil agreed to submit their respective claims to arbitration. Argentina invoked a map which was known as the *Mapa de las Cortes*, or Map of the Courts. It was prepared in 1749 during the tedious period of secret negotiations between Spain and Portugal. On that map, Spain and Portugal, the predecessor States, had marked the course of the boundary stipulated by the 1750 secret agreement with red lines. On 17 January 1751 the plenipotentiaries of Portugal and Spain signed various instruments at Madrid, among which were a Treaty of instruction to commissioners charged with the demarcation of the boundary; and a Protocol, warning the commissioners against the possible inaccuracies of the *Mapa de las Cortes*.[71] This Protocol provided in part as follows:

Whereas we have been governed by a manuscript geographical map in drawing up this treaty and the instructions for its execution; for this reason a copy of the said map is to be supplied to each party of the commissioners of each sovereign, for their guidance . . . We likewise declare that although according to the information of both courts we hold all things noted in the said map as very probable; admitting also that some of the territories demarcated have not been visited by persons now living, and that others have been taken from the maps of trustworthy persons who have travelled through them, though, perhaps, with little skill to represent them by sketch, on which account there may be some notable variations upon the ground, both in the situations of mountains, and in the origins and courses of rivers, and even in the names of some of them, because it is customary for each nation in America to give them different names, or for other reasons . . . the contracting sovereigns . . . have agreed, that any variation there . . . shall proceed as, in accordance with the treaty, the mind and intention of their majesties is manifested in the whole of it.[72]

Argentina claimed that the *Mapa de las Cortes* formed an indestructible judicial foundation, for it showed the Misiones as a Spanish territory. Brazil expressed doubts as to the accuracy and authenticity of the copy of this map submitted by Argentina.[73] It was alleged that in the collection of treaties by Borges de Castro a 'pretended copy' of this map was published, evidently altered in favour of Portugal: it altered the tributaries of the River Uruguay, changing the name of the Uruguay-Pita, one of the 'guides of the line of demarcation', to Yriboba, and transferring the name of the former to another river. It also bore on its back an inscription different from the true one. Argentina admitted that the original map had disappeared from the

[71] Ibid., p. 1998.
[72] Ibid.
[73] Ibid.

archives at Madrid during the occupation of Napoleon, but copies of it had been found in France, Spain and Portugal. The Arbitrator, President Grover Cleveland of the United States, decided in favour of the Brazilian claims. The map was not specifically mentioned in the award. Thus, the evidence of the *Mapa de las Cortes* was not decisive, but served mainly as a reference. Further, the Protocol warning against possible errors on that map prevented undue reliance being placed on the facts it purported to convey.

The Courts are definitely more cautious in admitting maps published by private persons than official maps. The leading authority on this subject is the *Labrador Boundary* case *(Boundary between Canada and Newfoundland)* (1927).[74] Lord Cave, who delivered the opinion of the Judicial Committee of the Privy Council, accurately stated the reasons:

Maps published by private persons must, of course, be received with caution, as such persons depend to a large extent upon information obtained from general and unauthoritative sources; but from a map issued or accepted by a public authority, and especially by an authority connected with one of the Governments concerned, an inference may not improperly be drawn.[75]

Similarly, in the *Island of Timor* arbitration *(Netherlands v. Portugal)* (1914), Charles Lardy, who acted as sole Arbitrator of the Permanent Court of Arbitration, stated that a private map 'could not be weighed in value with the two official maps signed by the commissioners or delegates of the two states'.[76] But, if the privately published map has satisfied the necessary conditions, it will nevertheless serve as evidence. In the *Palmas Island* case[77] Judge Huber emphasized that 'the first condition required of maps that are to serve as evidence on points of law is their geographical accuracy'.[78] Huber further stated that 'official or semi-official maps seem capable of fulfilling these conditions, as they would be of special interest in cases where they do not assert the sovereignty of the country of which the government has caused them to be issued'.[79] The existence of inaccuracies on any map which features in boundary proceedings will certainly diminish its probative value, although this may not affect its admissibility for other purposes. In the *Polish-Czechoslovakian Frontier* case *(Question of Jaworzina)* (1923), the PCIJ declared that maps and their tables cannot be regarded as conclusive proof independently of the text in the treaties and decisions.[80] However, the PCIJ concluded that in the case under discussion the maps 'confirm in a singularly convincing manner the conclusions drawn from the documents and from a legal analysis of them; and they are

---

[74] [1927] 2 DLR 401; 137 TLR 187.
[75] [1927] 2 DLR 401, 425.
[76] *American Journal of International Law*, 9 (1915), p. 240 at p. 259.
[77] *UNRIAA*, vol. 2, p. 829.
[78] Ibid., p. 852.
[79] Ibid.
[80] *PCIJ*, Series B, No. 8, p. 18.

certainly not contradicted by any document'.[81] In the *Minquiers and Ecrehos* case (*France* v. *UK*) (1953),[82] Judge Levi Carneiro, in his individual opinion, declined to take the evidence of maps into consideration. The issue in that case was sovereignty over a group of islets called the Minquiers and the Ecrehos. The UK cited the map drawn by Stieler, editions of 1905 and 1932, which depicts the disputed islets as British territory. The French Agent on the other hand submitted several other maps during the oral arguments, some of which showed the Ecrehos as British but made no reference to the Minquiers. Other maps submitted by France omitted both groups of islets, or in some cases showed the Ecrehos as falling outside the British sovereignty. Judge Carneiro remarked that evidence supplied by maps is not always decisive in the settlement of legal questions relating to territorial sovereignty. Such evidence, Judge Carneiro added, 'may, however, constitute proof of the fact that the occupation or exercise of sovereignty was well known'.[83] In view of the conflicts in the maps submitted by the parties, Judge Carneiro observed that 'a searching and specialized study would be required in order to decide which of the contending views in respect of maps should prevail. At any rate, maps do not constitute a sufficiently important contribution to enable a decision to be based on them.'[84] For these reasons, Judge Carneiro concluded that he could not take the evidence of maps into consideration.

In the *Frontier Land* case *(Belgium* v. *Netherlands)* (1959)[85] the Court relied on maps to determine whether the Belgian sovereignty which was established in 1843 over the disputed plots had been extinguished. The Court observed that 'Belgian military staff maps since their first publication in 1874 have shown these plots as Belgian territory. The plots were included in Belgian survey records from 1847 to 1852, when one plot for some reason was struck out but restored about 1890, since which time both have continued to appear therein.'[86] The Court concluded that the Belgian sovereignty over the disputed plots had not been extinguished. The *Frontier Land* case is one of the earlier cases where the parties placed reliance on surveys and maps; and where the Court placed particular emphasis on maps. The classical case where map evidence has played a significant function is the *Rann of Kutch (India* v. *Pakistan)* (1968).[87] In this case India relied heavily on surveys and maps, which were published by the Survey of India from 1907 onward with the increasing frequency. In the words of Counsel for Pakistan, India had based practically its 'entire case on maps'.[88]

---

[81] Ibid., p.33.
[82] *ICJ Reports*, 1953, p. 47.
[83] Ibid., p. 105.
[84] Ibid.
[85] *ICJ Reports*, 1959, p. 209.
[86] Ibid., p. 227.
[87] 50 ILR 2.
[88] Ibid., p. 106; see Wetter, 'The Rann of Kutch Arbitration', *American Journal of International Law*, 65 (1971), p. 346 at p. 351.

India claimed that the maps 'establish affirmatively' or they 'substantiate' or 'indicate' the position of the boundary, while the surveys could 'determine' a boundary, in the sense, explained in oral argument, of 'presenting pictorially' and thereby 'defining' an existing boundary.[89] Pakistan on the other hand claimed that it had produced maps mainly to demonstrate that the evidence derived from the maps on which India relied was not free from error.[90] Having examined the maps which formed the third and most convincing ground of India's case, the Chairman of the Commission concluded:

> When . . . the true extension of sovereignty over a territory became the subject of investigation and inquiry . . . the evidentiary value of the maps was lessened as far as the relevant boundaries were concerned, and they were made to yield to evidence of superior weight, particularly evidence of the exercise of jurisdiction.[91]

Another classical case where the maps were at the centre of the dispute is the *Temple of Preah Vihear (Cambodia v. Thailand)* (1962).[92] Cambodia alleged a violation on the part of Thailand of its territorial sovereignty over the region of the Temple of Preah Vihear and its precincts. Thailand replied by affirming that the area in question was situated on the Thai side of common boundary between the two countries and was under its sovereignty. The Temple of Preah Vihear is an ancient sanctuary and shrine. Although partially in ruins at the time of the dispute, the Temple had considerable artistic and archaeological interest, and was still used as a place of pilgrimage. It stands on a promontory of the same name, belonging to the eastern sector of the Dangrek range of mountains which, in a general way, constitutes the boundary between the two countries in that region—Cambodia to the south and Thailand to the north.[93] Until Cambodia attained its independence in 1953 it was part of French Indo-China, and its foreign relations, like those of the rest of French Indo-China, were conducted by France as the colonial Power. In principle the boundary of the area under discussion was laid down in the settlement made in the period 1904–8, between France and Siam, as Thailand was then called. The sovereignty over Preah Vihear depends on the Treaty of 13 February 1904, and upon events subsequent to that date.[94] However, the exact course of the boundary was, by virtue of Article 3 of that Treaty, to be delimited by a Franco-Siamese Mixed Commission. In due course that Commission was set up. It was composed of two sections, French and Siamese, sitting together. The Commission surveyed the Dangrek range, in which the Temple is situated. It prepared various maps. At that time, the Siamese Government did not

[89] 50 ILR 2, 105.
[90] Ibid., p. 106.
[91] Ibid., p. 515.
[92] *ICJ Reports*, 1962, p. 5; see also Verzijl, 'Case Concerning the Temple of Preah Vihear', *Nederlands Tijdschrift voor Internationaal Recht*, 9 (1962), pp. 229–63.
[93] *ICJ Reports*, 1962, p. 5 at p. 15.
[94] Ibid., p. 16, for translation of the relevant provisions of this Treaty.

possess adequate means of preparation and publication of maps, and therefore it had officially requested the French topographical officers to map the
region. The maps were printed and published by a well-known French
cartographical firm, H. Barrère. But before they were published another
Boundary Treaty was signed on 23 March 1907. The task of delimiting the
region under discussion was subsequently given to a second Mixed Commission set up under the Treaty of 1907. Eleven maps were in due course
communicated to the Siamese Government, as being those it had requested.
Amongst them was one of that part of the Dangrek range in which the
Temple is situated, and on it was depicted a boundary purporting to be the
outcome of the work of the delimitation and showing the whole Preah
Vihear promontory, with the Temple area, as being on the Cambodian
side. That map was filed by Cambodia as Annex I to its Memorial.

Cambodia relied principally on the Annex I map in support of its claim
to sovereignty over the Temple. Thailand, on the other hand, contested
any claim based on that map on these grounds: (a) it was not the work of
the first Mixed Commission, since that Commission had ceased to function
some months before the production of the map, and had therefore no binding character; (b) at Preah Vihear it embodied a material error; and (c)
Thailand had never accepted it or the boundary indicated on it, so far as
Preah Vihear was concerned, in such a way as to become bound thereby, or
alternatively, if it had accepted the map, it did so only under a mistaken
belief that the map was correctly drawn. The Court accepted the first contention, since the record did not show whether the map was based on any
decisions or instructions given by the Commission to the surveying officers
while it was still functioning.[95] However, the Court maintained that there
could be no reasonable doubt that the map was based on the work of the
surveying officers in the Dangrek sector, and identified the characters
which gave it authority:

> Being one of the series of maps of the frontier areas produced by French Govern-
> ment topographical experts in response to a request made by the Siamese author-
> ites, printed and published by a Paris firm of repute, all of which was clear from the
> map itself, it was thus invested with an official standing; it had its own inherent
> technical authority; and its provenance was open and obvious.[96]

The Court nevertheless concluded that in its inception, and at the moment
of its production, it had no binding character. But on point (c), the Court
viewed the matter differently and gave ample reasons for its decisive finding. The publication of the maps and their communication in August 1908
was regarded as an event of a certain importance: they were distributed on a
wide scale, even to leading geographical societies and Siamese legations
abroad and to all the members of the Mixed Commissions of 1904 and
1907. Had the Government of Siam disagreed with the map or had it had

---

[95] Ibid., p. 21.
[96] Ibid.

any serious questions to raise in regard to it, the Court noted, it should have acted accordingly on that occasion. Thus Thailand became bound by the map as a result of subsequent conduct. On the point of error, point (b), the Court invoked the general principles of international law. Thailand claimed that it was not aware of the error at the time of publication. The Court stated that it is an established rule of law that the plea of error cannot be allowed as an element vitiating consent if the party advancing it contributed by its own conduct to the error, or could have avoided it, or if the circumstances were such as to put that party on notice of a possible error. Thailand accepted the map, and therefore the plea of error was unacceptable.[97] In his separate opinion Judge Fitzmaurice stated:

[E]ven if Thailand admitted her acceptance of the map, it was open to her to argue that in a conflict between a treaty clause that says 'watershed' and a map that says something different, the former must prevail . . .

There is of course no general rule whatever requiring that a conflict of this kind should be resolved in favour of the map line . . . The question is one that must always depend on the interpretation of the treaty settlement, considered as a whole, in the light of the circumstances in which it was arrived at. So considered in the present case, I agree with the Court that, in this particular instance, the question of interpretation must be solved in favour of the map line.[98]

A recent case where the cartographic documentation had assumed what the Court described as 'unaccustomed proportion' is the *Frontier Dispute* case (1986).[99] The parties, Burkina Faso and Mali, submitted a considerable body of maps, sketches and drawings of the disputed territory. But the Court stated that 'special vigilance from the outset when examining the file of maps' was required, since none of those maps was annexed, referred to or even enclosed in the administrative document which the Court had to interpret.[100] The law of 4 September 1947 'for the re-establishment of the territory of Upper Volta', as Burkina Faso was formerly called, made no reference to any map; all it contained was a reference in general terms to the boundaries 'of the former colony . . . on 5 September 1932'.[101] Neither of the two parties had been able to identify the map, if there was one, which was used by the French lawmakers in 1947 'in order to obtain a clearer picture of those boundaries'. As regards a certain French Order 2336 of 1927 and its erratum, Mali had produced a map bearing the inscription 'New frontier of Upper Volta and Niger (according to the erratum of 5 October 1927 to the Order dated 31 August 1927)'. But that map offers no information as to which official body compiled it or which administrative authority approved the line shown on it. However, an official map that was annexed to a letter from the Governor-General of French West Africa dated

[97] Ibid., p. 26.
[98] Ibid., pp. 65–6.
[99] *ICJ Reports*, 1986, p. 554.
[100] Ibid., p. 584.
[101] Ibid.

19 February 1935 was found to be missing. Finally, a French Order 2728 AP of 27 November 1935 defined the boundaries the *cercle* of Mopti 'as transcribed on the maps annexed' thereto, but again the parties had been unable to find the maps in question. In such circumstances, the Court concluded that 'not a single map available to the Chamber can reliably be said to reflect the intentions of the colonial administration expressed in the relevant texts concerning the disputed frontier'.[102] It continued:

Thus, the Chamber is confronted with an unusual situation which does not ease its burden. It has no map available to it which can provide a direct official illustration of the words contained in the four texts already mentioned, which are essential to the case, even though their authors had intended two of these texts to be accompanied by such maps.[103]

Two of the maps produced by the parties were of overall significance, for the parties had devoted much attention to them. Burkina Faso in particular had referred expressly to them in its submission. These were: the 1:500,000 scale map of the colonies of French West Africa, 1925 edition, compiled by the Geographical Service of French West Africa at Dakar and printed in Paris by Blondel la Rougery; and the 1:200,000 scale map of West Africa, issued by the French Institut Géographique National (IGN), which was originally published between 1958 and 1960. The IGN submitted a Note to the Chamber explaining the delimitation depicted on these two maps. The latter map, according to that Note, of the Mali-Burkina Faso boundary had been surveyed before the two States became independent. The Note gave also the following explanation of how the boundaries were recorded on those maps:

Then, with the help of the text, the cartographers tried to locate the frontier in relation to the map base. Unfortunately, the inaccuracy of the texts made it impossible to draw a sufficiently reliable boundary in certain areas. Some names quoted in the texts could not be found, others referred to villages which had disappeared or been moved, or again the actual nature of the terrain (course of the rivers, position of mountains) appeared different from that described in the former itinerary surveys.

The actual frontier was, therefore, recorded in the light of information supplied by the heads of the frontier districts and according to information gathered on the spot from the village chiefs and local people.[104]

From this text the Court drew a conclusion that the IGN, which compiled the maps, was 'a body neutral towards the Parties' to the dispute. Referring specifically to the 1:200,000 scale map, it stated that 'although it does not possess the status of a legal title, [it] is a visual portrayal both of the available texts and of information obtained on the ground'.[105] However, it warned that that observation was not *ipso facto* sufficient to permit it to

---

[102] Ibid., p. 583.
[103] Ibid., pp. 583 ff.
[104] Ibid.
[105] Ibid., p. 586.

infer that the boundary depicted in successive editions of the IGN map corresponded entirely with the boundary inherited from the colonial administration. It had to consider how far the evidence offered by that map or any
other map corroborated the other evidence produced. The Court ruled that
it could not uphold the map evidence where it was contradicted by trustworthy information concerning the intentions of the colonial power—
France. It concluded that 'having regard to the date on which the surveys
were made and the neutrality of the source, the Chamber considers that
where all other evidence is lacking, or is not sufficient to show an exact line,
the probative value of the IGN map becomes decisive'.[106]

The question of maps was very central to the *Taba* award (Egypt-Israel
Arbitration Tribunal, 1988).[107] Briefly, the facts of this case are as follows.
Egypt and Israel concluded a Treaty of Peace on 26 March 1979. Article I
of this Treaty provides that '1. The state of war between the Parties will be
terminated and peace will be established between them . . .', and '2. Israel
will withdraw all its armed forces and civilians from the Sinai behind the
international boundary . . . and Egypt will resume the exercise of its full
sovereignty over the Sinai'. Further, Article II provides that the permanent
boundary between Egypt and Israel is 'the recognized international boundary between Egypt and the former mandated territory of Palestine'.[108] A
Joint Commission was established pursuant to Article IV of the Treaty of
Peace for the purpose of, *inter alia*, 'organizing the demarcation of the
international boundary as stipulated in Article IV (3)(d) of the Appendix to
Annex I to the above-mentioned Treaty of Peace'. In the course of the Joint
Commission's work the precise locations of some fourteen of the nearly 100
pillars demarcating the boundary could not be agreed upon prior to 25
April 1982, the date established pursuant to Annex I to the Treaty of Peace
for the final Israeli withdrawal behind the international boundary. On 25
April 1982, the parties agreed to submit the remaining technical questions
concerning the international boundary 'to an agreed procedure which will
achieve a final and complete resolution, in conformity with article VII of
the Treaty of Peace'. However, in the interim, each party agreed 'to move
behind the lines indicated by the other'.[109] Further, Article VII of the
Treaty of Peace provides that '1. Disputes arising out of the application or
interpretation of this Treaty shall be resolved by negotiations. 2. Any such
disputes which cannot be settled by negotiations shall be resolved by conciliation or submitted to arbitration'.[110] According to the Agreement of 25
April 1982 the representatives of the US Government 'will participate in
the negotiations concerning the procedural arrangement which will lead
to the resolution of the matters of the demarcation of the International

---

[106] Ibid.
[107] *International Legal Materials*, 27 (1988), p. 1421.
[108] Ibid., p. 1430.
[109] Ibid., p. 1430, para. 2.
[110] Ibid., p. 1430, para. 3.

Boundary between Mandated Palestine and Egypt in accordance with the Treaty of Peace, if requested to do so by the Parties'.[111] The negotiations were accordingly conducted, but the parties were unable to reach a solution. Consequently, the parties agreed on 11 September 1986 to submit to arbitration their differences regarding the location of fourteen of the pillars demarcating their international boundary between a point on the coast of the Mediterranean Sea near Rafah to a point called Ras Taba on the western shore of the Gulf of Aqaba.[112] The parties agreed that the locations of two other disputed pillars depended on the decision made by the arbitral tribunal regarding neighbouring disputed pillars.

For most of the disputed pillars the parties alleged the existence of remnants of original boundary pillars, and other types of physical markers erected in some cases by the United Nations Emergency Force (UNEF)— which was formed on 5 November 1956 to secure and supervise the cessation of hostilities between Israel and Egypt, that is, after the 'Sinai War'— and in other cases erected by the Survey of Israel in the 1950s and 1960s. However, in the absence of these markers, Egypt in particular based its claims on map evidence. An attempt by Israel to prove to the Tribunal that a British 1915 map was in error failed. That map was important because it showed a boundary pillar at the location claimed by Egypt for the final, crucial pillar at Taba, Pillar 91. Israel sought to show that, owing to an error by the map co-ordinator, in London, a marker at that location which was a trigonometrical point (used for survey purposes) was identified as a boundary pillar, and that this error was perpetuated in later maps. The Tribunal regarded this argument by Israel as speculative, and not proven, and in any event regarded the fact that since 1915 and throughout the mandate the marker was accepted as a true boundary pillar as decisive. Egypt systematically derived information concerning co-ordinates, elevation and distances regarding its disputed pillar locations to the west of Wadi Taba itself from its 1935–8 map of the Sinai. The Tribunal did not consider these map-based indications to be conclusive 'since the scale of the map (1:100,000) is too small to demonstrate a location on the ground as exactly as required in these instances where the distances between the disputed pillar locations are sometimes only of a few metres'.[113] Nevertheless, it

---

[111] Ibid., p. 1434, para. 17.

[112] Ibid., p. 1430, para. 3.

[113] Ibid., p. 1472, para. 184. The distances between the nine northernmost disputed pillars, viz., nos. 7, 14, 15, 17, 27, 46, 51, 52 and 56, are very small. In four instances the disputed pillars are less than six metres apart; in another four between 34 and 65 metres; and in one case about 145 metres. The Tribunal noted that in only two of these cases does the difference of the respective locations create a divergence of more than 20 metres between the boundary lines claimed by Egypt and Israel: ibid., p. 1472, para. 182. As the Tribunal stressed, on a map of the scale of 1: 000,000, 1 millimetre on the map represents 100 metres on the ground: ibid, p. 1473, para. 184. The above-stated nine pillars are situated in an uninhabited desert region where little evidence was available to assist the parties or the Tribunal in the establishment of the pillar locations. Further, 'despite the tribunal's request, the Parties did not even succeed in producing a coherent large-scale map showing the disputed locations of the nine pillars': ibid., p. 1472, para. 182.

admitted that those small scale maps 'can be of some assistance, for instance where they show straight lines through a number of boundary pillars. They will be taken into consideration in this respect'.[114] The Tribunal requested the parties to produce a 'coherent large-scale map', but they did not succeed in doing that. The Agreement of 1906 in particular stipulated that the course of the disputed pillar locations should follow a straight line. In these circumstances, where the parties disagreed on the significance of the map, the Tribunal declared that 'the straight line was the relevant criterion' on which it could rely.[115]

VII. MAPS AND THE CONDUCT OF STATES: THE BOTSWANA–NAMIBIA ALIGNMENT AND THE PRACTICE OF TRIBUNALS

(a) *Introductory Remarks*

The relevance of this heading has already been discussed.[116] The writer will rely on the map evidence to illustrate the fact that the problem concerning the Botswana-Namibia alignment—southern boundary of Caprivi Strip—has not yet been resolved. This article proceeds to discuss the nature of the problem and the claims of Germany and Great Britain, the then Colonial Powers in Namibia and Botswana respectively. There are two separate problems in this region. The writer has examined them under separate headings: first, the line between the 21° E and the Chobe River, and second, the boundary constituted by the Chobe to its junction with the Zambezi River. The case law has been considered to illustrate how tribunals found resolutions in similar situations.

(b) *The Line Situated between 21° E and the Chobe River*

1. *The nature of the problem*

The dispute as to the course of this line is based on the interpretation of Article III (2) of the Anglo-German Agreement (1890). So far as material Article III (2), paragraph 1, provides that the boundary follows the 21° E to the point of its intersection by the 18° S, and runs eastward along the last-mentioned parallel till it reaches the Chobe (Linyanti) River. However, Article III (2), paragraph 2, provides that 'it is understood that under this arrangement Germany shall have free access from her Protectorate to the Zambezi by a strip of territory which shall at no point be less than 20 English miles in width'. Consideration must be given to the northern boundary of Namibia in this region. According to the German-Portuguese

---

[114] Ibid., p. 1472, para. 184.
[115] Ibid., p. 1475, paras. 191, 192 and 193; p. 1476, para. 196.
[116] Above, p. 205.

Declaration of 30 December 1886, the boundary of Namibia runs from Andara,[117] along a straight line, to the Katima Rapids on the Zambezi. Andara, which is the southernmost point on the northern boundary of Namibia, is located about 18°1′26″ S, that is, south of the above-stated 18° S. Thus, the line described by Article III (2), paragraph 1, cuts the territory of Angola in the neighbourhood of Andara; consequently, there is no 'free access' to the Zambezi in this region. Moreover, the strip created by that line, in its eastward course, is less than 20 English miles in width at some points. In principle, the contracting parties—Germany and Great Britain—admitted that Article III (2), paragraph 1, which provides that the southern boundary of Caprivi Strip should run along the 18° S, is unworkable.

2. *The German claim*

The Imperial Government claimed that in settling the boundary question, Article III (2), paragraph 2, of the Anglo-German Agreement, which provides that there should be 'free access' to the Zambezi by means of a strip at no point less than 20 English miles wide, should come into effect. The provision of 'free access', Germany stated, was intended 'to prevent an encroachment of English territory on the German strip', in case the map used proved to be incorrect; but it was not intended to prevent the Strip in certain eventualities and according to geographical conditions from being more than 20 English miles in width.[118] The German Foreign Office in a Note from Schoen of 30 April 1910 communicated to the British Government declared that: 'In the opinion of the Imperial Government . . . the boundary between the 21st meridian and the Chobe . . . must be formed by a parallel of latitude lying 20 English miles south of the southernmost point of the German-Portuguese boundary in the neighbourhood of Andara.'[119]

The German Foreign Office criticized the British maps that showed the boundary of the Strip running to the Chobe along 'an oblique line parallel to and at a distance of 20 English miles from the northern boundary from Andara to Katima Rapids'.[120] Germany further claimed that as the course of the northern boundary of German South West Africa had already been defined by the Declaration of 30 December 1886, Article III (2), paragraph 2 (that is, the clause of 'free access'), would, if the British claim were correct, have been omitted. It would instead have been expressly stipulated that from the 21° E the boundary runs at a distance 20 miles from the northern boundary. The very fact that this simple form was not chosen, Ger-

---

[117] In this article, unless otherwise expressly stated, Andara refers to Sebanana Island which is also known as Old Andara. In modern maps, most of the cartographers depict the new site of Andara. For consideration of the dispute regarding Andara see below, n. 161.

[118] Memorandum from German Government, CO 879/104: African No. 948, p. 144; see also FO 371/15013, p. 147; FO 371/1501, pp. 148–9.

[119] CO 879/104: African No. 948, p. 83.

[120] Schoen, loc. cit. (previous note).

many claimed, but that it was considered necessary to introduce 'a special reservation in favour of Germany, goes to prove that the Parties intended to adopt a parallel of latitude'.[121] Furthermore:

[T]he actual form of Article 3 goes to prove that both Powers had in 1890 the intention of providing that the southern boundary of the German territory should be in any case a parallel of latitude. If for any reason this cannot be the 18th parallel of latitude, it must from analogous arguments and considerations be some other parallel which fulfils the conditions of para. 2 of No. 2.[122]

Apart from the 'natural boundaries' mentioned in Article III (2)—the Chobe and Zambezi Rivers—Germany claimed, 'nothing is mentioned there of any other than such artificial boundaries as are formed by degrees of latitudes and longitudes'.[123] It agreed in principle to refer the question of the boundary of the Strip to an Arbitrator. This arrangement was aborted by the First World War.[124]

3. The British claim

(i) The opinions of the Colonial Authorities in Bechuanaland. The British Colonial Office received various suggestions from the authorities in Bechuanaland as well as from the High Commissioner of South Africa, who was in fact responsible for the administration of Bechuanaland, regarding the settlement of the southern boundary of Caprivi Strip. In 1907 Lord Selborne, then High Commissioner of South Africa, repeatedly advised the Secretary of State to persuade the German Government to exchange Caprivi Strip for 'a corresponding piece of territory taken out of the Bechuanaland Protectorate'.[125] Lord Selborne claimed that the territory which he hoped that the German Government would be prepared to surrender was not in itself of any value either to Britain or to Germany. Politically, Selborne argued, the German Strip 'is most disadvantageous' to Britain. Lord Selborne claimed that 'such a strip, penetrating like a wedge between three British Administrations, is sure to be a source of trouble'.[126] Further, Lord Selborne claimed that the Strip could not be delimited

---

[121] Ibid.

[122] Memorandum of the German Government, CO 879/104: African No. 948, p. 144.

[123] Ibid.

[124] In July 1911 Captain Von Frankenberg, the Imperial Resident in Caprivi Strip, surveyed the area and erected a pole about 60 yards north of Headman Sehenge's 'village'—about 18° 15' 40″ S. Frankenberg noted that the pole was intended to mark the place where his instruments stood 'without prejudice as boundary to any future agreement between the governments or decision of arbitration'. In 1911 Frankenberg and Stigand, then Magistrate of 'Ngamiland', agreed as 'a convenient temporary measure' that the pole erected by the former should be observed as the boundary until the matter had been settled. In January 1931, the Resident Commissioner of Bechuanaland recommended that it be proposed to the Union that from a point 20 miles due south of Andara the boundary should run to Von Frankenberg's pole. Further, the Resident Commissioner observed that 'from the site of Frankenberg's pole, I do not think we have anything to lose if we agree to the boundary running due East with the latitude until it cuts the Chobe': ibid.

[125] Lord Selborne to Secretary of State (Confidential), 23 December 1907, FO 367/79, Folio 8448.

[126] Ibid. The three British Administrations were Bechuanaland, Northern Rhodesia and Southern Rhodesia.

without causing annoyance and irritation to the Barotse and Batawana Chiefs who lived in that area. For these reasons, Selborne requested the Colonial Office to propose one of the following solutions to the German Government, *viz.*, the Goold-Adams and Panzera solutions. This study proceeds to discuss them in outline only.

Major H.J. Goold-Adams was a Resident Commissioner in Bechuanaland. He suggested that Germany should renounce the right of 'free access' to the Zambezi, by means of a strip at no point less than 20 English miles, stipulated in Article III (2), paragraph 2, of the Anglo-German Agreement. In exchange for such a strip, the boundary of German South West Africa between the 22° S and 18° S would be extended eastward and run along the 21°15' E, instead of 21° E, so as to give an equivalent piece of territory to Germany, that is, about 3,500 square miles.[127] Alternatively, he suggested that Britain might agree to a strip of 40 miles south of the 18th parallel extending eastward from the 21° E to about 23° 30" E.[128]

Lieut.-Col. Francis W. Panzera a former Resident Commissioner at Mafeking, disagreed with the suggestions made by Goold-Adams. On 10 December 1907 Panzera advised the High Commissioner that Britain should aim at the 'acquisition of the whole of the tongue of the country now owned by Germany north of our borders'.[129] He stressed that Britain should not give a territory north of the 22° to Germany, as 'it would interfere with the vested interests of the white farmers'. He suggested that Caprivi Strip should be exchanged for the territory situated north of the Nossob River, south of the 22° S, west of the 21° E, and east of the 20° E. Panzera claimed that there were no recognized vested rights in the abovementioned territory, it was valueless and it caused considerable trouble to Britain.[130]

In addition to these proposals, the Resident Commissioner at Mafeking, in Bechuanaland, claimed that if the German interpretation were adopted the boundary would cut about four miles south of the Colonial Administration's Police Camp which was at Muhembo Drift on the west bank of the Okavango River.[131] The Resident Commissioner claimed that Muhembo Drift, where the Okavango River is about 200 to 250 yards wide, was the only spot in the region where their police could cross. The Police Camp was an 'exceptionally important station', as it enabled the Colonial Administration to control the border.[132] From the economic point of view the Police Camp was expensive; its construction cost £575.00.

---

[127] The size of the entire Strip east of the 21° E is about 10,573 square miles. Thus, the territory suggested by Goold-Adams is smaller. See *League of Nations Permanent Mandates Commission Minutes*, 1921–5, p. 57.

[128] FO 637/79, Folio 8448.

[129] Panzera to High Commissioner (Confidential), 10 December 1907, para. 10, FO 367/79. See also *The Colonial Office List*, 1907, p. 580.

[130] Panzera to High Commissioner, loc. cit. (previous note), para. 13.

[131] Despatch No. 2487, FO 371/15757, p. 240.

[132] Ibid. The Police Camp was also used to prevent the entry of 'diseased cattle' into Bechuanaland.

Lord Crewe, former Secretary of State for the Colonies, advised the Foreign Office not to communicate the above-stated suggestions, respecting the exchange of the Strip, to Germany. At the time in question the latter wanted to acquire sovereignty over Walvis Bay. The Colonial Office expressed fear that the suggestion of exchange might evoke a counter-proposal from Germany, especially the exchange of the Strip for Walvis Bay.[133]

(ii) *Solution of the High Commissioner for South Africa*. By 1931, when negotiations respecting the southern boundary of Caprivi Strip were in progress, the section of Zambezi River running from Katima Rapids to its confluence with the Chobe had not been delimited. Hugh Tweedie, then High Commissioner for South Africa, suggested an exchange of territory in order to secure title to the islands in the Zambezi, or to acquire title to the entire Strip. Tweedie claimed that if the islands in the Zambezi were delimited according to the solution suggested by the Government of the Mandated Territory,[134] only two islands of significant size would be allocated to the latter, namely, Nantungu and Isolionke. Further, Tweedie claimed that there were a number of islands 'which are of value for fishing or other purposes' which would fall into the Mandated Territory. In an attempt to secure the islands for 'Northern Rhodesia', then a British Colony, Tweedie suggested that 'the adjustment of the Southern boundary of the Strip so as to give the Mandatory Government Munembuana drift and the small piece of worthless Territory to the West of the point 20 miles due South of Andara might be an equitable and useful exchange'.[135] Tweedie claimed that the mutual adjustment of the boundary between Angola and the Mandated Territory in 1926, during the settlement of the boundary from the Kunene to the Okavango, had already established a precedent. The exchange of a portion of the strip for the islands, in his opinion, would provide a further precedent which might be of value in influencing the League of Nations to take a favourable view of 'a more comprehensive modification of the Northern and Western boundary between Bechuanaland and South West Africa if a mutual desire to remove the geographical anomaly formed by the Strip should become a subject for negotiation between the interested Governments at some future date'.[136] However, Tweedie concluded that there are objections 'to increasing the width of the Caprivi salient even if the surrender of only worthless sandy desert is involved'.[137] He claimed that the Zambezi Islands are of little more value than the desert, and that having regard to possible developments in the future it would be unwise to offer to surrender Munembuana Drift, particularly since by facilitating internal communications it would enhance the value of the Strip and render

---

[133] Letter No. 1280/1908 from Lord Elgin (signed H.W. Just) to FO, 10 March 1908, FO 367/79.
[134] FO 371/15757, p. 237.
[135] H.J. Tweedie to J.H. Thomas (DO), 2 April 1931, FO 371/15757, p. 237.
[136] Ibid., p. 238.
[137] Ibid.

its exchange for other territory at some later date more difficult. Tweedie, therefore, recommended that Britain should agree that 'West of the point 20 miles due South of Andara the boundary should follow a parallel of latitude and that in making this concession . . . we [Great Britain] should endeavour to obtain some insular concessions in the Zambesi'.[138] The High Commissioner's solution is a political one; it is not based on the interpretation of Article III (2) of the Anglo-German Agreement. Like Panzera and Goold-Adams, Tweedie's ultimate object was to secure British sovereignty over the entire Strip by means of exchange.

(iii) *Lord Crewe's solution regarding Caprivi Strip.* Lord Crewe, the then Secretary of State for the Colonies, agreed in principle that Britain should adhere to the notion of 'free access' to the Zambezi by means of a strip, described by Article III (2) of the Anglo-German Agreement. However, he rejected the above-mentioned German claim which stated that the boundary must follow 'a parallel of latitude lying 20 English miles south of the southernmost point of the German-Portuguese boundary in the neighbourhood of Andara'.[139] In view of the fact that the alignment defined by Article III (2), paragraph 1 (that is, running along the 18° S), did not create such a Strip, Lord Crewe suggested that recourse must be had to Article VI of the Anglo-German Agreement.[140] Article VI provides, *inter alia*, that 'all the lines of demarcation traced in Articles I to IV shall be subject to rectification by agreement between the two Powers, in accordance with local requirement'.[141]

Lord Crewe claimed that in delimiting the southern boundary of the Strip, the starting point should be Andara—the southernmost point on the northern boundary. The width of the Strip from Andara should be 20 English miles (32.18 km). From the point 20 miles south of Andara the boundary should run 20 miles south of and parallel to the Andara–Katima Rapids line, that is, the northern boundary, until it intersects the 18° S; then it follows the 18° S till it reaches the Chobe (Linyanti) River.[142]

The German Foreign Office as well as the Imperial Authorities in German South West Africa rejected the British claim.[143] Captain Streitwolf, then Imperial Resident at Caprivi Zipfel, for instance, commented that if the British claim were accepted Germany would lose about 48 km of the Chobe bank and a certain drift called Munembuana, which were, respectively, important for agricultural purposes and communication.[144]

Consideration must, however, be given to the fact that from the point where the line proposed by Lord Crewe intersects the 18° S to the Chobe,

---

[138] Ibid.; see also Letter from B.E.H. Clifford to Sir James Maxwell, 27 February 1931, FO 371/15757, p. 248.
[139] Above, p. 228.
[140] CO 879/104: African No. 948, p. 68.
[141] *BFSP*, 82 (1889–90), p. 42.
[142] CO 879/104: African No. 948, pp. 68, 142.
[143] Above, p. 228 (German claim).
[144] Letter from Streitwolf, 18 November 1909, FO 371/15013, p. 147.

the Strip would be more than 20 English miles in width. Furthermore, according to the available evidence, Lord Crewe, did not suggest a solution as to the delimitation of the section of the Strip lying between the point situated 20 miles south of Andara and the 21° E.

4. *Settlement of the boundary by the Union*

In March 1931 the Union, in its capacity as Mandatory Power, communicated to Britain that it had accepted the solution of the southern boundary of Caprivi Strip which was suggested by Lord Crewe.[145] It will be recalled that Crewe did not offer a solution to the portion of the Strip west of the point 20 miles south of Andara to its intersection of the 21° E. Therefore, it is suggested, there were four possible courses of this line. It could: (*a*) run parallel to the northern line—the Okavango River; (*b*) run along certain points situated 20 miles south of the Okavango River boundary; (*c*) follow a parallel; or (*d*) the line proposed by Lord Crewe could proceed till it intersects the 21° E. In view of this dilemma, H.D. Bodenstein, Secretary of External Affairs of the Union, observed:

The question now arises, however, as to whether the principle which it is proposed to apply to the eastern section should also be applied strictly to that portion of the boundary west of the twenty mile point South of Andara. If this is done a very awkward boundary will be created as it will have to run parallel to the Okavango River.[146]

In April 1931, the Union claimed that 'in view of the impossibility of demarcating such a boundary on the ground, the boundary west of the point 20 miles due South of Andara should follow a parallel of latitude or be formed by the extension westwards of the oblique line'.[147] However, Hugh J. Tweedie, the High Commissioner, suggested that in determining the course of the boundary of the Strip, consideration must be given to the delimitation of the Zambezi River.

The Colonial Authorities in Bechuanaland, it appears, were satisfied with the suggestion made by the Union, that the boundary west of a point lying 20 miles south of Andara should follow a parallel. B.E.H. Clifford noted:

As the Union . . . now conceded to Bechuanaland, without stipulating for a quid pro quo, the Territory formerly in dispute along the southern boundary of the strip between Muhembo Drift [on Okavango River] and the Chobe River, the High Commissioner has no longer anything to bargain with except a small strip of country, west of Muhembo which is practically worthless.[148]

Maps of Namibia published by South Africa consistently show the

---

[145] See above, p. 232.

[146] Despatch No. PM 21/63, of 5 March 1931, FO 371/256; see also J.B.M. Hertzog, Minister of External Affairs, to Secretary of Dominion Affairs, 23 July 1930, FO 371/15013, p. 143.

[147] H.J. Tweedie to J.H. Thomas (DO), 2 April 1931, FO 371/15757, p. 235.

[148] Clifford to Sir James Maxwell, FO 371/15757, p. 262; see also no. 653 from H.J. Tweedie, High Commissioner, 2 April 1931, FO 371/15757, p. 258.

southern boundary of Caprivi Strip west of the point 20 miles south of Andara following a parallel till it intersects the 21° E. As to the rest of the boundary of the Strip, these maps depict the boundary running along the line suggested by Lord Crewe, which has been discussed earlier.[149] The practice of Britain, then Colonial Power in Bechuanaland, had not been consistent. Similarly, the Government of Botswana does not adhere to this practice consistently.[150]

5. Claim of the Government of Botswana

The available evidence shows that since independence the Government of Botswana has not challenged the Botswana–Namibia alignment.[151] However, the map evidence indicates otherwise. For this reason, this article relies heavily on the official maps of the Government of Botswana. This evidence shows that the practice of Botswana respecting the line between the 21° E and the Chobe River has not been consistent. On some maps this alignment is depicted according to the solution which was accepted by the Union, that is, west of a point 20 miles south of Andara the line follows a

[149] See, for instance, van der Merwe (ed.), *National Atlas of South West Africa (Namibia)* (1983).

[150] See 'Sketch Map of the Bechuanaland Protectorate' published in *Annual Report on Bechuanaland Protectorate for the Year 1946* (London, HMSO, 1948); 'Map of Bechuanaland, 1965' in *Annual Report on Bechuanaland for the Year 1965* (London, HMSO, 1965); and 'Map of Botswana' in *1982 Botswana Agricultural Census, Planning and Statistics, Ministry of Finance and Development Planning* (Government Printer, April 1983), p. xii.

[151] On 22 November 1963—prior to the independence of Botswana—Mr Tsheko, a former elected member of the Bechuanaland Protectorate Legislative Council, proposed that the 'Government takes steps to resume responsibility for the administration of the Caprivi Strip': *Bechuanaland Protectorate Legislative Council Official Report* (Hansard 9), 3rd Session, 1st Meeting, Sitting from 18–26 November 1963, cols. 123–8, at col. 124. In his view the Strip 'is 20 miles wide at any given point': ibid., col. 123. His remarks show that he wished to achieve more than just administration; in fact he wanted Britain or a newly independent Botswana to claim title to the territory in question. Tsheko argued that Caprivi Strip 'was part and parcel of Ngamiland administered by the Chief and the District Commissioner for Ngamiland. The indigenous inhabitants of this Strip are one and the same as the inhabitants of Ngamiland and the Chobe. They have no connection whatsoever in language, custom or anything with the people of South West Africa': ibid. Further, he claimed that 'the people of South West Africa ["the African inhabitants"] have no interest whatsoever in this Strip because they know it has never belonged to them. The people in the Caprivi Strip are nowadays shocked when they are told they belong to the Government of South West Africa to which they never belonged as far as they know': ibid. Tsheko referred to the territory in question as 'this part of Bechuanaland', and stressed that 'South Africa has no right to administer this Strip which is not part of South West Africa': ibid., col. 124. In his view the Strip has some disadvantages. It 'cuts Bechuanaland completely from common frontage of two African States—Northern Rhodesia and Angola': ibid. 'Economically', he continued, 'the connection of Bechuanaland with Angola is very important because it affords us with access to sea coast in Angola for both our exports and imports. Connection with Northern Rhodesia on a wider frontage than at present is also very important economically. It will link this country with the rest of the African continent and will give an outlet to our beef market': ibid. Mr Masire, member of the Legislative Council, supported Tsheko's motion unreservedly, and declared: 'Here at any rate we have a territory which is wrongly occupied and which is so vital to our economy and . . . to our defence': ibid., col. 125. Masire urged the Council to 'press on Government to do something about this Caprivi Strip': ibid. Tsheko's motion was defeated: ibid., col. 128; see also *Africa Research Bulletin (Political, Social and Cultural)*, vol. 1, no. 1 (January 1964), p. 4. It would suffice to register that Messrs Tsheko and Masire lacked full knowledge of the legal issues relating to the delimitation of the territory situated between the 21° E and the Zambezi River, as well as the circumstances which led to the administration of Caprivi Strip as part of Bechuanaland in 1922.

parallel till it intersects the 21° E, and eastwards of this point it runs parallel to the northern boundary of Namibia—the Andara–Katima Mulilo line— till it intersects the 18° S and follows this parallel till it reaches the Chobe.[152] A further common practice is as follows: westward of a point 20 miles south of Andara the alignment is depicted running along a parallel till it reaches the 21° E. However, eastward of that point the alignment follows a straight line, which is neither parallel to the northern boundary of Namibia nor following a parallel, till it intersects the Chobe River. At the point where this line intersects the Chobe the 'Strip' is about 45 kilometres (28 miles) in width. There are numerous official maps similar to this.[153] The conclusion to be drawn from the practice of Botswana is that the problem concerning the alignment under discussion is outstanding. For this writer certain legal questions cast doubt on the application of the legal principles of estoppel and acquiescence.[154] However, the line accepted by the Union of South Africa constitutes the boundary at the moment.

6. *Map evidence*

Maps depicting the Botswana–Namibia alignment in the region of Caprivi Strip may be classified into several categories. The seven major classes are as follows. First, some cartographers depict the entire southern boundary of Caprivi Strip running along a parallel, that is, commencing from the 21° E, passing through a point 20 miles south of Andara to the Chobe River. Clearly, according to this class of maps, eastward and

[152] See the following maps: 'Botswana Population Density 1971', 'Botswana Population Distribution 1971' and 'Botswana Population Distribution 1971', scale 1:1,500,000, drawn by the Census Office, printed by Government Printer, Gaborone.

[153] See, for instance, *Report on the Population Census 1971*, published by Central Statistics Office (Government Printer, August 1972), figures 1 and 7.1; *Statistical Newsletter*, no. 2 (June 1972), Central Statistics Office, Ministry of Finance and Development Planning (Government Printer, Gaborone), p. 14; *Statistical Abstract 1974*, Central Statistics Office, Ministry of Finance and Development Planning (Government Printer); ibid., 1975 and 1976; *External Trade Statistics 1976*, Dept. of Customs and Excise, Central Statistics Office, Ministry of Finance and Development Planning (Government Printer), p. i; *1981 Population and Housing Census*, Census Administrative/Technical Report and National Statistical Tables, Central Statistics Office, Ministry of Finance and Development Planning (Government Printer), pp. 3a and 3b; *Statistical Bulletin*, September/December 1982, vol. 7, no. 3/4, Central Statistics Office, Ministry of Finance and Development Planning (Government Printer), p. 45; ibid., December 1983, vol. 8, no. 4, pp. 44 and 45; ibid., March 1984, vol. 9, no. 1, pp. 44, 45 and 46; ibid., June 1984, vol. 9, no. 2, pp. 46 and 47; ibid., December 1984, vol. 9, no. 4, pp. 45 and 46; ibid., March 1985, vol. 10, no. 1, pp. 45, 46 and 47; ibid., September 1985, vol. 10, no. 3, pp. 45 and 46; ibid., March 1986, vol. 11, no. 1, pp. 46, 47 and 48; ibid., June 1986, vol. 11, no. 2, pp. 51 and 52; *Botswana Country Profile 1985*, Central Statistics Office (Government Printer), p. 7, fig. 2.1.

[154] The solution concerning the southern boundary of Caprivi Strip which was accepted by the Union in 1931 raises important legal questions: Was the Union authorized by the League of Nations to settle the dispute? Article 7 of the Mandate for German South West Africa provides that 'the consent of the Council of the League of Nations is required for any modification of the terms of the present Mandate': *League of Nations Official Journal*, 2 (1921), January–August, p. 89. This writer did not find evidence showing that the Union Government was authorized to do so. For the present writer, the clause 'any modification' is broad. Clearly, it may include any adjustment of the boundaries. Further, did the Governments of the Union and Bechuanaland possess the capacity to settle the line in question? Can the maxim *nemo debet esse judex in propria sua causa* be raised? The writer does not intend to analyse these questions in this study.

westward of the point situated 20 miles south of Andara, the Strip is wider than 20 miles. As stated earlier, this practice reflects the German claim.[155] The second class of maps shows the line westward from a point 20 miles south of Andara running parallel to the Okavango River and terminates where it intersects the 21° E. From the former point, in its eastward course, the boundary is depicted running parallel to the northern boundary, that is, the straight Andara-Katima line, until it intersects the Chobe. The width of the Strip from the 21° E to the Chobe is 20 miles. Maps showing the boundary running parallel to the Okavango are not common.[156] In view of the natural geography of the Okavango River, demarcation of such a boundary running parallel to it is impossible. The third class of maps shows the section between the 21° E and the point 20 miles south of Andara following a parallel. Eastward of the last-mentioned point, the boundary is depicted running 20 miles south of and parallel to the Andara–Katima Rapids line, that is, the northern boundary of the Strip, until it reaches the Chobe.[157] The fourth class consists of maps depicting the line between a point 20 miles South of Andara and the 21° E following a parallel; then from the former point, in its eastward course, the line runs 20 miles south of and parallel to the Andara–Katima Rapids line until it intersects the 18° S; then it proceeds along the 18° S until it reaches the Chobe. This class indicates the settlement that had been accepted by the Union.[158] Fifth, there are cartographers who depict the line between a point 20 miles south of Andara and the Chobe running 20 miles south of and parallel to the Andara–Katima line. From the former point, in its westward course, the alignment proceeds following a straight line until it intersects the 21° E.[159] Sixth, some maps depict a curve (about) 20 miles south of Andara. From this curve, in its eastward and westward course the line is depicted as in class four. Finally, some maps depict a curve similar to class six. Westward and eastward of this curve the alignment is as in classes four and five, respectively.[160]

Clearly, there is no uniformity among cartographers as to the southern boundary of Caprivi Strip. The seven classes of maps discussed above indicate different schools of thought respecting the interpretation of Article III (2) of the Anglo-German Agreement. Some of the maps had been pub-

[155] See, e.g., 'Sketch Map of Bechuanaland Protectorate' in *Annual Report on Bechuanaland for the Year 1913–14* (No. 815), Cd. 7622–6.

[156] For this class see, e.g., the 'Map Illustrating the Partition of Africa (1870–1913)', scale 1:16,093,500, published by Stanford's Geographical Establishment, in London: MPI/377; CAB 29/1. This map, however, contains a disclaimer stating that the boundary of the Strip is approximate only.

[157] See, for instance, 'Map of the Republic of Botswana' in *1982 Botswana Agricultural Census, Planning and Statistics, Ministry of Finance and Development Planning* (Government Printer, April 1983), p. xii.

[158] The official UN Map of Namibia falls under this class.

[159] See 'Map of Bechuanaland, 1965' in *Annual Report on Bechuanaland for the Year 1965* (London, HMSO, 1965).

[160] See, e.g., 'Sketch Map of the Bechuanaland Protectorate', printed at the Ordnance Survey Office, Southampton, 1915, in *Annual Report on Bechuanaland Protectorate for the Year 1914–15* (No. 586), Cd. 7622–48.

lished by private persons, who depended to a large extent upon information obtained from general and unauthoritative sources. However, the official maps indicate the claims of the governments concerned at the time of their publication.

7. *Interpretation of Article III (2) of the Anglo-German Agreement*

By recurring to the language of Article III (2), paragraph 1, of the Anglo-German Agreement of 1890, it will be recalled that the boundary runs along the 21° E, northward 'to the point of its intersection by the 18th parallel of south latitude; it runs eastward along that parallel [18° S] till it reaches the River Chobe [Linyanti]; and descends the centre of the main channel of that river [Chobe] to its junction with the Zambezi, where it terminates'. Further, Article III (2), paragraph 2, adds that 'it is understood that under this arrangement Germany shall have free access from her Protectorate to the Zambezi by a strip of territory which shall at no point be less than 20 English miles in width'. We will illustrate that it was impossible for the contracting parties to establish a boundary running continuously from the 21° E, eastward, along the 18° S till it reaches the Chobe River. Having done that, we will trace the real intention of the contracting parties.

The northern boundary of German South West Africa was defined by the German-Portuguese Declaration of 30 December 1886, that is, prior to the conclusion of the Anglo-German Agreement (1890). In that region, the alignment follows the course of the Okavango River, to Andara (Sebanana Island),[161] and then it follows a straight line to the Katima Rapids on the

---

[161] A *caveat* is required at this juncture. There are two separate places known as 'Andara' in the region in question: the 'Old' and the 'New' Andara. Most of the modern maps depict only the latter. In 1886 a local ruler by the name of Andara had his *Kgotla*—residence—on Sebanana Island situated about 18° 1' 26" S. Both Sebanana Island and Andara's *Kgotla* were generally called 'Andara'. After his death he was succeeded by his son Libebe (Nandale). Libebe moved his *Kgotla* to Tahoe Island on the Okavango River, about three miles south-west of Sebanana Island. Tahoe Island eventually became known as 'Andara'. There is ample map evidence showing the old and new 'Andara', that is, respectively Sebanana and Tahoe Islands. The maps concerned were published in Germany, Great Britain and Portugal—the States which were involved in the delimitation of the region. (*a*) In the '*Kriegskarte von Deutsch Sudwest-Afrika*', published by Dietrich Reimer, Berlin, 1904, the original site of 'Andara' is marked 'Alt-Andara' while further downstream about three miles is shown the then existing site of 'Andara', where Andara's successor—Lebebe—took up his residence. (*b*) In the '*Karte de Gebiets Zwischen Okavango und Sambesi (Caprivi Zipfel) nach den Arfnachmen von Franz Seiner in der Jahren 1905–1906*', printed by Dietrich Reimer (Ernst Vohsen), Berlin, the original site is depicted as 'Andara (*fuherer Ort Insel*)' and the new site lower downstream as 'Libebe's'. (*c*) In a map described as 'Northern Portion Sketch Map of Ngamiland (including Western portion of Caprivi Strip) and Ghanzi', based upon traverses surveyed by Captain A.G. Stigand between 1910 and 1922, and published by the Geographical Section of the War Office in 1925, 'Andara' is depicted situated on Sebanana Island approximately in latitude 18° 1' 50" S, while the new site is shown further downstream as 'Litho's (late Libebe)' on Tahoe Island: FO 371/13429, File 2674. (*d*) In the '*Carta de Angola 1892*', scale 1:3,000,000; 70 x 62 cm, and the '*Carta de Angola 1900*', scale 1:3,000,000; 81 x 67 cm, both maps drawn by L. Coureico, engraved by A. Briesemeister Lith. da Ca. Nal. Editora., the new 'Andara' is marked 'Lebebe' to indicate that it is not the original 'Andara': Maps MFQ/488 (6) and (7), in FO 63/1390. Clearly, the name 'Andara' which is employed in the German-Portuguese Declaration (1886) does not refer to the new 'Andara': at the 'critical date' this site was known as Tahoe Island. The maps cited above are further evidence on this point. The dispute concerning the course of the Angola–Namibia alignment at Andara was resolved by the Caprivi Zipfel Boundary Commission in 1930. This Commission was established by

Zambezi. The territory lying northwards of this line—Angola—was under Portuguese sovereignty. Andara, which is the southernmost point on the northern boundary of Caprivi Strip, is situated about 18°1′26″ S. From the 21° E to a certain point approximately three miles west of Andara, the 18° S runs southward of the Okavango River, the northern limit of German South West Africa. The maximum width of the strip of territory between the Okavango and the 18° S in this region is about five miles. Moreover, from the above-stated point approximately three miles west of Andara, the 18° S, in its eastward course, runs northwards of Andara, for a total distance of approximately eight miles, thereby cutting the territory of Angola. After this distance, the 18° S runs south of the Andara–Katima line. But for a distance of about 96 miles, the strip between the Andara–Katima line and the 18° S is less than 20 miles in width. However, approximately 18 miles west of the Chobe, the width of such a strip is not less than 20 miles. Clearly, the boundary following the 18° S would be contrary to the real intention of the contracting parties, for the following reasons. First, such a line would partition the territory of Angola at Andara. At the time of delimitation, title to the territory north of Andara was already vested in Portugal. Therefore, the contracting parties could not have intended the boundary to run along the 18° S. Assuming the line were to terminate about three miles west of Andara, and to continue following the 18° S after a distance of about eight miles, in order to avoid cutting Angola, the delimitation would still be contrary to the intention of the contracting parties. Article III (2), paragraph 2, expressly states that Germany should have 'free access' to the Zambezi by a strip of territory at no point less than 20 English miles wide. In order to have 'free access' the strip of territory must run continuously, uninterrupted. Thus, such an assumption would not satisfy the requirement of 'free access'. Second, apart from a small portion of territory in the neighbourhood of the Chobe, the rest of the strip established by the boundary following the 18° S would be less than 20 miles in width. The present writer therefore maintains that in ascertaining the real intention of the parties, paragraph 1, which provides that there must be 'free access' by a strip of territory at no point less than 20 miles in width, must override paragraph 2, which designates the 18° S as the boundary.

The *travaux préparatoires* confirm these conclusions. Sir Percy Anderson, the British diplomat who drafted the Agreement under consideration

Great Britain (Colonial Power in Northern Rhodesia), Portugal (Colonial Power in Angola) and the Union of South Africa (then Mandatory Power in South West Africa). At the time in question Landsberg, the representative of the Union, relied heavily on the map evidence. He stated that Seiner, also a former German Representative in Caprivi Zipfel, in his map, scale 1:25,000, published in 1911, depicted the boundary as commencing at the northernmost point of Sebanana Island. Further, he relied on a map drawn by Von Frankenberg, a former German Representative in Caprivi Zipfel, which depicted the alignment as commencing from the northernmost point of Sebanana Island. He pointed out that Captain Streitwolf, the then Imperial Resident in Caprivi Zipfel, also depicted the boundary as running from the northerly point of the Sebanana Island: FO 371/15013, p. 187. It would suffice to register that the Commission agreed that Andara (Sebanana Island) should be part of the mandated territory.

with Dr Krauer, commented on the draft Article III, in a Note dated 28 June 1890, as follows:

The provision, inserted in the III rd Article, for a contingent rectification in order to give to Germany access to the Zambezi, is inserted because in certain maps Andara . . . is placed south of the 18th parallel; in all the best maps, however, including an excellent [sic] chart prepared by the Intelligence Department of the War Office, which has been our principal authority, it is placed well to the north of that parallel.[162]

According to this Explanatory Note, recourse must be had to Article III (2), paragraph 2—which provides for free access—in the event of the exact location of Andara being on the south of the 18° S. In such circumstances paragraph 2 would function as 'a contingent rectification', thereby securing to Germany a strip of territory at no point less than 20 miles wide. Since it is now certain that Andara is situated south of the 18° S, paragraph 1 must be ignored. Paragraph 2 is not, however, free from complications. It does not provide the precise course of the line: the clause 'shall at no point be less than 20 English miles' indicates but the minimum width of the strip, which has been agreed upon by the contracting parties. However, paragraph 3 of the same article throws light on the maximum agreed width of the Strip. This paragraph provides that 'the sphere in which the exercise of influence is reserved to Great Britain . . . includes Lake Ngami'. This clause was intended to provide for the contingency of the possible shifting on maps of the position of Lake Ngami. The *travaux préparatoires* confirm this interpretation. Sir Percy clarified the draft articles as follows:

The frontier traced in South-West Africa placed Ngamiland, with its lake and almost its entire water system, under British influence. The most trustworthy maps place the lake on the 23rd degree of east longitude, and its principal western affluent, the Tonga, to the east of the 21st degree up to the point of its intersection by the 18th parallel of south latitude.[163]

The precise location of Lake Ngami is 20°37' S, 22°40' E, and is thus further south of the disputed territory.[164] Clearly, Article III (2) contains two guidelines which are crucial in determining the course of the line running from the 21° E to the Chobe. First, such a line must establish a strip at no point less than 20 miles in width. Second, the line should not partition Lake Ngami, as the entire Lake must be an integral part of Botswana.
Paragraph 4 of the Article under discussion provides that 'the course of

---

[162] Sir Percy Anderson to Sir Edward Malet, 28 June 1890, *British Parliamentary Papers*, 1890, vol. 51, p. 19 at p. 20; Despatch No. 94 (very confidential) from Sir Edward Malet to Lord Kimberley, FO 64/1334; FO 881/6146, p. 52.

[163] FO 881/6146, p. 54.

[164] Lake Ngami is the shallow depression at the south-east corner of Okavango Swamps. The swamps and the lake are fed by the Okavango River. The lake is about 932 metres above sea level. In 1849, when David Livingstone came across it, he estimated it to be more than 275 km in circumference; but by 1950 it had become a sea of grass. During the severe drought in 1965–6 it dried up completely. It is rich in birdlife and contains barbel fish, which are able to survive in mud for months while the lake is dry: *Encyclopaedia Britannica* (15th edn., 1980), vol. 7, p. 312.

the above boundary is traced in general accordance with a Map officially prepared for the British Government in 1889'. The map mentioned in this paragraph is the 'Intelligence Division of the War Office Map No. 846'.[165] On that map, the 18° S is inaccurately depicted: it is shown as running about 40 miles south of the correct position of that parallel. Andara, which was the southernmost place on the northern boundary of German South West Africa, is shown situated approximately 40 miles north of the 18° S. However, the negotiators considered that map 'an excellent chart' and it had been their 'principal authority'. The entire course of the boundary, from the Orange to the junction of the Chobe with the Zambezi, is marked with a thick line on the map in question: following the 20° E until it intersects the 22° S; then it runs eastward along the 22° S to the point of its intersection by the 21° E; then it follows the 21° E northward to the point of its intersection by the 18° S; then it follows the 18° S eastward till it reaches the Chobe; and then it runs along the main channel of the Chobe to its junction with the Zambezi. Thus, the minimum width of the strip of territory, westward of the Chobe, which was intended for the so-called 'free access', according to this map is about 40 miles. In the neighbourhood of the Chobe, the Strip is approximately 80 miles in width. It is a general rule of interpretation that the context of a treaty comprises, in addition to the text, including its preamble and annexes, any instrument which was made by one or more parties in connection with the conclusion of the treaty and accepted by the other parties as an instrument related to the treaty.[166] The 'Intelligence Division of the War Office Map' has not been incorporated into the treaty; it has only been referred to. Nevertheless, in order to ascertain the intention of the parties, this map must be given the same effect as if it had been expressly made part of the Agreement.[167] The boundary would then run along the '18° S' shown on this map, as this represents the intention of the negotiators. Moreover, Article III (2) defines the entire boundary from the Orange to the Chobe in terms of parallels and longitudes. It would therefore appear that the contracting parties intended the southern boundary of Caprivi Strip to be constituted by a parallel. This interpretation satisfies the express conditions of Article III (2), paragraphs 2 and 3, which provide, respectively, that the Strip of territory for 'free access' should at no point be less than 20 miles in width, and that Lake Ngami should be part of Botswana. According to this interpretation, the minimum width of the strip between the 21° E and the Chobe River would be about 40 miles.

Alternatively, it may be argued that the parties intended the minimum width of the strip to be 20 miles, but not 40 which is indicated on the inaccurate Intelligence Division of the War Office Map. This argument may be

---

[165] See 'Map to Illustrate Article III of the Anglo-German Agreement of 1st July 1890', in Hertslet, *The Map of Africa by Treaty* (3rd edn., 1909), vol. 3.

[166] Article 31(2) of Vienna Convention on the Law of Treaties, 1969.

[167] See in particular *US* v. *State of Texas* (1896), 162 US 1, 37; *Noonan* v. *Braley* (1862), 67 US 2 Black, 499; *Cragin* v. *Powell* (1888), 128 US 691, 696; *Jefferis* v. *East Omaha Land Co.* (1890), 134 US 178; *McIver* v. *Walker* (1815), 13 US 9 Cranch, 173.

persuasive as this is the width expressly stated in the provision on 'contingent rectification'. Nevertheless, for the reasons stated earlier, the line intended by the parties should follow a parallel. In determining the precise course of the line in such circumstances, the first step would be to select the southernmost point on the northern boundary of Namibia in this region. It is certain that the point in question is Andara—Old Andara or Sebanana Island. The second task would be to locate a point situated exactly 20 miles south of Andara. The parallel that passes through this last-mentioned point would constitute the boundary between Botswana and Namibia. Thus, from this point, the boundary in its westward course would follow a parallel until it intersects the 21° E; and in its eastward course, the boundary would follow this parallel till it reaches the centre of the Chobe. As stated earlier, the line should not partition Lake Ngami.

There are some similarities between Article III (2) of the Anglo-German Agreement and Article III of the Treaty of 22 February 1819 between the USA and Spain. The latter caused a dispute and was subsequently interpreted in *US* v. *State of Texas* (1895).[168] Article III of this Treaty, so far as material, described the boundary between the two countries west of the Mississippi, in part, as follows: 'then following the course of the Rio Roxo, westward, to the degree of longitude 100 west from London and 23 from Washington . . . the whole being as laid down in Melish's Map of the United States, published at Philadelphia, improved to the first of January, 1818.'[169] As a matter of fact, Melish's Map located the 100th meridian inaccurately: it was far east of the place where the correct meridian is, when properly delineated. That meridian astronomically located is more than 100 miles further west than was indicated by the Melish Map. As a consequence, a tract of land lying between the Red River where the Indian territory and the State of Texas adjoin, east of 100th meridian, became a disputed territory. Both parties asserted title under the provisions of the above-mentioned Treaty. Texas claimed that it was within its boundary. As early as 1860, by legislative enactment, Texas created the county of Greer with boundaries that included the entire disputed territory, and it had ever since asserted its jurisdiction over both that territory and its inhabitants. The contention of the USA was that the terms of the Treaty could not be met except by going westward along and up the river called the Prairie Dog Town, a branch of the Red River to the point where that river intersects the 100th meridian. Texas insisted that, even if the Treaty were to be interpreted as referring to the true 100th meridian of longitude, and not to that meridian as located on the Melish Map of 1818, the course of the Rio Roxo westward from the intersection of the line extending north from the Sabine River to the Red River, takes the line, not westwardly along the Prairie Dog Town branch of the Red River, but northwardly and northwestwardly up the north branch of the Red River to the point where the latter branch

[168] 162 US 1.
[169] Ibid., p. 27.

crosses the true 100th meridian, between the 35th and 36th degrees of latitude. Therefore, Texas propounded the following proposition: that the
Treaty of 1819 having declared that the boundary should be as laid down
on Melish's Map, it was immaterial whether the location of the 100th meridian of longitude on that map was astronomically correct or not, or whether
the one or the other branch of Red River was or is the continuation of the
main river. Thus, according to Texas, the Map of Melish was conclusive
for the Contracting Parties, their privies and successors.[170] The evidence of
maps produced in this case was very voluminous.

The Court declared that the intention of the two governments—Spain
and the USA—as gathered from the words of the Treaty had to control,
and the entire instrument had to be examined in order to ascertain the real
intention of the contracting parties. For that purpose Melish's Map had to
be 'given the same effect as if it had been expressly made part of the treaty'.
In tracing the intention of the parties one of the principal questions was:
'Did the contracting parties intend [that] the words of the treaty should be
literally followed, if by so doing the real object they had in mind would be
defeated?'[171] Mr Justice Harlan, who delivered the opinion of the Court,
stated that the contracting parties certainly intended that the line should
run from the Gulf along the western bank of the Sabine River, and after it
reached Red River that it should follow the course of that river leaving both
rivers within the United States. But it could not be supposed that they
meant the Sabine river with any degree of latitude other than the true 32nd
degree of latitude, nor the crossing of the line extending along the Red
River westward with any meridian of longitude other than the true 100th
meridian.[172] In addition, the Court relied on the settlement of 1850
between Texas and the USA and other acts of the latter which stated that
the boundary should follow the 100th meridian. Thus, the two governments in 1850 intended the true 100th meridian and not that located on
Melish's Map.[173] Moreover, the USA had erected a monument at a spot
where the 100th meridian is intersected by the 36°30' north latitude. This
was done after an actual survey, and Texas had, by its legislation, recognized the true 100th meridian to be as located by the USA. In such circumstances the Court concluded that the 100th meridian mentioned in the
Treaty was the true meridian astronomically located.[174]

Clearly, Article III of the Treaty between the USA and Spain and
Article III (2) of the Anglo-German Agreement are not dissimilar. In both
articles the references were to rivers and degrees. Further, these articles
referred to maps which depicted the degrees inaccurately: Melish's Map
depicted the 100th meridian more than 100 miles further east, and the

---

[170] Ibid., p. 35.
[171] Ibid., p. 37.
[172] Ibid.
[173] Ibid., p. 39.
[174] Ibid., p. 88.

Intelligence Division of the War Office Map showed the 18° S running about 40 miles further south, than the correct locations. Therefore, in tracing the intention of the negotiators, the Intelligence Division of the War Office Map, which was referred to in Article III (2), paragraph 4, must be given effect as if it had been expressly made part of the Agreement. This interpretation has indeed been adopted in similar cases by the United States Supreme Court.[175] The correct parallel in the present circumstances would lead to a result which is unworkable, manifestly absurd and unreasonable, since it would run through the territory of Angola in the neighbourhood of Andara and it would not create a strip at no point less than 20 miles in width. In the present circumstances the correct degree would defeat the object of the Treaty. The contracting parties intended that the line should follow the parallel marked on the Intelligence Division of the War Office Map, and not the correct 18° S.

Furthermore, the question of the southern boundary of Caprivi Strip is not dissimilar to the *St Croix River* arbitration *(Great Britain* v. *USA)* (1798).[176] The facts of this case may be described, briefly, as follows. On 30 November 1782 Britain and the USA signed a Treaty of Peace, which *inter alia* laid down the boundaries between their respective territories.[177] The eastern boundary of the USA was declared by Article 2 of that Treaty to commence 'by a line to be drawn along the middle of the River St Croix, from its mouth in the Bay of Fundy to its source'. The British and American Commissioners, then negotiators of the Treaty of Peace, had before them and indeed used a map drawn in Britain by one Dr John Mitchell in 1755. On Mitchell's Map the St Croix River appeared as a stream of considerable volume, having its source in a lake called Kousaki and its mouth at the eastern head of what was then known as Passamaquoddy Bay. The greater part of Passamaquoddy Bay was depicted as having no separate designation; it appeared merely as a part of the Bay of Fundy. To the westward on the same map was another stream called the Passamadie (Passamaquoddy), emptying into a small bay or estuary of the same name.[178] But while Mitchell's Map was correct in representing two streams of the same magnitude as falling into the body of water commonly known as Passamaquoddy Bay, it did not give their true course or positions, nor was there in the region any river then commonly known as the St Croix. This name originated with the early French explorers, from whose charts it was transferred to later maps, on which it was given first to one stream and then the other; and in all the maps consulted by the negotiators of the Peace Treaty, including Mitchell's Map, the topography of the region was inaccurately depicted.[179] By a treaty of 19 November 1794, Britain and the USA agreed

[175] See *Noonan* v. *Braley* (1862), 67 US 2 Black, 499; *Cragin* v. *Powell* (1888), 128 US 691, 696; *Jefferis* v. *East Omaha Land Co.* (1890), 134 US 178; *McIver* v. *Walker* (1815), 13 US 9 Cranch, 173.

[176] Moore (ed.), *International Adjudications, Modern Series*, vols. 1 and 2 (1929/30).

[177] See Parry (ed.), *The Consolidated Treaty Series*, vol. 48 (1781–3), p. 223 (text).

[178] Moore, op. cit. above (n. 176), vol. 1, p. 6.

[179] Ibid.

to establish a Mixed Commission to decide the question: 'what river was truely indented under the name of the River Saint Croix mentioned in the treaty of Peace . . . and forming a part of the boundary therein described?'[180] At the time of the delimitation, no suggestion as to the error being on Mitchell's Map was made; therefore, the Contracting Parties did not express an understanding or agreement respecting contingent rectification. However, the Commissioners declared that the river intended under the name of the St Croix in the Peace Treaty was one whose mouth is in Passamaquoddy Bay at Joe's Point. The Commission defined the entire course of the boundary constituted by that river, that is, from its mouth to its source; and annexed a 'farther descriptive' map of its course on the award.[181]

The *St Croix River* case demonstrates that the existence of inaccuracy on a map, especially if the map had been annexed to the delimitation treaty or consulted by the negotiators, will certainly diminish its probative value. But it may not affect its admissibility for other purposes, particularly the elucidation of the real intention of the parties.[182] However, every case has to be treated according to its own merits. Therefore, notwithstanding that the above-mentioned Intelligence Division of the War Office Map is inaccurate as to the course of the 18° S, it can be invoked to establish the intention of the parties.

(c) *The Boundary constituted by the Chobe River*

1. *The geography of the Chobe*

The Chobe River rises in Central Angola, about 12°30′ S, 19° E, where it is known as the Kwando (Cwando). From its source it flows south-east till it reaches the 15° S, where it turns eastward and runs in that direction for nearly 100 km; it then continues flowing south-east. About 720 km (450 miles) from its source the Kwando intersects the northern boundary of Namibia. From this place, downstream to the neighbourhood of the 18° S, it is locally known as Mashi; then the rest of its course, that is, to its confluence with the Zambezi, is called Chobe or Linyanti. After the 18° S, the Chobe flows in several channels which eventually merge into one before it reaches the Zambezi. The total distance of the perennial river is about 735 km (457 miles); and its drainage basin is about 96,780 km² (37,367 miles²). The confluence of the Chobe and the Zambezi is about six miles.[183]

2. *Outline of the dispute*

According to Article III (2) of the Anglo-German Agreement (1890), the boundary 'descends the centre of the main channel of [the Chobe River] to

---

[180] Ibid., vol. 2, p. 373.
[181] Ibid., pp. 373–4.
[182] See Cukwurah, *The Settlement of Boundary Disputes in International Law* (1967), p. 217.
[183] *Encyclopaedia Britannica* (15th edn., 1980), vol. 5, p. 959.

its junction with the Zambezi, where it terminates'. It was, however, later discovered that the Chobe has more than one channel, and that these channels afterwards reunite before reaching the Zambezi. Two of these channels are almost of equivalent size. In one of the channels, about 10 miles west of its junction with the Zambezi, is situated an island known as Kasikili, which is about $1\frac{1}{2}$ square miles in area.[184] Initially, both German South West Africa and Bechuanaland considered the southern channel as the main one. Moreover the official maps published by Britain and Germany depicted the boundary following the southern channel, and Kasikili Island as an integral part of German South West Africa. After some years, the colonial authorities in Bechuanaland claimed that the northern channel is the main one; and subsequently claimed title to the southern channel and Kasikili Island. This claim is based on the provision of Article III (2), paragraph 1, of the Anglo-German Agreement, which expressly designated the 'centre of the main channel' of the Chobe as the boundary.

In 1911 Great Britain and Germany agreed in principle to refer the issue to a tribunal. In addition to the 'main channel' the tribunal had to define the course of the line between the Chobe and the 21° E, and decide 'whether the boundary to the east of Kaprivi Zipfel should be the *thalweg* of the Zambezi or its eastern or western bank'.[185] Great Britain wanted the issue to be referred to a 'strictly judicial tribunal', but not to a 'foreign sovereign'.[186] In January 1911 L. Harcourt, the then Secretary of State, requested the authorities in Bechuanaland to collect evidence from local sources in support of the British claim that the north channel is the main one. Harcourt requested also a map of the territory in question.[187] Before the delimitation, it appears, the territory in question had not been surveyed. An attempt was made by Captain Eason to survey the Chobe in 1913, but the rain delayed his work and the project was subsequently abandoned.[188] However, as a consequence of the First World War, Britain and Germany could not refer the issue to the tribunal.

3. *Claims respecting renunciation of the 'main channel'*

In 1949 the question of the 'main channel' was raised by a certain firm which intended to transport timber down the Chobe. In the same year the Union surveyed the territory and found that the 'main channel' is situated to the north of Kasikili Island. The Union noted that there had not been any change in the course of the 'main channel' within living memory. Notwithstanding the result of the survey, the Union claimed that the *status quo* should be maintained, that is, the southern channel should continue to

[184] Despatch No. 170 from E. Baring, High Commissioner for Bechuanaland, Basutoland and Swaziland, to Philip Noel-Baker, Commonwealth Relations Office, 6 June 1949, FO 371/73752, File 1082.
[185] Notes from FO to CO, dated 14 and 22 February, 22 May 1911, CO 879/107: African No. 969, pp. 19, 23, 49 respectively.
[186] Ibid.
[187] L. Harcourt to High Commissioner, 14 January 1911, CO 879/107: African No. 1015, p. 1.
[188] CO 879/114: African No. 1015, p. 1.

constitute the boundary between Bechuanaland and the Mandated Territory and Kasikili Island should be a portion of the latter territory.[189]

The Resident Commissioner of Bechuanaland stated that the above-mentioned South African proposal to set the boundary in the southern channel need not be resisted, provided the use of the northern channel, for navigation, was guaranteed for the people of Bechuanaland.[190] The Union was prepared to give such a guarantee. In June 1949 E. Baring, the High Commissioner for Bechuanaland, told the Commonwealth Relations Office that he considered, in the circumstances, that the proposal of the Union was acceptable.[191] The High Commissioner, in arriving at the conclusion that the southern channel should constitute the boundary, and that Kasikili Island should be part of the Mandated Territory, was influenced by maps produced by Germany and Great Britain where the boundary is depicted following the south channel.[192] Furthermore, he relied on the Joint Report.[193]

4. Construction of Article III (2) of the Anglo-German Agreement

The instrument concerning the boundary in this region will now be considered. Article III (2), paragraph 1, of the Anglo-German Agreement delimits the Chobe river in these words: 'descends the centre of the main channel of that river to its junction with the Zambezi, where it terminates.' The expression 'the main channel of' was inserted in this paragraph at the

---

[189] Despatch No. 170, loc. cit. above (n. 184), paras. 1–3; see also Despatch No. Y.4116/1 (Secret) from Mr Dundee, Commonwealth Relations Office, to J.R. Cotton, 22 August 1949, FO 371/73752, File 1082.

[190] Despatch No. 170, loc. cit. above (n. 184), para. 4.

[191] Ibid., para. 5.

[192] FO 371/73752, File 1082.

[193] In 1948 Messrs L.F.N. Trollope and N.V. Redman, respectively Magistrate of 'Eastern Caprivi Zipfel' and District Commissioner at Kasane in Bechuanaland, prepared a Joint Report respecting the main channel of the Chobe and Kasikili Island. The Report was produced after separate examination of the terrain and study of the aerial photographs. So far as material, it states:

'4. We express the opinion that the "main channel" [of the Chobe] lies in the waterway which would include the island [Kasikili] in question in Bechuanaland Protectorate.

5. On the other hand we are satisfied, after enquiring that since at least 1907, use has been made of the island by the Eastern Caprivi Zipfel [Namibian] tribesmen and that position still continues.

6. We know of no evidence of the island having been made use of, or claimed by the Bechuanaland Tribesmen or Authorities or of any objection to the use thereof by the Caprivi Tribesmen being made.

7. We record, however, the fact that the country on the Bechuanaland side of the boundary is for all practical purposes not tribally occupied': FO 371/73752, File 1082 (text of Joint Report), date 19 January 1948. Messrs Trollope and Redman recorded that they had neither arrived at, nor expressed, any joint opinion on the effect of their Report on the question of title to Kasikili Island as well as the main channel: Joint Report, loc. cit., para. 8. The British Foreign Office declared that it had no comments on the issue. However, the Commonwealth Relations Office (CRO) maintained that the 'slight alteration is of no intrinsic importance in itself and seems in substance unobjectionable'; and advised the High Commissioner to secure a guarantee of the use of the northern channel for navigation purposes. Further, it noted that the issue involved was not cession of a territory to the mandated territory: it was a confirmation of existing facts: Messrs Tait, Roberts-Wray, and Baxter (CRO), 371/73752, File 1082. From the political point of view, the CRO maintained that 'the publicity involved might arouse curiosity and subsequent criticism on the part of those who dislike the Union government's refusal to place South West Africa under trusteeship': J.R. Cotton to J.S. Gandee (restricted), CRO, 13 October 1949; see also C.I. Farr, CRO, to J.R. Cotton, FO, 12 September 1949, FO 371/73752.

request of Great Britain; the first draft articles did not identify the channel.[194] The question as to which is the main channel is a geographical one. However, the Court in the *Argentina-Chile Frontier* arbitration (1966)[195] specified certain guidelines which may be applied in determining the main channel. The Court states that 'the major channel can be determined on both historical and specific grounds. Tradition dictates the names of rivers, and sound evidence of traditional nomenclature—indigenous names given by first discoverers—would be decisive'.[196] The Court further noted that cartographers often use thick lines on maps, but such lines are determined by the breadth of the rivers; they do not indicate the major channels.[197] In the present circumstances, the surveys conducted by 'Bechuanaland' and the Union have established that the channel running north of Kasikili Island is the 'main channel' of the Chobe.[198] Moreover, it has been established that there has not been any change in the course of the 'main channel' of the Chobe within living memory. It was shown earlier that at Kasikili Island the main channel of this river had been inaccurately depicted on both British and German official maps. In addition to that the two Colonial Powers considered the south channel as the boundary between German South West Africa and Bechuanaland, and Kasikili Island as a portion of the former territory. This *status quo* was maintained during the mandate system. Indeed, it is still in existence. In the writer's opinion, there is no doubt that the boundary following the south channel at Kasikili is contrary to the clear provision of Article III (2), paragraph 1, of the Anglo-German Agreement. It is therefore concluded that in order to give effect to the terms of the Agreement under discussion, Botswana and Namibia, respectively the successor States to Great Britain and Germany, have to rectify the error, and agree upon the boundary constituted by the main channel. In such circumstances, Botswana would acquire sovereignty over Kasikili Island. However, assuming the States concerned intend to maintain the *status quo*, it is submitted that a formal arrangement is required.

The question of the Chobe is not dissimilar from the *Argentina-Chile Frontier* arbitration (1966).[199] The historical background of this case dates back to 30 August 1855, when Argentina and Chile concluded a Treaty which provided that the two countries should adopt the *uti possidetis*, that is, retain the territories they possessed in 1810, at the time of their independence from Spain. They agreed also to settle controversies by peaceful means, and to submit them to the arbitration of a friendly nation, in the event of disagreement. On 28 May 1902 the two countries submitted the question respecting the course of their boundary in the region of the River

[194] Telegram from Marquis of Salisbury to Sir Edward Malet, dated FO, 25 June 1890, FO 881/6156, p. 63; cf. draft articles, FO 881/6146, p. 54.
[195] *UNRIAA*, vol. 16, p. 109.
[196] Ibid., p. 177.
[197] Ibid.
[198] Above, n. 193 (Joint Report on Kasikili Island).
[199] *UNRIAA*, vol. 16, p. 109.

Encuentro to the arbitration of King Edward VII. The award was made on 20 November 1902. The award, so far as material, stated that the line should cross the Palena opposite the junction of the River Encuentro, and then follow the Encuentro along the course of its western branch to its source on the western slopes of Cerro Virgen.[200] A map, hereinafter the Award Map, was attached to this award. That Award Map was made up of maps submitted by Argentina. It depicted the boundary decided upon in the award with a solid red line, where the country had been adequately surveyed, and with pecked red line across unsurveyed areas. Most importantly, the Award Map depicted a section of the boundary as being not at the place indicated in the arbitral award, that is to say, opposite the mouth of the River Encuentro, but more to the east of this point, opposite the mouth of another different river which has its source in the vicinity of the Peak Herrero, so that it became impossible for the boundary to pass through the Virgin Peak. This mistake was reproduced from one of the maps which were submitted by Argentina. As a consequence of the error in the Award Map the sector of the boundary under discussion was wrongly demarcated in 1903. In addition to the Award Map, a series of official Chilean maps issued between 1913 and 1952 depicted the course of the boundary incorrectly. The 'Llanquihue Map' sent by Chile to Argentina on 26 December 1913 showed the boundary running in the north-south direction along a river named 'Rio Encuentro' through Cerro de la Virgen. Similarly, the Chilean *Carta Preliminar* of 1952 showed the boundary line taking a north-south direction along the last-mentioned course. Moreover, on this map the Cerro de la Virgen was incorrectly located, too far east, and the course of the River Engaño was incorrectly shown. It definitely did not follow the channel then referred to by Chile as the main or 'true Encuentro'. In reliance on these maps, Argentina claimed that Chile was precluded from contending that the boundary should follow the channel called by the former the Rio Falso Engaño and that it should not follow the Rio Encuentro and proceed through the Cerro de la Virgen. Chile's explanation of the erroneous cartography, extending over a period of 40 years, was that for a long time it remained in ignorance of the error in the Award Map; and that Argentina, which according to Chile was responsible for the error, failed to mention it. Accordingly, Chile claimed that Argentina was estopped from denying that the boundary should follow the course of the channel which has its source in the vicinity of the Cerro Herrero. The Court held that Argentina could not be held responsible for the error in the Award Map, nor was it under any legal duty to inform Chile or the Arbitrator of it when it became aware of it. In any case, the Chilean authorities were put on notice in 1913 that there was some difficulty in applying the 1902 award in the sector between Boundary Posts 16 and 17. The Court declared that the parties were not *ad idem* as to the extent of the river Encuentro, and there-

---

[200] Ibid., p. 142.

fore no claim of estoppel was made out by either party against the other.[201]
It concluded:

[T]he river which became the Encuentro as the result of the 1903 demarcation is
not the river which the Arbitrator had in contemplation when he pronounced the
Award; that is not the river shown on the Award Map; that the river now known as
the Encuentro, although it appears to be shown on the Award map, is not named
thereon; and that the course of that river, though in part inaccurately depicted on
that Map, is shown as having two channels. Nevertheless, there is no doubt that, as
a result of what happened in 1903, the river opposite Boundary 16 is the Encuentro
and has to be understood as such for the purpose of interpreting and fulfilling the
Award.[202]

Relying on the *Argentina-Chile* case, it would follow that the principles of
estoppel, admission and acquiescence are not applicable in the present circumstances. Thus, for the purpose of fulfilling the delimitation contemplated in Article III (2) of the Anglo-German Agreement, the boundary
should follow the northern channel which is indeed the main one.

In the *Taba* award (1988), with regard to the disputed boundary pillars
85, 86 and 87, Israel asserted that three places mentioned in Article 1 of the
agreement of 1906, viz., Wadi Taba, Jebel Fort and Jebel Fathi Pasha, had
been incorrectly identified on the ground by the persons who erected the
pillars and by Egypt.[203] The Tribunal examined two questions: 'First: Do
the locations of the existing boundary pillars . . . contradict the 1906
Agreement? Secondly: If such a contradiction exists, is it the line formed
by the pillars or the line described by the 1906 Agreement which prevails?'[204] Having examined several maps, the Tribunal concluded that the
locations of above-mentioned existing boundary pillars were not in contradiction with the 1906 Agreement.[205] Further, it declared that an examination of the second question was appropriate in view of a complete
exploration of the case. The Tribunal pointed out that Article 3 of the 1906
Agreement provides that the '[b]oundary pillars will be erected, in the presence of the Joint Commission, at intervisible points along the separating
line'.[206] The demarcation took place in two phases: first, the erection of
provisional telegraph poles in October 1906, and secondly, the replacement
of them by permanent masonry pillars between 31 December 1906 and
9 February 1907. Both operations were carried out in the presence of the
Egyptian and Turkish Commissioners or representatives. The evidence
showed that neither party claimed that the Agreement had not been correctly executed. On two later occasions, in 1909 and 1911, Turkish and
Egyptian officials co-operated in the rebuilding of certain boundary pillars.
The Tribunal concluded that:

[201] Ibid., p. 166.
[202] Ibid., p. 177.
[203] *International Legal Materials*, 27 (1988), p. 1478, para. 201.
[204] Ibid., p. 1478, para. 199.
[205] Ibid., p. 1481, para. 208.
[206] Ibid., para. 210.

If a boundary line is once demarcated jointly by the parties concerned, the demarcation is considered as an authentic interpretation of the boundary agreement even if deviations may have occurred or if there are some inconsistencies with the maps. This has been confirmed in practice and legal doctrine, especially for the case that a long time has elapsed since demarcation.[207]

In this context, the Tribunal cited the work of Professor Ress—*The Delimitation and Demarcation of Frontiers in International Treaties and Maps* (1985), pp. 435–7—where he states that: 'If the parties have considered over a long time the demarcated frontier as valid, this is an authentic interpretation of the relevant international title.'[208] Further, it referred to the well-known paragraph in the judgment of the International Court of Justice in the *Temple* case where the Court stated:

In general, when two countries establish a frontier between them, one of the primary objects is to achieve stability and finality. This is impossible if the line so established can, at any moment, and on the basis of a continuously available process, be called in question, and its rectification claimed, whenever any inaccuracy by reference to a clause in the parent treaty is discovered. Such a process could continue indefinitely, and finality would never be reached so long as possible errors still remained to be discovered. Such a frontier, so far from being stable, would be completely precarious.[209]

The Tribunal therefore concluded that the demarcated line would prevail over the Agreement if a contradiction could be detected. Clearly, this conclusion is based on legal principles such as admission, acquiescence, estoppel and recognition. The theoretical inaccuracy considered by the tribunal in the *Taba* award is slightly different from that of the Chobe River. First, the alignment constituted by the Chobe is not demarcated. Secondly, the parties intended the boundary to follow the 'main channel' as stipulated in the Agreement of 1890. Thirdly, the contradiction was discovered in 1948, that is, when Namibia was a mandate. At the time in question, and indeed after the termination of the mandate, South Africa—then Mandatory Power—did not intend to submit reports regarding Namibia to the United Nations. As stated earlier, the boundaries of the mandated territory could not be modified without the consent of the League of Nations, and later of the United Nations. In these circumstances it is not reasonable to raise the aforementioned legal principles. However, if the *status quo* continues for a

---

[207] Ibid., p. 1482, para. 210. Professor Lapidoth, a Member of the Tribunal, delivered a dissenting opinion. He declared that Professor Ress does not support an absolute preference for demarcation over delimitation. Further, he pointed out that of particular interest is Professor Ress's opinion that '[p]robably demarcation . . . only shifts the burden of evidence to the party which wants to argue that the demarcation was wrong': ibid., p. 1504, para. 30. Lapidoth added that 'the relative weight of the delimitation and demarcation depends on the circumstances of each case, i.e. the degree of precision and of detail in the delimitation agreement, the seriousness of the pre-delimitation survey, the degree of care with which the demarcation has been effected and reported, and of course whether it was undertaken unilaterally or bilaterally': ibid.

[208] Ibid.

[209] Ibid. See also *ICJ Reports*, 1962, p. 34.

long period after the independence of Namibia, it may be submitted that the line would prevail over the 1890 Agreement.

VIII. THE UNITED NATIONS MAP OF NAMIBIA: A CASE STUDY

(a) *Background and Scope of the Map*

On 20 December 1976 the General Assembly of the UN adopted Resolution 31/150 which, *inter alia*, requested the Secretary-General 'urgently to undertake, in consultation with the UNCN, the preparation of a comprehensive UN Map of Namibia reflecting therein the territorial integrity of the Territory of Namibia'.[210] Having completed the map the Secretary-General presented it to the General Assembly for approval.

The scale of the UN Map of Namibia is 1:4,000,000. It depicts international boundaries, intermittent and perennial rivers, landing strips and airports, railways, roads, towns and villages. With regard to the rivers, the courses of the international boundaries are not marked. Thus, it is impossible to determine the course of such lines in the cases of the Orange, Chobe, Zambezi, Okavango and Kunene Rivers from the evidence of this map. The eastern boundary is shown following 20° E, 22° S, then 21° E until it intersects a line running through a point situated 20 miles south of Andara. The rest of this eastern boundary, that is, the southern boundary of Caprivi Strip, follows the solution that was formally accepted by the Union in 1931. Similarly, the northern boundary, that is, the straight lines between the Kunene and Okavango Rivers, and between Andara on the latter river and the Katima Rapids, runs along the course defined by the agreements that had been concluded by Portugal and the Union in 1926 and 1931 respectively. Walvis Bay and all the islands lying along the coast—the Penguin Islands—are depicted as an integral part of Namibia. There is an inscription on it which provides that it 'represents an official United Nations map of Namibia and supersedes any other map on Namibia or South West Africa hitherto published by South Africa'. In addition the map contains a disclaimer which states that 'the delineation of the boundaries between Namibia and neighbouring countries and the names shown on this map do not imply official endorsement or acceptance by the United Nations as they are to be determined by the independent government of Namibia'.

(b) *The Legal Significance of the Map*

The map under consideration calls for an enquiry as to whether the UN is vested with the authority to make binding determinations respecting

---

[210] Resolution 31/150 was adopted by 125 votes to none with 4 abstentions (France, Federal Republic of Germany, the UK and USA): A/31/PV.105.

boundary regimes. Briefly, five propositions may be submitted in this context:

(1) As a general rule the UN cannot delimit territories except in special circumstances, or unless the express consent of the States concerned has been acquired;

(2) There may be an exception to (1) where the UN has a special responsibility over a territory;

(3) The UN may through its decision-making make determinations;

(4) It naturally follows that the UN may draw up a map;

(5) That leaves a closely related area as to whether the UN is settling the boundaries. Clearly the answer is in the negative. These have to be settled in accordance with the principles of international law by the States concerned.

Significantly, the disclaimer on the UN Map of Namibia testifies to the conclusion reached by this writer. It expressly states that the boundaries are to be settled by an independent government of that territory. The effect of this disclaimer is to avoid any assertion that the UN by publishing this map has become bound to accept the alignments depicted by virtue of legal concepts of estoppel, admission, acquiescence or recognition.[211] Similarly, the disclaimer would avoid the assertion that UN member States which share common boundaries with Namibia have become bound by virtue of these principles. This map was prepared for the purpose of the 'dissemination of information', and no request was made as to the delimitation. The boundaries depicted on this map are, therefore, provisional. Clearly, the territorial claims are beyond the scope of this disclaimer. The conclusion to be drawn is that the UN has settled the issue of title to Walvis Bay and the twelve Penguin Islands, which are situated between Walvis Bay and the Orange River, definitively.[212]

IX. CONCLUSIONS

The aforegoing consideration shows that official and unofficial maps are sources of evidence 'material for the purpose of determining the existence

---

[211] Above, p. 212 (consideration of disclaimer).

[212] South Africa claims title to Walvis Bay and to the following islands which are collectively known as the Penguin Islands, namely, Ichaboe, Hollandsbird, Mercury, Long, Seal, Penguin, Halifax, Possession, Albatross Rock, Pomona, Plum Pudding and Roastbeef (Sinclair's Island). The General Assembly of the UN maintains that these territories form an integral part of Namibia. The Penguin Islands have been depicted as part of the territory of Namibia on a number of official maps published by South Africa for a very long period. Interestingly, the available evidence shows that none of the maps published in the Reports concerning the mandated territory of South West Africa depicts the Penguin Islands as South African territories. These Reports were communicated by the Union of South Africa to the League of Nations. The maps in question have no disclaimers: see *Report on the Administration of South West Africa for the Years: 1918–1939; and 1946*. On recent official South African maps the islands are clearly marked, underlined in red, and contain a disclaimer stating that they form part of the Republic of South Africa. The present writer feels that there is room for an estoppel argument in the case of the Penguin Islands.

of an alignment and its status in terms of acceptance and recognition by the states concerned'.[213] However, the practice shows that tribunals are often reluctant to place much value on maps. As Weissberg rightly put it, 'this tendency has been particularly noticeable whenever the map describes a territory of which the authors have little knowledge, is geographically inaccurate, or is sketched in order to promote a country's claim'.[214] Further, this tendency may equally be noticed whenever the scale of map 'is too small to demonstrate a location on the ground as exactly required'.[215] The practice of the tribunals shows that maps are incorporated or appended to the judgments. In both cases the purpose of the maps may be the same. In the case concerning *Delimitation of the Maritime Boundary in the Gulf of Maine Area* (1984), for instance, the Chamber declared that 'the maps incorporated in the present Judgment were prepared on the basis of documents submitted to the Court by the Parties, and their sole purpose is to provide a visual illustration of the relevant paragraphs of the Judgment'.[216] Similarly, in the case concerning the *Continental Shelf (Libya/Malta)* (1985), the Court stressed that 'the only purpose of Map No. 1 appended to the present Judgment is to give a general picture of the geographical context of the dispute, and no legal significance attaches to the choice of scale or the presence or absence of any particular geographical feature'.[217] The study found that, in almost every boundary question, the cartographer's source of information is a matter of primary importance. Briefly, the conclusion to be drawn from the aforegoing is that map evidence plays a major part in boundary questions. Thus, the practice of tribunals has developed.

In some cases the parties place special reliance on the evidence of

[213] Brownlie, op. cit. above (n. 11), p. 5.

[214] Weissberg, 'Maps As Evidence in International Boundary Disputes: A Reappraisal', *American Journal of International Law* (1963), p. 781. The evidence shows that ignorance of certain geographical facts occasionally led the geographers to locate plateaux, mountains, lakes or rivers inaccurately, or to assign to them names by which they were not commonly or locally known. In other cases meridians and parallels had been wrongly depicted on maps. Some of these maps, however erroneous, had been used or consulted by negotiators of the delimitation treaties. As a consequence there are conflicts between the text of the treaty and the boundary illustrated on such maps. Further, in some circumstances unworkable delimitations had been established.

[215] *Taba* award, *International Legal Materials*, 27 (1988), p. 1472, para. 184. There are many small scale maps which depict a quadripoint—a convergence of four international boundaries—near Kazungula and the confluence of the Zambezi and Chobe Rivers. These boundaries are: Botswana–Namibia, Namibia–Zambia, Zimbabwe–Zambia and Botswana-Zimbabwe. As Professor Brownlie points out, this convergence is commonly shown 'since the scale of many maps leaves no choice': op. cit. above (n. 11), pp. 1099–107 (a detailed account). It has been reported that Botswana and Zambia share a common boundary of about 400 yards wide in this region: *The Times* (London), 11 November 1970.

[216] *ICJ Reports*, 1984, p. 246, at p. 269. The Maps incorporated in the judgment in this case are: (*a*) 'General Map of the Region, showing the starting-point for the delimitation line and the area for its termination'; (*b*) map showing the 'limits of fishery zones and continental shelf claimed by the Parties [Canada and the USA], at 1 March 1977'; (*c*) map depicting the 'delimitation lines proposed by the Parties before the Chamber'; and (*d*) the map showing the delimitation drawn by the Chamber. The map referred to in the dissenting opinion of Judge Gros is incorporated in the opinion in question. Further maps are appended to the judgment. See ibid., pp. 269, 285, 289, 346 and 390.

[217] *ICJ Reports*, 1985, p. 13, at p. 20. See the maps on pp. 21, 27, 54 and 171, published for illustrative purpose.

photographs of the disputed area. In the *Walfish Bay Boundary* case, for instance, Great Britain submitted about sixteen aerial photographs showing different views of the disputed area.[218] Notwithstanding that these photographs and Wrey's Map were clear, the Arbitrator decided to visit the disputed territory.[219] Recently, in the *Taba* award (1988), a number of photographs were introduced by both parties with the consent or at the request of the Tribunal.[220] In response to the testimony of an expert witness for Egypt that one of the photographs submitted by Israel might not be authentic, Israel requested leave to introduce additional witnesses in order to testify with regard to the authenticity of the series of photographs in question. The Tribunal decided, with one Member dissenting, that

---

[218] 'British Reply to the Memorandum Presented to the Arbitrator by the German Government', FO 881/9781.

[219] In the law of civil procedure provision is commonly made for members of the Court to visit the place or premises involved in cases where information gained by personal inspection may be of special value in elucidating disputed questions. Strictly speaking *descente sur les lieux* is not a matter of evidence: Sandifer, op. cit. above (n. 17), p. 343; Hudson, 'Visits by International Tribunals to Places Concerned in Proceedings', *American Journal of International Law*, 31 (1937), p. 696. Professor Cheng maintains that it 'presents considerable affinity with judicial notice', and may thus be regarded 'as a means for edifying the judicial knowledge': Cheng, *General Principles of Law as applied by International Courts and Tribunals* (1953), p. 304. The practice shows that international tribunals have resorted occasionally to this procedure of supplementing the evidence produced before them. In the *Ben Tillett* case (*Great Britain* v. *Belgium*) (1898) the Arbitrator visited the prison where Tillett had been held 'in order, by means of a full knowledge of the case, to solve certain questions which seemed doubtful to me': BFSP, 92 (1899–1900), pp. 105 and 78–109. An example of this is the King's Cross Fire Disaster inquiry (1987). On 18 November 1987 a wooden escalator at King's Cross, London's busiest underground station, caught fire. 31 people died and more than 50 were injured: *The Independent* (London), 19 November 1987, p. 1; *The Times* (London), 23 November 1987, p. 1. Mr Desmond Fennell, QC, Chairman of the inquiry, visited the spot on 24 November of the same year in order to 'understand the geography and gain a picture so I would be able to follow the narrative as it unfolds at the inquiry': *The Evening Standard* (London), 24 November 1987, p. 1. In the *Grisbadarna* case (1909)—delimitation of a certain part of the maritime boundary between Norway and Sweden—the Tribunal visited the disputed zone and embodied an account of it in the record of the proceedings: Scott, *Hague Court Reports* (1916), p. 122 at p. 125; *American Journal of International Law*, 4 (1910), p. 226. See also *Meerauge Boundary* arbitration (*Austria* v. *Hungary*) (1902), Martens, *Nouveau recueil general des traités*, 3rd series, vol. 3 (1910), p. 71; *Diversion of Water from the Meuse* (1937), PCIJ, Series A/B, No. 70; *Free Zones* case (1932), ibid., No. 46 at p. 99. In the *South West Africa* cases the ICJ rejected the proposal of *descente sur les lieux* made by Mr De Villiers, Agent of the Government of South Africa, on 30 March 1965: *South West Africa* cases, *ICJ Pleadings*, vol. 8 (1965), pp. 271, 280. De Villiers suggested an inspection *in loco* in Namibia, South Africa, the applicant States—Ethiopia and Liberia—and one or two additional sub-Saharan States of the Court's own choosing 'for a just and proper adjudication upon the factual aspects of the crucial issues regarding the promotion of well-being and progress': ibid., p. 278. Mr Gross, Counsel for the applicants, rejected the proposal in these words: 'The Applicants . . . respectfully submit that the proposal for the inspection *in loco* is unnecessary, expensive, dilatory, cumbersome and unwanted': *South West Africa* cases, ibid., vol. 9 (1965), p. 53. On 29 November 1965 the President announced that the Court had decided not to accede to the request made by Counsel for South Africa: *ICJ Reports*, 1966, p. 9. In the *Walfish Bay* case the Arbitrator visited the disputed territory 'in order to obtain impressions similar to those obtained by that officer [Captain Dyer] and to judge his intentions with the best guarantees of accuracy': *UNRIAA*, vol. 11, p. 294. The use of experts to obtain evidence must not be confused with *descente sur les lieux*. See *Corfu Channel* case, *ICJ Reports*, 1949, p. 151; Sandifer, op. cit. above (n. 17), p. 344. *Descentes sur les lieux* have considerable potential usefulness in boundary arbitration. More recently, in the *Taba* award (1988), the Tribunal visited the disputed territory in consultation with the parties: *International Legal Materials*, 27 (1988), pp. 1431, para. 5, and 1432, para. 7.

[220] See *International Legal Materials*, 27 (1988), pp. 1433, 1451, 1453, 1456, 1459, 1465 and 1467.

there was no reason at the time to grant the request. The original print of the challenged photograph was later submitted. Further, at the opening of the hearing, a short video film was presented by Israel.[221] Briefly, the conclusion to be drawn is that the evidence of photographs and video films is mainly admitted for illustrative purposes.

[221] Ibid., p. 1433, para. 12.

NUCLEAR ENERGY AND INTERNATIONAL LAW: AN ENVIRONMENTAL PERSPECTIVE*

By ALAN E. BOYLE‡

I. INTRODUCTION: INTERNATIONAL NUCLEAR POLICY

As the Chernobyl reactor accident in 1986 has shown, modern nuclear technology creates unavoidable risks for all States, whether or not they choose to use this form of energy. Every State, and the environment, is potentially affected by the possibility of radioactive contamination, the spread of toxic substances derived from nuclear energy, and the long-term health hazards consequent on exposure to radiation.[1]

In the early days of nuclear energy, it was widely believed that the benefits outweighed the risks, and could be shared by all.[2] This optimistic view was reflected in international policy. The International Atomic Energy Agency was created in 1956 with the object of encouraging and facilitating the spread of nuclear power.[3] Atomic energy, it was assumed, would contribute to 'peace, health and prosperity' throughout the world.[4] The prevalent belief then was that the health and environmental risks could be managed successfully by governments and the IAEA through co-operation on safety matters.

Successive declarations of international bodies maintained this belief in the dissemination of nuclear energy. In 1977, the UN General Assembly reaffirmed the importance of nuclear energy for economic and social development, and proclaimed the right of all States to use it and to have access to the technology.[5] The success of this early exercise in technology transfer

* © Alan E. Boyle, 1989.

‡ MA, BCL (Oxon.); Senior Lecturer, Faculty of Law, Queen Mary and Westfield College, University of London.

[1] See IAEA, *Summary Report on the Post Accident Review Meeting on the Chernobyl Accident* (Vienna, 1986); UKAEA, *The Chernobyl Accident and its Consequences* (London, 1987); NEA/OECD, *The Radiological Impact of the Chernobyl Accident in OECD Countries* (Paris, 1988); Report of the United Nations Scientific Committee on the Effects of Atomic Radiation, *UN General Assembly Official Records* (hereinafter GAOR), 37th Session (New York, 1982) and 41st Session (New York, 1986); *Report of the President's Commission on the Accident at Three Mile Island* (Washington, 1979).

[2] Agreed Declaration on Atomic Energy, Washington, 1945, *UN Treaty Series*, vol. 1, p. 123 (US, Canada, UK); UNGA Res. 1(1) (1945); President Eisenhower's 'Atoms for Peace Address', GAOR, 8th Session, 470th meeting, paras. 79–126; Szasz, *The Law and Practices of the IAEA* (Vienna, 1970), chs. 1 and 2; McKnight, *Atomic Safeguards* (New York, 1971), ch. 1.

[3] Statute, Arts. III (1)–(4), *UN Treaty Series*, vol. 276, p. 3; amended, 1961, ibid., vol. 471, p. 334; 1970, *US Treaties and Other International Agreements*, vol. 24, p. 1637.

[4] IAEA Statute, Art. III.

[5] UNGA Res. 32/50 (1977). See also Res. 36/78 (1981) and GAOR, 41st Session (1987), Report of the Preparatory Committee for the UN Conference for the Promotion of Industrial Co-operation in the Peaceful Uses of Nuclear Energy.

can be measured today in over 400 nuclear power plants operating in 26 countries.

(a) *The Acceptability of Nuclear Weapons*

There were fewer illusions about nuclear weapons. Non-proliferation beyond the five permanent members of the UN Security Council quickly became an international arms control policy, although not accepted by all.[6] Thus, a second role for the IAEA was to ensure that nuclear power was used for peaceful purposes only.[7] In 1968, the policy of non-proliferation and the powers of the IAEA were strengthened by the Nuclear Non-Proliferation Treaty.[8] Three nuclear powers and a large majority of UN members acknowledged 'the devastation that would be visited upon all mankind by a nuclear war', and agreed further measures intended to prevent the spread of nuclear weapons.[9] Although the treaty reaffirmed the belief that nuclear technology, including weapons technology, had beneficial peaceful applications which should be available to all, the linkage between non-proliferation and the peaceful uses of nuclear power has remained controversial for some States, such as India, and hindered agreement on further nuclear co-operation.[10]

The 1968 treaty did nothing to reduce the arsenals of existing nuclear weapons powers. At first the testing of those arsenals proceeded freely, without objection, even in the South Pacific where it was mainly carried out. In the 1950s the main reservations about these tests concerned disruption of local populations and interference with high seas freedoms.[11] The existence of a threat to health and the environment was recognized, however, by three nuclear powers, in the 1963 treaty which banned nuclear weapons tests in the atmosphere, outer space and under water.[12] But testing by France and China continued, prompting condemnation at the Stockholm Conference in 1972[13] and at the UN.[14]

[6] See Willrich, *International Safeguards and Nuclear Industry* (Baltimore, 1973); Potter, *Nuclear Power and Non-Proliferation*; Quester (ed.), *Nuclear Proliferation* (Madison, 1971); Willrich (ed.), *Civil Nuclear Power and International Security* (New York, 1968); Lamm, *The Utilization of Nuclear Energy and International Law* (Budapest, 1984); SIPRI, *Safeguards Against Nuclear Proliferation* (Stockholm, 1975).

[7] Statute, Arts. II, III. The EURATOM Treaty, 1957, *UN Treaty Series*, vol. 298, p. 169, provides for safeguards against diversion among European member States.

[8] *UN Treaty Series*, vol. 729, p. 161; Willrich, *Non-Proliferation Treaty* (Charlottesville, 1968); Fischer, *The Non-Proliferation of Nuclear Weapons* (New York, 1971); SIPRI, op. cit. above (n. 6).

[9] A comparable regime for South America was established by the Tlatelolco Treaty for the Non-Proliferation of Nuclear Weapons in Latin America, 1967, *UN Treaty Series*, vol. 634, p. 326; see Redick, in Quester, op. cit. above (n. 6), ch. 6.

[10] *GAOR*, 37th Session (1983), Report of the Preparatory Committee for the United Nations Conference for the Promotion of International Co-operation in the Peaceful Uses of Nuclear Energy; ibid., 40th Session (1986).

[11] McDougal and Schlei, *Yale Law Journal*, 64 (1955), p. 648; Margolis, ibid., p. 629.

[12] Treaty Banning Nuclear Weapons Testing in the Atmosphere, Outer Space and Under Water, 1963, *UN Treaty Series*, vol. 480, p. 43.

[13] A/CONF. 48/14/Rev. 1; Res. 3(1), 4 June 1972.

[14] UNGA Res. 3078 XXVIII (1973). Similar resolutions have been passed annually since 1955.

Australia and New Zealand failed in their attempt in 1974 to have the ICJ declare further French atmospheric tests illegal.[15] Their experience, reinforced by mounting evidence of the long-term effects of earlier tests in Australia and elsewhere,[16] eventually prompted the creation in 1985 of a South Pacific Nuclear Free Zone.[17] The prohibition among the parties of nuclear tests, or the dumping of radioactive waste at sea, within this zone, indicated the growing strength of regional and international opposition to such activities on environmental grounds.

(b) *The Emergence of Environmental Concern*

It was the popularity of nuclear power as an answer to the oil crisis of the 1970s which ultimately brought long-term health and environmental consequences to the forefront of international concern. The Stockholm Conference in 1972 had called for a registry of emissions of radioactivity and international co-operation on radioactive waste disposal and reprocessing.[18] It recognized that the latter was a growing problem, caused by the increasing use of nuclear power, but it could offer no solutions. A partial remedy was to ban oceanic dumping of nuclear waste, and in 1983 the parties to the London Dumping Convention[19] agreed to suspend oceanic dumping of all nuclear waste pending further assessment of health and environmental hazards, but no clear solution to the waste disposal issue has yet been found. Nuclear reactor accidents, at Three Mile Island in the United States, and Chernobyl in the Soviet Union, showed how serious were the risks for health, agriculture and the environment posed by nuclear power.[20] Spreading contamination over a wide area of Eastern and Western Europe, the accident at Chernobyl in 1986, like the sinking of the *Torrey Canyon* in 1967,[21] revealed the limitations of international policy for containing catastrophic risks.

Chernobyl cast doubt on the adequacy of national and international regulation of nuclear facilities. It showed how little agreement existed on questions of liability and State responsibility. It gave new importance to the interest of neighbouring States in the siting of nuclear power plants, the opportunities for consultation on issues of safety, and the right to prompt

---

[15] *Nuclear Tests* cases (*Australia v. France*), *ICJ Reports*, 1973, p. 99 (*Interim Measures*); *ICJ Reports*, 1974, p. 253 (*Jurisdiction*); (*New Zealand v. France*), *ICJ Reports*, 1973, p. 135 (*Interim Measures*); *ICJ Reports*, 1974, p. 457 (*Jurisdiction*); Prott, *Sydney Law Review*, 7 (1976), p. 433; Dugard, *Virginia Journal of International Law*, 16 (1976), p. 463; New Zealand Ministry of Foreign Affairs, *French Nuclear Testing in the Pacific* (Wellington, 1973); Dupuy, *German Yearbook of International Law*, 20 (1977), p. 375; MacDonald and Hough, ibid., p. 337; see below, n. 257.

[16] See Reports of the UN Scientific Committee on the Effects of Atomic Radiation, 1972, *GAOR*, 27th Session, Supplement No. 25; 1982, ibid., 37th Session, Supplement No. 45.

[17] South Pacific Nuclear Free Zone Treaty, 1985, *International Legal Materials*, 24 (1985), p. 1442.

[18] A/CONF. 48/14/Rev. 1, Rec. 75, *Action Plan for the Human Environment*.

[19] *International Legal Materials*, 11 (1972), p. 1291; Res. LDC 14(7), 1983. Annex I of the Convention had only prohibited dumping of high-level radioactive waste. See below, n. 101.

[20] See n. 1, above.

[21] See Brown, *Current Legal Problems*, 21 (1968), p. 113.

notification of potentially harmful accidents. It demonstrated, too, that the fundamentally benign view of nuclear power adopted in the 1950s now required modification, with new emphasis on stronger international control of safety matters.[22] For the first time, an international body, the Council of Europe, was prepared to describe nuclear energy as 'potentially dangerous', and to recommend a moratorium on construction of new facilities and the closure of those that did not meet international standards.[23] Few States have been willing to go this far; the predominant belief remains that through stronger international co-operation, the risks of nuclear energy can be contained and made environmentally acceptable.

II. The International Regulation of Nuclear Energy: The Role of International Organizations

Like oil tankers, nuclear installations are potentially hazardous undertakings which need regulation on grounds of health, safety and environmental protection. Because the consequences of failure to regulate adequately may affect other States and the global environment, international regulation— the setting of common standards, supervised by international institutions— offers the best means of ensuring generally accepted minimum standards of environmental protection. The benefits of this approach accrue to the international community, which gains protection from unilaterally chosen levels of risk, but the burdens fall on national governments, which lose the freedom to determine for themselves what standards provide an appropriate balance of safety and development in their own territories.[24]

For oil tankers, the choice of strong international regulation has been made. The minimum duties of flag States in matters of environmental protection are laid down in detail in international conventions, and given additional legal force by the Law of the Sea Convention.[25] A relatively strong scheme of enforcement exists. No similar choice has been made for nuclear installations. Here, instead, national sovereignty, and with it the freedom to set national standards, by and large prevails.[26] International bodies, including the IAEA, the OECD and the EEC, do have a responsibility for formulating international standards of health and safety regula-

---

[22] See IAEA General Conference, Special Session, 1986, IAEA Doc. GC (SPL.1)/4 and GC(SPL.1)/15/Rev. 1, in *International Legal Materials*, 25 (1986), pp. 1387 ff.; OECD Nuclear Energy Agency, 15th Report, *NEA Activities in 1986*, pp. 29 ff.; European Community, *20th General Report*, 1986, paras. 759–62. See Cameron *et al.* (eds.), *Nuclear Energy Law After Chernobyl* (London, 1988); Sands, *Chernobyl: Law and Communication* (Cambridge, 1988).

[23] Parliamentary Assembly Rec. 1068 (1988).

[24] Barkenbus, *International Organization*, 41 (1987), p. 475.

[25] Marine Pollution Convention, 1973 and 1978; UN Law of the Sea Convention, 1982, Arts. 211, 217, 218, 220.

[26] Barkenbus, loc. cit. above (n. 24), pp. 482, 486; Dickstein, *International and Comparative Law Quarterly*, 23 (1977), p. 426.

tion. But although these standards are often adopted into national law,[27] in the case of the IAEA and the OECD they are not as such binding on States in most instances, as will be seen, and lack the force of treaties like the MARPOL Convention. The result is that international regulation of nuclear energy, if it can be so called, is unsatisfactorily weak. It fails, for reasons explained below, to achieve the assurance of minimum standards of environmental protection[28] comparable to those on which other States are entitled to insist in the case of oil pollution. Without binding international standards, no comparable level of international enforcement is possible either.

(a) *IAEA and the Regulation of Nuclear Power*

The International Atomic Energy Agency was the product of compromise following failure to agree on United States' proposals for international management of all nuclear power by an international body.[29] Rather, its main tasks were to encourage and facilitate the development and dissemination of nuclear power,[30] and to ensure through non-proliferation safeguards that it was used for peaceful purposes only.[31] Setting standards for health and safety in collaboration with other international agencies was very much an incidental or secondary responsibility.[32]

The Chernobyl accident has called for significant alteration of the Agency's priorities. It provided the main forum for consideration of measures made necessary by the accident and member States endorsed the importance of the Agency's role in safety and radiological protection matters.[33] Among the recommendations of a review group were that the Agency should promote better exchanges of information among States on safety and accident experience, develop additional safety guidelines and enhance its capacity to perform safety evaluations and inspections on request.[34] The Convention on Assistance in cases of Nuclear Emergency

[27] See generally OECD/NEA, *Nuclear Legislation: Regulations Governing Nuclear Installations and Radiation Protection* (Paris, 1972); IAEA, *Experience and Trends in Nuclear Law* (Vienna, 1972); IAEA, *Nuclear Law for a Developing World* (Vienna, 1969); *Licensing and Regulatory Control of Nuclear Installations* (Vienna, 1975); Szasz, op. cit. above (n. 2), ch. 22; OECD, 'International Co-operation in the Field of Radioactive Transfrontier Pollution', *Nuclear Law Bulletin*, 14 (1974), p. 55.

[28] Barkenbus, loc. cit. above (n. 24), pp. 483, 486; Cameron *et al.*, op. cit. above (n. 22), at pp. 159 ff., 179 ff.

[29] Szasz, op. cit. above (n. 2), ch. 1; Potter, *Nuclear Power and Non-Proliferation* (Cambridge, Mass., 1982), ch. 2.; McKnight, op. cit. above (n. 2), ch. 1.

[30] Statute, Arts. II (1)–(4). In practice the development of the international nuclear industry has relied more heavily on assistance from other States than on the IAEA. See Cavers, *Vanderbilt Law Review*, 12 (1958), p. 68; Szasz, op. cit. above (n. 2), ch. 2; McKnight, op. cit. above (n. 2), ch. 2.

[31] Statute, Art. III (5).

[32] Statute, Art. III (6); Szasz, op. cit. above (n. 2), ch. 22.

[33] IAEA, 30th Conference, Special Session GC/SPL.1/Res. 1. See also statement of the Group of Seven on the implications of the Chernobyl Accident, *International Legal Materials*, 15 (1986), p. 1005; Handl, *Revue générale de droit international public*, 92 (1988), p. 5; Blix, *Environmental Policy and Law*, 18 (1988), p. 142.

[34] IAEA, *Summary Report on the Post Accident Review Meeting on the Chernobyl Accident* (1986).

also gives it the new task of co-ordinating assistance and responding to requests for help.[35]

Thus, despite the very different objectives it had in 1956, the Agency now attaches high importance to its nuclear safety role. Rather like the IMO after the *Torrey Canyon* disaster, it has acquired a new environmental perspective as perhaps the one positive result of Chernobyl.

(b) *Powers over Health and Safety*

The Statute requires the IAEA to establish 'standards' for protecting health and minimizing danger to life and property.[36] In addition, its health and safety document sets out a policy on the inclusion of safety standards in agreements with States.[37] This refers to 'standards, regulations, rules or codes of practice established to protect man and the environment against ionising radiation and to minimise danger to life and property'. 'Standards' may thus take a number of different forms, depending on their function, but all serve the same broad purpose of seeking to prevent harm to the environment and adverse effects on other States.

IAEA standards, regulations, codes of practice, guides and other related instruments cover such subjects as radiation protection, transport and handling of radioactive materials and radioactive waste disposal.[38] The Nuclear Safety Standards Programme, revised in 1988, sets basic minimum safety standards and guiding principles for the design, construction, siting and operation of nuclear power plants.[39] The important point is thus that the Agency has competence over a wide range of safety and health issues relating to all aspects of the use of nuclear energy: what it lacks is the ability to give these standards obligatory force.

(c) *The Legal Effect of IAEA Health and Safety Standards*

Nothing in the Statute confers any binding force on IAEA standards, or requires member States to comply with them.[40] While, under the Statute, the same is true of non-proliferation safeguards, in practice the IAEA

---

[35] See below, Section III (c).

[36] Art. III (6).

[37] Revised safety standards and measures (1976), INFCIRC/18/Rev. 1.

[38] Basic Safety Standards for Radiation Protection, 1981, summarized *Nuclear Law Bulletin*, 28 (1981), p. 38. These are sponsored jointly by the IAEA, WHO, ILO and OECD and are based on the ICRP's 1977 recommendations which seek to limit the incidence of radiation-induced fatal cancers and serious genetic disorders to a level accepted by society and to prevent other harmful disorders: Smith, *IAEA Bulletin*, 30 (1988), p. 42; see also Regulations on Safe Transport for Radioactive Materials, 1984; Principles for Establishing Intervention Levels for the Protection of the Public in the Event of a Nuclear Accident, 1985; Code of Practice for Management of Radioactive Waste from Nuclear Power Plants, 1985.

[39] The IAEA approved revised texts of five NUSS codes in 1988. According to the Director-General these establish 'the objectives and basic requirements that must be met to ensure adequate safety in the operation of nuclear power plants': *IAEA Bulletin*, 30 (1988), p. 58.

[40] Szasz, op. cit. above (n. 2), pp. 679 ff.

enjoys much stronger powers in that field as a result of the 1968 Non-Proliferation Treaty and regional agreements.[41]

The effect of the NPT treaty is to make obligatory the acceptance of non-proliferation safeguards through bilateral agreements with the Agency, and to allow periodic compulsory Agency inspection for the purpose of verification.[42] Compliance with the overall scheme of non-proliferation safeguards is monitored by the UN General Assembly and Security Council.

No comparable attempt has been made to require universal adherence to health and safety standards.[43] Safeguards agreements and safeguards inspections relate only to non-proliferation; they give the IAEA no power over health and safety.[44] Only where the Agency supplies materials, facilities or services to States does the Statute give it the power to ensure, through project agreements, that acceptable health, safety and design standards are adopted.[45] In such cases, but only in such cases, it also has the right to examine the design of equipment and facilities to ensure compatibility with its standards, and the right to send inspectors to verify compliance.[46] If these are not met, further assistance may be terminated and membership of the Agency withdrawn.[47] Considerable latitude is normally allowed, however, provided national practices meet the minimum criterion of offering an 'adequate' means of controlling hazards and ensuring effective compliance.[48]

These powers over safety relate only to materials or facilities supplied by[49] or through[50] the IAEA; States cannot be required to place their other facilities or materials under its standards merely because they seek its

[41] Above, nn. 8 and 9. For differences between statutory and NPT Safeguards, see Szasz, in Willrich (ed.), op. cit. above (n. 6), ch. 4, and McKnight, op. cit. above (n. 2), chs. 7 and 9. Non-Proliferation Safeguards must also be accepted when the IAEA provides assistance: Statute, Art. XII.

[42] Art. III, NPT Treaty. The terms of NPT safeguards agreements are set out in IAEA Doc. INFCIRC/153, 1972.

[43] Barkenbus, loc. cit. above (n. 24); Szasz, op. cit. above (n. 2), ch. 22; Cameron et al., op. cit. above (n. 22), pp. 4 ff.

[44] IAEA Doc. INFCIRC/153, paras. 46, 71–3; Szasz, op. cit. above (n. 2), pp. 662 f. See, e.g., Safeguards Agreement between the Agency, Israel and the USA, 1975, *Treaties and Other International Acts Series*, No. 8051, and others listed, Ruster and Simma, *International Protection of the Environment*, vol. 13, pp. 6468 ff. IAEA Doc. INFCIRC/153, para. 28, defines the objective of NPT safeguards as 'the timely detection of diversion of significant quantities of nuclear material from peaceful nuclear activities to the manufacture of nuclear weapons or of other explosive devices or for purposes unknown, and deterrence of such diversion by the risk of early detection'.

[45] Arts. III (6), XI, XII: IAEA Doc. INFCIRC/18/Rev. 1. The Agency does not in fact receive or supply materials as envisaged in Art. IX; it now arranges for others to do so.

[46] Statute, Art. XII; Inspectors' Doc. GC(V)INF. 39, Annex, paras. 9, 11.

[47] Statute, Art. XII. For the effect of material breach in terminating or suspending a treaty, see *Namibia* advisory opinion, *ICJ Reports*, 1971, pp. 16, 121; *ICAO Council* case, *ICJ Reports*, 1972, pp. 46, 67; Vienna Convention on the Law of Treaties between States and International Organizations, 1985, Art. 60; Vienna Convention on the Law of Treaties, 1969, Art. 60.

[48] INFCIRC/18/Rev. 1, paras. 2, 4.

[49] See, e.g., agreements listed in Ruster and Simma, *International Protection of the Environment*, vols. 12 and 26.

[50] See, e.g., trilateral agreements between the IAEA, the US and third countries: see agreements with Argentina, Peru, 1978, *US Treaties and Other International Agreements*, vol. 30, p. 1539; Indonesia, 1979, ibid., vol. 32, p. 361; Malaysia, 1980, ibid., p. 2610.

assistance, although they may do so voluntarily.[51] Where assistance is supplied under bilateral agreement without IAEA involvement, even these limited powers are lost, and the practice in such cases has been to provide only for safety consultations with the supplier State.[52]

In a few cases, other treaties do give IAEA standards greater legal standing. The High Seas Convention[53] requires States to take account of them in preventing pollution of the seas from dumping of radioactive waste. The 1972 London Dumping Convention[54] allows the IAEA to determine what high level waste is unsuitable for dumping at sea, and confirms the duty of States to take account of Agency standards when dumping low level waste. These are exceptional cases, however.

The process of adoption of IAEA health and safety standards confirms their limited legal status. In most cases they are not approved by the Agency's General Conference, in which member States are represented, but by the Board of Governors.[55] They will thus usually lack even the evidence of international support which approval by the IMO Assembly may confer on non-binding IMO recommendations.[56] It is thus difficult to describe them even as 'soft law', or to regard them as representing a standard of 'due diligence' for States to meet.[57] This point is particularly relevant when it comes to defining the content of States' obligations in customary law.

(d) *Assessing the Role of IAEA Standards*

Despite their non-binding character, IAEA health and safety standards are a significant contribution to controlling the risks of nuclear energy. Governments are consulted during the formulation stage[58] and in some cases drafting is carried out in co-operation with specialist bodies, such as the International Committee on Radiological Protection.[59] The Agency's standards thus reflect a large measure of expert and technical consensus, and it is for this reason, and not because of their legal status, that they have

---

[51] Statute, Arts. III (6), XII A; IAEA Doc. INFCIRC/18/Rev. 1, para. 25.

[52] See, e.g., US–Brazil Agreement, 1972, *US Treaties and Other International Agreements*, vol. 23, p. 2478; US–Thailand Agreement, 1974, *Treaties and Other International Acts Series*, No. 7850; FRG–Brazil Agreement, 1975, Ruster and Simma, *International Protection of the Environment*, vol. 13, pp. 6472 ff., and others listed at pp. 6415–29.

[53] *UN Treaty Series*, vol. 450, p. 82, Geneva, 1958, Art. 25. For regulations governing the operation of nuclear ships, see 1974 Safety of Life at Sea Convention, Annex, ch. 8 and Attachment 3.

[54] *International Legal Materials*, 11 (1972), p. 1291, Annex I and II. See IAEA, *Revised Definition and Recommendations concerning Radioactive Waste*, 1978, INFCIRC/205/Add.1/Rev. 1, *International Legal Materials*, 18 (1979), p. 826.

[55] Szasz, op. cit. above (n. 2), pp. 669 ff.

[56] Convention on the International Maritime Consultative Organization, 1948, *UN Treaty Series*, vol. 289, p. 48, Art. 16.

[57] See below, Section VI.

[58] Szasz, op. cit. above (n. 2), pp. 672 f.; IAEA, *Experience and Trends in Nuclear Law* (Vienna, 1972).

[59] The ICRP is a private association of scientific experts, comparable to ICES or SCAR: see Smith, *IAEA Bulletin*, 30 (1988), p. 42. For IAEA co-operation with other international bodies, see Szasz, op. cit. above (n. 2), ch. 12.

been influential and do serve as important guidelines for most States in regulating their nuclear facilities.[60]

At their thirtieth conference in 1986, prompted by the Chernobyl disaster, IAEA member States considered the question of obligatory international minimum safety standards for reactors, but reached no agreement.[61] Problems of reconciling many different national standards, and of modifying existing installations, an expensive and difficult task, mean that such agreement will not be easy. More fundamentally, it would require States to surrender their present national sovereignty in this field, and assumes that uniform standards for various types of reactor are possible and would enhance overall safety.[62] This assumption is not universally accepted. Instead the conference affirmed the responsibility of each State engaged in nuclear energy activities for ensuring nuclear and radiation safety, security and environmental compatibility, and the central role of the Agency in encouraging and facilitating co-operation on safety and radiological protection.[63] But it is clear that the opportunity which might have existed in the early stages of nuclear power for stronger international safety regulations has been missed, and that it may now be too late to move significantly in that direction.

(e) The IAEA as an International Inspectorate

The IAEA has very limited power to act as an international nuclear safety inspectorate. Compulsory inspections are possible only where an assistance agreement is in force, and in practice this power is rarely used.[64] The Agency can, if requested, provide safety advice and a review of safety practices at nuclear power stations, through its OSART programme, but up to 1987 only 23 such reviews had been carried out.[65] The Soviet Union has also sought a review of safety provisions at reactors of the Chernobyl type. Nevertheless, if unsafe practices are found, the Agency can only recommend, not enforce, changes.

One recommendation made in response to the Chernobyl accident was that States should make greater use of the OSART facility, and that the IAEA should enhance its capability for providing this service.[66] Even if the

---

[60] Szasz, op. cit. above (n. 2), pp. 673, 682 ff.; OECD, *Nuclear Legislation*; IAEA, *Experience and Trends in Nuclear Law*; IAEA, *Licensing and Regulatory Control of Nuclear Installations*, at pp. 3–10, 131–3; Cameron *et al.*, op. cit. above (n. 22), pp. 4, 159 ff.

[61] IAEA, 30th Conference, Special Session, 1986, *Environmental Policy and Law*, 16 (1986), p. 138. The conference called for the IAEA to consider the matter further: GC/SPL.1/RES/2. UNGA Res. 41/36 (1986) calls for the highest standards of safety in design and operation of nuclear plants.

[62] See Reyners and Lellouche, in Cameron *et al.*, op. cit. above (n. 22), pp. 16 f., 164 f. and 182 f.; Handl, *Revue générale de droit international public*, 92 (1988), pp. 5, 7 ff.

[63] Above, n. 33.

[64] Szasz, op. cit. above (n. 2), p. 696.

[65] *IAEA Bulletin*, 29 (1987), p. 12; Barkenbus, loc. cit. above (n. 24), pp. 484, 486; Franzen, *IAEA Bulletin*, 29 (1987), p. 13; Cameron *et al.*, op. cit. above (n. 22), pp. 184 ff. OSART stands for Operational Safety Review Team.

[66] IAEA, *Summary Report of the Post Accident Review meeting on the Chernobyl Accident*.

Agency cannot ensure compliance, making safety audits of this kind an international norm would provide a means of distinguishing good from bad safety performers, and bring international pressure to bear on the latter.[67] However, the present arrangements for inspection and oversight remain weak and reflect the prevailing reluctance to concede limitations on State sovereignty over nuclear operations within national borders. While the IAEA has shown its usefulness in co-ordinating responses to serious accidents and in acting as a forum for consideration of further measures, its role as an international inspectorate remains only a marginal guarantee of nuclear safety.

(f) Other International Bodies

1. EURATOM[68]

The Euratom Treaty was signed by EEC member States in 1957 for the purpose of creating a nuclear common market.[69] It continues to provide the basis of EEC competence in this field.[70] The treaty's objectives include the application of uniform safety standards to protect the health of workers and the general public against radiation.[71] Other provisions are intended to ensure non-diversion of nuclear materials for unintended purposes.[72] Safety is thus only one aspect of EEC nuclear responsibilities. Unlike the IAEA however, the EEC has power to require member States to implement safety directives and to ensure that they are enforced.[73]

Since 1959, Community directives have laid down basic radiation standards for health protection.[74] The object of these is to ensure that Community citizens are protected to internationally agreed levels, and that all exposures are adequately regulated and kept as low as is reasonably achievable.[75] Radioactivity levels are monitored by the Community through national reporting.[76] Following the Chernobyl accident the Community

---

[67] Barkenbus, loc. cit. above (n. 24), pp. 487 ff.; Council of Europe Parliamentary Recommendation 1068 (1988) calls for international inspection and monitoring of all nuclear installations.

[68] IAEA, *Nuclear Law for a Developing World*, pp. 39 ff.; Cavers, *Vanderbilt Law Review*, 12 (1958), p. 17 at pp. 31 ff.; Grunwald, in Cameron *et al.*, op. cit. above (n. 22), p. 33.

[69] Euratom Treaty, 1957, *UN Treaty Series*, vol. 298, p. 162, Art. 2 and Ch. IX.

[70] The Single European Act, 1986 (Cmnd. 9758), Art. 25, confers additional environmental competence on the Community, and requires action relating to the environment to be based on 'the principles that preventive action should be taken, that environmental damage should as a priority be rectified at source and that the polluter should pay'. See Glaesner, *Yearbook of European Law*, 6 (1986), p. 283.

[71] Arts. 2(b), 30, 31.

[72] Art. 2(e) and Ch. VII.

[73] Arts. 33, 38.

[74] Directives 76/579, *Official Journal*, No. L 187; 79/343, ibid. No. L 83; 80/836, ibid. No. L 246; 84/467, ibid. No. L 265; Rehbinder and Stewart, *Environmental Protection Policy* (New York, 1988), pp. 98 ff.

[75] 4th Environmental Action Programme (1986), Com. (86)485, p. 45.

[76] Art. 34, Euratom Treaty.

temporarily restricted the import of affected foodstuffs,[77] and it has now adopted regulations allowing it to specify permitted levels of radiation contamination in food.[78]

At present these are the only aspects of nuclear health and safety covered by Community law. Owing to opposition from some States, there are no rules setting standards for design, construction and operation of nuclear installations, or for radioactive emissions into air or water. The Community's 'Seveso' directive, which requires that adequate measures be taken to prevent the risk of major accidents at chemical plants or industrial enterprises, does not apply to nuclear installations and processing facilities.[79]

Faced with a reluctance on the part of some member States to allow the Community to regulate nuclear power more comprehensively, the main protection against nuclear risks which Community law and the Euratom treaty offer other States is the right of the Community to be consulted or notified in certain circumstances. Article 34 of the treaty obliges States to consult the Commission when they propose to conduct particularly dangerous nuclear experiments in their territories, and to obtain its consent if these are liable to affect other member States. This is stronger than the consultation requirements of customary international law to be considered in the next section, because it gives the Commission a power of veto, and suggests that such experiments will otherwise be unlawful.[80]

Article 37 also requires notification to be given to the Commission when radioactive substances are to be discharged which may contaminate other States, for example by disposal at sea or into rivers. In this case the Commission may only comment on the proposal.[80a] Neither article requires that other States be consulted at any stage. In that respect both are weaker than the customary law requirements. Finally, Community law requires nuclear States to give urgent notice to their neighbours of any accident which involves exposure of the population to radiation and to give information on how to minimize the consequences of the accident or of measures taken to deal with it.[81]

Euratom has the clear advantage over the IAEA that it can give legal force to its safety measures and it benefits from the wider and more explicit consultation requirements in cases of transboundary risks. But the safety measures it has adopted are limited in scope and some of those referred to

---

[77] Council Regs. 1707/86 and 3955/87.

[78] Council Reg. 3954/87.

[79] Directive 82/501, *Official Journal*, No. L 230, Art. 2(1); Rehbinder and Stewart, op. cit. above (n. 74), pp. 97 ff.; Cameron *et al.*, op. cit. above (n. 22), pp. 40 ff.

[80] See Section III (c) below, and n. 257.

[80a] In ECJ Case 187/87 (1988), *Land de Sarre* v. *Minister for Industry, Posts and Telecommunications*, the Advocate-General determined that Art. 37 required notification to be given before *authorization* of any discharge.

[81] Council Directive 80/836, *Official Journal*, No. L 246 (1980), Art. 45(5); Council Directive 87/600. See generally Cameron *et al.*, op. cit. above (n. 22), pp. 40 ff.

above were only adopted belatedly in response to the Chernobyl accident, which revealed little co-ordination or agreement among member States. The Community has no powers of independent inspection, and both the Euratom Treaty and Community law fall well short of creating an obligation for member States to submit nuclear installations to independent environmental or safety assessment by the Community.

The Commission does have power to propose further health and safety measures under the Euratom Treaty, covering the possible application of emission standards to nuclear installations, the harmonization of safety criteria, the transport of dangerous materials and the management of radioactive waste, and it has reviewed the adequacy of the policy of risk prevention through consultation and notification.[82] At present, however, the Euratom Treaty has proved little more effective than the IAEA Statute as a basis for regulating nuclear environmental risks, despite its apparent advantages.

2. *The OECD*

The OECD has been involved in nuclear safety matters through its Nuclear Energy Agency.[83] The aims of this organization are similar to those of the IAEA, without its safeguards role. They include encouraging the adoption of common standards for national nuclear legislation dealing with public health and the prevention of accidents.[84] Standards on such matters as radiation protection and waste management have been developed in collaboration with the IAEA and other bodies, but once again there is no power to compel compliance. The OECD has also been responsible for initiating a convention on third party liability.[85] The main achievements of the NEA appear to lie in the dissemination of information among States and the harmonization of national policies on a basis of consensus.[86]

3. *The ILO*

The ILO has sponsored a widely supported convention on protecting workers against radiation and it issues various non-binding recommendations on the subject.[87]

---

[82] European Communities, *20th General Report of the Commission*, 1986, paras. 759–62; *21st Report*, 1987, para. 692; 4th Environmental Action Programme (1986), Com. (86)485, p. 45.

[83] See Strohl, in IAEA, *Licensing and Regulatory Control of Nuclear Installations*, p. 135; OECD, *Nuclear Legislation*; Cameron *et al.*, op. cit. above (n. 22), pp. 6 ff.; Reyners, *European Yearbook*, 32 (1984), p. 1.

[84] ENEA Statute, Art. 1. Radiation protection norms were issued in 1962, 1968 and 1981.

[85] Convention on Third Party Liability in the Field of Nuclear Energy, 1960. See below, Section V.

[86] Cameron *et al.*, op. cit. above (n. 22), pp. 7 f.

[87] ILO Convention No. 115, Geneva, 1960: *UK Treaty Series*, No. 41 (1963), Cmnd. 2058. For the work of the ILO, the WHO and the International Committee on Radiological Protection, see OECD, *Nuclear Legislation*, pp. 11 ff. The Inter American Nuclear Energy Commission and the CMEA are reviewed in IAEA, *Nuclear Law for a Developing World*.

(g) *The Significance of International Regulation*

International regulation of the safety of nuclear power, and its potential environmental impact, is among the weakest examples of the regulation of major ultra-hazardous transboundary environmental risks. It gives minimal assurance of common standards, offers limited international inspection and oversight, and leaves to governments a largely unfettered discretion to determine their own balance of safety measures and economic interest. Moreover it relies heavily on voluntary compliance. This contrasts sharply with the growing strength of international regulation of other forms of pollution, and fails to match the seriousness of the potential transboundary damage which nuclear accidents may cause. As a result, principles of State responsibility or civil liability for nuclear damage remain of greater importance in this context than the emergent principle of international regulation. These principles are supplemented by a growing body of State practice concerning consultation, notification and assistance in cases of transboundary risk or emergency. It is on these aspects of international co-operation that the burden of protection from nuclear risks presently rests.

III. Customary Law Obligations Concerning Transboundary Pollution and Environmental Harm

International law does not allow States to conduct activities within their territories, or in common spaces, without regard for the rights of other States or for the protection of the environment.[88] This point is sometimes expressed by reference to 'principles of good neighbourliness', or the maxim *sic utere tuo, ut alienum non laedas*, but the contribution of customary law in environmental matters is neither as modest nor as vacuous as these phrases might suggest. Three important principles enjoy significant support.

(a) *A Duty to Control Sources of Harm*

First, States are required to take adequate steps to control and regulate sources of serious environmental pollution or transboundary harm within their territory or subject to their jurisdiction. Support for this principle of harm prevention can be found in a small number of arbitral and judicial

---

[88] See generally Kiss, in MacDonald and Johnston (eds.), *The Structure and Process of International Law* (The Hague, 1983), p. 1069; Schneider, *World Public Order of the Environment* (London, 1979); Handl, *Proceedings of the American Society of International Law*, 1980, p. 223; Brownlie, *Natural Resources Journal*, 13 (1973), p. 179; Birnie, *British Journal of International Studies*, 3 (1977), p. 169; Caldwell, *International Environmental Policy* (Durham NC, 1984); Quentin-Baxter, *Yearbook of the ILC*, 1980, vol. 2, pt. 1, pp. 256–62.

decisions and in more contemporary sources.[89] In the well known *Trail Smelter* arbitration,[90] a tribunal awarded damages to the United States and prescribed a regime for controlling emissions from a Canadian smelter which had caused air pollution damage. It concluded that 'no State has the right to use or permit the use of its territory in such a manner as to cause injury by fumes in or to the territory of another'.[91] The jurisprudence of the International Court supports a similar principle. In the *Corfu Channel* case,[92] the Court held Albania responsible for damage to British warships caused by a failure to warn them of mines in territorial waters. It indicated that it was 'every State's obligation not to allow knowingly its territory to be used for acts contrary to the rights of other States'.[93]

Continued international support for this broad principle that States must control sources of harm to others or to the global environment is reflected in United Nations resolutions,[94] in Principle 21 of the Stockholm Declaration of 1972,[95] in Articles 192 and 194 of the Law of the Sea Convention, 1982, in UNEP Principles,[96] and in the work of the International Law Com-

---

[89] See Dupuy, in OECD, *Legal Aspects of Transfrontier Pollution* (Paris, 1977), p. 345; Smith, *State Responsibility and the Marine Environment* (Oxford, 1988), pp. 36 ff., 72 ff.; Handl, *Natural Resources Journal*, 26 (1986), pp. 405, 427 ff.; Kirgis, *American Journal of International Law*, 66 (1972), pp. 290, 315.

[90] *American Journal of International Law*, 33 (1938), p. 182, and ibid. 35 (1941), p. 684. See Read, *Canadian Yearbook of International Law*, 1 (1963), p. 213; Rubin, *Oregon Law Review*, 50 (1971), p. 259; Kirgis, *American Journal of International Law*, 66 (1972), p. 290; Quentin-Baxter, *Yearbook of the ILC*, 1981, vol. 2, pt. 1, pp. 108 ff.; Smith, op. cit. (previous note), pp. 72 ff.

[91] *American Journal of International Law*, 35 (1941), p. 716. This finding relied on the *Alabama Claims* arbitration (1872), Moore, *International Arbitrations*, vol. 1, p. 485, and Eagleton, *Responsibility of States in International Law* (1928), p. 80, for the general proposition that 'A State owes at all times a duty to protect other States against injurious acts by individuals from within its jurisdiction', and on the evidence of US federal case law dealing with inter-state air and water pollution which, it held, 'may legitimately be taken as a guide in this field of international law . . . where no contrary rule prevails': *American Journal of International Law*, 35 (1941), at p. 714. Reliance on domestic case law by analogy was *not* required by the *compromis*, which called for application of US law and practice only in respect of issues of proof of damage, indemnity and the regime of future operations of the smelter: ibid., at p. 698. This is better treated as an invocation of the 'general principles of law' referred to in Art. 38(1) of the Statute of the ICJ. For criticism of the tribunal's approach see Rubin, loc. cit. (previous note), at p. 267; Goldie, *International and Comparative Law Quarterly*, 14 (1965), p. 1229; and for explanation, see Read, loc. cit. (previous note).

[92] *ICJ Reports*, 1949, p. 4.

[93] Ibid., at p. 22. See also *Nuclear Tests* case (*Australia* v. *France*), *ICJ Reports*, 1974, pp. 253, 388, *per* Judge de Castro; the *Lac Lanoux* arbitration (1957), 24 ILR 101, 123; and Brownlie, *System of the Law of Nations: State Responsibility, Part I* (Oxford, 1983), p. 182.

[94] GA Res. 2849 (XXVI) (1971); GA Res. 2995 (XXVII) (1972); GA Res. 2996 (XXVII) (1972); GA Res. 3281 (XXIX) (1974); GA Res. 34/186 (1979).

[95] *Report of the UN Conference on the Human Environment, Stockholm, 1972*, UN Doc. A/CONF. 48/14/Rev. 1.

[96] Principles of Conduct in the Field of the Environment concerning Resources Shared by Two or More States, Principle 3, UNEP/IG/12/2, 1978, *International Legal Materials*, 17 (1978), p. 1091. These recommendations were made without prejudice to the question of their legal status. The General Assembly 'took note' of them in Res. 34/186. See Adede, *Environmental Policy and Law*, 5 (1979), p. 66; Sand, in Dupuy (ed.), *The Future of the International Law of the Environment*, Hague Academy of International Law, 1984 Workshop (Dordrecht, 1985), pp. 51–72; Lammers, *Pollution of International Watercourses* (Dordrecht, 1984), pp. 335–8.

mission.[97] These instruments indicate also that the older formula referred to in the cases, which protected only States, has now been superseded by a wider principle which protects common spaces including the high seas, deep sea-bed and outer space, and also the atmosphere, from pollution.[98] Treaty definitions of pollution are increasingly refined,[99] while prohibitions of the discharge of persistent and highly toxic substances into the sea or the atmosphere are now so widely adopted that they should be regarded as a specific customary application of the general principle.[100] The dumping or discharge at sea or into the atmosphere of highly radioactive waste appears to fall into this category.[101]

Principle 21 of the Stockholm Declaration is particularly important, because it affirms both the sovereign right of States to exploit their own resources 'pursuant to their own environmental policies', and their responsibility 'to ensure that activities within their jurisdiction or control do not cause damage to the environment of other States or of areas beyond the limits of national jurisdiction'. Although, as Professor Sohn has observed, the first part of this principle comes 'quite close' to asserting that a State has unlimited sovereignty over its environment,[102] the totality of the provision, including its emphatic reference to responsibility for environmental

[97] See draft articles on International Watercourses, *Yearbook of the ILC*, 1984, vol. 2, pt. 1, p. 101; draft articles on International Liability for Injurious Consequences of Acts Not Prohibited by International Law, 1989, UN/Doc.A/CN.4/423; draft articles on State Responsibility, Art. 19, *Yearbook of the ILC*, 1980, vol. 2, pt. 2, p. 30; draft Code of Offences Against the Peace and Security of Mankind, ibid. 1986, vol. 2, pt. 2, pp. 441–4.

[98] Sohn, *Harvard International Law Journal*, 14 (1973), p. 423; Smith, op. cit. above (n. 89), pp. 76 ff. See also Vienna Convention for the Protection of the Ozone Layer, 1985; Arts. 145, 192, 194(1), UN Convention on the Law of the Sea, 1982; Outer Space Treaty, 1967; Moon Treaty, 1979; Convention on Antarctic Mineral Resource Activities, 1988, and Fleischer, in Bothe (ed.), *Trends in Environmental Policy and Law* (Gland, 1980), p. 321.

[99] See below, n. 142.

[100] See, e.g., Stockholm Declaration on the Human Environment, 1972, Principle 6; London Dumping Convention, 1972, Art. IV; Oslo Dumping Convention, 1972, Art. 5; Paris Convention for the Prevention of Marine Pollution from Land-Based Sources, 1974, Art. 4; Helsinki Convention on the Protection of the Marine Environment of the Baltic, 1974, Art. 6; Barcelona Convention for the Protection of the Mediterranean Sea Against Pollution, Protocol for the Prevention of Pollution by Dumping, 1976, Art. 4, and Athens Protocol for Protection Against Pollution from Land-Based Sources, 1980, Art. 5; Lima Convention for the Protection of the Marine Environment of the SE Pacific, Protocol for Protection Against Pollution from Land-Based Sources, 1981, Art. 4.

[101] Geneva Convention on the High Seas, 1958, Art. 25; London Dumping Convention, 1972, Annex I; Paris Convention for the Prevention of Marine Pollution from Land-Based Sources, 1974, Art. 5; Helsinki Convention, 1974, Annex II; Barcelona Convention, Protocol for the Prevention of Pollution by Dumping, 1976, Annex I; Protocol for Protection Against Pollution from Land-Based Sources, 1980, Annex I; Convention for the Protection of the Natural Resources and Environment of the South Pacific Region, 1987, Art. 10; Lima Convention, Protocol for Protection Against Pollution from Land-Based Sources, 1981, Annex I. The question whether sub-sea-bed disposal of radioactive waste is 'dumping' is controversial: see Art. 10 of the South Pacific Convention, 1987, and Welsch, *Environmental Policy and Law*, 12 (1984), p. 72. In 1983 the London Dumping Convention parties suspended dumping of low-level radioactive waste, although not required to do so by Annex I: see Res. LDC 14(7), and Forster, *Environmental Policy and Law*, 16 (1986), p. 7.

[102] Loc. cit. above (n. 98), at pp. 491 f.

damage, was regarded by many States present at the Stockholm Conference as reflecting international law.[103] It has remained a highly influential statement of principle in the subsequent development of law and practice on environmental matters,[104] despite difficulties in defining its precise content.

These difficulties can be briefly summarized. Chiefly, it is unclear whether the obligation is merely one of diligent conduct on the part of the State to prevent harm or pollution, or whether this obligation of prevention is absolute. This issue is explored in the context of State responsibility;[105] for the present it is sufficient to note that treaty formulations overwhelmingly favour the due diligence approach[106] and that the notion of an absolute obligation is based mainly on inferences from national law and international jurisprudence.[107]

Other questions arise. If the due diligence standard is accepted, what conduct is required to meet it? If the obligation of prevention is absolute, how is such an extensive obligation to be limited and made workable in practice? Finally, what degree of harm or injury is contemplated, and of what kind?

1. Due diligence

The advantages of due diligence as the required standard of conduct are its potential flexibility and the fact that it does not make the State an absolute guarantor of the prevention of harm.[108] Considerations of the effectiveness of territorial control, the resources available to the State and the nature of specific activities may all justify differing degrees of diligence.[109] Nevertheless, in general terms 'due diligence' implies the introduction of legislation and controls capable of effectively protecting other States, and it can

---

[103] Several States declared that Principle 21 accorded with existing international law: see Canadian and US Comments in UN Doc. A/CONF.48/14/Rev.1 at pp. 64–6. GA Res. 2996 (XXVII) (1972) asserts that Principles 21 and 22 of the Stockholm Declaration 'Lay down the basic rules governing the matter'. 112 States voted for this resolution; none opposed it. Eastern block States did not attend the Stockholm Conference and abstained on Res. 2996, but have supported subsequent treaties recognizing the normative character of Principle 21: see, e.g., Geneva Convention on Long Range Transboundary Air Pollution, 1979, and Vienna Convention for the Protection of the Ozone Layer, 1985. On the significance of Principle 21 and its relationship to earlier law see Dupuy, loc. cit. above (n. 89), pp. 345 ff., and Bothe (ed.), op. cit. above (n. 98), at pp. 366 ff.

[104] Dupuy, loc. cit. above (n. 89), p. 356; Jiménez de Aréchaga, *Recueil des cours*, 159 (1978–I), pp. 272 f.; Handl, *American Journal of International Law*, 74 (1980), p. 525.

[105] See below, Section IV.

[106] See below, Section IV (e).

[107] See below, Section IV (c).

[108] See generally OECD, *Legal Aspects of Transfrontier Pollution* (Paris, 1977), p. 380; Dupuy, ibid., at p. 369.

[109] See generally *Alabama Claims* arbitration (1872), Moore, *International Arbitrations*, vol. 1, p. 485; case concerning *US Diplomatic and Consular Staff in Tehran*, ICJ Reports, 1980, p. 3 at pp. 29–33; *Corfu Channel* case, ICJ Reports, 1949, p. 4 at p. 89, *per* Judge *ad hoc* Ecer; Dupuy, loc. cit. (previous note), at pp. 375 f.; Smith, op. cit. above (n. 89), pp. 38–41. Note Principle 23 of the 1972 Stockholm Declaration on the Human Environment which refers to standards which may be

be expressed as the conduct to be expected of a good government.[110] This formulation is relatively unhelpful in environmental matters because it lacks appropriate specificity.

A more useful approach to deciding what is required is to look to internationally agreed standards set out in treaties or in the resolutions and decisions of international bodies.[111] This is the technique used in the Law of the Sea Convention to define in detail what the content of States' obligations are with regard to the regulation of flag vessels and the protection of other States and the marine environment.[112] But as indicated earlier, no binding international standards can be said to exist for the precise regulation of national nuclear activities. At best, IAEA standards are a guide, but, lacking negotiated endorsement by States, it is hard to see them as an obligatory minimum.[113] Thus, expressed as a requirement of using diligent efforts to prevent harm to other States or pollution of the environment, Principle 21's application to nuclear energy is immediately problematical.

2. *Absolute prevention*

Viewing the matter as an absolute obligation stresses the fact of harm, rather than the conduct of the State in bringing it about or failing to prevent it.[114] An alternative way of making the same point is to postulate a duty of diligence so demanding that it amounts to an absolute obligation.[115]

One problem with these interpretations is that they may place unacceptable burdens on the freedom of States to carry out lawful activities within their own borders. For this reason some commentators limit this version of the principle to harm caused by ultra-hazardous activities, of which nuclear reactors are an obvious example.[116] An extreme view, that such activities may become impermissible, has led the ILC to develop a novel regime not based on the notion of breach of obligation but requiring compensation for harm resulting from lawful acts as part of an equitable balance of interests

---

'inappropriate and of unwarranted social cost for developing countries'. On the influence of this double standard in the Law of the Sea Convention, 1982, see Boyle, *American Journal of International Law*, 79 (1985), pp. 347, 353 ff.; Kindt, *Virginia Journal of International Law*, 20 (1979), p. 313.

[110] OECD, op. cit. above (n. 108), pp. 385 f.; Dupuy, ibid., pp. 369 ff.; Smith, op. cit. above (n. 89), pp. 36–42.

[111] Contini and Sand, *American Journal of International Law*, 66 (1972), p. 37; Dupuy, in Bothe (ed.), op. cit. above (n. 98), p. 369; Birnie, in Carroll (ed.), *International Environmental Diplomacy* (Cambridge, 1988), pp. 98 ff.; Jiménez de Aréchaga, loc. cit. above (n. 104), pp. 272 f.

[112] See, e.g., Arts. 210 and 211 which in effect incorporate the 1972 London Dumping Convention and the 1973 MARPOL Convention and in this way define the content of the obligation to control pollution from these sources. Compare Arts. 207 and 208, and see generally Van Reenen, *Netherlands Yearbook of International Law*, 12 (1981), p. 5; Vignes, *Annuaire français de droit international*, 1979, p. 712; Boyle, loc. cit. above (n. 109).

[113] Above, Section II and note 61.

[114] See below, Section IV.

[115] Smith, op. cit. above (n. 89), p. 41.

[116] See below, n. 241.

allowing the polluting activity to continue.[117] The conclusion that obligations of harm prevention make the activity itself impermissible is, however, widely regarded as misconceived.[118]

Absolute obligations of prevention also pose the question whether and in what sense harm must be a foreseeable possibility. To impose such an obligation for activities of whose existence or dangerous character States are unaware is undeniably extreme, and is inconsistent with what jurisprudence there is. In the *Corfu Channel*[119] case the Court stressed the importance of establishing Albania's knowledge of the risk to British ships as a condition of responsibility for the damage. Canada's knowledge of harmful activity in the *Trail Smelter* arbitration predated the US claim,[120] and cannot be taken as an irrelevant factor in the admission of responsibility. Nor has the ILC departed from this approach in its articles on 'International Liability', although it does consider it sufficient that the State should have known of the risk.[121] What may be justifiable is the proposition that once the existence of a potentially harmful activity is, or should be, appreciated, the test of foreseeability is met.[122] Thus, in quite general terms, the realization that nuclear reactors are potentially dangerous satisfies this requirement regardless of the circumstances of any individual accident, such as Chernobyl.

The final objection to absolute obligations of prevention is that they concentrate more on shifting the burden of proof and the burden of responsibility for loss back to the polluter than on the diligent control of dangerous activities, since conduct will be irrelevant to the performance of such obligations. Thus, even if arguments for absolute prevention are accepted, in practice the elaboration of standards of due diligence remains an essential complementary principle[123] and a better basis for international regulation.

3. *Harm or damage as the object of prevention*

Most interpretations of the principle under discussion refer to an obligation to prevent harm or damage to other States or to the global environment, and usually assume that this must reach some level of seriousness

---

[117] See Quentin-Baxter, *Yearbook of the ILC*, 1981, vol. 2, pt. 1, pp. 112–22; ibid. 1982, vol. 2, pt. 1, p. 60, para. 39; ibid. 1983, vol. 2, pt. 1, p. 206, paras. 19–22, and draft articles on International Liability, 1989, UN Doc. A/CN.4/423.

[118] See below, nn. 221, 222.

[119] *ICJ Reports*, 1949, p. 4 at pp. 17–20.

[120] See *American Journal of International Law*, 33 (1939), pp. 188–92, for details of earlier claims and of a reference in 1928 to the US-Canadian International Joint Commission.

[121] See Barboza, 4th Report, 1988, UN Doc. A/CN.4/413, p. 25, and 5th Report, draft Art. 3, 1989, UN Doc. A/CN.4/423.

[122] Barboza, loc. cit. (previous note).

[123] See Barboza, 2nd Report on International Liability, *Yearbook of the ILC*, 1986, vol. 2, pt. 1, p. 159, paras. 63–9; 4th Report, 1988, UN Doc. A/CN.4/413, p. 34, paras. 103–11. Draft Art. 8 amounts to an obligation of diligent control.

before it becomes wrongful.[124] Apart from obvious difficulties of definition and assessment of this threshold in individual cases, other formulations omit any qualifying reference to the level of harm or damage, and cast some doubt on the general assumption.[125]

More problematical is the view that this threshold is essentially relative and conditional on equitable considerations or a balance of interest.[126] This approach has the effect of converting an obligation to prevent harm into an obligation to use territory equitably and reasonably or into a constraint on abuse of rights.[127]

There is some support for equitable balancing as a test of the permissibility of pollution of shared resources, such as international watercourses,[128] and some commentators would apply the same approach to the obligation to prevent transboundary harm.[129] While States may choose to regulate transboundary pollution in this way,[130] neither the international case law nor treaty definitions of harm or damage support thresholds determined by equitable balancing outside the context of international watercourse law.[131] The only balancing of interests in *Trail Smelter* related not to the question

---

[124] The *Trail Smelter* arbitration, *American Journal of International Law*, 35 (1941), p. 716, talks of 'serious injury'; GA Res. 2995 (XXVII) (1972) refers to 'significant harmful effects'; ILC draft articles on International Liability, 1988, UN Doc. A/CN.4/413, and on International Watercourses, *Yearbook of the ILC*, 1984, vol. 2, pt. 1, p. 112, use the term 'appreciable injury', which is thought to mean less than serious.

[125] e.g. Principle 21 of the 1972 Stockholm Declaration and instruments based on it: see, e.g., Art. 194, UN Convention on the Law of the Sea, 1982; Art. 30, UNGA Res. 3281 (XXIX) (1974); Principle 3, UNEP Principles of Conduct Concerning Resources Shared by Two or More States, 1978, above, n. 96. Views differ on whether omission of an explicit threshold is intended to change earlier practice: compare Springer, in Carroll (ed.), op. cit. above (n. 111), p. 51, and Handl, loc. cit. above (n. 89), pp. 412 ff.

[126] Handl, *Canadian Yearbook of International Law*, 13 (1975), p. 156; id., *Natural Resources Journal*, 26 (1986), p. 405; Quentin-Baxter, *Yearbook of the ILC*, 1981, vol. 2, pt. 1, pp. 112–19; McCaffrey, ibid. 1986, vol. 2, pt. 1, pp. 133–4.

[127] On abuse of rights see Art. 300, UN Convention on the Law of the Sea, 1982; Art. 2, Geneva Convention on the High Seas, 1958; *Icelandic Fisheries* case, *ICJ Reports*, 1974, p. 3; Ago, *Yearbook of the ILC*, 1970, vol. 1, p. 178, para. 25, and p. 226, para. 31; Cheng, *General Principles of Law* (London, 1953), pp. 121–36; Kiss, *Encyclopedia of Public International Law*, vol. 7, p. 1; Brownlie, *Principles of Public International Law* (3rd edn., Oxford, 1979), pp. 442–5; Oppenheim, *International Law*, vol. 1 (8th edn., London, 1955), pp. 345–7.

[128] See ILC draft articles on International Watercourses, Arts. 6–9, *Yearbook of the ILC*, 1984, vol. 2, pt. 1, p. 101; *Lac Lanoux* arbitration (1957), 24 ILR 101; *Territorial Jurisdiction of the International Commission of the River Oder*, PCIJ, Series A, No. 23 (1929); Handl, *Revue belge de droit international*, 14 (1978), p. 40, and see also n. 126, above. The meaning and utility of the term 'shared resource' is controversial, however: see n. 156, below.

[129] Quentin-Baxter, 2nd Report on International Liability, *Yearbook of the ILC*, 1981, vol. 2, pt. 1, pp. 108 ff. See also McDougal and Schlei, at n. 258, below.

[130] Handl, loc. cit. above (n. 89), p. 447, argues that States have done so in the 1979 Geneva Convention on Long-Range Transboundary Air Pollution, but only for pollution *not* exceeding the customary threshold of serious harm enshrined in Principle 21.

[131] Bleicher, *Ecology Law Quarterly*, 2 (1972), p. 1, at p. 28; Handl, *Canadian Yearbook of International Law*, 13 (1975), pp. 177–80, agrees but argues that *Lac Lanoux* and precedents relating to international watercourses support a balancing test in that context. See also *Natural Resources Journal*, 26 (1986), pp. 421–7.

whether Canada was in breach of its obligation but to the determination of a regime for the future operation of the smelter.[132]

Nor is the case for making the customary threshold of serious harm dependent on a balance of interests a strong one.[133] The notion that States must act with due diligence to prevent serious harm is a formula which already allows for flexibility in individual cases and excludes liability for *de minimis* pollution. To add more variables would be subversive of efforts to establish minimum standards of environmental protection and prove too favourable to the polluter. Only if the obligation of prevention is an absolute one might it then be justifiable to resort to equitable manipulation of the threshold of harm in order to mitigate the rigours of an otherwise extreme rule.

Another possible limitation on the principle that harm must be prevented focuses on the type of interest protected, or on the type of harm which must occur. The *Trail Smelter* arbitration took a narrow view. Its concentration on property loss places no value on wider environmental interests such as wildlife, aesthetic considerations or the unity of ecosystems.[134] A more recent claim brought by Canada against the USSR in respect of environmental clean-up costs after the crash of a nuclear satellite was settled,[135] but in response to environmental damage in Western Europe after Chernobyl the Soviet Union maintained that the issue of 'material, moral and political damage' caused by nuclear accidents was not sufficiently studied.[136]

Treaty provisions sometimes refer to causing damage to the 'environment' of other States,[137] which suggests that ecological effects may be included, but the phrase is rarely defined.[138] Thus although there is a tendency to broaden the original, and clearly out-dated, approach in *Trail Smelter*, it is uncertain how far the obligation not to harm other States extends to environmental injury not quantifiable in material terms. For that

[132] Read, loc. cit. above (n. 90).

[133] Handl, loc. cit. above (n. 89), pp. 416–21.

[134] Rubin, loc. cit. above (n. 90), pp. 272–4. On this issue the tribunal was required to follow US law. US tort law is now more generous in allowing for ecological loss: see *Commonwealth of Puerto Rico v. SS Zoë Colocotroni*, 456 F Supp. 1327 (1978), and Halter and Thomas, *Ecology Law Quarterly*, 10 (1982), p. 5. The nuclear civil liability conventions remain very close to the *Trail Smelter* approach, however: see below, section V(i).

[135] Claim for Damage Caused by Soviet Cosmos 954, *International Legal Materials*, 18 (1979), p. 902. The Soviet Union accepted liability under the 1972 Convention on International Liability for Damage Caused by Space Objects.

[136] Proposed Programme for Establishing an International Regime for the Safe Development of Nuclear Energy, 1986, reprinted in Sands, op. cit. above (n. 22), p. 227.

[137] See, e.g., Art. 194(2), UN Convention on the Law of the Sea, 1982. The 1984 Protocol to the 1969 Convention on Civil Liability for Oil Pollution Damage allows recovery of the costs of environmental clean-up and reinstatement: see Jacobson and Trotz, *Journal of Maritime Law and Commerce*, 17 (1986), p. 467. The 1989 International Convention on Salvage provides for compensation for minimizing or preventing 'damage to the environment'.

[138] See, however, Convention for the Regulation of Antarctic Mineral Resource Activities, 1988. Art. 1(15) defines 'damage to the Antarctic environment or dependent or associated ecosystems' as 'any impact on the living or non-living components of that environment or those ecosystems, including harm to atmospheric, marine or terrestrial life beyond that which is negligible or which has been assessed and judged to be acceptable pursuant to this Convention'.

reason nuclear fallout without more is unlikely to amount to serious harm unless long-term effects are presumed,[139] but enough is now known of the impact of radiation to make this a possibility.[140]

There is less difficulty when the obligation is expressed in terms of preventing harm to the global environment or to common spaces, for here the almost invariable practice is to define harm in terms of 'pollution'.[141] Although several formulations are used, modern treaty definitions of pollution are considerably wider than the *Trail Smelter* approach, and usually include harm to living resources or ecosystems, and interference with amenities and legitimate uses of common spaces.[142]

The unifying feature of all current definitions is their focus on a detrimental alteration in quality, but this can be expressed broadly, in terms of environmental conservation or amelioration, or more narrowly, in terms of impact on useful resources. Threshold values remain important; some definitions are wide enough to cover any interference with quality while others apply only to irreversible change. Thus what 'pollution' means is significantly dependent on context and objective.[143] The widespread treaty prohibition on discharge or dumping of high level radioactive waste at sea indicates that this constitutes marine pollution regardless of any threshold level of interference.[144] The 1963 Nuclear Test Ban Treaty suggests a similar conclusion for atmospheric discharges.[145] Higher thresholds may be appropriate for land-based or sea-bed disposal, however, or for discharge of lower level waste.[146]

---

[139] See *Nuclear Tests* cases, *ICJ Reports*, 1974, p. 253. The applicants did not assert material damage but claimed that the deposit of potentially harmful radioactive fallout was a violation of their sovereignty. On the question whether this created a sufficient 'legal interest' to justify proceedings, see the joint dissenting opinion at pp. 369 ff., and Judge de Castro at pp. 388 ff. Handl, *American Journal of International Law*, 69 (1975), p. 50, argues that material damage to the State is required and that a mere intrusion or breach of sovereignty is insufficient.

[140] See above, nn. 1 and 16.

[141] See, e.g., UN Convention on the Law of the Sea, 1982, Art. 1(4); Paris Convention on Prevention of Marine Pollution from Land-Based Sources, 1974, Art. 1; Geneva Convention on Long-Range Transboundary Air Pollution, 1979, Art. 1; OECD Recommendation C(77) 28 on Implementing a Regime of Equal Access and Non-Discrimination, 1977. The 1985 Vienna Convention on the Ozone Layer does not refer to pollution but uses the phrase 'adverse effects' on the environment; see also n. 138, above.

[142] See Springer, *International and Comparative Law Quarterly*, 26 (1977), p. 531; Tomczak, *Maritime Policy and Management*, 8 (1984), p. 311.

[143] Springer, loc. cit. (previous note); Tomczak, loc. cit. (previous note). Compare principles 6 and 7 of the 1972 Stockholm Declaration on the Human Environment.

[144] See n. 101, above.

[145] Lammers, *Pollution of International Watercourses* (Dordrecht, 1984), pp. 319–27; Kirgis, loc. cit. above (n. 89), pp. 295 ff.; but compare Margolis, loc. cit. above (n. 11), and McDougal and Schlei, loc. cit. above (n. 11).

[146] See n. 101, above. The 1959 Antarctic Treaty is the only international prohibition of radioactive waste disposal on land.

(b) *Transboundary Co-operation*

1. *General principles*

A second principle, widely acknowledged, is that States are required to co-operate with each other in controlling transboundary pollution and environmental risks. In part, this principle can be supported by reference to the law relating to shared natural resources.[147] Article 3 of the Charter of Economic Rights and Duties of States indicates the essential points:

> . . . each State must co-operate on the basis of a system of information and prior consultation in order to achieve optimum use of such resources without causing damage to the legitimate interests of others.[148]

The requirement of prior consultation based on adequate information has a substantial pedigree of international support[149] and is a natural counterpart of the concept of equitable utilization of a shared resource, such as a watercourse.[150]

These points are confirmed by the award in the *Lac Lanoux* arbitration.[151] Here the Tribunal held that France had complied with its obligations under a treaty and customary law to consult and negotiate in good faith before diverting a watercourse shared with Spain. It noted that conflicting interests must be reconciled by negotiation and mutual concession.[152] This implied that France must inform Spain of its proposals, allow consultations and give reasonable weight to Spain's interests, but it did not mean that it could act only with Spain's consent:

> the risk of an evil use has so far not led to subjecting the possession of these means of action to the authorisation of States which may possibly be threatened.[153]

Spain's rights were thus of a procedural character only; it enjoyed no veto and no claim to insist on specific precautions. It was for France alone to determine whether to proceed with the project and how to safeguard Spain's rights.[154] Nevertheless, the obligation to negotiate is a real one and not a mere formality.[155]

---

[147] Riphagen, in Bothe (ed.), op. cit. above (n. 98), p. 343; Handl, *Revue belge de droit international*, 14 (1978), p. 40 at pp. 55–63.

[148] GA Res. 3281 (XXIX) (1974). See Brownlie, *Recueil des cours*, 162 (1979-I), p. 253. The resolution was opposed by some States on grounds unrelated to the present point. See *Texaco v. Libya*, *International Legal Materials*, 17 (1978), p. 1.

[149] See Bothe, op. cit. above (n. 98), p. 391; Utton, *Columbia Journal of Transnational Law*, 12 (1973), p. 56; Kirgis, *Prior Consultation in International Law* (Charlottesville, 1983).

[150] Handl, loc. cit. above (n. 147). Equitable utilization is regarded by most writers and by the ILC as the main principle of customary international water resources law. See Lipper, in Garretson *et al.* (eds.), *International Drainage Basins* (New York, 1967), p. 16; Jiménez de Aréchaga, loc. cit. above (n. 104), p. 192; McCaffrey, *Yearbook of the ILC*, 1986, vol. 2, pt. 1, pp. 110–13.

[151] 24 ILR 101 (1957). See McCaffrey, loc. cit. (previous note), at pp. 116–19.

[152] At p. 119.

[153] At p. 126.

[154] At pp. 140–1.

[155] See *North Sea Continental Shelf* cases, *ICJ Reports*, 1969, p. 3 at pp. 46–7, paras. 83–5; *Icelandic Fisheries* cases, *ICJ Reports*, 1974, p. 3 at pp. 32 ff.; Barboza, *5th Report on International Liability* (1989), UN Doc. A/CN.4/423, pp. 40 ff.; ILC, *Report to the UN General Assembly*, 42nd Session, Supplement No. 10 (1987), UN Doc. A/42/10, pp. 63 ff.

Despite doubts surrounding the term 'shared resource',[156] these procedural requirements—in effect an international right to a fair hearing and a formula for minimizing the risk of harm—are fully reflected in the ILC's codification of the law of international watercourses.[157] The same requirements are endorsed, in detailed form, in the 'Principles of Conduct' relating to shared natural resources adopted by UNEP in 1978.[158] These make it clear that effects on the environment, as well as on the resources of other States, are among the matters which must be taken into account in policies towards shared resources use.[159] UNEP's principles also require States to make environmental assessments before engaging in activities with shared resources likely to create a risk of significant environmental effects in other States.[160]

Thus although the concept of 'shared natural resources' and the legal implications of the term itself have proved controversial, the basic principle that States must co-operate in avoiding adverse effects on the environment of their neighbours through a system of impact assessment, notification, consultation and negotiation appears generally to be endorsed by the relevant jurisprudence, the declarations of international bodies and the work of the ILC.

2. Cases of transboundary risk

Nor are these co-operation requirements now confined only to the use of resources. Increasingly, the evidence points to their wider application to environmental risks or potentially harmful activities in general. Significantly, this proposition is borne out by State practice concerning consultation with States likely to be affected by nuclear installations near borders,[161] continental shelf operations,[162] long-range transboundary air

---

[156] The Executive Director of UNEP reported that the term included river systems, air sheds, enclosed and semi-enclosed seas, mountain chains, forests, conservation areas and migratory species: UN Doc. GC/44 (1975), para. 86. No agreement could be reached on a definition in UNEP's 1978 Principles of Conduct: see UNEP/IG. 12/2, 1978. Owing to opposition the term was removed from ILC draft articles on International Watercourses: *Yearbook of the ILC*, 1984, vol. 2, pt. 1, p. 110; ibid. 1986, vol. 2, pt. 1, p. 103.

[157] See draft Articles 10–14, ibid. 1984, vol. 2, pt. 1, pp. 113–16 and draft Articles 11–21, UN Doc. A/43/10, *Report of the International Law Commission to the General Assembly*, 43rd Session, 1988, pp. 114–38, and commentary at UN Doc. A/42/10, *Report of the International Law Commission to the General Assembly*, 42nd Session, 1987, pp. 33–47, where the rapporteur noted that the proposed rules had been acceptable to members. A six-month period for consultation was introduced with a commitment not to implement planned measures within that period. Compare Paris Convention on Prevention of Pollution from Land-Based Sources, 1974, Art. 9, however.

[158] Above, n. 96. See Principles 5–7.

[159] Principle 13.

[160] Principle 4.

[161] See below.

[162] Canada-Denmark Agreement for Co-operation Relating to the Marine Environment, 1983, *International Legal Materials*, 23 (1984), p. 269; Kuwait Protocol concerning Marine Pollution Resulting from Exploration and Exploration of the Continental Shelf, 1988, *Environmental Policy and Law*, 19 (1989), p. 32; UNEP Principles Concerning the Environment Related to Offshore Drilling and Mining within the Limits of National Jurisdiction, 1981, ibid. 7 (1981), p. 50.

pollution[163] and marine pollution from land-based sources.[164] UNEP guidelines now also call for prior impact assessment in the case of any activity likely to have a significant effect on the environment,[165] and there is growing evidence of this in treaties and State practice.[166]

The work of regional organizations and international codification bodies further supports the principle of transboundary co-operation in cases of environmental risk. Impact assessment, prior notice, consultation in good faith and negotiation are all called for in OECD and ILA principles on transfrontier pollution[167] and in the ILC's proposed articles on 'International Liability'.[168] In each case, the rules apply wherever there is a significant risk of transfrontier pollution.

Thus it has been possible to identify the main elements of the principle of transboundary co-operation and to suggest that, far from exclusive identification with shared natural resources, it applies to all cases of transboundary environmental risk affecting other States. This conclusion has particular importance with regard to the conduct of nuclear activities and the siting of nuclear installations. Unlike Principle 21 of the Stockholm Declaration, however, this form of co-operation is directed only at protecting States and does not benefit the global environment or common spaces.[169]

3. State practice on consultation in cases of nuclear risks

The evidence of bilateral agreements among a number of European States confirms that obligations of notification and consultation in cases of transboundary risk have been applied to planned nuclear activities, but only when these take place in border areas. Most of these treaties deal with installations within 30 km of the border.[170] All require a full exchange of

---

[163] Geneva Convention on Long-Range Transboundary Air Pollution, 1979, Arts. 5, 8.

[164] Paris Convention for the Prevention of Marine Pollution from Land-Based Sources, 1974, Art. 9; Athens Protocol to the Barcelona Convention for the Protection of the Mediterranean, 1980, Art. 12; Quito Protocol to the Lima Convention for the Protection of the Marine Environment and Coastal Area of the South-East Pacific, 1983, Art. 12; UNEP Montreal Guidelines for the Protection of the Marine Environment Against Pollution from Land-Based Sources, 1985, *Environmental Policy and Law*, 14 (1985), p. 77.

[165] Principles of Environmental Impact Assessment, 1987, *Environmental Policy and Law*, 17 (1987), p. 36. See Bonine, ibid., p. 5.

[166] e.g. UN Law of the Sea Convention, 1982, Art. 206; Convention for the Regulation of Antarctic Mineral Resource Activities, 1988, Art. 4; Convention for the Protection and Development of the Marine Environment of the Wider Caribbean Region, 1983, Art. 12; Convention for the Protection of the Natural Resources and Environment of the South Pacific Region, 1987, Art. 16; US-Mexico Agreement to Co-operate in the Solution of Environmental Problems in the Border Area, 1983, Art. 7, *International Legal Materials*, 22 (1983), p. 1025. In effect, the 1972 London Dumping Convention also requires prior environmental impact assessment before the grant of permits. See also Barboza, *5th Report on International Liability* (1989), UN Doc. A/CN.4/423, pp. 26–33.

[167] OECD Rec. C(74) 224 (1974), para. 6; Rec. C (77) 28 (1977), paras. 8–10; Rec. C(78) 77 (1978); Rec. C(79) 116 (1979), collected in *OECD and the Environment* (Paris, 1986); ILA, *Report of the 60th Conference*, p. 1, Arts. 4–6, Montreal Rules on Transfrontier Pollution.

[168] Draft Arts. 10–15, Barboza, loc. cit. above (n. 166).

[169] See above, n. 98.

[170] e.g. Agreement between Spain and Portugal on Co-operation in Matters Affecting the Safety of Nuclear Installations in the Vicinity of the Frontier, 1980, Ruster and Simma, *International Protection of the Environment*, vol. 27, p. 420; Netherlands-FRG Memorandum on Exchange of Information and

information on the proposed installation, intended to enable the other States to review the decision-making process and data and offer appropriate comments on safety and health protection. In most cases permanent commissions are established to review matters of joint interest affecting public health,[171] but these bodies have no power to impose limits on the freedom of action of any State. None of the treaties gives neighbouring States a veto, or suggests that the siting of nuclear installations near borders is impermissible or subject to any equitable balance of interests.[172]

Two conclusions follow from this: there is now a good case for treating transboundary consultation on border installations as a customary obligation, and the European treaties, with their relatively strong provisions on information exchange and institutional co-operation, provide a good model for use elsewhere.

(c) *Notification and Emergency Assistance*

1. *The general principle*

The third relevant principle concerns accidents and emergencies likely to cause transboundary harm. Here practice in a number of areas, including nuclear activities,[173] supports an obligation to give timely notification to States at risk, so that they can take appropriate protective measures. The *Corfu Channel* case[174] provides an early example of judicial support for this duty to warn. In that case British warships were damaged by mines in Albanian waters. Giving judgment for the United Kingdom, the Court noted:

> The obligations incumbent upon the Albanian authorities consisted in notifying for the benefit of shipping in general, the existence of a minefield in Albanian territorial waters and in warning the approaching British warships of imminent danger to which the minefield exposed them.[175]

Although the context of this case involved interference with freedom of maritime communication, the Court expressly based its conclusion on additional grounds of more general application, namely, elementary considerations of humanity and the obligation, referred to earlier, that a State

---

Consultation in Border Areas, 1977, ibid., p. 275; Denmark-FRG Agreement Regulating the Exchange of Information on the Construction of Nuclear Installations along the Border, 1977, *International Legal Materials*, 17 (1978), p. 274.

[171] e.g. Belgium-France Convention on Radiological Protection with regard to the Installations of the Ardennes Nuclear Power Station, 1966, *UN Treaty Series*, vol. 988, p. 288; Switzerland-FRG Agreement on Mutual Information on Construction and Operation of Nuclear Installations in Border Areas, 1982, [1983] *Bundesgesetzblatt* II, p. 734, and agreements listed at n. 170, above, between Spain-Portugal and Netherlands-FRG.

[172] Cameron *et al.*, op. cit. above (n. 22), pp. 73 ff.; but compare Handl, *Ecology Law Quarterly*, 7 (1978), p. 1, who argues that affected States are entitled to an equitable solution, i.e. more than consultation and negotiation, but less than a veto. See also n. 207, below.

[173] See below, Section IV.

[174] *ICJ Reports*, 1949, p. 4.

[175] Ibid., at p. 22.

should not knowingly allow its territory to be used for acts contrary to the rights of other States.[176] As we have seen, these include the right to protection from environmental harm.[177] For this reason it is legitimate to view *Corfu Channel* as authority for an obligation to give warning of known environmental hazards.

Treaties and State practice support this conclusion. It is unequivocally applied to marine pollution by the Law of the Sea Convention[178] and other treaties now widely ratified.[179] The same principle is found in treaties and the ILC's draft articles dealing with pollution of international watercourses,[180] in the ILA Montreal Rules on transfrontier pollution[181] and in the OECD principles.[182]

In all of these cases the object of notification is the same: States should be given sufficient information promptly enough to enable them to minimize the damage and take whatever measures of self-protection are permitted by international law. Modern treaties tend also to require States to make contingency plans for pollution emergencies and to co-operate in their response. A typical example of this is Article 199 of the Law of the Sea Convention. Practice in this respect is well developed in the maritime field at regional level,[183] but it is also the subject of a small number of bilateral arrangements.[184]

2. *State practice in cases of nuclear emergency*

The existence of a general obligation to notify other States and co-operate in cases where they are at risk of harmful consequences of accidents or incidents is confirmed both by regional practice in Western Europe and by two recent international conventions.

Most of the European treaties referred to in the last section contain provisions for the timely supply of information in cases of emergency and

---

[176] Ibid., at p. 22. Quentin-Baxter's view, at *Yearbook of the ILC*, 1980, vol. 2, pt. 1, p. 258, that this *dictum* refers only to innocent passage and not to acts which harm other States, seems unjustifiably narrow.

[177] Above, Section III (a).

[178] Arts. 198, 211(7).

[179] e.g. MARPOL Convention, 1973, Art. 8; Helsinki Convention on the Protection of the Marine Environment of the Baltic Sea, 1974, Annex 6; Barcelona Convention for the Protection of the Mediterranean Sea, Protocol on Co-operation in Case of Emergency, 1976, Art. 9; Cartagena Convention for the Protection and Development of the Marine Environment of the Wider Caribbean Region, 1983, Art. 11, and other treaties in the UNEP Regional Seas series. See Kiss, *German Yearbook of International Law*, 23 (1980), p. 231. See also Basle Convention on the Control of Transboundary Movement of Hazardous Wastes, 1989, Art. 13.

[180] e.g. Convention on the Protection of the Rhine Against Chemical Pollution, 1976, Art. 11; ILC, draft articles on International Watercourses, Art. 25, *Yearbook of the ILC*, 1984, vol. 2, pt. 1, p. 120.

[181] Art. 5: above, n. 167.

[182] Rec. C(74) 224 (1974), Annex, Part F.

[183] See n. 179, above. Protocols on Co-operation in cases of emergency are part of most UNEP Regional Seas Treaties. See also Agreement for Co-operation in Dealing with Pollution of the North Sea by Oil and Other Harmful Substances, 1983, Cmnd. 9104.

[184] e.g. US–Mexico Agreement to Co-operate in the Solution of Environmental Problems in the Border Area, 1983, with 1987 Annex II, *International Legal Materials*, 26 (1987), p. 19; Paris Convention for the Prevention of Marine Pollution from Land-Based Sources, 1974, Art. 13.

require radioactivity monitoring systems to be established to alert governments to the danger.[185] A small number also require co-operation in response to such an emergency.

Following the Chernobyl accident, the Soviet Union was criticized for failing to give adequate and timely information to other States likely to be affected by the disaster. Implicit in this criticism was a belief that such notification should reasonably be expected.[186] In addition to the practice of a growing number of States supporting such an obligation, the IAEA had developed guidelines on reporting of incidents and information exchange in 1985,[187] but these were non-binding.

One result of Chernobyl was the opening for signature of a Convention on Early Notification of Nuclear Accidents.[188] This imposes on parties a duty to notify other States likely to be affected by transboundary releases of 'radiological safety significance'. Information on the occurrence and on minimizing its radiological consequences must be supplied to enable other States to take all possible precautionary measures. The Convention specifies in detail what information is to be given and requires States to respond promptly to requests for further relevant information. It is much less clear, however, when a release acquires radiological safety significance; this provision is deliberately without objective definition, and thus leaves substantial discretion to States where incidents occur. The effectiveness of the Convention is also dependent on States possessing a basic radiological

---

[185] Agreement between Spain and Portugal, 1980, above, n. 170; Belgium-France Convention, 1966, above, n. 171; Agreement between France and Switzerland Concerning Exchange of Information in Case of Accidents, 1979, Ruster and Simma, *International Protection of the Environment*, vol. 27, p. 382; UK-France Exchange of Notes Concerning Exchanges of Information etc., 1983, *UK Treaty Series*, No. 60 (1983), Cmnd. 9041; Agreement between Switzerland and FRG Concerning Radiological Disaster Relief, 1978, Ruster and Simma, op. cit., vol. 27, p. 337; Agreement between France-FRG on Mutual Information in the event of Radiological Incidents, 1981, [1981] *Bundesgesetzblatt* I, p. 885; Agreement between France and Luxembourg on Exchange of Information in Case of Radiological Emergencies, 1983, *Nuclear Law Bulletin*, 34 (1984), p. 42. A further series of such agreements has been prompted by the Chernobyl accident: Agreement between Belgium and the Netherlands on Co-operation in Nuclear Safety, 1987, *Nuclear Law Bulletin*, 41 (1988), p. 42; Norway-Sweden Agreement on Exchange of Information and Early Notification Relating to Nuclear Facilities, 1987, *Environmental Policy and Law*, 17 (1987), p. 41; UK-Norway Agreement on Early Notification etc., 1987, Cm. 371; Finland-USSR Agreement on Early Notification of a Nuclear Accident, 1987, *Nuclear Law Bulletin*, 39 (1987), p. 54; FRG-GDR Radiation Protection Agreement, 1987, ibid. 40 (1987), p. 44; Brazil-Argentina Agreement on Early Notification and Mutual Assistance, 1987, ibid. 39 (1987), p. 36; Denmark-Sweden Agreement on Exchange of Information and Early Notification, 1986, ibid., p. 35; Denmark-Poland Agreement on Exchange of Information, 1987, ibid. 41 (1988), p. 49, and similar agreements with the FRG, USSR, UK and Finland. These are all intended to give effect to the provisions of the 1986 IAEA Notification Convention. See also EEC Council Directive 87/600, considered above at n. 81, and on the application of EEC law generally, see Cameron *et al.*, op. cit. above (n. 22), pp. 49 ff.

[186] Group of Seven, Statement on the Implications of the Chernobyl Nuclear Accident, 1986, *International Legal Materials*, 25 (1986), p. 1005; IAEA General Conference, Special Session, 1986, Doc. GC (SPL. 1), Res. 1.

[187] IAEA Doc. INFCIRC/321, Guidelines on Reportable Events etc., 1985.

[188] *International Legal Materials*, 25 (1986), p. 1369. See, generally, Cameron *et al.*, op. cit. above (n. 22), pp. 19 ff.; Adede, *The IAEA Notification and Assistance Conventions* (Dordrecht, 1987); Handl, *Revue générale de droit international public*, 92 (1988), pp. 5, 24 ff. In force 27 October 1986.

monitoring and assessment capability. Unlike bilateral treaties in Europe, the Convention does not require States to acquire this capability; where this is lacking, it is difficult to see how they will be able to respond effectively.[189]

Owing to superpower opposition, the Convention does not cover nuclear accidents involving military facilities, such as nuclear submarines, but the Soviet Union has given notice when two such vessels have run into difficulty, and the United Kingdom has undertaken to give such notice.[190] Since the Convention applies only to 'transboundary releases', it would seem that accidents whose consequences do not extend beyond national borders, or which occur wholly on the high seas, are also excluded.[191]

A number of States, including the Soviet Union and the United Kingdom, had declared that they would apply the Convention pending entry into force, and several agreements already apply its provisions bilaterally.[192] Although the Convention is open to criticism for the apparent looseness of its terminology and the range of excluded occurrences, it supports the conclusion that the principle of timely notification of nuclear accidents likely to affect other States is a customary obligation.

Assistance in cases of nuclear emergency is now also the subject of an IAEA Convention, which allows States to call for international help to protect 'life, property and the environment' from the effects of radioactive releases.[193] The IAEA is given a co-ordinating role and an obligation to respond to a request by making available appropriate resources. No explicit obligation to render assistance is placed on other States, however, even where an installation within their territory is the cause of harm, nor is there any provision for joint contingency planning comparable to that found in many maritime treaties.

Thus, in general, the Convention facilitates, but does not require, a response to nuclear accidents or emergencies. Its main achievement is to give assisting States and their personnel immunity from legal proceedings brought by the requesting State, and an indemnity for proceedings brought by others. However, these provisions are open to reservation.[194]

Like the small number of bilateral treaties which provide in more general

---

[189] Rosen, *IAEA Bulletin*, 29 (1987), pp. 34, 35.

[190] *International Legal Materials*, 25 (1986), p. 1369. The UK declaration specifically includes voluntary notification of military accidents; others refer to 'all' or 'any' accidents.

[191] Cameron *et al.*, op. cit. above (n. 22), p. 24.

[192] At least 12 States have made declarations, including all 5 Security Council members. See list at *International Legal Materials*, 15 (1976), p. 1395. These declarations are likely to be binding on States making them: see *Nuclear Tests* cases, *ICJ Reports*, 1974, pp. 253 and 457; *Military and Paramilitary Activities in and against Nicaragua* case, *ICJ Reports*, 1984, p. 392. See n. 185, above, for bilateral agreements.

[193] Convention on Assistance in the Case of a Nuclear Accident or Radiological Emergency, 1986, *International Legal Materials*, 25 (1986), p. 1377; see also IAEA Doc. INFCIRC/310, Guidelines for Mutual Emergency Assistance Arrangements etc., 1984. Assistance under the Convention was given to Brazil in 1987. See generally Cameron *et al.*, op. cit. above (n. 22), pp. 26 ff.; Adede, op. cit. above (n. 188).

[194] Arts. 8 and 10. Four States have excluded Art. 8; two have excluded Art. 10.

terms for emergency assistance,[195] the IAEA Convention leaves responsibility for making the request and taking or directing appropriate action in its territory with the State which needs help.[196] It creates no duty either to seek assistance or to stem the emergency. A failure to do so may of course incur State responsibility if it results in harm to others, in accordance with the general principles discussed below. But unlike maritime casualties, where States also have a recognized right of intervention or self-help to protect their own coasts,[197] there is no generally accepted basis in international law for intervention by neighbouring States seeking to avert the consequences of a nuclear catastrophe, such as Chernobyl. Any attempt to take unilateral preventive action within another State, or to render unrequested assistance in these circumstances, would in principle appear a violation of the source State's sovereignty.[198] The IAEA Convention, by leaving the requesting State the decisive role, does nothing to disturb this position. Assistance, as provided for in the instruments referred to here, is thus sharply different from intervention or self-protection. In short, it is not obligatory, it need not be sought and it cannot be given without consent.

(d) Customary Law: An Overview

The principles of harm prevention, co-operation in cases of transboundary risk, emergency notification and assistance form the core of customary law regulating the environmental impact of nuclear activities. Although there is now a wide consensus on the existence of an international customary obligation to protect the environment from pollution and other States from harm, the precise scope of this principle remains unsettled. While the evidence and arguments in favour of a due diligence analysis appear more compelling, support for a stronger obligation of prevention remains an important alternative view. This basic difference of approach is reflected in the application of the principle of State responsibility to nuclear accidents, to which we return in Section IV.

It has been possible, however, to draw conclusions regarding the permissibility of pollution of the seas and the atmosphere by high level radioactive particles and the prohibition of serious nuclear injury to other States. The second and third of the principles considered so far have also largely been

---

[195] e.g. Nordic Mutual Emergency Assistance Agreement in Connection with Radiation Accidents, 1963, *UN Treaty Series*, vol. 525, p. 76; Belgium-France Convention, 1966, above, n. 171; Belgium-France Agreement on Mutual Assistance in the Event of Catastrophic and Serious Accident, 1981, *Nuclear Law Bulletin*, 34 (1984), p. 42; France-FRG Agreement on Mutual Assistance in the Event of Catastrophic and Grave Disasters, 1977, [1980] *Bundesgesetzblatt* II, p. 33; FRG-Belgium Agreement on Mutual Emergency Assistance, 1980, [1982] *Bundesgesetzblatt* II, p. 1006.

[196] Art. 3.

[197] Convention on Intervention in Case of Maritime Casualties, 1969; UN Law of the Sea Convention, 1982, Art. 221.

[198] Compare the Security Council's condemnation of Israel's attack on an Iraqi nuclear reactor: UNSC Res. 487 (1981); see also IAEA Board of Governors Res. S/14532 (1981), *International Legal Materials*, 20 (1981), p. 963; *Corfu Channel* case, *ICJ Reports*, 1949, p. 4 at pp. 32–6; *Tehran Hostages* case, *ICJ Reports*, 1980, p. 3 at p. 43.

confirmed by the evidence of State practice and treaties dealing with nuclear transboundary risks and emergencies.

Certain conclusions which customary law does not yet appear to support are also worth noticing. In particular, it does not seem justifiable to conclude that States are debarred from creating sources of risk to others, even where these involve a possibility of nuclear injury. Diplomatic responses to the Chernobyl accident, considered below, make this point clear, since even now, no State has called on the Soviet Union to close reactors of this type.[199]

This conclusion has the important implication that, subject to the restraints imposed by the principles of customary law considered above, States are free to acquire and use nuclear technology or to site installations near borders.[200] The *Nuclear Tests* cases, which raised this issue directly, did not give an answer,[201] although one judge did assert that until damage occurs, 'each State is free to act within the limits of its sovereignty'.[202]

Those limits now clearly include controls on sources of risk and procedural obligations aimed at minimizing their potential for harm. The ILC rapporteurs have followed this trend in their reports on 'International Liability',[203] but unlike other formulations, they also envisage an obligation to negotiate a specific regime aimed at preventing, minimizing and compensating possible injury.[204] This approach is more than procedural; while not prohibiting all risk creation, it requires an equitable balance of interests as the price for undertaking risky activities.[205] All relevant factors, including the possibility of alternative sites and the adequacy of safety measures, would have to be considered in effecting a solution.[206] In extreme cases, an activity judged to pose an inequitable risk might become impermissible.[207]

Although a logical extension of the obligation to consult and take account of the interests of others, the equitable utilization of territory which this approach implies goes well beyond existing precedents dealing with the risk of transboundary harm.[208] Handl has argued that there is evidence of State

---

[199] Writers are divided on this issue: see Handl, *Ecology Law Quarterly*, 7 (1978), p. 1 at p. 8; Kirgis, loc. cit. above (n. 89), at p. 294; Reuter, *Recueil des cours*, 103 (1961–II), p. 592; Cameron *et al.*, loc. cit. above (n. 22), pp. 73 ff. On Chernobyl, see below, Section IV (f), and nn. 277–9.

[200] But compare Handl and Cameron, loc. cit. (previous note).

[201] *ICJ Reports*, 1973, p. 99 at p. 135; *ICJ Reports*, 1974, pp. 253 and 457. Note, however, that in its 1973 decisions the Court ordered France by way of interim measures to 'avoid nuclear tests causing the deposit of radioactive fallout' on the plaintiff's territory.

[202] *ICJ Reports*, 1973, p. 99 at p. 131, *per* Judge Ignacio Pinto.

[203] Schematic Outline, *Yearbook of the ILC*, 1983, vol. 2, pt. 1, p. 223, sections 2, 3; draft Arts. 7, 8, UN Doc. A/CN.4/413, 1988. See above, n. 117.

[204] Barboza, 2nd Report, *Yearbook of the ILC*, 1986, vol. 2, pt. 1, pp. 152 ff.

[205] See Schematic Outline referred to at n. 203, above.

[206] Schematic Outline, section 6.

[207] Handl, loc. cit. above (n. 199), at p. 35, argues that for activities carrying a risk of catastrophic effects, 'barring a special relationship between risk exposed states such as reciprocity of risk creation, or a sharing of the benefits to be derived from the proposed activity, such an activity should be considered impermissible'.

[208] See Section III (c), above, and n. 131.

practice in favour of an equitable approach,[209] but within the ILC this view remains controversial,[210] and it is not followed in other attempts at codification of environmental law.[211]

IV. RESPONSIBILITY AND LIABILITY FOR NUCLEAR DAMAGE AND ENVIRONMENTAL HARM

This article is not the place for an extended discussion of the complexities of the law of State responsibility. Only the main points of importance as they affect the use of nuclear energy and its impact on the environment need be considered. Since the Stockholm Conference in 1972, the attention of States has mainly centred on the international regulation of environmental problems, not on issues of State responsibility for environmental harm.[212] Yet this subject remains important both in providing a basis for remedying breaches of obligation by States and in allocating the costs of resulting environmental damage.[213]

(a) The Basis of Responsibility

The foundation of responsibility lies in the breach of obligations undertaken by States or imposed on them by international law;[214] in connection with nuclear activities responsibility will normally arise because of the breach of one or more of the customary obligations referred to earlier or on the basis of a breach of treaty.[215] Only the State's obligations are in issue

---

[209] Above, n. 199.

[210] See *Reports of the ILC to the UN General Assembly*, UN Doc. A/42/10, 1987, and A/43/10, 1988; and compare Barboza's 5th Report, 1989, UN Doc. A/CN.4/423. See Magraw, *American Journal of International Law*, 80 (1986), p. 305; Boyle, *International and Comparative Law Quarterly*, 39 (1990), p. 1, and below, n. 221.

[211] See ILA, Montreal Rules on Transfrontier Pollution, *Report of the 60th Conference*, 1982, pp. 1, 157. The ILA's approach is criticized by Quentin-Baxter, *Yearbook of the ILC*, 1983, vol. 2, pt. 1, p. 209.

[212] Most post-1972 treaties on environmental matters either leave for further development the implementation of principles on responsibility and liability for damage (see, e.g., Basle Convention on Control of Transboundary Movements of Hazardous Wastes, 1989, Art. 12) or omit all reference to responsibility (see, e.g., Paris Convention for the Prevention of Marine Pollution from Land Based Sources, 1974).

[213] See generally Brownlie, op. cit. above (n. 93); Jiménez de Aréchaga, in Sorensen (ed.), *Manual of Public International Law* (London, 1968), p. 539; Smith, op. cit. above (n. 89); Dupuy, *La Responsabilité internationale des états pour les dommages d'origine technologique et industrielle* (Paris, 1976); Hardy, *International and Comparative Law Quarterly*, 10 (1961), p. 739; Dupuy, loc. cit. above (n. 89), p. 345; Miatello, in Spinedi and Simma (eds.), *UN Codification of State Responsibility* (New York, 1987), p. 287.

[214] See Art. 3, draft articles on State Responsibility, pt. 1, *Yearbook of the ILC*, 1980, vol. 2, pt. 2, p. 30; Brownlie, op. cit. above (n. 93), pp. 37 f., 60–2; Jiménez de Aréchaga, loc. cit. above (previous note), at p. 534.

[215] On responsibility for breach of treaty, see *Chorzów Factory (Claims for Indemnity)* case, PCIJ, Series A, No. 9, p. 21 (1927); Rosenne, *Breach of Treaty* (Cambridge, 1985), p. 45.

here; the problem of attributing private conduct to States will seldom impinge on responsibility for non-performance of its own environmental duties.[216] Even where an activity causing harm is privately operated, as in the *Trail Smelter* case,[217] the issue remains one of the State's duty of control, co-operation or notification, which cannot be avoided by surrendering the activity itself into private hands.[218]

However, some writers argue that strict or absolute responsibility for harm is not based on any breach of obligation, but arises independently by operation of law, or of some principle of equity, sovereign equality or good neighbourliness.[219] Sometimes referred to as 'liability for risk', this theory of non-wrongful liability has been adopted by the ILC as the basis of its topic 'International Liability'. The argument here is that an alternative conceptual basis is needed to accommodate strict liability for lawful activities which cause harm without breach of an obligation of due diligence and to allow for a balance of interests without prohibition.[220]

The cogency of this analysis has been doubted. The case law, such as *Trail Smelter* or *Corfu Channel*, is clearly based on breach of obligation, not on some alternative thesis of liability.[221] Brownlie describes as fundamentally misconceived the Commission's distinction between wrongful and lawful activities causing harm. He notes that it is the content of the relevant rules which is critical and observes:

> The relations of adjacent territorial sovereigns are of course governed by the normal principles of international responsibility and these may sustain liability for the consequences of extra-hazardous operations.[222]

Thus on this view it is possible to encompass strict or absolute liability

---

[216] See Handl, *American Journal of International Law*, 74 (1980), p. 525; Jiménez de Aréchaga, loc. cit. above (n. 213), at pp. 560 ff. Compare draft Arts. 8, 11, *Yearbook of the ILC*, 1980, vol. 2, pt. 2, p. 30; Brownlie, op. cit. above (n. 93), pp. 159 ff., and case concerning *US Diplomatic and Consular Staff in Tehran*, *ICJ Reports*, 1980, p. 3.

[217] Above, n. 90.

[218] See especially Brownlie, op. cit. above (n. 93), pp. 152, 180 ff.; *Corfu Channel* case, *ICJ Reports*, 1949, p. 4; Jiménez de Aréchaga, loc. cit. above (n. 213), at p. 560.

[219] Jiménez de Aréchaga, loc. cit. above (n. 213), at p. 539; id., *Recueil des cours*, 159 (1978–I), p. 267 at p. 271; Reuter, *Recueil des cours*, 103 (1961–II), pp. 590–5; Handl, *Netherlands Yearbook of International Law*, 16 (1985), p. 46 at pp. 77–8, and see Goldie at n. 238, below.

[220] *Yearbook of the ILC*, 1980, vol. 2, pt. 1, p. 248; draft articles, UN Doc. A/CN.4/423, 1989. See above, n. 118, and Handl, loc. cit. above (previous note), p. 49 at p. 55. See also *Yearbook of the ILC*, 1969, vol. 2, pp. 229 ff., and paras. 79 and 83; ibid. 1973, vol. 1, pp. 7–14. For cogent criticism of the confusion of 'strict liability' with 'liability for risk' see Handl, loc. cit. above (n. 131), p. 164.

[221] Brownlie, op. cit. above (n. 93), p. 50; Akehurst, *Netherlands Yearbook of International Law*, 16 (1985), p. 8; Handl, loc. cit. above (n. 131), p. 156 at pp. 165–70; Hardy, loc. cit. above (n. 213), p. 751; cf. Magraw, loc. cit. above (n. 210). See also *Corfu Channel* case, *ICJ Reports*, 1949, p. 65, *per* Judge Badawi Pasha (dissenting):
'. . . it must be stressed that international law does not recognise objective responsibility based on the notion of risk, adopted by certain national legislations . . . The failure of Albania to carry out an international obligation must therefore be proved . . .'

[222] Brownlie, op. cit. above (n. 93), p. 50.

within the orthodox perspective of objective responsibility for breach of obligation.[223]

But would it matter if strict or absolute responsibility drew on some other basis, such as equity or sovereign equality, and not on breach of obligation? Rapporteur Quentin-Baxter argued that it would; in his view the reparation due for a breach of obligation entailed prohibition of the activity causing the harm, whereas this novel regime of risk liability would allow for continuation on an equitable basis.[224] The problem with this is that reparation for breach of obligation may not be as inflexible as Quentin-Baxter suggests.[225] Indeed the *Trail Smelter* case indicates the contrary. As Brownlie observes, 'the interaction of substantive laws and issues of reparation should be stressed'.[226] This conclusion, which reiterates a point familiar in most legal systems, confirms that it is unnecessary to depart from the thesis that in discussion of strict or absolute responsibility for harm, what matters is how the primary obligation itself is defined. But the possibility of alternative approaches must be recognized.

(b) *Fault and Strict or Absolute Responsibility*[227]

The point has already been made that the obligation to control sources of harm represented by Principle 21 of the Stockholm Declaration is capable of interpretation either as an obligation of due diligence or as one of absolute prevention of harm. The latter possibility may support strict or absolute responsibility for the fact of harm in international law, but the nature of such a principle must be considered.

The question cannot be reduced to a simple choice between 'fault' and some stricter standard of responsibility, since 'fault', as *Corfu Channel*[228] illustrates, can be used both subjectively, requiring intention or negligence on the part of the State or its agents,[229] and objectively, meaning simply the

---

[223] Smith, op. cit. above (n. 89), pp. 40–1, 124–5. But for a strong defence of the ILC's approach see Handl, loc. cit. above (n. 219). Use of the terms 'strict' or 'absolute' in this context merely signifies a difference of degree in the range of exculpatory factors which may negative responsibility. See further below, text at n. 321, where the same point arises in respect of civil liability.

[224] *Yearbook of the ILC*, 1981, vol. 2, pt. 1, pp. 115, 122; ibid. 1982, vol. 2, pt. 1, p. 60, para. 39. Compare Art. 6, Draft Articles on State Responsibility, ibid. 1984, vol. 2, pt. 1, p. 2, and Schematic Outline on International Liability, sections 4 and 5, ibid. 1983, vol. 2, pt. 1, p. 223. See also Barboza, ibid. 1986, vol. 2, pt. 1, p. 152, para. 31, and Handl, loc. cit. above (n. 219), at pp. 65 f.

[225] See Boyle, loc. cit. above (n. 210); Smith, op. cit. above (n. 89), pp. 124–6; Gray, *Judicial Remedies in International Law* (Oxford, 1987), pp. 222–3.

[226] Op. cit. above (n. 93), p. 234. See also Combacu and Allard, *Netherlands Yearbook of International Law*, 16 (1985), p. 81 at p. 108.

[227] For the difference between strict and absolute liability or responsibility see above, n. 223.

[228] *ICJ Reports*, 1949, p. 4.

[229] See the dissent of Judge Krylov, at p. 72, requiring *dolus* or *culpa*. See also Oppenheim, *International Law*, vol. 1 (8th edn., London, 1955), p. 343: 'An act of State injurious to another is nevertheless not an international delinquency if committed neither wilfully and maliciously nor with culpable negligence.'

breach of an international obligation.[230] Used in the former, subjective, sense, 'fault' is, as Handl observes, almost never the basis of responsibility in environmental disputes.[231] Jiménez de Aréchaga aptly explains the essential point:

> The decisive consideration is that unless the rule of international law which has been violated specifically envisages malice or culpable negligence, the rules of international law do not contain a general floating requirement of malice or culpable negligence as a condition of responsibility.[232]

Used in the objective sense, 'fault' is simply tautologous, unless the particular obligation itself incorporates subjective elements.[233]

This merely indicates that it is more productive to leave aside doctrinal arguments about the role and character of fault, and to concentrate instead on the essential point, that responsibility for a failure to prevent environmental harm will normally entail no more than the objective breach of an international obligation, however defined. Thus in choosing between diligent or absolute standards of responsibility, it is once more the definition of the primary obligation represented by Principle 21 of the Stockholm Declaration which is important, not the presence or absence of 'subjective' fault. Simply to show that *dolus* or *culpa* is not required is not enough to demonstrate that States are strictly or absolutely responsible for nuclear damage.[234]

(c) *The Views of Writers*

The argument that there is a relatively straightforward connection between responsibility and the fact of harm is put most strongly by writers such as Goldie and Schneider. They see *Trail Smelter*, *Corfu Channel* and *Lac Lanoux* as pointing to the emergence of strict liability as a principle of international law.[235]

Goldie's argument is a sophisticated one which draws on equity as the doctrinal basis of a system of strict liability for States. He treats risk creation as a form of expropriation of the adjacent State's use of its territory, and invokes the notion of unjust enrichment.[236] But the heavy reliance

---

[230] Jiménez de Aréchaga, loc. cit. above (n. 213), at pp. 534–7, and Handl, loc. cit. above (n. 131), p. 156 at pp. 162–7, prefer this interpretation of *Corfu Channel*. Brownlie, op. cit. above (n. 93), pp. 38–48, observes at p. 47: 'The approach adopted by the majority of the Court fails to correspond neatly with either the *culpa* doctrine or the test of objective responsibility.'

[231] Handl, loc. cit. above (n. 131), at p. 164.

[232] Loc. cit. above (n. 213), at p. 535.

[233] See Brownlie, op. cit. above (n. 93), pp. 44 ff.; Smith, op. cit. above (n. 93), pp. 15–20; Jiménez de Aréchaga, loc. cit. above (n. 213), at pp. 534–6; Hardy, loc. cit. above (n. 213), p. 754.

[234] Hardy, ibid., p. 755; Jiménez de Aréchaga, loc. cit. above (n. 104), p. 271; and Handl, loc. cit. above (n. 131), pp. 163 f., who criticizes Goldie for equating strict liability with the absence of intention or negligence: cf. Goldie, *International and Comparative Law Quarterly*, 14 (1965), p. 1189, and *Columbia Journal of Transnational Law*, 9 (1970), p. 283.

[235] Goldie, loc. cit. (previous note); Schneider, *World Public Order of the Environment* (London, 1975), ch. 6. See also Kelson, *Harvard International Law Journal*, 13 (1972), p. 197 at pp. 235 ff.

[236] *Netherlands Yearbook of International Law*, 16 (1985), p. 175 at pp. 204 ff.

Goldie places on inference from general principles of national law is the most questionable part of his thesis,[237] and his interpretation of the international case law is not widely accepted.[238]

Others, more plausibly, are more cautious. Jenks identifies ultra-hazardous activities as a distinct category for which strict or absolute responsibility is an exceptional principle justified as a means of shifting the burden of proof and ensuring a more equitable distribution of loss.[239] These arguments are of course especially relevant to nuclear activities; they do not allow States to escape responsibility by arguing that the harm was unavoidable. In defining what constitutes an 'ultra-hazardous' activity, most attempts focus more on the seriousness of the potential harm than on the likelihood of the risk occurring.[240] This is likely to include accidents at nuclear reactors, where the risk, though small, carries a foreseeable potential for very widespread and serious harm.[241] Beyond that, the boundaries of the category are more questionable. Does it, for example, cover activities whose effects are only cumulatively harmful, such as the continuous discharge of radioactive waste?[242]

An alternative approach to the definitional problem is to apply the category only to cases covered by specific agreement.[243] The only clear example of such an agreement is the 1972 Space Objects Liability Convention under which States bear direct and absolute responsibility for damage on earth.[244] Evidence of agreement on the inclusion of nuclear installations comes more questionably from civil liability treaties and national nuclear laws referred to below.[245]

Thus it is apparent that a strict or absolute standard of responsibility for failure to prevent harm enjoys some support among commentators as an exceptional principle applicable to ultra-hazardous activities, of which nuclear installations may be an example. But as a general principle, covering all sources of transboundary harm, it is the alternative thesis, that States are in general responsible for environmental damage only if it results from a want of due diligence, which is more cogently supported by writers

[237] On national law and civil liability treaties, see below, Section V.

[238] On *Trail Smelter* and *Corfu Channel*, see below, Section IV (d).

[239] *Recueil des cours*, 117 (1966–I), p. 105. See also Smith, op. cit. above (n. 89), pp. 112–25; Handl, loc. cit. above (n. 219), at pp. 68 ff., and loc. cit. above (n. 216); Hardy, this *Year Book*, 36 (1960), p. 223; Goldie, loc. cit. above (n. 93), p. 50.

[240] Jenks, loc. cit. (previous note); Handl, loc. cit. above (n. 216), at p. 555; Goldie, *International and Comparative Law Quarterly*, 14 (1965), p. 1189.

[241] Jenks, loc. cit. above (n. 239), at p. 195. On the question of foreseeability of the risk, see text at nn. 119–22, above.

[242] Jenks, loc. cit. above (n. 239), at p. 122, views *Trail Smelter* as a case of liability for ultra-hazardous activities. This is much broader than most interpretations. The ILC's draft articles on International Liability now apply to activities with a low probability of disastrous injury and to those with a high probability of minor injury: see below, n. 284.

[243] Jiménez de Aréchaga, loc. cit. above (n. 213), at p. 539.

[244] See Christol, *American Journal of International Law*, 74 (1980), p. 346; Foster, *Canadian Yearbook of International Law*, 10 (1972), p. 155; claim for damage caused by Cosmos 954, *International Legal Materials*, 18 (1979), p. 902.

[245] See Section V (e).

such as Dupuy, Handl and others.[246] They see this as the dominant theory supported by State practice.

Their main arguments point to the ambiguity or inconclusive character of much of the jurisprudence, and its misinterpretation by other writers, and they place more reliance on the evidence of treaty formulations of the obligation to prevent harm and the responsibility of States. They are sceptical also of strict or absolute responsibility as a general principle of law supported by national legal systems, but accept that in specific cases a system of liability for exceptionally dangerous activities not founded on a failure of due diligence may be appropriate.[247]

(d) *The Case Law*

This is certainly inconclusive. The final award of the tribunal in *Trail Smelter* required payment of further compensation if harm occurred notwithstanding Canada's compliance with the regime of control laid down,[248] and has thus been variously read as supporting either strict or absolute responsibility.[249] These concepts are often used interchangeably, as they will be in this article for the sake of convenience, but the point should be made at once that they differ significantly in the degree to which exculpation is permitted by international law. Strict responsibility places the burden of proof on the respondent but permits exculpation; absolute liability does not permit exculpation. Not all writers observe this basic distinction, but it indicates the difficulty of drawing firm conclusions from the *Trail Smelter* case. Since Canada's responsibility for damage was of course accepted by the parties at the outset, the award was not concerned with establishing a standard of responsibility in international law, but only with deciding what compensation was due and what the terms of future operation of the smelter should be.[250] In any event, as Dupuy points out, whatever the case decides, it must be read in the light of subsequent State practice, which in his view favours due diligence.[251]

The decision in the *Corfu Channel* case has suffered widely varied interpretations but in reality tells us only that States must make diligent efforts to warn other States of known hazards.[252] It permits no definitive conclu-

---

[246] Jiménez de Aréchaga, *Recueil des cours*, 159 (1978–I), p. 272; Smith, op. cit. above (n. 89); OECD, *Legal Aspects of Transfrontier Pollution*, p. 386, and Dupuy, ibid., at p. 353; Handl, loc. cit. above (n. 216), pp. 535 ff., and loc. cit. above (n. 89), pp. 427–30; Hardy, loc. cit. above (n. 213).

[247] See n. 239, above.

[248] *American Journal of International Law*, 35 (1941), p. 686 at p. 733.

[249] Goldie, loc. cit. above (n. 240), at p. 1227; Jenks, loc. cit. above (n. 239), at p. 122; Handl, loc. cit. above (n. 219), at p. 61.

[250] Handl, loc. cit. above (n. 131), pp. 167–8; Smith, op. cit. above (n. 89), at pp. 113 f.; Rubin, loc. cit. above (n. 90).

[251] Dupuy, in Bothe (ed.), op. cit. above (n. 98), at pp. 369, 373. Hardy, loc. cit. above (n. 240), pp. 751–2, appears to take the same view.

[252] See above, nn. 174–6; Brownlie, op. cit. above (n. 93), pp. 40–8; Handl, loc. cit. above (n. 131), pp. 165–6.

sions about the role of due diligence in cases of environmental injury, but it is difficult to reconcile the Court's efforts to establish what preventive steps the Albanian authorities could have taken with the view that States are strictly or absolutely responsible for injury.[253] Most of the debate about the role of fault in this case has centred on the choice between subjective and objective definitions of fault referred to earlier, not on the question whether the obligations of States are absolute or qualified by diligent conduct.[254]

For different reasons, the *Nuclear Tests* cases[255] are also unhelpful. Decided by the ICJ in 1974, they deal with a series of deliberate test explosions, not with operational pollution or nuclear accidents. The claimants did not seek reparation for proven damage, but only a judgment that there should be no further testing, no deposit of nuclear fallout in breach of their territorial sovereignty and no more interference with high seas freedoms.[256] The Court made no findings on any of these issues but dismissed the case on the ground that it no longer had any object, France having undertaken unilaterally to discontinue further atmospheric tests.[257] Only Judge de Castro made reference to the argument that nuclear testing may involve the breach of a State's obligation not to use its territory for acts contrary to the rights of other States.[258]

Although Principle 21 of the Stockholm Declaration now incorporates this obligation, it too is an inconclusive guide to the nature of responsibility for environmental damage, and must be interpreted within the framework of customary rules on which it is based.[259] Reviewing the proceedings of the Preparatory Committee for the Stockholm Conference, Handl concludes that they provide little or no support in favour of any specific theory

[253] *ICJ Reports*, 1949, p. 4 at pp. 22–3; and compare Judges Winarski, at pp. 53–6, and Badawi Pasha, at p. 65; see Hardy, loc. cit. above (n. 239), at p. 229; Smith, op. cit. above (n. 89), at pp. 112 f.

[254] See above, nn. 229–31.

[255] See above, n. 15.

[256] See *ICJ Pleadings*, 1978, vol. 1, pp. 479 ff., and vol. 2, pp. 264 ff.; Goldie, loc. cit. above (n. 236), at pp. 219 ff.; *ICJ Reports*, 1974, pp. 360 ff.

[257] On the question whether atmospheric testing is itself illegal, compare Judges Gros, *ICJ Reports*, 1974, at pp. 279 ff.; Petrén, at pp. 305 ff.; de Castro, at pp. 389 ff.; Barwick, at pp. 427 ff.: '. . . there is a radical distinction to be made between claims that violation of territorial and decisional sovereignty by the intrusion and deposition of radioactive nuclides . . . is unlawful according to international law, and the claim that the testing of nuclear weapons has become unlawful, according to customary law . . .': *per* Judge Barwick, at p. 248. See also *ICJ Pleadings*, 1978, vol. 1, pp. 500 ff.; vol. 2, pp. 264 ff. For the importance of proof of material injury, see above, n. 139, and for the view that testing constitutes prohibited pollution, see above, n. 145.

[258] *ICJ Reports*, 1974, p. 253 at p. 389. See Margolis, loc. cit. above (n. 11), at p. 642, and below, sub-section (f). McDougal and Schlei, loc. cit. above (n. 11), at pp. 690 ff., argue that responsibility for harm caused by nuclear tests must be judged by criteria of reasonableness and take account of the 'overriding utility of the tests to the free world'. See also *Nuclear Tests* cases, *ICJ Pleadings*, 1978, vol. 1, pp. 496 ff. On the question of equitable balancing as a test of responsibility, see above, text at nn. 128–33.

[259] Jiménez de Aréchaga, loc. cit. above (n. 104), at p. 272; Dupuy, loc. cit. above (n. 89), at pp. 355–8.

of liability, let alone a form of liability that is dependent on a link of causation in fact as the only prerequisite.[260]

(e) *Treaty Practice*

Only exceptionally does treaty practice adopt a form of responsibility for damage placed directly on States without more.[261] Most treaty obligations are expressed in terms of diligent control of sources of harm,[262] exemplified by Article 194 of the Law of the Sea Convention, which requires States to take 'all measures necessary' to protect other States against damage from marine pollution, and goes on to give practical content to the standard of diligence by specifying what these measures should consist of in some detail.[263] Articles 139 and 235 confirm that it is only for non-fulfillment of this and other obligations under the Convention and international law that the State is to be responsible.[264] There are comparable examples in treaties dealing with international watercourses and Antarctica.[265]

The tendency to avoid direct implication of the State in responsibility for damage is complemented in many cases by emphasizing the liability in national law of the relevant operator or company which caused it.[266] Significantly, this practice is adopted in treaties dealing with liability for nuclear damage.[267] These do not preclude the possibility of State responsibility for harmful nuclear activities, but their scheme involves States only as guarantors of the operator's strict liability, or in providing additional compensation funds. Moreover, the burden of this residual responsibility is either spread equitably across a group of nuclear States, as under the Brussels Supplementary Convention, or left in part to lie where it falls, by limiting liability. In neither case does the polluting State bear responsibility for the whole loss.[268] The extent of its exposure is further limited by the narrow definition given to nuclear damage.[269]

---

[260] Handl, loc. cit. above (n. 131), at p. 161; and loc. cit. above (n. 216), at pp. 535–40.

[261] Space Objects Liability Convention, 1972. See n. 244, above.

[262] See, e.g., Long Range Transboundary Air Pollution Convention, 1979, Art. 2; London Dumping Convention, 1972, Arts. II, IV; Paris Convention on the Prevention of Marine Pollution from Land-Based Sources, 1974, Art. 1; Vienna Convention for the Protection of the Ozone Layer, 1985, Art. 2. See generally Dupuy, in Bothe (ed.), op. cit. above (n. 98), p. 363.

[263] See above, nn. 111–12.

[264] See generally Handl, loc. cit. above (n. 216), at pp. 540–3, who notes the 'progressive de-emphasis' of the controlling State's direct liability for marine pollution damage in successive drafts of the Convention, and Pinto, *Netherlands Yearbook of International Law*, 16 (1985), p. 17 at pp. 28 ff.

[265] See Treaty Relating to the Co-operative Development of the Water Resources of the Columbia River Basin, 1961, Art. 18; Convention for the Regulation of Antarctic Mineral Resource Activities, 1988, Art. 8.

[266] See, e.g., Law of the Sea Convention, 1982, Annex III, Art. 22; Convention for the Regulation of Antarctic Mineral Resource Activities, 1988, Art. 8; 1969 International Convention on Civil Liability for Oil Pollution Damage with 1984 Protocol, and, generally, Handl, loc. cit. above (n. 216), at pp. 540 ff.

[267] See Section V for discussion of the conventions.

[268] See below, Section V (f).

[269] See below, Section V (i).

These factors make the nuclear liability conventions weak precedents for any particular theory or standard of State responsibility and are inconsistent with the view that States are absolutely or strictly responsible in international law for damage emanating from their territory.[270] As with national laws employing standards of strict or absolute liability contingent on compulsory insurance and limitation of exposure, it is difficult to treat complex schemes of loss distribution as indicating a standard of responsibility for States themselves in the less highly developed circumstances of international law.

(f) *State Claims*

State claims, or settlements involving damage caused by nuclear activities, provide little support for any one standard of responsibility and demonstrate the lack of international consensus on this point. In 1955 the United States in response to Japanese claims paid compensation to Japanese fishermen injured by one of its nuclear tests, but disclaimed any legal responsibility.[271] Japan and New Zealand reserved the right in diplomatic protests to hold the USA and France responsible for any loss or damage inflicted by further tests in the Pacific,[272] but made no claims. Canada asserted in 1979 that the standard of absolute responsibility for space objects, including those using nuclear power and causing the deposit of radioactive material, had become a general principle of international law, and it relied on this in a successful claim for compensation from the Soviet Union following the crash of Cosmos 954.[273] But this claim was supported by the 1972 Space Objects Liability Convention, to which both States were party;[274] the very different approach of the nuclear liability conventions undermines the relevance of this precedent.

Responses to the Chernobyl disaster provide the most telling evidence of State practice so far. This accident caused widespread harm to agricultural produce and livestock in Europe and affected wildlife, in some cases severely.[275] Clean-up costs were incurred and compensation was paid by several governments to their own citizens for produce which had to be

[270] Miatello, in Spinedi and Simma (eds.), *UN Codification of State Responsibility* (New York, 1987), pp. 306 ff.; Handl, loc. cit. above (n. 33), pp. 35 ff. *Contra*, Smith, op. cit. above (n. 89), pp. 114 ff.; Kelson, *Harvard International Law Journal*, 13 (1972), p. 197. Poor ratification of all but the Paris Convention is another factor lessening the significance of these conventions: see below, Section V (j).

[271] Settlement of Japanese claims for personal and property damage resulting from nuclear tests in the Marshall Island, 1955, *US Treaties and Other International Agreements*, vol. 1, p. 1, *Treaties and Other International Acts Series*, No. 3160; Whiteman, *Digest of International Law*, vol. 4, p. 553; Margolis, loc. cit. above (n. 11), McDougal and Schlei, loc. cit. above (n. 11).

[272] Whiteman, *Digest of International Law*, vol. 4, pp. 585 f.; *Nuclear Tests* cases, *ICJ Pleadings*, 1978, vol. 2, pp. 22–30. Australian notes on the subject made no reference to compensation, but did assert that the tests should be terminated: *Nuclear Tests* cases, *ICJ Pleadings*, 1978, vol. 1, pp. 22 ff.

[273] See above, n. 244.

[274] Canadian Claim, paras. 14–20.

[275] See above, n. 1.

destroyed or which was rendered unusable. Longer term evidence of health risks has yet to emerge, but could be serious.[276]

Despite this provable loss, no claims have been made against the Soviet Union by any affected State, although the possibility was considered by some governments.[277] Uncertainty over the basis for such a claim, reluctance to establish a precedent with possible future implications for States which themselves operate nuclear power plants, and the absence of any appropriate treaty binding on the Soviet Union are the main reasons for this inaction.[278] It is also unclear whether damage to the environment or the costs of precautionary measures taken by governments can be included. The Soviet Union has made no voluntary offer of compensation and has questioned the necessity for precautionary measures taken by its neighbours.[279]

The failure to demand, or to offer, compensation in this case shows the difficulty of reconciling doctrinal support for any standard of strict or absolute responsibility with the evidence of State practice, limited as it is. It points to the conclusion that responsibility for a failure of due diligence, that is, for causing avoidable loss only, provides a more convincing interpretation of the actual practice of States and the present state of customary law in cases of environmental damage.[280]

(g) *Developing Trends*

The arguments for using a standard more demanding than due diligence to shift the burden of unavoidable loss back to the polluter remain strong, particularly where the source is an ultra-hazardous activity, such as a nuclear power plant. In the absence of reciprocal acceptance of risk, making the victim suffer is not an attractive policy.[281] Nor in cases of nuclear accidents is due diligence an easy standard to administer. As we have seen, it is not possible to identify clearly accepted international standards defining the content of this duty in the case of nuclear activities. A heavy burden of proof will be placed on the State which has to establish a failure of due diligence; in the case of complex processes, such as the operation of nuclear reactors, this will be especially difficult unless liberal inferences of fact are allowed or the burden of proof is placed on the polluter.[282]

---

[276] NRPB, *A Preliminary Assessment of the Chernobyl Reactor Accident on the Population of the European Community* (1987), gives an estimate of 1000 deaths in the EEC. See also UKAEA, *The Chernobyl Accident and its Consequences* (London, 1987), sect. 7.

[277] West Germany, Sweden and the UK have reserved their position.

[278] Sands, op. cit. above (n. 22), p. 27.

[279] See above, n. 136.

[280] Handl, loc. cit. above (n. 33), at pp. 47 ff., argues that a stricter standard based on general principles of law should be adopted, however.

[281] See Quentin-Baxter, *Yearbook of the ILC*, 1981, vol. 2, pt. 1, pp. 113–18; Barboza, ibid. 1986, vol. 2, pt. 1, p. 160.

[282] Compare *Corfu Channel* case, *ICJ Reports*, 1949, p. 4, p. 18. On proposals for placing the burden of proof on the polluter, see McCaffrey, *Report of the ILC to the UN General Assembly*, 43rd Session, 1988, UN Doc. A/43/10, p. 68.

The desirability of international agreement on appropriate principles of responsibility for inter-State claims has been acknowledged by the Soviet Union following Chernobyl.[283] The ILC's proposed articles on 'International Liability' have since attracted some attention in the IAEA as a possible model. These provide reparation for injury on a strict liability basis that aims at restoring an equitable balance of interests between the parties. The articles now apply both to ultra-hazardous activities and to those with a higher probability of more minor but still appreciable injury.[284] However, the introduction of equitable balancing would inevitably tend to dilute the force of present customary obligations of responsibility for harm prevention, such as they are.

Another possibility is to rely on a reformed system of civil liability conventions, hoping that these will attract more support from States. But even this would not render recourse to State responsibility unnecessary in all cases, and for various reasons considered below, the two systems are better seen as complementary, not alternative.[285]

At present, however, it is difficult to conclude that State responsibility itself affords a sufficiently principled basis for the settlement of international claims arising out of nuclear damage. Without further agreement on the conditions and extent of its application, and on how the burden of reparation should be allocated, State responsibility is unlikely to supply answers which are either clear or predictable.

V. Civil Liability for Nuclear Damage

An alternative method for dealing with transboundary environmental damage is to facilitate civil liability proceedings by the individual victims. This requires removal of jurisdictional obstacles for foreign plaintiffs,[286] and shifts the burden of liability away from the State and on to private parties as operators of the industry or activity concerned. An important advantage of this approach is that by moving the issue away from responsibility in international law, it frees the injured party from reliance on diplomatic claims pursued by his government.[287]

(a) Equal Access and Non-Discrimination

The principle of equal access and non-discrimination is one form of this civil liability model of loss distribution. The foreign plaintiff is given access

---

[283] See above, n. 136.

[284] See 1989 draft articles in Barboza's 5th Report, 1989, UN Doc. A/CN.4/423, and see above, n. 221.

[285] See Section V (j), and Handl, loc. cit. above (n. 33), at pp. 41 ff.

[286] See McCaffrey, *California Western International Law Journal*, 3 (1973), p. 191; Ianni, *Canadian Yearbook of International Law*, 11 (1975), p. 258.

[287] On diplomatic claims see *Barcelona Traction* case, *ICJ Reports*, 1970, p. 3; *Nottebohm* case, *ICJ Reports*, 1955, p. 4; *Ambatielos* arbitration (1956), *UN Reports of International Arbitral Awards*, vol. 12, p. 83.

to judicial and administrative remedies on the same terms as nationals, and transboundary nuisances are treated like those within national borders. The OECD has endorsed this approach as a policy for transboundary environmental harm,[288] and it has also been adopted in several treaties which deal with nuclear risks.[289] National legal systems may also choose to follow this pattern independently of any treaty obligation.[290]

The idea that individuals should be given access to foreign remedies can also be seen as part of the development of international law regarding liability called for by Principle 22 of the Stockholm Declaration on the Human Environment, or as an application of the right to a decent environment proclaimed in a number of constitutions and endorsed by Principle 1 of the Declaration.[291]

Equal access has the major disadvantage that it does not guarantee the existence of appropriate legislation or require harmonization of laws on liability in different countries, but provides access only to whatever law States choose to adopt. Where the relevant legal systems differ widely in their substantive rules, equal access ceases to be a useful principle on which to rely.[292] It is for example unclear that proceedings in the Soviet Union arising out of Chernobyl would succeed even if equal access were available.[293]

(b) *The Need for a Special Regime of Civil Liability*[294]

The limited utility of equal access means that a more sophisticated model is desirable. This is offered by four international conventions which create a special regime of civil liability for nuclear risks. The Paris Convention of

---

[288] Recommendations C(74) 224; C(76) 55; C(77) 28, reprinted in OECD, *OECD and the Environment* (Paris, 1986); Smets, *Environmental Policy and Law*, 9 (1982), p. 110.

[289] Nordic Convention on the Protection of the Environment, 1974, Art. 1; Nuclear Liability Rules (US-Canada), 1976; Agreement on Third Party Liability in the Nuclear Field (Switzerland-FRG), 1986. For other applications of the principle see, e.g., Boundary Waters Treaty (US-Canada), 1909; UN Convention on the Law of the Sea, 1982, Art. 235(2); UNEP Principles of Conduct Concerning Shared Natural Resources, Art. 14, above, n. 96.

[290] See 1968 and 1978 EEC Conventions on Civil Jurisdiction and the Enforcement of Judgments; ECJ Case 21/76, *Handelskwerkerij Bier* v. *Mines de Potasse d'Alsace*, [1976] 2 ECR 1735; US-Canada Uniform Transboundary Reciprocal Access Act, 1982, implemented by legislation in New Jersey, Colorado and Montana, and see also *Michie* v. *Great Lakes Steel Division*, 495 F 2d 213 (1974).

[291] See Sohn, loc. cit. above (n. 98); Steiger *et al.*, in Bothe (ed.), op. cit. above (n. 98), p. 1; Gormley, *Human Rights and the Environment* (Leiden, 1976).

[292] Kiss, *Annuaire français de droit international*, 20 (1974), p. 808. See also Willheim, *Australian Yearbook of International Law*, 1976, p. 174.

[293] Soviet civil law allows for strict liability in cases of damage caused by sources of 'heightened danger'. See Butler, *Soviet Law* (2nd edn., London, 1988), p. 192, and Hardy, loc. cit. above (n. 239), at p. 235.

[294] See, generally, Miatello, in Spinedi and Simma (eds.), *United Nations Codification of State Responsibility* (1987), p. 287; IAEA, *Nuclear Law for a Developing World*, pp. 109–82; Hardy, loc. cit. above (n. 239); Cigoj, *International and Comparative Law Quarterly*, 14 (1965), p. 809; Reyners, in IAEA, *Licensing and Regulatory Control of Nuclear Installations*, p. 243; OECD Ad Hoc Group on Transfrontier Pollution, *Nuclear Law Bulletin*, 20 (1977), p. 50; IAEA, *Experience and Trends in Nuclear Law*, pp. 69 ff.; Arangio Ruiz, *Recueil des cours*, 107 (1962–III), pp. 497, 575 ff.; Fornassier, *Annuaire français de droit international*, 10 (1964), p. 303; Cameron *et al.*, op. cit. above (n. 22).

1960,[295] drafted by the OECD, applies to nuclear incidents within Western European member States. The Vienna Convention of 1963[296] offers a comparable scheme for global participation, while two more treaties deal with nuclear ships[297] and maritime carriage of nuclear materials.[298] Of these only the Paris Convention has attracted significant support among nuclear States.[299]

All four treaties seek to harmonize important aspects of liability for nuclear accidents and incidents in national laws, without requiring complete uniformity in every respect. They create a common scheme for loss distribution among the victims, focusing liability on the operator of a nuclear installation and based on the principle of absolute or strict liability. These two aspects distinguish the scheme from the principle of equal access to national remedies adopted by the OECD, and make it more beneficial to litigants, who are given the assurance of equitable compensation on proof of cause. At the same time, the scheme is intended to give the nuclear industry protection from unlimited, unpredictable liability involving multiple actions against suppliers, builders, designers, carriers, operators and States as potential defendants.[300]

The nuclear liability conventions thus reflect on the one hand an early recognition of the need for a stronger, more equitable system of loss distribution, appropriate to the serious risks of nuclear accidents, and on the other a desire to encourage the infant nuclear industry. Both points again distinguish nuclear pollution from transboundary air or water pollution, where equal access has remained the limit of State practice in civil liability matters.[301] While this special nuclear regime does not go so far as the

---

[295] *American Journal of International Law*, 55 (1961), p. 1083, amended by 1964 Additional Protocol, in IAEA, *International Conventions on Civil Liability for Nuclear Damage* (Vienna, 1976), p. 22; see also the 1963 Brussels Convention Supplementary to the Paris Convention, *International Legal Materials*, 2 (1963), p. 685. Both Conventions were amended by Protocols adopted 16 November 1982. The Protocol to the Paris Convention entered into force 7 October 1988. See Berman and Hydeman, *American Journal of International Law*, 55 (1961), p. 966; Arangio-Ruiz, loc. cit. above (n. 294), pp. 582 ff., and explanatory memorandum, *European Yearbook*, 8 (1960), p. 225.

[296] *International Legal Materials*, 2 (1963), p. 727; IAEA, *Civil Liability for Nuclear Damage*, *Official Records* (Vienna, 1964).

[297] Brussels Convention on the Liability of Operators of Nuclear Ships, 1962, *American Journal of International Law*, 57 (1963), p. 268; Hardy, *International and Comparative Law Quarterly*, 12 (1963), p. 778; Konz, *American Journal of International Law*, 57 (1963), p. 100; Szasz, *Journal of Maritime Law and Commerce*, 2 (1970), p. 541; Colliard, *Annuaire français de droit international*, 8 (1962), p. 41; Cigoj, loc. cit. above (n. 294). The Convention has six parties and is not in force. None of the States which licenses nuclear ships is a party.

[298] Brussels Convention Relating to Civil Liability in the Field of Maritime Carriage of Nuclear Material, 1971, IAEA, *International Conventions on Civil Liability etc.*, p. 55; Strohl, in IAEA, *Experience and Trends in Nuclear Law*, p. 89. Eleven parties, in force.

[299] The Vienna Convention has ten parties; only two possess nuclear facilities (Argentina and Yugoslavia). The USA, USSR, Japan and Canada are not parties. The Paris Convention has fourteen parties.

[300] Preamble to the Paris Convention, IAEA, *Conference on Civil Liability etc.*, pp. 66 f.; Berman and Hydeman, loc. cit. above (n. 295); Konz, loc. cit. above (n. 297), at p. 105; Cameron *et al.*, op. cit. above (n. 22), pp. 98 f.

[301] See nn. 288–90 above.

Convention on Liability for Damage Caused by Space Objects,[302] in that liability is not placed directly on the State, the influence of the nuclear example can be seen in later treaties dealing with liability for oil pollution.[303]

(c) The Scheme of the Conventions

Although there are variations, the overall scheme of the four conventions is based on the same five elements:

(i) Liability is absolute. No proof of fault or negligence is required as a condition of liability. Certain exceptions such as war, natural disaster or negligence of the victim may be allowed.[304]

(ii) Liability is channelled exclusively to the operator of the nuclear installation or ship, and all other potential defendants are protected.[305] In certain cases, however, a carrier or handler of nuclear material may be treated as an operator.[306]

(iii) Limitations may be placed on the total amount and duration of liability.[307]

(iv) Payment up to the prescribed limit of liability is supported by compulsory insurance or security held by the operator and guaranteed by the State of installation or registry.[308] Additional public funds are provided under a Convention Supplementary to the Paris Convention,[309] but not under the remaining three conventions.

(v) Rules determine which State or States have jurisdiction over claims, and all other recourse to civil proceedings elsewhere is precluded.[310]

This scheme draws partly on the example of early national nuclear legislation, notably the United States Price-Anderson Act of 1957.[311] In most

---

[302] See above, n. 244.

[303] 1969 International Convention on Civil Liability for Oil Pollution Damage with 1984 Protocol.

[304] Vienna Convention, Art. IV; Paris Convention, Arts. 3, 9; Brussels Convention on Nuclear Ships, Arts. II, VIII.

[305] Vienna Convention, Art. II; Paris Convention, Art. 3; Brussels Convention on Nuclear Ships, Art. II. The Convention Relating to Maritime Carriage, Art. I, channels liability to operators who would be liable under the Paris or Vienna Conventions, or under national laws which are at least as favourable to those suffering damage.

[306] Vienna Convention, Art. II(2); Paris Convention, Art. 4(d).

[307] Vienna Convention, Arts. V, VI; Paris Convention, Arts. 7, 8; Brussels Convention on Nuclear Ships, Arts. III, V.

[308] Vienna Convention, Art. VII; Brussels Convention on Nuclear Ships, Art. III; Paris Convention, Art. 10. Payment of sums due under the latter convention is guaranteed under the 1963 Supplementary Convention.

[309] 1963 Convention Supplementary to the Paris Convention, with Additional Protocols of 1964 and 1982, above, n. 295.

[310] Vienna Convention, Art. XI; Paris Convention, Art. 13; Brussels Convention on Nuclear Ships, Art. X.

[311] Atomic Energy Damages Act, 1957, 42 USC§2011–2284, as amended by the Price Anderson Amendments Act, 1988. See Cameron et al., op. cit. above (n. 22), chs. 9, 10; and Tomain, Nuclear Power Transformation (Bloomington, 1987), chs. 1 and 8. The Act imposes a liability ceiling, requires compulsory insurance and provides for Federal indemnity payments; it does not make operators exclusively liable, however, and it leaves the standard of liability to be settled by each state, but see n. 326, below.

cases, the treaties leave States considerable discretion to modify their basic elements, however. National laws may thus adopt different limitation periods or insurance and liability ceilings; they may extend the definition of nuclear damage, or choose not to relieve operators of liability in cases of grave natural disaster.[312] Some States have used this power to set much higher liability ceilings; a few, such as the Federal Republic of Germany, have now opted for unlimited liability in certain circumstances.[313]

Although fewer variations are allowed under the Brussels Convention on Nuclear Ships, none of the treaties requires complete uniformity of implementation. Rather, as the IAEA commentary on the Vienna Convention explains, the principal objectives are to enumerate minimum international standards which will be flexible and adaptable to a variety of legal, social and economic systems, while also designating which State will have exclusive legislative and jurisdictional competence.[314]

The conventions cover most, but not all, potential sources of nuclear damage. The Paris and Vienna Conventions apply to 'nuclear installations', a term broadly defined to include reactors, reprocessing, manufacturing and storage facilities, where nuclear fuel, nuclear material and radioactive products or waste are used or produced.[315] They also apply to the transport of nuclear material or the handling of nuclear waste.[316] The Brussels Convention covers nuclear powered ships, their fuel and incidental waste, but not the carriage of nuclear material by sea.[317] This latter is subject to other conventional regimes.[318] Most uses and by-products of civil nuclear power will thus fall under one or other of these headings, and only nuclear tests, nuclear weapons and peaceful nuclear explosions are excluded.

(d) Why Absolute Liability?

The combination of absolute liability with a ceiling on damages, supported by insurance and State indemnity, makes civil liability for nuclear risks unusual. An OECD study notes that these elements are found in national laws and are not new, but:

The originality of the system of nuclear liability lies rather in the fact that for the

---

[312] Vienna Convention, Art. IV (3) (*b*); Paris Convention, Art. 9. Germany and Austria reserved the right to exclude Article 9 in its entirety, thus making liability absolute; this is effected in the FRG by the Atomic Energy Act of 1985.

[313] See n. 350, below.

[314] IAEA, *Conference on Civil Liability etc.*, p. 67.

[315] Vienna Convention, Art. I; Paris Convention, Art. 1.

[316] Vienna Convention, Art. II; Paris Convention, Art. 4.

[317] Art. XIII.

[318] i.e. the Paris or Vienna Convention, or other conventions governing maritime cargoes, to the extent that these are not displaced in favour of the Paris and Vienna Conventions by the Convention on Maritime Carriage of Nuclear Material, 1972. See Strohl, in IAEA, *Experience and Trends in Nuclear Law* (Vienna, 1972), p. 89.

first time these various notions have been systematically applied to a whole industry and have been broadly accepted internationally.[319]

In these conventions the choice of strict or absolute liability was justified on several grounds: it would relieve Courts of the difficulty of setting appropriate standards of reasonable care, and plaintiffs of the difficulty of proving breach of those standards, in a relatively new, complex and highly technical industrial process; the risk of very serious and widespread damage, despite its low probability, placed nuclear power in the ultra-hazardous category; and it would be unjust and inappropriate to make plaintiffs shoulder a heavy burden of proof in respect of such an industry whose risks are only acceptable because of its social utility as a source of energy.[320] Thus the arguments are broadly comparable to those used in the case of State responsibility.

Whether liability is described as absolute or merely strict is a matter of degree.[321] The more exculpating factors are recognized, such as grave natural disasters or war, the less appropriate it becomes to use the term absolute. Liability is then strict in the limited sense that fault or negligence are not required; in effect the burden of proof is moved to the defendant. On this spectrum, the nuclear liability conventions[322] fall some way between those dealing with space objects, where few exonerations are allowed,[323] and those dealing with oil pollution, where liability is strict rather than absolute.[324]

The imposition of strict or absolute liability for nuclear incidents is supported by a substantial body of national legislation, including that of some States which are not parties to the conventions themselves.[325] There are significant exceptions however, including the Soviet Union, which has no specific legislation on the subject.[326] Reference to national tort laws or civil codes may also supply evidence of a general principle of strict or absolute liability for dangerous or unusual activities, but such principles do not

---

[319] OECD Environment Committee, 'Compensation for Nuclear Damage', *Nuclear Law Bulletin*, 20 (1977), p. 50.

[320] IAEA, *Conference on Civil Liability etc.*, p. 76; Cigoj, loc. cit. above (n. 294), pp. 831 ff.; OECD Environment Committee, loc. cit. (previous note), at p. 52; see, generally, Goldie, loc. cit. above (n. 240); Kelson, loc. cit. above (n. 235); Jenks, loc. cit. above (n. 240).

[321] Goldie, loc. cit. above (n. 240), at p. 1215; and loc. cit. above (n. 234), at p. 317.

[322] Goldie, loc. cit. above (n. 240), at p. 1215, regards these as being properly examples of absolute liability, because the possibility of exculpation is so limited.

[323] Convention on International Liability for Damage Caused by Space Objects, 1972, Art. II; Cosmos 954 Claim (Canada-USSR), *International Legal Materials*, 18 (1979), p. 902. See n. 244, above.

[324] See n. 303, above.

[325] See NEA, *Nuclear Legislation: Third Party Liability* (Paris, 1976). Non-parties with strict liability laws include Canada, Nuclear Liability Act, 1970; Japan, Acts Nos. 147 and 148 of 1961, Act No. 53 of 1971; Brazil, Act No. 6453, 1977, *Nuclear Law Bulletin*, 21 (1978), Supplement, p. 3; Switzerland, Act on Third Party Liability, 1983, ibid. 32 (1983), Supplement, p. 3.

[326] See n. 327, below. US Federal Law, 42 USC§2210, does not specifically impose strict liability but allows for a waiver of defences and of questions of negligence, contributory negligence and assumption of risk in indemnity cases. In *Duke Power Co.* v. *Environmental Study Group*, 438 US 59 (1978), this was held to establish the right to compensation without proof of fault.

invariably cover nuclear installations.[327] One important effect of the nuclear conventions is thus to clarify and harmonize the standard of liability.

(e) *The Channelling of Liability*

The channelling of all liability to the operator of nuclear installations or nuclear ships has the advantages of simplifying the plaintiffs' choice of defendant and establishing a clear line of responsibility,[328] since no one who is not an operator may be held liable for incidents falling within the terms of the conventions.[329] The possibility of transferring liability to a carrier of nuclear material[330] or a handler of radioactive waste[331] does not materially diminish this concentration of liability, although it provides for an alternative and more extended definition of who is an operator, and recognizes that there may be a need for special treatment in such cases.[332] Several operators may also be held jointly and severally liable for the same nuclear incident,[333] and the conventions provide rules for determining when liability for materials in transport passes from one operator to another, and when operators become or cease to be liable for material imported or exported.[334]

The choice of the operator as the focus of liability, rather than any other potential defendant, is based on the assumption that the operator of an installation or a ship is usually in the best position to exercise effective responsibility for it, and to secure adequate insurance.[335] This assumption is not universally shared, and German, Greek and Austrian reservations to the Paris Convention allow for persons other than the operator to be held

[327] Goldie, loc. cit. above (n. 240), at p. 1247; Kelson, loc. cit. above (n. 235); Hardy, loc. cit. above (n. 239). It is doubtful whether in the United Kingdom nuclear installations would be covered by *Rylands* v. *Fletcher* (1868), LR 3HL 330 (see *Dunne* v. *NW Gas Board*, [1964] 2 QB 806), or nuisance (see *Allen* v. *Gulf Oil*, [1981] 1 All ER 353), but liability for nuclear accidents is based on statute. Applicability of strict liability in the USA is a matter for state law: see *Silkwood* v. *Kerr McGee Corp.*, 464 US 238 (1984); Stason, *Vanderbilt Law Review*, 12 (1958), p. 93. For Soviet civil law, see n. 293, above.

[328] IAEA, *Conference on Civil Liability etc.*, p. 72; Hardy, loc. cit. above (n. 239), at pp. 247 ff.; Cigoj, loc. cit. above (n. 294), at pp. 822 ff.

[329] Vienna Convention, Art. IV (5); Paris Convention, Art. 6 (b); Brussels Convention on Nuclear Ships, Art. II (2).

[330] Vienna Convention, Art. II (2); Paris Convention, Art. 4 (d).

[331] Vienna Convention, Art. II (2); there is no comparable provision in the Paris Convention. See also Brussels Convention on Nuclear Ships, Art. II (4).

[332] See also Vienna Convention, Art. II (1); Paris Convention, Art. 4; Hardy, loc. cit. above (n. 239), at pp. 247 f.; IAEA, *Conference on Civil Liability etc.*, p. 74.

[333] Vienna Convention, Art. II (3), (4); Paris Convention, Art. 5(d); Brussels Convention on Nuclear Ships, Art. VII; IAEA, *Conference on Civil Liability etc.*, p. 75.

[334] Vienna Convention, Art. II (1): Paris Convention, Arts. 4(a), (b); IAEA, *Conference on Civil Liability etc.*, p. 73.

[335] Hardy, loc. cit. above (n. 239), at p. 247; Cigoj, loc. cit. above (n. 294), at p. 823; Konz, loc. cit. above (n. 297), at p. 105; Strohl, in IAEA, *Experience and Trends in Nuclear Law*, p. 72 at p. 89. But cf. the 1969 Convention on Civil Liability for Oil Pollution Damage, which places liability on the owner of the ship, rather than on the operator. However, this Convention allows a right of recourse against operators or others who cause damage intentionally *or recklessly*.

additionally liable.[336] The main argument for this is that it strengthens the incentive for all concerned, including manufacturers and suppliers, to behave responsibly.

To some extent the nuclear conventions accept this point, by allowing the operator a right of recourse against those who cause nuclear damage intentionally.[337] This is a narrow exception however, which still leaves the operator solely responsible for the negligence or carelessness of others,[338] unless broader indemnities can be voluntarily negotiated. For most European States, this arrangement has proved acceptable, since operators will be adequately protected by insurance. The criticism that denying wider recourse dilutes the incentive for others to behave responsibly[339] can be met in two ways; States are free to employ criminal law or civil penalties,[340] and the efficient control of construction and operational standards for nuclear installations is arguably a sufficient safety policy.[341]

It is important to note that it makes no difference for the purposes of channelling liability that the operator of a nuclear installation or ship will in many cases be a State or a State entity. The civil liability conventions ensure that States or their organs are precluded from invoking jurisdictional immunities, except in relation to the execution of judgments.[342] Thus, apart from this exception, States sued under the Conventions in their own Courts will be subject to the same liability, and enjoy the same defences, as other categories of defendants.[343]

(f) *Insurance and Limitation of Liability*

The scale of potential damage a nuclear accident could cause is likely to be well beyond the capacity of individual operators of nuclear installations to bear.[344] Ensuring adequate insurance cover or some other form of secur-

---

[336] Legislation in Austria and Germany has, however, remained within the terms of the Paris Convention on this point. For the position in the United States, see Cameron *et al.*, op. cit. above (n. 22), ch. 9.

[337] Vienna Convention, Art. X; Paris Convention, Art. 6 (*f*); Brussels Convention on Nuclear Ships, Art. II(6).

[338] Compare the broader right of recourse allowed under the 1969 Convention on Civil Liability for Oil Pollution Damage, above, n. 335.

[339] Pelzer, *Nuclear Law Bulletin*, 12 (1973), p. 46.

[340] IAEA, *Conference on Civil Liability etc.*, p. 83; this argument has been the focus of debate in the United States: see Cameron *et al.*, op. cit. above (n. 22), pp. 146 f.

[341] OECD Environment Committee, 'Compensation for Nuclear Damage', *Nuclear Law Bulletin*, 20 (1977), p. 50 at p. 76.

[342] Vienna Convention, Art. XIV; Paris Convention, Art. 13(*e*); Brussels Convention on Nuclear Ships, Art. X(3). The exclusion of jurisdictional immunities was opposed by Soviet bloc representatives at the Vienna Conference, and the inclusion of this provision is one reason for their failure to sign the Convention.

[343] See below, sub-section (g), for discussion of jurisdiction under the Convention.

[344] The Three Mile Island accident is thought to have cost US $1 billion; $52 million was paid out by insurers: Cameron *et al.*, op. cit. above (n. 22), pp. 151 ff. Estimates of the possible cost of a core meltdown in the United States reach $15 billion: US GAO Report, *Nuclear News*, September 1986. The

ity is therefore essential if victims are to have an assurance of compensation. The conventions require operators to hold liability insurance or other financial security, on terms specified by national authorities, unless the operator is itself a State.[345] Regardless of the operator's financial solvency, funds should thus be available in the event of an accident.

The assurance of compensation funding is further strengthened by placing an obligation on States to ensure that claims up to liability limits are met.[346] If insurance funds prove insufficient for this purpose, the State must step in and provide them. This is a unique feature of the nuclear conventions; it indicates an acknowledgement of the residual responsibility of States to compensate for damage caused by nuclear activities, where the operator is unable to do so, or is itself a State.[347]

Limitation of the amount of liability is intended primarily to make insurance easier to obtain. Without it, insurers might be reluctant to cover such potentially enormous risks, or to do so fully.[348] In return for this guarantee of compensation for plaintiffs, it also protects the industry itself from a burden of ruinous liability.[349] Since much will depend on the views of individual insurance markets, and their ability to pool risks internationally, the conventions set only minimum limits and allow States to fix higher ones, or to have no limit at all.[350]

The scheme adopted in the conventions is not intended to guarantee compensation for all harm in all cases, for by permitting liability limitation it necessarily envisages wider distribution of some of the loss among the public at large. The important question is whether these liability limits are adequate and strike the right balance between compensation and industry protection. The evidence suggests that the Vienna Convention in particular does not, and that it is unduly favourable to the nuclear industry. The Paris Convention, in contrast, arguably provides a more satisfactory balance by including governments in the provision of a broader compensation scheme.

The most obvious problem with the Vienna Convention is the disparity

---

Chernobyl accident may have caused damage in the USSR totalling $3 billion, including $1.2 billion in compensation payments: Shapar and Reyners, *The Nuclear Third Party Liability Regime in Western Europe: The Test of Chernobyl* (OECD, 1987).

[345] Vienna Convention, Art. VII; Paris Convention, Art. 10; Brussels Convention on Nuclear Ships, Art. III.

[346] See above, n. 308.

[347] See Miatello, in Spinedi and Simma (eds.), op. cit. above (n. 270), at pp. 297–9, 302–5. There is no comparable arrangement under the 1969 Convention on Civil Liability for Oil Pollution Damage.

[348] IAEA, *Conference on Civil Liability etc.*, p. 78; Hardy, loc. cit. above (n. 239), pp. 240 ff.; Cameron *et al.*, op. cit. above (n. 22), p. 109.

[349] IAEA, *Conference on Civil Liability etc.*, p. 78.

[350] Vienna Convention, Art. V; Paris Convention, Art. 7; IAEA, *Conference on Civil Liability etc.*, p. 78. Note that the Brussels Convention on Nuclear Ships, Art. III, sets a single obligatory limit, following the practice of maritime liability conventions. The Federal German Atomic Energy Act, 1985, is the first to abolish liability ceilings in a Paris Convention State, although for internal claims only. See Pfaffelhuber and Kučhuck, *Nuclear Law Bulletin*, 25 (1980), p. 70. Switzerland and Japan, who are not parties, also have unlimited liability. See Shapar and Reyners, *Nuclear Third Party Liability*, for comparative tables of national liability limits, and Deprimoz, *Nuclear Law Bulletin*, 32 (1983), p. 33.

between minimum levels of liability[351] and the more recent estimates of the cost of a catastrophic nuclear accident.[352] A large proportion of the loss caused by such an accident would fall on the public and on other States under this Convention if it were implemented at the minimum level of liability. Since only two nuclear States are presently party to the convention, this may be academic, but it is one reason why the promotion of wider ratification may be an inadequate response to the Chernobyl accident.

The limit set by the Brussels Convention on Nuclear Ships[353] is much higher than the level of insurance believed to be obtainable in 1962; the intention of States supporting this position was that in practice licensing States would have to provide the necessary additional compensation funds.[354] For this reason, the figure is also higher than the one adopted for large oil tankers in 1969, but unlike that scheme, the nuclear ships scheme is not supported by any additional compensation from industry sources.[355]

Although the Paris Convention liability limits are also low[356] compared to the probable cost of a serious accident, the scheme of the Convention is supported by a strong system of Stated-funded compensation at a level greatly above the convention's minimum limits.[357] The European scheme thus spreads the burden of compensation more broadly than the Vienna Convention; far from making the polluter and the victims bear the whole loss, it distributes this loss equitably in cases of serious accidents across the community of Western European States as a whole.

The scale of this redistribution can be seen in the figures. Beyond the operators' basic liability of 5 million SDRs a further 65 million SDRs are drawn from the contracting party in whose territory the nuclear installation is situated, and an additional 50 million from all other contracting parties.[358] This scheme thus offers far greater potential for meeting the real cost of a serious nuclear accident. It also enables individual States to transfer to the operator a substantially increased share of the risk in cases

---

[351] Art. V provides for US $5 million at 1963 values, worth approx. $58 million in 1988.

[352] See n. 344, above.

[353] Art. III: 1500 million gold francs.

[354] Konz, loc. cit. above (n. 297), at pp. 102 f.

[355] See the International Convention on Civil Liability for Oil Pollution Damage, Art. V, which sets a limit of 210 million gold francs; the 1971 International Convention on the Establishment of an International Fund for Compensation for Oil Pollution Damage, and voluntary schemes such as TOVALOP or CRISTAL provide additional sources of compensation from oil industry funds.

[356] Art. 7 establishes a normal level of 15 million SDRs. It leaves States the choice of setting higher or lower limits, taking account of the availability of insurance, but in no case lower than 5 million SDRs. 15 million SDRs is equivalent to approximately US $18.5 million at 1987 values.

[357] Brussels Supplementary Convention on Third Party Liability in the Field of Nuclear Energy, 1963, *UN Treaty Series*, vol. 1041, p. 358, as amended by a Protocol of 1982. See Lagorce, in IAEA, *Nuclear Law for a Developing World* (Vienna, 1969), p. 143; Fornasier, *Annuaire français de droit international*, 8 (1962), p. 762.

[358] Art. 3. The contribution made by other contracting States is calculated according to Art. 12. A 1982 protocol raises these figures to 170 million SDRs and 125 million respectively. It is not in force. 100 million SDRs is worth approximately US $123 million at 1987 values.

where he is at fault,[359] and has contributed to a general trend towards higher and more uniform liability ceilings in Europe or to their abolition altogether.[360]

Thus although all the nuclear conventions focus liability on the operator—the source of the damage or pollution—the Brussels Supplementary Convention clearly recognizes that this alone is insufficient, and unlike the other conventions it involves States in meeting substantial losses in excess of the operators's capacity to pay or cover through insurance. It cannot be said that any of the nuclear conventions implements fully the 'polluter pays' principle, or recognizes the unlimited and unconditional responsibility of States within whose borders nuclear accidents occur: what they do recognize, if imperfectly, is that the scale of possible damage has to be widely and equitably borne if nuclear power is to perform a viable social and economic role. This conclusion further weakens the already tenuous case for treating any of these agreements as evidence for the strict or absolute liability of the source State in international law for the full measure of any damage its nuclear activities may cause.

(g) *Bringing Claims under the Conventions*

The nuclear conventions simplify the jurisdictional issues which would otherwise arise under national law in bringing transboundary civil actions. First, they determine which State has jurisdiction over claims against operators or their insurers. In the case of nuclear installations, the location of the nuclear incident causing the damage, or, exceptionally, of the installation itself, is the deciding factor.[361] The object of this extended definition, and the reason jurisdiction does not simply follow the location of the installation, is to cater for incidents caused by material in transit.

Cases of multiple jurisdiction are to be dealt with either by agreement of the parties under the Vienna Convention,[362] or by a tribunal under the Paris Convention.[363] This tribunal would decide which Court was 'most closely related to the case in question'. In the case of ships, both the licensing States and the State or States where the damage occurs have jurisdiction.[364]

Secondly, judgments given by courts competent in accordance with the conventions must be recognized and enforced in other member States, with

---

[359] Art. 5(*b*). 'Fault' in this context is ambiguous. The 1985 Federal German Atomic Energy Act, s. 37, defines it as causing damage 'wilfully or by gross negligence'. The 1969 International Convention on Civil Liability for Oil Pollution Damage, as amended in 1984, denies the shipowner the right to limit his liability where he caused the damage 'recklessly' or 'with intent'. This suggests that 'fault' in Art. 5 does not cover simple negligence.

[360] OECD, 'International Co-operation in the Field of Radioactive Transfrontier Pollution', *Nuclear Law Bulletin*, 14 (1974), p. 55.

[361] Vienna Convention, Art. XI; Paris Convention, Art. 13.

[362] Art. XI (3).

[363] Art. 13 (*c*).

[364] Art. X.

certain limited exceptions which do not allow reconsideration of the merits of the case.[365] This facility is now of limited practical importance within most of Western Europe, since judgments will normally be recognized under EEC treaties,[366] but elsewhere it is an important further guarantee of access to compensation funds in transboundary cases.

Actions brought pursuant to all these conventions must commence within the appropriate limitation period, which in each case is ten years from the date of the nuclear incident, unless national law provides differently.[367] The period may be extended, or reduced, but in the latter case it must then be computed from the date on which the plaintiff knew or should have known of the damage and could identify the operator liable. Since it is characteristic of nuclear radiation that its effects on human health may not become apparent for many years after the event, a limitation period as short as ten years may leave victims to bear their own loss; not surprisingly, several States have now adopted periods of up to 30 years.[368]

(h) *Non-Party Claims*

None of the conventions categorically extends the benefit of its provisions to claimants who suffer damage in the territory of a non-contracting State, or to incidents which arise there. The Paris Convention gives parties the discretion to do so, but it is otherwise expressly inapplicable.[369] No consistent practice has been followed by contracting parties on this point, but several do allow non-party claims to be made.[370] A similar provision was deleted from the Vienna Convention after opposition to the notion that non-parties might benefit.[371] Both conventions provide jurisdictional rules for incidents occurring outside the territory of a party,[372] but these provisions are intended to resolve conflicts, not to extend the application of either instrument.

The Brussels Convention on Nuclear Ships applies to nuclear damage caused by an incident anywhere involving a nuclear ship of a contracting party,[373] but it is silent on the question whether this is intended to benefit a

[365] Vienna Convention, Art. XII; Paris Convention, Art. 13(*d*); Brussels Convention on Nuclear Ships, Art. XI (4).

[366] 1968 and 1978 Conventions on Civil Jurisdiction and the Enforcement of Judgments.

[367] Vienna Convention, Art. VI; Paris Convention, Art. 8; Brussels Convention, Art. V.

[368] FRG, Atomic Energy Act, 1985, s. 32; UK, Nuclear Installations Act, 1965; Switzerland, Act on Third Party Liability, 1983.

[369] Art. 3.

[370] FRG, Atomic Energy Act, 1985, s. 24(4); Denmark, Compensation for Nuclear Damage Act, 1974, s. 5(1); Finland, Nuclear Liability Act, 1972, s. 4; Netherlands, Act on Liability for Damage Caused by Nuclear Incidents, s. 26(1); Sweden, Nuclear Liability Act, s. 3; UK, Nuclear Installations Act, 1965, ss. 7, 12.

[371] *Conference on Civil Liability for Nuclear Damage*, Committee of the Whole, pp. 183 f.; Plenary, pp. 121 ff.

[372] Vienna Convention, Art. XI (2); Paris Convention, Art. 13(*b*).

[373] Art. XIII. A recommendation of the Steering Committee of the Paris Convention, made 25 April 1968, states that the Paris Convention is applicable to nuclear incidents on the high seas and to damage occurring on the high seas.

non-party. Following the normal principles of treaty law, it seems unlikely that either the Vienna or Brussels Nuclear Ships Conventions has created rights for non-party claimants.[374]

The major argument against allowing non-party claims is that with limited insurance funds to call on, adding more claimants will reduce the share available for those in contracting States, without reciprocal benefits. The Paris Convention necessarily accepts this result if its benefits are extended to non-parties, but such claimants are denied recourse to additional public funds provided under the 1963 Supplementary Convention.[375] Extension may be advantageous however; it permits operators to limit their liability to non-party claimants and it may facilitate transport of nuclear materials across non-party territories.[376] In effect it would create an equal access regime for those injured in non-party States, and for that reason extension would be consistent with OECD policy.[377]

None of these provisions is helpful in the case of accidents like Chernobyl, since the issue there involves the liability of a non-party operator rather than extension of benefits to non-party claimants. Non-party operators cannot be held liable under any of the conventions, and jurisdiction will in such cases be determined by ordinary rules of national law, with all the difficulties referred to earlier. Participation in the conventions by nuclear States—the source of potential defendants—is for this reason the best way of gauging international acceptance of the civil liability regime. That is what makes the Vienna Convention a particularly weak precedent, since so few nuclear States are parties to it.

(i) Nuclear Damage and the Environment

A common feature of the nuclear conventions is their relatively narrow definition of 'damage'. Like the *Trail Smelter* award their focus is on loss of life, personal injury or loss of or damage to property.[378] The Brussels and Vienna Conventions do allow parties to extend this definition, but the legislation of OECD States closely follows the provisions of the Paris Convention.[379] What is clearly missing is agreement on a broader environmental or ecological perspective.

Thus the kind of ecological damage to wildlife inflicted by the Chernobyl accident, or the harm to the marine environment which a nuclear incident

---

[374] Vienna Convention on the Law of Treaties, 1969, Art. 36; *Free Zones of Upper Savoy and the District of Gex* case (1932), *PCIJ*, Series A/B, No. 46.

[375] Art. 2(a). Art. 15 permits States to conclude agreements with non-parties for payment out of public funds, however.

[376] IAEA, *Conference on Civil Liability etc.*, p. 184, para. 55.

[377] See OECD recommendations on equal access to national remedies and non-discrimination, above, n. 288. See also Switzerland-FRG Agreement on Third Party Liability in the Nuclear Field, *Nuclear Law Bulletin*, 39 (1987), p. 51.

[378] Vienna Convention, Art. 1(1)(k); Paris Convention, Art. 3(a); Brussels Convention on Nuclear Ships, Art. 1(7); Holtz, *Nuclear Law Bulletin*, 40 (1987), p. 87. See above, text at n. 134.

[379] See OECD, *Nuclear Legislation: Third Party Liability* (Paris, 1976).

at sea might produce, does not easily fall within the conventions' terms. Here again, the 1969 Convention on Civil Liability for Oil Pollution Damage, as amended in 1984, offers a better model which provides for the costs of prevention measures taken to minimize damage and for reasonable measures of reinstatement of the environment.[380]

The nuclear conventions need a more realistic approach to environmental damage if the true costs of nuclear incidents are to be borne by the nuclear industry. Such additional environmental costs might be recoverable against States in international law, however, following the example of the Canadian claim for clean-up costs arising out of the Cosmos 954 crash.[381] If this is correct, it confirms that even in cases governed by one of the civil liability conventions, State responsibility for nuclear damage still has a role to play because of the narrowness of the conventions themselves.

(j) An Assessment of the Nuclear Conventions

Despite its novelty and sophistication, the most significant feature of the common scheme in these conventions is its lack of widespread international support. International willingness to agree to new conventions on notification and assistance following the Chernobyl accident has not been matched by any comparable interest in ratifying earlier liability conventions. This has prompted the IAEA to consider ways of encouraging greater participation. One measure already taken is the adoption of a joint protocol to prevent conflicts of law arising from the simultaneous application of the Paris and Vienna Conventions.[382]

At present, the Western European States who are parties to the Paris Convention represent the only significant grouping of nuclear States to have accepted an international agreement on civil liability. This is important since Western Europe has the world's greatest concentration of nuclear facilities and the highest likelihood of transboundary consequences arising from nuclear incidents.[383] But the spread of nuclear power worldwide, and the continental implications of major accidents, such as Chernobyl, makes the failure of the three global conventions to attract support a serious lacuna in the regulation of nuclear power. Of the ten parties to the Vienna Convention, only two possess nuclear facilities. Neither the USA nor the USSR has chosen to ratify it. Although the Brussels Convention on Nuclear Ships has six parties, it is not yet in force, because no State licensing such ships

---

[380] Art. 1(6). See Jacobsson and Trotz, *Journal of Maritime Law and Commerce*, 17 (1986), p. 467. Compare the Convention on Antarctic Mineral Resource Activities, 1988, Art. 1(15), and text at nn. 135–8, above.

[381] See above, nn. 135–6.

[382] IAEA Doc. N5/TC/643. It is hoped this Protocol will permit more States to ratify the Vienna Convention, including those who are at present party to the Paris Convention. See Busekist, *Nuclear Law Bulletin*, 43 (1989), p. 10, and Cameron *et al.*, op. cit. above (n. 22), pp. 112 ff. No East European State has signed the Protocol or the Vienna Convention.

[383] Approximately 120 of the world's 400 nuclear reactors are located in the 14 Paris Convention States.

has become a party.[384] The Convention on Maritime Carriage of Nuclear Material is in force, and has eleven parties, but these represent only a small proportion of world shipping tonnage. Overwhelmingly, those who operate nuclear installations or nuclear ships have failed to accept the international implications of making civil liability for nuclear damage easier to establish.

In the event of an accident causing damage, claimants in most countries will thus be forced either to resort to ordinary transboundary civil proceedings or to invoke State responsibility. Yet, as we have seen, there are serious obstacles to the former and much uncertainty over the content of the latter. Even if all four conventions were widely supported, they remain open to criticism in important respects. The narrowness of their environmental focus, the inadequacy of liability limits under the Vienna Convention, the shortness of the limitation period, the range of exceptions[385] and the possible dilution of a sense of responsibility on the part of operators of installations are the main points where reform may be desirable.[386]

More fundamentally, the OECD's Nuclear Energy Agency has pointed out that the use of unlimited liability and longer limitation periods by some States, notably West Germany, calls in question the basis of the scheme shared by all four conventions.[387] This may be desirable. Now that the nuclear industry is well established and its risks are better understood, it is harder to justify the exceptional level of State support and protection it presently enjoys in matters of civil liability.[388]

Despite these criticisms, the positive features of the four conventions as a model for other areas of environmental interest should be noted. They make individual access to legal remedies much easier than for any other form of transboundary environmental harm, and they eliminate or minimize difficult issues of proof and liability standards. They offer a scheme which ensures the availability of compensation funds regardless of the solvency of the defendant. The Paris Convention, benefiting from the supplementary provision of public funds, is particularly strong in this respect, and it sets an example which other liability conventions could usefully emulate.[389] The Conventions also offer a precedent for treating ultra-hazardous but socially desirable activities as risks which require exceptional provision for wider loss distribution, based only in part on the absolute or strict liability of the source of risk. However, lack of general international support

---

[384] Art. XXIV(1). Nuclear ships have been registered in the US, West Germany and the USSR.

[385] These include accidents caused by war, hostilities, civil disorder or grave natural disaster. Insurance cover is also unlikely to be available in such cases.

[386] OECD, 'Compensation for Nuclear Damage', *Nuclear Law Bulletin*, 20 (1977), p. 50; Shapar and Reyners, *Nuclear Third Party Liability*; Reyners, in IAEA, *Licensing and Regulatory Control of Nuclear Installations*, p. 243.

[387] OECD, *Nuclear Energy Agency, 15th Activity Report* (1986).

[388] See n. 386, above, and Pfaffelhuber and Kuchuk, *Nuclear Law Bulletin*, 25 (1980), p. 70.

[389] Cf. 1971 International Convention for the Establishment of an International Fund for Compensation for Oil Pollution Damage, 1971.

considerably weakens the value of that precedent as a basis for drawing inferences about the content of customary law.[390]

VI. CONCLUSIONS

This study points to four conclusions with wider significance for the international protection of the environment.

(1) The lack both of binding international standards for nuclear activities and of a strong system of international inspection and monitoring indicates the main weaknesses of the attempt at international regulation of nuclear risks through international institutions. Despite its influence on States, the ability of the IAEA to assure the environmental safety of nuclear power should not be exaggerated.

(2) Uncertainty regarding the content and character of the obligation to prevent serious harm to the environment diminishes the cogency of consensus on the existence of such an obligation. Both the standard of conduct required of States in controlling nuclear activities and the standard of responsibility for environmental damage require clarification by means of an international agreement.

(3) Neither the law of State responsibility, nor the alternative system of international conventions harmonizing principles of civil liability, provides a satisfactory basis for allocating the costs of transboundary environmental damage. Both systems indicate a failure to endorse the strict or absolute responsibility of 'source' States in cases of nuclear accidents, and may leave a heavy burden of loss to fall on 'victim' States.

(4) A customary law obligation to co-operate with neighbouring States in the management of transboundary environmental risks is firmly established. This obligation entails notification and negotiation aimed at limiting the risk when activities are planned in border areas, and requires environmental impact assessment and timely notification of accidents or environmental hazards. However, the evidence considered here does not show that activities involving transboundary risk are prohibited by international law, nor does it indicate that they may take place only on equitable terms agreed with States likely to be affected.

This article has tried to show that international environmental law has reached a level of sophistication well in advance of the award in the *Trail Smelter* case.[391] It has been suggested that the effectiveness of international institutions in implementing international standards for protecting the

---

[390] See above, text at nn. 267–70, for other objections.

[391] See generally Schneider, *World Public Order of the Environment* (London, 1973); Kiss, 'The International Protection of the Environment', in Macdonald and Johnston (eds.), *The Structure and Process of International Law* (The Hague, 1983); Caldwell, *International Environmental Policy* (Durham, 1984); Brownlie, *Natural Resources Journal*, 13 (1973), p. 179; Birnie, *British Journal of International Studies*, 3 (1977), p. 169; Bleicher, *Ecology Law Quarterly*, 2 (1972), p. 1; Hargrove (ed.), *Law, Institutions and the Global Environment* (Dobbs Ferry, 1972).

environment is now a more important perspective than older tort-based principles which merely redistribute the costs of transboundary nuisances. Nevertheless, in the control of nuclear energy, the basic structure of this legal system remains significantly unsettled, and the pace of progressive development through international agreements, State practice and international institutions has been uneven. A codification of principles for the use of nuclear energy comparable to Part 12 of the Law of the Sea Convention would still be a premature objective.

INTERNATIONALIZATION AND STABILIZATION OF CONTRACTS VERSUS STATE SOVEREIGNTY*

By ESA PAASIVIRTA‡

I. INTRODUCTION

MUCH of the academic discourse on State contracts has focused on the identification of the applicable law. There has been noticeably less effort to elaborate on the substantive aspects of that law. As an example one may refer to the approach adopted by the Institut de Droit International at its Athens session (1977). It is surprising that the Institut considered the question of the applicability of international law, for instance, as the proper law of State contracts, and at the same time excluded any consideration of the substantive consequences following the application of such law.[1]

This approach illustrates the emphasis of doctrinal discussion. A characteristic of the domain of State contracts is that international law has been introduced through the medium of conflict of laws, and the development of substantive law has been left to arbitral tribunals and thus has evolved on a case by case basis. The ICSID Convention[2] is another example of this 'instrumental' trend, for it provides a procedural framework rather than touching upon questions of substantive law. The Convention provides in Article 42(1) that, apart from the law of the host State, a tribunal shall also apply 'such rules of international law as may be applicable'. However, neither the Convention nor the preparatory work gives much guidance on the content of the substantive law.[3] In view of the fact that State contracts constitute a relatively new departure in international law, the above reference to 'applicable' rules may be seen as an indication of the quasi-legislative role which the tribunals play.[4]

---

* © Dr. Esa Paasivirta, 1990.

‡ Ph. D. (Cantab.); Associate Expert on Legal Aspects of Foreign Trade, International Trade Centre UNCTAD/GATT, Geneva. The views expressed herein are strictly personal and not necessarily shared by the UN or GATT or any of their related agencies.

[1] *Annuaire de l'Institut de Droit International*, 57 (1977), pt. 1, p. 202. The rapporteur, Professor van Hecke, stated merely that the options of international law, and the other non-municipal standards considered by the Institut, are 'utiles à dire': ibid., 58 (1978), pt. 2, p. 62.

[2] Convention on the Settlement of Investment Disputes between States and Nationals of Other States, Washington, 18 March 1965: *UN Treaty Series*, vol. 575, p. 159.

[3] The report of the Executive Directors provides: 'The term "international law" as used in this context should be understood in the sense given to it by Article 38(1) of the Statute of the International Court of Justice, allowance being made for the fact that Article 38 was designed to apply to inter-State disputes': *ICSID Documents Concerning the Origin and the Formulation of the Convention*, vol. 2, part 2 (1970), p. 1080.

[4] In discussing similar formulations, not infrequently used in international instruments on dispute settlement, Lauterpacht, *The Function of Law in the International Community* (1933), pp. 56–60, draws attention to the distinction between the 'existence' of a rule and its 'applicability'. A rule may exist, but still not be applicable, because it may lead to an unjust result.

Admittedly, it may be practicable to emphasize the 'instrumental' aspects, be they rules of procedure or of conflict of laws, and such an emphasis is probably explicable on the basis of past experience in the area of foreign investments. Several attempts have been made to provide comprehensive, universal, legal standards for investment protection, but they have failed to satisfy the diverse interests involved.[5] Against this background an approach such as the one adopted in the ICSID Convention may thus seem to be a 'stroke of genius' illustrating the 'unavoidable relativity of the distinction between form and substance in the reality of law as in any other sphere of human endeavour'.[6]

In general the above account suggests that in this area, which is so affected by conflicts of interest, arbitral tribunals as well as legal writers play a particularly prominent role in the formation of substantive law.[7] In this article three separate issues will be considered. In order to gain a proper perspective, it is useful first to draw attention to the great diversity of views of various authors on the consequences of the internationalization of State contracts. This will be followed by a discussion of stabilization clauses, and then of matters relating to State sovereignty and permanent sovereignty over natural resources.

II. ASSUMED EFFECTS OF INTERNATIONALIZATION

The aim of the present survey is to focus on the various views expressed by different writers. For these purposes a distinction between four different groups can be made.

Group I. The first group consists of those writers who have perceived the effect of internationalization as achieving a more or less absolute protection of the private party to a State contract. The underlying idea has been described as follows:

The main interest and motive of those who advocate the choice of public international law is the desire to ensure against the possibility of effect being given to a termination or modification of the agreement of the parties by an act of supervening legislation.[8]

Consequently, the internationalization of contracts has been perceived as a

---

[5] Among such attempts one may mention the Abs-Shawcross Draft Convention (1959) and the OECD Draft Convention (1967). See Schwarzenberger, *Foreign Investments and International Law* (1969), pp. 109–34, 153–69.

[6] Schwarzenberger, ibid., p. 152.

[7] There may not be anything particularly new in this. Historically speaking, the law of State responsibility has to a large extent been elaborated by international tribunals: Brownlie, *System of the Law of Nations: State Responsibility (Part I)* (1983), pp. 1–9.

[8] Suratgar, 'Considerations affecting Choice of Law Clauses in Contracts Between Governments and Foreign Nationals', *Indian Journal of International Law*, 2 (1962), pp. 273, 302.

way to 'deny effect'[9] to unilateral changes by States, the legal justification being the 'unrestricted application of the principle of *pacta sunt servanda*'.[10] Such an effect has been described as a 'detachment'[11] or an 'escape'[12] from the municipal legal systems or a ground to 'ignore'[13] the effects of the legal rules of States. F.A. Mann, one of the earliest contributors, refers to an internationalized contract and states that:

its existence and fate would be immune from an encroachment by a system of municipal law in exactly the same manner as in the case of a treaty between two international persons.[14]

Hence, the undertakings expressed in the terms of State contracts are 'international obligations' comparable to treaties.[15] Professor Kojanec suggests that it follows from the internationalization that 'the State cannot unilaterally modify the contractual system'.[16] Similarly Professor de Vries has concluded that 'the investors' contract rights cannot be adversely affected by the unilateral action of the host state'. For this reason it is recommended that 'the investor and his counsel should attempt to "internationalize" the contract'.[17] For Professor Garcia-Amador 'the purpose of "internationalization" of a contractual relation must be to "liberate" the relation from municipal law'.[18] He continues:

As in the case of treaties, when a contract or concession is governed by international law or by international principles, or provides for a mode of settlement of a genuinely international character, the rights of aliens derive from an 'international' source and the obligations of the State are necessarily also international. It follows that the mere non-performance of these obligations directly and immediately gives rise to state responsibility.[19]

---

[9] Ibid., p. 301.

[10] Ibid., p. 307. For this reason some lawyers have even doubted the applicability of the principle of *rebus sic stantibus* to State contracts. See Ray, 'The Law Governing Contracts Between States and Foreign Nationals', *Proceedings of the Institute of Private Investors Abroad* (1960), pp. 5, 65–9. On the same point another author, discussing the effects of the general principles of law as the proper law of the contract, has stated: 'If this situation exists, then—but only then—there is a case for unilateral alteration or abrogation of a contract': J.-F. Lalive, 'Unilateral Alteration or Abrogation by Either Party to a Contract Between a State and a Foreign National', *Private Investors Abroad* (1965), pp. 265, 278.

[11] Von Mehren and Kourides, 'International Arbitrations Between States and Foreign Private Parties: The Libyan Nationalization Cases', *American Journal of International Law*, 75 (1981), pp. 476, 510–11.

[12] Toriguian, *Legal Aspects of Oil Concessions in the Middle East* (1972), p. 242.

[13] Castberg, 'International Law in Our Time', *Recueil des cours*, 138 (1973-I), pp. 1, 10.

[14] Mann, *Studies in International Law* (1973), pp. 222–3.

[15] Ibid., p. 191. See also Shawcross, 'Problems of Foreign Investment in International Law', *Recueil des cours*, 102 (1961–I), pp. 335, 352–3.

[16] Kojanec, 'The Legal Nature of Agreements Concluded by Private Entities with Foreign States', in Kojanec (ed.), *Les Accords de commerce international, colloque 1968* (1969), pp. 299, 338 (footnote omitted).

[17] De Vries, 'The Enforcement of Economic Development Agreements with Foreign States', *University of Detroit Law Review*, 62 (1984), pp. 1, 20–1.

[18] Garcia-Amador, Fourth Report on State Responsibility, Doc. A/CN. 4/119, *Yearbook of the ILC*, 1959, vol. 2, p. 32, para. 127.

[19] Ibid., p. 33, para. 131.

J.-F. Lalive describes the effects in similar terms:

Il était difficile d'admettre qu'un Etat pût porter atteinte à des contrats 'interna-tionalisés', librement négociés et acceptés, contrats dont il avait lui-même, par une loi interne, prescrit la forme, dans le libre exercice de sa souveraineté.[20]

In his study in the principle of *pacta sunt servanda* Professor Wehberg concludes that

the principle is valid exactly in the same manner, whether it is in respect of con-tracts between states or in respect of contracts between states and private com-panies.[21]

And Professor Weil states that

le choix de droit international comme loi du contrat n'a souvent d'autre significa-tion que de rendre applicable à ce dernier certains principes de droit international, notamment *pacta sunt servanda*, de manière à faire regarder l'inéxecution du con-trat par l'Etat comme un acte illicite sur le plan international.[22]

The above views suggest a uniform perception of the function of inter-national law as the proper law of a contract. They imply basically that any acts of a State which contravene contractual provisions are unlawful in accordance with the applicable international law. The writers of the next group hold very different views on the matter.

Group II. The second group comprises those writers whose views are practically opposed to the first group. Professor Sereni analyses the sugges-tion that international law is the proper law of State contracts and rejects it bluntly:

Each legal system serves the purpose of regulating the status and relations of the social entities for which and among which it exists. An attempt at applying inter-national law to private relations would be tantamount to seeking to apply the matri-monial laws of France or England to relations between cats and dogs.[23]

Wolff states:

The choice of the law of nations as the proper law of contract includes the choice of all compulsory rules of that legal system, and therefore also the provision that only States can be subject to public international law.[24]

---

[20] Lalive, 'Contrats entre Etats ou enterprises étatiques et personnes privées. Développements récents', *Recueil des cours*, 181 (1983–III), pp. 9, 110.

[21] Wehberg, 'Pacta Sunt Servanda', *American Journal of International Law,* 53 (1959), pp. 775, 786.

[22] Weil, 'Problèmes relatifs aux contrats passés entre un Etat et un particulier', *Recueil des cours*, 128 (1969–III), pp. 94, 113–14; for similar views, see Böckstiegel, *Der Staat als Vertragspartner aus-ländischer Privatunternehmen* (1971), p. 308, who suggests such effects with respect to what the author sees as 'quasi-international law agreements'; Cohen-Jonathan, 'L'Arbitrage Texaco-Calasiatic c. gouvernement libyen', *Annuaire français de droit international*, 1977, pp. 452, 474.

[23] Sereni, 'International Economic Institutions and the Municipal Law of States', *Recueil des cours*, 96 (1959–I), pp. 129, 210.

[24] Wolff, 'Some Observations on the Autonomy of Contracting Parties in the Conflict of Laws', *Transactions of the Grotius Society*, 35 (1950), pp. 143, 150–1.

Even if it were possible to apply international law to contractual relations in the above sense, the author continues:

Indeed a State is able to bind itself towards another State not to exercise its power to legislate insofar as this would lead to a violation of duties which it has established by agreements of an international character. But this does not entail the consequences that a State can by a contract with an individual or with a company limited by shares bind itself to abstain from a full exercise of its right to legislate.[25]

Similar views have also been expressed by others.[26]

The common opinion of this group is that the use of international law, which governs relations between States, as the proper law of contract is inappropriate. Hence, no substantive consequences can reasonably be inferred.

Group III. The third group consists of those who do not reject the applicability of international law to State contracts but do not necessarily adopt the view that it confers absolute protection on the private party. These writers emphasize that the principles of law are not settled.

E. Lauterpacht, in discussing the role and effects of international law within the ICSID system, points out that the application of Art. 42(1) of the Convention is 'somewhat experimental' and 'unpredictable' and that much depends on arbitrators.[27] Similarly, Professor Schwarzenberger doubts whether an ICSID tribunal could apply rules of international law which were laid down in advance. The matter is ultimately left to each individual tribunal; hence, the composition of the tribunal is of importance.[28] Elsewhere, in considering the reluctance of States to opt for international arbitration in investment matters, this author explains: 'Among other reasons, this is due to the growing awareness of the truth that the rule of law means almost inevitably the rule of lawyers.'[29] Since the emergence of the notion of permanent sovereignty over natural resources and the New International Economic Order, Dr Delaume affirms, 'much uncertainty exists as to the precise status of international norms', and he continues:

Until such time as a consensus of opinion can be achieved in regard to the rules of international law applicable to the relations between foreign investors and host states (and not only developing nations), the effectiveness of 'internationalization' clauses is bound to remain uncertain. The difficulty is not that these clauses cannot

---

[25] Ibid., p. 151.

[26] 'Das Völkerrecht ist ein Recht für bestimmte Rechtssubjekte und auf diese zugeschnitten. Wendet man es auf die Beziehungen von Privatrechtssubjekten an, so erstreckt man es auf einen ganz anders strukturierten Bereich, für dessen Probleme es nicht geschaffen ist und denen es daher nicht gerecht werden kann': Sumampouw, 'Rechtswahl im Vertragsrecht', *Rabels Zeitschrift für ausländisches und international Privatrecht*, 30 (1966), pp. 334, 347; see also Zweigert, 'Vertrage zwischen staatlichen und nicht-staatlichen Partnern', *Berichte der Deutschen Gesellschaft für Völkerrecht*, 5 (1964), pp. 194, 210–11.

[27] Lauterpacht, 'The World Convention on the Settlement of International Investment Disputes', *Recueil d'études de droit international en hommage à Paul Guggenheim* (1968), pp. 642, 654–5.

[28] Schwarzenberger, op. cit., above (n. 5), at p. 144.

[29] Comment, in Kojanec (ed.), *Les Accords de commerce international, colloque 1968* (1969), at p. 343.

perform the normal function of stipulations of applicable law, but rather that the substantive rules to which they refer are still in a state of flux.[30]

It has been noted moreover that references in State contracts to the principles of international law

were generally construed to protect [investors] against . . . unilateral actions, but these principles are in a state of flux and it is by no means clear that they will continue to afford protection to the private party in the future.[31]

Group IV. Although their views are in some ways similar to those of the previous group, writers of the fourth group put a particular emphasis on international law as a general standard, instead of the narrower interpretation of it as the proper law of contract. These writers typically view the issue of the analogy between contracts and treaties as fallacious and warn of the danger of aprioristic thinking.[32] This approach, with its emphasis on the standards of international law, has been suggested by Judge Jiménez de Aréchaga:

We do not believe that there is an international law of contract, but even if it were so, international law contains the fundamental and overriding principle of the permanent sovereignty of the State over all its wealth and natural resources . . . [I]t is not the contract as such, but the situation as a whole which is governed by international law, whether or not the parties have so stipulated.[33]

Professor Verhoeven emphasizes that the application of treaty rules would be 'parfaitement abusif',[34] and considers it illusory to think that international law contains rules which would prevent a State from terminating or modifying its contract with a private party.[35] Another commentator has suggested recently that:

International law was not intended to regulate mutual contractual relations between States and private entities. However, investors might have an interest in

---

[30] Delaume, *Transnational Contracts: Applicable Law and Settlement of Disputes. Law and Practice*, Booklet 1 (issued January 1988), pp. 15–16.

[31] Crawford and Johnson, 'Arbitrating with Foreign States and Their Instrumentalities', *International Financial Law Review*, April 1986, pp. 11, 12; another commentator, assessing recent arbitral practice, concludes: 'Staaten haben das Recht ausländisches Viermogen innerhalb ihres Hoheitgebiets zur Förderung des offentlichen Wahls zu nationalisieren. Die Tendenz scheint dahin zu gehen, dass sich die Nationalisierung auch auf "internationalisierte" Verträge erstreckt; der Stand Völkerrechts ist jedoch noch nicht klar': Catranis, 'Probleme der Nationalisierung ausländischer Unternehmen vor internationalen Schiedsgerichten', *Recht der Internationalen Wirtschaft*, 1982, pp. 19, 26.

[32] Lalive, 'Sur une notion du "contrat international" ', *Festschrift Lipstein* (1980), pp. 135, 143, 154. The author emphasizes (p. 154) that the internationalisation of a State contract 'ne le rend *a priori* et en soi ni plus ni moins adaptable ou intangible, ni plus ni moins contraignant. Tout dépend du contenu, au moment critique, du droit applicable, quel qu'il soit.'

[33] 'International Law in the Past Third of a Century', *Recueil des cours*, 159 (1978–I), pp. 1, 308 (footnote omitted).

[34] Verhoeven, 'Arbitrage entre Etats et entreprises étrangères: Des règles spécifiques?', *Revue de l'Arbitrage*, 1985, No. 4, pp. 609, 624.

[35] 'Un tel espoir, il n'empêche, est *a priori* parfaitement illusoire. Il n'existe en effet présentement en droit des gens aucune règle qui interdise à un Etat de modifier ou de rompre le contrat qu'il a conclu avec un particulier étranger. Ce n'est point que le droit des gens autorise cette "déstabilisation". C'est simplement qu'il ignore de tels accords qu'il ne régit pas': ibid., p. 623.

there being a reference to international law, in order to ensure the application of standards that are not subject to unilateral amendment by the host country. If a nationalization occurs, for instance, this would become significant with respect to compensation laws which the state otherwise might amend. This does not mean that the parties' legal positions can be protected absolutely in every situation. Such a reference does not necessarily abolish the host country government's power, according to domestic law, to cancel the effect of the contractual clause by promulgating a general legal rule.[36]

It is appropriate at this point to make some comments on the positions of the above four groups. Historically, the first two groups precede the latter two.[37] The common feature between the first two is that both view the role of international law in the narrow sense of *lex contractus* rather than as a general standard. The difference, of course, is that whereas the first group expects the notion of internationalization to provide more or less absolute protection for the private party, the second does not regard it as having any legal effects at all.

The second group considers the use of international law as the applicable law of State contracts to be inappropriate. For these writers the system of international law is purely an inter-State system in which an individual or a company has no legal personality.[38] One should notice, however, that in recent arbitrations no tribunal has felt precluded from applying international law on such a basis, which implies a less State-centred conception of international law. The very existence of the ICSID system suggests the same (i.e. it would appear out-moded completely to exclude contracts from the province of international law). Nevertheless, the views of the second group of writers highlight the innovative way in which international law has been introduced into this domain as the proper law of contracts, and make one aware that the choice of applicable rules is a highly selective process.

It seems that the views of the first group are marginally better reflected in arbitral practice than those of the second group. It suffices for present purposes to note that here too the assumed legal consequences of internationalization of contracts relate to a preconception of the role of international law. The idea of international law as *lex contractus* is thought to provide the most powerful means of giving effect to the individual terms of a contract. As in the case of the treaties between States, the contractual relationship between a State and a foreign company is portrayed in terms of equality. By implication, it follows that the non-performance of contractual undertakings by a State constitutes an unlawful act pursuant to the applicable international law of contract. Ultimately, it seems to be the traditional liberal idea of the freedom of contract which induces the concept of the internationalization of State contracts.

[36] Bartels, *Contractual Adaptation and Conflict Resolution* (1985), p. 110.

[37] See Kuusi, *The Host State and the Transnational Corporation* (1979), p. 99.

[38] Not dissimilar doctrinal views may be traced in the *Aramco* (27 ILR 117) and *Sapphire* (35 ILR 136) awards. For these reasons, at least partly, the Tribunals were led to apply the general principles of law as a standard distinct from international law.

If it is correct to say that the approach of the first group of writers has aprioristic elements, the fourth group tends to be inductively orientated. That is, the rules of international law are investigated generally rather than selectively in order to establish analogies in accordance with preconceived ideas. Undoubtedly such an approach brings an element of uncertainty, which is reflected in the views of the third group of writers.

As the above account suggests, there are several ways in which one may think of the role and effects of international law *vis-à-vis* State contracts. To emphasize this point one may consider the following aggregation of related legal statements. In 1937 the American-Turkish Claims Commission, in referring to international disputes involving private contracts, stated that

the law of nations does not embrace any 'Law of Contracts', such as is found in the domestic jurisprudence of nations, and such cases are of course not actions on contracts in terms of domestic law.[39]

In 1945 Dr Lipstein wrote that

international law contains no branch dealing with contracts. If the breach of contract is to form the basis of a claim based on international law, it must constitute a tortious act in the nature of a denial of justice.[40]

Dr S. Friedman, writing in 1953, emphasized that

contracts cannot be the subject of international disputes since international law contains no rules respecting their form and effect.[41]

The most the International Court of Justice was able to say in 1970 on the institutions of municipal law in general was:

In this field international law is called upon to recognize institutions of municipal law that have an important and extensive role in the international field. This does not necessarily imply drawing any analogy between its own institutions and those of municipal law, nor does it amount to making rules of international law dependent upon categories of municipal law.[42]

Against this background it is surprising to find that in 1977 the Arbitrator in the *Texaco* case, Professor Dupuy, stated *ex cathedra*:

[C]ontracts between States and private persons can, under certain conditions, come within the ambit of a particular and new branch of international law: the international law of contracts.[43]

Has the law changed? The Arbitrator did not refer to new rules of cus-

---

[39] *United States of America on behalf of Ina M. Hofmann and Dulcie H. Steinhardt* v. *Republic of Turkey*, Nielsen, *American-Turkish Claims Settlement: Opinions and Report* (1937), pp. 286, 287.

[40] Lipstein, 'The Place of Calvo Clause in International Law', this *Year Book*, 22 (1945), pp. 130, 143.

[41] Friedman, *Expropriation in International Law* (1953), p. 156.

[42] *Barcelona Traction, Light and Power Company Limited* case, Judgment, *ICJ Reports*, 1970, p. 33, para. 38.

[43] 53 ILR at 447–8.

tomary international law. Nor does there exist a general treaty on the matter. If law is perceived statically as a separate objective reality, which has emanated from 'external' sources, it is difficult to reconcile the above statements. It rather seems that the discourse on an 'international law of contracts' is only comprehensible as a legal process involving (competing) values of social morality, economics and politics.

III. Stabilization Clauses—A Special Case?

Generally speaking, the aim of the internationalization of contracts is to stabilize the relationship between a State and a private party. This implies that in case of a dispute the range of applicable legal rules is not restricted to the law of the host State. The latter, which in most cases is the quite natural applicable law of contract, is often seen to pose risks to the private party, as the State may change it in accordance with its sovereign will.[44] Another technique to control the legal powers of a State is to insert so-called 'stabilization clauses' into contracts. The purpose of these clauses, it has been said, is 'to reach a compromise between the sovereign prerogatives of the State involved and the legitimate quest of the private party for stability of status consistent with sound business judgement'.[45] A brief survey of relevant contractual practice may be useful at this point.

A great variety of forms of provision are used. Sometimes a distinction is made between the stabilization clauses proper and the so-called 'intangibility clauses'.[46] An intangibility clause provides that any modification of a contract requires the mutual consent of the parties. A stabilization clause, in turn, aims at 'freezing' the law of a host State and thus preventing a State from using its legislative power to modify the contract in its own favour. An example of an intangibility clause occurs in the 1967 contract between the Ruler of Abu Dhabi and three Japanese companies which provided as follows:

The mutual consent of the Ruler and the Companies shall be required to annul, or modify, the provisions of this Agreement.[47]

A stabilization clause in the above sense was included in the well-known

---

[44] As put by Lord Radcliffe, the proper law 'not merely sustains but, because it sustains, may also modify or dissolve the contractual bond': *Kahler* v. *Midland Bank*, [1950] AC 24, 56.

[45] Delaume, *Transnational Contracts: Applicable Law and Settlement of Disputes. Law and Practice*, Booklet 8 (issued July 1983), p. 39.

[46] Weil, 'Les Clauses de stabilisation ou d'intangibilité dans les accords de développement économique', *Mélanges Rousseau* (1974), pp. 301, 307–9.

[47] Art. 33 of the Concession Agreement between the Ruler of Abu Dhabi and Maruzen Oil Co. Ltd., Daikyo Oil Co. Ltd. and Nippon Mining Co. Ltd., 6 December 1967, *Selected Documents of the International Petroleum Industry*, 1967, p. 137; also the Contract between the General Petroleum and Minerals Organization and AGIP Saudi Arabia SpA, 21 December 1967, Art. 21, ibid., p. 190; similar clauses were also included in the Libyan oil concessions which gave rise to the *BP*, *Texaco* and *Liamco* arbitrations, Clause 16 of which provided that the 'contractual rights expressly created by this concession shall not be altered except by mutual consent of the parties'. See respectively 53 ILR at p. 324; ibid. at p. 476; 62 ILR at p. 191.

Concession Agreement of 1933 between Iran and the Anglo-Iranian Oil Company. Article 21 of the Agreement laid down that the

Concession shall not be annulled by the Government and the terms therein contained shall not be altered either by general or special legislation in the future, or by administrative measures or any other acts whatever of the executive authorities.[48]

It is not unusual to find a combination of these provisions. The Petroleum Agreement of 4 February 1973 between the Sultan of Oman and the Sun Group stipulates in Article 22:

22.1 The Sultan shall not annul this Agreement by general or special legislation or by administrative measures or by any other act [except in the event of default by the other party].
22.2 The mutual written consent of the Sultan and the Sun Group shall be required to annul, amend or modify the provisions of this Agreement.
22.3 The Sultan agrees that no discriminatory laws or decrees affecting the Sun Group or its operations will be enacted.[49]

A stabilization clause of another type may be found in the Concession Agreement between the Government of the Republic of Liberia and the Liberia Iron and Steel Corporation of 2 June 1975. The choice of law provision in Article 21 states:

This Concession Agreement shall be governed, construed and interpreted in accordance with the laws of the Republic of Liberia excluding, however, any enactment passed or brought into force in the Republic of Liberia before or after the date of this Concession Agreement which is inconsistent with or contrary to the terms hereof.[50]

The above clauses vary in their scope of application. A wide and relatively detailed clause may be found in the 1977 Agreement between Mauritania and a consortium of foreign oil companies, which includes the following provision for a period of 25 years:

Le gouvernement garantit à la deuxième partie, pour la durée de la convention, la stabilité des conditions générales, juridiques, économiques, financières et fiscales dans lesquelles la deuxième partie exercera son activité, telles que ses conditions

---

[48] *Anglo-Iranian Oil Co.* case, *ICJ Pleadings*, 1952, p. 86.

[49] Cited in Delaume, op. cit. above (n. 30), Binder 1, Booklet 3.1. (issued April 1986), p. 25; see also the Production Sharing Agreement between the Republic of Togo and Oceanic Resources Ltd., 4 August 1977, Art. 30, ibid.; the Agreement between Kuwait and Kuwait Shell Petroleum Co., 15 January 1961, Art. 27, cited in Delaume, 'Des Stipulations de droit applicable dans les accords de prêt et de développement économique et de leur rôle', *Revue belge de droit international*, 1968, pp. 336, 356; the Joint Venture Agreement between AUXERAP and AQUITAINE, on the one hand, and the Government of Libya and LIPETCO, on the other hand, 30 April 1968, Art. 40 (III), *Selected Documents of the International Petroleum Industry*, 1968, p. 197; the Petroleum Concession Agreement between the Ruler of Abu Dhabi and Phillips Petroleum Co., American Independent Oil Co. and AGIP SpA, 21 January 1967, Art. 24, ibid., 1967, p. 165; a similar clause was the subject of careful consideration in the *Aminoil* award in 1982: 66 ILR 546.

[50] Fischer (ed.), *A Collection of International Concessions and Related Instruments* (hereinafter *CICRI*), vol. 1, p. 113; see also Jordan-Yugoslav Oil Concession Agreement, 8 March 1968, Art. 30, *Selected Documents of the International Petroleum Industry*, 1968, p. 335.

résultent de la législation et de la réglementation en vigueur à la date de signature de la convention ainsi que des dispositions de ladite convention.[51]

Such provisions are often addressed to defined areas, such as taxation,[52] corporate status or mining legislation.[53]

From the viewpoint of host States, the clauses discussed here are a means of attracting foreign investment. They are a part of the bargaining process as a whole. It is probably for these reasons, which involve a balancing of opposing interests, that some clauses seem ambiguous and cause difficulties of interpretation. This is the case, for instance, when the law of a State Party is at the same time chosen as the applicable law of the contract, as in the above cited Liberian contract of 1975. Another example is the Sales and Purchase Agreement of 1973 between Iran and a consortium of oil companies. It provided:

> This Agreement shall be interpreted in accordance with the laws of Iran. The rights and obligations of the Parties shall be governed by and according to the provisions of this Agreement. The termination before expiry date or any alteration of this Agreement shall be subject to the mutual agreement of the Parties.[54]

In a dispute involving the question of a subsequent legislative change, the relevance of the clause depends on whether the 'interpretation' in the first sentence is given a clearly different meaning from the 'rights and obligations', which are said to be 'governed' by the agreement. This would then imply that in a certain situation matters considered as interpretation are resolved by the law of the host State, whereas with regard to some other matters the question of the applicable law is left open. Such a view has

---

[51] Convention of Establishment Between the Islamic Republic of Mauritania and AGIP SpA, Getty Oil International (Mauritania) Inc., Hispánica de Petróleos SA (Hispanoil) and Phillips Petroleum International Corporation Mauritania Inc., 29 April 1977, Art. 4, *CICRI*, vol. 6, p. 279.

[52] For a detailed formulation of a tax clause, see the Foreign Investment Agreement between the Republic of Chile and the Foote Mineral Company of Pennsylvania, 25 March 1977, Clause 7 (9), *CICRI*, vol. 6, p. 27. A tax clause, but with a further extension of stabilizing the 'juridical terms of the present Convention', may also be found in the Investment Agreement between the Republic of Burundi and the Roumanian State enterprise GEOMIN, 16 May 1977, Art. 5(4), ibid., p. 329. Furthermore, tax clauses may be graded in the sense that the extent of stabilization is greater during the start-up period than during the time of commercial operation. This is the case in the Brazilian Model Service Contract for Onshore and Offshore Operations between Petróleos Brasileiros SA (PETROBRAS) and Private Contractors (1979), Art. 21(3): see Delaume, op. cit. above (n. 45), Binder 1, Booklet 3. (issued April 1986), p. 42. A clause freezing the relevant tax laws was the central issue in the *Revere* arbitration (1978), 56 ILR 258.

[53] For a clause concerning the corporate status, see *AGIP* award, *International Legal Materials*, 21 (1982), p. 727. A provision relating to mining legislation is included in the Concession Contract between the Government of Ecuador and Texas Petroleum Company, 21 February 1964, Art. 41, which states: 'The concessionary bind themselves especially to the Oil and Mining Laws, the provisions of which, as they are in force at the time of signature of this contract, are understood to be incorporated in the same and shall rule the relations between the parties in every aspect that had not been expressly agreed upon by them': Delaume, loc. cit. above (n. 49), at p. 358 (n. 59).

[54] Art. 29; Art. 28 contained a clause referring to international arbitration: *Selected Documents of the International Petroleum Industry*, 1973, p. 42.

recently been confirmed by the Iran-United States Claims Tribunal in the *Consortium* case.[55]

This might be the case in the following example of a Venezuelan oil contract which provided:

> This instrument cannot be modified in any way except in writing signed by the parties. This Agreement shall be governed by the laws of the Republic of Venezuela.[56]

An oil contract concluded in 1976 by the Government of Qatar also suggests a delicate balancing of interests. Article 33 reads:

> Without prejudice to the Government's prerogative of sovereign powers the mutual consent of the Parties hereto shall be required to annul, amend or modify the provisions of this Agreement.[57]

The last-mentioned contracts have two distinctive features. On the one hand, they refer to the law of the host State as the applicable law. On the other hand, the contracts include stabilization provisions and refer to international arbitration for dispute settlement. Thus, there are different interests involved, which different contract provisions aim to protect. It could be suggested that in fundamental matters, such as those concerning the very existence of a contract, the applicable law is in fact left to the arbitral tribunals to determine. Otherwise, stabilization provisions might remain completely meaningless (if their legal effect is assessed in accordance with the law of the State Party, subsequently amended), or one would be faced with the much criticized idea of a 'contract without law'.[58]

The legal effect of stabilization clauses may be viewed in two ways. First, the clauses may be dealt with in terms of substantive law. Secondly, one may approach them from the viewpoint of the conflict of laws. The latter approach will be considered first.

The present trend concerning international commercial arbitration allows much freedom in the choice of applicable conflict of laws rules. Arbitrators are not necessarily bound to apply any single national system of private international law. If a stabilization clause is perceived as a kind of

---

[55] *Iran–US Claims Tribunal Reports*, vol. 16, at p. 27.

[56] Agreement for the Purchase and Sale of Crude Oil and Petroleum Products between Petróleos de Venezuela and Exxon International Limited, 1 January 1976, Art. 15 (1), *CICRI*, vol. 2, p. 317. Art. 16 (1) contains an ICC arbitration clause.

[57] Exploration and Production Sharing Agreement between the Government of Qatar and Holcar Oil Co., 1 January 1976, Art. 33, ibid., p. 249. Art. 34 contains an arbitration clause providing that the place of arbitration is left at the discretion of the arbitrators. Art. 28 (B) states moreover that the applicable law is the law of Qatar.

[58] In a case where there is no arbitration clause and the disputes are settled by the courts of a host State, there is hardly any way to give effect to such clauses. This is due to the fact that State courts operate within clearly defined constitutional constraints so that in most cases it is unthinkable that they could stand against the will of a legislator in pursuance of its public interest. See also below, n. 74, and the accompanying text.

'negative' choice of law clause, providing that certain laws should *not* be applied, this leads to the question of whether the principle of autonomy of will should apply in a less forceful way than it does in the case of a 'positive' choice of law. If the matter is then addressed directly to an arbitral tribunal, as has been suggested,[59] it is difficult to ignore such provisions.

As an example of an arbitral framework which would allow this kind of thinking, one may take the UNCITRAL Model Law on International Commercial Arbitration of 25 June 1985. Article 28(1) provides:

The arbitral tribunal shall decide the dispute in accordance with such rules of law as are chosen by the parties as applicable to the substance of the dispute.[60]

The relevant report stated that, according to one view, the expression 'rules of law' was 'novel and imprecise'. On the other hand, the formula was seen to provide a necessary 'flexibility' as it allowed the parties to subject their relationship to the most suitable rules for their situation.[61] Even the other viewpoint, which had preferred the expression 'law', thought that a *dépeçage* of applicable law should be allowed.[62]

By treating stabilization clauses as negative choice of law clauses, complex questions of substance are avoided, in particular the issue of the binding force of contracts and how it relates to State sovereignty. While the above discussion suggests that a total rejection of the validity of stabilization clauses is difficult to maintain, an approach on the basis of conflict of laws alone is too narrow. It should go without saying that, even if the validity of stabilization clauses may be recognized as a negative choice of law, one ought not to draw conclusions which are too far-reaching from this.[63] Should one reject, *arguendo*, the effect of such clauses, wholly or partially, as a matter of substantive international law, this would restrict the use of conflict of laws techniques as well.

Expropriatory measures of the host State, affecting the performance of a contract on the State territory, are normally mandatory rules of that State. They cannot be ignored simply because they remain outside the proper law of the contract. Instead, such legal rules need to be taken into consideration, and applied selectively, within the confines of public international

---

[59] Tschanz, 'Contrats d'État et mesures unilatérales de l'État devant l'arbitre international', *Revue générale de droit international public*, 74 (1985), pp. 47, 57.

[60] Reproduced in *International Legal Materials*, 24 (1985), p. 1302.

[61] UNCITRAL Report Excerpts, ibid., pp. 1314, 1350–1.

[62] Ibid., p. 1351. For similar remarks with respect to the expression 'rules of law' in Art. 42 (1) in the ICSID Convention, see Delaume, 'La Convention pour le règlement des différends relatifs aux investissements entre Etats et ressortissants d'autres Etats', *Clunet*, 93 (1966), pp. 26, 48.

[63] It should be emphasized that the Institut de Droit International, which discussed the question of applicable law of State contracts at its Athens session (1979), abandoned, by a majority vote, the original draft article which referred to stabilization clauses. As the general perspective of the Institut was one of private international law, it was apparently felt that such a reference would have necessarily involved issues of substantive law, which had been left beyond the investigation. See *Annuaire de l'Institut de Droit International*, 58 (1959), pt. 2, pp. 92–6.

law, as 'directly' or 'immediately' applicable rules.[64] Assuming then that an enactment of an expropriatory decree regardless of a stabilization clause is considered as a part of the sovereign rights of the State, and thus an internationally lawful act *per se*, such a decree should be applied by an arbitrator as far as its effect of terminating the contract is concerned, though not necessarily to the extent that it deprives the private party of compensation.[65]

The last remarks lead to the question of the content of substantive international law on the matter. Three main positions may be distinguished.

First, there is the view that because of a specific contractual commitment to the contrary, a unilateral termination of a contract constitutes an internationally unlawful act. Under this view, the existence of a stabilization clause renders a contract different in kind and may result in the categorizing of a breach as unlawful, which it would not have been in the absence of such a clause. This was the view of the United Kingdom in the *Anglo-Iranian Oil Company* case, where it was submitted:

> The Government of the United Kingdom does not dissent from the proposition that a State is entitled to nationalize and, generally, to expropriate concessions granted to foreigners to the same extent as other property owned by foreigners. The exercise of that right, with regard to concessions and other property rights, is, however, subject to limitations clearly established by international practice and resting on well-recognized principles of international law. These limitations include, in particular, the principle that a State is not entitled to nationalize a concession if, by . . . a provision in the contract of concession it has expressly divested itself of the right to do so . . .[66]

---

[64] For support one may refer to the Draft Recommendations on the Law Applicable to International Contracts of 1980 by the Commission on Law and Commercial Practices of the International Chamber of Commerce. Art. 9 provides alternatively:
'Alternative 1.
Even when the arbitrator does not apply the law of a certain country as the law of governing the contract he may nevertheless give effect to mandatory rules of the law of that country if the contract or the parties have a close contact to that country and if and insofar as under its law those rules must be applied whatever be the law applicable to the contract. On considering whether to give effect to those mandatory rules, regard shall be had to their nature and purpose and to the consequences of their application or non-application.
Alternative 2.
Even when the arbitrator does not apply the law of a certain country as the law applicable to the contract he may nevertheless give effect to the mandatory rules of the law of that country if the contract or the parties have a close contact to the country in question especially when the arbitral award is likely to be enforced there, and if and insofar as under the law of that country those rules must be applied whatever be the law applicable to the contract':
reproduced in Lando, 'Conflict of Law Rules for Arbitrators', *Festschrift Zweigert* (1981), pp. 157, 176; a similar provision to the first alternative is adopted in Art. 7 (1) of the European Convention on the Law Applicable to Contractual Obligations, 1980; for arbitral practice, see Derains, 'Les Normes d'application immédiate dans la jurisprudence arbitrale internationale', *Mélanges Goldman* (1982), pp. 29, 38–40; see also the discussion in the *BP* award, 53 ILR 296.
[65] A not dissimilar approach is reflected also in Mayer, 'Mandatory Rules of Law in International Arbitration', *Arbitration International*, 2 (1988), pp. 274, 285, 292–3.
[66] *ICJ Pleadings*, 1952, p. 85. It was also claimed: 'In the case of a concession containing no clause in which the grantor State has expressly divested itself of the right of unilateral termination, there may even be an *implied* term that the concession may be terminated by lawful nationalization. In the other

Similar views are reflected among writers.[67] Most writers employ subjective arguments (i.e. referring to the will of the parties or the State's capacity to bind itself) suggesting that if a State can restrict the use of its prerogatives through a treaty, it can do so also through a contract.[68] This is sometimes combined with an objective argument, which emphasizes the legitimate expectations of the parties and principles such as good faith and estoppel.[69] Consequently, the stabilization clauses are seen to provide as it were a 'protection accrue, protection au second degré'.[70]

These views have been met with scepticism by others.[71] If the line of argument of the previous group was predominantly subjective, the second group typically resorts to objective arguments. A critic need only emphasize that State contracts are not treaties, because of the involvement of a private party.[72] Alternatively, it could be argued that there is no international customary rule which would make stabilization clauses a special case for the assessment of the legality of unilateral termination of a contract.[73] These views can also be criticized on the basis of the 'general principles of law', which are a source of law under Article 38(1)(c) of the Statute of the International Court of Justice. Instead of the loose rhetoric of *pacta sunt servanda*, which is prevalent, stricter considerations such as the constitutional principles of most legal systems tend to cast doubt on the ability of States to fetter their future legislative freedom by contracts.[74]

case, however, such as the present one, where there is an express term that the concession shall not be so terminated, there is clearly no room for the implied term as stated above: *expressum facit cessare tacitum*': ibid., p. 89.

[67] See Fischer, *Die Internationale Konzession* (1974), p. 410; Greenwood, 'State Contracts in International Law—The Libyan Oil Arbitrations', this *Year Book*, 53 (1982), pp. 27, 63; van Hecke, 'Contracts Between States and Foreign Private Persons', in Bernhardt (ed.), *Encyclopedia of Public International Law*, vol. 7, pp. 54, 56; Weil, loc. cit. above (n. 46), pp. 327–8; also White, *Nationalization of Foreign Property* (1961), p. 178 (though emphasizing time-limits in this respect).

[68] Weil, loc. cit. above (n. 22), at p. 233.

[69] Lalive, loc cit. above (n. 20), at pp. 59–60; also Weil, loc. cit. above (n. 46), at pp. 324–6.

[70] Lalive, loc. cit. above (n. 20), at p. 60; for a further discussion on the 'subjective' and 'objective'; ways of argument, see below, Section IV (b).

[71] Delaume, op. cit. above (n. 45), Booklet 8, p. 39; Goldman, 'Le Droit applicable selon la Convention de la B.I.R.D., du 18 mars 1965, pour le règlement des différends relatifs aux investissements entre Etats et ressortissants d'autre Etats', *Investissements étrangers et arbitrage entre Etats et personnes privées* (1969), pp. 133, 153.

[72] Delson, *The International Law Association, Report of the Forty-Eighth Conference, New York, 1958*, at p. 156; Friedmann, *Law in a Changing Society* (1959), p. 457.

[73] In the *Anglo-Iranian Oil Co.* case the British Government suggested the reverse. As an attempt to 'objectivize' the argument, it was claimed that the restriction of the exercise of sovereignty by contractual clauses was 'clearly established by international practice' and rested on 'well-recognized principles of international law'. See above, n. 66 and the accompanying text. Such a view is not, however, usually shared by writers. Mann, op. cit. above (n. 14), at p. 322, concludes: 'The Truth is that even in international law the express exemption from the effects of future legislation is redundant'; Foilloux, *La Nationalisation et le droit international public* (1962), pp. 302–3, emphasizes that the whole matter of distinguishing the stabilization clauses as a special case poses 'un faux problème'.

[74] 'It will have become clear to oil companies that the UK and Norwegian Governments are no more willing than their OPEC counterparts to stick rigidly to contracts that they deem unreasonably disadvantageous and that there is no absolute constitutional protection in either country for the principle of *pacta sunt servanda*': Daintith and Gault, 'Pacta Sunt Servanda and the Licensing and Taxation of North Sea Oil Production', *Cambrian Law Review*, 8 (1977), pp. 27, 42. For other such comparative

Moreover, stabilization clauses may be regarded as a derogation from the principle of State sovereignty in international law.[75]

In addition to the opposing viewpoints outlined above, a third position has emerged more recently. While it has the same origin as the second view, i.e. that stabilization clauses cannot make the legal situation different in kind as far as the question of international legality of unilateral termination is concerned, there is common ground with the first-mentioned view as well. On this new approach, stabilization clauses are not rendered meaningless, but are taken into consideration in the context of determining the amount of compensation. They gain a financial function. Judge Jiménez de Aréchaga, while rejecting the view that such provisions could deprive the State of legal power to terminate a concession, writes:

This does not mean that such stabilization clauses have no legal effect and may be considered as unwritten. An anticipated cancellation in violation of a contractual stipulation of such a nature would give rise to a special right to compensation; the amount of the indemnity would have to be much higher than in normal cases since the existence of such a clause constitutes a most pertinent circumstance which must be taken into account in determining the appropriate compensation. For instance, there would be a duty to compensate also for the prospective gains (*lucrum cessans*) to be obtained by a private party during the period that the concession still has to run.[76]

Whether stabilization clauses imply that lost future profits would always be recoverable, at least to their full extent, is uncertain, for, to date, the arbitral awards are unclear on this point. It suffices to say that this third position has certain advantages. On the one hand, it is easy to reconcile with the traditional view of the law of State responsibility, which does not consider contract breaches internationally unlawful *per se*. On the other hand, it gives effect to contractual practice. As stabilization clauses are a means of attracting foreign investors, they have an important market function. An outright rejection of all legal effects for such clauses may have undesirable policy implications, as such

studies, see Baloro, 'The Legal Status of Concession Agreement in International Law', *Comparative and International Law Journal of South Africa*, 19 (1986), pp. 410, 410–18; Flint, 'Foreign Investment and the New International Economic Order', in Chowdhury (ed.), *Permanent Sovereignty Over Natural Resources in International Law* (1984), pp. 144, 161–3; Wengler, 'Nouveaux aspects de la problématique des contrats entre Etats et personnes privées', *Revue belge de droit international*, 1978–9, pp. 415 ff. The problem is also displayed in the different emphases on this particular point between the *Texaco* and *Revere* cases. In the latter the Tribunal gave some effect to the constitutional principle that the State cannot fetter its future legislative freedom by a contract: 56 ILR at p. 281, 286. In the *Texaco* award, in turn, the only principles of Libyan law which were referred to were taken from the Civil Code ('The contract makes the law of the parties') or selectively chosen from the traditional Islamic law ('Muslims are bound by their contracts'): 53 ILR at pp. 472–3.

[75] Sornarajah, *The Pursuit of Nationalized Property* (1986), p. 93; in their comment on section 712 of the American Law Institute's *Restatement of the Foreign Relations Law of the United States* the reporters observed on stabilization clauses: 'Inclusion of such clauses may be resisted by some states, however, on the ground that they constitute a derogation from the state's sovereignty': *Restatement of the Law (Third)*, p. 215.

[76] Loc. cit. above (n. 33), at p. 307; see also Schachter, 'International Law in Theory and Practice', *Recueil des cours*, 178 (1982–V), pp. 9, 313–14; Geiger, 'Unilateral Change of Economic Development Agreements', *International and Comparative Law Quarterly*, 23 (1974), pp. 73, 99, 103.

investment could be unduly discouraged. Not dissimilar considerations, though expressed with caution and reservation, are reflected in the Secretary-General of the United Nations' report of 7 May 1981 on permanent sovereignty over natural resources:

A recurrent provision, even in very recent contracts, is the freezing of the tax regime applicable at the time of the negotiation. Some of the freezing clauses negotiated at present tie the hands of the Government for a very long period. Long and comprehensive 'freezing' clauses seem to run counter to the principle of permanent sovereignty over natural resources, although it may be conceivable that provisions to stabilize the fiscal regime for a reasonable period, so as to assure loan repayment, for example, can be found acceptable under specific conditions.[77]

An overview of contractual practice on stabilization clauses has been given above and, moreover, certain aspects relating to their legal effects have been considered. While stabilization clauses may not be a unique exception to the otherwise lawful termination of contracts, it would seem difficult to deprive them of all legal effect. In this respect, what has been considered above as the third position, put forward by Judge Jiménez de Aréchaga in particular, seems the most attractive. It is also in keeping with most arbitral practice. However, before this conclusion is too firmly adopted, the question of State sovereignty must be discussed.

IV. SOVEREIGNTY

(a) Sovereignty and Property

The original meaning of sovereignty is related to the idea of superiority. Etymologically, it stems from the Latin word '*supra*'. In legal and political theory the sovereign is the holder of ultimate power. In the modern world it is the State.[78]

In international law the most common meaning ascribed to sovereignty is the idea of independence. The classic definition given by Judge Huber in the *Island of Palmas* case (*Netherlands* v. *USA*) provides:

Sovereignty in the relations between States signifies independence. Independence in regard to a portion of the globe is the right to exercise therein, to the exclusion of any other State, the functions of a State.[79]

---

[77] E/C. 7/119, p. 24, para. 68. With regard to recent contractual practice relating to coal mining (in countries such as China, Colombia, Indonesia, Botswana and Tanzania) the Secretary-General's report of 7 April 1983 observes: 'In many of these contracts, Governments have delegated management to the mining companies. Fiscal regimes are comparatively favourable to companies and are generally protected by stabilization guarantees': E/C. 7/1983/5, p. 7.

[78] In general, see Wildhaber, 'Sovereignty and International Law', in Macdonald and Johnston (eds.), *The Structure and Process of International Law* (1983), pp. 425, 425–31.

[79] Permanent Court of Arbitration, 4 April 1928, *UN Reports of International Arbitral Awards*, vol. 2, pp. 829, 838. See also the individual opinion of Judge Anzilotti in the *Austro-German Customs Union* case, *PCIJ*, Series A/B, No. 41, p. 57 (advisory opinion of 5 September 1931).

Modern writers often emphasize that sovereignty is a relative notion.[80] From this perspective, it is 'sovereignty within law', giving effect to the idea of the rule of law in international society.[81] Indeed, a growing body of international regulation places restrictions of varying degrees on State behaviour in general. Not only is this true in the traditional relations between States ('external' sovereignty), but also within States ('internal' sovereignty). There is, moreover, the whole area of human rights, which sets standards for the treatment of individuals, aliens and nationals alike. Therefore, instead of emphasizing such ideas as independence or freedom, it is more realistic in view of the stage to which international law has evolved to perceive sovereignty as a legal power, or a bundle of powers regulated by law.[82] Hence, sovereignty is not an isolated 'thing', but a relational concept, a power among other powers.

Property, too, is often seen as providing a set of powers *vis-à-vis* other people (or States).[83] As such, it is a part of the same international legal structure as sovereignty. The relationship between the two sets of powers (i.e. sovereignty and property) has been a matter of continuous controversy in international law. The doctrinal debate has probably most often concerned the right of States to nationalize or expropriate foreign-owned property. In principle, such a right of action is recognized as a part of the legal powers inherent in statehood. However, these powers have not remained unfettered. Traditionally, it has been required that, in order to be lawful, a nationalization or expropriation has to be undertaken in the public interest, without discrimination, and with payment of compensation.[84] This implies that international law recognizes what is usually known as 'the social function of property'. Accordingly, property is not conceived purely as a des-

---

[80] Wildhaber, loc. cit. above (n. 78), at p. 473 and the authorities referred to therein.

[81] Larson, Jenks and others, *Sovereignty Within the Law* (1965), pp. 10–19.

[82] For an inspiring analysis, see Allott, 'Power Sharing in the Law of the Sea', *American Journal of International Law*, 77 (1983), pp. 1, 10–11, 26–7; cf. Kelsen, *General Theory of Law and State* (1949), pp. 348–9, who perceives national law as a 'delegation' by international law.

[83] Allott, loc. cit. (previous note), at p. 9.

[84] See, for instance, O'Connell, *International Law* (2nd edn., 1970), vol. 2, pp. 776–7; White, op. cit. above (n. 67), pp. 119–50, 183 ff. While the requirement of 'public interest' or 'public purpose' is often enumerated as one of the conditions for the lawfulness of expropriatory action, its practical relevance may turn out to be rather insignificant. In other words, in a system of sovereign States, the definition of 'public interest' in substantive terms tends to be elusive. Hence, it is the corporate definition which often subsists: public interest is what a State claims it to be. So, in the *Liamco* award, it was stated that '[m]otives are indifferent to international law, each State being free to judge for itself what it considers useful or necessary for the public good . . .': 62 ILR at p. 194. Alternatively, it may appear easier to argue in negative terms as the matter was put by the claimant in the *BP* arbitration: 'Whether the [Libyan] actions are characterised as not being for a public purpose, or as arbitrary or as abusive, is largely a question of terminology since the authorities often use them inter-changeably': *Memorial of the BP Exploration Company (Libya)*, part 2, 8 August 1972, p. 37, para. 140. Apart from discrimination, the absence of public purpose has only exceptionally constituted the reason for holding an expropriation to be unlawful. This was, however, confirmed in the *Walter Fletcher Smith* claim (*US* v. *Cuba*), Award of 2 May 1929 (C. Hale), *UN Reports of International Arbitral Awards*, vol. 2, pp. 913, 917. See also the *Letco* award, below, p. 346. Owing to the difficulties mentioned above, it has been suggested that expropriation should not be ruled unlawful solely on the ground of lack of a public purpose: White, op. cit. above (n. 67), at p. 150.

cription of a legal relationship between an owner and a thing, but rather within a wider societal context.[85] For this reason the notion of property is said to involve a 'tripartite' relationship: an owner, an object and a society.[86] This view is expressed in the UN Resolution 1803 (XVII) of 14 December 1962, which provides *inter alia*:

4. Nationalization, expropriation, or requisitioning shall be based on grounds or reasons of public utility, security or the national interest which are recognized as overriding purely individual or private interests, both domestic and foreign. In such cases the owner shall be paid appropriate compensation, in accordance with the rules in force in the State taking such measures in the exercise of its sovereignty and in accordance with international law.[87]

The idea of the social function of property not only relates to the immediate power relationship (lawful/unlawful acts *per se*), but most often its practical relevance bears on the standards of compensation. As Professor Brownlie suggests: 'It is all very well to say that nationalization is possible—providing prompt and adequate compensation is paid. In reality this renders any major economic or social programme impossible . . .'[88] Or, as Professor Rosalyn Higgins points out, in deciding on compensation one is really deciding where the loss shall lie. Is it to be borne by the individuals or by society?[89] As the question of compensation merits discussion beyond the scope of this article, it suffices to say that prima facie, the notion of 'appropriate' compensation goes further than 'full' compensation in giving effect to the idea of the social function of property.

Having described the relationship between sovereignty and poverty in general, it is necessary to consider whether it applies to contractual relationships.

(b) *The Exercise of Sovereignty and State Contracts—Polarity of Arguments*

In the earlier discussion on the effects of internationalization of contracts and stabilization clauses, the different forms of argument were mentioned. Ultimately, the notions of 'subjective' and 'objective' arguments address themselves to the question of State sovereignty and therefore some elaboration is required here.[90]

---

[85] Katzarov, *Théorie de la nationalisation* (1960), pp. 172–3; see also Seidl-Hohenveldern, 'The Social Function of Property and Property Protection in Present-Day International Law', in Karlshoven, Kuyper and Lammers (eds.), *Essays on the Development of the International Legal Order* (1980), pp. 77, 79.

[86] Kronfol, *Protection of Foreign Investment* (1972), p. 20.

[87] Reproduced in *International Legal Materials*, 2 (1963), p. 223.

[88] *Principles of Public International Law* (3rd edn., 1979), p. 537.

[89] 'The Taking of Property by the State: Recent Developments in International Law', *Recueil des cours*, 176 (1982–III), pp. 259, 277.

[90] For a comprehensive analysis of the game 'international legal argument', see Koskenniemi, 'Sovereignty: Prolegomena to a Study of the Structure of International Law as Discourse', *Juris Gentium*, vol. 4, nos. 1–2, pp. 71 ff.; id., *From Apology to Utopia: The Structure of International Legal Argument* (1989).

Sovereignty, in objectivist terms, is a principle of international law which provides for certain rights and powers.[91] Contracts, in turn, may be conceived as a type of property. This implies that, as far as the fundamental legal powers between the contracting parties are concerned, the same basic principles should apply as those which concern the international status of foreign-owned property in general. The core power relationship remains the same. In the context of expropriation, involving unilateral termination of contracts, this would imply that such action is lawful, provided that the above-mentioned general conditions (the requirement of public interest, non-discrimination, payment of compensation) are satisfied. This view is explicitly stated in the *Liamco* award and implied in a good number of other cases.

Instead of pursuing these ideas further, the focus will be on the subjective arguments—or, on the 'exercise' of sovereignty, as the conclusion of State contracts is often characterized. Some examples will be given below.

In the *Anglo-Iranian Oil Co.* case the following submission was made by the United Kingdom:

The right of expropriation for the purpose of nationalization or otherwise is admittedly an important right of sovereignty. Yet it does not follow that a State *cannot* for a defined period part with the *exercise* of that right in respect of any specific property or category of property or in relation to any class of persons. Thus, there is no doubt that State A *may* in a treaty concluded with State B bind itself not to nationalize in any circumstances . . . To give another example, the right to regulate immigration and the right to impose tariffs are important prerogatives of sovereignty. But a State *may* validly and with binding effect agree to a limitation or renunciation of these rights. The Government of the United Kingdom contends that with regard to nationalization or any other legislative measure affecting the property of foreigners, it is irrelevant that the limitation of the legislative freedom of the State—such as is most clearly expressed in Article 21 of the 1933 Concession Convention—is provided not in a treaty proper but in a contract with a foreign national.[92]

The *Aramco* Tribunal declared:

By reason of its very sovereignty within its territorial domain, the State possesses the legal *power* to grant rights which it forbids itself to withdraw before the end of the Concession, with the reservation of the Clauses of the Concession Agreement relating to its revocation. Nothing *can* prevent a State, in the exercise of its sovereignty, from binding itself irrevocably by the provisions of a concession and from granting to the concessionaire irretractable rights. Such rights have the character of acquired rights.[93]

---

[91] For a further discussion of the usage of sovereignty as a 'principle' of law, see id., 'General Principles: Reflections on Constructivist Thinking in International Law', *Oikeustiede-Jurisprudentia* (1985), pp. 117, 126–7, 142 ff.

[92] *ICJ Pleadings*, 1952, at p. 90 (emphasis added, footnotes omitted).

[93] 27 ILR at p. 168 (emphasis added).

Similar views are also expressed in *RCA* v. *China*. The Tribunal stated:

The Chinese Government *can* certainly sign away a part of its liberty of action, and this is also in the field of the establishment of international radio-telegraphic communications and of its cooperation therein. It *can* do so as well in an implicit manner, if a reasonable construction of its undertakings leads up to that conclusion.[94]

This line of argument appears most clearly in the *Texaco* award. In dealing with the notion of sovereignty, the Arbitrator first emphasized that the right to nationalize as such is unchallengeable as a rule of customary international law.[95] Nonetheless this was followed by an assertion for which no authority was cited, that 'the case is totally different where the State has concluded with a foreign contracting party an internationalized agreement'.[96] The Arbitrator went on to say that '[t]here is no doubt that in the exercise of its sovereignty, a State has the *power* to make international commitments'.[97] Regarding Libyan law, which was applicable as well as international law, it was held that 'the Libyan State *can* validly contract with subjects of foreign law'.[98] The public authority, the Tribunal added, 'is also *empowered* to enter into contracts . . .'. Moreover, '[t]here is no need to dwell at any great length on the existence and value of the principle under which a State *may*, within the framework of its sovereignty, undertake international commitments with respect to a private party. This rule results from the discretionary *competence* of the State in this area . . .'[99] In addition, treaties were invoked as an argument by analogy. Hence, the point was made that '[t]he right . . . *to undertake* commitments . . . with another State is unquestionable'. The Tribunal referred to the *Wimbledon* case, reiterating the view that 'sovereignty is not negated by the conclusion of a treaty but, quite the contrary, . . . the conclusion of a treaty is a *manifestation* of such sovereignty'.[100] While it was not suggested that a State contract should be equated with a treaty, the view expressed in the *Wimbledon* case had 'logically the same scope and significance' with respect to contracts.[101] The Tribunal concluded:

The result is that a State cannot invoke its sovereignty to disregard commitments freely undertaken through the exercise of this same sovereignty and cannot through

---

[94] *UN Reports of International Arbitral Awards*, vol. 3, at p. 1627 (emphasis added).

[95] 53 ILR at p. 469.

[96] Ibid., 470–1.

[97] Ibid., 471 (emphasis added).

[98] Ibid., 472 (emphasis added). In support of this, the Tribunal referred to the Koran ('Muslims are bound by their contracts') and Art. 147 (1) of the Civil Code ('The contract makes the law of the parties'): ibid.

[99] Ibid., 473 (emphasis added).

[100] Ibid. (emphasis added); for the *Wimbledon* case (*France, Great Britain, Italy and Japan* v. *Germany*), judgment of 17 August 1923, see *PCIJ*, Series A, No. 1 (1923) p. 25; similar formulation is also used in the *Exchange of Greek and Turkish Populations* (advisory opinion, 21 February 1925), *PCIJ*, Series B, No. 10 (1925), p. 21.

[101] 53 ILR 389, 473.

measures belonging to its internal order make null and void the rights of the contracting party which has performed its various obligations under the contract.[102]

The pattern of thought expressed in the *Texaco* award is closely followed in the *AGIP* case, decided by an ICSID Tribunal. Likewise, it was emphasized that State practice undoubtedly gives confirmation to the right of nationalization. In spite of this, the Tribunal continued, positive international law also recognizes that by concluding an international agreement with a private individual 'the State *exercises* sovereign powers from the moment that *consent* is freely given'.[103] Moreover, with regard to the stabilization clauses, the same idea was pursued further. As these clauses had been freely accepted by the State, the Tribunal emphasized that they 'do not affect the principle of its sovereign legislative and regulatory powers, since it retains both in relation to those, whether nationals or foreigners, with whom it has not entered into such obligations, and that, in the present case, changes in the legislative and regulatory arrangements stipulated in the agreement simply cannot be invoked against the other contracting party'.[104] This was the same as what in the *Texaco* award was described as the distinction between 'enjoyment and exercise' of sovereignty.[105]

Similar views are expressed by several writers. Thus, Professor Weil emphasizes that by concluding contracts with foreign companies 'un Etat, loin de limiter sa souveraineté, ne fait que l'exercer . . .'.[106] Elsewhere, the author elaborates further:

La thèse de 'inaliénabilité des prérogatives de souveraineté' comporte une certaine part de tautologie, toute la question étant précisément de savoir si l'Etat *peut* ou non renoncer valablement à certains éléments de sa compétence. Cette thèse se fonde au surplus sur une conception quelque peu dépassée de la souveraineté: il y a longtemps que l'on sait que c'est précisément par une *manifestation* de sa souveraineté que l'Etat *peut* se lier par un traité ou un contrat, et l'on ne voit pas pourquoi il en irait autrement de l'engagement de l'Etat de renoncer à exercer telle ou telle de ses prérogatives: le principe *Pacta sunt servanda* n'est pas une négation de la souveraineté. L'argument tiré du caractère soi-disant inaliénable de la souveraineté ne dépasse donc guère le stade des explications purement verbales.[107]

In discussing the notion of permanent sovereignty over natural resources,

---

[102] Ibid., 475.
[103] *International Legal Materials*, 21 (1982), at p. 735 (emphasis added).
[104] Ibid., pp. 735–6.
[105] 53 ILR at pp. 481–2.
[106] Weil, loc. cit. above (n. 22), at p. 122.
[107] Weil, 'Les Clauses de stabilisation ou d'intangibilité insérées dans les accords de développement économique', *Mélanges Rousseau* (1975), pp. 302, 324 (emphasis added). Similar argument has been relied on by many others. See, for instance, Fischer, op. cit. above (n. 67), at p. 410; Greenwood, loc. cit. above (n. 67), at p. 61; Higgins, loc. cit. above (n. 89), at p. 311; Kojanec, loc. cit. above (n. 16), at p. 338; Kissam and Leach, 'Sovereign Expropriation of Property and Abrogation of Concession Contracts', *Fordham Law Review*, 28 (1959–60), pp. 177, 199; Kronfol, op. cit. above (n. 86), p. 83; Shawcross, 'Problems of Foreign Investment in International Law', *Recueil des cours*, 102 (1961–I), pp. 335, 351; Schwarzenberger, 'The Protection of British Property Abroad', *Current Legal Problems*, 5 (1952), pp. 295, 313.

Dr J.-F. Lalive goes so far as to suggest that it might even 'vider la souveraineté de son contenu puisqu'un Etat ne pourrait plus s'engager durablement et valablement . . .'.[108]

As reflected in the above examples, the subjective viewpoint emphasizes the ability of a sovereign to bind itself. It relies on the assumptions that a State has the 'capacity' or 'power', so that it 'can' or 'may' conclude contracts and hence contractual obligations are actually a 'manifestation' of sovereignty, not its negation. The objective point of view perceives sovereignty in opposite terms. As an example one could cite the argument of the Government of Iran concerning the nationalization of the Anglo-Iranian Oil Company in 1951. In the so-called 'hot oil' litigation that followed before a Japanese Court, it was claimed successfully that:

> The Nationalization Law . . . naturally superseded the Concession Agreement and rendered it no longer valid. It was in the *exercise* of the sovereignty of an independent State that Iran enacted her industrial nationalization Law . . .'.[109]

The objective view emphasizes the sovereign's right to expropriate property, 'including contractual rights previously granted by itself', as was held by the ICSID Tribunal in the *AMCO* case.[110] If taken to its extreme, this would imply that a State may revoke its contracts at will.

A central feature of the legal discourse is that the opposing arguments tend to go in circles. A power of a sovereign to terminate contracts is turned into its power to conclude them, or *vice versa*. Facing this difficulty, tribunals may be tempted to avoid adopting a particular view on principle.[111] These problems are epitomized in the *Aminoil* arbitration. There the company pursued a predominantly subjective approach. It argued with regard to the stabilization clauses that, by 'exercising' its sovereignty, the host State had renounced its right of nationalization for a period of time.[112] The Government claimed the opposite.[113] Though it was the latter view which

---

[108] Lalive, 'Un Grand arbitrage pétrolier entre un gouvernement et deux sociétés privées étrangères', *Clunet*, 104 (1977), pp. 319, 343.

[109] *Anglo-Iranian Oil Co* v. *Idemitsu Kosan Kabushiki Kaisha*, District Court of Tokyo, 1953, 20 ILR 305, 307 (emphasis added); for a similar argument made on behalf of Iran before the International Court of Justice, see *Anglo-Iranian Oil Co.* case, *ICJ Pleadings*, 1952, at pp. 495–7.

[110] *International Legal Materials*, 24 (1985), at p. 1029.

[111] For instance by proceduralizing the issues, cf. Koskenniemi, loc. cit. above (n. 90), at p. 98.

[112] 'Just as a right in general to nationalize or to expropriate may be admitted to exist as a power of the State, it is submitted that the *exercise* of this right may be renounced for a period by virtue of the same sovereign power. Such a renunciation is a choice of means by the State as to the way in which it will exercise its powers—not a denial that such powers exist. When this course is elected—as clearly is the case in a contract with a foreign private party containing a guarantee or stabilization clause—it must be given effect. Good faith and respect for rights thus granted demand no less': *Pleadings* (Book 1), Aminoil Memorial, 2 June 1980, vol. I (text), p. 57 (emphasis sustained, footnote omitted).

[113] In considering the legality of the Nationalization Law (No. 124 of 1977), it emphasized sovereign prerogatives under constitutional law and the right to nationalize under international law, if the conditions of public interest, non-discrimination and the payment of compensation are fulfilled: *Pleadings* (Book 5), Government's Counter-Memorial, December 1980, pp. 133–484. On the matter of contractual undertakings it was stated: 'If the Government, acting in good faith, considers it to be in the best interests of the State to take over a private company operating within the State—whether it is in contractual relationship with that company or not—then the Government may do so, providing that it complies

finally prevailed, an element of ambiguity remains on the Tribunal's position on principle. It tried to pursue a kind of intermediate line, putting forward rather peculiar and unconvincing arguments as to the parties' intentions.[114]

Upon closer analysis of the subjective argument, the question arises as to how the binding force of contracts can be justified solely by reference to the will of the sovereign.[115] In terms of juridical logic, even if a State 'can' conclude contracts, it does not follow that it 'ought' not to revoke them. On the contrary, the opposite—that 'ought' implies 'can'—would be widely accepted.[116] Consequently, even if one characterizes the conclusion of a contract as an 'exercise' of sovereignty, the problem of its binding force still remains.

While the conclusions derived from the 'exercise' of sovereignty remain ambiguous, it does not mean that they should be ignored. Although uncertain, they are symptomatic and suggest that the phenomenon of State contracting involves issues of social morality requiring legal responses. That is, in the modern world it is accepted that power entails responsibility and this aspect gains further significance when States enter into contracts with private parties as a matter of large-scale social practice. However, to take these considerations into account requires a less technical approach.

Finally, it should be noted that the realms of subjective and objective arguments of sovereignty are not confined to isolated doctrinal argument but reflect corresponding viewpoints on related issues. What follows is the division of arbitral practice into two sets of cases with different responses on whether unilateral terminations of contracts should be considered internationally unlawful acts or not. Basically, this divison of views implies that there are two different contract models involved. The subjective approach is related to classical contract thinking, usually known as the will-theory of contracts. Indeed, the preoccupation with the aspect of the 'competence' or 'power' of a sovereign to conclude contracts, at the expense of more substantive legal issues, suggests that the will-theory is assumed as the self-evident starting point. A more objectivist emphasis of sovereignty, not limiting it to a power merely to conclude contracts, but considering it also as the basis for their lawful termination, forces one to a somewhat different view of contrac-

---

with its own constitutional requirements and with the requirements of international law . . . To this act of a sovereign government, the private company cannot oppose its contractual rights, entered into thirty years previously by the Ruler of a country which was then under foreign protection. This is so even if such rights are bolstered up by a clause (such as Article 17 of the original colonial-type 1948 Concession Agreement) declaring that they are to endure for the life of the contract, unless the private company agrees otherwise': ibid., p. 144.

[114] 66 ILR at p. 589.

[115] See generally Fitzmaurice, 'Some Problems Regarding the Formal Sources of International Law', *Symbolae Verzijl* (1958), pp. 153 ff.; Lauterpacht, *The Function of Law in International Community* (1933), pp. 407–23; more closely related to the present area, see also Verhoeven, 'Droit international des contrats et droit des gens', *Revue belge de droit international*, 14 (1978–9), pp. 209, 220, note 18. Therein similar difficulties are identified *vis-à-vis* the attempts to establish the international status of a private party through a unilateral contractual recognition of a State.

[116] On the latter, see Atiyah, *Promises, Morals and Law* (1981), pp. 155–7.

tual obligations, with less emphasis on the will of the parties. This is more appropriate to what is known as the reliance-theory of contracts.

V. Control over Natural Resources

The discussion of State sovereignty requires a special comment on the question of natural resources. The struggle over their control is probably best known to international law through the concept of 'permanent sovereignty over natural resources'. Since it first emerged in 1952, the notion has been one of the most frequently employed legal precepts in the debate on the relations between host States and transnational companies. Its origin and evolution owe much to the United Nations Resolutions.[117] Particular mention should be made of Resolutions 1803 (XVII) of 14 December 1962,[118] 3021 (S-VI) of 1 May 1974 (Declaration on the Establishment of a New International Economic Order)[119] and 3281 (XXIX) of 12 December 1974 (Charter of Economic Rights and Duties of States).[120] The latter two instruments consider permanent sovereignty within a wider context of economic and legal relations, whose reform has been vigorously advocated by developing countries. One should note, however, that the Charter, whilst in many respects reflecting the present customary law, has not gained full recognition as regards its treatment of foreign investment. In the hope of achieving a general consensus and compromise, Resolution 1803 is usually seen to represent a more broadly-based opinion.[121]

Although the UN Resolutions have provided the main medium for the propagation of the notion of permanent sovereignty, reference should also

[117] The first one was Resolution 626 (VII) of 21 December 1952, which stated that 'the rights of peoples freely to use and exploit their natural wealth and resources is inherent in their sovereignty and is in accordance with the purposes and principles of the Charter of the United Nations'. For detailed accounts of the UN resolutions, see Gess, 'Permanent Sovereignty Over Natural Resources', *International and Comparative Law Quarterly*, 13 (1964), pp. 398 ff.; Rosenberg, *Le Principe de souveraineté des États sur leurs ressources naturelles* (1983), pp. 100–224; Chowdhury, 'Permanent Sovereignty Over Natural Resources', in Hussain and Chowdhury (eds.), *Permanent Sovereignty Over Natural Resources. Principle and Practice* (1984), pp. 1 ff.

[118] Reproduced in *International Legal Materials*, 2 (1963), p. 223.

[119] Reproduced in ibid., 13 (1974), p. 715.

[120] Reproduced in ibid., 14 (1975), p. 251.

[121] *Aminoil* award, 66 ILR 546, 588; *Revere Copper*, 56 ILR 258, 279; *Sedco, Inc.* v. *National Iranian Oil Company and the Islamic Republic of Iran*, Iran-United States Claims Tribunal, interlocutory award No. ITC 59–129–3 of 27 March 1986, Chamber Three (Mangård, Brower, Ansari), *Iran-US Claims Tribunal Reports*, vol. 10, pp. 180, 186; *Amoco International Finance Corp.*, Award, ibid., vol. 15, at p. 223, para. 116. The controversy has been focused on Art. 2(2)(c) of the Charter, concerning expropriation. Though it provides for appropriate compensation, no reference other than to the law of a host State is made. In the roll-call vote this provision was given 104 in favour to 16 against, with 6 abstentions, whereas the Charter was adopted by 118 to 6, with 10 abstentions. For a close scrutiny of the voting patterns, see *Texaco* award, 53 ILR at pp. 487–93. In addition, authors have had doubts about its legal value. For instance, Brownlie, 'Legal Status of Natural Resources in International Law (Some Aspects)', *Recueil des cours*, 162 (1979–I), pp. 245, 268, refers to its 'strong programmatic, political and didactic flavour'. See also, Virally, 'La Charte des droits et devoirs économiques des Etats', *Annuaire français de droit international*, 1974, pp. 57, 68–70.

be made to other instruments such as the two International Human Rights Covenants of 1966, which clearly embrace the concept of permanent sovereignty over natural resources.[122] The human rights aspect ('people's rights') perceives the notion as part of the history of decolonization and parallel to the principle of national self-determination.[123]

There is no doubt nowadays that the concept of permanent sovereignty has been incorporated as a principle of international law. The uncertainty lies rather in its impact on the body of traditional international law. What are the so-called corollary rights? Faced with this question one may be inclined to either of two extremes—to minimize or maximize its legal content. On the one hand, it has been shown above that emphasis on the conclusion of contracts as an 'exercise' of permanent sovereignty causes the concept to become marginalized to the extent that it becomes almost meaningless. On the other hand, some have considered it as a peremptory rule of law (*jus cogens*).[124] This view—if adopted—would indeed give it legal relevance, but it has not gained sufficient support in practice.[125]

If the two 'extremes' are excluded, the meaning of permanent sovereignty appears to be difficult to define. In fact, any kind of stipulative definition of it seems quite out of place. This may not be very surprising in an area such as the one under discussion, which, for more than two decades, has been a real battlefield of legal ideas. Hence, the notion is often described in fairly broad terms.[126] Rather than defining the issue specifically,

---

[122] International Covenant on Economic, Social and Cultural Rights, Art. 1, para. 2; International Covenant on Civil and Political Rights, Art. 1, para. 2: 'All peoples may, for their own ends, freely dispose of their natural wealth and resources without prejudice to any obligations arising out of international economic co-operation based upon the principal of mutual benefit, and international law. In no case may a people be deprived of their own means of subsistence': reproduced in Brownlie, *Basic Documents in International Law* (3rd edn., 1983), pp. 258, 270. The principle is incorporated also in the Vienna Convention on Succession of States in respect of Treaties, 23 August 1978, Art. 13, reproduced in *American Journal of International Law*, 72 (1978), p. 971.

[123] Res. 1314 (XIII) of 12 December 1958 mentions it as 'a basic constituent' of the right to self-determination; also Resolution 3281 (XXIX) of 15 January 1975, Art. 1 (the Charter of Economic Rights and Duties of States). For an elaboration on this perspective in general, see Muchlinski, 'The Right to Economic Self-Determination', *Essays for Clive Schmithoff* (1983), pp. 73 ff.; Rosenberg, op. cit. above (n. 117), pp. 131–48.

[124] Jiménez de Aréchaga, loc. cit. above (n. 33), at p. 297; also Giardina, 'State Contracts: National Versus International Law', *Italian Yearbook of International Law*, 5 (1980–1), pp. 147, 164–5.

[125] For instance, see *Aminoil* case, *International Legal Materials*, 21 (1982), at p. 1021. The most elaborate discussion on the question may be found in the *Texaco* award. Interestingly, the Arbitrator did not reject the *jus cogens* aspect outright, but regarded it in temporal terms. Thus the relevant criterion was whether the State was 'alienated'—over a period of time—from its natural resources. However, this was found not to be the case here: 53 *ILR* at 482.

[126] The report of the Secretary-General on permanent sovereignty over natural resources, 25 February 1985, expresses the central idea, stating that the principle 'has been understood to imply the freedom of each country to dispose of its natural resources in accordance with its priorities, policies and objectives. It is also taken for granted that a country's natural resources shall be used to make the optimal contribution to national economic development': E/C. 7/1985/8 p. 4, para. 2; Brownlie, loc. cit. above (n. 121), at p. 271: 'Loosely speaking, permanent sovereignty is the assertion of the acquired rights of the host state, which are not defeasible by contract or, perhaps, even by international agreement'; Hossain and Chowdhury (eds.), *Permanent Sovereignty over Natural Resources*, vol. 13 (1984): 'At the core of the concept of permanent sovereignty is the inherent and overriding right of a state to control and dispose of the natural resources in its territory for the benefit of its own people.'

Resolution 1803 merely mentions nationalization, expropriation and compensation in this context (section 4). Moreover, it provides that 'foreign investment agreements freely entered into by, or between, sovereign States shall be observed in good faith . . .' (section 8).[127] It has been suggested that the real significance of the concept of permanent sovereignty can only be understood by examining its treatment on a case by case basis.[128] This is, in fact, the approach adopted in contemporary arbitral practice. Two questions arise in this context. The first concerns the scope of the notion of permanent sovereignty. The second relates to its actual implications in terms of law, which is considered further below.[129]

(a) *The Scope of Permanent Sovereignty over Natural Resources*

The question of who controls natural resources is a central issue in any discussion thereon. The concept of permanent sovereignty expresses the idea that natural resources should be controlled by the State in which they are located. The emphasis on the right to exercise permanent sovereignty stems from the past economic and political history of most developing countries. Since the process of decolonization, in particular, the shift of controlling power in favour of host States has been witnessed very often in favour of take-overs of foreign-owned activities in natural resource production. Many of the leading cases in recent arbitral practice arise out of this classic situation (for instance, *Texaco*,[130] *Liamco*,[131] *Aminoil*,[132] *BP*,[133] *Revere Copper*[134]). No arbitral tribunal has ever doubted that such situations give rise to issues within the scope of the concept of permanent sovereignty, although the views on the substantive legal consequences of this may vary. Conversely, certain activities can be readily excluded from the penumbra of the permanent sovereignty concept, namely those which do not directly relate to natural resources, such as certain types of manufacturing (*Benvenuti and Bonfant*[135]), various aspects of tourism (*SPP (Middle East) Ltd.* v. *Egypt (Pyramid Oasis)*[136] and *AMCO Asia*[137]) or

---

[127] This heterogeneity of elements within a single instrument results from the necessity of compromise between opposing interests. For a further discussion, see especially Rosenberg, op. cit. above (n. 117), pp. 209 ff.; also Sornarajah, op. cit. above (n. 75), at p. 121.

[128] Schachter, *Sharing of World's Resources* (1977), p. 125.

[129] p. 347.

[130] 53 ILR 389.

[131] 62 ILR 140.

[132] 66 ILR 546.

[133] 53 ILR 296.

[134] 56 ILR 258.

[135] *International Legal Materials*, 21 (1982), p. 740.

[136] Ibid. 22 (1983), p. 752.

[137] Ibid. 24 (1985), p. 1022. In this award Resolution 1803 of 1962 was mentioned, but clearly only as general evidence of the fundamental right to nationalize, which the award discussed *obiter*: ibid. at p. 1029.

transport and telecommunications (*RCA* v. *Czechoslovakia*;[138] *RCA* v. *China*[139]).

However, any attempt to narrow the scope of the notion further is considerably more difficult. On the other hand, it would seem inappropriate to extend the notion indiscriminately to all cases related to natural resources.

It is arguable that the notion of permanent sovereignty properly applies only to situations concerning control over the production itself—in other words, to what in business jargon are called 'upstream' rather than 'downstream' activities. One reason to restrict the notion thus may be found in the structural characteristics of international law. Production activities are usually (but not inevitably) located on the territory of a single State. Consequently, natural resource production is most susceptible to the exertion of entire legal (and political) control by that State. In other cases, such as transport or marketing, the activities do not necessarily take place within a single sovereign State. For this reason alone, any attempt to exert permanent sovereignty over 'all economic activities' (Charter of Economic Rights and Duties of States, Article 2 (1)) could certainly be perceived as 'too much of a good thing',[140] and might result in a clash between two States both purporting to exercise sovereignty.

Moreover, the treatment of 'downstream' activities as something beyond the proper scope of permanent sovereignty has support in the law of sovereign immunities. There are recent cases which seem to imply that a similarly narrow scope is appropriate, albeit not mandatory, in drawing the distinction between public acts (*jure imperii*) and private acts (*jure gestionis*) of States. Accordingly, in disputes closely related to production activities a plea of sovereign immunity may succeed, whereas in cases of sale of natural resources it has been refused in both European[141] and American

---

[138] *American Journal of International Law,* 30 (1936), p. 523.

[139] Ibid., p. 535.

[140] Stanford, 'International Law and Foreign Investment', in Macdonald, Johnston and Morris (eds.), *International Law and Policy of Human Welfare* (1978), pp. 471, 478.

[141] In the *National Iranian Oil Company Revenues from Oil Sales* case, Federal Republic of Germany, Federal Constitutional Court, 12 April 1983, 65 ILR 215, 221, the Court ruled: 'The funds had arisen in connection with *sales agreements* and therefore not in the course of sovereign activity' (emphasis added). A similar approach is reflected in the *National Iranian Oil Company Pipelines Contracts* case, Superior Provincial Court (Oberlandesgericht) of Frankfurt am Main, 4 May 1982, 65 ILR 212, 214. Referring to 'oil related activities', the defendant invoked sovereign immunity. In accordance with Res. 1803 of 1962, it was argued, the exploitation of oil was assigned to the 'inner sphere of sovereignty'. The Court, apparently considering that the various stages in the oil business are legally relevant, rejected the plea 'for the simple reason that the present case does not involve the *actual exploitation of oil resources* by the defendant in the attachment proceedings. The parties are in dispute over the financial performance of contracts for the building of oil and gas pipelines. In this respect, moreover, the defendant contracted with the plaintiff on a purely private commercial basis (contracts of work). It did not carry out any oil-related activities on a sovereign basis. The conclusion of the contracts for oil and gas pipelines was at most a preliminary step or a sequel to possible sovereign activity' (emphasis added). One may also mention the French decision in *Chilean Copper Corp.* v. *Braden Copper Co.,* 29 November 1972, Tribunal de grande instance de Paris, *International Legal Materials,* 12 (1973), pp. 182, 188. Following the nationalization of El Teniente copper mine, Braden had attached the proceeds of sales by the Chilean Copper Corp., to which its assets had been transferred. Chilean Copper

Court practice.[142] Although it was commonplace during the 1960s and 70s to nationalize or re-negotiate concessions relating to production activities, this did not threaten the position of transnational corporations in other areas such as marketing. Business has continued, even between the same parties, although often it is conducted somewhat differently.[143] In economic terms the distinction is valid, particularly with regard to the oil industry. It is axiomatic that whoever controls oil production controls the oil market. While States are not reluctant to share in any extra gains derived from their involvement in marketing, their primary focus has been to control production. Oil production has been the key to determining the price of oil.[144] Thus, it is—broadly speaking—at the 'upper' end of the process that the strong governmental interests lie. The involvement of foreign companies in the marketing function merely increases the price. It follows that the confrontation of two strongly opposed interests, typical in traditional concessions, is often far removed in the case of sales agreements.

Arbitral practice tends to follow that of the Courts in assuming a restrictive approach to the notion of permanent sovereignty. In the *AGIP* case, decided by an ICSID Tribunal, an Italian company which entered into an oil distribution agreement with the Government of the Congo in January 1974 was nationalized in April 1975. The Tribunal did not refer to the concept of permanent sovereignty over natural resources.[145] Nor was the

moved to vacate the attachment and invoked sovereign immunity. The Court stated that 'for the carrying out of its purpose the Chilean Copper Corporation proceeds specially in international transactions according to the ways and forms of private law of business; that thus the *contracts of sale* signed with Trefimetaux and the Groupement d'Importation des Metaux exclude any recourse to the methods which are usually connected with the public power . . .' (emphasis added).

[142] A highly complicated situation arose in *International Association of Machinists and Aerospace Workers* v. *Organization of Petroleum Exporting Countries et al.,* United States, Court of Appeals, Ninth Circuit, 6 July 1981, amended, 24 July 1981, 66 ILR 413. In this case the plaintiff brought an action against OPEC and its member States alleging that their price setting activities had violated United States anti-trust laws. The action against the member States had been dismissed by the District Court (63 ILR at 284) on the ground that control over natural resources is primarily a governmental function and as such entitled to sovereign immunity. The decision was confirmed, but the Court of Appeals preferred to base it on the act of State doctrine. It stated (p. 417) *inter alia*: 'The importance of the alleged price-fixing activity to the OPEC Nations cannot be ignored. Oil revenues represent their only significant source of income. Consideration of their sovereignty cannot be separated from their near total dependence upon oil. We find that these concerns are appropriately addressed by application of the act of State doctrine.' The case has been followed in *In the Matter of the Complaint of Sedco, Inc.,* US District Court for the Southern District of Texas, 1982, *International Legal Materials,* 21 (1982), pp. 318, 325 (emphasis added). It was ruled: 'The Court must regard carefully a sovereign's conduct with respect to its natural wealth. A very basic attribute of sovereignty is the control over its mineral resources and *short of actually selling these resources on the world market,* decisions and conduct concerning them are uniquely governmental in nature . . . Because the nature of Pemex' act in determining the extent of Mexico's natural resources was uniquely sovereign, this Court finds that the commercial activity exception to the FSIA, [sect.] 1605 (a)(2), is inapplicable to the facts presented by this case.'

[143] See generally, *Transnational Corporations in World Development: Third Survey* (1983), pp. 197, 209; Hossain, *Law and Policy in Petroleum Development* (1979), p. 40; Wälde, 'Third World Mineral Development in Crisis', *Journal of World Trade Law,* 19 (1985), pp. 3, 24–5: 'A characteristic feature of many compensation settlements is the continued presence of the nationalized investor, albeit in the role of a contractor supplying management, services and purchasing the output.'

[144] Luard, *The Management of the World Economy* (1983), p. 151.

[145] For a more comprehensive discussion of the case, see below, n. 159.

notion mentioned in the *Aramco* or *Sapphire* cases. The dispute in the former, although involving a traditional oil concession, did not concern the production itself; it was emphasized that the validity of the concession was not questioned, and that the dispute was 'strictly confined to the right of transportation by sea'.[146] The *Sapphire* case also concerned an oil concession agreement, concluded between the National Iranian Oil Company (NIOC) and a Canadian company in June 1958. The agreement distinguished between two periods: the first concerned prospecting activities and the second the extraction and sale of oil.[147] The project did not last into the second period as the disputes arose during the early stage of oil prospecting. By the end of 1958 NIOC had started claiming that prior consent was needed for every operation, which claim the court found contrary to the letter and spirit of the agreement. NIOC made baseless complaints and adopted an entirely negative attitude to the project. It also refused to take into consideration the expenses already incurred by the concessionaire. NIOC's conduct was held to constitute a flagrant breach of contract.[148]

From the point of view of permanent sovereignty it is arguable that prospecting activities are at most a 'preliminary step', prior to the actual production.[149] While it may be that in purely commercial terms natural resource activities form a unified whole, from the point of view of host States various stages may be perceived differently. In general the involvement of foreign companies in oil prospecting has not met with much discouragement from governments, at least in recent times. Foreign involvement in production, on the other hand, has been more problematic, as the State practice relating to large-scale nationalizations and re-negotiations of production activities from the middle of the 1960s up until 1980 suggests.[150] The fact that neither the *Aramco* nor the *Sapphire* award includes any explicit reference to the concept of permanent sovereignty is striking considering the dates of the awards (decided in 1958 and 1963

---

[146] 27 ILR at pp. 144–5, 177.

[147] 35 ILR at p. 137.

[148] Ibid., pp. 178–80.

[149] Cf. *National Iranian Oil Company Pipelines Contracts* case, above, n. 141; in the enforcement proceedings following the *Sapphire* award, NIOC's plea for sovereign immunity did not succeed. See *NV Cabolet* v. *National Iranian Oil Company*, Court of Appeal, The Hague, 28 November 1968, *International Legal Materials*, 9 (1970), p. 152. On the other hand, *In the Matter of the Complaint of Sedco*, loc. cit. above (n. 142), which also concerned oil exploration activities, sovereign immunity was granted. One may notice, however, that the dispute took place in the highly sensitive circumstances following the 1979 oil disaster in the Bay of Campeche which polluted the beaches of Texas. For a critical analysis of the case, see Delaume, 'Economic Development and Sovereign Immunity', *American Journal of International Law*, 79 (1985), pp. 319, 326–9.

[150] Since the late 1970s many of the Latin American countries, such as Brazil, Argentina and Chile, have awarded contracts for oil exploration to foreign companies. In Vietnam, also, exploration contracts with foreign companies have been negotiated. In Sri Lanka and Syria, where the States have retained their monopolies on petroleum exploration, such contracts have been signed with Western companies. The same has taken place in China and India. See *Permanent Sovereignty Over Natural Resources*, Report of the Secretary-General of 14 March 1979, E/C. 7/99, pp. 9–10; Report of 7 May 1981, E/C. 7/119, pp. 9–10; on the variation of interests depending on the stages of petroleum activities, see Hossain, op. cit. above (n. 143), at pp. 43–54.

respectively). Resolution 626 (VII) of 21 December 1952, the first United Nations instrument on the matter, had been passed well before the dates of these awards. In contrast, at least two municipal courts had by then referred to it in dealing with the classic case of nationalization of foreign-owned production activities.[151]

The main aim of the notion of permanent sovereignty has been to maintain national control over natural resources. It is sometimes regarded as a corollary to the principle of national self-determination. On a restrictive view, it would be difficult to disagree with the suggestion that the substitution of one private exploiter for another may be an exercise of permanent sovereignty over natural resources. However, viewed more broadly, in the final analysis the resource remains under the control of a foreign corporation, albeit quite possibly on terms which are enhanced from the State's point of view. In this sense, at least, such contractual abrogations appear alien to the exercise of permanent sovereignty over natural resources.

In general, such incidents happen not infrequently,[152] although the present discussion is confined to the scope of the notion of permanent sovereignty alone. A good example in this respect is the *Aramco* award. One

---

[151] This had occurred in the so-called 'hot oil' litigation following the Iranian nationalization of the Anglo-Iranian Oil Company. See *Anglo-Iranian Oil Company* v. *Idemitsu Kosan Kabushiki Kaisha*, High Court of Tokyo, 1953, 20 ILR at p. 313; *Anglo-Iranian Oil Company* v. *SUPOR Company*, Civil Court of Rome, 13 September 1954, 22 ILR 23, 40–1, where it was ruled: 'The General Assembly of the United Nations, at its meeting of December 21, 1952—less than one month after the date of the Iranian Law of November 26, 1952—passed a Resolution recommending that individual States should not be prevented from exploiting their natural resources. It is evident that the decision of the United Nations at that meeting, taking into consideration the date when it was taken and the international situation to which it related, constitutes a clear recognition of the international lawfulness of the Persian Nationalization Laws.' Six months after its adoption, the Resolution had also been invoked by Guatemala in support of her nationalization of a subsidiary of the United Fruit Company: Hyde, 'Permanent Sovereignty Over Natural Wealth and Resources', *American Journal of International Law*, 50 (1956), p. 854.

[152] In such a context it was stated in *Radio Corporation of America* v. *Czechoslovakia*, *American Journal of International Law*, 30 (1936), pp. 523, 534: 'When a public institution enters into an agreement with a private person or a private company, it must be assumed that the institution has intended by this agreement to benefit its citizens. But that this expectation sometimes proves to fail in not giving the country as large a profit as was expected, cannot be considered sufficient reason for releasing that public institution from its obligations as signatory of said agreement.' In *Radio Corporation of America* v. *China*, 13 April 1935 (*Hamel, Hubert, Furrer*), ibid., pp. 535, 541, the Tribunal emphasized 'utmost *bona fides*' in the case of a partnership or joint venture, and continued: 'Such a contract is violated if one of the parties initiates a direct joint activity on parallel lines with a competing third party. Even if not explicitly stipulated, such an obligation will then have to be implied.' In *Mojzesz Lubelski* v. *The State of Burundi*, *Jurisprudence du Port d'Anvers* (1969), p. 82, a three-year concession had been granted in 1965, which conferred on the company a right to buy gold and diamonds on the territory of the State. Only two weeks later this was cancelled by an administrative decision. The concession was considered to be an administrative contract governed by the law of Burundi. While the Tribunal admitted that its powers did not entail the review of the motives for cancellation (p. 91), it did take notice (p. 85) that '[l]e seul motif donné était l'existence "d'une autre convention passée entre le gouvernement précédent et un groupe de personnes"'. As an extreme case one could mention the situation where the very power to annul a contract would lie outside a government. With regard to such a situation the Permanent Court of International Justice has stated that 'the safeguard against ill-considered expropriation which exists when the initiative is in the hands of a State, which can only expropriate for reasons of public utility, was seriously impaired': *Mavrommatis Jerusalem Concessions* case, judgment of 26 March 1925, *PCIJ*, Series A, No. 5, p. 40.

should emphasize that in this case it was not simply a question of a confrontation of national interests with those of the company. The essence of the dispute was that a new contract concerning oil transportation had been concluded subsequently with another foreigner, Mr Aristotle Onassis.[153] It is possible that similar facts lay behind the *Sapphire* dispute as well, although the Tribunal did not elaborate on this point.[154] In the *Valentine Petroleum* arbitration, Valentine Petroleum and Chemical Corporation, an American company, signed a ten-year agreement with the Government of Haiti for exploration for oil and the establishment of oil refineries and petrochemical plants in Haiti.[155] The company was granted a contract of guarantee by the US Agency for International Development. In October 1964 there were press reports that the agreement had been annulled by a decree and that a similar concession had been granted to another foreign person, Sheikh Muhamed Fayed, for a period of fifty years. Shortly afterwards the staff of the company were arrested and subsequently returned to the United States.[156] Under the contract of guarantee the company submitted a claim against the Agency and the matter was referred to arbitration. The company's losses were held to be recoverable because the Tribunal found that the abrogation of the contract was wrongful in that it constituted expropriation of an arbitrary nature.[157] A similar situation appears in the *Letco* case. The ICSID Tribunal's *obiter dictum* suggests that had the unilateral reduction of the forest concession area been considered a nationalization, which was not at issue, the bona fide public purpose would have been missing. The Tribunal noted that the areas from which the plaintiff was ousted were given to other foreign companies which were run by people who were 'good friends' of the Liberian authorities. There was no indication of any 'stated policy on the part of the Liberian Government to take concessions of this kind into public ownership for the public good'.[158]

[153] The Tribunal noted: 'The Onassis Agreement is a contract, concluded by the State with a private individual or corporation . . . The second concessionaire cannot rely on any use, guaranteed to the public, of Aramco's Concession, but is a private individual who intervenes in his own interest in order to draw as much profit as possible from the vast and expensive operations of the first concessionaire. The creation of a state fleet is not at issue here. Satco tankships are not State Vessels. They belong to Mr Onassis and his companies and are merely registered in Saudi Arabia . . . ': 27 ILR at pp. 217–18.

[154] It found that 'while Sapphire International faithfully carried out its obligations, the defendant deliberately broke its own, by hiding behind reasons which it must have known were without validity, and once again taking up a wholly negative attitude and failing to perform duties which were clearly defined in the agreement of the parties. Such an attitude is a further breach of the obligations undertaken by NIOC, since the parties had expressly agreed to carry out their contract according to the rules of good faith and in a spirit of good will': 35 ILR at p. 181. Moreover, it was pointed out with respect to the lack of loyal collaboration on the part of NIOC: 'This behaviour was likely to convince the plaintiff that NIOC intended to avoid the contract by continuous and systematic obstruction, but without wishing to be the first one to denounce it': ibid., p. 185.

[155] 44 ILR at p. 79. This was the first arbitration within the United State Investment Guaranty Program.

[156] Ibid., pp. 82–5.

[157] Ibid., p. 89. Under the Investment Guaranty Program anticipated profits are excluded from recovery, though they may be included in the total claim against the expropriating State.

[158] *Liberian Eastern Timber Co. (Letco)* v. *Liberia, International Legal Materials,* 26 (1987), at p. 665.

(b) *The Effect of Permanent Sovereignty over Natural Resources*

If the present issues were to be approached from the viewpoint of the law of sovereign immunity, they could be reduced to a single question, that is, whether or not to grant immunity to the State. Likewise, simple solutions could be sought by attempting to analyse the situation in terms of lawful and unlawful acts and categories thereof. For instance, one may sometimes doubt the genuine necessity to take expropriatory action on the ground of the 'public interest' of a State.[159] To take another example, some acts might be considered arbitrary, particularly if the sole purpose of contract abrogation is to substitute one foreign company for another.[160] However, in an international system of sovereign States, which (by definition) are presumed to know what is in their own interest, difficulties readily arise if standards of lawful behaviour are based on grounds which are open to wide interpretation.[161] Consequently, in order to give legal effect to the above classifications, a more modest search, for differences of degree rather than overall substance, would seem more appropriate. The most convenient approach would then be to take account of the above distinctions as elements which influence the process of evaluation of compensation, along the lines of what might be called 'private law' and 'public law' approaches.

The 'private law' approach implies giving legal effect to the parties' expectations, as determined by the terms of their contract. Consequently, the recovery would not only involve the so-called *damnum emergens* but often the loss of profits would also be allowed. The parties' will as contractors is the focal point of consideration. As it was expressed in the *Amco* award: 'Whatever compensation the investor can hope to get, that means at the least that the nature of its rights was changed against its will . . .'.[162] Apart from this case, which also involved clearly unlawful acts, one should

---

[159] In the *AMCO Asia* case the Tribunal was at pains to emphasize that the State action must be 'a true nationalization . . . which aims to protect or to promote the public interest'. It did not, however, elaborate on this in substantive terms. Instead, it was found later, on formal grounds however, that the action was totally irregular, that is, that it had not been based on any legislative act by the Indonesian Parliament: ibid. 24 (1985), at pp. 1029–30. In the *AGIP* award similar considerations emerged. While it was not ruled that the decision of the State to revoke its contract and nationalize the oil distribution activities was taken in the absence of public interest, the Tribunal's approach suggests a salient critique of the measures. It was pointed out that to satisfy the public interest of the State, it was not necessary to resort to nationalization. Stressing that there was a contractual relationship between the State and AGIP, the Tribunal stated: 'Furthermore, the Government, which was not without responsibility for the economic difficulties experienced by the Company, was not legally in a position from the point of view of commercial law to act in such radical fashion against the Company. If it wished to protect its interests as a shareholder, the Government should have respected the legal procedures available to it, which in this case consisted either of having the board of directors call an extraordinary meeting of the Company, or regulating the judicial authority to pronounce its dissolution . . .': ibid. 21 (1982), at pp. 735, 737.

[160] Some writers have indicated that a State action which merely terminates a contract should be considered separate from nationalization. In this sense, Lalive, loc. cit. above (n. 20), at p. 58; similarly Schachter, loc. cit. above (n. 76), pp. 311–12, suggests, though with hesitation, that a simple non-performance of a contract without providing any legal remedy could constitute an arbitrary act.

[161] Above, n. 84.

[162] *International Legal Materials*, 24 (1985), at p. 1032.

refer generally to those disputes which, in terms of the above analysis, fall outside the ambit of the concept of permanent sovereignty over natural resources—in other words, disputes completely unrelated to natural resource activities, or falling outside the production activities themselves. In this respect, it suffices to say that there is a tendency in recent legal practice to compensate for the loss of future profits though not always to the full extent.

The 'public law' model would apply to long-term agreements concerning natural resource production, i.e. cases which lie at the heart of the concept of permanent sovereignty. According to this approach, not only the terms of a contract, but also wider considerations, relating to the dependence of national development on the natural resources, would be taken into account. The practical implication is that the recovery of lost profits is more restricted. The public law model is reflected in the *Liamco* and *Aminoil* awards in particular. Although the latter award may not be entirely unproblematic from a technical viewpoint, given the difficulties of reconciling the Tribunal's reasoning on quantification with the actual figures, the Tribunal nonetheless appears to have substantially accepted the validity of the contentions of the Kuwaiti Government in its policy argument:

> Oil, together with natural gas, is the only natural resource possessed by the desert State of Kuwait. It is a finite resource, upon which the welfare and prosperity of the people in large part depends. It proved too precious to be left in the hands of a private entrepreneur, concerned primarily with maximising its profits . . .[163]

Moreover, it continued:

> For the Tribunal to award compensation (or rather, damages) on the basis claimed by Aminoil would be as burdensome to the Government as it would be for the Government to relinquish all control or sovereignty over its natural resources. It would be tantamount to depriving the Nation for ever of all right over its oil reserves. This could not be a correct interpretation of international law, in a post-colonial era.[164]

Mindful of a similar approach in the *Liamco* award, in contrast to the *Texaco* case, one should also draw attention to the report of 7 May 1981 by the Secretary-General of the United Nations, which expresses a favourable comment *vis-à-vis* the former:

> The award in the *TEXACO/CALASIATIC* v. *The Libyan Arab Jamahiriya* case is still a subject of discussion. While some authorities note the arbitrator's reliance on international law, the principle of investment security and sanctity of contract, others note that the award is at variance with the opinion of States which regard State contracts with foreigners as being subject exclusively to national law. On the other hand, the award in the *LIAMCO* v. *The Libyan Arab Jamahiriya* case may

---

[163] *Pleadings* (Book 5), Government's Counter-Memorial, p. 151.
[164] Ibid., p. 160.

indicate a solution whereby the principle of permanent sovereignty over natural resources is affirmed.[165]

As has been shown above, contemporary international law recognizes that control over natural resources entails particularly strong considerations of public interest. Generally speaking, the ways in which the relations of 'public' and 'private' interests are arranged in law vary in cases from one society to another. Nevertheless, what has been discussed above with regard to international law is not wholly devoid of analogies in national law. In the area of State contracts one should mention particularly the notions of 'administrative' and 'public' contracts known in Continental and Anglo-American law respectively. Both cases reflect a necessary accommodation of public or State interests and the interests of individuals. Because of the involvement of public authorities such contracts have different characteristics as compared to ordinary private contracts. Notable among these is the right of the administration to terminate its contract unilaterally when public interests so require.[166] Also, there is a tendency in French doctrine, apparently of fairly recent origin, to consider mining concessions as administrative contracts.[167] The same view has been assumed in German doctrine as well.[168] Moreover, the public interest aspect may be reflected, to a greater or lesser degree, in the restriction of available remedies. In his classic work on public contracts, Professor Mitchell notes on English law:

> Finally, it must be remembered that the cause of interference with the contract is public necessity. While therefore it is perhaps reasonable to claim that the contractor should not lose, equally he should not be allowed to profit from the situation. In view of these factors, and of the cause of the interference with the contract, it might suffice if compensation were allowed solely for actual loss suffered without any

---

[165] E/C. 7/119, p. 28, para. 83.

[166] This may have been recognized by statutory provisions (Federal Republic of Germany, Italy, France) or generally acknowledged even in the absence of such provisions (France, Belgium). In Britain and the United States the same is achieved by the standard 'break'-clauses, which are regularly included in substantial government contracts. In the United States such a clause may even be incorporated by the operation of law if it has been wrongly omitted: Turpin, 'Public Contracts', *Encyclopaedia of Comparative Law*, vol. 7, chap. 4, pp. 56–7.

[167] de Laubadère, Moderne and Delvolvé, *Traité des contrats administratifs*, vol. 1 (1983), p. 332 ('La réponse ne peut être qu'affirmative'). The writers refer to the obligatory application of exorbitant contract terms imposed by public authorities as well as the exorbitant regime governing the concessions. Though they do not fall technically within the traditional categories of 'public service' or 'public works' concessions, the policy reason for the doctrinal development lies in the increased public interest in the matter: ibid., p. 330. Cf. *Texaco* case, where the role of stabilization clauses, in particular, was emphasized as an indication of the parties' intention not to refer to the doctrine of administrative contracts: 53 ILR at p. 478; the same conclusion was reached in the *Aramco* award on the ground that an oil concession was not technically a public service concession: 27 ILR at p. 169. On the other hand, the expert opinion submitted by the claimant in the *BP* award characterized oil concessions as administrative contracts according to Libyan law: 53 ILR at p. 324. In other cases oil concessions have been considered to have a mixed private and public nature: *Liamco* case, 62 ILR at p. 169; *Sapphire* award, 35 ILR at p. 171.

[168] Nicolayson, *Bewilligung und Förderabgabe nach dem Bundesberggesetz: unter besonderer Berücksichtigung der Förderung von Erdöl und Erdgas* (1982), pp. 20–1, 28.

element for loss of expectation of profit, whether the interference takes the form of a termination of an existing contract or of a considerable variation of one.[169]

In the United States, too, the recovery of lost future profits is excluded in the case of 'termination for convenience' clauses in public contracts.[170] On this point, the French doctrine seems to afford greater protection of private interests, for it would normally allow the recovery of loss of profit.[171]

In this article diverse but closely related matters have been discussed. At the outset, some of the assumptions which underlie the internationalization of State contracts were examined. This was followed by a brief survey of stabilization clauses and certain aspects concerning their efficacy. Finally, the notions of sovereignty and of permanent sovereignty over natural resources were dealt with. All of these separate issues underpin the discourse on the binding force of State contracts. However, it is unwise to consider them in isolation. In the event of a dispute, they generate simultaneous problems, and all these problems, in the final analysis, revolve around the central issue of how the law should accommodate, with justice, the conflict of interests between society as a whole and particular or sectional interests.

[169] Mitchell, *The Contracts of Public Authorities* (1954), p. 229; see also Higgins, 'The Availability of Damages for Reliance by a Government on Executive Necessity', *Festschrift Mann* (1977), pp. 21 ff.

[170] Turpin, loc. cit. above (n. 166), at p. 57; for more detailed studies, see Perlman and Goodrich, 'Termination for Convenience Settlements—The Government's Limited Payment for Cancellation of Contracts', *Public Contract Law Journal*, 10 (1978), pp. 1, 28; Andrews and Peacock, 'Terminations: An Outline of the Parties' Rights and Remedies', ibid. 11 (1980), pp. 269, 282.

[171] de Laubadère, Moderne and Delvolvé, *Traité des contrats administratifs*, vol. 2 (2nd edn., 1984), pp. 667–71; Vedel and Delvolvé, *Droit administratif* (9th edn., 1984), p. 356, comment on this point: 'Il semble que des éléments de moralité interviennent parfois dans la jurisprudence du Conseil d'Etat. Le *damnum emergens* est seul indemnisable quand c'est un événement indépendant de la volonté de l'Administration qui a motivé la résiliation. Au contraire, dans la mesure où il s'agit d'une nouvelle appréciation par l'Administration des besoins du service, la jurisprudence se montre plus large dans l'octroi des indemnités.'

NOTES

PARLIAMENTARY SOVEREIGNTY*
AND THE SUPREMACY OF COMMUNITY LAW

By MICHAEL AKEHURST‡

THE recent decision of the House of Lords in *Factortame Ltd. and others* v. *Secretary of State for Transport*[1] raises important issues concerning the relationship between the sovereignty of the British Parliament and the supremacy of European Community Law.

EEC regulations establishing the Community's common fisheries policy allocated fishing quotas to each member State. A number of foreign nationals (especially Spanish nationals) formed companies in the United Kingdom; the ships owned by these companies were eligible for registration as British ships under the Merchant Shipping Act 1894, and were thus entitled to participate in catching the UK's quota of fish. Part II of the Merchant Shipping Act 1988 changed the rules governing the nationality of British ships; as a result, ships owned by British companies controlled by foreign nationals were no longer eligible for registration as British ships.

The applicants in the present case were companies controlled by Spanish nationals, whose right to register their ships as British had been taken away by the 1988 Act. They sought, by an application for judicial review, to challenge the legality of Part II of the 1988 Act on the grounds that it violated their rights under European Community law. The Secretary of State for Transport argued, first, that Community law did not restrict the sovereign right which every State had, under international law, to decide who was entitled to be a national of that State or what vessels were entitled to fly its flag, and, second, that the 1988 Act was fully in accordance with the EEC's common fisheries policy. The Divisional Court asked the Court of Justice of the European Communities to give a preliminary ruling, under Article 177 of the EEC Treaty, on the question whether there was a conflict between Community law and the 1988 Act. The Divisional Court also granted the applicants interim relief, by ordering that 'pending final judgment . . . the operation of Part II of the Merchant Shipping Act 1988 . . . be disapplied and the Secretary of State be restrained from enforcing the same in respect of any of the applicants . . .'.[2] The Secretary of State appealed against this order to the Court of Appeal, which allowed the appeal and set aside the order for interim relief.[3] The applicants appealed to the House of Lords against the decision of the Court of Appeal.

---

* © Estate of Professor Michael Akehurst, 1990.

‡ Late Professor of International Law, Keele University.

[1] [1989] 2 All ER 692; [1989] 2 WLR 997.

[2] [1989] 2 CMLR 353, 357–92.

[3] [1989] 2 CMLR 353, 392–409.

Lord Bridge, with whom the other Law Lords agreed, said that, 'as a matter of English law', an English court had no power to make an order for interim relief suspending the application of a British Act of Parliament until the Court of Justice of the European Communities had decided whether or not that Act was contrary to Community law. He conceded that an English court 'may in its discretion properly decline to exercise its jurisdiction to grant an interim order in aid of the enforcement of disputed legislative measures in a situation where . . . it is necessary to invoke the court's jurisdiction in order to secure their enforcement'; for instance, if the applicants had been prosecuted for violating the 1988 Act, an English court could grant a stay of the prosecution proceedings until the Court of Justice of the European Communities decided whether or not the 1988 Act was contrary to Community law. But the interim relief sought by the applicants was of an entirely different nature.

[T]he provisions of Part II of the 1988 Act require no assistance from the court for their enforcement. Unambiguous in their terms, they simply stand as a barrier to the continued enjoyment by the applicants' vessels of the right to registration as British fishing vessels. . . . [A]n order granting the applicants the interim relief which they seek will only serve their purpose if it declares that which Parliament had enacted to be the law from 1 December 1988, and to take effect in relation to vessels previously registered under the 1894 Act from 31 March 1989, not to be the law until some uncertain future date. Effective relief can only be given if it requires the Secretary of State to treat the applicants' vessels as entitled to registration under Part II of the 1988 Act in direct contravention of its provisions. Any such order, unlike any form of order for interim relief known to the law, would irreversibly determine in the applicants' favour for a period of some two years rights which are necessarily uncertain until the preliminary ruling of the European Court has been given. If the applicants fail to establish the rights they claim before the European Court, the effect of the interim relief granted would be to have conferred on them rights directly contrary to Parliament's sovereign will and correspondingly to have deprived British fishing vessels, as defined by Parliament, of the enjoyment of a substantial proportion of the United Kingdom quota of stocks of fish protected by the common fisheries policy. I am clearly of the opinion that, as a matter of English law, the court has no power to make an order which has these consequences.[4]

Lord Bridge added

that, as a matter of English law, the absence of any jurisdiction to grant interim injunctions against the Crown is an additional reason why the order made by the Divisional Court cannot be supported.[5]

However, Lord Bridge went on

to consider the submission made on behalf of the applicants that, irrespective of the position under national law, there is an overriding principle of Community law which imposes an obligation on the national court to secure effective interim protection of rights having direct effect under Community law where a seriously arguable claim is advanced to be entitled to such rights and where the rights claimed will in substance be rendered nugatory or will be irremediably impaired if not effectively protected during any interim period which must elapse pending determination of a dispute as to the existence of those rights.[6]

---

[4] [1989] 2 All ER 692, 702D–703C.
[5] Ibid., at p. 709A.
[6] Ibid., at p. 709B.

He found that none of the previous decisions of the Court of Justice of the European Communities gave a clear ruling on the question

whether, in relation to the grant of interim protection in the circumstances of the instant case, Community law *overrides* English law and either empowers or obliges an English court to make an interim order protecting the putative rights claimed by the applicants.[7]

He therefore proposed, and the other Law Lords agreed, that the following questions should be referred to the Court of Justice of the European Communities for a preliminary ruling under Article 177 of the EEC Treaty:

(1) Where—(i) a party before the national court claims to be entitled to rights under Community law having direct effect in national law (the rights claimed), (ii) a national measure in clear terms will, if applied, automatically deprive that party of the rights claimed, (iii) there are serious arguments both for and against the existence of the rights claimed and the national court has sought a preliminary ruling under Article 177 whether or not the rights claimed exist, (iv) the national law presumes the national measure in question to be compatible with Community law unless and until it is declared incompatible, (v) the national court has no power to give interim protection to the rights claimed by suspending the application of the national measure pending the preliminary ruling, (vi) if the preliminary ruling is in the event in favour of the rights claimed, the party entitled to those rights is likely to have suffered irremediable damage unless given such interim protection, does Community law either (a) oblige the national court to grant such interim protection of the rights claimed or (b) give the court power to grant such interim protection of the rights claimed?

(2) If question 1(a) is answered in the negative and question 1(b) in the affirmative, what are the criteria to be applied in deciding whether or not to grant such interim protection of the rights claimed?

The House of Lords adjourned further consideration of the applicants' appeal until the Court of Justice of the European Communities had given a preliminary ruling on these questions.[8]

The questions referred by the House of Lords to the Court of Justice of the European Communities dealt only with the issue of interim relief. There remained in the background the question of substance, namely, whether the 1988 Act did conflict with Community law. As regards the situation which would arise if the Court of Justice of the European Communities decided this question in favour of the applicants, the Divisional Court[9] and two of the three judges in the Court of Appeal[10] thought that Community law would override the 1988 Act, because Community law was the higher law. By contrast, Lord Bridge's approach was, at first sight at least, more cautious:

By virtue of s. 2(4) of the 1972 [European Communities] Act, Part II of the 1988 Act is to be construed and take effect subject to directly enforceable Community rights and those rights are, by s. 2(1) of the 1972 Act, to be recognised and available in law, and . . . enforced, allowed and followed accordingly . . . This has precisely the same effect as if a section were incorporated in Part II of the 1988 Act which in terms enacted that the provisions with respect to registration of British fishing vessels were to be without prejudice to the directly enforceable Community rights of nationals of any member state of the EEC. Thus it is common ground that, in so far as the applicants succeed before the European

[7] Ibid., at p. 710B (italics added).
[8] Ibid., at pp. 710C–711B.
[9] [1989] 2 CMLR 353, 373–4, 380–1.
[10] Ibid., pp. 403–4 (Bingham LJ) and 408 (Mann LJ). The third member of the Court, Lord Donaldson MR, did not discuss this issue.

Court in obtaining a ruling in support of the Community rights which they claim, those rights will prevail over the restrictions imposed on registration of British fishing vessels by Part II of the 1988 Act and the Divisional Court will, in the final determination of the application for judicial review, be obliged to make appropriate declarations to give effect to those rights.[11]

In other words, the 1988 Act must be interpreted in the light of the European Communities Act, and must therefore be interpreted as not applying to Community nationals. By treating the question as one of interpretation only, Lord Bridge provided a neat way of avoiding any conflict between Community law and English law.[12] However, to interpret the 1988 Act as not applying to Community nationals is a singularly bold interpretation; if Lord Bridge had looked at *Hansard* (something which English judges are not supposed to do when they interpret Acts of Parliament), he would have seen that the relevant provisions of the Act were aimed mainly against Spanish nationals,[13] and an amendment which would have exempted Community nationals (subject to certain conditions) from the operation of those provisions was not adopted.[14]

Besides, it is not clear that Lord Bridge did regard the issue as one of interpretation only. In the passage which has just been quoted, he said that the applicants' rights under Community law would *prevail* over the restrictions imposed on the registration of British fishing vessels by the 1988 Act. It may be possible to explain this statement as meaning only that the 1988 Act should be interpreted as containing an implied exception in favour of Community nationals, and that this exception prevailed over the general words in the Act in the same way that any exception in an Act of Parliament prevails over the general words in that Act. However, elsewhere in his speech, he recognized the possibility that there could be a principle of Community law which '*overrides* English law and either empowers or obliges an English court to make an interim order protecting the putative rights claimed by the applicants'.[15] One of the rules of English law which would be overridden by such a principle of Community law is the rule that an English court has no power to make an order declaring 'that which Parliament had enacted to be the law from 1 December 1988 . . . not to be the law until some uncertain future date'.[16] This rule of English law is not simply a technical limitation on the power of English courts to grant interim relief; it is an essential part of the fundamental principle of Parliamentary sovereignty. Thus it would appear that Lord Bridge, and the other

[11] [1989] 2 All ER 692, 700J–701B.
[12] In the *Factortame* case the applicants relied on EEC regulations and articles of the EEC Treaty which had direct effect. If they had invoked EEC directives the position would probably have been different; in *Duke* v. *GEC Reliance Ltd.*, [1988] 2 WLR 359, the House of Lords held that the obligation to interpret Acts of Parliament in conformity with EEC directives applied only if the Act in question had been passed for the purpose of implementing the directive. The decision in the *Duke* case conflicts with the decision of the Court of Justice of the European Communities in *Officier van Justitie* v. *Kilpinghuis Nijmegen BV*, [1989] 2 CMLR 18, 27, which held that the duty of national courts to interpret national legislation in the light of relevant EEC directives applies whenever a national court is 'applying . . . national law and *in particular* the provisions of a national law specifically introduced in order to implement the directive' (emphasis added) (i.e. the duty is not limited to the particular case of a national law specifically passed in order to implement the directive).
[13] *Hansard*, HL Debates, vol. 489, col. 1331; vol. 490, cols. 570–80; HC Debates, vol. 126, col. 552.
[14] *Hansard*, HL Debates, vol. 490, cols. 575–80.
[15] [1989] 2 All ER 692, 710B (italics added).
[16] Ibid., at p. 703A, C.

Law Lords who agreed with him, are prepared to allow Community law to override the sovereignty of the British Parliament.

Such an approach would be fully in accordance with the principle laid down by the Court of Justice of the European Communities in the *Simmenthal* case that 'a national court which is called upon . . . to apply provisions of Community law is under a duty to give full effect to those provisions, if necessary refusing of its own motion to apply any conflicting provision of national legislation, even if adopted subsequently, and it is not necessary for the [national] court to request or await the prior setting aside of such provision by legislative or other constitutional means'.[17] This principle has been accepted by the courts in most member States of the EEC.[18]

Community law was made part of English law by the European Communities Act 1972, and therefore, even according to traditional ideas of Parliamentary sovereignty, Community law will override rules of the common law and Acts of Parliament passed before 1972 in so far as they conflict with Community law. But, if an Act passed by the British Parliament after 1972 conflicts with Community law, the traditional principle of Parliamentary sovereignty, whereby a later Act overrides an earlier Act in the event of conflict, will lead to results which are diametrically opposed to the *Simmenthal* principle.

Nevertheless, it seems that English courts are showing some degree of willingness to move away from traditional ideas of Parliamentary sovereignty. In *Macarthys Ltd.* v. *Smith*, Lord Denning said:

[T]he provisions of Article 119 of the EEC Treaty take priority over anything in our English statute on equal pay which is inconsistent with Article 119.[19] That priority is given by our own law. It is given by the European Communities Act 1972 itself. Community law is now part of our law: and, whenever there is any inconsistency, Community law has priority. It is not supplanting English law. It is part of our law which *overrides any other part which is inconsistent with it.*[20]

In *Aero Zipp Fasteners* v. *YKK Fasteners (UK) Ltd.*, Graham J said *obiter* that the European Communities Act had 'enacted that relevant Common Market law . . . should, where there is a conflict, override English law'.[21] In *Re an*

---

[17] [1978] ECR 629, 645–6.

[18] Lasek and Bridge, *Law and Institutions of the European Communities* (4th edn., 1987), pp. 335–58.

[19] The Court of Appeal treated the case as one of conflict between the European Communities Act (and Community law) and a *later* Act of the British Parliament, because the relevant provisions of the Equal Pay Act 1970 had been inserted in it by the Sex Discrimination Act 1975. But it is submitted that the Court of Appeal was wrong in thinking that there was a conflict between Community law and the Acts of 1970 and 1975. The case involved a form of discrimination which was prohibited under Article 119 of the EEC Treaty, but was not prohibited by the 1970 and 1975 Acts. But those Acts did not authorize or require such discrimination any more than they prohibited it; they were simply silent on this issue, thereby leaving a gap in English law, which could be filled by Community law, without raising any issue of conflict between Community law and Acts of Parliament.

[20] [1981] QB 180, 200 (italics added). Lawton LJ agreed (ibid., p. 201), and Cumming-Bruce LJ expressed similar views (ibid., p. 201). See also the *obiter dictum* by Lord Denning in *Shields* v. *E. Coomes (Holdings) Ltd.*, [1978] 1 WLR 1408, 1415 ('If . . . a tribunal should find any ambiguity in the statutes or any inconsistency with Community law, then it should resolve it by giving the primacy to Community law'). But compare his conflicting *obiter dictum* in *Felixstowe Dock and Railway Company* v. *British Transport Docks Board*, [1976] 2 CMLR 655, 664–5.

[21] [1973] CMLR 819, 820.

Absence in Ireland, the National Insurance Commissioner held that provisions of an EEC regulation on social security 'override' a provision of the Social Security Act 1975, which limited entitlement to social security benefits.[22] In *Marshall* v. *Southampton and South West Hants. Health Authority* an industrial tribunal found that there was a conflict between Community law, which entitled the plaintiff to adequate compensation, and the Sex Discrimination Act 1975, which placed such a low limit on compensation as to make it inadequate; the tribunal, invoking the principle of the supremacy of Community law, decided to 'ignore the limit' contained in the 1975 Act and to award the plaintiff the compensation to which she was entitled under Community law.[23]

Professor Hood Phillips[24] has argued that such cases are concerned only with *interpreting* English statutes to make them conform with Community law. But it is respectfully submitted that this explanation is unconvincing. Lawyers in general, and judges in particular, are trained to use words carefully; and, when judges use words like 'priority', 'override', 'supremacy' and 'ignore', they are not the sort of words which judges use when they are doing nothing more than interpreting Acts of Parliament.

However, there are limits to the willingness of English courts to accept the supremacy of Community law. In *Garland* v. *British Rail Engineering Ltd.*, the House of Lords said:

> The instant appeal does not present an appropriate occasion to consider whether . . . anything short of an *express positive statement* in an Act of Parliament passed after January 1, 1973, that a particular provision is intended to be made in breach of an obligation assumed by the United Kingdom under a Community treaty, would justify an English court in construing that provision in a manner inconsistent with a Community treaty obligation of the United Kingdom. . . .[25]

This statement clearly implies that English courts will apply an Act of Parliament which contains an express positive statement that it is intended to violate Community law.[26] Similarly, in *Macarthys Ltd.* v. *Smith*, Lord Denning MR said: 'If the time should come when our Parliament deliberately passes an Act with the intention of repudiating the [EEC] Treaty or any provision in it or intentionally of acting inconsistently with it *and says so in express terms* I should have thought that it would be the duty of our courts to follow the statute of our Parliament.'[27] In the same case Lawton LJ said: 'Parliament's recognition of European Community law . . . by one enactment can be withdrawn by another' (but he immediately added that there was 'nothing in the Equal Pay Act . . . to indicate that Parliament intended to amend the European Communities Act 1972, or to limit its application').[28]

---

[22] [1977] 1 CMLR 5, 9–10.
[23] [1988] 3 CMLR 389, 400–2.
[24] *Law Quarterly Review*, 95 (1979), p. 167, and 96 (1980), p. 31.
[25] [1983] 2 AC 751, 771 (italics added).
[26] But the *Factortame* case answers the question which the House of Lords left open in *Garland*, and makes clear that nothing short of such an express positive statement will justify an English court in construing an English statute in a manner inconsistent with the UK's obligations under Community law.
[27] [1979] 3 All ER 325, 329 (italics added). But he added: 'Unless there is such an intentional and express repudiation of the [EEC] Treaty, it is our duty to give priority to the Treaty.'
[28] Ibid., at p. 334.

Thus the position appears to be that English courts will apply an Act of Parliament which expressly states that it is intended to violate or repudiate a rule of Community law, or to repeal, amend or limit the application of the European Communities Act; but in all other cases they will recognize the supremacy of Community law over the sovereignty of the British Parliament.

THE COMMERCIAL LAW OF NATIONS AS REFLECTED BY CMND. 1 TO 10,000*

By F.A. MANN‡

I

IN the course of more than 30 years since the commercial law of nations was subjected to scrutiny in the pages of this *Year Book*[1] its development was not appreciably promoted either by judicial or arbitral decisions or by academic contributions. In fact, apart possibly from certain aspects of the *Barcelona Traction* case,[2] there was probably no decision by an international tribunal that could properly be described as pertaining to the customary commercial law of nations. In view of the chilling defeats which Great Britain suffered at the hands of Monsieur Cassin[3] and Belgium at the hands of the International Court of Justice[4] it is perhaps not surprising that States have hesitated to initiate truly international proceedings on commercial as opposed to territorial disputes. The well-known arbitral awards[5] involving questions relating to State contracts, their repudiation as well as the confiscation of the assets created by them, have doubtless greatly assisted in developing the law, but none of them is free from grave and ill-considered defects nor entitled to be treated as laying down international law: they were, of course, awards made under the control of local law and are, therefore, a source of international law in the same way, but not necessarily with the same authority, as decisions of municipal tribunals; in fact, if they did not have the quality of a national award they could not be enforceable in national Courts. As regards academic work no major piece of an analytical character has come to the writer's notice, although odd points of detail have from time to time been explored by learned authors; by way of example one may mention Sir Joseph Gold's interesting discussion of the meaning and the implications of the term 'pledge' in a treaty or of the 'finality' of a decision by an organ of an international body.[6]

Yet the States' treaty practice has continued to an ever-increasing extent, so much so that it is quite impossible to follow the developments worldwide. This is a cause for much regret, for treaties, as we know, are indications of State practice

---

* © Dr. F.A. Mann, 1990.

‡ CBE, FBA; Honorary Professor of Law in the University of Bonn; Solicitor of the Supreme Court; Member of the Institut de Droit International.

[1] Vol. 33 (1957), p. 20, reprinted in *Studies in International Law* (1973), p. 140. A German translation appeared under the title *Betrachtungen über ein Völkerhandelsrecht (Baden-Baden, 1982)*.

[2] *ICJ Reports*, 1970, p. 3.

[3] Case of the *Diverted Cargoes* (Greece v. United Kingdom) decided by an Award which was published in *Revue critique de droit international privé*, 1956, p. 278, and (in English) in 22 ILR 280. It is discussed on p. 47 of the article referred to in n. 1 above.

[4] See n. 2, above.

[5] See, e.g., *Texaco v. Libya*, 53 ILR 398.

[6] *International and Comparative Law Quarterly*, 16 (1967), p. 289, at pp. 289, 310. On the latter point see, e.g., the English decisions *Re Wynn*, [1952] Ch. 271, or *Re Gilmore*, [1957] 1 QB 574: the word 'final' does not necessarily exclude the jurisdiction of the courts.

and a primary source of international law, so that their collection and analysis would have great value. Even if they do not lay down the law, they are expressive of it, and provide evidence of custom, or at least of standards. Moreover, as Wilfred Jenks said somewhere many years ago, there exists a great need for a collection of forms and precedents in international practice. The prevailing treaty practice strongly supports this demand, for it continuously causes concern and surprise at the light-heartedness with which treaties are drafted. Thus the numerous commodity agreements which have been concluded since the end of the Second World War fail to deal with the liability for the debts of the international organization which they created, as the creditors of the International Tin Council have experienced to their grave misfortune.[7] Or, while leases usually deal with the tenant's right of ingress and egress, the treaties relating to Berlin did not spell out the Western Powers' right of access by land or air, so that in 1948 the Berlin air lift had to be mounted and even today the legal position is not entirely free from precariousness.[8] These, however, are typical aspects of treaty practice, and at the same time so obvious and so elementary, that one would like to find an answer to the question why treaty practice so radically differs from what in private law is self-evident to any draftsman.

In these circumstances it is perhaps helpful to survey British practice in the commercial field for the period from 8 November 1956 to 31 October 1986, during which Her Majesty's Stationery Office published Cmnd. 1 to 10,000. By no means every one of these documents was looked at or relates to what may fairly be described as the commercial law of nations. Even so, three large boxes were required to collect relevant treaties without there being any certainty that the collection is complete. Fortunately many of the relevant treaties are of little interest. But there is enough material that requires and justifies renewed publication and a certain amount of discussion. This must largely be descriptive in character and does not throw up any real problems, that is to say, any problems which have arisen in practice. A lawyer's analytical mind can, of course, discover or create problems which could have arisen and the solution of which could have caused great difficulties. But this would have been an artificial type of legal research, although in certain respects the need for clarification and analysis may be so plain that some purely theoretical discussion cannot be avoided. This, therefore, is an article which, on the whole, records rather than analyses, which in the eyes of many readers deals with facts rather than law and which is likely to bore rather than to fascinate. Yet it is submitted that it may serve a useful purpose not only for the reasons already indicated, but also on account of the effect it may have upon others. They may come across material for further research or they may be induced to collect similar material published in countries other than Britain. Such undertakings could well lead to the creation of an encyclopedia of international forms and precedents, which might well produce some uniform practice, particularly if it were accompa-

---

[7] See, in particular, the decision in the case of *Maclaine Watson & Co. Ltd.* v. *Department of Trade and Industry*, [1988] 3 WLR 1033, particularly at pp. 1088, 1126 *per* Kerr and Nourse LJJ respectively. The question of the liability of members of an international organization was, in the Anglo-American literature, first raised in this *Year Book*, 42 (1967), p. 145, at p. 160, reprinted in *Studies in International Law* (1973), p. 553, at p. 572, but sadly neglected by most later writers. It is almost unbelievable that *A Handbook of International Organizations* published by the Hague Academy of International Law in 1988 does not even mention it.

[8] See, in particular, the very helpful book by Hendry and Wood, *The Legal Status of Berlin* (1987).

nied by a thoughtful explanation of unsettled problems. It is for this reason that a publication seems justifiable that describes, but does not primarily aim at strictly legal discussion.

It will be obvious to the reader that more than one view may be taken of the question whether a particular treaty comes within the meaning of a commercial law of nations or, if so, is of sufficient interest to warrant mention. A choice had to be made and if it is open to criticism this may not necessarily lack justification. The present writer can only offer to lend his material to any serious student who wishes to review it afresh.

The treaties which will be considered are limited to arrangements made between the United Kingdom and another State and recording such transactions as in view of their nature and terms could have been entered into by private persons. This test excludes treaties by which the contracting parties acting as sovereigns prepare the basis for business to be done, not by themselves, but by private parties, their subjects. Trade Agreements laying down the conditions upon which nationals of the contracting States may trade are an example of documents which regulate the trade of third parties, but do not bring about trade between the two States themselves. Nor does, for example, an Agreement between the UK and France concerning the protection of alcoholic beverages (Cmnd. 6301) or a tripartite arrangement between the UK, the United States of America and Burma concerning the use of American raw cotton (Cmnd. 724, 738, 2060, 2061) come within the scope of the following discussion which is strictly limited to States as traders.

II

(a) *Agency*

As will appear later, there are very many treaties, usually called Agreements, relating to loans made by or to the UK. But there is one such Agreement which is remarkable, because under it the UK appointed the Inter-American Development Bank, an international organization,[9] its agent, and, as we know,[10] in international law agency is a rare occurrence. By the Agreement of 18 April 1966 made in Washington the UK financed certain exports, presumably to assist British industry. The Agreement is in the following terms:[11]

WHEREAS the Government of the United Kingdom of Great Britain and Northern Ireland (hereinafter generally referred to as 'the Government') have indicated their desire to make a further contribution to the economic development of countries which are members of the Inter-American Development Bank through the extension of aid for this purpose;

WHEREAS the purpose of the Inter-American Development Bank (hereinafter generally referred to as 'the bank') is to contribute to the development of its member countries;

WHEREAS in the view of the Government and of the members of the Bank, the Bank is an appropriate multilateral institution through which such United Kingdom aid could be made available;

WHEREAS the Bank, in compliance with general policy directives from its Board of

---

[9] *UN Treaty Series*, vol. 389, p. 69, Treaty No. 5593.

[10] Sereni, *Recueil des cours*, 73 (1948–II), p. 69; Verdross-Simma, *Universelles Völkerrecht* (3rd edn., 1984), section 660 with further references.

[11] Cmnd. 3047.

Governors, has determined that close co-operation with the Government for administration of United Kingdom aid to its member countries would strengthen the efforts of the Bank to foster the development of such countries;

Now, THEREFORE, the parties hereto agree as follows:

ARTICLE 1

Basic Authorization of the Bank

On behalf of the Government and subject to the provisions of this Agreement, the Bank is authorized, as administrator, to make loans to any government, entity, or person in the member countries of the Bank, to assist in financing projects, which are consistent with the general lending policies of the Bank.

ARTICLE 2

Amounts Available

For the purpose of this Agreement, the Government shall make available £4,142,800 (four million one hundred and forty-two thousand eight hundred pounds sterling) to finance approved projects in member countries of the Bank.

ARTICLE 3

Terms of Loans

(a) Loans shall have maturities of from fifteen (15) to twenty-five (25) years with a grace period for the beginning of amortization payments of from nil to seven (7) years.

(b) The applicable rate of interest for each loan shall be agreed with the Government prior to the signing of each loan agreement.

(c) Consistent with its normal procedures, the Bank is authorized to require each borrower to pay to the Bank a commission of up to $\frac{1}{2}$ of 1 per cent per annum, payable in such currency as may be determined by the Bank, on amounts committed or outstanding to compensate it for services rendered on loans made under this Agreement.

(d) Amortization and interest shall be payable in pounds sterling.

ARTICLE 4

Expenditure of Funds in the United Kingdom

Funds made available under this Agreement shall be used only for the purchase in the United Kingdom of goods of United Kingdom manufacture and United Kingdom services. For the purpose of this Article the Government will indicate the definitions of United Kingdom goods and services to be adopted.

ARTICLE 5

Responsibility for Selection of Projects

The Bank shall have the primary responsibility for selecting, processing and approving loan projects and, subject to the provisions of this Agreement, for establishing terms and conditions for loans, using its normal policies, procedures, and staff, provided, however, that the Bank shall consult the Government at an early stage in the selection of projects and thereafter from time to time during the processing and approval of projects, and shall obtain their consent to the terms of any loan agreement before signing such agreement. The Bank shall furnish to the Government such information and documentation as the latter shall reasonably request.

ARTICLE 6

Loan Agreements

Loan agreements shall be signed by the Bank on behalf of the Government. In loan projects where the Bank is also extending a loan from its own resources, separate agreements shall be signed by the borrower and the Bank with respect to the commitment of the Bank's resources and United Kingdom funds.

ARTICLE 7

Disbursements under Loans

The Bank shall be responsible for the collection and examination of contract and payment documents in respect of which disbursements are to be effected in accordance with the provisions of loan agreements and for ensuring compliance with Article 4 of this Agreement in accordance with the requirements of the Government. The disbursements of funds provided under loan agreements shall be made from special accounts to be opened by the Bank in London for that purpose. To the extent that payments fall due under loan agreements the Government will from time to time make payments into these accounts. All loan agreements shall provide for the borrower to submit the documentation required by the Government to the Bank. With respect to each disbursement, the Bank shall submit to the Government (through the Ministry of Overseas Development) such documents as may be agreed upon from time to time.

ARTICLE 8

Records of the Bank

The Bank shall maintain separate records and accounts of funds provided under this Agreement and shall make such of these records and accounts available to the Government as the latter may reasonably request, and in any event shall furnish to the Government, within sixty (60) days after the end of each fiscal year of the Government, an audited statement of account, including the status of each loan made hereunder with funds provided under this Agreement.

ARTICLE 9

Project Supervision

The Bank, on behalf of the Government, shall have the responsibility for project supervision and control but shall keep the Government informed with respect to the implementation of each project financed with funds made available under this Agreement.

Standard of Care

The Bank shall exercise the same care in the discharge of its functions under this Agreement as it exercises with respect to the administration and management of its own affairs.

ARTICLE 11

Transferability of Obligations

Contracts entered into by the Bank on behalf of the Government shall contain provisions permitting the transfer of obligations arising thereunder from the Bank to the Government.

ARTICLE 12

Payments on Loans

All monies received in repayment of loans out of Government funds, or by way of interest thereon, shall be paid to the Bank, which, except as specified in Article 3(c) of the Agreement, shall transfer such funds to the Government (through the Ministry of Overseas Development) within fifteen (15) days after their receipt by the Bank.

ARTICLE 13

Bank not Obligated

Loans made by the Bank under this Agreement shall not constitute part of the Bank's own resources or involve any financial obligation on the part of the Bank.

ARTICLE 14

Consultation

(a) The Government and the Bank shall consult with each other from time to time on all matters arising out of this Agreement.

(b) The Government shall from time to time designate an officer through whom such consultation may be effected and who shall be authorized to give the consent specified in Article 5 of this Agreement.

ARTICLE 15

Entry into Force, Amendment and Termination

(a) This Agreement shall enter into force on signature thereof.

(b) This Agreement may be extended to cover any additional funds which the Government may from time to time make available for the purposes of the Agreement.

(c) Either party may at any time propose revisions to this Agreement, particularly if it is extended to cover additional funds.

(d) If it appears to either party that the co-operation envisaged by this Agreement can no longer appropriately or effectively be carried out, this Agreement may be terminated at the initiative of such party on ninety-one (91) days' notice in writing.

(e) Upon termination of this Agreement, unless the parties agree on another course of action, any contracts entered into by the Bank on behalf of the Government shall be transferred to the latter and any funds or other property held hereunder by the Bank shall be returned to the Government and the Bank's administration on its behalf shall be considered terminated.

(f) In any discussion of termination, due consideration shall be given to the disposition of loans in process.

It will be noted that the Agreement is not stated to be subject to a particular legal system. It seems likely, therefore, that it is governed by public international law. The agent's standard of care is defined by Article 10 as *diligentia quam in suis*. But otherwise the agent's rights and obligations are not defined; if public international law is applicable they could only be derived from the general principles of law recognized by civilized nations. Thus it may be assumed that in selecting projects in accordance with Article 5 the Bank was under a duty of fidelity or that, in acting as an administrator for the purpose of making loans to a government, an entity or person, the Bank was debarred from accepting a secret commission. Article 11 is not free from obscurity, because it is difficult to see how the contracts made by the Bank with borrowers could impose upon it obligations which it would have to assign to Britain. The assignment of rights is apparently not contemplated inasmuch as all payments by the borrowers are to be made to the Bank (Article 12).

The Bank incurred 'certain expenditures on capital and semi-capital goods and services bought in the United Kingdom'. Accordingly part of the sum mentioned in Article 2 of the above agreement was to be 'disbursed by the Government and repaid by the Bank' under a further agreement of 10 December 1969 reading as follows:[12]

Her Majesty's Ambassador at Washington to the President of the Inter-American Development Bank

British Embassy,
Washington,
10 December, 1969.

Sir,

I have the honour to refer to the Agreement signed at Washington on 18 April 1966 between the Government of the United Kingdom of Great Britain and Northern Ireland ('the Government') and the Inter-American Development Bank ('the Bank') providing for the administration by the Bank of certain funds to be made available by the Government for economic assistance to countries which are members of the Bank ('the 1966 Agreement'). I also have the honour to refer to recent discussions between the Government and the Bank regarding arrangements for reimbursing the Bank in respect of certain expenditures on capital and semi-capital goods and services bought in the United Kingdom. As a result of those discussions the Government has agreed to support such arrangements and I therefore have the honour to propose an Agreement supplementary to the 1966 Agreement, in the following terms:

1. The sum of £1,121,800 (one million one hundred and twenty one thousand eight hundred pounds sterling), being that part of the sum of £4,142,800 (four million one hundred and forty two thousand eight hundred pounds sterling) not yet committed by the

---

[12] Cmnd. 4508.

Government under the 1966 Agreement, shall be disbursed by the Government and repaid by the Bank on the terms of this Agreement. The sum to be disbursed under this Agreement shall hereinafter be referred to as 'the fund'.

2. The fund shall be used only for reimbursing the Bank for disbursements by it in respect of purchases by its borrowers of capital or semi-capital goods and services in the United Kingdom since 1 January 1969. For the purpose of this paragraph the Government will indicate the definitions of such goods and services to be adopted, which in any event shall be of a suitable development nature.

3. (a) In order to qualify for reimbursement under the preceding paragraph the Bank shall submit to the Government at agreed intervals details of such disbursements. Each submission shall be accompanied by such documents as may be agreed from time to time.

(b) The Government shall notify the Bank whether or to what extent such disbursements are eligible for reimbursement.

4. Reimbursement shall be effected by payments made by the Government into a special account which the Bank shall open in London for that purpose. Sums so received shall be included in the Bank's ordinary capital resources and may be exchanged for the currency of any other country without restriction.

5. The total payments from the fund shall be repaid by the Bank in sterling in London in accordance with the following provisions:

INSTALMENTS

Date due	Amount £
30 June 1972	8,500
31 December 1972...	8,500
30 June 1973	17,000
31 December 1973...	17,000
30 June 1974	25,500
31 December 1974...	25,500
30 June 1975 and on the 30 June in each of the succeeding 14 years	34,000
31 December 1975 and on the 31 December in each of the succeeding 13 years...	34,000
31 December 1989...	33,800

6. The Bank shall pay to the Government in sterling in London interest on payments from the fund in accordance with the following provisions:

(a) The rate of interest in respect of each of such payments shall be eight and seven eighths per cent per annum.

(b) Interest shall be calculated in respect of each payment, on the basis of a 365 day year, on the balance of the instalments for the time being outstanding, provided that no interest shall be payable on any balance of the instalments outstanding during a period of four years from 31 December 1969.

(c) Subject to the preceding sub-paragraph, interest shall be paid on 30 June and on 31 December in each year.

7. The Bank shall be free to repay the whole or any part of the instalments outstanding, together with accrued interest, at any time.

It is, however, particularly interesting to note that in 1971 the earlier structure was completely changed. An Agreement between the UK and the Inter-American Development Bank[13] established the United Kingdom Development Fund for Latin America (Article 1) and appointed the Bank Administrator of the Fund 'on behalf of the Government and subject to the provisions of this Agreement' (Article 2). Some of the provisions are the same as those agreed upon in 1966, but some are significantly different and are therefore set forth as follows:

ARTICLE 3

Purpose of the Fund

The Fund shall be used to provide loans to any government of, or entity or person in, the developing countries which are members of the Bank to assist in the financing of goods and services for projects which are designed to promote the economic and social development of such member countries of the Bank being projects which are consistent with the general lending policies of the Bank.

ARTICLE 4

Terms of Loans

(a) Loans from the Fund shall have maturities of twenty-five (25) years with a grace period for the beginning of amortization payments of four (4) years.

(b) Loans from the Fund shall bear interest at the rate of 3 per cent annum.

(c) Consistent with its normal procedures, the Bank is authorized to require each borrower to pay to the Bank a commission of up to $\frac{1}{2}$ of 1 per cent per annum on amounts committed or outstanding on loans to compensate it for services rendered under this Agreement.

(d) Consistent with its normal procedures, the Bank is authorized to require each borrower to pay to the Bank a one-time charge of 1 per cent of the loan amount as a contribution towards the cost of special supervision and inspection of loans.

(e) Amortization, interest and commissions shall be payable in pounds sterling.

ARTICLE 5

Responsibility for Selection of Projects

The Bank shall have responsibility for selecting, processing and approving loan projects and, subject to the provisions of this Agreement, for establishing terms and conditions of loans, using its normal policies, procedures, and staff, provided, however, that the Bank shall consult the Government at an early stage in the selection of projects and shall obtain their consent to the use of the Fund for the respective loan project before granting any loan. The Bank shall furnish to the Government such information and documentation as the latter shall reasonably request.

---

[13] Cmnd. 4783.

ARTICLE 6

Loan Agreements

Loan agreements shall be signed by the Bank as Administrator of the Fund. In loan projects or programmes where the Bank is also extending a loan from its own resources, separate agreements shall be signed by the borrower and the Bank with respect to the commitment of the Bank's resources and the resources of the Fund.

ARTICLE 7

Resources of the Fund

(a) The Fund shall be constituted by the following resources:

(i) two million pounds sterling (£2,000,000) to be contributed by the Government;

(ii) any additional contributions to the Fund by the Government.

(b) Cash balances of the Fund shall be held in a special account in pounds sterling to be opened by the Bank in London for that purpose. The account shall be denominated 'Inter-American Development Bank—United Kingdom Development Fund for Latin America' (hereinafter called 'the Fund Account').

(c) The Government shall deposit, within thirty (30) days of signing this Agreement, a non-interest bearing non-negotiable promissory note for two million pounds sterling (£2,000,000) with the bank holding the Fund Account. The Bank may draw against this promissory note for disbursement on specific sub-loans at such time or times as shall be agreed by the Government and the Bank.

(d) All monies received in repayment of loans from the Fund or by way of interest thereon, shall be paid to the Bank, which shall transfer such monies to the Government through the Foreign and Commonwealth Office (Overseas Development Administration) within thirty (30) days after their receipt by the Bank.

ARTICLE 8

Separation of Assets

The assets and accounts of the Fund shall be kept separate and apart from all other assets and accounts of the Bank and shall be separately designated in appropriate manner.

ARTICLE 9

Use of Loan Funds

(a) Loans from the Fund may be used only for payments for goods and services originating in the United Kingdom or in such other countries as are members of or significant contributors to the Bank.

(b) The policies and procedures applied to loans from the Fund shall in all other respects be consistent with the normal policies and procedures applied by the Bank to loans from its ordinary capital resources.

Article 10

Disbursements under Loans

Disbursements from the Fund shall be effected by the Bank in accordance with its normal disbursement procedures.

Article 11

Records of the Bank

The Bank shall maintain separate records and accounts of funds provided under this Agreement and shall make such of these records and accounts available to the Government as the latter may reasonably request, and in any event shall furnish to the Government an annual report containing information about the operations of the Fund and the status and progress of each loan made with funds provided under this Agreement.

Article 12

Project Supervision

The Bank, as Administrator of the Fund, shall have the sole responsibility for project inspection and supervision and for this purpose may require a contribution from each loan to be paid to the Bank consistent with its general practice and as set forth in Article 4 (*d*).

It will be noted that according to Article 6 the Bank is now the contracting party of loan agreements and that, accordingly, the former Articles 11 and 12 have disappeared. Article 7 introduces the mechanism of a promissory note, but while Article 7(*d*) deals with the repayment of monies received by the Bank from borrowers, nothing is said about the Bank's duty to recover such monies or the expenses which may be incurred in connection with proceedings (if any). In both respects general principles will have to be resorted to: the Bank will be bound to act with the standard of care which it exercises in respect of its own affairs and, since it acts as Administrator 'on behalf of the Government', it will probably be subject to the instructions of the Government, but have a right of indemnity. These, it is realized, are assertions, but it is believed that all representative systems of law are likely to agree.

(b) *Lines of Credit*

One speaks of a line of credit in cases in which a borrower is entitled to call upon the lender for a loan of money as and when the need arises, so that he does not have to pay interest before he needs and receives the money. A line of credit in this sense of not more than $500 million was the subject-matter of an Agreement of 25 February 1957 between the UK and the Export-Import Bank of Washington.[14] It reads as follows:

THIS AGREEMENT made and entered into this 25th day of February 1957, by and between the The Government of the United Kingdom of Great Britain and Northern

---

[14] Cmnd. 104. For a similar Agreement see Cmnd. 2610.

IRELAND (hereinafter referred to as the 'United Kingdom'), and EXPORT-IMPORT BANK OF WASHINGTON (hereinafter referred to as 'Eximbank'), an agency of the United States of America.

WITNESSETH:

WHEREAS, to enable the United Kingdom to finance dollar requirements for United States commodities, materials, equipment and services and its dollar requirements for petroleum, petroleum products and related services, the United Kingdom has requested a credit up to Five Hundred Million Dollars ($500,000,000) from Eximbank to be secured by the pledge of certain collateral on the terms and conditions hereinafter set forth; and

WHEREAS, the extension of such credit will facilitate exports and imports and the exchange of commodities between the United States and the United Kingdom;

Now, THEREFORE, in consideration of the premises and mutual covenants herein contained, it is agreed that:

ARTICLE I

Line of Credit

Eximbank hereby establishes in favour of the United Kingdom a line of credit of not to exceed Five Hundred Million Dollars ($500,000,000) against which Eximbank will make advances from time to time, subject to the terms and conditions hereinafter stated, to assist the United Kingdom in financing its dollar requirements for United States commodities, materials, equipment and services, and its dollar requirements for petroleum, petroleum products and related services.

ARTICLE II

Advances

Subject to the provisions of Article VI and all other conditions precedent contained herein, upon the written request of the United Kingdom, Eximbank will make advances from time to time for the account of the United Kingdom in a bank in the United States designated by the United Kingdom. As a condition to the making of each such advance the United Kingdom with its request will furnish to Eximbank the following documents:

(a) A duly executed promissory note, substantially in the form annexed hereto as Exhibit A, in the principal amount of the advance requested, as provided in Article IV hereof;

(b) A certificate of the Bank of England, substantially in the form annexed hereto as Exhibit B, certifying that payments as described therein in an amount at least equivalent to the amount requested by the United Kingdom have been made for the purposes of this Agreement subsequent to December 31, 1956;

(c) A true copy of an Instruction substantially in the form annexed hereto as Exhibit C from the Bank of England on behalf of the United Kingdom to Agency Bank of Montreal, New York City, to transfer collateral as set forth in Article VI and to furnish Eximbank with a confirmation of such transfer when effected.

ARTICLE III

Availability

No advances will be made under this Agreement by Eximbank subsequent to February 28, 1958, except to the extent Eximbank may consent in writing.

ARTICLE IV

Notes

1. Each such advance will be evidenced by the promissory note of the United Kingdom in the principal amount of such advance. Each of such notes shall be dated as of its date of issue, shall be payable to the order of Export-Import Bank of Washington, at the office of the Export-Import Bank of Washington, Washington, D.C., or such commercial bank or other financial institution in the United States as may be satisfactory to Eximbank, and shall be payable as to both principal and interest in lawful money of the United States of America. Each such note shall bear interest at the rate of four and one-half per cent ($4\frac{1}{2}\%$) per annum, payable semiannually. The principal amount of each of such notes shall be paid in ten (10) semiannual installments according to the following schedule:

Months after date of note	Per cent of face of note
36	7
42	8
48	8
54	11
60	11
66	11
72	11
78	11
84	11
90	11
	100

Interest shall be computed on the basis of actual number of days, using a factor of 365 days and will be payable only from the date of each advance.

2. The form and text of each note issued hereunder shall be satisfactory to Eximbank and substantially that of Exhibit A Annexed hereto, and shall be printed or lithographed.

3. Eximbank agrees not to negotiate or transfer any note or notes issued hereunder nor to dispose of any participations in any of said notes unless the United Kingdom consents in writing to such transfer or participations.

ARTICLE V

Tax Exemption

The notes issued pursuant hereto, and the proceeds and income of any such note shall be exempt from taxation for any purposes by or within the United Kingdom of Great Britain and Northern Ireland or by any political subdivision or taxing authority thereof.

ARTICLE VI

Pledge of Collateral

1. All advances made under this credit shall be secured by the pledge of collateral consisting of securities selected by the United Kingdom from the list of securities held by Agency Bank of Montreal, New York City, for Bank of England Special Account (as initially filed with Eximbank under letter from Agency Bank of Montreal, New York City, dated December 21, 1956, and as such list may be revised from time to time through additions, sales or purchases by or on behalf of the United Kingdom). At the time of each advance the United Kingdom agrees to direct or cause to be directed Agency Bank of Montreal, New York City, to deliver to Eximbank or its nominee, as collateral security for any and all advances made hereunder, so much of said securities as equals in Market Value, as hereinafter defined, One Hundred Twenty per cent (120%) of the amount of such advance. The United Kingdom will advise Eximbank from time to time of changes in said list of securities.

2. If at any time the aggregate Market Value of all the collateral is less than the then unpaid principal amounts of such note or notes, the United Kingdom, upon request in writing from Eximbank, agrees to deliver to Eximbank or its nominee, to be held as part of the collateral hereunder, additional collateral of a Market Value at least equal to such deficiency. In the event the United Kingdom fails to pledge such additional collateral as herein provided within sixty (60) days after being requested to do so by Eximbank, then the United Kingdom agrees to prepay forthwith a sufficient amount of the outstanding principal balance so that the Market Value of the collateral then pledged shall at least equal the then outstanding amount of principal after such prepayment has been made.

3. If at any time the aggregate Market Value of all the collateral amounts to more than One Hundred Twenty per cent (120%) of the then unpaid principal amounts of such note or notes, then upon the request of the United Kingdom, Eximbank will cause to be released from the pledge so much of said securities selected by the United Kingdom as equals in Market Value the amount of such excess.

4. The Market Value of the securities set forth in the list herein referred to, as revised from time to time, shall be determined by J. P. Morgan & Co. Incorporated quarterly, (i) if such securities are listed on a national securities exchange in the United States, then on the basis of the last sale price on such exchange on the date of such valuation or failing such price, the last bid price, or (ii) if not so listed, then on such basis as J. P. Morgan & Co. Incorporated in their discretion shall determine. A copy of such list and valuation thereof shall be delivered to Eximbank. For the purposes of this Agreement the Market Value of the collateral shall be deemed to be the latest such quarterly valuation as determined by J. P. Morgan & Co. Incorporated.

ARTICLE VII

Collateral

1. All securities at the time of their delivery to Eximbank or its nominee as part of the collateral shall be duly endorsed in blank for transfer or accompanied by proper instruments of assignment in blank, with such signature guaranties as may be deemed necessary by Eximbank, but, unless and until an event of default as hereinafter set forth shall have occurred and shall not have been cured by the United Kingdom or waived in writing by Eximbank, no transfer of record title of any of the collateral shall be made by Eximbank except with the consent in writing of the United Kingdom and no rights of ownership in or to the collateral shall be exercised by Eximbank.

2. From time to time the United Kingdom may sell any of the collateral. Such sales may

be made in such manner and in such place, and either publicly or privately, and through such agent or agents as the United Kingdom may deem advisable. In addition certain of said collateral may be redeemed from time to time. In case of any such sale or redemption, Exim-bank shall cause to be released the part of the collateral so sold or redeemed upon receipt by it of the net proceeds of the sale or redemption as certified in writing to it by the United Kingdom, the date of such release and delivery of securities to be the date specified in said writing. The net proceeds of any such sale or redemption shall be applied upon receipt by Eximbank to the reduction of the principal of any note or notes outstanding at the time of such sale or redemption in the same manner as provided in paragraph 1 of Article VIII.

3. The United Kingdom reserves the right to substitute for any of such securities held as collateral other securities of equal Market Value.

4. Unless and until an event of default as hereinafter set forth shall have occurred and shall not have been cured by the United Kingdom or waived in writing by Eximbank, the United Kingdom shall have and enjoy all rights arising out of ownership of the pledged securities including, but not limited to, the right to vote the pledged securities with the same effect as though they were not subject to this pledge and the United Kingdom shall have the right to receive all dividends whether paid in cash or in stock or other payments (including rights, if any) made upon or in respect of such shares as though such shares were not subject to this pledge.

ARTICLE VIII

Prepayment and Installment Payment: Release of Collateral

1. The United Kingdom may prepay at any time all or from time to time a part of the unpaid principal (without premium) of any of such notes with accrued interest upon at least ten (10) days written notice to Eximbank of its intention so to do. Such partial prepayments will be applied to the latest maturing installments of principal of the note or notes on which such prepayments are being made.

2. Notwithstanding the provisions of Paragraph 3 of Article VI, in the event of any such partial prepayment (unless an event of default as hereinafter set forth shall have occurred with respect to any of such notes and not have been cured by the United Kingdom or waived in writing by Eximbank), Eximbank agrees to release or cause to be released from pledge under such notes and this Agreement and to deliver or cause to be delivered to the order of the United Kingdom, such amount of collateral selected by the United Kingdom, the Market Value of which shall bear the same proportion to the total Market Value of all collateral pledged hereunder and not heretofore released, as the amount of such prepayment bears to the total principal amount outstanding and unpaid hereunder at the time of such prepayment; provided, however, that such release of collateral shall not reduce the total Market Value of all collateral which remains pledged hereunder below an amount equal to One Hundred per cent (100%) of the total principal amount outstanding and unpaid hereunder after such prepayment has been made.

3. Notwithstanding the provisions of Paragraph 3 of Article VI, at the time of payment of each installment of principal due on the notes hereunder, Eximbank similarly agrees to release and deliver collateral selected by the United Kingdom; the amount of such collateral to be released at the time of each such payment shall be determined on the same proportionate basis and shall be subject to the same limitation as is provided in paragraph 2 above, with respect to releases in the event of prepayment.

4. At the time of each prepayment or installment payment or reduction of principal pursuant to Article VII, Section 2, Eximbank will stamp each note with respect to which

payment is made to evidence the reduction by the amount of such payment in the principal amount of such note which remains outstanding and unpaid.

ARTICLE IX

Default

If any one or more of the following events of default shall have happened and shall not have been cured by the United Kingdom or waived in writing by Eximbank, as provided in Article X hereof, with respect to each of such notes, viz.:

1. Failure to pay any installment of principal of any of such notes, within sixty (60) days after the due date thereof;

2. Failure to pay any installment of interest on any of such notes, within sixty (60) days after the date thereof; or

3. Failure by the United Kingdom to perform or observe any other covenant or condition which it has agreed to perform or observe hereunder for a period of sixty (60) days after the date on which notice in writing of such failure, requiring the United Kingdom to remedy the same, shall be given to the United Kingdom by Eximbank;

then Eximbank at its option may declare by notice in writing to the United Kingdom the principal of all such notes to be due and payable immediately and upon any such declaration the same shall become and be due and payable immediately, anything in this Agreement or in such note or notes contained to the contrary notwithstanding.

Upon the nonpayment of the principal of all such notes declared due as aforesaid, the securities constituting the collateral pledged under Article VI hereof shall at its option be transferred into the name of Eximbank and Eximbank directly or acting through its nominee is empowered to sell, assign, collect and convert into money and deliver the whole or any part of the collateral at public or private sale, without demand, advertisement or notice of the time or place of sale or of any adjournment thereof which are hereby expressly waived. After deducting all expenses of such sale or sales, Eximbank shall apply the residue of the proceeds thereof to the payment of such notes and unpaid interest thereon at the rate specified in such notes, returning the excess, if any, to the United Kingdom.

ARTICLE X

Waiver Provisions

Eximbank may waive in writing the observance by the United Kingdom of any of the terms and provisions of this Agreement or of any note or notes issued hereunder, but no such waiver or any failure on the part of Eximbank to insist on any such terms and provisions shall operate as a waiver thereof in respect to any subsequent act or transaction hereunder, or of any other terms or provisions hereof. No delay on the part of Eximbank in exercising any power or right hereunder shall operate as a waiver thereof, nor shall any single or partial exercise of any right or power hereunder preclude other or further exercise thereof or the exercise of any other power or right.

ARTICLE XI

Final Payment

Upon payment in full of the principal of and interest on all the notes issued hereunder and advances incurred or made pursuant to Article XII hereof, Eximbank shall release or cause to be released from pledge under such notes and this Agreement and shall deliver or cause to be delivered to the order of the United Kingdom the then remaining collateral and the remaining note or notes, and thereupon this Agreement shall terminate.

Article XII

Costs and Expenses

The United Kingdom shall pay all transfer taxes and expenses of any nature in connection with or arising out of this Agreement or any transaction contemplated thereby, including the expenses of Eximbank and the reasonable fees and expenses of Agency Bank of Montreal, New York City, incurred under this Agreement, including all expenses in connection with the administration, supervision, preservation, protection of, or realization on default upon the collateral. In event of failure of the United Kingdom to pay, Eximbank is authorized to pay at any time any or all of such expenses on behalf of the United Kingdom and add the amount of such payment to the amount of the indebtedness.

Article XIII

Commission and Fees

The United Kingdom hereby represents and warrants that no commission fee, or payment of any kind has been or will be paid to any person, firm or corporation in connection with the application which has resulted in the extension of the financial assistance by Eximbank provided for in this Agreement or in connection with any negotiations incident thereto, except reasonable compensation for bona fide professional, technical, or other comparable services incident to presenting the merits of the application or to the establishment of the credit or operations hereunder; and the United Kingdom covenants that upon request of Eximbank the amount of payments made to any such person, firm or corporation for services in connection herewith will be disclosed to Eximbank.

Article XIV

Legal Opinions and Authorizations

Prior to and as a condition of the first advance under the credit, Eximbank shall be furnished with the following without cost to it:

(a) An opinion or opinions of counsel demonstrating to the satisfaction of the General Counsel of Eximbank, or counsel designated by him (1) that the United Kingdom has taken all action necessary and appropriate under its laws and regulations to authorize it to incur the indebtedness contemplated by the credit; (2) that this Agreement has been validly signed and entered into by the United Kingdom and is binding upon it in accordance with its terms; (3) that the notes, when and as signed and issued pursuant hereto, will constitute the valid and binding obligations of the United Kingdom in accordance with their terms; and (4) that the delivery of such collateral pursuant to the agreement to pledge as provided in Article VI will constitute a valid and effective pledge;

(b) Evidence of the authority (1) of the person or persons who will sign this Agreement on behalf of the United Kingdom; (2) of the person or persons who will date and sign the promissory notes to be issued hereunder; and (3) of any other person or persons who will act as the representative or representatives of the United Kingdom in connection with the operation of the credit; together with the authenticated specimen signature in duplicate of each such person.

From time to time thereafter, Eximbank shall be furnished without cost to it such additional opinion or opinions of counsel and such additional evidences of authority, authenticated specimen signatures, documents and other information as it may reasonably request.

ARTICLE XV

Notices, Demands and Deliveries

Unless otherwise provided in this Agreement, all notices, demands and deliveries to be given or made to the United Kingdom or Eximbank shall be given or made, as the case may be, at The British Embassy, Washington, D.C., or Export-Import Bank of Washington, Washington, D.C.

Either party may take such action as may be required or permitted under this Agreement through its duly authorized agents or representatives.

ARTICLE XVI

Applicable Law

All questions with respect to the execution or interpretation of this Agreement and the notes or with respect to performance or non-performance hereunder or thereunder shall be interpreted according to New York law.

In Witness Whereof, the parties hereto have caused thus Agreement to be duly executed in duplicate in Washington, District of Columbia, United States of America, on the date first mentioned above.

The Government of the United Kingdom
of Great Britain and Northern Ireland

By HAROLD CACCIA,

*Her Majesty's Ambassador Extraordinary and
Plenipotentiary at Washington*

Export-Import Bank of Washington
By SAMUEL C. WAUGH,
President

The Collateral Note mentioned in the Agreement is Exhibit A:

$.....................
No.....................

Collateral Note

Dated......................................

For Value Received, The Government of the United Kingdom of Great Britain and Northern Ireland (the Government) hereby promises to pay to Export-Import Bank of Washington (the Bank) or order against this promissory note the principal sum of.. Dollars ($.....................) in installments as hereinafter provided and to pay interest from the date on which the principal sum has been deposited to the credit of the Government in...Bank on..................................and semiannually thereafter at the rate of four and one-half per cent ($4\frac{1}{2}\%$) per annum on the unpaid principal balance of this note from time to time outstanding.

For the prompt payment of principal and interest on this promissory note in accordance with its terms the Government hereby pledges its full faith and credit.

Both the principal of and interest on this note are payable at the office of...in the City of New York, New York, in lawful money of the United States of America, without deduction for or on account of any present or future taxes, duties or other charges imposed or levied against this note or the proceeds or holder hereof by or within the United Kingdom of Great Britain and Northern Ireland or any political subdivision or taxing authority thereof.

The principal of this promissory note shall be payable in ten (10) consecutive semiannual installments in the amounts and at the times set forth in the following schedule of payments:

Installment Number	Date Due	Amount
1		
2		
3		
4		
5		
6		
7		
8		
9		
10		

This note is one of a series of notes issued under and pursuant to the terms of the Agreement dated February 25, 1957 between the Government and the Bank, and is subject to the conditions and entitled to the benefits thereof. As provided in the Agreement, the undersigned shall have the right to prepay, without penalty or premium, all or any part of the principal of this promissory note, with accrued interest on the amount so prepaid.

This note together with all other notes issued pursuant to said Agreement, is secured by the pledge with Agency Bank of Montreal, New York City, New York, as custodian for the Bank of certain collateral as set forth in said Agreement to which reference is made for a description of the rights and obligations of the parties in the premises.

Upon the happening of an event of default which shall not have been cured by the undersigned or waived by the Bank as specified in said Agreement, the entire unpaid principal amount of and interest accrued on this note and all other notes issued pursuant to said Agreement shall become due and payable immediately at the option and upon the demand of the holder hereof.

The non-exercise by the holder hereof of any of its rights hereunder in any particular instance shall not constitute a waiver thereof in that or any subsequent instance.

This note shall be non-negotiable and non-transferable except with the consent in writing of the Government.

THE GOVERNMENT OF THE UNITED KINGDOM
OF GREAT BRITAIN AND NORTHERN IRELAND

By..

As has been pointed out on a previous occasion,[15] this is, of course, a highly unusual Agreement, for it is governed by the law of New York. It is not, therefore,

[15] *Studies in International Law* (1973), p. 241.

a treaty within the meaning of the Vienna Convention[16] and the same applies to the promissory note which is expressed to be 'subject to the conditions and entitled to the benefits' of the Agreement. Accordingly it does not appear either in the *UK Treaty Series* or in the *United Nations Treaty Series*. Yet it seems that in law the Bank's 'contractual liabilities constitute general obligations of the United States'.[17] If in truth the United States should be party to the Agreement, it would be an example of those commercialized inter-State arrangements which are a pre-eminent aspect of the commercial law of nations.

This feature is even more strikingly illustrated by the next Agreement, which was made on 3 November 1969 between the UK and the Export-Import Bank and provided for a line of credit not exceeding $100 million. Its text is as follows:[18]

THIS AGREEMENT, made and entered into as of the 3rd day of November 1969, by and between The Government of The United Kingdom of Great Britain and Northern Ireland (hereinafter called 'Borrower') and the Export-Import Bank of the United States (hereinafter called 'Eximbank'), an agency of the United States of America.

WITNESSETH:

WHEREAS, the Borrower has entered or will enter into arrangements (hereinafter called 'Purchase Arrangements') with the Department of Defense, United States of America (hereinafter called 'DOD'), for the purchase from the DOD of certain aircraft including related articles and services (said purchases being hereinafter collectively called 'Purchase Program'); and

WHEREAS, the Borrower has requested Eximbank to establish a line of credit in its favor to assist the Borrower in financing payments required to be made by the Borrower to the DOD from July 1, 1969, through March 31, 1972, inclusive, under the Purchase Arrangements for or towards the acquisition in the United States from United States suppliers of that portion of the Purchase Program which consists of equipment, components, and articles of United States manufacture and services of United States origin; and

WHEREAS, the establishment of the line of credit requested will facilitate exports and imports and the exchange of commodities between the United States of America and the United Kingdom;

Now, THEREFORE, the parties hereto agree as follows:

ARTICLE I

Line of Credit

Eximbank hereby establishes in favor of the Borrower a line of credit (hereinafter called 'Credit') in the principal amount of One Hundred Million Dollars (US$100,000,000), United States currency, against which Eximbank will make disbursements from time to time, subject to the terms and conditions hereinafter set forth, to assist the Borrower in financing payments required to be made by the Borrower to the DOD from July 1, 1969, through March 31, 1972, inclusive, under Purchase Arrangements satisfactory to Eximbank

---

[16] Article 2 defines a treaty as an international agreement concluded between States in written form and governed by international law. It may well be that this definition is too narrow. The Convention was published in Cmnd. 7964.

[17] See footnote 3 of the paper referred to in n. 15, above.

[18] Cmnd. 4226.

for or towards the acquisition in the United States from United States suppliers of that portion of the Purchase Program which consists of equipment, components, and articles of United States manufacture and services of United States origin.

Article II

Repayment of Credit

The Borrower covenants and agrees to repay the principal amount of the Credit, and to pay interest thereon, subject to the following terms and conditions:

(a) *Principal and Interest*. The Borrower shall repay each disbursement under the Credit in fourteen (14) approximately equal installments, the first of which shall be due and payable on the 31st day of December following the close of the fiscal year of Eximbank in which the disbursement was made with the remaining thirteen installments due and payable successively semiannually thereafter. In addition to the foregoing amounts, the Borrower shall pay interest semiannually on the 30th day of June and the 31st day of December at the rate of six per cent (6%) per annum on the principal amount of the Credit disbursed and outstanding from time to time, said interest to accrue from the dates of the respective disbursements under the Credit and to be computed on the basis of the actual number of days using a 365-day factor. Interest shall not be charged for the date on which any principal payment is made on the amount of such principal payments. All payments of principal and interest hereunder shall be made to the order of Eximbank at the Federal Reserve Bank of New York in the City of New York, State of New York, United States of America.

(b) *Promissory Notes*. Further to evidence the obligation of the Borrower to pay the amount specified in subparagraph (a) of this Article, the Borrower shall within thirty (30) days following the close of each fiscal year of Eximbank issue and deliver to Eximbank a negotiable promissory note in the form of Annex 'A' to this Agreement in the principal amount of the disbursements made under the Credit by Eximbank during the preceding fiscal year. Each note shall be dated as of the first day of July of the year preceding the year of issue, printed or lithographed on one side of one sheet of bank note or safety paper and be in form and substance satisfactory to Eximbank. Although notes shall bear interest from their date of issue, appropriate adjustment will be made so that interest is charged only from the dates of the respective disbursements. (The term 'Notes' shall mean the promissory note or notes evidencing the principal amount of the disbursements under the Credit outstanding at any one time.)

(c) *Prepayments*. The Borrower shall have the right, upon payment of all accrued charges for interest, to repay at any time in advance of maturity, without premium or penalty, all or part of the principal amount of the Credit at the time outstanding, and of the Notes; provided, that any such prepayments shall be applied to the Notes in the inverse order of their issue and to the installments of said Notes in the inverse order of their maturity.

(d) *Application of Payments*. All payments by the Borrower on or in respect of the principal of and interest on the Credit, and of the Notes, shall be applied first to accrued interest and then to the repayment of principal.

(e) *Commitment Fee*. The Borrower shall on the 30th day of June and the 31st day of December of each year pay to the order of Eximbank in United States currency at the Federal Reserve Bank of New York in the City of New York, State of New York, United States of America, a commitment fee computed at the rate of one-half of one per cent ($\frac{1}{2}$ of 1%) per annum on the undisbursed, uncancelled or unexpired balance of the Credit outstanding, from time to time, using a 365-day factor; said commitment fee to accrue from July 26, 1969, through March 31, 1972.

Article III

Disbursement Procedures

A. *Disbursement to DOD.* When all conditions precedent to the first utilization of the Credit have been fulfilled, Eximbank will, upon receipt of the following form and substance satisfactory to it, make disbursements from time to time on behalf of the Borrower to the account of the DOD for the purpose of financing payments required to be made by the Borrower (i) under Purchase Arrangements satisfactory to Eximbank and (ii) in conformity with the purposes for which the Credit has been established:

(1) *Request.* A request signed by a duly authorized representative of the Borrower for a disbursement in the amount specified in the statement required by subparagraph (2) below:

(2) *DOD Statement.* A statement of the DOD (a) identifying the Purchase Arrangement(s) under which disbursement is being requested by the Borrower; (b) verifying that the amount of the requested disbursement is due under said Purchase Arrangement(s) and specifying the due date thereof; and (c) certifying that the amount of the requested disbursement will be applied for or towards the acquisition in the United States from United States suppliers of that portion of the Purchase Program which consists of equipment, components, and articles of United States manufacture and services of United States origin;

(3) *Additional Information.* Such additional documents and information as Eximbank may from time to time reasonably request.

B. *Disbursements to Borrower.* When all conditions precedent to the first utilization of the Credit have been fulfilled, Eximbank will, upon receipt of the following in form and substance satisfactory to it, make disbursements from time to time to the account of the Borrower at a financial institution in the United States designated by the Borrower and acceptable to Eximbank to reimburse the Borrower for payments made by the Borrower to the DOD (i) under Purchase Arrangements satisfactory to Eximbank and (ii) in conformity with the purposes for which the Credit has been established:

(1) *Request.* A request signed by a duly authorized representative of the Borrower for a disbursement in the amount specified in the statement required by subparagraph (2) below;

(2) *DOD Statement.* A statement of the DOD (a) identifying the Purchase Arrangement(s) under which disbursement is being requested by the Borrower; (b) verifying that the amount of the requested disbursement was paid under said Purchase Arrangement(s) and specifying the date on which said payment was due; and (c) certifying that an amount equal to the amount of the requested disbursement has been or will be applied for or towards the acquisition in the United States from United States suppliers of that portion of the Purchase Program which consists of equipment, components, and articles of United States manufacture and services of United States origin;

(3) *Additional Information.* Such additional documents and information as Eximbank may from time to time reasonably request.

C. *Reports.* Within thirty (30) days following the date upon which the Department of Defence has submitted the final United States certified costs of the total orders covered by the lines of credit, the Borrower shall submit or cause to be submitted to Eximbank an expenditure report which shall set forth, on a cumulative basis through March 31, 1972, an itemized statement of (1) all expenditures in connection with the Purchase Program, said expenditures to be segregated as between those financed by Eximbank and those financed out of other funds, as well as between United States currency and other currencies, and (2) the amount (hereinafter called 'Excess Disbursement'), if any, by which the aggregate of all funds disbursed by Eximbank exceeds the aggregate of such funds utilized through March 31, 1972, for or towards the acquisition in the United States of that portion of the Purchase Program which consists of equipment, components and articles of United States manufacture and services of United States origin irrespective of whether such Excess Disbursements shall have been caused by (a) the utilization of such funds for or towards other than the acquisition in the United States of that portion of the Purchase Program which consists of equipment, components, and articles of United States manufacture and services of United States origin, (b) adjustments or refunds, or (c) any reason of whatsoever nature; said report to be satisfactory in form and substance to Eximbank, and to bear or be accompanied by evidence of the approval of a duly authorized representative of the Borrower.

D. *Repayment of Excess Disbursements.* The Borrower shall on the first repayment date of principal following the due date of the report required by paragraph C of this Article, make a repayment to Eximbank in advance of maturity on the principal amount of the Credit and the Notes at the time outstanding in an amount equal to the aggregate of the Excess Disbursements outstanding as of March 31, 1972; provided that any such repayment as aforesaid shall be applied to the Notes in the inverse order of their issue and to the installments of said Notes in the inverse of their maturity.

ARTICLE IV

Representations and Warranties

The Borrower represents and warrants as follows:

(a) *Authority.* The Borrower has full power, authority and legal right to incur the indebtedness and other obligations provided for in this Agreement and the Notes, to execute and deliver this Agreement and the Notes, and this Agreement does, and the Notes when issued hereunder will, constitute valid and binding obligations of the Borrower in accordance with the respective terms hereof and thereof.

(b) *Legal Action.* The Borrower has taken all action required under the laws and regulations of the Borrower, or of any political subdivision, department or agency thereof, to authorize the execution and delivery of this Agreement and the Notes.

(c) *Full Faith and Credit.* All covenants of the Borrower contained in this Agreement constitute, and the Notes when issued hereunder will constitute, unconditional direct obligations of the Borrower, for the payment and performance of which the full faith and credit of the Borrower is pledged.

ARTICLE V

Events of Default

In case one or more of the following events (hereinafter called 'Event of Default') shall have occurred and be continuing, that is to say:

(a) A default shall have occurred in the payment of any amount required under this Agreement, the Notes, or any other agreement between Eximbank and the Borrower; or

(b) A default shall have occurred in the performance of any other covenant or agreement on the part of the Borrower under this Agreement, the Notes, or any other agreement between Eximbank and the Borrower, and such default remains unremedied for a period of thirty (30) days after written notice thereof shall have been given to the Borrower by Eximbank; or

(c) Any representation or warranty made by the Borrower under this Agreement, the Notes, or any other agreement between Eximbank and the Borrower proves to be incorrect in any material respect and has not been corrected within thirty (30) days after written notice thereof shall have been given to the Borrower by Eximbank;

then and in each and every case, Eximbank may, upon written notice to the Borrower, make immediately due and payable the entire principal amount of the Credit at the time outstanding, or any Notes evidencing such amount, together in each case with accrued interest thereon to the date of payment.

ARTICLE VI

Availability, Cancellation and Suspension

A. *Availability*.   Except to the extent that a duly authorized officer of Eximbank may otherwise consent in writing, Eximbank shall not be obligated to make disbursements under the Credit subsequent to the close of business on March 31, 1972, and any part of the Credit which shall not have been disbursed on or before said date may be cancelled by Eximbank without the requirement of notice to the Borrower.

B. *Cancellation*.   The Borrower may by written notice to Eximbank cancel all or part of the Credit which shall not have been disbursed.

C. *Suspension*.   If an Event of Default shall occur and be continuing, then and in each and every case, Eximbank may, upon written notice to the Borrower, suspend all further disbursements under the Credit; thereafter, Eximbank shall not be obligated to make further disbursements until it (i) shall have received evidence that the cause or causes of the suspension have been eliminated or corrected in a manner satisfactory to Eximbank, and (ii) shall have notified the Borrower in writing that the suspension has been removed.

D. *Continuation of Rights and Obligations*.   Notwithstanding any cancellation or suspension pursuant to this Article, all the provisions of this Agreement and the Notes, and the rights and obligations of either party with respect to disbursements made prior to such cancellation or suspension, shall continue in full force and effect.

ARTICLE VII

Legal Opinions and Other Documents

Prior to and as a condition precedent to the first utilization of the Credit by the Borrower, Eximbank shall be furnished with the following in form and substance satisfactory to it:

(a) *Legal Opinion*.   An opinion or opinions of Her Majesty's Procurator-General and Solicitor for the Affairs of Her Majesty's Treasury or in his absence of an Assistant Treasury Solicitor verifying the representations and warranties of the Borrower set forth in subparagraphs (a) through (c) of Article IV hereof; provided that, such opinion or opinions shall refer to all pertinent laws, ordinances, regulations, decrees, resolutions, and other relevant documents.

(b) *Evidence of Authority*.   Evidence of the authority of the person or persons (i) who have signed this Agreement on behalf of the Borrower; (ii) who will execute the Notes on behalf of the Borrower; and (iii) who will sign the requests for disbursements and other documents required or permitted by this Agreement and who will otherwise act as the representative or representatives of the Borrower in connection with the operation of the Credit.

(*c*) *Specimen Signatures*.   The authenticated specimen signature of each person named pursuant to subparagraph (*b*) above.

Thereafter, prior to and as a condition precedent to disbursements by Eximbank with respect to any given Purchase Arrangement, the Borrower shall submit or cause to be submitted to Eximbank a certified or conformed copy of the Purchase Arrangement in question, said Purchase Arrangement to be satisfactory in form and substance to Eximbank.

In addition, Eximbank shall be furnished with such additional legal opinions, evidences of authority, authenticated specimen signatures, documents, and other information as Eximbank may from time to time reasonably request.

Article VIII

Miscellaneous Provisions

A. *Taxes*.   The Borrower covenants and agrees that:

(*a*) the execution, issuance, and delivery of this Agreement and the Notes, and the payment of principal and interest hereunder and thereunder, shall be exempt from all present and future taxes, duties, fees, restrictions, and other charges of whatsoever nature now or hereafter levied or imposed (i) under the laws of the Borrower or laws in effect in its territories or (ii) by the Borrower or by any political subdivision, taxing authority, department, or agency thereof; and

(*b*) the principal and interest payable under this Agreement and the Notes shall be paid without deduction for or on account of such taxes, duties, fees, restrictions, and charges.

B. *Marine Transportation*.   Any item or items, the purchase of which is to be financed in whole or in part under this Agreement and which shall be exported by ocean vessel to the United Kingdom shall be transported from the United States in vessels of United States registry, as required by Public Resolution No. 17 of the 73rd Congress of the United States, except to the extent that a waiver of such requirement is obtained from the United States Maritime Administration.

C. *Expenses*.   All statements, reports, certificates, opinions and other documents or information furnished to Eximbank under this Agreement shall be supplied by the Borrower without cost to Eximbank. Further, the Borrower hereby agrees to reimburse Eximbank on demand for all out-of-pocket costs and expenses incurred by Eximbank in connection with the enforcement, protection or preservation of any right or claim of Eximbank in connection with this Agreement or the Notes.

D. *Sale of Notes*.   Eximbank agrees not to negotiate or transfer the Credit or the Notes nor to dispose of any participations therein without the prior written consent of the Borrower; provided, however, that the foregoing shall not apply to the sale of participations in the Credit or the Notes (i) if such participations constitute interests in a pool of Eximbank loans, which pool includes the Credit or the Notes, and (ii) such participations are guaranteed by Eximbank.

E. *Exchange of Notes*.   Upon the request of Eximbank made at any time or from time to time more than thirty (30) days after the final date for making disbursements as provided in paragraph A of Article VI hereof, the Borrower shall issue and deliver to Eximbank, in exchange for any Notes theretofore issued to Eximbank hereunder, its new Notes in such denominations as Eximbank may specify, dated the date to which interest shall have been paid on the Notes surrendered, and in an aggregate principal amount equal to the aggregate of disbursements against, less the aggregate of any repayments of principal made upon, the Notes surrendered. The new Notes issued pursuant hereto shall conform to the requirements of subparagraph (b) of Article II hereof and shall be substantially in the form of Annex 'A' to this Agreement, except for such modifications as Eximbank may specify to give effect to any of the provisions of this paragraph E. The new Notes shall be dated so that no gain or loss of interest or acceleration or delay of interest payments will result.

F. *Notices*.   All notices, demands and deliveries to be given or made to the Borrower or Eximbank shall be given or made, as the case may be, at the Embassy of the Borrower, Washington, District of Columbia, United States of America, or at the principal office of Eximbank, Washington, District of Columbia, United States of America, or at such other place as may be designated in writing by the respective parties hereto.

G. *Waiver*.   No failure or delay on the part of Eximbank to exercise any right, power, or privilege under this Agreement or the Notes shall operate as a waiver thereof, nor shall any single or partial exercise of any right, power, or privilege under this Agreement or the Notes preclude any other or further exercise thereof or the exercise of any other right, power, or privilege.

IN WITNESS WHEREOF, the parties hereto have caused this Agreement to be duly executed in duplicate in Washington, District of Columbia, United States of America, on the date first mentioned above.

THE GOVERNMENT OF THE UNITED KINGDOM
OF GREAT BRITAIN AND NORTHERN IRELAND
By EDWARD E. TOMKINS

EXPORT-IMPORT BANK OF THE UNITED STATES
By WALTER C. SAUER

It will be noticed that this Agreement does not say anything about the governing law. Is it, therefore, governed by international law, because it is in fact made between two States, or is it made with a corporation created under the law of the District of Columbia and perhaps governed by the creditor's law? Or do established principles of the conflict of laws[19] attribute such weight to the identity of the borrower that English law should be held to be applicable? There is no compelling argument to be adduced in support of any one of these three possibilities, but it is believed that international law as expressed by the general principles of law recognized by civilized nations is most likely to prevail.

(c) *Loans*

So far loans to the UK as borrower have been considered. Loans made by the UK are usually in very much simpler form. It seems that they are invariably made to provide assistance in carrying out agreed projects which are to be built by British firms or with British materials; frequently such loans are called development loans. They are usually made free of interest and repayable by instalments. Their princi-

---

[19] Dicey and Morris, *Conflict of Laws* (11th edn., 1987), p. 1187.

pal characteristic is that they do not make any provision for default: nothing is said about proceedings to recover the loan, the consequences of the failure to pay an instalment or any liability to interest during a period of default. It cannot be assumed that the contingency of default was not at any time within the contemplation of the parties or at least of the lender. But courtesy invariably prevailed over legal prudence.

Very many such arrangements were made with Jordan and it is, therefore, perhaps useful to treat them as representative. A typical Agreement is that of 4 May 1960.[20] It reads as follows:

British Embassy,

Your Excellency, Amman, May 4, 1960.

I have the honour to refer to our recent discussions concerning proposals for an interest-free loan by the Government of the United Kingdom of Great Britain and Northern Ireland to the Government of the Hashemite Kingdom of Jordan during the financial year ending the 3rd of March, 1961. Acting upon instructions from Her Majesty's Principal Secretary of State for Foreign Affairs I now have the honour to propose the following terms:—

(a) The Government of the United Kingdom will advance to the Government of the Hashemite Kingdom of Jordan an interest-free loan of a sum of £500,000 during the financial year ending the 31st of March, 1961.

(b) The loan shall be spent in the course of the said financial year on the development of the Desert Road between Amman and Ma'an.

(c) The amount shall be repaid by the Government of the Hashemite Kingdom of Jordan to the Government of the United Kingdom in ten equal instalments of £50,000 beginning on the 1st of April, 1966.

If the foregoing terms are acceptable to the Government of the Hashemite Kingdom of Jordan I have the honour to suggest that the present Note and Your Excellency's reply in that sense should be regarded as constituting an agreement between the two Governments in this matter.

Please accept, &c.
C. H. JOHNSTON.

Altogether 15 such Agreements were made between 1949 and 1965. In 1967 all earlier arrangements providing for the repayment of loans were terminated and new terms were agreed. The principal ones were to the effect that Jordan was to pay 45 equal half-yearly instalments of £277,500 each.[21]

Other development loans were made on more elaborate terms. By way of example one may refer to an Agreement made with Turkey in 1967:[22]

British Embassy,

Your Excellency, Ankara, 21 April, 1967

I have the honour to refer to the discussions concerning development aid from the Government of the United Kingdom of Great Britain and Northern Ireland to the Government of the Republic of Turkey and to inform Your Excellency that the Government of the United Kingdom are prepared to conclude an Agreement with the Turkish Government on this question. The position of the Government of the United Kingdom with regard to the provision of finance and the commitments of that Government and of the Government of

[20] Cmnd. 1090.
[21] Cmnd. 3363, where the earlier financial agreements are enumerated.
[22] Cmnd. 3374.

Turkey as regards associated matters shall be as respectively set out in part A and part B below:

A.   The Government of the United Kingdom declare that it is their intention, acting by the Ministry of Overseas Development (hereinafter referred to as 'the Ministry'), to make available to the Government of Turkey by way of an interest-free loan a sum not exceeding £2,500,000 (two million five hundred thousand pounds sterling) for the purchase in the United Kingdom of the equipment and services hereinafter mentioned.

B.(1) The Government of the United Kingdom shall adopt the arrangements and procedures described in the following paragraphs of this Note in so far as they relate to things to be done by or on behalf of that Government. The Government of Turkey shall adopt the arrangements and procedures so described in so far as they relate to things to be done by or on behalf of that Government.

(2) (a) For the purposes of these arrangements the Government of Turkey shall, by a request in the form set out in Annex A to this Note, open a special account (hereinafter referred to as 'the Account') with a bank in London (hereinafter referred to as 'the Bank'). The Account shall be operated solely for the purposes of the loan and in accordance with the instructions contained in the said request.

(b) As soon as the Account is opened and before taking any other step required by these arrangements for obtaining any part of the loan, the Government of Turkey shall furnish the Ministry with a copy of the Government's instructions to the Bank given in accordance with the foregoing provisions of this paragraph. The Government of Turkey shall at the same time and so often as any change is made therein, notify the Ministry of the names of the officers who are duly authorised to sign on its behalf the Payment Authorities hereinafter provided and shall furnish a specimen signature in duplicate of each such officer.

(c) The Government of Turkey shall ensure that the Bank forwards monthly to the Ministry a statement of receipts to and payments from the Account.

(d) Unless the Ministry otherwise agree payments into the Account will not be made after the 30th June 1969.

(3) Save to the extent (if any) to which the Ministry may otherwise agree drawings from the loan shall be used only—

(a) for payments under a contract for the purchase in the United Kingdom (which expression in this letter shall be deemed to include the Channel Islands and the Isle of Man) of capital or quasi-capital equipment wholly produced or manufactured in the United Kingdom or for work to be done or for services to be rendered in the United Kingdom by persons ordinarily resident or carrying on business in the United Kingdom or for two or more of such purposes only, being a contract which—

(i) provides for payment in sterling to persons carrying on business in the United Kingdom; and

(ii) is approved on behalf of the Government of Turkey and accepted by the Ministry for financing from the loan; and

(iii) is entered into after the date of this Note and before the 31st December, 1968;

(b) to reimburse any bank in the United Kingdom for payments made by means of letters of credit which are confirmed, opened or advised after the date of this Note for the purpose of contracts complying with the conditions specified in sub-head (*a*) of this paragraph, provided that each such letter of credit or the instructions and any subsequent amendment thereof for the confirming, opening or advising of the letter of credit is endorsed in writing by the Ministry to show the amount that may be paid out of the Account in respect of that letter of credit;

(*c*) for payment of sterling bank charges payable in the United Kingdom to any bank in the United Kingdom in respect of letters of credit referred to in this paragraph.

(4) (*a*) Where the Government of Turkey proposes that part of the loan shall be applied to a contract, that Government shall ensure that there are forwarded at the earliest opportunity to the Ministry:

(i) a copy of the contract, or of a notification thereof in the form set out in Annex B to this Note; and

(ii) two copies of a certificate from the contractor concerned in the United Kingdom in the form set out in Annex C to this Note.

(*b*) The Government of Turkey shall ensure that the Ministry is informed if at any time a contract which has been submitted in accordance with the foregoing provisions of this paragraph is amended or if liability is incurred or is to be incurred thereunder to a greater or lesser amount than the amount specified in the contract certificate and in either of these cases the Government of Turkey shall ensure that there are forwarded as soon as possible to the Ministry the relevant supplementary or revised documents.

(5) (*a*) After the Ministry has considered the documents forwarded, in respect of any contract in pursuance of the procedure described in the foregoing provisions of this Note and any additional information which it may request from the Government of Turkey for this purpose (and which that Government shall then supply), the Ministry shall notify that Government in the form set out in Annex C(i) to this Note whether and to what extent it accepts that payments or reimbursements may be made from the loan.

(*b*) To the extent that the Ministry accepts that a contract may be financed from the loan it shall, on receipt of a request from the Government of Turkey, in the form set out in Annex C(ii) to this Note, giving details of contractual payments made or about to be made, make payments in sterling into the Account and each such payment shall constitute a drawing on the loan.

(6) Withdrawals from the Account shall be made only in the manner and subject to the conditions set out in this paragraph:

(*a*) for payments due under a contract in the cases to which paragraph (3)(*a*) refers, withdrawals shall be made in accordance with Payment Authorities in the form shown in Annex D hereto duly signed on behalf of the Government of Turkey and countersigned by the Ministry. Each Payment Authority forwarded to the Ministry for counter-signature shall be accompanied by Payment Certificates from the Suppliers concerned in the form shown in Annex E hereto and the invoices referred to therein.

(*b*) for reimbursement to a bank in the cases to which paragraph (3)(*b*) refers, withdrawals shall be made only on receipt by the Bank of letters of credit which have been endorsed in writing by the Ministry and are supported by a Payment

Certificate from the Supplier in the form shown in Annex E hereto and the invoices referred to therein; and provided that

(i) the amount of reimbursement in respect of any one contract, excluding the sterling bank charges referred to in paragraph (3)(c) above, shall not exceed the amount specified in relation to that contract in the notification in the form set out in Annex C(i); and

(ii) the Bank shall forward to the Ministry the relevant Payment Certificates and invoices immediately any such reimbursements have been made; and

(iii) where the amount shown in paragraph (ii) of a Payment Certificate exceeds the amount specified in paragraph 4 of the Contract Certificate relating to that contract the Government of Turkey, at the request of the Ministry, shall pay an amount equal to the difference into the Account.

(c) for payments in the cases to which paragraph (3)(c) refers, the Bank shall debit the Account and inform the Ministry of the amounts so debited and give details of the contract to which each payment relates;

(d) photocopies or duplicates of invoices may be submitted instead of the originals for the purpose of this paragraph.

(7) If any monies that have been paid out of the Account are subsequently refunded either by the Supplier or by a guarantor the Government of Turkey shall, so long as there are payments or reimbursements to be made from the Account, pay an equivalent of such sums into the Account and, in any other case, apply the refunds to the reduction of the balance of the loan outstanding.

(8) The Government of Turkey shall repay to the Ministry in pounds sterling in London the total sum borrowed under the arrangements set out in this Note, such repayment to be made by instalments paid on the dates and in the amounts specified below, except that if, on the date when any such instalment is due to be paid, there is then outstanding less than the amount specified for that instalment only the amount then outstanding shall be paid:—

INSTALMENTS

Due	Amount £
1st October 1969	10,200
1st April 1970	10,200
1st October 1970	20,400
1st April 1971	20,400
1st October 1971	30,600
1st April 1972	30,600
1st October 1972	40,800
1st April 1973	40,800
1st October 1973	51,000
1st April 1974	51,000
1st October 1974	61,000
and on the 1st October in each of the succeeding 17 years ...	61,000
1st April 1975	61,000
and on the 1st April in each of the succeeding 16 years.. ...	61,000
1st April 1992	59,000

(9) Notwithstanding the provisions of paragraph (8) of this Note, the Government of

Turkey shall be free at any time to repay to the Ministry in pounds sterling in London the whole or any part of the loan that is still outstanding.

(10) The Government of Turkey shall ensure that foreign shipping lines, including British lines, will be given the opportunity to compete for the shipping of goods under contracts financed by funds provided under this Agreement and that when Turkish vessels are used this will be solely on commercial grounds.

2. If the foregoing proposals are acceptable to the Government of the Republic of Turkey, I have the honour to suggest that the present Note together with Your Excellency's reply in that sense shall constitute an Agreement between the two Governments which shall enter into force on the date of your reply and the Agreement shall be referred to as the United Kingdom/Turkey Loan, 1967.

I avail myself of this opportunity to renew to Your Excellency the assurances of my highest consideration.

Her Majesty's Ambassador
for and on behalf of the
Government of the United Kingdom.

ROGER ALLEN.

An Agreement of this type which in substance was employed for loans to numerous other countries[23] may give rise to many difficult questions. Who is liable if money is withdrawn by a fraudulent official and used for his own purposes? What happens if drawings are used for purposes other than those mentioned in paragraph B(3)(a)? If goods are shipped on a vessel belonging to a Panama company the share capital of which belongs to Turkish nationals is this a foreign shipping line within the meaning of clause B(10)? Yet no arrangements for the decision of disputes are made nor is the applicable legal system defined. English law obviously applied to the relationship between the Bank on the one hand and the British Government and Turkey on the other. Does it also apply to the relationship between Britain and Turkey? An affirmative answer would clearly simplify matters very considerably. The only element which perhaps permits a slight indication in favour of a municipal system of law rather than public international law may be found in the fact that the Agreement is made between the two Governments rather than the two States of which the Governments are agents. But this is a very common lack of legal precision which is probably an insufficient foundation for drawing any inferences. The real contracting parties are the States and therefore it is regrettably more likely that public international law applies.

This problem is perhaps even more obscure in the case of a credit facility

---

[23] Afghanistan: Cmnd. 4597; Bolivia: Cmnd. 6313, 6443; Brazil: Cmnd. 5572; Cambodia: Cmnd. 4174; Ceylon: Cmnd. 4815; Chile: Cmnd. 5406; Colombia: Cmnd. 5318, 5436 (as amended by Cmnd. 5901), 5448, 5497; Costa Rica: Cmnd. 5436; Ecuador: Cmnd. 4344 (as amended by Cmnd. 5234), 5378, 5503, 6110, 6673; Egypt: Cmnd. 6172, 5473 (as amended by Cmnd. 5923); Ethiopia: Cmnd. 4859 (as amended by Cmnd. 5295), 4895, 4896, 4994, 5408, 5521; Honduras: Cmnd. 8230; Indonesia: Cmnd. 3770, 3969, 3980, 4335, 4759, 4760, 5374, 5559, 5881; Khmer Republic: Cmnd. 6045; Mozambique: Cmnd. 7074, 7366; Nepal: Cmnd. 5528; Nicaragua: Cmnd. 5739 (as amended by Cmnd. 6166); Pakistan: Cmnd. 3777, 5278, 5550, 5837; Peru: Cmnd. 3379, 3805, 5507, 5896, 6125, 6237, 6689; Philippines: Cmnd. 8096; Portugal: Cmnd. 7546; Sudan: Cmnd. 4962, 5291, 5562; Thailand: Cmnd. 6716; Turkey: Cmnd. 3811, 3876, 4472 (as amended by Cmnd. 4586), 4602, 4778, 4868, 5842, 6738, 7482, 8209, 8997; Vietnam: Cmnd. 5271; Yugoslavia: Cmnd. 8988.

extended to Yugoslavia by means of promissory note. The Agreement reads as follows:[24]

Foreign Office, S.W.I,
February 3, 1959.

Your Excellency,

I have the honour to propose that, in order to give effect to the decision of Her Majesty's Government in the United Kingdom to make available to the Government of the Federal People's Republic of Yugoslavia a credit of £3,000,000 for the purchase of capital and semi-capital goods, manufactured in the United Kingdom, Her Majesty's Government in the United Kingdom acting through the Export Credits Guarantee Department shall, subject to such conditions as may be agreed between the Secretary of the Export Credits Guarantee Department and the competent authority of the Yugoslav Government, purchase Promissory Notes of the Government of the Federal People's Republic of Yugoslavia up to a total of £3,000,000. These Promissory Notes shall be issued by the State Secretariat for Financial Affairs of the Yugoslav Government, shall be expressed in pounds Sterling and shall become payable in ten equal and consecutive half-yearly amounts over a period from the 30th of June, 1964 to the 31st December, 1968. Each Promissory Note shall carry interest at a rate related to that charged by Her Majesty's Treasury at the date of issue of the Note on a loan for a comparable period out of the Consolidated Fund. Such interest shall be calculated from the date of issue until the date of payment of the Note and shall be payable half-yearly on the 30th of June and the 31st of December in each year.

2.   I have further to propose that, if the provisions set forth above are acceptable to the Government of the Federal Republic of Yugoslavia, this Note, together with Your Excellency's reply to that effect, shall constitute an Agreement between the two Governments which shall come into force on this day's date.

I have, &c.,
SELWYN LLOYD.

The text of the promissory note issued in pursuance of the Agreement does not seem to have been published. We know that it was to be issued by the State Secretariat for Financial Affairs to the Yugoslav Government, i.e. by the State of Yugoslavia. But who was the payee? If it was the Export Credits Guarantee Department, then the note may well have been subject to English law. Was it a negotiable instrument? Where was it issued? If a municipal system of law applied, the place of issue may be highly significant.[25]

Finally there exists a type of Loan Agreement which in truth is a method of ensuring payments to British private creditors of debtors in the borrower country the foreign exchange resources of which render external payments difficult: the British Government provides money for the immediate benefit of British creditors and accepts repayment at a future date. The following is an Agreement with Brazil,[26] but similar Agreements were made for instance with Argentina[27] and Ghana:[28]

The Government of the United Kingdom of Great Britain and Northern Ireland (hereinafter referred to as 'the United Kingdom Government') and the Government of the United States of Brazil (hereinafter referred to as 'the Brazilian Government'):

[24] Cmnd. 722, and also Cmnd. 1539.
[25] See Bills of Exchange Act 1882, s. 72.
[26] Cmnd. 1463.
[27] Cmnd. 3215.
[28] Cmnd. 4763.

Considering that the United Kingdom Government are desirous of joining with other Western European Governments in providing financial assistance to Brazil by way of the consolidation and refinancing of Brazil's medium term commercial debts:

Have agreed as follows:

ARTICLE I

In this Agreement, the expression 'medium term commercial debts' shall mean debts falling due after the 31st of May, 1961, from the Brazilian Government or persons or corporations resident in Brazil to persons or corporations resident in the United Kingdom, under contracts for the supply of goods and/or services which provide for payment to be made within a period exceeding six months from the date of delivery of the goods or satisfactory performance of the services undertaken under the said contracts.

ARTICLE II

The United Kingdom Government shall make available to the Brazilian Government a loan of £2,500,000 to assist the Brazilian Government to provide the full amount of exchange required to meet payments due between the 1st of June, 1961, and the 31st of December, 1965, in respect of medium term commercial debts.

ARTICLE III

The loan shall be paid to the Brazilian Government in four instalments as follows:

Date	Instalment
1st October, 1961 .	£600,000
31st December, 1961	£600,000
30th June, 1962 ...	£650,000
31st December, 1962	£650,000

ARTICLE IV

(a) The Brazilian Government shall pay interest to the United Kingdom Government on each instalment at a rate to be determined by Her Majesty's Treasury having regard to the cost of borrowing by the United Kingdom Government at the date on which the instalment is advanced.

(b) Such interest shall be calculated on the balance of each instalment outstanding and shall be payable in sterling on the 30th of June and the 31st of December in each year; the first payment in respect of interest shall be made on the 31st of December, 1961.

ARTICLE V

(a) The Brazilian Government shall make repayment to the United Kingdom Government of the sums advanced in accordance with Article III of the present Agreement as follows:

Date							Amount
30th June, 1965 ...	...	...	...	...	...	...	£200,000
31st December, 1965	...	...	...	...	...	...	£200,000
30th June, 1966 ...	...	...	...	...	...	...	£400,000
31st December, 1966	...	...	...	...	...	...	£500,000
30th June, 1967 ...	...	...	...	...	...	...	£600,000
31st December, 1967	...	...	...	...	...	...	£600,000

(*b*) These amounts shall be applied in each case to the reduction of the oldest outstanding instalment of the loan.

ARTICLE VI

The present Agreement shall come into force on the date of signature thereof.

IN WITNESS WHEREOF the undersigned, being duly authorised thereto by their respective Governments, have signed the present Agreement.

DONE in duplicate at Rio de Janeiro, this 21st day of July, nineteen hundred and sixty-one, in the English and Portuguese languages, both texts being equally authoritative.

<table>
<tr><td>On behalf of the Government of the United Kingdom of Great Britain and Northern Ireland:</td><td>On behalf of the Government of the United States of Brazil:</td></tr>
<tr><td>G. A. WALLINGER</td><td>CLEMENTE MARIANI</td></tr>
<tr><td>Ambassador Extraordinary and Plenipotentiary.</td><td>Minister of Finance.</td></tr>
</table>

(d) *Grants*

'Grants' seems to be the diplomatic word for gifts: the British Government makes money available, but does not obtain repayment.

Sometimes the terms expressing the parties' intention are fairly clear. An example is the UK–Sudan Grant Agreement 1976 which reads as follows:[29]

16 February, 1976.

Your Excellency,

I have the honour to refer to the recent discussions concerning development aid from the Government of the United Kingdom of Great Britain and Northern Ireland to the Government of the Democratic Republic of the Sudan and to inform Your Excellency that the Government of the United Kingdom are prepared to conclude an Agreement with the Government of the Democratic Republic of the Sudan in the following terms. The position of the Government of the United Kingdom with regard to the provision of finance and the commitment of that Government and the Government of the Democratic Republic of the Sudan as regards associated matters shall be as respectively set out in Part A and Part B below.

A.　　The Government of the United Kingdom declare that it is their intention to make available to the Government of the Sudan by way of financial assistance a sum not exceeding £4,000,000 (four million pounds sterling), (hereinafter referred to as 'the grant'), towards the cost of development projects to be agreed.

[29] Cmnd. 6502.

B.(1) The Government of the United Kingdom shall adopt the arrangements and procedures described in the following paragraphs of this Note insofar as they relate to things to be done by or on behalf of that Government. The Government of the Sudan shall adopt the arrangements and procedures so described insofar as they relate to things to be done by or on behalf of that Government.

(2) (a) For the purposes of these arrangements the Government of the Sudan shall, by a request in the form set out in Annex A to this Note open a special account (hereinafter referred to as 'the Account') with a bank in London (hereinafter referred to as 'the Bank'). The Account shall be operated for the purposes of the grant and in accordance with the instructions contained in the said request.

(b) As soon as the Account is opened and before taking any other step required by these arrangements for obtaining any part of the grant, the Government of the Sudan shall furnish the Government of the United Kingdom and the Crown Agents for Overseas Governments and Administrations, 4 Millbank, London SW1P 3SD (hereinafter referred to as the 'Crown Agents') with a copy of their request in accordance with the provisions of sub-paragraph (a). The Government of the Sudan shall at the same time and so often as any change is made therein, notify the Government of the United Kingdom and the Crown Agents of the names of the officers who are duly authorised to sign on its behalf the Payment Authorities, Payment Orders and Requests for Drawing hereinafter provided and shall furnish a specimen signature in duplicate for each such officer.

(3) (a) Where the Government of the Sudan propose that part of the grant shall be allocated to the costs (as described in paragraph B(4)) of a project they shall forward to the Government of the United Kingdom through the British Embassy a description of the project and its location and shall provide such further details as the Government of the United Kingdom may require.

(b) The Government of the United Kingdom shall notify the Government of the Sudan whether their proposal to allocate part of the grant to the costs of a project is accepted, the amount of the grant accepted as provisionally allocated towards the offshore sterling costs and local costs and any special conditions attached to such acceptance. If the project has not previously been agreed between the Government of the Sudan and the Government of the United Kingdom, the acceptance of the Government of the United Kingdom of a proposal under this sub-paragraph shall constitute the agreement of the project.

(c) For the purposes of this Agreement 'offshore sterling costs' are defined as costs payable outside the Sudan, and 'local costs' (which include import duty, sales tax or any other tax levied directly in the Sudan) as costs payable in the Sudan. It is the intention of the Government of the United Kingdom that not more than 40% of the grant overall shall be determined in the exchanges of letters relating to each individual project.

(4) Save and to the extent (if any) to which the Government of the United Kingdom may otherwise agree, drawings from the grant shall be used only:

(a) for payments under a contract for the purchase in the United Kingdom (which expression in this Note shall be deemed to include the Channel Islands and the Isle of Man) of goods wholly produced or manufactured in the United Kingdom, or in the case of chemical and allied products, goods which are duly declared to be of United Kingdom origin on the form set out in Annex C (Chemicals) to this Note, or for work to be done or for services to be rendered by persons ordinarily resident or carrying on business in the United Kingdom or for two or more such purposes, being a contract which:

(i) provides for payment in sterling to persons carrying on business in the United Kingdom; and

(ii) is approved on behalf of the Government of the Sudan and accepted on behalf of the Government of the United Kingdom for financing from the grant; and

(iii) is a contract entered into after the date of this Note and before 31 March 1979.

(b) for reimbursing the Government of the Sudan a proportion of payments made for an accepted project by them being payments of costs incurred in the Sudan in respect of:

(i) the purchase of goods wholly produced or manufactured in the Sudan; or

(ii) the purchase in the Sudan, with the prior approval of the Government of the United Kingdom, of goods wholly produced or manufactured in the United Kingdom; or

(iii) the costs of services rendered by citizens of the United Kingdom and Colonies, or citizens of the Sudan,

in such proportion and in respect of such goods and services as are accepted by the Government of the United Kingdom for financing from the grant.

(c) for payment of sterling bank charges payable in the United Kingdom to the Bank in respect of their services on behalf of the Government of the Sudan in connection with this agreement.

(5) (a) Where the Government of the Sudan proposes that part of the grant shall be applied to a contract, that Government shall ensure that there are forwarded to the Crown Agents acting on behalf of the Government of the United Kingdom at the earliest opportunity:

(i) a copy of the contract, or a notification thereof in the form set out in Annex B to this Note; and

(ii) two copies of a certificate from the United Kingdom contractor concerned in the form set out in Annex C and Annex C (Chemicals) (whichever is appropriate) to this Note.

(6) (a) After the Crown Agents, acting on behalf of the Government of the United Kingdom, have considered the documents obtained in pursuance of the procedure described in the foregoing provisions of this Note, they shall decide whether and to what extent a contract is eligible for payment from the grant, and shall notify the Government of the Sudan in the form set out in Annex C(i) to this Note whether and to what extent it accepts that a contract is eligible for payment from the grant.

(b) To the extent that the Crown Agents acting on behalf of the Government of the United Kingdom so accept a contract or transaction and agree to payment from the Account and to the extent that reimbursement of costs incurred by the Government of the Sudan is properly due from the Account, they shall on receipt of a Request of Drawing from the Government of the Sudan, in the form set out in Annex C (ii) to this Note, arrange payments in sterling into the Account, and each such payment shall constitute a drawing on the grant.

(*c*) Unless the Government of the United Kingdom otherwise agrees, payments into the Account shall not be made after the 30 September 1980.

(7) Withdrawals from the Account shall be made only in the manner and subject to the conditions set out in this paragraph:

(*a*) for payments due under a contract in the cases to which paragraph B(4)(*a*) refers, withdrawals shall be made in accordance with Payment Authorities in the form shown in Annex D hereto duly signed on behalf of the Government of the Sudan and countersigned on behalf of the Government of the United Kingdom. Each Payment Authority shall be forwarded in duplicate to the Crown Agents acting on behalf of the Government of the United Kingdom for countersignature and shall be accompanied by Payment Certificates from the contractors concerned in the form shown in Annex E hereto and the invoices (or a photocopy or duplicate of such invoices) referred to therein or the invoices only for contracts in respect of which a Contract Certificate in the form shown in Annex C (Chemicals) hereto has been provided.

(*b*) for reimbursements to the Government of the Sudan in the cases to which paragraph B(4)(*b*) refers, withdrawals shall be made in accordance with Payment Orders in the form shown in Annex D (i) to this Note duly signed on behalf of that Government and countersigned on behalf of the Government of the United Kingdom. Each Payment Order shall be forwarded in duplicate to the Government of the United Kingdom for countersignature and shall be accompanied by a claim from the Government of the Sudan in the form shown in Annex F to this Note.

(*c*) for payments to which paragraph B(4)(*c*) refers, the Bank shall debit the Account from time to time, and inform the Government of the Sudan of the amount so debited.

(8) (*a*) If any monies that have been paid out of the account are subsequently refunded by a contractor or by a guarantor, the Government of the Sudan shall pay an equivalent of such sums into the account. If the account should at that time be closed, the money shall be disposed of as mutually agreed between our respective governments.

(*b*) Any balance remaining in the account six months after the date of the last credit to the account in accordance with paragraph 6 of this Note shall be applied as mutually determined between our respective governments.

(9) Goods shall be shipped and insured in accordance with normal commercial competitive practice and not be directed to ships or companies of any particular flag or country. Provided payments for these services are made in sterling in the United Kingdom they may be met from the grant.

(10) The Government of the Sudan shall ensure the provision of such finance additional to the aid finance provided in accordance with the arrangements set out in this Note, as may be needed to complete each project.

(11) The Government of the Sudan shall supply to the Government of the United Kingdom an annual statement in triplicate in respect of local costs incurred on each approved project. The statement shall be countersigned by the appropriate audit authority of the Sudan and shall show the drawings made and the actual expenditure incurred during each financial year of the Government of the Sudan for the purposes of sub-paragraph B(4)(*b*) of this Note and shall certify that the expenditure was incurred in accordance with the terms and conditions on which the project was accepted for financing from the grant. Such statements shall be forwarded to the

Government of the United Kingdom as soon as possible and, in any event, not later than 12 months after the end of each Sudanese financial year.

(12) In relation to goods and services provided with finance from the grant the Government of the Sudan shall permit officers from the British Embassy and other servants or agents of the Government of the United Kingdom to visit any project for which any part of the grant is allocated or made available and shall furnish such officers, servants or agents with such information relating to the projects and the progress and financing thereof as the latter may reasonably require.

In this case the Crown Agents act on behalf of the British Government and if they accept a contract and receive a request for drawing from the Government of the Sudan, then they arrange for sterling payments into the Sudan's account with a London bank.[30] This, therefore, is simply a subsidy which the UK pays for the benefit of the Sudan as donee and the British contractor whose commercial activities are supported with the consequence, for instance, that unemployment is reduced.

There are other occasions on which the grant is combined with a loan. This happened, for instance, in the case of the UK–Laos Electrification Grant and Loan Agreement 1974:[31]

> *British Embassy,*
> *Vientiane.*
>
> Your Excellency,   *25 June, 1974.*

I have the honour to refer to the Second Nam Ngum Development Fund Agreement 1974([1]) (hereinafter referred to as the 'Fund Agreement') to which the Government of the United Kingdom of Great Britain and Northern Ireland and the Provisional Government of National Union of Laos are signatories and to inform Your Excellency that the Government of the United Kingdom are prepared to conclude an Agreement in the following terms with the Provisional Government of National Union of Laos in regard to the contribution by the Government of the United Kingdom. The position of the Government of the United Kingdom with regard to the provision of finance is set out in Part A below and the commitments of that Government and the Provisional Government of National Union of Laos as regards associated matters shall be as set out in Part B.

([1]) Treaty Series No. 45 (1975), Cmnd. 5955.

'A. The Government of the United Kingdom declare that it is their intention to make available to the Asian Development Bank (hereinafter referred to as 'the Administrator'), acting on behalf of the Provisional Government of National Union of Laos, by way of financial assistance a sum not exceeding £80,000 (eighty thousand pounds) sterling towards the foreign exchange components costs of the rural electrification works for BAN THALAT, PHONE HONG and BAN KEUN villages, Laos (hereinafter referred to as 'the project'). Of the total sum intended to be made available (hereinafter referred to as the 'UK Aid') 40 per cent will be provided as a grant and 60 per cent in the form of an interest-free loan. It is the intention of the Government of the United Kingdom that funds should be applied in these proportions to each drawing approved for financing under this Agreement.

B.(1) The Government of the United Kingdom shall adopt the arrangements and procedure described in the following paragraphs of this Note insofar as they relate to

[30] Clause B(6)(*b*).
[31] Cmnd. 5956.

things to be done by or on behalf of that Government. The Provisional Government of National Union of Laos shall adopt the arrangements and procedures so described insofar as they relate to things to be done by or on behalf of that Government.

(2) (a) In accordance with the terms of the Fund Agreement:

(i) The Asian Development Bank (ADB) shall act as Administrator of the UK Aid, and

(ii) The project shall be executed by the Electricité du Laos (EDL) in accordance with the terms of a Project Agreement, to be signed on 26 June 1974 between Laos EDL and ADB, and

(iii) Payments approved against the UK aid shall be made payable to the Fund administered by the ADB.

(b) For the purpose of these arrangements, the Administrator shall open a special account (hereinafter referred to as 'the Account') with a bank in London (hereinafter referred to as 'the Bank'). The Account shall be operated only for the purposes of the UK Aid and in accordance with the instructions of the Administrator.

(3) Save to the extent (if any) to which the Government of the United Kingdom and the Administrator may otherwise agree, drawings from the loan (which will be applied for by the Administrator) may be used as provided in part A only for payments to be made in sterling or other freely convertible currency to persons ordinarily resident or carrying on business in the United Kingdom for

(i) the purchase in the UK of goods produced or manufactured in the UK (which expression in this Note shall be deemed to include the Channel Islands and the Isle of Man) or

(ii) work done or services rendered by persons ordinarily resident or carrying on business in the UK

in accordance with arrangements made between the Government of the United Kingdom and the Administrator.

(4) Upon entry into force of the Fund Agreement, the Administrator shall notify the Government of the United Kingdom of the amount of the loan required to cover estimated disbursements on the Project prior to 30 June 1974. The Administrator, before the beginning of each semi-annual period commencing 1 July 1974 and each 1 January and 1 July thereafter, shall notify the Government of the United Kingdom of the amount of the loan required to cover estimated disbursements on the Project during the semi-annual period in question. Payment of the amounts specified in such notification shall be made at the time specified therein into the Account by the Crown Agents for Overseas Governments and Administration 4 Millbank London S.W.1 (hereinafter referred to as 'the Crown Agents'), and each such payment shall constitute a drawing on the loan and grant in the proportions aforesaid. At the end of each semi-annual period the Administrator shall submit to the Crown Agents a statement of all disbursements from the Account during the semi-annual period in question supported

(i) where the disbursement relates to payment for goods or services related to goods by a certificate from the EDL consultants in the form set out in Appendix A to this Note, giving details of the payments made to the United Kingdom suppliers;

(ii) where the disbursement relates to payments other than for goods or services related to goods, by a certificate from the EDL consultants in the form set out in Appendix B to this Note giving details of the payments made in sterling in the United Kingdom for services provided in or from the United Kingdom.

Each certificate in the form of Appendix A shall be accompanied by copies of invoices from the United Kingdom contractor endorsed to the effect that the goods supplied have been produced or manufactured in the United Kingdom. Each certificate in the form of Appendix B shall be accompanied by copies of the relevant invoices or accounts from the person concerned who must be a person ordinarily resident or carrying on business in the United Kingdom. After the last payments have been made the Administrator shall ensure that any unspent balance remaining shall be returned to the Government of the United Kingdom through the Crown Agents in reduction of the loan and grant in the prescribed proportion.

(5) The Provisional Government of National Union of Laos shall repay to the Government of the United Kingdom in pounds sterling in London the proportion of the total sum made available in accordance with this Note which represents a loan, such repayment to be made by instalments paid on the dates and in the amounts specified below, provided that if, on the date when any such instalment is due to be paid, there is then outstanding less than the amount specified for that instalment only the amount then outstanding shall be paid:

INSTALMENTS

Date due	Amount £
9 October 1981 and on 8 October in each of the succeeding 17 years	1,335
8 April 1982 and on 8 April in each of the succeeding 16 years	1,335
8 April 1999	1,275

(6) Notwithstanding the provisions of part B(5) above, the Provisional Government of National Union of Laos shall be free at any earlier time to repay to the Government of the United Kingdom in pounds sterling in London the whole or any part of the loan outstanding.'

On the other hand the financial arrangements relating to development loans which the UK concluded with China in 1986 are much less clear:[32]

ARTICLE I

Financial Arrangements

(1) The form of the financial arrangements shall be the provision of certain sums by way of Government Grants (hereinafter referred to as 'Government Grants') supplied through the Overseas Development Administration of the Government of the United Kingdom (hereinafter referred to as 'ODA') to enable certain bank loans (hereinafter referred to as 'the Loans') to be provided on the terms set out in paragraph (1) of Article 3 of this Agreement.

(2) The Loans, which shall be supported also by the United Kingdom Export Credits Guarantee Department (hereinafter referred to as 'ECGD') shall not exceed in aggregate £300,000,000 (three hundred million pounds sterling) and shall be made by banks acceptable to the Government of the United Kingdom and the Government of China (hereinafter

[32] Cmnd. 9865.

referred to as 'the Lending Banks') to the Bank of China which is authorised by the Government of China to be the borrower (hereinafter referred to as 'the Borrower'). The Loans shall be eligible for financial support under this Agreement provided the terms for this Agreement are met.

ARTICLE 2

Procedures and Practices

(1) The Government of the United Kingdom and the Government of China shall consult and assess the suitability of individual projects for funding. If a project satisfies the criteria of both Governments, Notes shall be exchanged as set out in Appendix A, approving the project for funding and stating the amount of Loan funds to be provided through the Lending Bank or Banks. Four projects which have been identified as suitable for further consideration are recorded in Appendix B.

(2) After the Exchange of Notes and subject to the conditions set out in this Agreement, the Government of China shall in respect of the relevant project authorise the Chinese purchaser approved by the Ministry of Foreign Economic Relations and Trade of the Government of China (hereinafter referred to as 'MOFERT') to negotiate contracts (hereinafter referred to as 'the Contracts'), to be approved by ODA and MOFERT with companies registered in and carrying on business in the United Kingdom (hereinafter referred to as 'United Kingdom companies').

(3) The Government of the United Kingdom shall, on the request of the Government of China, arrange through ECGD with the Lending Banks for the terms set out in paragraph (1) of Article 3 of this Agreement to be applied to the Loan agreement signed by the Borrower and the Lending Bank and shall subsequently make the necessary payments due from the Government Grants to implement and sustain the said terms.

(4) Grant allocations made to any project within the scope of this Agreement shall be agreed between the Foreign Administration acting on behalf of MOFERT and the British Embassy in Peking acting on behalf of ODA.

ARTICLE 3

Terms and Conditions

(1) Subject to the conditions in paragraph (1) of Article 2 of this Agreement, the terms of the Loans shall be twenty years' maturity, including five years' grace period for principal and repayment over fifteen years in equal semi-annual instalments. The rate of interest in respect of each drawing shall be five per cent per annum commencing from the draw-down date of the relevant drawing. Interest shall be payable at intervals not exceeding six months. For Loans in respect of projects with a scheduled commissioning period of more than four years the Government of the United Kingdom will be prepared to consider an extension of the grace period for principal of up to two years after the scheduled commissioning date, subject to a maximum grace period of seven years, within the twenty years' maturity.

(2) Unless the Government of the United Kingdom accepts otherwise, goods financially supported under this Agreement shall be produced in and supplied from the United Kingdom (and shall hereinafter be referred to as 'United Kingdom Goods') and services financially supported under this Agreement shall be provided by persons normally resident in the United Kingdom (and shall hereinafter be referred to as 'United Kingdom Services'). One hundred per cent of the value of the United Kingdom Goods and the United Kingdom Services provided under the Contracts shall be financed by the Loans.

(3) The approved texts of the Contracts and the Loan agreements shall not be amended without the prior approval of ODA, ECGD, MOFERT and the Borrower.

(4) The Government Grants and the Loans shall not be used to meet the cost of any fiscal levies directly or indirectly imposed in the People's Republic of China except to the extent that British personnel who are normally resident in the United Kingdom and who are working in China for the purpose of the Contracts are liable to any such fiscal levies imposed in the People's Republic of China.

(5) Goods purchased under the Contracts shall be shipped and insured in accordance with normal commercial competitive practice by ships or companies of any flag or country acceptable to both Governments. This provision shall be stated explicitly in the Contracts.

(6) The Loans eligible for support under this Agreement shall be for capital goods and related services which shall be used only for civilian purposes.

(7) The Contracts shall contain a clause extending to the personnel or representatives of the Government of the United Kingdom sufficient access to permit a proper examination and assessment of procurement efficiency.

(8) The Government of China shall permit the personnel or representatives of the Government of the United Kingdom to visit any sites or locations where projects which are being financed under the Loans are being carried out, and shall furnish them with such information as they require regarding the projects, their progress, and financing.

(9) The Government of China shall ensure the provision of such additional finance, including local costs, that may be required to complete approved projects.

(10) If a project is suspended or terminated before completion the Government of the United Kingdom and the Government of China shall consult on measures to resolve the problems, including treatment of any Government Grants already paid or to be paid, and agree on appropriate action. Such consultations shall not affect the rights and obligations of the respective parties to the Contracts and the Loan agreements.

(11) The Government of China shall ensure that:

(a) all goods and services for which payment has been financed under the Loans are employed for the purposes for which and by the user for whom they were supplied, for as long as their being so employed remains feasible and the items purchased will be used for civilian purposes only;

(b) all reasonable precautions are taken to protect any Loan funds paid out for the Contracts in advance of work being carried out.

(12) Any sums payable to the Chinese purchaser by or on behalf of United Kingdom companies in relation to goods and services for which finance is made available under the Loans shall be paid to the appropriate Lending Bank which shall inform the Borrower and shall use such sums to reduce the Loan advances already made.

(13) Unless the Government of the United Kingdom accepts otherwise, the Contracts and the Loans must become effective by 31 March 1989 in order to be eligible for funding.

ARTICLE 4

Entry into Force

This Agreement shall come into force on the date of its signature.

One gathers that English banks were intended to make loans not exceeding £300 million to the Bank of China, the borrower. Such loans were supported by the Export Credits Guarantee Department, but in addition the UK was to provide 'certain sums by way of Government Grants . . . to enable certain bank loans . . . to be provided' on agreed terms (Article 1). What is unclear is when, to whom and to what extent payments 'by way of Government Grants' are to be paid. Are the grants a type of guarantee? Or are they intended to finance the difference in the rate of interest between the rate of 5% referred to in Article 3 and the current rate? In view of the participation of the Export Credits Guarantee Department the former possibility seems unlikely. Article 2(3) mentions the UK duty to 'make the necessary payments due from the Government Grants to implement and sustain' the terms mentioned in Article 3(1). Perhaps this does point to the difference in the rate of interest.

However this may be, it is probably free from doubt that, while the relationship between the English lending banks and the Bank of China are presumably governed by some municipal system of law, the rights and duties of the UK and of China itself are subject to public international law. But there are many clauses in the Agreement which can lead to difficulties so that the absence of any jurisdiction clause appears remarkable.

(e) *Loan of Goods*

After considering loans of money it is appropriate to turn to the loan of goods. There do not seem to be many of such cases, but an interesting example is an Agreement between the UK and Lebanon made in 1958.[33] It reads as follows:

Ministère des Affaires Etrangères,
May 19, 1958.

Your Excellency

I have the honour to refer to the free loan, in November, 1956, from the Government of the United Kingdom of Great Britain and Northern Ireland to the Government of the Republic of the Lebanon of the arms, ammunition and equipment set forth in the Annex to the present Note and to propose that the said loan shall be subject to the following terms:—

1. The Lebanese Government undertake:—

(a) not to dispose by sale or gift of any of these arms, ammunition or equipment to any third party, without prior consultation with the Government of the United Kingdom;

(b) to return to the Government of the United Kingdom any of these arms, ammunition or equipment which at any time they may no longer require;

(c) (i) to return, not later than the 1st of January, 1967, the arms, equipment, and such accessories as have not been expended by that date (but not ammunition which shall be deemed expendable at the discretion of the Lebanese Government) or, in agreement with and on behalf of the Government of the United Kingdom, to dispose of them locally;

(ii) not to sell, or otherwise dispose of the said arms, equipment or accessories save for the benefit of specified States, administrations, or persons or to associations or persons, natural or juridical, having a residence or place of business in the Lebanon;

(iii) in any case not to dispose of them either directly or indirectly to the profit of the enemy;

[33] Cmnd. 518.

(d) to pay the cost of transport back to the United Kingdom (or to some other place to be agreed upon with the Government of the United Kingdom provided that the cost of transport is not more than it would be for transport to the United Kingdom) of any arms, equipment or accessories which the Lebanese Government are required to return in accordance with paragraphs (b) and (c) above;

(e) to make good to the Government of the United Kingdom the cost of repairing damage (except for fair wear and tear and damage resulting from enemy action) to equipment, other than that which has been expended as provided for in paragraph (c)(i) above, which is found, on the 1st January, 1967, to be damaged, and to replace equipment other than ammunition and expended accessories, which has been lost or destroyed at that date, other than by enemy action;

(f) to enter into negotiations with the Government of the United Kingdom as to the terms on which any of the arms, equipment, ammunition and accessories, which the Lebanese Government wish to keep after the 1st January, 1967, may be sold to them.

2.   An Anglo-Lebanese commission shall be set up to study the question of compensation for the losses referred to in paragraph 1(e) above whilst taking into account the accepted usages and the eventualities foreseen in the arrangements set out herein.

If the foregoing proposal is acceptable to the Government of the United Kingdom I have the honour to suggest that the present Note, together with its Annex, and Your Excellency's reply in that sense, should be regarded as constituting an agreement between the two Governments in this matter.

CHARLES MALIK.

It is noteworthy that 'the enemy' referred to in clause 1(c)(iii) is not identified and that clause 1(e) uses language ('except for fair wear and tear') which clearly originates in English municipal law. The loan is gratuitous, but in so far as compensation for losses is concerned account is to be taken of 'the accepted usages and the eventualities foreseen in the arrangements set out herein'. The term 'accepted usages' again would seem to refer to municipal law, for nothing similar appears to exist in public international law. But whether usages in the UK or in Lebanon are being envisaged is unexplained, though one is inclined to hold the former to be applicable.

A different type of loan of goods is represented by the Agreement between the UK and the United Arab Republic relating to the Tutankhamen Exhibition at the British Museum in 1972.[34] The Agreement between the two States, to which an Agreement between the Cairo Museum and the British Museum was annexed, reads as follows:

ARTICLE 1

(1) There shall be held at the British Museum in London for a period of six months, commencing in April/May 1972, an Exhibition of relics of the period of Tutankhamen belonging to the Cairo Museum.

(2) Annex A to this Agreement contains a list of objects to be exhibited and their individual valuation. It shall not be subject to alteration or modification except with the consent of the British Museum and of the Cairo Museum.

[34] Cmnd. 4898. See also the Agreement between the UK and China for the Exhibition of Terracotta Figures of 2 August 1985, Cmnd. 9698.

(3) The Government of the United Arab Republic shall take the necessary steps to authorise the exhibition in London of the objects referred to in paragraph 2 of this Article.

(4) The objects to be exhibited shall be furnished by the Government of the United Arab Republic, as a loan, solely for the purpose of the Exhibition. The Government of the United Kingdom, for their part, undertake to respect the rights of the Cairo Museum and the Government of the United Arab Republic in the objects to be exhibited and undertake, within the limits of their legal powers, to protect these objects against any form of sequestration, seizure or any form of prejudice to the rights of the Cairo Museum or the Government of the United Arab Republic, whether on the part of another government or an individual. The Government of the United Kingdom further undertake to co-operate in the implementation of arrangements for the physical security and protection of the objects, from the time of their arrival in the United Kingdom until the time of their departure from the United Kingdom, under the agreement between the British Museum and the Cairo Museum, a copy of which is attached to this Agreement at Annex B.

ARTICLE 2

(1) The Government of the United Kingdom shall arrange for the payment, in sterling, of the net proceeds of the Exhibition, after deduction of all expenses incurred in connection with it, to the fund administered by the United Nations Educational, Scientific and Cultural Organisation for the restoration of the temples at Philae.

(2) The Government of the United Arab Republic shall not be charged by the Government of the United Kingdom or the British Museum with any expenses or have any financial obligations of any sort towards them in connection with the Exhibition.

ARTICLE 3

(1)(a) The Government of the United Kingdom shall, subject to the necessary Parliamentary approval which the Government of the United Kingdom undertake to seek, indemnify the Government of the United Arab Republic up to a limit of £9,060,000 in respect of any loss or damage to the objects listed in Annex A to this Agreement, other than loss or damage resulting from the actions or omissions of the Government of the United Arab Republic, or of the Cairo Museum, from the time of the removal of the objects from the Cairo Museum to the time of their arrival at the Cairo Museum on their return from London. This indemnity shall extend to any loss or damage suffered by the Government of the United Arab Republic as the result of any decision, order or procedure in the United Kingdom preventing the objects from being returned to the United Arab Republic at the end of the Exhibition. The circumstances giving rise to the proceedings initiated against the Government of the United Arab Republic shall not be considered as constituting an action or omission on their part within the meaning of this sub-paragraph. The Government of the United Kingdom shall inform the Government of the United Arab Republic of the granting of the Parliamentary approval referred to above before the removal of the objects from the Cairo Museum.

(b) Sub-paragraph (a) notwithstanding, this indemnity shall exclude any loss or damage, caused during transit between the Cairo Museum, and the British Museum, both before and after the Exhibition, as a result of any war or hostilities or other warlike operations.

(2) The Government of the United Kingdom shall arrange for the insurance of the objects, to the valuation specified in Annex A to this Agreement, against the risks specified in sub-paragraph (b) of paragraph (1) of this Article. Evidence of such insurance shall be produced to the Director of the Cairo Museum before the departure of the objects. The

premium payable for such insurance, and any other expenses incurred in connection there-with, shall be a charge against the proceeds of the Exhibition in accordance with paragraph (1) of Article 2. No charge in connection with such insurance shall fall on the Government of the United Arab Republic.

(3) Should the indemnity set out in paragraph (1) of this Article be called upon, the Government of the United Arab Republic shall ensure that the Government of the United Kingdom are subrogated to any rights, which the Government of the United Arab Republic or persons under its jurisdiction may have, to recover compensation for the loss or damage in question.

ARTICLE 4

Any other arrangements for the holding of the Exhibition such as packing, unpacking and transport of the objects to be exhibited, the participation of representatives of the Cairo Museum, the production of any representation or copy of any of the objects to be exhibited, together with any other matters, will be the subject of arrangements to be made between the Cairo Museum and the British Museum.

ARTICLE 5

Any dispute between the two Governments concerning the interpretation or execution of this Agreement shall be settled by direct negotiations between the two Governments. If agreement is not reached as a result of such negotiations, either Government may submit the dispute to a Committee of Arbitration, composed of three members. Each Government shall nominate an arbitrator within a period of two months from the receipt of the notice of the submission of the dispute to arbitration. The two arbitrators selected shall, within one month of their nomination, choose a third arbitrator, who shall not be a national of either Government, to act as chairman of the Committee of Arbitration. If the periods of time referred to above are not respected, each Government shall have the right, in default of any further agreement between the two Governments on other means of arriving at a solution, to request the President of the International Court of Justice to make the necessary nomination. The Committee shall take its decision by a majority of votes. Its decision shall be final and binding.

ARTICLE 6

This Agreement shall enter into force on signature.

For once one notices a jurisdiction clause, but perhaps the most interesting clause is Article 1(4) according to which the UK undertook 'within the limits of their legal powers to protect these objects against any form of sequestration, seizure or any form of prejudice'. Suppose another government or an individual has started proceedings and obtained an injunction in England to claim an item included in the exhibition. What could or would the UK have done? Would it have to pay off the claimant? Would it have to finance the defence? Could it have been required to pass legislation? It is likely that the answers are in each case in the affirmative, so that the UK would have discharged its obligations only if Parliament had either passed or rejected legislation. Only in the case of rejection would the Government's legal powers have been exhausted. On the other hand the settlement of accounts would have been an accountancy problem and would have been unlikely to give rise to legal problems of any substance.

(f) *Sales*

In 1957 the UK sold four destroyers to Turkey on the following terms:[35]

British Embassy,
Istanbul, August 26, 1957.

Your Excellency,

I have the honour to refer to the discussions between representatives of the Government of the United Kingdom of Great Britain and Northern Ireland and the Government of the Turkish Republic concerning the purchase of certain ships of the British Reserve Fleet by the Turkish Government. As a result of these discussions agreement was reached in principle in the following terms:—

(1) The Government of the United Kingdom will make available to the Turkish Government four 'M' Class destroyers of the British Reserve Fleet and will arrange for the immediate transfer of title to these ships, which will then be at the risk of the Turkish Government.

(2) The Government of the United Kingdom will refit the vessels within an estimated maximum cost of £500,000 per ship, and provide them with initial stores and spares, on a scale recommended by the British Admiralty and agreed by representatives of the Turkish Government.

(3) The Government of the United Kingdom will make the necessary payments, as and when required, in connexion with the cost of refitting and the provision of initial stores and spares, direct from the sum to be made available in paragraph (4) below.

(4) The Government of the Turkish Republic have deposited the sum of £100,000, and the Government of the United Kingdom undertake to grant to the Turkish Government a loan of £2,900,000, towards the total purchase price of the hulls, the cost of refitting them, and the initial stores and spares.

(5) Interest at the rate of 5% per annum will be payable commencing, in respect of that part of the loan applicable to each destroyer, from the date on which each destroyer sails from the United Kingdom.

(6) The sum of £2,900,000 loaned to the Turkish Government under the provisions of paragraph (4) above, together with simple interest thereon calculated in accordance with paragraph (5), and outstanding on the first day of January, 1968 (hereinafter referred to as the 'principal sum') shall be repaid by the Government of the Turkish Republic to the Government of the United Kingdom in pounds sterling by means of ten equal half-yearly instalments, payable on the first day of July and on the first day of January, of such amount as will secure the repayment by the first day of January, 1973, of the principal sum.

(7) The Turkish Government will insure the ships against loss or damage and make them available to the Government of the United Kingdom for the initial refit. In the event of any claims being made against insurance for loss or damage to the ships while being towed to the refitting ports or during the period they are undergoing refit, the Turkish Government will remit to the Government of the United Kingdom any insurance monies received. Monies made available in respect of loss will be debited to the total amount of the loan outstanding at that date, while monies made available in respect of damage will be put by the Government of the United Kingdom towards the cost of making good that damage.

I now have the honour upon instructions from Her Majesty's Principal Secretary of State for Foreign Affairs to inform your Excellency that the above terms are acceptable to the Government of the United Kingdom, and if they are likewise acceptable to the Government of the Turkish Republic to propose that this Note, together with your Excellency's reply in

[35] Cmnd. 260.

that sense, should be regarded as constituting an agreement between the two Governments in this matter which shall enter into force on this day's date.

I have, &c.

JAMES BOWKER.

It will be noticed that, although agreement between the Parties was stated to have been 'reached in principle', the Note and the reply to it were 'regarded as constituting an agreement' between the two States. In private law there might well be an argument for suggesting that an agreement 'in principle' was so incomplete as to exclude the existence of a legally binding contract. But, it is submitted, no such argument would have any force in the present case. Furthermore, it will be noted that the purchase price was financed by a loan of £2,900,000 at $5\frac{1}{2}\%$ p.a. repayable over a period ending in 1973, but these terms were substantially altered in 1959[36] and 1967,[37] so that, in particular, the principal sum lent to Turkey became £4,482,187 and was repayable by means of twenty half-yearly instalments beginning on 1 July 1968.

However, the treaty does not in any way address the problems arising from the fact that the destroyers were to be refitted and the money lent to Turkey was to be paid direct to the yard. One could imagine many problems relating to quality, time of delivery and other aspects, which in private law would probably be dealt with very meticulously. That the treaty with Turkey does not include any such terms nor any jurisdiction clause will strike the private lawyer as remarkable.

Another treaty of a not altogether dissimilar character was made with Ghana in 1972.[38] In 1965 the UK had lent to Ghana £3,714,390 to pay for a frigate which was then being built by Yarrow & Co. Ltd. of Glasgow. But in 1972 the UK and Ghana entered into the following treaty whereby the former took over the frigate and converted the loan into a grant:

British High Commission,
Accra.

Sir,
13 March, 1972.

I have the honour to inform you that, as agreed between the Prime Minister of the United Kingdom of Great Britain and Northern Ireland and the Prime Minister of Ghana in their discussions of the 24th of August, 1971, the Government of the United Kingdom is prepared to take over the frigate belonging to the Government of Ghana, which is at present lying in the Clyde, and to waive the outstanding balance of the loan for the purchase of this frigate made to the Government of Ghana by the Government of the United Kingdom under the terms of the agreement set forth in my predecessor's Note of the 14th of April, 1965.

If this is acceptable to the Government of Ghana the Government of the United Kingdom propose that the frigate should pass from Ghanaian to British ownership with effect from the 24th of August, 1971, and that the Government of Ghana should be excused those payments in respect of the frigate due to the Government of the United Kingdom or to Messrs. Yarrow and Company Limited as detailed in the Annex attached to this Note. Any refund or rebate due from Messrs. Yarrow and Company Limited to the Government of Ghana in respect of any payment relating to the frigate made by that Government before the 24th of August would become payable to the Government of the United Kingdom. The outstanding

---

[36] Cmnd. 751.
[37] Cmnd. 4241.
[38] Cmnd. 5005.

capital sum of £3,803,125.95 would be converted by the Government of the United Kingdom from a loan into a grant.

Except as mentioned in paragraph 2 above, the Government of the United Kingdom would not become responsible for the payment of any costs incurred (including agency fees incurred in efforts to dispose of the vessel) by the Government of Ghana prior to the date of this Note in respect of the frigate.

If the foregoing proposals are acceptable to the Government of Ghana, I have the honour to suggest that this Note and your reply thereto shall constitute an Agreement in this matter between the two Governments which shall enter into force on the date of your reply.

I have the honour to be,

Sir,

Your obedient Servant,

H. S. H. STANLEY

Finally it is appropriate to mention a somewhat unusual Agreement between the UK and Italy[39] whereby the Italian Air Force was appointed 'the representative' of the Royal Air Force for the sale of certain materials and the Italian Government was given 'the option to purchase any material put for sale at a price to be agreed with the Royal Air Force'—an option which in private law would probably be so uncertain as to render it invalid in the absence of a jurisdiction clause:

The Government of the United Kingdom of Great Britain and Northern Ireland and the Government of the Republic of Italy:

Considering that the Government of the United Kingdom acting through the command of the Royal Air Force in Italy envisages the disposal of waste material, surplus material and stores and scrap in Italy, which is the property of the Government of the United Kingdom, and desires to dispose of such material in Italy or by export direct from Italy;

Convinced that the disposal of such material will be beneficial both to the Italian economy and to the Command of the Royal Air Force in Italy;

Noting that the Government of the Republic of Italy agrees that the Command of the Royal Air Force in Italy may dispose of such scrap, waste material, surplus material and stores, which is the property of the United Kingdom, have agreed as follows:

Article I

The Command of the Royal Air Force shall be free to sell any of its waste material, surplus material, surplus stores and scrap (hereinafter referred to as 'material') which arise from its operations in Italy and for which it has no further use, in accordance with the following Articles.

Article II

The Command of the Royal Air Force, shall notify the Italian Government of the type, quantity, approximate value, location and proposed point of sale in Italy of any material it wishes to offer for sale.

[39] Cmnd. 6516.

Article III

If so requested the Italian Air Force will act as the representative of the Royal Air Force for these sales. Such sales shall be effected in accordance with the principles normally adopted for the sale of similar material which is the property of the Italian Government, following a procedure which is to be agreed between the appropriate authorities of the Italian Air Force and the Royal Air Force.

Article IV

The lira revenue which accrue to the Royal Air Force from these sales may be used for any expenditure in Italy by the Royal Air Force, or the Government of the United Kingdom, or it may be converted into sterling for transfer to the United Kingdom in accordance with the existing currency arrangements.

Article V

The Italian Government shall have the option to purchase any material put up for sale at a price to be agreed with the Royal Air Force. If this option is not exercised within thirty days of the notification referred to in Article II, the Royal Air Force shall have the right to continue with the proposed sale to any other purchaser.

Article VI

The Italian Government shall consider in each case the desirability of importing materials and equipment. If no objection is received within thirty days of the notification referred to in Article II, the Royal Air Force shall have the right to continue with the proposed sale as set out below.

Article VII

For the import of material to Italy:

(a) Sales may be made to any persons, firms or other non-governmental organisations authorised to transact business in Italy;

(b) An import licence shall be obtained by the purchaser from the Government of Italy in each case;

(c) The Royal Air Force shall ensure that the materials sold are not released to the purchaser without the necessary clearance from the Italian Customs authorities;

(d) The Italian Government shall grant all technical and administrative facilities compatible with Italian legislation for the import of material;

(e) The import of material to Italy shall be limited to an aggregate sale value not exceeding 60,000,000 lire in any calendar year, this sum being exclusive of any sales to Italian Government organisations. This sum may be increased for a particular calendar year by agreement between the appropriate authorities of the Italian Government and the Royal Air Force.

ARTICLE VIII

For the export of material from Italy:

(*a*) Export sales may be made by the Royal Air Force to any foreign persons, firms or other organisations without restriction as to type, quantity or value of the material. Such sales to persons, firms or other organisations authorised to transact business in Italy shall be subject to the specific approval of the Italian Government in each case. If no objection is received from the Italian Government within thirty days of the day of despatch of the request of the Royal Air Force such request will be considered as granted automatically;

(*b*) Export sales made under the terms of this Agreement shall be subject to the existing Italian Customs procedures and regulations but the materials shall not be subject to Italian Customs duties.

ARTICLE IX

Each Contracting Party reserves the right to request, at least two months in advance, re-negotiation of any clause of this Agreement.

ARTICLE X

This Agreement shall come into force upon signature and shall continue in force unless either of the Contracting Parties shall notify the other in writing at least two months in advance of its intention to terminate the Agreement.

In witness whereof the undersigned, being duly authorised thereto by their respective Governments, have signed this Agreement.

Done in duplicate at Rome this 29th day of January 1976 in the English and Italian languages, both texts being equally authoritative.

For the Government of the United Kingdom of Great Britain and Northern Ireland:	For the Government of the Republic of Italy:
GUY MILLARD	CESIDIO GUAZZARONI

(g) *Trust*

Treaties frequently speak of, and thus seem to create, a trust in the sense which is familiar to private law not only in the Anglo-Saxon countries, but also in civil law systems. Yet it is by no means certain that, when treaties employ the term, they contemplate anything like the institution known to municipal laws. For more than a century we have known that the term may be used 'in the higher sense' and indicate 'mere governmental obligations'.[40] It is in each case a matter of construction, and may raise a very difficult problem. As an example one may mention the Agreement concerning the Voluntary Contributions to save the Temples of Philae.[41] It reads as follows:

---

[40] *Kinloch* v. *Secretary of State for India* (1882), 7 App. Cas. 619; *Tito* v. *Waddell (No.2)*, [1977] Ch. 106, 210 ff.

[41] Cmnd. 5033.

CONSIDERING that, as already proclaimed on several occasions by the General Conference of Unesco, the monuments of Nubia, now endangered by the construction of the Aswan High Dam which the United Arab Republic has undertaken in order to ensure the country's economic development and to promote the welfare of its peoples, form part of the cultural heritage of the entire human race.

NOTING that the salvage project adopted by the Government of the United Arab Republic, involving the dismantling of the temples and their reconstruction on a small island close to the original site, has been subsequently recommended by the various competent technical committees, and accepted by the Executive Committee of the Campaign to Save the Monuments of Nubia,

ANXIOUS to play a part in ensuring that the temples of Philae survive to be admired and treasured by future generations,

RESPONDING to the appeals for international co-operation launched for this purpose by the United Nations Educational, Scientific and Cultural Organization,

The Contracting Member States and Associate Members of Unesco agree as follows:

ARTICLE I

1. Every Contracting Member State or Associate Member of Unesco undertakes to contribute to the execution of the project to save the temples of Philae by making a contribution in kind or by paying into the Trust Fund established for this purpose by the Director-General of the United Nations Educational, Scientific and Cultural Organization, hereinafter referred to as 'the Director-General', the amounts set forth in the Annex to this Agreement, in the currency, on the dates and under the conditions specified in the said Annex.

2. The Director-General will not transmit any amount that may have been deposited with him to the competent authorities of the United Arab Republic, nor will he take any steps to make contributions in kind available to these authorities, until such time as the Government of the United Arab Republic has finally given an assurance that it will undertake the operations to save the temples of Philae and take the necessary measures for their satisfactory completion and that it will conclude for that purpose, with one or more contractors, the contract for the work described in the specifications drawn up by the Ministry of Culture of the United Arab Republic (Salvage of the Temples of Philae).([1])

ARTICLE II

1. The Director-General will obtain all the necessary particulars regarding the payment dates with which the United Arab Republic will have to reckon in executing the contract referred to in Article I, paragraph 2. He will also receive periodical progress reports.

2. He will pay the amounts which he receives in conformity with the terms of Article I, paragraph 1, and in accordance with the procedure laid down in the Agreement between Unesco and the Government of the United Arab Republic concerning the safeguarding of the temples of Philae to the appropriate authorities of the United Arab Republic, taking the time-table of payments due and the progress of work into account.

([1]) The U.A.R. concluded a contract for the execution of the Philae project on 3 June 1971.

Article III

The Director-General will communicate a periodical information report, at least every six months, to the Contracting Member States and Associate Members of Unesco concerning the implementation of this Agreement and the progress of the operations to save the temples of Philae.

Article IV

This Agreement will bear the date of 19 December 1970 and will remain open to the signature of all the Member States and Associate Members of Unesco.

Article V

This Agreement shall enter into force for each Contracting Member State or Associate Member of Unesco upon its signature or, if it is signed subject to ratification or acceptance, on the date of the deposit of an instrument of ratification or acceptance with the Director-General.

Article VI

The Director-General will hold at the disposal of Contracting Member States and Associate Members of Unesco the sums which the latter have contributed under this Agreement if the Government of the United Arab Republic does not conclude the contract for the work described in the specifications drawn up by the Minister of Culture (Salvage of the Temples of Philae).

Article VII

The Director-General shall inform the Member States and Associate Members of Unesco of the signatures affixed to this Agreement, as well as of the deposit of the instruments of ratification or acceptance mentioned in Article V of this Agreement.

Article VIII

In accordance with Article 102 of the Charter of the United Nations, this Agreement will be registered at the United Nations Secretariat, at the request of the Director-General.

Article IX

This Agreement, except for its annex, is drawn up in Arabic, English, French, Russian and Spanish, all five texts being equally authentic.

Done in Cairo this nineteenth day of December 1970 in a single copy, which will be deposited in the Archives of the United Nations Educational, Scientific and Cultural Organization and certified copies of which will be communicated to all signatory Member States and Associate Members, as well as to the United Nations.

In faith whereof, the undersigned representatives, duly authorized to that effect, have signed this Agreement.

Could Egypt enforce the trustee's obligations under this Agreement? Could the contributories insist upon the use of the funds for the specific purpose for which they were given? It seems likely that both questions should be answered in the affirmative. The reason probably lies in the specificity of the objects as well as the beneficiary.

Such characteristics are missing in the case of the Agreement between the UK[42] and Mauritius concerning the Ilois:[43]

The Government of the United Kingdom of Great Britain and Northern Ireland (herein-after referred to as the Government of the United Kingdom) and the Government of Mauritius,

Desiring to settle certain problems which have arisen concerning the Ilois who went to Mauritius on their departure or removal from the Chagos Archipelago after November 1965 (hereinafter referred to as 'the Ilois');

Wishing to assist with the resettlement of the Ilois in Mauritius as viable members of the community;

Noting that the Government of Mauritius has undertaken to the Ilois to vest absolutely in the Board of Trustees established under Article 7 of this Agreement, and within one year from the date of the entry into force of this Agreement, land to the value of £1 million as at 31 March 1982, for the benefit of the Ilois and the Ilois community in Mauritius;

Have agreed as follows:

ARTICLE 1

The Government of the United Kingdom shall *ex gratia* with no admission of liability pay to the Government of Mauritius for and on behalf of the Ilois and the Ilois community in Mauritius in accordance with Article 7 of this Agreement the sum of £4 million which, taken together with the payment of £650,000 already made to the Government of Mauritius, shall be in full and final settlement of all claims whatsoever of the kind referred to in Article 2 of this Agreement against the Government of the United Kingdom by or on behalf of the Ilois.

ARTICLE 2

The claims referred to in Article 1 of this Agreement are solely claims by or on behalf of the Ilois arising out of:

(a) all acts, matters and things done by or pursuant to the British Indian Ocean Territory Order 1965, including the closure of the plantations in the Chagos Archipelago, the departure or removal of those living or working there, the termination of their con-tracts, their transfer to and resettlement in Mauritius and their preclusion from returning to the Chagos Archipelago (hereinafter referred to as 'the events'); and

(b) any incidents, facts or situations, whether past, present or future, occurring in the course of the events or arising out of the consequences of the events.

---

[42] Here as so often the Agreement is described as having been made between the Government of the UK and the Government of Mauritius. In truth the contracting parties are the UK and Mauritius. In the exercise of the treaty-making power the Government is only an agent, not a party.

[43] Cmnd. 8785.

ARTICLE 3

The reference in Article 1 of this Agreement to claims against the Government of the United Kingdom includes claims against the Crown in right of the United Kingdom and the Crown in right of any British possession, together with claims against the servants, agents and contractors of the Government of the United Kingdom.

ARTICLE 4

The Government of Mauritius shall use its best endeavours to procure from each member of the Ilois community in Mauritius a signed renunciation of the claims referred to in Article 2 of this Agreement, and shall hold such renunciations of claims at the disposal of the Government of the United Kingdom.

ARTICLE 5

(1) Should any claim against the Government of the United Kingdom (or other defendant referred to in Article 3 of this Agreement) be advanced or maintained by or on behalf of any of the Ilois notwithstanding the provisions of Article 1 of this Agreement, the Government of the United Kingdom (or other defendant as aforesaid) shall be indemnified out of the Trust Fund established pursuant to Article 6 of this Agreement against all loss, costs, damages or expenses which the Government of the United Kingdom (or other defendant as aforesaid) may reasonably incur or be called upon to pay as a result of any such claim. For this purpose the Board of Trustees shall retain the sum of £250,000 in the Trust Fund until 31 December 1985 or until any claim presented before that date is concluded, whichever is the later. If any claim of the kind referred to in this Article is advanced, whether before or after 31 December 1985, and the Trust Fund does not have adequate funds to meet the indemnity provided in this Article, the Government of Mauritius shall, if the claim is successful, indemnify the Government of the United Kingdom as aforesaid.

(2) Notwithstanding the provisions of paragraph (1) of this Article the Government of the United Kingdom may authorise the Board of Trustees to release all or part of the retained sum of £250,000 before the date specified if the Government of the United Kingdom is satisfied with the adequacy of the renunciations of claims procured pursuant to Article 4 of this Agreement.

ARTICLE 6

The sum to be paid to the Government of Mauritius in accordance with the provisions of Article 1 of this Agreement shall immediately upon payment be paid by the Government of Mauritius into a Trust Fund to be established by Act of Parliament as soon as possible by the Government of Mauritius.

ARTICLE 7

(1) The Trust Fund referred to in Article 6 of this Agreement shall have the object of ensuring that the payments of capital (namely £4 million), and any income arising from the investment thereof, shall be disbursed expeditiously and solely in promoting the social and economic welfare of the Ilois and the Ilois community in Mauritius, and the Government of Mauritius shall ensure that such capital and income are devoted solely to that purpose.

(2) Full powers of administration and management of the Trust Fund shall be vested in a

Board of Trustees, which shall be composed of representatives of the Government of Mauritius and of the Ilois in equal numbers and an independent chairman, the first members of the Board of Trustees to be named in the Act of Parliament. The Board of Trustees shall as soon as possible after the end of each year prepare and submit to the Government of Mauritius an annual report on the operation of the Fund, a copy of which shall immediately be passed by that Government to the Government of the United Kingdom.

ARTICLE 8

This Agreement shall enter into force on the twenty-eighth day after the date on which the two Governments have informed each other that the necessary internal procedures, including the enactment of the Act of Parliament and the establishment of the Board of Trustees pursuant to Articles 6 and 7 of this Agreement, have been completed.

It is difficult to maintain that this Agreement as such, i.e. independently of any law of Mauritius, creates anything in the nature of a trust in the sense of private law.

(h) *Use of Land*

Numerous treaties, particularly between the UK and the USA, concern the use of land and of facilities built on land. Frequently the Agreements include terms of a peculiarly sovereign nature in that they provide for fiscal exemptions, criminal jurisdiction, the use of currency, the importation and exportation of materials and similar matters. Examples are the Agreement concerning the Establishment of a Station for Space Vehicle Tracking and Communications on Antigua,[44] or the Agreement concerning the Bahamas Long-Range Proving Ground.[45] But there are also Agreements which more closely correspond to leases in private law with which every lawyer is familiar. Thus one finds the agreement regarding a proposed road through the Naval Air Station in Bermuda, which was made in 1971[46] and is a consequence of the famous Agreement of 27 March 1941[47] for the grant of a lease of 99 years in exchange for 50 destroyers.[48] The 1971 Agreement reads as follows:

Embassy of the United States of America,
London.
January 28, 1971.

Sir,

I have the honour to refer to the Agreement relating to the Bases leased to the United States of America, signed on March 27, 1941, as amended and to recent discussions between representatives of the Government of the United States and the Government of Bermuda regarding a proposed road through the United States Naval Air Station, Bermuda (formerly known as the United States Kindley Air Force Base, Bermuda).

I now have the honour to inform you that the Government of the United States is prepared to enter into an agreement in the following terms, for making available an area within the United States Naval Air Station for the construction by the Government of Bermuda, at its expense, of the proposed road and for the use of the proposed road by vehicular and pedestrian traffic:

---

[44] Cmnd. 3289.
[45] Cmnd. 8109, 9810, and 3421.
[46] Cmnd. 4634.
[47] Cmnd. 6259.
[48] For the circumstances surrounding the Agreement see Churchill, *The Second World War*, vol. 2 (1949), pp. 353 ff.

(1) The area to be made available to the Government of Bermuda shall comprise the area located generally as shown on the map annexed to this Note described in metes and bounds and geographical co-ordinates on the United States Air Force Drawing No. PBD 1968–1 prepared and held in the United States Naval Air Station Civil Engineer's Office and in constructional detail on the three sheets of Drawing No. 5/10/41 prepared and held in the Public Works Department of Bermuda including all such portions of the United States Military Road called 'Swalwell Drive' as are located therein. The area made available shall be used by the Government of Bermuda for the construction thereon, at its own expense, of the proposed road between the road used by the Government of Bermuda known as 'Kindley Field Road' and the public road known as 'St. David's Road' as is shown on the said Drawings, in which road shall be incorporated, with such realignments as may be appropriate or necessary, the said portions of Swalwell Drive and which road shall be for the use of vehicular and pedestrian traffic passing thereover between the Kindley Field Road and St. David's Road and which when constructed shall also be known as 'St David's Road'.

(2) The Government of Bermuda shall not be required to pay rent to the Government of the United States for the area made available.

(3) The Government of Bermuda shall have control and jurisdiction over the area made available in the same manner and to the same extent as it would if the area were outside the leased area and shall relieve the Government of the United States from responsibility for the road, including its maintenance and traffic control.

(4) The United States military authorities shall have the right to use the proposed road and to determine, so as to prevent interference with United States military activities at the base, the manner and location of the construction and installation of any works, fixtures, and facilities on the area made available.

(5) Before the area made available is used by or with the authority of the Government of Bermuda for the traffic purposes aforesaid the Government of Bermuda shall in accordance with guidelines and criteria agreed between the United States military authorities and the Government of Bermuda, construct at its own expense:

(a) a dividing fence along the southern boundary of the area made available;

(b) a new roadway to be called 'Swalwell Drive' to the south of such dividing fence located generally as shown on the three sheets of Drawing No. 5/10/41; and

(c) the new traffic complex shown on Sheet 1 of the said Drawing together with a new gatehouse, bus shelter and telephone kiosk to be located generally as shown on the said Sheet.

(6) The Government of Bermuda shall hold harmless the Government of the United States its agents and employees from all claims for injury to, or death of, persons or damage to, or destruction of, property, arising from the construction of any works, fixtures or facilities contemplated by these arrangements, unless such injury, death or damage results from the gross negligence or wilful misconduct of an employee of the Government of the United States.

(7) The use of the area made available for the purpose specified herein shall not be considered to diminish in any way the military nature and importance of the United States Naval Air Station. Except as expressly provided herein, these arrangements shall not, in any manner derogate from the provisions of the Agreement relating to the Bases leased to the United States of America, signed on March 27, 1941 as modified by the following instruments:

the Agreement concerning the Opening of Certain Military Air Bases in the

Caribbean Area and Bermuda to Use by Civil Aircraft, dated February 24, 1948; the
Agreement modifying the Agreement relating to the Bases leased to the United States
of America of March 27, 1941, effected by the Exchange of Notes dated July 19 and
August 1, 1950; the Agreement on the Provision of Civil Airport Facilities at the
Kindley Air Force Base, Bermuda, effected by the Exchange of Notes dated March 23
and April 25, 1951; the Agreement extending the Area of the Civil Air Terminal in
Bermuda, effected by the Exchange of Notes, dated May 25, 1960 and the Agreement
regarding additional Civil Airport facilities at the United States Kindley Air Force
Base, Bermuda, effected by the Exchange of Notes dated June 4, 1968.

(8) The United States military authorities and the Government of Bermuda or any authority designated by that Government in that behalf may conclude supplementary
arrangements in implementation of this agreement in accordance with its intent and
purposes.

If the foregoing is acceptable to the Government of the United Kingdom of Great Britain
and Northern Ireland, I have the honour to propose that this Note and your reply to that
effect shall constitute an Agreement between our two Governments which shall enter into
force on the date of Your Excellency's reply and shall remain in force until the expiration of
the lease of the United States Naval Air Station.

W. H. ANNENBERG.

A much more elaborate Agreement between the UK and the US is the San
Diego Garcia Agreement of 1978:[49]

Foreign and Commonwealth Office
London

Sir,   *25 February, 1976.*

I have the honour to refer to the Agreement constituted by the Exchange of Notes dated
30 December 1966 between the Government of the United Kingdom of Great Britain and
Northern Ireland and the Government of the United States of America concerning the availability of the British Indian Ocean Territory for defence purposes and to the Agreement
constituted by the Exchange of Notes dated 24 October 1972 between the two Governments
concerning a limited United States naval communications facility on Diego Garcia, British
Indian Ocean Territory. Pursuant to paragraph 2(b) of the former Agreement, I now convey
the approval in principle of the Government of the United Kingdom to the development of
the present limited naval communications facility on Diego Garcia into a support facility of
the United States Navy and propose an Agreement in the following terms:

(1) *Scope of the facility*

(a) Subject to the following provisions of this Agreement, the Government of the
United States shall have the right to develop the present limited naval communications
facility on Diego Garcia as a support facility of the United States Navy and to maintain
and operate it. The facility shall consist of an anchorage, airfield, support and supply
elements and ancillary services, personnel accommodation, and transmitting and receiving services. Immovable structures, installations and buildings for the facility may, after
consultation with the appropriate administrative authorities of the United Kingdom, be
constructed within the specific area shown in the plan attached to this Note. The specific
area may be altered from time to time as may be agreed by the appropriate administrative
authorities of the two Governments.

(b) During the term of the Agreement the Government of the United States may conduct on Diego Garcia such functions as are necessary for the development, use, mainten-

[49] Cmnd. 6413.

ance, operation and security of the facility. In the exercise of these functions the Government of the United States, members of the United States Forces and contractor personnel shall have freedom of access to that part of Diego Garcia outside the specific area referred to in sub-paragraph (a), but the Government of the United States may erect or construct immovable structures, installations and buildings outside the specific area only with the prior agreement of the appropriate administrative authorities of the Government of the United Kingdom.

(c) Delimitation of the specific area shall, subject to the provisions of the BIOT Agreement and after consultation with the appropriate United States authorities with a view to avoiding interference with the existing use of the facility, in no way restrict the Government of the United Kingdom from constructing and operating at their own expense their own defence facilities within that area, or from using that part of Diego Garcia outside the specific area.

(2) *Purpose*

The facility shall provide an improved link in the United States defence communications, and furnish support for ships and aircraft owned or operated by or on behalf of either Government.

(3) *Consultation*

Both Governments shall consult periodically on joint objectives, policies and activities in the area. As regards the use of the facility in normal circumstances, the Commanding Officer and the Officer in Charge of the United Kingdom Service element shall inform each other of intended movements of ships and aircraft. In other circumstances the use of the facility shall be a matter for the joint decision of the two Governments.

(4) *Access to Diego Garcia*

(a) Access to Diego Garcia shall in general be restricted to members of the Forces of the United Kingdom and of the United States, the Commissioner and public officers in the service of the British Indian Ocean Territory, representatives of the Governments of the United Kingdom and of the United States and, subject to normal immigration requirements, contractor personnel. The Government of the United Kingdom reserves the right, after consultation with the appropriate United States administrative authorities, to grant access to members of scientific parties wishing to carry out research on Diego Garcia and its environs, provided that such research does not unreasonably interfere with the activities of the facility. The Commanding Officer shall afford appropriate assistance to members of these parties to the extent feasible and on a reimbursable basis. Access shall not be granted to any other person without prior consultation between the appropriate administrative authorities of the two Governments.

(b) Ships and aircraft owned or operated by or on behalf of either Government may freely use the anchorage and airfield.

(c) Pursuant to the provisions of the second sentence of paragraph (3) of the BIOT Agreement, ships and aircraft owned or operated by or on behalf of a third government, and the personnel of such ships and aircraft, may use only such of the services provided by the facility, and on such terms, as may be agreed in any particular case by the two Governments.

(5) *Protection and security*

Responsibility for protection and security of the facility shall be vested in the Commanding Officer, who shall maintain a close liaison with the Commissioner. The two Governments shall consult if there is any threat to the facility.

(6) *Shipping, navigation and aviation facilities*

The Government of the United States shall have the right to install, operate and maintain on Diego Garcia such navigational and communications aids as may be necessary for the safe transit of ships and aircraft into and out of Diego Garcia.

(7) *Radio frequencies and telecommunications*

(*a*) Subject to the prior concurrence of the Government of the United Kingdom, the Government of the United States may use any radio frequencies, powers and band widths for radio services (including radar) on Diego Garcia which are necessary for the operation of the facility. All radio communications shall comply at all times with the provisions of the International Telecommunications Convention.

(*b*) The Government of the United States may establish such land lines on Diego Garcia as may be necessary for the facility.

(8) *Conservation*

As far as possible the activities of the facility and its personnel shall not interfere with the flora and fauna of Diego Garcia. When their use is no longer required for the purposes of the facility, the two Governments shall consult about the condition of the three islets at the mouth of the lagoon with a view to restoring them to their original condition. However, neither Government shall be under any obligation to provide funds for such restoration.

(9) *Anchorage dues and aviation charges*

Collection of dues and charges for use of the anchorage and airfield at Diego Garcia which may be levied by the Commissioner shall be his responsibility. Aircraft and ships owned or operated by or on behalf of the Government of the United States shall be permitted to use the anchorage and airfield without the payment of any dues or charges.

(10) *Meteorology*

The Government of the United States shall operate a meteorological facility on Diego Garcia and supply such available meteorological information as may be required by the Government of the United Kingdom and the Government of Mauritius to meet their national and international obligations.

(11) *United Kingdom Service element*

The United Kingdom Service element on Diego Garcia shall be under the Command of a Royal Navy Officer who shall be known as the Officer-in-Charge of the United Kingdom Service element.

(12) *Finance*

(*a*) The Government of the United States shall bear the cost of developing, operating and maintaining the facility. However, in relation to United Kingdom personnel attached to the facility, the Government of the United Kingdom shall be responsible for their pay, allowances and any other monetary gratuities, for the cost of their messing, and for supplies or services which are peculiar to or provided for the exclusive use of the United Kingdom Services or their personnel and which would not normally be provided by the Government of the United States for the use of its own personnel.

(*b*) Except in relation to the United Kingdom Service personnel attached to the facility, logistic support furnished at Diego Garcia by either Government, upon request, to the other Government, shall be on a reimbursable basis in accordance with the laws, regulations and instructions of the Governments furnishing the support.

(13) *Fisheries, oil and mineral resources*

The Government of the United Kingdom will not permit commercial fishing in the lagoon or oil or mineral exploration or exploitation on Diego Garcia for the duration of this Agreement. Furthermore, the Government of the United Kingdom will not permit commercial fishing or oil or mineral exploration or exploitation in or under those areas of the waters, continental shelf and sea-bed around Diego Garcia over which the United Kingdom has sovereignty or exercises sovereign rights, unless it is agreed that such activities would not harm or be inimical to the defence use of the island.

(14) *Health, quarantine and sanitation*

The Commanding Officer and the Commissioner shall collaborate in the enforcement on Diego Garcia of necessary health, quarantine and sanitation provisions.

(15) *News broadcast station*

The Government of the United States may establish and operate a closed circuit TV and a low power radio broadcast station to broadcast news, entertainment and educational programmes for personnel on Diego Garcia.

(16) *Property*

(*a*) Title to any removable property brought into Diego Garcia by or on behalf of the Government of the United States, or by a United States contractor, shall remain in the Government of the United States or the contractor, as the case may be. Such property of the Government of the United States, including official papers, shall be exempt from inspection, search and seizure. Such property of either the Government of the United States or of a United States contractor may be freely removed from Diego Garcia, but shall not be disposed of within the British Indian Ocean Territory or Seychelles unless an offer, consistent with the laws of the United States then in effect, has been made to sell the property to the Commissioner and he has not accepted such offer within a period of 120 days after it was made or such longer period as may be reasonable in the circumstances. Any such property not removed or disposed of within a reasonable time after termination of this Agreement shall become the property of the Commissioner.

(*b*) The Government of the United States shall not be responsible for restoring land or other immovable property to its original condition, nor for making any payment in lieu of restoration.

(17) *Availability of funds*

To the extent that the carrying out of any activity or the implementation of any part of this Agreement depends upon funds to be appropriated by the Congress of the United States, it shall be subject to the availability of such funds.

(18) *Representative of the Commissioner*

The Commissioner shall designate a person as his Representative on Diego Garcia.

(19) *Supplementary arrangements*

Supplementary arrangements between the appropriate administrative authorities of the two Governments may be made from time to time as required for the carrying out of the purposes of this Agreement.

(20) *Definitions and interpretation*

(*a*) For the purposes of this Agreement
'BIOT Agreement' means the Exchange of Notes dated 30 December 1966, between the Government of the United Kingdom of Great Britain and Northern Ireland and the

Government of the United States of America concerning the availability of the British Indian Ocean Territory for defence purposes;

'Commanding Officer' means the United States Navy Officer in command of the facility;

'Commissioner' means the officer administering the Government of the British Indian Ocean Territory;

'Diego Garcia' means the atoll of Diego Garcia, the lagoon and the three islets at the mouth of the lagoon.

(b) Questions of interpretation arising from the application of this Agreement shall be the subject of consultation between the two Governments.

(c) The provisions of this Agreement shall supplement the BIOT Agreement and shall be construed in accordance with that Agreement. In the event of any conflict between the provisions of the BIOT Agreement and this Agreement the provisions of the BIOT Agreement shall prevail.

(21) *The Diego Garcia Agreement 1972*

This Agreement shall replace the Agreement constituted by the Exchange of Notes dated 24 October 1972 between the Government of the United Kingdom of Great Britain and Northern Ireland and the Government of the United States of America concerning a limited United States naval communication facility on Diego Garcia, British Indian Ocean Territory.

(22) *Duration and termination*

This Agreement shall continue in force for as long as the BIOT Agreement continues in force or until such time as no part of Diego Garcia is any longer required for the purposes of the facility, whichever occurs first.

2. If the Government of the United States of America also approves in principle the development of the facility subject to the above terms, I have the honour to propose that this Note and the plan annexed to it, together with your reply to that effect, shall constitute an Agreement between the two Governments which shall enter into force on the date of your reply and shall be known as the Diego Garcia Agreement 1976.

I have the honour to be
with high consideration
Sir
Your obedient Servant
ROY HATTERSLEY

It will be noted that the Agreement speaks of approval 'in principle'. Yet there cannot be any doubt that it is far from a mere agreement to make an agreement. It would be inappropriate to attribute to these words any qualifying effect such as a private lawyer might be inclined to read into them.

The use of the airfield at Wideawake in Ascension Island was agreed by a treaty of 1956,[50] but in 1962 the UK was granted landing rights for military aircraft[51] (which, it will be remembered, became a matter of great strategic importance during the Falklands crisis):

[50] Cmnd. 9810.
[51] Cmnd. 1869.

British Embassy,
Washington, D.C.
August 29, 1962.

Sir,

I have the honour to refer to the technical discussions which have recently taken place between representatives of the Government of the United Kingdom of Great Britain and Northern Ireland and the Government of the United States of America concerning the use of the Airfield at Wideawake in Ascension Island by aircraft of the Royal Air Force. In these discussions agreement was reached in principle upon the following provisions:—

(*a*) Notwithstanding the provisions of Article IV (2) of the Agreement of the 25th of June, 1956, concerning the Extension of the Bahamas Long Range Proving Ground by the Establishment of Additional Sites in Ascension Island:

    (i) the Government of the United Kingdom shall have the right to land United Kingdom military aircraft at Wideawake Airfield upon receipt by the United States Commanding Officer at the Airfield of at least 24 hours advance notification of the arrival of any single aircraft and at least 72 hours advance notification of the arrival of groups of two or more aircraft;

    (ii) in the event that additional logistic, administrative or operating facilities at the Airfield are considered by the Government of the United Kingdom to be necessary in connexion with its use by United Kingdom military aircraft, the Government of the United States shall permit the Government of the United Kingdom to establish, maintain and use such facilities in accordance with arrangements to be agreed between the United Kingdom and United States authorities.

(*b*) Arrangements shall be made between the United Kingdom and United States authorities to ensure that the operation of the Long Range Proving Ground and the use of Wideawake Airfield by United Kingdom military aircraft are carried out in such a way as to avoid interference with one another.

(*c*) The Governments of the United Kingdom shall reimburse the Government of the United States for any readily identifiable additional cost to the latter arising out of the use of Wideawake Airfield by United Kingdom military aircraft, including costs related to claims arising out of or incident to such use, subject to the terms of the Exchange of Notes of the 23rd of October 1946/23rd of January 1947 between the two Governments for Mutual Forbearance concerning Claims against Members and Civilian Employees of their respective Armed Forces.

I now have the honour to confirm that the above provisions are acceptable to the Government of the United Kingdom and to propose that, if they are likewise acceptable to the Government of the United States, the present Note and your reply to that effect should be regarded as constituting an Agreement between the two Governments in this matter, which shall enter into force on this day's date and shall continue in force for the duration of the Agreement of the 25th of June, 1956, referred to above.

I avail, etc.
HOOD.

(i) *Joint Ventures*

Numerous treaties, usually described as co-operation or co-production agreements, have been concluded, which in private law would be known as joint ventures. In the present context one does not think of treaties which are so described, but lay down sovereign rights and duties and are, therefore, outside the scope of this survey. The Mutual Defence Assistance Agreement between the USA and the UK of 27 January 1950 as amended and supplemented[52] is a prime example, and, apart from multilateral treaties, there are many Agreements of a similar type such as the Agreement with the Federal Republic of Cameroon on commercial and economic co-operation,[53] with Yugoslavia on co-operation in the fields of applied science and technology,[54] with Brazil and with El Salvador on technical co-operation,[55] with Cuba on the development of economic and industrial co-operation,[56] with Qatar on technical co-operation,[57] with China on economic co-operation,[58] with the Hellenic Republic on applied scientific and technological co-operation.[59]

The type of treaty which is relevant to the present discussion is represented by Films Production Agreements with France,[60] Italy,[61] Canada[62] and Norway.[63] The last-mentioned Agreement, excluding the Annex, reads as follows:

ARTICLE 1

For the purpose of this Agreement:

(1) a 'co-production film' shall be a theatrical film made by one or more United Kingdom makers (hereinafter referred to as 'the United Kingdom co-producer') in conjunction with one or more Norwegian makers (hereinafter referred to as 'the Norwegian co-producer') and made in accordance with the terms of an approval given by the competent authorities of each Contracting Party acting jointly;

(2) 'nationals' means:

(a) in relation to the United Kingdom of Great Britain and Northern Ireland, Commonwealth citizens;

(b) in relation to the Kingdom of Norway, Norwegian citizens;

(3) 'residents' means:

(a) in relation to the United Kingdom of Great Britain and Northern Ireland, persons ordinarily resident in the United Kingdom;

(b) in relation to the Kingdom of Norway, persons ordinarily resident in Norway;

(4) 'Great Britain' means England, Wales and Scotland;

(5) 'Member State' means any country that is a Member State of the European Economic Community;

(6) 'competent authorities' means the authorities designated by the Government of the United Kingdom of Great Britain and Northern Ireland and the Government of the Kingdom of Norway respectively.

[52] Cmnd. 7894, 8480; Cmnd. 198, 714, 1612, 1863.
[53] Cmnd. 2133.
[54] Cmnd. 3979.
[55] Cmnd. 3816, 3813.
[56] Cmnd. 6327.
[57] Cmnd. 6607.
[58] Cmnd. 7594.
[59] Cmnd. 9594.
[60] Cmnd. 2898, 3349.
[61] Cmnd. 3434.
[62] Cmnd. 6380.
[63] Cmnd. 9007.

ARTICLE 2

A co-production film shall be entitled to the full enjoyment of all the benefits which are or may be accorded in Great Britain and Norway respectively to national films.

ARTICLE 3

In approving projects for co-production films for the purpose of this Agreement, the competent authorities of each Contracting Party acting jointly shall apply the rules set out in the Annex, which forms an integral part of this Agreement.

ARTICLE 4

Each of the Contracting Parties shall provide facilities in the United Kingdom or Norway as the case may be in accordance with the terms of Articles 1 to 22 inclusive and Annex B of the Customs Convention on the Temporary Importation of Professional Equipment, done at Brussels on 8th June 1961('), for the temporary admission and re-export of all cinematographic equipment (within the meaning of the Convention) necessary for the making of co-production films.

(') Treaty Series No. 62 (1963), Cmnd. 2125.

ARTICLE 5

Each of the Contracting Parties shall permit the nationals or residents of the other Contracting Party and citizens of a Member State to enter and reside in Great Britain or Norway as the case may be for the purpose of making or exploiting a co-production film, subject only to the requirement that they comply with the laws and regulations relating to entry and residence.

ARTICLE 6

There shall be a Mixed Commission composed of representatives of the Contracting Parties to supervise and review the working of the Agreement and, where necessary, to make proposals to the Contracting Parties for its modification. The Mixed Commission shall meet within one month of a request being made by either Contracting Party. Its meetings shall be held alternately in Great Britain and Norway.

ARTICLE 7

Each of the Contracting Parties shall notify the other of the completion of any procedure required by its constitutional law for giving effect to this Agreement, which shall enter force from the date of receipt of the later of these notifications.

ARTICLE 8

This Agreement shall remain in force for a period of three years from the date of its entry into force. Either Contracting Party wishing to terminate it shall give written notice of termination to the other, three months before the end of that period and the Agreement shall then terminate at the end of the three years. If no such notice is given the Agreement shall automatically remain in force for successive periods each of three years unless it is terminated in writing by either Contracting Party three months before the end of any period of three years, when it will terminate at the end of that period.

In witness whereof, the undersigned, being duly authorised thereto by their respective Governments, have signed this Agreement.

Done in duplicate at London this 8th day of December 1982, in the English and Norwegian languages, both texts being equally authoritative.

For the Government of the United Kingdom of Great Britain and Northern Ireland:	For the Government of the Kingdom of Norway:
MALCOLM RIFKIND.	ALV HELTNE.

There exist even more treaties relating to the exploitation of nuclear power. One of the most important[64] is an Agreement with the USA relating to the disposition of rights in atomic energy inventions:

Washington, September 24, 1956

The Government of the United Kingdom of Great Britain and Northern Ireland, the Government of Canada, and the Government of the United States of America;

Recognising that the rights, title and interests in certain inventions and discoveries (known as Combined Policy Committee inventions) resulting from wartime co-operation of the Governments of the United Kingdom, Canada, and the United States are held in a fiduciary capacity at present; and

Believing (1) that it is desirable at this time to make the final disposition of the rights, title and interests in those inventions and discoveries, and (2) that mutual benefit will result from the interchange of rights, title and interests in existing inventions and discoveries in the field of and related to atomic energy which are the subject of patents or patent applications by one Government in the country of one or both of the other Governments.

Have agreed as follows:—

Article I

The term 'Government' or 'Governments' in this Agreement shall be deemed to include—

1. In the case of the United States, the United States Atomic Energy Commission;
2. In the case of the United Kingdom, the United Kingdom Atomic Energy Authority;
3. In the case of Canada, the Atomic Energy Control Board, Atomic Energy of Canada Limited, Eldorado Mining and Refining Limited, National Research Council, and the Department of Mines and Technical Surveys.

[64] Cmnd. 20.

ARTICLE II

It is desirable to make final and ultimate disposition of the rights, title and interests in the Combined Policy Committee inventions, thereby terminating the fiduciary provision heretofore applying. To that end, the Government or Governments employing the inventor or inventors shall own the entire rights, title and interests in any such Combined Policy Committee invention which is the subject of patent or patent application in one or more of the three countries.

ARTICLE III

In addition, it is desirable and to the mutual benefit to exchange certain rights, title and interests in all inventions or discoveries in the field of atomic energy which are the subject of patents or patent applications by one Government in the country or countries of either one or both of the other two Governments as of November 15, 1955.

ARTICLE IV

With respect to any invention or discovery within the scope of Articles II and III, each Government, within the limits of its ownership as of November 15, 1955—

1. Shall transfer and assign to the other Government or Governments such rights, title and interests as the assigning and transferring Government may own in the other's country, subject to the retention by the assigning and transferring Government of a non-exclusive, irrevocable, paid-up licence to make, use and have made or used such invention or discovery by or for the assigning and transferring Government or for purposes of mutual defence.

2. Shall accord the right to a non-exclusive, irrevocable, paid-up licence to the other Governments to make, use, and have made or used such invention or discovery by or for such other Government or Governments or for purposes of mutual defence in all countries.

3. Shall not discriminate against nationals of the other Government or Governments in the grant of licences in any patents or patent applications owned by each Government or in which each Government acquires ownership or rights under this Agreement, but shall accord licences to nationals of the other Government or Governments on the same or as favourable terms as it accords licences to its own nationals (including its Government-owned or controlled corporations when such corporations practise the invention or discovery in the performance of services for a party other than the licensing Government).

4. Shall waive any and all claims against the other Government or Governments for compensation, royalty or award as respects any invention or discovery within the scope of Articles II and III, and release the other Governments with respect to any claim on any such invention or discovery.

ARTICLE V

This Agreement shall come into force on the date of signature.

In witness whereof, the undersigned, duly authorised, have signed this Agreement.

Done at Washington this twenty-fourth day of September, 1956 in three original texts.

For the Government of the United Kingdom of Great Britain and Northern Ireland:

ROGER MAKINS.

For the Government of Canada:

A. D. P. HEENEY.

For the Government of the United States of America:

C. BURKE ELBRICK.
LEWIS L. STRAUSS.

In so far as the US is concerned there followed an Agreement on the Civil Uses of Atomic Energy[65] which consolidated eight earlier Agreements:

The Government of the United Kingdom of Great Britain and Northern Ireland, on its own behalf and on behalf of the United Kingdom Atomic Energy Authority, and the Government of the United States of America (including the United States Atomic Energy Commission);

Considering that they have for several years been engaged in atomic energy programmes within their respective countries and from the inception of these programmes have collaborated closely in certain fields;

Considering that the use of atomic energy for peaceful purposes is a major objective of each of these programmes;

Believing that mutual benefit would result from further co-operation between them; and

Recognising that for the present their main efforts in the field of atomic energy will be directed to defence but desiring also to promote the development of atomic energy for peaceful purposes;

Have agreed as follows:

ARTICLE I

Scope of Agreement

A.   Subject to the provisions of this Agreement, the availability of material and personnel, and the applicable laws, regulations and licence requirements in force in their respective countries, the Parties shall assist each other in the achievement of the use of atomic energy for peaceful purposes. It is the intent of the Parties that such assistance shall be rendered on a reciprocal basis.

B.   The disposition and utilisation of atomic weapons and the exchange of restricted data relating to the design or fabrication of atomic weapons shall be outside the scope of this Agreement.

C.   The exchange of restricted data under this Agreement shall be subject to the following limitations:

(i) It shall extend only to that which is relevant to current or projected programmes.

[65] Cmnd. 4694.

(ii) Restricted data which is primarily of military significance shall not be exchanged, except as provided in Article I *bis*.

(iii) The development of submarine, ship, aircraft, and certain package power reactors is presently concerned primarily with their military use, and there may be future types of reactors the development of which is concerned primarily with their military use. Accordingly, restricted data pertaining primarily to any of these types of reactors will not be exchanged, except as provided in Article I *bis*.

(iv) Restricted data on specific experimental power, demonstration power, or power reactors will not be exchanged unless the reactor is currently in operation in the receiving country or is being considered seriously for construction by the receiving country as a source of power or as an intermediate step in a power production programme. There shall, however, be exchanged such general information, including restricted data, on design and characteristics of various types of reactors as is required to permit evaluation and comparison of their potential use in a power production programme.

D.   This agreement shall not require the exchange of any information which the Parties are not permitted to communicate because the information is privately developed and privately owned or has been received from another government.

E.   The Parties will not transfer or export, or permit the transfer or export, under this agreement of any material, equipment or device which is primarily of a military character.

ARTICLE I *bis*

Exchange of Information on Reactors of Primarily Military Significance

A.   At such time as any one of the types of reactors referred to in Article I C. (iii) warrants application to civil uses, restricted data on that type shall be exchanged as may be agreed, subject to the provisions of Article I.

B.   In the meantime, and subject to the provisions of Article I, classified and unclassified information on the development, design, construction, operation and use of military package power reactors and reactors for the propulsion of naval vessels, aircraft, or land vehicles, for military purposes shall be exchanged to the extent and by such means as may be agreed. Each Party will use its best efforts to ensure that any classified information received from the other Party pursuant to this paragraph will be used only in connection with reactors intended for military use, until such time as it has been agreed under paragraph A. of this Article to exchange restricted data on the type of reactor to which such classified information pertains or such information has been removed from the category of classified information by the Party from which it has been received.

ARTICLE II

Exchange of Information between the Commission and the Authority

Subject to the provisions of Article I, classified information in the specific fields set out below and unclassified information shall be exchanged between the Commission and the Authority with respect to the application of atomic energy to peaceful uses, including research and development relating to such uses and problems of health and safety connected therewith. The exchange of information provided for in this Article shall be accomplished through the various means available, including reports, conferences and visits to facilities. The following are the fields in which classified information shall be exchanged:

A. *Reactors*

1. Fields of exchange:

(*a*) Reactor physics, including theory of and pertinent data relating to neutron bombardment reactions, neutron cross sections, criticality calculations, reactor kinetics, and shielding.

(*b*) Reactor engineering—theory of and data relating to such problems as reactor stress and heat transfer analysis insofar as these are pertinent to the over-all design and optimisation of the reactor.

(*c*) Properties of reactor materials—effects of operating conditions on the properties of reactor materials, including fuel, moderator and coolant.

(*d*) Specification for reactor materials—final form specifications including composition, shape, and size, and special handling techniques of reactor materials including source material, special nuclear material, heavy water, reactor grade graphite, and zirconium.

(*e*) Reactor components—general performance specifications of reactor components.

(*f*) Over-all design and characteristics, and operational techniques and performance, of research, experimental power, demonstration power, and power reactors.

2. Detailed designs, detailed drawings and applied technology of reactors of the types referred to in sub-paragraph 1 (*f*) of this paragraph and of related components, equipment and devices in this field shall not be exchanged except as may be agreed.

3. The exchange of information under this paragraph shall include and be limited to information from the following sources and shall be accomplished in such a manner as to maintain a reciprocal basis of exchange:

(*a*) Information developed by and for the Commission and information developed by and for the public and private utility groups in the United States with the assistance of the Commission;

(*b*) Information developed by and for the Authority and information developed by and for the United Kingdom Electricity Supply Authorities with the assistance of the Authority.

B. *Uranium and Thorium*

Geology, exploration techniques, chemistry and technology of extracting uranium and thorium from their ores and concentrates, the chemistry, production technology and techniques of purification and fabrication of uranium and thorium compounds and metals, including design, construction and operation of plants.

C. *Properties of Materials*

Physical, chemical, and nuclear properties of all elements, compounds, alloys, mixtures, special nuclear material, byproduct material, other radioisotopes, and stable isotopes and their behaviour under all conditions.

D. *Technology of Production and Utilisation of Materials*

1. Technology of production and utilisation, from laboratory experimentation up to pilot plant operations but not including design and operation of pilot plants except as may be agreed, of all elements, compounds, alloys, mixtures, special nuclear material, byproduct material, other radioisotopes, and stable isotopes relevant to paragraphs A. and E. of this Article.

2. This paragraph shall not be construed as including—

(a) the exchange of restricted data pertaining to design, construction, and operation of production plants for the separation of U–235 from other uranium isotopes;

(b) the exchange of restricted data on the design, construction, and operation of specific production plants for the separation of deuterium from the other isotope of hydrogen until such time as the Party wishing to receive the information shall determine that the construction of such plants is required; the Commission will, however, supply the Authority with heavy water as provided in Article III A. and Article IV;

(c) the exchange of restricted data pertaining to the design, construction, and operation of production plants for the separation of isotopes of any other element, except as may be agreed;

(d) the exchange of restricted data pertaining to the underlying principles, theory, design, construction, and operation of facilities, other than reactors, capable of producing significant quantities of isotopes by means of nuclear reactions except as may be agreed.

E. *Health and Safety*

The entire field of health and safety as related to any of the fields within which information is to be exchanged in accordance with the provisions of this Article; in addition those problems of health and safety which affect the individual, his environment, and the civilian population as a whole and which arise from nuclear explosion (excluding such test data as would permit the determination of the yield of any specific weapon or nuclear device and excluding any information relating to the design or fabrication of any weapon or nuclear device).

ARTICLE III

Research Materials and Research Facilities

A. *Research Materials*

Materials of interest in connexion with any subject of agreed exchange of information as provided in Article II subject to the provisions of Article I, including source material, special nuclear material, byproduct material, other radioisotopes, and stable isotopes shall, except as provided in paragraph E. of Article I, be exchanged for research purposes in such quantities and under such terms and conditions as may be agreed when such materials are not available commercially to the Party wishing to receive them.

B. *Research Facilities*

Under such terms and conditions as may be agreed, specialised research facilities and reactor testing facilities shall be made available for mutual use consistent with the limits of space, facilities, and personnel conveniently available, except that it is understood that neither Party will be able to permit access by personnel of the other Party to facilities which are primarily of military significance.

ARTICLE IV

Materials for Purposes other than Research

A. In connexion with any subject of agreed exchange of information as provided in Article II subject to the provisions of Article I, specific arrangements may be agreed between the Parties from time to time for the sale and purchase, under such terms and conditions as may be agreed, of quantities, greater than those required for research, of materials other than special nuclear materials.

B. In connexion with any subject of agreed exchange of information as provided in Article II subject to the provisions of Article I, specific arrangements may be agreed between the Parties from time to time under which special nuclear material required for developmental purposes, including use in research and experimental reactors, may be exchanged for other materials under such terms and conditions as may be agreed.

C. 1. In addition to transfers of special nuclear material for the purposes provided elsewhere in this Agreement, irradiated special nuclear material of United States origin may be transferred under such terms and conditions as may be agreed by the Parties to the United Kingdom for chemical reprocessing. Under such terms and conditions as may be agreed by the Parties, the United Kingdom also may convert or fabricate, or both, material transferred pursuant to the preceding sentence. In connexion with such conversion and fabrication services, the United States may agree,

(a) to transfer to the United Kingdom uranium including its compounds in such amounts and at such enrichment in the isotope U–235 as when blended with the reprocessed uranium will permit the fabrication of replacement fuel;

(b) to transfer to the United Kingdom uranium including its compounds in such amounts and at such enrichment in the isotope U–235 as may be required for replacement fuel and to accept the reprocessed uranium as a credit against the transfer;

(c) to permit the blending of the reprocessed uranium with United Kingdom material; and

(d) to permit the re-enrichment of the reprocessed uranium in United Kingdom facilities.

Upon completion of any of the services mentioned in this paragraph C.1 such transferred material may be transferred to another nation or group of nations pursuant to the terms of Article IX hereof or retained in the United Kingdom for applications otherwise within the scope of this Agreement or the Agreement between the Parties for Co-operation in the Civil Power Applications of Atomic Energy signed at Washington on June 2, 1966.

C. 2. On such terms and conditions as may be agreed by the Parties, transfers may also take place between their respective countries of special nuclear material for the performance in the country of the recipient of conversion or fabrication services or both. Upon completion of such services, such transferred material may be retained in the recipient country for applications otherwise within the scope of this Agreement or the Agreement between the Parties for Co-operation in the Civil Power Applications of Atomic Energy, signed at Washington on June 2, 1966; transferred to another nation or group of nations pursuant to the terms of Article IX hereof; or returned to the country of origin.

D. The Commission will sell to the Government of the United Kingdom in such quantities and under such terms and conditions as may be agreed up to a net quantity of 2,400 kilograms of U–235 in uranium enriched in the isotope U–235 to satisfy United Kingdom requirements for fuelling reactors in its civil research and development programmes. This net amount shall be the gross quantity of contained U–235 in enriched uranium sold to the United Kingdom under this paragraph during the period of this Agreement less the quantity of such contained U–235 in recoverable uranium which has been returned to the Government of the United States of America or transferred to any other nation or group of nations with the approval of the Government of the United States of America during the term of this Agreement. The enriched uranium so supplied may contain more than twenty per cent

(20%) U–235 upon request and at the discretion of the Commission if there is a technical or economic justification in a particular case for higher enrichment.

ARTICLE V

Transfer of Equipment and Devices

With respect to any subject of agreed exchange of information as provided in Article II subject to the provisions of Article I, equipment and devices may be transferred from one Party to the other under such terms and conditions as may be agreed, except as provided in paragraph E. of Article I. It is recognised that such transfers will be subject to limitations which may arise from shortages of supplies or other circumstances existing at the time.

ARTICLE VI

Permissive Arrangements for Materials, including Equipment and Devices, and Services

A. Within the fields specified in paragraph B. of this Article, persons under the jurisdiction of one Party shall be permitted to make arrangements to transfer and export materials, including equipment and devices and rights owned by them therein, to and perform services for the other Party and such persons under its jurisdiction as are authorised by it to receive and possess such materials and utilise such services, provided that any classified information the disclosure of which would be involved shall fall within the fields specified in paragraph B. and subject to:

(1) the provisions of paragraph E. of Article I;

(2) applicable laws, regulations and licence requirements;

(3) approval of the Party to the jurisdiction of which the person making the arrangement is subject if the materials or services are classified or if the furnishing of such materials or services requires the communication of classified information.

B. To the extent necessary in carrying out the arrangements made under paragraph A. of this Article, classified information in the following fields, subject in each case to the provisions of Article I, may be communicated by the person furnishing the material or services to the Party or person to whom such material or service is furnished:

(1) the subjects of agreed exchange of information as provided in Article II;

(2) the development, design, construction, operation, and use of research, experimental power, demonstration power, and power reactors;

(3) the development, design, manufacture, and use of equipment and devices of use in connexion with the fields described in this paragraph.

ARTICLE VII

Patents

A. With respect to any invention or discovery employing information which has been communicated under this Agreement by one of the Parties to the other in accordance with Article I *bis* or Article II and made or conceived thereafter but during the period of this Agreement, and in which invention or discovery rights or owned by the Government of the United Kingdom, or by the Government of the United States or any agency or corporation owned or controlled by either, each Party:

(1) agrees to transfer and assign to the other Party all right, title, and interest in and to any such invention, discovery, patent application or patent in the country of that other Party, to the extent owned, subject to a royalty-free, non-exclusive, irrevocable licence for the governmental purposes of the transferring and assigning Party and for purposes of mutual defence;

(2) shall retain all right, title, and interest in and to any such invention, discovery, patent application or patent in its own or third countries but shall, upon request of the other Party, grant to that other Party a royalty-free, non-exclusive, irrevocable licence for the governmental purposes of such other Party in such countries, including use in the production of materials in such countries for sale to the other Party by a contractor of such other Party; each Party may deal with any such invention, discovery, patent application or patent in its own country and all countries other than that of the other Party as it may desire, but in no event shall either Party discriminate against citizens of the country of the other Party in respect of granting any licence under the patents owned by it in its own or any other country;

(3) waives any and all claims against the other Party for compensation, royalty or award as respects any such invention or discovery, patent application or patent and releases the other Party with respect to any such claim.

B. (1) No patent application with respect to any classified invention or discovery employing information which has been communicated under this Agreement may be filed by either Party or any person in the country of the other Party except in accordance with agreed conditions and procedures.

(2) No patent application with respect to any such classified invention or discovery may be filed in any country not a party to this Agreement except as may be agreed and subject to Article IX.

(3) Appropriate secrecy or prohibition orders shall be issued for the purpose of giving effect to this paragraph.

Article VIII

Classification Policies

Agreed classification policies shall be maintained with respect to all information, materials, equipment and devices exchanged under this Agreement. The parties intend to continue the present practice of consultation with each other on the classification of these matters.

Article IX

Guarantees

The Parties guarantee that:

A. All classified material, equipment, devices and classified information exchanged under this Agreement shall be safeguarded in accordance with the applicable security arrangements between the Commission and the Authority.

B. No material, equipment or device transferred pursuant to this Agreement shall be used for atomic weapons or for research on or development of atomic weapons, or for any other military purpose.

C. No material, equipment, device, or restricted data transferred pursuant to this

Agreement, and no equipment or device which would disclose any restricted data transferred pursuant to this Agreement, shall be transferred to any unauthorised person or beyond the jurisdiction of the country receiving it, without the written consent of the Party to this Agreement from which or by permission of which it was received. Such consent will not be given on behalf of the Government of the United States unless the transfer in respect of which it is requested is within the scope of an agreement for co-operation made in accordance with Section 123 of the United States Atomic Energy Act of 1954.

Article IX *bis*

Responsibility for Use of Information, Material, Equipment and Devices

The application or use of any information (including design drawings and specifications), material, equipment or device, exchanged or transferred between the Parties under this Agreement shall be the responsibility of the Party receiving it, and the other Party does not warrant the accuracy or completeness of such information and does not warrant the suitability of such information, material, equipment, or device for any particular use or application.

Article X

Definitions

For the purposes of this agreement:

'Atomic weapon' means any device utilising atomic energy, exclusive of the means for transporting or propelling the device (where such means is a separable and divisible part of the device), the principal purpose of which is for use as, or for development of, a weapon, a weapon prototype, or a weapon test device.

'The Authority' means the United Kingdom Atomic Energy Authority.

'Byproduct material' means any radioactive material (except special nuclear material) yielded in or made radioactive by exposure to the radiation incident to the process of producing or utilising special nuclear material.

'Classified' means a security designation of 'Confidential' or higher applied under the laws and regulations of either the United Kingdom or the United States to any data, information, materials, services or any other matter, and includes 'restricted data'.

'The Commission' means the United States Atomic Energy Commission.

'Equipment and devices' and 'equipment or device' means any instrument, apparatus, or facility and includes any facility, except an atomic weapon, capable of making use of or producing special nuclear material, and component parts thereof.

'Person' means any individual, corporation, partnership, firm, association, trust, estate, public or private institution, group, government agency or government corporation other than the Commission and the Authority.

'Pilot plant' means a device operated to acquire specific data for the design of a full-scale plant and which utilises the process, or a portion thereof, and the type of equipment which would be used in the full-scale production plant.

'Reactor' means an apparatus, other than an atomic weapon, in which a self-supporting fission chain reaction is maintained by utilising uranium, plutonium, or thorium or any combination of uranium, plutonium, or thorium.

'Restricted data' means all data concerning (1) design, manufacture, or utilisation of atomic weapons; (2) the production of special nuclear material; or (3) the use of special nuclear material in the production of energy, but shall not include data declassified or removed from the category of restricted data by the appropriate authority.

'Special nuclear material' means (1) plutonium, uranium enriched in the isotope 233 or in the isotope 235, and any other material which the Commission or the Authority determines to be special nuclear material; or (2) any material artificially enriched by any of the foregoing.

Article XI

Period of Agreement

This Agreement shall enter into force on the date on which each government shall receive from the other Government written notification that it has complied with all statutory and constitutional requirements for the entry into force of such Agreement and shall remain in force for a period of twenty-one years.

III

At the end of this survey it will be apparent that its descriptive and factual character is such as to render it impossible to submit precise conclusions. It does, however, seem appropriate to add two final remarks.

On the one hand it will be noticed that nothing has been said about the legal character, in particular the personality, of international trading organizations. The reason is that the problem and all its implications have arisen in the litigation relating to the International Tin Council in which the present writer was heavily engaged. It would, therefore, be inappropriate if he were to discuss the great problems arising in it either at the present time or, perhaps, at all. Suffice it to say that, in effect, the House of Lords did not treat the International Tin Council as an international organization at all, but (*mirabile dictu*) as a body 'which is created by United Kingdom legislation',[66] and ignored the treaty as non-justiciable. On the other hand, by a truly exemplary decision relating to the Arab Organization for Industrialization founded by a treaty of 29 April 1975, the Swiss Federal Tribunal construed the treaty in the light of common sense and found the Organization to be so similar to a limited company that the liability of the constituent States was excluded. It is likely that the latter decision[67] will be treated as persuasive.

On the other hand a point of a more general character has to be made. The treaties considered in this paper will probably require interpretation in numerous respects. But the interpretation of treaties in the light of the Vienna Convention has so far resulted in the most general comments only. What is needed is a careful and imaginative discussion of the implications of Articles 31 and 32. What does the tautologous expression 'object and purpose' mean? What is meant and, indeed, added to the process of interpretation by the reference to good faith? Such and similar questions have been discussed in great detail in many systems of municipal law and it may well be that international law could learn a great deal from them. A full commentary on the Vienna Convention will, it is hoped, profit from the material made available in this article. It may provide some of the illustrations without which that commentary would have little value.

[66] *J.H. Rayner (Mincing Lane) Ltd.* v. *Department of Trade and Industry,* [1989] 3 WLR 969, at p. 1011.

[67] 19 July 1988, not yet reported.

REVIEWS OF BOOKS

The Law of the International Civil Service (as Applied by International Tribunals). By C. F. AMERASINGHE. Oxford: Clarendon Press, 1988. xii + 635 pp. (Volume I), xviii + 700 pp. (Volume II). £60 each.

This work represents a major discourse on the employment law rights of the staff of the main international organizations of the world as they have been interpreted and applied by the relevant administrative tribunals. As such, the book covers a very wide range of detailed material concerning some 70 international organizations, agencies, commissions, committees, offices and other bodies in all, although focusing on the main examples of the United Nations, its agencies, including in particular the World Bank, and the European Community institutions. The work comes from an authoritative source as the author is the Executive Secretary of the Administrative Tribunal of the World Bank, and is an established author in the field and an international lawyer of high standing.

The book comes in two volumes which reflect the manner in which the subject-matter has been treated. Part I, in Volume I, deals with the 'General Principles' of administrative review. Under this heading are covered the nature and origin of the law governing staff rights in international organizations and the origins and structures of the various procedures which exist to enforce those rights; the sources of the law applied by those tribunals; the general principles of their jurisdictional competence and the nature and scope of the control they have exercised over the administrations concerned; the remedies available and the costs awarded; as well as the procedural aspects of the bringing of an action before such a tribunal.

Part II, and Volume II, contain a more detailed description of the law as it has been applied, concerning such matters as the nature of temporary and more permanent employment situations; the conditions governing termination of employment; the application of disciplinary measures; the classification and grading of posts; transfer and reassignments; promotion; salaries; and the right of association.

The appendices contain the texts of the Statutes of the tribunals of the United Nations, the ILO and the World Bank, plus the Rules of the World Bank Administrative Tribunal, the Staff Regulations and Rules of the United Nations and the Council of Europe, and the Principles of Employment of the World Bank. Perhaps for reasons of length, the equivalent texts for the European Community institutions are not included. A table lists alphabetically by name the decisions and judgments of the tribunals concerned, and the structure of the text itself is supplemented by a detailed index, which is a necessary means of access to a work of this nature.

The book treats a large subject not hitherto—to the knowledge of this reviewer—approached in such a comprehensive and yet detailed manner. Presented as it is in a clear structural framework, and in the lucid style of the author, the book constitutes a rich source from which the practitioner and others with professional interests in the subject-area will be able to draw. There is included ample material for comparison and contrast and for the analysis of the direction in which the relevant laws of the various organizations are developing. If regular up-dating were to follow, the work could easily become a standard text on the subject.

The work should have an obvious and immediate value to practitioners advising clients on the law governing their employment in the organizations covered; those involved in the running of the administrations concerned; the members or judges of the administrative panels, boards, tribunals and other bodies involved; not to mention the staff members themselves and those interested in studying the development of this area of employment law.

The text, although structured so as to enable the comparison and contrast of the material covered, is essentially descriptive and does not itself attempt any systematic comparative or critical analysis. In the same way, while the work provides a wealth of information on which conclusions could be drawn as to the existence, or desirability, of a common employment law of international organizations, no attempt is made by the author to discuss this aspect of the subject. While, as Dr Christine Gray (volume 56 of this *Year Book* at page 40) has observed in connection with the award of remedies by these tribunals, the search for uniformity can be taken too far and the case for inter-organizational consistency exaggerated, there may yet be room for some further study of the *rationale* on which common or divergent rules have been, or could be, founded.

The scope and detail of the panorama provided by this book may well provoke further interest in these aspects of the subject which could provide a greater academic input to the continuing debates within some, at least, of the organizations concerned as to the overall direction of the future development of their staff rights law.

While the book focuses on the substantive law of the staff rights within the organizations, one chapter is also devoted to the constitutions of the procedures for administrative review concerned. This chapter naturally focuses on the roles of the tribunals concerned within each procedure, paying less attention to the usually preceding stage of executive decision-making or any subsequent stage of judicial or other review. With respect to the United Nations procedure, the functions of the Committee on Applications for Review of the Judgments of the United Nations Administrative Tribunal and the further role attributed to the International Court of Justice might perhaps have warranted further explanation, given the political controversy which has for years surrounded this *sui generis* development of an otherwise relatively straightforward judicial procedure. (For some comments on the most recent pronouncements from the International Court on this subject see Professor P. Tavernier, *Annuaire français de droit international*, 33 (1987), p. 211.)

The omission of any detailed explanation of the background to and character of these aspects of the United Nations procedure may be explained by the minimal impact which these additional stages in this particular procedure have had on the substantive law concerned. Nevertheless, they are aspects of the procedure which have been the subject of considerable political, judicial and administrative controversy, involving both the General Assembly and the International Court, over the years. Moreover, they remain currently under review within the United Nations.

One related aspect of the subject which the book, as a more technical practitioners' text, does not seek to cover is the wider question of the influence which political pressure has exerted, from time to time, on administrative decision-making on staff rights, the judicial resolution of disputes arising from such decisions, as well as the consequences for the development of the legal procedures involved. Such pressures have, of course, been much less evident in some organizations than others and have fluctuated in their nature and importance over the years in the organizations where they have been evident. Certainly such considerations have played a considerable role in moulding many important aspects of the United Nations procedure as well as substantive staff rights, for example in relation to the application of the principle of 'acquired rights' to new staff rules introduced each year by the Secretary-General before the General Assembly has had an opportunity to consider their impact.

However, these are essentially issues which might find their place in a work of a different nature from that under review; and their exclusion from this largely more technical work does not detract from the enormous value of the book as a work of reference and a more general source on employment law in international organizations.

J. I. STOODLEY

Droit international. By DOMINIQUE CARREAU. Paris: Éditions A. Pedone, 1986. 615 pp. + indexes. F 180.

There certainly is no lack of introductory textbooks to international law. Mercifully, Professor Carreau has not undertaken to write another one in the traditional fashion. Instead of attempting to cover all matters of substantive international law in a single volume, the book, according to its preface, 'plus modestement . . . donne une méthode pour appréhender le droit international: il entend montrer son processus et formation, d'application et de contrôle . . .' .

This is, of course, in and of itself a challenging task and a worthwhile endeavour indeed, considering the doctrinal confusion which is still prevailing in the structural analysis of international law, and which is seldom clarified in student introductions.

The book opens with a brief historical synopsis of international relations since biblical times, laying the groundwork for an understanding of the classical Westphalian system and leading up to the current, more complex, international society. Carreau soon admits to the transnational perspective of international law pioneered by Jessup and others, although international law still is 'un système juridique imparfait et incomplet' (p. 34). Nevertheless, this imperfect legal order dominates all other forms of law in the author's opinion.

Although this finding is by no means radical in the context of the usual discussions about the relationship between international and municipal law, he expands its application to new reaches. For Carreau, there also exists a hierarchy among different kinds of international law, and he is not referring to the familiar question of ranking the sources of law enumerated in Article 38(1) of the ICJ's Statute.

Of course, the introduction of *jus cogens* and of *erga omnes* principles to safeguard basic interests of world order does indicate that a hierarchy of norms is developing. Already Article 103 of the UN Charter serves as a convenient illustration. But the author suggests a theory extending much further. In his view, conventions aiming at universal membership always prevail over regional ones, which, in turn, prevail over bilateral agreements. The examples he cites in support of this challenging idea relate mostly to the special case of *jus cogens* principles. Instead of furnishing a more general analysis, the author declares that: 'Le principe de superiorité s'explique là encore pour des raisons de logique juridique' (p. 81).

It certainly makes perfect sense to assume, along with Carreau, that regional norms cannot conflict with rules which apply to all members of international society, since then those rules would obviously lose their universal character (p. 78). In fact, this conclusion is already inherent in the definition of the terms used. But, unfortunately, it must be doubted whether international law really complies with the rigid dictates of formal structural logic and with the abstract application of scientific terminology. With a few exceptions, including some conventions of a constitutional kind, the legal 'quality' of treaty obligations is not necessarily determined by the number of States which subscribe to them.

If a State was to agree to an obligation contrary to undertakings it has already made in a previous treaty, either one of two results can be envisaged. On the one hand, there might be a violation of the prior undertaking, regardless of whether or not the new obligation is enshrined in a convention with universal aspirations. If, on the other hand, there is no objection by the signatories of the first agreement, it rather seems that traditional rules, like that of *lex posterior derogat legi priori*, reflected in Article 59 of the Vienna Convention on the Law of Treaties, would apply.

When dealing with the law of treaties in the following section, the author gives an excellent overview of the relevant provisions of the Vienna Convention, which will be most helpful to all students eager to disentangle and understand its carefully crafted provisions. Carreau also offers a comprehensive discussion of treaties involving non-State entities, soft law and unilateral acts. He even covers unilateral acts of international organizations. In that context, it might be interesting to ask whether international organizations generally produce 'unilateral acts' proper. Outside of purely administrative functions, international organizations—possibly in contrast to the truly supra-national ones—seem rather to function as a transmission belt for the will of their various member States. Those States, say in the organs of the United Nations, negotiate to some extent what actions the organization is to take. Perhaps it is therefore something of a contradiction in terms to group the decisions taken 'by' international organizations under the heading of unilateral acts.

Carreau's treatment of customary law is also very interesting. Rather than denigrating the role of custom in the light of ever increasing codification efforts, he sees it as 'une produit de nécessités de la vie internationale' (p. 243), which is of increasing importance in several areas, gradually overcoming the limitations imposed by the strait-jacket of classical positivist doctrine.

After a clear exposition of the nature of general principles of law and of subsidiary sources, the author turns to the question of the application of the law. He begins, however, with a discussion of the subjects of international law. Since the principle of effectiveness in international law dictates that the law emanates from the acts of its subjects, this section might well have fitted into the introductory chapter. A student might find it easier to follow the discussion of the law-creating nature of acts of non-traditional subjects of international law after having been introduced to their status in the international system first.

Leaving aside these minor quibbles, the substance of the chapters which follow, covering all aspects of the implementation of legal obligations, will be most enlightening to the beginner. When dealing with responsibility for the violation of international obligations, however, the important ILC draft articles on the subject are only mentioned in passing.

In subsequent sections, Carreau provides an excellent discussion of questions concerning the application of international law in domestic *fora*, emphasizing the French legal system.

Finally, in the chapter on the enforcement of international obligations, the author advocates the right of 'intervention', or the unilateral use of force in extreme cases of the violation of essential principles of international order (p. 514). The few instances he cites to establish this justification for the use of force are all highly controversial, and in most of those cases even the States involved argued self-defence rather than self-help. It may of course be true that the unilateral use of force is permissible outside the narrow limitations of self-defence. But such a potentially dangerous exception to the prohibition of the use of force should not be re-introduced casually.

Overall, this book recommends itself for student use, to be read along with one of the traditional introductory textbooks which often neglect the important doctrinal questions addressed by Carreau. Generally, the work succeeds in presenting complex and controversial issues in all their relevant aspects without running the risk of confusing the uninitiated reader. On occasion, the author's own innovative views would deserve to be explained and supported at greater length.

MARC WELLER

International Economic Sanctions: Improving the Haphazard US Legal Regime. By BARRY E. CARTER. Cambridge: Cambridge University Press, 1989. xiv + 290 pp. £25.

The sub-title to this book is important, for it indicates the focus of the book. This is not a book about economic sanctions in general, nor is it concerned with the legality of economic sanctions in international law. Its purpose is more restricted, but nevertheless important, namely to examine the record of sanctions imposed by the US, and their effectiveness, and further to examine the legal basis of the measures taken in US law. The author then makes suggestions for improving and rationalizing what he describes as a 'haphazard' legal regime.

In successive chapters he examines non-emergency laws, the systems of export and import controls, controls over private financial transactions, controls via international financial institutions, emergency laws, the controversial issue of extra-statutory Presidential powers, problems of liaison with Allied Powers and, in his concluding chapter, he makes his recommendations for re-structuring the US system.

There are, however, two chapters of more general interest to the international lawyer. Chapter Two gives an overview of the history and effectiveness of sanctions, and concludes more optimistically than is common about the efficacy of sanctions. The US has been generally successful in applying sanctions designed to de-stabilize foreign governments (for example, Chile's Allende in 1971, or the Dominican Republic's Trujillo in 1961), but less successful in disrupting the 'military adventures' of foreign States. And the risk of failure has obviously increased with the relative decline of US economic power, or in circumstances in which the target State has been helped by the Soviet Union (as Cuba was). There are other fortuitous circumstances. If Iran had not had over 12 billion dollars in investments in the USA the effectiveness of US sanctions against that country would have been far less, simply because there would not have been the assets to seize.

Chapter Seven also has a considerable amount of interest. It makes the point that organizations like the World Bank or the IMF, because of their apolitical character, do not provide a very helpful vehicle for US sanctions policies. There are useful case-studies on Nicaragua, Ethiopia, South Yemen and Chile which bring out the evidence for the author's conclusions.

D.W. BOWETT

Conflict of Laws. By J. G. COLLIER. Cambridge: Cambridge University Press, 1987. xlvi, 377 + (index) 9 pp. Hardback, £40; paperback, £15.

This is a book 'chiefly intended' (Preface) for the undergraduate student of the conflict of laws. So it is as a students' text that it should be judged. And if the students I teach are any guide, they feel that it serves their needs adequately. We have, alas, seen the last edition of Morris (*The Conflict of Laws*, 3rd edition, 1984, by J.H.C. Morris) by Dr Morris himself. But this book seems set fair to take Morris's place as the students' favourite. They bring Collier to supervisions, they quote great chunks from him in essays, and they look quizzical when one suggests that this book might contain less than the final word on every topic. The influence of this book on the undergraduate teaching of the conflict of laws will doubtless be considerable. The author deserves our congratulations.

But what is this influential book like? It combines brevity with breadth of scope. Practically every topic that an undergraduate might wish or need to know about is discussed within the compass of a mere 377 pages. The latest edition of Cheshire and North (*Private International Law*, 11th edition, 1987, by P. M. North and J. J. Fawcett) does much the same task in 922 rather larger pages. So the book is crammed full of useful information; and the author's vivid, down to earth style makes it, generally, a delight to read.

Unlike Morris, Mr Collier follows the more traditional approach of introducing the student to the unique conceptual problems of *renvoi*, characterization and the incidental question at the beginning of the text rather than postponing discussion of these questions until the closing chapters of the book. On balance, I think that Mr Collier's approach is preferable. Although unsympathetic critics are wont to suggest that these conceptual problems are both difficult and irrelevant, students can grasp them even at an early stage; and a sound grasp of these matters enlightens and enlivens consideration of the more conventional choice of law topics.

Having cleared the conceptual problems out of the way, the book proceeds to canter through jurisdiction and foreign judgments and then on to the choice of law aspects of the law of obligations, property, succession and family law. Then come two chapters (that could easily have come in the introductory part) dealing with substance and procedure and the exclusion of foreign laws. The final part of the book consists of two chapters, one dealing with the 'reasons for and basis of the conflict of laws' and the other with 'public international law and the conflict of laws'.

Brevity, however, is only a virtue to the extent that it does not introduce ambiguity or lead to a superficial consideration of matters that should be considered more fully. And the incautious student may be led by Collier to accept as orthodox some views that are at least open to question.

Let me make this concrete with the example of Mr Collier's treatment of *Regazzoni v. K. C. Sethia (1944) Ltd.*, [1958] AC 301 (HL). He says in his most substantial account of this case that the implications of *Regazzoni* mean 'that if I contract to purchase 1,000 copies of the Holy Bible from the Cambridge University Press, and, to the latter's knowledge, I intend to distribute them to persecuted Christians in Agnostica (a country not actually at war with Her Majesty), and it is illegal to distribute Bibles in Agnostica by the law of that land, then if the Press delivers the Bibles to me and I refuse to pay, the court will refuse to order me to do so. This is, of course, preposterous' (at p. 176).

Indeed it is preposterous but it is not a result that is necessarily implied by *Regazzoni*. True some of the judgments delivered in that case are open to such readings (especially Denning LJ's judgment in the Court of Appeal and the speeches of Lord Keith and Lord Somervell in the House of Lords) but the remaining judges in the House of Lords (Viscount Simonds, Lord Reid and Lord Cohen) recognized that the principle that the English courts will not enforce contracts where the parties contemplate the breach of the law of a foreign and friendly country was limited to illegalities committed or to be committed *in the foreign country*. Thus in the example posed by Collier, the contract can obviously be performed entirely outside Agnostica; thus the contract can be enforced in England and the result is no longer preposterous.

Should not some discussion along these lines have been included? Given the debate on the continent over whether the public laws of legal systems other than the *lex fori* or the *lex causae* should in certain circumstances be applied, should not this aspect of the law have been explored properly? And has not the otherwise admirable brevity of Mr Collier's book denied this discussion to students?

Perhaps this is a trivial criticism of the book; views will inevitably differ on what is important and how cases should be interpreted. But behind the restrictions imposed by brevity lies in my view a weightier and more profound point. Mr Collier is often, quite rightly, very critical of judicial decisions on this branch of the law. But how is this to be remedied? Only by educating counsel and judges; and the best way of educating them is by educating the law students that will in due course become counsel and judges. The students reading Mr Collier's book will be the judges and practitioners of tomorrow; and his book is playing a crucial part in moulding their understanding of the nature of this subject.

But what will be their understanding of the subject? In Mr Collier's book only rarely are any cases other than English cases cited, nor are any other comparative sources worth mentioning discussed. References to academic writing are sparse and haphazard. Theoretical discussions are reduced to a bare and superficial minimum. The student relying on this book will gain a non-comparative and non-theoretical approach to the subject. But, in my opinion, that is exactly what is wrong with the conflict of laws in England: it is non-comparative and non-theoretical. Mr Collier's book could have been influential in remedying this; disappointingly it is not.

Christopher Forsyth

Repertory of International Arbitral Jurisprudence. Volume I (1794–1918); Volume II (1919–1945). Edited by Vincent Coussirat Coustere and Pierre Michel Eisemann. Dordrecht: Martinus Nijhoff, 1988. 540 pp. (Volume I) + 860 pp. (Volume II). £125.

Few libraries now contain the entirety of what is truly a vast reservoir of arbitral awards, and the *UN Reports of International Arbitral Awards* are filling that gap. But an analysis of this vast body of law is another matter. It was done for the Permanent Court of Arbitration (*Fontes juris gentium*), and Edvard Hambro did it for the International Court. But, until this publication, the task had not been attempted for arbitral awards. It is, indeed, a formidable undertaking, executed with great skill and intelligence, for which international lawyers will be indebted to the editors for many years to come.

The editors have sensibly included 'transnational' awards, between States and private entities, when these have involved questions of international law. The criterion for selection is the juridical content of an award, not the political importance of the case. And, of course, what is set out is only that part of the award that contains the statement of legal principle.

The system of presentation is orthodox and therefore readily usable. It covers sources ('international normative framework'), the State, other subjects, maritime areas and airspaces ('areas'), intercourse, coercion, State responsibility and settlement of disputes. There is, in any event, a good, detailed analytical index.

D. W. BOWETT

Die Kompetenzen des UN-Menschenrechtsausschusses im Staatenberichts-verfahren. By H.-M. EMPELL. Frankfurt am Main: Peter Lang Verlag, 1987. viii + 294 pp.

It is the small print which counts. This basic truth is certainly applicable to human rights law. In few other areas do States display more care and caution when drawing up international instruments. The relationship between a State and its subjects, after all, used to lie solely within the domestic jurisdiction of States, protected from outside influence by the heavy armour of sovereignty. Hence it took over a quarter of a century to produce and bring into force the two UN Human Rights Covenants.

And yet, despite the tremendous labour which went into drafting both treaties, the extent of the obligations incurred by States which have signed and ratified them is by no means clear. This applies especially to the definition of the functions and powers of the Human Rights Committee, which is part of the implementation machinery of the Covenant on Civil and Political Rights. In fact, agreement on the competence of the Committee has eluded even its very members, who represent 'the different forms of civilization and . . . the principal legal systems' (Article 31 of the Covenant).

Fortunately, Hans-Michael Empell has undertaken to disentangle the legal complexities involved in at least one aspect of the Committee's activities. He focuses on the reporting procedure under Article 40 of the Covenant.

After a short general introduction, Empell quickly addresses the issues under dispute, such as the right of the Committee to request further information from States after they have submitted their initial reports, the use of information submitted by other UN agencies or NGOs, and the precise nature of the Committee's own reports. In all instances, the author first introduces the wording of the relevant paragraph of the Covenant together with the differing interpretations which have been suggested. He then surveys the scholarly debate on the issue in light of the *travaux préparatoires* and the actual practice of the Committee. Where appropriate, he also provides a comparative analysis of other United Nations human rights procedures, before finally reaching his own conclusion.

Overall, this methodical and thorough approach has resulted in a very balanced work. In fact, its main virtue lies in the fact that it simply ignores the twin evils of rhetoric and ideology which still seem to pervade the discussion of human rights questions occasionally. Instead, we are presented with a technical contribution to the literature which is not afraid to advocate a restrictive interpretation of the Committee's mandate in some aspects, while defending a broader approach in others, in accordance with the deep and dispassionate analysis by the author.

It could possibly have been worthwhile if Empell had added a concluding chapter of a slightly more speculative nature. There is no general assessment of the relevance and value of the Committee's performance under the reporting procedure so far, and of its place in the ever growing jungle of mechanisms for the implementation of human rights, both inside and outside the UN. This, however, in no way detracts from the value of the book, which will certainly be of interest to specialists in human rights law. Perhaps the author could even be encouraged to summarize his conclusions in an article in either English or French, to make sure his contribution can be fully appreciated by all those most concerned with the issues he discusses.

MARC WELLER

Relevant Circumstances and Maritime Delimitation. By MALCOLM D. EVANS. Oxford: Oxford University Press, 1989. xiv + 253 pp. £32.50.

This is another book in the series of *Oxford Monographs in International Law,* a series which grows in stature with each new publication. Certainly this is an excellent addition. It is a highly intelligent piece of work, demonstrating real familiarity with the sources, both literary and judicial, and revealing considerable subtlety of analysis. Moreover, in concentrating on 'relevant circumstances', the author has grasped the essential truth that it is these which will determine the delimitation rather than abstract theories about 'equity' or the basis of title. He believes that the delimitation process can be viewed as a whole, for the result will be the same whether one starts from the premises of conventional or of customary law.

The first two chapters review the evolution of criteria for shelf and EEZ delimitation, and in the third chapter the author discusses the interrelationship of the shelf and EEZ regimes. His conclusions are challenging, but controversial. Essentially he gives priority to the shelf regime, for he accepts that shelf rights are inherent, and he even accepts the Court's 1969 view that, essentially, the shelf boundary is pre-existing, so that the Court's task is to identify it rather than establish it. From this it follows, in the author's view, that, since an EEZ has to be *claimed,* such a claim could not be made in an area in which shelf rights already appertained to another State by virtue of 'natural prolongation':

. . . where there is, in geological terms, a common continental shelf, irrespective of any claims to an EEZ that either party might make, the essential question is the location of the sea-bed boundary which defines the extent of the respective rights of the parties *and which the EEZ boundary must respect*

(p. 57, emphasis added). Time will tell whether Courts will give the shelf boundary this sort of priority. It is equally conceivable that in cases where the real resources at issue are water-column resources (i.e. fish), and where coasts are less than 400 miles apart, the physical structure of the shelf will be ignored and it will be the EEZ boundary which takes priority.

A fourth chapter on 'The Delimitation Process' concludes Part One. The author rejects the idea that there is utility in cataloguing 'equitable principles' and turns, instead, to 'relevant circumstances', correctly pointing out that these can both determine the appropriate method of delimitation and require some modification of that method. In a section entitled 'a new approach' (pp. 87–90), he sets out a very useful framework for analysis of any given delimitation problem.

Part Two turns to the different categories of relevant circumstances. In Chapter 5 the author discusses natural prolongation, geology and geomorphology and concludes, rightly, that geology and geomorphology must now be regarded as having little relevance to delimitation, and that 'natural prolongation' has become a geographical rather than a physical concept.

Chapter 6 turns to geography. This is correctly seen as the prime factor, and the author examines concepts such as the 'relevant area', 'relevant coasts', and unusual features such as islands to which he declines to attach special rules except, perhaps, to say that only dependent islands can be 'relevant circumstances' (p. 137). It is the effect of geographical features upon the delimitation which is important, not the type of feature in question.

Then, in Chapter 9, he turns to factors consequent upon geography, such as coastal lengths, seaward extension and encroachment, and then notes that, in choosing base-lines or base-points for the purposes of constructing a delimitation line, the Court does not necessarily adopt the lines or points used by the parties for purposes of measuring the outer-limit of their territorial sea.

In the concluding chapters the author turns to a variety of other factors: geo-political interests, political status, defence and security interests, navigational interests, economic factors, the presence of natural resources, and conduct. He approves, in general, the indifference of the Courts to economic factors, even evidence of pre-existing economic dependence, more particularly in shelf delimitations but even in EEZ delimitations. To this reviewer this has always seemed an extraordinary conclusion, given that the whole purpose of the EEZ is to secure the economic interests of the coastal State. The extreme 'test case' would be a delimitation between two equal coasts, the one totally uninhabited (and the offshore resources unexploited) and the other heavily populated and heavily dependent on those resources.

Chapter 18, on proportionality, is less impressive than most, being a series of comments, case by case, on how proportionality was used. The author doubts that proportionality should have played any role in *Malta/Libya* and concludes: 'Proportionality is simply a means of seeing whether the chosen equitable criterion is truly reflected in the resulting delimitation, for use only where the circumstances permit' (p. 231). One suspects that, in the seclusion of the Judges' conference room, if not in the text of the judgments, proportionality has a much greater role.

Chapter 19 concludes on the topic 'Third Parties and Delimitation'. He is rightly critical of the 'extraordinary decision' by the Court in *Malta/Libya*. He might well have gone further and noted the extreme difficulty of dealing with disputed boundaries in areas claimed by more than two parties, given that litigation is essentially structured on a pattern for *bilateral* confrontation.

All in all, an excellent book. It is good to see Ph.D theses of this quality and maturity finding their way to press.

D. W. BOWETT

Epochen der Völkerrechtsgeschichte. By WILHELM G. GREWE. Baden-Baden: Nomos Verlagsgesellschaft, 1984. 897 pp. + indexes. DM 138.
Fontes Historiae Iuris Gentium. Volume II (1493–1815). Edited by WILHELM G. GREWE. Berlin: Walter de Gruyter Verlag, 1988. 741 pp.

Good things are worth waiting for, and it certainly took a while until this magnificent history of international law was finally published. The book had already been finished in its basic conception by the end of World War II. Adverse circumstances made its immediate publication impossible. The author then entered the German foreign service and became one of Bonn's leading diplomats. It took exactly forty years until the work was finally updated and ready for publication.

The author himself suggests that this book should be viewed as an introductory text. And, indeed, the work will certainly entice people who are not experts in international law or history to read and enjoy it. Full historical background information is given to ease the understanding of important developments, and the relevance of legal conceptions is explained for the novice. There are even a number of reproductions of contemporary documents and historical paintings. But the work is certainly more than a student introduction. It is possibly the best and most comprehensive history of international law which has appeared for almost a century.

The book begins with a brief introduction to the relations among the political entities of the ancient world. The first chapter, dealing with the medieval system, is, according to the author, also designed as a mere introduction, leading up to the first period of true international law, the Spanish Age. Typically, even this introduction amounts to a substantial treatment of the period.

In each of the subsequent parts, the reader is guided through an era of international law with great care and precision. Generally, there is an introduction to the political framework of the historic system, a survey of the advance in legal doctrine, and a collection of specialized chapters on particular legal issues of outstanding importance at the time, like the *jus ad bellum*, arbitration, the law of the sea, and so on.

It has to be admitted that extra-European legal systems and colonial questions are only touched upon briefly, but the Eurocentrism of the book is obviously dictated by a need for clear focus to give coherence and structure to the vast amount of material that is covered. The division of the book into six distinct periods (medieval; Spanish; French; British; transitional period of the League of Nations; United Nations: superpower rivalry and the rise of the Third World) provides for additional clarity, and is well justified throughout the text in terms of substance.

The collection of treaties and other interesting documents in the Series of *Fontes Historiae Iuris Gentium* is organized similarly. The first volume to appear, Volume II, covers the Spanish and French periods, beginning with the Treaty of Tordesillas and ending with the abdication of Napoleon. While the editor obviously had to limit the amount of material which could be included, the selection has been made with great care, and even the expert will find interesting bits and pieces he or she had hitherto found elusive.

All treaties and documents have been reproduced in their original language, together with a German and English translation, or at least a content summary. Some of the documents regrettably had to be abbreviated, but they are all accompanied by references to the original source.

In short, this collection promises to be an indispensable reference work for all who share an interest in the history of international law and who just do not have the space to accommodate Martens' *Recueil* and the entire *Consolidated Treaty Series* on their book-shelves.

MARC WELLER

The Shatt-al-Arab Boundary Question: A Legal Reappraisal. By KAIYAN HOMI KAIKOBAD. Oxford: Clarendon Press, 1988. xix + 159 pages. £25.

The course of the international boundary in the Shatt-al-Arab has long been a source of friction between Iran and Iraq. Several treaties in the nineteenth and early twentieth centuries, culminating in the Treaty of 4 July 1937, set the boundary on the Iranian bank, leaving within Iraq all of the waters of the Shatt, with the exception of small areas abutting the Iranian ports of Mohammara (now Khoramshar) and Abadan. Despite the 1937 Treaty, Iran remained reluctant to accept that boundary. A period of tension and military clashes between the two States ensued in the late 1960s and 1970s, during which time Iran purported to denounce the 1937 Treaty. That conflict was brought to a peaceful conclusion after the intervention of the United Nations, and in 1975 a new boundary was agreed by Iran and Iraq in the Baghdad Treaty. That Treaty and its protocols established the frontier in the *thalweg* of the Shatt. It also included, as what it termed 'the indivisible elements of an overall settlement', confirmation of the Iran-Iraq land boundary and a duty to control the frontier so as to prevent cross-border subversion. In 1980 Iraq purported to abrogate the 1975 Treaty, on a variety of grounds including Iran's alleged support for Kurdish insolvency in Iraq in violation of the 1975 Treaty. Those events were the backdrop to the long and bitter conflict which broke out between the States in 1980.

This short and scholarly study of legal questions relating to the boundary in the Shatt is certain to become an indispensable text for scholars and practitioners alike. Half of the 118 pages of text consists of a detailed history of the boundary from the sixteenth century onwards, with particular emphasis on the negotiations leading up to the series of treaties between 1847 and 1947. Dr Kaikobad has drawn extensively on archival material in the India Office library and his detailed account of these papers, liberally supplemented with maps and documentary annexes, is a substantial contribution to legal scholarship, albeit a contribution likely to appeal more to the specialist than to the general reader. The second half of the text consists of an analysis of the main legal issues. Dr Kaikobad argues cogently to the conclusions that Iran's objections to the 1937 Treaty were misconceived, but that Iraq's claims that Iran had by its àctions abrogated, or entitled Iraq to abrogate, the 1975 Treaty were also mistaken, and that the Treaty survived even the outbreak of war between the two States. Some readers may wish that he had included a fuller consideration of the impact of the principle of self-determination upon boundary questions, in the light of the *Western Sahara* case, but few would wish to challenge the reasoning or conclusions which he so ably presents. This is a fine work of scholarship on a question which combines the highest political importance with an unusual degree of legal complexity, and it deserves to find its way into all international law libraries.

A. V. LOWE

International Law, Chiefly as Interpreted and Applied in Canada. By H. M. KINDRED, J.-G. CASTEL, D. J. FLEMING, W. C. GRAHAM, A. L. C. DE MESTRAL, I. A. VLASIC and S. A. WILLIAMS. 4th edition. Toronto: Edmond Montgomery Publications Ltd., 1987. xlix + 958pp. (including appendix and index). $96.

This is a new version of a casebook which in its previous editions was wholly the work of Professor Castel. It is divided into eleven major sections which cover international legal persons, the creation and ascertainment of international law, the application of international law (including the peaceful settlement of disputes), inter-State relations (recognition and diplomatic and State immunities), jurisdiction over territory, nationality, personal jurisdiction, State responsibility, human rights, the law of the sea, and a final chapter entitled 'From sovereignty to common interest', which includes material relating to environmental law and collective disarmament. There is no chapter on treaties because the relevant material is in the long chapter on sources, and no chapter on the use of force because this is treated as part of the rights and duties of States and therefore forms part of the even longer chapter on international legal persons. An appendix contains the United Nations Charter and Statute of the International Court.

One of the difficulties of editing a collection of cases and materials is to know what to leave out. Here the authors have chosen to provide substantial extracts from a limited selection of material, rather than a multitude of fragments from a larger number. This is a wise choice, and while it means that instruments such as the American Convention on Human Rights had to be omitted, what is included is long enough to be useful. It seems odd, however, that Article 1 of three of the major human rights instruments is missing and a pity that the interesting extracts from decisions of the United Nations Human Rights Committee do not include an account of the facts of one of the more serious cases, to provide a contrast with the rather different jurisprudence of the European Convention.

The distinctive feature of the book is, of course, the emphasis on Canadian material of all kinds, ranging from matter which will be of primary interest to Canadian lawyers, such as discussion of the treaty-making power, to case law and practice of more general relevance. In the latter category old favourites like the *Trail Smelter* and *The Caroline* are joined by the *Gulf of Maine* case and a number of Canadian cases before the United Nations Human Rights Committee. Because Canadian practice is now so extensive and because the authors provide a large amount of non-Canadian material, the book is in no sense parochial, but, on the contrary, conveys a good general picture of its subject.

The materials included are therefore well-chosen and for the most part are also up to date. In places, however, more might have been done to present the latest information. If the status of the Montego Bay Convention can be given as of November 1986, it is hard to see why we should be told that the African Charter of Human and Peoples' Rights is not yet in force, or that 'as of 1 January 1984' 31 States had ratified the Optional Protocol to the Covenant on Civil and Political Rights (p. 662).

As with other casebooks, the cases and materials are linked by authors' notes and these, while not providing extended exposition, are usually accurate and helpful. Occasionally the need to make a point concisely produces a dogmatic statement which could mislead. For example the view that the implementation machinery of the Covenant on Economic and Social Rights is 'virtually non-existent' (p. 645) is ill-judged, while the view that when dealing with an obdurate State, a reference to the Human Rights Committee 'is of no practical value' (p. 663) seems somewhat overstated. For the reader who wishes to seek other views or follow up a point, however, the authors provide a very useful set of references to the literature.

When reviewing a work of this kind it is easy to criticize an omission here and there, or challenge the authors' expression of a certain point of view. Quibbling aside, this is a book which, like its predecessors, provides the student with an excellent collection of source material and an instructive account of international law from a Canadian perspective.

J. G. MERRILLS

Das interamerikanische System zum Schutz der Menschenrechte. By JULIANE KOKOTT. Heidelberg: Springer Verlag/Max-Planck-Institut für ausländisches öffentliches Recht und Völkerrecht, *Beiträge zum ausländischen öffentlichen Recht und Völkerrecht,* No. 92, 1986. xii + 166 pp. DM 78.

There has been a long-standing need for a German-language introduction to the human rights system in the Americas. Juliane Kokott, one of the leading German experts in the field, has made an effort to satisfy this demand with her short book. She covers most institutional aspects of interest, beginning with a historic overview which is essential for an understanding of the fluidity and flexibility of the inter-American human rights machinery.

The author then turns to questions of structure and procedure of both Commission and Court. In this part of the book there are frequent references to and comparisons with the system of the European Convention. No real attempt has been made, however, to achieve an in-depth comparative analysis. Still, occasional references to the more familiar European system will certainly ease the reader's way towards an understanding of complex problems of procedure.

A clearer distinction between the process under the American Convention on Human Rights and that applicable to States not yet party to it could perhaps have been helpful to avoid confusion among the uninitiated. It would also have been interesting if the author could have included a survey or even a brief analysis of the substantive human rights provisions which have evolved in the Americas. Kokott frequently, and quite properly, reminds us of the importance of social and cultural influences in the development of that law, but she denies the reader the chance to sample a taste of its real flavour. There is a short review of the Inter-American Court's jurisprudence, but at the time of writing there was of course little ground to cover in terms of substance.

On the whole, Kokott has succeeded in presenting a lucid introduction to the formal aspects of the inter-American system. Unfortunately she has limited herself to a very concise format and left little room for the application of her well-proven analytical capabilities. The book therefore does not quite live up to the standard of depth which can usually be expected from works published under the auspices of the Heidelberg Max-Planck-Institute. It might have fitted better into a series of more widely available and less expensive introductory texts.

MARC WELLER

Vorbehalte zu multilateralen völkerrechtlichen Verträgen. By ROLF KÜHNER. Heidelberg: Springer Verlag/Max Planck Institut für ausländisches öffentliches Recht und Völkerrecht, *Beiträge zum ausländischen öffentlichen Recht und Völkerrecht,* No. 91, 1986. xi + 307 pp. + index. DM 98.

The Vienna Convention on the Law of Treaties is perhaps the most important attempt at codification of international law yet. It was created through decades of meticulous labour in the International Law Commission and especially through the efforts of its distinguished rapporteurs, it is slowly achieving a reasonable rate of acceptance among States, and many of its provisions have been declared to reflect customary international law. In fact, there is a tendency to regard the Convention *per se* as the embodiment of international custom as it relates to the law of treaties.

Rolf Kühner has undertaken to challenge this simplistic view in his monograph on reservations to multilateral treaties. He introduces this thorny subject by first distinguishing true reservations from related unilateral acts, such as interpretative declarations. Then he offers a historical survey of State practice and doctrine leading up to the adoption of the Vienna Convention. The amount of material used to frame the issue is impressive. Some of his assessments, including his perhaps over harsh views on the majority opinion in the highly influential ICJ case concerning *Reservations to the Convention on the Prevention and Punishment of the Crime of Genocide,* indicate Kühner's willingness to question doctrine which, at first sight, appears thoroughly convincing. This approach comes to full fruition when he analyses the applicable provisions of the Vienna Convention, and the relevant *travaux préparatoires,* at length, after having given a general synopsis of its negotiating history.

The strength of this detailed investigation lies in the overwhelming amount of State practice digested by the author. His attempt to distil this evidence into categories of custom which can be compared to the provisions of the Vienna Convention and to the multitude of theories concerning reservations is most laudable. It allows Kühner to establish where the Convention actually codifies customary law, and where progressive development has taken place. Furthermore, the author is able to demonstrate whether or not State practice has followed the new rules instituted by the Convention. On that basis the author concludes that the Vienna Convention has not really clarified the status of the law pertaining to reservations. From his vantage point, the codification is not the end, but merely the starting point for further analysis and discussion.

While nobody would deny the tendency of codification efforts to re-awaken dormant disputes about doctrine, one cannot help but wonder whether the author does not on occasion over-emphasize the relevance of some of the points which were possibly left unresolved in the Vienna Convention. In fact, it sometimes appears as if his penetrating powers of thought might have led him to embark upon an intellectual odyssey, when a much simpler rationale could be found in support of specific provisions. His position concerning reservations which are not in line with the object and purpose of a treaty might be an example.

On the whole, however, this study is a welcome addition to the other well-known works on the subject. Like all books published in the prestigious Max Planck series, it includes a short English summary, although this particular one rather lacks elegance and clarity. The last fifty pages of the work are taken up by a helpful documentary annex.

MARC WELLER

International Economic Law: Basic Documents. Edited by PHILIP KUNIG, NIELS LAU and WERNER MENG. Berlin: Walter de Gruyter & Co., 1989. xvi + 691 pp. DM 228.

This is a well-devised collection. Part One gives mainly the multilateral treaties relevant to the institutions concerned with international economics (although there are, in addition, the three central General Assembly resolutions on sovereignty over natural resources, the Declaration of a New International Economic Order, and the Charter on Economic Rights and Duties). Part Two gives some prominent examples of instruments regulating the economy, including many of the GATT and OECD texts, but also some of the Codes and Guidelines on Multinationals, International Investments, Competition and, finally, Transportation.

The problem facing the editors is clearly that of deciding which documents to exclude, because of space and cost. So, although one can think of documents which might well have been usefully included, the question is really whether documents now included would be best left out to make room for other candidates. The judgment of the editors on this point seems sound.

The only substantive suggestion this reviewer would make is the following. It would have been well worth an extra fifty pages to have some editorial guidance or comment. It is, of course, true that there is a good Introduction of four pages, but I envisage more a short note giving the background to each document. For example, why was the 1965 ICSID Convention necessary, and how far has it proved successful? Or how does the Air Services Transit Agreement of 1944 fit into the scheme of the Chicago Convention, and relate to the many bilateral agreements?

No doubt, if this book is used in connection with a good lecture course, such editorial comments are unnecessary. But not all readers may be so well-served.

D. W. BOWETT

Conflict and Peace in the Modern International System. By EVAN LUARD. 2nd (completely revised) edition. London: Macmillan Press, 1988. xii + 328 pp.

This book has considerable interest for the international lawyer because it places the most fundamental rules—those relating to the restraint of force—in the wider setting of international relations. Moreover it demonstrates a breadth of knowledge and a degree of perception, clearly the result of reflection over a long period of time, which is unusual. There is no evidence of 'special pleading', and its sincerity is apparent. It would therefore make excellent pre-course reading for international law students.

A first chapter on 'External Wars' demonstrates some remarkable changes over the past hundred or so years in the nature of war. Territorial expansion is no longer the prime motivating force, and there is a general fear of a major, global conflict. States fight limited wars with limited (i.e. non-nuclear) means and major powers clash indirectly rather than directly, by intervening in wars between or within other States.

As regards the legal rules on the restraint of the use of force, the author is sceptical about the value of definitions of 'aggression', because in practice such definitions are always subjectively applied. There is a real need for 'objective' evaluation, which necessarily means via international bodies or institutions, and it is here that the UN has singularly failed, for its record is not one of objectivity and impartiality (p. 57). Mr Luard concludes that greater objectivity might be attained if the UN concentrated more on restoring peace and less on the allocation of responsibility or guilt for war (p. 64). He argues that restoration of the *status quo* will not suffice, for many conflicts are a form of challenge to the *status quo*, and it is the need for peaceful change that has to be recognized. All of this is true. However, it needs to be added that some conflicts stem from deeply-felt antagonisms, and the views of people often take a very long time to change (India/Pakistan, the Middle East, South Africa, the Iran/Iraq war, the Falklands war), so that governments cannot negotiate change which will be unacceptable to their people. They must first educate their people on the need for change.

Chapter 2, on 'Frontiers', shows that, as sources of conflict, these have increased since 1945 (in contrast to wars of territorial expansion). And the author is clearly right in showing that self-determination is no panacea. But the suggestion that the UN might help by publishing a definitive atlas showing the frontiers (p. 89), or by establishing a permanent Commission on Frontiers, is not likely to find much support within the UN itself, for it would lead to endless acrimony.

Chapter 3, on 'Colonies', notes their decline as a source of conflict, but finds it difficult to assess the effect of the UN's role in bringing this about.

Chapter 4, on 'Civil Wars', touches upon the most common source of conflict in the world today. Mr Luard demonstrates that, since 1945, the traditional rules of law on assistance to either governments or revolutionaries by outside Powers have rarely been applied. But he treats the contemporary rules with less than his usual thoroughness. The General Assembly's Resolution on Non-Intervention of 1965 is relegated to a footnote and, surprisingly, he makes no mention of self-determination in this connection. He certainly sees the utility of UN supervision of elections, so as to resolve disputes about the legitimacy of one faction's claim to govern over another, but this precept of political action finds legal support in the principle of self-determination. Thus, one can argue that it is always illegal to intervene against a government supported by the majority of the people.

Nevertheless, the author is right in regarding agreements on arms control as largely incidental to situations of civil strife—the main cause of international conflicts (Chapter 5). He is equally sceptical about measures for agreed disarmament as a direct means for curbing international conflicts, since these, too, have but minimal effect on civil conflicts (Chapter 6).

The remaining chapters have a different character, for they are in effect essays on the different components of international society. Chapter 7, on 'Authority', criticizes the UN for its unpredictability and makes the point that authority rests on respect, and respect is not likely to be accorded to a body which acts in an unpredictable, or seemingly unprincipled, manner. Mr Luard favours weighted voting in the General Assembly, based on population, to bring more realism to its actions.

Chapter 8, on 'Law', reveals some misunderstanding of the role of law. The lack of provision for 'peaceful change' is not a defect of the legal system, as Mr Luard supposes (p. 247), but of the political system. The prime movers in 'peaceful change' ought to be the political organs, namely the General Assembly and Security Council, not the International Court. And it is axiomatic that in the realm of disputes threatening world peace the solution has to be political rather than legal. Thus Mr Luard's disappointment at the minimal role played by the law results from too high an expectation of what the law can achieve. To take a parallel, no one expects the solution to the problems in Northern Ireland to be provided by the law and the courts. Why should we expect the situation to be different in relation to world peace?

There is an interesting final chapter on 'Opinion'. Mr Luard is sceptical about the effectiveness of public opinion in securing world peace. He suggests that the simple desire for peace is, in itself, ineffective: it has to be harnessed to the principles that will ensure peace (p. 282). Yet he finds that the principles of international law are not understood by world opinion, and thus they lack the backing of world opinion which is necessary to make the law effective. This is largely true, but the fault lies with governments which rarely explain their policies in terms of what the law requires, but rely on what expediency dictates or what will be 'popular' with that public opinion.

D. W. Bowett

The Law of Deep Sea-Bed Mining. By Said Mahmoudi. Stockholm: Almqvist & Wiksell International, 1987. 361 pp. + index. SEK 520,00.

Solidarity cannot be achieved by legislation. This conclusion may safely be deduced from the experience of the Third United Nations Conference on the Law of the Sea (UNCLOS III). The Conference, it was hoped by the less developed nations, was to provide for the equitable sharing of the resources of the sea-bed. But this grandiose scheme under the principle of 'common heritage of mankind' had already been cut down significantly in the negotiations of the Convention. It was weakened further by the refusal of significant industrialized nations under the leadership of the United States to sign the Convention. And, some would say, the dramatic fall in world market prices for certain minerals might have rendered the cumbersome and possibly inefficient UNCLOS III regime for sea-bed mining obsolete.

Said Mahmoudi, in his substantive study on the subject, takes a different view. To his mind, the framework established by the Convention remains both valid and practicable. He bases this assessment on a detailed study of the applicable general international law and the *travaux préparatoires* of UNCLOS III.

Mahmoudi sets out to establish that the principle of common heritage of mankind is indeed part of current international law. First he turns to the traditional notions of *res nullius* and *res communis* and discusses both concepts at length. However, for all the detail in his presentation, some essential elements have been left out. For example, there is no mention of the *Behring Sea* arbitration.

Having found neither *res nullius* nor *res communis* applicable to deep sea mining, the author then traces the development of the common heritage principle. Again, his presentation is rich in detail. Of course, the actual behaviour of relevant States remains mostly outside UNCLOS III. This is evidenced in the licensing of national mining enterprises, or the negotiation of 'mini treaties' which purport to divide the spoils of the sea-bed among a few technologically advanced nations. Mahmoudi seeks to overcome this difficult fact by referring to State practice of another kind. He provides a barrage of citations from statements of various delegations during the negotiations leading up to the adoption of the Convention, emphasizes the package-deal principle and argues that UN General Assembly resolutions on the common heritage principle have had some sort of law-creating effect. In short, he argues on the basis of what is known as 'soft law', but, considering the inherent weakness of his position, he makes his case quite convincingly.

However, the author himself is forced to admit that the common heritage principle remains largely undefined. Still, he concludes confidently, and controversially, that this principle nevertheless renders illegal the exploitation of the sea-bed outside of the UNCLOS III regime. On that basis, he analyses the machinery provided for the implementation of the Convention in some detail.

While many commentators would echo Western concerns over the forced transfer of technology, the complex and costly registration procedures, or the provisional nature of the protection for pioneer investors, Mahmoudi is unperturbed. To him, the organizational structure of the Convention represents simply the more concrete manifestation of the common heritage principle. In fact, he is not convinced that the Convention's system does enough to satisfy the needs of the less developed nations. Nevertheless, he concludes that it would be unrealistic to expect a result different from that achieved in UNCLOS III.

Overall, Mahmoudi presents a very substantial rationalization of the standpoint taken by the Group of 77 nations. He thus provides us with a well researched and ably presented piece of advocacy. While there is room for disagreement on the substance of his conclusions, it will be difficult to ignore his book in the discussion about deep sea mining, which is bound to continue well into the next decade.

MARC WELLER

International Sports Law. By JAMES A. NAFZIGER. Ardsley-on-Hudson, New York: Transnational Publishers Inc., 1988. xiv + 250 pp. $45.

There is no doubt that sport is being attended by an increasing number of problems which involve the law to a greater or lesser extent. These involve violence at sports grounds; misbehaviour, sometimes outside the actual sports ground, by fans and supporters; trademark infringements; anti-trust and taxation law; the use of drugs; contracts between professional sportsmen and their clubs; television rights; injuries on the playing field; and many others. Recourse to courts to resolve sports disputes is becoming more common, e.g. *Reel* v.

Holder, [1979] 1 WLR 1252; [1981] 1 WLR 1226, noted in this *Year Book*, 50 (1979), p. 217, and 52 (1981), p. 301. Most sports issues are of course determined by national courts applying national law. Some issues, however, involve the application of private international law, and an increasing number raise questions of public international law as well.

It is for this reason that Professor Nafziger's pioneering work is to be welcomed, even if it is the first word, rather than the last word, on the subject. There is now a wide range of international sports, and obviously more research needs to be carried out. As might be expected, Professor Nafziger's work begins with a study of the Olympic Games of the ancient Greek period and then moves on to the revival of the Olympic Games through the influence of Baron Pierre de Coubertin at Athens in 1896. Games were then held at Paris (1900), St Louis (1904), London (1908) and Stockholm (1912). Naturally the First World War caused an interruption, but the Games were revived at Antwerp in 1920. In this early period the main problems were the exclusive employment of judges by the host country and the distinction between amateurs and professionals. After the post-war revival of the Games, things proceeded fairly smoothly until the Berlin Games of 1936, which were exploited for propaganda purposes by the Nazis. The Second World War naturally caused another interruption, but the Games were revived again at London in 1948. Since then the Games have been held regularly at four-year intervals without interruption, although frequently subject to boycotts promoted for political reasons. Separate winter games were started at Chamonix in 1924, and winter games were held in the same year as the summer games until 1986, when the International Olympic Committee (IOC) decided that it would be better to hold the winter games half way through each four-year Olympiad rather than in the same year as the summer games. The new system will become effective in 1994, when winter games will be held after the summer games have been held at Barcelona in 1992. Naturally, for climatic reasons, winter games are not necessarily held in the same country as the summer games. For example, in 1948, the summer games were held in London and the winter games in St Moritz. In 1980, a difficult year for the Olympic movement, the summer games were held in Moscow, though subject to boycott, and the winter games were held at Lake Placid in New York. An important distinction between the ancient games and the modern games is that the former were held at a single site (Olympia), whereas the modern games move from place to place, the choice of venue usually being hotly contested and controversial. There is some support for holding the games once again at a single site, which would be Athens, but it remains to be seen whether that view will attract sufficient support to be implemented in practice.

The organization of the IOC, which was founded in 1894, is, from the perspective of an international lawyer, rather similar to that of the Red Cross. The IOC, which is one of the oldest international non-governmental organizations in the world, is composed of three bodies: an Executive Board of eleven members; a Plenary Session which meets at least once a year; and a Secretariat, which is located at Lausanne. The broader Olympic Movement consists of the IOC, the International Federations governing individual sports; National Olympic Committees; the organizing committee for a particular Olympiad; and the Olympic Congress which meets every eight years and has advisory functions only. There are 29 International Federations, the best known being the International Amateur Athletic Federation (IAAF) and the International Federation of Association Football (FIFA). The whole system is regulated by the Olympic Charter which provides that the IOC is 'a body corporate under international law having juridical status and perpetual succession'; that its headquarters are in Switzerland; that it is not formed for profit; and that among its aims are 'to make the Olympic Games ever more worthy of their glorious history and of the high ideals which inspired their revival by Baron Pierre de Coubertin and his associates'. A Court of Arbitration for Sport (CAS) was founded in 1983. Its jurisdiction is optional but its judgments are binding. The CAS, which applies Swiss law unless a particular arbitration agreement provides otherwise, also has power to render advisory opinions. The whole Olympic system thus operates on the fringe of public international law.

Recent events, particularly the situation in South Africa, have made the relation between international law and international sports even closer. South African athletes were prevented from attending the Olympic Games of 1964 at Tokyo by the operation of the IOC's own rules. Subsequently the IOC decided by a majority vote that South Africa had made sufficient progress in deleting racism from athletics to warrant South African participation in the Mexican games of 1968, but under pressure from the Supreme Council for Sports in Africa, representing 33 African States, had to rescind this decision. The General Assembly of the United Nations supported the new IOC stand, and in 1977 adopted an International Declaration against Apartheid in Sports.

Thus, contrary to a widely held view that politics should be kept out of sport, politics was beginning to impinge upon sport, and this tendency was confirmed by the decision of the Carter Administration to organize a boycott of the 1980 Moscow Games in consequence of the Soviet incursion into Afghanistan. The boycott was not very successful, and a retaliatory boycott of the 1984 Los Angeles Games by the USSR was no more successful. Fortunately the 1988 Games in Seoul were less affected by boycotts, and, although it would be dangerous to prophesy, it does now seem that generalized boycotts are unlikely to achieve their objectives and are therefore less likely to occur. But boycotts of South Africa continue, and pressure is still applied against teams or individuals maintaining sports contacts with that country.

All these matters are lucidly covered by Professor Nafziger, although there will be less general interest in the chapter which he devotes to the Amateur Sports Act passed by the United States Congress in 1978. The book is inclined to place more emphasis on Olympic sports than on other sports such as cricket and rugby which do not form part of the Olympic programme. It also places more emphasis on the practice of the United States than that of other countries. But Professor Nafziger has blazed a trail which deserves to be followed by other authors, and it is to be hoped that eventually there will emerge a compendium of international sports law which will be of great interest to international lawyers as well as being of particular value to sports administrators.

D. H. N. JOHNSON

The Laws of Armed Conflicts: A Collection of Conventions, Resolutions and Other Documents. 3rd Edition. Edited by DIETRICH SCHINDLER and JIRI TOMAN. Dordrecht: Martinus Nijhoff Publishers, 1988. xvii + 958 pp. £124.25.
The Law of Naval Warfare: A Collection of Agreements and Documents with Commentaries. Edited by NATALINO RONZITTI. Dordrecht: Martinus Nijhoff Publishers, 1988. xviii + 888 pp. (including index). £117.

The publication of a new edition of Schindler and Toman's collection of documents on the law of armed conflict will be welcomed by everyone with an interest in this subject. By far the most comprehensive collection of documents on the law of armed conflict, the book is not confined to the treaties currently in force but includes the texts of some earlier treaties, such as the 1929 Geneva Prisoners of War Convention in force during World War Two, and a number of documents, such as the General Assembly resolutions on nuclear weapons, which are of considerable interest, even though they lack binding force. The new edition includes the text of the 1980 Weapons Convention, the most important omission from the previous edition. Although the price of this volume means that students will almost certainly opt for one of its less expensive rivals, Schindler and Toman will remain the most important collection of documents for anyone engaged in research into the law of armed conflict.

Unlike the law of land warfare, agreements on which occupy most of Schindler and Toman's book, the law of naval warfare has eluded attempts at systematic reform. The result is that the law is to be found in a bewildering mass of treaties dealing with specific points, many of which were drafted before World War One, and widely divergent State practice. The shortcomings of this law were vividly illustrated during the Gulf conflict, which gave rise to long overdue debate about both the content of the existing law and the possibilities for reform.

Ronzitti's *Law of Naval Warfare* is a major contribution to this debate. Twenty-four authors, from a wide variety of backgrounds, have collected and analysed the principal agreements and other documents relating to the laws of naval warfare. All of the treaties currently in force relating to naval warfare are included, along with a number of agreements which never entered into force, such as the 1909 London Declaration which is the subject of an excellent study by Frits Kalshoven, or which were never intended to be formally binding, such as the Oxford Manual on the Law of Naval Warfare of 1913. The standard of the analyses is, for the most part, very high. Most of the authors have engaged in extensive research in the *travaux préparatoires* of the treaties which they analyse and have a good understanding of their subsequent interpretation and application. The result is a very thorough study of the texts, their interpretation and current legal standing and the areas in which they are thought to be deficient.

Yet this is only part of the story. Much of the modern law of naval warfare is to be found not in international agreements but in customary law, derived from State practice and frequently deviating very significantly from the written law. Moreover, much of the traditional law of naval warfare concerns the rights and duties of neutrals, and it must be questioned here how far that law has survived the impact of the United Nations Charter and the changes in the attitudes of States towards conflicts in which they are not directly involved. Some of these issues are discussed in the most interesting introductory essay by Natalino Ronzitti, which identifies many of the most difficult issues which any attempt to explain, let alone reform, the law of naval warfare must face.

The book is really a preparatory work for future studies of the law of naval warfare and will be invaluable to anyone involved in such work. It deserves a wide audience amongst those interested in the law of armed conflict or the law of the sea.

CHRISTOPHER GREENWOOD

International Arbitration: Three Salient Problems. By STEPHEN M. SCHWEBEL. Cambridge: Grotius Publications Ltd., 1987. xviii + 303 pp. £33; US$59.

While student textbooks on international law continue to present the topic of international dispute settlement as if recourse to the International Court of Justice were the normal means for the judicial resolution of disputes, it is perfectly plain that this is a perspective which, if it ever had any truth, belongs to a phase of international law which is now waning fast. The last twenty years have seen a great increase in the numbers of international arbitral tribunals established to decide issues, many of which arise from disputes between States and non-State entities such as multinational companies, which in earlier times might have been settled by inter-State proceedings before the International Court. It is therefore particularly gratifying that a Judge of the International Court of Justice, one of the outstanding international lawyers of the present generation, should have devoted such care and scholarship to the examination of some of the central problems concerning the international arbitral process.

Judge Schwebel's monograph, derived from the course of Lauterpacht lectures which he delivered at Cambridge University in 1983, tackles three of the most topical of these problems. He begins with the question whether an arbitration clause can survive the termination of an agreement in which it is included—the question of the 'severability' or 'autonomy' of the arbitration clause. After a careful review of international judicial and arbitral practice, and of the rules for arbitration adopted by bodies such as the International Chamber of Commerce and UNCITRAL, he concludes that the severability of the arbitral clause is sound in principle and supported by practice and doctrine, with the result that a tribunal may properly be established to decide issues under an agreement which one of the parties asserts not to be binding upon it. Judge Schwebel suggests that this might be so whether or not the agreement in which the arbitration clause appears is, or ever was, itself valid, as long as the agreement was actually concluded. The rationale is that the parties must have intended to provide for the resolution of disputes not only over the interpretation and application of the agreement but also over the validity of the agreement. Some may find this difficult to accept as a matter of strict logic in the case of agreements void *ab initio*, and might wish to distinguish between different grounds for the initial nullity. For example, nullity deriving from the lack of authority of an agent to bind the State might be thought to give rise to different questions from nullity deriving from patent constitutional limitations upon the power of the State to commit itself to arbitration: the arguments for upholding an arbitration clause are perhaps rather different, and stronger, in the latter case than in the former. However, none can fail to be impressed by the cogency and elegance of Judge Schwebel's reasoning.

The second chapter considers whether the refusal of a State to comply with an obligation to arbitrate assumed in a contract with an alien may be considered a denial of justice. He concludes that it may, and offers a powerful rebuttal of Dr Mann's claim that no denial of justice occurs when a refusal to arbitrate is grounded in general legislation, not specifically directed against a contracting alien, adopted after the arbitration agreement. He also demonstrates that in such cases no exhaustion of local remedies is required before the denial can be pursued on the international plane.

The final, and much the longest, chapter is entitled 'The Authority of Truncated Tribunals', and it addresses the sadly common phenomenon of the withdrawal of State-appointed arbitrators from tribunals established pursuant to an obligation to arbitrate. This practice, made familiar by events in the Iran-US Claims Tribunal in recent years but having a history that goes back to the dawn of modern arbitration under the Jay Treaties of 1794, he considers to be unlawful, and not to impair the authority of the truncated tribunal or the right of the remaining arbitrators to deliver a valid award. His examination of State practice and doctrine is as comprehensive and incisive as in the rest of the monograph, but does not give the same overwhelming support to his thesis as does the practice surveyed in the earlier chapters. Nonetheless, readers will surely accept the underlying view that any other conclusion is so destructive of the rule of law in international relations as to be scarcely acceptable.

This is an exceptionally fine work, consummately crafted and argued with great consideration for the views of those who oppose his theses. Happily, the publishers have lavished equal care on the production of the book, which is of the highest quality. There can be no doubt that this will remain for many years a classic treatment of these issues, of the greatest value to scholar and practitioner alike, and a model of the standards to which legal scholarship should aspire.

A. V. LOWE

Corporations in and under International Law. By IGNAZ SEIDL-HOHENVEL-DERN. Cambridge: Grotius Publications Ltd., 1987. xviii + 138 pp. £25.

International law is no longer a set of legal rules addressed exclusively to sovereign States. It can and does apply to many types of corporations. It is these two principles that Seidl-Hohenveldern concisely maintains and develops in this book.

The book is divided into two parts—corporations in international law and corporations under international law. In regard to Part One, the examination centres on the control and protection of private corporations and also their nationalization, together with the resultant issue of lifting the corporate veil. Not surprisingly, heavy reliance is made on the International Court of Justice decisions in the *Nottebohm* and *Barcelona Traction* cases. The author argues that a State is protecting its own interests in proffering diplomatic protection to shareholders of corporations and that economic realities and a promotion of respect for international law require a more frequent lifting of the corporate veil to allow this protection. The difficult problem of the control of transnational corporations is then analysed. Control of these corporations by the United Nations is proposed, as offering scrutiny without self-interest and without incurring the distrust inherent in a State seeking to enforce extra-territorial legislation. However, this proposal does not overcome the principal objection by many jurists that a corporation must be subject to some State's national law, as it has to be incorporated in a State.

The most lengthy chapter concerns nationalization and the lifting of the corporate veil. Using material and case law from Europe and the United States, a strong argument is put that the doctrine of severance should apply here so that the right of each shareholder in the assets of the corporation is localized wherever there are assets of the corporation. This right is thus severed from its fictional location at the seat of the corporation and so assets outside the nationalizing State are still available to the 'residual' or 'split' corporation. This can be supported as consistent with the doctrine of territoriality. However, the author seems prepared to accept that the amount of compensation to be paid is to be determined in accordance with the standard established under the Constitution of the Federal Republic of Germany (i.e. 'the compensation shall be determined after just consideration of the interests of the general public and the participants') and insufficient consideration is given to the various General Assembly resolutions dealing with the principles of compensation or to decisions in international arbitrations, such as *Aminoil* v. *Kuwait* or even the Libyan oil arbitrations.

State-owned corporations are examined, with particular reference to reliance by these corporations on *jure imperii* State acts to avoid contracts and also to responsibility by the State-owned corporation for its State's acts. The views given are straightforward, for example, 'a fair deal to foreign business partners is more likely to protect socialist property in the long run' (p. 60).

In Part Two of the book, the author deals with the role of member States in, and their responsibility for, international organizations: interaction of the international organization with third States; its succession and division; the effect of national law on international organizations; and common inter-State enterprises. Here it is reaffirmed that international law can and does apply to corporations (essentially being international organizations) and not exclusively to sovereign States. It can be argued that in stating that 'only entities established by States are subjects of international law' (p. 70), he does not go far enough, as there are strong arguments for a broader view of the subjects of international law. However, the explanation for the application of international law to international organizations is that 'none of the States divest themselves of that part of their own power in favour of the organization. The power is retained by the States but it is dormant. The temporary vacuum is filled by the organization, which thereby avails itself of a legislative and executive power of its own' (p. 71). Consistent with this position, it is shown that the States parties to a treaty setting up an international organization can ignore the terms of the treaty and alter the constitution of that organization by agreement between them; and that international organizations, except the United Nations, do not have objective personality and so require recognition by third States.

The chapter on international organizations in domestic law confirms that these organizations have personality in national law, at least in regard to their activities in a State. It is concluded that the treaty establishing the international organization is the national law of the organization. However, the resultant issue of de-localization of contracts (where the proper law of the contract is not any national law) is too briefly discussed. Common inter-State enterprises, their legal personality and independence, are then examined together with the piercing of their corporate veils to attach liability to the member States. The author's view that member States of a common inter-State enterprise should be jointly and severally responsible for the acts of the enterprise will now need to be reconsidered in light of the decisions in the *International Tin Council* cases.

This book is clearly and concisely written. Seidl-Hohenveldern has here provided the solid, practical groundwork for the consideration of the place of corporations in and under international law.

ROBERT McCORQUODALE

United Nations Codification of State Responsibility. Edited by MARINA SPINEDI and BRUNO SIMMA. New York: Oceana Publications Inc., 1987. 430 pp. $75.

The long gestation of the ILC's work on State Responsibility has meant that access to it has become more difficult, involving reference to the *Yearbooks* of the Commission over nearly twenty years. This new volume is of great help. It reproduces as appendices the articles adopted on first reading (based on Ago's drafts), the two drafts proposed by Riphagen, a detailed synopsis of the ILC proceedings for each of the above, and an extensive bibliography.

In addition, the book has eight essays on controversial issues of State responsibility. It omits the topic of liability for lawful acts because the ILC gives it separate treatment, which is perhaps a pity. The editors express some surprise at the relative lack of academic interest in the ILC's work. But this is not so surprising when one considers the very long period that has already elapsed and the lack of any promise that the work will soon reach completion.

However, the eight essays are excellent, and they make a contribution irrespective of the ultimate fate of the ILC's work. Tanzi examines the question whether damage is a necessary constituent of a wrongful act. He examines the problem largely as one arising from violations of obligations owed *erga omnes* (although the problem could equally arise under a simple, bilateral treaty where a breach produced no material damage). However, he also argues for the award of pecuniary damages in cases where no material loss has been suffered, even though there is little support for the idea in State practice. One has to ask what the purpose of such an award of damages might be. If it is not to compensate an injured party, it is presumably intended as a deterrent. But this implies that the Court's finding that a wrong has been committed is not in itself a sufficient deterrent.

Hazem Atlam questions whether the ILC was right to deal with traditional revolutionary groups and national liberation movements on the same footing. He maintains the difficult thesis that an act may be lawful or unlawful, depending on whether it was committed by an insurrectionist or a liberation movement. This 'preferential' treatment for liberation movements, struggling against racist or colonialist regimes, is clearly controversial. Most insurrectionist or revolutionary movements would advocate the 'justice' of their cause in terms just as ethical as any liberation movement. His proposition that, on achieving success and becoming the new government, a liberation movement ought not to be liable for the wrongs of the predecessor colonialist government is less controversial, but still too wide. Why should they not compensate for requisitions of property of 'neutrals' which is retained for use by the new government? Unjust enrichment has a role.

Mazzeschi tackles the less sensitive question of responsibility for breach of treaty, and the remedies of termination or suspension. He sees this responsibility as part of the general law of State responsibility, and not a special category arising from breach of treaties. Accordingly he tends to disagree with Riphagen and to see the remedies of termination and suspension as part of the wider right of reprisals. Similarly he doubts whether 'third' States, i.e. States parties to a multilateral treaty but not directly injured by the breach, can react by suspension or termination only by virtue of the special regime of Article 60 of the Vienna Convention.

Wolfram Karl writes on the time factor in the law of State responsibility. He sensibly points out certain inconsistencies in the ILC drafts, and has interesting observations on the role of *jus cogens*. Manfred Mohr treats the distinction between international 'crimes' and 'delicts', mainly by way of describing the ILC's work, but he usefully stresses that the concept has little to do with 'criminality' in the accepted sense: it rather indicates an area of responsibility in which States have a broader range of reactions to choose from.

The two essays by Alland, on self-defence and countermeasures, and Malanczuk, also on self-defence and countermeasures, contain some measure of overlap. The difference is one of approach: Alland is concerned with them as sanctions, whereas Malanczuk is concerned with them as circumstances precluding wrongfulness. Both are excellent, but it is Malanczuk who deals more directly with the Court's judgment in *Nicaragua* v. *US*. He accepts, following Ago and the Court, that self-defence exists only in relation to an armed attack, and that for other delicts the remedy is 'countermeasures'. This is now the accepted wisdom and, whatever one's doubts as to the realism of this distinction, it must be accepted as the law.

A final article by Miatello on responsibility for the use of nuclear energy offers a good, comprehensive account of this topic, and actually does touch on liability for lawful acts.

The quality of these articles by young European academics (plus Atlam from Cairo) is most reassuring. One need have no fears for international law scholarship in Europe over the near future.

D. W. Bowett

Völkerrechtlicher Vertrag und Drittstaaten (Berichte der Deutschen Gesellschaft für Völkerrecht, Heft 28). By C. Tomuschat, H.-P. Neuhold and J. Kropholler. Heidelberg: C. F. Müller Juristischer Verlag, 1988. 179 pp. DM 84.

Conference reports tend to lack structure, coherence and depth. Thankfully, the book under review is an exception. The first two of the three articles it incorporates, all dealing with the controversial and topical issue of third party obligations in international law, can be regarded as substantial contributions to the literature. This review will not cover the third paper by Jan Kropholler on private international law and third States, as he himself admits that this subject is 'of no significant relevance' (p. 106).

All contributions, which were originally presented at the annual gathering of the German International Law Society in 1987, are accompanied by short summaries in English. As an added bonus, the book includes the critical comments of some of the more illustrious members of the Society.

The first lecture is by Christian Tomuschat of Bonn University. He opens with an acknowledgement of the long-standing positivist viewpoint which denies third party obligations arising from treaties. But on the other hand, he recognizes claims asserting universally binding objective legal regimes, obligations *erga omnes* or *jus cogens*. He briefly surveys the potential sources of such legal principles of a constitutional kind, pointing to the recent trend in ICJ jurisprudence to presume, without much apparent analysis, an identity of treaty stipulations and of general customary law. The author does not consider it necessary to challenge the doctrinal soundness of this perhaps not entirely uncontroversial approach.

Tomuschat next analyses whether there are areas of policy which would require further legal regulation on a truly universal basis. With respect to international peace and security, he finds that the ICJ's *Nicaragua* Judgment and the UN deliberations leading to the adoption of General Assembly Resolution 2625 (XXV) have closed possible gaps in the law governing the use of force (p. 23). This conclusion seems to stand in slight contradiction to his earlier finding (at p. 21) that the General Assembly has failed to develop practicable rules of an *erga omnes* character, since its broad and mostly political definitions yield imprecise and ambiguous norms to which States are not really committed.

The author does, however, find room for constitutional international legal regulation where the appropriation of natural resources outside areas of national jurisdiction, especially deep sea mining, is concerned. The attempt of the less developed nations to declare the results of UNCLOS III binding on all States, regardless of whether or not they have signed or ratified the Convention, indicates to him a trend towards the more concrete manifestation of (nascent?) customary principles of world order in future law-making treaties.

Examining some of the quasi-universal treaties dealing with global problems, Tomuschat does not find that these instruments are generally binding on non signatories. For example, he categorically denies a customary prohibition of nuclear weapons proliferation for States outside the NPT. Nevertheless, massive political and economic pressure should be applied to ensure that such States do not acquire nuclear weapons, the author argues. This possibly contradictory conclusion is justified with reference to the world order principles which are the object of the treaty.

The precise definition of such principles, as proposed by Tomuschat, is as follows: they are essential high value goals established in quasi-universal instruments that are open to all and have been embraced by representative members of all five regional groups of States. Near universal acceptance would suffice, and even persistent objection would not bar the extension of these obligations to non-parties. The author finds examples of such principles in the enumeration of international crimes in Article 19 (3) of the ILC draft on State responsibility.

More controversially, he proposes that the UN Security Council might be used to enforce compliance with these essential rules of world order, including areas like the protection of the environment. Tempting as the idea might seem in the current atmosphere of revitalization of the UN's organs, it is not clear whether the Council would be best suited to take on such broad responsibilities, or whether individual States would wish to submit to its supervision.

In the absence of guaranteed implementation, however, Tomuschat's essential principles, and his insistence on their enforcement, might actually tempt States to take actions that would undermine world order as it is currently understood. Measures even more controversial than, say, the unilateral use of force to wipe out a suspect nuclear power station in a Middle Eastern country, might inaugurate an era of destructive unilateralism which finds its justification in other 'essential principles' that are claimed to be practically necessary, morally true and of obvious and unchallengeable universal validity.

Professor Neuhold of Vienna, in his more traditionalist contribution, is struck by a certain contradiction in the Vienna Convention on the Law of Treaties. While Article 34 enshrines the static principle of the non-applicability of treaty obligations to third States, the Convention at the same time establishes the concept of *jus cogens*, which is based on the nebulous acceptance and recognition of legal rules 'by the international community of States as a whole'.

The author is particularly startled by the fact that a State cannot be bound against its will through treaties or general customary law, while even persistent objection will not exempt it from the application of *jus cogens* which, after all, might restrict its sovereignty much more dramatically. For example, he finds it 'odd' (p. 64) to suppose that South Africa should be bound by an obligation to refrain from the exercise of *apartheid*, reprehensible as that practice may be.

This view somewhat overlooks the very essence of the concept of *jus cogens*. These obligations towards international society are being proposed precisely because their importance is deemed to be so great as to override the particular interests of individual States, even if they object.

Neuhold himself does, on the other hand, recognize the need for community rules to govern 'space-ship earth' (p. 52). But he suggests with some justification that the dogmatic foundation of such constitutional principles, and the actual support of States that they enjoy, is too weak. He is weary of over-zealous efforts to establish more and more largely undefined *jus cogens* rules.

Tomuschat's suggestions might be helpful in this context. He seeks to introduce more objective criteria for the identification of the content of *jus cogens* and *erga omnes* principles. This endeavour will become increasingly necessary, since notions of global interests are bound to gain even further in relevance as the century closes.

MARC WELLER

Die Friedenswarte. Volume 66, Nos. 3–4 (1986). Berlin: Berlin Verlag, 1988. 389 pp.

Die Friedenswarte used to be one of Germany's leading journals concerned with international law and relations. For some time now there has been an attempt to steer it back to the position of prominence it once enjoyed. The volume under review will assist in this endeavour only to a certain degree.

The book opens with the concluding part of F. Münch's survey of activities which were inspired by the occasion of the four-hundredth anniversary of Hugo Grotius in 1983. Münch asserts that nowadays Grotius is interpreted in very different and sometimes contradictory ways. From this very fact he deduces that the great jurist remains relevant today.

Schindler's contribution is in fact the transcript of a laudatory speech given in honour of Professor von der Heydte in 1987. Schindler points to the sad fact that, despite recent and detailed codifications of the laws of war, States appear to be increasingly reluctant to apply them. Nevertheless, he expresses the hope that States will slowly grow into the advanced legal structure which they have established.

Ferenc Majoros, the editor of the volume, provides the only substantial and more scholarly article. He addresses automatic reciprocity of reservations as established in Article 21 of the Vienna Convention on the Law of Treaties. That article has come under attack since, in 1981, the Institut de Droit International adopted a resolution apparently rejecting automatic reciprocity. Majoros argues forcefully against these attempts to undo the clear Vienna formula. While he is openly polemic in his approach, his contribution is well researched as far as it goes. A second, concluding part has been promised for the next issue.

Next, the implications of political culture for international negotiations are analysed briefly by Eberhard Schulz. He offers very short (one page) studies on complex cases, including the SALT and CSCE negotiations, each of which might merit a treatment of book-length in itself.

Joachim Hofmann presents a clear exposition of select aspects of the jurisprudence of the Court of Justice of the European Communities. The article is descriptive and does not attempt an analysis of any sort.

The last contribution to be surveyed here is by Theo Vogler. He argues that formal extradition is not dead, despite the other forms of legal assistance between States which have gained in importance lately. He also focuses on the trend towards increased co-operation in the execution of sentences according to humanitarian principles.

In addition to a number of book reviews, the following notes are included in the book: Heinrich Vogel on Western economic ties with the small States of Eastern Europe; Gerhard Ritter on the 1917 revolution; and Götz Mavius on the Balkan Wars of 1912/13.

MARC WELLER

DECISIONS OF BRITISH COURTS DURING 1989 INVOLVING QUESTIONS OF PUBLIC OR PRIVATE INTERNATIONAL LAW

A. Public International Law*

International organization—International Tin Council—Council insolvent and defaulting on debts—whether member States liable to Council's creditors—personality of Council in international law and English law—whether Council the agent of its members—status of treaties in English law—doctrine of non-justiciability— Sixth International Tin Agreement 1982—International Tin Council–United Kingdom Headquarters Agreement 1972—International Tin Council (Immunities and Privileges) Order 1972—International Organizations Act 1968

Case No. 1. J.H. Rayner (Mincing Lane) Ltd. v. Department of Trade and Industry and others; Maclaine Watson & Co. Ltd. v. Department of Trade and Industry, [1989] 3 WLR 969, [1989] 3 All ER 523, HL; *Case No. 2. Maclaine Watson & Co. Ltd. v. International Tin Council,* [1989] Ch. 253, [1988] 3 WLR 1169, [1988] 3 All ER 257, CA; [1989] 3 WLR 969, [1989] 3 All ER 523, HL. The House of Lords has dismissed appeals by creditors of the International Tin Council (the ITC) from two judgments of the Court of Appeal striking out the creditors' principal claims.[1] The judgment of the House of Lords is the latest phase in litigation which has been going on since the ITC announced, in November 1985, that it could not meet debts estimated at between £700 million and £900 million.

1. Background

The ITC is an international organization which, at the relevant time, was operating under the Sixth International Tin Agreement 1982 (ITA6),[2] a treaty to which the EEC and some twenty-three States,[3] including the United Kingdom, were parties, representing a majority (although a much smaller one than under past tin agreements) of the principal tin producer and consumer countries. The ITC's chief object was to promote an orderly market in tin by matching production and consumption and stabilizing prices. To this end it operated a system of floor and ceiling prices for tin, maintained by the use of a buffer stock of tin, financed by contributions and loans from member States. If the market price of tin rose above the ceiling price, the ITC's Buffer Stock Manager would sell part of his reserves to depress the price; if the market price dropped below the floor price, he bought into the buffer stock until prices on the markets rose again.

Article 16 of ITA6 provided that the ITC should have legal personality,

---

* © C. J. Greenwood, 1990.

[1] The Court of Appeal judgment in the direct actions is discussed in this *Year Book*, 59 (1988), at p. 267. See also 58 (1987), p. 399. The decision of the Court of Appeal in the receivership action is noted below, p. 471. Two other decisions of the Court of Appeal are considered below at p. 473.

[2] Cmnd. 8646.

[3] See this *Year Book*, 58 (1987), p. 399 at n. 2.

including 'the capacity to contract, to acquire and dispose of movable and immovable property and to institute legal proceedings'. The management of the buffer stock was governed by Articles 21 and 22, which provided that the buffer stock was to be financed by contributions from the member States in proportion to their share of worldwide tin production or consumption, by government guarantees or undertakings from the member States and by borrowing. Under Article 22 the member States were to be liable to the ITC up to the extent of their guarantees or undertakings. ITA6 said nothing about whether the members of the ITC might be held liable for any debts incurred by the ITC. The headquarters of the ITC were established in London and operated under the terms of a Headquarters Agreement concluded in 1972 between the ITC and the United Kingdom.[4] That agreement was given effect in English law by the International Tin Council (Immunities and Privileges) Order 1972 ('the 1972 Order'), a statutory instrument made under the International Organizations Act 1968. Article 4 of the Order stated that the ITC was 'an organization of which Her Majesty's Government in the United Kingdom and the governments of foreign sovereign powers are members'. Article 5 provided that the ITC should have 'the legal capacities of a body corporate', while Article 6 conferred upon the ITC 'immunity from suit and legal process' subject to certain exceptions, including, in particular, an action for the enforcement of an arbitration award. Neither ITA6 nor the Headquarters Agreement, however, was made part of English law.

It seems that for much of the life of ITA6 the ITC had difficulty maintaining the floor price of tin, owing in part to the ITC's inability to control production in non-member States such as Bolivia and China. The Buffer Stock Manager was forced to enter the market on an ever-increasing scale (in the last full year for which figures are available the turnover of the ITC was £3 billion) until, on 24 October 1985, he informed the London Metal Exchange that the ITC could not meet its commitments. Most of these commitments were owed to commodity brokers, with whom the ITC had bought and sold tin, and banks, which had lent the ITC money. The principal difference between these two groups of creditors was that the brokers' contracts with the ITC included arbitration clauses so that they were able to obtain arbitration awards against the ITC, whereas there were no such clauses in most of the loan agreements between the ITC and the banks.

2. *The litigation*

The ITC's lack of funds meant that its creditors devoted most of their energies to securing payment from the members of the ITC. The present appeals, while involving several different actions, concerned two separate attempts to establish liability on the part of the members.

In the 'direct actions' (*J.H. Rayner (Mincing Lane) Ltd.* v. *Department of Trade and Industry and others* and *Maclaine Watson & Co. Ltd.* v. *Department of Trade and Industry*) various banks and brokers[5] proceeded directly against the Depart-

---

[4] Cmnd. 4398

[5] There were four groups of direct actions:

(1) In *J.H. Rayner (Mincing Lane) Ltd.* v. *Department of Trade and Industry and others* ('the *Rayner* action'), the plaintiffs, who had concluded contracts for the sale of tin with the ITC, obtained an arbitration award for some £16.3 million against the ITC under the arbitration clauses in the contracts.

(2) In *Arbuthnot Latham Bank Ltd.* v. *Commonwealth of Australia and others* and five similar actions ('the *Six Banks* actions'), the plaintiffs claimed a total of approximately £29.5 million as money lent to the ITC under loan contracts. Except in the case of one bank, the loan contracts did not include provision for arbitration.

ment of Trade and Industry (representing the United Kingdom) and the other members, arguing that they were liable for the contract and judgment debts of the ITC.[6] Before the House of Lords the creditors advanced four different arguments in support of this contention:[7]

(1) that, so far as English law was concerned, the ITC was not a legal entity distinct from its members but merely a collective trading name under which the members did business ('submission A');

(2) that, even if the ITC possessed a separate legal personality in English law, that personality did not exclude the liability of the members for debts incurred by the ITC ('submission B(1)');

(3) that, as an international organization, the ITC derived its personality from public international law under which the members of an international organization remained liable for the debts of the organization, in the absence of an express provision to the contrary in the treaty constituting the organization ('submission B(2)'); and

(4) that the constitution of the ITC was such that it had contracted as agent for its members ('submission C').[8]

Each of these submissions was alternative to, and independent of, the others. In separate proceedings Staughton J[9] and Millett J[10] rejected the creditors' contention that the members of the ITC were liable for the debts of the organization and ordered that their actions be struck out. The Court of Appeal (Kerr, Nourse and Ralph Gibson LJJ)[11] dismissed the creditors' appeals, although Nourse LJ considered that the appellants should have succeeded on submission B(2).

In the 'receivership action' (*Maclaine Watson & Co. Ltd.* v. *International Tin Council*) one broker, who had obtained an arbitration award against the ITC and then converted it into a judgment, sought the appointment of a receiver by way of

---

(3) In *Amalgamated Metal Trading Ltd. and others* v. *Department of Trade and Industry and others* ('the *Multi-Brokers* action'), nine metal brokers claimed a total of approximately £105 million. The plaintiffs had concluded contracts for the sale of tin with the ITC and had subsequently obtained arbitration awards against the ITC under the arbitration provisions in the contracts.

In each case the plaintiffs sued the Department of Trade and Industry ('DTI'), representing the United Kingdom, and the other 22 member States of the ITC. In the *Rayner* and *Six Banks* actions the plaintiffs also sued the Commission of the European Communities. In the *Multi-Brokers* action the plaintiffs sued the European Economic Community (rather than the Commission) and the ITC itself, as well as the DTI and the other member States. The plaintiffs in all the actions contended that the members of the ITC were liable for debts incurred by, or in the name of, the ITC.

(4) In *Maclaine Watson & Co. Ltd.* v. *Department of Trade and Industry* ('the *Maclaine Watson* direct action'), another tin trading company brought proceedings against the DTI to enforce a judgment for over £6 million which had been entered against the ITC. The plaintiffs contended that the members of the ITC were jointly and severally liable for the debt.

[6] There was no appeal from the decision of the Court of Appeal in another action involving an attempt to wind up the ITC. See *In re International Tin Council*, [1987] Ch. 419, noted below at p. 473.

[7] Although these submissions were essentially the same as those made in the Court of Appeal, the arguments in support of them had been refined by the time the cases reached the House of Lords.

[8] This submission, known as 'constitutional agency', should not be confused with the 'factual agency' arguments which were the subject of other proceedings which have not yet been reported. See below, p. 471.

[9] [1987] BCLC 667; 77 ILR 55. See this *Year Book*, 59 (1988), p. 267.

[10] [1987] BCLC 707; this *Year Book*, loc. cit.

[11] [1989] Ch. 72; this *Year Book*, loc. cit.

equitable execution over the assets of the ITC. Maclaine Watson argued that those assets included a right on the part of the ITC to be indemnified by, or to obtain contributions from, the members. The receiver would enforce that right and thus ensure that the ITC was put in funds. At first instance Millett J[12] held that although the court had the power to appoint a receiver, that power should not be exercised on the facts of this case, since any rights which the ITC might have had against its members were not justiciable in an English court. An appeal was unanimously dismissed by the Court of Appeal (Kerr, Nourse and Ralph Gibson LJJ).[13]

3. The direct actions

Submission A: did the ITC possess separate personality in English law? Submission A was summarized by Lord Oliver in four propositions:

(1) Persons who join together in trade in the United Kingdom are, prima facie, jointly and severally liable for the debts which they incur and they cannot exclude this liability by agreement between themselves. (2) States engaging in collective trading are no different from other traders. (3) Their prima facie liability can be displaced only by incorporation (either by statute or by charter), by express statutory provision or by demonstrating the creation of an association under foreign law having a status which excludes liability of the membership. (4) The Order in Council does not incorporate the ITC but merely confers capacities and immunities.[14]

Lords Templeman and Oliver, with whom the rest of their Lordships agreed, thought this submission foundered on the proper interpretation of the 1972 Order. It was true that the Order did not incorporate the ITC: that had been a central feature of the decisions of the lower courts in another of the ITC cases.[15] That did not mean, however, that the Order did not confer some kind of legal personality upon the ITC. Lord Templeman considered that any other conclusion was inconsistent with the wording of the Order, since the ITC could not exercise the capacities of a body corporate, as provided by Article 5 of the Order, and yet be treated as if it were an unincorporated association.

Lord Oliver reached the same conclusion on the text of the Order. He added, however, that even if the Order had been ambiguous in this respect, reference to ITA6 and the Headquarters Agreement (which the Order had been intended to implement) required that the Order be interpreted as conferring separate legal personality upon the ITC. Both treaties expressly provided that the ITC should have legal personality. The result, Lord Oliver considered, was that:

. . . the effect of the Order in Council was to create the ITC (which, as an international legal persona, had no status under the laws of the United Kingdom) a legal person in its own right, independent of its members.[16]

Submission B (1): the nature of the ITC's personality in English law. As an alternative to submission A, the creditors argued that even if the ITC did possess separate legal personality in English law, that personality was of such a nature that the members of the ITC were liable in respect of contracts concluded by the ITC. The essence of this submission was that the fact that the ITC possessed a person-

---

[12] [1988] Ch. 1. See this *Year Book*, 58 (1987), p. 418.
[13] See below, p. 471.
[14] [1989] 3 WLR at 1003.
[15] *In re International Tin Council*; see below, p. 473.
[16] [1989] 3 WLR at 1008.

ality distinct from that of its members did not mean that that personality had to be the same as that of a limited company. There was no reason why an entity should not be clothed with a different form of legal personality, one of the attributes of which was that its members would be liable for its debts. Such 'mixed entities' existed in the laws of many countries, including Scotland. This submission received short shrift. Lord Oliver accepted that Parliament could, if it wished, have conferred upon the ITC a personality of this kind but found nothing in the 1972 Order to suggest that it had done so. On the contrary, he considered that all the indications in the Order were that the intention had been to treat the ITC in the same way as a body corporate. Suggestions that a contrary intention might be divined from ITA6 or the Headquarters Agreement he dismissed as fanciful.[17]

Submission B (2): the personality of the ITC in international law. The essence of this submission was that the ITC, as an international organization, derived its legal personality from international law. The creditors maintained that the English courts therefore had to look to international law to determine the nature of its legal personality, in the same way as they would look to the law of France in order to ascertain the nature of the legal personality possessed by a French company.[18] Under international law, it was argued, the legal personality of an international organization did not exclude the liability of its members for the debts incurred by that organization.

In order to succeed on this submission, the creditors had to establish three propositions. First, they had to show that Article 5 of the 1972 Order did not create the ITC as a legal person but merely recognized and gave effect to a personality which already existed and was derived from international law. Secondly, it was necessary to establish that the English courts could apply the rules of international law which defined the attributes of that personality and, in particular, the rules which determined whether the members were liable for the ITC's debts. Finally, the creditors had to show that there was a rule of international law which provided that the members of an international organization were liable for the debts of that organization, at least in the absence of any exclusion of liability in the treaty creating the organization.

Submission B(2) had a measure of success in the Court of Appeal, where Nourse LJ largely accepted it and Kerr LJ, who eventually rejected the second proposition on which it was based, expressed sympathy for other parts of it.[19] The House of Lords, however, unanimously rejected the first proposition, which constituted the premiss on which the whole submission was based. Lord Oliver was prepared to accept that when a foreign company did business in England the question whether its members were liable for its debts had to be determined by reference to the law of the place of incorporation, but he rejected the notion that the position of an international organization was analogous to that of a foreign company. When a company was incorporated in France, French law made that company a legal person distinct from its members and it could assert that personality in England by,

---

[17] Ibid. at 1010.
[18] Rule 174 of Dicey and Morris, *The Conflict of Laws* (11th edn., 1987), vol. 2, p. 1134, states that:
'(1) The capacity of a corporation to enter into any legal transaction is governed both by the constitution of the corporation and by the law of the country which governs the transaction in question.
(2) All matters concerning the constitution of a corporation are governed by the law of the place of incorporation'.
[19] See this *Year Book*, 59 (1988), p. 267.

for example, becoming party to contracts there. By contrast, when the ITC was created as an international organization, the legal personality which it thus acquired was one which Lord Oliver considered could be asserted only on the plane of international law. The 1972 Order thus went far beyond a recognition of the ITC as an existing legal person; it was the act which conferred upon the ITC a personality which it could assert in English law and without which it would have been unable to function at all on the plane of English law. As Lord Oliver put it,

> Whilst it is, of course, not inaccurate to describe Article 4 of the Order as one which 'recognizes' the ITC as an international organization, such 'recognition' is of no consequence in domestic law unless and until it is accompanied by the *creation* of a legal persona. Without the Order in Council the ITC had no legal existence in the law of the United Kingdom and no significance save as the name of an international body created by a treaty between sovereign States which was not justiciable by municipal courts. What brought it into being in English law was the Order in Council and it is the Order in Council, a purely domestic measure, in which the constitution of the legal persona is to be found and in which there has to be sought the liability of the members which the appellants seek to establish, for that is the act of the ITC's creation in the United Kingdom.[20]

In Lord Oliver's eyes, therefore, the ITC as an international legal person was an entity separate and distinct from the ITC as a legal person in English law, so that even if there were a rule of international law under which the members of an international organization were liable for the debts of the organization, that would not avail the banks and brokers, since they were the creditors not of the international organization known as the ITC but of the separate entity created by the 1972 Order:

> Let it be assumed, for the moment, that the international entity known as the ITC is, by the treaty, one for the engagements of which the member States become liable in international law, that entity is not the entity which entered into the contracts relevant to these appeals. Those contracts were effected by the separate *persona ficta* which was created by the Order in Council.[21]

The correct analogy, he considered, was not with the position of a French company directly engaged in business in England but with a French company which established an English subsidiary through which it did business in England.

One can understand why this approach commended itself to their Lordships. By anchoring the ITC firmly in the familiar ground of English law, the House of Lords was able to avoid examining an area of international law almost wholly unexplored prior to the present litigation and one in which almost any decision would have been intensely controversial. Nevertheless, their Lordships' approach is highly artificial. Nobody who worked for, or dealt with, the ITC in London imagined that the body which employed them or concluded contracts with them was anything other than the international organization created by ITA6. The analogy with the foreign company doing business in England through a locally incorporated subsidiary is particularly inapposite. In its judgment in *In re International Tin Council*,[22] in respect of which there was no appeal to the House of Lords, the Court of Appeal had held that the ITC had not been incorporated in English law so as to fall within the winding-up jurisdiction of the English courts. This conclusion

---

[20] [1989] 3 WLR at 1012. See also the opinion of Lord Templeman, ibid., p. 982.
[21] Ibid. at 1011.
[22] *In re International Tin Council.* See below, p. 473.

was reached in part because of the status of the ITC as an international organiz-ation. On that basis, it is respectfully submitted, the decision made perfect sense. In the light of Lord Oliver's judgment, however, it seems that what the creditors in *In re International Tin Council* were seeking to wind up was not the international organization known as the ITC but rather the English law entity through which that organization did business in England. Nevertheless, it is inconceivable that the House of Lords would have allowed an appeal in the winding-up case, had one been entered. The effect of their Lordships' approach is thus that the ITC as an English entity created by the 1972 Order traded in England on a very substantial scale indeed without being subject either to the rules of English law regarding insolvent associations or to the principles of international law regarding liability for the debts of an insolvent international organization.

Moreover, even the appearance of simplicity in their Lordships' approach is deceptive. If the effect of the 1972 Order was to create the ITC as a legal persona in English law, distinct from the entity of the same name which existed under inter-national law, presumably separate entities were also created under the laws of other member States which gave effect to Article 16 of ITA6. The result appears to be that several different bodies, each known as the ITC and all controlled by persons who seem to have thought that these bodies were in fact a single entity, stalked the world. If such is the case, the approach adopted by the House of Lords can scarcely be said to simplify the picture.[23]

Having rejected the first proposition on which submission B(2) was based, it was not strictly necessary for the House of Lords to consider the other two proposi-tions. Nevertheless, Lord Templeman and Lord Oliver went on to hold that, even if the personality of the ITC had been derived from international law rather than from the 1972 Order, any principle of international law imposing liability upon the members for the ITC's debts would have been non-justiciable in the English courts. Lord Templeman held that

> The courts of the United Kingdom have no power to enforce at the behest of any sover-eign State or at the behest of any individual citizen of any sovereign State rights granted by treaty or obligations imposed in respect of a treaty by international law.[24]

Similarly, Lord Oliver opined that any rights arising against the member States 'are founded, created and regulated in and can be ascertained only by reference to ITA6'.[25] Since ITA6 had not been 'incorporated' into English law by Parliament, it could not be enforced by the English courts.

The basis for this part of the judgment is not entirely clear. If the suggestion had been that ITA6 imposed upon the members of the ITC a liability towards the ITC's creditors, that liability would clearly have been non-justiciable in English law. It is a well-established principle of the United Kingdom constitution that the Crown cannot alter English law by the act of concluding a treaty. Unless Parlia-ment chooses to provide for alterations to the law in order to give effect to a treaty, therefore, a treaty cannot create rights,[26] remove existing rights,[27] or impose obli-gations in English law. The creditors, however, did not suggest that ITA6 imposed

---

[23] See *Arab Monetary Fund* v. *Hashim*, below, p. 475.
[24] [1989] 3 WLR at 983.
[25] Ibid. at 1012.
[26] See, e.g., *Malone* v. *Metropolitan Police Commissioner*, [1979] Ch. 344.
[27] See, e.g., *Walker* v. *Baird*, [1892] AC 491.

liability upon the members. Their argument was that the principles of customary international law regarding the personality of international organizations included a principle that the members of an international organization were liable for its debts unless they expressly excluded that liability by a clear provision in the treaty creating the organization.[28] What the English courts were being asked to enforce, therefore, was not a right created by ITA6 but a right derived from the general international law which formed the legal background against which ITA6 was concluded. Reference to ITA6 was necessary, on this argument, only to establish that an international organization possessing legal personality had been created, to ascertain the identity of its members and to determine whether those members had exercised the right given them by the general law to exclude their liability. That liability, if not excluded, arose from a source outside the treaty.[29] In these circumstances there was no question of the treaty purporting to alter English law, any more than the French legislature can be said to alter English law merely because a corporation established under French law does business in England.

It seems, therefore, that the present decision goes beyond the traditional constitutional principle that treaties cannot alter English law unless Parliament so ordains and reflects some broader principle that 'unincorporated treaties' (i.e. treaties to which Parliament has not given legislative effect) cannot be taken into account at all by an English court, even to ascertain the nature of an international organization which engages in trade in this country. The only exception would be that reference may be made to such treaties as an aid to the interpretation of ambiguous legislation. Otherwise, as Lord Templeman put it, 'English judges cannot meddle with unincorporated treaties'.[30]

In places, however, the opinions delivered by Lords Templeman and Oliver indicate a still broader rationale for their decision about non-justiciability. Both opinions contain suggestions that the reason why any obligation which international law might impose upon the members of the ITC would not be justiciable in an English court was that a rule of international law of this kind was inherently unsuitable for application by an English court (or, presumably, any other national court). Thus, Lord Templeman appeared to think that it was irrelevant whether the principle said to impose liability upon the members was contained in ITA6 or in general international law:

. . . if there existed a rule of international law which implied in a treaty or imposed on sovereign States which enter into a treaty an obligation (in default of a clear disclaimer in the treaty) to discharge the debts of an international organization established by that treaty, the rule of international law could only be enforced under international law. Treaty rights and

---

[28] The appellants submitted, in the alternative, that under international law the members of an international organization were liable for the debts of the organization irrespective of whether the constituent treaty contained a clause excluding liability.

[29] It is true that the position might have been different if ITA6 had contained an express provision that the members *were* liable for the debts of the organization. Had the creditors sought to rely solely upon such a provision and that provision had not been given effect in the 1972 Order, then the creditors would have been seeking to enforce a right derived from a treaty and the constitutional principle discussed in the preceding paragraph would have barred adjudication of their claim. On that hypothesis the creditors would have been arguing that the treaty had altered English law by creating a right which would not otherwise have existed. If, however, customary international law imposed liability on the members of an international organization in the absence of express exclusion, then whether the treaty was silent or contained a provision that members were liable would make no difference. The important point in that case would be that the treaty did not exclude a right derived from the customary law.

[30] [1989] 3 WLR at 986.

obligations conferred or imposed by agreement *or by international law* cannot be enforced by the courts of the United Kingdom.[31]

This broader rationale for non-justiciability goes beyond any constitutional rule regarding the effects of treaties and touches on the heart of the relationship between international law and English law.

It must therefore be asked why a principle of international law which imposed liability on the members of an insolvent international organization—if, indeed, such a rule existed—should not be applied by a national court. It can be conceded that some disputes involving the activities of international organizations are not suitable for adjudication in a municipal court, even if they do concern the rights of private parties. Thus, a municipal court is not the best forum to determine a tort claim arising out of the use of force by a United Nations peacekeeping force. However, the ITC is a very different organization from the United Nations. While its objectives may have been those of high economic policy, its *modus operandi* was to deal in tin on national markets by means of ordinary commercial contracts, governed by municipal law. Nor had it ever been intended to operate in any other way. In the circumstances, it is difficult to see why questions about the liability of its members for debts arising under those contracts should be inherently unsuitable for adjudication by a national court.

One objection, advanced by Lord Templeman, is that any such principle which imposed joint and several liability on the member States must include a right of contribution between them. It was common ground that this right between the member States would be enforceable only on the international plane and could not be made the subject of an order by the English courts. Lord Templeman considered, therefore, that it would be unjust for the English courts to enforce the liability of the members to the creditors since the judgment would be likely to bear almost exclusively upon the United Kingdom which would then have to enforce its right of contribution against the other members through diplomacy or international proceedings without the assistance of the English courts. It was more logical, he thought, that the whole question of who should pay what and to whom should be settled on the international plane.[32] Yet is the result which Lord Templeman feared really so unjust or his preferred solution so logical? Of course there would be an element of unfairness if the ITC's creditors, having obtained from an English court a judgment in their favour against the members, were to enforce that judgment against one of the members, and that member was then left with no recourse but the uncertainties of diplomacy and international dispute settlement to enforce its right of contribution against the other members. Nevertheless, that State would be in a far stronger position to seek payment on the international plane than would the ITC's creditors. The methods of asserting international claims are designed for use by States and are largely closed to private parties unless a State is prepared to assert a claim on their behalf. Most of the ITC's creditors were nationals of one or other of the member States. Who, then, would be able (or willing) to bring an international claim on their behalf? Lord Templeman's approach amounts to saying that, because a sovereign State, which does have access to all the methods of asserting an international claim, might not obtain

---

[31] Ibid. at 983–4 (emphasis added).
[32] Ibid. at 984.

justice from the use of those methods, the ITC's creditors, which enjoyed no such access, should be forced to seek redress through those methods.

The judgment of the House of Lords in the direct actions has expanded the notion of non-justiciability in English law without giving any clear indication of whether the rationale for that doctrine is the constitutional separation of powers or the impropriety of national courts (whatever the constitution under which they operate) deciding certain questions of international law. In so far as the rationale for non-justiciability is to be found in wider considerations of the role of national courts in deciding questions of international law, the doctrine is of uncertain scope and rests on no very clearly articulated considerations of policy. The result is likely to haunt much future litigation.

The third proposition advanced by the creditors, namely that there is a principle of international law which imposes liability upon the members of an international organization for the debts of that organization unless they have expressly excluded their liability in the treaty creating the organization, raises the most interesting questions of international law. In view of the rejection of the first two propositions on which submission B(2) was based, however, the House of Lords did not find it necessary to decide whether there was in fact such a principle of international law. Nevertheless, considerable doubt was expressed regarding the existence of this principle. Lord Templeman stated that 'no plausible evidence was produced of the existence of such a rule of international law before or at the time of ITA6 in 1982 or thereafter',[33] while Lord Oliver considered that 'the "authorities" to which your Lordships were referred, which consisted in the main of an immense body of writings of distinguished international jurists, totally failed to establish any generally accepted rule of the nature contended for'.[34]

Since there had been very little discussion, prior to the collapse of the ITC, of the legal consequences of an international organization becoming insolvent, there was very little 'authority' of any kind for or against the proposition advanced by the creditors. There is no doubt, therefore, that had the House of Lords reached a different conclusion with respect to the first two propositions it would have been confronted with an extremely difficult question of law. The caution with which their Lordships viewed this question is thus understandable. Nevertheless, insofar as the opinions delivered in the House of Lords touched upon the content, rather than the applicability, of international law, there is an unsatisfactory character to them. Thus, Lord Oliver stated that:

A rule of international law becomes a rule—whether accepted into domestic law or not— only when it is certain and is accepted generally by the body of civilized nations; and it is for those who assert the rule to demonstrate it, if necessary before the International Court of Justice. It is certainly not for a domestic tribunal in effect to legislate a rule into existence for the purposes of domestic law and on the basis of material that is wholly indeterminate.[35]

Leaving aside the obvious fact that the creditors could not have brought a case before the International Court of Justice, if international law confers personality upon an organization then it must contain principles about the nature of that personality. In particular, it must contain either a principle that the members will be liable for the debts of the organization or one which states that they are not so

---

[33] Ibid. at 983.
[34] Ibid. at 1014.
[35] Ibid.

liable. To reject one principle would necessarily have entailed adopting the other. Moreover, it was not merely the principle put forward by the creditors which was novel. Since, as Lord Oliver said, the material available was indeterminate, to have accepted either principle would have been to break new ground in a difficult area.

Submission C: the constitutional agency argument. The final submission advanced by the creditors was that the constitution of the ITC was such that the ITC had acted at all relevant times as the agent of its members. This submission was known as the 'constitutional agency' argument to distinguish it from the quite distinct 'factual agency' argument (the subject of separate proceedings) in which the claim that the ITC had acted as agent was based upon the facts of the various transactions.

The constitutional agency argument failed on its merits in the Court of Appeal, where a majority of the court was prepared to look at ITA6 to determine the factual question whether it created a relationship of principal and agent but considered that the terms of ITA6 did not support the contention that the treaty had authorized the ITC to contract only as the agent of its members. In addition, some of the contracts contained express disclaimers of agency. In the House of Lords, Lord Oliver held that submission C had to be dismissed for the reasons given by the Court of Appeal. However, both he and Lord Templeman went further and held that even to look at ITA6 only to determine whether or not it created a relationship of principal and agent between the members and the ITC would infringe the principle of non-justiciability. Lord Oliver's reasons are very similar to those already discussed in relation to submission B(2). He held that the rights and obligations of the members towards the ITC and towards one another had to be derived from the treaty and, as such, were not justiciable in English law. It followed that the whole agency submission required the court:

. . . to embark upon the exercise of interpreting the terms of the treaty and ascertaining, on the basis of that determination, the rights of the members in international law and the consequences in municipal law of the rights so determined.[36]

That, in Lord Oliver's eyes, was exactly what the principle of non-justiciability prevented. His decision on this point is further evidence that the House of Lords saw the principle of non-justiciability as going beyond the constitutional principle that treaties could not alter English law.

The position of the EEC. One of the arguments advanced by the EEC in the direct actions was that the EEC was entitled to the same kind of immunity under common law as that accorded to a sovereign State by the State Immunity Act 1978. This argument was unanimously rejected by the Court of Appeal. The decision of the House of Lords on the matters discussed above made it unnecessary to consider this argument, but Lord Oliver seems to have regarded the matter as open.[37]

4. *The receivership action*

The appeal in the receivership action (*Maclaine Watson & Co. Ltd.* v. *International Tin Council*) also foundered on the non-justiciability principle both in the Court of Appeal and in the House of Lords. All three members of the Court of Appeal held that the rights which Maclaine Watson intended that the receiver

---

[36] Ibid. at 1015–6. See also Lord Templeman at 985.
[37] Ibid. at 1017.

should enforce were non-justiciable, but they reached that conclusion for different reasons. Ralph Gibson LJ based his judgment on the decision of the House of Lords in *Buttes Gas and Oil Co.* v. *Hammer (No. 3)*.[38] Kerr LJ and Nourse LJ, on the other hand, rejected the idea that the principle in *Buttes* (which Kerr LJ described as 'act of State non-justiciability') was applicable to State acts performed in a commercial context. They held that any rights which the ITC might have had against its members had to be derived from ITA6 and were thus non-justiciable under the constitutional principle that a treaty could not create rights enforceable in the English courts.[39]

Lords Templeman and Oliver dismissed Maclaine Watson's appeal for the same reasons as those given by Kerr and Nourse LJJ and thus found it unnecessary to consider act of State non-justiciability. The limitations imposed upon the *Buttes* doctrine by the majority of the Court of Appeal, which it is respectfully submitted are entirely correct, have not, therefore, been rejected.

5. *Conclusions*

The decision of the House of Lords, especially in respect of the direct actions, reflects a rigidly dualist picture of the relationship between international law and English law. Their Lordships evidently considered that international law was all about relations between States and had very little to do with the work of the English courts. An international organization created under international law could exist as a legal person only on the Olympian level of international relations. To come down to earth and move amongst men it had to be given an entirely distinct legal personality by the 1972 Order. Whether the States which created the international organization were placed by international law under obligations to that organization's creditors was considered to be a question wholly unsuitable for adjudication in an English court. The reluctance of the House of Lords to be drawn into a particularly difficult area of international law is, perhaps, understandable. Yet questions of law which reach the House of Lords generally have an element of difficulty about them. In avoiding the ones which arose in this case the House of Lords has adopted an approach to the relationship of international law and municipal law which is markedly at variance with that adopted by the courts of many other countries, which is in some respects highly artificial and which one member of the House of Lords, who reluctantly supported it, considered left the creditors to suffer grave injustice.[40]

Any assessment of whether the creditors were badly treated must, however, take into account the settlement reached in the aftermath of their Lordships' decision. According to press reports, the ITC and its creditors have agreed upon a settlement under which the creditors will receive £182.5 million in settlement of all claims. Since the full extent of the ITC's liabilities was never established in the proceedings and it is unclear how far the creditors were able to mitigate their losses by the sale of tin held as security, it is impossible to say what percentage of the ITC's debts will be paid. Nevertheless, the conclusion of the settlement, which cannot have been an easy task, is a positive achievement. It is understood that, fol-

---

[38] [1982] AC 888.
[39] [1989] Ch. 253 at pp. 284 ff.
[40] Lord Griffiths, [1989] 3 WLR at 986.

lowing the conclusion of this settlement, all the remaining litigation against the ITC and its members, at least in the English courts,[41] has been discontinued.

Another positive development is that the *Institut de droit international* has taken on the task of trying to articulate the principles of international law which would form a code of bankruptcy for international organizations, the need for which was graphically illustrated by the tin litigation. One can only hope that the years which this project is likely to take to reach fruition will not see another insolvency on the scale of that concerning the ITC.

International organization—International Tin Council—Council insolvent and defaulting on debts—petition to wind up the Council—immunities of Council—Sixth International Tin Agreement 1982—International Tin Council–United Kingdom Headquarters Agreement 1972—International Tin Council (Immunities and Privileges) Order 1972—International Organizations Act 1968

Case No. 3. In re International Tin Council, [1989] Ch. 309, [1988] 3 WLR 1159, [1988] 3 All ER 359, CA. This case concerned an attempt by one of the ITC's creditors, which had obtained an arbitration award against the ITC, to have the organization wound up under Section 665 of the Companies Act 1985. The judgment of Millett J at first instance has already been noted in this *Year Book*.[42] The Court of Appeal unanimously upheld his decision to strike out the winding-up petition. Millett J held that although the ITC fell within the literal meaning of the term 'association' in Section 665, Parliament could not have intended to subject an international organization to the winding-up jurisdiction of the English courts. He also held that the immunity from suit and legal process conferred on the ITC by Article 6 of the 1972 Order included immunity from the winding-up process. That process could not be regarded as simply an 'enforcement' of the arbitration award in the petitioner's favour and did not, therefore, fall within the exception to immunity for which the Order provided in the case of proceedings to enforce an arbitration award against the ITC. In a brief judgment Nourse LJ, with whom Kerr and Ralph Gibson LJJ agreed, adopted the reasoning of Millett J.

International organization—International Tin Council—Council insolvent and defaulting on debts—enforcement of arbitration award against assets of Council—order that Council officers disclose nature, location and value of assets—Sixth International Tin Agreement 1982—International Tin Council—United Kingdom Headquarters Agreement 1972—International Tin Council (Immunities and Privileges) Order 1972—International Organizations Act 1968

Case No. 4. Maclaine Watson & Co. Ltd. v. International Tin Council (No. 2), [1989] Ch. 286, [1988] 3 WLR 1190, [1988] 3 All ER 376, CA. The one case in which a creditor of the ITC succeeded in the Court of Appeal was *Maclaine Watson & Co. Ltd v. International Tin Council (No. 2)*, the 'disclosure of assets' case. In this case, Maclaine Watson sought to enforce an arbitration award against the ITC first by converting it into a judgment (for some £6 million) and then by

---

[41] In addition to the litigation in the English courts, there are decisions of courts in Canada, Malaysia, the Netherlands and New York. The decision of the Court of Justice of the European Communities in an action brought by Maclaine Watson & Co. Ltd. against the Commission of the European Communities was still pending at the time of going to press.

[42] 58 (1987), at pp. 406–18.

levying execution against the assets of the ITC. This process required Maclaine Watson to ascertain the location, nature and value of the ITC's assets. To that end it sought an order for the examination of the ITC as a judgment debtor under RSC Order 48 rule 1 and, in the alternative, a mandatory injunction requiring the ITC to disclose full particulars of its assets, both inside and outside the United Kingdom. At first instance, Millett J held that Order 48 did not apply to an unincorporated association such as the ITC, but he granted the mandatory injunction sought.[43] The Court of Appeal unanimously dismissed the ITC's appeal, rendering it unnecessary to consider a cross-appeal by Maclaine Watson against the decision regarding Order 48.

Most of the brief judgment of the Court of Appeal (delivered by Kerr LJ) is concerned with questions of English procedural law. The court did, however, consider two questions of international law. First, it reaffirmed Millett J's decision that the injunction did not violate the immunity of the ITC's officials. Like Millett J, the Court of Appeal accepted that the immunity granted to the Executive Chairman of the ITC by the 1972 Order ('the like immunity from suit and legal process . . . as . . . in respect of a diplomatic agent') precluded his being required to give evidence. However, the Court of Appeal held that the immunity from suit and legal process conferred upon other officials of the ITC 'in respect of things done or omitted to be done by them in the course of the performance of their official duties' did not prevent their being ordered to give evidence about the assets of the ITC.

Secondly, the Court of Appeal considered an argument, left open in the lower court, that the order granted by Millett J should be modified to ensure that the ITC and its officials were not required to do anything which would disclose information derived from the archives of the ITC, the inviolability of which was guaranteed by Article 7 of the 1972 Order. The Court accepted, as the House of Lords had done in *Shearson Lehman Bros.* v. *Maclaine Watson & Co. Ltd. (No. 2)*,[44] that the purpose of Article 7 was to protect the confidentiality of the contents of the ITC's archives, but felt it unnecessary to amend Millett J's order. The Court of Appeal appears to have thought that the ITC could comply with the order, provided that it was willing to adopt a less obstructive attitude, without any violation of the inviolable. The Court of Appeal was plainly less than impressed with the attitude to the litigation of the ITC and its members. At the conclusion of his judgment in the disclosure of assets case, Kerr LJ said, in reference to all the Tin appeals:

Having heard all these appeals consecutively and expressing ourselves as moderately as we can, we have formed the clear impression that the ITC has given no sufficient thought as to how it should set about meeting its obligations in an orderly manner, having regard to its special position in the law. Wherever the original responsibility may lie for its collapse in 1985, due to gross mismanagement or worse, the ITC is now insolvent, with debts totalling hundreds of millions of pounds. Its obligations are now to its creditors. It has successfully resisted Maclaine Watson's attempts to procure an orderly distribution of its assets to its creditors by the appointment of a liquidator or a receiver. The way in which it has resisted the present proceedings, designed to assist in the enforcement of a debt to which there is no answer whatever, speaks for itself. In our view this conduct is unbecoming to an international organization, to those who constitute it and to those who are responsible for its actions. The ITC's present duty is to undo to the greatest possible extent the damage to its

[43] See this *Year Book*, 58 (1987), at pp. 424–9.
[44] See below, p. 476.

creditors by ensuring that its assets are used to pay its debts, without any further prevarication. And its members are, in our view, at least morally obliged to put the ITC in funds to ensure that its creditors are ultimately paid in full.[45]

International organization—Arab Monetary Fund—personality in international law—whether capable of recognition in English law—capacity to sue and be sued— Arab Monetary Fund Agreement 1976

Case No. 5. Arab Monetary Fund v. *Hashim and others*, [1990] 1 All ER 685, Ch. D (Hoffman J). The decision of Hoffman J in *Arab Monetary Fund* v. *Hashim* is a vivid illustration of the problems to which the House of Lords' judgment in the Tin cases can give rise. The Arab Monetary Fund (the AMF) is an international organization created by the Arab Monetary Fund Agreement 1976, the parties to which, at the relevant time, were twenty Arab States and the Palestine Liberation Organization. The Agreement provided that the AMF was to have 'independent juridical personality and . . . in particular the right to own, contract and litigate'. The United Kingdom was not a member of the AMF and no Order in Council had been made under the International Organizations Act 1968 in respect of the AMF. The AMF brought an action in the High Court in London against its former Director-General, Dr Hashim, whom it accused of embezzling some US $50 million of its funds, and against various other defendants accused of complicity. The defendants moved to strike out the action on the ground that the AMF did not exist as a legal person in English law and therefore could not be party to proceedings before the English courts.

The logical answer to that argument would be that English law could recognize the existence of an entity created under international law, just as it recognizes the existence of an entity created under the laws of a foreign State. Hoffman J stated that, but for the decision in the Tin cases, he would have accepted this conflict of laws approach, although with the qualification (added by Dr F.A. Mann[46]) that the organization concerned must be recognized by the United Kingdom Government:

> The recognition of an international organization at the level of international law must be a matter for the Executive and it would be rather odd if the English courts recognized the existence in domestic law of an international organization which Her Majesty's Government declined to recognize in international law.[47]

This requirement might have presented a problem since the Government does not generally make pronouncements about recognition with respect to international organizations. Moreover, in a 1978 statement the Minister of State at the Foreign and Commonwealth Office had expressed the view that the capacity of a financial entity created by treaty to sue or be sued in the English courts did not depend upon recognition by the Government.[48] Nevertheless, Hoffman J went on to hold that the 1978 statement was a clear indication, of which he could take judicial notice, that the Government would recognize the legal personality of the AMF. He also rejected the defendants' submission that for the court to recognize the international

---

[45] [1989] Ch. 286 at 308.
[46] 'International Corporations and National Law', this *Year Book*, 42 (1967), p. 145.
[47] [1990] 1 All ER 685 at 688.
[48] This *Year Book*, 49 (1978), pp. 346–8.

legal personality of an organization created by treaty would infringe the principle of non-justiciability in *Buttes Gas and Oil* v. *Hammer (No. 3)*.[49]

The court was, however, precluded from following this logical approach by the decision of the House of Lords in *J.H. Rayner (Mincing Lane) Ltd.* v. *Department of Trade and Industry* that the legal personality which an international organization derived from its constituent treaty existed only on the level of international law so that a further grant of legal personality was necessary for it to function on a municipal law plane.[50] Hoffman J thus felt himself constrained to hold that, since the AMF Agreement had been incorporated into the law of Abu Dhabi (where the AMF had its headquarters), he could recognize the AMF as an entity existing under Abu Dhabi law.

The result—that the AMF is recognized as a legal person with capacity to sue in the English courts—is satisfactory but the method of arriving at that result (which Hoffman J himself described as 'unappetising') is absurd. A body which is plainly an international entity has to be treated as though it were a creation of Abu Dhabi law, which it plainly is not. It is true that the 1978 statement stated that

> . . . on the assumption that the entity concerned enjoys, under its constitutive instrument or instruments *and under the law of one or more member States or the State wherein it has its seat or permanent location*, legal personality and capacity to enter into transactions of the type concerned governed by the law of a non-member State, the Foreign and Commonwealth Office . . . would be willing officially to acknowledge that the entity concerned enjoys such legal personality and capacity and to state this.[51]

However, it is one thing to state that the international legal personality of an international organization will only be given effect in the laws of a non-member State if that personality has also been accepted under the laws of at least one member country. It is an entirely different matter to hold that the courts of the non-member State will ignore the international legal personality of the organization and treat the organization as a person constituted under the laws of one of the member States. Yet that is what the English courts now seem constrained to do.

More seriously, the legal personality of a particular international organization may well be embodied in the laws of several member States (and, indeed, non-member States). The effect of the judgments in *Rayner* and *Hashim* is that the organization has a separate personality in each such State. Which of those personalities is the one which the English courts recognize? That granted by the law of the State where the organization has its headquarters, or (which will not necessarily be the same) the office from which the contract in question was concluded, or some distillation of all these personalities? No wonder Hoffman J described these questions as ones of 'Trinitarian subtlety'.[52]

International organization—International Tin Council—inviolability of archives—comparison with archives of diplomatic mission—Sixth International

---

[49] [1982] AC 888.

[50] See above, p. 461 at 466.

[51] Loc. cit. above (n. 48) (emphasis added).

[52] [1990] 1 All ER 685 at 692. In a separate judgment in the same proceedings (*Arab Monetary Fund* v. *Hashim*, [1989] 1 WLR 565), Morritt J held that there was no privilege against self-incrimination in relation to possible offences under foreign law. Dr Hashim could not, therefore, resist an order for disclosure in connection with the grant of a *Mareva* injunction on the ground that he might become liable to criminal penalties in Iraq.

Tin Agreement 1982—International Tin Council–United Kingdom Headquarters Agreement 1972—International Tin Council (Immunities and Privileges) Order 1972—International Organizations Act 1968

Case No. 6. Shearson Lehman Brothers Inc. and another v. *Maclaine Watson & Co. Ltd., International Tin Council Intervening (No. 2)*, [1988] 1 WLR 16, HL. Following the collapse of the ITC[53] the London Metal Exchange took various steps to re-establish order in the tin market. Shearson Lehman Brothers objected to these measures and commenced proceedings against the Committee of the Exchange and against a number of metal brokers with which it had contracts. All the parties in these proceedings intended to produce in evidence a large number of documents emanating from, or connected with, the ITC and relating to the ITC's trading activities. These documents had come into the possession of the parties by a variety of means, including disclosure in the United States under the Freedom of Information Act and publication in the United Kingdom by the House of Commons Select Committee on Trade and Industry. It was agreed that they must originally have been disclosed to third parties by (*a*) Member States of the ITC or the members of their delegations to the ITC; (*b*) organizations with observer status at the ITC; or (*c*) officers or members of the staff of the ITC, who may or may not have been acting with authority in making the disclosure.

The ITC intervened in the proceedings to claim that some of these documents were inadmissible. The questions of principle raised by this plea were tried as a preliminary issue, with the result that the rulings given in court were made on a hypothetical basis, the actual provenance of the various documents remaining to be determined. The ITC relied on Article 7(1) of the 1972 Order, which provided that:

> The Council shall have the like inviolability of official archives as in accordance with the 1961 Convention Articles is accorded in respect of the official archives of a diplomatic mission.

The ITC maintained that the guarantee of inviolability meant more than simply that the ITC itself could not be required to produce documents from its archives in court and extended to protection of the confidentiality of those archives. This contention was accepted by Webster J, at first instance,[54] by the Court of Appeal[55] and the House of Lords.[56] In almost every other respect, however, the three courts differed.

At the heart of the case lay two problems: what documents were capable of forming part of the archives of the ITC and did they cease to be part of those archives when disclosed to a member State or a third party? The ITC submitted that:

> . . . all documents relating in any way to the business of the ITC which originate within the ITC and therefore commence life as documents which belong to the ITC retain that character unimpaired when they are communicated to constituent members or their representatives . . .

with the result that any ITC document, even if subsequently disclosed by the

---

[53] See above, p. 461.
[54] 77 ILR 107 at 121–2.
[55] Ibid. at 131.
[56] [1988] 1 WLR 16 at 27.

delegation of one of the member States, was inviolable and thus inadmissible in the action.[57]

Webster J accepted that a document which formed part of the ITC's archives did not lose that character merely because it was transmitted to a member State or a third party. Archival documents remained inviolable at any time and wherever they might be.[58] However, he took a fairly narrow view of what constituted the archives of the ITC. He rejected the suggestion that the ITC's archives were comparable to those of the diplomatic mission of a foreign State. The ITC, he held, was an international organization, not a sovereign State, and its functions were primarily commercial and economic, so that its rights of confidentiality were correspondingly less extensive than those accorded to a diplomatic mission. In particular, he held that the protection of Article 7 of the 1972 Order did not extend to documents relating to the commercial activities of the ITC.[59] The Court of Appeal disagreed with this part of Webster J's ruling. Mustill LJ thought that the distinction between documents relating to trading activities and other ITC documents was probably based upon an analogy, which he considered to be unsound, with the restrictive theory of sovereign immunity.[60] The Court of Appeal was plainly right to reject Webster J's approach to this question. The fact that a State may not enjoy immunity from the jurisdiction of the courts in an action relating to its commercial activities does not mean that documents concerning those activities which are contained in diplomatic archives are not inviolable.

Both the Court of Appeal and the House of Lords, however, rejected the ITC's submission that a document continued to form part of its archives even when it had been communicated to a member State or to an organization with observer status. In support of that argument the ITC had argued that, for the purposes of its internal affairs, no distinction could be drawn between the ITC and its members. Since the other actions concerning the ITC had turned on the fact that the ITC was, as regards the outside world, a separate legal person from its members, this argument was, to say the least, ironic and it is not surprising that in the House of Lords, Lord Bridge, with whom the rest of their Lordships agreed, confessed that he found it difficult to follow. In view of the clear provision in ITA6 that the ITC was to have legal personality, he was not disposed to accept the argument, but he held that it was unnecessary to consider it in any detail, since the provisions of the 1972 Order made clear that once documents had passed into the possession of a member State, it was the member State, not the ITC, which enjoyed any inviolability in respect of that document and which was able to waive that inviolability. If a member State had chosen to disclose those documents so that they subsequently came into the hands of the parties to the present action, the ITC could not rely upon the 1972 Order to prevent their use in the action.[61]

---

[57] Ibid. at 25.
[58] 77 ILR 107 at 122–3.
[59] Ibid. at 116–19.
[60] Ibid. at 137.
[61] [1988] 1 WLR 16 at 26. Article 14(1) of the 1972 Order provided that:
'Except in so far as in any particular case any privilege or immunity is waived by the government of the member country or by the intergovernmental organization whom they represent, representatives of member countries of the council and of intergovernmental organizations participating in the International Tin Agreement . . . shall enjoy:–
. . .

So far as the documents which had been disclosed by officers or members of staff of the ITC were concerned, the House of Lords considered that the critical question was whether the persons disclosing those documents had done so with actual or ostensible authority. According to Lord Bridge:

> The underlying purpose of the inviolability conferred is to protect the privacy of diplomatic communications. If that privacy is violated by a citizen, it would be wholly inimical to the underlying purpose that the judicial authorities of the host State should countenance the violation by permitting the violator, or any one who receives the document from the violator, to make use of the document in judicial proceedings.[62]

It followed that the inviolability conferred by the Order did not empower the ITC to prevent the production in court of documents disclosed by its officers or staff with actual authority. Even where the disclosure had not been authorized, Lord Bridge held that there was a presumption that an officer or employee of the ITC acting in the course of his employment had at least ostensible authority to disclose documents. To rebut that presumption the ITC would have to show both the absence of actual authority and that there was something in the circumstances of the disclosure to put the recipient of the document on inquiry. The only documents which, the House of Lords considered, were inadmissible in the proceedings were any which had been disclosed without actual or ostensible authority. Moreover, Lord Bridge rejected a submission by the ITC that the rule in *Juan Ysmael & Co. Inc.* v. *Government of the Republic of Indonesia*[63] meant that the ITC had only to assert an interest in the documents concerned (perhaps supported by prima facie evidence that they formed part of the ITC's archives and had been disclosed without authority) to bar adjudication of the claim. Lord Bridge held that the principle in *Juan Ysmael* had been designed to protect a sovereign which was resisting a claim against it, not to facilitate the assertion of a claim by a State or organization. Since the rule in *Juan Ysmael* has, in any event, a distinctly dated ring about it in view of the developments in the law of sovereign immunity, the refusal to extend it is most welcome.

The judgments in this case are not always easy to follow. In particular, the judgment of the House of Lords fails properly to distinguish between the right of the ITC to prevent a violation of its archives under Article 7 and its right to prevent a breach of confidence under the general law. Nevertheless, the result in the case is plainly correct. The suggestion that documents given by the ITC to the member States remained part of the ITC's archives was untenable. It was the States which controlled the ITC, not the other way round. Once a document had passed into the hands of a member State it was therefore for that State to determine whether or not to waive inviolability in respect of it. For the English courts to have refused to allow the use in proceedings between two of the ITC's creditors of documents which had been disclosed by a member State or an employee of the ITC possessing at least ostensible authority would have been absurd.

(b) while exercising their functions and during their journeys to and from the place of meetings convened by the council . . . the like inviolability for all their official papers and documents as is accorded to the head of a diplomatic mission . . . '
Lord Bridge held that the reference to 'official papers and documents' meant documents concerning ITC business and included documents emanating from the ITC ([1988] 1 WLR 16 at 26).
[62] Ibid. at 27.
[63] [1955] AC 72.

Refugee status—well-founded fear of persecution—whether objective test—whether applicant must show that there is real risk of persecution—Immigration Act 1971— Convention relating to the Status of Refugees 1951

Case No. 7. *R* v. *Secretary of State for the Home Department, ex parte Sivakumaran,* [1987] 3 WLR 1047, CA; [1988] 2 WLR 92, [1988] 1 All ER 193, HL. In *R* v. *Secretary of State for the Home Department, ex parte Bugdaycay*[64] the House of Lords held that it was for the Home Secretary, not the courts, to determine whether an applicant for asylum qualified for refugee status, although the courts retained a supervisory jurisdiction to ensure that the Secretary of State did not misdirect himself in any way. *R* v. *Secretary of State for the Home Department, ex parte Sivakumaran* raised the question whether the Secretary of State had misdirected himself as to the proper definition of a refugee.

Article 1(A)(2) of the United Nations Convention relating to the Status of Refugees 1951[65] provides that the term 'refugee' applies to any person who

. . . owing to well-founded fear of being persecuted for reasons of race, religion, nationality, membership of a particular social group or political opinion, is outside the country of his nationality and is unable or, owing to such fear, is unwilling to avail himself of the protection of that country . . .

Sivakumaran turned on the meaning to be attributed to the phrase 'well-founded fear'. The Secretary of State maintained that it meant that not only must the applicant have a subjective fear of persecution for one of the Convention reasons but also that that fear must be objectively justified. In other words, an applicant was entitled to treatment as a refugee only if an examination by the Secretary of State of the conditions in the country to which the applicant feared return revealed a real prospect that the applicant would be persecuted. In the present case the Secretary of State considered that the applicants, a group of Sri Lankan Tamils, had no real reason to fear persecution in Sri Lanka and accordingly determined that they were not entitled to refugee status.

The Court of Appeal disagreed with the test propounded by the Secretary of State. Lord Donaldson MR held that:

Fear is clearly an entirely subjective state experienced by the person who is afraid. The adjectival phrase 'well-founded' qualifies, but cannot transform, the subjective nature of the emotion. The qualification will exclude fears which can be dismissed as paranoid, but we do not understand why it should exclude those which, although fully justified on the face of the situation as it presented itself to the person who was afraid, can be shown objectively to have been misconceived.[66]

He gave the example of a man who is threatened by a robber brandishing a realistic imitation firearm. The man's fears, Lord Donaldson held, were objectively misconceived since the 'weapon' was in fact harmless, but most people would describe his fear as 'well-founded'. The Court of Appeal therefore held that it was not necessary for the applicant to show that a real risk of persecution actually existed in the country concerned. All that Article 1(A)(2) required was that there should be good reason for the applicant's fear 'looking at the situation from the point of view of one of reasonable courage circumstanced as was the applicant for refugee status'.[67] It followed that whether an applicant's fears were well-founded had to be

---

[64] [1987] AC 514; noted in this *Year Book,* 58 (1987), p. 429.
[65] Cmd. 9171.
[66] [1987] 3 WLR 1047 at 1052.
[67] Ibid.

determined on the facts known to the applicant, rather than on the results of an examination by the Secretary of State of conditions in the country concerned.

A third approach was suggested by counsel for the United Nations High Commissioner for Refugees, who was allowed to intervene in the proceedings before the House of Lords. He accepted that whether an applicant's fear of persecution was well-founded had to be determined on the basis of the objective facts ascertained by the Secretary of State (rather than the facts as the applicant imagined them to be). He then maintained, however, that the question was not whether those facts disclosed an actual risk of persecution but whether, on the basis of those facts, a reasonable man in the position of the applicant would think that there was a risk (a test not unlike that which the courts apply in the criminal law to determine whether a defendant is acting under duress).[68] It was this approach which had been adopted by the United Nations High Commissioner in the *Handbook on Procedures and Criteria for determining Refugee Status* (1979).[69]

The subjective approach adopted by the Court of Appeal received short shrift from the House of Lords. The Court of Appeal's decision was based, at least in part, upon a misunderstanding of the decision of the United States Supreme Court in *Immigration and Naturalization Service* v. *Cardoza-Fonseca*.[70] The Supreme Court's decision in that case was really only authority for the proposition that it was sufficient for the applicant to show that there was a real risk of persecution; he did not have to show that it was more likely than not that he would be persecuted. The Supreme Court had not held that the applicant need not show that the risk was objectively justified. The House of Lords readily accepted that the test to be applied was that of the 'real risk of persecution' and not the 'more likely than not' test. However, since the Secretary of State in *Sivakumaran* had accepted that only a real risk of persecution need be shown, *Cardoza-Fonseca* was not really in point. Moreover, the House considered that the Court of Appeal's approach was difficult to reconcile with other provisions of the Convention, such as Article 1(C)(5), which envisaged that a person would lose his refugee status if 'the circumstances in connection with which he was recognized as a refugee have ceased to exist'.

The House of Lords also rejected the interpretation advanced by the High Commissioner. Lord Goff maintained that this test would require the Secretary of State to ask himself 'the purely hypothetical question whether, if the applicant knew the true facts, and was still (in the light of those facts) afraid, his fear could be described as plausible and reasonable'.[71] Lord Goff rejected the argument that the High Commissioner's approach was supported by the *travaux préparatoires* of the Convention, although he did not go into detail. He also refused to regard the passage in the *Handbook* as authoritative, describing it as no more than 'a statement of the point of view espoused by the High Commissioner'.[72]

The decision of the House of Lords that an applicant for asylum need not show that it is more likely than not that he will face persecution if returned to his country of origin but need only demonstrate a reasonable degree of likelihood of persecution is most welcome. That the House did not feel able to accept the High Commissioner's approach to determining whether a fear of persecution was

---

[68] See *R* v. *Howe*, [1987] AC 417.
[69] Paragraphs 37–50.
[70] (1987) 94 L Ed 2d 434; 79 ILR 610.
[71] [1988] 2 WLR 92 at 104.
[72] Ibid.

well-founded will doubtless cause regret to many concerned that the United Kingdom may be hardening its heart to refugees in the face of a substantial increase in the numbers claiming refugee status. It is true that, as Lord Goff pointed out, the tests formulated by the Secretary of State and the High Commissioner will lead to the same result in most cases and if the Secretary of State is correct in his assessment of the likelihood of persecution, no harm will be done. Nevertheless, there is some force in the High Commissioner's view that a State which is eager not to prejudice its relations with another country will find it easier to allow refugee status to someone fleeing from that country if the grant of refugee status is not seen as involving a finding that there really was a likelihood of persecution in the latter country. It must be remembered that, just as the English courts in *Sivakumaran* made much of the Supreme Court's decision in *Cardoza-Fonseca*, so courts in other States are likely to follow the interpretation of Article 1(A)(2) adopted by the House of Lords.[73]

C. J. Greenwood

B. Private International Law[*]

Jurisdiction: aspects of service of process upon an absent defendant

Case No. 1. Order 11, rule 1(1), of the Rules of the Supreme Court lists the principal cases in which, with leave of the court, service of a writ out of the jurisdiction is permissible. Included in the list is the case (r. 1(1)(d)(iii)) in which 'the claim is brought to enforce, rescind, dissolve, annul or otherwise affect a contract, or to recover damages or obtain other relief in respect of a breach of contract, being (in either case) a contract which . . . is by its terms, or by implication, governed by English law'. Rule 4(2) of the Order provides that leave shall not be granted 'unless it shall be made sufficiently to appear to the Court that the case is a proper one for service out of the jurisdiction'.

The facts giving rise to the recent Court of Appeal decision in *Seashell Shipping Corporation* v. *Mutualidad de Seguros del Instituto Nacional de Industria (The Magnum)*[1] were that a Spanish company had insured a ship, which it owned, with the defendants (Musini), who were Spanish insurers carrying on business wholly in Spain. Later the shipowners let the ship to the plaintiffs (Seashell), who sought a quotation from the defendants for a continuation of cover except for war risks. Cover was confirmed on certain terms. The cover did not include war risks, which were covered by another insurer. Subsequently the ship sustained damage as a result of a collision. Some of that damage was repaired, but there was considerable damage remaining unrepaired when the vessel was hit by a missile and became a constructive total loss. The plaintiffs' claim in respect of that loss was settled by their separate war risk insurers, but they claimed to be entitled to recover against the defendants in respect of the earlier and unrepaired damage. The defendants

---

[73] Three other decisions concerning public international law are considered elsewhere in this volume. *R* v. *Secretary of State for Transport, ex parte Factortame*, [1989] 2 WLR 997 is discussed in a note by Professor M. Akehurst, above, p. 351. *Holmes* v. *Bangladesh Biman Corporation*, [1989] AC 1112, and *Libyan Arab Foreign Bank* v. *Bankers Trust*, [1989] QB 728, are noted below at pp. 499 and 502 respectively.

[*] © P.B. Carter, 1990.

[1] [1989] 1 Lloyd's Rep. 47.

refused to pay, and the plaintiffs sought and obtained leave to serve them *ex juris*. Leggatt J set aside the writ and service thereof on the ground that, although the plaintiffs, Seashell, had a good arguable case that the contract was governed by English law and was therefore within Order 11, r. 1(1)(d)(iii),[2] the case was not a 'proper one' within Order 11, r. 4(2).[3]

The Court of Appeal allowed the plaintiffs' appeal, and an application for further appeal to the House of Lords was refused. The leading judgment in the Court of Appeal (in which Stocker and May LJJ concurred) is that of Parker LJ. It illustrates and clarifies several aspects of law and practice relating to service *ex juris*, but at the same time manifests a feature which could provoke misgivings.

It is first to be observed that, as his Lordship noted,[4] it was common ground that, if the contract between the parties was governed by English law, then the plaintiffs' claim was sustainable; but that, if it was governed by Spanish law, their claim would fail.

The threshold question raised by the facts of the case was, of course, the identity of the proper law of the contract between the parties. Only if this was found to be English law could the case come within Order 11, r. 1(1)(d)(iii), and only then could the further question arise as to whether it had been 'made sufficiently to appear to the Court that the case is a proper one for service out of the jurisdiction', as mandated by r. 4(2).

In every case in which leave to serve *ex juris* pursuant to Order 11, r. 1(1), is sought, it is for the applicant to show that the case comes within one of the listed categories. It has been emphasized many times that his obligation is to show that the case is clearly within the category upon which he relies, and that any doubts on this score should be resolved in favour of the defendant. At the same time an apparent dilemma can be posed if an issue to be determined in this jurisdictional context is identical (or virtually identical) with an issue which will fall to be determined in adjudicating upon the merits, should the Court take jurisdiction. In the case of *The Magnum* determination of the proper law of the contract was not only a prerequisite for the granting of leave to serve the defendant *ex juris*: it was also an issue central to the merits. This potential dilemma, of requiring a court to appear to prejudge the merits at an application (often made *ex parte*) for leave to serve an absent defendant, is resolved by resort to the concept of the 'good arguable case'. This problem seems to have been foreshadowed by, for example, Lloyd J in *Atlantic Underwriting Agencies Ltd.* v. *Compagnia di Assicurazione di Milano SpA*[5] when he said:

A plaintiff seeking leave to serve out need only show a good arguable case on the merits. But when it comes to bringing the case within one of the heads of R.S.C., Order 11, he must do more than that. He must show that the case comes clearly within one of the heads of R.S.C., Order 11; and further that the case comes not merely within the letter but also within the spirit of the rule.

In the particular context of r. 1(1)(d)(iii) the phrase 'is by its terms, or by implication, governed by English law' is in effect taken to mean no more than that there is a good arguable case that this is so. The plaintiff has to show clearly that his case

---

[2] Above.
[3] Above.
[4] Ibid. 48.
[5] [1979] 2 Lloyd's Rep. 240, 245.

comes within the letter and the spirit of the head, but the head as construed in this sense. In *The Magnum* the Court of Appeal, confirming the trial judge on this point, found that there was at least a good arguable case that English law was the proper law of the parties' contract.

The Court then had to consider whether it had been made 'sufficiently to appear' to it 'that the case was a proper one for service out of the jurisdiction'. Lord Justice Parker, citing[6] some words of Lord Goff in *Spiliada Maritime Corporation* v. *Cansulex Ltd.*[7] saw this as depending upon where the action should be tried 'suitably for the interests of all the parties for the ends of justice'. His Lordship said:

> . . . it is for the plaintiff who seeks to make a foreign defendant defend himself in the Courts here to make it, using the words of r. 4(2), 'sufficiently to appear to the Court' that England is clearly the forum where the case may more suitably be tried for such interests and ends.[8]

The Court found that the plaintiff in the instant case had discharged this burden, and the appeal was accordingly allowed. Parker LJ noted that this did involve departure from the practice advocated by Lord Templeman in the *Spiliada* case[9] that appeals against a trial judge's exercise of discretion in Order 11 cases should be rare and that an appeal court should be slow to interfere. The instant case was seemingly seen as such a rare case.

Parker LJ acknowledged that

> In the present case Musini's place of residence is clearly a matter of importance. They carry on business wholly in Spain and were sought out by Seashell. It is of the more importance because Seashell are Panamanian, not seeking to use their own Courts but rather to use the English Courts, whose jurisdiction to entertain the action at all stems exclusively from the fact that the putative proper law of the contract is English law.[10]

His Lordship further acknowledged[11] that 'subject to one qualification' the outcome of the proceedings on the merits, whether heard in England or in Spain, would depend upon the final holding as to the proper law. The one qualification envisaged by Parker LJ was the possibility that, even if a Spanish court were to hold that English law was the proper law, it might nevertheless hold the plaintiffs disentitled to recover on overriding grounds of Spanish public policy. The importance attached by the Court to this possibility is symptomatic of the general tenor of its holding, which seems to have been that England was the most appropriate *forum* because (and in effect only because) it was the forum in which a particular party was likely to succeed on the merits, this being seen by an English court as the proper outcome. However, it may be asked, does this not raise the spectre of latter-day judicial chauvinism? It is an approach which would seem not to lie too easily with the admonishment of Lord Wilberforce in the House of Lords in *Amin Rasheed Corporation* v. *Kuwait Insurance*[12] that 'It is not appropriate, in my opinion, to embark upon a comparison of the procedures, or methods, or reputation or standing of the courts of one country as compared with those of another'.

---

[6] [1989] 1 Lloyd's Rep. 47, 49.
[7] [1987] AC 460.
[8] [1989] 1 Lloyd's Rep. 47, 49.
[9] [1987] AC 460, 465.
[10] [1989] 1 Lloyd's Rep. 47, 49.
[11] Ibid.
[12] [1984] AC 50, 72.

It is a little difficult to see why, if such restraint is (very properly) to be exercised with regard to adjectival matters, it should not be similarly appropriate with regard to substantive matters.

Perhaps, in other and appropriate circumstances, an argument might be made that, in deciding whether to grant leave, a factor properly to be taken into account could be that the likely finding in a foreign court would be, not simply at variance with what would probably happen in English proceedings, but so manifestly contrary to English public policy (as applied in a private international law context) as to be unacceptable. However, the instant case could scarcely be regarded in this way, because the ground, upon which it was feared that a Spanish court (even if it found the proper law to be English) might prevent the plaintiffs from succeeding, was that for them to do so would mean that, having already been paid by the war risk insurers on a constructive total loss, they would then, to the extent of the unrepaired damage, be receiving double compensation.

The reasoning in *The Magnum* could be seen as marking a shift away from notions of *forum non conveniens*, the appropriate *forum*, and the natural *forum*, and to evaluation of the likely outcome in one *forum* (foreign) as compared with another (English)—such evaluation leading to an operative preference for the latter.

The location of a tort for the purposes of service of process out of the jurisdiction

Case No. 2. Order 11, rule 1, of the Rules of the Supreme Court lists as one of the 'Principal cases in which service of a writ out of jurisdiction is permissible' that in which, in the action begun by the writ, 'the claim is founded on a tort and damage was sustained, or resulted from an act committed, within the jurisdiction'.[13] Until 1987 the wording of the corresponding provision was: 'Where the action is founded on a tort committed within the jurisdiction'.[14] This latter had been construed as requiring that the 'substance of the cause of action arose' within the jurisdiction.[15] The wording of the new sub-paragraph in fact largely reflects the interpretation that has been placed upon the relevant category of Special Jurisdiction allowed under the Brussels Convention on Jurisdiction and the Enforcement of Judgments in Civil and Commercial Matters. The actual wording there is: 'in matters relating to tort, delict or quasi-delict, in the courts of the place where the harmful event occurred'.[16] The 'place where the harmful event occurred' has been construed by the European Court of Justice in *Handelskwerkerij G.J. Bier BV* v. *Mines de Potasse d'Alsace SA*[17] as referring both to the place where the tortious act occurred and to the place where the damage was suffered. There has thus been achieved a rough correspondence between (1) the test to be applied when the issue is as to whether (in a case not within the scope of the Convention) the Court has power to allow service upon an absent defendant, and (2) that to be applied when the issue is as to whether (in a case within the scope of the Convention) a person

---

[13] RSC Order 11, r. 1(1)(f).

[14] Pre-1987 RSC Order 11, r. 1(1)(h).

[15] For instance, in *Castree* v. *E.R. Squibb & Sons Ltd*. Ackner LJ (with whom the other members of the Court of Appeal agreed) spoke of 'applying the test which is accepted on all sides to be the appropriate test, namely, to look back over the series of events constituting the tort and ask the question where in substance the cause of action arose . . .' ([1980] 1 WLR 1248, 1252).

[16] Article 5(3). See the Civil Jurisdiction and Judgments Act 1982, Schedule 1.

[17] (Case 21/76) [1978] QB 708.

may exceptionally be sued in a Contracting State other than the Contracting State in which he is domiciled.

The position in the former of these two contexts has been clarified and refined in several ways, but, in the view of the present writer, distorted in another way, in the recent Court of Appeal case of *Metall und Rohstoff AG* v. *Donaldson Inc.*[18] The facts giving rise to the litigation were somewhat complex, as was the lengthy course of the litigation itself. The situation, so far as relevant to the instant aspect of the matter, was in brief summary as follows. The plaintiffs, a Swiss company, traded on the London Metal Exchange through brokers, A.M.L. The plaintiffs' chief aluminum trader had instructed A.M.L. to open a number of accounts under various names; and, with the assistance of a number of employees of A.M.L., had traded fraudulently. A.M.L., its American parent company (A.C.L.I.) and the American holding company (D.L.J.) all knew that this trading was without the plaintiffs' knowledge. A.M.L. nevertheless in order to protect itself closed the plaintiffs' accounts and seized certain of their assets. The plaintiffs subsequently obtained judgment against A.M.L. for over £50m., but had been able to recover only £6.7m. (and no costs) because A.M.L. had become insolvent. The plaintiffs then commenced proceedings against A.C.L.I. and D.L.J. The plaintiffs claimed damages for conspiracy but without alleging that the purpose of the conspiracy had been to harm them. They also claimed damages under various other heads: inducing breach of contract, abuse of the process of the court, accounting as constructive trustees and procuring breaches of trust.

The plaintiffs obtained an order to serve the writ out of the jurisdiction. Gatehouse J decided that this order should be set aside in respect of the claims based upon abuse of the process of the court and inducing breach of trust, but that otherwise it should stand. The Court of Appeal allowed the defendants' appeal in part, holding that the only cause of action available to the plaintiffs was that founded on inducement or procurement of breaches of contract, and that in respect of that claim leave had been properly granted.

Before dealing with the specific but central question of the interpretation to be placed upon RSC Order 11, r. 1(1)(f), Slade LJ, who delivered the judgment of the Court of Appeal, considered two more general aspects of Order 11, r. 1. His Lordship re-iterated that a plaintiff seeking leave under the Order bears a threefold burden. First, he must show that the claim he wishes to pursue is a good arguable claim on the merits: the court must be satisfied that the plaintiff, if given leave, has a 'good chance' of succeeding on the merits.[19] Secondly, 'the plaintiff must show a strong probability that the claim falls within the letter and the spirit of the sub-head or sub-heads of Order 11, r. 1(1), relied on. This requirement is treated strictly, since if leave is given (and, if challenged, upheld) it will never thereafter be investigated.[20] Thirdly, 'the plaintiff must persuade the court that England is the forum in which the case can most suitably be tried in the interests of all the parties and for the ends of justice'.[21] These lucidly stated propositions were not disputed in the instant case. They are separate and distinct propositions. However, as has already been indicated[22] in the commentary upon *Seashell Shipping Corpora-*

---

[18] [1989] 3 WLR 563.
[19] Ibid. 579.
[20] Ibid. 579.
[21] Ibid. 580.
[22] p. 484 above.

tion v. *Mutualidad de Seguros del Instituto Nacional de Industria (The Magnum)*,[23] difficulties may arise from interaction between the first and second proposition. In the instant case, the importance of the second proposition at the procedural level was emphasized and elaborated in that the Court of Appeal held that the plaintiff seeking leave is bound by, and limited to, the specific legal basis he has pleaded as giving rise to a cause of action. He cannot (with the possible exception of a claim referred to in an affidavit of evidence) rely on the pleaded facts as disclosing a different and unpleaded basis for his claim. Accordingly, even on the assumption that there is such a tort as maliciously instituting legal proceedings (upon which reliance had been placed as an alternative to abuse of the process of the court), the issue could not be raised in Order 11 proceedings because the plaintiffs had not raised it nor identified it in their pleadings.

Turning to the interpretation of Order 11, r. (1)(f), Slade LJ first isolated what the Court saw as three separate conditions imposed by it: (1) that the claim be founded upon a tort; and either (2) that the damage was sustained within the jurisdiction, or (3) that it resulted from an act committed within the jurisdiction.

Rejecting the argument that satisfaction of the second condition involved showing that all the damage had been sustained within the jurisdiction, his Lordship said: 'It is enough if some significant damage had been sustained in England'.[24] Presumably it is not only enough but also essential that some *significant* damage had been sustained in England. Dealing with the third condition, and rejecting the argument that it requires that all the acts necessary to establish liability take place within the jurisdiction, the learned judge said:

> In our view [it] requires the court to look at the tort alleged in a common sense way and ask whether damage has resulted from substantial and efficacious acts committed within the jurisdiction (whether or not other substantial and efficacious acts have been committed elsewhere); if the answer is yes, leave may (but of course need not) be given. But the defendants are, we think, right to insist that the acts to be considered must be those of the putative defendant, because the question at issue is whether the links between him and the English forum are such as to justify his being brought here to answer the plaintiffs' claim.[25]

The flexibility introduced into these two conditions manifested by the use of the key phrases 'some significant damage' and 'substantial and efficacious acts' can be seen as a partial restoration of the pre-1987 test involving looking back 'over the series of events constituting the tort' so as to 'ask the question where in substance the cause of action arose'.[26] Indeed, there is room for the view that, having regard to the many and diverse types of possible tort actions, and to the almost infinite variety of fact situations that may give rise to some form of tortious liability, the generality of that former test is more appropriate than a test in the formulation of which two factors (the locations of the defendant's acts and of damage to the plaintiff) are singled out, even if these factors are themselves flexibly interpreted.

It is concerning the Court of Appeal's treatment of what is seen as the first of the three above-mentioned conditions, namely that the claim is founded on a tort, that the present writer ventures to voice serious doubts. The Court saw this requirement as posing the question as to 'what law is to be applied in resolving whether the

[23] [1989] 1 Lloyd's Rep. 365.
[24] [1989] 3 WLR 563, 582.
[25] Ibid.
[26] *per* Ackner LJ in *Castree* v. *E.R. Squibb and Sons Ltd.*, [1980] 1 WLR 1248 at p. 1952.

claim is "founded on a tort"?'.[27] The Court's answer to this question seems to have been:

> In our judgment, in double locality cases our courts should first consider whether, by reference exclusively to English law, it can properly be said that *a tort has been committed within the jurisdiction of our courts*. In answering this question, they should apply the now well familiar 'substance' test previously applied in such cases as *Distillers Co. (Biochemicals) Ltd.* v. *Thompson* [1971] A.C. 458, *Castree* v. *E.R. Squibb & Sons Ltd.* [1980] 1 W.L.R. 1248 and *Cordoba Shipping Co. Ltd.* v. *National State Bank, Elizabeth, New Jersey* [1984] 2 Lloyd's Rep. 91. If on the application of this test, they find that the tort was in substance committed in this country, they can thenceforth wholly disregard the rule in *Boys* v. *Chaplin* [1971] A.C. 356; the fact that some of the relevant events occurred abroad will thenceforth have no bearing on the defendant's liability in tort. On the other hand, if they find that the tort was in substance committed in some foreign country, they should apply the rule and impose liability in tort under English law, only if both (a) the relevant events would have given rise to liability in tort in English law if they had all taken place in England, and (b) the alleged tort would be actionable in the country where it was committed.[28]

The formulation of the question posed and this apparent response to it seem clearly based upon the assumption that, in order to obtain leave under Order 11, r. 1(1)(f), one of the things that a plaintiff must show is that (if the material facts are proved) a tort has as a matter of law *actually* been committed. If the alleged tort was committed in England the case is outside the scope of the rule in *Boys* v. *Chaplin*; if, on the other hand, it was committed abroad resort must be had to that rule. In locating the alleged tort for this purpose (in effect a choice of law purpose) the court is to look exclusively to English law and, in so doing, is to borrow the 'substance' test which had been evolved in the context of interpreting the pre-1987 Order 11, r. 1(1)(h).

This line of reasoning, in addition to introducing a new dimension of complexity, is, in the present writer's respectful submission, based upon a faulty initial assumption. That assumption is that the wording of heading (f), 'the claim is founded on tort', means that a tort has been committed. What, it is submitted, it should be taken to mean is simply that the plaintiff's claim raises what is to be characterized as a tort issue. Characterization is a matter for English law as the *lex fori*. Choice of law issues are not raised. Consideration of the rule in *Boys* v. *Chaplin* (or of any other choice of law rule) is, therefore, in this context always irrelevant.

In the pre-1987 Order 11, r. 1(1), the corresponding wording 'the action begun by the writ is founded on a tort'[29] was not materially different; and it was seemingly assumed to have the same significance as it is suggested should now be accorded to the wording of the present rule 1(1)(f). It is to be noted, too, that the corresponding wording of Article 4 of the Brussels Convention, namely 'may . . . be sued (3) in matters relating to tort, delict or quasi-delict . . . ',[30] clearly does not imply that liability under the relevant choice of law rule must be established.

It is to be noted, too, that, if the approach taken by the Court of Appeal in relation to the wording of heading (f) under rule 1(1) is accepted, it should be equally acceptable in relation to some other headings. For example, if, relying upon heading (e), 'the claim is brought in respect of a breach committed within the

---

[27] [1989] 3 WLR 563, 582.
[28] Ibid. 590 (original emphasis).
[29] p. 485 above.
[30] p. 485 above.

jurisdiction of a contract made within or out of the jurisdiction', a plaintiff seeks leave to serve an absent defendant, he will have to show that a breach of a valid contract had *actually* been committed within the jurisdiction.

For the avoidance of doubt, it may be emphasized that the problem now under consideration is quite distinct from that referred to[31] in the commentary on *Seashell Shipping Corporation* v. *Mutualidad de Seguros del Instituto Nacional de Industria (The Magnum).*[32] That problem was one that may arise if a precondition for the exercise of the power to grant leave *ex juris* involves the same issue as may arise on the merits, for example, as to whether the proper law of a contract is English law for the purposes of an Order 11, r. 1(1)(d)(iii), application. The problem currently under consideration is as to whether the word 'claim', which prefaces all but two of the now nineteen heads under Order 11, r. 1(1), is in effect to be construed as meaning valid claim.

Had the approach suggested here been followed in *Metall und Rohstoff AG* v. *Donaldson Inc.*, the conclusion, that the plaintiffs' claim alleging inducement to procure breaches of contract came within Order 11, r. 1(1)(f), would, of course, still have been reached—but by a shorter and analytically less hazardous route. So, too, the holding that the plaintiffs had no claim under English law in conspiracy would have been unchanged: a plaintiffs' claim based upon an agreement the purpose of which was not to injure him is not to be characterized as a claim in tort under English law. By a parity of reasoning rejection of the plaintiffs' claims based upon tortious abuse of the process of the court, and upon constructive trust and procuring a breach of trust, would seemingly be unaffected.

The Brussels Convention—actions in rem—*suit in the State of domicile—Article 57*

Case No. 3. In the recent Admiralty case of *The Deichland*[33] the Court of Appeal had to deal with what were in effect three separate points arising out of the Civil Jurisdiction and Judgments Act 1982, the primary purpose of which was, of course, to give effect in the law of the United Kingdom to the provisions of the 1968 Convention on Jurisdiction and the Enforcement of Judgments in Civil and Commercial Matters ('the Brussels Convention').[34]

The facts of *The Deichland* may be summarized as follows. In January 1986 the plaintiffs had shipped a cargo of steel coils on board the *Deichland* from Glasgow to La Spezia. Deich Navigation SA (Deich), the disponent owners of the vessel (to whom it was chartered under a demise charter), were a Panamanian corporation whose central management and control were exercised in the Federal Republic of Germany. A year later, i.e. in January 1987, the plaintiffs issued a writ *in rem* in respect of damage to the cargo alleged to have occurred during the voyage. The defendants were named as 'the owners and/or the demise charterers' of the *Deichland*. The writ was not served on the vessel until November 1987, by which time the demise charter had ended and the vessel was in different ownership. In June 1988 the demise charterers sought to have the writ set aside and a declaration that the court had no jurisdiction over the defendants. The trial judge dismissed the motion. On appeal Deich contended that the plaintiffs' action should have been brought in the Federal Republic of Germany, where, it contended, it was

---

[31] p. 483 above.
[32] [1989] 1 Lloyd's Rep. 365.
[33] [1989] 3 WLR 478.
[34] The text of the Convention, as amended, is set out in Schedule 1 to the Act.

domiciled. In support of this contention reliance was placed upon the Civil Jurisdiction and Judgments Act 1982 and in particular upon Article 2 of the Brussels
Convention. That Article, so far as it was material, runs as follows: 'Subject to the
provisions of this Convention, persons domiciled in a contracting State shall, whatever their nationality, be sued in the courts of that State'. It was common ground
that, unless the provision could be successfully invoked, the High Court would
have jurisdiction to hear this action *in rem*.

The plaintiffs argued, *inter alia*, that so long as the action remained solely *in
rem*, Deich Navigation SA was not a defendant and that therefore Article 2 was not
applicable. Neill LJ put their case thus:

> The plaintiffs' case is based on the proposition that an action in rem is an action against
> the ship itself and that the owners or charterers, as the case may be, of the ship only incur
> some personal liability if they enter an appearance. In that event the action will proceed both
> as an action in rem and as an action in personam: see *The August 8* [1983] 2 A.C. 450.
> Unless and until an appearance is entered, however, the claim is against the res alone and
> Deich not a defendant in a relevant sense although so described in the writ.[35]

After surveying the development of the English action *in rem*, Neill LJ turned to
the relevant provisions of the Brussels Convention and the 1982 Act. Having
alluded to section 3 of the Act which relates to the way in which the Convention is
to be interpreted, his Lordship pointed out[36] that it is clear in the Preamble to the
Convention that one of its objects was 'to determine the international jurisdiction'
of the contracting States. He also drew attention[37] to the fact that Title 1 of the
Convention, in defining its scope, provides that the Convention should 'apply in
civil and commercial matters whatever the nature of the court or tribunal'. His
Lordship then singled out a provision in Article 5 as being particularly significant.
That Article lists cases of 'Special Jurisdiction' in which a person domiciled in one
contracting State may be sued in another contracting State. The seventh case so
listed runs thus:

> . . . (7) as regards a dispute concerning the payment of remuneration claimed in respect of
> the salvage of a cargo or freight, in the court under the authority of which the cargo or
> freight in question: (*a*) has been arrested to secure such payment, or (*b*) could have been so
> arrested, but bail or other security has been given; provided that this provision shall apply
> only if it is claimed that the defendant has an interest in the cargo or freight or had such an
> interest at the time of salvage.[38]

Finally Neill LJ made reference to part of Article 57 to the effect that 'This Convention shall not affect any conventions to which the Contracting States are or will
be parties and which, in relation to particular matters, govern jurisdiction or the
recognition or enforcement of judgments . . . '.[39]

Rejecting the plaintiffs' contention that, so long as the action remained solely *in
rem*, Article 2 had no application on the ground that Deich was not being 'sued',
his Lordship said:

> I have come to the conclusion that the right approach when one is considering the effect of
> an international convention is to take account of the purpose or purposes of the convention.

[35] Ibid. 483.
[36] Ibid. 486.
[37] Ibid. 486.
[38] Set out by Neill LJ at p. 486.
[39] Set out by Neill LJ at p. 487.

Plainly the 1968 Convention was intended, inter alia, to regulate the circumstances in which a person domiciled in one contracting state might be brought before the courts of another contracting state 'in civil and commercial matters'. Accordingly it seems to me that all forms of proceedings in civil and commercial matters were intended to be covered except in so far as some special provisions such as article 57 might otherwise prescribe. Furthermore it seems to me that paragraph (7) in article 5, which confers a special jurisdiction in the case of claims for remuneration in respect of the salvage of cargo or freight, contemplates that this special jurisdiction may be exercised by proceedings either in rem or in personam.[40]

The fact that in the present case the vessel was no longer chartered to Deich was not material because 'looking at the reality of the matter it is Deich who is interested in contesting liability and against whom the plaintiffs would wish to proceed *in personam* if an appearance is entered'.[41] His Lordship concluded his consideration of this issue with a welcome observation which can have wider significance:

By English law an Admiralty action in rem has special characteristics . . . I do not consider, however, that the rules relating to such actions and governing the rights of a plaintiff to levy execution can affect the substance of the matter when the court is faced with an international Convention designed to regulate the international jurisdiction of national courts.[42]

Stuart-Smith LJ and Sir Denys Buckley concurred in holding that Deich was being 'sued' for the purposes of Article 2 of the Convention. The former said: 'In my judgment the Act of 1982 and the 1968 Convention provide a comprehensive code . . . Articles 1, 2, 3 and 57 are clearly intended as it seems to me to apply to actions in rem'.[43] Sir Denys Buckley said:

It is true that in an action in the High Court which is exclusively in rem against a ship, the plaintiff cannot recover any relief against the party who could be made liable on the same ground of complaint in an action in personam unless that party elects to enter an appearance to the writ in rem. If he does enter such an appearance unconditionally he becomes liable in that action as though it had been commenced in personam. This is a peculiarity of our rules of procedure and practice. The underlying complaint, however, is the same whether the action be framed in personam or in rem.[44]

He continued that in the instant case, 'The cause of action alleged is precisely that which would be alleged in an action in personam against Deich in respect of the same ground of complaint'.[45] His Lordship concluded that to hold that Deich was not being 'sued' would appear to him to conflict with the policy of the Convention which he took to be that (except where otherwise provided in the Convention) 'disputes of a litigious character between parties domiciled in different contracting states shall be resolved in the courts of the state in which that party is domiciled against whom a complaint is made'.[46]

The second matter with which the Court of Appeal had to deal in *The Deichland* arose from the plaintiff's further contention that Deich Navigation SA was not domiciled in the Federal Republic of Germany (a contracting State) but in Panama.

Article 53 of the Convention provides:

[40] Ibid. 487.
[41] Ibid.
[42] Ibid.
[43] Ibid. 497.
[44] Ibid. 500.
[45] Ibid. 501.
[46] Ibid.

For the purposes of the Convention, the seat of a company or other legal person or association of natural or legal persons shall be treated as its domicile. However, in order to determine that seat, the court shall apply its rules of private international law.

The relevant rule of British private international law is set out in section 42 of the 1982 Act. It provides:

. . . (2) The following provisions of this section determine where a corporation or association has its seat—(a) for the purposes of Article 53 (which for the purposes of the 1968 Convention equates the domicile of such a body with its seat); . . . (6) Subject to sub-section (7), a corporation or association has its seat in a state other than the United Kingdom if and only if—(a) it was incorporated or found under the law of that state and has its registered office or some other official address there; or (b) its central management and control is exercised in that state.

Sub-section (7) provides that a corporation or association shall not be regarded as having its seat in a contracting State, other than the United Kingdom, if the courts of that State would not regard it as having its seat there.

The material facts in the instant case were not disputed. Deich was incorporated in the Republic of Panama. The central management and control of Deich was exercised in the Federal Republic of Germany. The courts of the Federal Republic would regard Deich as having its seat there. The plaintiffs' contention was that a corporation or association can only have one seat, Deich's seat being in Panama by virtue of section 42(6)(a) of the Act. The contention was emphatically rejected by Neill and Stuart-Smith LJJ, although Sir Denys Buckley expressed some doubts. Neill LJ said:

It seems to me to be quite clear from section 42(3) [which makes parallel alternative provision with regard to a seat within the United Kingdom] and section 42(6) [above] that for the purposes of the Act of 1982 a corporation may satisfy the statutory test in relation to more than one state.[47]

His Lordship went on to mention that Articles 21 and 22 of the Convention are in fact designed to deal with cases where related actions are being brought in the courts of different contracting States. Sir Denys Buckley declined to express an opinion as to whether a corporation or association could have its seat in more than one *contracting State*, and indeed, found it unnecessary to do so for the purposes of the instant appeal as Panama is not a contracting State.

The third issue before the Court of Appeal derived from the plaintiffs' further argument that, even if a German court would have jurisdiction, an English court could also exercise jurisdiction by virtue of Article 57 of the 1968 Convention. That Article is in the following terms:

This Convention shall not affect any conventions to which the Contracting States are or will be parties and which, in relation to particular matters, govern jurisdiction or the recognition or enforcement of judgments . . . .

When the United Kingdom acceded to the 1968 Convention it was (and still is) a party to the 1952 International Convention for the Unification of Certain Rules relating to the Arrest of Seagoing Ships (implemented by sections 20 and 21 of the Supreme Court Act 1981). Article 7 of that 1952 Convention provides that the courts of the country in which a ship is arrested shall have jurisdiction to determine

47 Ibid. 488.

the case on its merits. It was common ground that, if it were not for the 1968 Convention, the jurisdiction of the High Court in the instant case would have to be based upon sections 20 and 21 of the Supreme Court Act 1981. Section 9 of the 1982 Act, so far as material, provides:

(1) The provisions of Title VII of the 1968 Convention (relationship between that convention and other conventions to which contracting states are or may become parties) shall have effect in relation to—(*a*) any statutory provision, whenever passed or made, implementing any such other convention in the United Kingdom; and (*b*) any rule of law so far as it has the effect of so implementing any such other convention, as they have effect in relation to that other convention itself.

The scope of Article 7 of the 1952 Convention is limited to cases of 'arrest'. *The Deichland* had not been arrested. To the extent that the High Court's jurisdiction under sections 20 and 21 was available even in the absence of actual arrest it could not, therefore, be said to be 'implementing' the 1952 Convention. Accordingly Article 57 of the 1968 Convention could have no bearing upon the facts of the instant case. Neill LJ said:

It is common ground that if it were not for the 1968 Convention the High Court would have jurisdiction to try this action and that this jurisdiction is derived from section 20 and section 21 of the Act of 1981 (formerly section 1 and section 3 of the Act of 1956). In my view, however, as the jurisdiction given by article 7 of the 1952 Convention is governed by the word 'arrest' it is not permissible for the purpose of applying section 9 of the Act of 1982 to treat any part of the High Court's jurisdiction other than the 'arrest' jurisdiction as being based on a statutory provision implementing the 1952 Convention.[48]

The general approach of the Court of Appeal to all of the three issues presented to it in *The Deichland* is intellectually sympathetic (as distinct from merely emotionally sympathetic, let alone unsympathetic) to the international dimension. The Brussels Convention is no longer seen as something of an anomaly, albeit an important one, but rather as an intrinsic, albeit distinctive, ingredient of *forum* jurisprudence. This is as welcome as it is important: it bodes well for the future,— especially as, not only is the future likely to embrace the 1988 Lugano Parallel Convention (already signed by a number of EEC and EFTA members), but also it could hold out possibilities of even wider political and geographic scope.

The willingness of the Court to look behind the historic pattern of English law so as to be able to hold that Deich was being 'sued' is clearly indicative of its general approach.

Again, holding that a corporation or association can have its seat, and thus be regarded as domiciled, in more than one place accords with the realities of international trade. The actual decision in *The Deichland*, if narrowly regarded, was that domicile in a non-contracting State (Panama) did not preclude domicile for Convention purposes in a contracting State (Germany). This was as far as Sir Denys Buckley was able to go. The majority was, however, clearly willing to contemplate the possibility of a corporation or association having a domicile in more than one contracting State. Sir Denys Buckley's reservations seem to have stemmed from the circumstance that analogous questions could arise, as to the possibility of a corporation or association domiciled in the United Kingdom being regarded as domiciled elsewhere as well, or as to the possibility of a corporation or association having a domicile in one part of the United Kingdom being regarded as

[48] Ibid. 491.

domiciled in another part as well. His Lordship thought that in such analogous cases 'different considerations may possibly apply which we have not explored'.[49] He added, however, that: 'If I thought it necessary to decide this question on section 42(6) at this stage, I should, as at present advised, be inclined to do so in Deich's favour'.[50] It is submitted, with respect, that, even if different considerations might bear upon a holding of concurrent domicile in two parts of the United Kingdom (although why even this is so is not immediately obvious), it is hard to see why a differentiation should be made, either on the basis that one of the countries involved is the United Kingdom, or on the basis that (as in *The Deichland* itself) one of them is a non-contracting State.

Finally it may be observed that the Court of Appeal's strict and sophisticated interpretation of Article 57 and of section 9, with a consequential denial of jurisdiction to the English Admiralty court,[51] again manifests a willingness to accord primacy to the policies and to the purposes of the Brussels Convention.

Provision of evidence for foreign courts—foreign revenue laws

Case No. 4. The facts giving rise to the two consolidated appeals recently dealt with by the House of Lords in *In re Norway's Application (Nos. 1 and 2)*[52] were as follows. A county tax committee in Norway had raised a supplementary retrospective tax assessment against the estate of the deceased, a Norwegian who had resided in Norway, on the ground that he had failed to declare a large part of his assets. These assets were alleged to include the assets of a Panamanian company. Shares in that company formed part of a trust, and it was alleged that the deceased was a settlor, or in control, of that trust, and that he was accordingly the beneficial owner of the assets of the Panamanian company. The deceased's estate brought an action in Norway against the State of Norway seeking to have the assessment set aside. The Norwegian court addressed letters rogatory to the English High Court requesting the oral examination of two witnesses in England. Lazards appear to have acted as bankers to the trust. One of the witnesses was a director of Lazards, and the other was one of their senior employees, who had been an official of the Panamanian company. The State of Norway made its application to a Master in Chambers under the Evidence (Proceedings in Other Jurisdictions) Act 1975, section 1, for an order requiring the two witnesses to give the evidence sought; and the deceased's estate supported the application. The matter eventually reached the House of Lords, the Court of Appeal having held that the court had no jurisdiction under the Act because the Norwegian proceedings were not 'proceedings in a civil or commercial matter' for the purposes of the Act. Both the State of Norway and the deceased's estate appealed. The House of Lords allowed the appeal.

The leading judgment (in which Lords Keith of Kinkel, Brandon of Oakbrook,

---

[49] Ibid. 499.

[50] Ibid.

[51] The consequences of this approach need not be as dire as counsel had suggested for, as Stuart-Smith LJ pointed out at p. 497: 'If a plaintiff for some reason is determined to litigate in the English Admiralty Court he can easily secure this; either he arrests the ship, or he secures express agreement by the defendant owner or demise charterer to submit to the jurisdiction of the English court to avoid arrest, no doubt at the same time obtaining security. In the present case the plaintiffs did neither of these things'.

[52] [1989] 2 WLR 458.

Griffiths and Lowry concurred) is that of Lord Goff of Chieveley. His Lordship identified four issues that had emerged in the course of argument:

First, the State of Norway challenged the decision of the Court of Appeal that the English court had no jurisdiction to entertain its application. The witnesses, while seeking to uphold the decision of the Court of Appeal on that point, submitted, in the alternative, that the State of Norway's application should in any event be dismissed, either as 'tax-gathering' and as such inconsistent with the well-known principle in *Government of India* v. *Taylor* [1955] A.C. 491; or on the ground that it constituted an illegitimate 'fishing expedition'; or because it compelled the witnesses to break their duty of confidentiality as bankers.[53]

Having found in favour of the State of Norway (and the deceased's estate) on the first two issues, Lord Goff dealt quite shortly with the last two, namely those concerned with 'fishing' and with confidentiality.

The allegation of 'fishing' related to only one of the letters of request. His Lordship, rejecting this allegation, took the view that it 'was in substance a request for what, by English law, would be regarded as assistance in obtaining evidence'.[54]

With regard to the breach of confidence argument Lord Goff said:

It is accepted on both sides that the question of confidentiality can only be answered by the court undertaking a balancing exercise, weighing on the one hand the public interest in preserving the confidentiality owed by the witnesses as bankers to their customers, and on the other hand the public interest in the English courts assisting the Norwegian court in obtaining evidence in this country.[55]

The trial judge had performed this balancing exercise, and as a result had rejected the submission made by the two witnesses but had made an order subject to certain conditions. The Court of Appeal had unanimously decided not to disturb the judge's exercise of discretion on the point. 'In these circumstances', said Lord Goff, 'it would require cogent reasons to persuade your Lordships to interfere with the judge's decision. For my part, I do not consider that your Lordships should, in the present case, take that unusual step.'[56]

The principal interest of the case lies in the way in which the first and second of the issues listed by Lord Goff were dealt with by the House.

The first of these was as to whether the proceedings in the Norwegian court were civil proceedings within section 1(*b*) of the 1975 Act, bearing in mind the definition of 'civil proceedings' in section 9(1) of that Act. Section 1 provides that one of the pre-conditions, for the exercise by a United Kingdom court of powers conferred upon it by the Act to grant an application for the obtaining of evidence, is that the court is satisfied'....(*b*) that the evidence to which the application relates is to be obtained for the purposes of civil proceedings which either have been instituted before the requesting court or whose institution before that court is contemplated...'. Section 9(1) provides: 'In this Act—"civil proceedings", in relation to the requesting court, means proceedings in any civil or commercial matter...'.

After noting that a major purpose of the 1975 Act was to give effect to the Hague Convention of 1970 relating to the Taking of Evidence Abroad in Civil and Commercial Matters, Lord Goff drew attention to the fact that the Act was not the first piece of legislation dealing with jurisdiction to provide evidence in response to a

[53] Ibid. 463.
[54] Ibid. 479.
[55] Ibid.
[56] Ibid. 480.

request by a court sitting in another jurisdiction, and that indeed the expression 'civil or commercial matter' was used in the earliest statute concerned with the subject, namely the Foreign Tribunals Evidence Act 1856. His Lordship felt able to have recourse to earlier legislation for the purpose of construing the 1975 Act because that Act was passed, not only for the purpose of accommodating the 1970 Hague Convention, but also in order to consolidate in one statute the relevant powers of superior courts in various parts of the United Kingdom previously contained in a multiplicity of Acts of Parliament. Moreover, the scope of the 1975 Act, like some of its predecessors, extends beyond countries party to the 1970 Convention. Lord Goff concluded: 'In these circumstances, in considering the scope of the jurisdiction conferred by the Act of 1975, it is, in my opinion, both legitimate and appropriate to have regard to the legislative history of the Act'.[57] His Lordship then surveyed in some detail the relevant parts of the earlier legislation. He considered, too, the pattern of other international conventions dealing with the subject matter and to which the United Kingdom has been and/or still is a party. Finally his Lordship added that:

It is, in my opinion, important to bear in mind, when ascertaining the jurisdiction conferred on the courts of the United Kingdom by the Act, its impact upon the relationship between the courts of this country and the courts of Commonwealth countries, with whom, as fellow members of the largest legal family in the world, we enjoy the closest of legal ties.[58]

His Lordship was thus, for a variety of reasons, unable to accept that the expression 'proceedings in any civil or commercial matter' in section 9(1) of the 1975 Act should be accorded a new and more restricted meaning. In this context he added:

Lastly the Act provides, consistently with the law as it has stood for over 100 years (since section 24 of the Act of 1870), for courts in the United Kingdom to have jurisdiction to assist courts in other countries by obtaining evidence in criminal proceedings. This power has nothing to do with private law at all; and it would be surprising if Parliament was expressly to perpetuate the power in relation to criminal proceedings, which are par excellence proceedings brought by the foreign state itself, and at the same time be held, by reference to section 9(1), to have restricted the meaning of the words 'civil or commercial matter' by excluding from them what are recognised (in varying forms) as public law cases by the law of certain states. Indeed, the argument for the witnesses leads to the remarkable conclusion that, if penal proceedings in the requesting court are categorised as criminal proceedings, the English court can assist under section 5; but if they are not criminal proceedings, the English court has no jurisdiction to assist.[59]

His Lordship considered the position in some civil law jurisdictions, but concluded that it was difficult to identify by reference to such systems any internationally acceptable definition of the words 'civil or commercial matters'.[60] His Lordship continued: 'There remains therefore the question how they should be construed; and to answer that question it is first necessary to consider by reference to which system of law this question should be answered'.[61] Lord Goff held, con-

---

[57] Ibid. 466.
[58] Ibid. 469.
[59] Ibid. 470–1.
[60] His Lordship added, too, (p. 472) that no assistance could be drawn from the 1968 Convention on Jurisdiction and the Enforcement of Judgments in Civil and Commercial Matters (the 'Brussels Convention').
[61] Ibid. 473.

sistently with what had been the approach taken pursuant to the 1856 Act, that jurisdiction can only be established if the relevant proceedings are regarded as proceedings in a civil or commercial matter both under the law of the requesting State and under the law of the United Kingdom.

In the instant case the trial judge had concluded on the evidence before him that under Norwegian law the proceedings in Norway would be classified as proceedings in a civil matter. In this context Lord Goff noted that the judge's conclusion was

consistent with the view expressed by Lord Diplock in the *Westinghouse* case [1978] A.C. 547, 633–634, that in the ordinary way the English court should be prepared to accept the statement of the requesting court that the evidence is required for the purpose of civil proceedings. It is appropriate that the requesting court should have regard to its own ordinary approach to these matters, without indulging in an analysis which is inappropriate in its own system. In this way, the Act of 1975 can be made to work sensibly in relation to all countries in the world, common law countries and civil law countries alike, without requiring any of them to act in any way which is foreign to its own way of thinking; and expert evidence will, in the vast majority of cases, be unnecessary.[62]

Turning to the position under English law, his Lordship said:

I have no doubt that, under English law, the words in section 9(1) should be given their ordinary meaning, so that proceedings in any civil matter should include all proceedings other than criminal proceedings, and proceedings in any commercial matter should be treated as falling within proceedings in civil matters. On this simple approach, I do not see why the expression should be read as excluding proceedings in a fiscal matter; so that the High Court can have jurisdiction in respect of such a matter under the Act of 1975.[63]

The only comment now submitted on this aspect of the holding in *In re Norway's Application (Nos. 1 and 2)* is that, even if support had not been found in historical precedent based on earlier legislation and in other quarters, and even if there had been evidence of the existence of an internationally acceptable definition of 'civil or commercial matters' indicating the contrary, the case for nevertheless treating 'civil proceedings' in section 1 of the 1975 Act as covering fiscal matters would still have been very strong,—very strong both in point of statutory construction and in point of policy. The relevant wording of section 1 is itself unqualified. Moreover, section 9(1) defines 'civil proceedings' as 'proceedings in *any* civil *or* commercial matter'.[64] As for policy considerations, it would (as Lord Goff pointed out)[65] be remarkable indeed if the Act as a whole were to be seen as applying, not only to foreign civil 'private law' cases, but also to foreign criminal proceedings,[66] and yet not to foreign revenue cases.

The second major issue before their Lordships' House, was as to whether the application fell within inhibitions concerning the enforcement of foreign revenue laws which received the *imprimatur* of the House in *Government of India* v. *Taylor*.[67] In this context his Lordship first took the opportunity to clarify (i.e. correct) the formulation of the relevant Rule in *Dicey and Morris*.[68] That Rule (Rule

[62] Ibid. 474–5.
[63] Ibid. 475.
[64] Italics supplied.
[65] Ibid. 471.
[66] See section 5 of the Act.
[67] [1955] AC 491.
[68] *The Conflict of Laws* (11th edn., 1987), p. 100.

3) runs as follows: 'English courts *have no jurisdiction* to entertain an action: (1) for the enforcement, either directly or indirectly, of a penal, revenue or other public law of a foreign state; (2) founded upon an act of state'.[69] Lord Goff said that, whatever its theoretical basis, 'the rule cannot, in my view, go to the jurisdiction of the English court. What the English court does is simply to decline in such cases to exercise its jurisdiction, and on that basis the relevant proceedings will be either struck out or dismissed.'[70] There was, therefore, no basis upon which the *jurisdiction* conferred by section 1 of the 1975 Act could be read as being qualified by the principle associated with *Government of India* v. *Taylor*.

There remained, however, the further question as to whether

> . . . given that the jurisdiction is unqualified, the English courts should decline to exercise that jurisdiction in the case of letters of request for assistance in relation to civil proceedings concerned with the enforcement of the revenue laws of the requesting state. It can be argued that they should decline to do so, as a matter of judicial discretion, on the basis that direct or indirect enforcement of foreign revenue laws constitutes an invasion of the sovereignty of this country, and is contrary to a fundamental rule of English law.[71]

His Lordship's use of the phrase 'as a matter of discretion' is to be noted and welcomed.

To the extent that the application was being made or supported by the taxpayer (here the deceased's estate), to grant it might be seen as not involving the enforcement, direct or indirect, of a foreign revenue law. However, as the State of Norway was also seeking the assistance of the English court, the general issue had to be faced. Lord Goff said: 'It is plain that the present case is not concerned with the direct enforcement of the revenue laws of the State of Norway. Is it concerned with their indirect enforcement? I do not think so.'[72] The distinction between indirect enforcement and mere recognition has long been regarded as somewhat elusive.[73] At one time it might have appeared that the distinction had crystallized into a rule of thumb the gist of which was that an English court will not proceed in a way which makes it significantly more likely that the tax will be paid. However, on this basis it would seem that the granting of the application made by the State of Norway would involve indirect enforcement of the Norwegian revenue law. Lord Goff avoids this conclusion by invoking a further limitation upon the scope of the doctrine. That limitation is in terms of territoriality. His Lordship said: 'I cannot see any extra-territorial exercise of sovereign authority in seeking the assistance of the courts of this country in obtaining evidence which will be used for the enforcement of the revenue laws of Norway in Norway itself'.[74] To illustrate his point Lord Goff continued:

> Let it be supposed, for example, that in *Attorney-General of New Zealand* v. *Ortiz* [1984] A.C. 1, the case was not one of New Zealand seeking to enforce its claim in this country, but of seeking the assistance of the English courts to obtain evidence to enforce its claim in New Zealand. I find it very difficult to imagine that such an application would have been refused.[75]

---

[69] Italics supplied.
[70] [1989] 2 WLR 458, 476–7.
[71] Ibid. 477.
[72] Ibid. 478.
[73] See, e.g., Carter, *Cambridge Law Journal*, 48 (1989), pp. 417 ff.
[74] [1989] 2 WLR 458, 478.
[75] Ibid.

In the modern world justification for anything approaching a blanket refusal on the part of British courts to enforce foreign revenue laws *per se* is far from clear. Indeed, authority for the doctrine before the decision of the House of Lords in *Government of India* v. *Taylor* was slender. There are three ways in which the decision and the reasoning in *In re Norway's Application (Nos. 1 and 2)* would appear to mark welcome curtailment of its scope. First, it is made clear that it does not go to the jurisdiction of the English court. Secondly, the application of the doctrine would appear to be discretionary rather than mandatory. Thirdly, indirect enforcement will be countenanced provided it is likely to be effective only in the foreign country concerned.

Statutes in private international law

Case No. 5. There is a generally accepted and quite strong, although not irrebuttable, presumption that a *forum* statute is not to be accorded what may be loosely designated 'extra-territorial' effect. This means that the provisions of a statute will usually be regarded as inapplicable in a private international law case in which the *lex causae* is other than the domestic law of the *forum*. The operation of this presumption will accord in the great majority of cases with the likely intention of the legislature.

The operation of the presumption will, of course, be severely curtailed if the prime purpose of a statute is to change a rule of private international law; such a statute was, for example, the Foreign Limitation Periods Act 1984, the general effect of which was that questions of limitation must be characterized for choice of law purposes as substantive rather than (as had been the position at common law) procedural. Moreover, and apart from statutes of that explicit and relatively rare type, the presumption, not being irrebuttable, may be rebutted in relation to a particular statute. In the final analysis the matter is one of statutory construction. A statute, although essentially concerned with the domestic law of the *forum*, may be interpreted as having wider applicability. It may be construed as having effect in some cases in which the *lex causae* is foreign. A particular problem liable to arise in this context derives from the draftsman's use of general words. Should such words be accorded a literal interpretation, thereby giving the provision in which they occur 'extra-territorial' effect? To do so would often thwart the likely intention of the legislator. An illustration of this danger can be seen in the case of *Re Cutcliffe's Will Trusts*.[76] There the court was concerned with the interpretation of section 75(5) of the Settled Land Act 1925, which (re-enacting section 22(5) of the Settled Land Act 1882) provides that capital money arising under the Act, while remaining uninvested or unapplied, and securities on which an investment of any such capital money is made 'shall for all purpose of disposition, transmission and devaluation be considered as land'. The phrase 'all purposes' was held to include the purposes of characterization, and thus of choice of law, in private international law. The phrase, particularly the use of the word 'all', literally construed, could hardly be more general; but there is certainly room for the view that in 1882,[77] when drawing up a long and complex statute effecting major changes in the English

---

[76] [1940] Ch. 565.
[77] i.e. 14 years before even the first edition of *Dicey* had been published!

law of real property, neither Parliament nor the draftsmen gave a single thought to problems of the conflict of laws.

In the recent case of *Holmes* v. *Bangladesh Biman Corporation*[78] the House of Lords has had occasion to address itself to the general problem. In that case the plaintiff was the widow and the executor of a passenger who had been killed when an aircraft operated by the defendant airline had crashed on an internal domestic flight in Bangladesh. Her action was brought under the Fatal Accidents Act 1976 on behalf of herself and her children, and under the Law Reform (Miscellaneous Provisions) Act 1934 on behalf of her husband's estate. The defendant airline's liability not being in dispute, the only issue was as to the amount of damages recoverable. Under the law of Bangladesh they would be limited to £913. On the other hand, if an Order made in 1967 pursuant to the Carriage by Air Act 1961 were to be applied, damages might be recovered up to £83,763. The House of Lords (reversing the trial judge and the Court of Appeal) unanimously held that the 1967 Order was not applicable and that the law of Bangladesh fell to be applied. Damages were thus restricted to £913.

The House reached this conclusion on the basis of construction of section 10(1) of the 1961 Act. That sub-section authorized delegated legislation by Order in Council in relation to 'carriage by air...of such descriptions as may be specified in the Order'. These words, the House of Lords held, should despite their generality be construed as not covering carriage in which the places of departure and of destination and any agreed stopping places were all within the territory of a single foreign State. It naturally followed that the 1967 Order made pursuant to the Act could not be given a wider scope. The plaintiff could not, therefore, rely upon the Order in the instant case.

The Preamble to the Carriage by Air Act 1961 runs thus:

An Act to give effect to the Convention concerning international carriage by air known as 'the Warsaw Convention as amended at The Hague, 1955', to enable the rules contained in that Convention to be applied, with or without modification, in other cases and, in particular, to non-international carriage by air; and for connected purposes.

Although the facts of *Holmes* v. *Bangladesh Biman Corporation* clearly fell outside the scope of the Warsaw and Hague Conventions, the question was as to whether they nevertheless fell within the wider scope of the Act.

The key words in section 10(1) of the Act, 'carriage by air', are, of course, themselves unqualified. The House of Lords, having cited a considerable, if somewhat sporadic, range of authority, reiterated that this circumstance does not preclude qualification. Amongst the authority cited both by Lord Bridge of Harwich[79] and by Lord Jauncey of Tullichettle[80] were words of Brett LJ and of Cotton LJ in *Ex parte Blain*[81] (a case concerned with jurisdiction). Brett LJ said:

It is said that the case is literally within the words of the statute, and so, no doubt, it is. But does it follow that, because a case is literally within the words of a statute of any country, therefore it is within the jurisdiction of the courts of that country? Certainly not.[82]

---

[78] [1989] AC 1112.
[79] Ibid. 1128.
[80] Ibid. 1147.
[81] (1879) 12 Ch.D. 522.
[82] At p. 528.

Cotton LJ said:

All we have to do is to interpret an Act of Parliament which uses a general word, and we have to say how that word is to be limited, when of necessity there must be some limitation.[83]

The principal and sufficient source of necessity must be the need to comply with the presumed intention of the legislator.

The unexpressed intention of the legislator may often be elusive. However, that intention in relation to facts such as those presented in the instant case would seem relatively clear. All the significant elements, except the circumstance that the plaintiff's husband was only a visitor to Bangladesh, were exclusively connected with that country. Lord Bridge did, however, consider what the position would have been in several alternative and less clear-cut non-Convention cases. He concluded that section 10(1) should be construed so as to cover (1) cases in which the place of departure, the place of destination, and any agreed stopping place, are all within the United Kingdom or other British territory, and (2) cases in which at least one of these places is in a foreign State and at least one is in the United Kingdom or other British territory. On the other hand, not only cases (such as the instant case) in which all of the relevant places are in a single foreign country, but also those in which the places of departure and destination are in different foreign States with no agreed stopping place in the United Kingdom or other British territory, should be regarded as outside the scope of the section. To the extent that these conclusions represent *obiter dicta* they do not as a matter of authority preclude the possibility of further elaboration in future so as to take account in some situations of factors such as the nationality, domicile and residence of the passenger, the nationality and place of business of the airline and the identity of the proper law of the contract of carriage. On the other hand it must be recognized that the dominant theme running through Lord Bridge's analysis is territoriality: *locus regit actum*.

In the light of their Lordships' holding in *Holmes* v. *Bangladesh Biman Corporation* that section 10 of the Carriage by Air Act 1961 was not applicable in the circumstances of the case, it was seen as automatically following that the domestic law of Bangladesh fell to be applied. It is perhaps permissible for a commentator to reflect upon why this should be so.

The plaintiff's action under the Fatal Accidents Act 1976 was seemingly framed in tort. The only issue was as to the extent of compensation. Could an argument be put that this issue ought to have been determined by reference to English domestic law in the same way as this type of issue was determined in *Boys* v. *Chaplin*?[84] If reliance were to be placed upon the reasoning in that case of Lord Guest, that of Lord Donovan or that of Lord Pearson, the argument would seem to be a strong one. (Lord Guest had seen the issue as one of procedure; Lord Donovan had seen fit to invoke the rule that only remedies known to the *forum* are available; and Lord Pearson had held that, as the act was not justifiable under Maltese law, the *lex loci delicti*, the *lex fori* fell to be applied.) On the other hand, if (as could well be desirable[85]) the true *ratio* of *Boys* v. *Chaplin* is to be found in the judgment of Lord Wilberforce supported by that of Lord Hodson, the *Holmes* case is clearly distinguishable on its facts. Whereas in *Boys* v. *Chaplin* both parties were British

---

[83] At pp. 531–2.
[84] [1971] AC. 356.
[85] See comments in this *Year Book*, 52 (1981), pp. 22–6.

nationals, domiciled and usually resident in England, the only connection with Malta being that the accident occurred there, in the *Holmes* case, the *locus delicti* was Bangladesh and the defendant was a Bangladesh airline, the only connection with England seemingly being that the plaintiff and her deceased husband were English. In *Boys* v. *Chaplin* the 'centre of gravity' of the fact situation was in England, but in *Holmes* v. *Biman Corporation*, it was in Bangladesh.

Moreover, could a further point be taken regarding the application of the law of Bangladesh? In the *Holmes* case Lord Bridge at the beginning of his judgment said: 'Under the terms of the contract between Mr. Holmes and the airline and in accordance with the relevant Bangladesh legislation applicable to carriage by air in Bangladesh the damages the widow could recover would be limited to £913'.[86] The proper law of the contract of carriage was clearly the law of Bangladesh. To the extent that, as indicated by Lord Bridge, the limitation upon recovery was contractual, an issue could be raised akin to that which was before the Court of Appeal in *Sayers* v. *International Drilling Co.*[87] There the Court of Appeal appears to have held that the extent to which tortious liability, which arises in the course of the performance of a contract, can be limited by contract is to be determined by reference to the proper law of the contract. Even if, therefore, in the absence of a contractual limitation, recovery would have been allowable by reference to English law, the limitation imposed under the Bangladesh contract would override this. Lord Bridge's express reference to 'the terms of the contract' in this connection perhaps suggests that it was to the law of Bangladesh *qua* proper law of the contract that resort was in effect being had. On this assumption the holding accords with the holding of the majority of the Court of Appeal in the *Sayers* case.

Contract: interaction of the proper law and the lex loci solutionis

Case No. 6. In the recent case of *Libyan Arab Foreign Bank* v. *Bankers Trust Co.*[88] Staughton J said:

There is no dispute as to the general principles involved. Performance of a contract is excused if (i) it has become illegal by the proper law of the contract, or (ii) it necessarily involves doing an act which is unlawful by the law of the place where the act has to be done.[89]

With these words may be contrasted the wording of *Dicey and Morris*'s Rule 184, Exception 1. That Exception runs thus:

A contract (whether lawful by its proper law or not) is, in general, invalid in so far as the performance of it is unlawful by the law of the country where the contract is to be performed (*lex loci solutionis*).[90]

This in its turn is to be contrasted with words of Diplock LJ (as he then was) in *Mackender* v. *Feldia AG*:[91]

A fortiori a contract which is not illegal by its proper law, but requires for its performance an act to be done which would be illegal under the law of the country where the act is

---

[86] [1989] AC 1112, 1124.
[87] [1971] 1 WLR 1176.
[88] [1989] QB 728.
[89] Ibid. 743.
[90] Dicey and Morris, *The Conflict of Laws* (11th edn., 1987), p. 1218.
[91] [1967] 2 QB 590.

required to be done, is not void. It is a contract which is, in a particular respect only, unenforceable in the English courts. This is to be contrasted with an agreement which under its proper law is illegal and incapable of giving rise to legally enforceable rights and liabilities under that law. Since the foreign proper law must be looked to for the legal effects of the agreement, such an agreement may properly be said to be void, i.e., not to be a contract at all.[92]

These three statements taken together contain and imply some contradictions. Before commenting more specifically upon the *Libyan Arab Bank* case itself, the following rationalization is submitted.

First, as regards illegality under the proper law, principle surely requires that a *forum* should endeavour to treat the effects of such illegality in the same way as they would be treated under the proper law itself. This should be so whether the effect under that law is to render the contract a total nullity, to render it only partially void by virtue of some such doctrine as severance, or in the case of a subsequent illegality to regard the contract as discharged and, if so, on what terms. Staughton J's unqualified statement that performance is excused if a contract has become illegal by its proper law must therefore be regarded as no more than a useful generalization.

More controversial is the situation in which the contract is and remains entirely valid and lawful under the proper law, but performance of it, in the words of Staughton J, 'necessarily involves doing an act which is unlawful by the law of the place where the act has to be done'.[93] In such circumstances according to the *Dicey and Morris* Exception the contract is to this extent 'in general, invalid'. This is in direct conflict with the Diplock analysis in *Mackender* v. *Feldia AG*[94] and differs from Staughton J's statement that in such circumstances 'performance' is 'excused'.

One approach to the problem would be to look to the proper law in order to ascertain the effect of illegality under the *lex loci solutionis*. There is, however, seemingly little support for this approach, which would involve introduction of a type of *renvoi* into the private international law of contract.

Given, therefore, that the English *forum* must itself determine the matter, it is, of course, to be remembered that it is barely credible that an English court would ever in its discretion order specific performance in the circumstances under consideration. The true question is as to whether damages should be available. Why, it could pertinently be asked in this context, should a party to a contract (entirely valid under its proper law), who has perhaps already had some benefit from the other party's performance, not be required to make money compensation in lieu of performance, this latter being prohibited by the *lex loci solutionis*? There could occasionally be an answer in terms of public policy, but this will not be the common case. The pertinence of the general question is high-lighted where the contractual obligation itself is to pay money,—but to do so in one place rather than another. This was the policy precipice from which Staughton J was able to step back in *Libyan Arab Foreign Bank* v. *Bankers Trust Co.*

The simplified facts of that case were as follows. The plaintiffs, a Libyan bank, had a call account with the London branch of the defendants, an American bank. They also had a demand account with the defendant bank's New York branch. The contractual arrangements were that the plaintiffs would maintain a peg balance of

[92] Ibid. 601.
[93] [1989] QB 728, 743.
[94] Above.

$500,000 in the New York account; and that each day in the morning and again at 2 p.m. funds would be transferred to or from London in order to maintain this balance. Transfers due under this arrangement were not in fact made at 2 p.m. on 7 January 1986 or at 2 p.m. on 8 January 1986. At 4 p.m. on the latter date the President of the United States signed an executive order freezing all Libyan property in the United States or in the possession or control of United States persons including overseas branches of United States persons. The plaintiff bank instituted proceedings in England demanding *inter alia* (1) payment of $131m., this being the balance actually standing to the credit of the London account at the close of business on 8 January 1986, and (2) payment of a further $161m., this being the net loss to the London account resulting from the failures to transfer on 7 and 8 January 1986. Alternatively, they claimed (*inter alia*) that their contract with the Bankers Trust had been frustrated with the consequence that they were entitled to the sums claimed by virtue of the Law Reform (Frustrated Contracts) Act 1943, or as a restitutionary remedy at common law.

Staughton J's judgment is interesting and important in several ways.

First, his Lordship held that, although the contract out of which the proceedings arose was a single contract, it was a contract with a split proper law, being governed in part by English law and in part by the law of New York. Having rejected both the notion of two separate contracts as being 'artificial and unattractive', and the 'device of a collateral contract' as involving 'some cost to logic and consistency', the learned judge said: 'It is possible, although unusual, for a contract to have a split proper law'.[95] The splitting of the proper law in the instant case was a consequence of Staughton J's application of the general rule that a 'contract between a bank and its customer is governed by the law of the place where the account is kept, in the absence of agreement to the contrary'.[96] Considerations of simplicity, clarity and policy will usually indicate that the proper law of a contract be regarded as a single identifiable law. This has been emphasized more than once in English case law. For instance, Lord MacDermott said in the House of Lords in *Kahler* v. *Midland Bank Ltd.*: 'The courts of this country will not split the contract...readily and without good reason'.[97] At the same time there must occasionally be situations in which these considerations are largely negatived. The contract under consideration in *Libyan Arab Foreign Bank* v. *Bankers Trust Co.* provides an illustration. It is to be remembered, too, that parties can, even in a situation of this type, avoid splitting by a clear and reasonable contractual choice of a single applicable law. In the instant case, had the parties made an express, or otherwise clear, choice of the law of New York as the law governing the whole pattern of their contractual transaction, effect could have been given to that choice. In the absence of such a choice Staughton J was able to 'hold that the rights and obligations of the parties in respect of the London account were governed by English law'.[98]

The learned judge held that the plaintiffs' claim under the contract should succeed. He was, therefore, able to deal quite briefly with what he saw as their 'paradoxical' alternative argument that the contract had been frustrated, and that they were entitled to succeed by virtue of the Law Reform (Frustrated Contracts) Act 1943. Questions relating to discharge of contractual obligations, including dis-

[95] Ibid. 747.
[96] Ibid. 746.
[97] [1950] AC 24, 42.
[98] [1989] QB 728, 748.

charge by frustration or its foreign equivalent, are governed by the proper law. The application of this principle could *prima facie* present difficulty in the case of a contract with more than one proper law. The plaintiffs' argument was obviously based upon the assumption that the relevant proper law was English law, and Staughton J seems to have dealt with the matter on this assumption. He held that the contract had not been discharged because the effect of the Presidential order was merely to suspend rather than to extinguish the defendants' obligation to repay. Presumably (*sed quaere*) his Lordship would have taken the same view even if there had been clear and uncontradicted expert evidence that under the law of New York the effect of the Presidential decree was to discharge the contract totally. The logic of two proper laws would be partial 'total' discharge of contractual obligations!

The plaintiffs' alternative claim to restitution at common law, seemingly also being dealt with by reference to English common law, was similarly rejected: the consideration given by the defendants had not wholly failed because their obligation 'to repay one day, and meanwhile to credit interest to the account'[99] remained.

The central interest and importance of *Libyan Arab Foreign Bank* v. *Bankers Trust Co.* lies in Staughton J's holding that the plaintiffs were entitled under the contract to repayment of the sums of $131m. and $161m., the Presidential decree notwithstanding. The issue here was, in Staughton J's words, as to whether repayment 'necessarily involves doing an act which is unlawful by the law of the place where the act has to be done'.[100] However, as his Lordship observed, there may 'be difficulty in ascertaining when performance of a contract "necessarily involves" doing an illegal act in another country'.[101] The payment of damages in England, even if it results from a failure to do something which would be illegal by the law of the place where it ought to have been done, will not *itself* involve doing something illegal in the place (England) where it is done. Staughton J, however, did not question conventional doctrine, namely that the effect of illegality under the *lex loci solutionis* is that performance is excused and not that an obligation to pay damages is substituted. Nevertheless, in the instant case, in so far as the plaintiffs' demand was for payment in cash (this being an assertion of a bank customer's fundamental right) in London, no illegal action in New York was 'necessarily involved'.

It is to be noted that had payment in cash in London not constituted valid performance of the defendants' obligation, the position could well have been different. Indeed Staughton J indicated[102] that, if the only permitted payment had been by issue of a banker's draft or banker's payment by the defendants to the plaintiffs, and even if that issue was in London and the instrument were cleared through dollar clearing, some action in New York could ultimately be required.

With regard to the position more generally, it is perhaps a matter for remark that, in the case of a contract entirely valid and lawful by its proper law, if the sum claimed is payable in the *forum* in accordance with the terms of the contract, it may be recovered there, but if the claim (perhaps for an identical sum) takes the form of a claim for damages resulting from failure to discharge an obligation elsewhere it cannot be entertained.

---

[99] Ibid. 772.
[100] Ibid. 743. See above.
[101] Ibid. 743.
[102] Ibid. 763.

A further matter dealt with[103] by Staughton J related to the currency in which payment was to be made. His Lordship noted that the contract contained no express term (and held that none could be implied) to the effect that payment could not be made in sterling. In these circumstances (at least) payment could be made in sterling if it was impracticable to pay in dollars.[104]

P. B. CARTER

[103] Ibid. 764–6.

[104] It would be churlish for this commentator not to admit that he has found it impracticable to do full justice within the confines of a short case note to the meticulously careful and detailed consideration of the various issues set out in Staughton J's 40-page judgment.

DECISIONS ON THE EUROPEAN CONVENTION ON HUMAN RIGHTS DURING 1989*

Right to respect for private life (Article 8)—the meaning of 'necessary in a democratic society' in Article 8(2)—the margin of appreciation in matters of morality—the meaning of 'victim' in Article 25—just satisfaction (Article 50)

Case No. 1. Norris case.[1] The Court held by 8 votes to 6 that the existence of legislation penalizing private homosexual activity between adults in the Republic of Ireland violated the applicant's rights under Article 8 of the European Convention. The Court also held unanimously that the Government should pay the applicant the sum of IR £14,962.49, less 7,390 French francs, in respect of his costs and expenses.

The applicant, Mr David Norris, was an active homosexual who had been campaigning for homosexual rights in Ireland since 1971 and was instrumental in setting up the Irish Gay Rights Movement in 1974. In 1977 he began proceedings in the Irish courts to contest the constitutionality of legislation under which certain homosexual acts committed between consenting adult males were criminal offences. The claim was unsuccessful and in 1980 the Supreme Court ruled that the legislation in question was constitutional.

In his application to the Commission in 1983 Mr Norris complained that the legislation violated his right to respect for his private life under Article 8 of the Convention, although he had never been charged with any offence under it. In its report in March 1987 the Commission concluded by 6 votes to 5 that there had been a breach of Article 8. The Commission then referred the case to the Court.

Before the Court could address the substantive issue, it first had to deal with an objection to the admissibility of the claim under Article 25. This provides that:

> The Commission may receive petitions . . . from any person . . . claiming to be the victim of a violation by one of the High Contracting Parties of the rights set forth in this Convention . . .

The Government argued that since Mr Norris had not been prosecuted for his homosexual activities (which were well known), he could not claim to be the 'victim' of any violation of his rights, but was seeking a review *in abstracto* of the law which it was not within the power of the Court or the Commission to supply.

It is clear from the Court's jurisprudence that Article 25 may not be used as the basis for an *actio popularis*, or to support a claim made *in abstracto* that a law contravenes the Convention. However, the Court has also often made the point that Article 25 'entitles individuals to contend that a law violated their rights by itself, in the absence of an individual measure of implementation, if they run the risk of being directly affected by it'.[2] The Court, like the Commission, considered that

---

* © Professor J.G. Merrills, 1990. My thanks are due to the Registrar of the Court for his co-operation in the preparation of these notes.

[1] European Court of Human Rights (ECHR), judgment of 26 October 1988, Series A, No. 142. This case was decided by the plenary Court.

[2] Judgment, para. 31. See also the *Johnston* case, Series A, No. 112, and this *Year Book*, 58 (1987), p. 463, and the *Marckx* case, Series A, No. 31, and this *Year Book*, 50 (1979), p. 260.

this was the situation here, just as it was in the *Dudgeon* case[3] in 1981, which concerned identical legislation then in force in Northern Ireland. It was true that there had been no prosecutions under the Irish legislation in recent years and that the risk of prosecution in the applicant's case appeared to be minimal. However, there was no stated policy that the legislation would not be enforced, and a law which remained on the Statute book could be enforced at any time. In the light of this, and the domestic court's finding that one of the effects of criminal sanctions is to put homosexuals under stress, the Court concluded that the applicant could be said to 'run the risk of being directly affected' by the legislation and thus qualified as a 'victim' for the purposes of Article 25.

The main point in the case concerned Article 8 which provides:

1. Everyone has the right to respect for his private . . . life . . .
2. There shall be no interference by a public authority with the exercise of this right except such as is in accordance with the law and necessary in a democratic society . . . for the protection of . . . morals . . .

The first question was whether Mr Norris had suffered an interference with his right to respect for his private life, contrary to Article 8(1). The Government submitted that he had not, and once more drew attention to the fact that the legislation was not enforced. The Court, however, decided that in this respect Mr Norris' position was again indistinguishable from that of the applicant in the *Dudgeon* case and therefore concluded that the maintenance in force of the legislation was enough to constitute an interference with the applicant's right to respect for his private life.

The next and most important question was whether the maintenance in force of the impugned legislation was 'necessary in a democratic society' for the protection of morals, which the applicant recognized was its legitimate aim. According to the Court's case law, to fulfil such a condition the interference must answer a pressing social need and be proportionate to the aim pursued. In the *Dudgeon* case the Court had rejected the argument that attitudes towards homosexuality demonstrated a pressing social need in Northern Ireland, and so in the present case the Irish Government adopted a different line of argument. Suggesting that the established criteria might be appropriate for testing restrictions imposed in the interests of national security, public order or the protection of public health, the Government submitted that they could not be applied to determine whether an interference was necessary for the protection of morals. For, according to the Government, the moral fibre of a democratic nation is a matter for its own institutions and so when dealing with a moral issue a Government should be allowed a wide degree of tolerance in its compliance with Article 8.

The Court, relying on its previous jurisprudence,[4] rejected the argument. Although it acknowledged that the national authorities enjoy a wide margin of appreciation in matters of morals, it was not prepared to grant the virtually unlimited discretion which the Government's argument appeared to demand. Emphasizing that it is the Court's duty to review a State's observance of its obligations, even in matters of morals, the Court found that the Government had adduced no convincing evidence to support retaining the impugned legislation. On

---

[3] ECHR, judgment of 22 October 1981, Series A, No. 45, and this *Year Book*, 52 (1981), p. 343.

[4] See the *Dudgeon* case (n. 3, above), the *Handyside* case, Series A, No. 24, and this *Year Book*, 48 (1976–7), p. 381, and more recently the *Müller* case, Series A, No. 133, and this *Year Book*, 59 (1988), p. 389.

the contrary, the authorities had refrained from enforcing the law without apparent injury to moral standards or provoking a demand for stricter enforcement. In these circumstances it could not be maintained that there was a 'pressing social need' for the legislation. Accordingly, since the interference was unjustified, there had been a breach of Article 8.

There remained the issue of just satisfaction under Article 50 which provides:

> If the Court finds that a decision or a measure taken by a legal authority or any other authority of a High Contracting Party is completely or partially in conflict with the obligations arising from the present Convention, and if the internal law of the said Party allows only partial reparation to be made for the consequences of this decision or measure, the decision of the Court shall, if necessary, afford just satisfaction to the injured party.

The applicant sought compensation for damage of an unspecified amount and reimbursement of his costs and expenses. On the compensation point the Court explained that to fulfil Article 53[5] it would be necessary for Ireland to amend its domestic legislation. In view of this the Court concluded that its finding of a breach of Article 8 constituted adequate just satisfaction without the need for compensation. As to costs and expenses, the applicant claimed that the taxed costs which he received in respect of the national proceedings did not fully cover his actual expenditure. However, since those costs had been assessed in accordance with the law of Ireland, the Court held that it had no power to reassess them. The applicant also claimed a sum in respect of the proceedings before the Convention institutions. The Court decided that the amount claimed satisfied the criteria laid down in its case law and unanimously awarded that sum, less the amount already received in legal aid.

The decision in this case contains no surprises, following as it does the Court's treatment of similar issues in the *Dudgeon* case. The six members of the Court who dissented did so on the ground that the applicant could not be regarded as a victim, an argument which the majority rightly rejected. The Government's argument that there is room for a substantial margin of appreciation in moral matters is, of course, correct up to a point, but, as the Court indicated, can hardly protect legislation which is not being enforced.

Trial within a reasonable time (Article 6(1))—the scope and criteria of State responsibility—just satisfaction (Article 50)

Case No. 2. Martins Moreira case.[6] The Court held unanimously that Portugal had violated Article 6(1) of the Convention because the length of civil proceedings had exceeded a reasonable time. The Government was also ordered to pay the applicant 2,000,000 escudos compensation and 435,000 escudos, less 5,180 French francs, in respect of his costs and expenses.

In 1975 the applicant was seriously injured when the car in which he was travelling as a passenger was involved in a road accident. In December 1977 he began

---

[5] Article 53 provides: 'The High Contracting Parties undertake to abide by the decision of the Court in any case to which they are parties.'

[6] ECHR, judgment of 26 October 1988, Series A, No. 143. The Court consisted of the following Chamber of Judges: Ryssdal (President); Gölcüklü, Pinheiro Farinha, Sir Vincent Evans, Macdonald, Carrillo Salcedo, Valticos (Judges).

proceedings in the courts in Portugal against the driver of the other vehicle, its owner, the latter's insurance company and the company for which the driver and owner of the other car were working. In October 1982 the court of first instance upheld the applicant's claim in part and ordered the defendant to pay damages. In May 1985 an appeal by the applicant on the issue of quantum was upheld and the award of damages increased. In February 1987 a further appeal on the same issue was again upheld and an unspecified sum awarded to cover future loss arising from the applicant's inability to work. In October 1987 the applicant asked the court to order the payment of the part of the damages award which had already been calculated, but problems were encountered when it emerged that the defendant company was subject to insolvency proceedings. Because of the difficulties of enforcement, at the time the European Court decided the case the applicant had not yet requested the award of the portion of the damages which still had to be calculated.

In his application to the Commission in July 1984 Mr Martins Moreira submitted that the length of the proceedings amounted to a violation of his rights under Article 6(1) of the Convention. In its report in October 1987 the Commission unanimously upheld this submission. The Commission and the Government then referred the case to the Court.

According to Article 6(1):

> In the determination of his civil rights and obligations . . . everyone is entitled to a . . . hearing within a reasonable time by a . . . tribunal . . .

The question for the Court was whether the time taken to hear the applicant's action for damages was 'reasonable' within the meaning of this article.

In accordance with its established practice, the Court began by determining the period to be taken into consideration. It decided that this ran from November 1978, when Portugal accepted the right of individual application, to the enforcement proceedings which began in October 1987 and had not yet been completed. The Government had argued, and the Commission accepted, that the period ended with the Supreme Court's judgment in February 1987, but the Court, though adopting a wider view, noted that even this first stage had taken eight years and three months.

The Court then proceeded to apply the various criteria laid down in its case law to the particular facts. It noted that while the case in itself was not complex, problems had been encountered in obtaining an expert medical opinion. In the Court's view, however, these were merely procedural difficulties which could not justify the length of the proceedings. The Government also relied on the applicant's behaviour, but the Court found this to be an inadequate justification. Though recognizing that the applicant could have assisted the medical experts by providing them with documents more expeditiously, it found that his failure to do so had not prolonged the proceedings unduly. A number of delays were attributed to the judicial authorities and particularly to the first instance court which had an excessive work-load. The Court held that these called for remedial measures which had not been taken. In particular it rejected the Government's argument that the duration of the proceedings compared favourably with the position in other States of the Council of Europe, a submission which the Court suggested had not been substantiated and which in any case was unacceptable because:

> It could lead to the acceptance of unsatisfactory practices if they are sufficiently general,

whereas, according to the case-law of the Court, the circumstances of each case must be taken into account . . . and, in any event compliance with Article 6(1) of the Convention must be ensured.[7]

The Court noted that the length of the proceedings had been due above all to the difficulties which the applicant had encountered in obtaining an orthopaedic examination. He had requested this in October 1979 but getting it had taken almost two years, most of which had been taken up with administrative steps. The domestic court had initially requested various public institutions to carry out the examination, but without success. Finally it had turned to the Lisbon Institute of Forensic Medicine whose doctors had only been able to draw up an interim report since no orthopaedic experts were available. Orthopaedic experts had been appointed by the court in May 1981 and had begun their work, which took about fifteen days, in June.

The Court recognized that there was force in the Government's argument that it was impossible to determine precisely how much the applicant's health had been affected by the accident without some lapse of time. It pointed out, however, that acceptance of this argument would mean that those whose need was greatest on account of the gravity of their injuries would be deprived of their right to obtain justice within a reasonable time. It also rejected the Government's submission that only the judicial authorities could incur international responsibility, explaining that:
                                                                                          •

This argument runs counter to the established case-law of the Court. In ratifying the Convention, the Portuguese State undertook the obligation to respect it and it must, in particular, ensure that the Convention is complied with by its different authorities . . .[8]

Here all the institutions concerned, including the Lisbon Institute of Forensic Medicine, were public bodies and the State was under a duty to provide means for them to carry out their objectives. In any case, the Court added, the applicant's orthopaedic examination was carried out in the context of judicial proceedings and the domestic court consequently retained responsibility for ensuring that it was conducted speedily. The Court therefore concluded that there had been a violation of Article 6(1).

The issue of just satisfaction under Article 50 was quickly dealt with. The Court considered that because of the delay Mr Martins Moreira had suffered a loss of opportunity with regard to the possibility of recovering the entirety of his debt. He had also suffered non-pecuniary injury on account of uncertainty and anxiety as to the outcome of the domestic proceedings and the effect of this on his finances and health. He was therefore awarded the sum mentioned earlier as compensation. In respect of the costs and expenses incurred in Portugal the Court awarded him a further amount, together with a more substantial sum in respect of the fees of the two lawyers who represented him at Strasbourg, less the amount already received as legal aid.

The length of domestic proceedings was also in issue in *Bock* (Case No. 9), *Neves e Silva* (Case No. 12), *Oliveira Neves* (Case No. 13), *Unión Alimentaria Sanders SA* (Case No. 18) and *H* v. *France* (Case No. 23), below.

---

[7] Judgment, para. 54.
[8] Ibid., para. 60.

Right to liberty (Article 5(1))—application to reference of a child to a psychiatric hospital by a parent—the scope of State responsibility—the meaning of 'deprived of liberty' in Article 5(1)

Case No. 3. Nielsen case.[9] In this case, which concerned a mother's reference of her son to a psychiatric hospital in Denmark, the Court held by 9 votes to 7 that Article 5 of the Convention was not applicable.

The applicant, Jon Nielsen, was born in Denmark in 1971. His parents were not married and under the law as it then stood only his mother had parental rights over him. In 1978 the law was changed and his father was able to apply to have the parental rights transferred to him. The father's application was, however, refused by the Danish courts. Father and son then went into hiding. In October 1979 the police found Jon Nielsen and returned him to his mother, who arranged for him to be placed in the Department of Child Psychiatry at a Danish hospital. In December 1979 the child disappeared from the hospital and resumed living with his father. In November 1982 the father again applied for a transfer of parental rights, but was again unsuccessful. The father was then arrested, charged with depriving the mother of her parental rights, and subsequently convicted.

In September 1983 the mother, advised by the local Social Welfare Committee, her family doctor, and Professor T, the Chief Physician in the State Hospital's Child Psychiatric Ward, requested that her son be admitted to the Ward, since it was clear that he did not wish to stay with her. The applicant was admitted to the Ward by Professor T and the Social Welfare Committee recorded its approval. In February 1984, on the day the applicant was due to be discharged and returned to his mother, he again disappeared. He was found by the police early in March and at his mother's request was sent back to the Child Psychiatric Ward, where he stayed until the end of the month.

While the applicant was in hospital his representatives tried to challenge the lawfulness of his detention before the Danish courts, but the action was dismissed on the ground that he had been admitted to hospital at his mother's request and not by virtue of the compulsory procedure applicable to the mentally ill. After an investigation of the case from the medical point of view the National Health Authority concluded that no ground could be found for criticizing the Child Psychiatric Ward, either with regard to the medical evaluation of the applicant, or with regard to the treatment he received whilst in hospital.

In his application to the Commission in 1984 Jon Nielsen claimed that his placement in the Child Psychiatric Ward and subsequent detention there violated his rights under Articles 5(1) and 5(4) of the Convention. In its report in March 1987 the Commission concluded, by 11 votes to 1 and 10 votes to 2 respectively, that there had been a breach of both provisions. The Commission and the Government then referred the case to the Court.

The main issue in this case concerned the scope of Article 5(1) of the Convention which provides:

Everyone has the right to liberty and security of person. No one shall be deprived of his liberty save in the following cases and in accordance with a procedure prescribed by law . . .

---

[9] ECHR, judgment of 28 November 1988, Series A, No. 144. This case was decided by the plenary Court.

The questions for the Court were first, whether the State could be regarded as responsible for the applicant's committal to hospital, and secondly, whether during the period which he spent in hospital, the applicant could be said to have been 'deprived of his liberty'.

As regards the issue of responsibility, the Court recalled that the protection of Article 5 clearly extends to minors. It pointed out, however, that the present case concerned a minor's placement in hospital at the request of his mother, who at the time was sole holder of parental rights. The significance of this, the Court explained, was that family life in the Contracting States encompasses a broad range of parental rights and responsibilities with regard to the care and custody of minor children, and family life in this sense is recognized and protected in Article 8 of the Convention. With this as the relevant background the Court proceeded to reject the argument of the Commission that the State was responsible under Article 5 for the placement of the applicant in hospital. In the Court's view neither the Chief Physician's power to refuse admission, nor the social authorities' involvement and powers,[10] altered the mother's position as the sole person with the power under Danish law to refer the applicant to hospital and to remove him from there. By comparison with the mother's parental powers, the Court considered that the assistance rendered by the authorities was of a limited and subsidiary nature. It therefore concluded that Article 5 was inapplicable in so far as it concerned deprivation of liberty by the authorities of the State.

The other question was whether the applicant's detention in hospital constituted a deprivation or restriction of his liberty, stemming from the exercise of his mother's parental rights. To resolve this issue the Court considered the applicant's situation while in the Ward, taking into account, among other matters, the type, duration, effects and manner of implementation of the disputed measures. The Court began by pointing out that the domestic authorities all considered that the mother's decision to commit the applicant to hospital was a lawful exercise of parental powers and also well founded. It was satisfied that the mother, who took her decision after receiving medical advice, had as her objective the protection of the applicant's health, which was certainly a proper purpose for the exercise of parental rights. The Court also found that the treatment given to the applicant was appropriate. Treatment was needed and that given involved talks and environmental therapy, not medication. Pointing out that the restrictions on the applicant's freedom were not very different from those which might be imposed on a child in an ordinary hospital, the Court added that the duration of the treatment, though substantial, did not exceed the average period of therapy at the Ward and that the restrictions imposed were relaxed as the treatment progressed.

The Commission's view that there had been a deprivation of liberty was based on the fact that the case involved the detention in a psychiatric ward of a twelve year old boy who was not mentally ill and who, when he had disappeared from hospital, was found and returned by the police. Although the Court accepted that parental rights are not unlimited, and that the State must provide safeguards against abuse, it viewed the situation here quite differently. Having regard to the factors previously mentioned, to the fact that the hospital was not actually used for the treatment of mentally ill persons and that the applicant himself was not referred on this

---

[10] According to the applicant, Danish law gave the social authorities the power to have him taken into care, should the mother arrange for him to be discharged from hospital against their wishes.

basis,[11] the Court decided that the restrictions imposed on him could not be considered to be of a nature or of a degree similar to the cases of deprivation of liberty specified in Article 5(1).

Finally, the Court observed that at the relevant time the applicant was at an age when it would be normal for a decision to be made by a parent, even against the wishes of a child, and that the intervention of the police would have been appropriate for the return of any runaway child, even to parental custody. In the light of the above the Court concluded that the restrictions on the applicant in hospital did not amount to a deprivation of liberty within the meaning of Article 5, but were a responsible exercise by his mother of her custodial rights in the interests of the child. Article 5 was accordingly not applicable.

This was a difficult case and the Court went to unusual lengths to justify its conclusions. Even so, seven judges expressed their disagreement with various aspects of its reasoning. All seven agreed with the Commission that the circumstances of the applicant's detention amounted to a deprivation of liberty and six of them considered that since the applicant had no way of challenging his detention there had been a breach of Article 5(4).[12] In addition three of the dissenting judges[13] held that there had been a violation of Article 5(1) because the State could not disclaim responsibility for the acts of its officials. Whether, as two members of the Court suggested, the decision to admit the applicant constituted an abuse of psychiatry[14] is open to argument, but the Court's view that the case was in essence no different from a routine hospital referral does not seem very convincing.[15] Judge Carrillo Salcedo was surely nearer the mark when he suggested that the real issue was 'the absence in Danish law of adequate procedures for judicial review in connection with the committal of a child to psychiatric hospital by the parent with custody, where . . . the child in question is not mentally ill and there are disagreements concerning custody'.[16]

Although the applicant narrowly lost his case in the European court, on the domestic front the story has a happy ending. In 1984 his father made a further attempt to have the parental rights transferred to him and on this occasion was successful. Jon Nielsen now lives with his father.

Right to liberty (Article 5(1))—right to be brought promptly before a judge or other judicial officer (Article 5(3))—right to take proceedings to test the lawfulness of detention (Article 5(4))—right to compensation for unlawful arrest or detention (Article 5(5))

Case No. 4. Brogan and others case.[17] The Court held by 12 votes to 7 that the four applicants in this case were victims of a violation of Article 5(3) of the Conven-

---

[11] The Ward was, however, used for the care of children suffering from psychiatric disorders. The medical evaluation of the applicant by Professor T was that he was 'trapped in a neurotic state requiring treatment'.

[12] Joint dissenting opinion of Judges Thór Vilhjálmsson, Pettiti, Russo, Spielmann, De Meyer and Valticos. Judge Carrillo Salcedo, though not formally associated with this opinion, may also have shared this view. For the text of Article 5(4) see Case No. 4, below.

[13] Judges Pettiti, De Meyer and Carrillo Salcedo.

[14] See the joint dissenting opinion of Judges Pettiti and De Meyer.

[15] For a forceful expression of this point see the separate opinion of Judge Pettiti.

[16] Dissenting opinion of Judge Carrillo Salcedo.

[17] ECHR, judgment of 29 November 1988, Series A, No. 145B. This case was decided by the plenary Court.

tion because they had not been brought promptly before a judge or other judicial officer, following their arrest on suspicion of involvement in terrorist activities in Northern Ireland. The Court also found by 13 votes to 6 that because the applicants did not have an enforceable right to compensation for the violation of Article 5(3), there had been a violation of Article 5(5). Various other claims under Article 5 were rejected and the Court ruled that it was unnecessary to examine the applicants' complaint under Article 13.

In the autumn of 1984 the four applicants were arrested under section 12 of the Prevention of Terrorism (Temporary Provisions) Act 1984 on the basis of a reasonable suspicion that they had been involved in the commission, preparation or instigation of acts of terrorism connected with affairs in Northern Ireland. 'Terrorism' is defined in the 1984 Act as 'the use of violence for political ends', including 'the use of violence for the purpose of putting the public or any section of the public in fear'. In each case the initial period of 48 hours' detention permitted by the legislation was extended by a decision of the Secretary of State for Northern Ireland. The applicants were held for periods of five days and eleven hours, six days and sixteen and a half hours, four days and six hours, and four days and eleven hours respectively. All four were questioned about specific terrorist incidents, but none of them was charged or brought before a judicial authority before his release.

The legislation granting the special powers under which the applicants were arrested was originally introduced in 1974 as a response to the emergency situation in Northern Ireland and the attendant level of terrorist activity. Since the introduction of those powers the need for their continuation has been constantly monitored by Parliament and their operation regularly reviewed by independent bodies. The authors of these reviews concluded that in view of the problems inherent in the prevention and investigation of terrorism, the continued use of the special powers of arrest and detention was indispensable. The suggestion that decisions extending the detention should be taken by the courts was rejected, because, amongst other reasons, the information grounding these decisions was highly sensitive and could not be disclosed to the persons in detention or their legal advisers.

In their applications to the Commission in 1984 and 1985, the applicants complained of various breaches of Article 5 and also of Article 13. In its report in May 1987 the Commission concluded that there had been certain violations of Articles 5(3) and 5(5), but no breaches of Articles 5(1) and 5(4), and that no separate issue arose under Article 13. The Commission and the Government then referred the case to the Court.

Article 5(1) of the Convention provides:

Everyone has the right to liberty and security of person. No one shall be deprived of his liberty save in the following cases and in accordance with a procedure prescribed by law:

. . .

(c) the lawful arrest or detention of a person effected for the purpose of bringing him before the competent legal authority on reasonable suspicion of having committed an offence . . .

The applicants maintained that the deprivation of liberty they suffered by virtue of section 12 of the 1984 Act failed to comply with this provision because they were not arrested on suspicion of an 'offence', nor was the purpose of their arrest to bring them before a lawful authority. However the Court, like the Commission, rejected these arguments. The Court acknowledged that the Act did not require an arrest to be based on suspicion of a specific offence, but on suspicion of involvement in 'acts of terrorism'. Nevertheless it ruled that the statutory definition of terrorism was fully consonant with the Convention's concept of an offence. Moreover, within a few hours of his arrest each applicant had been questioned about his involvement in specific offences.

The applicants' other point was rejected on the ground that although they had been neither charged, nor brought before a court, the requisite purpose could exist independently of its achievement. Evidence on which to base charges may have been unobtainable, or in view of the nature of the suspected offences, impossible to produce in court without endangering the lives of others. There was no reason to believe that the applicants' detention was not intended to further the police investigation by confirming or dispelling the suspicions which grounded their arrest. Thus the conditions for lawful arrest and detention set out in Article 5(1)(c) had been satisfied.

The most important issue in this case concerned Article 5(3) which provides:

Everyone arrested or detained in accordance with the provisions of paragraph 1(c) of this Article shall be brought promptly before a judge or other officer authorized by law to exercise judicial power . . .

The applicants submitted that whilst in custody under the 1984 Act they had been denied their right to be brought promptly before a judge or other judicial officer.

The Court began by observing that in accordance with its previous jurisprudence, and the use of the word '*aussitôt*' in the French text, it regarded the word 'promptly' as importing only a limited degree of flexibility. Moreover,

Whereas promptness is to be assessed in each case according to its special features . . . , the significance to be attached to those features can never be taken to the point of impairing the very essence of the right guaranteed by Article 5(3), that is to the point of effectively negativing the State's obligation to ensure a prompt release or a prompt appearance before a judicial authority.[18]

Turning to the particular facts, the Court recognized that the investigation of terrorist offences in Northern Ireland presents the authorities with special problems. Account was also taken of the safeguards of ministerial control, the constant monitoring of the need for the legislation by Parliament and the regular review of its operation. The Court therefore accepted that 'the context of terrorism in Northern Ireland'[19] had the effect of prolonging the permissible period of police custody prior to appearance before a judge or other judicial officer. Furthermore, the difficulties of judicial control over decisions to arrest and detain suspected terrorists might require certain procedural precautions.

Notwithstanding the above, the Court decided that even the shortest of the four periods of detention, which was the four days and six hours spent in police custody by one of the applicants, fell outside the strict constraints as to time permitted by the notion of promptness. To regard the special features of the case as important enough to justify such a long period of detention would, said the Court, seriously weaken the individual's procedural guarantee and 'entail consequences impairing

---

[18] Judgment, para. 59.
[19] Ibid., para. 61.

the very essence of the right to prompt judicial control protected by Article 5(3)'.[20] The Court concluded that none of the applicants was either brought 'promptly' before a judicial authority or released 'promptly' following his arrest. The fact that the arrest and detention of the applicants were motivated by the legitimate aim of protecting the community was not enough. There had therefore been a violation of Article 5(3).

The remaining issues can be dealt with quite briefly. Article 5(4) of the Convention provides:

> Everyone who is deprived of his liberty by arrest or detention shall be entitled to take proceedings by which the lawfulness of his detention shall be decided speedily by a court and his release ordered if the detention is not lawful.

The Court explained that this provision, which has been subject to extensive interpretation,[21] guaranteed the applicants a judicial review bearing upon the procedural and substantive conditions which were essential for the lawfulness, in the sense of Article 5(1)(c), of their deprivation of liberty. The remedy of *habeas corpus*, which the applicants chose not to use, permitted the courts in Northern Ireland to examine compliance with the procedural requirements of the 1984 Act and also the reasonableness of the suspicion grounding the arrest, as well as the legitimacy of the purpose behind the arrest and the ensuing detention. In these circumstances the Court decided that there had been no violation of Article 5(4).

The final provision to be considered[22] was Article 5(5), which lays down that:

> Everyone who has been the victim of arrest or detention in contravention of the provisions of this Article shall have an enforceable right to compensation.

The Government submitted that the entitlement to compensation referred to here is confined to a deprivation of liberty which was unlawful under domestic law or arbitrary. The Court, however, rejected the argument. The text of Article 5(5) referred to arrest or detention 'in contravention of the provisions of this Article'. The Government admitted that the violation of Article 5(3) which the Court had identified could not give rise either before or after the present judgment to a claim for compensation enforceable in the domestic courts. Accordingly, there had also been a breach of Article 5(5) in respect of all the applicants.

This was the first of a number of cases involving the United Kingdom to be decided in the period under review[23] and, though concerned with somewhat narrower issues than those to be considered shortly, the decision contains a number of points of interest. At the beginning of the judgment the Court stated that it had taken note of the growth of terrorism in modern society and had 'already recognized the need, inherent in the Convention system, for a proper balance between the defence of the institutions of democracy in the common interest and the protection of individual rights'.[24] Despite this declaration, and a pointed observation that the absence of a notice of derogation under Article 15 did not preclude 'proper

---

[20] Ibid., para. 62.

[21] See, for example, the *Ashingdane* case, Series A, No. 93, and this *Year Book*, 56 (1985), p. 348, and subsequently the *Weeks* case, Series A, No. 114, and this *Year Book*, 58 (1987), p. 470.

[22] The Court, like the Commission, considered that it was unnecessary to examine the case under Article 13.

[23] See also *Chappell* (Case No. 11), *Gaskin* (Case No. 21), and *Soering* (Case No. 22), below.

[24] Judgment, para. 48.

account being taken of the circumstances of the case',[25] the decision proved extremely controversial. Ten members of the Court delivered dissenting opinions. Seven judges maintained that the exigencies of the situation, when viewed in the light of the Court's previous case law, meant that there had been no violation of Article 5(3), and six of them said that it followed from this that there was no violation of Article 5(5) either.[26] On the other hand, three members of the Court considered the judgment too limited and held that there had also been a violation of Article 5(1).[27] This is, of course, not the first occasion on which a government's response to the threat posed by terrorism has been challenged, and, as we have explained elsewhere,[28] such cases tend to split the Court along predictable lines.

On the question of just satisfaction under Article 50 the Court decided unanimously that as the applicants had not submitted any claim for reimbursement of costs and expenses and the Court did not have to consider the matter on its own motion, there was no call to examine this aspect of the application. As regards the issue of compensation for damage, on the other hand, the Court held that this was not yet ready for decision and must be reserved for later consideration. The final stage of the proceedings is described as Case No. 15 below.

Right to a fair and public hearing (Article 6(1))—the meaning of 'impartial' in Article 6(1)

Case No. 5. *Barberá, Messegué and Jabardo* case.[29] The Court held by 10 votes to 8 that there had been a violation of Article 6(1) of the Convention because the applicants had not received a fair trial when they were convicted of murder in Spain. It held unanimously, however, that there had been no violation of Article 6(2).

In 1980 the applicants were arrested in Barcelona following the killing of a Catalan businessman by a terrorist organization.[30] While in police custody they signed a statement acknowledging that they had taken part in the killing. Subsequently, in proceedings before the investigating judge, they retracted their confessions and alleged that they had been subjected to ill-treatment. In January 1982, after a hearing in Madrid which lasted only one day, the three were convicted and sentenced. Mr Barberá and Mr Messegué were convicted of murder and sentenced to thirty years' imprisonment and Mr Jabardo was convicted of aiding and abetting a murder and sentenced to twelve years and one day. Appeals by the applicants on points of law were unsuccessful, except in the case of Mr Jabardo, whose sentence was

[25] Ibid.

[26] See the joint dissenting opinion of Judges Thór Vilhjálmsson, Bindschedler-Robert, Gölcüklü, Matscher and Valticos, and the partly dissenting opinion of Judge Sir Vincent Evans. Judge Martens dissented on the issue of Article 5(3) alone and explained this conclusion in a fully reasoned opinion which repays close attention.

[27] See the joint dissenting opinion of Judges Walsh and Carrillo Salcedo and the partly dissenting opinion of Judge Pinheiro Farinha.

[28] See Merrills, *The Development of International Law by the European Court of Human Rights* (1988), pp. 216–25.

[29] ECHR, judgment of 6 December 1988, Series A, No. 146. This case was decided by the plenary Court.

[30] The killing was particularly unpleasant. The victim, who was 77 years old, was held at gun-point in his home while an explosive device was attached to his chest. He was informed that unless he paid a large ransom within 25 days he would be killed by it. A few hours later, however, the device exploded, killing him instantly. The police investigation concentrated on an organization known as the 'Catalan Peoples' Army' with which the applicants were evidently associated.

reduced to six years for assisting armed gangs. A further appeal to the Constitutional Court was ruled inadmissible.

Their application to the Commission in 1983 was declared admissible in so far as it related to Articles 6(1) and 6(2) of the Convention. In its report in October 1986 the Commission unanimously expressed the opinion that there had been a violation of Article 6(1) and found that it was unnecessary to consider the complaints of the first two applicants under Article 6(2). The Commission and the Government then referred the case to the Court.

The relevant part of Article 6(1) provides:

In the determination . . . of any criminal charge against him, everyone is entitled to a fair and public hearing within a reasonable time by an independent and impartial tribunal established by law. . . .

The applicants' first point was that the court which had tried them was not impartial because of the political sympathies and attitude of the presiding judge and because the membership of the tribunal had been changed at the last moment. The Court rejected these complaints; the first because the applicants had failed to exhaust domestic remedies, and the second because, although they were entitled to raise the issue, the circumstances surrounding the tribunal's change of membership were not such as to raise doubts about its impartiality.

The applicants' main argument was that they had not received a fair and public trial. This required the Court to examine their case in some detail, including the way in which the evidence was taken and the conduct and background of the proceedings.

The applicants, who had been in prison in Barcelona, were transferred to Madrid on the night preceding their trial and arrived in the capital early in the morning, a few hours before the hearing began. The Court considered that this was regrettable and 'undoubtedly weakened their position at a vital moment when they needed all their resources to defend themselves and, in particular, to face up to questioning at the very start of the trial and to consult effectively with their counsel'.[31] The Court considered that the change in composition of the domestic court was also open to criticism. Recalling that two judges had been substituted at short notice, the Court decided that defence counsel had grounds for fearing that the new judges would be unfamiliar with the investigation file of the case, which ran to some 1,600 pages.

Turning to the conduct of the trial, the Court explained that the taking and presentation of evidence must always be considered in the light of Article 6(2), which incorporates the presumption of innocence, and Article 6(3), which guarantees the rights of the defence, including the right to call and examine witnesses. While the Court was satisfied that the last requirement had been fulfilled, it found that in its interim submissions the prosecution had not specified in detail the particular facts on which it proposed to rely, an omission which had made the task of the defence more difficult.

As far as the voluminous written evidence was concerned, the parties had agreed, under what is known as the *por reproducida* procedure, that it need not be read out and the Court accepted that in this respect the defence had waived the need for publicity. It pointed out, however, that the adoption of the expedited procedure did not mean that the applicants accepted all the written evidence, nor that

[31] Judgment, para. 70.

they had waived their right to challenge it. On the contrary, they had challenged parts of it in their subsequent appeals and the Court held that in order to decide whether their trial was fair it must itself examine how the disputed evidence had been procured and presented. Finding that the investigation stage of the case had been conducted in a way which made it difficult for the applicants to understand the case against them, the Court concluded that deficiencies in the proceedings at the trial stage had not been compensated for by procedural safeguards during the earlier stages.

The Court was also critical of the use made of the evidence of a key witness whose incriminating statement was on the file but whom the applicants had never been given an opportunity to examine. It also had reservations about the accuseds' confessions, which had been obtained during a long period of custody in which they had been held incommunicado, and about weapons, documents and other evidence found at the applicants' homes, but which had not been produced at the trial and which the defence had therefore not been able to challenge in an effective manner.

Having regard to the above factors, the Court concluded that the proceedings in question, taken as a whole, did not satisfy the requirements of a fair and public hearing. Consequently there was a violation of Article 6(1). The Court found, however, that there had been no violation of Article 6(2) and reserved the question of just satisfaction under Article 50.

Eight judges voted against the Court's decision.[32] In a joint dissenting opinion they explained that although the proceedings were admittedly unsatisfactory in certain respects, the majority judgment exaggerated the significance of certain factors, while minimizing the applicants' failure to safeguard their interests by using the opportunities offered by the Spanish system. In their view neither the belated transfer of the applicants to Madrid, nor the change in the membership of the bench, had had an appreciable effect, whilst the brevity of the final hearing was partly attributable to the applicants' unwillingness to analyse and impugn the relevant documentation until later. Underlying their disagreement with the majority can be seen the idea that though the Court has a duty to enforce the Convention, it must resist the temptation to retry criminal cases, or to substitute its own assessment of the evidence for that of the domestic court. As the closeness of the decision in the present case demonstrates, however, this is one of those incontrovertible principles of Strasbourg law which it is easier to state than to apply.

Right to a fair trial (Article 6(1))—application to alleged assurance relating to a reduced charge

Case No. 6. Colak case.[33] In this case, which concerned a criminal trial in the Federal Republic of Germany, the Court held unanimously that there had been no violation of Article 6(1) of the Convention.

In April 1979, in the course of a brawl in a Frankfurt restaurant, the applicant, a Turkish national, injured a compatriot by a knife thrust to the abdomen. Shortly afterwards he was arrested by the police and charged with attempted murder. At

---

[32] The dissenters were Judges Bindschedler-Robert, Thór Vilhjálmsson, Gölcüklü, Matscher, Walsh, Russo, Valticos and Torres Boursault.

[33] ECHR, judgment of 6 December 1988, Series A, No. 147. The Court consisted of the following Chamber of Judges: Ryssdal (President); Matscher, Pettiti, Macdonald, Russo, Bernhardt, Carrillo Salcedo (Judges).

his trial before the Frankfurt Assize Court the applicant was officially informed that there was a possibility that he could be convicted on the lesser charge of causing grievous bodily harm. In addition, Mr Colak claimed that in a conversation outside the court-room the President of the court had told his lawyer that he would indeed be convicted on the lesser charge, that the court would not change its position, and that if it did so, his counsel would be given due notice. Subsequently, however, the President of the court stated that he could no longer recall details of this conversation. In February 1981 the applicant was convicted and sentenced to five years' imprisonment for attempted murder. Appeals by the applicant, in which he claimed that he had been misled by the alleged assurance from the President, were dismissed by the German courts.

In his application to the Commission in 1982 Mr Colak submitted that the Assize Court's failure to inform him that it had changed its position, following the President's alleged assurance, meant that he had been denied a fair trial, contrary to Article 6(1). In its report in October 1987 the Commission expressed the opinion that there had been no violation of this provision. The Commission then referred the case to the Court.

In *Barberá, Messegué and Jabardo* (Case No. 5), as we have just seen, the application of the Convention's guarantee of a fair trial required an elaborate investigation and divided the Court. The present case was much simpler and produced no such difficulty. In the first place, on the evidence available it was impossible to establish with certainty whether the alleged conversation had ever taken place. The Court therefore decided that it did not have 'sufficient information to enable it to rule on this disputed issue of fact'.[34] Aware, perhaps, that this was a somewhat unsatisfactory conclusion, but not wishing to address the issue of standard of proof, the Court made a second point. This was that even if the President of the Assize Court did have a conversation with the applicant's lawyer (a possibility which the Court said could not be excluded), there was no way of establishing its content. Moreover,—and here the Court moved from evidential to substantive considerations—assuming a conversation had taken place in the terms alleged, the applicant's right to a fair trial had not been infringed because the President could not speak on behalf of his fellow judges:

The applicant's lawyer knew that the Assize Court would make its ruling after its deliberations, solely on the basis of the issues raised during the hearing. Accordingly, he should have satisfied himself that the President's alleged appraisal of the situation did indeed reflect the views of the Court itself. It was open to him to seek formal confirmation of those views.[35]

The Court therefore found that there had been no violation of Article 6(1).

Right to liberty (Article 5(1))—the meaning of 'any obligation prescribed by law' in Article 5(1)(b)—the scope of Article 5(1)(c)—right to compensation for unlawful arrest or detention (Article 5(5))—just satisfaction (Article 50)

Case No. 7. Ciulla case.[36] The Court held by 15 votes to 2 that the application of preventive measures against a suspected drug trafficker in Italy had violated Article 5(1), and by 11 votes to 4 that there had also been a violation of Article 5(5) of the

[34] Judgment, para. 30.
[35] Ibid., para. 31.
[36] ECHR, judgment of 22 February 1989, Series A, No. 148. This case was decided by the plenary Court.

Convention. It held unanimously, however, that the judgment constituted adequate just satisfaction and that no award of compensation under Article 50 was necessary.

Between 1982 and 1986 the applicant, who was an Italian national, was prosecuted for various drug offences. On 8 May 1984, during separate but parallel 'preventive' proceedings under Law No. 1423 of 1956, the President of the Milan District Court ordered his arrest and detention pending a decision on an application for a compulsory residence order. The President's order was made because it was thought that there was a danger that the applicant might abscond. When the application for a compulsory residence order was granted on 24 May the applicant's detention immediately ended. The next day, however, the police took him to the place appointed for his compulsory residence. At the time the case was heard by the European Court the applicant was serving a sentence of nine years' imprisonment for drug offences.

In his application to the Commission in 1984 Mr Ciulla claimed that his detention under Law No. 1423 had involved violations of Articles 5(1) and 5(5) of the Convention. In its report in May 1987 the Commission expressed the opinion that there had been a breach of both provisions. The Commission then referred the case to the Court.

The relevant part of Article 5(1) provides:

Everyone has the right to liberty and security of person. No one shall be deprived of his liberty save in the following cases and in accordance with a procedure prescribed by law

. . .

(b) the lawful arrest or detention of a person for non-compliance with the lawful order of a court or in order to secure the fulfilment of any obligation prescribed by law;

(c) the lawful arrest or detention of a person effected for the purpose of bringing him before the competent legal authority on reasonable suspicion of having committed an offence or when it is reasonably considered necessary to prevent his committing an offence or fleeing after having done so;

. . .

After rejecting the Government's preliminary objection that the applicant had failed to exhaust his domestic remedies, the Court considered first whether his detention could be justified under Article 5(1)(b). The Government's submission was that the authorities' action was intended 'to secure the fulfilment of [an] obligation prescribed by law', namely the obligation to live in a designated locality imposed by the compulsory residence order. The difficulty, however, was that the obligation in question did not arise until May 1984 and so did not exist when the preventive proceedings were taken. Since the Court has previously indicated that for the purposes of Article 5(1)(b) an obligation must be incumbent on the applicant at the time of the disputed detention and not afterwards,[37] it rejected the Government's argument.

In relation to Article 5(1)(c) the Government submitted that there was a 'reasonable suspicion' that the applicant had 'committed an offence' and also that it had been 'reasonably considered necessary to prevent his committing an offence'. These arguments too were rejected, on the ground that this sub-paragraph permits deprivation of liberty only as a part of criminal proceedings. Although the Government maintained that there were affinities between the criminal proceedings and

---

[37] See the *Guzzardi* case, Series A, No. 39, and this *Year Book*, 51 (1980), p. 335.

the preventive procedure provided for in Law No. 1423, the Court held that the latter was designed for purposes different from those of criminal proceedings, with the result that the deprivation of liberty which sometimes preceded the making of a compulsory residence order could not be equated with pre-trial detention. As to detention having been considered necessary to prevent the commission of an offence, the Court said that even if this was correct, the fact would remain that the custodial order had not been made in the context of criminal proceedings. For as the terms of the order indicated, the arrest of the applicant on 8 May had been designed to obviate the risk that he might 'evade any preventive measure that might be taken'.

The Court therefore concluded that since the applicant's detention had not been justified, there had been a breach of Article 5(1).

The other issue in the case concerned Article 5(5), which has been quoted in Case No. 4, and which provides for an enforceable right to compensation for those arrested or detained in contravention of Article 5. Having reviewed the relevant Italian case law, the Court held that the effective enjoyment of this right was not ensured with a sufficient degree of certainty and therefore concluded that there had also been a breach of this provision.

In examining the applicant's claim for compensation under Article 50 the Court found that Mr Ciulla had not provided any particulars or prima facie evidence as to the nature and extent of the alleged damage in respect of his detention. Although the Court accepted that he might have sustained some non-pecuniary damage, it considered that the finding of violations of Article 5 amounted in itself to just satisfaction.

Four judges dissented on the issue of Article 5(5) and pointed out some of the difficulties in applying this provision.[38] Judge Valticos and Judge Matscher went further and maintained that there had been no breach of Article 5(1) because it was 'artificial' to consider the detention of the applicant in isolation from the other proceedings in which he was involved. As in *Brogan* (Case No. 4) and *Barberá, Messegué and Jabardo* (Case No. 5), criticism of the Court's approach may well have been coloured by the particular facts. The Court, it should be noted, stated that it did not 'underestimate the importance of Italy's struggle against organised crime', but observed that 'the exhaustive list of permissible exceptions in paragraph 1 of Article 5 of the Convention must be interpreted strictly',[39] a principle which has been consistently followed in its jurisprudence.

Freedom of expression (Article 10)—application to magazine article likely to damage a lay judge's reputation—the meaning of 'necessary in a democratic society' in Article 10(2)

Case No. 8. Barfod case.[40] In this case, which, concerned Denmark, the Court held by 6 votes to 1 that the applicant's conviction for defaming two members of the High Court of Greenland did not constitute a violation of Article 10 of the Convention.

[38] See the dissenting opinion of Judge Valticos, approved by Judge Matscher, and the joint partly dissenting opinion of Judges Bindschedler-Robert and Gölcüklü.

[39] Judgment, para. 41.

[40] ECHR, judgment of 22 February 1989, Series A, No. 149. The Court consisted of the following Chamber of Judges: Ryssdal (President); Cremona, Bindschedler-Robert, Gölcüklü, Matscher, Walsh (Judges); Gomard (*ad hoc* Judge).

In 1979 the Government of Greenland decided to tax Danish nationals who work on American bases in Greenland. A number of those affected challenged this decision in the courts, maintaining that it was illegal because they had no right to vote in elections in Greenland and were not eligible to receive any benefits there. The case was heard by the High Court of Greenland which, in accordance with its usual practice, was composed of one professional judge and two lay judges, both of whom happened to be Government employees. In its judgment the High Court unanimously upheld the Government's case and this decision was subsequently confirmed on appeal.

In August 1982 the applicant, who worked in Greenland but was not affected by the new tax, wrote an article for the magazine *Grønland Dansk* criticizing the High Court. In it he expressed the opinion that the two lay judges were legally disqualified and questioned their power and their ability to deal impartially with a case against their employer. His article also included the following passage:

> Most of the local government's members could on the other hand afford the time to watch that the two Greenlandic lay judges—who are by the way both employed directly by the local government, as director of the museum and as consultant in urban housing affairs—did their duty, and that they did. The vote was two to one in favour of the local government and with such a bench of judges it does not require much imagination to guess who voted how.[41]

When the article was published the professional judge considered that this observation on the lay judges might damage their reputation in the eyes of the public and hence impair confidence in the legal system. As head of the Greenland judiciary he therefore reported Mr Barfod's remarks to the police and asked for a criminal investigation. As a result, the applicant was subsequently prosecuted for defamation under the Greenland Penal code and, on being convicted by a District Court, fined 2,000 Danish crowns.

Mr Barfod appealed but in July 1984 the High Court, sitting with a different professional judge, confirmed his conviction. The High Court stressed that the statement that the two lay judges 'did their duty' was, in the context of the article, a serious accusation which was likely to lower them in public esteem. It did, however, agree with the accused that the lay judges should have considered themselves disqualified and ought to have withdrawn from the case, and also that he had been correct to point this out.

The applicant applied to the Commission in March 1985 relying *inter alia* on Article 10 of the Convention. In its report in July 1987 the Commission expressed the opinion by 14 votes to 1 that this article had been violated. The Commission and the Danish Government then referred the case to the Court.

Article 10 of the Convention provides:

1. Everyone has the right to freedom of expression. This right shall include freedom to hold opinions and to receive and impart information and ideas without interference by public authority and regardless of frontiers . . .
2. The exercise of these freedoms, since it carries with it duties and responsibilities, may be subject to such formalities, conditions, restrictions or penalties as are prescribed by law and are necessary in a democratic society . . . for the protection of the reputation or rights of others . . . or for maintaining the authority and impartiality of the judiciary.

---

[41] Judgment, para. 9. The statement that the vote was two to one was an error. As indicated earlier, the High Court of Greenland was unanimous.

It was clear that the applicant's conviction by the courts in Greenland constituted an 'interference by public authority' with his freedom of expression. Accordingly, the case turned on whether that conviction could be justified under Article 10(2). Since the applicant accepted that the interference was 'prescribed by law' and that its aims were the protection of the reputation of others, and, indirectly, the maintenance of the authority of the judiciary, the only question was whether the interference was 'necessary in a democratic society' for achieving these aims.

The difficulty of the case stemmed from the fact that Mr Barfod's article contained two elements. Firstly, there was the criticism of the composition of the domestic court which, as we have seen, was found to be justified. Secondly, however, there was his statement that the lay judges 'did their duty' which implied that they cast their votes as Government employees, rather than as independent and impartial judges. The key point, when the case was considered under Article 10, turned out to be whether the two elements could be separated. To the applicant and the Commission the elements had to be considered together. Because the statement as a whole concerned matters of public interest, they maintained that the test of 'necessity' had to be strictly applied. On this view even if the article could be interpreted as an attack on the lay judges, which was denied, the general interest in allowing public debate about the functioning of the judiciary outweighed the interest of the two judges in being protected from criticism. To the Government, on the other hand, the two elements were separate. Whereas Mr Barfod's criticism of the court's composition was justified, his accusation against the two judges was false and defamatory. Emphasizing the national authorities' margin of appreciation, the Government submitted that as the accusation did not contribute to the formation of public opinion which was worthy of safeguarding in a democratic society, Mr Barfod could be punished without transgression of Article 10.

The Court agreed with the Government. Having regard to the circumstances of the conviction, the Court was satisfied that the interference had neither the aim, nor the effect, of restricting the applicant's right to criticize the composition of the domestic court. The Court observed that:

It was quite possible to question the composition of the High Court without at the same time attacking the two lay judges personally. In addition, no evidence has been submitted to the effect that the applicant was justified in believing that the two elements of criticism raised by him . . . were so closely connected as to make the statement relating to the two lay judges legitimate. The High Court's finding that there was no proof of the accusation against the lay judges . . . remains unchallenged; the applicant must accordingly be considered to have based his accusations on the mere fact that the lay judges were employed by the Local Government, the defendant in the 1981 tax case. Although this fact may give rise to a difference of opinion as to whether the court was properly composed, it was certainly not proof of actual bias and the applicant cannot reasonably have been unaware of that.[42]

It therefore decided that 'the State's legitimate interest in protecting the reputation of the two lay judges was accordingly not in conflict with the applicant's interest in being able to participate in free public debate on the question of the structural impartiality of the High Court'.[43] Having regard also to the fact that the domestic court took into account the context of the impugned statement when deciding the amount of the applicant's fine, the Court decided that there had been no violation of the Convention.

[42] Ibid., para. 33.
[43] Ibid., para. 34.

Although this is not the first case in which the Court has allowed a government to rely on Article 10(2), the result here is surely questionable. It will be recalled that in the *Sunday Times* case[44] the Court made the vital point that freedom of expression is a fundamental principle to which Article 10(2) provides only limited exceptions. Moreover, in that case and more recently in the *Lingens* case,[45] it has stressed the crucial role of a free press in a democracy. In its report in the present case, which was endorsed by Judge Gölcüklü in his dissenting opinion, the Commission observed that 'For the citizen to keep a critical control of the exercise of public power it is essential that particularly strict limits be imposed on interferences with the publication of opinions which refer to activities of public authorities, including the judiciary'.[46] In the face of such persuasive considerations, the decision of the Court to reject Mr Barfod's claim is more than a little surprising.

Trial within a reasonable time (Article 6 (1))—just satisfaction (Article 50)

Case No. 9. *Bock* case.[47] The Court held unanimously that the Federal Republic of Germany had violated Article 6(1) of the Convention because the applicant's divorce proceedings had not been concluded within a reasonable time. The Court also ordered the Government to pay the applicant 10,000 Deutschmarks as compensation for non-pecuniary damage and 12,000 Deutschmarks in respect of his costs and expenses.

In March 1974 the applicant, who was a senior civil servant in the Federal Republic, filed a petition for divorce before the Düsseldorf Regional Court. When his wife responded by claiming that he was mentally ill,[48] the court decided that it was necessary to investigate his capacity to take legal proceedings. In July 1977, before the issue of capacity had been resolved, the divorce laws were changed and Mr Bock's case was transferred to the newly established Family Court in Düsseldorf.

In December 1978 the Family Court granted the divorce petition. However, on appeal its judgment was quashed on the ground that it had failed to examine the applicant's alleged lack of capacity. In June 1980, at a rehearing of the case, the Family Court again granted the divorce, having refused to take further evidence on the applicant's mental state. In September 1980, on appeal by the wife, the second judgment was also quashed and the case referred back for a further rehearing. In July 1981 the Family Court heard evidence from a medical expert which indicated that the applicant was not mentally ill. In February 1982 the Family Court therefore pronounced the divorce for the third time. The wife again appealed against this judgment and the applicant cross-appealed. In May 1983, having heard further medical evidence, the Court of Appeal dismissed the appeal and the cross appeal, stating that no doubts now existed as to the applicant's mental capacity. The judgment was served on the parties in June 1983.

---

[44] ECHR, judgment of 26 April 1979, Series A, No. 30, and this *Year Book*, 50 (1979), p. 257.

[45] ECHR, judgment of 8 July 1986, Series A, No. 103, and this *Year Book*, 57 (1986), p. 463.

[46] Dissenting opinion of Judge Gölcüklü, para. 4.

[47] ECHR, judgment of 29 March 1989, Series A, No. 150. The Court consisted of the following Chamber of Judges: Ryssdal (President); Bindschedler-Robert, Pettiti, Sir Vincent Evans, Bernhardt, De Meyer, Valticos (Judges).

[48] In 1974 and 1976 Mrs Bock instituted separate proceedings in the German courts relating to her husband's mental capacity. As a result of the first set of proceedings the applicant was temporarily committed to a mental hospital and secured his release only after challenging this decision in the courts.

In October 1983 the Federal Constitutional Court dismissed a constitutional complaint by the applicant which was mainly concerned with the length of the divorce proceedings. In July 1983 the applicant lodged a further constitutional complaint concerning certain ancillary matters determined by the final divorce decree. This complaint was dismissed in January 1984.

In July 1982 Mr Bock applied to the Commission which declared the application admissible only in respect of a complaint under Article 6(1) concerning the length of the divorce proceedings. In its report in November 1987 the Commission, with only one dissentient, expressed the opinion that there had been a violation of Article 6(1). The Commission then referred the case to the Court.

In accordance with its usual practice the Court began by considering the relevant time period. It was clear that this started with the initiation of proceedings in 1974, but there was disagreement as to whether the final stage before the Constitutional Court could be taken into account. This kind of issue has arisen before[49] and the Court explained that the conclusion to be drawn from its case law is that, where a constitutional decision will affect the result of a case before the ordinary courts, such proceedings are relevant. In the present case, however, the Court held that the substantive issue could be decided by taking into account only the actual divorce proceedings. Accordingly, the relevant period was from March 1974 to June 1983.

To assess the reasonableness of the length of the proceedings the Court reviewed the various stages in the litigation with particular reference to the time devoted to establishing the applicant's mental state, which was of course a special feature of the case. On the assumption that doubts as to the applicant's mental health could be legitimately entertained, the Court found that the Regional Court failed to ensure a speedy taking of evidence on this issue. Indeed, at the time the case was transferred the divorce petition itself had still to be examined, although attestations by two doctors as to Mr Bock's soundness of mind were in existence, against one contrary diagnosis whose author had been disqualified for bias. The Court therefore considered that there had been an undue delay at this stage, although it added that the conduct of both the applicant and his wife were contributory factors.

Turning to the proceedings in the Family Court, the Court considered that the first hearing could have been arranged more quickly. It wondered why the Court of Appeal could not have resolved the issue of capacity instead of referring it back, but concluded that the domestic court was in the best position to decide what action was required under German Law.

The second set of proceedings in the Family Court lasted from March to July 1980. The Court noted that this was not a lengthy period, but pointed out that failure to comply with the Court of Appeal's decision as to expert evidence led to a further appeal. Although the Government put forward the ingenious argument that 'no State can guarantee that its judges will not make mistakes',[50] the Court rightly ruled that the Family Court's error was a further source of delay.

In the third set of proceedings the case was pending before the Family Court from October 1980 to February 1982, during which time the necessary expert psychiatric evidence was obtained. The Court found that this period was not excessive, but criticized the fifteen-month delay in obtaining a further decision from the

[49] See, for example, the *Eckle* case, Series A, No. 51, and this *Year Book*, 53 (1982), p. 317.
[50] Judgment, para. 44.

Court of Appeal. Pointing out that by this time there was an even greater obligation to act expeditiously, the Court concluded that this final period was excessive.

Reviewing the evidence as a whole, the Court explained that the case was unusual because the delay in resolving Mr Bock's petition resulted not from a lack of judicial activity, as in so many cases, but rather from an excess of it. In this connection the Court made a point of general importance when it observed that:

In principle national courts have to proceed on the basis that a representative or actual plaintiff is not suffering from mental incapacity. Should any reasonable doubt arise in this regard, they have to clarify *as soon as possible* the extent to which he is competent to conduct legal proceedings.[51]

As the Court explained, in the present case doubts persisted in the national courts as to Mr Bock's soundness of mind, although by the time of the final divorce judgment no less than five reports attested to his competence, against one which did not, but whose author had been disqualified. Finding that these doubts over a period of nine years had caused the applicant hardship and represented 'a serious encroachment on human dignity',[52] the Court concluded that, in view of 'the particular diligence required in cases concerning civil status and capacity',[53] there had been a violation of Article 6(1).

As just satisfaction under Article 50 the applicant sought compensation in respect of the damage he had allegedly suffered and reimbursement of his costs and expenses. The Court decided that the excessive length of the proceedings was highly detrimental and, considering the matter on an equitable basis, awarded the applicant the sum of 10,000 Deutschmarks as compensation for non-material loss. It held, however, that no compensation was called for in respect of alleged material loss. As far as costs and expenses were concerned, the Court decided that the excessive length of the domestic proceedings must have involved the applicant in expenses over and above those of an ordinary divorce petition and awarded him 10,000 Deutschmarks in this respect. In addition, the applicant represented himself before the Strasbourg institutions and did not receive legal aid. He claimed various travelling and other expenses arising out of these proceedings and the Court awarded him a further sum of 2,000 Deutschmarks to cover his expenditure under this head.

Right to take proceedings to challenge the lawfulness of detention (Article 5(4))— equality of arms—just satisfaction (Article 50)

Case No. 10. Lamy case.[54] The Court held unanimously that Belgium had violated Article 5(4) of the Convention when a person was committed for trial without being able to inspect his case file. As just satisfaction under Article 50 the Government was ordered to pay the applicant 100,000 Belgian francs in respect of his costs and expenses.

This case originated in an application against Belgium lodged with the European Commission by a Belgian citizen in 1983. The applicant was the manager of a pri-

---

[51] Ibid., para. 47 (emphasis added).
[52] Ibid., para. 48.
[53] Ibid., para. 49.
[54] ECHR, judgment of 30 March 1989, Series A, No. 151. The Court consisted of the following Chamber of Judges: Ryssdal (President); Cremona, Thór Vilhjálmsson, Pettiti, Russo, De Meyer, Carrillo Salcedo (Judges).

vate limited company which built industrial buildings and which was declared bankrupt by a Belgian court in November 1982. In February of the following year he was arrested and charged with fraudulent bankruptcy. He appeared before the local *chambre du conseil*, which upheld the warrant for his arrest issued by the investigating judge. The warrant was also upheld by the Liège Court of Appeal and in May 1983 a further appeal to the Court of Cassation was dismissed. When the *chambre du conseil* first confirmed the arrest warrant, and when the case was heard by the Court of Appeal, neither Mr Lamy, nor his counsel, had access to the file on his case.

In his application to the Commission Mr Bock claimed that he was the victim of a violation of several paragraphs of Article 5 and also of Article 6(3)(b). In its report in October 1987 the Commission expressed the opinion that there had been a violation of Article 5(4), though not of Article 6(3)(b), and that it was unnecessary to consider his other complaints. The Commission then referred the case to the Court.

Article 5(4) of the Convention, which has been quoted earlier,[55] guarantees those deprived of their liberty by arrest or detention the right to take proceedings by which the lawfulness of the detention can be judged. The argument that this provision had been violated in the present case rested on the proposition that to comply with the requirements of Article 5(4) the domestic review of detention must involve objective, adversarial, proceedings in which the principle of equality of arms is respected. In Mr Bock's submission the authorities' refusal to give him access to his file had put him at a serious disadvantage with the result that the requirements of procedural fairness had not been satisfied.

In Belgian law the file on a suspected person is opened by the investigating judge and added to as the case against the suspect is built up. The Government maintained that the reason why the defence was denied access to the file was that it was being constantly added to and as a practical matter could not be held at the registry for consultation. The Government also submitted that Mr Lamy had had the benefit of adversarial proceedings because he was notified of the case against him and was able to participate in the proceedings. Although he had not had access to the case file, this was unnecessary since, according to the Government, the principle of equality of arms had no relevance to applications for provisional release.

The Court rejected the Government's arguments. It found that access to the case file was essential for the defence to be able to challenge the lawfulness of the arrest warrant effectively, and in an important statement of principle held that:

> The appraisal of the need for a remand in custody and the subsequent assessment of guilt are too closely linked for access to documents to be refused in the former case when the law requires it in the latter case.[56]

Whereas the prosecution was familiar with the whole file, the applicant had been denied the chance to challenge the reasons relied on to justify a remand in custody. There had been a failure to respect the principle of equality of arms and so the procedure was not truly adversarial. There had therefore been a violation of Article 5(4).

The applicant also relied on Article 5(2), which provides for an arrested person to be informed of the reasons for his arrest, Article 5(3), which provides for a

[55] See Case No. 4.
[56] Judgment, para. 29.

prompt judicial hearing, and Article 6(3)(b), which guarantees adequate time and facilities for the preparation of a defence. As regards the first two provisions, however, the Court found the applicant's arguments to be unfounded and, ruling that his submissions in relation to Article 6(3)(b) were essentially the same as those it had accepted in relation to Article 5(4), agreed with the Commission that this provision need not be considered.

As just satisfaction under Article 50 the applicant claimed a substantial sum in respect of damage allegedly suffered. However, the Court found that there was no evidence that the applicant would have been released earlier if he had been able to inspect the file and so held that he had suffered no pecuniary loss. As regards non-pecuniary loss, on the other hand, it decided that the judgment provided adequate satisfaction. On the matter of costs and expenses the Court awarded only one third of the sum claimed in view of the applicant's failure to provide the Court with the necessary details.

Right to respect for private life and home (Article 8(1))—application to search authorized by 'Anton Piller order'—the meaning of 'in accordance with the law' and 'necessary in a democratic society' in Article 8(2)

Case No. 11. Chappell case.[57] In this case, which concerned the United Kingdom, the Court held unanimously that the execution of a court order under which the applicant was required to submit to a search of his premises in furtherance of civil proceedings had not given rise to a breach of Article 8 of the Convention.

The applicant, Mr Chappell, operated a club for the exchange of video cassettes in the town of Frome. His business came to the notice of two film companies and two organizations which had been formed to protect film producers and distributors from activities in breach of copyright. Following a report from a private investigator, these four bodies began proceedings for breach of copyright and, as a preliminary step in the action, obtained an 'Anton Piller order' from the High Court. Such orders are made without the defendant's being heard or notified, but incorporate various provisions to safeguard his position.[58]

The order obtained by the plaintiffs in this case required Mr Chappell to permit up to five of their representatives to enter his premises for the purpose of searching for and removing unlicensed copies of films, the copyright of which was owned by the plaintiffs, along with certain related documents. As well as being used for his business activities, the premises which were to be searched were occupied by Mr Chappell as his home.

The investigator had informed the police that he had seen on the premises material which he considered to be obscene. The police therefore obtained a warrant to search the premises and seize any pornographic video films. On 2 March 1981, in accordance with a prearranged plan, the police and the plaintiffs' solicitors entered Mr Chappell's premises together. The police served their warrant and began their search. The solicitors then served the Anton Piller order on the applicant, and after he had taken legal advice, proceeded to execute it, at the same time

[57] ECHR, judgment of 30 March 1989, Series A, No. 152. The Court consisted of the following Chamber of Judges: Ryssdal (President); Bindschedler-Robert, Walsh, Sir Vincent Evans, Macdonald, Bernhardt, Spielmann (Judges).

[58] An outline of the nature and conditions of Anton Piller orders, together with information relating to their execution and the remedies available to the defendant, will be found in paragraphs 10 to 24 of the judgment.

as the police search. The searches were made by five representatives of the plaintiffs and eleven or twelve police officers and a substantial quantity of material was removed.

Subsequent proceedings in the High Court and the Court of Appeal concluded with the dismissal of applications by Mr Chappell for discharge of the order and the return of items seized under it. The courts did, however, criticize certain aspects of the procedure followed in relation to the simultaneous searches. The action for breach of copyright was later stayed by a court order made with the parties' consent. This order restrained Mr Chappell from any dealings with unlicensed copies of the plaintiffs' films, directed that the material seized under the Anton Piller order be returned to him after erasure of films from the cassettes, and released both sides from any liability or claim arising from the subject-matter of the action and its pursuit by the plaintiffs.

In his application to the Commission in 1982 Mr Chappell raised a variety of complaints concerning the terms, content and manner of service of the Anton Piller order and invoked several articles of the Convention. In its report in October 1987 the Commission reviewed the application under Article 8 and expressed the opinion by 6 votes to 5 that there had been no violation of the applicant's rights. The Commission then referred the case to the Court.

Article 8 of the Convention provides:

1. Everyone has the right to respect for his private life . . ., his home and his correspondence.
2. There shall be no interference by a public authority with the exercise of this right except such as is in accordance with the law and is necessary in a democratic society . . . for the protection of the rights and freedoms of others.

The United Kingdom Government accepted that there had been an interference with Mr Chappell's right to respect for his private life and his home. The applicant, for his part, accepted that the interference had the legitimate aim of protecting the rights of others, namely the plaintiffs' copyright. The questions for the Court were therefore whether the interference was 'in accordance with the law' and, if so, whether it was 'necessary in a democratic society' for achieving its aim.

To be 'in accordance with the law' an interference with an applicant's right must satisfy a number of conditions.[59] First of all it must have some basis in domestic law. The Court found that as regards Anton Piller orders in general this condition was satisfied because whatever the precise basis on which such orders were made, the concept of law includes unwritten or common law. As regards the particular order in this case the applicant submitted that the grant and the execution of it were contrary to English law. The Court, however, rejected this argument, explaining that the issue of legality had been examined in detail by the English courts. A further requirement is that the law should be accessible and foreseeable. No difficulty arose as to former, and as regards foreseeability the Court held that the criteria for granting this form of relief are now sufficiently well settled. A final condition, mentioned by the Court in the *Olsson* case,[60] is that the law is not arbitrary in its operation. Having regard to the various safeguards attached to the order in the present case, the Court found that this requirement too was satisfied.

Turning to the issue of whether the interference was 'necessary in a democratic

[59] See the *Sunday Times* case, Series A, No. 30, and this *Year Book*, 50 (1979), p. 257.
[60] ECHR, judgment of 24 March 1988, Series A, No. 130, and this *Year Book*, 59 (1988), p. 380.

society', the Court observed that the need for the order arose from the nature and scope of the applicant's business. The order was accompanied by safeguards in the form of limitations on its scope and undertakings by the plaintiffs, while remedies were available to Mr Chappell in the event of improper execution. Moreover, the fact that implementation of the order was left to the plaintiffs' solicitors did not mean that the High Court was unable to exercise sufficient supervision.

The Court agreed with the applicant that there were aspects of the actual execution of the order which were open to criticism: the applicant had not been given a proper opportunity to refuse the plaintiffs entry at the door and the premises had been searched simultaneously by sixteen or seventeen people. However, these shortcomings, which had been criticized by the English courts, were in the European Court's view not so serious that the execution of the order could be regarded as disproportionate to the legitimate aim pursued. Accordingly, since the interference with the applicant's right had been justified, there was no violation of Article 8.

The judgment in this case is a straightforward application of established principles in what ought to be an unusual type of situation. While there are advantages for plaintiffs who can arrange for implementation of an Anton Piller order to coincide with the execution of a search warrant, if the safeguards which should surround both are to be effective, a clear separation between the two is plainly desirable.

Trial within a reasonable time (Article 6(1))—the meaning of 'contestation' *and* 'civil rights and obligations' *in Article 6(1)—just satisfaction (Article 50)*

Case No. 12. Neves e Silva case.[61] The Court held unanimously that there had been a violation of Article 6(1) of the Convention because a civil action instituted by the applicant in Portugal had not been resolved within a reasonable time. As just satisfaction under Article 50 the Court ordered the Government to pay the applicant 500,000 escudos in respect of non-material damage and 400,000 escudos in respect of his costs and expenses.

In 1962 Mr Neves e Silva, who was one of the owners and the managing director of the company *Molda Plásticos*, sought authorization to use an automatic machine for the manufacture of plastic fibres. He was unsuccessful. In 1963 his company amended its articles of association and a new company was set up, *Indústrias de Plástico Póvoa Mar*, in which he held 30 per cent of the share capital. Between 1968 and 1971 he made numerous further attempts to obtain the desired authorization, but the competent authorities rejected his requests, although they accepted applications from two other shareholders and from competitors.

In May 1972 Mr Neves e Silva brought an action in the Lisbon Administrative Court for damages against the State, a chief engineer of the Directorate General for Industry, and the two rival shareholders in the company. In March 1984 the Administrative Court declared the action time-barred and therefore extinguished. In October 1985 an appeal to the Supreme Administrative Court was dismissed. A further appeal to the same court in plenary session also failed.

In his application to the Commission in October 1984 Mr Neves e Silva com-

---

[61] ECHR, judgment of 27 April 1989, Series A, No. 153. The Court consisted of the following Chamber of Judges: Ryssdal (President); Pinheiro Farinha, Pettiti, Walsh, Sir Vincent Evans, Spielmann, Valticos (Judges).

plained that the administrative courts had not heard his case within a reasonable time and that as a consequence there had been a breach of Article 6(1) of the Convention.[62] In its report in December 1987 the Commission expressed the unanimous opinion that this provision had been violated. The Commission and the Government then referred the case to the Court.

Before the Court the Portuguese Government challenged the application on the merits, but also raised two objections to admissibility. One, that because Mr Neves e Silva was a minority shareholder he failed to qualify as a 'victim' within the meaning of Article 25, was quickly disposed of. Although this submission derived some support from a previous decision of the Commission,[63] the Court pointed out that since the only issue was whether the applicant's case was heard within a reasonable time, his status as a minority shareholder was irrelevant.

The other objection was more substantial. This was that Article 6(1) was inapplicable because the Lisbon court did not have to decide a 'dispute' (*contestation*) concerning 'civil rights and obligations'. This is a type of objection which the Court has often had to consider and here, as in many previous cases, the attempt to restrict the scope of the Convention was unsuccessful. On the question of whether the domestic court had had to determine a '*contestation*' the Court recalled that Article 6(1) extends to disputes which can be said on arguable grounds to be recognized under domestic law, irrespective of whether they are also protected under the Convention.[64] These conditions were satisfied in the present case. The applicant had genuine grounds for considering that the conduct of a public official could have incurred the liability of the State. In finding that the right relied on was statute-barred, the domestic court had resolved a '*contestation*' concerning Mr Neves e Silva's right to compensation for the wrongful conduct of the administrative authorities. Such a right was a 'civil right' notwithstanding the origin of the dispute in a matter involving administrative discretion, and therefore fell within Article 6(1).

Having disposed of the preliminary objections, the Court turned to the substantive issue. It decided that the period to be taken into consideration ran from November 1978, when Portugal became a party to the Convention, to June 1985 when the Supreme Court's judgment was notified to the parties. To decide whether this period of six years and seven months was unreasonable the Court applied the criteria laid down in its extensive case law. It noted that the case was not particularly complex and attached no weight to an argument that the applicant had lengthened the proceedings. As far as the conduct of the domestic courts was concerned, the Court noted that efforts had been taken to improve the functioning of the administrative courts and tribunals.[65] However, since Portugal's ratification of the Convention the applicant had had to wait more than six years for a decision which merely found that the right relied on was statute-barred. In the Court's view the delays in these proceedings, which it noted were begun in 1972, could not be regarded as the consequence of a temporary crisis or justified thereby. There had therefore been a violation of Article 6(1).

As just satisfaction in respect of non-pecuniary loss the applicant claimed a large sum which the Government regarded as unreasonable. The Court agreed and,

---

[62] For the text of Article 6(1), see Case No. 2, above.

[63] *Yarrow v. United Kingdom* (1983), *Decisions and Reports*, No. 30, p. 155.

[64] See, for example, *H v. Belgium*, Series A, No. 127B, and this *Year Book*, 59 (1988), p. 371.

[65] In this respect the position of the administrative courts was different from that of the civil courts as described in *Martins Moreira* (Case No. 2).

though prepared to accept that he had incurred some damage in the form of mental stress, reduced the sum awarded to a small fraction of the claim. The claim in respect of costs and expenses was not disputed by the Government and was allowed in full.

Trial within a reasonable time (Article 6(1))—friendly settlement (Rule 48(2))

Case No. 13. Oliveira Neves case.[66] Following a friendly settlement between the Portuguese Government and the applicant, the Court decided unanimously to strike this case out of its list.

In 1979 the applicant, who ran a poultry business, dismissed S who was one of her employees. In March 1980 S brought an action in the Portuguese courts claiming that her dismissal was void and seeking arrears of salary and various amounts as compensation. In April 1985 the domestic proceedings were concluded with a finding in favour of S.

In her application to the Commission in June 1985 Mrs Oliveira Neves complained that the length of the proceedings in the Oporto Labour Court violated Article 6(1) of the Convention. In its report in December 1988 the Commission unanimously expressed the opinion that this article had indeed been violated. The Commission then referred the case to the Court.

In March 1989 the Court was informed that the Government and the applicant had reached a friendly settlement in the following terms:

Article 1—Mrs Oliveira Neves agrees to accept the sum of 1,300,000 escudos as compensation from the Portuguese Government, constituting full and final reparation for all the material and non-material damage alleged in this case and also covering all the lawyers' fees and other costs incurred.

Article 2—Mrs Oliveira Neves undertakes, subject to the payment of the aforementioned sum, not to proceed with the case pending before the Court and not to institute any subsequent proceedings in this connection against the Portuguese State, in the domestic or international courts.

Article 3—Mrs Oliveira Neves accepts that this sum of 1,300,000 escudos will be paid by the Portuguese Government immediately following the decision of the European Court of Human Rights to strike the case out of its list . . .

In view of the settlement the Government requested the Court to strike the case off the list in accordance with Rule 48(2) of the Rules of the Court which provides:

When the Chamber is informed of a friendly settlement, arrangement or other fact of a kind to provide a solution of the matter, it may, after consulting, if necessary . . . the Delegates of the Commission and the applicant, strike the case out of the list.

The Commission had no objection and the applicant regarded the settlement as in her interests. Therefore the only question was whether considerations of public policy necessitated a continuation of the proceedings. The Court ruled that they did not. Recalling that it had recently reviewed the reasonableness of the length of civil proceedings in Portugal in *Martins Moreira* (Case No. 2) and *Neves e Silva* (Case No. 12) and had examined the same issue elsewhere in *Bock* (Case No. 9) and many earlier cases, the Court explained that this extensive jurisprudence had

---

[66] ECHR, judgment of 25 May 1989, Series A, No. 153B. The Court consisted of the following Chamber of Judges: Ryssdal (President); Cremona, Bindschedler-Robert, Gölcüklü, Pinheiro Farinha, Spielmann, Martens (Judges).

already clarified the nature and extent of the obligations undertaken by the Contracting States.

Accordingly, the Court decided that it was appropriate to strike the present case out of the list.

Right to a hearing before an 'impartial' tribunal (Article 6(1))—exhaustion of domestic remedies (Article 26)—just satisfaction (Article 50)

Case No. 14. Hauschildt case.[67] In this case, which concerned Denmark, the Court held by 12 votes to 5 that there had been a breach of Article 6(1) of the Convention because the applicant was tried on criminal charges by tribunals whose impartiality was capable of appearing open to doubt. As just satisfaction under Article 50 it unanimously awarded him £20,000 in respect of his costs and expenses.

In January 1980 the applicant, Mr Hauschildt, was arrested and charged with various economic offences. He was remanded in custody by the Copenhagen City Court judge and his detention was subject to regular judicial control at intervals which never exceeded four weeks. He was held continuously in custody both before and during his trial, which began in the City Court in April 1981. Most of the orders prolonging Mr Hauschildt's detention on remand were made by the City Court judge who subsequently heard the case. In November 1982 the applicant was convicted and sentenced to seven years' imprisonment. He then appealed. Both before and during the trial on appeal decisions concerning his continued detention on remand were taken by some of the High Court judges who determined the appeal. In March 1984 the High Court confirmed the finding of guilt on six counts out of eight and reduced the sentence to five years' imprisonment. However, in view of the time which Mr Hauschildt had already spent in detention, he was released immediately.

In his application to the Commission in August 1980 Mr Hauschildt complained of various violations of the Convention. In its report in July 1987 the Commission expressed the opinion by 9 votes to 7 that as regards the only complaint which it had found admissible, which related to Article 6(1), there had been no breach of the Convention. The Commission then referred the case to the Court.

The only substantive question for the Court to consider was whether the two courts which heard the applicant's case were 'impartial', as Article 6(1) of the Convention requires. It is clear from the Court's case law that for the purpose of the Convention the impartiality of a court or tribunal must be examined in two ways: according to a subjective test, that is on the basis of the personal convictions of the judge, as in *Barberá, Messegué and Jabardo* (Case No. 5); and by applying an objective test, which means ascertaining whether the judge was so placed as to exclude any legitimate doubt as to his impartiality. In the present case there was no evidence of personal bias; the question was therefore whether the objective test was satisfied.

The Court recalled that in applying the objective test appearances are important because 'What is at stake is the confidence which the courts in a democratic society must inspire in the public and above all, as far as criminal proceedings are concerned,

---

[67] ECHR, judgment of 24 May 1989, Series A, No. 154. This case was decided by the plenary Court.

in the accused'.[68] In deciding whether there was a legitimate reason to fear that a particular judge lacked impartiality, the Court said that it had to establish whether the applicant's apprehensions on this score could be regarded as 'objectively justified'.[69] It then made the important point that the mere fact that a trial judge, or an appeal judge, had also made pre-trial decisions in the case could not in itself be held to justify fears as to his partiality.

The Court found, however, that in the present case there were special circumstances which put it into a different category. On numerous occasions before the opening of the two trials, both the City Court judge and certain of the High Court judges had based their decision that Mr Hauschildt should be detained on remand on section 762(2) of the Administration of Justice Act. This provision required the judge to be satisfied that there was a 'particularly confirmed suspicion' that the accused had committed the crime. This stipulation has been officially explained as requiring 'a very high degree of clarity' as to the question of guilt. As a result, said the Court, 'the difference between the issue the judge has to settle when applying this section and the issue he will have to settle when giving judgment at the trial becomes tenuous'.[70] The Court therefore concluded that in the circumstances the impartiality of the tribunals in question was capable of appearing to be open to doubt and that the applicant's fears in this respect could be considered objectively justified. Accordingly, it decided that there had been a breach of Article 6(1).

Although the Court upheld Mr Hauschildt's complaint, his request for just satisfaction under Article 50 was less successful. His claim for compensation for material damage was rejected on the ground that there was no causal link between it and the violation of Article 6(1). In addition, his claim in respect of non-pecuniary damage was rejected because the Court held that the finding of a violation in itself constituted adequate just satisfaction. The Court also rejected the applicant's claim for reimbursement of costs and expenses incurred outside Strasbourg, and for the proceedings before the Convention institutions it awarded him less than four-fifths of the sum claimed.

Five judges dissented from the Court's conclusion on Article 6(1).[71] Like the majority of the Commission, they considered that in the absence of evidence of personal bias, the judges concerned should be regarded as capable of distinguishing between their roles at different stages of the trial process and that the case therefore fell under the general rule permitting the exercise of multiple functions. Three of the dissenting judges were also of the view that the case should have been held inadmissible for failure to exhaust domestic remedies.[72] The Government maintained that under the rules relating to the composition of the bench in Denmark it is always open to an accused person to argue that a judge should be disqualified on grounds of previous involvement in a case. Mr Hauschildt had not invoked this provision because his legal advisers considered that such an argument could not succeed. Without deciding which view of Danish law was correct, the Court held that the Government had not demonstrated that the remedy in question was available and effective.

---

[68] Judgment, para. 48.
[69] Ibid.
[70] Ibid., para. 52.
[71] See the joint dissenting opinion of Judges Thór Vilhjálmsson, Palm and Gomard, para. 2, and the joint dissenting opinion of Judges Gölcüklü and Matscher.
[72] See the joint dissenting opinion of Judges Thór Vilhjálmsson, Palm and Gomard, para. 1.

Just satisfaction (Article 50)—costs and expenses—non-pecuniary damage—finality of judgments (Article 52)

Case No. 15. Brogan and others case (Application of Article 50).[73] The Court unanimously dismissed the applicants' claim for financial compensation and held that in view of its earlier judgment it could not consider a claim for reimbursement of their costs and expenses.

In its judgment on the merits (Case No. 4) the Court held that Article 5(3) of the Convention had been violated because none of the four applicants had been brought promptly before a judge or other judicial officer, following their arrest on suspicion of involvement in terrorist activities in Northern Ireland. It also found that there had been a breach of Article 5(5) because under the law of Northern Ireland the applicants did not have an enforceable right to compensation for the violation of Article 5(3). However, the Court rejected the applicants' claims under Articles 5(1) and 5(4). As regards the issue of just satisfaction it will be recalled that the Court decided that there was no need to examine the application of Article 50 in relation to the reimbursement of costs and expenses, since the applicants had not submitted any claim in this respect. The question of the claim for compensation for loss suffered, which they had presented, was reserved.

In the present proceedings the applicants sought reimbursement of the costs and expenses incurred in the proceedings before the Convention institutions and compensation for non-pecuniary loss. In a brief judgment the Court held that it was not open to it to consider the first claim because this had been settled by the 1988 judgment and Article 52 of the Convention states that 'The judgment of the Court shall be final'. As regards the issue of damage, it accepted that the applicants might have suffered some non-pecuniary damage as a result of the breaches of Articles 5(3) and 5(5). However, having regard to the circumstances of the case, and in particular the reasons for its dismissal of the applicants' claim under Article 5(1), the Court considered that the findings in its earlier judgment constituted sufficient just satisfaction.

Meaning of 'independent and impartial' tribunal (Article 6(1))—just satisfaction (Article 50)

Case No. 16. Langborger case.[74] The Court held by 17 votes to 3 that there had been a violation of Article 6(1) of the Convention because the Swedish court which heard a case brought by the applicant relating to his tenancy lacked the attributes of independence and impartiality. As just satisfaction under Article 50, the Government was ordered to pay the applicant 63,475 Swedish crowns in respect of his costs and expenses.

The applicant was the tenant of a flat in a town near Stockholm. His lease contained a clause stipulating that the rent must be fixed by negotiation between a landlords' union and a tenants' union, which is the usual arrangement in Sweden. Tenants are, however, entitled to apply to the courts to have such a clause deleted and, if successful, can then negotiate their rent individually with their landlord. In 1983 Mr Langborger applied to the local Rent Review Board, and subsequently to

[73] ECHR, judgment of 30 May 1989, Series A, No. 152B. This case was decided by the plenary Court.

[74] ECHR, judgment of 22 June 1989, Series A, No. 155. This case was decided by the plenary Court.

the Housing and Tenancy Court, to have the negotiation clause removed, but on each occasion was unsuccessful. Both organs were composed of professional judges and lay assessors nominated by a landlords' and a tenants' association. In his argument before these organs the applicant maintained that in view of their composition they were incapable of deciding his case impartially, but here also his arguments were rejected.

In his application to the Commission in 1984 Mr Langborger put forward a variety of submissions based on the Convention. In its report in October 1987 the Commission expressed the unanimous opinion that there had been a violation of Article 6(1) as regards a lack of impartiality, that there had been no violation of Articles 8 and 11, nor of Article 1 of Protocol No. 1, and that it was unnecessary to consider the complaint under Article 13, or under Article 6(1) as regards the requirements of a public hearing and a public pronouncement of the judgment. The Commission then referred the case to the Court.

The essence of the applicant's argument was that the lay assessors who were present in the bodies which had decided his case were unsympathetic to his submissions because they had close links with their respective associations. Although his objection was directed against both the Rent Review Board and the Housing and Tenancy Court, the European Court decided that it need only examine the latter, as this was the last national organ to decide the questions of fact and law which were in dispute.

The Housing and Tenancy Court which heard Mr Langborger's case was composed of two professional judges and two lay assessors. The Court noted that the independence and impartiality of the professional judges was not in issue. As regards the lay assessors, it found that it was difficult to separate the issues of impartiality and independence and so considered both together.[75] The Court observed that the lay assessors appeared in principle well qualified to take part in the adjudication of disputes between landlords and tenants and the specific issues which might arise in such cases. It recognized, however, that their independence and impartiality might be open to doubt in a particular case, although it accepted that there was no reason to question their personal impartiality in the present proceedings.

The crucial issue was the assessors' 'objective impartiality' and the question whether they presented an appearance of independence. Here the Court found that they had been nominated by, and had close links with, two associations with an interest in upholding negotiation clauses. Although the assessors were appointed to act independently, since the applicant sought the deletion of such a clause from his lease, he could legitimately fear that the lay assessors had a common interest contrary to his own. Thus the balance of interests, inherent in the Housing and Tenancy Court's composition in other cases, was liable to be upset when it came to decide Mr Langborger's claim. As the presence of the professional judges could not alter this situation, there had been a violation of Article 6(1).

The Court, like the Commission, decided that other claims either were insubstantial or need not be considered. It was therefore left only with the issue of 'just satisfaction' under Article 50. Here the Court rejected an unusual request by the applicant for remuneration for his own work on the case, together with further

---

[75] In his concurring opinion Judge Martens suggested that it would have been better to rule that no issue arose as regards independence and to decide the case only by reference to the issue of impartiality.

claims in respect of pecuniary and non-pecuniary damage, which it found had not been proved. As regards the applicant's costs and expenses, the Court pointed out that it had declared only one of his complaints to be well-founded and on this account awarded a sum of just over half the amount claimed.

Three judges dissented on the ground that the presence of the professional judges in the Housing and Tenancy Court ensured that its independence and impartiality were guaranteed.[76] This reasoning is, however, contrary to the Court's previous jurisprudence[77] and unsatisfactory in principle. They were on stronger ground when they drew attention to the difficulties which too strict an interpretation of the concept of impartiality could present in fields where it is common to find judicial bodies which include in their membership lay persons with specialized knowledge and expertise. In this respect it is significant that while the Court upheld Mr Langborger's claim, it did not condemn the Swedish system entirely, but emphasized the special features of the case. It follows that to meet the Court's standard of impartiality and independence it would be enough to provide for any case in which a negotiation clause is challenged to be heard by a chamber of the Housing and Tenancy Court from which interested lay assessors are excluded.

Right to respect for family life (Article 8(1))—application to decisions relating to a child in care—right of access to the courts (Article 6(1))—just satisfaction (Article 50)

Case No. 17. Eriksson case.[78] This case concerned a number of complaints against Sweden brought by Mrs Cecilia Eriksson, on behalf of herself and her daughter Lisa. The Court held unanimously that as regards both applicants there had been a violation of Article 8 of the Convention by reason of a prohibition on the mother from removing her daughter from her foster home and restrictions on their access to each other. It also held unanimously that as regards the mother there had been a violation of Article 6(1) because no judicial remedy was available to challenge the restrictions on access, and by 15 votes to 5 that this also constituted a violation of the same provision as regards the daughter. In respect of other complaints examined it found that the articles invoked either had not been violated or were not applicable. As just satisfaction under Article 50 Sweden was ordered to pay 200,000 Swedish crowns to Cecilia Eriksson and 100,000 Swedish crowns to Lisa Eriksson in respect of non-pecuniary damage and 100,000 Swedish crowns to Cecilia Eriksson in respect of her legal costs and expenses.

In March 1978, when Mrs Eriksson's daughter Lisa was less than a month old, she was taken into public care and placed in a foster home. This was because conditions at home were unsatisfactory, Mrs Erkisson having been convicted of possessing stolen goods and narcotics, for which offences she had been sentenced to 14 months' imprisonment. During her time in prison Mrs Erkisson underwent a religious conversion and in January 1983, because conditions in the mother's home

---

[76] See the dissenting opinion of Judge Pinheiro Farinha and the joint dissenting opinion of Judges Pettiti and Valticos.

[77] In 1984, for example, the Court held that the Tyrol Regional Real Property Transactions Authority was not an 'independent' tribunal because one of its seven members was a civil servant in a subordinate relationship to one of the parties. See the *Sramek* case, Series A, No. 84, and this *Year Book*, 55 (1984), p. 392.

[78] ECHR, judgment of 22 June 1989, Series A, No. 156. This case was decided by the plenary Court.

had considerably improved, the Social District Council terminated care. Nevertheless, the Council prohibited Mrs Eriksson from removing her daughter from the foster home, although in the light of its long-term aim that they should be reunited, it decided that she should have a limited right of access to Lisa.

Mrs Eriksson challenged the prohibition on removal before the administrative courts but was unsuccessful. In August 1985 the Social District Council resolved 'not to decide at present on the access and the frequency of access'. In this decision the Council noted that it could not indicate any avenues of appeal since there were no legal provisions on which a decision on access could be based. In 1987 the Social District Council introduced an action before the District Court requesting that custody of Lisa be transferred to the foster parents. At the time the case was heard by the European Court these proceedings were still pending.

In her application to the Commission in December 1984 Mrs Eriksson and her daughter complained of violations of numerous articles of the Convention. In its report in July 1988 the Commission expressed the opinion that there had been a violation of both applicants' rights under Article 8 and a breach of Article 6(1) in respect of the claim for access to Lisa. Various other complaints were rejected. The Commission and the Government then referred the case to the Court.

The relevant part of Article 8 of the Convention provides:

1. Everyone has the right to respect for his . . . family life . . .
2. There shall be no interference by a public authority with the excerise of this right except such as is in accordance with the law and is necessary in a democratic society . . . for the protection of health . . . , or for the protection of the rights and freedoms of others.

Mrs Eriksson raised no complaint as regards the initial decision to take Lisa into care or its implementation. Her complaint was that the authorities had violated her right to respect for family life when they had prohibited her from removing Lisa from the foster home, maintained the prohibition in force for more than six years, imposed restrictions on access and failed to reunite the applicants. The Court found that the prohibition on removal and its subsequent maintenance in force amounted to an interference with the applicant's right to respect for family life. As regards the other measures the Court found that the same was true for the restrictions on access. These interferences, however, all had legitimate aims since they were designed to protect Lisa's health and rights. The question was therefore whether the disputed measures complied with the other requirements of Article 8(2).

As regards the prohibition on removal the Court considered that the scope of the discretion conferred on the authorities by the relevant legislation was reasonable and acceptable. It therefore met the requirement that an interference should be 'in accordance with the law' in general, and also satisfied this requirement as regards its application in the particular case. However, this did not apply to the restrictions on access. In a decision in 1988 the Swedish Supreme Administrative Court found that such restrictions had no legal basis. The decision to restrict Mrs Eriksson's access to her daughter was therefore not 'in accordance with the law'.

Turning to the question of whether the prohibition on removal could be regarded as 'necessary in a democratic society', the Court observed that this requirement might well be regarded as satisfied as far as the original decision to impose a prohibition was concerned. However, as regards the maintenance in force of the prohibition and the restrictions on access, the Court stated that in cases like this 'a mother's right to respect for family life under Article 8 includes a right to the taking of measures with a view to her being reunited with her child'.[79] It appeared, however, that under Swedish law Mrs Eriksson had no enforceable visiting rights while the prohibition on removal was in force. The Court also found that she had in fact been denied sufficient opportunities of meeting her daughter to promote the lifting of the prohibition on removal and the reunification of mother and daughter. The resulting stress in the relations between the applicants, and the uncertainty with regard to Lisa's future, had already lasted for more than six years, causing great anguish to both of them. Notwithstanding Sweden's margin of appreciation, the Court concluded that in these circumstances there had been a violation of the mother's rights under Article 8.

Mrs Eriksson's complaint under Article 6(1) was that she had been denied a right of access to a court to challenge the restrictions on access to Lisa. The Court upheld this complaint because in its decision in 1988 the Supreme Administrative Court had recognized that no administrative appeal lay against a decision by the Social Council to restrict access. While it was true that Mrs Eriksson could challenge the prohibition on removal, and had in fact done so, the Court explained that 'in cases of the present kind, the question of access is quite distinct from the question of whether or not to uphold the prohibition on removal'.[80] The Court therefore decided that the judicial remedies available were not adequate and held that there had been a breach of Article 6(1).

The daughter's complaints were dealt with more briefly. Mrs Eriksson, acting as her daughter's legal guardian and natural parent, alleged that Lisa had been a victim of the same violations of Articles 8 and 6(1) as herself. On the basis of the reasons given in respect of Mrs Eriksson the Court agreed. The decision in respect of Article 8 was unanimous, and that in respect of Article 6(1) by a majority of 15 votes to 5.

Since the Court, like the Commission, rejected the applicants' other complaints,[81] there remained only the question of just satisfaction under Article 50. The applicants each claimed 5,000,000 Swedish crowns for non-pecuniary damage, but the Court agreed with the Government that these claims were excessive and awarded much smaller sums. It also awarded a reduced sum to Mrs Eriksson in respect of her legal costs and expenses.

This is the latest case in what is now a series of decisions subjecting the arrangements for protecting the interests of children who are taken into care, and those of their parents, to scrutiny at Strasbourg.[82] The fact that on most issues the Court was unanimous indicates that the problems here were relatively straightforward,

---

[79] Judgment, para. 71.

[80] Ibid., para. 81.

[81] Their other complaints, which were rejected unanimously, were that they had not received a 'fair hearing', 'within a reasonable time', contrary to Article 6(1); that there had been an additional violation of their right of access to the courts, in view of the circumstances in which Mrs Eriksson had been forced to withdraw an appeal; that they were victims of a breach of Article 2 of Protocol No. 1 because Mrs Eriksson was allegedly prevented from giving Lisa an education according to the beliefs of the Pentecostal movement; and that they had no effective remedy under Article 13 in respect of certain of the rights which they claimed.

[82] For earlier cases of this type see the *Olsson* case, Series A, No. 130, and this *Year Book*, 59 (1988), p. 380, and *O, H, W, B and R* v. *United Kingdom*, Series A, Nos. 120 and 121, and this *Year Book*, 58 (1987), p. 484.

but the question of the daughter's position under Article 6(1), on which the Court was divided, raises an unusual and interesting point. The judges who dissented drew attention to the fact that Lisa had never shown any interest in reuniting with her mother, but, on the contrary, wished to remain with her foster parents.[83] Although they found that this did not affect her position under Article 8, they considered that it made it somewhat unreal to regard her as the victim of a violation of her right to a court under Article 6. There is something to be said for this view. While there are many issues on which the position of parents and children under the Convention will be identical, this cannot be assumed, and where, as here, the facts suggest otherwise a distinction between their respective claims ought to be made.

Trial within a reasonable time (Article 6(1))—just satisfaction (Article 50)

Case No. 18. Unión Alimentaria Sanders SA case.[84] In this case which concerned Spain, the Court held unanimously that there had been a violation of Article 6(1) because civil proceedings instituted by the applicant company had not been concluded within a reasonable time. The Government was ordered to pay the applicant 1,500,000 pesetas as compensation for pecuniary damage and 220,171 pesetas in respect of costs and expenses.

In May 1979 Unión Alimentaria Sanders SA, a limited company in the food industry, brought an action in Barcelona for the recovery of a debt. By an order in December 1981 the case, which concerned a contract for the rearing of pigs, was declared ready for decision. In October 1983, as no judgment had yet been delivered, the applicant company appealed to the Constitutional Court. In January 1985 this appeal was dismissed. In the meantime in December 1983 the first instance court had allowed some of the applicant's claims. However, on appeal by the applicant the Court of Appeal varied this judgment in May 1986. In October 1986 the applicant petitioned the court of first instance to have the judgment enforced. When the European Court gave its decision in July 1989 these proceedings were still pending.

In its application to the Commission in July 1985 the company complained that the length of the domestic proceedings had exceeded a reasonable time and that this constituted a violation of Article 6(1) of the Convention. In its report in October 1988 the Commission expressed the opinion by 13 votes to 1 that this provision had been violated. The Commission and the Government then referred the case to the Court.

The period to be considered began in July 1981, which was when the Spanish declaration accepting the right of individual petition took effect. Although the proceedings had still to be concluded, the Court considered that for the purposes of the case it was necessary only to examine the course of the proceedings up to September 1986, when the Court of Appeal's judgment was notified to the parties. The relevant period was therefore five years, two months and thirteen days.

In assessing the reasonableness of this period the Court began by noting that the case was not complex and that the applicant had shown diligence in carrying out its

---

[83] Partly dissenting opinion of Judges Thór Vilhjálmsson, Bindschedler-Robert, Matscher, Palm and Foighel.

[84] ECHR, judgment of 7 July 1989, Series A, No. 157. The Court consisted of the following Chamber of Judges: Ryssdal (President); Cremona, Thór Vilhjálmsson, Matscher, Macdonald, De Meyer, Carrillo Salcedo (Judges).

part of the procedures and had attempted to expedite matters by complaining of the delay. The Court then turned to the main point in issue which was the conduct of the domestic courts. Here it noted that there had been two periods of almost total inactivity amounting to more than three and a half years. This, said the Court, could be justified only by very exceptional circumstances. The Government drew attention to the increase in the volume of litigation, following the restoration of democracy in Spain, and claimed that the necessary remedial action had been taken. The Court, while expressing its appreciation of the authorities' efforts, pointed out that when a State is faced with a serious crisis it may not be enough to deal with cases according to their urgency and importance, but more fundamental action may be required.

Reviewing the situation in Spain, the Court found that the backlog in the relevant courts, which had been foreseeable, was the result not only of measures to improve access to the courts as a part of constitutional reform, but also of increased migration to Catalonia, and to Barcelona in particular. Since the backlog of work had become 'organisationally in-built',[85] the measures taken had proved insufficient and belated even at the time. Although they had slightly reduced the length of proceedings in the Court of Appeal, they had had no effect in the court of first instance. The Court therefore held that there was no excuse for the delay and concluded that there had been a violation of Article 6(1).

As just satisfaction under Article 50 the applicant company claimed a sum for pecuniary damage which it left to the Court's discretion. Making its assessment on an equitable basis, the Court awarded the amount mentioned earlier and a further sum in respect of costs and expenses.

Right to a fair trial (Article 6(1))—rights of the defence (Articles 6(3)(b) and 6(3)(d))—just satisfaction (Article 50)

Case No. 19. Bricmont case.[86] In this case, which concerned criminal proceedings in Belgium, the Court held by 5 votes to 2 that the failure of the authorities to arrange a confrontation between Mr Bricmont and a person seeking civil damages against him constituted a breach of Article 6(1) of the Convention. A number of other claims under Article 6 were rejected. As just satisfaction under Article 50 the Government was ordered to pay the applicant 274,335.95 Belgian francs in respect of his costs and expenses.

Between 1969 and 1977 the first applicant, Mr Bricmont, was the lawyer of Prince Charles, formerly Regent of the Kingdom of Belgium, who also entrusted him with certain work relating to the management of part of his fortune. Mrs Bricmont, the second applicant, assisted her husband in this work. In 1977 the Prince, who had recently appointed a new agent to manage his affairs, lodged a criminal complaint against Mr and Mrs Bricmont, accusing them of having cheated him of his assets. The applicants were acquitted at first instance, but in March 1983 were convicted on various charges by the Brussels Court of Appeal. In January 1984 the Court of Cassation dismissed an appeal by them on points of law.

The applicants' complaints all related to the procedure adopted by Belgian courts and in particular to their handling of various important matters of evidence.

[85] Judgment, para. 41.
[86] ECHR, judgment of 7 July 1989, Series A, No. 158. The Court consisted of the following Chamber of Judges: Ryssdal (President); Cremona, Matscher, Pinheiro Farinha, Macdonald, Russo, De Meyer (Judges).

On two occasions the President of the Brussels Court of Appeal took unsworn evidence from Prince Charles and in July 1979 the latter appeared as a complainant and civil party before the investigating judge of the Brussels *tribunal de première instance*. In October of the same year a confrontation was arranged between the Prince and Mr Bricmont. However, although there was no legal impediment to his doing so,[87] the Prince did not appear at the hearings before the court of first instance because of his poor state of health.

In 1980 Mr and Mrs Bricmont sought to have evidence taken from two witnesses, C and G, but the *chambre du conseil* did not consider it necessary to call them. A statement was subsequently taken from C by the Cannes police, acting under letters rogatory issued by the office of the Brussels Crown Prosecutor. In 1982 the applicants applied for another witness, M, to be examined on oath, and produced a statement from C in which he said he was available to give evidence. However, no action was taken as regards either witness. At the request of the Brussels investigating judge, searches were made in France and Switzerland in an attempt to trace the books of various companies, but these searches were unsuccessful and no audit was ordered of the Prince's financial affairs.

Finally, a gouache by the Prince, entitled 'Storm over Cannes', was not ordered to be produced at the trial, despite a request from the applicants, who claimed that since the painting had been dedicated to them by the Prince, it showed that he was well disposed towards Mrs Bricmont and thus could help to prove the authenticity of a disputed deed of gift.

In their applications to the Commission in 1984 Mr and Mrs Bricmont claimed *inter alia* that the various deficiencies in the judicial investigations constituted a breach of several aspects of Article 6. In its report in October 1987 the Commission expressed the opinion that in certain respects there had been a violation of Article 6(1) and also of Article 6(3)(d), but not of Article 6(3)(b). The Commission then referred the case to the Court.

The parts of Article 6 which the Court was concerned with in this case provide:

1. In the determination of . . . any criminal charge against him, everyone is entitled to a fair . . . hearing . . . by [a] . . . tribunal . . .

. . .

3. Everyone charged with a criminal offence has the following minimum rights:

. . .

(b) to have adequate time and facilities for the preparation of his defence;

. . .

(d) to examine or have examined witnesses against him and to obtain the attendance and examination of witnesses on his behalf under the same conditions as witnesses against him.

Recalling that the guarantees of paragraph 3 represent aspects of the concept of a fair trial contained in paragraph 1, the Court decided that it was appropriate to examine the applicants' complaints in the light of the two paragraphs taken together.

Its first task[88] was to consider the manner in which evidence was taken from

---

[87] Under the Code of Civil Procedure princes of the blood cannot be summoned as witnesses unless a special royal decree has authorized them to appear in court. In the present case, however, a decree had been issued in August 1981 which would have enabled the Prince to give evidence if his health had permitted him to do so.

[88] Before dealing with the merits the Court briefly rejected a preliminary objection based on the alleged non-exhaustion of domestic remedies, which it held the Government was estopped from raising.

Prince Charles and the failure to arrange a confrontation between him and the applicants on all the charges. Here the applicants alleged that the Prince's unsworn evidence was taken in accordance with a prearranged understanding between the Crown Prosecutor's Office and the investigating judge. The Court, however, noted that while the procedure adopted had given rise to certain misgivings, it had not been repeated. It added that there are 'objective reasons'[89] for having special regulations for taking evidence from, and questioning, high-ranking persons of State, and unanimously concluded that such regulations do not conflict with Article 6.

The applicants further submitted that there should have been a confrontation between them and the Prince on all the charges if their trial was to be fair. On this point the Court noted that at each stage of the proceedings the applicants had asked for a confrontation with the Prince, but that no confrontation had been arranged for the benefit of Mrs Bricmont, while the confrontation arranged for her husband had dealt with only two of the five charges against him. Given that the judicial investigation was secret, Mr Bricmont had not at that time had access to the criminal file and could not question the Prince on all the charges, yet—and this was the crucial point—the criminal proceedings against the applicants had been based on the Prince's accusations.

The Court explained that the exercise of the rights of the defence, which is an essential part of the right to a fair trial, 'required in principle that the applicants should have an opportunity to challenge any aspect of the complainant's account during a confrontation or an examination, either in public or, if necessary, at his home'.[90] However, the Court still had to determine whether the Court of Appeal had relied on the Prince's accusations in order to convict the applicants. In the light of the judgment in March 1983, the Court decided that in holding three counts to have been proved the Court of Appeal had relied on the Prince's accusations without Mr Bricmont ever having had an opportunity to have evidence taken from the Prince in his presence on all the charges. It therefore decided that on those three charges he had been convicted after proceedings which infringed his rights of defence as secured by Article 6. As regards Mrs Bricmont, on the other hand, the Court decided that there had been no violation because the Court of Appeal did not refer to the Prince's submissions, but relied on other evidence.

The applicants' second complaint concerned the Belgian courts' failure to examine the witnesses, G, C, and M. The Court, however, considered that it did not need to discuss the position of G and C because G had died at an early stage and the applicants had not applied to the Court of Appeal for evidence to be heard from C. As regards M, the Court pointed out that it is normally for the national courts to decide whether it is necessary or advisable to call a witness. There might be exceptional circumstances which could prompt the Court to conclude that failure to hear a witness constituted an infringement of Article 6, but in the present case there were insufficient grounds for that conclusion. There had therefore been no breach of Articles 6(1) and 6(3)(d) taken together.

The applicants' third complaint concerned the failure to have the Prince's accounts audited. On this issue the Court acknowledged that an audit would have been desirable. It noted, however, that the applicants themselves maintained that most of the disputed transactions had been carried out without being properly

[89] Judgment, para. 77.
[90] Ibid., para. 81

recorded and through companies which observed a rule of secrecy. In these circumstances the Belgian courts could reasonably have believed that an audit would serve no useful purpose. The applicants could therefore not complain of this decision and had, indeed, never clearly requested an audit. Accordingly, there had been no breach of Article 6(1) and Article 6(3)(b) taken together.

The final complaint concerned the gouache 'Storm over Cannes'. However, the applicants' difficulty here was that prior to their appearance before the European Court they had never given any details of the text of the dedication on which they had sought to rely. With regard to this point the Court therefore concluded that they could not claim to be the victims of a breach of paragraphs 1 and 3(b) of Article 6, taken together.

Since the Court had found no violation of Mrs Bricmont's rights, the issue of just satisfaction under Article 50 only needed to be considered in relation to her husband. As regards pecuniary damage, he claimed a large sum for deprivation of his professional income. The Court, however, found that no causal connection had been established between the violation of the Convention and the alleged damage and so rejected this claim. As regards non-pecuniary damage, Mr Bricmont claimed compensation for the 981 days he was held in detention and 'the Belgian Government's attitude'.[91] The Court, however, considered that the judgment itself constituted sufficient just satisfaction and so rejected this claim also. As compensation for costs and expenses the applicant claimed various amounts in respect of proceedings in Belgium and Canada.[92] The Court held that no award could be made for the latter, but as regards the proceedings in Belgium awarded a proportion of the costs incurred. In addition Mr Bricmont was awarded an equitable sum in respect of the cost of the Strasbourg proceedings, together with a proportion of the costs incurred by Mrs Bricmont.

On most of the issues in this case the Court was unanimous, but four judges delivered dissenting opinions. Judges Matscher and De Meyer held that there was no infringement of the rights of the defence because when the proceedings were viewed as a whole, the Belgian courts had acted reasonably in not arranging further confrontations with the Prince. For Judges Pinheiro Farinha and Russo, on the other hand, there was not only a violation stemming from the failure to arrange further confrontations, but also a violation of both applicants' rights stemming from the failure to carry out an audit of the Prince's finances. Whatever one's conclusion on these specific points, the case confirms the observation made earlier in *Barberá, Messegué and Jabardo* (Case No. 5) that certain issues which can arise under Article 6 require the Court to investigate judicial proceedings in the Contracting States with a greater than usual attention to their detail.

Meaning of 'criminal charge' and 'civil rights and obligations' in Article 6(1)—right to a court (Article 6(1))—right to the peaceful enjoyment of possessions (Article 1 of Protocol No. 1)—just satisfaction (Article 50)

Case No. 20. Tre Traktörer Aktiebolag case.[93] The Court held by 6 votes to 1 that the withdrawal of a company's licence to serve alcoholic beverages in its res-

---

[91] Ibid., para. 98.

[92] Mr Bricmont was extradited from Canada in July 1988.

[93] ECHR, judgment of 7 July 1989. Series A, No. 159. The Court consisted of the following Chamber of Judges: Ryssdal (President); Cremona, Thór Vilhjálmsson, Pinheiro Farinha, Macdonald, Bernhardt, Palm (Judges).

taurant had involved a breach of Article 6(1) of the Convention, but no breach of Article 1 of Protocol No. 1. The Swedish Government was ordered to pay the applicant 60,000 Swedish crowns under Article 50 in respect of its costs and expenses.

The applicant in this case was a company, *Tre Traktörer Aktiebolag*, which ran a restaurant in Helsingborg for which it had been granted a licence to serve alcoholic drinks. In November 1982 the County Administrative Board informed the company that it was considering withdrawing the licence in view of certain discrepancies in the restaurant's book-keeping. However, when the Board came to decide the matter in January 1983 it resolved to admonish the company instead. The Social Council of Helsingborg, which wished the licence to be revoked, appealed against the Board's decision to the National Board of Health and Welfare. In July 1983 the latter quashed the decision and referred the matter back to the County Administrative Board. Later in the month the County Board revoked the licence with immediate effect. A request from the applicant to the National Board for a stay of execution was refused.

In its application to the Commission in October 1985 the company alleged that the withdrawal of its licence had involved breaches of various provisions of the Convention, including Article 6(1) and Article 1 of Protocol No. 1. In its report in November 1987 the Commission concluded that there had been a violation of Article 6(1), though not of the Protocol. The Commission then referred the case to the Court.

Article 6(1) of the Convention provides:

> In the determination of his civil rights and obligations, or of any criminal charge against him, everyone is entitled to a fair and public hearing . . . by an independent and impartial tribunal established by law . . .

The applicant's complaint was that the Swedish courts had no power to review the decisions of the two Boards relating to its drinks licence. However, Article 6(1) does not require a judicial procedure to be available in respect of all domestic decisions, only those which involve the determination of 'civil rights and obligations' or of 'any criminal charge'. Consequently, before the Court could consider the adequacy of Swedish law, it first had to decide whether Article 6(1) was applicable.

The Court rejected the argument that withdrawing the applicant's licence constituted the determination of a 'criminal charge'. Although this could be regarded as a severe measure, it did not have the character of a penal sanction. Accordingly, Article 6(1) was not applicable in this respect.[94] Whether the decision involved a determination of 'civil rights and obligations', on the other hand, raised more complex considerations, and on this point the Court agreed with the applicant. The extensive jurisprudence on this kind of issue[95] indicates that it is first necessary to establish that a dispute exists over a right. Here the Court rejected the Government's view that no serious dispute of fact or law concerning a right had arisen. It considered that the applicant could maintain on arguable grounds that under Swedish law it was entitled to run its restaurant with the licence, unless the

---

[94] It followed from this conclusion that Article 6(2), which concerns the presumption of innocence, and Article 7, which prohibits retrospective criminal law, both of which had been invoked by the company, were not applicable either.

[95] See, for example, the *Pudas* case and the *Boden* case, Series A, No. 125, and this *Year Book*, 59 (1988), p. 365, *H* v. *Belgium*, Series A, No. 127, and this *Year Book*, 59 (1988), p. 371, and the *Neves e Silva* case (Case No. 12, above).

conditions of the licence were contravened, or there was a statutory ground for revocation.

The second requirement was that the right in question was a 'civil' right. On this issue, which has frequently been the subject of argument in previous cases, the Court began by noting that the withdrawal of the licence had adverse effects on the goodwill and value of the restaurant. Whilst the Court recognized that the distribution of alcoholic beverages in Sweden involved features of public law, it pointed out that the serving of alcohol in restaurants and in bars was mainly performed by private persons and companies, which conducted a private commercial activity based on a contractual relationship with their customers. In these circumstances the Court concluded that the dispute in question did concern a civil right and that Article 6(1) was therefore applicable.

The question of compliance with the Convention was straightforward. The decisions of the National Board of Health and Welfare on the revocation of licences were not open to review on grounds of lawfulness by either the ordinary or the administrative courts. Moreover, the Court agreed with the applicant and the Commission that neither the National Board, nor the County Board, qualified as a 'tribunal' for the purpose of Article 6(1). The Court therefore concluded that there had been a violation of this provision.

The other issue in the case concerned Article 1 of Protocol No. 1, which provides:

Every natural or legal person is entitled to the peaceful enjoyment of his possessions. No one shall be deprived of his possessions except in the public interest and subject to the conditions provided for by law and by the general principles of international law.

The preceding provisions shall not, however, in any way impair the right of a State to enforce such laws as it deems necessary to control the use of property in accordance with the general interest or to secure the payment of taxes or other contributions or penalties.

The Court ruled that this provision was applicable because the economic interests connected with the running of the restaurant could be regarded as 'possessions' and its goodwill and value had been adversely affected by the withdrawal of the licence. However, it decided that the withdrawal of the licence did not amount to a deprivation of property, because the applicant retained certain economic interests in the restaurant. The withdrawal thus constituted a control of the use of property, rather than a deprivation, and called for consideration under the second paragraph. Turning to the issue of compliance with the paragraph's requirements, the Court observed that by subjecting the sale of alcohol to a licensing system the Swedish Parliament was implementing national policy in this field. It was therefore established that the aim was to control the use of property in the general interest. As regards the specific measures which had been taken in the present case, the Court held that there was nothing in the relevant decisions to suggest that they were contrary to Swedish law, or to support the applicant's contention that the revocation of its licence had a different purpose from that of the legislation. The Court therefore concluded that the withdrawal of the licence was lawful and pursued the general interest.

The other requirement was proportionality. Here the Court agreed with the Commission that the revocation of the licence was a severe measure in the particular circumstances. However, it observed that this had to be weighed against the general interest of the community and, in this context, as the Court has previously emphasized,[96] States enjoy a wide margin of appreciation. Although the two Boards could have taken less drastic measures, the Court, in the light of the aim of Swedish social policy, found that on the present facts Sweden had not failed to strike a fair balance between the economic interests of the applicant company and the general interest of society. Accordingly, the Court decided that there had been no breach of Article 1 of Protocol No. 1.

As just satisfaction for the violation of Article 6(1) the applicant claimed over three million Swedish crowns for the pecuniary damage it had allegedly suffered. The Court, however, rejected the claim. In spite of its reference to the adverse effects of the licensing decision on the company's economic interests in earlier parts of the judgment, the Court held that no causal link had been shown between the alleged pecuniary damage and the violation of the Convention. The applicant was therefore given nothing under this head. The Court did, however, give the applicant something in respect of its costs and expenses, although the sum awarded on an equitable basis was only half of the original claim.

Right to respect for private and family life (Article 8)—access to confidential records—positive obligations—freedom to receive information (Article 10)—just satisfaction (Article 50)

Case No. 21. Gaskin case.[97] In this case, in which the applicant was a person who had been brought up in the care of an English local authority, the Court held by 11 votes to 6 that the procedures followed in relation to access to the applicant's case records failed to secure respect for his private and family life as required by Article 8 of the Convention. As just satisfaction under Article 50 the Court held by 9 votes to 8 that the United Kingdom must pay the applicant £5,000 for non-pecuniary damage suffered and £11,000, less 8,295 French francs, in respect of his costs and expenses.

The applicant, who was born in 1959, was received into care in September 1960 by Liverpool City Council when his mother died. He remained in care under the Children Act 1948 until he reached the age of 18 in December 1977. While he was in care he was boarded out with various foster parents and a record of this was maintained by the local authority in accordance with the Boarding-Out of Children Regulations 1955. In 1979 Mr Gaskin, who alleged he was ill-treated while in care, wished to bring proceedings against the local authority for negligence and applied under the Administration of Justice Act 1970 for discovery of the local authority's case records relating to his period in care. In 1980 the High Court refused discovery on the grounds that case records compiled pursuant to the 1955 Regulations were private and confidential. This decision was confirmed by the Court of Appeal.

Between 1980 and 1983 various committees of the City Council adopted resolutions on the release of child care records. However, these could not be implemented because they were challenged in the courts by a member of the Council who considered that they went too far. Finally, in November 1983, the Council

---

[96] See, for example, the *James* case, Series A, No. 98, and this *Year Book*, 57 (1986), p. 450, and earlier the *Sporrong and Lönnroth* case, Series A, No. 52, and this *Year Book*, 53 (1982), p. 319. For discussion of the Court's treatment of the margin of appreciation in this context see Merrills, *The Development of International Law by the European Court of Human Rights* (1988), pp. 140–3.

[97] ECHR, judgment of 7 July 1989, Series A, No. 160. This case was decided by the plenary Court.

adopted a further resolution which provided that information in the applicant's file should be made available to him if the contributors to the file gave their consent to disclosure. This policy conformed to a circular issued by the DHSS earlier in the year. The applicant's case record consisted of 352 documents contributed by 46 persons. In May 1986 copies of 65 documents supplied by 19 persons were sent to the applicant's solicitors, these being the only documents whose authors had consented to disclosure.

In his application to the Commission in February 1983 Mr Gaskin complained that the refusal of Liverpool City Council to give him access to his case records violated his rights under Articles 8 and 10 of the Convention. In its report in November 1987 the Commission rejected the claim under Article 10, but concluded, by 6 votes to 6 with a casting vote by the acting President, that the procedures and decisions relating to access did amount to a violation of Article 8. The Government and the Commission then referred the case to the Court.

The main issue in this case was the scope of the right to respect for 'private and family life' which is guaranteed by Article 8.[98] The Government's first argument was that the applicant's personal file did not form part of his private life and so could not enjoy the protection of the Convention. The Court, like the Commission, had no difficulty in rejecting this view and held that the file did relate to Mr Gaskin's 'private and family life' in such a way that the question of access to it fell within the ambit of Article 8.

A more contentious issue was the application of Article 8 in the circumstances of the case. Mr Gaskin did not challenge the fact that information was compiled and stored about him and did not allege that any use of it was made to his detriment. His claim was that he had not been given unimpeded access to that information. The Court consequently observed that by refusing him access to his complete case records the United Kingdom could not be said to have 'interfered' with the applicant's private or family life. The substance of the complaint was not that the State had acted, but that it had failed to act. The question was therefore whether the United Kingdom was in breach of a positive obligation flowing from Article 8.

According to the Court's case law, 'although the essential object of Article 8 is to protect the individual against arbitrary interference by the public authorities, there may in addition be positive obligations inherent in an effective "respect" for family life'.[99] Was there such a positive obligation in the present case? According to the Government, the proper operation of the child-care service depended on information supplied by professional persons and bodies, and others. If the confidentiality of these contributors was not respected their co-operation would be lost and this would have detrimental consequences. The Government pointed out that there was no blanket refusal of access to case records since access was given to confidential information in so far as the consent of the contributor could be obtained. The applicant, on the other hand, drew attention to the fact that under the Access to Personal Files Act 1987, and its associated regulations, information of the kind he sought would in future be made available by public authorities. Although, as the Government pointed out, the new regulations would not apply to records compiled

---

[98] For the text of Article 8, see Case No. 17, above.
[99] See the *Johnston* case, Series A, No. 112, para. 55.

before April 1989, this change of policy did seem to weaken the Government's case.

Confronted with the delicate task of identifying the 'fair balance that has to be struck between the general interest of the community and the interests of the individual',[100] the Court decided that persons in Mr Gaskin's position have a vital interest in receiving the information necessary to know and understand their childhood and early development. Although a system which made access to child-care records dependent on the contributors' consent could in principle be regarded as compatible with Article 8, the Court considered that the interests of an individual seeking access to his records must be properly secured when a contributor to the records is not available or improperly refuses consent. In the Court's view in such a case the principle of proportionality required that an independent authority ought to decide whether access to the record should be granted. As no such system was available to Mr Gaskin, the majority of the Court concluded that the procedures followed had failed to secure respect for the applicant's private and family life. There had therefore been a breach of Article 8.

Since the Court unanimously held that Article 10 did not impose an obligation on the Government to impart the information in question to the applicant, the only remaining issue was the question of just satisfaction under Article 50. Mr Gaskin sought a large sum in respect of loss of earnings, but the Court, not surprisingly, dismissed this claim on the ground that the effect of any procedural deficiencies on the applicant's future earnings was entirely speculative. Although the claim for pecuniary damage was rejected, the Court by a narrow majority upheld a claim for non-pecuniary damage in view of the emotional distress and anxiety which the applicant could have suffered on account of the absence of an independent review procedure. Mr Gaskin's claims in respect of the costs and expenses of the domestic and European proceedings were accepted, though both were reduced, the former because the Court held that only costs incurred subsequently to the termination of the domestic proceedings could be considered, and the latter because it considered that the claim was not reasonable as to quantum.

This was one of the most difficult cases the Court had to decide in the period under review and, as the division of opinion in the Court and the Commission indicates, the issue as regards the extent of positive obligations under Article 8 was finely balanced. Five of the dissenting judges rejected the Government's argument that the records in Mr Gaskin's file did not relate to his private and family life, but agreed with its submission that by writing a letter to each contributor the local authority had gone as far as it reasonably could in meeting his request for access.[101] As they pointed out, although the majority had taken a different view, demanding a more elaborate procedure implicitly recognizes that access to this kind of record can only be given selectively and is quite different from deciding that someone in the applicant's position has a right of access to the whole of his file, regardless of the issue of confidentiality. It would likewise be wrong to see this decision as establishing any general right of access to information on the basis of Article 8 of the

[100] See the *Rees* case, Series A, No. 106, para. 37.

[101] Joint dissenting opinion of Judges Ryssdal, Cremona, Gölcüklü, Matscher and Sir Vincent Evans. The other member of the Court to vote against the decision, Judge Walsh, stated in his dissenting opinion that he did not regard Article 8 as applicable. He considered that the case did raise an issue under Article 10, but held that the conduct of the authorities in withholding the information from Mr Gaskin could be justified.

Convention, for the Court itself expressly disclaimed any such intention.[102] The judgment is, however, a step towards greater openness in an area where the importance and sensitivity of what is at stake indicate that a degree of judicial caution is well justified.

Freedom from inhuman or degrading treatment or punishment (Article 3)—application to extradition of a suspect to a non-European State—status of the death penalty and the 'death row phenomenon'—right to legal assistance (Article 6(3)(c))—right to an effective remedy (Article 13)—just satisfaction (Article 50)

Case No. 22. Soering case.[103] This case, to which both the United Kingdom and the Federal Republic of Germany were parties, concerned the imminent extradition of a German national from the United Kingdom to the United States, where he feared that he would be sentenced to death for capital murder and become subject to the 'death row phenomenon'. The Court held unanimously that in the event of a decision to extradite the applicant being implemented, there would be a breach of Article 3 of the Convention. On the other hand, the Court rejected the applicant's complaints under various paragraphs of Article 6 and under Article 13. As just satisfaction under Article 50, the British Government was ordered to pay the applicant £26,752.80 and 5,030.60 French francs, plus any value added tax, in respect of his costs and expenses.

The applicant was a German national who moved to the United States with his parents when he was eleven years old. At the time of the case he was in detention in the United Kingdom awaiting extradition to the United States. The extradition request had been made in July 1986 and was based on the terms of an extradition treaty between the two countries. The extradition was requested so that Mr Soering could be tried for murdering the parents of his girlfriend at their home in Bedford County, Virginia. At the time of the killing, which the applicant admitted and in which his girlfriend was also involved,[104] he was eighteen years old.

In March 1987 the Government of the Federal Republic of Germany also sought Mr Soering's extradition to stand trial for the alleged murders. If convicted there the applicant could not be executed as the death penalty has been abolished in the Federal Republic. In May 1987 the British Government informed the German Government that they proposed to consider the earlier United States request in the normal way.

In June 1987 the extradition hearing was held at Bow Street Magistrates' Court. Mr Soering put forward psychiatric evidence that at the time of the killing he was suffering from a mental abnormality which substantially impaired his responsibility for his acts. The court decided, however, that there was sufficient evidence to justify extradition and committed him to await the Home Secretary's order for his return to the United States. An application to the courts for an order of *habeas corpus* was unsuccessful and in August 1988 the Home Secretary signed the warrant ordering Mr Soering to be surrendered to the United States authorities.

Under Virginia law the death penalty may not be imposed unless one of two aggravating circumstances ('future dangerousness' of the defendant and 'vileness'

---

[102] Judgment, para. 37.
[103] ECHR, judgment of 7 July 1989, Series A, No. 161. This case was decided by the plenary Court.
[104] The woman in question, who was a US citizen, was extradited to the United States in May 1987. In August she pleaded guilty to the charge of being an accessory to the murder of her parents and was sentenced to 90 years' imprisonment.

of the crime) is proved by the prosecution beyond reasonable doubt at a separate sentencing hearing. The Supreme Court of Virginia automatically reviews every case in which a death sentence is passed. Virginia law recognizes a defence of insanity, but has no defence of diminished responsibility. The imposition of the death penalty is not precluded by a defendant's age, but age, along with other factors such as the defendant's mental state, can be taken into account as a mitigating factor at the sentencing stage.

In June 1987 the Attorney for Bedford County, who was responsible for conducting the prosecution against Mr Soering, gave an undertaking to the British Government that if the applicant were to be convicted of capital murder, as charged, he would indicate to the judge at the sentencing stage that it was the wish of the United Kingdom that the death sentence should not be imposed or carried out. It was clear, however, that in his capacity as prosecutor the Attorney maintained his intention to seek the death penalty.

If the applicant were to be sentenced to death he would be held on 'death row' at the Mecklenburg Correctional Centre, where a particularly stringent custodial regime is operated. The average time spent by an inmate on death row in Virginia is 6 to 8 years. The automatic appeal to the Supreme Court is normally completed within 6 months. The delays are mainly accounted for by the exercise of collateral challenges by the condemned men in the State and Federal Courts. The means of execution used in Virginia is electrocution.

Mr Soering's application against the United Kingdom was lodged with the European Commission in July 1988. During its examination of the case the Commission indicated to the Government, as an interim measure, that it was desirable not to extradite the applicant to the United States. In its report in January 1989 the Commission expressed the opinion that there had been a breach of Article 13, but no breach of either Article 3 or Article 6. The case was referred to the Court by the Commission and the United Kingdom Government in January 1989. In February it was also referred by the Government of the Federal Republic, acting under Article 48(b) of the Convention which enables a State whose national is alleged to be the victim of a violation of the Convention to bring a case before the Court. This is the first case in which a Government not associated with the proceedings before the Commission has taken advantage of this provision, and as a result of its use the Federal Republic became a party to the case. In January 1989, following requests for an interim measure from the Commission and the applicant, the Court indicated to the British Government that it would be advisable not to extradite the applicant, pending the outcome of the case.

In the proceedings before the Court the main issue concerned Article 3, which provides:

No one shall be subjected to torture or to inhuman or degrading treatment or punishment.

The first question was whether extradition by a Contracting State can involve the responsibility of that State under Article 3 for ill-treatment which the extradited person may suffer in the receiving country. The Court recognized the force of the British Government's point that the Convention does not govern the action of States which are not parties to it, nor does it purport to be a means of requiring contracting States to impose the standards of the Convention on others. It also accepted that the object of extradition is to prevent fugitive offenders from evading justice. On the other hand, it is a well-established principle that the provisions of

the Convention must be 'interpreted and applied so as to make its safeguards practical and effective',[105] and the Court observed that the 'absolute prohibition of torture and of inhuman or degrading treatment or punishment under the terms of the
Convention shows that Article 3 enshrines one of the fundamental values of the
democratic societies making up the Council of Europe'.[106] Although it is not normal for the Convention institutions to pronounce on the existence or otherwise of
potential violations of the Convention, a departure from this rule was necessary in
order to ensure the effectiveness of the safeguard provided in Article 3. The Court
therefore concluded that:

> . . . the decision by a Contracting State to extradite a fugitive may give rise to an issue
> under Article 3, and hence engage the responsibility of that State under the Convention,
> where substantial grounds have been shown for believing that the person concerned, if
> extradited, faces a real risk of being subjected to torture or to inhuman or degrading treat-
> ment or punishment in the requesting country.[107]

The next question was the bearing of this principle on the facts of the case. The
Court found that there were substantial grounds for believing that if the applicant
was returned to Virginia, he would run a real risk of a death sentence and consequently of exposure to the 'death row phenomenon', which allegedly constituted
inhuman and degrading treatment or punishment. The Court acknowledged that
in view of the applicant's age and mental state it could not assume that if he was
convicted of capital murder, he would necessarily be sentenced to death. It noted,
however, that the undertaking given by the Attorney for Bedford County did not
elimate the risk of the death sentence being imposed. Moreover the Attorney had
clearly expressed his intention of seeking a death sentence and:

> If the national authority with responsibility for prosecuting the offence takes such a firm
> stance, it is hardly open to the Court to hold that there are no substantial grounds for believ-
> ing that the applicant faces a real risk of being sentenced to death and hence experiencing the
> 'death row phenomenon'.[108]

The Court therefore concluded that Article 3 was applicable.

The third and final question was whether Mr Soering's exposure to the 'death
row phenomenon' would actually involve treatment or punishment contrary to
Article 3. According to the Court's case law, ill-treatment must achieve a minimum
level of severity if it is to contravene Article 3 and the assessment of this threshold
depends on the circumstances of the particular case.[109] In view of the terms of
Article 2(1) of the Convention,[110] the applicant did not attempt to argue that the
death penalty *per se* violates Article 3 and the Court, in a notable *obiter dictum*,
agreed that such an argument would be untenable. However, the applicant, with
whom the Federal Government substantially agreed, maintained that the constituent features of the 'death row phenomenon', when considered cumulatively, constituted such serious treatment that his extradition would contravene Article 3. He

---

[105] Judgment, para. 87.
[106] Ibid., para. 88.
[107] Ibid., para. 91.
[108] Ibid., para. 98.
[109] See *Ireland* v. *United Kingdom*, Series A, No. 25, and this *Year Book*, 49 (1978), p. 301, and the
Tyrer case, Series A, No. 26, and this *Year Book*, 49 (1978), p. 306.
[110] Article 2(1) provides: 'Everyone's right to life shall be protected by law. No one shall be deprived
of his life intentionally save in the execution of a sentence of a court following his conviction of a crime
for which this penalty is provided by law.'

also relied on the possibility of extradition or deportation to the Federal Republic, which he undertook not to oppose, and which he claimed accentuated the disproportionality of the Home Secretary's decision. The Commission and the United Kingdom Government, on the other hand, suggested that the degree of severity contemplated by Article 3 would not be attained.

The Court, after reviewing the facts described earlier, expressed its conclusion on this point as follows:

> For any prisoner condemned to death, some element of delay between imposition and execution of the sentence and the experience of severe stress in conditions necessary for strict incarceration are inevitable. The democratic character of the Virginia legal system in general and the positive features of Virginia trial, sentencing and appeal procedures in particular are beyond doubt. The Court agrees with the Commission that the machinery of justice to which the applicant would be subject in the United States is in itself neither arbitrary nor unreasonable, but, rather, respects the rule of law and affords not inconsiderable procedural safeguards to the defendant in a capital trial . . .
>
> However, in the Court's view, having regard to the very long period of time spent on death row in such extreme conditions, with the ever present and mounting anguish of awaiting execution of the death penalty, and to the personal circumstances of the applicant, especially his age and mental state at the time of the offence, the applicant's extradition to the United States would expose him to a real risk of treatment going beyond the threshold set by Article 3. A further consideration of relevance is that in the particular instance the legitimate purpose of extradition could be achieved by another means which would not involve suffering of such exceptional intensity or duration.[111]

The Court therefore concluded that the decision to extradite the applicant would, if implemented, give rise to a breach of Article 3.

The applicant also complained of various other violations of the Convention. These included an allegation that his extradition to the United States would violate Article 6(3)(c) (the right to legal assistance), and a claim under Article 13 which guarantees the right to an effective remedy. The Court rejected both submissions. On the first point it said that it could not rule out the possibility that 'an issue might exceptionally be raised under Article 6 by an extradition decision in the circumstances where the fugitive has suffered or risks suffering a flagrant denial of a fair trial in the requesting country'.[112] However, having made this significant observation, the Court ruled that in the present case there was no such risk. As regards Article 13, where the Commission had upheld the applicant's claim, the Court came to a different conclusion. Having examined the principles on which judicial review is exercised in English law, it was satisfied that the courts can review the reasonableness of an extradition decision in the light of the kinds of considerations relied on by Mr Soering in his submissions relating to Article 3. The Court therefore concluded that the applicant did have a remedy satisfying Article 13 in the form of an application for judicial review.

As just satisfaction with regard to the ruling on Article 3 the applicant did not claim damages, but invited the Court to give directions relating to the implementation of its judgment. The Court agreed that the judgment constituted adequate just satisfaction, but following its usual practice, pointed out that the execution of judgments is the responsibility of the Committee of Ministers. The Government suggested that costs and expenses should be awarded on a reduced basis because

---

[111] Judgment, para. 111.
[112] Ibid., para. 113.

some of the applicant's arguments had been rejected. However, since he had succeeded on the crucial issue of Article 3, the Court decided that he merited full reimbursement.

The decision in this case, which it is worth noting was unanimous, has far-reaching implications. The ruling that extradition (and presumably deportation) can give rise to an issue under Article 3 confirms the Commission's case law but is a point which the Court had not dealt with previously. The suggestion that the same principle could be relevant to Article 6 is consistent with its underlying rationale and naturally raises the possibility of further extensions. On the issue of Article 3 the decision is a useful addition to the Court's limited jurisprudence on the meaning of 'inhuman or degrading treatment'[113] and, though concerned with a very specific situation, will no doubt be closely studied in future cases. The statement that the death penalty as such is not a violation of Article 3 was challenged by one judge,[114] but is clearly correct. To abandon accepted canons of interpretation in order to promote humanitarian objectives is not only wrong but, as the result of the present case demonstrates, often also unnecessary.

Trial within a reasonable time (Article 6(1))—right to a fair trial (Article 6(1))— just satisfaction (Article 50)

Case No. 23. H v. France.[115] The Court held unanimously that France had committed a breach of Article 6(1) of the Convention because civil proceedings brought by the applicant were not concluded within a reasonable time. However, a claim that the applicant had also been denied a fair trial, contrary to the same article, was dismissed. As just satisfaction under Article 50 the Court awarded the applicant 50,000 French francs as compensation for non-pecuniary damage and 40,000 French francs in respect of his costs and expenses.

In 1961 the applicant, a primary school supply teacher, spent nearly four months in a psychiatric clinic in Strasbourg where he was diagnosed as schizophrenic and given an unauthorized treatment with amphetamines. The treatment caused a reaction known as 'amphetamine shock' and, although he subsequently tried to resume work, he was forced to retire owing to ill health and from 1964 onwards received a disability pension.

In 1974 H began proceedings against the hospital administration, claiming damages for the serious health problems which he alleged the treatment given to him in the clinic had caused. He also applied for an expert to be appointed to examine him. The Strasbourg Administrative Court dismissed both these claims in 1978 and in 1981 his appeal was dismissed by the *Conseil d'État*.

In his application to the Commission in 1982 H claimed that he had been denied a fair trial, contrary to Article 6(1), and that the length of the proceedings had exceeded a reasonable time. In its report in March 1988 the Commission rejected the first claim, but accepted the second. The Commission then referred the case to the Court.

As regards the length of the proceedings, H maintained that the period to be considered began in May 1973 when he applied to the Legal Aid Office at the Stras-

---

[113] See n. 109, above.
[114] Concurring opinion of Judge De Meyer.
[115] ECHR, judgment of 24 October 1989, Series A, No. 162. The Court consisted of the following Chamber of Judges: Ryssdal (President); Thór Vilhjálmsson, Gölcüklü, Pettiti, Macdonald, Carrillo Salcedo, Valticos (Judges).

bourg Administrative Court. This was disputed by the Government. Given the total length of the proceedings on the merits, the Court found that it was unnecessary to decide whether the preliminary procedure also came within the scope of Article 6(1). It therefore confined its review to the period from the start of the action in the Administrative Court in June 1974, to the notification of the *Conseil d'État*'s judgment in January 1982. The relevant period was therefore just over seven years and seven months.

Recalling that the reasonableness of this period had to be assessed in the light of the particular circumstances and the criteria laid down in its case law, the Court noted that the case was not complex and that the actions of H's lawyer might, to some extent, have prolonged the proceedings before the Administrative Court. The Government explained that there had also been a backlog of cases awaiting trial in the Administrative Court, but failed to show that this was a temporary situation, or that remedial action had been taken. The European Court therefore concluded that the length of the first phase of the proceedings—about four years—was excessive.

The *Conseil d'État* gave its judgment just over three years after it had been seised of the case. Despite certain delays, the Court concluded that this period of time was not excessive. Considering the proceedings as a whole, the Court said that it was 'not unaware of the difficulties which sometimes delay the hearing of cases by national courts and which are due to a variety of factors'.[116] It emphasized, however, that Article 6(1) lays down that cases must be heard 'within a reasonable time' and that in so providing 'the Convention underlines the importance of rendering justice without delays which might jeopardise its effectiveness and credibility'.[117] Assessing the circumstances of the case as a whole, the Court concluded that the proceedings before the Strasbourg Administrative Court had exceeded a reasonable time and that there was therefore a breach of Article 6(1).

The other issue under Article 6(1) concerned the fairness of the proceedings before the French courts and specifically the rejection of the applicant's request for the appointment of an expert witness. The Administrative Court had based its decision on this point on the ground that as no causal link had been established between the drug treatment and the alleged damage, the action for compensation could not succeed. H, however, maintained that his purpose in requesting an expert opinion was precisely to establish this link. The Court noted that in reaching its decision the Administrative Court had taken documentary evidence into account, in particular a medical certificate which H had obtained in 1974, but which the French court found did not assist his case. In the light of this the Court decided that the Administrative Court could reasonably hold that it was not necessary to test the accuracy of its conclusion by means of an expert opinion.

In the proceedings before the *Conseil d'État* H had specified the purpose of the expert opinion he sought by asking the court to instruct an expert to give an opinion on, among other matters, the causal link between the drug treatment and his subsequent ill-health. The European Court observed that in these circumstances the decision not to order an expert opinion might seem open to criticism. The Court pointed out, however, that the *Conseil d'État* had available to it the parties' pleadings and other documents which they had supplied. Furthermore,

---

[116] Judgment, para. 58.
[117] Ibid.

during the domestic proceedings the applicant had failed to explain why, when he had been informed of the amphetamine treatment, he had waited for more than two and a half years before applying for legal aid. The Court concluded that the *Conseil d'État* was entitled to take the view that it had enough information to be able to give judgment on the basis of the evidence before it. Accordingly, the fact that it had not ordered an expert opinion had not infringed the applicant's right to a fair trial.

On the issue of Article 50 the Court noted that the only basis on which the applicant could be granted just satisfaction was the failure to try the case within a reasonable time, as required by Article 6(1). It dismissed his claim in respect of pecuniary damage on the ground that there was no evidence that the length of the proceedings had reduced his chances of establishing a causal link between his health problems and the drug treatment complained of. However, it awarded him a sum as compensation for non-pecuniary damage in view of the prolonged uncertainty caused by the protracted litigation. As far as costs and expenses were concerned, the Court noted that the bulk of the costs in the French courts were incurred in connection with the merits of the claim and could not be recovered. For the rest the Court assessed the applicant's legal costs and travel and subsistence expenses and awarded him a sum on an equitable basis.

Two judges disagreed with the Court's conclusion on the fair trial issue. In their view it was 'unfair and even illogical'[118] for the *Conseil d'État* to refuse the applicant the possible benefit of an expert opinion, especially as the treatment administered had not been prescribed and was carried out without the patient's consent. As we have already seen, the difficulty in cases of this kind stems from the need to ensure that the guarantee of a fair trial in Article 6(1) is effective, while at the same time ensuring that the European Court is not obliged to retry the case and so turned into a tribunal of fourth instance. In *Barberá, Messegué and Jabardo* (Case No. 5), which concerned criminal proceedings, the Court gave the benefit of the doubt to the applicant. Perhaps the facts that the present case involved civil proceedings, and that the applicant had already succeeded on the reasonable time point, account for a decision in which it appeared to lean the other way.

Right to the peaceful enjoyment of possessions (Article 1 of Protocol No. 1)—the meaning of 'contestation' and 'civil rights and obligations' in Article 6(1)—right to a court (Article 6(1))—just satisfaction (Article 50)

Case No. 24. Allan Jacobson case.[119] In this case, which concerned planning regulations in Sweden, the Court held unanimously that there had been a violation of Article 6(1) of the Convention, but not of Article 1 of Protocol No. 1. As just satisfaction under Article 50 the Government was ordered to pay the applicant 80,000 Swedish crowns in respect of his costs and expenses.

In 1974 the applicant bought a house and some land in a suburb of Stockholm. The property was covered by a 'subdivision plan' which restricted further building until sufficient water and sewage facilities had been provided. Since 1965 the property had also been subject to a series of building prohibitions, lasting one or two years each, pending the preparation of a town plan by the municipality. New build-

---

[118] Partly dissenting opinion of Judges Macdonald and Carrillo Salcedo.
[119] ECHR, judgment of 25 October 1989, Series A, No. 163. The Court consisted of the following Chamber of Judges: Ryssdal (President); Gölcüklü, Walsh, Bernhardt, De Meyer, Valticos, Palm (Judges).

ing prohibitions continued to be issued regularly. The Government and the applicant disagreed as to whether the property was also subject to the regulations for
non-planned areas.

Following his purchase of the property, the applicant made a number of unsuccessful requests to the authorities. In 1975 he requested authorization to divide the
property into two units; in 1980 and 1984 he applied for an exemption from the
building prohibition and for a building permit to construct a second house; and in
1983 and 1984 he applied to have decisions to renew the prohibition invalidated.
Except for the decision relating to the 1975 application, the authorities' decisions
on these various requests were not subject to judicial review.

In his application to the Commission in 1984 Mr Jacobson claimed that the limitations on the use of his property violated several provisions of the Convention. In
its report in October 1987 the Commission concluded that there had been a breach
of Article 6(1) in view of the absence of judicial control, though not of Article 1 of
Protocol No. 1. The Commission then referred the case to the Court.

Article 1 of Protocol No. 1, which has been quoted earlier,[120] guarantees the
peaceful enjoyment of possessions. The Court had no hesitation in ruling that the
protracted use of the building prohibitions interfered with Mr Jacobson's rights in
this respect and so came within the scope of the article. However, it also found that
the applicant's right of property was never threatened by expropriation or similar
measures. It was only his use of the property which was subject to control, pending
the preparation of a town plan. Thus, as in *Tre Traktörer Aktiebolag* (Case
No. 20), the question was whether the interference with the applicant's use of his
property could be justified as lawful and 'in accordance with the general interest'
under the second paragraph of Article 1.

In view of the fact that its power to review compliance with domestic law is
limited, the Court saw no reason to doubt that the interference was in accordance
with Swedish law, despite the applicant's allegations to the contrary. Moreover, it
found nothing to suggest that the impugned prohibitions were not aimed at facilitating town planning, a purpose within the general interest as envisaged in Article
1. Since this was therefore a lawful interference for a legitimate purpose, the crucial question was whether it satisfied the test of proportionality.

The Court acknowledged that for a very long time the applicant had been left in
a state of uncertainty over whether he could develop his property. However, in
view of the restrictions of the 'subdivision plan' he could not be said to have
acquired an unconditional right to build a second house. Neither could it be said
that the impugned prohibitions affected any unconditional right to divide the property, since the rules governing such divisions were to a large extent the same as
those applicable to building permits. The Court considered that Mr Jacobson
could not reasonably have been unaware of the state of the law when he bought the
property. Moreover, it noted that he had been able to live on the property throughout and that there were various procedures available for weighing the public interest against that of the individual.

Pointing out that it seemed to be agreed that the planning situation in the area
was very complex, the Court held that bearing the above considerations in mind,
and having regard to the State's margin of appreciation, the interference with the
applicant's right could not be regarded as disproportionate to the municipality's

---

[120] See Case No. 20, above.

legitimate aim in planning the area. There had therefore been no violation of Article 1 of Protocol No. 1.

The other issue in the case concerned the applicant's right to a court under Article 6(1).[121] As in Case No. 20, where this provision was quoted, the main question was whether it was applicable, and specifically whether the facts of the case disclosed the existence of a 'dispute' (*contestation*) relating to 'civil rights and obligations'.

The Court, following its approach in the earlier case, rejected the Government's submission that no serious dispute of fact or law concerning a right had arisen. It considered that the applicant could maintain on arguable grounds that he had a right to obtain a permit to build a second house, subject to meeting the conditions laid down in the relevant legislation. It also found that the proceedings whereby he challenged the lawfulness of the building prohibitions were directly decisive for the exercise of this right, notwithstanding the fact that the prohibitions also affected the rights of many other property owners.

The next question was whether the aforementioned right was a 'civil' right. Here the Court found that the right which the applicant claimed, namely to build a second house, was of a 'civil nature' for the purposes of Article 6(1). It held that this conclusion was not affected by the general character of the building prohibitions, nor by the classification of the planning procedure as part of public law. Accordingly, the dispute in question did concern a civil right and Article 6(1) was applicable.

The issue of compliance was easily decided. Under Swedish law a dispute regarding the lawfulness of the protracted use of building prohibitions could only be decided by the Government as final arbiter. Such decisions were not subject to review by any body which could be regarded as a 'tribunal' for the purposes of Article 6(1). There had therefore been a breach of this provision.

Although the situation in this case was very different from that which the Court examined in *Tre Traktörer Aktiebolag*, it is clear that on all significant points the Court closely followed the previous decision. This parallel was carried further when it turned to the issue of just satisfaction under Article 50. The applicant claimed a substantial sum as compensation for pecuniary damage, but, as in the earlier case, the Court refused to award anything under this head on the ground that there was no causal link between the alleged damage and the breach of Article 6(1). Mr Jacobson was, however, awarded a sum on an equitable basis in respect of his costs and expenses.

Right to have the lawfulness of detention determined 'speedily' (Article 5(4))—just satisfaction (Article 50)

Case No. 25. Bezicheri case.[122] The Court held unanimously that Italy had committed a breach of Article 5(4) of the Convention because an application for release from detention on remand had not been examined speedily.

---

[121] As well as the provisions discussed in the text, the applicant also relied on Article 13 and at an earlier stage Articles 17 and 18. The Court, however, held that in view of its conclusion on Article 6(1) it was unnecessary to consider the case under Article 13 and, as the other articles had not been relied on before the Court, decided that it was unnecessary to consider these on its own initiative.

[122] ECHR, judgment of 25 October 1989, Series A, No. 164. The Court consisted of the following Chamber of Judges: Ryssdal (President); Thór Vilhjálmsson, Gölcüklü, Matscher, Pinheiro Farinha, Russo, Martens (Judges).

In May 1983 the applicant, who was a lawyer, was arrested and detained on remand on suspicion of having participated in a murder. In June the investigating judge dismissed a first application for release. In December he rejected a second application which Mr Bezicheri had made in July and in which he claimed that there was insufficient evidence to justify his detention. Subsequent appeals to the Pisa Regional Court and the Court of Cassation were dismissed in January 1984 and July 1984 respectively. The applicant was finally released in June 1985 and the proceedings against him were eventually discontinued.

In his application to the Commission in January 1985 Mr Bezicheri raised a variety of complaints, only one of which, an alleged violation of Article 5(4), was found to be admissible. In its report in March 1988 the Commission expressed the opinion that this article had been violated. The Commission then referred the case to the Court.

Article 5(4) of the Convention, which has been quoted in Case No. 4, entitles those who are deprived of their liberty by arrest or detention to take proceedings by which the lawfulness of such detention shall be decided 'speedily'. Mr Bezicheri's complaint was that the delay in examining his application of July 1983 entailed a breach of this provision.

The Government argued that the July application was a request for additional investigative measures rather than an attempt to contest the lawfulness of the detention, but the Court disagreed. Having disposed of this preliminary point, it considered whether, after the rejection of his June application, Mr Bezicheri was entitled to make a new application in July which would also be subject to Article 5(4). It decided that he was, on the ground that an interval of a month between applications was not unreasonable, since the Convention assumes that detention on remand is of strictly limited duration. The Government then argued that instead of making a fresh application, Mr Bezicheri should have contested the rejection of the first application, or applied to a special court with jurisdiction to hear cases concerning detention on remand. The Court, however, found this submission unconvincing because, among other reasons:

. . . the simultaneous or successive use of two procedures, which were legally distinct but ultimately directed towards the same end, could have resulted in a loss of time that would scarcely have been consistent with the requirement that proceedings be conducted 'speedily' and would in any event have been contrary to the applicant's interests.[123]

The crucial issue was therefore the Court's assessment of the delay in processing the July application. Here the Court accepted that the judge assigned to the case had required a certain amount of time to carry out his inquiries. It noted, however, that these investigations had extended over a period which was incompatible with the requirements of Article 5(4). Although the investigating judge had, according to the Government, been labouring under an excessive workload at the material time, the Court, as in previous cases where this point has been raised, dismissed it by observing that 'the Convention requires the Contracting States to organise their legal systems so as to enable the courts to comply with its various requirements . . . .'.[124]

Having found that the examination by the investigating judge was not conducted 'speedily', the Court held that it was unnecessary to consider the subsequent

[123] Judgment, para. 21.
[124] Ibid., para. 25.

proceedings before the Regional Court and the Court of Cassation. Its conclusion was therefore that there had been a breach of Article 5(4).

The issue of just satisfaction under Article 50 was soon dealt with. Mr Bezicheri claimed a large sum as compensation for pecuniary damage. The Court found, however, that this was based on circumstances unrelated to the breach of Article 5(4) and dismissed the claim. He also claimed a large sum for non-pecuniary damage. The Court accepted that the failure to conduct the review of his application speedily must have caused him some damage of this kind, but decided that the judgment itself constituted adequate satisfaction. Mr Bezicheri had waived his right to recover the costs and expenses borne by him before the Convention organs and so these did not need to be considered. He had sought the repayment of the fees of the lawyers who represented him in the national courts, but the Court held that this claim was not related in any way to the proceedings concerning the examination of the application of July 1983, which alone was the subject of the case at Strasbourg. In the end therefore the Court decided to award the applicant nothing by way of just satisfaction.

Freedom of expression (Article 10)—application to a trade publication—domestic competition law—the margin of appreciation—role of the Court's President (Rule 20(3))

Case No. 26. Markt intern Verlag GmbH and Klaus Beermann case.[125] In this case, which concerned the Federal Republic of Germany, the Court decided by 9 votes to 9, with the casting vote of the President, that there had been no violation of Article 10 of the Convention.

The applicants in this case were *markt intern*, a publishing firm run by journalists, and the firm's editor-in-chief, Mr Klaus Beermann. The aim of *markt intern* is to defend the interests of small and medium-sized retail businesses against the competition of large scale distribution companies by publishing information which the former can use. In November 1975 an article by Mr Beermann appeared in an information bulletin which *markt intern* produced for the chemist and beauty-product retail trade. It described an incident involving an English mail-order firm ('the Club') which had failed to reimburse a customer who was dissatisfied with one of its products. To enable an assessment to be made of the business practices of that firm the article also invited the specialist retailers to inform *markt intern* of any similar experiences.[126]

The Club instituted proceedings in the Hamburg Regional Court, which ordered *markt intern* to refrain from repeating some of the statements in the article. The Hanseatic Court of Appeal quashed the judgment, but on a further appeal the Federal Court of Justice found that the statements in question, though not alleged to be inaccurate, were contrary to 'honest practices' and therefore infringed section 1 of the 1909 Unfair Competition Act. In February 1983 the Federal Constitutional Court declined to entertain the applicant's appeal.

In their application to the Commission in July 1983 *markt intern* and Mr Beermann claimed that the domestic injunction constituted a violation of their right to freedom of expression contrary to Article 10 of the Convention. In its report in

---

[125] ECHR, judgment of 20 November 1989, Series A, No. 165. This was the Court's two hundredth judgment and was given by the plenary Court.

[126] The text of the article, which was neutral in tone, is reproduced in para. 11 of the judgment.

December 1987 the Commission expressed the opinion by 12 votes to 1 that there had been a violation of this provision. The Commission and the Government then referred the case to the Court.

The text of Article 10 has been quoted in Case No. 8 above, and the Court had no difficulty in deciding that the present case fell within its scope. Although the disputed publication had clearly been addressed to a limited circle of tradespeople and not to the public as a whole, it conveyed information of a commercial nature which 'cannot be excluded from the scope of Article 10(1) which does not apply solely to certain types of information or ideas or forms of expression . . . '.[127] The question therefore was whether the interference with the applicants' freedom of expression, which the injunction plainly was, could be justified by the criteria set out in Article 10(2).

The Court decided that the injunction was 'prescribed by law' because the domestic court's judgment was based on section 1 of the 1909 Act, and the case law and commentaries concerning the concept of 'honest practices' had established its meaning with sufficient precision. It also decided that the injunction was intended to protect the reputation and the rights of others which are, of course, legitimate aims under Article 10(2). The critical issue was thus whether restraining the applicants could be regarded as 'necessary in a democratic society' for attaining these aims.

The Court's starting point in considering this question was the respondent's margin of appreciation, which it described as:

. . . essential in commercial matters and, in particular, in an area as complex and fluctuating as that of unfair competition. Otherwise, the European Court of Human Rights would have to undertake a re-examination of the facts and all the circumstances of each case. The Court must confine its review to the question whether the measures taken on the national level are justifiable in principle and proportionate . . . [128]

The Court observed that in order to establish whether the interference was proportionate, it must weigh the requirements of the protection of the reputation and rights of others against the publication of the information in question. In so doing it must look at the impugned court decision in the light of the case as a whole.

Developing this reasoning, the Court stated that in a market economy a business undertaking necessarily exposed itself to close scrutiny by its competitors. Its commercial strategy and the way it honoured its commitments might both give rise to criticism from consumers and the specialized press. In order to carry out its task the specialized press had to be able to disclose facts which could be of interest to its readers and contribute to the openness of business activities. This principle was, however, subject to some important qualifications:

However, even the publication of items which are true and describe real events may under certain circumstances be prohibited: the obligation to respect the privacy of others or the duty to respect the confidentiality of certain commercial information are examples. In addition, a correct statement can be and often is qualified by additional remarks, by value judgments, by suppositions or even insinuations. It must also be recognised that an isolated incident may deserve closer scrutiny before being made public; otherwise an accurate description of one such incident can give the false impression that the incident is evidence of a general practice. All these factors can legitimately contribute to the assessment of statements

---

[127] Judgment, para. 26.
[128] Ibid., para. 33.

made in a commercial context, and it is primarily for the national courts to decide which statements are permissible and which are not.[129]

Turning to the particular facts, the Court noted that the disputed article was written in a commercial context. Although *markt intern* was not itself in competition with the Club, it had intended, legitimately, to protect the interests of chemists and beauty-product retailers. According to the Federal Court of Justice, however, the applicants were not justified in reporting the incident when the Club had already agreed to carry out an immediate investigation. Moreover, in the Federal Court's opinion the applicants should have recognized that such premature publication was bound to have adverse effects on the Club's business. In the light of these findings and 'having regard to the duties and responsibilities attaching to the freedom guaranteed by Article 10',[130] the Court found that the final decision of the Federal Court of Justice did not go beyond the margin of appreciation left to the national authorities. The Court therefore decided, after the President had exercised his casting vote, that there had been no violation of Article 10.

The judgment just described demonstrates an extremely unsatisfactory approach to Article 10 and in the present writer's view is one of the Court's least convincing decisions on this, or any other, article of the Convention. The eight judges who delivered dissenting opinions[131] considered that the narrow interpretation of the concept of freedom of expression and the correspondingly wide scope given to the margin of appreciation cannot be reconciled with the Court's emphasis in its previous case law of the fundamental importance of this right and the strong presumption against its limitation. This is certainly true and a comparison between the judgment in the *Sunday Times* case[132] and that in the present case is particularly instructive. Judge Martens made the further point that to treat an article in the press as subject to the law relating to unfair competition 'is to place that organ of the press in a legal position which is fundamentally different from that to which it is entitled under Article 10 of the Convention'. Thus the whole basis of the domestic court's approach was flawed and there was no room for the margin of appreciation 'because this margin cannot justify assessments incompatible with the freedoms guaranteed under the Convention'.[133] This too can be regarded as a well-founded criticism.

Right to a fair trial (Article 6(1))—right to examine witnesses (Article 6(3)(d))

Case No. 27. Kostovski case.[134] The Court held unanimously that the Netherlands had committed a breach of Article 6(3)(*d*), taken together with Article 6(1)

---

[129] Ibid., para. 35.

[130] Ibid., para. 37.

[131] Judges Gölcüklü, Pettiti, Russo, Spielmann, De Meyer, Carrillo Salcedo and Valticos gave a joint dissenting opinion and Judges Pettiti and De Meyer also delivered individual dissenting opinions. Judge Martens gave an individual dissenting opinion which was approved by Judge Macdonald.

[132] ECHR, judgment of 26 April 1979, Series A, No. 30, and this *Year Book*, 50 (1979), p. 257. See also Merrills, *The Development of International Law by the European Court of Human Rights* (1988), pp. 122–5.

[133] Dissenting opinion of Judge Martens, para. 5.

[134] ECHR, judgment of 20 November 1989, Series A, No. 166. This case was decided by the plenary Court.

of the Convention, because the applicant had been convicted of a criminal offence on the basis of reports of statements by two anonymous witnesses.

In August 1981 the applicant, who had a long criminal record, escaped from prison in the Netherlands with others and remained on the run until April 1982. In January 1982 three masked men held up a bank in the town of Baarn. Shortly afterwards the police were visited by two persons who made statements implicating the applicant and others in the robbery. Owing to fear of reprisals, these witnesses indicated that they wished to remain anonymous. Subsequently, an examining magistrate interviewed one of the witnesses in the absence of the public prosecutor, the applicant and his defence counsel. The witness confirmed his (or her) previous statement. Later the applicant's lawyer was given an opportunity to submit written questions to the witness, but the majority of the questions were either not put, or not answered, in order to preserve the witness's anonymity.

In September 1982 the Utrecht District Court convicted the applicant and his co-accused of armed robbery and sentenced each of them to six years' imprisonment. The anonymous witnesses, whose identity was known to the prosecutor, were not heard at the trial. However, the District Court based its finding of guilt on reports drawn up by the police and the examining magistrates which dealt with the hearings of the witnesses, and which the court admitted as evidence and regarded as decisive and reliable. In May 1983, after a retrial before the Amsterdam Court of Appeal, which also admitted the reports as evidence, Mr Kostovski and his co-accused were again convicted and given the same sentence as before. The applicant's subsequent appeal to the Supreme Court was dismissed in September 1984.

In his application to the Commission in March 1985 Mr Kostovski complained that he had been the victim of a violation of Article 6(3)(d) of the Convention which guarantees the right of an accused to examine, or to have examined, the witnesses against him. In its report in May 1988 the Commission expressed the unanimous opinion that this provision, read in conjunction with Article 6(1), had been violated. The Commission and the Government then referred the case to the Court.

It will be recalled that in *Bricmont* (Case No. 19), the Court pointed out that the specific guarantee to be found in Article 6(3)(d) is one aspect of the general right to a fair trial guaranteed by Article 6(1) and therefore considered it appropriate to take the two provisions together. In the present case the Court adopted the same approach and, pointing out that its task was not to decide whether the statements of the anonymous witnesses had been properly admitted, decided that the only question was whether the proceedings considered as a whole, including the way in which the evidence was taken, were fair.

In principle, the Court explained, all the evidence has to be produced in the presence of the accused at a public hearing with a view to adversarial argument. However, statements obtained at the pre-trial stage could be used as evidence provided the rights of the defence had been respected. As a rule, those rights required that the accused be given, at some stage in the proceedings, an adequate and proper opportunity to challenge and question a witness against him.

In the Court's view such an opportunity had not been given in the present case. At no stage could the anonymous witnesses be questioned directly by the applicant or his representative. In addition, the written questions had been restricted by the decision to preserve the witness's anonymity. Indeed, this had compounded the applicant's difficulty because 'if the defence is unaware of the identity of the person it seeks to question, it may be deprived of the very particulars enabling it to demonstrate that he or she is prejudiced, hostile or unreliable'.[135] Moreover, the Court did not consider that the procedures followed by the judicial authorities had counterbalanced the handicaps suffered by the defence. The trial courts did not see, and could not form their own impression of the reliability of, the anonymous witnesses, and only one of the witnesses had been heard by an examining magistrate, who was unaware of his identity.

The Government maintained that the use of anonymous evidence was a necessary response to the increasing intimidation of witnesses. The Court said that it did not 'underestimate the importance of the struggle against organised crime', but observed that 'the right to a fair administration of justice holds so prominent a place in a democratic society . . . that it cannot be sacrificed to expediency'.[136] The use of anonymous statements as sufficient evidence to found a conviction, as here, was a different matter from reliance on anonymous informants at the investigation stage. The former had involved limitations on the rights of the defence which were irreconcilable with the guarantees in Article 6.

The Court therefore concluded that since Mr Kostovski could not be said to have received a fair trial, there had been a violation of Article 6(3)(d), taken together with Article 6(1). The question of just satisfaction under Article 50 was reserved.

Right to be informed of a criminal charge (Article 6(3)(a))—right to prepare a defence (Article 6(3)(b))—friendly settlement (Rule 49(2))

Case No. 28. Chichlian and Ekindjian case.[137] The Court decided to strike this case, which concerned France, out of the list. It reached this decision unanimously in accordance with Rule 49(2) of the Rules of Court, following the conclusion of a friendly settlement between the Government and the applicants.

In 1981 criminal proceedings were brought against the two applicants for infringement of a particular article in a 1968 decree concerning financial relations with foreign countries. At first instance they were acquitted, but the Toulouse Court of Appeal found them guilty of an offence under another article of the same decree, which was relied on by the Customs authorities for the first time in the appellate proceedings. The Court of Cassation dismissed the applicants' appeal on a point of law in 1983.

The applicants lodged an application with the European Commission in April 1984, complaining that their conviction had been obtained in conditions which contravened Article 6(3)(a) (right to be informed of the nature and cause of the accusation) and Article 6(3)(b) (right to have adequate time and facilities to prepare a defence) of the Convention. In its report in March 1989 the Commission expressed the unanimous opinion that these provisions had been violated. The Commission then referred the case to the Court.

In November 1989 the Registrar received from each of the applicants a signed declaration, the text of which had been proposed to them by the Government, in the following terms:

---

[135] Judgment, para. 42.
[136] Ibid., para. 44.
[137] ECHR, judgment of 29 November 1989, Series A, No. 162B. The Court consisted of the following Chamber of Judges: Ryssdal (President); Cremona, Matscher, Pettiti, Valticos, De Meyer, Martens (Judges).

I . . . declare that I accept the sum of 100,000 francs which the French Government have offered to me in the case brought against them before the European Court of Human Rights . . .

I acknowledge that the payment of this sum shall constitute full and final compensation for all the pecuniary damage alleged by me in [my] application and shall also cover in their entirety the lawyers' fees and other expenses incurred by me in this case.

I therefore agree, subject to the payment of this sum, to withdraw from these proceedings and to refrain from taking any further action in this matter against the French State in the national and international courts.

I note that the French Government will pay to me the sum in question as soon as the Court has decided to strike the case out of its list.

. . .

As we have seen in Case No. 13, the Court's function in situations of this kind is to consider whether it is appropriate to strike a case out of its list in accordance with Rule 49(2) of the Rules.[138] Accordingly, the Court took formal note of the friendly settlement. It then observed that there were no reasons of public policy to justify continuation of the proceedings, since the dispute here was mainly concerned with questions of a factual nature and did not raise any important issue as to the interpretation of the Convention. It therefore decided to strike the case out of the list.

J.G. MERRILLS

[138] Formerly Rule 48(2). The Rules of the Court were renumbered in April 1989. Case No. 13 was decided under the old system.

UNITED KINGDOM MATERIALS ON INTERNATIONAL LAW 1989*

Edited by GEOFFREY MARSTON[1]

[*Editorial note*: Attention is drawn to the editorial note in UKMIL 1983, p. 361. The publication schedule of the present edition of UKMIL has permitted the citation of the definitive column references in the bound volumes of the Parliamentary Debates.]

INDEX[2]

* Editorial arrangement and comments © Geoffrey Marston, 1990. Copyright in the materials cited is in the original copyright holders.

[1] LLM, Ph.D. (Lond.): Lecturer in Law, University of Cambridge; Fellow of Sidney Sussex College. The assistance of Mr M.C. Wood, Legal Counsellor, Mr J.J. Rankin, Assistant Legal Adviser, and Dr G. Plant, formerly Assistant Legal Adviser, Foreign and Commonwealth Office, is gratefully acknowledged.

[2] Based on the *Model Plan for the Classification of Documents concerning State Practice in the field of Public International Law* adopted by the Committee of Ministers of the Council of Europe in Resolution (68) 17 of 28 June 1968.

Abbreviations

HC Debs	*Hansard*, House of Commons Debates (6th series)
HL Debs	*Hansard*, House of Lords Debates (5th series)
Cmnd.	Command Paper (5th series)
Cm.	Command Paper (6th series)
UKMIL	*United Kingdom Materials on International Law*
TS	*United Kingdom Treaty Series*
EC	European Community

Part One: II. A. *International law in general—relationship between international law and municipal law—in general*

In moving the approval in the House of Lords of the Merchant Shipping Act 1988 (Amendment) Order 1989, the Government spokesman, Viscount Davidson, stated:

Before I move the Motion, I feel that it would be helpful and would perhaps save some time if I answered more fully some of the points which were raised last week on the occasion of the Question of the noble Lord, Lord Stoddart of Swindon. He asked whether it was not intolerable that a court sitting in a foreign land could instruct the British Parliament to alter an Act of Parliament. I cannot accept this. The relationship between Community and national law was considered at the time of our accession. In joining the European Community we accepted an obligation to comply with Community law. This includes compliance with orders from the European Court of Justice. It is now a fact of life within the Community that Community law prevails over any conflicting provisions of national law. The European Communities Act 1972 provides machinery for giving effect to Community law. Hence the draft Order in Council that we are debating tonight.

(HL Debs., vol. 511, cols. 1450–1: 25 October 1989)

Part One: II. D. 1. *International law in general—relationship between international law and municipal law—implementation of international law in municipal law—treaties*

(See Part Eight: IV. (Antarctic Minerals Bill), Part Nine: VIII. and Part Nine: XV. D., below)

In moving the second reading in the House of Commons of the Multilateral Investment Guarantee Agency Bill, the Minister for Overseas Development, Mr Chris Patten, stated:

. . . we should not underestimate the value of the Bill. Britain is the second largest investor in the developing world. From 1982 to 1986, our private investments totalled £6,727 million. International investment insurance is therefore particularly important for us. In ratifying the Multilateral Investment Guarantee Agency convention we shall be discharging an obligation that we implicitly accepted at the Venice economic summit earlier this year, and which we reaffirmed during the Commonwealth Finance Ministers' meeting in September.

The Bill is required to enable the United Kingdom to ratify the convention establishing MIGA, which is an international organisation associated with the World Bank, and is intended to promote foreign direct investment in developing countries, primarily by offering would-be investors insurance against non-commercial risks. The Chancellor of the Exchequer signed the convention establishing the agency on behalf of the United Kingdom in April 1986. In order to become members of the agency, we need to ratify the convention; and before we can ratify, legislative provision is needed to give effect in domestic law to our obligations under this convention.

(HC Debs., vol. 123, col. 155: 24 November 1987)

In the course of a speech in the UN Commission on Human Rights on 8 March 1989, the UK representative, Miss D.L. Walker, stated:

Her delegation wished to draw the Commission's attention in particular to the problem of child abduction and the distress it caused to the children and families concerned. In an effort to resolve that problem, her Government had passed two Acts in 1984 and 1985 on the question, which had enabled it to ratify, in 1986, the Hague Convention on the Civil Aspects of International Child Abduction and the European Convention on Recognition and Enforcement of Decisions concerning Custody of Children and on Restoration of Custody of Children.

(E/CN. 4/1989/SR. 54, p. 13)

In moving the second reading in the House of Lords of the Criminal Justice (International Co-operation) Bill, the Minister of State, Earl Ferrers, stated:

If the Bill is enacted in due course, the provisions which are contained in Part I will enable us to ratify the European Convention on Mutual Assistance in Criminal Matters. This is a step which will be widely welcomed among the international community.

I turn now to Part II of the Bill. The purpose of this part is to make the legislative changes which are necessary in order to enable the United Kingdom to ratify the United Nations Convention against Illicit Traffic in Narcotic Drugs and Psychotropic Substances. This convention—which is known for the purposes of the Bill as the Vienna Convention—was adopted in Vienna on 20th December by a plenipotentiary conference which was attended by representatives of 106 states. On the following day, together with representatives of 42 other states, I had the honour of signing the convention on behalf of Her Majesty's Government.

(HL Debs., vol. 513, col. 1217: 12 December 1989)

In reply to a question about the delay in introducing the Bill, the Minister of State observed:

The United Kingdom takes the view that there is no point in ratifying a convention until there is in place all the legislation and procedures which are necessary to implement it fully. The convention was signed last December; therefore this is the first parliamentary session in which we are able to introduce a programmed Bill. In the meantime, as I have described to your Lordships, we have been at the forefront, having implemented most of the convention. This has been fully recognised by the international community. I hope therefore that the noble Lord will not think that we have been unduly laggardly.

The procedure is that we in the United Kingdom first put our own legal house in order. We then ratify the convention. Others sometimes ratify the convention first and then sort out their own legislation afterwards. Ratification is done by an order in council. Then the instrument of ratification is deposited with the Secretary General of the United Nations, because it is a United Nations convention.

(Ibid., col. 1232)

In moving the second reading in the House of Lords of the Contracts (Applicable Law) Bill, the Lord Advocate, Lord Fraser of Carmyllie, stated:

The Bill incorporates into United Kingdom law a convention between member states of the European Community on the law applicable to contractual obligations which was opened for signature in Rome in 1980 and signed on behalf of the United Kingdom in December 1981. All nine states which belonged to the Community in 1989 have signed the convention, and Greece has now also signed it. The Greek accession to the Rome Convention is contained in the Luxembourg Convention of April 1984 and the Bill enables the United Kingdom also to give effect to that convention.

Your Lordships may wonder why it has taken so long for the United Kingdom to ratify the Rome Convention of 1980. The answer lies principally in the need to work out what powers the European Court of Justice should have to interpret the convention. A compromise was eventually reached in December 1988, when two protocols were signed in Brussels conferring jurisdiction similar to that which the European Court has under the European Judgments Convention. The need for a second protocol arose out of constitutional difficulties of the Irish Republic. The Bill gives effect to the first, substantive protocol, but there is no need for it to give effect to the second.

(HL Debs., vol. 513, col. 1257: 12 December 1989)

Part Two: I. *Sources of international law—treaties*

(See also Part Three: I.C. 4. (item of 21 June 1989) and II. A. 1.(b)., below)

The following extract is taken from the Foreign and Commonwealth Office Treaty Section's *Instruction Manual*, prepared in May 1988 for internal use:

NOMENCLATURE: TYPES OF TREATY DOCUMENTS

1. The Vienna Convention on the Law of Treaties 1969 defines a treaty as 'an international agreement concluded between States in written form and governed by international law, whether embodied in a single instrument or in two or more related instruments and whatever its particular designation'.

2. International agreements have a variety of names although there is no juridical distinction between them. The titles most frequently used are:

  (a) *Treaty*. In the past this has usually been reserved for the more important political agreements such as Treaties of Peace, Friendship and Alliance but in recent years it has been used for major treaties on disarmament and space matters, eg the Treaty banning Nuclear Weapons Tests in the Atmosphere, in Outer Space and Under Water, 1963, the Treaty on Non-Proliferation of Nuclear Weapons, 1968 and the Treaty on Principles Governing the Activities of States in the Exploration and Use of Outer Space, including the Moon and other Celestial Bodies, 1967, as well as the Treaty of Rome establishing the European Economic Community, 1957 and the Treaties of 1972, 1979 and 1985 for the Accession to the European Communities by the United Kingdom, Republic of Ireland and Denmark, Greece, and Spain and Portugal respectively.

  (b) *Convention*. This term is frequently, though not necessarily employed for agreements to which a large number of countries are parties and especially those of a law-making type, eg Vienna Convention on the Law of Treaties, 1969 and Vienna Convention on State Succession in respect of Treaties, 1980; in the field of bilateral relations it is often applied to formal instruments of a technical or social character, eg Conventions on Social Security and Double Taxation.

(c) *Agreement*. This is an instrument which may be said to be less formal than a Treaty or Convention and usually is more limited in scope and has fewer parties than a Convention. Simple agreements are often not subject to ratification but come into force on signature. Exchanges of Notes may also constitute agreements (see (e) below).

(d) *Protocol*. This usually denotes an agreement amending or supplementing an existing Agreement.

(e) *Exchange of Notes*. Notes exchanged between the Ambassador or High Commissioner of one State and the Minister for Foreign Affairs of the State to which he is accredited can constitute an international agreement between the two Governments. Similarly Notes can be exchanged between an Ambassador or Permanent Representative to an international organisation and the Secretary General of that organisation constituting an agreement.

In addition to the terms described above, there are a number of other terms used to describe agreements which are more rarely used. They are:–

(f) *Decision*. Since United Kingdom membership of the European Communities we have been obliged to publish in the Treaty Series Decisions of the Representatives of the Governments of Member States of the European Coal and Steel Community, meeting within the Council, which have the force of legally binding instruments, eg TS 50/1980, Cmnd. 7936—Decision Allocating Supplementary Revenue for 1980.

(g) *Pact*. This is generally the name given to an agreement setting out the terms of a political or defence arrangement between two or more powers, eg the Baghdad Pact on Mutual Cooperation between Turkey and Iraq, 1955, to which the United Kingdom and other States acceded. This was later renamed as the Central Treaty Organisation (CENTO)—TS 39/1956, Cmd. 9859.

(h) *Charter*. A term used to describe a multilateral treaty laying down certain fundamental principles to which a large number of States are invited to subscribe, eg Charter of the United Nations (TS 67/1946, Cmd. 7015).

(i) *Covenant*. The use of this term is very similar to Charter and the only well known examples are the Covenant of the League of Nations and in more recent time the two Covenants on Economic, Social and Cultural Rights and Civil and Political Rights adopted by the General Assembly of the United Nations in December, 1966 (TS 6/1977, Cmnd. 6702).

(j) *Constitution or Statute*. The basic instrument establishing an international organisation, eg Constitution of UNESCO or Statute of the Council of Europe (TS 36/1961, Cmnd. 7778).

(k) *Articles of Agreement*. A type of agreement very similar to a Constitution, eg the establishment in 1945 of the International Bank for Reconstruction and Development (IBRD) and the International Monetary Fund (IMF) (TS 21/1946, Cmd. 6885).

(l) *Regulations*. This term is used in cases where the constitution of a technical specialised agency makes provision for the adoption of regulations and these may themselves constitute a treaty instrument or require separate approval or acceptance eg International Health Regulations of the World Health Organisation (TS 18/1971, Cmnd. 4650) and International Regulations for Preventing Collisions at Sea annexed to the Convention on Safety of Life at Sea, 1960 ('SOLAS') (TS 23/1966, Cmnd. 2956). (The 1960 SOLAS Regulations were later superseded by those annexed to the 1974 Convention which were an integral part of the Convention (see TS 46/1980, Cmnd. 7874).)

(m) *Modus vivendi* is used to describe an instrument recording an agreement of a temporary or provisional character intended to be replaced by a treaty of a more permanent nature.

Some other very common designations are *Memorandum of Understanding*, *Agreed Minute* and *Arrangement*, none of which is normally regarded by HMG as having the status of a treaty although the second of these categories is often so regarded by other Governments.

(n) *Memorandum of Understanding* is a form frequently used, particularly by the Ministry of Defence, to record informal international arrangements between States on matters which are inappropriate for inclusion in binding agreements either because of their technical complexity or their confidentiality. They may be drawn up as a single document signed on behalf of two or more Governments or may consist of an exchange of notes or letters recording an understanding reached between two governments.

(o) *Agreed Minute* usually records briefly decisions reached between two delegations and is sometimes to be followed by a full agreement on the subject discussed or may be annexed to an agreement to deal with administrative details eg UK/USSR biennial Agreements on Relations in the Scientific, Educational and Cultural Fields (TS 61/1985, Cmnd. 9663).

(p) *'Arrangement'* sometimes results from the translation into English of the text of an agreement which has been negotiated in French. The French word 'arrangement' meaning in English 'agreement' should not be confused with the English word 'arrangement', a term used to denote an understanding which does not constitute an international agreement and would not therefore appear in the Treaty Series.

3. Special mention should also be made of the term *Final Act*, which is normally used to designate a document which constitutes a formal statement or summary of the proceedings of an international conference, enumerating the treaties drawn up as a result of their deliberations together with any resolutions adopted by the conference. Very often one or more draft treaties adopted by the conference are annexed to the Final Act. Signature of an instrument of this nature does not in itself entail any expression of consent to be bound by the treaties so enumerated, which require separate signature and to the extent necessary ratification, eg Final Act of the Intergovernmental Conference on the Convention on Dumping of Wastes at Sea, 1972 (Miscellaneous 54/1972, Cmnd. 5169). The Final Act of a conference is not always published.

4. In connection with treaties concluded by the European Communities a Final Act is often appended to an Agreement and usually covers a series of declarations by one or more parties relating to specific articles of the Agreement. There are numerous examples in the European Communities Series of Command Papers.

5. The term '*procès-verbal*' is another term which is used but as far as Treaty Section is concerned its use is limited to instruments setting out agreed corrections to a treaty already signed. Strictly speaking it denotes the detailed record of the proceedings of a conference.

(Text provided by the Foreign and Commonwealth Office (some cross-references deleted))

The following passage is extracted from a later part of the *Manual of Instructions*:

Different forms in which treaties may be concluded.

Before the Second World War, important treaties were normally concluded by *Heads of State*, and those of lesser importance by *governments*, whereas the tendency since that time has been for an increasing number of multilateral treaties of all classes to be drawn up between *States*. The change has come about principally because of the large number of treaties concluded under United Nations auspices in the inter-state form. The Heads of State form has ceased to be used for multilateral treaties except for some concluded under the auspices of the European Economic Community, eg the series of Lomé Conventions between the EC States and the African, Caribbean and Pacific states and the Treaties of Accession by new member states to the Community. The Third and most recent Lomé Convention is published in European Communities Series No. 19/1985, Cmnd. 9511. Extradition treaties and Consular Conventions were traditionally in Heads of State form but are now more often drafted in inter-state or -governmental form. Sometimes the other State's constitutional law or practice requires the highest level of formality and therefore the Heads of State form is used (eg UK/Austria Social Security Convention, 1980—TS 25/1981, Cmnd. 8048). Treaties of Friendship are drawn up in Heads of State form, eg Treaty of Friendship and Co-operation with Brunei, 1979 (Miscellaneous No. 5/1979, Cmnd. 7496) and because of its importance the Channel Fixed Link Treaty of 1986 was in this form (see France No. 1/1986, Cmnd. 9745).

(Ibid.)

In reply to a question, the Parliamentary Under-Secretary of State, Foreign and Commonwealth Office, wrote:

A high degree of autonomy for Hong Kong is provided for in the Sino-British joint declaration of 1984, an international agreement binding under international law. We have the right to satisfy ourselves that the Basic Law fully and faithfully reflects the provisions of the joint declaration. We intend to live up to our commitments under the joint declaration and we look to the Chinese to do the same.

(HC Debs., vol. 154, Written Answers. col. *523*: 15 June 1989)

In the course of a speech to the UN General Assembly on 27 September 1989, the Secretary of State for Foreign and Commonwealth Affairs, Mr John Major, stated:

By treaty, Hong Kong will revert to China in 1997. By treaty, Hong Kong will also preserve its traditional freedoms and way of life. That treaty, the Sino-British

Joint Declaration of 1984, is binding. It has been registered as such at the United Nations by both Britain and China.

(A/44/PV. 8, p. 48)

In reply to a question on the subject of Hong Kong, the Minister of State, Foreign and Commonwealth Office, wrote in part:

The Sino-British joint declaration is an internationally binding agreement registered by both Governments with the United Nations.

(HC Debs., vol. 158, Written Answers, col. *146*: 18 October 1989)

Part Two: II. *Sources of international law—custom*

(See Part Four: VII. (item of 20 February 1989), and Part Nine: I. B. (item of 11 July 1989), below)

Part Two: VIII. *Sources of international law—restatement by formal processes of codification and progressive development*

(See Part Three: I. A. 2. (item of 20 February 1989), below)

Part Two: X. *Sources of international law—acquisition, retention and loss of rights*

The following paragraph appeared in a Joint Statement issued on 19 October 1989 by the British and Argentine delegations to discussions in Madrid on the subject of bilateral relations:

Both governments agreed that:
(1) Nothing in the conduct or content of the present meeting or of any similar subsequent meetings shall be interpreted as:
    (a) A change in the position of the United Kingdom with regard to sovereignty or territorial and maritime jurisdiction over the Falkland Islands, South Georgia and the South Sandwich Islands and the surrounding maritime areas:
    (b) A change in the position of the Argentine Republic with regard to sovereignty or territorial and maritime jurisdiction over the Falkland Islands, South Georgia and the South Sandwich Islands and the surrounding maritime areas:
    (c) Recognition of or support for the position of the United Kingdom or the Argentine Republic with regard to sovereignty or territorial and maritime jurisdiction over the Falkland Islands, South Georgia and the South Sandwich Islands and the surrounding maritime areas.
(2) No act or activity carried out by the United Kingdom, the Argentine Republic or third parties as a consequence and in implementation of anything agreed to in the present meeting or in any similar subsequent meetings shall constitute a basis for affirming, supporting, or denying the position of the United Kingdom or the Argentine Republic regarding the sovereignty or territorial and maritime jurisdiction over the Falkland Islands, South Georgia and the South Sandwich Islands and the surrounding maritime areas.

(Text provided by the Foreign and Commonwealth Office)

Part Three: I. A. 1. *Subjects of international law—States—international status—sovereignty and independence*

In a statement issued on 12 June 1989 by the Twelve Member States of the EC on the subject of Lebanon, it was stated in part:

The Twelve reiterate their support for the independence, sovereignty, unity, and territorial integrity of Lebanon, as expressed in their previous statements on the tragic situation prevailing in that country.

(Text provided by the Foreign and Commonwealth Office)

Part Three: I. A. 2. *Subjects of international law—States—international status—non-intervention and non-use of force*

(See also Part Twelve: II., below)

In the course of a debate on the case of Mr Alan Rees, whose extradition was sought by the Federal Republic of Germany in respect of alleged crimes committed in Bolivia against German nationals, the Minister of State, Foreign and Commonwealth Office, Mrs Lynda Chalker, stated:

. . . it is internationally accepted practice that the officials or representatives of one state cannot intervene in the judicial proceedings of another sovereign state. We in the United Kingdom would not tolerate attempted foreign intervention in our judicial system, and I suspect that no other country would welcome it either.

(HC Debs., vol. 146, cols. 1109–10: 8 February 1989)

In the course of a statement made on 16 February 1989, a spokesman for the Foreign and Commonwealth Office referred to the statement made by Ayatollah Khomeini in Iran on 14 February 1989 about the book *The Satanic Verses* by Mr Salman Rushdie. He went on:

Our Chargé in Tehran had a meeting at the Ministry of Foreign Affairs . . . He expressed our grave concern at the incitement to violence against the author and publishers of Satanic Verses made by Ayatollah Khomeini.

Mr Browne did not receive satisfaction on this question. We have therefore summoned the Iranian Chargé to the FCO to protest in the strongest terms at the Ayatollah's statement. We recognise that Moslems and others may have strong views about the contents of Mr Rushdie's book. However, no-one has the right to incite people to violence on British soil or against British citizens. This is incompatible with the UN Charter and constitutes interference in our internal affairs contrary to the UK/Iran agreement and joint statement of 10 November 1988. Ayatollah Khomeini's statement is totally unacceptable.

(Text provided by the Foreign and Commonwealth Office)

On 20 February 1989, in the UN Commission on Human Rights, the Twelve Member States of the European Community delivered a common statement on human rights which contained the following passage:

The codification of universally accepted norms in which this Commission has been involved is one of the most significant achievements of the United Nations.

Starting with the 1966 Covenants, a comprehensive conventional framework has been developed, aimed at securing an even stronger commitment.

Consequently, the Twelve attach essential importance to the respect of human rights and fundamental freedoms in their relations with other countries. Moreover, it is our firm conviction that raising human rights issues and expressing concern for violations of internationally recognized rights cannot be considered interferences in internal affairs. As the International Court of Justice has pointed out, 'The principles and rules related to fundamental rights of the human being represent obligations for governments towards the international community as a whole'.

(Text provided by the Foreign and Commonwealth Office)

In the course of a debate on the subject of relations with Iran, the Secretary of State for Foreign and Commonwealth Affairs, Sir Geoffrey Howe, stated:

On 14 February, Ayatollah Khomeini made a statement inciting Moslems to violence against Mr. Salman Rushdie, the author, and the publishers of 'The Satanic Verses'. That was totally incompatible with Iran's obligations under the United Nations Charter, and with respect for our sovereignty and the rule of law. We protested in the strongest terms and put an immediate freeze on the intended gradual build-up of our staff in Tehran.

. . .

Britain is able to have normal relations with many countries that do not share our ideals or democratic way of life. We were ready to do the same with Iran. But we can do so only if Iran respects accepted standards of international behaviour—in particular, respect for the sovereignty and law of other states as laid down in the Charter of the United Nations. Iran has disregarded those standards in the most flagrant and menacing way. The response of the Government and of the other member countries of the European Community is firm and clear. Before normal relations can be restored, Iran must meet her international obligations—in particular, by renouncing the use or threat of violence against citizens of other countries.

(HC Debs., vol. 147, cols. 839–40: 21 February 1989; see also ibid., vol. 148, col. 895: 8 March 1989)

Speaking on 27 February 1989 in the UN Commission on Human Rights, the UK representative, Mr H. Steel, stated in respect of the same matter:

I shall use only the measured language of my own Secretary of State, Sir Geoffrey Howe. Speaking yesterday after a meeting of the Foreign Ministers of the Twelve Member States of the European Community, he said the following:

'We all view these threats with grave concern. We share a sense of outrage at the incitement to murder on British soil, now repeated by Ayatollah Khomeini despite the apology made by the author on 18 February.

'Fundamental principles are at stake—freedom of expression, religious tolerance, the paramount need to uphold the law. The statements of Ayatollah Khomeini are contrary to the Charter of the United Nations, and constitute unwarranted interference in our internal affairs. We all condemn this incitement to violence.'

I will quote also one other passage, this time from the Declaration made by the Foreign Ministers of the Twelve.

'The Foreign Ministers view these threats with the gravest concern. They condemn this incitement to murder as an unacceptable violation of the most elementary principles and obligations that govern relations among sovereign states. They underline that such behaviour is contrary to the Charter of the United Nations . . . '.

(Text provided by the Foreign and Commonwealth Office; see also E/CN. 4/1989/ SR. 39, p. 15)

In the course of a speech on 7 March 1989 in the UN Commission on Human Rights, the UK representative, Mr H. Steel, observed:

One other general observation before I come to the situation in particular countries. It is an observation which is relevant to what is said about particular countries. Contrary to what some delegations may contend—indeed, have contended— the consideration by this Commission of the human rights situation in a particular country, and the action of any delegation in drawing the Commission's attention to that situation, is not an improper interference in that country's internal affairs. It is the legitimate carrying out of our duty under Articles 55 and 56 of the Charter, and in pursuance of the mandate given to this Commission under Article 68 of the Charter to which I referred when I began this statement, to promote the human rights of human beings, individual human beings, even when that is unwelcome to, or calls into question, the actions of their own governments.

(Text provided by the Foreign and Commonwealth Office; see also E/CN. 4/1989/ SR. 52, pp. 4–5)

In the course of a press conference held on 7 March 1989, a spokesman for the Foreign and Commonwealth Office remarked in the context of the threats uttered by Iranian authorities against Mr Rushdie:

Incitement to murder was a violation of the most elementary principles and obligations that governed relations between sovereign States.

(Text provided by the Foreign and Commonwealth Office)

In the course of his reply to a question on the subject of two British nationals imprisoned in Peru, the Minister of State, Foreign and Commonwealth Office, wrote:

It would be contrary to internationally accepted practice for us to seek to interfere in the judicial process of an independent sovereign state. We would not tolerate such interference in our own judicial processes.

(HC Debs., vol. 157, Written Answers, col. 863 : 27 Jul7 1989)

Part Three: I. A. 3. *Subjects of international law—States—international status—domestic jurisdiction*

(See also Part Three: I. A. 2., above and Part Four: VII. (item of 20 February 1989), below)

In reply to the question whether Her Majesty's Government will make representations to the authorities in Grenada for the restoration of a constitutional court system, the Parliamentary Under-Secretary of State, Foreign and Commonwealth Office, wrote:

No. As an independent Commonwealth country, it is for Grenada to determine its own judicial system.

(HC Debs., vol. 156, Written Answers, col. *363*: 10 July 1989)

Part Three: I. B. 1. *Subjects of international law—States—recognition— recognition of States*

(See also Part Three: I. B. 5., below)

In reply to the question 'what criteria Bophuthatswana would need to satisfy in order to be recognised by Her Majesty's Government as an independent nation state', the Minister of State, Foreign and Commonwealth Office, Mrs Lynda Chalker, stated:

The same criteria that have been followed by successive British Governments and which are based on international law. Other factors, including relevant United Nations resolutions, are also taken into account.

(HC Debs., vol. 152, col. 852: 10 May 1989)

The Minister was then asked:

Why does my right hon. Friend not agree that, in international law, Bophuthatswana does fulfil the criteria laid down for recognition? It has a definable territory, a permanent population, a government, and the capacity to enter into relations with other states. Does not my right hon. Friend's policy have the rather ludicrous effect of driving Bophuthatswana to stay inside the sphere of influence of South Africa and thus strengthen apartheid, while the Government's policy is to woo South Africa's neighbours away from South Africa's sphere of influence and weaken apartheid? Cannot my right hon. Friend see the total inconsistency of the Government's policy?

The Minister replied in part:

I take up my hon. and learned Friend on what he said about the criteria for recognition. He subtly altered the wording of the third criterion, which involves independence in external relations. That is one of our criteria. These criteria have been used by successive British Governments and are recognised by international law. I know that my hon. Friend has been researching Judge Friedman's views and I understand that under the terms of the Montevideo convention, they may be different. Our prime cause must be to help South Africa get rid of apartheid throughout the territories, including Bophuthatswana. Until there is a democratic system in South Africa, we cannot consider change.

(Ibid., cols. 852–3)

[*Editorial note*: It may be assumed that the reference by the Minister of State in the above reply to the views of Judge Friedman is to the judgment in the courts in Bophuthatswana in February 1989 in the case of *State* v. *Banda and others*, [1989] 4 SA 517]

In the course of a debate on the subject of Cyprus, the Minister of State, Mr William Waldegrave, stated:

To those who believe that we should be according the same treatment to Mr. Denktash, who is the Turkish-Cypriot leader, as we give to President Vassiliou, I say that we recognise only one state in Cyprus, whose Government is now headed by Mr. Vassiliou. Mr. Denktash made it difficult for us to give him the access that he used to have to Ministers when the so-called 'Turkish Republic of Northern Cyprus' was declared in November 1983. We can have no truck with separatism and must guard against any action that might be construed by one side or the other as conferring recognition on an illegal entity.

(HC Debs., vol. 153, col. 1273: 26 May 1989)

In reply to a question, the Parliamentary Under-Secretary of State, Foreign and Commonwealth Office, wrote:

The normal criteria that we apply for recognition as a state are that it should have, and seem likely to continue to have, a clearly defined territory with a population, a Government who are able of themselves to exercise effective control of that territory, and independence in their external relations. Other factors, including some United Nations resolutions, may also be relevant.

(HC Debs., vol. 160, Written Answers, col. *494*: 16 November 1989)

Part Three: I. B. 2. *Subjects of international law—States—recognition— recognition of governments*

(See also Part Three: I. B. 5., below)

In the course of a reply to an oral question on the subject of Kampuchea, the Secretary of State for Foreign and Commonwealth Affairs, Sir Geoffrey Howe, stated:

Britain was, in fact, one of the first to withdraw recognition from the Pol Pot regime. The policy which we and others share at the United Nations and elsewhere on the seating of the coalition Government of democratic Kampuchea does not in any sense mean recognition as a Government or support for Pol Pot. That is not the position either after the United Nations General Assembly has adopted resolution after resolution condemning the atrocities committed by the Khmer Rouge.

(HC Debs., vol. 148, cols. 877–8: 8 March 1989)

The Secretary of State for Foreign and Commonwealth Affairs, Sir Geoffrey Howe, stated during a visit to Islamabad, Pakistan, that he had met there members of the 'interim government' of Afghanistan. He went on:

It is in fact premature to talk of recognition of the interim government in the light of our own policy to recognize States and not governments.

(Interview broadcast on BBC Television: 28 March 1989; *ex relatione* G. Marston)

In reply to a question on the subject of regimes in Kampuchea/Cambodia, the Parliamentary Under-Secretary of State, Foreign and Commonwealth Office, wrote in part:

We recognise states, not Governments, and have dealings with neither the CGDK nor the PRK. We currently foresee no change in this policy.

(HC Debs., vol. 154, Written Answers, col. *137*: 7 June 1989; see also ibid., vol. 156, Written Answers, col. *536*: 12 July 1989)

In the course of an oral answer, the Secretary of State for Foreign and Commonwealth Affairs, Sir Geoffrey Howe, stated in part:

We have no substantive dealings with the Kabul regime, which has been rejected by a majority of the Afghan people.

(HC Debs., vol. 156, col. 966: 12 July 1989)

In the course of a debate on the subject of Cambodia, the Minister of State, Foreign and Commonwealth Office, Mr William Waldegrave, stated:

The hon. Member . . . raised the often misunderstood question of the recognition of Governments and of credentials. Since 1980, Britain has recognised states and not Governments. One advantage of that is that we do not have to judge between competing claimants in circumstances of civil war or conflict. But in 1979, the position was different. Our criterion then for recognition of a Government was whether or not it had effective control over the greater part of the country. That was not a moral criterion, simply a descriptive criterion, and it led us to abandon recognition of the Khmer Rouge Government in 1979.

As we now recognise states not Governments, our only judgment is whether there is a Government within a country with which we are able to deal. Obviously the extent of that Government's ability of themselves to control their territory, will be one consideration. So will the assessment of British interests. At present, we recognise no Government in Cambodia.

There is also the separate issue of Cambodian credentials at the United Nations, which is mentioned in the motion. It is clear that the credentials committee could find no technical or legal reason for debarring the Cambodian delegation from this year's General Assembly. It is equally clear that, if there had been a vote in the General Assembly, the so-called coalition Government of Democratic Kampuchea would have won it overwhelmingly. This has not, therefore, been the most profitable pressure point on which to concentrate.

As I have said, neither our recognition of the reality of the situation, nor any other action of ours implies recognition of the coalition Government of Democratic Kampuchea or any other party as the legitimate Government in Cambodia. A dispute over credentials might also have split the unity of the Association of South-East Asian Nations which we hoped would be the principal vehicle for diplomatic progress towards a settlement in Cambodia.

(HC Debs., vol. 160, col. 46: 13 November 1989)

Part Three: I. B. 5. *Subjects of international law—States—recognition— non-recognition*

(See also Part Three: I. B. 1. and 2., above)

In the course of answering oral questions on the subject of Tibet, the Parliamentary Under-Secretary of State, Foreign and Commonwealth Office, Mr Timothy Eggar, stated:

The Dalai Lama is, of course, welcome to visit this country, but he is regarded by some as the leader of a Tibetan Government in exile, which is recognised neither by Her Majesty's Government nor by any other Government. A meeting with Ministers would, therefore, be open to misconstruction.

(HC Debs., vol. 144, col. 838: 11 January 1989)

In reply to a question, the Parliamentary Under-Secretary of State, Foreign and Commonwealth Office, wrote:

Since 1950, successive British Governments have dealt with the Government of the People's Republic of China as the sole legal Government of China. Accordingly there can be no question of [the Secretary of State for Foreign and Commonwealth Affairs] meeting representatives of the authorities in Taiwan.

(Ibid., Written Answers, col. 704: 11 January 1989)

In a speech in explanation of vote in the UN Security Council on 11 January 1989, the UK Permanent Representative, Sir Crispin Tickell, stated:

With regard to the request that has just been approved, as a result of which the Alternate Permanent Observer of Palestine will take part in the current debate in the Council, the United Kingdom abstained, as it did in the past when similar proposals were made regarding the participation of the Palestine Liberation Organization in the Council's proceedings. Our abstention on this occasion—and in the future if the same proposal should be made again—does not mean that the United Kingdom has recognized the State of Palestine, as proclaimed unilaterally by the Palestine National Council on 15 November 1988 in Algiers. Our abstention should not be taken as implying any change in my Government's position on that matter.

(S/PV. 2841, pp. 7–8)

In reply to a question, the Minister of State, Foreign and Commonwealth Office, wrote:

We do not recognise the state of Palestine declared by the PNC in Algiers. Our contacts with Palestinians do not and cannot amount to Government-to-Government dealings. We regard the persons with whom such contacts take place not as governmental representatives but as Palestinian leaders. Accordingly, such contacts do not and cannot affect our position of not having recognised the state of Palestine.

(HC Debs., vol. 146, Written Answers, col. 436: 3 February 1989)

The following note verbale dated 28 April 1989 was transmitted to the Director General of the World Health Organisation by the Permanent Mission of Spain to the United Nations in Geneva on behalf of the Twelve Member States of the EC:

The Twelve Member States note that in paragraph 3 of Resolution A/RES/43/177 of 1988 the General Assembly of the United Nations decided that, effective as of 15 December 1988, 'the designation "Palestine" should be used in place of the designation "Palestine Liberation Organisation" in the United Nations system, without prejudice to the observer status and functions of the Palestine Liberation Organisation within the United Nations system, in conformity with relevant United Nations resolutions and practice'.

The Twelve Member States further note that Article 6 of the Constitution of the World Health Organisation provides that 'States' may apply to 'become Members and shall be admitted as Members when their application has been approved by a simple majority vote of the World Health Assembly'.

The Twelve Member States of the European Community recall that no member of the Community has recognised the Palestine Liberation Organisation/Palestine as a State.

(Text provided by the Foreign and Commonwealth Office)

In reply to a question on the above subject, the Parliamentary Under-Secretary of State, Foreign and Commonwealth Office, wrote:

We are in close touch with a wide range of fellow members of the World Health Organisation, including European Community and Western partners in Geneva.

The Twelve member states of the European Community have made their position clear in a formal note to the director general of the World Health Organisation. No member of the European Community has recognised the Palestine Liberation Organisation/Palestine as a state. Accordingly, we do not accept that the Palestine Liberation Organisation satisfies the criteria for membership of the World Health Organisation.

We have also strongly advised the Palestine Liberation Organisation not to pursue its application.

(HC Debs., vol. 152, col. 191: 4 May 1989)

In reply to a question, the Minister of State, Foreign and Commonwealth Office, wrote:

In common with every country except South Africa we do not recognise the 'independence' of Bophuthatswana. Our training and scholarships programmes are available to individual applicants from Bophuthatswana as from elsewhere in South Africa.

(HC Debs., vol. 153, Written Answers, col. 642: 25 May 1989)

In reply to a question, the Minister of State, Foreign and Commonwealth Office, wrote:

We have not recognised the 'state of Palestine' declared by last November's Palestine National Council. Accordingly, we do not believe that 'Palestine' satisfies the criteria for membership of UN agencies. We have advised the PLO against pursuing these applications.

(HC Debs., vol. 154, Written Answers, col. 471: 14 June 1989)

In reply to a question, the Parliamentary Under-Secretary of State, Foreign and Commonwealth Office, wrote:

We do not recognise the 'Turkish Republic of Northern Cyprus' and have no formal dealings with its authorities. The British high commissioner in Nicosia nevertheless has informal contacts with Mr. Denktash and we are thus able to protect the interests of British nationals.

Whilst we are not aware of any instances of the outright expropriation of property by those authorities, we are continuing to press for all outstanding claims for compensation from our citizens to be dealt with expeditiously and for the remaining difficulties facing those attempting to establish their freehold title to property to be resolved.

(HC Debs., vol. 154, Written Answers, col. *474*: 14 June 1989)

In reply to a question, the Minister of State, Foreign and Commonwealth Office, wrote in part:

The Government do not recognise any claim to an independent Kurdish state, although we acknowledge the Kurds' cultural identity.

(HC Debs., vol. 159, Written Answers, col. *63*: 30 October 1989)

In reply to the question what steps Her Majesty's Government had taken to overcome import restrictions on whisky exported to Taiwan, the Parliamentary Under-Secretary of State for Corporate Affairs wrote:

The authorities in Taiwan are well aware of United Kingdom concerns. Her Majesty's Government have no dealings with the Taiwanese authorities but United Kingdom concerns on this and other matters are put across very clearly in Taipei and London by the Anglo-Taiwan trade committee, a private organisation set up to promote British exports to Taiwan.

(HC Debs., vol. 159, Written Answers, col. *348*: 3 November 1989)

In reply to a question, the Parliamentary Under-Secretary of State, Foreign and Commonwealth Office, wrote:

There are a number of territories not recognised by the United Kingdom as independent sovereign states:
North Korea
Taiwan
Turkish Republic of Northern Cyprus
Micronesia
Palestine
Saharan Arab Democratic Republic
Transkei, Ciskei, Venda and Bophuthatswana (the South African 'homelands').

(HC Debs., vol. 160, Written Answers, col. *119*: 14 November 1989)

In reply to a question, the Minister of State, Foreign and Commonwealth Office, wrote in part:

Successive British Governments have never recognised de jure the forcible incorporation of the former Baltic states in the Soviet Union. It follows that we respect the right of the peoples of Estonia, Latvia and Lithuania to say what their own future should be.

(HC Debs., vol. 162, Written Answers, cols. *323–4*: 29 November 1989)

In reply to a question, the Minister of State, Foreign and Commonwealth Office, wrote:

No country in the world except South Africa recognises the independence of Bophuthatswana. Bophuthatswana does not meet the criteria for recognition as an independent state that have been followed by successive British governments. The criteria are based on international law, and are that a state should have and seem likely to continue to have:
  (i) a clearly defined territory with a population;
  (ii) a government who are able of themselves to exercise effective control of that territory; and
  (iii) independence in their external relations.
There are also exceptional cases when other factors, including relevant United Nations resolutions, may be taken into account. These considerations apply to the question of recognition of Bophuthatswana.

(HL Debs., vol. 513, cols. 844–5: 5 December 1989)

Part Three: I. C. 4. *Subjects of international law—States—types of States—dependent States and territories*

The following letter, dated 7 January 1988, was sent by the Secretary of State for Foreign and Commonwealth Affairs, Sir Geoffrey Howe, to the Governor of Hong Kong:

I have the honour to refer to the draft Agreement for the purpose of providing the framework for air services between Hong Kong and Switzerland, the text of which was negotiated during the period from July 1986 to November 1987.

The United Kingdom Government remains responsible for the external relations of Hong Kong until 30 June 1997. However, the United Kingdom Government hereby entrusts to you authority:
  (a) to conclude the said Agreement;
  (b) in accordance with prior specific authorisations in that behalf from the United Kingdom Government, to agree and confirm amendments to the said Agreement;
  (c) to carry into effect and to exercise the other powers conferred upon a contracting party by the said Agreement.
Further, with the prior agreement of the United Kingdom Government, you may terminate the said Agreement in accordance with its terms.

If action is required to be taken relating to the international conventions referred to in the said Agreement it shall be taken either by the United Kingdom Government, or as appropriate, by the Hong Kong Government acting under the authority of the United Kingdom Government.

Following the coming into force of the said Agreement, the United Kingdom Government will register it on behalf of the Hong Kong Government.

(Special Supplement No. 5 to the *Hong Kong Government Gazette*, vol. 130 (1988), p. E 15)

See also letters in similar terms dated 12 September 1986 in respect of an air services agreement between Hong Kong and the Netherlands

Government (Special Supplement No. 5 to the *Hong Kong Government Gazette*, vol. 129; see also UKMIL 1987, pp. 515–16); 6 June 1988 in respect of an air services agreement between Hong Kong and Canada (Special Supplement No. 5 to the *Hong Kong Government Gazette*, vol. 130, p. E 201); 5 December 1988 in respect of an air services agreement between Hong Kong and Brunei Darussalam (Special Supplement No. 5 to the *Hong Kong Government Gazette*, vol. 141, p. E 17).

The following extract is taken from the Foreign and Commonwealth Office Treaty Section's *Instruction Manual*, prepared in May 1988 for internal use.

1. *The United Kingdom dependent territories as Contracting Parties*. Dependent territories do not possess the capacity to enter into treaty relations with other dependent territories or States, although the Governments or Administrations of the United Kingdom dependent territories do on occasions conclude treaties with the consent and authority of the Government of the United Kingdom, a recital of such consent and authority being written into the treaty in question. (See TS 57/1957, Cmnd. 250.) Alternatively, the Government of the United Kingdom may treat both on its own behalf and on behalf of the Government of a United Kingdom dependent territory. Where the Government or Administration of a dependent territory is expressed as a party to a treaty, the Government of the United Kingdom is, from a legal standpoint, ultimately responsible for fulfilling the obligations of the treaty.

2. *Entrustments*. Some territories which have reached an advanced stage of constitutional development are given authority to conclude treaties in certain fields. This is called an entrustment.

3. *Ratification*. Such entrustments can include ratification, where this is required. [An example] is a draft ratification prepared for the Governor of Bermuda to sign under delegated authority from the UK.

4. *Publication*. Agreements concluded by territories under entrustment need not be published as a UK Command Paper. If, however, the UK acts on behalf of a territory (alone, without the UK becoming a party) the text should be published in the Miscellaneous Series of Command Papers. This rarely happens but an example was the International Arrangement regarding Trade in Textiles, 1975 (Miscellaneous No. 18/1975, Cmnd 6205) and the two Protocols extending the period of validity of the Arrangement in 1978 and 1981 (see Miscellaneous Nos. 19/1978 and 25/1984, Cmnd 7259 and 9408) which the UK accepted on behalf of Hong Kong. (Despite its title the said 'Arrangement' is an agreement). If, of course, the agreement is concluded by the UK on behalf of a territory, it should be published in the country and/or Treaty Series in the same way as any bilateral treaty. The UK has concluded a series of agreements with the United States on behalf of several territories in the West Indies which have all been published in the Treaty Series, eg TS 70/1984, Cmnd 9344 (Cayman Islands), TS 20/1987, Cm 136 (Turks and Caicos Islands).

5. *Hong Kong* has concluded a number of agreements with the consent and authority of the United Kingdom. Hong Kong was given an entrustment to conclude an Air Services Agreement with the Netherlands in 1986. This was the first of many treaties which will be concluded by Hong Kong as it develops its own network

of agreements prior to attaining its new status in 1997 as a Special Administrative Region of the People's Republic of China.

(Text provided by the Foreign and Commonwealth Office (some cross-references deleted))

In reply to a question, the Parliamentary Under-Secretary of State, Foreign and Commonwealth Office, wrote:

The British Antarctic Territory was established as a separate dependent territory in 1962. Since then, as a matter of convenience, the territory has been administered by an high commissioner resident in Stanley. Following consideration of the future administrative needs of the territory, we have decided that from 1 July this year the administration of the BAT will be repatriated to London and that the commissioner will be a senior official of the Foreign and Commonwealth Office. The present high commissioner has been informed and is informing the Falkland Islands Councillors. The British Indian Ocean Territory has been similarly administered from London since 1977.

(HC Debs., vol. 145; Written Answers, col. *473*: 24 January 1989)

The Foreign and Commonwealth Office submitted a memorandum on the subject of progress in implementing the Sino-British Joint Declaration of 1984 on Hong Kong to the Foreign Affairs Committee of the House of Commons for its meeting of 22 March 1989. The memorandum read in part as follows:

I. BACKGROUND TO THE NEGOTIATION OF THE JOINT DECLARATION

1. Under the Treaty of Nanking (1842) and the Convention of Peking (1860), Hong Kong Island, the southern part of the Kowloon Peninsula and Stonecutters Island were ceded to Britain in perpetuity. The rest of the territory of Hong Kong (comprising 92 per cent of the total land area) was leased to Britain for 99 years from 1 July 1898 under a further Convention signed in Peking in that year. This leased area, consisting of the area north of Kowloon up to the Shenzhen River and 235 adjacent islands, is known as the New Territories.

2. The Chinese Government has consistently taken the view that the whole of Hong Kong is Chinese territory. For many years its position was that the treaties relating to Hong Kong were unequal ones left over from history; that the question should be settled peacefully through negotiation when the time was ripe; and that pending a settlement the status quo should be maintained. It made it clear that in its view the settlement of the question of Hong Kong was a matter of China's sovereign right.

3. The expiry of the New Territories' lease on 30 June 1997 made it necessary to tackle the question of the future as soon as possible after China's emergence from the Cultural Revolution. It was clear that the remaining 8 per cent of Hong Kong's land area would not be viable without the New Territories, which contain most of the territory's agriculture and industry, its power stations, and its airport and container port. Moreover, by the late 1970s, concern about Hong Kong's future, both locally and amongst foreign investors, began to grow. The inability of the Hong Kong Government to grant new land leases in the New Territories extending beyond 1997 was a particular problem which was becoming progressively more serious. Simply to have ignored the 1997 deadline was not an option: the legal

instrument under which the New Territories was governed was due to expire in 1997; and uncertainty as to what would happen thereafter would have led to an erosion of confidence as the reality of Hong Kong's uncertain future became closer and clearer.

4. Against this background, the British Government resolved to remove the uncertainty imposed by the 1997 deadline. The visit of the Prime Minister to China in 1982 provided an appropriate opportunity to open discussions with the Chinese Government about Hong Kong's future. As a result of that visit, the two sides agreed that talks would begin 'with the common aim of maintaining the stability and prosperity of Hong Kong'.

II. The Negotiation of the Joint Declaration

5. The negotiations lasted two years, from September 1982 to September 1984, when the documents comprising the Agreement were initialled. The negotiations fell into two phases: an initial phase, conducted through the British Embassy in Peking; and a second phase of formal talks, which began in July 1983 and consisted of 22 rounds of negotiations over 14 months, supplemented by informal contacts, and in the final four months by full-time discussion of draft texts tabled by the two sides. The Foreign Secretary, Sir Geoffrey Howe, was closely involved at every stage in the second phase of the talks and intervened personally at several important points in the negotiations.

6. The negotiations were complex and difficult. The British side initially argued hard for the retention of British administration in Hong Kong after 1997 as the surest way of maintaining the prosperity and stability of the territory. After protracted discussion, however, it became clear that the continuation of British administration in any form was unacceptable to the Chinese Government and that the talks would break down if the British Government continued to insist on it. Since most of Hong Kong would in any case under the Treaty pass under Chinese jurisdiction in 1997, the only way forward was to explore the possibility of negotiating arrangements under Chinese sovereignty which would command sufficient confidence to ensure Hong Kong's future stability and prosperity.

7. From October 1983, the two sides began to examine in detail how to devise arrangements which would secure for Hong Kong after 1997 a high degree of autonomy under Chinese sovereignty; and which would enable Hong Kong, as a Special Administrative Region of the People's Republic of China, to preserve its existing way of life and the essential elements of its present system. A great deal of work was required in order to turn this concept—that of 'one country two systems'—into a written agreement that embodied such arrangements with sufficient clarity and precision to be acceptable to the British Government. The Foreign Secretary paid two visits to Peking in April and July 1984, during both of which substantial progress was made. That paved the way to final agreement: the texts were initialled on 26 September 1984.

III. Consultation with the People of Hong Kong

8. The negotiations were conducted on a strictly confidential basis. But the British Government had made it clear from the outset that any agreement on Hong Kong's future would have to be acceptable to the people of Hong Kong. The Governor of Hong Kong was a member of the British negotiating team. Members of the Executive Council, the Governor's closest advisers, were kept fully informed of

developments. The Foreign Secretary consulted the Executive Council before each
of his visits to China. Our negotiating position was helpfully and decisively
influenced by their advice. The Governor and members of the Executive Council
visited London on several occasions, for talks with the Prime Minister and other
Ministers; and British Ministers paid a series of visits to the territory to keep in
direct touch with opinion there, including in particular with Members of the Legislative Council.

9. After the Joint Declaration was initialled in September 1984, an Assessment
Office was set up in Hong Kong to analyse and assess the views of Hong Kong
people on the draft. To ensure complete impartiality, the work of the Assessment
Office was overseen by two eminent independent monitors. The Assessment Office
found that the draft had been widely accepted by the people of the territory: there
was general recognition that a document containing such detailed and comprehensive provisions for Hong Kong's future was the best that could have been achieved
in the circumstances. It exceeded the expectations of many people, who had
assumed from statements made by the Chinese authorities before the negotiations
began that any agreement on Hong Kong's future would be couched in very
general terms. The Agreement was widely welcomed internationally as a major
diplomatic achievement.

IV. CONSULTATION WITH THE BRITISH PARLIAMENT

10. The British Parliament took a close interest in the progress of the negotiations and in the Joint Declaration itself. There were debates on Hong Kong in
October and November 1983 and in May 1984. The draft Agreement was presented to Parliament in a White Paper in September 1984. In thorough and
wide ranging debates in December 1984, the overwhelming majority of speakers
expressed the view that the agreement was an excellent one which provided a
sound basis for a stable and prosperous future for Hong Kong after 1997. The
Joint Declaration was signed by the British and Chinese Governments on 19
December 1984. The Hong Kong Act 1985, providing for the ending of British
sovereignty and jurisdiction over Hong Kong on 30 June 1997, was passed by
Parliament and received the Royal Assent on 24 April 1985.

11. The Agreement entered into force on 27 May 1985, when instruments of
ratification were exchanged in Peking between the British and Chinese Governments. On 12 June 1985 it was registered at the United Nations by the two governments, in accordance with the normal practice.

V. ANALYSIS OF THE JOINT DECLARATION

12. The Agreement consists of a Joint Declaration by the two governments and
three Annexes. The Annexes have the same status as the Joint Declaration. Associated with the Agreement is a separate Exchange of Memoranda on the status after
1997 of Hong Kong British Dependent Territories citizens.

13. The Joint Declaration sets out the essentials of what had been agreed by
the two governments. It outlines the policies of the Chinese Government
towards Hong Kong after 1997, which are further elaborated in Annex I.
Paragraph 7 stipulates that the two governments agree to implement the

Joint Declaration and Annexes. It has the effect of making them legally binding on both parties.

(*Parliamentary Papers*, 1988–89, HC, Paper 281–ii, pp. 1–2)

In the course of a debate on the subject of events in China, the Secretary of State for Foreign and Commonwealth Affairs, Sir Geoffrey Howe, stated:

It is an important feature of the joint declaration that the Government of the People's Republic of China recognise, without qualification, the responsibility of Her Majesty's Government for the administration of Hong Kong until 1997, which is a responsibility that we shall continue to discharge to the fullest of our ability. It is also important for my right hon. Friend to remind the House and, through the House, the Government of the People's Republic of China of their responsibilities in the years that extend beyond 1997, under the joint declaration for a full span of 50 years, but in practice and aspiration way beyond that into the future.

(HC Debs., vol. 154, cols. 34–5: 6 June 1989)

In reply to a question, the Parliamentary Under-Secretary of State, Foreign and Commonwealth Office, wrote:

The relationship between the Falkland Islands and the European Economic Community is governed by part four of the Treaty of Rome and Council decision 86/283/EEC on the association of overseas countries and territories with the EEC. These provisions are not affected by the Single European Act.

(HC Debs., vol. 154, Written Answers, col. *356*: 13 June 1989)

In the course of a debate on the subject of Hong Kong, the Minister of State, Foreign and Commonwealth Office, Lord Glenarthur, stated:

I noted the suggestion . . . about trusteeship, but the pitfall to that idea lies, I believe, in China's views about its ultimate sovereignty over Hong Kong. That is why we have told the Chinese very clearly that we shall fulfil our obligations under the joint declaration. We insist that they continue to fulfil theirs. Not only is there a solemnly binding international obligation on them to do so, but also it is manifestly in their own interests that they should.

(HL Debs., vol. 509, col. 256: 21 June 1989)

In the course of a debate on the subject of fishing by Northern Ireland fishermen in waters near the Isle of Man, the Parliamentary Secretary to the Ministry of Agriculture, Fisheries and Food, Mr David Mellor, stated:

. . . the Isle of Man is a dependency of the Crown and has its own legislature, judiciary and system of Government. However, its legislation must receive Royal Assent from the Queen in Council. Its Tynwald is probably the oldest legislature in continuous session in the world. The United Kingdom Government are, nevertheless, responsible for defence and foreign affairs and have ultimate responsibility for the good government of the Isle of Man.

(HC Debs., vol. 163, col. 1134: 13 December 1989)

Part Three: I. E. *Subjects of international law—States—self-determination*

(See also Part Four: VII. (item of 20 February 1989), below)

In reply to a question, the Minister of State, Foreign and Commonwealth Office, Lord Glenarthur, stated:

. . . there are two basic principles for settlement which have been long advocated. One is the right of all states in the region, including Israel, to a secure existence; the other is the Palestinians' right to self-determination.

(HL Debs., vol. 503, col. 696: 25 January 1989; see also, e.g., HC Debs., vol. 146, col. 964: 8 February 1989, and ibid., vol. 154, Written Answers, col. *469*: 14 June 1989)

In the course of a speech on 7 February 1989 in the UN Commission on Human Rights, the UK representative, Mr H. Steel, stated:

I do not need to repeat at any length the comments which I made last year, and which the United Kingdom delegation has made on a number of occasions, about the extreme importance which the right to self-determination has—has not merely for us, the United Kingdom, but has objectively, so to speak—an importance which is symbolized by the prominence given to it by its being invoked in Article 1 (as well as Article 55) of the Charter and by its enunciation in the common Article 1 of the two International Covenants. But I do want to say—because it needs to be said on every occasion when we discuss this topic—that the draftsmen of the Charter and of the two Covenants knew exactly what they were saying when they defined the right to self-determination as the right of peoples. It is the right of each people to be free to determine its own destiny; a right which can be infringed by a people's own government as well as by a foreign government or authority; an enduring, ever-operative right which can never be exhausted; a right which, even once acquired, requires perpetual vigilance in its defence.

(Text provided by the Foreign and Commonwealth Office: see also E/CN. 4/1989/ SR. 11, pp. 6–7)

The following extract is from a note verbale dated 28 April 1989 transmitted to the Director General of the World Health Organization by the Permanent Mission of Spain to the United Nations in Geneva on behalf of the Twelve Members States of the EC:

The Twelve attach particular importance to the recent evolution in the policy of the PLO. They welcome the acceptance by the PLO of Security Council Resolutions 242 and 338 as a basis for an International Conference and of the right of Israel to exist. Respect for this principle goes together with that of justice for the peoples of the region, in particular the right of self-determination of the Palestinian people, with all that this implies.

(Text provided by the Foreign and Commonwealth Office)

In reply to a question, the Minister of State, Foreign and Commonwealth Office, wrote in part:

Our consideration of Gibraltar's future is governed by the commitment, renewed by successive Governments, that we would never enter into arrangements under which the people of Gibraltar would pass under the sovereignty of another state against their freely and democratically expressed wishes.

(HC Debs., vol. 156, Written Answers, col. *318*: 7 July 1989)

In the course of a debate on 18 October 1989 in the Sixth Committee of the UN General Assembly on the subject of methods of preventing international terrorism, the representative of France, on behalf of the Twelve Member States of the EC, stated:

> Les Etats membres de la Communauté réaffirment, à cet égard, leur opposition à la tenue d'une conférence internationale ayant pour objet de définir le terrorisme et d'opérer une distinction entre le terrorisme et la lutte des peuples pour leur libération nationale, qui risquerait de nuire aux progrès déjà réalisés par la coopération internationale contre le terrorisme, en envenimant un débat qui doit rester technique. Un tel exercice ne ferait que perpétuer l'idée fausse, à laquelle les Douze se sont toujours opposés, selon laquelle il y aurait un lien entre le terrorisme et l'exercice du droit à l'autodétermination.

(Text provided by the Foreign and Commonwealth Office; for the translation in English see A/C.6/44/SR. 21, p. 16)

Part Three: II. A. 1. (b). *Subjects of international law—international organizations—in general—legal status—powers, including treaty-making power*

(See also Part Three: II. A. 1. (c), below)

The Foreign and Commonwealth Office addressed a memorandum, dated 4 December 1989, to the Joint Committee of the House of Commons and House of Lords on Statutory Instruments which was considering the draft European Communities (Definition of Treaties) (European School) Order 1989 and the draft European Communities (Privileges of the European School) Order 1989. The memorandum read in part:

1. The Committee have asked on what grounds the FCO consider the agreement between the United Kingdom Government and the Governors of the European School at Culham to be an international agreement or otherwise to be a treaty.

2. The intention of the United Kingdom Government and the Board of Governors was to enter into an agreement binding in international law. The agreement was accordingly drawn up in standard treaty form and laid before Parliament as a Treaty. It will be published in the Treaty Series and registered with the United Nations Secretariat. In the considered view of Her Majesty's Government, the European School has the legal capacity to enter into such an international agreement. The Board of Governors of the European School have concluded agreements with a number of other European Community States. All these agreements are in treaty form and have been processed as such under the domestic law of the Member States concerned.

(*Parliamentary Papers*, 1989–90, HC, Paper 29–ii, p. 10)

The following extract from the Committee's report indicates the background and reaction to the question:

The two Orders go together. The Definition of Treaties Order designates as a Community treaty, under section 1(3) of the European Communities Act 1972, an Agreement between the United Kingdom Government and the Board of Governors of the European School at Culham. The Privileges Order, to be made under section 2(2) of the European Communities Act, gives effect to the Agreement, which is an agreement to confer privileges on the School and its staff as respects income tax, customs charges and other matters. It did not seem to the Committee that an agreement between the Government and the governors of a school in the United Kingdom could, in the ordinary way, be regarded as an international agreement. They accordingly sought elucidation on this point from the Foreign and Commonwealth Office by asking on what grounds that department took the view that the Agreement in this case was an international agreement or was otherwise a treaty. The Department's reply is contained in a memorandum which is printed in Appendix IV. The material part of the memorandum states as follows:

'The intention of the United Kingdom Government and the Board of Governors was to enter into an agreement binding in international law. The agreement was accordingly drawn up in standard treaty form and laid before Parliament as a Treaty. It will be published in the Treaty Series and registered with the United Nations Secretariat. In the considered view of Her Majesty's Government, the European School has the legal capacity to enter into such an international agreement'.

The Committee do not find this reply very illuminating. In addition to the intention of the parties there must, it seems to the Committee, also be some objective element that governs the question whether an agreement can be regarded as a treaty. Both parties must have capacity to enter into an international agreement. Clearly the Government has such capacity. The essential question in this case is whether the Board of Governors of the European School at Culham also has it. The Department's memorandum states baldly that in the Government's view the School has such capacity (and the Committee take it that the Government regards the Board of Governors as in the same position). The memorandum does not, however, indicate why the Government takes that view. Perhaps it is material that the Board of Governors is composed of Ministers of the Member States of the European Community, but the Government have made no claim on this basis.

(Ibid., p. 4)

Part Three: II. A. 1. (c) *Subjects of international law—international organizations—in general—legal status—privileges and immunities*

(See also Part Three: II. A. 1. (b)., above)

In the course of a speech in the UN Security Council on 7 November 1989 on the subject of Israeli activities in the occupied territories, the UK Permanent Representative, Sir Crispin Tickell, stated:

We are particularly concerned about the situation of the United Nations Relief and Works Agency for Palestine Refugees in the Near East (UNRWA). In his speech to the Special Political Committee on 24 October the Commissioner-General stated that UNRWA had obstacles placed in its way by the Israeli authorities. We should not forget that UNRWA provides basic services for the most needy elements in the Palestinian population. In particular, my Government deplores the recent raids by the Israeli Defence Force on UNRWA premises in the West Bank and Gaza Strip. These appear to be a violation of the privileges and immunities of a respected United Nations body. The Israeli authorities have still not responded to the protest made by UNRWA on 20 October. We hope that a reply will be forthcoming soon.

(S/PV. 2889, pp. 19–20)

In the course of a debate in the Fifth Committee of the UN General Assembly on the subject of the privileges and immunities of officials of the UN and its specialized agencies, the representative of France, on behalf of the Twelve Member States of the EC, stated on 16 November 1989:

Le statut juridique, les privilèges et les immunités des fonctionnaires sont régis par l'Article 105 de la Charte des Nations Unies qui dispose notamment que les fonctionnaires 'jouissent . . . des privilèges et immunités qui leur sont nécessaires pour exercer en toute indépendance leurs fonctions en rapport avec l'Organisation'.

Dans le cas des fonctionnaires de l'ONU, ce principe a été développé dans la Convention de 1946 sur les privilèges et immunités des Nations Unies, à laquelle, faut-il le rappeler, plus de 120 Etats Membres sont actuellement parties.

Concernant les organisations ou institutions spécialisées, des dispositions pertinentes ont été incluses dans les accords de siège conclus avec les gouvernements des pays hôtes.

Des accords types en matière d'assistance régissent les conditions dans lesquelles le PNUD et ses agents oeuvrent dans les pays en développement.

Bien entendu, ces privilèges et immunités sont accordés non pas à titre personnel, mais dans l'intérêt des organisations. Toute entrave à leur exercice normal constitue un obstacle à l'accomplissement de la mission confiée par la communauté internationale aux organisations du système des Nations Unies.

. . .

Le rapport A/C.5/44/11 indique que, malgré les appels répétés du Secrétaire Général, malgré les efforts constants déployés par lui et les directeurs des agences et organisations concernées, en dépit des nombreuses résolutions adoptées par les organes compétents et l'Assemblée Générale, la situation reste alarmante. Nous regrettons une nouvelle fois que le nombre d'arrestations et de détentions de fonctionnaires des Nations Unies ait augmenté dans les dernières années, en totale contradiction avec les principes établis par la Charte et les conventions internationales, et particulièrement dans différentes régions du Moyen Orient, ainsi que le souligne le Secrétaire Général dans son rapport.

. . .

Le rapport A/C.5/44/11 relève des cas très graves de détention arbitraire, d'arrestation et d'enlèvement de fonctionnaires internationaux, de violations des droits de l'homme, de restrictions à l'exercice des libertés fondamentales.

Les Douze appuient les efforts sans relâche déployés par le Secrétaire Général et les Directeurs des institutions spécialisées qui, le plus souvent, par la rapidité de leurs interventions ont pu faire prévaloir le droit international.

Mais nous voudrions aussi exprimer la profonde émotion que nous avons ressentie à la nouvelle, encore non confirmée, de l'assassinat du Lieutenant-colonel

Higgins et indiquer une nouvelle fois notre vive préoccupation face à la détention de M. Alec Collet, enlevé au Liban en 1985, dont le cas est mentionné à l'annexe I du rapport. Les Etats Membres de la Communauté Européenne condamnent fermement de tels actes de terrorisme. Nous attendons en outre l'avis consultatif que doit rendre prochainement la Cour Internationale de Justice sur le cas de M. Dumitru Mazilu.

Nous notons que ces cas ne sont pas les seuls et que les atteintes aux privilèges et immunités des fonctionnaires peuvent prendre des formes multiples et variées, comme l'adoption de législations contraires au statut des fonctionnaires internationaux. Le rapport du Secrétaire Général en donne de nombreux exemples.

Les Douze renouvellent leur appel aux gouvernements concernés afin que soit mis fin rapidement à de telles exactions et à de telles situations, et que les fonctionnaires internationaux puissent exercer leurs fonctions sans contraintes d'aucune sorte. Nous appuyons les efforts constants du Secrétaire Général en vue de faire appliquer les accords internationaux relatifs aux privilèges et immunités des organisations internationales et de leur personnel. Nous l'assurons de notre entière coopération et nous encourageons les Etats membres à faire de même.

(Text provided by the Foreign and Commonwealth Office; for the translation in English see A/C.5/44/SR.42, pp. 14–15)

The Foreign Office addressed a memorandum, dated 4 December 1989, to the Joint Committee of the House of Commons and House of Lords on Statutory Instruments which was considering the draft European Communities (Definitions of Treaties) (European School) Order 1989 and the draft European Communities (Privileges of the European School) Order 1989. The memorandum read in part:

It should first be noted that the proposed Orders do not confer any immunities on the European School or its staff. They confer only certain privileges and exemptions. Article 28 is couched in very broad terms and, it is submitted, can quite properly be interpreted to include the kind of privileges and exemptions which it is proposed to confer. The Committee might like to note that the European Court of Justice held in the *Hurd* case, that by virtue of the general obligation in Article 5 of the EEC Treaty, the United Kingdom was bound not to levy tax upon the salaries paid by the European School at Culham to its teachers, when the burden of that taxation would be borne by the Community budget. This decision of the ECJ was given effect to expressly by Article 9 of the Agreement, which is in turn reflected in Article 7(c) of the draft Order on the Privileges of the European School. It is the understanding of this Department that the other European Schools enjoy similar privileges and exemptions.

(*Parliamentary Papers*, 1989–90, HC, Paper 29–ii, p. 4)

Part Three: II. A. 2. (c) *Subjects of International law—international organizations—in general—participation of States in international organizations—obligations of membership*

In reply to a question, the Minister of State, Foreign and Commonwealth Office, wrote:

The international coffee agreement (1983) expires on 30 September 1989.

Intensive discussions have taken place since mid-1988 but have failed to result in a consensus on the content of a new agreement. On 3 July the International Coffee Council will consider two draft resolutions for extension with economic provisions. If neither resolution obtains the required majority, the Council may adopt a resolution providing for the 1983 agreement to be extended without economic provisions. With its Community partners the United Kingdom has supported the principle of extension of the 1983 agreement as part of a transition to a new agreement.

It has been the practice to lay the text of any agreed resolution for extension of an international commodity agreement before Parliament for 21 sitting days before the United Kingdom deposits an instrument of acceptance with the United Nations. Given the parliamentary recess, there will not be 21 sitting days between 3 July and 1 October. We cannot wait until Parliament sits again in the autumn, because under the terms of article 68 of the current ICA, contracting parties who have not notified the United Nations of their acceptance by 1 October 1989 will cease to be members of the ICA.

I have therefore decided to place in the Library of the House today copies of the two draft resolutions to be considered by the Council on 3 July. Once the final text of the Council resolution is known, I will ensure that it is laid before Parliament for as much of the usual 21-day period as possible.

(HC Debs., vol. 155, Written Answers, col. *580*: 30 June 1989)

In reply to a subsequent question, the Under-Secretary of State, Department of Trade and Industry, wrote in part:

The International Coffee Council on 3 July resolved (resolution number 347) to extend the international coffee agreement (1983) without quotas and virtually all its other economic provisions for a period of two years from 1 October 1989. The Council also resolved to suspend the quota system with effect from 4 July.

(Ibid., vol. 157, Written Answers; cols. *1171–2*: 28 July 1989)

Part Three: II. A. 3. *Subjects of international law—international organizations—in general—legal effect of acts of international organizations*

In the course of replying to questions on the subject of uranium coding on supplies imported from Namibia, the Parliamentary Under-Secretary of State, Department of Energy, Baroness Hooper, stated:

. . . if my noble friend is referring to the Security Council Resolutions 283 and 301, as a matter of law, our view is the same as that of successive British Governments. The Security Council cannot take decisions that are generally binding on member states unless there has been a determination of the existence of a threat to peace, a breach of the peace or an act of aggression. We therefore believe that it is up to us to decide what arrangements we make for trading with Namibia.

(HL Debs., vol. 509. col. 126: 20 June 1989)

Part Three: II. B. 4. *Subjects of international law—international organizations—particular types of organizations—other types of organizations*

In moving the second reading in the House of Lords of the Pakistan Bill, the Minister of State, Foreign and Commonwealth Office, Lord Brabazon of Tara, stated:

. . . the purpose of the Bill before us today is no more than to modify existing domestic legislation to place Pakistan on the same footing as other Commonwealth countries. Pakistan has duly rejoined the Commonwealth, with effect from 1st October. The Bill involves purely technical amendments to a number of Acts in order to apply them to Pakistan. The Bill deals with Pakistan's relationship with the Commonwealth Institute. It reinstates the right of the Government of Pakistan to appoint a trustee to the Board of the Imperial War Museum. It makes some amendments to our legislation so that Pakistan forces are included in the definition of Commonwealth forces, with implications for their legal status when, for example, training in this country. It makes provision for the exercise of command and discipline when British forces and Commonwealth forces are serving together and for attachment of members of one force to another. It also ensures that the arrangement for reciprocal enforcement of judgments with Pakistan will continue in force.

The immigration and electoral implications of Pakistan's return to the Commonwealth have been dealt with separately by an Order in Council made on 2nd August, which added Pakistan to the list of Commonwealth countries given in Schedule 3 to the British Nationality Act 1981.

(HL Debs., vol. 514, cols. 356–7: 21 December 1989)

Part Three: III. D. *Subjects of international law—subjects of international law other than States and organizations—mandated and trust territories, Namibia*

(See also Part Three: II. A. 3., above)

In reply to questions on the subject of Palau, the Government spokesman in the House of Lords, Lord Reay, stated:

. . . Palau is a group of islands in the south-west Pacific to the north of Indonesia. It has a population of 15,000. Its capital is Koror. Between the wars it was a mandated territory under the League of Nations administered by Japan. After the last war it became a United Nations trust territory and was administered by the United States of America together with what are now the Marshall Islands, the Federated States of Micronesia and the northern Marianas.

. . . our policy is to see the trusteeship for the Trust Territory of the Pacific Islands, which includes Palau, terminated in accordance with the UN charter and the freely expressed wishes of the inhabitants of the trust territory.

. . . we believe that the policy I have stated is correct, given the fact that we are members both of the trusteeship council and of the Security Council. The trusteeship agreement can be terminated only by the United Nations Security Council. As Members both of the trusteeship council and the Security Council, we see it as being our duty to ensure that the proper procedures under the United Nations charter for terminating the agreement are followed.

. . . In 1983 Palau chose to enter into a compact of free association with the United States. That would bring self-government to Palau, leaving responsibility for security and defence to the United States. The compact would permit the transit of nuclear material. However, the courts of Palau found that to be in conflict with the country's constitution which it had freely adopted in 1979. In order to resolve the dilemma various referenda have been held to enable the constitution to be amended and the compact implemented. However, none has yet attained the required 75 per cent. majority. The next referendum is likely to be held next year.

(HL Debs., vol. 511, cols. 1022–3, *passim*: 19 October 1989)

Part Four: I. *The individual (including the corporation) in international law—nationality*

The extension on 1 January 1989 by the UK Government of the Convention on the Transfer of Sentenced Persons, 1983, to the British Virgin Islands was accompanied by the following declaration:

In accordance with Article 20, paragraph 2, I hereby declare, on behalf of the Government of the United Kingdom, that the application of the Convention on the Transfer of Sentenced Person shall extend to the British Virgin Islands.

I further declare in accordance with Article 3, paragraph 4, of the said Convention, that, for the purposes of the said Convention, the term 'National' means, in relation to the British Virgin Islands, a person who is a British Citizen, or a British Dependent Territories Citizen by virtue of a connection with the British Virgin Islands or any other person whose transfer to the British Virgin Islands appears to the Officer for the time being administering Government of the British Virgin Islands to be appropriate having regard to any close ties which that person has with the British Virgin Islands.

(TS No. 80 (1988); Cm. 702, p. 9)

In reply to a question, the Parliamentary Under-Secretary of State, Foreign and Commonwealth Office, wrote:

The nationality of Vietnamese refugees and boat people in Hong Kong will be governed by the nationality laws of Vietnam, or of any other state whose nationality they might claim.

Persons born in Hong Kong before 1 January 1983, including those born to Vietnamese refugees, were born 'British subjects: citizens of the United Kingdom and Colonies' under the British Nationality Act 1948. On 1 January 1983, such persons became British Dependent Territories Citizens under the British Nationality Act 1981, which came into force on that date. After that date, persons born to Vietnamese refugees or boat people in Hong Kong do not have British nationality by virtue of their birth there.

(HC Debs., vol. 152, Written Answers, col. *306*: 8 May 1989)

In reply to a question on the right of settlement within the EC, the Minister of State, Foreign and Commonwealth Office, wrote:

EC nationals have the right to reside in the other member states of the Community in accordance with the Treaties. It is for each Member State to define who are its own nationals for Community purposes. The provisions of the EC treaty relating to the free movement of persons apply to European territories for whose external relations a member state is responsible, such as Gibraltar. Citizens of the following overseas territories are also defined as nationals by the member states concerned:

United Kingdom —Falkland Islands
France —St. Pierre et Miquelon, Mayotte and the overseas Departments and Territories
Netherlands —Aruba
—Netherlands Antilles
Portugal —Macau

(HC Debs., vol. 152, Written Answers, col. *481*: 11 May 1989)

In reply to a question, the Minister of State for Defence Procurement wrote:

The United Kingdom memorandum associated with the Sino-British Joint Declaration of 1984 states that 'British Dependent Territories Citizens (BDTCs) will cease to be BDTCs with effect from 1st July 1997, but will be eligible to retain an appropriate status which, without conferring right of abode in the UK, will entitle them to use passports issued by the Government of the UK'. No other statements of intention in respect of nationality and right of abode have been made by the Government to the Chinese Government.

(HL Debs., vol. 510, col. 901: 19 July 1989)

In reply to a series of questions, the Minister of State, Foreign and Commonwealth Office, wrote:

The British memorandum associated with the Sino-British Joint Declaration on the question of Hong Kong makes clear that from 1 July 1997 those British Dependent Territories Citizens (BDTCs) from Hong Kong, who have by then elected to become BN(O)s and to travel on BN(O) passports, will be entitled to consular services and protection in third countries. The Chinese memorandum indicates that such passports may continue to be used from 1 July 1997, although, in accordance with normal practice in cases of dual nationality, BN(O)s will not be entitled to consular protection by the United Kingdom Government in the Hong Kong Special Administrative Region, or in other parts of China.

. . .

The Chinese memorandum to the Sino-British Joint Declaration states that under Chinese nationality law, all Hong Kong Chinese are Chinese nationals. The British memorandum makes clear that all Hong Kong British Dependent Territories Citizens will, from 1 July 1997, be eligible to retain an appropriate status which will entitle them to continue to use passports issued by the Government of the United Kingdom. It also provides that that status will be acquired by BDTCs only if they hold, or are included in, a BN(O) passport issued before 1 July 1997, except that eligible persons born on or after 1 January 1997, but before 1 July 1997, may obtain or be included in such a passport up to 31 December 1997.

. . .

In accordance with the exchange of memoranda associated with the Sino-British Joint Declaration on Hong Kong, all persons who on 30 June 1997 are, by virtue of a connection with Hong Kong, British Dependent Territories Citizens (BDTCs) under the law in the United Kingdom, will cease to be BDTCs with effect from 1 July 1997, but will be eligible to retain the status of British Nationals (Overseas).

At the same time, under the nationality law of the People's Republic of China, all Hong Kong Chinese compatriots, whether they are BDTCs or not, are Chinese nationals.

(HC Debs., vol. 158, Written Answers, col. 76 : 17 October 1989)

In reply to the question whether Her Majesty's Government 'will cite the occasions where the UK has engaged in treaty making or other international agreement which complies with Article 10 of the UN Convention on Reduction of Statelessness', the Parliamentary Under-Secretary of State, Foreign and Commonwealth Office, wrote:

When the United Kingdom has transferred territory by treaty in the circumstances envisaged in the United Nations convention since 1966, the date when the convention became binding on the United Kingdom, appropriate arrangements for nationality have been made in compliance with that article.

(Ibid., col. 80 : 17 October 1989)

Part Four: V. *The individual (including the corporation) in international law—statelessness, refugees*

(See also Part Four: VII., below)

In reply to the question

What steps [Her Majesty's Government] are taking to protect the interests and human rights of refugees and asylum-seekers in the European preparations for 1992; and what definitions of 'persecution' and 'genuine fears concerning life and liberty' they seek to have agreed, in the light of our obligations under the United Nations Convention on the Status of Refugees (1951),

the Minister of State, Home Office, wrote:

Discussions on a wide range of issues relating to asylum are continuing in the EC Ad Hoc Working Group on Immigration established during the United Kingdom Presidency. These include the question of which state should be responsible for examining asylum applications.

All member states of the Community are signatories to the 1951 United Nations Convention on Refugees, and discussions in the Community are based on the assumption that we shall continue to carry out in full our individual obligations under the Convention. Discussions have not sought separately to define the terms quoted in the Question.

(HL Debs., vol. 503, col. 228: 18 January 1989)

In reply to the question

How [Her Majesty's Government] expect that refoulement of genuine refugees contrary to the 1951 United Nations Convention on Refugees will be prevented after 1992; and what progress has been made within the European Community on negotiations concerning asylum-seekers, the same Minister wrote in part:

All member states are signatories of the 1951 UN Convention, and as such are committed not to permit the refoulement of refugees. There is no reason to think that this will cease to be the case after 1992.

(HL Debs., vol. 508; col. 494: 24 March 1989)

In reply to a question, the Parliamentary Under-Secretary of State, Foreign and Commonwealth Office, wrote:

We have no plans to suspend the return of fugitives to Hong Kong. My right hon. Friend the Home Secretary can only order the return of a fugitive when all court proceedings in the United Kingdom have been concluded. If a fugitive offender is returned to Hong Kong under the Fugitive Offenders Act before 1997, that would be for an offence against Hong Kong laws. It would not be for offences against the law of the PRC. The case would be heard by the Hong Kong courts. Under the joint declaration Hong Kong will retain its separate legal system after 1997, and will not be relying on the PRC criminal code.

(HC Debs., vol. 154, Written Answers, col. 524: 15 June 1989)

In reply to a question on the subject of Mr Ozberk, from Turkey, the Minister of State, Home Office, wrote:

Under the 1951 United Nations Convention on Refugees, the practice is that it is the responsibility of the individual signatory state to decide whether applicants meet the criteria for recognition as refugees. In this case, after recognition was refused, the applicant twice sought and was refused leave by the High Court for judicial review of that decision before the London Office of the United Nations High Commissioner for Refugees (UNHCR) intervened.

While any representations from that source are always—like the original applications themselves—considered with particular care, the representations did not in this instance include any information which had not previously been before the Home Office or the High Court, nor did they otherwise appear to identify grounds for accepting that the convention criteria were satisfied. Although regretting, therefore, that a difference of opinion should persist, the Government has co-operated with the UNHCR's London office in their efforts to arrange for Mr. Ozberk to go to a country other than Turkey (and accordingly he left for Italy at 1 p.m. this afternoon).

(HL Debs., vol. 511, col. 1548: 25 October 1989)

In the course of a statement on the subject of Vietnamese boat people in Hong Kong, the Secretary of State for Foreign and Commonwealth Affairs, Mr Douglas Hurd, stated:

This morning, Hong Kong time, a group of 51 boat people were returned to Vietnam by aircraft from Hong Kong. All 51 had been screened under a thorough process agreed with the United Nations High Commissioner for Refugees and they did not qualify for refugee status under the terms of the 1951 United Nations convention on refugees and the 1967 protocol. The repatriation was conducted in line with procedures used worldwide to remove people refused permission to remain in a territory. No firearms were carried. No force was used.

At the international conference on Indo-Chinese refugees in Geneva in June, the international community agreed that refugees would be resettled in other countries, and that those who did not qualify as refugees would not be resettled and should return to Vietnam. I stress that the criteria for establishing who qualifies as a refugee are not decided by Britain, or by the Hong Kong authorities alone, but by agreement with the UNHCR.

(HC Debs., vol. 163, col. 857: 12 December 1989)

During a debate on the statement, the Secretary of State remarked:

There is no discrimination. The crucial test tests who is a refugee. We apply the same test in the United Kingdom, as I know from my last job. The same test is being applied in Hong Kong. It is not a test laid down by us but by the United Nations in the 1951 convention. The test is whether an individual has a well-founded fear of being persecuted for reasons of race, religion, nationality, membership of a particular social group or political opinion. That is the United Nations' test. We apply it in Britain and it is being applied in Hong Kong.

(Ibid., cols. 859–60)

Part Four: VI. *The individual (including the corporation) in international law—immigration and emigration, extradition, expulsion and asylum*

(See also Part Four: V. (items of 18 January and 24 March 1989), above)

The Foreign and Commonwealth Office issued a press release on 29 June 1989 which read in part as follows:

We and our European partners have consistently urged the Israeli authorities to refrain from the deportation of Palestinians. Such action is against international law and defies Security Council Resolution 607 which was approved unanimously.

(Text provided by the Foreign and Commonwealth Office)

In reply to a question, the Secretary of State for the Home Department wrote in part:

I will shortly lay before Parliament a statement of changes in the immigration rules which will include provisions requiring Turkish nationals to obtain visas before travelling to the United Kingdom. The necessary written notice of one month under the 1960 agreement for the abolition of visas (Cmnd. 1043) was given to the Turkish Government on 23 May. The new visa regime will come into effect on 23 June.

(HC Debs., vol. 154, Written Answers, col. 45: 6 June 1989)

In reply to a question on the subject of Chinese students presently studying in the UK, the Minister of State, Home Office, wrote:

Any application for asylum will be considered in accordance with the UN 1951 convention relating to the status of refugees.

In addition, while the situation in China remains uncertain, we shall look sympathetically at any application by a Chinese national to extend their stay, depending on their individual circumstances.

(HC Debs., vol. 154, Written Answers, col. 327: 12 June 1989)

In reply to a question, the Minister of State, Home Office, wrote in part:

Asylum applications continue to be decided under the criteria of the 1951 convention. There is no question of granting refugee status in cases which do not qualify under the convention in order to reduce the backlog of outstanding applications.

(HC Debs., vol. 155, Written Answers, col. *323*: 26 June 1989)

In the course of a debate on the subject of immigration, the Secretary of State for the Home Department, Mr Douglas Hurd, stated:

I refer to the treatment of refugees, with particular reference to that part of the immigration laws which deals with the Turkish Kurds. The United Nations 1951 convention defines the test of asylum, the granting of refugee status, as 'owing to a well-founded fear of being persecuted for reasons of race, religion or nationality, membership of a particular social group or political opinion.' That definition is about 38 years old and it was devised for different circumstances, but it holds up very well. The United Nations draftsmen drafted the definition well and the test is still valid in changed circumstances.

(HC Debs., vol. 156, col. 381: 5 July 1989)

In the course of a debate on the subject of Jens Soering, accused of murder in USA, the Minister of State, Home Office, Mr John Patten, stated:

. . . I want to underline certain key issues raised by the case. The first is the importance that the United Kingdom attaches to its extradition agreements. They are a major factor in our responses to serious crime and we are committed to the principle of co-operation between jurisdictions.

(HC Debs., vol. 157, col. 643: 20 July 1989)

In reply to the question under what circumstances can persons be extradited from Peru and charged with offences in UK, the Minister of State, Home Office, wrote:

Persons may be extradited from Peru if they are accused or convicted of offences committed within the jurisdiction of the United Kingdom which are deemed to be extraditable under the terms of the Extradition Act 1870 and the bilateral treaty of 1907 between the United Kingdom and Peru.

(HC Debs., vol. 157, Written Answers, col. *1171*: 28 July 1989)

In reply to a question on the subject of Turkish Kurds, the Minister of State, Home Office, wrote:

By 11 October the asylum applications from 592 Turkish nationals had been considered in detail. The results of this consideration are that 71 met the criteria of the 1951 UN convention and have been recognised as refugees; 243 have been given leave to remain in the United Kingdom on an exceptional basis; 24 departed voluntarily before a final decision was reached; 172 have been notified of a provisional decision that they do not qualify for asylum and further information/representations are awaited; 36 did not qualify for asylum or leave to enter under the immigration rules, were refused entry and returned to Turkey.

In addition, a further 207 have made voluntary departures after withdrawing their claims for asylum.

(HC Debs., vol. 158, Written Answers, col. *611*: 26 October 1989)

In reply to a question, the Minister of State, Foreign and Commonwealth Office, wrote:

The joint declaration makes provision for us and the Government of the People's Republic of China to ensure the continued application of international rights and obligations affecting Hong Kong. The Chinese authorities have agreed that before 1997 we should authorise Hong Kong to conclude its own extradition agreements, designed to continue in force after 30 June 1997. These agreements will contain traditional safeguards for fugitive criminals. In addition, Hong Kong's domestic law will continue to provide traditional safeguards for fugitive criminals.

(HC Debs., vol. 159, Written Answers, col. *58*: 30 October 1989)

In the course of replying to questions on the subject of the repatriation of Vietnamese boat-people in Hong Kong, the Minister of State, Foreign and Commonwealth Office, Lord Brabazon of Tara, stated:

. . . the problem is that no other country in the world is prepared to accept any of these people who have not been screened out as regards genuine refugee status. The Geneva Conference in June therefore came to the conclusion that there was no other option for them—other than to stay in Hong Kong, which would be completely unsatisfactory—than to return to their own country.

(HL Debs., vol. 513, col. 860: 6 December 1989)

Part Four: VII. *The individual (including the corporation) in international law—protection of human rights and fundamental freedoms*

(See also Part Three: I.A. 2. (item of 20 February 1989), above and Part Fourteen: I.B. 8., below)

In reply to a question, the Parliamentary Under-Secretary of State, Foreign and Commonwealth Office, wrote:

. . . the Minister of State raised the subject of human rights with the Turkish ambassador on 12 December 1988. We continue to urge the Turkish Government to maintain the improvement in human rights there has been in recent years and to respect and abide by the terms of the relevant international human rights conventions to which Turkey is a signatory.

(HC Debs., vol. 145, Written Answers, col. *256*: 19 January 1989; see also HC Debs., vol. 146, Written Answers, col. *584*: 7 February 1989 and HL Debs., vol. 505, cols. 3–4: 13 March 1989)

In reply to a question, the Minister of State, Foreign and Commonwealth Office, wrote:

We can see no justification for the Soviet authorities' continued refusal to allow Boris and Galina Lifshitz to emigrate. Her Majesty's embassy in Moscow raised the case with the Russians in December and we will be raising it again at the UK-USSR bilateral human rights talks on 26 January.

(HC Debs., vol. 145, Written Answers, col. *362*: 20 January 1989)

In reply to a question, the Minister of State, Foreign and Commonwealth Office, wrote in part:

We are seriously concerned at continuing allegations of the use of napalm and of the bombing of civilians in Tigray, and have raised the matter with the Ethiopian Government. We shall express our concern under Item 12(D) at the UN Human Rights Commission.

(HL Debs., vol. 503, col. 977: 30 January 1989)

In reply to a question, the Minister of State, Foreign and Commonwealth Office, wrote:

We have made frequent representations to the South African Government, both bilaterally and with our European partners, to express our concern about human rights abuses including reports of maltreatment of both children and adults. We have made clear our view that the South African Government should release all those detained without charge.

(HC Debs., vol. 146, Written Answers, col. *110*: 31 January 1989)

In reply to a question, the Minister of State, Foreign and Commonwealth Office, wrote:

We press the Soviet Authorities at every possible opportunity about long-term refusenik cases such as Boris Chernobilsky. The most recent occasion was at the United States-USSR bilateral talks on human rights on 26 January.

(HC Debs., vol. 146, Written Answers, col. *434*: 3 February 1989; see also ibid., vol. 157, Written Answers, col. *4*: 17 July 1989)

In reply to a question, the Minister of State, Foreign and Commonwealth Office, wrote:

I summoned the ambassador of Romania on 30 January to protest about the infringement of the rights both of Her Majesty's ambassador in Romania and the Romanian citizen, Mrs Doina Cornea. We will continue to protest strongly about Romanian policies, which run counter to their obligations under the Vienna CSCE agreement, at every suitable opportunity.

(HC Debs., vol. 146, Written Answers, col. *436*: 3 February 1989; See also ibid, vol. 148, Written Answers, col. *550*: 8 March 1989; and vol. 154, Written Answers, col. *469*: 14 June 1989)

In reply to a question, the Parliamentary Under-Secretary of State, Foreign and Commonwealth Office, wrote in part:

We have in the past few weeks made representations at a high level about a wide range of human rights issues in Chile.

(HC Debs., vol. 146, Written Answers, col. *732*: 8 February 1989)

In reply to a question, the Minister of State, Foreign and Commonwealth Office, wrote:

[The Secretary of State for Foreign and Commonwealth Affairs] raised Czechoslovakia's handling of human rights in my speech last month at the conclusion of the CSCE follow-up meeting in Vienna. I also expressed our concern to the Czechoslovak ambassador on 31 January.

(Ibid., col. *733*)

In reply to a question on the subject of East Timor, the Parliamentary Under-Secretary of State, Foreign and Commonwealth Office, wrote:

With our European partners, we have regularly conveyed to the Indonesian Government our views on the importance of respecting human rights and expressed our concern, on humanitarian grounds, in individual cases. There is evidence that respect for human rights in East Timor has improved in recent years.

(Ibid., col. *742*)

In the course of a speech on 10 February 1989 to the UN Commission on Human Rights, the UK representative, Mr H. Steel, stated:

. . . the South African system of apartheid, where racial discrimination is institutionalised at every level, offends against the United Nations Charter and all the relevant instruments. I say that, on behalf of my Government, as a plain statement of law.

(Text provided by the Foreign and Commonwealth Office; see also E/CN. 4/1989/ SR. 17, p. 5)

In the course of a speech on 13 February 1989 in the UN Commission of Human Rights, the UK representative, Mr H. Steel, stated:

First, then, the question of economic, social and cultural rights. It is sometimes hinted—indeed, sometimes expressly stated—by some delegations that the concept of economic, cultural and social rights is an unreal concept, an artificial construction. Or it is suggested that, if they do exist, they operate on an inferior plane to civil and political rights. Let me say, categorically and unambiguously, that that is not the position of the United Kingdom Government. If we had not thought that economic, cultural and social rights were real, we should not have ratified the Covenant on Economic, Cultural and Social Rights, since it is not the practice of the United Kingdom Government to undertake international legal obligations in which they do not believe or which they do not intend to comply with scrupulously. Nor, of course, would that attitude be consistent with our faithful observance of our undertaking, under Part IV of the Covenant, to submit regular reports to ECOSOC on our observance of the Covenant and to give full co-operation to the Committee on Economic, Social and Cultural Rights in its scrutiny of those reports.

. . .

The point that we do make about economic, cultural and social rights—it is of course equally true about civil and political rights, but it is scarcely in question in that context—is that the rights which we have undertaken to respect are the rights of individuals, of human persons; they are not the rights of Governments or States.

This is not merely a quibble, a piece of lawyer's pedantry. As we see it, it goes to the very essence of those rights and it has a significant bearing on the spirit in which Governments approach them and therefore on the measures which they take to implement them.

(Text provided by the Foreign and Commonwealth Office; see also E/CN. 4/1989/ SR. 20/Add. 1, p. 3)

The following protest was made on 14 February 1989 to the Soviet authorities in Berlin in respect of an attempted escape from the Soviet Sector of Berlin to the British Sector. The escapee was said to have swum 'to the western bank of the [River Spree], which is British Sector territory, and to hold on to it. He was then pulled by the hair out of the water on to a GDR patrol boat and taken away'. The protest went on:

The action of the GDR border guards was a blatant violation of human rights. Once again those responsible have shown their total disregard for civilised values. This incident is rendered even more serious by the fact that the young man had already reached the British Sector.

The British commandant, in association with the French and US commandants, protests most strongly against this incident and calls on those responsible finally to put an end to such outrageous incidents.

A press statement about this incident was issued on 15 February 1989 as follows:

Representatives of the British Military Government today called on the Soviet Embassy to protest about the incident yesterday in which a young man who had swum across the Spree was removed from British Sector territory by the guards on board a GDR patrol boat.

Explaining that they were acting in association with the US and French authorities, they emphasised that it was unacceptable and inconsistent with Four Power practice and co-operation in Berlin that an individual should be forcibly removed from the Western Sectors. They expressed concern about the future welfare of the young man and made clear their expectation that he should be permitted to return to the Western Sectors.

(Texts provided by the Foreign and Commonwealth Office)

On 20 February 1989, the Twelve Member States of the EC delivered a common statement on human rights to the UN Commission on Human Rights. In the course of the common statement it was declared:

We call upon all States that have not yet done so, to become party to both Covenants, and stress the importance of making the procedure of their specific monitoring bodies as effective as possible. But even for those States not being party to any human rights Convention, compliance with human rights and fundamental freedoms as embodied in the Charter of the United Nations, the Universal Declaration of Human Rights, and as reflected by international customary law, is nevertheless a universal obligation.

The Twelve consider that a great deal of progress has been achieved on the route towards full recognition of human rights in the last 40 years, due in large measure to the efforts of the United Nations. Old disputes—about Article 2,7 of the

Charter, for example—have been shelved. Decolonization and the enshrinement of the right of peoples to self-determination have changed the face of the world. A new awareness of each person's rights as an individual and as a member of a political and cultural community is present today in every corner of our planet. A new solidarity among peoples is also a major new development. At the same time we experience a widespread growth of non-governmental organizations concerned with human rights, a good number of which contribute highly to the work of this Commission. Governments engaged in human rights abuses have to confront the fact that individuals have acquired substantial rights under international law.

(Text provided by the Foreign and Commonwealth Office)

In reply to a question on the subject of human rights in Bangladesh, the Parliamentary Under-Secretary of State, Foreign and Commonwealth Office, wrote:

We have made clear to the Bangladesh Government the concern felt in this country about human rights issues. They were discussed most recently during the visit of President Ershad.

(HC Debs., vol. 147, Written Answers, col. 620: 22 February 1989)

In reply to a question, the Parliamentary Under-Secretary of State, Foreign and Commonwealth Office, wrote in part:

We have on several occasions conveyed to the Peruvian authorities our concern about reported abuses of human rights.

(HC Debs., vol. 148, Written Answers, col. 560: 8 March 1989)

In reply to a question, the Minister of State, Foreign and Commonwealth Office, wrote in part:

We take suitable opportunities to discuss the maintenance of high standards of human rights with the Kenyan Government.

(HL Debs., vol. 505, col. 3: 13 March 1989; see also HC Debs., vol. 155, Written Answers, col. 288: 26 March 1989)

In reply to a question, the Minister of State, Foreign and Commonwealth Office, wrote:

We have repeatedly made clear to the Government of Iraq our concern at their failure to respect human rights in their country. On 9 March, we co-sponsored a draft resolution on human rights in Iraq in the United Nations Commission on Human Rights, and voted against Iraq's successful motion to take no action on that draft. Our representative at the Commission made clear our concern in his statement.

(HC Debs., vol. 149, Written Answers, col. 144: 14 March 1989)

In reply to a question, the Parliamentary Under-Secretary of State, Foreign and Commonwealth Office, wrote in part:

We are concerned about human rights in China. Our general aim is to encourage the Chinese Government to continue their programme of economic, social and political reforms, in the belief that in the long run this will lead to the development of a stable and democratic society in China, which is essential for the respect of human rights.

(Ibid.)

In reply to a question, the Parliamentary Under-Secretary of State, Foreign and Commonwealth Office, wrote in part:

We condemn human rights abuses whenever they may occur. We are aware of allegations of ill-treatment by SWAPO of detainees held in their camps in Angola and Zambia. This is primarily a matter for the United Nations High Commissioner for Refugees to investigate, but we have raised the issue with SWAPO. We have also made known our concern to the office of the high commissioner.

(HC Debs., vol. 149, Written Answers, col. 625: 22 March 1989)

Following an unsuccessful attempt to escape from the Soviet Sector to the British Sector of Berlin, the following press statement was issued on 17 April 1989:

The Allied Commandants call on those responsible for preventing freedom of movement to the Western Sectors to end their blatant disregard for human rights, to act in accordance with commitments so recently reaffirmed at the Vienna CSCE Conference and to give details of the fate of the young man who this morning disappeared in his bid for freedom.

(Text provided by the Foreign and Commonwealth Office)

In reply to a question, the Minister of State, Foreign and Commonwealth Office, wrote:

The Chinese Government are aware of our dismay at recent events in Tibet. In addition to the bilateral contacts we have had with the Chinese Government about this, the Ambassadors of the Troika in Peking have made a demarche on behalf of the Twelve concerning the situation in Tibet in the context of the commitment of the Chinese authorities to ensure full respect for human rights.

(HL Debs., vol. 506, col. 1264: 25 April 1989; see also HC Debs., vol. 153, Written Answers, cols. 771–2: 26 May 1989)

In reply to a question, the Minister of State, Foreign and Commonwealth Office, wrote:

We have repeatedly made clear to the Iraqi authorities our concern at the abuses of human rights in Iraq. Both the United Kingdom and Iraq have ratified the international covenant on civil and political rights which prohibits the use of the death penalty against minors. The Iraqis know that we expect them to abide by their international obligations.

(HC Debs., vol. 151, Written Answers, col. 684: 28 April 1989)

In a statement issued on 6 June 1989 in Madrid by the Twelve Member States of the EC on the subject of events in China, it was stated in part:

Continuing repressive actions, in violation of universally recognised human rights principles, will greatly prejudice China's international standing and compromise the reform and open-door policies which the European Community and its member States have actively supported.

(Text provided by the Foreign and Commonwealth Office)

At a press conference held at the Foreign and Commonwealth Office on 14 June 1989, the following statement by the Minister of State, Foreign and Commonwealth Office, Mrs Lynda Chalker, on the subject of ethnic Turks expelled from Bulgaria was read:

We view this new Bulgarian policy of expulsion with deep and growing concern. It appears to be wholly at odds with Bulgaria's CSCE commitments, including those recently entered into at the Vienna Follow-Up Meeting. We consider the Turkish minority in Bulgaria should be free to choose to live where they wish and should not be subjected to harassment.

(Text provided by the Foreign and Commonwealth Office)

In reply to a question, the Minister of State, Foreign and Commonwealth Office, wrote:

We have made no recent representations to the Iraq or Turkish Governments concerning specific Kurdish asylum cases though no one can be in any doubt about our concern over human rights and the problem of Kurdish refugees.

(HC Debs., vol. 154, Written Answers, col. 464: 14 June 1989; see also ibid., vol. 158, Written Answers, col. 490: 25 October 1989)

The Foreign and Commonwealth Office submitted a memorandum on human rights in Hong Kong to the HC Foreign Affairs Committee for its meeting on 14 June 1989. It read in part as follows:

BACKGROUND

1. In 1976 Her Majesty's Government ratified the International Covenant on Civil and Political Rights (ICCPR) and the International Covenant on Economic, Social and Cultural Rights (ICESCR) with certain reservations, and extended the Covenants to 10 British dependent territories including Hong Kong.

APPLICATION OF THE COVENANTS

2. There are no particular provisions in the Covenants prescribing how effect should be given to them. Article 2(2) of the ICCPR states that: 'Where not already provided for by existing legislative or other measures, each State Party to the present Covenant undertakes to take the necessary steps . . . to adopt such legislative or other measures as may be necessary to give effect to the rights recognised in the present Covenant'. Article 2(1) of the ICESCR has a similar provision that reads 'each State Party to the present Covenant undertakes to take steps . . . with a view to achieving progressively the full realisation of the rights recognised in the present Covenant by all appropriate means, including particularly the adoption of legislative measures'.

3. At present, the two Covenants are implemented in Hong Kong, as they are in the UK, through a combination of common law, legislation and administrative rules. Thus, for example, *Article 10* of the ICESCR (substantially repeated in

Article 23 of the ICCPR) declares that the family is the natural fundamental group unit of society; marriage is to be entered into freely; special protection should be taken on behalf of children and young persons including limits on their employment. Various Ordinances including the Marriage Ordinance, the Employment Ordinance and the Protection of Women and Young Persons Ordinance give effect to this article in Hong Kong. *Article 9* of the ICCPR provides that everyone has the right to liberty and security of person; no one shall be subjected to arbitrary arrest or detention and any one arrested or detained on a criminal charge shall be entitled to trial within a reasonable time. The common law remedies relating to *habeas corpus* and false imprisonment ensure the availability of these rights in Hong Kong. Further, in addition to legislative provisions, the Police General Orders, which are administrative rules, set limits on the powers of police officers, for example, to stop and search for offensive weapons. *Article 17* of the ICCPR provides *inter alia* for protection against unlawful attacks on an individual's honour or reputation. This is covered by the common law governing libel and slander. *Article 26* of the ICCPR is concerned with equality before the law, this right has been guarded jealously by the legal profession and practice directions, issued by the Chief Justice, are important administrative rules which give effect to this article.

4. This system of protecting human rights through various complementary means is not specific, but is constantly evolving through new legislation, developments in common law and equity and refinement of administrative practices. Legislation and rules are kept under constant review so that any remaining inadequacies may be exposed and remedied, and positive improvements made. The system has worked well and Hong Kong has a good record on human rights.

(*Parliamentary Papers*, 1988–89, HC, Paper 281–ii, p. 348)

In reply to a question, the Parliamentary Under-Secretary of State, Foreign and Commonwealth Office, wrote:

The international covenant on civil and political rights was extended to Hong Kong, with certain reservations, in 1976. It is at present implemented in Hong Kong, as in the United Kingdom, through a combination of common law, legislation and administrative rules. We are now considering with the Hong Kong Government as a matter of priority whether to enact a human rights ordinance, and if so, what form it should take.

(HC Debs., vol. 154, Written Answers, col. *523*: 15 June 1989)

In reply to a question, the Parliamentary Under-Secretary of State, Foreign and Commonwealth Office, wrote in part:

We have made a number of representations about human rights to the Paraguayan authorities over the last five years.

(HC Debs., vol. 156, Written Answers, col. *14*: 3 July 1989)

In reply to a question, the Parliamentary Under-Secretary of State, Foreign and Commonwealth Office, wrote:

We have made a number of representations about human rights in China in recent years. As regards the most recent events, my right hon. and learned Friend the Secretary of State for Foreign and Commonwealth Affairs said in his statement to the House on 6 June that he had summoned the Chinese chargé d'affaires on 5 June to make clear to him that the British Government and people deeply deplored the action of the Chinese authorities in suppressing the democratic aspirations of the Chinese people. Representations have also been made on behalf of all EC members.

(HC Debs., vol. 156, Written Answers, cols. *315–6*: 7 July 1989; see also ibid., col. 965: 12 July 1989)

In reply to a question, the Parliamentary Under-Secretary of State, Foreign and Commonwealth Affairs, wrote:

Over 85 countries are parties to the Slavery Convention of 1926 (as amended by the Protocol of 1953), and 102 countries to the supplementary convention on the abolition of slavery, the slave trade and institutions and practices similar to slavery.

Since 1974, a United Nations working group on slavery has met annually to review the problems of slavery, including child slavery, and has recommended remedial action.

We hope that the draft United Nations convention on the rights of the child will shortly be adopted and will further strengthen international efforts to combat child slavery in all its forms.

(HC Debs., vol. 156, Written Answers, col. *550*: 12 July 1989)

In reply to the question how many representations Her Majesty's Government had made complaining about the denial of human rights in Brunei in the last five years, the Parliamentary Under-Secretary of State, Foreign and Commonwealth Office, wrote:

None. We expressed concern about certain aspects of human rights in Brunei at the United Nations Commission on Human Rights. The Brunei Government are aware of our concern.

(HC Debs., vol. 156, Written Answers, col. *674*: 14 July 1989)

In reply to a similar question in respect of Burundi, the Parliamentary Under-Secretary of State wrote:

We have made a number of representations to the Burundi authorities about human rights over the last five years. Following the ethnic violence last August we made a demarche to the Government of Burundi in concert with our EC partners. We are pleased to note the recent efforts of the Burundi Government to improve the human rights situation.

(Ibid.)

In reply to a question, the Parliamentary Under-Secretary of State, Foreign and Commonwealth Office, wrote:

We receive frequent representations about human rights violations affecting Bulgaria's Turkish minority. We have long had a policy of taking all appropriate opportunities of expressing our concern to the Bulgarian authorities, both bilaterally and in multilateral fora.

(HC Debs., vol. 157, Written Answers, col. 6: 17 July 1989; see also ibid., vol. 158, Written Answers, col. 545: 26 October 1989)

In the course of a debate on the subject of Jens Soering, accused of murder in the USA, the Minister of State, Home Office, Mr John Patten, stated:

Soering sought first to challenge the decision to extradite him to America. He did that in the domestic courts in Britain and then by application to the European Commission of Human Rights. Before the Commission, Soering's principal contention was that, if he was surrendered to the United States, there was serious reason to believe that he would be subjected to inhuman or degrading treatment or punishment in contravention of article 3 of the convention. This would arise, he suggested, from the exceptional and inordinate delay before carrying out the death penalty in Virginia. In a number of cases in that state's jurisdiction, delay has been substantial—five to eight years.

The Government acceded to the request of the President of the Commission not to remove Soering while it considered his application on this ground.

What happened is now history and is in the judgment, which is in the Library. The Commission decided by a narrow margin that the extradition of Soering to the United States of America would not give rise to a breach of the convention. The case was then referred to the court by the Commission and subsequently by the United Kingdom Government and the Government of the Federal Republic of Germany. The judgment of the court was delivered on 7 July. The court held unanimously that Soering's extradition would violate article 3 of the convention.

. . .

I want to respond, however, to the specific points raised by my hon. Friend [Mr Taylor]. He suggested in particular that the United Kingdom should simply ignore the views of the European Court of Human Rights—tell it to 'jump in the lake' was his graphic phrase. But we are talking of international obligations binding upon the United Kingdom. Each of the parties to the European convention of human rights has undertaken to abide by the decision of the court in any case to which they are parties. The House will recall that this country took a leading role in the evolution of the convention, and successive Governments have been scrupulous in complying with the judgments of the court.

My hon. Friend also referred implicitly to a recent case in which the United Kingdom felt obliged to derogate from the convention, following a judgment of the court. I want to point out why derogation was correct in that case and would not be correct in the case that my hon. Friend has raised. The circumstances were very different. That case concerned detention in Northern Ireland under the Prevention of Terrorism Act 1974. In that case, we derogated from our obligations under article 5 of the convention. Derogation in respect of particular articles of the convention is expressly provided for in article 15, which states: 'in time of war or other public emergency threatening the life of the nation.' We believe that there is an emergency in the Northern Ireland case. That is not the position in the case we are discussing tonight.

I must also point out to my hon. Friend that no derogation is permitted from certain articles of the convention, including article 3 on inhuman or degrading treatment or punishment. Under the convention, we cannot derogate in the same way as we are able to derogate in the case to which my hon. Friend referred.

(HC Debs., vol. 157, cols. 642–3: 20 July 1989)

In reply to a question, the Minister of State, Foreign and Commonwealth Office, wrote:

We have not taken up the question of human rights in Israel proper but have made repeated representations to the Israelis about human rights in the occupied territories.

(HC Debs., vol. 157, Written Answers, col. *599*: 25 July 1989)

In reply to a question, the Minister of State, Foreign and Commonwealth Office, wrote in part:

We have made a number of representations about human rights to the Colombian authorities over the last five years.

(HC Debs., vol. 157, Written Answers, col. *724*: 26 July 1989)

In reply to a similar question, the same Minister wrote in part:

We have made a number of representations to the Bahraini authorities about human rights over the past five years.

(Ibid.)

In a statement issued in August 1989, the Foreign and Commonwealth Office observed in part:

We have reminded the Czechoslovak authorities again of Britain's opposition to the use of force against those who exercise their legitimate political rights. We look to the Czechoslovak Government to allow their citizens to exercise freely all the rights accorded to them under the CSCE process.

(Text provided by the Foreign and Commonwealth Office)

In reply to the question how many regional treaties similar to the European Convention for the Protection of Human Rights and Fundamental Freedoms are in existence, the Minister of State, Foreign and Commonwealth Office, wrote:

There are two other major regional treaties. The American convention on human rights entered into force in 1978 and is interpreted and applied by the Inter-American Commission on Human Rights and (in the case of those States Parties which have recognised its jurisdiction) the Inter-American Court of Human Rights. States parties to the convention are from the Latin American and Caribbean regions. The African charter on human and peoples' rights came into force in 1986 and is interpreted and applied by the African Commission on Human and Peoples' Rights. It is open to members of the Organization of African Unity.

(HC Debs., vol. 158, Written Answers, col. *146*: 18 October 1989)

In reply to a question, the Minister of State, Foreign and Common-wealth Office, wrote:

The question of human rights and particularly the Kurds has recently been raised with the Turkish Government, who claimed that efforts to solve remaining problems would continue. Members of Her Majesty's embassy in Ankara have visited all three refugee camps since January. Her Majesty's embassy maintains contacts with representatives of a wide political spectrum in Turkey.

We regularly make clear to the Iraqi Government our concerns about Iraq's human rights record. We have no diplomatic relations with Iran or Syria and have made no direct representations to them, but we continue to make our views on human rights known to those Governments by our statements at international meetings.

(HC Debs., vol. 158, Written Answers, col. 640: 27 October 1989)

In reply to a question, the Minister of State, Foreign and Common-wealth Office, wrote:

Persons imprisoned in Hong Kong will, in accordance with the provisions of the joint declaration relating to the continuity of laws, remain subject to Hong Kong law. The joint declaration also provides that the International Covenant on Civil and Political Rights as applied to Hong Kong shall remain in force after 1997. In this connection it is noteworthy that article 15 of the Covenant prohibits the impo-sition of a heavier penalty than that applicable when the offence was committed.

(HC Debs., vol. 159, Written Answers, col. 58: 30 October 1989)

In the course of a debate in the Third Committee of the UN General Assembly on the subject of the elimination of all forms of religious intoler-ance, the UK representative, Mr M. Raven, stated on 14 November 1989:

. . . my Government is totally opposed to all forms of religious intolerance and dis-crimination based on religion. We have long supported the United Nations Declar-ation on Religious Intolerance and continue to stand by it. This Declaration is a standard which all governments should seek to follow.

(Text provided by the Foreign and Commonwealth Office; see also A/C.3/44/SR. 41, p. 6)

In an interview broadcast on BBC radio on 20 November 1989, the Minister of State, Mr William Waldegrave, stated that he had protested to the Czech Ambassador over the police suppression of public gatherings in Prague. He recalled that the Ambassador had in turn complained that the UK protest was an interference in Czech internal affairs. The Minister observed:

The Czechs have agreed that we have authority to question them on this matter by signing the Helsinki Final Act.

(*Ex relatione* G. Marston)

In a statement issued by the Twelve Member States of the European Community on 21 November 1989, it was written in part:

The Twelve appeal to the Czechoslovak Government to honour the commitments which it freely entered into, particularly those contained in the Helsinki Final Act and the Vienna Closing Document.

(Text provided by the Foreign and Commonwealth Office)

At a press conference held by the Foreign and Commonwealth Office on 24 November 1989, it was stated:

On November 17, officials of the Bucharest Embassies of the United States, the United Kingdom, Canada, and the Netherlands attempted to visit the United Nations Special Rapporteur for Human Rights and Youth, Mr Dumitru Mazilu. Since the preparation of his report, which is sharply critical of the Government of Romania's human rights practices, Mr Mazilu has been under virtual house arrest. The Romanian Government intervened to prevent the proposed visit to him by the four Western Embassy officers. This obstruction of diplomatic contact with a Romanian citizen and UN official is a violation of internationally accepted standards of human rights and Romania's CSCE obligations. The four concerned Governments deplore in the strongest terms this unwarranted interference in the work of their Embassies in Bucharest. They will continue to support Mr Mazilu and others who are being deprived of their fundamental human rights by the Romanian Government.

(Text provided by the Foreign and Commonwealth Office)

At a press conference held on 19 December 1989, a spokesman for the Foreign and Commonwealth Office stated in part:

Although the Romanian authorities are seeking to place obstacles in the way of information about events, it now seems clear that they violently suppressed a peaceful demonstration in Timisoara on 16/17 December. We condemn this in the strongest possible terms. It represents a very serious violation of Romania's commitments under the Helsinki and Vienna agreements. We summoned the Romanian Ambassador this morning to tell him so. We urgently call upon the Romanian Government to end their policies of repression and allow their citizens the freedom to exercise their fundamental human rights in accordance with Romania's CSCE commitments.

(Text provided by the Foreign and Commonwealth Office)

The Twelve Member States of the EC made a statement on 19 December 1989 on the subject of Romania, which read in part:

The Ministers of Foreign Affairs of the Twelve are deeply dismayed by the news of the Romanian authorities' violent and brutal repression of popular demonstrations.

They condemn in the strongest terms the attitude of a regime which, turning its back on all the commitments concerning human rights to which it has subscribed in the CSCE framework, is capable only of repressing by force the legitimate aspiration of the Romanian people to freedom.

(Text provided by the Foreign and Commonwealth Office)

Part Five: IV. *Organs of the State—diplomatic agents and missions*

At a press conference held on 30 January 1989, the spokesman of the Foreign and Commonwealth Office issued the following statement:

. . . at 11.30 am this morning Mr Waldegrave [Minister of State] had summoned the Romanian Ambassador to deliver a strong protest about an incident in Cluj on 27 January in which the British Ambassador was forcibly prevented from meeting Mrs Doina Cornea. In the course of the incident the British Ambassador and his party were man-handled by Romanian militiamen.

Mr Waldegrave told the Romanian Ambassador that we were shocked by this incident and that it was unacceptable for a diplomat to be prevented from conducting his legitimate business in this way. Such actions were extraordinary coming barely two weeks after the conclusion of the Vienna meeting of the CSCE, at which all participants had committed themselves to establishing and maintaining direct personal contacts between their citizens. Mr Waldegrave sought an apology and an assurance that such events would not be repeated.

The Romanian Ambassador undertook to look into the incident.

At a press conference held on 21 February 1989, the spokesman issued the following statement about a meeting between the Minister of State and the Romanian Ambassador held earlier on that day:

—Responding to the matters raised with him by Mr Waldegrave on 30 January, Mr Soare said his government rejected the account of the incident involving the British Ambassador in Cluj on 27 January. Mr Arbuthnott had infringed traffic regulations. The Romanian authorities also rejected the requests concerning Mrs Cornea whose activities were a matter for the Romanian authorities alone.

—Mr Waldegrave expressed profound regret at this response. There was no question of the British Ambassador having broken Romanian law and it was deeply discourteous of the Chief of Protocol to refuse to see Mr Arbuthnott about his treatment by the militia man.

In reply to a question, the Minister of State, Foreign and Commonwealth Office, wrote:

Of those territories recognised by the United Kingdom as independent sovereign states, the United Kingdom does not have an embassy, a high commission, or a consulate-general accredited to the following:

Albania
Argentina
Bhutan
Cambodia
Iran
Libya
Syria

The United Kingdom does not have diplomatic relations with Albania or Cambodia.

The United Kingdom does not have diplomatic relations with the Kingdom of Bhutan but maintains friendly contacts and conducts official business with its embassy in New Delhi.

Iran broke diplomatic relations with the United Kingdom in March this year. British interests are represented by the Swedish embassy in Tehran, where there are no United Kingdom staff.

There are British interest sections with United Kingdom staff in the embassies of protecting powers in Argentina, Libya and Syria.

The staff of the British embassy of Afghanistan have been withdrawn for security reasons.

There are no plans at present to establish additional representative offices.

(HC Debs., vol. 152, Written Answers, col. 275: 5 May 1989)

In reply to a question, the Parliamentary Under-Secretary of State, Foreign and Commonwealth Office, wrote:

There has been an exchange of notes with the Liberian Government through its embassy in London about Mr Osman's appointment as Liberian ambassador-at-large to the European Community and his status in the United Kingdom. It is for the courts to decide whether Mr Osman has any diplomatic immunity, in accordance with the Diplomatic Privileges Act 1964 and the facts presented to them.

(HC Debs., vol. 153, Written Answers, col. 248: 18 May 1989; see also UKMIL 1988, pp. 479–84)

Part Five: V. *Organs of the State—consular agents and consulates*

In the course of a debate on the subject of the detention in Iran of a United Kingdom citizen, Mr Roger Cooper, the Parliamentary Under-Secretary of State, Foreign and Commonwealth Office, Mr Timothy Eggar, stated:

Once Roger's detention had been confirmed we made repeated representations for consular access to him in prison. I have from time to time had to emphasise from the Dispatch Box the very real limitations on the level of assistance which our consular representatives abroad can offer British citizens in trouble. However, access for consular authorities to prisoners abroad is a fundamental right under the terms of the Vienna convention on consular relations. Iran is a signatory to that convention, as are we, but the Iranian Foreign Ministry told us only that the question of access to Roger Cooper was no longer within its gift. That attitude and approach was not and is not acceptable from a country which is a signatory to the Vienna convention. My hon. Friend is absolutely right to stress the fact that Roger's detention contravenes the Vienna convention on consular relations.

Since the start of Roger's detention we have pressed repeatedly for access to him and for the Iranian authorities to fulfil the terms of their international obligations. But it was not until August 1986 that our consul was granted a sight of Roger and then only a sight, through a glass screen. Since that viewing, if that is the way to describe it, and until August last year, British officials were only permitted to visit Roger on one occasion.

(HC Debs., vol. 145, cols. 461–2: 18 January 1989)

On 7 August 1989, the French Ambassador in Rangoon, speaking on behalf of the Governments of the EC, drew to the attention of the Burmese Government the statement issued by the EC Secretariat on 26 July 1989. In this statement the Twelve Member States of the European Community expressed concern at the 'persistent and extensive impediments to the exercise of fundamental freedoms in Burma'. The French Ambassador on behalf of the Twelve also drew the attention of the Burmese authorities to the case of Dr Michael Aris, a British citizen who arrived in Burma on 22

July. While the British Consul had received a letter from Dr Aris, consular access to him had so far been denied, which was a violation of international practice.

(Material provided by the Foreign and Commonwealth Office)

The following item appeared in the report of a press conference held by the Foreign and Commonwealth Office on 19 October 1989:

Spokesman said that Mr Waldegrave [Minister of State, Foreign and Commonwealth Office] had asked the Iraqi Ambassador to call this morning. Mr Waldegrave had told the Ambassador of HMG's continuing serious concern about the lack of consular access to Mrs Parish and Mr Bazoft, despite many requests by Ministers and others. Mr Waldegrave had reminded the Ambassador that the two had now been held for more than a month and that, under the provisions of the Vienna Convention on Consular Relations, we were entitled to exercise our right to access to a British subject without delay.

Mr Waldegrave had said that HMG could not accept the link which had been made by the Iraqi authorities between access and the conclusion of investigations into the alleged activities of the two detainees. We urged the Iraqi authorities to resolve this problem speedily and to grant consular access without further delay in accordance with accepted international practice.

The Ambassador had had no information which had not already been conveyed to HMG by the Iraqi authorities but undertook to report to his Government immediately.

(Text provided by the Foreign and Commonwealth Office)

Part Five: VII. *Organs of the State—armed forces*

In reply to a question, the Minister of State for Defence Procurement wrote:

. . . the stationing of US forces in the United Kingdom is governed by a number of agreements between the British and US Governments, including the Churchill-Truman understanding of 1952. These agreements remain in force. They will be formally reaffirmed with the new United States administration in the near future.

(HL Debs., vol. 503, Written Answers, col. 1651: 8 February 1989)

In moving the consideration in the HC Second Standing Committee on Statutory Instruments of the draft Visiting Forces and International Headquarters (Application of Law) (Amendment) Order 1989, the Minister of State for the Armed Forces, Mr A. Hamilton, said in part:

Members of the Committee will know that Spain joined the NATO Alliance following its 1986 referendum, a move welcomed on all sides. Members of our armed forces who visit Spain on duty are therefore now covered by the provisions of the NATO status of forces agreement of 1951 which allows them, for instance, to exercise their own military discipline. I understand that the Spanish have taken the necessary steps to implement in their own law their obligations under that agreement. The order before us today is part of the process that enables us to do the same in respect of Spanish forces who may come to the United Kingdom on duty and to put them on the same footing as all the other NATO countries, except Iceland which has no armed forces of its own.

The order adds Spain to the list of those countries to which the Visiting Forces and International Headquarters (Application of Law) Order 1965 applies. That order was made under section 8 of the Visiting Forces Act 1952, which provides for certain statutory powers, privileges and exemptions that apply in the case of home forces to be extended to visiting forces. The extension of this order to Spain will, for example, mean that if a Spanish service man needed to carry a firearm in the United Kingdom—perhaps for a joint exercise—he would from a legal point of view be regarded in the same way as a British or other NATO service man in respect of firearms legislation. Many of the other provisions of the 1965 order, such as those relating to planning, are less likely to have much direct relevance to Spain, which is likely to have only very small numbers of service men visiting the United Kingdom on exchange. None the less it is important that we treat forces from all NATO countries that may visit the United Kingdom in the same fashion from a legal point of view.

An order is also being made, with the intention that it should come into force at the same time, under section 1 of the Visiting Forces Act. This section 1 order, which does not require parliamentary approval, will add Spain to the list of countries to which the Visiting Forces Act as a whole applies. That will allow the Spanish service authorities, among other things, to exercise their own jurisdiction over their visiting forces here.

(HC Second Standing Committee on Statutory Instruments, etc., 12 July 1989, cols. 3–4)

Part Five: VIII. A. *Organs of State—immunity of organs of State— diplomatic and consular immunity*

The CSCE Information Forum (Immunities and Privileges) Order 1989 (1989 No. 480) was made on 15 March 1989 and came into force on 13 April 1989. It confers privileges and immunities upon the representatives of the sovereign Powers at the Conference on Security and Co-operation in Europe (CSCE), which was held in the United Kingdom from 18 April to 12 May 1989, and upon certain members of their official staffs.

Article 2 of the Order reads as follows:

2.—(1) For the purposes of this Order, there are hereby specified the representatives of the sovereign Powers at the CSCE Information Forum.

(2) Except in so far as in any particular case any privilege or immunity is waived by the Governments of the sovereign Powers whom they represent, the persons specified in the preceding paragraph shall enjoy:—

  (a) immunity from suit and legal process in respect of things done or omitted to be done by them in their capacity as representatives;

  (b) while exercising their functions and during their journeys to and from the place of meeting, the like inviolability of residence, the like immunity from personal arrest or detention and from seizure of their personal baggage, the like inviolability of all papers and documents, and the like exemption or relief from taxes (other than customs and excise duties or value added tax) as are accorded to the head of a diplomatic mission; and

(c) while exercising their functions and during their journeys to and from the place of meeting, the like exemptions and privileges in respect of their personal baggage as in accordance with Article 36 of the Vienna Convention on Diplomatic Relations, which is set out in Schedule 1 to the Diplomatic Privileges Act 1964(. . .), are accorded to a diplomatic agent.

(3) Section 6(3) of the Act and Part IV of Schedule 1 to the Act shall not operate so as to confer any privilege or immunity on the official staff of a representative other than delegates, deputy delegates, advisers, technical experts and secretaries of delegations.

(4) Neither this Article nor section 6(3) of the Act and Part IV of Schedule 1 to the Act shall operate so as to confer any privilege or immunity on any person as the representative of the United Kingdom or as a member of the official staff of such a representative or on any person who is a British citizen, a British Dependent Territories citizen, a British Overseas citizen or a British National (Overseas) or who is permanently resident in the United Kingdom.

In reply to the question whether foreigners holding diplomatic passports, but not accredited in the UK, are exempted from normal entry procedures when visiting this country, the Minister of State, Home Office, wrote:

Possession of a diplomatic passport does not, in itself, afford the holder any special status or entitlement.

Under the Immigration Act 1971, certain persons, including members of diplomatic missions in the United Kingdom who meet the requirements of section 8(3) of that Act as amended by the Immigration Act 1988, are entitled to exemption from immigration control. Members of the family forming part of the household of such members similarly benefit.

Certain members of diplomatic missions which are not based in the United Kingdom who are passing through this country while proceeding to take up or return to their posts, or who are returning to their own countries are, with their families, treated as being exempt from immigration control in order to meet the requirements of article 40 of the Vienna convention on diplomatic relations.

(HC Debs., vol. 150, Written Answers, col. *551*: 12 April 1989)

In reply to a question, the Parliamentary Under-Secretary of State, Foreign and Commonwealth Office, wrote:

Forty-four alleged serious offences by persons entitled to immunity were drawn to the attention of the Foreign and Commonwealth Office in 1988. 'Serious offences' are defined in accordance with the report to the Foreign Affairs Committee 'The abuse of diplomatic immunities and privileges (1985)' as offences falling into a category which could in certain circumstances attract a penalty of six months or more; we are advised that very few of the alleged offences would have been likely to attract a custodial sentence. The majority involved drinking and driving and shoplifting.

Fourteen diplomats were withdrawn from their posts in Britain in 1988 following alleged offences.

(HC Debs., vol. 151, Written Answers, col. *101*: 18 April 1989)

In reply to an oral question, the Attorney-General, Sir Patrick Mayhew, stated:

Individuals enjoying diplomatic immunity may not by law be prosecuted unless there is a waiver of that immunity on behalf of the diplomat's own state. Whether it is appropriate to seek such a waiver is a matter for my right hon. and learned Friend the Foreign Secretary.

The question whether a diplomat should be prosecuted will, subject to waiver, be determined by reference to the code of Crown prosecutors.

(HC Debs., vol. 154, col. *552*: 12 June 1989)

According to an item in the *Daily Telegraph*, 28 July 1989, the UK vice-consul in Auckland, New Zealand, had avoided a breath-test by pleading diplomatic immunity when stopped for speeding. A spokesman of the Foreign and Commonwealth Office is reported to have said that the vice-consul was entitled only to consular immunity, which applied only so long as he was carrying out his consular duties. The spokesman added that the vice-consul would pay a fine for the speeding offence.

In the course of a discussion on 26 October 1989 in the Sixth Committee of the UN General Assembly on the subject of the International Law Commission's draft articles on the status of the diplomatic courier and the diplomatic bag not accompanied by diplomatic courier, the UK representative, Mr A. Aust, remarked:

Paragraph (10) of the Commentary on paragraph 4 of [draft] Article 22—which deals with waiver of immunity—explains that the provision has been extended. It now provides that the 'double waiver' requirement would also apply in criminal proceedings. In other words, a State, having waived immunity for criminal proceedings to be instituted, would have to make a further waiver before a sentence could be imposed and carried out. This is contrary to the position under the Vienna Conventions on Diplomatic Relations and on Consular Relations. In the view of my delegation, a 'double waiver' is both unreasonable and impracticable given the nature of criminal proceedings.

. . . [draft] Article 28, which deals with the protection of the diplomatic bag, is probably the most important provision. We are frankly very disappointed at the outcome. Paragraph 1 now provides specifically that a diplomatic bag shall be exempt from examination through electronic or other technical devices. This is a significant departure from existing law. It will do nothing to help curtail abuse of the bag. Instead it could make the problem worse.

I would also mention my delegation's misgivings about paragraph (8) of the Commentary on [draft] Article 24, which deals with identification of the diplomatic bag. The Commentary says that the question of the size and weight of the bag should be determined by agreement between the sending and receiving States. My Government has never accepted—or imposed—a limitation on the size or weight of the diplomatic bag.

(Text provided by the Foreign and Commonwealth Office; see also AC.6/44/SR. 25, p. 8)

In the course of a debate on 21 November 1989 in the Sixth Committee of the UN General Assembly on the subject of relations with the Host

State, the representative of France, on behalf of the Twelve Member States of the EC, stated:

En ce qui concerne plus particulièrement les questions de transport et d'application du code de la route, les douze Etats membres de la Communauté Européenne souhaitent rappeler à nouveau l'importance qu'ils attachent à l'application de l'Article IV de l'accord de siège de 1947 et de l'Article 31 de la Convention de Vienne de 1961 suivant lesquels les agents diplomatiques bénéficient de l'immunité de juridiction pénale, civile et administrative vis-à-vis de l'Etat accréditaire. Ils attendent du pays hôte qu'il prenne les mesures appropriées pour s'acquitter complètement des obligations auxquelles il est, à cet égard, tenu.

(Text provided by the Foreign and Commonwealth Office; for the translation into English see A/C.6/44/SR. 44, p. 3)

In reply to a question, the Parliamentary Under-Secreatary of State, Foreign and Commonwealth Office, wrote that there were no plans for the 'non-intrusive searching of diplomatic bags entering and leaving the United Kingdom'.

(HC Debs., vol. 164, Written Answers, col. *390*: 21 December 1989)

Part Five: VIII. B. *Organs of the State—immunity of organs of the State— immunity other than diplomatic and consular*

In the course of a debate on the subject of immunity from taxation in a House of Commons Standing Committee discussing the Finance (No. 2) Bill, the Paymaster General, Mr Peter Brooke, stated:

When the hon. Gentleman spoke on the general subject of sovereign immunity, he asked about the criteria, the dividing line and who monitored it. The provisions for sovereign immunity are operated by the Board of Inland Revenue, based on legal advice on the application of international law. Ministers are not involved in decisions on individual cases.

The hon. Gentleman drew attention to the fact that sovereign immunity is a concept of very long standing. It has its origins in the general principle of international law that sovereigns and the public property belonging to them are treated as being not subject to the municipal laws of foreign states. In accordance with that principle, the income, profits and gains of sovereigns, foreign states and integral parts of foreign Governments arising in the United Kingdom are immune from United Kingdom tax. Again, I think that I have common cause with the hon. Gentleman.

The hon. Member for Dunfermline, East asked about the Government's basic attitude to sovereign immunity. As I have said, we benefit from sovereign immunity under other countries' tax regimes, including the management of the foreign currency holdings that make up our own Reserves. Foreign investment in the United Kingdom and through United Kingdom financial institutions is certainly of benefit to us. If the sovereign bodies operate in the United Kingdom via companies resident here, those companies will of course be taxed in the normal way. Sovereign immunity applies only to the dividends and interest remitted abroad.

(HC Standing Committee A, Finance Bill (No. 2), cols. 577–8, *passim*: 21 June

1988; see also *R* v. *Inland Revenue Commissioners, ex parte Camacq Corporation and another*, [1990] 1 All ER 173, 181)

In reply to a question, the Financial Secretary to the Treasury wrote in part:

In the year to 31 March 1988, tax of approximately £119 million was refunded to sovereign immune bodies . . .

(HC Debs., vol. 136, Written Answers, col. *525*: 5 July 1988)

During a discussion in the Sixth Committee of the UN General Assembly on the subject of the International Law Commission's report and draft articles on jurisdictional immunities of States and their property, the UK representative, Sir Arthur Watts, stated on 7 November 1989:

On the subject of *Jurisdictional Immunities of States and their Property*, my delegation notes that there are apparently still sharply divided views on the underlying doctrinal basis for this subject, as is indicated in paragraphs 409 to 411 of the Commission's Report. In my Government's view the contemporary position is clear: international law has developed in such a way that the old rule of absolute immunity is now obsolete. It is in our view now well-settled that those who find themselves involved in a dispute with a foreign State, acting in a non-sovereign capacity, should be able to have that dispute determined by the ordinary process of law.

A particularly important provision is *paragraph 3 of Article 2*, concerning the test to be applied to determine whether an activity is commercial (at paragraph 423 of the Commission's Report). The Special Rapporteur has struggled hard— and we very much appreciate his efforts—in an attempt to meet the concerns of those who wish to refer to the 'purpose' of a transaction in determining whether immunity may be claimed, and those on the other hand who believe that subjective factors such as 'purpose' should not be introduced. The United Kingdom falls very much into the latter group. We shall clearly need to look very carefully at the text which the Commission eventually produces on this important point.

(Text provided by the Foreign and Commonwealth Office; see also A/C.6/44/SR. 35, pp. 19–20)

Part Five: IX. *Organs of the State—protecting powers*

At a press conference held by the Foreign and Commonwealth Office on 13 March 1989, the spokesman stated that Her Majesty's Government had agreed to the appointment of Pakistan as the protecting power for Iranian interests in the UK under Article 45 of the Vienna Convention on Diplomatic Relations.

(Text provided by the Foreign and Commonwealth Office)

On 27 July 1989, the United Kingdom concluded with Sweden an Agreement concerning the Assumption of Responsibility for the Protection of the Diplomatic and Consular Interests of the United Kingdom in the Islamic Republic of Iran. A background note, issued by the Foreign and Commonwealth Office, read in part as follows:

This Agreement is at Swedish initiative. Sweden looks after the interests of some 10 countries and the Swedish Parliament last year passed legislation requiring the Government to conclude bilateral agreements with the countries whose relations it is protecting. This agreement is the first of its kind and will serve as a model for Sweden's negotiations with other commissioning countries. It covers administrative, humanitarian and consular interests, but not commercial relations. It formalises our existing arrangements with Sweden.

British interests were protected in Iran by Sweden from 1980–1988, when the British Embassy was re-opened. After the closure of the Embassy this year, Sweden again resumed responsibility for our interests.

(Foreign and Commonwealth Office Press Release 1989/No. 109)

Part Six: I. A. *Treaties—conclusion and entry into force—conclusion, signature, ratification and accession*

(See also Part One: II.D.1., above)

The following extract is taken from the Foreign and Commonwealth Office Treaty Section's *Instruction Manual*, prepared in May 1988 for internal use.

23. *Ratification and Entry into Force*
Some agreements enter into force on signature but the majority require ratification or some other procedure to bring them into force.

24. *Bilaterals*. If subject to ratification the treaty provides for the exchange of instruments of ratification, usually in the opposite capital from that in which signature took place. The treaty may enter into force on the day the exchange takes place or a specified number of days or months afterwards, according to the constitutional or legislative requirements of the parties.

25. Many bilateral agreements enter into force on the exchange of notifications that their constitutional requirements or legislative procedures have been completed eg some Investment Protection Agreements and some Double Taxation Conventions—two examples of each are the Investment Protection Agreements with Egypt (TS 97/1976, Cmnd 6638) and Indonesia (TS 62/1977, Cmnd 6285) and the Double Taxation Conventions with The Gambia (TS 51/1982, Cmnd 8717) and India (TS 2/1982, Cmnd 8442). It should be noted in connection with Double Taxation conventions that the entry into force of the Convention is not the same as its 'having effect'. The former is its status under international law, the latter its operation internally within the two states affected.

26. *Multilaterals* are usually but not always signed subject to ratification: They may enter into force in any of the following ways:
    (a) on the deposit of all instruments of ratification;
    (b) on the deposit of a given number of ratifications;
    (c) at the end of a given period following the deposit of a given number of ratifications;
    (d) at the end of a given period following the deposit of a specified number of ratifications provided that certain States are included among those which have ratified;

(e) on a specified date following the deposit of ratifications or accessions by States holding a given percentage of conference votes;

(f) on a specified date, regardless of the number of ratifications or accessions that may have been deposited by that date.

27. A treaty may come into force on ratification subject to certain given circumstances. For instance, its entry into force may be conditional upon the entry into force of another treaty; or subject to certain events due to occur at a future date, as in the case of the 1954 Convention on the Presence of Foreign Forces in the Federal Republic of Germany which entered into force only after the admission of the Federal Republic of Germany to the North Atlantic Treaty (see TS 77/1955, Cmd 9617).

28. To meet a situation in which certain States may not be in a position to ratify or accede to a treaty before the date of its initial entry into force, the formal articles usually provide for a treaty to enter into force for each State subsequently ratifying on the date of deposit of its instrument of ratification or of accession, or after a fixed period following such deposit.

29. Although a treaty may be subject to ratification so that it does not enter into force definitively until such time as ratifications have been exchanged or a specified number deposited, the signatory Governments may desire to bring it into practical operation immediately on signature or provisionally on receipt by the depositary of a sufficient number of undertakings to ratify. Commodity agreements often provide for provisional entry into force in this way eg International Coffee Agreement 1983 (TS 27/1986, Cmnd 9775), International Agreement on Olive Oil and Table Olives, 1986 (Miscellaneous No. 10/1987, Cm 203).

30. If a treaty provides for ratification but makes no express provision for entry into force, it will be deemed to come into force on the date of the exchange of ratifications, or on the deposit of the last of the ratifications required.

31. Entry into force can never be retroactive either generally or for any particular State in the absence of express provision to that effect.

The following extract (with some cross-references deleted) is taken from later in the *Manual*:

Definition. The Vienna Convention on the Law of Treaties, Article 2 1(b) defines 'ratification', 'acceptance', 'approval' and 'accession' as 'the international act so named whereby a State establishes on the international plane its consent to be bound by a treaty'. Ratification, acceptance and approval are confirmation of signature whereas 'accession' is a method whereby a state may become a party to a treaty which has closed for signature.

Preliminaries to Ratification

1. *United Kingdom Constitutional Position: Parliamentary and Legislative Requirements*

(1) Ratification is a prerogative of the Crown exercised on the advice of the Secretary of State for Foreign and Commonwealth Affairs after consulting, where necessary, the Departments of Her Majesty's Government concerned with the implementation of the treaty.

(2) Formal Parliamentary approval of treaties is not normally required except in the case of treaties of alliance or those entailing the cession of territory or the voting of money from public funds, when ratification is subject to the approval of Parliament (usually in the form of a Bill). Treaty provisions, however, are not self-executory in the law of any part of the United Kingdom, and it is accordingly the practice of Her Majesty's Government to ensure, before ratifying a treaty, that they have the necessary statutory power to enable them to give effect to its provisions, or if the existing law is inadequate, that the necessary enabling legislation is passed. The ratification of the treaty is, in such circumstances, deferred until the enabling legislation has been enacted.

(3) In accordance with an undertaking given to Parliament in 1924, the text of every treaty concluded in respect of the United Kingdom which is subject to ratification is laid before Parliament for a period of 21 Parliamentary working days before it is ratified. This is known as the *Ponsonby Rule*, which is not a legal or constitutional requirement. Ample opportunity is thus given for debating the provisions of a treaty, if Parliament so desires. Since most treaties of importance are made subject to ratification, Parliament is, in effect, able to exercise substantial control in these matters. The Government of the day bear the added responsibility of affording opportunity for debate, where it sees fit, in respect of those treaties which are not subject to ratification.

(4) The Rule applies not only to treaties which are subject to ratification but also to all treaties to which the United Kingdom becomes a party by accession or acceptance. It can also apply to some amendments even when those amendments are not in the form of a treaty instrument, if they require the making of a statutory instrument.

. . .

(5) Texts of treaties are presented to Parliament to fulfil requirements of the Ponsonby Rule by means of *Command Papers*.

(Text provided by the Foreign and Commonwealth Office)

Part Six: I. B. *Treaties—conclusion and entry into force—reservations and declarations to multilateral treaties*

(See Part Eight: II. A. (items of 27 August 1987 and 13 January 1988), below)

On 9 February 1987, the Democratic Republic of Yemen acceded to the Convention on the Prevention and Punishment of the Crime of Genocide, 1948, with the following reservation:

In acceding to this Convention, the People's Democratic Republic of Yemen does not consider itself bound by Article IX of the Convention, which provides that disputes between the Contracting Parties relating to the interpretation, application or fulfilment of the Convention shall be submitted to the International Court of Justice at the request of any of the parties to the dispute. It declares that the competence of the International Court of Justice with respect to disputes concerning the interpretation, application or fulfilment of the Convention shall in each case be subject to the express consent of all parties to the dispute.

(TS No. 47 (1987); Cm. 217, p. 9)

On 30 December 1987, the UK Government deposited with the UN Secretary-General the following objection to the above reservation:

The Government of the United Kingdom of Great Britain and Northern Ireland have consistently stated that they are unable to accept reservations in respect of Article IX of the said Convention; in their view this is not the kind of reservation which intending parties to the Convention have the right to make.

Accordingly the Government of the United Kingdom of Great Britain and Northern Ireland do not accept the reservation entered by the People's Democratic Republic of Yemen against Article IX of the Convention.

(TS No. 78 (1988); Cm. 562, p. 6)

On 19 November 1987, the UK acceded to the International Convention for the Unification of certain Rules concerning the Immunity of State-owned Ships with Supplementary Protocol, 1926, on behalf of Guernsey, Jersey and the Isle of Man. The instrument of accession contained the following reservation:

We reserve the right to apply Article 1 of the Convention to any claim in respect of a ship which falls within the Admiralty jurisdiction of Our courts, or of Our courts in any territory in respect of which We are party to the Convention.

We reserve the right, with respect to Article 2 of the Convention, to apply in proceedings concerning another High Contracting Party or ship of another High Contracting Party the rules of procedure set out in Chapter II of the European Convention on State Immunity, signed at Basle on the Sixteenth day of May, in the Year of Our Lord One thousand Nine hundred and Seventy-two.

In order to give effect to the terms of any international agreement with a non-Contracting State, We reserve the right to make special provision

    (a) as regards the delay or arrest of a ship or cargo belonging to such a State, and

    (b) to prohibit seizure of or execution against such a ship or cargo.

(TS No. 78 (1988); Cm. 562, p. 20)

The following letter, dated 28 January 1988, was sent to the Secretary-General of the Council of Europe by the UK Permanent Representative:

I have the honour to refer to my letter of 26 March 1987 in which I gave notice of the withdrawal of the reservations made at the time of the ratification of the Convention on the Conservation of European Wildlife and Natural Habitats in respect of Northern Ireland (*see* Treaty Series No. 47 (1987), Cm 217, p. 4).

In giving notice of the withdrawal I took the opportunity to revise the reservations in respect of Great Britain. Unfortunately, in the course of this revision a reservation in respect of the use against seals of semi-automatic weapons with a magazine capable of holding more than two rounds of ammunition was inadvertently added to the amended list of Reservations to Article 22 of the Convention.

The addition is contrary to the provisions of Article 22 and I hereby formally withdraw it. I have pleasure in enclosing a further revised version of the list of reservations for Great Britain.

(TS No. 78 (1988); Cm. 562, p. 3: see also UKMIL 1987, pp. 577–8)

On 25 February 1988, the UK Government registered the following declaration with the Secretariat General of the Council of Europe in respect of the First Protocol to the Convention for the Protection of Human Rights and Fundamental Freedoms, 1950:

In accordance with Article 4 of the said Protocol I hereby declare, on behalf of the Government of the United Kingdom, that the Protocol shall apply to:

The Bailiwick of Guernsey
The Bailiwick of Jersey
Anguilla
British Virgin Islands
Cayman Islands
Gibraltar
Montserrat
St. Helena
St Helena Dependencies
Turks and Caicos Islands,

being territories for whose international relations the Government of the United Kingdom are responsible, subject to the following reservations:

1. In view of certain provisions of the Education (Guernsey) Laws and of the Education Ordinance of Gibraltar, the principle affirmed in the second sentence of Article 2 is accepted by the United Kingdom only so far as it is compatible with the provision of efficient instruction and training, and the avoidance of unreasonable public expenditure in Guernsey and Gibraltar.

2. The principle affirmed in the second sentence of Article 2 is accepted by the United Kingdom only insofar as it does not affect the application of the following legal provisions:

   (i) the common law of Anguilla which permits the imposition by teachers of moderate and reasonable corporal punishment;

  (ii) section 26 of the Education Act 1977 of the British Virgin Islands (which permits the administration of corporal punishment to a pupil only where no other punishment is considered suitable or effective and only by the principal or any teacher appointed by the principal for that purpose);

 (iii) section 30 of the Education Law 1983 of the Cayman Islands (which permits the administration of corporal punishment to a pupil only where no other punishment is considered suitable or effective and only by the principal or any teacher appointed in writing by him for that purpose);

 (iv) the common law of Montserrat which permits the imposition by teachers of moderate and reasonable corporal punishment;

  (v) the law of St. Helena, which permits the administration by teachers of reasonable corporal punishment; and section 6 of the Children and Young Persons Ordinance 1965 of St. Helena (which states that the right of a teacher to administer such punishment is not affected by the provisions of that section which relate to the offence of cruelty to children);

 (vi) the law of St. Helena Dependencies, which permits the administration by teachers of reasonable corporal punishment; and section 6 of the Children and Young Persons Ordinance 1965 of St. Helena (which states that the right of a teacher to administer such punishment is not affected by the provisions of that section which relate to the offence of cruelty to children);

(vii) the common law of the Turks and Caicos Islands which permits the administration by teachers of reasonable corporal punishment; and section 5 of the Juveniles Ordinance (Chapter 28) of the Turks and Caicos Islands (which states that the right of a teacher to administer such punishment is not affected by the provisions of that section which relate to the offence of cruelty to juveniles).

(TS No. 78 (1988); Cm. 562, pp. 7–8)

Part Six: I. D. *Treaties—conclusion and entry into force—'without prejudice' provisions*

In the Exchange of Notes between the Governments of the UK and South Africa on 22 September 1989 concerning the regulation of the terms of settlement of the salvaging of the wreck of HMS *Birkenhead* (see Part Nine: XV. A. 3., below), the following provision is included:

This settlement is without prejudice to the respective legal positions of our two Governments.

(TS No. 3 (1990); Cm. 906)

Part Six: II. A. *Treaties—observance, application and interpretation—observance*

(See also Part Two: I. (items on Hong Kong) and Part Four: VII. (item of 20 July 1989), above)

In the course of a debate on the subject of African elephants, the Parliamentary Under-Secretary of State for the Environment, Mrs Virginia Bottomley, stated:

Hong Kong has strictly adhered to all of the conservation and enforcement measures called for by CITES and recently has strengthened its controls on the import of worked ivory. The only ivory which may legally be imported into Hong Kong at present is that which comes from a CITES-approved source and is subject to the issue of a licence.

(HC Debs., vol. 153, col. 1298: 26 May 1989)

In reply to a question, the Economic Secretary to the Treasury wrote in part:

Trade is not normally allowed in Indian elephant ivory under the convention on international trade in endangered species of fauna and flora (CITES). Similar strict controls will now apply to African elephant ivory following agreement this week at the CITES conference.

In the United Kingdom, strict controls were introduced on imports of ivory from 9 June 1989. From 17 August 1989, these controls have been applied in the European Community under Commission Regulation 2496/89.

(HC Debs., vol. 158, Written Answers, col. 286: 23 October 1989)

In reply to a question, the Minister of State for Health wrote:

Infractions of the CITES controls would be matters for the CITES Secretariat. The United Kingdom strictly implements the provisions of the convention on international trade in endangered species of wild fauna and flora (CITES) under which commercial trade in hawksbill and green turtles is already prohibited. We have not raised the matter with the Japanese Government.

(HC Debs., vol. 158, Written Answers, col. *302*: 23 October 1989)

In the course of a debate on 18 October 1989 in the Sixth Commission of the UN General Assembly on the subject of methods of preventing international terrorism, the representative of France, on behalf of the Twelve Member States of the EC, referred to treaties against terrorism and continued:

Il va de soi que l'adhésion à ces conventions ou leur ratification supposent en parallèle la volonté de les appliquer de bonne foi et ne saurait atteindre son plein effet que dans le respect du principe de droit international *pacta sunt servanda*.

(Text provided by the Foreign and Commonwealth Office; for the translation in English see A/C.6/44/SR. 21, p. 16)

Part Six: II. B. *Treaties—observance, application and interpretation— application*

On 22 March 1989, the Governments of the UK and Ghana signed an Agreement for the Promotion and Protection of Investments. Article 1 of the Agreement reads in part:

(e) 'territory' means:
    (i) in respect of Ghana: the present territory of the Republic of Ghana including the territorial sea and any maritime area situated beyond the territorial sea of Ghana which has been or might in the future be designated under the national law of Ghana in accordance with international law as an area within which Ghana may exercise rights with regard to the sea-bed and subsoil and the natural resources;
    (ii) in respect of the United Kingdom: Great Britain and Northern Ireland, including the territorial sea and any maritime area situated beyond the territorial sea of the United Kingdom which has been or might in the future be designated under the national law of the United Kingdom in accordance with international law as an area within which the United Kingdom may exercise rights with regard to the sea-bed and subsoil and the natural resources . . .

(Cm. 811; see also Cm. 909 (Agreement for the Promotion and Protection of Investments signed on 27 October 1989 between the Governments of the UK and Guyana))

Part Six: II. C. *Treaties—observance, application and interpretation— interpretation*

In reply to the question whether 'the development of lasers, particle beams, pellets and electromagnetic weapons in orbit would be compatible with the terms of the Outer Space Treaty', the Minister of State for Defence Procurement wrote:

Under Article IV of the Outer Space Treaty, states parties to the treaty undertake not to place in orbit around the earth any object carrying nuclear weapons or any other kinds of weapon of mass destruction. Whether placing in orbit the objects or systems to which the noble Lord refers would be compatible with the terms of the treaty depends upon whether they would fall into either of these prescribed categories.

(HL Debs., vol. 504, col. 1133: 1 March 1989)

In reply to a further question on the same matter, the Government Minister in the House of Lords wrote:

If any of the objects referred to in the noble Lord's recent Question were deployed in space, it would be for the parties to the Outer Space Treaty to decide whether or not they fell into the categories described in the Answer to that Question. Any dispute about interpretation of the treaty would be subject to the usual methods of peaceful settlement of disputes.

(HL Debs., vol. 505, col. 224: 15 March 1989)

Part Six: II. D. *Treaties—observance, application and interpretation— treaties and third States*

In reply to the question

Whether in Her Majesty's Government's view the adoption by the US of a 'broad' interpretation of the Anti-Ballistic Missile Treaty, is in the British interest; and, if not, what steps they are taking to inform the US Government of their views,

the Parliamentary Under-Secretary of State, Department of Energy, wrote:

The US Administration has declared that all its SDI-related activities are being conducted within the 'narrow' interpretation of the treaty. The British interest is best served if the parties to the treaty observe their obligations under it. Interpretation of what those obligations are is a matter for the parties: and, as a non-party, we have no locus to interpret it.

(HL Debs., vol. 508, col. 496: 24 May 1989)

Part Six: IV. C. *Treaties—invalidity, termination and suspension of operation—termination, suspension of operation, denunciation and withdrawal*

In a letter dated 26 June 1987 to the Secretary-General of the Council of Europe, the UK denounced its acceptance of Article 8(4)(a) of the European Social Charter, to be effective from 26 February 1988.

(TS No. 61 (1988); Cm. 286, p. 10)

The following extract is taken from the Foreign and Commonwealth Office Treaty Section's *Instruction Manual*, prepared in May 1988 for internal use.

Duration, Denunciation, Withdrawal, Termination, Amendment

32. It is common practice for all treaties to contain termination or denunciation provisions of some kind, unless they fall into a category of 'law-making' treaties in which fundamental principles of future conduct are permanently laid down, or by which a new international organisation of a permanent nature is established, eg the United Nations Charter and the Statute of the International Court of Justice (TS 67/1946 Cmd 7015). There is a whole Section in the 1969 Vienna Convention on the Law of Treaties (Section 3—Articles 54–64) on Termination and Suspension of the Operation of Treaties (TS 58/1980, Cmnd 7964). A similar series of articles is included in the 1986 Convention on the Law of Treaties between States and International Organisations or between International Organisations (Miscellaneous No. 11/1987, Cm 244). . . . Such provisions range from a simple provision whereby each party of a bilateral treaty may terminate its participation in the treaty by simple notification in writing to the other party, to more elaborate provisions laying down special conditions governing the termination of multilateral treaties and the circumstances in which they may cease to have effect.

(Text provided by the Foreign and Commonwealth Office)

The following press notice, No. 432, was issued by the Department of Transport on 16 October 1989:

The UK's resignation as Managing Government of and as a party to the Red Sea Lights Agreement [597 UNTS 159] was announced today by Cecil Parkinson, Secretary of State for Transport. The Agreement covers the operation of two navigation lights in the Southern Red Sea, managed by the UK on behalf of the 15 contracting Governments.

Following a recent review, most signatory Governments to the Agreement concluded that the lights are no longer needed for their international shipping. The British Government shares this view and accordingly has resigned its position as Managing Government to take effect from 31 March 1990. Its withdrawal from the Agreement as a participating Government will take effect from 31 March 1991. If no successor managing Government is appointed by the contracting Governments, the Agreement will lapse before that date.

The position locally has now changed unexpectedly in that the lights administered by the Red Sea Lights Company, which acts as the UK's managing agent, are no longer operating. Other lights are now operating at the same locations, and these are understood to have been put up by the Yemen Arab Republic. Accordingly, the UK has advised other signatory Governments and the marine community that the lights now operating are not the responsibility of the UK and other signatory Governments to the Red Sea Lights Agreement. An appropriate Notice to Mariners has been issued.

Part Six: V. *Treaties—depositaries, notification, correction and registration*

(See also Part One: II. D. 1. (item of 12 December 1989), Part Two: I. (item of 18 October 1989), Part Three: I. C.4. (item of 22 March 1989, paragraph 11), above and Part Six: II. A. (item of 27 September 1989), below)

The following extract is taken from the Foreign and Commonwealth

Office Treaty Section's *Instruction Manual*, prepared in May 1988 for internal use.

REGISTRATION OF TREATIES WITH THE UNITED NATIONS

1. The international practice of registering and publishing the texts of treaties originated with the League of Nations, which laid the obligation on its Member States with the intention of discouraging the conclusion of secret agreements. The League of Nations Treaty Series volumes are now in the possession of the United Nations which endorsed the principle of registration in Article 102 of the Charter (see TS No. 67/1946 Cmd 7015) which reads as follows:

'Every treaty and every international agreement entered into by any Member of the United Nations after the present Charter comes into force shall as soon as possible be registered with the Secretariat and published by it.'

Article 102(2) of the Charter states that 'no party to any such treaty or international agreement which has not been registered in accordance with the provisions of paragraph (1) of this Article may invoke that treaty or agreement before any organ of the United Nations.' This means that a treaty or international agreement which has not been registered cannot be invoked before the International Court of Justice.

2. Considering it advisable to establish rules for the application of Article 102 of the Charter, the General Assembly adopted the Regulations which govern the registration of treaties . . .

3. *Filing and Recording.* In addition to accepting for registration all treaties submitted to it by Members of the United Nations, the Secretariat, in accordance with Articles 10 and 11, of the Regulations, *'files and records'* the following:

(a) treaties or international agreements entered into by the United Nations itself or by one or more of its Specialised Agencies;

(b) treaties or international agreements transmitted by a Member of the United Nations which were entered into before the coming into force of the Charter, but which were not included in the Treaty Series of the League of Nations; and

(c) treaties or international agreements transmitted by a party not a Member of the United Nations entered into before or after the coming into force of the Charter which were not included in the Treaty Series of the League of Nations.

4. It should be noted that Members of the United Nations are not only obliged to register all treaties which they conclude, but that Article 2 of the Regulations obliges them to register 'any *subsequent action* which effects a change in the parties' to a treaty which has been registered, 'or in the terms, scope or application thereof.'

5. In principle each Member of the United Nations is under an equal obligation to see that its treaties are registered, but, in order to avoid swamping the Secretariat with certified copies of the same treaty, it has become the practice in the case of multilateral treaties to provide in the treaty for one of the parties, usually the depositary authority, to effect registration, thus relieving the other parties of the responsibility. Similarly, the Secretary-General of the United Nations and the administrative heads of the Specialised Agencies will register *ex-officio* any treaty to which their Organisation may become a party.

6. In the case of bilaterals the parties sometimes agree in advance which of them will register but usually the United Kingdom proceeds with registration as soon as

convenient. If the other party has already registered the UN Secretariat informs us in due course. In special cases joint registration is possible.

7. The meaning of 'a treaty' or 'international agreement' for the purposes of Article 102 of the Charter has never been defined by the United Nations Secretariat. The decision as to which of the international agreements they have concluded fall into the registrable category is left to the Member States of the United Nations, the Secretariat accepting every instrument submitted to them for registration unless they have serious reason to doubt its status as an instrument registrable under Article 102.

8. In order to reach a decision on whether an international agreement constitutes a registrable instrument, there are four distinct but related issues to be considered:—

(a) Is the agreement in question one which, in form and in substance, fulfils the essential requirements of an 'international agreement' within the meaning of Article 102 of the Charter?

(b) Assuming that the answer to (a) is in the affirmative, did the parties to the agreement have the capacity to conclude such an agreement?

(c) Is the agreement in question one which fulfils the formal requirements of an international agreement, as distinct from a unilateral statement of policy or intentions or a memorandum of understanding not intended to bind governments?

(d) Is the particular agreement in question one which in substance fulfils the requirements of an international agreement, ie is it an agreement which involves continuing obligations in the sphere of international law rather than in the sphere of municipal law?

An Agreement which fulfils the formal requirements of an international agreement may still be non-registrable if it does not fulfil the substantive requirements of an international agreement. Similarly, an agreement which fulfils the substantive requirements of an international agreement may be non-registrable if it has been drafted in a form which does not fulfil the formal requirements of an international agreement.

9. It is sometimes thought that the form of an agreement in some way affects the obligation to register under Article 102 of the Charter. This is not the case. Provided the arrangement is in some written form and embodies in fact a binding engagement to do or to refrain from doing something definite, and operates within the sphere of international law, it does not matter what the document is called or how it is concluded. It is just as necessary to register letters exchanged informally between the representatives of governments, if they embody obligations intended to be binding, as it is to register a formal treaty between Heads of States.

10. An international agreement in the registrable category is only required to be registered when it has entered into force.

Non-registrable documents with an agreement

11. Under the Charter, therefore, anything which creates a future international obligation must be registered, and consequently it is impossible to have a confidential agreement creating a future international obligation. It is sometimes possible, on the other hand, to draw up in connexion with a published agreement a confidential letter, or agreed minute, which explains in greater detail the effect of the published document. Similarly, it is possible to exchange confidential letters

embodying understandings which are not intended to constitute international obligations to do or not to do some particular thing, but are rather declarations of policy or of attitude.

12. Documents recording the following types of transactions would *not* constitute registrable instruments:—

(a) A final settlement of a claim where one Government pays another in full, leaving no continuing obligation.

(b) Commercial transactions of the type that private persons or companies could make and which are governed by some municipal law or by private international law rather than public international law, eg an Export Credits Guarantee Department contract or an agreement under which the Crown leased a piece of land to a foreign Government.

(c) An interpretative commentary relating, for example, to what a party understands by a particular provision or what it can do or intends to do in fulfilment of the provision. Provided such commentaries do not alter the agreed obligation or affect the substance of the actual agreement, they would not require to be registered.

13. While it is comparatively easy to decide that an instrument is in the registrable category it is usually much more difficult to conclude that it is in the non-registrable category and careful drafting is required to ensure that an 'agreement' which is to remain confidential is not so worded as to attract the obligation to register it. In all cases of doubt about the status of an agreement, the legal adviser should be consulted.

14. There are sometimes differences of opinion or interpretation between two parties as to what is registrable and what is not. For example, the USA and the USSR regard Agreed Minutes as registrable whereas the United Kingdom does not.

(Text provided by the Foreign and Commonwealth Office (some cross-references deleted))

Part Six: VI. *Treaties—breach*

In reply to the question 'whether the International Labour Organisation . . . has held Her Majesty's Government to be in breach of normal [sic] conventions on eight counts', the Government spokesman in the House of Lords, the Earl of Dundee, wrote:

. . . the United Kingdom reports at specified intervals on the conventions of the International Labour Organisation which it has ratified. Following these reports and other documentation such as criticisms from trade unions, the Committee of Experts has questioned aspects of the United Kingdom's application of various conventions. The United Kingdom Government will be responding to these points.

. . .

The one matter that the ILO committee fully recognises is that these are complex legal issues. The Government of the United Kingdom are fully confident that we have in no way breached Convention No. 87, or indeed Convention No. 93, which is the other convention referred to.

(HL Debs., vol. 508, col. 717: 6 June 1989)

Part Seven: II. B. *Personal jurisdiction—exercise—military jurisdiction*
(See Part Five: VII. (item of 12 July 1989), above)

Part Eight: II. A. *State territory and territorial jurisdiction—territorial jurisdiction—territorial sovereignty*
(See also Part Two: X., above)

The Argentine Republic made the following declaration, dated 8 May 1987, on its accession to the Convention abolishing the Requirement of Legalisation for Foreign Public Documents, 1961:

The Argentine Republic rejects the extension of the application of the Convention abolishing the requirement of legalisation of foreign public documents, adopted at The Hague on 5 October 1961, to the Falkland Islands, South Georgia and South Sandwich Islands which was notified to the Ministry of Foreign Affairs of the Kingdom of the Netherlands by the United Kingdom of Great Britain and Northern Ireland on 24 February 1965, and reaffirms its sovereign rights over the Falkland Islands, South Georgia and South Sandwich Islands, which form an integral part of its national territory.

The United Nations General Assembly has adopted Resolutions 2065 (XX), 3160 (XXVIII), 31/49, 37/9, 38/12, 39/6, 40/21 and 41/40 which recognise the existence of a sovereignty dispute over the Falkland Islands and urges the Argentine Republic and the United Kingdom of Great Britain and Northern Ireland to maintain negotiations in order to obtain a peaceful and lasting settlement of the dispute as soon as possible, using the good offices of the Secretary-General of the United Nations who is to report to the General Assembly on the progress achieved.

The Argentine Republic likewise rejects the extension of the Convention to the so-called 'British Antarctic Territory', which took place on the same date, and reaffirms the rights of the Republic to the Argentine Antarctic Sector, including those rights relating to its sovereignty or corresponding maritime jurisdiction. Furthermore, it recalls the safeguards regarding claims to territorial sovereignty contained in Article IV of the Antarctic Treaty signed in Washington on 1 December 1959 to which the Argentine Republic and the United Kingdom of Great Britain and Northern Ireland are Parties.

(TS No. 47 (1987); Cm. 217, pp. 20–1)

By a communication to the Netherlands Government as depositary, dated 27 August 1987, the UK Government wrote in response:

The Government of the United Kingdom of Great Britain and Northern Ireland cannot accept the declaration made by the Argentine Republic as regards the Falkland Islands and South Georgia and the South Sandwich Islands. The Government of the United Kingdom of Great Britain and Northern Ireland have no doubt as to United Kingdom sovereignty over the Falkland Islands and South Georgia and the South Sandwich Islands and, accordingly, their right to extend the application of the Convention to the Falkland Islands and South Georgia and the South Sandwich Islands.

The Government of the United Kingdom of Great Britain and Northern Ireland also cannot accept the declaration made by the Argentine Republic as regards the

British Antarctic Territory. The Government of the United Kingdom of Great Britain and Northern Ireland have no doubt as to the sovereignty of the United Kingdom over the British Antarctic Territory and, accordingly, their right to extend the application of the Convention to the British Antarctic Territory. The Government of the United Kingdom draw attention to Article IV of the Antarctic Treaty, to which the Governments of the United Kingdom and Argentina are parties. Article IV freezes claims to Antarctic territory South of 60 degrees South latitude.

(TS No. 79 (1988); Cm. 597, p. 14)

On depositing its ratification, dated 8 August 1986, of the International Covenant on Economic, Social and Cultural Rights, 1966, the Argentine Republic made the following objection:

The Argentine Republic rejects the extension, notified to the Secretary-General of the United Nations on 20 May 1976 by the United Kingdom of Great Britain and Northern Ireland, of the application of the International Covenant on Economic, Social and Cultural Rights, adopted by the General Assembly of the United Nations on 16 December 1966, to the Malvinas, South Georgia and South Sandwich Islands, and reaffirms its sovereign rights to those archipelagos, which form an integral part of its national territory.

The General Assembly of the United Nations has adopted resolutions 2065(XX), 3160 (XXVIII), 31/49, 37/9, 38/12, 39/6 and 40/21 in which it recognizes the existence of a sovereignty dispute regarding the question of the Falkland Islands (Malvinas) and urges the Argentine Republic and the United Kingdom of Great Britain and Northern Ireland to pursue negotiations in order to find as soon as possible a peaceful and definitive solution to the dispute, through the good offices of the Secretary-General of the United Nations, who shall inform the General Assembly of the progress made.

(TS No. 61 (1987); Cm. 286, pp. 10–11)

By a communication to the Secretary-General of the UN as depositary, dated 13 January 1988, the UK Government wrote in response:

The Permanent Representative wishes to inform the Secretary-General that the Government of the United Kingdom of Great Britain and Northern Ireland rejects the statements made by the Argentine Republic, regarding the Falkland Islands and South Georgia and the South Sandwich Islands, when ratifying the International Covenant on Economic, Social and Cultural Rights and the International Covenant on Civil and Political Rights . . .

The Government of the United Kingdom of Great Britain and Northern Ireland has no doubt as to British sovereignty over the Falkland Islands and South Georgia and the South Sandwich Islands and its consequent right to extend treaties to those territories.

(TS No. 79 (1988); Cm. 597, pp. 6–7)

On 11 April 1988, the Ministry of Foreign Affairs of the Netherlands received from Argentina a communication relating to the acceptance by the UK of the Argentine accession to the Convention on the Taking of Evidence Abroad in Civil or Commercial Matters, 1970. The communication read:

With respect to the acceptance by the United Kingdom of Great Britain and Northern Ireland of the adhesion of the Argentine Republic to the Hague Convention on the Taking of Evidence Abroad in Civil or Commercial Matters, declared by Note dated February 12, 1988, the Argentine Government rejects the pretended acceptance of said Convention formulated for the Malvinas Islands, South Georgia Islands and South Sandwich Islands and reaffirms the sovereignty of the Argentine Republic over said islands, that are an integral part of the national territory.

(TS No. 79 (1988); Cm. 597, p. 14)

The UK Government responded with the following Note dated 6 July 1988:

The Government of the United Kingdom of Great Britain and Northern Island have no doubt as to the United Kingdom's sovereignty over the Falkland Islands or South Georgia and the South Sandwich Islands and are fully entitled to include those territories within the scope of application of international agreements to which they are a party. The United Kingdom, therefore, cannot accept the Argentine declaration which purports to question the right of the United Kingdom to extend the Convention to the Falkland Islands or South Georgia and the South Sandwich Islands; nor can it accept that the Government of the Argentine Republic has any right in this regard.

(TS No. 80 (1988); Cm. 702, p. 8)

In 'notes to editors' attached to Press notice No. 432 issued on 16 October 1989 (Part Six: IV. C., above), the Department of Transport stated in part:

The lights at Jabal al Tair and Abu Ali were among four built by the Ottoman Empire and first exhibited in 1903. Turkey renounced her rights and titles to the islands in the Treaty of Lausanne, and their sovereignty has since remained undetermined. The two lights have been managed by Britain since 1915, when the former Turkish islands were occupied by the Royal Navy during the First World War. For a period in the 1930s Germany, Italy and the Netherlands contributed to the costs of managing the lights, but this ended with the Second World War.

Part Eight: II. C. *State territory and territorial jurisdiction—territorial jurisdiction—concurrent territorial jurisdiction*

The following statement was made on 15 January 1989 by the delegation of the UK at the meeting of representatives of the participating States of the Conference on Security and Co-operation in Europe:

On behalf of the Governments of the United Kingdom, the United States of America and France, I wish to state that the points of agreement which have emerged at the Vienna talks in respect of the mandates for the Negotiation on Conventional Armed Forces in Europe and for the Negotiations of Confidence- and

Security-building Measures do not and cannot in any way affect the Quadripartite rights and responsibilities relating to Berlin and Germany as a whole. I request that this statement be entered in the Journal of the Day.

(Text provided by the Foreign and Commonwealth Office)

The following letter, dated 27 April 1989, was sent to the Director-General of the International Atomic Energy Authority by the UK Mission to the UN in Vienna:

On behalf of the Governments of the United Kingdom of Great Britain and Northern Ireland, the United States of America and France, I have the honour to refer to the Note Verbale No. 279 dated 24 June 1988 from the Permanent Mission of the Union of Soviet Socialist Republics, contained in Notification No. 230–N 4.11.4/F 1.32 of 5 July 1988, concerning the extension to the Western Sectors of Berlin of the arrangements between the Federal Republic of Germany and the International Atomic Energy Agency in respect of the design work to be performed and meetings to be held pursuant to the ITER Agreement at the Institute for Plasma Physics Garching, Federal Republic of Germany.

In a communication to the Government of the Union of Soviet Socialist Republics, which is an integral part (Annex IVA) of the Quadripartite Agreement of 3 September 1971, the Governments of France, the United Kingdom and the United States, without prejudice to the maintenance of their rights and responsibilities relating to the representation abroad of the interests of the Western Sectors of Berlin, confirmed that, provided that matters of security and status are not affected and provided that the extension is specified in each case, international agreements and arrangements entered into by the Federal Republic of Germany may be extended to the Western Sectors of Berlin in accordance with established procedures. For its part, the Government of the Union of Soviet Socialist Republics in a communication to the Governments of the Three Powers, which is similarly an integral part (Annex IVB) of the Quadripartite Agreement, affirmed that it would raise no objections to such extension.

The established procedures referred to above, which were endorsed in the Quadripartite Agreement, are designed *inter alia* to afford the authorities of the Three Powers the opportunity to ensure that international agreements and arrangements entered into by the Federal Republic of Germany which are to be extended to the Western Sectors of Berlin are extended in such a way that matters of security and status are not affected. When authorizing the extension of the above-mentioned arrangements to the Western Sectors of Berlin, the authorities of the Three Powers took such steps as were necessary to ensure that matters of security and status were not affected. Accordingly, the Berlin declaration made by the Federal Republic of Germany in accordance with established procedures is valid and the arrangements apply to the Western Sectors of Berlin subject to Allied rights and responsibilities.

(Text provided by the Foreign and Commonwealth Office)

The US Department of State, Washington, communicated the following note dated 3 July 1989:

The Secretary of State presents his compliments to Their Excellencies, Messieurs and Mesdames the Chiefs of Mission of the Governments concerned with the Statute of the International Atomic Energy Agency signed at United Nations Headquarters under date of October 26, 1956, and has the honor to refer to the note of the Department of State dated 28 July 1988, which transmitted the note of the Soviet Union dated 16 October 1987, regarding the amendment of Article VI A 1 of the statute of the International Atomic Energy Agency and, on behalf of the Governments of the United States, France, and the United Kingdom has the honor to state the following:

The Three Powers reject as without foundation the Soviet assertion that the extension to the Western sectors of Berlin of the IAEA statute and the subject amendment thereto was unlawful. They reaffirm the position set out in the Notes No. 68 of 28 March 1974 and No. 46 of 28 March 1974 from the Embassies of France and the United Kingdom of Great Britain and Northern Ireland respectively. In a communication to the Government of the Union of Soviet Socialist Republics, which is an integral part (Annex IV A) of the Quadripartite Agreement, the Governments of France, the United Kingdom and the United States, without prejudice to the maintenance of their rights and responsibilities relating to the representation abroad of the interests of the Western sectors of Berlin, confirmed that, provided that matters of security and status are not affected and provided that the extension is specified in each case, international agreements and arrangements entered into by the Federal Republic of Germany may be extended to the Western sectors of Berlin in accordance with established procedures. For its part, the Government of the Union of Soviet Socialist Republics in a communication to the Governments of the Three Powers, which is similarly an integral part (Annex IV B) of the Quadripartite Agreement, affirmed that it would raise no objection to such extension.

The established procedures referred to above, which were endorsed in the Quadripartite Agreement, are designed inter alia to afford the authorities of the Three Powers the opportunity to ensure that international agreements and arrangements entered into by the Federal Republic of Germany which are to be extended to the Western sectors of Berlin are extended in such a way that matters of security and status are not affected. When authorizing the extension of the above-mentioned arrangements to the Western sectors of Berlin, the authorities of the Three Powers took such steps as were necessary to ensure that matters of security and status were not affected. Accordingly, the Berlin declaration made by the Federal Republic of Germany in accordance with established procedures is valid and the arrangements apply to the Western sectors of Berlin, subject to Allied rights and responsibilities.

The Three Powers also reject the Soviet assertion that the use of the formula 'Land Berlin' is incompatible with the provisions of the Quadripartite Agreement. In approving the Constitution of Berlin, the Allied Kommandatura made no reservation with regard to Article 1, paragraph 1, which provided that Berlin is both a German Land and a city. There is therefore no reason why international agreements to which the Federal Republic of Germany is a party should not be applied to the Western sectors of Berlin in accordance with established procedures endorsed by the Quadripartite Agreement, using the formula 'Land Berlin'. It will be recalled that Article 1, paragraph 2 of the Constitution of Berlin, which provides that Berlin is a Land of the Federal Republic of Germany, continues to be suspended.

Regarding other communications on the subject, the Three Powers would add that states which are not parties to the Quadripartite Agreement are not competent to comment authoritatively on its provisions.

The Three Powers request that the Department of State circulate the contents of this note to all countries that are parties to the IAEA statute.

(Text provided by the Foreign and Commonwealth Office)

The following press statement was issued by the British Military Government in Berlin on 5 October 1989:

The Allied Commandants have noted with great concern the recent action of the GDR authorities in turning back permanent residents of West Berlin and other persons who wished to cross the sector boundary between the Western and Soviet Sectors of Berlin. These actions by the GDR authorities are contrary to provisions of the Quadripartite Agreement and arrangements implementing it, and seriously infringe the principle of freedom of movement throughout Berlin. The Allied Commandants expect the Soviet Embassy to take the necessary steps to rectify this situation.

The following press statement was issued by the British Military Government in Berlin on 7 October 1989:

GDR military units participated today in a demonstration in Berlin. Their equipment included main battle tanks, armoured fighting vehicles, rocket carrying vehicles and launchers, and artillery pieces. The Allied Commandants condemn the continuation of these military displays which are provocative and a violation of the demilitarised status of the city.

(Text provided by the Foreign and Commonwealth Office)

Part Eight: II. D. *State territory and territorial jurisdiction—territorial jurisdiction—extra-territoriality*

(See also Part Eleven: II. D. 2. (items on war crimes inquiry), below)

In reply to a question, the Minister for Trade wrote:

There is no extraterritorial control on United Kingdom high technology as such. But when an element of United States origin, either physical or intellectual, is present the United States Government make claims, which we have rejected on many occasions, on the ground that United Kingdom sovereignty is infringed. We have made representations on the extraterritorial aspects of United States export controls on technical data, in connection with the review currently being undertaken by the United States Department of Commerce. We have also reached an understanding with the United States on export controls for supercomputers which respects our position on extraterritoriality.

(HC Debs., vol. 136, Written Answers, col. *481* : 5 July 1988)

The following letter, dated 29 September 1988, was sent by the UK Ambassador to the USA, Sir Antony Acland, to Senator Robert C. Byrd and the other members of the Senate Foreign Relations Committee:

I am writing to you about the 'Anti-Apartheid Act Amendments of 1988', S2756, on which the Senate Foreign Relations Committee have recently submitted their report. A number of provisions in this Bill are of concern to the British Government. I enclose a copy of a Diplomatic Note communicated formally to the Department of State in June of this year, following approval of the House version of this Bill.

The British Government is, of course, firmly opposed to apartheid. Where we differ with some is on the best means of ending it. We do not support the introduction of punitive economic sanctions, for instance, because we do not think they would work. By undermining the South African economy, they would damage rather than promote the interests of black South Africans (and the economies of neighbouring countries), and they would be counter-productive by stiffening the resistance of the South African Government and the white community to peaceful change.

But the aspect of the present Senate bill to which I would like to draw your particular attention today is its extraterritorial scope, which I outline in the accompanying enclosure. There would be strong reaction here if the British Parliament were to consider legislation claiming to control the activities of companies incorporated in the United States and trading from the United States, or to impose penalties on US companies in the United Kingdom for trade carried out legitimately elsewhere. Accordingly, the British Government feel strongly that the provisions of this type in the present bill, S2756, would constitute an unjustified assertion of US jurisdiction over companies in the United Kingdom. Moreover, discriminatory actions taken under the bill would be inconsistent with the United States' international obligations to its trading partners, notably under the GATT and the OECD principles of national treatment. Such provisions could hardly fail to lead to serious trade and political conflicts. Accordingly, the British Government welcome the deletion from the bill of the provision which would have denied the issue of oil, gas and coal leases to foreign companies with investments in South Africa.

. . .

The enclosure read as follows:

EXTRATERRITORIAL IMPLICATIONS OF ANTI-APARTHEID ACT AMENDMENTS OF 1988

The Senate Bill, as it now stands, would have a number of extra-territorial implications. Specifically, it would:

(a) prohibit re-exports from foreign countries of all goods and technology of US origin, including foreign-produced items which are the product of US technology;

(b) prohibit foreign companies owned or controlled by US citizens or corporations from re-exporting from foreign countries any goods or technology to South Africa, as well as from transporting crude oil and refined products to South Africa, either directly or by an affiliate, including a foreign affiliate;

(c) prohibit investment in South Africa by such companies;

(d) impose import and government contracting penalties on any foreign company deemed by the US to have taken significant commercial advantage of any sanction or prohibition imposed under the legislation.

The Diplomatic Note, No. 117 dated 8 June 1988, read as follows:

Her Britannic Majesty's Embassy . . . have the honour to refer to the Bill approved by the House Foreign Affairs Committee on 3 May, 1988, and cited as the 'Anti-Apartheid Act Amendments of 1988', and also to recent representations made by the Delegation of the Commission of the European Community and the Embassy of the Federal Republic of Germany as Presidency of the European Community. Her Majesty's Government have studied the proposals put forward in the Bill and are very concerned at the extraterritorial reach of some of the claims incorporated in these proposals. The United States authorities will be aware of the consistent view of the British Government that any extraterritorial extension of US jurisdiction prejudicial to the sovereignty of another jurisdiction is objectionable both as a matter of law and of policy. The United States authorities are therefore urged to do everything possible to avoid potential conflicts when enacting any new powers by respecting and accommodating the legitimate interests of other states.

Her Majesty's Government reserve the right to make further more detailed comments.

(Texts provided by the Foreign and Commonwealth Office; see also UKMIL 1988, p. 509)

In the course of a debate on the subject of unitary taxation, the Financial Secretary to the Treasury, Mr Peter Lilley, stated:

I must straight away reaffirm both the Government's opposition to worldwide unitary tax and their support for the aims and objectives of the Unitary Tax Campaign and other bodies which have campaigned against worldwide unitary tax. The British Government are opposed to worldwide unitary taxation because it is contrary to accepted international tax principles, manifestly unfair and damaging to international investment. It is contrary to the accepted international principles, which indicate that each country should levy tax only in respect of profits which arise in that country's jurisdiction. It is manifestly unfair, since it can result in international companies paying tax to more than one Administration in respect of the same profits—and even paying taxes in a country where they are making losses simply because they are making profits elsewhere, in another country. It is damaging because it is bound to discourage the flow of international investment, which is mutually beneficial to host and source countries, as well as undermining normal relations between tax authorities.

That is why the British Government have pursued their opposition to worldwide unitary taxation as vigorously as possible through all appropriate channels—directly to the Californian state authorities, jointly with the United States Federal Government whose support in this matter we greatly welcome; in conjunction with our European Community partners; in supporting British companies in their court actions; and in taking legislative power to strengthen our bargaining position. Those pressures and the sustained work of the Unitary Tax Campaign have not been without effect. Barclays won a notable victory when the Californian Superior Court ruled its worldwide unitary taxation unconstitutional. Unfortunately, however, the United States legal mills grind slow and the final outcome is far from sure.

(HC Debs., vol. 164, col. 175: 18 December 1989)

Part Eight: III. B. *State territory and territorial jurisdiction—acquisition and transfer of territory—transfer*

(See Part Four: I. (second item of 17 October 1989), above)

Part Eight: IV. *State territory and territorial jurisdiction—regime under the Antarctic Treaty*

(See also Part Three: I. C. 4. (item of 24 January 1989) and Part Eight: II. A. (items of 8 May 1987, 27 August 1987 and 13 January 1988), above)

In reply to a question, the Parliamentary Under-Secretary of State, Foreign and Commonwealth Office, wrote:

We are following with close attention the construction of the French airstrip at Point Geologie in the French-claimed sector of Antarctica. The information required under the Antarctic treaty concerning French activities this austral summer has already been approved by the French authorities.

The French are constructing their airstrip under the terms of article VII. 2 of the agreed measures on the conservation of antarctic fauna and flora, which permit such activities to the minimum extent necessary for the establishment, supply and operation of Antarctic stations. Observance of the agreed measures is subject to review, and this can be done during the normal course of Antarctic treaty meetings, the next of which will take place in Paris in May.

I understand that a number of the members of Greenpeace involved in the recent airstrip protest were British subjects.

Under the Antarctic treaty, consultative members have the right to designate observers to carry out inspections in all areas of Antarctica including all stations operated by treaty members.

The United Kingdom is a founder-member of the Antarctic treaty system, and a full consultative party.

(HC Debs., vol. 145, Written Answers, col. 576: 25 January 1989)

In moving the second reading in the House of Lords of the Antarctic Minerals Bill, the Minister of State, Foreign and Commonwealth Office, Lord Glenarthur, stated:

The main purpose of the Bill is to enable the United Kingdom to ratify the convention on the regulation of Antarctic mineral resource activities, adopted at Wellington on 2nd June 1988 and signed on behalf of the United Kingdom on 22nd March 1989. The Bill will prohibit mineral activities in Antarctica by British companies and nationals, except prospecting activities authorised by the United Kingdom Government or another contracting party to the minerals convention, and will enable the Secretary of State to grant licences for prospecting activities in accordance with the convention.

. . .

The Antarctic treaty makes no provision concerning the mineral resources of Antarctica. From the outset of the minerals convention negotiations, Britain has shared the view of its Antarctic treaty partners that it would be difficult, perhaps even impossible, to reach agreement to regulate minerals activity in the political circumstances peculiar to Antarctica once commercially viable quantities of minerals had been located.

. . .

The convention established two permanent institutions: a commission on which will be represented all Antarctic treaty consultative parties and other qualified states; and a scientific, technical and environmental advisory committee composed of all parties to the convention. If an area of the Antarctic is opened for exploration and development, the commission shall also establish a regulatory committee composed of 10 members of the commission, including the claimant or claimants (if any) whose territory is included in the area.

. . .

I should like to say a few words in explanation of Clause 14. This clause empowers Her Majesty the Queen by Order in Council to confer on specified courts in England and Wales criminal or civil jurisdiction in respect of matters arising under the law of the British Antarctic territory. This clause is not directly related to the convention or its implementation, but it owes its inclusion to the prospect of mineral activities in the British Antarctic territory, however remote they may now appear.

There is at present very little risk of serious crime or need for civil litigation in the territory. But if mineral activities were to commence on any significant scale the risk would obviously increase. It would be impractical for a court actually sitting in the territory to deal with any but the most trivial cases. Alternative venues must therefore be found. The most obvious one is the Falkland Islands, and powers already exist in the British Settlements Acts to provide for its courts to try matters arising under territory law. But no powers exist to allow United Kingdom courts to do the same, and there may be circumstances in which this country would be the most appropriate forum. Clause 14 is designed to fill this gap in case the need should arise at some time in the future.

As I said, the main purpose of the Bill is to enable the United Kingdom to ratify the Antarctic Minerals Convention. The convention fills an important and long-awaited gap in the Antarctic treaty system, the continued success and stability of which will be secured by the convention's early entry into force.

(HL Debs., vol. 506, cols. 926–31, *passim*: 20 April 1989)

During the debate on the motion, the same Minister stated:

Perhaps I may clear up one point in connection with the idea of a world park. . . . The point dealt with the United Nations' control of Antarctica. I must say to the noble Lord that the Antarctic Treaty has worked effectively now for over a quarter of a century. United Nations' moves to replace the treaty might risk unravelling demilitarisation and nuclear control provisions. When it comes to UN resolutions, it is possible that they could be prejudicial to the good management of Antarctica. It is not the United Nations' role to oversee international treaties negotiated outside its ambit. We and the treaty partners have registered our common disapproval by taking the unusual step of not participating in successive UN General Assembly votes on the matter.

. . .

My noble friend Lord Craigton questioned the inclusion of Clause 14 in the Bill, and asked for an assurance that no other revisions of the Antarctic treaty laws are necessary or intended within the next two or three years. I readily give such an assurance. Although the Antarctic treaty is open to review as from 1991, there is no obligation upon the parties to do so. Even if there were such a review, which is far from certain, we cannot yet predict whether there would need to be primary legislation to amend the Antarctic Treaty Act 1967. In those circumstances we thought it a sensible precaution to seek the powers provided in Clause 14. While I understand my noble friend's doubts, I hope that I explained in my earlier remarks the connection that Clause 14 has, if only indirectly, with the convention and the prospect of minerals activity in the British Antarctic territory. I also pointed out that the Falkland Islands will remain an alternative venue for the trial of cases arising under British Antarctic territory law. . . .

My noble friend Lord Morris asked whether the South Orkney Islands fell within the ambit of the Bill and the convention, in the general welcome that he gave the Bill and his remarks about the speed with which it has come forward. The answer in short is, yes. He asked whether the definition of the Antarctic and the continental shelf would include South Georgia. The short answer to that is, no. . . .

In summary, the Bill will enable the United Kingdom to ratify the Antarctic minerals convention to fill a gap within the Antarctic treaty system and to fulfil our commitment to the treaty. Following careful consideration, the Government are convinced that the convention meets our interests in strengthening the Antarctic treaty system as the guarantor of peace and stability in the region. It will adequately provide for the orderly regulation of any minerals activity that may take place there and protect the unique Antarctic environment.

(Ibid., cols. 942–5, *passim*: 20 April 1989)

During the third reading of the above Bill in the House of Commons, the Parliamentary Under-Secretary of State, Foreign and Commonwealth Office, Mr Timothy Eggar, stated:

The Bill is the vehicle for Britain's ratification of the convention. We consider it vital that we play our part to bring that convention into force, not just because we believe that it is a remarkable international achievement—as, indeed, it is—and not just because we think that it offers the best chance of preventing possible disastrous exploitation of Antarctic mineral resources, but because unless it is implemented in a timely manner the voluntary moratorium on Antarctic minerals activity will definitely be put at risk. . . .

A fragile consensus—a consensus with no legally binding force—is all that currently inhibits mineral activity in the Antarctic. That consensus is conditional. If it ever became clear that the convention was unlikely to come into force, it would be only a matter of time before one of the parties decided that the conditions on which it had agreed to the moratorium no longer applied and that the moratorium was no longer valid. We already know that at least one country had engaged in prospecting activity under the guise of scientific research. We simply cannot run that risk.

Without the Bill and the convention, there is a real risk of a mining free-for-all, of heightened tension and possibly conflict, and of the collapse of the Antarctic treaty system which has served so well to keep Antarctica peaceful and stable for more than 30 years.

(HC Debs., vol. 157, col. 149: 17 July 1989)

The Bill was enacted on 21 July 1989 as the Antarctic Minerals Act (1989 c. 21) 'to make provision with respect to the exploration and exploitation of mineral resources in Antarctica; to enable proceedings with respect to matters arising under the law of the British Antarctic Territory to be brought in England and Wales; and for connected purposes'. Section 1 of the Act reads in part as follows:

Exploration and exploitation

1.—(1) Except as provided by section 2 below, a person to whom this section applies shall not carry on in Antarctica any activities for, or for purposes connected with, the exploration or exploitation of mineral resources.

(2) This section applies to United Kingdom nationals, Scottish firms, and bodies incorporated under the law of any part of the United Kingdom.

(3) Her Majesty may by Order in Council extend the application of this section to bodies incorporated under the law of any of the Channel Islands, the Isle of Man or any colony.

(4) In this Act—
  'Antarctica' means the following areas—
        (a) the continent of Antarctica (including all its ice shelves);
        (b) all Antarctic islands, that is to say, islands south of 60° South Latitude; and
        (c) all areas of continental shelf which are adjacent to that continent or those islands,
  and for this purpose 'continental shelf' shall be construed in accordance with the rules of international law . . .

Part Nine: I. A. *Seas, waterways, ships—territorial sea—delimitation, baselines*

The Territorial Sea (Limits) Order 1989 (Statutory Instruments 1989 No. 482), which amended slightly the co-ordinates set out in the Territorial Sea (Limits) Order 1987 (Statutory Instruments 1987 No. 1269), came into force on 6 April 1989. It provided in part as follows:

2. The seaward limit of the territorial sea adjacent to the United Kingdom between Point 1 and Point 6 indicated in the Schedule to this Order shall consist of a series of straight lines joining, in the sequence given, Points 1 to 6 indicated in the Schedule to this Order.

3. The seaward limit of the territorial sea adjacent to the United Kingdom shall be the median line where the baselines from which the breadth of the territorial sea adjacent to the United Kingdom is measured are less than 24 nautical miles from the baselines from which the breadth of the territorial sea adjacent to the Isle of Man is measured.

4. In this Order—
      (a) 'straight line' means a loxodromic line;
      (b) all positions given by means of co-ordinates are defined on European Datum (1st Adjustment 1950);
      (c) 'median line' is a line every point of which is equidistant from the nearest points of the baselines from which the breadth of the territorial sea adjacent to the United Kingdom and the Isle of Man respectively is measured.

SCHEDULE
LIST OF POINTS

Point	Position of Point	
1	50°49′30″95N	01°15′53″43E
2	50°53′47″00N	01°16′58″00E
3	50°57′00″00N	01°21′25″00E
4	51°02′19″00N	01°32′53″00E
5	51°05′58″00N	01°43′31″00E
6	51°12′00″72N	01°53′20″07E

An Explanatory Note attached to the Order, though not a part of it, reads:

This Order provides for the seaward limit of the territorial sea adjacent to the United Kingdom in the Straits of Dover and in the vicinity of the Isle of Man. The limit in the Straits of Dover is constituted by straight lines joining the points indicated in the Schedule and follows the line defined in the Agreement of 2nd November 1988 between the Government of the United Kingdom and the Government of the French Republic (Cm. 557) relating to the Delimitation of the Territorial Sea in the Straits of Dover. The limit in the vicinity of the Isle of Man is the median line.

On 1 November 1989, the following Orders in Council were made in pursuance of the powers conferred upon the Crown by the Colonial Boundaries Act 'and all other powers enabling Her in that behalf'; the Falkland Islands (Territorial Sea) Order 1989 (Statutory Instruments 1989 No. 1993), the St. Helena and Dependencies (Territorial Sea) Order 1989 (Statutory Instruments 1989 No. 1994), the South Georgia and South Sandwich Islands (Territorial Sea) Order 1989 (Statutory Instruments 1989 No. 1995), and the Turks and Caicos Islands (Territorial Sea) Order 1989 (Statutory Instruments 1989 No. 1996). All the Orders came into force on 1 January 1990.

Each of the above Orders in Council contains a s. 2 in common form:

The boundaries of the [dependent territory] are hereby extended to include, as territorial sea, that part of the sea which is situated within 12 nautical miles measured from the baselines as established by article . . . of this Order, together with the seabed of the territorial sea and its subsoil.

Article 3 of the Falkland Islands (Territorial Sea) Order 1989 reads:

3.—(1) Except as otherwise provided in paragraphs (2) to (4) of this article, the baselines from which the breadth of the territorial sea adjacent to the Falkland Islands is measured shall be the low-water line along the coast of all islands comprised in the Colony of the Falkland Islands.

(2) For the purposes of this article a low-tide elevation which lies wholly or partly within the breadth of sea which would be territorial sea if all low-tide elevations were disregarded for the purpose of the measurement of the breadth thereof and if paragraphs (3) and (4) of this article were omitted shall be treated as an island.

(3) The baseline from which the breadth of the territorial sea is measured between Cape Carysfort (East Falkland), Cape Percival (West Falkland) and

MacBride Head (East Falkland) shall consist of the series of loxodromes drawn so as to join successively, in the order in which they are there set out, the points identified by the co-ordinates of latitude and longitude in the first column of the Schedule to this Order, each being a point situate on the low-water line on or adjacent to the feature named in the second column of that Schedule opposite to the co-ordinates of latitude and longitude of the point in the first column.

(4) The provisions of paragraph (3) of this article shall be without prejudice to the operation of paragraph (2) of this article in relation to any island or low-tide elevation which for the purposes of that paragraph is treated as if it were an island, being an island or low-tide elevation which lies to seaward of the baseline specified in paragraph (3) of this article.

Article 4 of the Falkland Islands (Territorial Sea) Order 1989 reads:

In this Order—
  (a) 'island' means a naturally formed area of land surrounded by water which is above water at mean high-water spring tides;
  (b) 'low-tide elevation' means a naturally formed area of drying land surrounded by water which is below water at mean high-water spring tides; and
  (c) 'nautical miles' means international nautical miles of 1,852 metres.

An explanatory note, which is not part of the Order, reads in part as follows:

The effect of the Order is to establish around all of the Falkland Islands (including Beauchene Island) a territorial sea extending to 12 nautical miles from the appropriate baselines.

Article 3 of the St. Helena and Dependencies (Territorial Sea) Order 1989 reads:

3.—(1) Except as otherwise provided in paragraph (2) of this article and in article 4 of this Order, the baseline from which the breadth of the territorial sea adjacent to St. Helena and its Dependencies is measured shall be the low-water line along the coast of all islands comprised in the Colony of St. Helena and its Dependencies.

(2) For the purposes of this article a low-tide elevation which lies wholly or partly within the breadth of sea which would be territorial sea if all low-tide elevations were disregarded for the purpose of the measurement of the breadth thereof shall be treated as an island.

Article 4 of the St. Helena and Dependencies (Territorial Sea) Order 1989 reads:

4. In the case of the sea adjacent to a bay, the baseline from which the breadth of the territorial sea is measured shall—
  (a) if the bay has only one mouth and the distance between the low-water lines of the natural entrance points of the bay does not exceed 24 nautical miles, be a straight line joining the said low-water lines;
  (b) if, because of the presence of islands, the bay has more than one mouth and the distances between the low-water lines of the natural entrance points of each mouth added together do not exceed 24 nautical miles, be a

series of straight lines across each of the mouths drawn so as to join the said low-water lines;

(c) if neither paragraph (a) nor (b) of this article applies, be a straight line 24 nautical miles in length drawn from low-water line to low-water line within the bay in such a manner as to enclose the maximum area of water that is possible with a line of that length.

Article 5 of the St. Helena and Dependencies (Territorial Sea) Order 1989 reads:

5. In this Order—
(a) 'bay' means an indentation of the coast such that its area is not less than that of the semi-circle whose diameter is a line drawn across the mouth of the indentation, and for the purposes of this definition the area of an indentation shall be taken to be the area bounded by the low-water line around the shore of the indentation and the straight line joining the low-water lines of its natural entrance points, and where, because of the presence of islands, an indentation has more than one mouth the length of the diameter of the semi-circle referred to shall be the sum of the lengths of the straight lines drawn across each of the mouths, and in calculating the area of an indentation the area of any islands lying within it shall be treated as part of the area of the indentation;
(b) 'island' means a naturally formed area of land surrounded by water which is above water at mean high-water spring tides;
(c) 'low-tide elevation' means a naturally formed area of drying land surrounded by water which is below water at mean high-water spring tides; and
(d) 'nautical miles' means international nautical miles of 1,852 metres.

An explanatory note, which is not part of the Order, indicates that the Order applies to the islands of St. Helena, Ascension, Tristan da Cunha, Gough Island, Nightingale Island and Inaccessible Island.

Article 3 of the South Georgia and South Sandwich Islands (Territorial Sea) Order 1989 reads:

3.—(1) Except as otherwise provided in paragraphs (2) to (4) of this article, the baseline from which the breadth of the territorial sea adjacent to South Georgia and South Sandwich Islands is measured shall be the low-water line along the coast of all islands and territories comprised in South Georgia and South Sandwich Islands by virtue of the South Georgia and South Sandwich Islands Order 1985.

(2) For the purposes of this article a low-tide elevation which lies wholly or partly within the breadth of sea which would be territorial sea if all low-tide elevations were disregarded for the purpose of the measurement of the breadth thereof and if paragraph (3) and (4) of this article were omitted shall be treated as an island.

(3) The baseline from which the breadth of the territorial sea is measured around the island of South Georgia and the islands in its immediate vicinity shall consist of the series of loxodromes drawn so as to join successively, in the order in which they are there set out, the points identified by the co-ordinates of latitude and longitude in the first column of the Schedule to this Order, each being a point

situate on the low-water line on or adjacent to the feature named in the second column of that Schedule opposite to the co-ordinates of latitude and longitude of the point in the first column:

Provided that the baseline between points 19 and 20 of that Schedule shall be the low water line as laid down in paragraphs (1) and (2) of this article.

(4) The provisions of paragraph (3) of this article shall be without prejudice to the operation of paragraph (2) of this article in relation to any island or low-tide elevation which for the purposes of that paragraph is treated as if it were an island, being an island or low-tide elevation which lies to seaward of the baseline specified in paragraph (3) of this article.

Article 4 of the South Georgia and South Sandwich Islands (Territorial Sea) Order 1989 reads:

In this Order—
  (a) 'island' means a naturally formed area of land surrounded by water which is above water at mean high-water spring tides;
  (b) 'low-tide elevation' means a naturally formed area of drying land surrounded by water which is below water at mean high-water spring tides; and
  (c) 'nautical miles' means international nautical miles of 1,852 metres.

An explanatory note, which is not part of the Order, reads in part as follows:

In particular, it defines the baseline from which the breadth of the territorial sea is measured as generally the low-water line, except that around South Georgia and other islands in its immediate vicinity a series of straight baselines joining specified points is provided for. The effect of the Order is to establish around South Georgia (including Shag Rocks, Black Rock, Clerke Rocks and the Office Boys) and all islands in the South Sandwich Islands a territorial sea extending to 12 nautical miles from the appropriate baselines.

Articles 3, 4 and 5 of the Turks and Caicos Islands (Territorial Sea) Order 1989 read:

3.—(1) Except as otherwise provided in paragraph (2) of this article and article 4 of this Order, the baseline from which the breadth of the territorial sea adjacent to the Turks and Caicos Islands is measured shall be the low water line along the coast of all islands comprised in the Colony of the Turks and Caicos Islands.

(2) For the purpose of this article a low-tide elevation which lies wholly or partly within the breadth of sea which would be territorial sea if all low-tide elevations were disregarded for the purpose of the measurement of the breadth thereof and if article 4 of this Order were omitted shall be treated as an island.

4.—(1) The baseline from which the breadth of the territorial sea is measured between North West Point, Providenciales and Company Point, West Caicos; between South West Point, West Caicos and the south-easterly point of Toney Rock; and between the north-easterly point of Toney Rock and Drum Point, East Caicos shall consist of the series of loxodromes drawn so as to join successively, in the order in which they are there set out, the points identified by the co-ordinate of latitude and longitude in the first column of the Schedule to this Order, each being a point situate on the low water line on or adjacent to the feature named in the second column of that Schedule opposite to the co-ordinates of latitude and longitude of the point in the first column.

(2) The provisions of paragraph (1) of this article shall be without prejudice to the operation of article 3 of this Order in relation to any island or low-tide elevation which for the purposes of that article is treated as if it were an island, being an island or low-tide elevation which lies to seaward of the baseline specified in paragraph (1) of this article.

   5. In this Order—

     (a) 'island' means a naturally formed area of land surrounded by water which is above water at mean high-water spring tides;

     (b) 'low-tide elevation' means a naturally formed area of drying land surrounded by water which is below water at mean high-water spring tides; and

     (c) 'nautical miles' means international nautical miles of 1,852 metres.

An explanatory note, which is not part of the Order, reads in part as follows:

In particular, it defines the baseline from which the breadth of the territorial sea is measured as generally the low water line, but between North West Point, Providenciales and Company Point, West Caicos; between South West Point, West Caicos and Toney Rock—SE; and between Toney Rock—NE and Drum Point, East Caicos a series of straight lines joining specified points lying on the seaward side of the Turks and Caicos group of islands are used.

In its press release relating to the above four Orders in Council, the Foreign and Commonwealth Office issued the following background note:

Generally accepted international law provides for a maximum of twelve nautical miles as the breadth of the territorial sea (but it is open to states to choose less than twelve miles). The territorial sea around the UK was extended from three to twelve nautical miles in 1987, but no similar extension was made in the case of the Channel Islands or the UK Dependent Territories, as there was considered to be no general need to do so. Since then, extensions around the Dependent Territories have been considered on a case by case basis.

The Orders define the baselines from which the territorial sea is measured in each case as generally the low-water line. In the cases of the Falkland Islands, South Georgia and Turks and Caicos Islands, some straight baselines have been drawn, in accordance with international law (Article 4 of the Convention on the Territorial Sea 1958).

(Foreign and Commonwealth Press Release No. 150/1989)

On 19 December 1989, the Cayman Islands (Territorial Sea) Order 1989 (Statutory Instruments 1989 No. 2397) was issued in pursuance of the powers conferred upon the Crown by the Colonial Boundaries Act 1895 'and all other powers enabling Her in that behalf'. Article 2 of the Order, which came into force on 1 January 1990, reads:

2. The boundaries of the Colony of the Cayman Islands are hereby extended to include, as territorial sea, that part of the sea which is situated within 12 nautical

miles of the Cayman Islands, measured from the baselines as established by article 3 of this Order, together with the seabed of the territorial sea and its subsoil.

The Order continues:

3.—(1) Except as otherwise provided in paragraph (2) of this article and in articles 4 and 5 below, the baseline from which the breadth of the territorial sea adjacent to the Cayman Islands is measured shall be the low-water line along the coast, including the coast of all islands comprised in the territory.

(2) For the purposes of this article a low-tide elevation which lies wholly or partly within the breadth of sea which would be territorial sea if all low-tide elevations were disregarded for the purpose of the measurement of the breadth thereof shall be treated as an island.

4.—(1) In the case of the sea adjacent to a coast off which there are fringing reefs, the baseline from which the breadth of the territorial sea is measured shall be the sea-ward limit of the low-water line of the fringing reefs.

(2) Where there is a break or passage through the fringing reefs referred to in paragraph (1) of this article, the baseline from which the breadth of the territorial sea is measured shall be a straight line joining the seaward entrance points of that break or passage.

5. In the case of the sea adjacent to a bay, the baseline from which the breadth of the territorial sea is measured shall—

    (a) if the bay has only one mouth and the distance between the low-water lines of the natural entrance points of the bay does not exceed 24 nautical miles, be a straight line joining the said low-water lines;

    (b) if, because of the presence of islands, the bay has more than one mouth, and the distances between the low-water lines of the natural entrance points of each mouth added together do not exceed 24 nautical miles, be a series of straight lines across each of the mouths drawn so as to join the said low-water lines;

    (c) if neither paragraph (a) nor (b) of this article applies, be a straight line 24 nautical miles in length drawn from low-water line to low-water line within the bay in such a manner as to enclose the maximum area of water that is possible with a line of that length.

6. In this Order—

    (a) 'bay' means an indentation of the coast such that its area in not less than that of the semi-circle whose diameter is a line drawn across the mouth of the indentation, and for the purposes of this definition the area of an indentation shall be taken to be the area bounded by the low-water line around the shore of the indentation and the straight line joining the low-water lines of its natural entrance points, and where, because of the presence of islands, an indentation has more than one mouth the length of the diameter of the semi-circle referred to shall be the sum of the lengths of the straight lines drawn across each of the mouths, and in calculating the area of an indentation the area of any islands lying within it shall be treated as part of the area of the indentation;

    (b) 'fringing reefs' means reefs attached directly to, or located in the immediate vicinity of, the coast or any coastal lagoon;

    (c) 'island' means a naturally formed area of land surrounded by water which is above water at mean high-water spring tides;

(d) 'low-tide elevation' means a naturally formed area of drying land surrounded by water which is below water at mean high-water spring tides; and

(e) 'nautical miles' means international nautical miles of 1,852 metres.

An explanatory note, not part of the Order, reads:

This Order extends the boundaries of the Colony of the Cayman Islands so as to include, as territorial sea, the sea within twelve nautical miles of the baselines of the Cayman Islands, together with its seabed and subsoil, and makes other provisions in this connection. In particular, it defines the baseline from which the breadth of the territorial sea is measured as generally the low-water line, except where there are fringing reefs or bays.

The following notice was issued by the Hydrographic Division of the Navy on 1 January 1990:

ADMIRALTY NOTICES TO MARINERS

12. TERRITORIAL WATERS AND FISHERIES JURISDICTION CLAIMS.

Former Notice 1991/89 is cancelled.

The following list shows the breadth of sea (measured from the appropriate baselines) claimed respectively as territorial waters and as being under the state's jurisdiction for fishing. The information is compiled from various, sometimes unofficial, sources; the absence of a limit from this list indicates that the information is not held.

The claims are published for information only. Her Majesty's Government does not recognise claims to territorial waters exceeding twelve miles or to fisheries jurisdiction exceeding two hundred miles.

Albania[1]	15**	15	Cambodia[1]	12	200
Algeria[8]	12**	12	Cameroon*	50	
Angola	20	200	Canada[1]	12	200
Antigua and Barbuda[2]*	12**	200	Cape Verde Islands[2]*	12	200
Argentina	200	200	Chile[1]	12	200
Australia[1]	3	200	Chinese People's		
Australian Antarctica	3	12	Republic[1]	12**	
			Colombia[1]	12	200
Bahamas*	3	200	Comoros[2]	12	200
Bahrain*	3		Congo	200	200
Bangladesh[4]	12**	200	Costa Rica	12	200
Barbados	12**	200	Cuba[1]*	12	200
Belgium	12	200	Cyprus*	12	12
Belize*	3	3			
Benin	200	200			
Brazil*	200**	200	Denmark[1]	3**	200
Brunei	12	200	Djibouti	12	200
Bulgaria	12**	200	Dominica	12	200
Burma[1]	12**	200	Dominican Republic[1]	6	200

Ecuador[1]	200	200
Egypt[1]*	12**	200
El Salvador	200	200
Equatorial Guinea	12**	200
Ethiopia[1]	12	
Fiji[2]*	12	200
Finland[1]	4**	12
France[1]	12	200
French Antarctica	12	
Gabon	12	200
Gambia*	12	200
Germany (East)[1] [11]	12**	
Germany (West)[1] [10]	3	200
Ghana*	12	200
Greece	6	6
Grenada	12**	200
Guatemala	12	200
Guinea[1]*	12	200
Guinea Bissau[1]*	12	200
Guyana	12**	200
Haiti	12	200
Honduras	12	200
Iceland[1]*	12	200
India	12**	200
Indonesia[2]*	12	200
Iran[1]	12**	50
Iraq*	12	
Irish Republic[1]	12	200
Israel	6	6
Italy[1]	12	12
Ivory Coast*	12	200
Jamaica*	12	12
Japan[11]	12	200
Jordan	3	3
Kenya[1]*	12	200
Kiribati[2]	12	200
Korea (North)	12**	200
Korea (South)[1]	12[6]**	
Kuwait*	12	
Lebanon	12	
Liberia	200	200
Libya[5]	12**	20

Madagascar[1]	12**	200
Malaysia[1]	12	200
Maldives[3]	12**	up to 200
Malta[1]	12**	25
Mauritania[1]	12	200
Mauritius[1]	12**	200
Mexico[1]*	12	200
Monaco[3]	12	12
Morocco	12	200
Mozambique	12	200
Namibia	12	200
Nauru	12	200
Netherlands	12	200
Netherlands Antilles	12	12
New Zealand	12	200
Nicaragua	200**	200
Nigeria*	30**	200
Norway[1]	4	200
Oman[1]*	12	200
Pakistan	12**	200
Panama	200	200
Papua New Guinea[2]	12	200
Peru	200	200
Philippines[2] [3]*	12	200
Poland[8]	12**	12
Portugal[1]	12	200
Qatar	3	to median lines
Romania	12**	200
St. Kitts-Nevis	12	200
St. Lucia*	12	200
St. Vincent and the Grenadines[2]	12**	200
Sao Tome and Principe[2]*	12	200
Saudi Arabia[1]	12	
Senegal[1]*	12	200
Seychelles	12**	200
Sierra Leone	200	200
Singapore	3	3
Solomon Islands[2]	12	200

Somalia*	200**	200
South Africa	12	200
Spain[1]	12	200
Sri Lanka	12**	200
Sudan*	12**	
Suriname	12	200
Sweden[1] [11]	12**	200
Syria	35**	
Taiwan	12	200
Tanzania[1]*	12	200
Thailand[1]	12	200
Togo*	30	200
Tonga[3]	12	200
Trinidad and Tobago[2]*	12	200
Tunisia[1] [9]*	12	12
Turkey[1]	12[7]**	12[7]
Tuvalu	12	200
UAE		up to 73
Abu Zabi	3	
Ajman	3	
Dubayy	3	
Fujayrah	12	
Ra's al Khaymah	3	
Ash Shariqah	12	
Umm al Qaywayn	3	
UK[1]	12	200
Anguilla	3	200
Bermuda	12	200
British Antarctic Territory	3	3
British Indian Ocean Territory	3	12
British Virgin Islands	3	200
Cayman Islands	12	200
Cyprus (Sovereign Base Areas)	3	3
Falkland Islands[1]	12	150
Gibraltar	3	3
Hong Kong	3	3
Montserrat	3	200
Pitcairn	3	200
St. Helena and Dependencies	12	200
South Georgia[1]	12	12
South Sandwich Islands	12	12
Turks and Caicos Islands[1]	12	200
Uruguay	200	200
USA	12	200
USSR[1]	12**	200
Vanuatu[2]	12	200
Venezuela[1]	12	200
Vietnam[1]	12**	200
Western Samoa	12	200
Yemen Arab Republic	12**	36
Yemen People's Democratic Republic[1]*	12**	200
Yugoslavia[1]*	12	12
Zaire*	12	200

Limits of dependent territories have not been listed unless they differ from those of the metropolitan state.

[1] employs straight baseline systems along all or part of the coast.
[2] claims all waters within the archipelago.
[3] claims waters within limits defined by geographic co-ordinates not related to distance from coastline.
[4] claims straight baseline system between points along the 18 metre depth line.
[5] claims all water south of 32°30'N. in Gulf of Sirte as internal waters.
[6] claims 3 miles in Korea Strait.
[7] claims 6 miles in Aegean Sea.

[8] fishery limit extends beyond 12 miles to limits to be agreed.

[9] fishery limit extends to 50 metre isobath off Gulf of Gabes.

[10] special claim extends limit to include deep water anchorage west of Helgoland.

[11] reduced limits in some straits.

* Indicates a state which has ratified the U.N. Law of the Sea Convention 1982. The Convention does not come into force until one year after 60 instruments of ratification or accession have been deposited.

** Indicates a state which requires prior permission or notification for entry of warships into territorial sea. The United Kingdom government does not recognise this requirement.

Hydrographic Department.   (*HH. 085/012/01*).

(Annual Summary of Admiralty Notices to Mariners in Force on 1 January 1990, pp. 94–6)

Part Nine: I. B. *Seas, waterways, ships—territorial sea—legal status*

In reply to the following question

Whether [Her Majesty's Government's] claimed 12 nautical miles territorial sea round Rockall is recognised as such by (a) the United States, (b) the other adjacent states, and (c) the European Community; and whether the claim is in accordance with UNCLOS provisions,

the Minister of State for Defence Procurement wrote:

The 12 nautical miles territorial sea around Rockall is consistent with the terms of the UN Law of the Sea Convention and with the rules of customary international law. We have no reason to believe that this position is not recognised by the international community in general, although it is not recognised by the Republic of Ireland.

(HL Debs., vol. 510, col. 250: 11 July 1989)

The following question was later asked:

Further to [the] Answer of 11th July . . . , whether they will specify, as asked in the original Question, whether their claim to 12 nautical miles of territorial sea round Rockall is recognised as such by the United States of America, the other adjacent states (other than the Republic of Ireland, to which [the] Answer referred) and the European Community.

In reply, the Minister of State for Defence Procurement wrote:

It is not our practice to ask other Governments whether they recognise maritime limits around our territory which are in accordance with international law. As already stated, we have no reason to doubt that our claim is recognised by all those referred to in the Question bar the Republic of Ireland.

(Ibid., col. 1666: 27 July 1989)

In the course of a debate on the subject of fishing by Northern Ireland fishermen in the waters near the Isle of Man, the Parliamentary Secretary to the Ministry of Agriculture, Fisheries and Food, Mr David Maclean, stated:

. . . Parliament passed the Territorial Sea Act 1987 which extended the breadth of territorial waters adjacent to the United Kingdom from three to 12 miles. The provision to do the same for the Isle of Man and the Channel Islands was not implemented immediately.

Implementation is not a simple matter because it may involve transferring jurisdiction over rights on the exploitation of the sea bed or of other marine resources and the ability to try criminal acts within 12 miles of the shore. Implementation has therefore been the subject of discussion between the Isle of Man, the Home Office and Government Departments with an interest in, for example, oil, coal and mineral extraction. We have also discussed fisheries. The right hon. Gentleman will appreciate that fisheries are a special issue. We are dealing basically with a hunting industry catching migrating natural resources. We are dealing with important traditional rights in fishing grounds from which some United Kingdom communities, including those in County Down, take some or all of their catches. We are dealing with obligations to Irish, French and Belgian fishermen who have traditionally fished these waters as well. We are also dealing with ensuring that any measures are compatible with the common fisheries policy—with all our Community obligations, the need to manage fisheries and the need to manage them in a non-discriminatory manner.

Officials have therefore explored whether, if the territorial sea is extended to 12 miles around the Isle of Man, the essential features I have just outlined, can be safeguarded.

(HC Debs., vol. 163, col. 1133: 13 December 1989)

Part Nine: III. *Seas, waterways. ships—internal waters, including ports*

(See Part Nine: I. A. (Orders in Council made on 1 November and 19 December 1989), above)

In reply to the question what steps were Her Majesty's Government taking to ensure that the memorandum of understanding on port State control was strictly enforced to a uniform and high level throughout the EC, the Parliamentary Under-Secretary of State, Department of Transport, wrote:

Each signatory country of the memorandum of understanding (MOU) should achieve an annual total of inspections corresponding to 25 per cent. of the estimated number of individual foreign merchant ships which enter its ports during a 12-month period. The United Kingdom has always exceeded the 25 per cent. figure of inspection of foreign flag vessels since the memorandum became operational. United Kingdom representatives have always endorsed the efforts of the secretariat of the port state control committee to encourage signatories of the memorandum, which include all littoral EEC countries, to achieve the 25 per cent. inspection rate.

(HC Debs., vol. 159, Written Answers, col. *94*: 30 October 1989)

Part Nine: IV. *Sea, waterways, ships—straits*

The Air Navigation (Second Amendment) Order 1987 (Statutory Instruments 1987, No. 2062), which came into force from 1 January 1988, provides, *inter alia*, for the insertion into the Air Navigation Order (Statutory Instruments 1985, No. 1643) of the following Article 91A:

Aircraft in transit over certain United Kingdom territorial waters

91A.—(1) Where an aircraft, not being an aircraft registered in the United Kingdom, is flying over the territorial waters adjacent to the United Kingdom within part of a strait referred to in paragraph (4) of this article solely for the purpose of continuous and expeditious transit of the strait, only the following articles of and Schedules to this Order shall apply to that aircraft:—

article 14 and Schedule 6, to the extent necessary for the monitoring of the appropriate distress radio frequency, article 64(1)(a), (b) and (e), article 64(2), (3) and (4), together with the regulations made thereunder, article 94 and Part A of Schedule 13.

(2) The powers conferred by the provisions referred to in paragraph (1) of this article shall not be exercised in a way which would hamper the transit of the strait by an aircraft not registered in the United Kingdom, but without prejudice to action needed to secure the safety of aircraft.

(3) In this article 'transit of the strait' means overflight of the strait from an area of high seas at one end of the strait to an area of high seas at the other end, or flight to or from an area of high seas over some part of the strait for the purpose of entering, leaving or returning from a State bordering the strait and 'an area of high seas' means any area outside the territorial waters of any State.

(4) The parts of the straits to which this article applies are specified in Schedule 14 to this Order.

Schedule 14 reads as follows:

SCHEDULE 14   Article 91A(4)

PARTS OF STRAITS SPECIFIED IN CONNECTION WITH THE FLIGHT OF AIRCRAFT IN TRANSIT OVER UNITED KINGDOM TERRITORIAL WATERS

(1) The following parts of the straits named hereafter are hereby specified for the purposes of article 91A(4) of this Order–

(a) In the Straits of Dover, the territorial waters adjacent to the United Kingdom which are (i) to the south of a rhumb line joining position 51°08′23″ north latitude: 1°23′00″ east longitude and position 51°22′41″ north latitude: 1°50′06″ east longitude, and (ii) to the east of a rhumb line joining position 50°54′33″ north latitude: 0°58′05″ east longitude and position 50°43′15″ north latitude: 0°51′39″ east longitude;

(b) In the North Channel, the territorial waters adjacent to the United Kingdom which are (i) to the north of a rhumb line joining position 54°13′30″
north latitude: 5°39′28″ west longitude and position 54°09′02″ north latitude: 5°18′07″ west longitude, (ii) to the west of a rhumb line joining
position 54°26′02″ north latitude: 4°51′37″ west longitude and position
54°38′01″ north latitude: 4°51′16″ west longitude, and (iii) to the east of
(a) a rhumb line joining position 55°40′24″ north latitude: 6°30′59″ west
longitude and position 55°29′24″ north latitude: 6°40′31″ west longitude
or (b) a rhumb line joining position 55°24′54″ north latitude: 6°44′33″
west longitude and position 55°10′15″ north latitude: 6°44′33″ west longitude;

(c) In the Fair Isle Channel, the territorial waters adjacent to the United
Kingdom which are (i) to the north of a rhumb line joining position
59°10′54″ north latitude: 2°01′32″ west longitude and position 59°33′27″
north latitude: 2°38′35″ west longitude, and (ii) to the south of a rhumb
line joining position 59°51′06″ north latitude: 0°52′10″ west longitude
and position 59°51′06″ north latitude: 1°46′36″ west longitude.".

(2) The parts of each of the Straits specified in paragraph (1) are shown hatched
on Charts A, B and C respectively.

Part Nine: VIII. *Seas, waterways, ships—continental shelf*

In moving the second reading of the Petroleum Royalties (Relief) and
Continental Shelf Bill in the House of Lords, the Parliamentary Under-
Secretary of State, Department of Energy, Baroness Hooper, stated:

I turn now to the second purpose of this Bill, which is to enable the United
Kingdom to implement the agreement which has recently been negotiated with the
Irish Republic on the delimitation of the continental shelf. This is dealt with in
Clause 3.

It is very much to be welcomed that it has proved possible to resolve issues concerning conflicting claims to the continental shelf which have been outstanding for
25 years. The Republic of Ireland has agreed to give up some of its original claim
and so have we . . . Agreeing boundaries will open up new opportunities for the oil
industry and, potentially, for the offshore supplies industry.

The short clause is needed because, without it, the Government do not have the
power to de-designate areas that have once been designated. The clause makes it
clear that the power it confers can only be used to implement this particular agreement with the Irish Republic. I can assure noble Lords that there is no possibility
of its being used in any other context.

(HL Debs., vol. 503, col. 179: 17 January 1989)

In moving the second reading of the Continental Shelf Bill in the House
of Lords, the Minister of State for Defence Procurement, Lord Trefgarne,
stated:

As your Lordships will recall, Section 3 of the Petroleum Royalties (Relief) and
Continental Shelf Act 1989 was debated in this House in January. The purpose of
Section 3 was to implement the recent agreement with the Republic of Ireland on

the delimitation of the Continental Shelf. It gave power to amend by Order in Council the Continental Shelf (Designation of Additional Areas) Order 1974, to the extent necessary to give effect to the agreement. As a result of an unfortunate oversight, power was not taken in Section 3 to amend the Continental Shelf (Designation of Additional Areas) Order 1971. Line B, agreed with the Irish, runs through the area designated by that order of 1971 as its south western corner. This was not noticed until after Royal Assent when a large scale map was prepared during the drafting of the order to be made under Section 3. There is therefore no alternative to a further Bill.

The House has already approved the policy of implementing the agreement with the Republic of Ireland. However, the wording of Section 3 does not achieve the legislative purpose. It is slightly too narrow. The purpose of the Bill is simply to amend Section 3, so as to take power to modify the order of 1971. This would allow the agreement to be implemented.

(HL Debs., vol. 510, cols. 1041–2: 21 July 1989)

On 19 December 1989, the Continental Shelf (Designation of Areas) Order 1989 (Statutory Instruments 1989 No. 2398) was made. The Order, made in exercise of powers conferred on the Crown by s. 1(7) of the Continental Shelf Act 1964 and s. 3 of the Petroleum Royalties (Relief) and Continental Shelf Act 1989 'and of all other powers enabling Her in that behalf' was accompanied by an explanatory note, not part of the Order, which reads as follows:

This Order:
  (a) designates further areas of the continental shelf in the Irish Sea, in the South-Western Approaches and to the west of Scotland, up to Lines A and B defined in the Agreement between the United Kingdom and the Republic of Ireland signed on 7th November 1988, as areas in which the rights of the United Kingdom with respect to the sea bed and subsoil and their natural resources are exercised; and
  (b) amends the Continental Shelf (Designation of Additional Areas) Orders 1971 and 1974 by omitting therefrom certain areas situated on the Irish side of Line B,
thereby giving effect to that Agreement.

Part Nine: IX. *Seas, waterways, ships—exclusive fishery zone*

(See also Part Nine: I. A. (Admiralty Notice of 1 January 1990), above)

In reply to a question, the Parliamentary Under-Secretary of State, Foreign and Commonwealth Office, wrote:

Conservation in the waters around South Georgia is covered by the convention for the conservation of Antarctic marine living resources (CCAMLR). Under pressure from the United Kingdom and others CCAMLR recently banned all fishing around South Georgia for mackerel ice fish (the primary endangered species) until November 1989.

(HC Debs., vol. 145, Written Answers, col. *12*: 16 January 1989)

Part Nine: XIV. *Seas, waterways, ships—international regime of the sea in general*

In the course of a speech in the UN General Assembly on 28 November 1989, the representative of France, on behalf of the Twelve Member States of the European Community, stated:

The States members of the European Community note with great satisfaction that at the summer session of the Preparatory Commission of the International Sea-Bed Authority and the International Tribunal for the Law of the Sea many States recognized the need for a universally acceptable United Nations Convention on the Law of the Sea. We are indeed convinced of the importance and value of that Convention, which was adopted in 1982 and has done so much towards maintenance of a legal order to regulate the seas and oceans. This importance can be increased only by universal acceptance of the Convention and by its entry into force, with the support of all States.

(A/44/PV. 62, pp. 29–30)

Part Nine: XV. A. 3. *Seas, waterways, ships—ships—legal status—warships*

On 22 September 1989 an Exchange of Notes took place between the UK Ambassador in South Africa and the South African Foreign Minister concerning the regulation of the terms of settlement of the salvaging of the wreck of *HMS Birkenhead*. The background to the Exchange of Notes was explained in a document issued by the Foreign and Commonwealth Office as follows:

HMS Birkenhead was a Royal Naval troop ship which sank off the Cape Colony in February 1852 with the loss of 445 lives. Over the years, there have been several unsuccessful attempts by South African marine archeologists to salvage the vessel, which was reputed to have been carrying 240,000 gold sovereigns.

Recent advances in diving technology now allow easier access to this and other wrecks around the world. We have therefore agreed with the South African authorities practical arrangements allowing the South Africans to continue salvage operations without prejudice to our legal position regarding ownership of the wreck. The Agreement, the first of its kind, also safeguards the wreck's status as a military grave. We hope that it will form the basis of any future agreements the UK may seek to conclude with other countries to protect wrecks of other Royal Naval vessels.

The interests of the regiments whose men were on the ship will be safeguarded as will the sanctity of any human remains remaining in or near the vessel.

The South African Government's arrangement with the salvors provides for a 50/50 division of artefacts after payment of the salvors. This means that HMG would receive 25% of any large gold finds: we would not expect 100% in view of the need to pay the salvors.

The text of the UK letter, which was acknowledged in identical terms by the South African letter, reads as follows:

I have the honour to refer to recent discussions between our two Governments about the question of the wreck of the Birkenhead and to propose a settlement of all outstanding issues in the following terms:

The wreck of the Birkenhead shall, as a military grave, continue to be treated at all stages with respect. In particular, the South African Government shall seek to ensure that the salvors treat reverently and refrain from disturbing or bringing to the surface any human remains which may be discovered at the site of the wreck or in its vicinity. British military historians shall have temporary access for research purposes to salvaged artefacts designated for South African museums.

The South African Government shall as far as possible ensure that representative examples of salvaged artefacts identifiable with a particular British regiment or institution are offered without charge to that regiment (or its successor) or to such institution.

The British Government shall not enter into any salvage contract in respect of the Birkenhead and shall not object to the South African Government maintaining its existing salvage arrangements in regard to the wreck under the applicable South African legislation.

If any gold coin (apart from the coins considered to have been in private ownership) were to be recovered, such coin (after deduction of the share due to the salvors in accordance with the existing salvage arrangements) would be shared equally between our two Governments.

In order to facilitate the implementation of these arrangements, consultations shall be held as necessary between representatives of our two Governments, the salvors and other South African institutions concerned.

This settlement is without prejudice to the respective legal positions of our two Governments.

If the above is acceptable to the Government of the Republic of South Africa, I have the honour to propose that this letter and Your Excellency's reply to that effect shall constitute an agreement between our two Governments in this matter which shall enter into force on the date of Your Excellency's reply.

(TS No. 3 (1990); Cm. 906)

In a Press Release issued on the same day containing the above letters and background document, the Foreign and Commonwealth Office stated:

The Agreement reflects HMG's position that the Crown maintains rights and interests in ships of the Royal Navy which have sunk, wherever they may be and without time limit.

(Foreign and Commonwealth Office Press Release No. 131)

Part Nine: XV. B. *Seas, waterways, ships—ships—nationality*

In moving the approval in the House of Commons of the draft Merchant Shipping Act 1988 (Amendment) Order 1989, the Minister for Aviation and Shipping, Mr Patrick McLoughlin, stated:

The order gives effect to an interim order of the president of the European Court of Justice made on 10 October 1989. The interim order by the court requires the United Kingdom to suspend, until judgment in the main proceedings, the application of the British nationality requirements for registration of certain fishing vessels set out in section 14(1), (2) and (7) of the Merchant Shipping Act 1988. The affected fishing vessels are those that were fishing under the British flag up to 31 March 1989 with a licence granted under the Sea Fish (Conservation) Act 1967.

The court order is in restricted terms. It requires the United Kingdom to suspend the application of the British nationality requirements as a condition for the registration of fishing vessels as British fishing vessels to the extent that, at present, the owners, charterers, managers and operators of such vessels must either be British nationals, or in the case of a company, have at least 75 per cent. of its shares legally and beneficially owned by British nationals and at least 75 per cent. of its directors as British nationals.

The benefit of the court order is restricted to nationals of the European Community. It does not affect the requirement that such persons must be resident and domiciled in the United Kingdom. Moreover, it does not affect the requirement that the vessels should be managed and their operations directed and controlled from within the United Kingdom. We do not know how many additional fishing vessels will now become eligible for registration on the United Kingdom fishing vessel register. That will depend on how many have been ineligible for registration by reason only of the nationality requirements that are changed by the order.

It might help if I fill in some of the background here. Part II of the Merchant Shipping Act 1988 introduced a new register of British fishing vessels. The main intention of this register was to restrict sea fishing rights so that the fishing quotas granted to the United Kingdom under the common fisheries policy benefited the genuine United Kingdom fishing fleet and the British communities dependent upon fishing. There were at the time a large number of fishing vessels that were fishing against the United Kingdom quotas, operating largely out of Spanish ports, and which had only a nominal British connection.

The fishing vessel register came into full effect on 1 April 1989, but vessels could transfer to it from old registers on or after 1 December 1988. Since then the overwhelming proportion of the United Kingdom fishing fleet, numbering over 10,000 vessels, has been registered in circumstances where my right hon. Friend the Secretary of State has been satisfied that they comply with the requirements of the Act. One hundred and twenty one have been refused registration primarily because they have not been able to demonstrate that beneficial ownership is British or that the vessels are managed, directed and controlled from the United Kingdom.

In the meantime the European Commission on 10 August 1989 instituted an action under article 169 of the EEC treaty alleging that the United Kingdom had, in its imposition of the nationality requirement in sections 13 and 14 of the 1988 Act, failed to fulfil its obligations under the EEC Treaty. The United Kingdom is defending these proceedings.

The Commission also brought an application for interim measures under article 186 of the treaty asking the court 'to order the United Kingdom to suspend, as regards nationals of the other Member States, the nationality requirements enshrined in sections 13 and 14 of the Merchant Shipping Act'.

Judgment in respect of that application was delivered on 10 October and the order concerns that judgment alone. My hon. and learned Friend the Solicitor-General robustly argued the case for the United Kingdom on the grounds that among other things, interim relief ought not to be ordered where the Commission's case on the incompatibility of the nationality conditions with Community law was weak. In particular, he argued that a state has the right and duty under international law to prevent the abuse of its flag and to lay down the conditions for registration of ships that will fly its flag. He further submitted that the nationality requirements at issue were both consistent with international law and necessary to uphold the system of national quotas under the common fisheries policy, which are based on nationality.

The House will remember that the common fisheries policy was negotiated in minute detail by Ministers from each member state in a whole series of monthly meetings in Brussels when this system was set up in 1982–83. However, the court accepted the Commission's view that there was a prima facie case against the United Kingdom on the nationality issue and also that in the meantime certain 'quota hoppers', particularly Spanish vessels that had hitherto fished against United Kingdom quotas, were suffering loss. The court, therefore, made its interim order to limit the loss of these fishermen pending the outcome of the main action—provided that they were able to satisfy the other conditions for registration to which I have already referred.

(HC Debs., vol. 158, cols. 997–8: 25 October 1989; see also HL Debs., vol. 511, cols. 1448–51, 1462–4: 25 October 1989)

Part Nine: XV. D. *Seas, waterways, ships—ships—jurisdiction*

In introducing a debate on the subject of the draft Merchant Shipping (Safety at Work Regulations) (Non-UK Ships) Regulations 1988, the Minister for Public Transport, Mr Michael Portillo, stated:

> The purpose of the regulations is to extend to foreign ships when in United Kingdom ports the following 1988 merchant shipping regulations: the Merchant Shipping (Means of Access) Regulations 1988—S.I. 1988 No. 1637; the Merchant Shipping (Safe Movement on Board Ship) Regulations 1988—S.I. 1988 No. 1641; the Merchant Shipping (Guarding of Machinery and Safety of Electrical Equipment) Regulations—S.I. 1988 No. 1636; the Merchant Shipping (Entry into Dangerous Spaces) Regulations 1988—S.I. No. 1638 and the Merchant Shipping (Hatches and Lifting Plant) Regulations 1988—S.I. 1988 No. 1639.
>
> Those five sets of regulations laid before Parliament on 30 September 1988 already allow some action to be taken against foreign ships, including their detention, to ensure the safety of those working on board. However, they do not provide for the prosecution of foreign employers and masters in respect of breaches of those regulations. That is because the particular International Labour Organisation Convention 147 which those regulations implement does not provide for this measure. The regulations that we are debating today rectify this omission, thereby ensuring even-handed treatment of all ships, whether British or foreign, in UK ports by invoking the power available under section 21(1)(c) of the Merchant Shipping Act 1979, which allows for the regulation of foreign ships whether provided for by conventions or not.
>
> The purpose of all the 1988 safety at work regulations is, together with the 1988 docks regulations which were laid before Parliament on 20 October, to replace the existing 1934 docks regulations with ones giving recognition to the technological changes which have taken place since those early days. The need for improved and modern dock regulations was acknowledged internationally by the International

Labour Organisation in its convention concerning occupational safety and health in dock work, convention 152, adopted at the ILO conference on 25 June 1979. It replaced the earlier Protection against Accidents (Dockers) Convention 32 of 1932. Our merchant shipping safety at work regulations, together with the docks regulations, will in due course enable ratification by the UK of ILO Convention 152.

By mirroring closely, where appropriate, the provisions of the 1988 docks regulations, the merchant shipping regulations allow the transition from the domain of one set of regulations to another to be achieved as smoothly as possible. The 1988 docks regulations made under the Health and Safety at Work etc. Act 1974 also provide for the prosecution of masters of foreign ships, as did the 1934 regulations. Not all the requirements of the five sets of merchant shipping regulations will apply in full to foreign ships. The exceptions are, however, minor and are made simply because no provision is made for those particular requirements in ILO Convention 152.

We believe that it is important, if there is to be confidence in the safe operation of ships in UK ports, that we seek to ensure that those ships comply with long-recognised international standards.

(HC Sixth Standing Committee on Statutory Instruments, etc.: 15 December 1988, cols. 3–4)

In reply to a question, the Minister for Public Transport wrote:

Under the international convention for the prevention of pollution from ships 1973, and its protocol, no oil or oily mixtures may be discarded within prescribed distances from land; and ships are required to be so designed, equipped and operated that when a discharge is permitted the oil content has to be kept to the minimum specified. We have taken a number of positive measures to enforce the convention. Ships in the United Kingdom port are inspected to check that their pollution prevention equipment and operational practices are satisfactory. Reception facilities are made available to receive oil residues retained on board. At sea, as from April last year surveillance aircraft have been employed by the United Kingdom to undertake regular patrols over the shipping lanes around the United Kingdom to detect and deter ships discharging oil in contravention of the convention.

(HC Debs., vol. 146, Written Answers, col. 363: 2 February 1989)

In moving the consideration by the HC Fourth Standing Committee on Statutory Instruments of the draft Merchant Shipping (Weighing of Goods Vehicles and Other Cargo) (Application to Non-UK Ships) Regulations 1989, the Minister for Public Transport, Mr Michael Portillo, stated in part:

The regulations would extend to foreign ships when in UK ports, provisions similar to regulations that are already in force for UK ships. The regulations for UK ships are the Merchant Shipping (Loading and Stability Assessment of Ro/Ro Passenger Ships) Regulations 1989, SI 1989 No. 100 which came into force on 20 February 1989, and the Merchant Shipping (Weighing of Goods Vehicles and Other Cargo) Regulations 1988, SI 1988, No. 1275 which came into force on 1 February 1989. The draft regulations before us today are required to be made by affirmative procedure. The requirement of the enabling legislation is that orders applying to foreign ships must be made by affirmative procedure unless the requirement is the subject of international agreement.

. . .

The regulations before us apply to all non-UK ships, so it does not matter whether they happen to be flags of convenience or any other flag.

. . . European countries are parties to the Paris memorandum on port state control, which calls for a system of inspection of ships in the ports of each signatory state to ensure compliance with several safety and pollution conventions. Naturally, we can detain vessels that fail to comply.

(HC Fourth Standing Committee on Statutory Instruments, etc., 22 March 1989, cols. 3, 13–14, *passim*)

On 20 February 1989, an Exchange of Notes between the UK Government and the Government of Vanuatu concerning the use of British controlled ships registered in Vanuatu entered into force (TS No. 48 (1989); Cm. 814). On 17 March 1989, an Exchange of Notes between the UK Government and the Government of Liberia concerning the use of United Kingdom controlled ships registered in Liberia entered into force (TS No. 39 (1989); Cm. 788). The texts of the agreements were substantially similar. The material part of the agreement with Liberia reads as follows:

The Minister responsible for merchant shipping in the Republic of Liberia, shall whenever requested by the Government of the United Kingdom of Great Britain and Northern Ireland, waive the exercise of the sovereign authority of Liberia over a Liberian vessel where the following circumstances exist:
(a) The vessel is owned directly or indirectly by a person who is:
    (i) A British citizen, a British Dependent Territories citizen, a British National (Overseas), a British Overseas citizen, or a British subject under the British Nationality Act 1981; or
    (ii) A body incorporated or constituted under the law of any part of the United Kingdom or of any Territory for the international relations of which the United Kingdom is responsible; and
(b) The property in the vessel is divided into shares whereof the greater parts are owned by persons described by sub-paragraph (a) above; and
(c) There exists a state of war or other hostilities involving the United Kingdom or the threat of such war or other hostilities; and
(d) There is in force in respect of the vessel a contract of commitment between the owner of the vessel and the competent authorities of the United Kingdom which has been approved by the Government of Liberia in accordance with the applicable Liberian legislation.
The Government of the Republic of Liberia in waiving its sovereign authority shall allow the control of such a vessel to be committed to the Government of the United Kingdom in the circumstances mentioned aforesaid. In the event that any of the circumstances referred to in sub-paragraphs (a), (b), (c) or (d) no longer exists in relation to a vessel, this agreement shall cease to apply to that vessel.
It is further understood and agreed between the two Governments that no Liberian flag vessel will be accepted as entered in a war risks association under such

contract of commitment unless the contract in question has first been approved in writing as required by the Liberian Maritime Regulations.

The background to the agreements was explained in a letter sent to the Clerk of the HC Defence Committee by the Private Secretary to the Secretary of State for Defence. This read in part:

HMG and the governments of three 'open register' countries (Bahamas, Liberia and Vanuatu) have entered into agreements under which those countries have undertaken not to attempt to prevent British beneficially owned ships on their registers from being made available to HMG in the event of hostilities involving the UK. DTp and the FCO are currently reviewing which other 'open register' countries could reasonably be approached.

Final arrangements are being made for a 'Contract of Commitment' between British owners with ships on these registers and HMG under which the ship owner undertakes to make the ship available in the event of hostilities, and in return HMG undertakes to provide reinsurance against Queen's Enemy Risks through one of the British Mutual War Risks Associations. This method had been adopted because Liberia has insisted on the prior agreement of shipowners to their ships being requisitioned. Approaches will be made initially to UK owners, followed where practicable by owners resident in dependent territories, the majority of which are in Hong Kong.

Until such time as owners have been approached and have agreed, or not as the case may be, to sign these Contracts of Commitment it is not possible to assess accurately the numbers and types of ships likely to be available.

(*Parliamentary Papers*, 1988–89, HC, Paper 495, p. 8)

Part Nine: XVI. *Seas, waterways, ships—marine scientific research*

The following passage was included in a communication dated 20 May 1988 from the UK Permanent Mission to the UN in New York to the UN Office for Ocean Affairs and the Law of the Sea:

2. In order to comply with Government Regulations, applications to carry out marine scientific research within the territorial sea, the 200 mile fishery zone or on the continental shelf of the United Kingdom should be submitted through diplomatic channels to the Maritime, Aviation and Environment Department of the Foreign and Commonwealth Office at least three months prior to the commencement of the research cruise. The application should include details of the vessel and the dates and nature of the proposed research using a standard application form [not reproduced].

3. Conditions, other than the basic requirement to provide details of the results of a cruise within 12 months and to invite the participation of a British observer, are only placed on any proposed research cruise in order to take care of practical circumstances (e.g. bottom trawling equipment should not be used in the vicinity of fixed gear or within a mile of cables on the seabed). Copies of cruise reports should be sent to the Foreign and Commonwealth Office within 12 months of the completion of the cruise (or an explanation of the delay given within that period).

(*The Law of the Sea: National Legislation, Regulations and Supplementary*

Documents on Marine Scientific Research in Areas under National Jurisdiction,
UN Office for Ocean Affairs and the Law of the Sea, 1989, p. 270)

Part Ten: III. *Air space, outer space—outer space*
   (See Part Six: II. C., above)

Part Eleven: II. A. 1. *Responsibility—responsible entities—States—*
elements of responsibility

   In reply to a question on the subject of compensation for economic
damage done to upland farming by the radioactive fall-out from the Chernobyl accident, the Secretary of State for Foreign and Commonwealth
Affairs wrote in part:

   The position with regard to compensation remains as stated in the reply . . . of
21 July 1989 . . .
   (HC Debs., vol. 158, Written Answers, col. *293*: 23 October 1989; see UKMIL
1986, p. 600)

   In reply to the question 'whether the Australian Government have
sought any financial compensation from the United Kingdom to offset payments they agreed to make, on 4 September, to Australian service men con-
taminated by radioactive fallout from United Kingdom nuclear weapons
tested in Australia in the 1950s', the Minster of State for the Armed Forces
wrote:

   We have not received any such request from the Australian Federal Government, nor would we expect to do so.
   (HC Debs., vol. 159, Written Answers, col. *376*: 3 November 1989)

Part Eleven: II. A. 2. *Responsibility—responsible entities—States—*
executive acts

   (See also Part Six: IV. C. (item of 16 October 1989), above)

   In reply to a question on the subject of the death outside the Libyan
Mission in London in 1984 of Woman Police Constable Fletcher, the
Minister of State, Foreign and Commonwealth Office, wrote:

   We continue to take every opportunity to remind the Libyans of our claim for
compensation for the life and career of WPC Fletcher.
   (HC Debs., vol. 154, Written Answers, col. *473*: 14 June 1989)

   In reply to a question, the Minister of State, Foreign and Commonwealth Office, wrote:

. . . the Minister of State spoke to the Iraqi Ambassador on Wednesday 14th June
to express our concern at allegations of an Iraqi policy of mass deportations of
Kurds from Qala Diza and other settlements in north Iraq. The ambassador
responded that some localised resettlement was taking place on security and humanitarian grounds. We continue to press the Iraqis to allow foreign diplomats and
journalists access to the areas in question to see for themselves what the truth is.

On the evidence available to us we do not believe that these actions constitute genocide as defined under the Convention on the Prevention and Punishment of the Crime of Genocide.

(HL Debs., vol. 509, col. 727: 27 June 1989)

Part Eleven: II. A. 6. *Responsibility—responsible entities—States—reparation*

In reply to a question on the subject of compensation paid to former prisoners of war in Japanese captivity, the Parliamentary Under-Secretary of State, Foreign and Commonwealth Office, wrote:

. . . The question of compensation was dealt with in the 1951 treaty of peace with Japan. The total sum made available to the United Kingdom for compensation was £4,816,473, including £174,871 contributed by the Thai Government for work done on the Burma-Siam railway.

(HC Debs., vol. 145, Written Answers, col. *661*: 26 January 1989; see also item of 25 October 1989, below)

On 22 March 1989, the Governments of the UK and Ghana signed an Agreement for the Promotion and Protection of Investments. The Agreement includes the following Articles:

Article 7

Expropriation

(1) Investments of nationals or companies of either Contracting Party shall not be nationalised, expropriated or subjected to measures having effect equivalent to nationalisation or expropriation (hereinafter referred to as 'expropriation') in the territory of the other Contracting Party, except where for a public purpose related to its internal needs, a Contracting Party expropriates the investments of nationals or companies of the other Contracting Party, the following conditions shall be complied with:
  (a) The measures shall be accompanied by provision for the payment of compensation amounting to the full and genuine value of the investment expropriated immediately before the expropriation or before the impending expropriation became public knowledge whichever is the earlier.
  (b) The compensation shall be effectively realizable and freely transferable.
  (c) The compensation shall be paid without undue delay. If the compensation is not paid within six months, it shall after that date attract interest at the normal commercial rate until the date of payment.

(2) A national or company affected shall have a right, under the law of the Contracting Party making the expropriation, to prompt review, by a judicial or other independent authority of that Party, of his or its investment in accordance with the principles set out in paragraph (1) of this Article.

(3) Where a Contracting Party expropriates the assets of a company which is incorporated or constituted under the law in force in any part of its own territory, and in which nationals or companies of the other Contracting Party own shares, the provisions of paragraphs (1) and (2) of this Article shall apply.

ARTICLE 8

Repatriation of Investment and Returns

Each Contracting Party shall, in respect of investments, guarantee to nationals or companies of the other Contracting Party the unrestricted transfer to the country where they reside of their investments and returns. Transfers of currency shall be effected without undue delay in the convertible currency in which the capital was originally invested or in any other convertible currency agreed by the investor and the Contracting Party concerned. Unless otherwise agreed by the investor, transfers shall be made at the rate of exchange applicable on the date of transfer pursuant to the exchange regulations in force.

(Cm. 811)

On 27 October 1989, the Governments of the UK and Guyana signed an Agreement for the Promotion and Protection of Investments. The Agreement includes the following Articles:

ARTICLE 5

Expropriation

(1) Investments of nationals or companies of either Contracting Party shall not be nationalised, expropriated or subjected to measures having effect equivalent to nationalisation or expropriation (hereinafter referred to as 'expropriation') in the territory of the other Contracting Party except for a public purpose related to the internal needs of that Party on a non-discriminatory basis and against prompt, adequate and effective compensation. Such compensation shall be equivalent to the genuine value of the investment expropriated immediately before the expropriation or at the time the proposed expropriation became public knowledge, whichever is the earlier, shall include interest at a normal commercial rate until the date of payment, shall be made without delay, be effectively realisable and be freely transferable. The national or company affected shall have a right, under the law of the Contracting Party making the expropriation, to prompt review, by a judicial or other independent authority of that Party, of his or its case and of the valuation of his or its investment in accordance with the principles set out in this paragraph.
(2) Where a Contracting Party expropriates the assets of a company which is incorporated or constituted under the law of any part of its own territory, and in which nationals or companies of the other Contracting Party own shares, it shall ensure that the provisions of paragraph (1) of this Article are applied to the extent necessary to guarantee prompt, adequate and effective compensation in respect of their investment to such nationals or companies of the other Contracting Party who are owners of those shares.

ARTICLE 6

Repatriation of Investment and Returns

(1) Each Contracting Party shall in respect of investments guarantee to nationals or companies of the other Contracting Party the unrestricted transfer of their investments as well as any returns which are yielded after the entry into force of this Agreement.
(2) Transfers shall be effected without delay in the convertible currency in which

the capital was originally invested or in any other convertible currency agreed by the investor and the Contracting Party concerned. Unless otherwise agreed by the investor transfers shall be made at the rate of exchange applicable on the date of transfer pursuant to the exchange regulations in force.

(Cm. 909)

Following discussions between the delegations of the British and Argentine Governments held in Madrid, a joint statement was issued on 19 October 1989 which read in part:

Each Government undertook not to pursue any claim against the other, including nationals of the other, in respect of loss or damage arising from the hostilities and all other actions in and around the Falkland Islands, South Georgia and the South Sandwich Islands before 1989.

(Text provided by the Foreign and Commonwealth Office)

In reply to the question whether further representations would be made to the Egyptian Government regarding its failure to return to Mr Douglas Forsyth control and possession of his villa in Egypt, the Parliamentary Under-Secretary of State, Foreign and Commonwealth Office, replied:

No. Mr. Forsyth's father accepted compensation from funds provided by Egypt under the 1959 agreement for the presence of a sitting tenant when the villa was handed back.

(HC Debs., vol. 158, col. 835: 25 October 1989; see also UKMIL 1985, pp. 508–9)

In reply to the question whether reconsideration would be given to the claims of ex-prisoners of war involved in building the Siam to Burma railway in 1941, the Parliamentary Under-Secretary of State, Foreign and Commonwealth Office, wrote:

No. The question of compensation for the suffering and damage caused by Japan during the war was dealt with in the 1951 treaty of peace with Japan. While recognising the very great debt owed by this country to those who fought against the Japanese, there are no grounds to reopen the issue now.

(HC Debs., vol. 158, Written Answers, col. *491*: 25 October 1989)

Part Eleven: II. A. 7. (a). (i). *Responsibility—responsible entities— States—procedure—diplomatic and consular protection—nationality of claims*

On 22 March 1989, the Governments of the UK and Ghana signed an Agreement for the Promotion and Protection of Investments. Article 1 of the Agreement reads in part:

(c) 'nationals' means:
　　(i) in respect of the Republic of Ghana: physical persons deriving their status as Ghanian nationals from the law in force in the Republic of Ghana;
　　(ii) in respect of the United Kingdom: physical persons deriving their

status as United Kingdom nationals from the law in force in the United Kingdom;
(d) 'companies' means:
   (i) in respect of the Republic of Ghana: any corporations, firms and associations incorporated or constituted under the law in force in the Republic of Ghana;
   (ii) in respect of the United Kingdom: corporations, firms and associations incorporated or constituted under the law in force in any part of the United Kingdom . . .

(Cm. 811; see also Cm. 909 (Agreement for the Promotion and Protection of Investments signed on 27 October 1989 between the Governments of the UK and Guyana))

Part Eleven: II. A. 7. (b). *Responsibility—responsible entities—States— procedure—peaceful settlement*

In reply to a succession of questions, the Minister of State, Foreign and Commonwealth Office, wrote:

The Foreign Compensation Order 1987 (1987/2201) was laid before Parliament subject to negative procedure. It was made on 18th December 1987, laid before Parliament on 8th January 1988 and came into force on 1st March 1988.

. . .

We received the sum of £23,468,008 from the People's Republic of China and agreed to pay to the People's Republic of China the sum of US$3,800,000. Those sums were received and paid in two equal instalments on 5th August 1987 and 5th August 1988 respectively. At the end of September the amount held in the China Fund was £23,127,134.70. We have agreed to waive our own claims so that all the money in the China Fund will be available for distribution to private claimants.

The agreements between the United Kingdom and the People's Republic of China signed in Beijing on 5th June 1987 mutually settled all claims arising before 1st January 1980, including claims in respect of property as well as bonds. No sums are still owed to the United Kingdom by China in respect of claims arising before 1st January 1980.

. . .

The deadline for the submission of bond claims was 30th June 1988.

A total of 1941 ordinary bond claims were received by the Foreign Compensation Commission, with an estimated face value of £13 million. One thousand, seven hundred and seventeen of these claims have been determined, 127 rejected and 97 remain to be determined. An interim dividend of 5 per cent. of the value assigned by the commission to a bond was paid earlier this year to 1591 bond claimants. The amount paid was £425,723.99 on bonds with a face value of £8,514,480.

In addition to bond claims, 995 property claims were received by the Foreign Compensation Commission. It is anticipated that final payments will be made to all successful claimants in the autumn of next year.

The Foreign Compensation Commission calculates the amount of a final payment when all claims including property claims against the China Compensation Fund have been determined. It is only then that the commission is able to make an assessment of the amount payable in relation to the amount of each claim and the funds available for distribution. The percentage payment in respect of sterling bonds is made on the sterling face value of the bonds.

The administrative expenses of the commission in determining claims against the fund are deducted from the fund. No charges are made by HM Treasury.

(HL Debs., vol. 511, cols. 902–4, *passim*: 18 October 1989; see also UKMIL 1987, pp. 624–7)

In reply to a question on the subject of the implementation of the Foreign Compensation (Union of Soviet Socialist Republics) (Distribution) Order 1987, the Minister of State, Foreign and Commonwealth Office, wrote:

. . . the Secretary of State for Foreign and Commonwealth Affairs has approved interim payments to successful property and bond claimants against the Russian fund of 30 per cent. of the value assigned by the Foreign Compensation Commission to a successful property claim and 20 per cent. of the value assigned by the Commission to a bond. The interim payments will be made on or after 15th December 1989. Successful bond claimants received a first interim payment of 10 per cent. of the value assigned to a bond in November 1987.

As of 17th November 1989, all bond claims but one and 2,123 out of 2,635 property claims made against the Russian Fund had been determined by the Foreign Compensation Commission. It is expected that the final distribution from the fund will be announced during the first half of 1990 and that it may exceed 15 per cent. of the value assigned by the Commission to a property claim or bond. This would result in a total pay-out from the fund of 45 per cent. of the value assigned to a claim.

(HL Debs., vol. 513, col. 233: 23 November 1989)

Part Eleven: II. D. 2. *Responsibility—responsible entities—individuals, including corporations—responsibility of individuals*

In reply to a question, the Secretary of State for the Home Department wrote:

There is no internationally agreed definition of terrorism. For practical purposes we rest on the definition in the Prevention of Terrorism (Temporary Provisions) Act 1984 and in the Prevention of Terrorism (Temporary Provisions) Bill currently before the House.

(HC Debs., vol. 145, Written Answers, col. 775: 27 January 1989)

The Secretary of State for the Home Department, Mr Douglas Hurd, made the following statement in the House of Commons:

. . . I should like to make a statement about the report of the war crimes inquiry.

I set up the inquiry in February 1988 to consider allegations that persons who are now British citizens or resident in the United Kingdom committed war crimes during the second world war and to advise whether the law of the United Kingdom should be amended to enable prosecutions for war crimes to take place in this country.

The report as submitted to me was in two parts. The main report contains the inquiry team's analysis and conclusions. The second part contains detailed material on individual cases. The inquiry team intended that the main report should be published. I am today publishing it in full and without amendment. I also accept the expert view of the inquiry team that publishing the material in the second part about individual cases would risk prejudicing any proceedings which might be instituted. I am sure that the House will see the wisdom of that distinction and understand why I cannot comment on individual cases.

I believe that the House will find the main report a full and impressive document. It takes a broad view of the historical context affecting the territories and peoples of eastern Europe, of the conduct of successive British Governments during and after the last war and of the legal and other issues. The team visited the Soviet Union and interviewed a large number of possible witnesses. I am most grateful to Sir Thomas Hetherington, formerly Director of Public Prosecutions, and Mr William Chalmers, formerly Crown Agent for Scotland, for their authoritative analysis.

The inquiry deals with allegations of horrific killings on a large scale—crimes which would constitute violations of the internationally agreed laws and customs of war. The allegations are not about actions committed in the heat of war. They concern individuals allegedly holding quite senior positions in paramilitary units operating in territories occupied by the German forces, whose task was the systematic murder of civilians.

The inquiry examined in detail seven cases. It concluded in respect of four that there was sufficient evidence to mount a criminal prosecution. One of the individuals concerned has since died. The inquiry went on to recommend that further investigations should take place in respect of the other three cases. In addition, of the nearly 300 further cases drawn to the attention of the inquiry, it recommends further investigation of 75 and that attempts should be made to trace a further 46.

The inquiry recommends that there should be a change in the law to permit the prosecution in this country of acts of murder and manslaughter committed as war crimes in Germany or German-occupied territory during the period of the second world war, by persons who are now British citizens or who are resident in the United Kingdom. Certain procedural changes, including the taking of evidence by live television link from persons outside the United Kingdom, are proposed to facilitate the trial of such cases.

The members of the inquiry were aware of the danger of creating retrospective legislation and have tried to meet that objection. They are addressing actions which they are satisfied constituted at the time clear breaches of international law, and which would constitute offences triable in British courts now, had the persons concerned been British citizens at that stage.

The inquiry reached its recommendation on legislation and prosecution in this country after examining and rejecting other courses of action. In particular, it discussed but did not recommend extradition of the individuals concerned to stand trial in the Soviet Union. It set out in the report the arguments for and against extradition. The Government find the arguments against extradition to the Soviet Union convincing.

The inquiry's recommendations raise important issues of principle and practicality. It can be argued that it is no service to the memory of the victims of these crimes to resurrect, after so many years, the horror of what they endured. One can question what will be achieved by prosecuting old men so long after the events.

The practical difficulties of conducting trials include the age and frailty of witnesses, the problems of assembling the evidence, which is available in the Soviet Union, if at all, in a form in which it can be convincingly presented to a jury in Britain, and the problem of establishing identity and other key elements beyond reasonable doubt when witnesses' memories are more than 40 years old. The report deals with all those matters.

On the other hand it will be argued that, in the words of the report: 'The crimes committed are so monstrous that they cannot be condoned . . . To take no action would taint the United Kingdom with the slur of being a haven for war criminals.' Other countries that have uncovered similar evidence have acted to enable the alleged offenders to be brought to trial, sometimes making broader changes in the law than recommended in this report. Despite the practical problems of conducting a trial, the experienced inquiry team consisting of a former Director of Public Prosecutions and a former Crown Agent, reached the view that there would be sufficient evidence in three cases to mount a prosecution if there were jurisdiction. If and when the time comes for assessing the evidence, the prosecuting authorities of the day will need to make their own assessment of particular cases.

We are impressed by the force of argument that led the inquiry to its clear conclusion that legislation was required, but we want to hear the views of Parliament before taking a final view on the principle of legislation. This is a matter, after all, on which the views of Parliament will be decisive. The Government will provide an opportunity for each House to debate the implications of the report and the action that should be taken in response to it. The debates will take place in the autumn once there has been a proper opportunity to study the report and reflect upon it. In the light of the views expressed in those debates, the Government will take a final decision on whether to bring forward a Bill on the lines proposed by the inquiry.

(HC Debs., vol. 157, cols. 733–4: 24 July 1989)

In response to questions following his statement, the Secretary of State remarked:

. . . the proposal in the inquiry would not make anything criminal which is not now criminal. Instead, it would bring within the jurisdiction of our courts certain allegations of crimes which are not at the moment within their jurisdiction because those concerned did not live here at the time of the crime although they now live here and in some cases are British citizens. That is the scope of the change.

. . . When the hon. Gentleman studies the report, he will see why the inquiry came down in favour of a narrow extension of the law. It was anxious to avoid the accusation of retrospection and, therefore, to confine the scope of any change in the law to allegations of crimes which clearly and beyond any doubt were crimes and were criminal at the time they were committed, and not as a result of any international instruments that may have been entered into since 1945.

(Ibid., cols. 736–7: 24 July 1989)

The Secretary of State for the Home Department, Mr Douglas Hurd, wrote the following letter, dated 1 August 1989, to the Deputy Leader of the Opposition, Mr Roy Hattersley MP:

During the exchanges following my statement on the War Crimes Inquiry last Monday, you asked me to consider the case for general war crimes legislation which would make possible the prosecution of criminals from any war who have taken refuge in Britain.

Obviously the Government will take full account of this suggestion, along with other views on the nature and extent of possible war crimes legislation which may be expressed over the coming months. But a good deal of what you were seeking is achieved already by the Geneva Conventions Act 1957 which gives the British courts jurisdiction over grave breaches of those Conventions, committed anywhere in the world after 31 July 1957. Such 'grave breaches' include wilful killing and torture.

The 1957 Act gave effect to the four Geneva Conventions made under the auspices of the International Red Cross in 1949. (The Conventions are described in detail in paragraphs 5.30 to 5.33 of the Report.) They go wider than the 1907 Hague Conventions—which enshrined the concept of offences against the rules and customs of war, on which the present Inquiry based its proposals—in that they extend to acts committed during the course of civil wars and peaceful annexations. This is to say, they were addressed to some of the offences which Nuremberg defined as crimes against humanity.

Since 1957, therefore, the perpetrators of war crimes (widely defined) have been liable to prosecution in this country. I recognise that this does not meet the whole of your concern. The Inquiry's recommendations were directed narrowly to war crimes committed in Germany or German-occupied territory during the period of the Second World War—so that (if their proposals are accepted as they stand) the British courts would not have jurisdiction over offences committed outside that geographical area during the Second World War, or committed anywhere between 1945 and 1957.

I doubt in practice whether this is a serious gap. It seems unlikely that it would in fact exclude from prosecution anyone who might otherwise have faced charges. My present view is that the 1957 Act provides an adequate war crimes measure: as I said to the House, I believe we should face problems of retrospection if we were to attempt to do more.

(Text provided by the Foreign and Commonwealth Office)

In the course of a debate in the Sixth Committee of the UN General Assembly on the subject of a draft Code of Crimes against the Peace and Security of Mankind prepared by the International Law Commission, the UK representative, Sir Arthur Watts, stated on 1 November 1989:

As regards *war crimes*, we think it is important to include the concept of gravity, and suggest that the solution to this problem, as well as that of a list of crimes, could be assisted by having regard to the important concept of 'grave breaches' as that term is understood in the Geneva Conventions and the 1977 Protocols.

Turning to *crimes against humanity*, my delegation has real doubts about the inclusion of a number of items under this head. Even as regards those crimes whose inclusion in a Code would be generally uncontroversial, such as genocide, important questions of definition remain to be resolved. We are not, for example, convinced that it is desirable to depart, as the draft Code does, from the definition of genocide in the 1948 Convention.

(Text provided by the Foreign and Commonwealth Office; see also A/C.6/44/ SR.29, pp. 12–13)

In moving that the House of Lords took note of the report of the War Crimes Inquiry, the Minister of State, Home Office, Earl Ferrers, stated in part:

We have before us a report by two very eminent people, which says that legislation should be introduced to make it possible for some people, who are at present resident in the United Kingdom, to be liable for prosecution for atrocities which they are alleged to have committed during the war when they were not resident in the United Kingdom and when they did not come under the United Kingdom's jurisdiction. I have no hesitation in saying to your Lordships that this is a weighty decision to make, and the Government would like to have the benefit of your Lordships' views before deciding whether or not to introduce legislation.

I think that it would be right to make clear that, were alleged atrocities to be committed now, the United Kingdom law would since 1957 permit action to be taken against those who perpetrated them, even if the atrocities had been committed by non-British citizens outside the United Kingdom. This follows the Geneva Conventions Act 1957 and the Genocide Act 1969. What we are considering therefore today is whether there is a need to alter the law in order to take action in respect of acts which particular individuals may have committed at a time—unlike now—when their actions, although contrary as they then were to international law, were not subject to the jurisdiction of the United Kingdom courts.

(HL Debs., vol. 513, col. 604: 4 December 1989)

Part Twelve: II. *Pacific settlement of disputes—modes of settlement*

Following discussions between the delegations of the British and Argentine Governments held in Madrid, a joint statement was issued on 19 October 1989, which read in part:

The two Governments confirmed their commitment to respect fully the principles of the Charter of the United Nations, in particular:
—the obligation to settle disputes exclusively by peaceful means: and
—the obligation to refrain from the threat or use of force.

(Text provided by the Foreign and Commonwealth Office)

Part Twelve: II. G. 1. *Pacific settlement of disputes—modes of settlement—arbitration—arbitral tribunals and commissions*

The following statement was issued on 28 June 1989 by the relevant UK and US authorities:

Despite consultations between Governments, it has not proved possible to resolve a dispute between them as regards Heathrow Airport user charges.

Accordingly, the US Government has requested formal arbitration on this issue under Article 17 of the US/UK Air Service Agreement. In the absence of a negotiated solution the parties consider this the most appropriate means of settling the dispute.

The US has selected Fred Fielding Esq., as an arbitrator; the UK has selected

Jeremy Lever, QC. The two arbitrators selected Professor Isi Foighel of Denmark as the Chairman of the arbitration panel.

The first hearing was held on June 28/29, 1989 in The Hague to discuss procedural matters. The Parties have agreed not to discuss publicly the proceedings while the arbitration is in progress.

(Text provided by the Foreign and Commonwealth Office)

On 22 March 1989, the Governments of the UK and Ghana signed an Agreement for the Promotion and Protection of Investments. The Agreement contains the following Articles:

ARTICLE 10

Settlement of Disputes between an Investor and a Host State

(1) Disputes between a national or company of one Contracting Party and the other Contracting Party concerning an obligation of the latter under this Agreement in relation to an investment of the former which have not been amicably settled shall, after a period of three months from written notification of a claim, be submitted to international arbitration if either party to the dispute so wishes.

(2) Where the dispute is referred to international arbitration, the investor and the Contracting Party concerned in the dispute may agree to refer the dispute either to:

 (a) the International Centre for the Settlement of Investment Disputes (having regard to the provisions, where applicable, of the Convention on the Settlement of Investment Disputes between States and Nationals of other States, opened for signature at Washington DC on 18 March 1965 and the Additional Facility for the Administration of Conciliation, Arbitration and Fact-Finding Proceedings); or

 (b) an international arbitrator or *ad hoc* arbitration tribunal to be appointed by a special agreement or established under the Arbitration Rules of the United Nations Commission on International Trade Law.

(3) If after a period of three months from written notification of the claim there is no agreement to one of the above alternative procedures, the parties to the dispute shall be bound to submit it to arbitration under the Arbitration Rules of the United Nations Commission on International Trade Law as then in force. The parties to the dispute may agree in writing to modify these Rules.

ARTICLE 11

Disputes between the Contracting Parties

(1) Disputes between the Contracting Parties concerning the interpretation or application of this Agreement should, if possible, be settled through the diplomatic channel.

(2) If a dispute between the Contracting Parties cannot thus be settled, it shall upon the request of either Contracting Party be submitted to an arbitral tribunal.

(3) Such an arbitral tribunal shall be constituted for each individual case in the following way: within two months of the receipt of the request for arbitration, each Contracting Party shall appoint one member of the tribunal. Those two members shall then select a national of a third State who on approval by the two Contracting

Parties shall be appointed Chairman of the tribunal. The Chairman shall be appointed within two months from the date of appointment of the other two members.

(4) If within the periods specified in paragraph (3) of this Article the necessary appointments have not been made, either Contracting Party may, in the absence of any other agreement, invite the President of the International Court of Justice to make any necessary appointments. If the President is a national of either Contracting Party or if he is otherwise prevented from discharging the said functions, the Vice-President shall be invited to make the necessary appointments. If the Vice-President is a national of either Contracting Party or if he also is prevented from discharging the said function, the Member of the International Court of Justice next in seniority who is not a national of either Contracting Party shall be invited to make the necessary appointments.

(5) The arbitral tribunal shall reach its decision by a majority of votes. Such decision shall be binding on both Contracting Parties. Each Contracting Party shall bear the cost of its own member of the tribunal and of its representation in the arbitral proceedings. The cost of the Chairman and the remaining costs shall be borne in equal parts by the Contracting Parties. The tribunal may, however, in its decision direct that a higher proportion of costs shall be borne by one of the two Contracting Parties, and this award shall be binding on both Contracting Parties. The tribunal shall determine its own procedure.

(Cm. 811; see also Cm. 909 (Agreement for the Promotion and Protection of Investments signed on 27 October 1989 between the Governments of the UK and Guyana))

Part Twelve: II. H. 1. *Pacific settlement of disputes—modes of settlement—judicial settlement—the International Court of Justice*

In the course of a debate in the Sixth Committee of the UN General Assembly on the subject of the report of the UN Special Committee on the Charter of the UN and on the strengthening of the role of the organization, the UK representative, Mr A. Aust, stated on 5 October 1989:

In connection with the subject of peaceful settlement of disputes I wish to say something about the proposal, made in document A/44/191, for a United Nations Decade of International Law. The Decade would have several purposes, perhaps the most important, from the point of view of the Sixth Committee, would be the promotion and enhancement of peaceful methods for the settlement of disputes between States, including resort to the International Court of Justice, and compliance with its judgments. Other relevant objectives would be promoting respect for international legal principles against the threat or use of force, and public education for a better understanding of international law. All these objectives are most commendable. The Decade could play an important role in the continuing process of building confidence in international law and existing dispute settlement mechanisms.

The most important of these is, of course, the International Court of Justice. In my speech in this Committee last year on the current items I outlined various ways in which the role of the International Court of Justice could be enhanced. I should like to recall them briefly.

Firstly, more States could accept the compulsory jurisdiction of the Court. We are encouraged to note that since the last General Assembly two States, both developing countries, have accepted the compulsory jurisdiction of the Court. Recently, Poland announced its intention of also doing so.

Secondly, there could be increased adherence to the optional protocols to multilateral conventions which confer jurisdiction on the Court. We are pleased to note that recently more European States have accepted certain of these optional protocols, or announced their intention of doing so.

Thirdly, more conventions could have, as a matter of course, articles providing for the compulsory jurisdiction of the Court. In this connection, we are pleased to note the recent withdrawal by some European States of their reservations to some of these provisions, and their intention to consider withdrawing others.

Fourthly, there could be a general convention providing for the compulsory jurisdiction of the Court, on the lines of The Hague Convention of 1899 or the General Act of 1928.

(Text provided by the Foreign and Commonwealth Office; see also A/C.6/44/SR.10, pp. 7–8, and UKMIL 1988, pp. 565–6)

In reply to the question whether the UK Government would support an extension of the Court's jurisdiction to 'Fourth world nations' such as the Kurds, the Parliamentary Under-Secretary of State, Foreign and Commonwealth Office, Mr T. Sainsbury, stated:

The hon. Gentleman raises an interesting idea, but one which appears clearly to be outside the terms of reference of the International Court of Justice, which is concerned with disputes between member States. I suspect that there would be no little difficulty in defining which or what organisations or bodies should come under the hon. Gentleman's 'Fourth world' definition, and who would be responsible for deciding which should qualify.

(HC Debs., vol. 158, col. 840: 25 October 1989)

In reply to further questions, Mr Sainsbury observed in part:

I must repeat that the International Court of Justice is concerned with disputes between States, not matters involving individuals.

(Ibid., col. 841)

In the course of a debate on 1 November 1989 in the UN General Assembly on the subject of the International Court of Justice, the UK representative, Sir Arthur Watts, stated:

The United Kingdom has been a consistent and a staunch supporter of the Rule of Law in international relations. The Rule of Law—and the rule of international law in particular—is indispensable to the maintenance of international peace and security. It is the counterpart to the principle of non-use of force enshrined in the Charter of this Organisation.

That same Charter declares as one of its Principles that Member States 'shall settle their international disputes by peaceful means', establishes the International Court of Justice as 'the principal judicial organ of the United Nations', records the 'consideration that legal disputes should as a general rule be referred by the parties to the International Court of Justice', and provides that 'all Members of the United Nations are *ipso facto* parties to the Statute' of that Court.

The international Rule of Law requires no less. Indeed, it requires more. It requires in particular not only that there should exist a Court to which legal disputes can be referred, but that access to that Court should in reality be available to all States which seek it for the settlement of their international legal disputes. The international community still has some way to go in this respect. But it is possible to be optimistic.

Although the jurisdiction of the Court depends on the consent of the parties, it is possible for that consent to be given in advance, by a declaration accepting as compulsory the Court's jurisdiction. The United Kingdom is proud of its record as a State which has always accepted the compulsory jurisdiction of the Court, just as it previously accepted the compulsory jurisdiction of its predecessor under the League of Nations, the Permanent Court of International Justice.

(Text provided by the Foreign and Commonwealth Office; see also A/44/PV.43, pp. 11–13)

Part Twelve: II. I. 2. *Pacific settlement of disputes—modes of settlement—settlement within international organizations—organizations other than the UN*

In the course of a debate on the subject of Lebanon, the Parliamentary Under-Secretary of State, Foreign and Commonwealth Office, Mr Timothy Eggar, stated:

We believe that, for as long as the Arab League is pursuing its initiatives, it should be allowed a free hand before the international community considers alternative approaches. This is in keeping with article 52 of the United Nations charter, which says that every effort should be made to achieve pacific settlement of local disputes through regional organisations before referring them to the Security Council. In any case, it is clear we should have to think very carefully before involving the Security Council actively in what is essentially an internal Lebanese issue.

(HC Debs., vol. 153, col. 297: 16 May 1989)

Part Thirteen: I. C. *Coercion and use of force short of war—unilateral acts—pacific blockade*

In the course of a debate on the subject of Lebanon, the Minister of State, Foreign and Commonwealth Office, Mr William Waldegrave, stated:

It is true our own ships and those which carried our flag, along with American ships and those which sought the protection of the American flag, did enable the complement of British and, ultimately more important in the scale of events, American naval forces to continue their passage to and fro in the Gulf. There is a long history of blockades in the Levant. In recent years, too, the Israelis have intervened on many occasions to stop ships. They have searched ships widely if they believed that that was necessary for their security. We deplore blockades and my hon. Friend is right to say that on many occasions international law is being flouted.

(HC Debs., vol. 157, col. 1465: 28 July 1989)

Part Thirteen: I. D. *Coercion and use of force short of war—unilateral acts—intervention*

In reply to a question, the Minister for Overseas Development wrote:

We shall not consider Government-to-Government aid for reconstruction until Vietnam has fully withdrawn from its illegal occupation of Cambodia.

(HC Debs., vol. 149, Written Answers, col. *626*: 22 March 1989)

In reply to a question, the Minister of State, Foreign and Commonwealth Office, wrote:

Complete withdrawal by Vietnam from its illegal occupation of Cambodia is a crucial prerequisite for considering these questions.

(HC Debs., vol. 150, Written Answers, col. *195*: 5 April 1989)

In a statement on the subject of the US armed intervention in Panama, the Secretary of State for Foreign and Commonwealth Affairs, Mr Douglas Hurd, observed in part:

We welcome the establishment of democratic Government in Panama. We fully support the American action to remove General Noriega, which was undertaken with the agreement of the leaders who clearly won the elections held last May. Noriega's arbitrary rule was maintained by force. We and many others have repeatedly condemned Noriega and called for the election result in Panama to be respected. Every peaceful means of trying to see the results of the democratic elections respected had failed.

(HC Debs., vol. 164, col. 357: 20 December 1989)

In reply to questions on the subject, the Secretary of State said:

It is not a question of the United States intervening to impose a Government. A Government was elected but that election was set aside. . . . Independent observers . . . observed the election and upheld the result. However, it was then set aside.

Constant efforts have been made—not just by the United States, but by many others also—to have the democratic results restored, but all those efforts have failed. More recently, an American officer has been murdered, threats and attacks have been made on others and General Noriega has declared that his country must be regarded as in a state of war with the United States. Having added up those considerations they appear to us to be strong and sufficient.

The Secretary of State was then asked:

Whatever the provocation, is it not a vital principle, always worth upholding, that countries should invade others only under the terms of international law? Does the right hon. Gentleman agree that, having had a declaration by General Noriega of a state of war between the two countries and having had threats to the lives of American service men who had every right to be in Panama, it is under the terms of the charter that the Americans should now rest their case, not on the restoration of democracy, however desirable?

He replied:

The right hon. Gentleman is right to stress the two latter points, on which, as I have said, we rest our belief that the reasons were strong and sufficient. However, one cannot get away from the political context, and I do not think that the right hon. Gentleman would want us to do so. We are not talking about a military ruler being imposed by the United States; we are talking about a military ruler being deposed and a democratically elected president being able to take up his position.

(Ibid., cols. 359–60, *passim*)

The statement of the Secretary of State was repeated in the House of Lords by the Minister of State, Foreign and Commonwealth Office, Lord Brabazon of Tara (HL Debs., vol. 514, col. 273: 20 December 1989). In reply to a question, he stated:

We are unanimous in condemning General Noriega as a brutal dictator. As regards US action and its legality, the root of the problem was General Noriega's defiance of his own people and his refusal to accept the result of the May election. It is clear that President Endara endorsed the American action. General Noriega is said to have said that they were in a state of war with the United States. President Bush said that he took action only as a last resort and for four reasons: to protect American lives; to defend democracy; to arrest an indicted drugs trafficker; and to defend the integrity of the Panama Canal treaties. Surely there is no suggestion that General Noriega represented legality.

All 279 independent observers from 21 countries formally declared that the May election was won overwhelmingly by the opposition alliance headed by President Endara. No doubt there will be a great deal of debate by lawyers about the legal aspects. The fact is that it was General Noriega who by his actions brought about the US action.

(HL Debs., vol. 514, col. 274)

In reply to the question

. . . if it is true that the United States intends to remove General Noriega from Panama by force, if they can locate him and take him to the United States for trial, is that in accordance with international law?

the Minister of State said:

. . . I am afraid that I cannot answer that question.

(Ibid., cols. 276–7)

During a debate on the US invasion of Panama in the UN Security Council on 20 December 1989, the UK representative, Mr T.L. Richardson, stated:

As my Government has already made clear, we fully support the action taken by the United States. That action was undertaken with the agreement and support of the Panamanian leaders who had won last May's election, and has at last enabled them to assume their rightful functions. General Noriega's rule was illegal and arbitrary. The establishment of a legal and democratically elected Government in Panama can only be beneficial for Panama itself and for peace and security in the region. In our view, the Security Council should do its utmost to encourage progress in that direction.

(S/PV. 2899, pp. 26–7)

Part Thirteen: I. E. *Coercion and use of force short of war—unilateral acts—other unilateral acts, including self-defence*

Following the repression of demonstrations in China, the Secretary of State for Foreign and Commonwealth Affairs, Sir Geoffrey Howe, stated in part:

In present circumstances, however, there can be no question of continuing normal business with the Chinese authorities.

Her Majesty's Government have therefore decided on the following action.

All scheduled ministerial exchanges between Britain and China have been suspended. The visit of the Chinese Minister of Justice, who was due to arrive here tomorrow, has been cancelled. My right hon. Friend the Minister of Agriculture, Fisheries and Food has also cancelled his forthcoming visit to China.

The proposed visit of their Royal Highnesses the Prince and Princess of Wales to China in November clearly cannot take place so long as those responsible for the atrocities over the past weekend remain in control of the Chinese Government.

All high-level military contacts with China have been suspended.

All arms sales to China have been banned.

(HC Debs., vol. 154, col. 30: 6 June 1989)

Following discussions between the delegations of the British and Argentine Governments held in Madrid, a joint statement was issued on 19 October 1989, which read in part:

. . . the British delegation announced the British Government's decisions:
. . . to align the limits of the [Falkland Islands] Protection Zone with those of the Conservation Zone.

(Text provided by the Foreign and Commonwealth Office)

At a press conference held by the Foreign and Commonwealth Office on 10 November 1989, it was stated:

. . . our decision, announced at the Madrid meeting last October, to align the limits of the Falkland Islands Protection Zone with those of the Falkland Islands Conservation Zone, would take effect from 1 December 1989.

(Text provided by the Foreign and Commonwealth Office)

Part Thirteen: II. A. *Coercion and use of force short of war—collective measures—regime of the UN*

(See also Part Fourteen: I. B. 10. (item of 25 January 1989), below)

In reply to a question on the subject of the UN arms embargo on arms exports to South Africa, the Minister of State, Foreign and Commonwealth Office, stated:

We faithfully implement the United Nations arms embargo. It is for the United Nations Security Council arms embargo committee to investigate alleged breaches by other countries. We would deplore any breach shown to have occurred.

(HC Debs., vol. 149, Written Answers, col. *448*: 20 March 1989)

Part Thirteen: II. B. *Coercion and use of force short of war—collective measures—collective measures outside the UN*

In reply to a question, the Minister of State, Foreign and Commonwealth Office, wrote:

In 1986 EC member states agreed to a series of measures against Libya including a ban on the export of arms and other military equipment; these are still in force. On 20 February 1989 the EC deplored a regulation controlling the export of 8 chemical weapon precursors. Discussion continues among the Twelve about possible further measures to counter chemical weapon proliferation in Libya and elsewhere.

(HC Debs., vol. 147, Written Answers, col. *852*: 24 February 1989)

Part Fourteen: I. B. 7. *Armed conflicts—international war—the laws of war—humanitarian law*

(See Part Fourteen: I. B. 8., below)

Part Fourteen: I. B. 8. *Armed conflicts—international war—the laws of war—belligerent occupation*

In the course of a debate on the subject of the Middle East and the territories occupied by Israel, the Secretary of State for Foreign and Commonwealth Affairs, Sir Geoffrey Howe, stated:

The occupation is illegal and does not contribute at all to the prospects for peace.

(HC Debs., vol. 144, col. 825: 11 January 1989)

In the course of a speech on 2 February 1989 to the UN Commission on Human Rights, the UK representative, Mr H. Steel, stated:

There has been no improvement in the human rights situation in the Occupied Territories since this Commission last considered it exactly 12 months ago. Indeed, it has got worse. I must again make clear, as I did last year and as my delegation will continue to do so as long as the need exists, not only that the occupation of the Territories is a wrong which should be brought to an end at the earliest possible moment but that, until that happens, the Government of Israel has both a legal and a moral duty to respect scrupulously the human rights of the inhabitants. Specifically, it must apply in the Territories all the provisions of the relevant human rights conventions and we see no room for doubt that these include the provisions of the Fourth Hague Convention of 1907 and the Fourth Geneva Convention of 1949. That is the firm view of the Government of the United Kingdom. It is a view which we share with our partners in the European Community.

Under Article 27 of the Fourth Geneva Convention, the Government of Israel has an unambiguous and inescapable obligation to treat the population of the Occupied Territories humanely at all times. Quite apart from the specific requirements of Article 27—indeed, quite apart from any question of the application of that Convention—we cannot believe that the obligation to act humanely towards a population under its control is one which the Government of any civilised State (I am tempted to say least of all the Government of Israel) would wish to deny. I have to say that we do not think that it is an obligation which the Government of Israel consistently respect.

Humane or inhumane treatment aside, there are certain Israeli practices in the Occupied Territories which directly contravene specific provisions of the Fourth Geneva Convention. I refer in particular to the Israeli policy of financing and encouraging settlements in the Territories. This clearly contravenes Article 49 of the Convention. It is therefore with grave concern that my Government views the recent statement by the Israeli Government—as recent as December last year—of its intended support for a further eight settlements. We say unequivocally that this policy is illegal and we call on the Government of Israel to put an immediate end to it.

(Text provided by the Foreign and Commonwealth Office; see also E/CN. 4/1989/ SR.6, pp. 17–18)

In the course of a speech in the UN Security Council on 7 February 1989 the UK Permanent Representative, Sir Crispin Tickell, referred to casualties in the territories under Israeli occupation and continued:

These events, brought about by a cycle of violence and counter-violence, have drawn new attention to the fundamental problems underlying the conflict. The Council's resolutions 242 (1967) and 338 (1973) remain unfulfilled. There has been little progress towards giving them effect. However events are explained or interpreted, the Israeli Government still continues to occupy territories which are not part of Israel. The ultimate solution to the problem, to be resolved at an international conference, will have to take account of the right of the Palestinians to self-determination. In the meantime the military occupation of the territories lays heavy responsibility on Israel in terms of international law.

My Government's views on this subject have been expressed many times. We look to the Israeli Government to abide fully by its obligations under the Fourth Geneva Convention, including the obligation under Article 27 which requires it to treat the population of the occupied territories humanely at all times. We do not accept that the need to maintain law and order should be used as a pretext to override the specific and unambiguous obligations placed upon the occupying Power under the terms of the Convention.

(S/PV. 2849, p. 26; see also S/PV. 2867, p. 18; 9 June 1989)

In reply to a question on the same subject, the Minister of State, Foreign and Commonwealth Office, wrote:

We continue to take all appropriate opportunities to remind the Israeli authorities of their obligation to administer the occupied territories in accordance with international law and human rights standards.

(HC Debs., vol. 146, Written Answers, col. 729 : 8 February 1989)

In the course of a common statement on human rights delivered on 20 February 1989 to the UN Commission on Human Rights, the Twelve Member States of the EC observed:

The Twelve have repeatedly stated at the United Nations their position on the human rights situation in the occupied territories, which has seriously deteriorated in the past fourteen months, with the unnecessary loss of life and human rights abuses that the repression of the Palestinian uprising has brought about. The Twelve reiterate that the Fourth Geneva Convention is applicable in this case.

(Text provided by the Foreign and Commonwealth Office)

In reply to a question, the Minister of State, Foreign and Commonwealth Office, wrote:

We have frequently exercised our right as a contracting party to the fourth Geneva convention to raise with the Israeli Government breaches of the convention in the occupied territories. Questions of prosecuting under the 1957 Geneva Conventions Act are a matter for the prosecuting authorities.

(HC Debs., vol. 157, Written Answers, col. *1165*: 28 July 1989)

In reply to a question on the subject of the Gaza Strip and the West Bank, the Minister of State, Foreign and Commonwealth Office, wrote:

. . . the Secretary of State for Foreign and Commonwealth Affairs discussed the situation in the occupied territories with the Israeli Foreign Minister on 25 September and underlined our concern that, pending their withdrawal, the Israelis should administer the territories in accordance with international law and their human rights obligations.

(HC Debs., vol. 158, Written Answers, col. *492*: 25 October 1989)

In the course of a speech in the UN Security Council on 7 November 1989, the UK Permanent Representative, Sir Crispin Tickell, stated:

Israel has continued to deport individuals from the occupied territories, in breach of its obligations under the Fourth Geneva Convention and in repeated defiance of this Council's resolutions.

(S/PV. 2889, p. 21)

In reply to a question, the Minister of State, Foreign and Commonwealth Office, wrote:

Diplomatic and consular staff in Tel Aviv and Jerusalem are free to move throughout the occupied territories, including that part of Jerusalem which Israel illegally annexed de facto in 1967, while having regard to any restrictions imposed by the Israeli authorities in accordance with Israel's responsibilities as a military occupier of these territories under international law, in particular the fourth Geneva convention of 1949.

(HC Debs., vol. 162, Written Answers, col. *96*: 27 November 1989)

Part Fourteen: I. B. 10. *Armed conflicts—international war—the laws of war—nuclear, bacteriological and chemical weapons*

In the course of his reply to a question on the subject of the recent international conference on chemical weapons in Paris, the Parliamentary Under-Secretary of State, Foreign and Commonwealth Office, wrote:

We particularly welcome the concluding conference declaration which was adopted by consensus by all 149 States participating. It specifically recognises the important and continuing validity of the 1925 Geneva protocol and contains an undertaking by all not to use CW. It also expresses support for the Geneva negotiations for a global ban on CW, and the role of the UN Secretary-General in investigating allegations of use.

(HC Debs., vol. 144, Written Answers, col. *763*: 13 January 1989)

In reply to a question, the Parliamentary Under-Secretary of State, Department of Trade and Industry, wrote:

Methyl phosphonyl difluoride is not itself a nerve gas of lethal character: it can however be used in the preparation of the nerve gas Sarin.

Following the first confirmation in March 1984 of the use of chemical weapons in the Gulf conflict, controls were imposed on exports of methyl phosphonyl difluoride from the United Kingdom to all destinations under the Export of Goods (Control) Order. No licences have been issued for the export of this substance to Iran or Iraq since the imposition of controls in 1984.

(HC Debs., vol. 145, Written Answers, col. *443*: 23 January 1989)

In reply to a question, the Minister of State, Foreign and Commonwealth Office, wrote in part:

We are committed to the achievement of a comprehensive global and verifiable ban on chemical weapons as the only effective means to halt the spread of these weapons and to ensure the destruction of existing stockpiles.

Pending the conclusion of such a convention, 19 western countries (the 'Australia Group') meet regularly to exchange information and to concert action on export controls on chemical weapon precursors. Members of the group also circulate to national industries a longer warning list of other chemicals which might have relevance to the manufacture of chemical weapons.

Security Council Resolution 620 of 26 August 1988, sponsored by the United Kingdom called upon all states 'to continue to apply, to establish or to strengthen strict control of the export of chemical products serving for the production of chemical weapons'.

(HC Debs., vol. 145, Written Answers, cols. *575–6*: 25 January 1989)

In reply to a question, the Minister of State, Foreign and Commonwealth Office, Lord Glenarthur, stated in part:

. . . the use of chemical weapons in war is already banned under the 1925 Geneva Protocol to which over 120 states, including the United Kingdom, are party. Negotiations aimed at achieving a global, comprehensive and verifiable ban on the development, production and possession as well as use of chemical weapons continue at the conference on disarmament in Geneva. Progress has been made, but complex issues remain to be resolved particularly concerning verification.

(HL Debs., vol. 503, col. 985: 31 January 1989)

In reply to a question, the Minister of State, Department of Trade and Industry, wrote in part:

We have made clear to the Iraqi Government our condemnation of the use of chemical weapons and we expect the Government of Iraq to honour their pledge not to use these weapons in the future.

(HC Debs., vol. 146, Written Answers, col. *417*: 3 February 1989)

In reply to a question on the subject of the Intermediate Nuclear Forces Agreement, the Minister of State for Defence Procurement wrote:

The interpretation of the treaty is a matter for the parties to the treaty. However, it is our understanding that the treaty demands the elimination of all ground-launched missiles and launchers with a range between 500km and 5,500km as well as certain support facilities and structures.

(HL Debs., vol. 503, col. 1423: 6 February 1989)

In reply to a question, the Minister of State, Foreign and Commonwealth Office, wrote:

We continue to subscribe to the NATO policy that our security will depend for the foreseeable future on an appropriate mix of nuclear and conventional weapons. We fully observe our obligations under the 1968 non-proliferation treaty including those relating to the non-transferral of nuclear weapons technology.

(HC Debs., vol. 154, Written Answers, col. *32*: 6 June 1989)

In reply to the question what was Her Majesty's Government's attitude towards the possession of nuclear weapons by USSR, USA, France and the People's Republic of China, the Minister of State, Foreign and Commonwealth Office, wrote:

All four countries are recognised nuclear weapons states as defined by the non-proliferation treaty. We, therefore, recognise their right to possess nuclear weapons.

(HC Debs., vol. 155, Written Answers, col. *33*: 19 June 1989)

In reply to a question on the subject of the coding of uranium imported from Namibia, the Parliamentary Under-Secretary of State, Department of Energy, Baroness Hooper, stated:

. . . the Euratom authorities which place the coding on the material that comes to this country are governed by the terms of the Euratom Treaty. We in this country are bound by the terms of the UK-Euratom-IAEA safeguards agreement and our terms as treaty members. I can assure the noble Lord that the terms of both the treaty and the agreement are fully complied with. I can only say once again that it is not for the receiving country to change the coding placed upon imports by the Euratom authorities.

(HL Debs., vol. 509, col. 127: 20 June 1989)

In reply to the question

Whether, in view of the value [Her Majesty's Government] place in nuclear weapons in Europe, they support the development of nuclear weapons by the governments of India and Pakistan, the Minister of State, Foreign and Commonwealth Office, Lord Glenarthur, wrote:

No. As a depositary power of the NPT, we have consistently made clear our commitment to the principle of non-proliferation of nuclear weapons.

(HL Debs., vol. 509, col. 298: 21 June 1989)

In reply to the question whether Her Majesty's Government would make it their policy 'to implement those provisions of (*a*) the Genocide Act 1969, (*b*) the Geneva Convention Act 1957, (*c*) the Nuremberg principles, (*d*) the Geneva protocol 1977 and (*e*) all other customary and conventional law which would make it an offence to use, or to plan to use, weapons of mass murder', the Minister of State, Foreign and Commonwealth Office, wrote:

While the use of certain weapons of mass destruction is controlled or prohibited by international treaty, there is no treaty dealing specifically with the use of nuclear weapons. However, any such use would be governed by the applicable laws of war, as is the case with other weapons. Since the use of nuclear weapons would, according to the circumstances, be lawful, so the deterrent threat of their legitimate use is similarly lawful. The enforcement of the Acts of Parliament referred to is a matter for the Director of Public Prosecutions.

(HC Debs., vol. 159, Written Answers, col. *292*: 2 November 1989)

Part Fourteen: I. B. 12. *Armed conflicts—international war—the laws of war—termination of war, treaties of peace, termination of hostilities*

Following discussions between the delegations of the British and Argentine Governments held in Madrid, a joint statement was issued on 19 October 1989, which read in part:

The two Governments noted that all hostilities between them had ceased.

(Text provided by the Foreign and Commonwealth Office)

APPENDICES

I. MULTILATERAL AGREEMENTS SIGNED BY THE UNITED KINGDOM IN 1989[1]

Title	Place and Date	UK Signature	Text[2]
1987 Amendments to the Annex of the Protocol of 1978 relating to the International Convention for the Prevention of Pollution from Ships, 1973 (Resolution MEPC.29(25))	London, 1.12.1987	1.4.1989 (entry into force)	
Amendments to the International Convention for the Safety of Life at Sea, 1974, concerning Passenger Ro-Ro Ferries (Resolution MSC.11(55))	London, 21.4.1988	22.10.1989 (entry into force)	
Convention on the Regulation of Antarctic Mineral Resource Activities	Wellington, 2.6.1988	22.3.1989	Misc. No. 6 (1989) (Cm. 634)
Convention on Jurisdiction and the Enforcement of Judgments in Civil and Commercial Matters	Lugano, 16.9.1988	18.9.1989	
Joint Protocol relating to the application of the Vienna Convention and the Paris Convention	Vienna, 21.9.1988	21.9.1988	Misc. No. 12 (1989) (Cm. 774)
Amendment to Article 26 of the Statute of the Council of Europe	Strasbourg, 16.11.1988	16.11.1988 (entry into force)	TS No. 51 (1989) (Cm. 843)
Convention concerning the Construction and Operation of a European Synchrotron Radiation Facility	Paris, 16.12.1988	16.12.1988	Misc. No. 1 (1990) (Cm. 911)

1 Information supplied by the Foreign and Commonwealth Office. The table includes some agreements signed by the United Kingdom before 1989, where information was not previously available. The information is correct as at January 1990, although in some cases information available since that time has been included.

2 Publication is in various series of UK Command Papers, namely: Misc. = Miscellaneous Series; TS = Treaty Series; Cm. = Command Paper number.

Title	Place and Date	UK Signature	Text
First Protocol on the Interpretation by the Court of Justice of the European Communities of the Convention on the Law applicable to Contractual Obligations, opened for signature in Rome on 19.6.1980	Brussels, 19.12.1988	19.12.1988	Misc. No. 7 (1989) (Cm. 682)
Second Protocol conferring on the Court of Justice of the European Communities certain Powers to interpret the Convention on the Law applicable to Contractual Obligations, opened for signature at Rome on 19.6.1980	Brussels, 19.12.1988	19.12.1988	Misc. No. 8 (1989) (Cm. 681)
Basel Convention on the Control of Transboundary Movements of Hazardous Wastes and their Disposal	Basel, 22.3.1989	6.10.1989	
Convention on Insider Trading	Strasbourg, 20.4.1989	13.9.1989	Misc. No. 5 (1990) (Cm. 981)
Third Additional Protocol to the Protocol to the European Agreement on the Protection of Television Broadcasts	Strasbourg 20.4.1989	18.12.1989 (definitive signature)	
Additional Protocol No. 4 to the Revised Convention for Rhine Navigation of 17.10.1868, as amended on 20.11.1963	Strasbourg, 25.4.1989	25.4.1989	Misc. No. 7 (1990) (Cm. 987)
Amendment to Article 26 of the Statute of the Council of Europe	Strasbourg, 5.5.1989	5.5.1989 (entry into force)	TS No. 52 (1989) (Cm. 842)
European Convention on Transfrontier Television	Strasbourg, 5.5.1989	5.5.1989	
Convention on the Accession of the Kingdom of Spain and the Portuguese Republic to the Convention on Jurisdiction and the Enforcement of Judgments in Civil and Commercial Matters and to the Protocol on its Interpretation by the Court of Justice, with the Adjustments made to them by the Convention on the Accession of the Kingdom of Denmark, of Ireland and of the UK and the Adjustments made to them by the Convention on the Accession of the Hellenic Republic	Donostia–San Sebastian, 26.5.1989	26.5.1989	

Title	Place and Date	UK Signature	Text
Protocol to the Convention on Insider Trading of 20.4.1989	Strasbourg, 11.9.1989	13.9.1989	Misc. No. 5 (1990) (Cm. 981)
Anti-Doping Convention	Strasbourg, 16.11.1989	16.11.1989 (definitive signature)	
Protocol to the Convention on the Elaboration of a European Pharmacopoeia	Strasbourg, 16.11.1989	16.11.1989	
Protocol [further] amending the Convention for the Prevention of Marine Pollution by Dumping from Ships and Aircraft, done at Oslo on 15.2.1972	Oslo, 5.12.1989	5.12.1989	

II. BILATERAL AGREEMENTS SIGNED BY THE UNITED KINGDOM IN 1989[1]

Country and Title	Place and Date	Text[2]
ANGOLA Exchange of Notes concerning Certain Commercial Debts (The UK/Angola Debt Agreement No. 1 (1987))	Luanda, 6/26.7.1989	TS No. 5 (1990) (Cm. 920)
ARGENTINA Exchange of Notes between the Swiss Confederation, on behalf of the Government of the UK, and the Federative Republic of Brazil, on behalf of the Government of the Republic of Argentina, concerning Certain Commercial Debts (The UK/Argentina Debt Rescheduling Agreement (1985))	Paris, 16.2.1989	TS No. 50 (1989) (Cm. 839)
Exchange of Notes between the Swiss Confederation, on behalf of the Government of the UK, and the Federative Republic of Brazil, on behalf of the Government of Argentina, concerning Certain Commercial Debts (The UK/ Argentina Debt Agreement No. 2 (1987))	Paris, 24.10.1989	

[1] Information supplied by the Foreign and Commonwealth Office. The table includes some agreements signed by the United Kingdom before 1989, where information was not previously available. The information is correct as at January 1990, although in some cases information available since that time has been included.

[2] Publication is in various series of UK Command Papers, including Treaty Series (TS). Cm. = Command Paper number.

Country and Title	Place and Date	Text
BOLIVIA		
Exchange of Notes concerning Certain Commercial Debts (The UK/Bolivia Debt Agreement No. 2 (1988))	La Paz, 27.9/ 20.11.1989	TS No. 23 (1990) (Cm. 1035)
BRAZIL		
Exchange of Notes amending the UK/ Brazil Loan Agreement 1973 signed at Brasilia on 20.11.1973, as amended	Brasilia, 20.7.1989	TS No. 63 (1989) (Cm. 1056), p. 3
Agreement amending the UK/Brazil Loan Agreement 1973	Brasilia, 21.8.89	TS No. 16 (1990) (Cm. 969)
Exchange of Notes concerning Certain Commercial Debts (The UK/Brazil Debt Agreement No. 3 (1988))	Brasilia, 28.12.1989	TS No. 40 (1990) (Cm. 1095)
BRUNEI DARUSSALAM		
Exchange of Notes concerning the Reference of Appeals to the Judicial Committee of Her Majesty's Privy Council from the Supreme Court of Brunei Darussalam	Bandar Seri Begawan, 27.6.1989	Miscellaneous No. 17 (1989) (Cm. 890)
CHINA, PEOPLE'S REPUBLIC OF		
Exchange of Notes amending the Agreement concerning the Financial Arrangement relating to Development Loans, signed at London on 15.5.1986 (The UK/China Development Loans Arrangement 1986 (Amendment No. 1))	Peking, 31.3.1989	TS No. 62 (1989) (Cm. 988), p. 3
CONGO		
Agreement for the Promotion and Protection of Investments	London, 25.5.1989	
COSTA RICA		
Exchange of Letters further amending the UK/Costa Rica Loan 1973 (The UK/Costa Rica Loan 1973 Debt Rescheduling Agreement (Consolidation 1985))	San José, 3.11.1989	
DENMARK		
Exchange of Notes agreeing to the indefinite suspension of the activity of the Mixed Commission established under Article 14 of the Cultural Convention signed at London on 2.5.1974	Copenhagen, 14.8.1989	
DOMINICA		
Exchange of Notes concerning the extension to the Bailiwicks of Jersey and Guernsey and to the Isle of Man of the Agreement for the Promotion and Protection of Investments signed at Roseau on 23.1.1987	Roseau, 25.9/4.10. 1989	TS No. 64 (1989) (Cm. 1076), p. 5

Country and Title	Place and Date	Text
ETHIOPIA Exchange of Notes further amending the Air Services Agreement signed at London on 7.7.1958	Addis Ababa, 5.4/ 22.9.1988	TS No. 13 (1989) (Cm. 683)
FINLAND Exchange of Notes concerning the 1925 Agreement for the Reciprocal Exemption from Income Tax in certain cases of Profits accruing from the Business of Shipping, which shall cease to have effect, and the 1935 Agreement for Reciprocal Exemption from Income Tax on Profits or Gains arising through an Agency, which shall be terminated	London, 12.10/ 1.11.1988	
Exchange of Notes abrogating certain Articles of the Treaty of Commerce and Navigation signed at Helsinki on 14.12.1923	Helsinki, 15.9/ 17.11.1989	
GHANA Exchange of Notes amending the British Expatriates Supplementation (Ghana) Agreement 1971 (The British Expatriates Supplementation (Ghana) Agreement 1971/1986)	Accra, 20.2/ 16.3.1987	TS No. 63 (1989) (Cm. 1056), p. 5
Agreement for the Promotion and Protection of Investments	Accra, 22.3.1989	Ghana No. 1 (1989) (Cm. 811)
GREECE Exchange of Notes amending the Agreement on the International Carriage of Goods by Road signed at London on 26.2.1974	Athens, 2/7.2.1989	TS No. 14 (1989) (Cm. 689)
GUYANA Agreement for the Promotion and Protection of Investments	London, 27.10.1989	TS No. 47 (1990) (Cm. 1120)
HONDURAS Exchange of Notes amending the UK/Honduras Loan 1980, signed at Tegucigalpa on 11.9/24.12.1980	Tegucigalpa, 15.3/ 9.5.1985	TS No. 61 (1989) (Cm. 949), p. 7
Exchange of Notes further amending the UK/Honduras Loan 1980, signed at Tegucigalpa on 11.9/24.12.1980	Tegucigalpa, 8/ 24.3.1988	TS No. 61 (1989) (Cm. 949), p. 7
IRELAND, REPUBLIC OF Exchange of Notes further amending the Route Schedules annexed to the Air Services Agreement signed at London on 5.4.1946	London, 1/6.5.1987	TS No. 57 (1989) (Cm. 898)

Country and Title	*Place and Date*	*Text*
ITALY		
Exchange of Notes terminating Article 28 and amending Article 29 of the Consular Convention signed at Rome on 1.6.1954	Rome, 18.10.1988	Italy No. 1 (1989) (Cm. 798)
Agreement concerning Collaboration in the Exploitation of the Spallation Neutron Source Isis for Condensed Matter Research	London, 9.10.1989	TS No. 9 (1990) (Cm. 944)
JAMAICA		
Exchange of Notes amending the Agreement on Certain Commercial Debts signed at Kingston on 12.8.1987/16.3.1988 (The UK/Jamaica Debt Agreement No. 3 (1987))	Kingston, 11.4/ 2.5.1989	TS No. 62 (1989) (Cm. 988), p. 13
Exchange of Notes concerning Certain Commercial Debts (The UK/Jamaica Debt Agreement No. 4 (1988))	Kingston, 18.5/ 14.6.1989	TS No. 8 (1990) (Cm. 943)
JORDAN		
Exchange of Notes cancelling the UK/ Jordan Loan Agreement (No. 2) 1987, signed at Amman on 6.1.1988	Amman, 2/ 15.11.1989	TS No. 21 (1990) (Cm. 1000)
LIBERIA		
Exchange of Notes concerning the use of UK Controlled Ships registered in Liberia	Monrovia, 16.2/ 17.3.1989	TS No. 39 (1989) (Cm. 788)
MADAGASCAR		
Exchange of Notes amending the UK/ Madagascar Debt Agreement No. 5 (1986), signed at Antananarivo on 13.5/3.6.1987	Antananarivo, 15/ 28.12.1988	TS No. 62 (1989) (Cm. 988), p. 14
MALAWI		
Agreement concerning Certain Commercial Debts (The UK/Malawi Debt Agreement No. 3 (1988))	Lilongwe, 23/ 27.1.1989	TS No. 31 (1990) (Cm. 1062)
MALAYSIA		
Exchange of Notes further amending the Route Schedules annexed to the Agreement for Air Services between and beyond their respective Territories signed at London on 24.5.1973	Kuala Lumpur, 18.5/13.6.1989	TS No. 44 (1989) (Cm. 807)
Agreement on Mutual Assistance in relation to Drug Trafficking	Kuala Lumpur, 17.10.1989	
MALTA		
Agreement on the Development of Friendly Relations and Co-operation	Valletta, 15.3.1989	TS No. 46 (1989) (Cm. 808)
Exchange of Notes concerning the Establishment of an English Language Resource Centre in Valletta	Valletta, 11.8.1989	TS No. 4 (1990) (Cm. 933)

Country and Title	Place and Date	Text
MEXICO		
Exchange of Notes constituting an Agreement concerning the bicultural college 'Greengates School'	Mexico City, 21.11.1988	
Exchange of Notes constituting an Agreement concerning the bicultural school 'El Colegio Britanico (The Edron Academy) AC'	Mexico City, 21.11.1988	
MISCELLANEOUS		
Agreement between the Government of the UK and the European Space Agency concerning the Establishment and Use of an Ariane Downrange Station on Ascension Island (with Exchange of Letters)	London, 27.11.1989	TS No. 27 (1990) (Cm. 1042)
MOROCCO		
Exchange of Notes concerning Certain Commercial Debts (The UK/Morocco Debt Agreement No. 3 (1987))	Rabat, 16.11.1988	TS No. 18 (1989) (Cm. 703)
Exchange of Notes concerning Certain Commercial Debts (The UK/Morocco Debt Agreement No. 4 (1988))	Rabat, 27.7/ 31.8.1989	TS No. 11 (1990) (Cm. 953)
NETHERLANDS		
Protocol further amending the Convention for the Avoidance of Double Taxation and the Prevention of Fiscal Evasion with respect to Taxes on Income and Capital Gains, signed at The Hague on 7.11.1980, as amended by the Protocol, signed at London on 12.7.1983	The Hague, 24.8.1989	
NIGERIA		
Exchange of Notes concerning Certain Commercial Debts (The UK/Nigeria Debt Agreement No. 2 (1989))	Lagos, 23.8.1989	TS No. 60 (1989) (Cm. 924)
Agreement concerning the Investigation and Prosecution of Crime and the Confiscation of the Proceeds of Crime	London, 18.9.1989	Nigeria No. 1 (1989) (Cm. 901)
NORWAY		
Exchange of Notes concerning the Export of Uranium to Norway	Oslo, 23/27.11.1989	TS No. 29 (1990) (Cm. 1049)
POLAND		
Exchange of Notes concerning Certain Commercial Debts (The UK/Poland Debt Agreement No. 4 (1987))	Warsaw, 27.10.1989	TS No. 17 (1990) (Cm. 971)
SAINT LUCIA		
Agreement for Air Services between and beyond their respective Territories	Castries, 31.8.1989	TS No. 58 (1989) (Cm. 888)

Country and Title	Place and Date	Text
SENEGAL		
Exchange of Notes concerning Certain Commercial Debts (The UK/Senegal Debt Agreement No. 7 (1989))	Dakar, 20/ 25.11.1989	TS No. 41 (1990) (Cm. 1096)
SINGAPORE		
Exchange of Notes further amending the Agreement for Air Services between and beyond their respective Territories, signed at Singapore on 12.1.1971, as amended	Singapore, 30.8/ 17.10.1989	TS No. 42 (1990) (Cm. 1097)
SOMALIA		
Exchange of Notes concerning Certain Commercial Debts (The UK/Somalia Debt Agreement No. 2 (1987))	Mogadishu, 20.1.1988/26.1.1989	TS No. 20 (1989) (Cm. 714)
SOUTH AFRICA		
Exchange of Notes concerning the Regulation of the Terms of Settlement of the Salvaging of the Wreck of 'HMS Birkenhead'	Pretoria, 22.9.1989	TS No. 3 (1990) (Cm. 906)
SOVIET UNION		
Agreement for the Promotion and Reciprocal Protection of Investments	London, 6.4.1989	
SPAIN		
Agreement concerning the Prevention and Suppression of Drug Trafficking and the Misuse of Drugs	Madrid, 26.6.1989	Spain No. 1 (1989) (Cm. 830)
SWEDEN		
Agreement concerning the Assumption of Responsibility for the Protection of the Diplomatic and Consular Interests of the UK Government in the Islamic Republic of Iran by the Government of the Kingdom of Sweden	London, 27.7.1989	TS No. 45 (1989) (Cm. 809)
Agreement concerning the Restraint and Confiscation of the Proceeds of Crime	Stockholm, 14.12.1989	
SWITZERLAND		
Exchange of Notes concerning Safeguards and Assurances relating to the Transfer of Nuclear Material from the UK to Switzerland	Berne, 7/10.11.1989	TS No. 28 (1990) (Cm. 1050)
TOGO		
Exchange of Notes concerning Certain Commercial Debts (The UK/Togo Debt Agreement No. 6 (1988))	Accra/Lomé, 9.12. 1988/31.1.1989	TS No. 31 (1989) (Cm. 754)
TRINIDAD AND TOBAGO		
Exchange of Notes concerning Certain Commercial Debts (The UK/Trinidad and Tobago Debt Agreement No. 1 (1989))	Port of Spain, 21.7.1989	TS No. 7 (1990) (Cm. 942)

Country and Title	Place and Date	Text
TUNISIA		
Agreement for the Promotion and Protection of Investments	Tunis, 14.3.1989	TS No. 18 (1990) (Cm. 976)
Exchange of Notes further amending the UK/Tunisia Air Services Agreement done at London on 22.6.1971	Tunis, 25.10.1989	TS No. 26 (1990) (Cm. 1041)
UNITED STATES OF AMERICA		
Exchange of Notes further extending the Narcotics Co-operation Agreement with respect to the Turks and Caicos Islands signed on 18.9.1986	Washington, 19.1.1989	TS No. 61 (1989) (Cm. 949), p. 27
Exchange of Notes further extending the Narcotics Co-operation Agreement with respect to Montserrat signed in London on 14.5.1987	Washington, 28.2.1989	TS No. 61 (1989) (Cm. 949), p. 27
Exchange of Notes further extending the Narcotics Co-operation Agreement with respect to British Virgin Islands signed in London on 14.4.1987	Washington, 10.5.1989	TS No. 62 (1989) (Cm. 988), p. 20
Exchange of Notes further extending the Agreement in the form of an Exchange of Letters concerning the Cayman Islands and Matters connected with, arising from, related to, or resulting from any Narcotics Activity referred to in the Single Convention on Narcotic Drugs, 1961, as amended by the Protocol amending the Single Convention on Narcotic Drugs, 1961, signed in London on 26.7.1984	Washington, 25.5.1989	TS No. 62 (1989) (Cm. 988), p. 20
Exchange of Notes further amending the Agreement concerning Air Services, signed at Bermuda on 23.7.1977, as amended	Washington, 25.5.1989	TS No. 41 (1989) (Cm. 792)
Exchange of Notes concerning the Licensing of their respective Airlines to operate International Air Services	Washington, 25.5.1989	TS No. 42 (1989) (Cm. 793)
Exchange of Notes further extending the Narcotics Agreement with respect to Anguilla, signed at Washington on 11.3.1987	Washington, 23.6.1989	TS No. 62 (1989) (Cm. 988), p. 20
Exchange of Notes further extending the Narcotics Co-operation Agreement with respect to the Turks and Caicos Islands, signed on 18.9.1986	Washington, 20.7.1989	TS No. 63 (1989) (Cm. 1056), p. 15

Country and Title	*Place and Date*	*Text*
Exchange of Notes exempting from Income Tax, on a reciprocal basis, Income derived by Residents of the Isle of Man and the United States for the International Operation of Ships	Washington, 1/ 15.8.1989	TS No. 54 (1989) (Cm. 883)
Exchange of Notes further extending the Narcotics Co-operation Agreement with respect to Montserrat signed at London on 14.5.1987	Washington, 30.8.1989	TS No. 63 (1989) (Cm. 1056), p. 16
Exchange of Notes further extending the Narcotics Co-operation Agreement with respect to the British Virgin Islands signed at London on 14.4.1987	Washington, 9.11.1989	TS No. 64 (1989) (Cm. 1076), p. 26
Exchange of Notes further extending the Agreement in the form of an Exchange of Letter concerning the Cayman Islands and Matters connected with, arising from, related to, or resulting from any Narcotics Activity referred to in the Single Convention on Narcotic Drugs, 1961, as amended by the Protocol amending the Single Convention on Narcotic Drugs, 1961, signed in London on 26.7.1984	Washington, 28.11.1989	TS No. 64 (1989) (Cm. 1076), p. 25
Exchange of Notes further extending the Narcotics Co-operation Agreement with respect to Anguilla, signed at Washington on 11.3.1987	Washington, 21.12.1989	
VANUATU Exchange of Notes concerning the use of British Controlled Ships registered in Vanuatu	Port Vila, 20.2.1989	TS No. 48 (1989) (Cm. 814)
Agreement in support of Upper Air Observations at Bauerfield, Vanuatu	Port Vila, 7.4.1989	TS No. 35 (1989) (Cm. 766)
YUGOSLAVIA Exchange of Notes further amending the Agreement on Certain Commercial Debts, signed at Belgrade on 29.7.1987 (The UK/ Yugoslavia Debt Agreement No. 3 (1986))	Belgrade, 11.1.1989	TS No. 14 (1990) (Cm. 957)
Exchange of Notes concerning Certain Commercial Debts (The UK/Yugoslavia Debt Agreement No. 4 (1988))	Belgrade, 11.1.1989	TS No. 38 (1989) (Cm. 785)
ZAIRE Exchange of Notes concerning Certain Commercial Debts (The UK/Zaire Debt Agreement No. 7 (1986))	Kinshasa, 11.7/ 5.12.1989	
Exchange of Notes concerning Certain Commercial Debts (The UK/Zaire Debt Agreement No. 8 (1987))	Kinshasa, 11.7/ 9.12.1989	

III. United Kingdom Legislation during 1989 Concerning Matters of International Law[1]

The Antarctic Minerals Act (1989 c. 21) makes provision with respect to the exploration and exploitation of mineral resources in Antarctica. It provides for licensing and other controls of prospecting activities in Antarctica, for criminal and civil liability in respect of such activities, and for powers of arrest and evidentiary matters. The Act gives effect to certain articles of the Convention on the Regulation of Antarctic Mineral Resource Activities of 2 June 1988 (Miscellaneous No. 6 (1989); Cm. 634). It also provides that Her Majesty may by Order in Council confer on any court in England and Wales such criminal and civil jurisdiction in respect of matters arising under the law of the British Antarctic Territory as Her Majesty thinks fit. (See Part Eight: IV., above.)

The Brunei Appeals Act (1989 c. 36) makes provision for effect to be given by Order in Council to a proposed agreement between the Government of the United Kingdom and the Government of Brunei Darussalam for the reference of appeals from the Supreme Court of Brunei Darussalam to the Judicial Committee of the Privy Council. (The agreement was concluded by an Exchange of Notes dated 27 June 1989: Miscellaneous No. 17 (1989); Cm. 890.)

The Continental Shelf Act (1989 c. 35) amends Section 3 of the Petroleum Royalties (Relief) and Continental Shelf Act 1989 (see below) so as to include therein a reference to the Continental Shelf (Designation of Additional Areas) Order 1971 and the area designated by that Order. (For the reasons for this amendment, see Part Nine: VIII., above.)

The Extradition Act (1989 c. 33) consolidates the law relating to extradition and replaces, with certain amendments, the Extradition Act 1870, the Fugitive Offenders Act 1967, Part I of the Criminal Justice Act 1988 (which never entered into force) and certain other statutory provisions relating to extradition (although extradition to and from the Republic of Ireland continues to be governed by the Backing of Warrants (Republic of Ireland) Act 1965). The main innovations are contained in Section 9(4) and (8), which allows arrangements to be made for extradition to a foreign State in the absence of a demonstration of a prima facie case by the foreign State, and Section 10, which allows an appeal by way of case stated by a foreign State which seeks to challenge a refusal of the court of committal to commit a fugitive.

The Petroleum Royalties (Relief) and Continental Shelf Act (1989 c. 1) by Sections 1 and 2 confers on holders of petroleum licences granted under the Petroleum (Production) Act 1934 exemption from royalties payable to the Crown in respect of oil fields in the Southern Basin of the North Sea and onshore oil fields. It provides in Section 3 that Her Majesty may by Order in Council amend the Continental Shelf (Designation of Additional Areas) Order 1974 (made under the Continental Shelf Act 1964) so as to give effect to the Agreement of 7 November 1988 between Her Majesty's Government in the United Kingdom and the Government of the Republic of Ireland in relation to the continental shelf adjacent to the two countries. (See Part Nine: VIII., above; see also the Continental Shelf Act 1989, above.)

The Prevention of Terrorism (Temporary Provisions) Act (1989 c. 4) re-enacts with certain amendments the Prevention of Terrorism (Temporary Provisions) Act 1984, which expired on 21 March 1989. As was the case with the 1984 Act, certain provisions of the Act apply to international terrorism, and these include Part III of the Act, which deals with financial assistance for terrorism. This Part extends the definition of existing offences of contributing to terrorism and creates a new offence of assisting in retention or control of terrorist funds. (For the effects of the 1984 Act, see this *Year Book*, 55(1984), pp. 540–1, 604.)

[1] Compiled by C. A. Hopkins.

TABLE OF CASES[1]

[1] The figures in heavier type indicate the pages on which cases are reviewed.

INDEX